KU-705-900

# WHO'S WHO IN ART

# AN APPEAL

## TO

# ARTISTS

## AND

# AGENTS

Applications for inclusion in *Who's Who in Art* are always sympathetically considered. If you know of an artist who you think should be included an entry form will be sent on request. Ten lines are inserted free of charge and there is no obligation whatsoever to purchase a copy of the book. Any information that should be added to existing entries should be sent to the Editor immediately. *Who's Who in Art* is revised every two years.

# WHO'S WHO IN ART

## TWENTY-EIGHTH EDITION

*Biographies of leading Men and Women
in the world of Art today-Artists,
Designers, Craftsmen, Critics, Writers,
Teachers and Curators, with an Appendix of
Signatures*

THE      ART      TRADE      PRESS      LTD
HAVANT                                         HANTS

Distributed exclusively in the United States of America, its possessions, Canada and Mexico by The Gale Research Co., Book Tower, Detroit, Michigan 48226, U.S.A.

©

THE ART TRADE PRESS LTD., 1998

9 BROCKHAMPTON ROAD, HAVANT, HANTS

*First Published.* . . . . . . . . . . *1927*
*Sixth Edition (Reset).* . . . . . . *1952*
*Twenty-Eighth Edition.* . . . . . *1998*

ISBN 0-900083-17-4

Printed in Great Britain by
Unwin Brothers Limited, Old Woking, Surrey

# CONTENTS

PUBLISHERS NOTES . . . . . . ix

AIMS AND ACTIVITIES OF ACADEMIES, GROUPS,
SOCIETIES, ETC . . . . . . . xi

BIOGRAPHIES . . . . . . . . 1

APPENDIX I   MONOGRAMS AND SIGNATURES . 643

II  OBITUARY . . . . . 689

III ABBREVIATIONS . . . . 692

# PUBLISHER'S NOTES

IN COMPILING *Who's Who in Art* it is our aim to produce a comprehensive list of biographical details of living artists in Britain and Ireland today.

Overseas artists are represented but we have decided not to add any new names, so that their numbers will gradually dwindle, until we are left with artists in or from the British Isles.

*Who's Who in Art* embraces exponents of all forms of painting and drawing, graphic art and sculpture in their widest forms and in any mediums.

One of the criticisms always levied at "Who's Who"-type publications is that many famous names are excluded. The omission of well-known names is most regrettable, but we are limited to those artists who wish their names to appear.

If by any chance there are any artists of repute in Britain today who have never been approached by us, we can only apologize for the oversight and hope that if they should read these Publisher's Notes they will inform us of the omission so that they may appear in the next edition of *Who's Who in Art*, which will be published in 2000.

All the entries in the last edition have been submitted to the individuals concerned and any corrections or additions sent in by them have been incorporated in the *Twenty-Eighth Edition*. We have approached numerous additional artists, and many new names appear for the first time. We always welcome applicants and names of artists recommended by others.

Exactly the same procedure has been followed as in the compilation of former editions. We gratefully acknowledge the kind assistance of all who have contributed information, including the various societies, art galleries and numerous individuals who have helped us in this edition.

This is the first edition that we have produced on our own database and we have made some minor changes to the formatting of artists' entries. We have decided to omit references to parentage which do not seem to be relevant and we have agreed to accept "E mail" addresses, but not telephone numbers.

Unfortunately, several months must elapse between the closing dates for accepting revision of entries and final publication and we regret any late changes which are not reflected in this edition.

# AIMS AND ACTIVITIES OF ACADEMIES, GROUPS, SOCIETIES, ETC.

## Armed Forces Art Society

Annual Exhibition in the National Army Museum. All who are currently serving or have ever served in any branch of the Royal Navy, the Army or the Royal Air Force (including auxiliary, territorial, volunteer and reserve units and the Women's branches of the services) and/or their spouses, are eligible to submit works for the exhibition as Members or Associates of the Society.

*Chairman:* Col. C. D. A. Blessington, The Oast House, Peelings Manor, Hankham, nr. Pevensey, East Sussex BN24 5AP.

## British Society of Painters
### (In Oils, Pastel and Acrylics) (1987)

Formed to promote the very best in works of art in these media. Society formed of Hon. Fellows, Fellows and Members, in a very short time has become a leading Society in the field with twelve Fellows and fifty members; promoting all that is best in traditional values, allowing artists in any media to compete unrestricted in open exhibition - showing their works alongside those of the Fellows and Members - with the opportunity of being selected for Membership. (Membership on merit - restricted by selection).

Major Prize "The Old Masters Award", presented annually. Also many other prestigious prizes. Exhibitions bi-annually, Spring and Autumn at the Kings Hall/Winter Gardens Complex, Ilkley, West Yorkshire - central geographical position, equi-distant from Scotland, the South, the West Country and the East Coast. Applications for exhibition to the Director.

*Hon. Fellows*: David Shepherd, O.B.E., F.R.S.A., Terence Cuneo, O.B.E., Rowland Hilder, P.P.R.I., R.S.M.A., O.B.E. *The First International Hon. Fellow*: The late Pietro Annigoni. *Secretary*: Margaret Simpson, Briargate, 2 The Brambles, Ilkley, W. Yorkshire LS29 9DH. *Tel:* 01943-609075.

## The British Watercolour Society

Only the second major Art Society to leave London; formerly The Royal Water-colour Society Art Club, reverted its title to that of The British Watercolour Society (1911) which became defunct in 1961. The aims of The Society are to promote all that is best in the traditional values of watercolours, allowing watercolourists to compete in unrestricted open exhibition, showing their works alongside those of the Members and Associate Members - membership restricted by selection.

Several thousands of pounds in prizes annually - two Exhibitions per year,

Summer and Christmas, at The Kings Hall/Winter Gardens Complex, Ilkley, West Yorkshire - central geographical position equi-distant from Scotland, the South, the West Country and the East Coast. Applications to The Director.

*Hon. Members:* Sir Robin Philipson, R.S., P.P.R.S.A., R.S.W., Rowland Hilder, P.P.R.I., R.S.M.A., O.B.E., Edith Hilder, W. J. L. Baillie, R.S.A., P.R.S.W., W. Heaton-Cooper, R.I. *President:* Kenneth Emsley, M.A. (Cantab), L.L.M., F.R.S.A. *Secretary:* Margaret Simpson. *Director:* Leslie Simpson, F.R.S.A.,Briargate, 2 The Brambles, Ilkley, W. Yorkshire LS29 9DH. *Tel:* 01943-609075.

## The Chartered Society of Designers

The Chartered Society of Designers is the professional body representing the interests of designers. Its function is to promote high standards of design, to foster professionalism and to emphasise designers' responsibility to Society, to the client and to each other.

Established in 1930 and granted its Royal Charter in 1976, it represents product, interior, fashion, textile and graphic designers, design educators and design managers.

The CSD provides a wide range of member benefits and services including events, training, seminars, a regular newsletter, a reference library, and information service, a wide range of specialist publications and professional services, and its journal.

The CSD is the British member of BEDA, Bureau of European Design Associations, and of the three international design organisations.

*Director:* Brian Lymbery. *Address*: 32 Saffron Hill, London EC1N 8FH. *Tel:* 0171-831 9777. *Fax:* 0171-831 6277.

## Chelsea Art Society

Exhibition held annually at The Main Hall, Chelsea Old Town Hall, Kings Rd., London SW3.

*President:* Julian Barrow. *Vice-President*: Sheila Donaldson Walters. *Hon. Secretary:* Heather Wills-Sandford. *Hon. Treasurer:* Ronald Webster. *Council:* Julian Barrow, Sheila Donaldson Walters, F.R.S.A., Dennis Gilbert, N.E.A.C., David Griffin, Christopher Keays, Ann Langford Dent, Ann Mavroleon Dixon, Gwen Mandley, Sally McGill, Alison Musker, James Parfitt, Diana Whelan, A.R.B.S., Katherine Yates. *Address:* Hon.Secretary, 50 Bowerdean St., London SW6 3TW. *Tel*: 0171-731 3121.

## European Group

When Britain officially became a part of Europe and joined the E.E.C. the European Group was formed. Its first major exhibition was held at The Mall Galleries, F.B.A. London, 1974. Since then the Group has staged major exhibitions in a different member country of the E.E.C. each year. Its intention is to exhibit the work of well known artists from member European countries together with work by guest artists. The aim of the European Group is to contribute towards friendship and understanding between European countries.

*President*: Charles White, D.F.A. (Lond.), F.R.S.A., S.G.A., F.F.P.S. *Co-ordinator:* Prof. Roger Dornseiffer, C.E.P. Luxembourg. *Secretary General:* Heinz Webeler, Zimmerplatzweg 6, 55599 Wonsheim, West Germany.

## Federation of British Artists

The Federation of British Artists was incorporated on 13 Feb., 1961 with the following objects: (1) To provide adequate and modern facilities for art exhibitions, conferences, lectures, etc., at a reasonable cost to societies and individual artists. (2) By using the accommodation to the utmost extent, to reduce the costs to the art societies, thus enabling each society to retain its individual character and raise the standard of its exhibitions by being more selective. (3) To sponsor or help to sponsor exhibitions of work by younger or deserving painters, to enable them to become better known to the public. (4) To provide a central forum for the arts and to establish a representative body which would speak with authority. (5) To provide a central source of information on all contemporary art matters.

The Federation is a charity and incorporates the majority of London art societies, including the Royal Institute of Oil Painters, The Royal Institute of Painters in Watercolours, The Royal Society of British Artists, The Royal Society of Marine Artists, The Royal Society of Portrait Painters, The Hesketh Hubbard Art Society, The New English Art Club, The Pastel Society (incorporating The Pencil Society), The Society of Wildlife Artists.

The Singer and Friedlander and the Laing Group Awards for the Best Oil Painting and the Best Water-colours of the year are presented at Annual Exhibitions.

In addition, the Federation organises annually many exhibitions and important One Man Shows or group exhibitions.

No financial aid is given to the Federation which maintains itself upon the proceeds of its own activities.

*Chairman of Governors:* Ronald Maddox, P.R.I. *Address:* 17 Carlton House Terr., London SW1Y 5BD. *Tel:* 0171-930 6844.

## Free Painters and Sculptors (F.P.S.)

This FPS was founded in 1952 when painter members of the ICA formed an individual group devoted to the principle of a 'free association of painters for mutual assistance, without regard to style, with no theory held in common, but believing in vital experiment and friendship'. Initially known as the Free Painters Group, the name was changed in the mid-Sixties to the Free Painters and Sculptors to include sculptors who had become an integral part of the Group.

In 1972 the FPS opened the Loggia Gallery in Buckingham Gate where exhibitions of members' work, either in group or one-person shows, are held throughout the year. Group exhibitions are also held in galleries out of London.

Membership is £15 annually. Persons interested in the visual arts are welcomed and applications will be submitted to the Executive Committee. Full membership is awarded to practising artists whose work is of the required standard. Fellowship is awarded to Full members solely on the quality of their work.

The Free Painters and Sculptors is an Incorporated body and is registered as an Educational Charity.

*Chairman:* Robert de Quin. *Hon. Secretary:* Lee Campbell. *Address:* 15 Buckingham Gate, London SW1E 6LB. *Tel:* 0171-828 5973.

## Glasgow Art Club

This Club was formed in 1867 to advance the cause of and stimulate interest in art in all its branches by means of exhibitions of works of art, life classes, the acquisition of Publications on art, lectures on art subjects, and by such other means as the Council may decide from time to time. Consequently, the Club's Membership comprises painters, sculptors and architects as Artist Members and ladies and gentlemen interested in art as Lay Members. To be admitted to Artist membership, candidates must submit examples of their work for the approval of the Artist Members. Painters, sculptors and members pay on admission an entry fee of £5.

*Secretary:* Leslie J. McIntyre, C.A., Messrs. Wylie & Bisset, 135 Wellington St., Glasgow G2 2XE. *Tel:* 0141-248 3904. *Fax:* 0141-226 5047.

## Hesketh Hubbard Art Society

Founded as RBA Art Club under the auspices of the Royal Society of British Artists. Members meet on Monday or Friday evenings to draw from the model throughout the year. New members admitted any Monday or Friday after a folio of work is inspected. No tuition unless specially requested. The Mall Galleries, The Mall, SW1.

*President:* Simon Whittle. *Chairman:* Colin McMillan. *Address:* 17 Carlton House Terr., London SW1Y 5BD. *Tel:* 0171-930 6844.

## The Hilliard Society of Miniaturists

Society founded in 1982. Membership of approximately 250 worldwide consisting of Patrons and Artists. Annual exhibition in May/June. Society dinner and lunch at that time. Seminars various parts of England. Two Newsletters a year. Full Exhibiting Artists entitled to use H.S. (H.S.F.- Founder member).

*Enquiries:* Mrs. S. M. Burton, Burwood House, 15 Union St., Wells, Somerset BA5 2PU.

## The International Guild of Artists

Now exclusively restricted to 20 leading artists as Hon. Fellows and Fellows of the Society. Lesser activities have been suspended for 1992.

*Principal:* I.G.A., Briargate, 2 The Brambles, Ilkley, W. Yorkshire LS29 9DH. *Tel:* 01943-609075.

Ultimate aim of the Guild to promote the British Watercolour Society, Society of Miniaturists, British Society of Painters, Yorkshire Artists Exhibition. The four major National Societies annually on show at The Kings Hall/Winter Gardens Complex, Ilkley, West Yorkshire.

## Ipswich Art Society

*President:* Colin Moss. *Chairman:* Myra Finch.

Founded in 1874, the objects were to encourage a love of Art and to promote its study and practice. Today most Members are professionals and those joining as Friends, skilled amateurs. The main open exhibition is held in May/June, three others are scheduled in 1998, and the programme includes lectures, excursions, etc.

Enquiries to Mary Warsop, Membership Secretary, 46 Crabbe St., Ipswich IP4 5HS.*Tel:* 01473-255 542.

## The National Acrylic Painters' Association

This Association, founded in 1985, is for all practising artists and painters, who wish to explore the potential of the acrylic medium. A person is elected into either full or associate membership. It is recognised that acrylic paint is but a medium amongst others, yet that as a painting substance it has a flexibility that renders it extremely versatile.

*Founder and Director:* Kenneth J. Hodgson. *Patrons:* Adrian Henri, P.P.N.A.P.A., Brendan Neiland, R.A., Rt. Rev. David Sheppard, Dr. Sally Bulgin. *President::* A. Alwyn Crawshaw, S.E.A., B.W.S., F.R.S.A. *Vice-President:* Professor Arthur Hughes, Editor of The Artist Magazine. In 1995 the Association established a U.S.A. division. The President is Gerald Brommer, N.W.S., author, and the Vice-President Sandy Carpenter, Editor of The Artist Magazine, U.S.A. The Director is Linda S. Gunn.

*Further information and details of membership obtainable from:* National Acrylic Painters' Association, 134 Rake Lane, Wallasey, Wirral, Merseyside L45 1JW.

## National Society of Painters, Sculptors and Printmakers

The National Society was formed in 1930 to escape rigid traditionalism by allowing Member Artists to exhibit a diversity of the best of creative art with full freedom of expression. The objects of the Society are to advance the awareness of the public by promoting, demonstrating or teaching painting, sculpture and printmaking and to hold an annual exhibition in London (and secondary exhibitions from time to time) of the work of artists of every creed and outlook representing all aspects under one roof without prejudice or favour to anyone.

Membership is in two categories: Members (N.S.) and Associate Members (A.M.N.S.). Members are elected on merit from among those Associates who have had at least two works selected for the annual exhibition for three years. Application information may be requested from the Hon. Secretary.

A Newsletter is sent to Members and Associates twice a year.

*President:* Denis C. Baxter, U.A., F.R.S.A. *Hon. Secretary:* Gwen Spencer. *Address:* 122 Copse Hill, Wimbledon, London SW20 0NL.


## Nature in Art

NATURE IN ART is a museum of fine, decorative and applied art inspired by nature. It opened to the public in May 1988 and in June 1988 HRH Princess Alexandra attended a celebration of the opening. Nature in Art is the first of its kind anywhere in the world. It is housed in a fine, early Georgian mansion set in its own grounds and is owned and managed by Nature in Art Trust, registered charity 1000553.

Nature in Art is readily accessible from M5 (J11 and 11A) and the centre of Gloucester (both 10 minutes by car). The entrance is on A38 in Twigworth, one mile North of A40.

Art inspired by nature, from all periods and parts of the world in any medium, including works by living artists, is included in the permanent collection. All aspects of nature are included (but domestic, farm and sporting animals etc. are excluded). Temporary exhibitions are held regularly and the permanent collection on show is regularly changed.

Nature in Art was one of six museums "specially commended" in the National Heritage Museum of the Year Awards, 1989. The museum is fully registered.

Handicapped people are specially welcome. Facilities include free car parking, meals and light refreshments all day, library and reference collection of slides and other information, childrens play area, shop, studios and nature garden with open air sculptures. Different artists are in residence February/November and courses and demonstrations on a wide range of art techniques are arranged. A new conference/education centre opened in 1994.

Open Tuesday-Sunday and Bank Holidays 10am-5pm. Closed other Mondays, (except by special arrangement when the facilities of Wallsworth Hall can be privately hired), and on Dec. 24, 25 and 26. Full details are available from the Deputy Director.

*Patron:* H.R.H. Princess Alexandra. *President:* Lady Scott. *Hon. Director:* Dr. David H. Trapnell. *Address:* Wallsworth Hall, Twigworth, Gloucester GL2 9PA. *Tel:* 01452-731422. *Fax:* 01452-730937.

## Nature in Art Trust

Established as a Registered Charity (No. 1000553) in 1982, the Trust owns and manages Nature in Art. This centre has been created to exhibit, study and teach fine, decorative and applied art inspired by nature in all media from all national origins and all historical periods depicting any living (or previously living) wild thing. The facilities of Nature in Art are described under that title.

Friends of the Trust receive a regular Newsletter, *Nature in Art*, free admission to all regular activities of the Society, use of the library etc. Individual and gallery membership (for commercial and institutional galleries) is available. Further details from the Membership Secretary, Nature in Art (q.v.).

*Patron:* H.R.H. Princess Alexandra. *President:* Lady Scott. *Chairman:* Dr. David H. Trapnell. *Address*: Wallsworth Hall, Twigworth, Gloucester GL2 9PA. *Tel*: 01452-731422. *Fax:* 01452-730937.

## New English Art Club

The New English Art Club was founded in 1886. Its origin was a wave of foreign influence in the person of a number of students who had worked in the Parisian schools. The New English Art Club came into existence as a protest against a false concept of tradition, and it stands today against an equally false rejection of tradition. The annual exhibition is held in the Mall Galleries, The Mall, SW1, when the work of non-members is considered for display, November/December.

*Hon. Secretary:* William Bowyer, R.A., R.W.S., R.P. *Hon. Treasurer:* David Corsellis. *Keeper:* Charlotte Halliday, R.B.A. *Assistant Keeper:* Jacqueline Rizvi. *Address:* 17 Carlton House Terr., London SW1Y 5BD. *Tel:* 0171-930 6844.

## Newlyn Art Gallery

Newlyn Art Gallery plays an important role in the South-West as one of the leading venues for contemporary art. The programme reflects current U.K. and international art practice and includes regular shows from locally-based artists. As an educational charity Newlyn Art Gallery aims to promote and encourage greater understanding and enjoyment of contemporary art. Throughout the year we present nine major exhibitions and associated educational events.

*Director:* Emily Ash. *Education Officer:* Amanda Colquhoun. *Address:* Newlyn, Penzance, Cornwall TR18 5PZ. *Tel:* 01736-3637150. *Fax*: 01736-331578.

## Pastel Society

Founded 1898. Annual exhibition open to all artists who work in any `dry' medium, i.e. pastel, pencil, charcoal, chalk, conté, sanguine, etc., at The Mall

Galleries, The Mall, SW1, usually August/September.

*President:* Thomas Coates. *Vice-President:* Moira Huntly. *Secretary:* Bria
Gallagher. *Treasurer:* John Ivor Stewart. *Address:* 17 Carlton House Terr
London SW1Y 5BD. *Tel:* 0171-930 6844.

## Royal Academy of Arts

The Royal Academy was founded in 1768 under the patronage of George II
Sir Joshua Reynolds was the first President. It was to be a "Society for promot
ing the arts of design". Since that date it has fulfilled this role through promo
tion of the work of living artists with an unbroken series of Summe
Exhibitions, held annually since 1769. It provides post-graduate training for 6(
students in the Royal Academy Schools, which were established at the founda
tion. The Academy continues to administer trust funds for the benefit of artist
and for the promotion of the visual arts, and has a distinguished Library. Loa
exhibitions, of great international importance, date from the 1870's. The Roya
Academy receives no direct Government subsidy. It is an independent, self
supporting institution, under the patronage of the Crown, and its activities ar
directed by its Members (Painters, Engravers, Sculptors and Architects) wh
serve in rotation on the Council. The President is elected annually.

The Royal Academy is supported by sponsorship, through the subscription
of its 70,000 Friends, and of its Corporate Members, through an active fund
raising programme and through retail sales of art books and specially commis
sioned works and a fine art framing service.

*President:* Sir Philip Dowson, C.B.E. *Keeper:* Leonard McComb
*Treasurer*: Michael Kenny. *Secretary:* David Gordon. *Address:* Burlingto
House, Piccadilly, London W1V 0DS. *Tel:* 0171-439 7438.

## Royal Birmingham Society of Artists

The Royal Birmingham Society of Artists is a non-profit-making society
unique in the Midlands for possessing its own spacious exhibition galleries
Specially designed for art exhibitions and opening on to Birmingham's busies
central street, these galleries are well illuminated by day and night.

The galleries are available for hire for exhibitions and for evening meetings
Schedules for the three Open Exhibitions - oil and sculpture in February, water
colour and craftwork in May, and pastel and drawing in December - may b
obtained from the Secretary by sending a stamped addressed envelope si
weeks before the sending-in days. A more prestigious Prize Exhibition is hel
in June with a top prize of £1000 for painting donated by the R,B.S.A., an
many other cash prizes for sculpture, ceramics, etc. that are specially donate
by Birmingham industries. The Society also holds a Members and Associate
exhibition in the Autumn, and hosts for Birmingham the Singe
Friedlander/Sunday Times Water-colour Competition. There is also a flourish
ing Friends of the R.B.S.A. who hold two exhibtions a year at the gallery.

For details apply to the Hon. Secretary, 69a New St., Birmingham B2 4DU

*Tel*: 0121-643 3768. *Fax:* 0121-644 5298.

## Royal Cambrian Academy of Art

The Royal Cambrian Academy of Art was founded in 1881, and granted its Royal Charter in 1882. The Headquarters have been in Conwy since 1886. In 1993 the Academy moved from Plas Mawr to its new purpose built Gallery, where Exhibitions are held throughout the year. The main open Exhibition is the Annual Summer Exhibition, and forms for this exhibition and membership of the Academy, may be obtained from the Gallery.

*President:* Kyffin Williams, O.B.E., M.A., R.A. *Vice-President:* Dr. Ivor Davies. *Hon. Treasurer:* George Spafford. *Hon. Secretary:* Ann Lewis. *Curator:* Ms.Vicky Macdonald. *Address:* Crown Lane, Conwy LL32 8BH. Gallery open 11 a.m.-5p.m. daily except Monday. *Tel:* 01492-593413.

## Royal Glasgow Institute of the Fine Arts

This Institute was founded in 1861, and has now over 1,500 Members. Its object is "to promote a taste for art generally, and more especially to encourage contemporary art; to further the diffusion of artistic and aesthetic knowledge, and to aid the study, advancement and development of art in its applications." Towards the attainment of this object, the Institute holds open annual exhibitions in the McLellan Galleries, Glasgow, and shows approximately 400 works in all mediums. The Membership fee is an initial payment of £35. Annual subscription £15.

*President:* Dr. Kenneth G. Chrystie, LL.B. (Hons.). *Secretary:* R.C. Liddle, C.A., Oswald St., Glasgow G1 4QR. *Tel:* 0141-248 7411.

## Royal Hibernian Academy

The Academy was incorporated by Charter of King George IV in 1823 with the intention of encouraging the fine arts in Ireland by giving Irish artists the opportunity of exhibiting their works annually. It was reorganized under a new Charter in 1861 and enlarged to thirty Constituent Members, and up to the present time has consistently fulfilled its original aims.

In 1824 Francis Johnston, P.R.H.A., endowed the Academy with a house and exhibition gallery in Lower Abbey St. This was later enlarged by his widow, and again by Sir Thomas Jones, P.R.H.A., who erected a school for the study of the antique and living model, where many of the future artists received their training. The Academy House and Exhibition Galleries were destroyed by fire during the Easter Rising, 1916, and the Academy was without premises until 1939, when it acquired the house and garden of 15 Ely Place with the intention of erecting an exhibition hall when it had the funds to do so. In 1969 the late Mr. Matthew Gallagher undertook to build a new gallery for the Academy on the site. The building was well advanced at the time of his death four years later.

On Thomas Ryan becoming President in 1982 it was decided to attempt the completion of a building left derelict for over 12 years. The Academy attempted this on its own, but it was not until a committee of business interests was set up that funds were engendered and work resumed. The first Academy exhibition was held in the partially completed exhibition rooms in 1986. Since then completion of other phases of the operation has allowed the building to serve a variety of exhibition and display purposes. Though there is still work to be done to finish the building, the facilities available make it the finest exhibition amenity in Ireland and its rooms are used for R.H.A. exhibitions as well as local, national and international displays. Thomas Ryan retired as President in 1992 having seen the advancement of the Academy building from a concrete shell to a serviceable institution.

The Academy has encouraged and developed art in Ireland since its foundation. It has given the Irish artist his status; and the present position of Irish Art can be said to be the outcome of the encouragement it has afforded to Irish men and women of talent and the part it has taken in art affairs generally in the country. There is hardly an Irish artist of note living or dead who has not been a member of the Academy or who has not benefited in one way or another by its activities.

*President*: Arthur Gibney. *Treasurer:* Peter Collis. *Secretary:* Brett McEntagart. *Keeper:* Liam Belton. *Address:* 15 Ely Place, Dublin 2.

## Royal Institute of Oil Painters

Founded in 1883 as the Institute of Painters in Oil Colours. The annual exhibition, which is open to all artists, subject to selection, is held in the Mall Galleries, The Mall, SW1.

*President:* Frederick Beckett. *Vice-President:* Richard Bains, R.B.A. *Hon. Treasurer:* Muriel Temkin. *Hon. Secretary:* Brian Bennett. *Address:* 17 Carlton House Terr., London SW1Y 5BD. *Tel:* 0171-930 6844.

## The Royal Institute of Painters in Water-colours

Formed in 1831 as the "New Society of Painters in Water-colours," a title which was afterwards changed to the "Institute of Painters in Water-colours." Shortly after the opening of the 1884 Exhibition the command of Queen Victoria was received that the Society should henceforth be called "The Royal Institute of Water-colours."

The honour of a diploma under the Royal Sign Manual was given to the members on August 29, 1884, by virtue of which they rank as *Esquires.*

Members are limited to 100. Annual Open Exhibition, March, at The Mall Galleries, The Mall, SW1.

*President:* Ronald Maddox, F.C.S.D., F.S.A.I. *Vice-President:* Peter Folkes, R.W.A. *Hon. Secretary:* Tony Hunt, A.R.W.A. *Exhibitions Secretary:* Richard Boden. *Address:* 17 Carlton House Terr., London SW1Y 5BD. *Tel:* 0171-930 6844.

## Royal Scottish Academy

The Academy is an independent body incorporated by Royal Charter for the furtherance of art in Scotland and for educational purposes. Annual exhibitions of contemporary art: Mid-April to July; special Festival exhibitions: August to mid-September.

*President:* William J. L. Baillie, P.R.S.A., P.P.R.S.W., R.G.I. H.R.A., H.R.H.A., H.R.W.A., H.R.B.S., H.B.W.S., D.A.(Edin.). *Secretary:* Ian McKenzie Smith, O.B.E., D.A., R.S.A., P.R.S.W., F.R.S.A., F.S.S., F.M.A., F.S.A.Scot., LL.D. *Treasurer:* James Morris, R.S.A., D.A., A.R.I.B.A., F.R.I.A.S. *Librarian:* Peter Collins, R.S.A. *Administrative Secretary:* Bruce Laidlow. *Address:* The Mound, Edinburgh EH2 2EL. *Tel:* 0131-225 6671. *Fax:* 0131-225 2349.

## Royal Scottish Society of Painters in Water-colours

This Society was founded in 1878, and in 1888 Queen Victoria conferred on it the title "Royal." In its first Exhibition twenty-five artists showed their works; today there are 106 exhibiting Members. The object of the Society is to encourage and develop the art of painting in water-colours and the appreciation of this art, and toward the attainment of that object exhibitions of water-colour painting are held annually. While these are normally held in Edinburgh, they have on occasion been held in Glasgow, Aberdeen, Dundee and Perth. Candidates for Membership must be sponsored by Members of the Society, and must submit works for the consideration of the Members at an election meeting. The entrance fee is £30.00 and the annual subscription £45.00.

*Secretary:* Roger C. C. Frame, C.A. *Address:* 29 Waterloo St., Glasgow G2 6BZ. *Tel:* 0141-226 3838. *Fax:* 0141-221 1397.

## Royal Society of British Artists

This Society was founded in 1823, incorporated by Royal Charter in 1847 and constituted a Royal Society in 1887. Membership is limited to 200. Associate Membership is by invitation. Annual exhibition held each year, when the work of non-members is admitted at The Mall Galleries, The Mall, SW1.

*President:* Colin Hayes, R.A. *Vice-President:* Albert Carter, R.B.A. *Hon. Secretary:* John Wilkinson. *Hon. Treasurer:* Leigh Parry. *Keeper:* Alfred Daniels. *Address:* 17 Carlton House Terr., London SW1Y 5BD. *Tel:* 0171-930 6844.

## Royal Society of British Sculptors

The Royal Society of British Sculptors (R.B.S.) a registered charity, was founded in 1904 with the purpose of "the promotion and advancement of the art of sculpture." The R.B.S. provides services to sculptors and encourages the appreciation of sculpture, in all its forms. The Society disseminates technical, aesthetic, legal, national and international information which assists artists in the pursuit of excellence in their work. It actively encourages the exchange of ideas by organising workshops, lectures and exhibitions.

The R.B.S. provides a network of advice and knowledge through its 300 professional members. And through its marketing subsidiary The Sculpture Company, it provides a comprehensive resource centre, which enables easy access to the work of contemporary sculptors, for exhibition, loan, purchase or commission.

*President:* John Mills, P.R.B.S., A.R.C.A. *Vice-President:* Derek Morris, V.P.R.B.S. *Hon. Treasurer:* Tracy Long. *Address:* 108 Old Brompton Rd., S Kensington, London SW7 3RA. *Tel:* 0171-373 5554. *e-mail:* rbs@sculpture-company.demon.co.uk

## Royal Society of Marine Artists

Founded 1939, following a major exhibition entitled "Sea Power" under the patronage of King George V and opened by Winston Churchill. First exhibition was not until 1946 owing to the war. Initially known as The Society of Marine Artists, the right to use the title "Royal" was granted by H.M. The Queen in 1966.

Membership in two categories: Artist Members and Lay Members who are not necessarily painters but wish to further marine painting. The latter are admitted for a subscription of £15.00 p.a. and are given many advantages i.e. invitation to annual party, Private Views, prizes of pictures and first choice of pictures for sale. Open exhibition annually at The Mall Galleries, The Mall SW1 Oct./Nov.

*President:* Mark Myers. *Vice-President:* Bert Wright, R.S.M.A. *Hon. Secretary:* Sonia Robinson, R.S.M.A. *Hon. Treasurer:* Geoff Hunt. *Address:* 17 Carlton House Terr., London SW1Y 5BD. *Tel:* 0171-930 6844.

## Royal Society of Miniature Painters, Sculptors and Gravers

This Society was founded in 1896 and its aim is to promote the fine art of miniature painting or any allied craft. The annual exhibition will usually be held in November (handing-in day in September) at the Westminster Gallery, Westminster Central Hall, Storey's Gate, London SW1H 9NH.

The Gold Bowl Award was established in 1985 and is one of the highest accolades for miniature art in the world. Non-members may submit work.

Membership is by selection after establishing a consistently high standard of work. (A.R.M.S. - Associate Member, R.M.S. - Full Member).

*President:* Suzanne Lucas, F.L.S. *Hon. Treasurer:* Alastair MacDonald *Hon. Secretary:* Pauline Gyles.

For further information contact the *Executive Secretary:* Mrs. Pamela Henderson, 1 Knapp Cottages, Wyke, Gillingham, Dorset SP8 4NQ. *Tel:* 01747-825718.

## Royal Society of Painter-Printmakers

The Royal Society of Painter-Printmakers was founded in 1880. The Society was granted a Royal Charter in 1911. Eminent Past-Presidents have been Sir F. Seymour Haden, Sir Frank Short, Malcolm Osborne and Robert Austin. All the well-known printmakers have exhibited with the Society, whose annual exhibition caters for and encourages all forms of printmaking. An election of Associates is held annually.

As part of its aim to promote a knowledge and understanding of original printmaking, the Society organises courses, talks and tours.

*President:* Prof. David Carpanini. *Secretary:* Judy Dixey. *Address:* Bankside Gallery, 48 Hopton St., Blackfriars, London SE1 9JH. *Tel:* 0171-928 7521. *Fax:* 0171-928 2820.

## Royal Society of Portrait Painters

This Society was founded in 1891 and has for its object the promotion of the fine art of portrait painting. The annual exhibition is held during April/May in The Mall Galleries, The Mall, SW1 and non members may submit work in any medium, except miniatures or sculpture, to the Selection Committee.

*President:* Daphne Todd. *Vice-President:* Trevor Stubley. *Hon. Treasurer:* Andrew Festing. *Hon. Secretary:* Paul Brason. *Address:* 17 Carlton House Terr., London SW1Y 5BD. *Tel:* 0171-930 6844.

## Royal Ulster Academy of Arts

*President:* Richard Croft, P.R.U.A. *Secretary:* Harry Reid, 23 Ranfurly Ave., Bangor, Co. Down BT20 3SJ. *Treasurer:* Neil McKibbin, A.C.A. All communications to *Secretary.*

## Royal Water-Colour Society

The Royal Water-Colour Society, which is next in seniority to the Royal Academy, was founded in 1804. It has numbered amongst its distinguished Members John Varley, Peter de Wint, David Cox, John Sell Cotman, Samuel Prout, Samuel Palmer, Ambrose McEvoy and D. Y. Cameron to mention but a few. Two exhibitions are held annually - in the spring and autumn. These exhibitions are confined to the works of Members. An annual exhibition open to all water-colour painters working in Britain is held in the summer. There is an annual election of Associates.

As part of its educational remit, the Society organises courses, talks, tours and other events on the subject of water-colour.

*President:* John Doyle, M.B.E. *Secretary:* Judy Dixey. *Address:* Bankside Gallery, 48 Hopton St., Blackfriars, London SE1 9JH. *Tel:* 0171-928 7521.

*Fax:* 0171-928 2820.


## Royal West of England Academy

The Academy was founded in 1844. Election to Membership (R.W.A.) is by postal ballot. The Academy is an independent, self-supporting institution, founded to assist professional artists, sculptors and architects, through exhibitions and other activities. The principal exhibitions are organised on behalf of its Members, but because of its excellent galleries, exhibitions from other sources are accepted, subject to their standards and the approval of the R.W.A. Council. An open exhibition is held every autumn; information may be obtained from the Secretary.

*President:* Peter Thursby, P.R.W.A., F.R.B.S. *Academy Secretary:* Rachel Fear. *Address*: Queen's Rd., Clifton, Bristol BS8 1PX. *Tel:* 0117-973 5129. *Fax:* 0117-923 7874.


## St. Ives Society of Artists

Holds exhibitions of new works by Members in its Nor'way Gallery between March and November, and at Christmas, and occasional one-man and group shows in its Mariners Gallery.

*President:* Lord St. Levan. *Secretary and Curator:* Judy Joel. *Address:* Old Mariners Church, Norway Sq., St. Ives, Cornwall TR26 1NA.


## Scottish Artists' Benevolent Association

This Association was formed in 1889, and gives assistance to distressed deserving artists, their widows and dependants. Each year it disburses over £10,000. Membership is open to anyone and the subscription payable is £25 (Life).

*Secretary:* R. C. Liddle, C.A. *Address:* Second Floor, 5 Oswald St., Glasgow G1 4QR. *Tel:* 0141-248 7411.


## Society of Botanical Artists

The Society of Botanical Artists is an International Society, founded in 1985. Holds an open exhibition in the Westminster Gallery, Westminster Central Hall, Storey's Gate, London SW1H 9NH each year March/April with other exhibitions of members' work. Combines art and science and strives to enhance botanical art by proper promotion. Newsletter and Social meetings for members.

*Founder President:* Suzanne Lucas, F.L.S. *Hon. Treasurer:* Pamela Davis. *Hon. Secretary:* Paula Joyce. Enquiries to *Executive Secretary:* Mrs. Pamela Henderson, 1 Knapp Cottages, Wyke, Gillingham, Dorset SP8 4NQ. *Tel:* 01747-825718.

### Society of Designer Craftsmen

The Society of Designer Craftsmen was founded in 1888 as The Arts and Crafts Exhibition Society with Walter Crane and William Morris among its most prominent members, each of whom was to serve as President. Its aim is to strengthen the professional standards and status of designer-makers in Great Britain and to stimulate public awareness by bringing works of fine craftsmanship before the public through major comprehensive exhibitions and specialised displays. In 1960 the Society assumed its present title as representative of the largest body of independent professional crafts practitioners in Britain. It lays great emphasis on helping young graduates at the outset of their careers by arranging assessments of their work and offering Licentiateship of the Society (L.S.D.C.) to those whose work is of a high standard and by organising an annual exhibition for the most outstanding of them, which makes them eligible for the T.S.B. and Marlow awards and the possibility of becoming a Distinction Licentiate.

Applications for election as Members (M.S.D.C.) are considered on a regular basis thoughout the year by a Selection Committee, which meets to examine the individual craft pieces submitted. Fellowship of the Society (F.S.D.C.) may be awarded by a majority vote of the Fellows on Council.

Annual subscriptions: Fellows, £50; Members, £40; Licentiates, £25; Associates, £20. *Hon. Secretary:* Richard O'Donoghue. *Address:* 24 Rivington St., London EC2A 3DU. *Tel:* 0171-739 3663.

### Society of Equestrian Artists

Founded in 1978/79, the Society of Equestrian Artists exists to encourage the study of equine art and by its mutual assistance between members, to promote a standard of excellence in its practise, worthy of the subject's importance in British artistic traditions.

Membership consists of Friends, who may be artist or non-artist, Associates and Full Members who have attained a consistently high standard in their work. Annual Exhibitions August/September at Christie's, St. James's, London.

*President:* vacant. *Vice-Presidents:* Frank Wootton, O.B.E., John N.Thompson. *Chairman:* Group Captain Philip Gibson, O.B.E. *Hon. Treasurer:* Keith Chesworth. *Hon. Secretary:* John Collins, 63 Gordon Cl., Knowle Green, Staines TW18 1AP. *Tel:* 01784-889669.

### Society of Graphic Fine Art
(formerly Society of Graphic Artists)

The Society was founded in 1919 to promote fine drawing skills whether with brush, pen, pencil, charcoal or any of the forms of original Printmaking. Newly elected Members remain Associates for a period of three years. The Society holds Annual Open Exhibition in central London and are increasing their out-of-town Exhibitions.

The 77th Annual Exhibition will take place at the Art Connoisseur Gallery, 95-97 Crawford St., London W1 from 15-26th September 1998. Receiving Day 15th August at Art Moves of Chelsea.

*President:* Jean Canter. *Vice-Presidents:* Michael J. Taylor, Dip.Arch., R.I.B.A., F.S.A.I., Valerie Warren, S.W.A., F.S.A.I. *Hon. Treasurer:* David Brooks, U.A., N.A.P.A., B.A.*(Hons.).Secretary:* Mrs. Sharon Curtis, 15 Willow Way, Hatfield, Herts. AL10 9QD.

## Society of Miniaturists
(Founded London, May 1895)

The oldest Miniature Society in existence and the first major Society to leave London - its main aim is to promote the traditional, ancient and precise art of miniature painting that goes back many centuries. The Society holds two Exhibitions per year, Summer and Christmas, at The Kings Hall/Winter Gardens, Ilkley, West Yorkshire - a central geographical position equi-distant from the South, Scotland, West Country and the East Coast.

A major prize is presented at each Exhibition for the best miniature. Non-members can exhibit alongside Members work - applications to the Director.

*President:* Kenneth Emsley, M.A. (Cantab), L.L.M., F.R.S.A. *Secretary:* Margaret Simpson. *Director:* Leslie Simpson, F.R.S.A., Briargate, 2 The Brambles, Ilkley, W. Yorkshire LS29 9DH. *Tel:* 01943-609 075.

## Society of Scottish Artists

The S.S.A. was founded in 1891 to represent the adventurous spirit in Scottish art. Today the S.S.A. has over 500 members throughout Britain of which 150 are elected Professional members. Associate and Ordinary membership is also available by payment of an annual subscription.

The main focus of the Society is its Annual Exhibition which traditionally takes place in the Royal Scottish Academy in Edinburgh in the Autumn. Submission of work is open to both members and non members, who undergo the same selection procedures, ensuring that each Annual Exhibition is unique, challenging and innovative.

For details about the Annual Exhibition (available from August) or about membership,contact the Secretary.

*President:* Gwyneth Leech. *Secretary:* Susan Cornish, 11a Leslie Pl., Edinburgh EH4 1NF. *Tel:* 0131-332 2041.

## Society of Wildlife Artists

Founded in 1964 to foster contact and co-ordinate activities among the many wildlife artists resident in this country and to improve both the standard and recognition of their work. The Society is supported by a number of Lay

Members interested in the Society's work but not necessarily artists themselves. An annual exhibition is held in The Mall Galleries, The Mall, SW1 during June/July and this is open to non-members who may submit work.

*President:* Bruce Pearson. *Hon. Vice-Presidents:* Robert Gillmor, Roger Tory Peterson and Keith Shackleton. *Hon. Secretary:* Andrew Stock. *Address:* 17 Carlton House Terr., London SW1Y 5BD. *Tel:* 0171-930 6844.

## Society of Women Artists

This Society was founded in 1855 for the encouragement of women painters and sculptors, etc. Annual Exhibitions February/March at the Westminster Gallery, Westminster Central Hall, Storey's Gate, London SW1H 9NU. Open to all women artists.

*Patron:* Princess Michael of Kent. *President:* Barbara Tate, R.M.S., A.S.A.F.(HC), F.S.B.A., F.R.S.A. *Vice-Presidents:* Susan Millis, S.E.A., Muriel Owen, U.A., N.D.D., A.T.D., F.R.S.A., Joyce Rogerson, R.M.S., Joyce Wyatt, R.M.S., Hon. U.A., A.S.A.F.(HC). *Hon. Treasurer:* Susan Millis, S.E.A. *Hon. Secretary:* Joyce Rogerson, R.M.S. *Executive Secretary:* E. Davies, Willow House, Ealing Green, Ealing, London W5 5EN.

## The Society of Wood Engravers

Founded in 1920 by Gibbings, Gill, Hagreen, Raverat et al., and revived, after a brief lapse, in 1984, the Society promotes the practice and appreciation of wood engraving and related relief printmaking arts through an annual, open, touring exhibition, occasional publications and a regular newsletter. It is an international contact organisation for those interested in the subject. Subscription (£15 p.a.) is open to all, artists, collectors or enthusiasts. Membership is by election.

*Chairman:* Ian Stephens, R.E. *Hon. Treasurer:* Simon Brett, R.E. *Secretary:* Hilary Paynter, R.E., P.O. Box 355, Richmond, Surrey TW10 6LE.

## Ulster Society of Women Artists

The Ulster Society of Women Artists was founded in 1957 by Gladys Maccabe, M.A.(Hon.), R.O.I., F.R.S.A., for which she had long felt there was a need. This was to include painting, sculpture and other visual arts.

The aims of the Ulster Society of Women Artists are: (1) To promote and encourage a high standard of art in Ulster. (2) To maintain such a standard in exhibitions that election to membership be considered a mark of distinction. (3) To seek out and encourage talent.

The Society always welcomes new members. Those interested in joining may submit work to the Election Committee. Applications to the Hon. Secretary.

*Patron:* Her Grace, The Duchess of Abercorn. *President:* Shelagh Boucher,

B.A.,A.T.D., U.S.W.A. *Vice-President:* Maureen Cashell, U.S.W.A., *Hon. Treasurer:* Sara S. McNeill, D.A., F.I.L.S., U.S.W.A. *Hon. Secretary:* Elizabeth Morrow, D.A., U.S.W.A., U.W.S., 33 Kensington Gdns., South Belfast BT5 6NN.


## United Society of Artists

Founded in 1921, the aim of the Society is to exhibit work of professional quality in oils, water-colours, pastels (with particular reference to drawing) and sculpture. Venues in London and throughout Britain. Election of new members is based on work submitted. `U.A. News and Views' is a newsletter edited and produced by the President.

*President:* Leo Illesley Gibbons-Smith, V.P.S.G.F.A. *Vice-Presidents:* Constance Nash, N.D.D., A.T.D., Margaret Ballardie, Roy Chaffin. *Secretary:* David Headon, Holmdene, 2 Wade Court Rd., Havant, Hants. PO9 2SU.


## Yorkshire Artists Exhibition

Now recognised as the largest event of its kind in Great Britain, with between 1,000 and 1,500 paintings by over 200 artists on show, bi-annually. Exhibitions Spring and Autumn at The Kings Hall/Winter Gardens Complex, Ilkley, West Yorkshire.

The Exhibitions attract leading artists from all over Britain and abroad. Established over ten years, it is well supported by the art-buying public and commercial galleries, etc.

Application for entry to: The Director.

*Hon. Patron:* David Shepherd, F.R.S.A., O.B.E. *Director:* Leslie Simpson, F.R.S.A., Briargate, 2 The Brambles, Ilkley, W. Yorkshire LS29 9DH. *Tel:* 01943-609075.

# WHO'S WHO IN ART

## A

**AARONS, Andrew,** N.D.D. (1958), Postgrad.Dip. Printmaking (1991); painter/printmaker in oil and etching, art historian, teacher; senior lecturer, Anglia University, Cambridge; *b* London, 1 Feb., 1939. *m* Paula. one *s*. one *d*. *Educ:* Camberwell School of Art, Junior Dept. (1951-54). *Studied:* Camberwell School of Art (1954-58). *Exhib:* solo shows in Europe, Canada and U.S.A. *Work in collections:* Berlin Museum; C.B.C. Toronto; York University, Toronto; Barclays Bank; Bank of Mexico; Cambridge University. *Commissions:* Bodilly Suite; Sporting Etchings: Newmarket & Bloodstock; Serigraphs of Newmarket Life. *Publications:* Two Nations in a New Land; A History of Canadian Painting; Is this Art; Journal of Progressive Judaism. *Signs work:* "AARONS" normally followed by year. *Address:* 16 Huntingdon Rd., Cambridge CB3 0HH.

**ABBASSY, Samira,** B.A.(Hons.) (1987); painter in oil on paper, canvas and board, gouache on paper; *b* Ahwaz, Iran, 29 May, 1965. *m* Guy Buckles. *Educ:* Hillview School for Girls, Tonbridge; West Kent College of F.E. *Studied:* Maidstone College of Art and Design, Canterbury College of Art. *Exhib:* Mercury Gallery, East West Gallery London. *Work in collections:* South East Arts. *Publications:* book jackets: Landscape Painted with Tea by Milorid Pavich, The Ice Factory by Russell Lucas. *Clubs:* Rye Soc. of Artists. *Signs work:* "Samira Abbassy." *Address:* c/o Mercury Gallery, 26 Cork St., London W1X 1HB.

**ABELL, Roy,** R.B.S.A., A.R.C.A. (Silver Medal, Painting, First Class Hons. 1957); oils, water-colour, etching; Head of School of Painting, Birmingham College of Art; Course Director B.A. Fine Art, Birmingham Polytechnic (retd.); *b* Birmingham, 21 Jan., 1931. *m* Mary Patricia. two *s*. one *d*. *Educ:* Waverley Grammar School, Birmingham (Jack Davis). *Studied:* Birmingham College of Art (1947-52, Harold Smith, Fleetwood-Walker); Royal College of Art (1954-57, Carel Weight, Ruskin Spear, John Minton). *Exhib:* Young Contemporaries, R.A., John Moores; one-man exhbns.: National Museum of Wales, Ikon, Oriel (Cardiff), Thackeray (London), Tegfryn (Menai), Birmingham Centenary Artist 1989. *Work in collections:* National Museum of Wales, A.C.G.B., Art Galleries of Birmingham, Bradford, Lichfield, Walsall, University of Wales, University of Central England. *Signs work:* "Roy Abell." *Address:* 204 Birmingham Rd., Sutton Coldfield, Birmingham B72 1DD.

**ABRAHAMS, Ivor,** R.A., Sir Winston Churchill Fellow (1989); sculptor in bronze; *b* Lancs., 10 Jan., 1935. *m* Evelyne. two *s*.(one decd.). *Educ:* Wigan Grammar School. *Studied:* St. Martin's School of Art (Frank Martin, Anthony Caro), Camberwell School of Art (Prof. Karel Vogel). *Exhib:* Kölnischer Kunstverein, Cologne (1973), Ikon Gallery, B'ham (1976), Yorkshire Sculpture Park, Wakefield (1984). *Work in collections:* A.C.G.B.; Bibliotheque National, Paris; British Council; Denver Museum, Colorado; Metropolitan Museum, N.Y.; V. & A.; Wilhelm Lembruck Museum, Duisburg; Boymans Museum, Rotterdam, etc. *Publications:* E.A. Poe (1975), Oxford Gardens Sketchbook (1976). *Clubs:* Chelsea Arts, Colony. *Signs work:* "Ivor Abrahams." *Address:* 67 Bathurst Gdns., London NW10 5JH.

**ABRAHAMS, Ruth,** N.D.D. (Painting) (1955), Cert. R.A.S. (1959), Leverhulme award; painter in oil and water-colour on canvas and paper; part-time lecturer, Loughborough College of Art; *b* London, 11 Mar., 1931. *m* formerly to David Willetts. one *s*. *Educ:* Dagenham Grammar School, Essex. *Studied:* St. Martin's School of Art (1951-55, Frederick Gore, Bateson Mason), R.A. Schools (1955-59, Peter Greenham, R.A.). *Exhib:* Young Contemporaries, London Group, John Moores, R.A., Middlesbrough Drawing Biennale (1980); work selected for Sunday Times water-colour competition (1990). *Work in collections:* Durham University, J. Walter Thompson. *Signs work:* "R.A." or "Ruth Abrahams." *Address:* Pear Tree Cottage, 1 Allington Rd., Sedgebrook, nr. Grantham, Lincs.

**ACHESON, Joseph,** B.A. Lond., Dip. F.A., Lond., M.S.I.A.D.; artist in oil, gouache, line; Tutor, Universities of London, Surrey and the Open University; Capt., R.A. (1942-46); *b* Marylebone, London, 30 Dec., 1918. *m* Eileen Veronica Adie. two *d*. *Educ:* U.S.A.; Canada; England. *Studied:* Slade School and Courtauld Institute, London (1946-65), and subs. France, Italy, Greece, U.S.A. *Exhib:* R.A., R.P.S., Arts Council, private galleries. *Work in collections:* Min. of Works, Army, Football Assoc. and public bodies, and for leading publishers and industrial concerns (1958-92). *Signs work:* "Joseph Acheson." *Address:* Littleworth Cross Lodge, Seale, nr. Farnham, Surrey.

**ACKROYD, Jane V.M.,** B.A.(Hons.), M.A., R.C.A. (Sculpture); sculptor in mild steel; *b* London, 25 Feb., 1957. *m* David Annesley. one *s*. *Educ:* Godolphin and Latymer School, London. *Studied:* St. Martin's School of Art (1975-79, Adrian de Montford, David Annesley, Anthony Caro); R.C.A. (1980-83, Philip King, Bryan Kneale). *Exhib:* International Garden Festival Liverpool (1984), Serpentine Gallery (1984), Anti-Thesis Angela Flowers Gallery (1986), R.A. Summer Exhbn. (1988, 1989); one-man shows Anderson O'Day (1988). *Work in collections:* A.C.G.B., Contemporary Arts Soc., Leics. Educ. Authority, London Docklands Development Corp. *Commissions:* 'Herring Gull' Limehouse, 'Moonlight Ramble' Haymarket London. *Signs work:* "Jane Ackroyd." *Address:* 77 Park Ave. North, London N8 7RS.

**ACKROYD, Norman,** R.A. (1991); painter/etcher; *b* Leeds, 26 Mar., 1938.

*Educ:* Cockburn High School, Leeds. *Studied:* R.C.A. (1961-64). *Exhib:* extensively in Europe and U.S.A. *Work in collections:* Tate Gallery, V. & A., Museum of Modern Art, N.Y., National Galleries of Scotland, Canada, S. Africa, Norway, The Rijksmuseum and Stedelijk Amsterdam, The Albertina Vienna, Musee d'Art Historie Geneva, British Council, Leeds, Manchester, Sheffield, Hull, Glasgow, Aberdeen, Norwich, Preston, Bradford, Newcastle, and other city A.G's. *Publications:* Thirty minute film on etching for B.B.C., writing for Studio International. *Signs work:* see appendix. *Address:* 1 Morocco St., London SE1 3HB.

**ADAIR:** see PAVEY, Don.

**ADAIR, Hilary,** N.D.D. (1963), A.T.C. (1965), R.E. (1991); painter/printmaker in water-colour, acrylic, oil, etching, silkscreen; *b* Sussex, 29 May, 1943. *m* Julian Marshall. two *s. Educ:* Chichester High School for Girls. *Studied:* Brighton College of Art (1960-61; 1964-66, J. Dickson), St. Martin's School of Art (1961-63, F. Gore, A. Reynolds). *Exhib:* British Council, R.A., Sue Rankin Gallery, Jill Yakas Gallery Athens, R.W.A., Concourse Gallery, The Barbican, Bankside Gallery. *Work in collections:* Arts Council, Gray's Library, Eastbourne, Lancs., Oldham and Stoke-on-Trent Educ. Authorities. *Signs work:* "Hilary Adair" on prints, "Adair" on paintings. *Address:* Halse Cottage, Winsford, nr. Minehead, Som. TA24 7JE.

**ADAM-TESSIER, Maxime,** sculptor; *b* Rouen, France, 2 June, 1920. *Work in collections:* museums of Modern Art, Paris, São Paulo, Le Havre and Rouen. Steel Relief, Metro Station, La Defense. *Signs work:* see appendix. *Address:* 3 rue Schoelcher, 75014 Paris, 14.

**ADAMS, Anna:** see BUTT, Anna Theresa.

**ADAMS, Hervey,** R.B.A. (1932); art master, Berkhamsted School, 1937-40, Tonbridge School, 1940-63 (Lecturer on Painting); landscape painter in oils and water-colour; *b* 15 Feb., 1903. *m* Iris Gabrielle Bruce. *Educ:* Charterhouse. *Studied:* with Bernard Adams, 1928-30. *Exhib:* R.A., R.B.A., Leicester Galleries. *Publications:* The Student's Approach to Landscape Painting (Pitman), Art and Everyman (Batsford), 18-19th Century Painting in Europe (Medici), The Adventure of Looking (Bell). *Signs work:* "Hervey Adams." *Address:* The Priory Nursing Home, Priory Fields, Horsley, Stroud, Glos. GL6 0PT.

**ADAMS, Ken Praveera,** M.A. (1958), Dip. F.A. (1964), Dip. A.T. (1986); artist, painter, sculptor and composer of music; *b* Northumberland, 1 Sept.,1933. *Educ:* Balliol College, Oxford. *Studied:* Slade School of Fine Art. *Exhib:* London, Suffolk, Amsterdam, Dusseldorf, Paris. *Work in collections:* Museum Sztuki, Lodz, Poland. *Publications:* Leonardo Vol. 12 (1979) Commentary on Sculptures. *Signs work:* "Ken Praveera Adams" or "K.P.A." or intermediate forms. *Address:* 19 Dartmouth Park Rd., London NW5 1SU.

**ADAMS, (Dorothea Christina) Margaret,** A.R.M.S. (1990), R.M.S.

(1992), H.S. (1989); Suzanne Lucas award H.S. (1989), Hon. Men. R.M.S. Gold Bowl award (1991); portrait miniature painter in water-colour on ivorine; *b* Haslemere, 17 Feb., 1918. *m* Stanley V. Adams, O.B.E. (decd.); two *s.* four *d.* Harry E. Gaze (1996). *Educ:* St. Mary's School, Colchester, The Grove School, Hindhead. *Studied:* Farnham School of Art, Bloomsbury Trade School. *Exhib:* R.M.S., H.S. *Signs work:* "Margaret Adams" and see appendix. *Address:* 2 St. Nicholas Park, Penn Hill, Yeovil, Som. BR20 1SX.

**ADAMS, Marina,** A.L.I. (1968); landscape architect in private practice: drawings in ink, water-colour, gouache, crayon; *b* Athens, 27 Aug., 1940. *m* (1964) Robert John Adams, dissolved (1980). one *s.* one *d. Educ:* Pierce College, Athens; Landscape Architecture Dip. L.A. Reading University (1959-62). *Exhib:* R.A. Summer Exhbn. (1987, 1988, 1989, 1990, 1992, 1993, 1994). *Signs work:* "Marina Adams." *Address:* 3 Pembroke Studios, Pembroke Gdns., London W8 6HX.

**ADAMS, Norman,** A.R.C.A., R.A.; painter; Prof. of Painting and Keeper, Emeritus, Royal Academy, London; Prof. of Fine Art, Newcastle University (1981-86); *b* London, 9 Feb., 1927. *m* Anna Butt. two *s. Studied:* Harrow Art School, and R.C.A. *Exhib:* R.A., Tate Gallery, City Art Galleries of Bradford, Leeds, York; also Rome, Paris, Brussels, Pittsburgh. *Work in collections:* Official purchases: C.A.S., Arts Council, National Gallery, N.Z., Tate Gallery, most provincial galleries, various education committees. Murals in public buildings. Décor for Sadler's Wells and Covent Garden. *Publications:* work repro.: magazines, etc. *Signs work:* "Norman Adams," "N.A." *Address:* Butts, Horton-in-Ribblesdale, Settle, Yorks. BD24 0HD; and Royal Academy of Arts, Piccadilly, London W1V 0DS.

**ADAMSON, Crawfurd,** D.A. (1975); painter in oil and pastel; *b* Edinburgh, 24 Mar., 1953. *m* Mary Phimister. one *s.* one *d. Educ:* Royal High School, Edinburgh. *Studied:* Duncan of Jordanstone College of Art (1971-76, Alberto Morrocco, David McLure, Jack Knox). *Exhib:* 12 one-man shows since 1984 (seven in London); group shows in U.K., U.S.A., Spain, France, Japan, Monaco. *Work in collections:* Metropolitan Museum of Art, N.Y. *Publications:* exhibition catalogues (1991, 1995). *Signs work:* "Crawfurd Adamson." *Address:* c/o Jill George Gallery, 38 Lexington St., London W1R 3HR.

**ADAMSON, George Worsley,** R.E., M.C.S.D.; illustration, humour, design; *b* N.Y.C., 7 Feb., 1913. two *s. Studied:* Wigan and Liverpool City Schools of Art. *Exhib:* Walker A.G.; R.A.; Arts Council Exhbn.; American Inst. of Graphic Arts: covering Punch; British humour, Paris, Los Angeles; illustrations to Ted Hughes Poems Word Perfect/Ginn. *Work in collections:* V. & A., B.M., Imperial War Museum, Air Ministry Coll., Ulster Museum, Exeter Museum, Ashmolean. *Publications:* work repro.: British Airports Authority magazine, Nursing Times. Publication planned: Humour/100 illustrations on three Italian cities. *Address:* 46 Bridge Rd., Countess Weir, Exeter, Devon EX2 7BB.

**AIERS, Pauline Victoria,** painter and printer in oil, pastel, charcoal, mono-print, collagraph; *b* Inverness, 1926. *m* David Aiers (decd.). one *s.* one *d. Educ:* West Heath School, Sevenoaks. *Studied:* Warsaw Beaux Arts (1947-48), Ju I. Hsiung, Philippines (1959-62), Morley College (1984-85), with Oliver Bevan, London (1984-89). *Exhib:* solo shows: Lionel Wendt Gallery, Colombo, Gallery 47 and Wine Gallery, London, National Museum of Fine Arts, Malta; two person: Hyde Park Gallery, London, Riverside Gallery, Richmond; others, Singapore Art Soc., Spirit of London, Royal Festival Hall, Camden Annual, Southwark Cathedral, Gallery 10, Flying Colours Gallery, International Arts Fair, Islington, Art for Sale. *Work in collections:* National Museum of Fine Arts, Malta. *Signs work:* "P.A." *Address:* 13 Harefield, Hinchley Wood, Surrey KT10 9TG.

**AINLEY, John Anthony,** retired Head Teacher; Diploma in Child Development; M.Sc., Diploma in the Visual Arts; *b* Sheffield, 1931. married; two children. *Clubs:* Secretary of Leatherhead Art Club. *Address:* Bridleside, Farm Ct. Rd., Leatherhead, Surrey KT22 8NY.

**AINSCOW, George Frederick,** Paris Salon gold and silver medallist (1980, 1981); textile designer, artist in water-colour and oil; *b* Manchester, 10 Feb., 1913. *m* (1) Margaret Shackleton (decd.); (2) Marjorie Standring. one *s.* one *d. Educ:* Derby St. School, Rochdale. *Studied:* Rochdale College of Art (1929-33, G.Wheeler, Principal). *Exhib:* R.A., R.I., R.B.A., N.E.A.C., Preston A.G., R.W.S. Open; one man shows, Rochdale A.G., Mall Galleries, Salford A.G., Oldham A.G. *Work in collections:* R.A.F. Museum, Hendon, Bury A.G., work in private collections. *Signs work:* "G.F. Ainscow." *Address:* 4 Saxonholme Rd., Castleton, Rochdale, Lancs. OL11 2YA.

**AITCHISON, Craigie,** painter in oil; *b* 13 Jan., 1926. *Studied:* Slade School of Fine Art. *Commissions:* Four panels for Truro Cathedral. *Publications:* Art of Craigie Aitchison by Gillian Williams. *Signs work:* "Craigie Aitchison." *Address:* c/o Royal Acadamy of Arts, Burlington House, London W1.

**AIVALIOTIS, Sharon Firth,** R.E., B.A.(Hons.) (1979), Postgrad. Dip. (Printmaking) (1980); artist/printmaker in mezzotint, all intaglio processes and graphite; part-time lecturer, St. Martin's School of Art and Design; *b* Trinidad, 2 Apr., 1951. *m* Stak Aivaliotis. *Studied:* St. Martin's School of Art (1975-79, Albert Herbert), Slade School of Fine Art (1979-80, Bartolomeo Dos Santos). *Exhib:* solo shows: Jill George Fine Art London since 1985; many mixed shows nationally and internationally. *Work in collections:* V. & A., Library of Congress Washington D.C., Whitworth Gallery Manchester, Ferens A.G. Hull. *Publications:* The Mezzotint: History and Technique by Carol Wax (Thames and Hudson). *Signs work:* "Sharon Firth Aivaliotis" or "S. Aivaliotis." *Address:* 22 Brownlow Mews, London WC1N 2LA.

**ALEXANDER, Elsie W. M.,** A.M.N.S. (1977); artist in oil on canvas; retired company director; *b* Ware, Herts., 13 Feb., 1912. *m* Herbert John Alexander, Ph.D. one *d. Educ:* Grammar School, Ware. *Studied:* pastel and abstract painting at Montclair State College, N.J. (1958); graphic art with Hyman J. Warsager; also pupil of the late Victor Askew, R.O.I., F.I.A.L. (1972 73). *Exhib:* City of London (awarded vellum and freedom, Worshipful Co. of Painters and Stainers, freedom, City of London), Leicester, Chelsea, Cornwall Norfolk; one-man show, Mill Hill (1971). First prize winner of She comp (Chelsea, 1968). *Clubs:* Buckingham Art Soc., Wine Trade Art Soc. *Sign work:* "ALEXANDER." *Address:* 20 Parkside Drive, Edgware, Middx.

**ALEXANDER, Gregory,** R.W.S. (1984), B.A. (1981); artist in water-colour and oil; *b* Ramsgate, Kent, 14 May, 1960. *m* Francesca Rigony. *Studied* Canterbury College of Art (1976-78), W. Surrey College of Art (1978-81). *Exhib:* R.W.S., N.E.A.C., R.A. Summer shows, and over 12 one-man exhbns in England and Australia. *Work in collections:* R.W.S. Diploma, A.N.Z. Bank Melbourne. *Publications:* Kipling's The Jungle Book (Pavilion 1991), Tale from the African Plains (Pavilion 1994), Step by Step Water-colour Painting (Weidenfeld & Nicolson 1994). *Signs work:* "Gregory Alexander." *Address* 1/73 Abbott St., Sandringham, Melbourne, Victoria 3191, Australia; U.K Address: 1 Joann's Ct., Stephen Cl., Broadstairs, Kent CT10 1NY.

**ALEXANDER, Hazel,** sculptor in bronze and cold cast bronze; *b* Newcastle-on-Tyne, 1 Feb., 1912. *m* John Alexander. one *s.* three *d. Educ* Smarts College. *Studied:* Luton Art School (1936), Camden Inst. (1970, Joan Armitage), and Fred Kormis. *Exhib:* Mall Gallery, Ben Uri Gallery, Bristo Cathedral (Amnesty), St. Paul's Cathedral, Festival Hall. *Work in collections* Cambridge University Library, All England Lawn Tennis Club (Member Lounge), Museum of Israel Defence Forces, King Solomon Hotel, Elat Wimbledon Museum, Wolfson-Poznansky Home, London, Ben Uri Gallery private collections in England, France, Italy, Germany, U.S.A., Israel. *Sign work:* "Hazel Alexander." *Address:* 34 West Heath Rd., Hampstead, London NW3 7UR.

**ALEXANDER, Naomi,** N.D.D. (1959), R.O.I. (1982), S.F.G.A. (1985) asst. mem. British Picture Restorers Assoc.; Publicity Officer, R.O.I.; old mas ter conservator; Cornelissen, Stanley Grimm, and Visions prize; *b* 1938. one *d Studied:* Hornsey College of Art (1954-59), Central School of Art (1961-63 post graduate. *Exhib:* R.A., Spink, Mercury Gallery, N.E.A.C., R.B.A., R.O.I. R.P., Fosse and David Messum Galleries, municipal galleries in Britain, Young Contemporaries, Mall Galleries, Llewellyn Alexander Gallery, Centur Gallery, Richmond Gallery; one-man shows Ben Uri, Sheila Harrison, Sheridan Russell Gallery. *Work in collections:* V. & A.; Japanese Broadcasting Assoc. Salomon Bros. Bank, Tokyo; Morgan Grenfell Bank, N.Y.; Christies, Tel Aviv; The Yeungling Collection, Arizona; Merryfield Gallery; Oscar Woollens; Sir Richard Storey; Katharine, Viscountess Macmillan; 2nd Royal Tank Regt.; Su Han of Oman; Paintings in Hospitals. *Publications:* The Art Review, Royal Academy Illustrated, Graves Encyclopedia of R.A. Exhbns The Observer, Artist and Illustrator, House and Garden, The Bread-givers by ezierska, Tableaux, Mail on Sunday, Quarto Publications - Encyclopaedia of ainting Techniques - Harper Collins publications. *Signs work:* "Naomi lexander." *Address:* 6 Bishops Ave., Hampstead, London N2 0AN.

**ALEXANDRI, Sara,** Dip. of Royal Academy of Fine Arts in Painting Florence, Italy); art teacher; landscape, flower and figure painter in oil and ater-colour; etcher; *b* Kherson, Russia, 22 Oct., 1913. *m* Michael Perkins. one *Educ:* High School, Palestine, and privately in Italy and Switzerland. *tudied:* Royal Inst. d'Arte, Florence, and Royal Academy of Fine Arts, lorence (1936-40, 1946-47). *Exhib:* R.A., R.B.A., W.I.A.C., R.W.A., Paris alon, foreign and main provincial galleries. *Signs work:* "S. ALEXANDRI" or S. Alexandri." *Address:* 28 Gensing Rd., St. Leonards-on-Sea, Sussex.

**ALFORD, John,** N.D.D., A.T.D., R.B.A., N.E.A.C.; painter in oil and ater-colour; Director of Art, Shrewsbury School (retd. 1989); *b* Tunbridge Vells, 14 Oct., 1929. *m* Jean. one *s.* two *d. Educ:* Reading School. *Studied:* amberwell School of Art (1949-53, Gilbert Spencer, Richard Eurich, Bernard unstan). *Exhib:* R.A., R.W.A., R.B.A., R.S.M.A., N.E.A.C.; numerous one-an shows in England, S. Africa, France, Canada. *Work in collections:* At ome and abroad, Reading A.G., Shropshire C.C. *Commissions:* several for the oyal Navy and Royal Canadian Navy. *Signs work:* "John Alford." *Address:* 7 Porthill Rd., Shrewsbury, Shropshire SY3 8RN.

**ALLCOCK, Annette,** painter in oil and gouache, greeting card designer, lustrator; *b* Bromley, Kent, 28 Nov., 1923. *m* James Allcock. one *s.* one *d. :duc:* various private schools. *Studied:* West of England College of Art Stanley Spencer). *Exhib:* R.A., R.W.A., Bath Contemporary Arts Fair. *Work in ollections:* Japan. *Publications:* work repro.: illustrating childrens books. igns work:* "Annette Allcock." *Address:* 22 South St., Corsham, Wilts. SN13 HB.

**ALLINSON, Sonya Madeleine,** M.F.P.S. (1989); artist in oil, acrylic, ouache, collage, pen and wash; *b* London. *Studied:* St. Martin's School of Art; andscape scholarship from R.A.; R.A. Schools. *Exhib:* one-man shows: ederation of British Artists, Cirencester Workshops, Everyman, Axiom entre for the Arts, Cheltenham, Sheffield; mixed: R.A., Leicester Galleries, .W.A., R.B.A., New English, Tooth's, Heal's, Brighton, Fosse, Manor House, )elahaye, Loggia, R.W.A., Bloomsbury, Anderson Galleries, Waterman Fine rt, Masters Fine Art, Bath, Gloucester City A.G. *Work in collections:* Britain, rance, Holland, Israel, U.S.A., S. America. *Clubs:* Cheltenham Group, F.P.S. igns work:* "Allinson" or "S.M. Allinson." *Address:* 13 Cleevemont, Evesham .d., Cheltenham GL52 3JT.

**ALLISON,, Jane,** 1st Class B.A. Hons. (1980), Slade Higher Dip. (1982); ortrait painter in oil/pastel; *b* Woking, 21 Mar., 1959. *m* John Tatchell reeman. one *s. Studied:* Chelsea School of Art (1977-80, Norman Blamey), lade School of Fine Art (1980-82). *Exhib:* B.P. Portrait Award, Royal Library, Vindsor Castle, St. Pancras Hospital, University of Surrey. *Commissions:* Sir

George Edwards, O.M., F.R.S., Lord Robens, Lord Mishcon, Sir Christophe
Collet, Prof. P.S. Boulter, Lord Nugent, etc. *Signs work:* "Jane Allison.
*Address:* 12 Sydney Rd., Guildford, Surrey GU1 3LJ.

**ALLSOPP, Bruce,** B.Arch. 1st Class Hons. (1933), A.R.I.B.A. (1935
A.M.T.P.I. (1938), F.R.I.B.A. (1955), F.S.A. (1968); author, painter an
designer; Chairman of the Society of Architectural Historians (1960); Master c
the Art Workers Guild (1970); Chairman of the Independent Publishers Guil
(1971); *b* Oxford, 4 July, 1912. *m* Florence Cyrilla Woodroffe, A.R.C.A
(decd.). two *s. Educ:* Manchester Grammar School. *Studied:* Liverpoc
University. *Exhib:* London and provincial galleries. *Clubs:* Athenaeum. *Sign*
*work:* "Bruce Allsopp" or "B.A.," the "A" lower than the "B." *Address*
Ferndale, Mount View, Stocksfield, Northumberland NE43 7HL.

**ALSOP, Roger Fleetwood,** S.G.F.A. (1991); painter in water-colour, cray
on, oil; *b* Skipton, 1946. *Educ:* Queen's Boys' Sec. Mod., Wisbech. *Studied*
Cambridge School of Art (1966-72). *Exhib:* Amalgam Gallery, Barnes, Ro
Miles Gallery, Zella Nine Gallery, Old Fire Engine House, Ely. *Commissions*
Medici Soc., Mercedes-Benz, Right Now magazine. *Signs work:* "Roge
Alsop." *Address:* 4 St. John's Villas, London N19 3EG.

**ALSOP, Will,** A.A.dip. (1973), S.A.D.G. (1973), William Van Allen Meda
(1972), Bernard Webb Rome Scholarship (1973); architect, artist, lecturer, vis
iting professor at Universities of Ball State Indiana, Royal Melbourne Institut
of Technology, New South Wales Institute of Technology, San Francisc
Institute of Art, Tulane New Orleans, Bremen Academy for Art and Music
Hannover University and currently Vienna University. Tutor in Sculpture, S
Martin's School of Art; *b* Northampton, 12 Dec., 1947. *m* Sheila Bean. *Studied*
Northampton School of Art (1967). Proprietor: Alsop & Störmer, Architects
*Clubs:* Reform. *Signs work:* "William Alsop." *Address:* 72 Pembroke Rd
London W8.

**AMBRUS, Victor Gyozo Laszio,** A.R.C.A. (1960), R.E. (1973), F.R.S.A
(1978); Library Assoc., Kate Greenaway Gold Medal (1966 and 1975); bool
illustrator, graphic designer; visiting lecturer, Graphic Design; *b* Budapest, 1*
Aug., 1935. *m* Glenys Rosemary, A.R.C.A. two *s. Educ:* St. Imre Gramma
School, Budapest. *Studied:* Hungarian Academy of Fine Art, Budapest; R.C.A.
London. *Exhib:* R.A., R.E., Biennale: Bratislava; Bologna, Italy, Belgium
Japan, Belgrade, New York. *Work in collections:* University of Souther
Mississippi, U.S.A.; Library of Congress, U.S.A.; O.U.P., London. Prizes: R.A
Arts' Club Prize (1996) Summer Exhbn.; P.S. Prize (1995); Daler Rowne
Prize; World Wildlife Prize (1994); Mall Galleries. *Publications:* The Roya
Navy, British Army, Royal Air Force, Merchant Navy, Three Poor Tailors
Brave Soldier Janos, The Little Cockerell, The Sultan's Bath, Hot Water fo
Boris, Country Wedding, Mishka, Horses in Battle, Under the Double Eagle
O.U.P.: Dracula (1980), Dracula's Bedtime Storybook (1982), and Blackbear
(1983) author and illustrator. *Signs work:* "V.G. Ambrus." *Address:* 5*

ooksbury Rd., Farnham, Surrey GU10 1QB.

**AMERY, Shenda,** A.R.B.S. (1984); sculptor in bronze; Council mem.
B.S.; *b* England, 1937. *m* Sheikh Nezam Khazal. two *s. Educ:* Municipal
ollege, Southend-on-Sea (H.N.C. chemistry). *Exhib:* R.A., Paris Salon, Mall
alleries, Locus Gallery, Osbourne Studio Gallery, Orangery, Holland Pk.,
hran Gallery, Iran, Kessel Long Gallery, Scottsdale, Ariz. *Commissions:*
rtrait bust : Rt. Hon. John Major M.P., Prime Minister, H.H. Queen Noor of
rdan, Baroness Thatcher, Prime Minister, Dr. Lee, King Hussein of Jordan,
e Earl of Bessborough, Sir Francis Dashwood, President Roh Tae Woo of S.
orea, Sir John Richards, Mayor Herb Drinkwater. *Clubs:* Arts. *Signs work:*
henda Amery." *Address:* 25a Edith Grove, London SW10 0LB.

**ANDERSON, Douglas Hardinge,** R.P.; portrait painter and wildlife artist in
ls; *b* 8 Aug., 1934. *m* Veronica née Markes. one *s.* two *d. Studied:* under
etro Annigoni in Florence. *Exhib:* R.P., R.A. Paintings in private collections
orldwide. *Clubs:* Turf. *Signs work:* "Douglas Anderson." *Address:* 56036
laia, (Pisa), Italy.

**ANDERSON, James,** B.A.; East of England art show Under-30 award
993); printmaker, painter, writer, teacher; *b* Cambridge, 3 Mar., 1965. *Educ:*
orcester College, Oxford. *Studied:* Central School of Art and Design. *Exhib:*
ixed and solo shows in Oxford, Bristol, London, Svendborg Denmark, Lvov
kraine. *Work in collections:* Museum of History of Religion, Lvov, Ukraine.
gns work: "J.W. ANDERSON." *Address:* 18c Digby Cres., London N4 2HR.

**ANDERSON, Margaret Denise,** A.R.M.S., H.S., M.M.A.S.; portrait and
imal painter of miniatures in water-colour and pastels; *b* Newport, Gwent, 29
ec., 1926. *m* Michael Anderson (decd.). two *s. Educ:* privately. *Studied:*
ewport Polytechnic (1944). *Exhib:* R.A., P.S., R.M.S. *Work in collections:*
ewellyn Alexander Galleries London, Beaulieu Fine Arts Beaulieu, Orchid
ne Arts Lymington. *Signs work:* "Margaret Anderson." *Address:* 314 Everton
d., Everton, nr. Lymington, Hants. SO41 0JX.

**ANDERTON, Eileen,** A.R.M.S., S.M., H.S., F.R.S.A.; Gold Medal (1981)
ccademia Italia delle Arti e del Lavoro, Gold plaque (1986) Premio d`Italia
arga Djoro; freelance artist in body-colour, water-colour, mixed media; *b*
radford, Yorks., 26 April, 1924. *Educ:* Bradford Girls' Grammar School.
udied: Bradford Art School (1939-44) under John Greenwood and Vincent
nes. *Exhib:* Cartwright Hall, Bradford, Wakefield, Halifax, S.W.A., Royal
ater-colour Soc. Gallery; one-man show at Bradford Library Gallery. *Work in
llections:* Bradford University. *Clubs:* Bradford Arts. *Signs work:* "E.
nderton." *Address:* 4 Braybrook Ct., Keighley Rd., Bradford BD8 7BH.

**ANDREW, Keith,** R.C.A. (1981); artist, painter/printmaker in water-colour,
mpera, etching; elected V.P. Royal Cambrian Academy (1993); *b* London, 26
n., 1947. *m* Rosemary. two *s. Educ:* Picardy Secondary, Erith, Kent. *Studied:*
avensbourne College of Art and Design (1963-67, Mike Tyzack, John
urgess). *Exhib:* R.A. Summer Exhbn. (1981), Mostyn A.G., Llandudno, Oriel

Cardiff (1982), Bangor A.G. (1982), Aberystwyth Arts Centre (198
Williamson A.G., Birkenhead (1982), National Eisteddfod Swansea (1982) a
Anglesey (1983), Oriel Mold (1983), Tegfryn Gallery, Anglesey (1983); gro
exhbn. 'Through Artists Eyes'. *Work in collections:* National Library of Wal
Contemporary Art Soc. for Wales, University of Wales, Amoco, Oce
Transport, British Gypsum, Milk Marketing Board. *Signs work:* "Ke
Andrew." *Address:* Gwyndy Bach, Llandrygarn, Tynlon P.O., Holyhea
Anglesey LL65 3AJ, Wales.

**ANDREWS, Carole,** S.B.A.; Founder Presidents Hon. Award S.B.
(1995); professional artist in water-colour; tutor for mid-Surrey Educ.;
Worcester Park, Surrey, 13 Jan., 1940. *m* Peter Leonard. two *d. Studied:* Sutt
College of Liberal Arts (Philip Meninsky, Ken Bates). *Exhib:* Mall Galleri
(1983-86), Westminster Central Hall (1986-95), The Guildhall, Londe
Alexandra Palace, Turner A.G., Denver, U.S.A. Work in private collectio
*Publications:* work repro.: Limited edn. and volume prints, illustration f
Coalport and Wedgwood porcelain. *Signs work:* "Carole Andrews." *Addre.*
129 Chapel Way, Epsom Downs, Epsom, Surrey KT18 5TB.

**ANDREWS, Marcia,** painter in oils; *b* London. *m* Edward Andrews. one
one *d. Educ:* St. Andrews; New City, London. *Exhib:* London, Mexico City a
Paris. *Work in collections:* University of Surrey; Medway Council Libra
Loan Service; private collections at home and abroad. *Signs work:* ")
ANDREWS," "M. Andrews" or "M.A." *Address:* 40 Robin Hood L.
Walderslade, Chatham, Kent ME5 9LD.

**ANDREWS, Mrs. Pauline Ann,** graphic artist and designer in Bournemou
; *b* Bournemouth, 4 Mar., 1968. *m* Jonathan Lawrence Andrews. *Edu.*
Stourfield and Beaufort Schools, Bournemouth. Work includes book illust
tion, leaflet, poster, card and badge design and production in addition to norm
commercial work. Also undertakes drawings and sketches as Fine art. *Addre.*
99 Carbery Ave., Southbourne, Bournemouth BH6 3LP.

**ANGADI, Patricia,** artist in oil; *b* Hampstead, 23 Sept., 1914. *m* Aya
Angadi, Indian author and lecturer. three *s.* one *d. Educ:* Prior's Fie
Godalming. *Studied:* Heatherleys (1933-37). *Exhib:* R.P., W.I.A.C., S.W.A
R.B.A., R.O.I., Goupil Galleries, Paris Salon, N.E.A.C., Utd. Artists, Camd
Arts Centre. *Work in collections:* Portraits of James Maxton, M.P., by Glasgo
People's Gallery, C. E. M. Joad by Birkbeck College, Baron Reuter by Reute
Press Museum, Aachen. *Publications:* novels: The Governess, The Do
Thing, The Highly Flavoured Ladies, Sins of the Mothers, Playing for Re
Turning the Turtle (Gollancz). *Signs work:* "Angadi" in red. *Address:* 3.
Belsize Park, London NW3 4DX.

**ANGEL, Marie,** A.R.C.A. (1948); calligrapher, illustrator; *b* 1923. *Edu.*
Croydon School of Art (1940-45), R.C.A. Design School (1945-48). *Exhi.*
R.A., S.S.I., and widely in U.S.A.; one-man shows: San Francisco (1967), Ca
del Libro (1975). *Work in collections:* Harvard College Library, Hunt Botanic

ibrary, Casa del Libro, San Francisco Library and V. & A. *Publications:* A
estiary, A New Bestiary, Two Poems by Emily Dickinson, An Animated
lphabet (Harvard); illustrated: The Tale of The Faithful Dove, The Tale of
uppenny by Beatrix Potter; Catscript, Cherub Cat, Angel Tiger; author: The
rt of Calligraphy, Painting for Calligraphy. *Signs work:* "Marie Angel,"
Angel" or "M.A." *Address:* Silver Ley, 33 Oakley Rd., Warlingham, Surrey
R6 9BE.

**ANNAND, David,** sculptor in clay, bronze resin, bronze, mixed media; *b*
sch, Aberdeenshire, 30 Jan., 1948. *m* Jean. one *s.* one *d. Educ:* Perth
cademy. *Studied:* Duncan of Jordanstone College of Art, Dundee (Scott
utherlands). *Exhib:* Royal Scottish Academy, Open Eye, Edinburgh, etc. *Work*
 *collections:* throughout the world, including Edinburgh, Dundee, Perth,
anberra, Wisconsin, Hong Kong. *Commissions:* "Deer Leap" Dundee
echnology Pk.; "Man Feeding Seagulls" Glasgow Gdn. Festival; "Grey
eron" Edinburgh Botanic Gdns.; "Cranes" British High Commission Hong
ong; "Naeday Sae Dark", Perth. Awards: Royal Scottish Academy: Latimer
976), Benno Schotz (1978), Ireland Alloys (1982); Sir Otto Beit medal,
.B.A. (1987). *Signs work:* "David A. Annand," a tiny frog on a lily leaf.
ddress: Pigscrave Cottage, The Wynd, Kilmany Cupar, Fife KY15 4PU.

**ANSCHLEE:** see SCHLEE, Anne H.

**ANSELMO, (Anselmo Francesconi),** painter in oil, acrylic on canvas,
rawing and etching, sculptor in clay for bronze; *b* Lugo (Ravenna), Italy, 29
ly, 1921. *m* Margherita Francesconi. *Educ:* Lugo. *Studied:* Liceo Artistico,
avenna; School of Fine Art, Bologna; Brera, Milan. *Exhib:* one-man shows:
atherine Viviano, N.Y., Engelberths, Geneva, Galleria d'Eendt, Amsterdam,
usée d'Art et d'Histoire, Geneva, Fine Art Faculty, University of Teheran,
an, Galleria Toninelli, Milan, Galleria Giulia, Rome, Bedford House Gallery,
ondon, stained glass windows and murals for two churches - Canton de
riburg, Switzerland, Mussavi Art Center, N.Y., Fante di Spade, Milano,
useum of Bagnacavallo, Museum of Bulle, Switzerland, Palazzo Trisi - Lugo,
alazzo Corradini, Ravenna, etc. *Work in collections:* Musée d'Art et
Histoire, Geneva; Musée Cantonale de Lausanne; Cabinet delle Stampe,
astello Sforzesco, Milan; Museum of Fine Art, N.Y.; Museum of Fine Art,
uffalo. *Signs work:* "Anselmo." *Address:* 8b Berkeley Gdns., London W8
AP.

**APPELBEE, Leonard,** A.R.C.A. (1938); artist in oils, wood-engraver, lith-
grapher and writer of verse; *b* London, 13 Nov., 1914. *m* Frances Macdonald,
ainter. one *d. Studied:* Goldsmiths' College (1931-35, Clive Gardner), R.C.A.
935-38, Barnett Freedman). *Exhib:* Wildenstein (1947), Leicester Galleries
948, 1951, 1955, 1962), Fine Art Soc. (1968), Plymouth City A.G. (1977),
.A., Scottish Academy, Welsh Academy, Salon 1970 (silver medal). *Work in*
ollections: Tate Gallery; National Galleries of N.S.W. and Victoria, Australia;
berdeen, Carlisle, Southport, Preston, Reading, Newport, Coventry galleries;

Arts Council; M. of S.; M. of W.; Contemporary Art Soc., British Council, e¹ *Publications:* published, designed and illustrated, book of verse 'That Voic (1980). At present, painting landscape, portrait, etc. *Signs work:* "LEONAR APPELBEE", from 1971 "APPELBEE." *Address:* Rosemount, Toll R‹ Kincardine-on-Forth, Fife FK10 4QZ.

AP **RHYS PRYCE, Vivien Mary,** F.R.B.S.; sculptor in modelling clay a¹ wax for bronze; *b* Woking, 1 Nov., 1937. *Educ:* Claremont School, Esh‹ Surrey. *Studied:* City and Guilds of London Art School. *Exhib:* R.A., R.W.*/* Jonathan Poole Gallery, London, and various provincial galleries. *Work in cc lections:* National Gallery of New Zealand, Wellington, University of Exe¹ (water sculpture), Nymans Gdns., Handcross, Sussex (fountain). *Signs wor* Impress of signet ring (Lion's head). *Address:* 15 North St., Calne, Wilts. SN¹ 0HQ.

**ARCHAMBAULT, Louis,** sculptor, B.A. (1936), D.E.B.A. (193⁹ R.A.I.C. Allied Arts Medal (1958), O.C. (1968), R.C.A. (1968), C.C.*/* Diplôme d'honneur (1982); *b* Montreal, 4 Apr., 1915. *m* Mariette Provost. fo¹ children. Teaching career: Musée des Beaux-Arts, Montreal; Ecole des Beau⁻ Arts, Montreal; University of British Columbia, Vancouver; Université ‹ Québec, Montreal; Concordia University, Montreal. *Exhib:* group: Festiva Britain (1951), 10th and 11th Milan (1954-57), XXVIIIth Venice (195⁶ Brussels Universal (1958), Pittsburgh International (1958), Montreal Expo 6 300 Years of Canadian Art, National Gallery, Ottawa (1967), etc.; one-ma Canada, France, England. *Work in collections:* National Gallery, Ottaw. Musée du Québec, Quebec City; Musée d'art contemporain and Musée d‹ Beaux Arts, Montreal; Art Gallery of Ontario, Toronto; Winnipeg A.G Winnipeg; Museo Internazionale della Ceramica, Faenza, Italy; Sun Life buil‹ ing, Quebec City; Place des Arts, Montreal; Malton Airport, Toront‹ Scarborough College, Toronto; Macdonald Block, Queen's Park, Toront‹ Federal Food and Drug building, Longueuil, Quebec; Canadian Imperial Bar of Commerce, Montreal; Canada Council Art Bank, Ottawa; Justice Cou building, Quebec City, etc. *Commissions:* Canadian Pavilion, Brussells (1958 Canadian Pavilion, Expo 67, Montreal, etc. *Signs work:* "Louis Archambault *Address:* 278 Sanford Ave., St. Lambert, Quebec, Canada J4P 2X6.

**ARCHER, Cyril James,** R.I.; self taught artist in water-colour; retd. comp‹ ny director; *b* London, 7 Aug., 1928. *m* Betty. two *s. Educ:* West Ha¹ Municipal College. *Exhib:* numerous galleries in London, south of Englan‹ also one-man shows. *Work in collections:* England, U.S.A., Canada, Midd‹ and Far East, Japan. Limited Editions etc. *Clubs:* Sussex Water-colour So‹ *Signs work:* "ARCHER." *Address:* 4 Willowbrook Way, Hassocks, W. Susse BN6 8QD.

**ARCHER, Frank Joseph,** R.W.S. (1976), R.E. (1960), A.R.C.A. (193⁷ Rome Scholar (1938); painter in oil, water-colour, tempera, etching; Retd Head, School of Fine Art, Kingston College of Art/Polytechnic;

Walthamstow, 1912. *m* Celia Cole. one *s.* one *d. Educ:* Eastbourne Grammar School. *Studied:* Eastbourne School of Art, Brighton College of Art, R.C.A., British School at Rome. *Exhib:* R.A., R.W.S., R.E., London and provincial galleries. *Work in collections:* Whitworth, Manchester, Rochdale, Graves, Eastbourne. *Signs work:* "Frank Archer." *Address:* Flat 1 Stonydown, 8 Milnthorpe Rd., Eastbourne, E. Sussex.

**ARCHER, Patricia Margaret Alice,** Slade Dip., A.T.D., F.M.A.A.; retd. medical artist in various media; Head of Dept. of Medical Illustration, Guy's Hospital Medical School (1964-83); *b* London. *Educ:* Convent Collegiate School, Sacred Heart of Mary, Chilton, Bucks. *Studied:* Ruskin School of Drawing, Slade School of Fine Art (1944-47), Inst. of Education, London (1947-48). *Exhib:* Medical Artists' Assoc., London (1952, 1964, 1970, 1989, 1993); one-man shows, London Hospital (1955), Medical Picture Show, Science Museum (1978). *Publications:* illustrated books on medicine and surgery. *Clubs:* Fellow, Medical Artists' Assoc., Hon. Sec. (1964-68), Chairman (1984-86) and (1990-93), Vice-Chairman (1986-1988) and (1993-1995), Archivist (1986-); Founder Associate, Inst. of Medical Illustrators (1969). *Signs work:* "ARCHER." *Address:* Rangemore, Park Ave., Caterham, Surrey CR3 6AH.

**ARDAGH, Elisabeth (now Mrs. Tredgett),** elected Hon. Senior mem. R.O.I. (1994); artist in oil, acrylic, gouache; *b* Brighouse, Yorks., 26 Mar., 1915. *m* L.V. Ardagh (decd.). one *d. Educ:* Godolphin School, Salisbury. *Studied:* Farnham (1934-36), Otway McCannel), Chelsea Polytechnic (1936-37, sculpture under Henry Moore), Wimbledon (1937-39, painting under Gerald Cooper). *Exhib:* F.P.S., N.S., R.O.I., R.A. *Clubs:* Overseas. *Signs work:* "Ardagh." *Address:* 40 Orchard Ave., Chichester, W. Sussex PO19 3BG.

**ARDIZZONE, Charlotte,** N.E.A.C., N.D.D., R.W.A., Byam Shaw Dip. (1st); artist in oil; *b* London, 24 Oct., 1943. one *d. Educ:* Rye St. Antony School, Oxford. *Studied:* Byam Shaw Art School under Maurice de Sausmarez. *Exhib:* one-man shows: Blond Fine Art, Bohun Gallery, Curwen Gallery, Drian Gallery, Sally Hunter Fine Art. *Work in collections:* National Gallery, Australia, National Gallery, Warsaw, Dublin University, Nuffield Foundation. *Clubs:* N.E.A.C., R.W.A. *Signs work:* "Charlotte Ardizzone," and "CA" joined. *Address:* The Old School, Whinburgh, Norfolk NR19 1QR.

**ARKLESS, Lesley Graham,** B.A. Hons.; painter/illustrator in oil, gouache, water-colour; M.A. Museums and Galleries in Education (1993); Head of Education, Design Museum, London; *b* Northumberland, 30 Jan., 1956. *m* John M. Butterworth. two *s.* one *d. Educ:* Church High School for Girls, Newcastle-upon-Tyne. *Studied:* West Surrey College of Art and Design (1974-78). *Exhib:* Ash Barn Gallery, Petersfield, St. Edmund's Art Centre, Salisbury, National Museum of Wales, 'Pictures for Schools', Astoria Theatre, London, Le Havre Municipal Gallery, Sanderson's Gallery, London. *Publications:* author and illustrator: 'What Stanley Knew' (Andersen Press, London). *Signs work:* "LES-

LEY ARKLESS." *Address:* 2 Nun's Walk, Winchester, Hants.

**ARLOTT, Norman Arthur,** S.WL.A.; freelance wildlife illustrator in water-colour, author; *b* 15 Nov., 1947. *m* Marie Ellen. one *s.* two *d. Educ:* Stoneham Boys School. *Exhib:* Annual S.WL.A., London, widely in U.K., also U.S.A. *Publications:* over fifty, including Norman Arlott's Bird Paintings, and many commonwealth stamp issues, i.e. Bahamas, Jamaica, British Virgin Islands. *Signs work:* "Norman Arlott." *Address:* Hill House, School Rd., Tilney St. Lawrence, Norfolk PE34 4RB.

**ARMFIELD, Diana M. (Mrs. Bernard Dunstan),** A.R.A. (1989), R.A. (1991), R.C.A. (Wales) (1992), M.C.S.D., Hon. P.S., N.E.A.C., R.W.A., R.W.S.; painter, retired textile and wallpaper designer; taught at Central School, and Byam Shaw Art School; *b* Ringwood, Hants, 1920. *m* Bernard Dunstan, R.A. three *s. Educ:* Bedales, Slade School, Central School. *Studied:* Bournemouth Art School. *Exhib:* Festival of Britain; one-man shows, Browse and Darby, National Eisteddfod Wales, Albany Gall. Cardiff, U.S.A. etc. *Work in collections:* V. & A., R.W.A., Govt. picture collection, Contemporary Art Soc. for Wales, National Trust, Reuters, Yale Centre for British Art, Faringdon Collection, B.M., H.R.H. Prince of Wales, Lancaster City Gallery, Mercury Asset Management Collection. *Commissions:* H.R.H. Prince of Wales, Reuters. *Publications:* The Art of Diana Armfield by Julian Halsby (David & Charles, 1995). Artist in Residence: Perth (1985), Jackson Hole, U.S.A. (1989). *Clubs:* Arts. *Signs work:* "D.M.A." *Address:* 10 High Park Rd., Kew, Richmond, Surrey TW9 4BN.

**ARMITAGE, Joshua Charles,** freelance artist in black and white and colour; *b* Hoylake, Cheshire, 26 Sept., 1913. *m* Catherine Mary Buckle (decd.). two *d. Studied:* Liverpool School of Art (1929-36). *Work in collections:* twelve water-colour drawings for the United Oxford and Cambridge University Club. *Publications:* work repro.: Punch, The Countryman, etc. 100th Open Championship at Royal Birkdale and illustrations for many books for adults and for children. Many water-colour drawings with golf as the subject. Long association with Penguin Books editions of P.G. Wodehouse. *Clubs:* Royal Liverpool Golf. *Signs work:* "Ionicus." *Address:* 34 Avondale Rd., Hoylake, Cheshire L47 3AS.

**ARMITAGE, Kenneth,** C.B.E. (1969); sculptor; *b* 18 July, 1916. *Exhib:* works shown in North and South America, France, Italy, Germany, Austria, Yugoslavia, Malta, Cyprus, Gibraltar, Israel, Lebanon, Ethiopia, Spain, Portugal, Australia, New Zealand, Sarawak, Sebah, Malaysia, Singapore, Bermuda, Jamaica, Trinidad, Cuba, Argentina, Peru, Venezuela, Chile, Brazil, Japan, Finland, Norway, Sweden, Denmark, Poland. Works in major public collections throughout the world. *Address:* 22a Avonmore Rd., London W14 8RR.

**ARMOUR, Mary,** A.R.S.A. (1941), R.S.W. (1956), R.S.A. (1958), R.G.I. (1977), LL.D. (Glasgow) 1982; Hon. Pres.: Glasgow School of Art (1982),

Royal Glasgow Inst. (1983); Hon. Fellowship: Paisley University (1989), Glasgow School of Art (1993); P.A.I. (1995); artist in oil, water-colour; *b* Blantyre, Lanarkshire, 27 Mar., 1902. *m* William Armour. *Educ:* Low Blantyre Public School; Hamilton Academy. *Studied:* Glasgow School of Art under D. Forrester Wilson, R.S.A., Maurice Grieffenhagen, R.A. (1920-25). *Exhib:* R.A., R.S.A., S.S.A., Royal Glasgow Institute. *Work in collections:* Glasgow Municipal Gallery, Greenock A.G., Victoria (Australia), Paisley A.G., Aberdeen A.G., Perth A.G., Edinburgh A.G. *Publications:* work repro.:The Studio. *Signs work:* "Mary Armour." *Address:* Priory Park Residential Home, 19 Main Rd., Castlehead, Paisley PA2 6AJ.

**ARN or ARNEAL:** see NEAL, Arthur Richard.

**ARNETT, Joe Anna,** painter in oil; *b* Texas. *m* James D. Asher. *Educ:* Baylor University and University of Texas. *Studied:* Art Students' League, N.Y. (1979-83), University of Texas (1970-72). *Exhib:* Salmagundi Club, American Artist Professional League, Artists of America, Denver (1988, 1995), Katherine Lorillard Woolfe Art Club, Catto Gallery, London (1987-92), Zaplin-Lampert Gallery, Santa Fe, N.M., Art Asia (1994) Hong Kong. *Signs work:* "J.A. Arnett." *Address:* P.O. Box 8022, Santa Fe, New Mexico 87504-8022, U.S.A.

**ARNOLD, Gordon C.,** A.R.C.A.; artist in water-colour; *b* Sheffield, 30 Mar., 1910. *Studied:* Liverpool School of Art (Will Penn, R.O.I., R.P., R.C.A., G. Wedgwood, R.E.). *Exhib:* one-man shows: Birkenhead A.G., Warrington A.G., Bootle A.G., Wrexham Library, Weaver Gallery, Weaverham, Pratts Hotel, Bath, etc. *Work in collections:* Williamson A.G., Birkenhead, Warrington A.G., Liverpool Corp. Library, etc. *Signs work:* "Gordon Arnold." *Address:* 58 Fairfield Terr., Newton Abbot, Devon TQ12 2LH.

**ARNOLD, Phyllis Anne,** R.M.S. (1988), A.R.M.S. (1983), S.M. (1976-86), U.S.W.A. (1982), P.U.S.W.A. (1988-91), P.U.S.M. (1987-93), U.W.S. (1984), H.S. (1985); miniaturist, artist in water-colour, ink and gouache; Hunting Group finalist (1980, 1981, 1983), R.M.S. Memorial Gold Bowl (1988); *b* Belfast, 1938. *m* Michael J. Arnold, C.Eng. two *s*. *Educ:* Victoria College, Wallace High School. *Studied:* self taught, entered Commercial Art Dept. Short Bros & Harland (1956-58). *Exhib:* S.M., R.M.S., R.A., U.S.W.A., H.S., U.W.S., R.U.A. *Work in collections:* Ulster Museum, Belfast. *Signs work:* "P.A. ARNOLD" or "P.A.A." for miniatures, see appendix. *Address:* Phyllis Arnold Studio, Deepwell House, Lowry Hill, Bangor, Co. Down, N. Ireland.

**ARNUP, Sally,** A.R.C.A. (1954); sculptor in bronze; *b* London, 15 July, 1930. *m* Mick Arnup, A.R.C.A. two *s*. two *d*. *Studied:* Kingston School of Art (1943-50, H. Parker), Camberwell School of Art (1951, Dr. Vogel), Royal College of Art (1952-55, John Skeaping). *Exhib:* Tryon Gallery (1973, 1976, 1981), U.S.A. (1977, 1980, 1986, 1987), Drobak Norway (1976), Wexford Festival (1974, 1978, 1982, 1986), York Festival (1969, 1976, 1978, 1980, 1984, 1988, 1992), Florence (1983), Edinburgh Festival (1988), Stamford Art

Centre (1987, 1990), Holland & Holland (Paris, London 1994, 1995). *Work in collections:* H.M. The Queen, Burton Agnes. *Clubs:* R.B.S. *Signs work:* "ARNUP." *Address:* Studios Holtby, York YO1 3UA.

**ARRIDGE, Margaret Irene Chadwick,** N.S. (1988), F.S.B.A. (1988), A.R.M.S.; artist in water-colour, pastel, oil, private teacher; *b* Salisbury, Wilts., 13 Feb., 1921. *m* I.M.C. Farquharson, M.A., F.I.A. one *s. Educ:* Croydon High School. *Studied:* Chelsea School of Art (Bernard Adams, Violet Butler, miniaturist). *Exhib:* R.A., Paris Salon, Mall Galleries; one-man shows Johannesburg. *Signs work:* "M. Arridge." *Address:* 5 Dudley Rd., Parkwood, Johannesburg 2193, S.A.

**ARTHUR, Harry H. Gascoign,** F.L.A. (1948), F.R.S.A. (1949), F.I.Mgt. (1974), Mem. Museums Assoc. (1949); lecturer, writer and broadcaster on the arts; W.E.A. lecturer on art, architecture and art history; Director of Libraries, Museums and Arts, Wirral (1974-80); formerly held libraries and arts posts at Bath, Bristol and Blackpool; Librarian and Curator, Buxton (1949-50), Director of Libraries and Arts, Wigan (1950-68), Borough Librarian and Director, Williamson A.G. and Museum, Birkenhead (1968-74); *b* Bristol, 30 June, 1920. *m* Kathleen Joan Fuge. one *s.* one *d. Educ:* Bristol Cathedral School. *Studied:* West of England College of Art. *Publications:* History of Haigh Hall; Guide to the Williamson A.G. and Museum; Guide to the Wirral Maritime Museum; Lee Tapestry Room. *Address:* 20 Christchurch Rd., Oxton, Birkenhead, Wirral, Merseyside L43 5SF.

**ASCHAN, Marit Guinness,** enamellist and painter; President, Artist Enamellers since foundation 1968; *m* C. W. Aschan. one *s.* one *d. Exhib:* R.A., Leicester Galleries, Lincoln Center, N.Y., Worshipful Company of Goldsmiths, etc.; one-man shows, Beaux Arts, International Faculty of Arts, The Leicester Galleries, Roy Miles, Saga Gallery, London; The Minories, Colchester; Lilienfeld Gallery and Van Diemen-Lilienfeld Galleries, Bodley Gallery, N.Y.; Waldhorn Company Inc., New Orleans; Galerie J. Kraus, Paris; Inter Art Gallery, Caracas, Venezuela; Oslo Kunstforening, Galleri Galtung, Oslo; etc. *Work in collections:* V. & A., central enamel of Louis Osman Cross, Exeter Cathedral; Worshipful Company of Goldsmiths, London; Oppé Coll., Brooklyn Museum; New York University Art Coll.; Fordham University Art Coll.; Yale University A.G.; Nelson Gallery and Atkins Museum, Kansas; North Carolina State Museum of Art, Raleigh; Rochester A.G., N.Y.; University of Kansas Museum of Art, New Orleans Museum of Art; Parrish Art Museum, Southampton, N.Y.; Weatherspoon A.G., University of North Carolina; Finch College A.G.; The Housatonic Museum, Bridgeport, Connecticut; The Snite Museum of Notre Dame University; The Ian Woodner Family Collection, N.Y.; The Royal Norwegian Embassy, London; Kunstindustrimuseet, Hans Rasmus Astrup Coll. Oslo, etc. *Clubs:* Chelsea Arts. *Address:* (residence) 25 Chelsea Park Gdns., London SW3; (studio) Moravian Close, 381 King's Rd., London SW10.

**ASHBY, Derek Joseph,** D.A. (Edin.); artist in oil painting and steel and aluminium; lecturer in drawing and painting, Gray's School of Art, Aberdeen; *b* 24 June, 1926. *m* Mairi Catriona. one *s*. one *d*. *Educ:* Oldham High School. *Studied:* Edinburgh College of Art (1948-51) under Gillies, Henderson, Blyth; R.A. Schools (1953-55) under Rushbury. *Exhib:* R.S.A., Aberdeen Artists, S.S.A. *Work in collections:* Scottish Arts Council. *Clubs:* A.A.S., S.S.A. *Signs work:* "Derek Ashby." *Address:* Old Invery, Auchattie, Banchory, Kincardineshire AB31 6PR.

**ASHE, Faith:** see WINTER, Faith.

**ASHER, James,** artist in water-colour, oil, lithograph; *b* Butler, Missouri, 14 Apr., 1944. *m* Joe Anna Arnett. one *s*. one *d*. *Educ:* Central Missouri University. *Studied:* The Art Center College of Design, Los Angeles, Calif. *Exhib:* Catto Gallery, London, Zaplin-Lampert Gallery, Santa Fe, N.M., Artists of America, Denver (1991-1995). *Signs work:* "James Asher." *Address:* P.O. Box 8022, Santa Fe, New Mexico 87504-8022, U.S.A.

**ASHMORE, Lady, Patricia,** P.S. (1953); landscape and portrait painter in pastel, oil and water-colour; *b* Horsham, 13 July, 1929. *m* Vice Admiral Sir Peter Ashmore. one *s*. three *d*. *Educ:* North Foreland Lodge. *Studied:* Chelsea Polytechnic (portrait painting with Sonia Mervyn). *Exhib:* Pastel Exhbn. (annually), Women Artists, Sussex Artists Assoc. (member and exhibitor), Kentish Artists Annual Exhbn. for Charities. *Signs work:* "Patricia Ashmore." *Address:* Netherdowns, Sundridge, Sevenoaks, Kent TN14 6AR.

**ASHTON-BOSTOCK, David A.,** F.I.A.L. (1960), N.D. (1950), intermed. (1949); artist in oil and interior decorator; Fellow of I.D.D.A. Ltd.; *b* London, 17 Feb., 1930. *m* Victoria Rosamond White (divorced). one *d*. *Educ:* Wellington College. *Studied:* Maidstone College of Art (1947-50) under A. G. Cary and W. Eade, Byam Shaw School of Art (1953-54) under P. E. Philips. *Exhib:* United Artists, Nat. Soc., R.B.A., N.E.A.C., R.O.I., Paris Salon, Summer Salon, Chelsea Artists, City of London Artists, Ridley Art Club, Hambledon Galleries (Blandford). *Publications:* work repro.: La Revue Moderne, Queen, Country Life, Times, Sunday Express, Christmas cards, posters. *Signs work:* "Ashtock." *Address:* Danes Bottom Place, Wormshill, nr. Sittingbourne, Kent ME9 0TS; 28 Sutherland St., London SW1V 4LA.

**ASSHETON-STONES, Christopher John ,** P.S.; painter in pastel, designer, lecturer; Council mem. Pastel Soc.; *b* Ceylon, 19 Apr., 1947. *m* Penelope Barlow. one *d*. *Educ:* Shrewsbury School, Keele University. *Studied:* Exeter College of Art, Bournemouth and Poole College of Art. *Exhib:* Paris Salon, R.W.A., R.O.I., R.S.M.A., P.S., etc. *Publications:* author of Working with Pastel, and Towns and Buildings in Pastel (published in G.B., U.S.A. and Australia); Video publications: Discovering Pastel; Developing Pastel; Instruction videos: Discovering Pastel and Developing Pastel. *Signs work:* "CJA-STONES" and date. *Address:* The Lane Hall, Weasdale, Newbiggin-on-Lune, Kirkby Stephen, Cumbria CA17 4LY.

# WHO'S WHO IN ART

**ATHERTON, Barry,** N.D.D., D.A. (Manc.) Dist. (1965), Leverhulme Scholarship (1965-66), R.A.S.Cert. (1969); artist in mixed media; Lecturer in Fine Art, Glasgow School of Art; *b* England, 1944. *m* Linda. two *s. Studied:* Manchester College of Art and Design (Norman Adams), R.A. Schools (Edward Bawden). *Exhib:* New Academy Gallery (1990, 1992, 1994, 1997), Mistral Galleries (1996). *Work in collections:* Aberdeen A.G., University of Strathclyde, Glasgow Caledonian University, also private and corporate collections. *Clubs:* N.E.A.C., S.S.A. *Signs work:* no signature, identification on the back. *Address:* 235 Nithsdale Rd., Glasgow G41 5PY.

**ATKIN, Ann,** *b* Lindfi0eld, Sussex, 1937. graduate of Brighton College of Art and Royal Academy Schools. Founded The Gnome Reserve in N. Devon in 1979, followed shortly by The Wild Flower Garden. Organic abstract paintings celebrating nature and life. *Exhib:* Young Contemporaries, R.A. Summer Exhbn.; solo show: Beaford Centre. *Work in collections:* Dartington Hall Trust (Oct. 1992). Paintings discussed on ''Hayes on Saturday' Radio 2 (May 1993), and shown on GMTV (May 1993 and March 1995). To be included in The Guinness Book of Records (1998). *Signs work:* see appendix. *Address:* Warren Cottage, Abbots Bickington, N. Devon EX22 7LQ.

**ATKIN, Peter,** U.A. (1968); artist in water-colour; Past President, Northampton Town and Country Art Soc.; *b* Wallasey, 16 Aug., 1926. *m* Joyce Wood. one *s.* one *d. Educ:* Stamford School, Lincolnshire; no formal art training, instruction from the late Wilfred R. Wood of Barnack, nr. Stamford. *Exhib:* R.B.A., R.I., U.A., Britain in Water-colour, N.S.; one-man shows, York Galleries and Municipal Gallery, Northampton, Savage Fine Art, Northampton. *Signs work:* "PETER ATKIN." *Address:* 1 High St., Collingtree, Northampton NN4 0NE.

**ATKIN, Ron,** F.R.S.A.; painter in water-colour and oil; *b* Leics., 3 Feb., 1938. *Studied:* Loughborough College of Art (1954-57), R.A. Schools (1957-61). *Exhib:* regularly at R.A.; mixed shows: Roland, Browse and Delbanco. *Work in collections:* Lincoln College Oxford, Dartington Trust, Devon C.C. Schools Museum Service, Alexander Theatre, B'ham, Plymouth City Museum and A.G. Shortlisted for a Gulbenkian Printmakers award; featured in first and second edition of Dictionary of British Art Volume VI, 20th century painters and sculptors; also in Debrett's. *Signs work:* "Atkin" or "Ron Atkin." *Address:* Wild Flower Cottage, Abbots Bickington, Devon EX22 7LQ.

**ATKINSON, Anthony,** A.R.C.A. (1954); painter in oil; Dean, Colchester Inst.; *b* 1929. *m* Joan Dawson. one *s.* one *s-d. Educ:* Wimbledon College. *Studied:* Royal College of Art. *Exhib:* R.A., Leicester Galleries; one-man: Minories, Colchester, Leighton House, London, Gainsborough's House, Sudbury, Mercury Theatre, Colchester, British Council, Kuwait, Phoenix, Lavenham, Coach-House Gallery, Guernsey, Phoenix, Highgate, Hayletts, Colchester, Chappel Gallery. *Work in collections:* Essex Museum; Ernst & Young; Essex C.C, Colchester Hospital, etc. *Publications:* work repro.: Shell,

London Transport, G.P.O. *Signs work:* "ATKINSON." *Address:* Coach House, Great Horkesley, Colchester, Essex CO6 4AX.

**ATKINSON, Eric Newton,** N.E.A.C., R.C.A.; painter in oils and collage; Nat. Dipl. (1st hons., painting), R.A. Drawing Medal, Silver Medal for Painting; Dean, Faculty of Arts, Fanshawe College, London, Canada; *b* W. Hartlepool, 23 July, 1928. *m* Muriel H. Ross. one *s.* one *d. Educ:* Dyke House, W. Hartlepool. *Studied:* W. Hartlepool College of Art and R.A. Schools. *Exhib:* Redfern Gallery, Tate Gallery, Austin Hayes, York, Leeds Univ., Wakefield and Middlesbrough city galleries, Zwemmer Gallery, Corcoran Gallery, Rothman Gallery, Kingpitcher Gallery, Capponi Gallery, Pollock Gallery, Mendal Gallery, Carnegie Mellon, U.S.A. *Work in collections:* National Portrait Gallery, Contemporary Art Soc., M. of W., Leeds, Leicester, Wakefield, Hereford and Kendal A.G., Leeds City A.G. Collection, McIntosh Gallery U.W.O., Government Art Collection, U.K. *Signs work:* "Eric Atkinson." *Address:* 69 Paddock Green Cres., London N6J-3P6, Ontario, Canada.

**ATKINSON, Kim,** M.A. (R.C.A.) (1987); S.W.L.A. (1992); artist in water-colour, oil, printmaking, drawing; *b* Bath, 1962; partner Gwydion Morley. *Studied:* Falmouth School of Art (Foundation); Cheltenham College of Art (B.A. Painting); Royal College of Art (M.A. Natural History Illustration). *Exhib:* Wales, England, Europe, America. *Publications:* Birds in Wales (Poyser, 1994) (illustrations); chapter in Watercolour Masterclass by Lawrence Wood (Collins, 1993). *Signs work:* "Kim Atkinson." *Address:* Ty'n Gamdda, Uwchmynydd, Pwllheli, Gwynedd LL53 8DA.

**ATKINSON, Ted,** D.F.A. (Lond., 1952), R.E. (1988), F.R.B.S., F.R.S.A. (1957), Slade Prize Winner (1952); sculptor; Head of Sculpture School, Coventry University (1968-83); *b* Liverpool, 21 Mar., 1929. *Educ:* Oulton School, Liverpool. *Studied:* Liverpool College of Art and Slade School, Slade Post-graduate Scholar (1952-53). *Work in collections:* Arts Council, London, Ashmolean Museum, Oxford, Dallas Art Museum, Kunst Academie, Dresden, Fitzwilliam Museum, Cambridge, Museum of Modern Art, N.Y., Seattle Art Museum, etc.; public sculptures in Coventry, Dusseldorf, Hamburg, Univ. Birmingham. One of six sculptors chosen to represent Britain at Expo 88 Brisbane. *Address:* 4 De Vere Pl., Wivenhoe, Essex CO7 9AX.

**ATTREE, Jake (Jonathan),** Dip.A.D. (Painting) (1972), R.A. Schools Post-Grad. Cert. (1977); Landseer prize, Creswick prize, David Murray Scholarship; painter; *b* York, 13 Oct., 1950. *m* Lindsay Knight. *Educ:* Danesmead, York. *Studied:* York College of Art (1966-68), Liverpool College of Art (1969-72), R.A. Schools (1974-77). *Exhib:* regular one person and group shows include R.A. Summer Exhbn. (1975, 1985), Serpentine Summer (1982), Maastricht, Dortmund (1992), Leeds City A.G. (1993), Michael Richardson Contemporary Art, London, Dean Clough Halifax (1994). *Work in collections:* Leeds City Council, City of Dortmund, Grays A.G. Hartlepool, Sheffield University,

Nuffield Trust. *Publications:* illustrated At This Time and The Purblind Man by John Holmes. Studio: Dean Clough, Halifax HX3 5AX. *Signs work:* usually unsigned, unless requested, then "J. Attree." *Address:* 33 Titus St., Saltaire, Shipley BD18 4LU.

**AUERBACH, Frank Helmut,** painter; *b* Berlin, 29 Apr., 1931. *Educ:* privately. *Studied:* St. Martin's School of Art; R.C.A. *Exhib:* one-man shows: Beaux-Arts Gallery (1956, 1959, 1961, 1962, 1963); Marlborough Fine Art (1965, 1967, 1971, 1974, 1983, 1987, 1990, 1997); Marlborough, N.Y. (1969, 1982, 1994); retrospective, Hayward Gallery (1978), Venice Biennale (1986) (joint winner Golden Lion), Hamburg (1986), Essen, Madrid (1987), Rijksmuseum Vincent Van Gogh, Amsterdam (1989), Yale Center for British Art, New Haven (1991), National Gallery, London (1995). *Work in collections:* Metropolitan Museum, N.Y.; Museum of Modern Art N.Y.; Los Angeles County Museum; National Gallery of Australia; B.M.; Tate Gallery, London; and many other museums; British Council; Arts Council; Contemporary Art Society, etc. *Address:* c/o Marlborough Fine Art Ltd., 6 Albemarle St., London W1X 4BY.

**AULD, John Leslie M.,** D.A. Belfast, A.R.C.A., N.R.D., F.I.A.L.; art teacher, designer-craftsman in goldsmiths' work; head, Art Dept., Municipal Tech. College, Londonderry (1940-46); Senior Lecturer, Glasgow School of Art (retd. 1979); *b* Belfast, 21 Jan., 1914. *m* Doreen M. W. Auld (née Sproul). one *s. Educ:* Methodist College, Belfast. *Studied:* Belfast Coll. of Art (1931-35); Royal Coll. of Art (1935-39). *Exhib:* London, Brussels, Paris, New York, Stockholm, Arts Council, etc. *Work in collections:* Goldsmiths' Company, London; New York City Corpn.; University of Glasgow. *Commissions:* crozier: R.C. Bishopric Motherwell; font & ewer: Bearsden Parish Church; altar vases: Knightswood Parish Church, Glasgow. *Publications:* Your Jewellery. *Signs work:* "J. L. AULD," but see appendix. *Address:* Flat 20, 41 Dundas Ct., East Kilbride G74 4AN.

**AVATI, Mario,** Prix de la Critique, Paris (1957), Gold Medal First International Prints Exhbn., Florence (1966), Prix du Lion's Club (1972), Grand Prix des Arts de la Ville de Paris (1981); painter/printmaker in mezzotint; *b* Monaco, 27 May, 1921. *m* Helen. *Educ:* College de Grasse, France. *Studied:* Ecole des Arts Decoratifs, Nice, Ecole des Beaux Arts, Paris. *Exhib:* one-man shows worldwide. *Work in collections:* museums in Europe, America, Asia, Oceania. *Publications:* 12 'Livres de Luxe' illustrated with original prints. *Clubs:* Soc. Les Peintres-Graveurs Paris, La Jeune Gravure Contemporaine Paris, Royal Soc. of Painter-Printmakers, London. *Signs work:* "AVATI." *Address:* 12 Cite Vaneau, Paris, France F75007.

**AYERS, Eric,** A.R.C.A., M.S.I.A.; consultant designer; *b* 12 Aug., 1921. *m* Duffy Rothenstein (née Fitzgerald). *Educ:* Balgowan Grammar School, Beckenham. *Studied:* The School of Photoengraving and Lithography, London, E.C.1, Beckenham School of Art, R.C.A. *Exhib:* Design in Business Printing

Exhibition, Festival of Britain (Dome of Discovery); Milwaukee Library, Wisconsin (U.S.A.); C. of I.D. "100 Good Catalogues"; R.A. Summer Shows. *Work in collections:* Museum of Modern Art, N.Y., B.M. Dept. of Prints and Books, V. & A. Dept. of Prints and Books, O.U.P. Library. *Commissions:* Collaborated with David Hockney's artist's book 'Grimms Fairy Tales' 1969/1970), Henry Moore's artist's book 'W.H. Auden Poems' (1971/1972), Patrick Caulfield's artist's book 'The poems of Jules Laforge' (1972/1973), Claes Oldenburgh's Multiple, 'London Knees' 1966, etc. *Publications:* work repro.: Graphis, Graphis Annual, Design Magazine. No. 142 1960. Article, "Do Posters Work?" Taught at London College of Printing, Senior Lecturer Camberwell School of Art, Graphic Arts Department (1972-1983), Fellow, Fine Art Dept., University of Newcastle, (1966-1967), Director and Art Director, since conception, of Editions Alecto (1963-1968). *Signs work:* "ERIC AYERS." *Address:* 4 Regent Sq., London WC1H 8HZ.

**AYRES, Gillian,** O.B.E., A.R.A.; painter; taught at Bath Academy, St. Martin's; Head of Painting, Winchester School of Art since 1978; *b* Barnes, London, 3 Feb., 1930; two children. *Educ:* St. Paul's Girls' School. *Studied:* Camberwell School of Art. *Exhib:* group shows: Musée d'Art Moderne; Bienale de Paris, Paris (1959); Situation, London (1960-61); one-man shows, Gallery One (1956), Kasmin Gallery (1965-66, 1969), Hayward Gallery (1972), Kasmin/Knoedler (1979), Knoedler London (1979, 1982, 1985, 1987), Knoedler New York (1985), R.A. British Art (1987), London, and Stuttgart, Germany. Awarded Japan International Art Promotion Association Award 1963). *Work in collections:* Tate Gallery, Museum of Modern Art, N.Y. *Signs work:* "Gillian Ayres." *Address:* Tall Trees, Gooseham, nr. Bude, Cornwall.

**AYRTON, Millicent,** M.B.E. (1946), R.Cam.A. (1948); painter in oil and water-colour, teacher; Past Chairman and Founder, Deeside Art Group; *b* Hoylake, Ches., 23 Nov., 1913. *m* Bertram Ayrton (decd.). one *s. Educ:* The Westlands, Acton Reynold, Salop. *Studied:* Liverpool Art College (1930-35, Will C. Penn, R.O.I.). *Exhib:* R.A., Liverpool Academy, Royal West Academy, R.Cam.A. *Work in collections:* Liverpool University, Birkenhead Williamson Gallery, Stafford University. *Publications:* A Northern School by Peter Davies, Liverpool Seen by Peter Davies. *Signs work:* "M.E. AYRTON." *Address:* The Anchorage, Townfield Rd., West Kirby, Merseyside L48 7EY.

# B

**BACK, Ken,** Cert. R.A.S. (dist.) (1967), N.D.D. (1964); painter in oil and ink; part-time art lecturer; *b* Guildford, 2 Apr., 1944. *m* Corinne Jones, artist (decd.). one *s.* one *d. Educ:* Astor School, Dover. *Studied:* Dover, Folkestone and Canterbury Colleges of Art (1959-64), R.A. Schools (1964-67, Peter Greenham, Charles Mahoney). *Exhib:* R.A., Piccadilly Gallery, Park Walk

Gallery, London, Chappel Galleries, Colchester, etc. *Work in collections* Europe and U.S.A. *Signs work:* "K.W. BACK" or "K.B." *Address:* White Cottage, The Moor, Dickleburgh, nr. Diss, Norfolk IP21 4NT.

**BACKHOUSE, David John,** R.W.A., F.R.B.S.; sculptor in bronze; Corsham, Wilts., 5 May, 1941. *m* Sarah Barber. one *s.* two *d. Educ:* Lord Weymouth School, Warminster. *Studied:* West of England College of Art. *Work in collections:* R.W.A., British Steel Corp., Royal Opera House, Covent Garden, Morgan Crucible Co., Mercantile and General Reinsurance Co. Haslemere Estates, Telford Dev. Corp., City of Bristol, Tesco plc, J. Sainsbury plc., Standard Life, and private collections throughout Europe and in U.S.A. Studio: Lullington Studio, Lullington, Frome, Som. BA11 2PW. *Signs work* "Backhouse," and see appendix. *Address:* The Old Post Office, Lullington Frome, Som.

**BAFFONI, Pier Luigi,** N.S. (1975), R.O.I. (1979); artist in oil, water-colour and pastel; *b* Turin, Italy, 11 Aug., 1932. *m* Mary Bainbridge. *Educ:* College of the Missioni Consolata, Turin. *Studied:* College of Art, Turin (1954-58) under Luigi Guglielmino and privately from Alessandro Pomi of Venice. *Exhib:* one man shows, Italy, Hertford, Cambridge, Bedford, Hitchin; mixed shows, Biennale of Castelfranco Veneto, Bologna, Mall Galleries, London. *Work in collections:* Montebelluna Town Hall, Bedfordshire Educ. Art Loan Service. *Signs work:* "P. L. Baffoni." *Address:* 140 Station Rd., Lower Stondon, Beds SG16 6JH.

**BAGHJIAN, Manouk,** artist in water-colour, pastel, oil; *b* Nicosia, Cyprus, 7 Jan., 1929; married. one *s.* one *d. Educ:* Armenian High School, Cyprus. *Studied:* Richmond A.E.C. *Exhib:* Gulbenkian Hall Kensington, Clarendon Gallery Holland Pk., Chiswick Library, Pinacoteca Tossa de Mar, R.S.M.A. Mall Galleries (1989, 1990, 1991, 1994, 1995, 1996), B.B.C. Bush House, Hogarth Club W4, Hertford Art Soc. (1995), Chelsea Art Soc. (1995). *Work in collections:* 8 Turnham Green Terr., London W4. *Clubs:* Ealing Art, Richmond Art Soc. *Signs work:* "Manouk." *Address:* 213 Popes La., London W5 4NH.

**BAILE de LAPERRIERE, Charles,** editor; *b* Le Mans (France), 17 Sept. 1939. *Educ:* Ecole Pascal (Paris), College St. Esprit (Beauvais). *Publications* edited: Royal Academy Exhibitors 1971-89, The Royal Scottish Academy Exhibitors 1826-1990 4 Vols., The Society of Women Artists Exhibitors 1855 1996 4 Vols., The Royal Society of Marine Painters 1946-1996, Silver Auction Records. *Clubs:* Arts, London, Scottish Arts, Edinburgh. *Address:* Hilmarton Manor, Calne, Wilts. SN11 8SB.

**BAILEY, Caroline,** B.A.(Hons.), M.A.; artist in water-colour, gouache, oil; *b* Chester, 5 Aug., 1953. *m* Philip Curzons. two *d. Educ:* St. Dominic's High School, Stoke on Trent. *Studied:* Manchester Polytechnic (1972-76, Hugh Barret, Anne Bradley, Bronwen Hargreaves). *Exhib:* Solomon Gallery Dublin, Minarenton Gallery London, Foyer Gallery Royal Exchange Theatre Manchester, Lowen Gallery Stoke on Trent, Castlegate House Cumbria, Manor

House Gallery Oxon., The Gallery Manchester, John Noott Gallery Worcs., also Open Exhbns. R.W.S., R.I. *Work in collections:* Irish Management Inst. *Signs work:* see appendix. *Address:* c/o John Noott Galleries, 14 Cotswold Ct., Broadway, Worcs. WR12 7AA.

**BAILEY, Julian,** B.F.A. Oxon. (1985), R.A.Dip. (M.A.) (1988); artist in oil and pastel; *b* Cheshire, 8 Apr., 1963. *m* Sophie Cullen, ceramist. one *d. Educ:* Malvern College. *Studied:* Ruskin School of Art (1982-85), R.A. Schools (1985-88, Jane Dowling, Norman Blamey, R.A.). *Exhib:* R.A., New Grafton Gallery, Browse & Darby. *Work in collections:* National Trust (F.F.A.), New College, Oxford. *Signs work:* "J.B." or "JULIAN BAILEY." *Address:* 16 Pembridge Mews, London W11 3EQ.

**BAILEY, Terence Robert,** N.D.D. (1958), A.T.D. (1962), R.B.S.A. (1991); painter in oil; Senior lecturer, Northumberland C.H.E. (1962-79); *b* Wolverhampton, 21 Dec., 1937. *m* Kate (Valerie Ann Browning). three *s. Educ:* Wolverhampton Technical High School. *Studied:* Wolverhampton College of Art (1954-58), Bournemouth College of Art (1962). *Exhib:* Northern Painters (1966), Northern Art Exhbn. (1978), prize winner R.B.S.A. Open (1986), R.P., R.O.I., regularly at R.B.S.A.; several one-man shows. Winner in Alexon "Women on Canvas" portrait competition (1990). *Work in collections:* Northumberland C.C., Northern Arts, National Library of Wales, R.B.S.A.; many private collections. *Signs work:* "Terry Bailey." *Address:* Dovey Studio, Aberdyfi, Gwynedd LL35 0LW.

**BAILLIE, William James Laidlaw,** P.R.S.A., P.P.R.S.W., R.G.I., H.R.A., H.R.H.A., H.R.W.A., H.B.W.S., H.F.R.B.S., H.S.S.A., D.Litt., D.A.Edin. (1950); painter in oil and water-colour; President, Royal Scottish Academy; *b* Edinburgh, 1923. *m* Helen Baillie. one *s.* two *d. Educ:* Dunfermline High School, Fife. *Studied:* Edinburgh College of Art (1941-42; (War Service 1942-46) 1946-50, Gillies, Maxwell, Rosoman, Philipson, MacTaggart), Diploma 1950. *Exhib:* one-man shows: Edinburgh, Harrogate, Newcastle, Salisbury, London, etc. *Work in collections:* Aberdeen, Edinburgh, Glasgow, Kansas, U.S.A. etc. *Clubs:* Scottish Arts and New Club. *Signs work:* "W.J.L. Baillie." *Address:* 6a Esslemont Rd., Edinburgh EH16 5PX.

**BAIN, Julia Mary,** M.F.P.S. (1985), Mem. Chelsea Art Soc. (1984); Woodrow Award (1986); sculptor in terracotta, wax and bronze; *b* London, 22 June, 1930. *m* David Bain, F.R.C.S. three *s.* one *d. Educ:* The Legat School of Russian Ballet. *Studied:* I.L.E.A. Chelsea/Westminster (1978-81), Sir John Cass College (1981-83). *Exhib:* F.B.A. (1983-89), R.B.A., S.W.A., N.S., F.P.S. Trends, Art of Living S.P.S., Chelsea Art Soc.; one-man shows, Windsor Festival (1981, 1986, 1989), Century Gallery, Datchet (1990, 1995), The Deanery, Windsor Castle (1993, 1995). Work in private collections. *Signs work:* "J.B." *Address:* The Studio, Hadleigh House, Sheet St., Windsor, Berks. SL4 1BN.

**BAIN, Peter,** painter in oil; *b* London, 15 December, 1927. *m* Jennifer. four *s. Studied:* Bath Academy of Art. *Signs work:* "Bain." *Address:* Tiled Cottage, Old Bosham, Sussex PO18 8LS.

**BAINES, Richard John Manwaring,** M.A., R.O.I., R.D.S., N.D.D. A.T.D., V.P.R.O.I. (1997); Dartington Crystal Award (1996); painter, writer, lecturer, critic and broadcaster (radio & TV); previously Senior lecturer/Head of Academic Studies, London College of Fashion, London Inst.; *b* Hastings, 1940. *m* Maureen Gregory. two *s.* one *d. Studied:* Regent St. Polytechnic, Goldsmiths' College, Birmingham Polytechnic. *Exhib:* R.O.I., R.B.A., N.S., R.E., Painter-Etchers, London and provinces; one-man exhbns. Hastings (1968, 1987). *Work in collections:* County Borough of Hastings, Manx Museum, London Inst. *Commissions:* Royal Arms and mural restorations, All Saints Church, Hastings. *Publications:* Mainly design history. *Clubs:* East Sussex Arts (Past President). *Signs work:* see appendix. *Address:* 138 St. Helens Rd., Hastings TN34 2EJ.

**BAINES, Valerie,** A.R.M.S. (1985), F.S.B.A. (1988), F.L.S. (1991); V.P.S.B.A. (1996); Botanical artist, miniature painter and natural history illustrator in water-colour and oil; *b* Romford, 1935. *m* Brian Norman. one *s. Educ:* Roxeth Mead School, Harrow on the Hill; Royal College of Music. *Studied:* Harrow Art School. *Exhib:* R.A., R.M.S., S.B.A., R.H.S. Westminster Galleries, Mall Galleries, Alpine Gallery, Medici Gallery, Llewellyn Alexander Gallery, International Botanical Art, Carnegie Mellon University Pittsburgh. *Work in collections:* Carnegie Mellon University Botanical Library Pittsburgh, Port Lympne Kent. *Publications:* The Naturalist's Garden by John Feltwell (Ebury Press, 1987), Botanical Diary (St. Michael, 1989), The Story of Silk by J. Feltwell (Allen Sutton 1990), The Big Book (Collins, 1991), Meadows by J. Feltwell (Allen Sutton 1992), Glorious Butterflies, Butterfly Conservation (1993), Gardens and Butterflies Calendar, Butterfly Conservation (1998). *Signs work:* "V.B." and "V. BAINES." *Address:* Shreives Oak, 16 Medway Rd., Gillingham, Kent ME7 1NH.

**BAIRSTOW, Elizabeth Ann,** F.S.B.A., S.W.A.; professional artist in water-colour, gallery owner; *b* White River, S.Africa, 11 Apr., 1938. *m* Dr. D.G. Gourley. three *s. Educ:* New Hall, Chelmsford. *Exhib:* Dorset County Museum (1984), Tate Gallery (1983), Mall Galleries, Westminster Gallery. *Work in collections:* The Bairstow Gallery, Cerne Abbas. *Publications:* illustrated, Piddle Valley Book of Country Life. *Signs work:* "Elizabeth Bairstow" or "E.A.B." *Address:* The Bairstow Gallery, Cerne Abbas, Dorset DT2 7JG.

**BAKER, Christopher William,** B.A.Hons. (Fine Art, 1978), P.G.C.E. (1981), R.B.A. (1981); etcher, oil on canvas, dramatic landscape paintings; Tutor, West Dean College; *b* Essex, 27 May, 1956. *Educ:* Kingham Hill School, Oxon. *Studied:* West Surrey College of Art and Design (1974-75, M. Fairclough), Glos. College of Art and Design (1975-78, D. L. Carpanini), Exeter University. *Exhib:* R.W.A., R.B.A., Mall Galleries, Phoenix Gallery, Highgate, Burstow Gallery, Brighton College, Wyckeham Gallery, ockbridge. *Work in collections:* Coventry Adult Educ., Oundle School, rtham House. *Publications:* work repro.: The Artist, Quattro Publications. *gns work:* "Christopher Baker." *Address:* 110 Fitzallan Rd., Arundel, W. ssex.

**BAKER, Hilary Jayne,** B.A.Hons. Fine Art (1984); artist, drawings in char- al, etchings and oil paintings, principal subjects - the figure and reportage ortraiture; *b* Cheltenham, 1 Mar., 1962. *Educ:* Cheltenham Grammar School. *udied:* Sheffield Art College (1981-84), Cheltenham Art College (1980-81). *xhib:* one-man shows: Ogle Gallery, Cheltenham (1986), Brewery Court allery, Cirencester (1985), Iris Ryman Gallery, Marbella (1990). *Work in col- ctions:* portrait, Gen. Sir John Hackett, in N.P.G.; many private collections in rope, U.S.A., Australia. *Signs work:* see appendix. *Address:* Harford House, aunton, Cheltenham, Glos. GL54 3AG.

**BALDWIN, Arthur Mervyn,** N.D.D. (1955), Rome Scholarship, Sculpture, )60; sculptor in metals and synthetics; self employed artist and restorer; 1978, tired defeated by lack of public appreciation - now restores antique watches r which service people happily pay; *b* Immingham, Lincs., 1 Feb. 1934. *m* atrica Mary. two *s*. *Educ:* Humberstone Foundation School, Old Clee, Lincs. *udied:* Grimsby School of Art, Leicester College of Art. *Work in collections:* ational Museum of Wales, Arts Council (Wales); Städtischen unstammlungen, Ludwigshafen. *Signs work:* sculpture unsigned; drawings c. signed "MERVYN BALDWIN." *Address:* 18 The Walk, Cardiff CF2 3AF.

**BALDWIN, Gordon,** O.B.E. (1992), N.D.D. (1952), Central Dip. (1953); ramist; *b* Lincoln, 1932. *m* Nancy Chandler. one *s*. two *d*. *Educ:* Lincoln chool. *Studied:* Lincoln School of Art (1949-51, Toni Bartl), Central School f Art and Design (1951-53, Dora Billington). *Work in collections:* V. & A.; outhampton A.G.; Crafts Council; Leicester Educ. Authority; Usher Gallery, incoln; Abbots Hall, Keswick; Paisley A.G.: Boymans van Beuningen, otterdam; Bellrive Museum, Zurich; Penn. State University, U.S.A.; ateshead A.G.; Swindon A.G.; Museum of Art, Melbourne; Museum of Art, erth; Knukke-Heiste, Keramion, W. Germany; Octagon Centre, Idah., U.S.A. ddress: Rylands House, Greathales St., Market Drayton TF9 1JN.

**BALDWIN, Martyn John,** Dip.A.D.; painter in oil; *b* Edgware, 18 May, 959. *Educ:* Downer Grammar School. *Studied:* Harrow School of Art (1979- 3). *Exhib:* R.A., N.P.G. *Signs work:* "M. Baldwin" or "BALDWIN." *Address:* lat 3, 132 Headstone Rd., Harrow HA1 1PF.

**BALDWIN, Nancy,** painter; *b* Sunderland, 3 Mar., 1935. *m* Gordon aldwin. one *s*. two *d*. *Educ:* St. Joseph's Convent, Lincoln. *Studied:* Lincoln chool of Art (1949-52, Toni Bartl), Central School of Art and Design (1952- 4, Dora Billington). *Exhib:* Reading Gallery, Thames Gallery, Windsor, The allery, Eton College, Cross Keys Gallery, Beaconsfield, Salix, Windsor, xford Gallery, City Museum and Gallery, Stoke-on-Trent, Midland Group, ottingham, Ikon, Birmingham, Holsworthy, London, Carmel College Gallery,

Bohun Gallery, Henley, Ellingham Mill, Bungay; prize winner Midland Vie (1980). *Work in collections:* Ashmolean Museum, Oxford and private colle tions in U.K., Italy, Switzerland, Belgium, Hong Kong, France, U.S. *Address:* Rylands House, Greathales St.,Market Drayton TF9 1JN.

**BALFOUR, Maria,** Medal Winner, Internationale Academie de Lutec Paris (1977); painter in oil; self taught artist; *b* 27 June 1934. *m* Lord Balfour Inchrye. one *d. Educ:* America and Great Britain. *Exhib:* Loggia Gallery (197 1980, 1985), Paris Salon, Galerie Internationale, N.Y., Chelsea Art Soc Kensington & Chelsea Artists; R.I. Galleries, Medici Galleries, Lloyds Bar (Pall Mall) in aid of Mental Health Foundation (1990), exhbns. with oth artists in aid of British Diabetic Assoc., Southwold, Suffolk (1995). *Work collections:* New Zealand, S. Africa, Belgium, Holland, U.S.A., British Isle Israel and Italy. *Commissions:* crest for Bridal Kneeler to celebrate 250th ye of founding of Guy's Hospital (1976). *Address:* 4 Marsh End Flats, Ferry Rc Walberswick, Suffolk IP18 6TH.

**BALL, Gerald,** R.C.A. (1979); painter in water-colour and tempera; Ashton-under-Lyne, 24 May, 1948. *m* Ann. *Educ:* Hartshead Comprehensiv *Studied:* Ashton-under-Lyne C.F.E. *Exhib:* R.W.S., Richard Hagen, Ltd., R. Manchester Academy, Agnews, Tegfryn Gallery, Bourne Gallery, Lion ar Lamb Gallery, Walker Galleries, Crossing Gate Gallery. *Work in collection* Coleg Harlech. *Signs work:* "GERRY BALL." *Address:* Old Golderwel Golderfield, Pudleston, Leominster, Herefordshire HR6 0RG.

**BALL, Robert,** A.R.C.A. (1942), R.E. (1943), R.B.S.A. (1943), F.R.S. (1950), R.B.A. (1979), A.R.W.A. (1988); British Inst. Scholarship fe Engraving (1937); teacher of painting, drawing and anatomy, Birmingha College of Art (1942); Princ. Stroud School of Arts and Crafts (Jan., 1953 teacher of painting, Glos. College of Art (1959-81); artist in oil, water-colou drawing, etching, line-engraving, mezzotint, aquatint, and wood-engraving; Birmingham, 11 July, 1918. *m* Barbara Minchin. one *s.* two *d. Studie* Birmingham Junior School of Art (1930-33), Birmingham College of A (1933-40); R.C.A. (1940-42). *Exhib:* R.A., R.W.A., R.E., R.B.S.A., R.B. *Work in collections:* V. & A., Ashmolean, Gloucester, Dudley, Hunteria Walsall, Cheltenham and Birmingham Museums. *Publications:* illustrate Cotswold Ballads by Mansell. *Signs work:* "Robert Ball." *Address:* Beth-sha Kingsmead, Painswick, Glos. GL6 6US.

**BALMER, Barbara,** A.R.S.A. (1973), R.S.W. (1966), R.G.I. (1988 painter in oil and water-colour; *b* B'ham, 23 Sept., 1929. *m* George Macki R.D.I., R.S.W. two *d. Educ:* Solihull High School for Girls. *Studied:* Coventr School of Art; Edinburgh College of Art. *Exhib:* one-man shows: Demarc Gallery, Edinburgh (1965-70), Scottish Gallery, Edinburgh (1975, 1980, 198: 1988), Posterngate Gallery, Hull (1983), Stirling Gallery (1976), Ush Gallery, Lincoln (1984); Retrospective '55-'95 Touring Exhbn. (1995-96 *Work in collections:* Glasgow City A.G., Edinburgh City Art Centre, Aberde

A.G., Perth A.G., S.N.P.G., S.A.C., Usher Gall. Lincoln, Coventry A.G., Dundee A.G., Leicester City Museum. *Signs work:* "Barbara Balmer." *Address:* 32 Broad St., Stamford, Lincs. PE9 1JP.

**BALMER, Derek Rigby,** R.W.A.; painter in oil and acrylic; *b* Bristol, 28 Dec., 1934. *m* Elizabeth Mary Rose. one *s.* one *d. Educ:* St. Gabriel's Convent, Waterloo House, Sefton Pk. *Studied:* West of England College of Art (Dennis Darch, Derek Crowe, Paul Feiler). *Exhib:* Arnolfini (four), New Art Centre, Leicester Gallery, R.W.A. Represented by Anthony Hepworth Fine Art Bath, and Gisela Van Beers London, Dutch Dealers: Smelik and Stokking The Hague. *Clubs:* Chelsea Arts. *Signs work:* "Balmer" or "Derek Balmer." *Address:* Mulberry House, 12 Avon Grove, Sneyd Pk., Bristol 9.

**BANEY, Ralph R.,** F.R.B.S. (1984), M.F.A. (1973), Ph.D. (1980), A.T.C. (1962), Who's Who in American Art (1973); Professor of Art; sculptor in wood, bronze, ceramic, fibreglass; *b* Trinidad, 22 Sept., 1929. *m* Vera. one *s. Educ:* Naparima College, Trinidad. *Studied:* Brighton College of Art (1957-62, A.J.J. Ayres), University of Maryland, U.S.A. (1971-76, Ken Campbell). *Exhib:* Washington County Museum, O.A.S. Gallery, Washington D.C.; Sculpture House, N.Y.C.; Georgetown University. *Work in collections:* H.M. The Queen; Washington County Museum of Fine Arts, Hagerstown, Md.; Central Bank, Trinidad. *Clubs:* R.B.S., Sculptors Guild Inc. N.Y., Washington Sculptors Group. *Signs work:* "R. BANEY." *Address:* 5203 Talbot's Landing, Ellicott City, Md. 21043, U.S.A.

**BANKS, Brian,** painter in acrylic, oil, mixed media; *b* London, 21 Oct., 1939. *m* Christine, divorced 1974. two *s.* one *d. Educ:* Sir Walter St. John's Grammar School, London. *Studied:* St. Martin's (1956-57), Peter de Francia, Edward Middleditch, James Dring; privately with John Flavin, A.R.C.A. (1958). *Exhib:* one-man shows: Colin Jellicoe Gallery, Manchester; Ansdell Gallery, London; Zaydler Gallery, London; Fermoy Art Gallery, King's Lynn; Conway Hall, London; Leigh Gallery, London, (1984, 1985), Trinity Arts Centre, Tunbridge Wells. Represented by Leigh Gallery, Bloomsbury, London. *Work in collections:* Britain, Australia, France, U.S.A., Denmark. *Signs work:* "BANKS" (year). *Address:* 8 Ravenet Ct., Battersea Pk. Rd., London SW11 5HE.

**BANKS, Nancy,** U.A., M.F.P.S.; sculptor in bronze, direct plaster, terracotta; *b* St. Helens, 12 Feb., 1923. *m* John Banks, M.Eng., F.Eng. two *s. Educ:* Nutgrove, Rainhill, Lancs. *Studied:* Sir John Cass College of Art (Clive Duncan). *Exhib:* Mall Galleries, R.B.A., U.A., N.S., R.M.S., S.W.A., S.P.S., Barbican, Bloomsbury, Guildhall, Alpine, Weighouse galleries, I.E.E., Blackheath, Usher, Lincs., Worthing Museum and A.G., M.A.S.-F. *Work in collections:* U.K., U.S.A., Japan, Spain. *Clubs:* L.L.L.C. *Signs work:* "N. BANKS" or "Nancy Banks." *Address:* B.1. Marine Gate, Marine Drive, Brighton, E. Sussex BN2 5TQ.

**BANNISTER, Geoffrey Ernest John,** served Royal Navy Minesweepers

(1942-46); E.V.T. instructor in Commercial Art (Royal Navy, 1945-46); artist/designer, figure, scraper-board, water-colour, oils.; *b* Birmingham, 15 Jan., 1924. *m* Beryl Parr Robinson, 1949 (deceased, 1966); one *s*. one *d*.; remarried, 1967, Susan Jennefer Peters. two *s*. *Educ:* St. Philip's Grammar School. Proprietor, Minster Print & Packaging. Commissions for portraits, animals, landscapes in oils. *Clubs:* Great Barr Golf, Catenian Assoc. *Signs work:* "Geoff Bannister." *Address:* Crossways, 811 Sutton Rd., Aldridge, Walsall, W. Midlands WS9 0QJ.

**BARANOWSKA, Janina,** artist in oil; *b* Poland, 28 Oct., 1925. *m* Maksymilian Baranowski. one *s*. *Educ:* In Poland, Middle East and Scotland. *Studied:* Borough Polytechnic under Prof. Bomberg (1947-50), School of Art at the Polish University of Stefan Batory in London (1951-54). *Exhib:* One-man shows: Drian Gallery, Grabowski Gallery, Raymond Duncan Galleries, Alwin Gallery, Grand Prix Rencontre Lyon, France, Det Lille Galleri, Norway, State Galleries in Krakow and Poznan, Poland, Royal Festival Hall, London, Dixon Gallery - University of London, Bloomsbury Gallery, Woburn Fine A.G., Polish Cultural Inst. Mixed exhib.: R.A., Burlington Gallery, Cassel Gallery, R.B.A. Galleries, New Vision Centre, Walker's Galleries, Whitechapel A.G., Edinburgh. *Publications:* Editor of Contemporary Polish Artists in G.B. (1983). *Clubs:* W.I.A.C., Group 49, I.A.L., I.A.A. - U.K. National Com., A.P.A. in G.B. (Chairman), N.S.P.S. (Mem.). *Signs work:* "Baranowska." *Address:* 20 Strathmore Rd., London SW19 8DB.

**BARBER, Raymond,** A.C.F.I., A.M.II.M., City and Guilds, London Inst. (1943), E.M.E.U. (1937), S.S.I.A. (1945); Course Tutor at Footwear Dept Wellingborough Technical College; Footwear Section Head (retd.); *b* 30 Sept., 1921. *Educ:* Kettering Rd. Inst., Northampton, College of Technology, Northampton, Leicester College of Technology. *Exhib:* Walsall, London, in conjunction with "Leather, Footwear and Allied Industries" Export Corp., Ltd.; Quality Footwear Exhib., Seymour Hall, London. *Clubs:* N.C.T.S.A., N.G.C., N.S.M.E. *Signs work:* "Renny." *Address:* 10 Wantage Cl., Moulton, Northampton NN3 7UY.

**BARBER KENNEDY, Mat,** B.A.(Hons.) (1984), M.A. (1988), R.I. (1994); painter in mixed media collage using water based media, water-colour, acrylic, ink; *b* Hornchurch, Essex, 7 Oct., 1962. *m* Sherry Kennedy. *Educ:* Coopers Company and Coborn School. *Studied:* Royal College of Art (Derek Walker, Kit Alsop). *Exhib:* annual Spring show at Mall Galleries, regular events at galleries in England and America. *Signs work:* see appendix. *Address:* 1906 S. Halsted, Chicago, Illinois 60608, U.S.A. *Email:*71322.2143 @ compuserve.com

**BARCLAY, Sir Colville,** Bart., M.A.; painter in oil and water-colour; *b* London, 7 May, 1913. *m* Rosamond Elliott. three *s*. *Educ:* Eton and Oxford. *Studied:* Ruskin School, Oxford. *Exhib:* R.B.A., R.A., London Group, Brighton and Bradford A.G. *Work in collections:* L.C.C. Schools, Arts Council, Bradford

City Art Gallery. *Signs work:* "Barclay." *Address:* Pitshill, nr. Petworth, Sussex GU28 9AZ.

**BARKER, Clive,** sculptor in bronze and chrome; *b* Luton, Beds., 29 Aug., 1940. *m* Rose Bruen. two *s. Educ:* Beech Hill Secondary Modern. *Studied:* Luton College of Technology and Art (1957-59) under Clifford Barry, A.R.C.A. *Exhib:* Robert Fraser Gallery, Hanover Gallery, Musee d'Art Moderne, Museum of Modern Art, N.Y., Palais des Beaux-Arts, Palazzo Strozzi, etc. *Work in collections:* Arts Council of Gt. Britain, British Council, V. & A., Tate Gallery, etc. *Publications:* Pop Art Re-defined (Thames & Hudson), Image as Language (Penguin), Pop Art (Studio Vista), Art in Britain 1969-70 (Dent), Objekt Kunst (Dumont). *Signs work:* "Clive Barker." *Address:* 6 The Clocktower, Heath St., Hampstead, London NW3.

**BARKER, Dale Devereux,** A.R.E., B.A. (Hons.) (1984), H. Dip. F.A. (Slade) (1986); artist, printmaker; *b* Leicester, 4 Feb., 1962. *m* Rebecca Weaver. *Educ:* Alderman Newton's Grammar School, Leicester. *Studied:* Loughborough College of Art and Design, Leicester Polytechnic and Slade (Stanley Jones). *Exhib:* 16 solo exhbns. *Work in collections:* Tate Gallery, V. & A., Ashmolean, New York Public Library, Harvard University. *Commissions:* Clifford Chance, British Rail, Lloyds Insurance. *Publications:* Published own collaborative books with poets Martin Stannard (G.B.), Paul Violi (U.S.) and Kenneth Koch (U.S.). *Signs work:* "D.D. Barker." *Address:* 'Untitled', The Bungalow, Capel Grove, Capel St. Mary, Suffolk IP9 2JS.

**BARKER, David,** Dip. A.D. (1966), A.T.C. (1967), Hon. R.E. (1995), Prof. Lu Xian Academy of Fine Arts, China (1997); Senior lecturer/ research translator; University of Ulster,Prof., Lu Xian Academy of Fine Arts, Mem. International Exchange Com., China National Academy of Fine Arts; drawing/silk screen; *b* Dorchester, 11 Jan.,1945. *m* Catherine Elizabeth (née Grover). one *s.* two *d. Educ:* University of London (1962-67), University of Leeds (1988). *Publications:* An English - Chinese Glossary of Printmaking Terms (1995), The Chinese Arts Academies Printmaking Exhibition (1993), The Techniques of the Chinese Print (in preparation). *Signs work:* "David Barker." *Address:* University of Ulster, Faculty of Art and Design, York St., Belfast BT15 1ED.

**BARKLAM, Harold,** A.R.C.A. (1936); artist in oil, water-colour; art lecturer, Derby College of Art; art teacher, Lowestoft School of Art (1946-50); *b* Tipton, Staffs., 14 Jan., 1912. *m* Marjorie Hale. one *d. Educ:* Ryland Memorial School of Art, W. Bromwich, R.C.A. and College of Art, Birmingham. *Exhib:* Birmingham A.G., Derby A.G., Norwich Castle, Nottingham Castle. *Publications:* oil paintings of Dunster Castle, Hardwicke Hall, Serlby Hall, Berkeley Castle, Blithfield Hall, Ingestre Hall; mural paintings entitled "Children's Games" painted for Lady Bagot of Blithfield Hall. *Signs work:* "H. BARKLAM." *Address:* 9 Eastwood Drive, Littleover, Derby.

**BARLOW, Bohuslav,** Dip.A.D.(Hons.) (1970), S.G.F.A.; artist mainly in oil, some pastel; *b* Bruntal, Czechoslovakia, 8 July, 1947. *Educ:* St. Mary's Grammar School, Blackburn. *Studied:* Manchester (1966), Central School of Art, London (1967-70). *Exhib:* R.A., R.E., P.S., International Contemporary Art Fairs. Work in many Northern municipal collections, Manchester Academy. *Work in collections:* Leeds City Council, Coopers & Lybrand, N. Rothschild, Royal Family of Saudi Arabia. *Commissions:* Four large murals for M.E.P.C. plc., Bronte Soc. *Publications:* Visual Alchemy - Bohuslav Barlow. Opened own gallery in Todmorden 1997. *Clubs:* Manchester Academy. *Signs work:* "B. Barlow." *Address:* 262 Rochdale Rd., Todmorden, Lancs. OL14 7PD.

**BARLOW, Gillian,** B.A. (1970), M.A. (1971), P.G.C.E. (1972), R.H.S. Gold medal (1994); artist in water-colour on paper, gouache on vellum; *b* Khartoum, Sudan, 10 Dec., 1944. *Educ:* Ashford School for Girls, Kent; University of Sussex. *Studied:* Slade School (1962-63, Patrick George, John Aldridge). *Exhib:* solo shows: British Council, Bombay; Hudson View Gallery, N.Y.; Vassar College, N.Y.; Blond Fine Art, London; Spinks Fine Art, London; numerous mixed shows. *Work in collections:* Hunt Inst. of Botanical Documentation, Pittsburgh, U.S.A.; Vassar College, N.Y.; Lady Margaret Hall, Oxford; Boscobel Restoration, N.Y.; British Council, India; Shirley Sherwood Botanical Painting Collection, London; Royal Horticultural Soc. London. *Signs work:* see appendix. *Address:* 33a Moreton Terr., London SW1V 2NS.

**BARNARD, Roger,** B.A. Fine Art (1974); artist, participatory set-ups some include video; painting, drawing, photography, holography, writing; *b* London, 4 Nov., 1951. *Educ:* Chichester High School for Boys. *Studied:* West Sussex College of Design (1970-71), North Staffs. Polytechnic (1971-74). *Exhib:* one-man shows, Tate Gallery, Air, Scottish Arts Council Gallery, Third Eye Centre, South Bank London, Truro, etc.; mixed shows, Tate, Serpentine, Hayward, Air, Holborn Underground Comp., Whitechapel, Arts Council of G.B. touring exhbn., Coventry, Chichester, Third Eye Centre, Osaka Triennale '90' (Painting), '91' (Print) Japan, etc. *Work in collections:* Royal Inst. of Cornwall County Coll., Contemporary Art Centre Osaka, Japan; private collections in U.K., U.S.A., France, Germany; U.C.H. London. *Commissions:* Organisations, incl. British Refugee Council, and private individuals. *Signs work:* paintings since 1970 unsigned, drawings dated, some signed "R. Barnard." *Address:* 151 Archway Rd., London N6 5BL.

**BARNDT, Helen Grace,** artist in sepia ink, oil, tempera; *b* 1928. *Work in collections:* Dr. J. Trenton Tully, Ronald M. Tully, Victor Hansen. *Commissions:* Commissioned by: Dr. J. Trenton Tully for the Metaphysical Research Society of Denver, Colorado (1968-92) for series of religious oil paintings, ceiling murals and interior designs; paintings - Denver Museum of Natural History (1993). *Signs work:* "H. G. Barndt" and "H.G." *Address:* Apt 9, 940 E. 8th Ave., Denver, Colorado. 80218.

**BARNES, Ann Margaret,** B.Ed.(Hons.) (1973), M.F.P.S. (1974), A.M.N.S.

(1978), F.R.S.A. (1995); artist in airbrush on botanical themes, head teacher; *b* London, 1951. *Educ:* Wimbledon County School for Girls; Stockwell College of Education, Bromley. *Exhib:* F.P.S., N.S., Soc. of Botanical Artists; one-man shows: London, Chiswick, Leatherhead, Henley, Croydon, Morden. *Signs work:* "A. Barnes." *Address:* 16 Mount Pleasant, Ewell, Epsom, Surrey KT17 1XE.

**BARNES-MELLISH, Glynis Lily,** B.A.Hons. Fine Art (1975), Advanced Combined Fine Art Dip. (1983); portrait painter in water-colour; *b* Bromley, Kent, 10 June, 1953. one *d*. *Educ:* The William School, Letchworth. *Studied:* St. Albans School of Art (1971-72, 1981-83), W. Surrey College of Art and Design (1972-75). *Exhib:* annually R.I., S.W.A., P.S. *Work in collections:* Self portrait - Lee Valley University. *Publications:* The Artist, Hodder & Stoughton, Penguin Books. Limited Edition Prints (Solomon & Whitehead Ltd.). *Clubs:* S.W.A., Cambridge Drawing Soc. *Signs work:* "Mellish." *Address:* 16 Lytton Ave., Letchworth, Herts. SG6 3HT.

**BARNS-GRAHAM, Wilhelmina,** D.A. (Edin.), D. Litt. St. Andrews (1992); painter in oil, acrylic, gouache; *b* St. Andrews, Fife, 8 June, 1912. *Exhib:* London, Edinburgh, Oxford, St. Ives, Penzance, Leeds, Cumbria, Orkney, Germany, St. Andrews, Wakefield, Perth, Kendal, Glasgow, Exeter, Truro, Dundee. *Work in collections:* English Arts Council; S.A.C.; British Council; B.M.; V. & A.; Contemporary Art Soc.; Scottish National Gallery; Government Coll.; Tate Gallery; Edinburgh City Coll.; New South Wales A.G., Australia; Universities of Michigan U.S.A., Aberdeen, Cambridge, Edinburgh, Manchester; Museums of Glasgow, Ayr, Birmingham, Dundee, Hull, Hove, Kirkcaldy, Leeds, Plymouth, Sheffield; Educ. authorities of Cornwall, Herts., Leeds, W. Riding. *Clubs:* Chelsea Arts; Founder Mem. Penwith Soc. of Arts (1949). *Signs work:* W. Barns-Graham." *Address:* 1 Barnaloft, St. Ives, Cornwall TR26 1NJ.; Balmungo, St. Andrews, Fife KY16 8LW.

**BARRATT, Mary H.,** B.A. (1969); painter in oil; part time art lecturer; *b* Annesley Woodhouse, Notts., 27 Mar., 1948. *m* Michael Ian Barratt. *Studied:* Loughborough College of Art and Design (1966-69, Philip Thompson, Colin Saxton). *Exhib:* 359 Gallery, Nottingham, Crucible Theatre, Sheffield, Rufford Country Pk., Ollerton, Merlin Gallery, Sheffield, Pierrepont Gallery Thoresby Park, Newark. *Signs work:* "M. Barratt." *Address:* 7 Craigston Rd., Carlton-in-Lindrick, Worksop, Notts. S81 9NG.

**BARRETT, Franklin Allen,** chartered accountant (retd.); mem. English Ceramic Circle; Chairman Church Stretton and S. Shropshire Arts Festival (1979-81); *b* Edgbaston, Birmingham, 4 Apr., 1906. *m* Winifred Mary Webb. one *s*. *Educ:* King Edward's Grammar School, Five Ways, Birmingham. *Publications:* Caughley and Coalport Porcelain (F. Lewis); Worcester Porcelain (Faber and Faber); Lund's Bristol & Worcester Porcelain (Faber and Faber); papers in English Ceramic Circle Transactions; co-author (with A. L. Thorpe), Derby Porcelain (Faber and Faber); contributor to English Porcelain,

1745-1850 (Ernest Benn), Joint Editor (with A. L. Thorpe), Pinxton China Factory, Exley (Cook-Steel, Derby), revised edition 'Honey Old English Porcelain' (Faber and Faber, 1977). *Address:* Mallards Keep, Alison Rd., Church Stretton, Salop. SY6 7AT.

**BARRETT, Priscilla,** freelance illustrator and wildlife artist in watercolour, pastels, pencil, pen and ink; *b* S. Africa, 4 May, 1944. *m* Gabriel Horn. *Educ:* Universities of Cape Town and Stellenbosch. *Exhib:* solo exhbns. in Cambridge, also exhib. London, Brighton, Lavenham. *Publications:* Collins Field Guide - Mammals of Britain and Europe; European Mammals; Evolution and Behaviour; The Domestic Dog; Running with the Fox; The Wolf; A Year in the Life: Badger; A Year in the Life: Tiger; RSPCA Book of British Mammals. *Signs work:* "Priscilla Barrett." *Address:* Jack of Clubs, Lode, Cambridge CB5 9HE.

**BARRETT, Roderic,** artist in oil; visiting lecturer, Central School of Art and Design (1947-68); invited to P.E.A., Exeter, U.S.A. (1957-58); tutor, Royal Academy Schools (1968); *b* 8 Jan., 1920. *m* Lorna Blackmore. two *s.* one *d. Educ:* St. Christopher's School, Letchworth. *Studied:* Central School of Arts and Crafts (1936-40). *Exhib:* One-man shows: London (1954, 1956, 1964, 1966, 1970, 1976, 1978, 1980), The Barbican (1996), Cambridge (1947, 1963, 1966), Exeter, N.H., U.S.A. (1957), Boston, U.S.A. (1958), Oxford Gallery (1971, 1975, 1981), The Minories Colchester (1962, 1974, 1984, 1997), Chilham (1969, 1972), Harlow (1974, 1984), University of Essex (1966), University of Southampton (1975), University of Warwick (1975), Norwich Museum (1974), Ipswich (1987), Phoenix Gallery (1988), Chappel (1993), London Group, Wildensteins, Beaux Arts, Manchester, Cardiff, Aldeburgh, Bath Festival, Bristol City Art Gallery, Brussels, Zürich, Nice, Holland, Boston Arts Festival, U.S.A. Princetown U.S.A., Worcester Museum, U.S.A., Chicago, U.S.A., New York, European Parliament Strasburg (1995), etc. *Work in collections:* V. & A., Lamont Gallery, U.S.A., University of Essex, University of Southampton, Essex Museum, Southend A.G., Christchurch Mansion, Ipswich; in private collections in France, England, Belgium, Italy, Eire, U.S.A. *Signs work:* "R.B." *Address:* Rooks End, Church Lane, Stanway, Colchester, Essex CO3 5LR.

**BARRIE, Mardi,** M.A., D.A. (1953), R.S.W. (1969); painter in oil, acrylic/water medium; *b* Kirkcaldy, Fife, 25 Apr., 1931. *Educ:* Kirkcaldy High School. *Studied:* Edinburgh University and Edinburgh College of Art (Prof. D. Talbot Rice, W.G. Gillies). *Exhib:* regularly in group and solo exhbns. since 1963; principal private galleries include Scottish Gallery, Edinburgh, Macaulay Gallery, Stenton, Thackeray Gallery, London, Bruton Gallery, Somerset. *Work in collections:* U.K. and abroad, including H.R.H. Duke of Edinburgh, R.S.A., S.A.C., Glasgow A.G., Scottish National Gallery of Modern Art. *Signs work:* "Mardi." *Address:* Studio 5, 33 Melville St., Edinburgh EH3 7JF.

**BARTLETT, Charles,** P.P.R.W.S., R.E., A.R.C.A.; artist in oil and water-colour, printmaker; *b* Grimsby, 23 Sept., 1921. *m* Olwen Jones. one *s. Educ:* Eastbourne Grammar School. *Studied:* Eastbourne School of Art, R.C.A. *Exhib:* two one-man shows in London; major Retrospective Exhbn. (1997), Bankside Gallery, London. *Work in collections:* V. & A. Museum, National Gallery of S. Australia, Arts Council of Great Britain, numerous public and private collections in Britain and abroad. *Publications:* Monograph: Charles Bartlett, Painter and Printmaker. *Clubs:* The Arts. *Signs work:* "Charles Bartlett." *Address:* St. Andrew's House, Fingringhoe, nr. Colchester, Essex CO5 7BG.

**BARTLETT, Paul Thomas,** R.B.A. (1981), R.A. Schools P.G. Cert./M.A. (1980), B.A.Hons. Fine Art (Falmouth 1976), B'ham Poly.: F.E.T.C. (1987), P.G. Dip. hist. art/design (1990), B.P.S. (1993), R.B.S.A. (1997). Prizes: Turner Gold Medal, Landseer Life Painting, Sir James Walker; scholarships: David Murray, Elizabeth Greenshield; painter/printmaker/lecturer; *b* B'ham, 7 July, 1955. *Exhib:* (major Prizes): Stowells Trophy, Royal Overseas League, Spirit of London, Mid Art, Mid 25, Hunting Group, R.B.A., R.B.S.A., Alexon Women on Canvas; other exhbns.: R.A., V. & A., N.P.G., I.C.A. *Publications:* work repro.: Alan Hutchison, Quarto, Dorling Kindersley. *Signs work:* "Paul Bartlett" or " P.T.B." *Address:* 144 Wheelers Lane, Kings Heath, B'ham. B13 0SG.

**BARTOLO, Maria,** painter in mixed media, including wax and varnish; *b* Cardiff, 7 Dec., 1967. *Educ:* Oaklands R.C. Comprehensive. *Studied:* City and Guilds of London Art School (Roger de Grey). *Exhib:* The Discerning Eye, Mall Galleries, Christie's, Sotheby's, R.A. Summer Show, Barbican. *Work in collections:* Art Council, De Beers. *Publications:* work repro.: R.A. magazine, C.V. magazine, Evening Standard Newspaper (four edns.). Winner of Evening Standard prize. *Address:* 23a Milner Sq., London N1.

**BARTOLOME, Jaime,** painter; 1958 Press Assoc., Barcelona, 1st Prix; 1970 Grand Prix New York, Nice (France), 2nd Prix; 1971 Grand Prix Paques, Nice, 2nd Prix; *b* Santander, Spain, 4 Apr., 1927. *Educ:* Barcelona. *Exhib:* Individual show in Barcelona, 1958-62-64-65 and 1969, Bilbao, 1966, Madrid, Palma, Mallorca, 1967; group shows in Barcelona, Madrid, Alicante, München, Italy, Sweden, Hong Kong, France. *Work in collections:* Museum of Modern Art, Barcelona. *Clubs:* Circulo Artistico "Saint Lluc," Instituto Estudios Hispanicos, Barcelona. *Signs work:* "Bartolomé." *Address:* Studio, Diputación, 321, Barcelona, Spain.

**BARTON, Patricia:** see MYNOTT, Patricia.

**BASIA:** see WATSON-GANDY, Basia.

**BASKO, Maurice P. Duviella,** Dip. Salon Automne, France; Prize, Figuratif Chateau of Senaud, France; painter in oil and water-colour, art researcher; restoration of paintings; art expert; *b* Biarritz, 30 Sept., 1921. three *d. Educ:* Jules Ferry College, Biarritz. *Studied:* Academy Frochot, Paris. *Exhib:* Museum of Modern Art, Paris, Salon Automne, Salon Bosio, Grand Prix, Pont

Aven, Salon Art Libre, Paris, Salon Versailles, France, Paris Gallery, N.Y., Galerie Colise, Paris, Fontainebleu Gallery, N.Y.; one-man shows: Paris, N.Y., Lyon, Mallorca, Vichy, Cannes, Biarritz. *Work in collections:* Guggenheim Museum, N.Y., Albertina Museum, Vienna, Museum of Modern Art, Miami, Public Library, N.Y.; and more than 400 works in private collections. *Publications:* 5000 painter's signatures (famous painters) all world, all periods. President of Biarritz Art Festival since 1991. *Signs work:* "BASKO" and sometimes "Duviella." *Address:* Résidence Arverna/Bloc C, 26 Ave. Lahouze, 64200 Biarritz, France.

**BATCHELOR, Bernard Philip,** R.W.S.; painter in water-colour and oil; *b* 29 May, 1924. *Studied:* St. Martin's and City and Guilds of London Art schools gaining City and Guilds Painting medal and a David Murray Scholarship. Subject matter relates mainly to town or landscapes with figures, coastal scenes, etc. *Work in collections:* many in private collections here and abroad; also M.O.W., Museum of Richmond and Richmond Parish Charity Lands. *Address:* 50 Graemesdyke Ave., East Sheen, London SW14 7BJ.

**BATEMAN, Robert McLellan,** O.C., R.C.A., D.Litt., D.Sc., Ll.D., D.F.A.; artist in oil and acrylic; *b* Toronto, 24 May, 1930. *m* Birgit Freybe Bateman. four *s.* one *d. Studied:* University of Toronto (1950-54, Carl Schaeffer). *Exhib:* major one-man shows in museums throughout Canada and U.S.A. incl. Smithsonian Institution, Washington D.C. (1987) and the Joslyn Fine Arts Museum, Nebraska (1986); Tryon Gallery, London (1975, 1977, 1979, 1985); Le Conseil International de la Chasse et de la Conservation de Gibier, Monoco-extensive tour of Europe (1982). *Work in collections:* the late Princess Grace of Monaco, H.R.H. Prince Philip, H.R.H. Prince Charles, H.R.H. Prince Bernhard, Hamilton Art Museum, Canada, Leigh Yawkey Woodson Art Museum, U.S.A. etc. *Commissions:* numerous. *Publications:* numerous articles, four major books and seven films on Robert Bateman. *Clubs:* Life membership in numerous clubs and conservation organizations. *Signs work:* "Robert Bateman." *Address:* Box 115, Fulford Harbour, B.C. Canada V8K 2P2.

**BATES, Joan Elliott,** D.F.A. (Lond. 1952); painter, draughtsman and printmaker; *b* Sheffield, 22 Jan., 1930. *m* John F. Bates. three *s. Studied:* Sheffield College of Art (1947-49), Slade School of Fine Art (1949-52, Prof. William Coldstream). *Exhib:* R.A. Summer Exhbns., Hunting Award finalist, N.E.A.C., R.W.S., R.O.I., R.E., etc. and in numerous galleries in London and the provinces. *Work in collections:* Paintings in Hospitals, The House of Commons. *Publications:* work repro.: Harper Collins, Anness Publishing, etc. Awards: Laing Painting Competition 3rd prize (1981) 2nd prize (1984), Cornelissen award (1986). *Signs work:* "J. Elliott" or "J.E." *Address:* 17 Marlow Mill, Mill Rd., Marlow, Bucks. SL7 1QD.

**BATES, Patricia Jane,** B.Ed. (Lond.) (1976), M.F.P.S. (1980); artist in oil, oil collage, mixed media, sculpture, printmaking; *b* Surbiton, 8 Jan., 1927. *m* Martin Colin Bates. one *s.* one *d. Educ:* Priors Field, Godalming. *Studied:*

Bartlett School of Architecture (1944-46), Epsom School of Art (1947-48), Byam Shaw (1952-53). *Exhib:* one-man shows: Loggia Gallery, London, Cranleigh Art Centre; mixed shows: Mall Galleries, London, Guildford, Westcott Gallery, Mill Gallery, Coverack, Cornwall. Work auctioned: East African Wildlife Soc. Kenya. *Work in collections:* England and many other countries. *Signs work:* "PAT BATES" or "PAT SIMON BATES." *Address:* Brackenhurst, Wonham Way, Gomshall, Guildford, Surrey GU5 9NZ.

**BATTERBURY, Helen Fiona,** self-taught artist in water-colour; *b* Stockton-on-Tees, 30 July, 1963. *m* Paul Batterbury. two *s.* one *d. Educ:* Durrants School, Watford. *Exhib:* S.Eq.A., S.WL.A., S.W.A., Wildlife Art Soc., numerous mixed exhbns.: Century Gallery, Thoresby Hall, Newport Gallery. *Commissions:* Commissioned as equestrian artist primarily. *Publications:* wrote and illustrated article The Horse in Watercolour for Leisure Painter magazine (Jan. 1997); paintings reproduced in many sporting magazines as promotions for exhbns. *Clubs:* S.W.A., Wildlife Art Soc. *Signs work:* "Fergusson." *Address:* Pelham House, Worksop College, Worksop, Notts. S80 3AP.

**BATTERSHILL, Norman James,** R.B.A. (1973), R.O.I. (1976), P.S. (1976), F.S.I.A.D. (1968); R.O.I. Stanley Grimm award (1989); landscape painter in oil, pastel, acrylic and water-colour, author, tutor; *b* London, 23 Apr., 1922. two *s.* three *d. Exhib:* R.A., R.B.A., R.O.I., N.E.A.C., P.S., etc., numerous one man shows etc. *Work in collections:* Ciba Geigy, Beechams, Post Office, Southern Gas, etc. *Publications:* Light on the Landscape, Draw Trees, Drawing and Painting Skies, Draw Landscape, Draw Seascapes (Pitman Publishing), Working with Oils, Painting Flowers in Oils, Painting Landscapes in Oils, Drawing for Pleasure, Teach Yourself to Draw (Search Press Ltd., London; and Pentalic Corp. U.S.A.), Painting and Drawing Water (A. & C. Black Ltd., 1984), Learn to Paint Trees (Collins, 1990), Painting Gardens (Batsford 1994), painting Landscapes in Oils (Batsford 1997). *Signs work:* "Norman Battershill." *Address:* 1 Lovells Cottages, Burton St., Marnhull, Sturminster Newton, Dorset.

**BAWTREE, John Andrew,** D.Arch (Kingston, 1977), A.R.B.A. (1982), R.B.A. (1984); Greenshield Foundation Award (1978, 1980); painter in oil on canvas; *b* Cheam, Surrey, 1 Nov., 1952. *Educ:* Bradfield College, Berks. (1966-70). *Studied:* Kingston Polytechnic School of Architecture (1970-73, 1975-77). *Exhib:* R.A., R.B.A.; one-man: Caius College, Cambridge, Christ Church, Oxford, British Council, Oman, Aldeburgh Cinema Gallery, Falcon House, Boxford, Piers Feetham Gallery, London, Melitensia Gallery, Malta. *Work in collections:* Greenshield Foundation, Montreal, Foreign and Commonwealth Office, Muscat. *Clubs:* Chelsea Arts. *Signs work:* "John Bawtree." *Address:* Pine View, Peasenhall, Suffolk IP17 2HZ.

**BAXTER, Ann W.,** N.D.D.(Hons.) (1955), S.E.A.; winner, British Sporting Art Trust Sculpture Prize (1990), joint winner (1986) and President's Medal

(1994); freelance sculptor in wood, stone and bronze; *b* Leeds, Nov., 1934. *m* W.L.J. Potts (decd.). one *s. Educ:* Leeds Girls' High School. *Studied:* Leeds College of Art (1950-55, Harry Phillips). *Exhib:* S.E.A. annually, Open exhbns.: Leeds City A.G., Cartwright Hall Bradford, Wakefield City A.G., and widely in U.K. in private and public galleries. *Work in collections:* York City A.G., and private collections in U.K., U.S.A., Europe and Australia. Breeds Arabian horses. *Signs work:* "A.W. Baxter." *Address:* Ivy Farm, Roecliffe, Boroughbridge, York YO5 9LY.

**BAXTER, Denis Charles Trevor,** F.R.S.A., U.A. (1986), Mem. Printmakers Council (1981), N.S. (1987), President, N.S. (1989); teacher, lecturer, artist in oil and etching; *b* Southsea, 1 Mar., 1936. *Educ:* Ryde School, I.O.W. *Studied:* Bournemouth and Poole College of Art (1964-65); Stockwell College, Bromley, Kent (1965-68). *Exhib:* R.A., R.W.A., R.E., N.E.A.C., P.S., N.S., U.A. *Work in collections:* Canada, France, Germany, Japan, Switzerland, U.K., U.S.A. *Clubs:* Chelsea Arts. *Signs work:* "Denis Baxter" or "D.B." *Address:* 20 Church Rd., Southbourne, Bournemouth, Dorset BH6 4AT.

**BAYLY, Clifford John,** R.W.S. (1981), N.D.D. (1950); painter in oils, acrylic, water-colour, illustrator, lecturer, writer. Four times prizewinner in national competitions (1992/93, 1996); *b* London, 1927. *m* Jean Oddell. two *s.* one *d. Studied:* St. Martin's and Camberwell Schools of Art (Sir William Coldstream, Prof. Sir Lawrence Gowing). *Exhib:* R.A., R.W.S., various galleries in U.K., also Malta, Sydney, Melbourne and Adelaide, Australia. *Work in collections:* State Bank of S. Australia, Westpac Bank, T.V. South, Tricentrol, London, Chevron U.K. *Commissions:* Winchester Hospital. *Publications:* children's educational books, books on painting and drawing techniques. *Signs work:* "CLIFFORD BAYLY." *Address:* The Stables, Oaks Farm, High St., Staplehurst, Tonbridge, Kent TN12 0BH.

**BAYNES, Pauline Diana,** M.S.I.A.; designer and illustrator; *b* 1922. *Studied:* Farnham School of Art and Slade. *Publications:* books illustrated include: A Treasury of French Tales, Farmer Giles of Ham and Tom Bombadil (Allen and Unwin), Arabian Nights and Fairy Tales of the British Isles (Blackie), seven Narnia Books by C. S. Lewis (Bles and Bodley Head), Sister Clare, Miracle Plays, St. George and the Dragon (Houghton Mifflin, U.S.A.), Dictionary of Chivalry (Longmans), Kate Greenaway Medal (1968), Companion to World Mythology (Kestrel Books, 1979). *Signs work:* "PAULINE BAYNES" - occasionally with a small bird - see appendix. *Address:* Rock Barn Cottage, Dockenfield, nr. Farnham, Surrey GU10 4HH.

**BAYS, Jill,** N.D.D. (1951), S.W.A. (1988), B.A. (Open)(1985); artist in water-colour and oil, teacher; *b* Ambala, India, 24 Nov., 1931. *m* Bernard Bays. two *d. Educ:* Sir William Perkins', Chertsey. *Studied:* Guildford School of Art (1947-51). *Exhib:* R.I., S.WL.A., S.W.A., numerous shared exhbns. with husband and others. *Publications:* The Watercolourist's Garden (David and Charles, 1993), Flowers in the Landscape (David and Charles,1995). *Signs* *work:* "Jill Bays." *Address:* Bayswater, Hamm Ct., Weybridge, Surrey KT13 3YB.

**BAZAINE, Jean,** painter; *b* Paris, 1904. *Educ:* L. ès L. *Exhib:* Galerie Carré and Maeght, Paris, Retr. exhbn., Berne (1958), Eindhoven (1959), Hanover, Zürich, Oslo (1963), Paris (1965), Athènes, London, Edinburgh (1977), Oslo (1983), Maeght's Foundation (1987); repr. Biennele de Venice, São Paulo and Carnegie (member of the jury, 1952). *Work in collections:* most important museums in Europe and America. *Publications:* Notes sur la peinture l'aujourd'hui (ed. Seuil, Paris, 1948), Exercise de la peinture (ed. Seuil, 1973). Awards: Prix National des Arts (1964). Executed stained-glass windows for the church of Assy (1946), Saint Séverin, Paris (1966), Cathedrale St. Die (1986), Chapelle de la Madeleine Bretagne, Chapelle de Berlens Suisse, Chapelle St. Dominique Paris; ceramic mural and windows at Audincourt (1951-54); ceramic mural at U.N.E.S.C.O. (1960); Maison de l'O.R.T.F., Paris (1963), Se'nat, Paris (1986), Subway 'Cluny' (1987). *Address:* 36 r. P. Brossolette 92140 Clamart.

**BEAUMONT, Sarah Elizabeth,** B.A. (Hons.) (1988), A.M.N.S. (1997), N.A.P.A. (1997); painter in oil and acrylic; *b* London, 10 Sept.,1966. *Educ:* City of London School for Girls, EC1; University of Lancaster (1985-88). *Exhib:* R.A., S.W.A., N.S., group shows include Scott Gallery, Lancaster, Westminster Gallery, London, The Atrium Gallery, Whiteley's, London, Mariots, Bristol, Mall Galleries, London, R.A. *Commissions:* various for public bldgs. including the Millfield Theatre, London. *Clubs:* Fine Art Trade Guild. *Signs work:* "S.E Beaumont." *Address:* P.O Box 11801, London N20 0EA.

**BEAUVAIS, Walter John,** artist in oil and water-colour; *b* Datchet, Bucks., 14 Mar., 1942. *m* Anne Veronica. one *s.* one *d. Educ:* Staines Grammar School. *Studied:* under Arnold Beauvais in his London, Paris and Rome studios. *Exhib:* regular annual exhbns. both national and international. *Work in collections:* two royal and many international. Gallery affiliation: John Campbell Gallery, 164 Walton St., London SW3 2JL. *Clubs:* Chelsea Arts. *Signs work:* see appendix. *Address:* 1 The Dell, Bishopsgate Rd., Englefield Green, Surrey TW20 0XY.

**BECK, Stuart,** R.S.M.A. (1980); artist in water-colour and oil; former technical illustrator and graphic designer; *b* London, 18 June, 1903. *m* Jane Gwendoline (decd.). one *s.* one *d. Studied:* Rochester School of Art (1919-21). *Exhib:* R.S.M.A., R.B.A., S.G.A., etc. Abroad: R.S.M.A. (Vancouver 1982), Paris (1984), New Zealand (1984), R.S.M.A. (Mystic Seaport, U.S.A. 1987), Dusseldorf (1987). *Work in collections:* National Maritime Museum, Hull, R.N.L.I. Museum, Poole. *Publications:* How to Draw Fishing Craft; How to Draw Pleasure Craft; Ships, Boats and Craft; A Dash of Salt (autobiography). *Signs work:* "STUART BECK." *Address:* 22 Parish Ct., Emsworth Rd., Lymington, Hants. SO41 9BS.

**BECKER, Haidee,** draughtsman, painter in oil; *b* Los Angeles, Calif., 13 Jan., 1950. one *s.* one *d. Educ:* French Lycée. *Studied:* with Uli Nimptsch, R.A.,

Elizabeth Keys, Adrian Ryan. *Exhib:* R.P., H.A.C., R.A., Ben Uri, Roland Browse & Delbanco, New Grafton, C.D. Soar & Son, Odette Gilbert Gallery Timothy Tew Galerie, Atlanta, Georgia; managed by Anne Berthoud, 4 Stanley Cres., W11 2NB. *Work in collections:* N.P.G. *Signs work:* "Becker." *Address:* 46 Glebe Pl., London SW3 5JE.

**BECKERLEY, Tracy,** M.A. (1989), B.A.(Hons.) (1986), Higher Dip. in Visual Art (1987), Art Foundation Dip. (1983); artist in gouache, paper making printmaking; and healer; visiting lecturer, Lincoln Art School and Brooks University; *b* Bournemouth, 10 Dec., 1963. *Studied:* Harrow C.H.E. (1982-83 Brian Pummer), Gwent C.H.E. (1983-86, Roy Ascot), Oxford Polytechnic (1986-87, Ivor Robinson), Chelsea School (1988-89, Tim Mara). *Exhib* Whitechapel Open (1994); mixed shows in East-West Gallery, Todd Gallery Concourse Gallery Barbican, Flowers East, Overseas League House Whitworth Gallery, Business Design Centre. *Signs work:* "Beck." *Address.* Suite 22, Sparkford House, Battersea Church Rd., London SW11 3NQ.

**BEECROFT, Glynis:** see OWEN, Glynis.

**BEESON, Jane,** Arnolfini Open Competition prize winner, 1963; painter in P.V.A., oil and enamel; *b* Weybridge, Surrey, 10 Apr., 1930. *m* Christopher Beeson. three *s.* one *d. Studied:* Kingston School of Art, Surrey (1949-51) Beaux Arts, Paris (1951-52), under Brianchon; Slade, London (1953). *Exhib.* John Moore's (1961); London exhib., Rowan Gallery and New Art Centre Arnolfini, Bristol. *Work in collections:* "Mauve and Yellow" bought by Director, Ferens Art Gallery, Hull. *Signs work:* "J. Beeson." *Address:* Ford Farm, Manaton, S. Devon.

**BEILBY, Pauline Margaret,** N.D.D. (1950); portrait and equestrian sculptor in clay, textile designer, freelance; *b* Bramcote, Notts., 21 June, 1927. *m* Keith David Barnes, lace manufacturer. two *s. Educ:* Nottingham Girls' High School. *Studied:* Nottingham College of Arts and Crafts under A. H. Rodway A.R.C.A., F.R.S.A., principal. *Signs work:* see appendix. *Address:* Burleigh House, 15 Albemarle Rd., Woodthorpe, Notts. NG5 4FE.

**BELL, Catherine,** B.A. (1985), painter in water-colour; *b* Tadcaster, 30 Nov., 1951. *m* Derek Ogle. *Educ:* Wakefield Girls' High School, University of Sussex. Elected mem. S.B.A. (1995), winner of Joyce Cumming Presentation Award for Botanical Painting (1994), elected mem. Yorkshire Water-colour Soc. (1995). *Exhib:* R.I. and R.W.S., many mixed exhbns., one-woman shows at Harrogate and Leeds. Work in corporate collections. *Signs work:* "C. Bell." *Address:* 11 Neville Terr., The Groves, York YO3 7NF.

**BELL, Stanley Fraser,** D.A. (Mural Design) Glasgow (1970); artist in mixed media reliefs and painted murals; former Senior Lecturer, Glasgow School of Art; *b* Glasgow, 12 Jan., 1928. *m* Catherine MacDonald. one *s. Studied:* Glasgow School of Art (1966-70). *Exhib:* Scottish Young Contemporaries (1969, 1970, 1971), The Clyde Group, Edinburgh (1971), John Player Bienalle 2 Touring Exhbn. (1971), 'With Murals in Mind' Acheson

House, Edinburgh (1974), 'Un Certain Art Anglais' Paris, Brussels (1979). *Work in collections:* large scale exterior murals in Glasgow. *Clubs:* Glasgow Art. *Signs work:* "Stan Bell." *Address:* 419 North Woodside Rd., Glasgow G20 6NN.

**BELLANY, John,** C.B.E. (1994), D.A. (Edin.), M.A. (Fine Arts), A.R.C.A., R.A., Hon. R.S.A.; artist in oil, water-colour, etching; *b* Port Seton, Scotland, 18 June, 1942. *m* Helen. two *s.* one *d. Educ:* Preston Lodge, Prestonpans, Scotland. *Studied:* Edinburgh College of Art (1960-65), R.C.A. (1965-68). *Exhib:* one-man shows in major galleries and museums throughout the world. *Work in collections:* National Galleries of Scotland, N.P.G., Tate Gallery, V. & A., M.O.M.A. (N.Y.), Metropolitan Museum (N.Y.), etc. *Publications:* John Bellany - Retrospective (Scottish National Gallery of Modern Art), John Bellany by John McEwen (Mainstream), John Bellany as Printmaker by Prof. Duncan Macmillan. *Signs work:* "John Bellany." *Address:* c/o Royal Academy of Arts, Piccadilly, London W1V 0DS.

**BELSEY, Hugh Graham,** B.A. (1976), M.Litt. (1981); museum curator; Curator, Gainsborough's House; *b* Hemel Hempstead, 15 May, 1954. *Educ:* University of Manchester and The Barber Inst. of Fine Arts, Birmingham. *Publications:* articles for art periodicals and exhbn. catalogues. *Address:* Gainsborough's House, 46 Gainsborough St., Sudbury, Suffolk CO10 6EU.

**BELSKY, Franta,** A.R.C.A., F.R.B.S., P.S.P.S., Hon. Doc., Fulton, Westminster College, Missouri; *b* Brno, 1921. *m* Margaret C. Owen (d. 1989). *Studied:* sculpture: Prague Academy, R.C.A. *Work in collections:* The Queen, Queen Mother, Universities, N.P.G., Europe and U.S.A., c. councils, ind. and pte. companies, e.g., "Joy-ride," Stevenage; "Triga," Tattersalls, Knightsbridge; "Lesson," Bethnal Green; "Astronomer Herschel," Slough; "Oracle," Temple Way, Bristol; "Totem," Arndale Centre, Manchester; Admiral Cunningham, Trafalgar Square; Mountbatten Memorial, Horse Guards Parade; Winston Churchill statue, Fulton, Missouri; Winston Churchill sculpture, Prague; Harry S. Truman, Pres. Library, Independence; Lord Cottesloe, National Theatre; fountains: Shell Centre, London; "Leap," Jamestown Harbour, London Dockland; R.A.F. Memorial, Prague (1995). Monograph (Zwemmer, 1992). *Address:* 4 The Green, Sutton Courtenay, OX14 4AE.

**BELTON, Liam,** R.H.A. (1993), A.N.C.A. (1971); painter in oil, keeper of Royal Hibernian Academy (1995); *b* Dublin, 1947. *m* Sharon Lynch. two *s.* one *d. Educ:* Synge Street. *Studied:* National College of Art, Dublin (1966-72). *Exhib:* five one-man shows, various group shows throughout Ireland. *Work in collections:* Dept. of Labour, E.S.B., G.P.A., National Self-Portrait Collection, K.P.M.G., Craig Gardner, Sisks, Elm Park Hospital, An Post., A.I.B., O.P.W., Haverty Trust. Member of A.A.I. and S.S.I. *Signs work:* "Liam Belton, R.H.A." *Address:* 18 Whitethorn Rd., Artane, Dublin 5, Ireland.

**BELTRAN, Felix,** B.A., B.Sc.; American Inst. of Graphic Arts, N.Y. (1961),

Internationale Buchkunst Ausstellung, Leipzig (1971), Bienale Uzite Grafiky, Brno (1972), International Print Biennale, Listowel (1980); painter, printmaker, illustrator; Titular Prof. Universidad Autónoma Metropolitana, México; *b* Havana, 23 June, 1938. *m* Lassie Sobera. one *d*. *Educ:* Colegio Cubano Arturo Montori, Havana. *Studied:* School of Visual Arts, N.Y., American Art School, N.Y. *Exhib:* Rousski Gallery, Sofia; Galerie Manes, Praha; Sala Ocre, Caracas; Galería Elisava, Barcelona. *Work in collections:* Museo de Arte Contemporaneo, Panamá; Brooklyn Museum, N.Y.; Museo de Bellas Artes, Caracas; Muzeum Sztuki, Lodz; National Museum, Stockholm; Museum Narodowe, Warsaw. *Publications:* Desde el Diseño (Havana, 1970), Artes Plásticas (Havana, 1982). *Clubs:* World Print Council, San Francisco, Print Club, Philadelphia, L'Accademia d'Europa, Parma, Assoc. Internationale des Arts Plastiques, Paris. *Signs work:* see appendix. *Address:* Apartado M-10733, México 06000 DF, México.

**BENHAM, Clive Graham,** R.B.S.A., City and Guilds (1951); teacher/artist in wood (wood carving, sculpture and cabinet making), painting; Retd. Head of Dept. Careers Education; V.P.R.B.S.A. (1984-87); *b* Melbourne, Australia, 23 Sept., 1929. *m* Doreen Hazel. two *s*. *Studied:* Moseley Rd. School of Art, B'ham College of Arts and Crafts (A. Gregory), Aston Technical College (now Central University). *Exhib:* joint shows, lectures and demonstrations in Wales and the Midlands. *Clubs:* Chairman and organiser 'Winter Salon' Group of Artists. *Signs work:* "C. Graham Benham." *Address:* 53 Spiceland Rd., Northfield, Birmingham B31 1NL.

**BENJAMIN, Anthony,** N.D.D., R.E., F.R.S.A.; artist in sculpture, painting and print-making; *b* 29 Mar., 1931. *Studied:* F. Leger Studio, Paris (1951), Atelier 17 (1957). *Work in collections:* Museum of Modern Art, N.Y.; Tate Gallery, London; V. & A., London; Museum of Modern Art, Japan; Museum of Modern Art, Poland; Museum of Modern Art, Yugoslavia; Albright-Knox Gallery, U.S.A.; J. Hershon Museum of Contemporary Art, U.S.A.; Norwich Castle Museum, etc. *Publications:* Empty Swings (Two Printers Press, 1965). Dealers: Gimpel Fils, London, Mira Godard, Toronto. *Signs work:* see appendix. *Address:* The Green, Kelling Village, Holt, Norfolk NR25 7EN.

**BENNETT, Brian Theodore Norton,** M.A. Oxon. (1954), R.O.I. (1973), P.R.O.I. (1987), N.S. (1985), Hon. U.A. (1985); landscape painter in oil; Director of Art, Berkhamsted School; *b* Olney, Bucks., 1927. *m* Margrit Elizabeth Brenner. *Educ:* Magdalen College School, Oxford and Magdalen College, Oxford. *Studied:* Ruskin School of Art, Oxford (1950) part-time; Regent St. Polytechnic (1956) evening classes. *Exhib:* R.A., R.B.A., R.O.I., R.S.M.A., etc. *Publications:* Choir Stalls of Chester Cathedral (1965), Oil Painting with a Knife (1993). *Signs work:* "Brian Bennett" or "B.T.N.B." *Address:* 18 Upper Ashlyns Rd., Berkhamsted, Herts. HP4 3BW.

**BENNETT, David Stuart,** B.A. (Hons.) (1992); M.A. (R.C.A.) (1995), S.WL.A. (1992); artist in water-colour and oil; *b* Doncaster, 11 Dec., 1969.

*udied:* Leeds Polytechnic (1989-92), Royal College of Art, London (1993-5). *Exhib:* one-man shows: England; mixed exhbns. America, Holland, Spain, ance, Ireland. *Publications:* Artist for nature publications, Flight of Cranes to xtremadura. *Signs work:* "David Bennett." *Address:* 16 Pearl St., Harrogate G1 4QW.

**BENNETT, June,** N.D.D., A.T.D.; painter/jeweller in silver and gold; *b* range over Sands. *m* Michael Bennett. two *s. Educ:* Ulverston G.S. *Studied:* ancaster and Leicester Colleges of Art. *Exhib:* Goldsmiths Hall, Midland roup Gallery, Nottingham, Park Square Gallery, Leeds, Mignon Gallery, ath, Ashgate Gallery, Farnham; one-man shows, Castlegate House Gallery, ockermouth (1988, 1989, 1991, 1993, 1994). *Work in collections:* Jewellery: bbot Hall Gallery, Kendal, Shipley A.G.; Paintings: Carlisle Museum and .G., Copeland C.C. Painting full time from 1987. *Signs work:* "June Bennett," .B." and Sheffield Assay Office hallmark. *Address:* The Hollies, Port arlisle, Cumbria. CA5 5BU.

**BENNETT, Michael,** N.D.D., A.T.D.; painter in oils; *b* Windermere, 1934. June Steer. two *s. Educ:* Windermere Grammar School. *Studied:* Lancaster d Leicester Colleges of Art. *Exhib:* one-man shows: Park Square Gallery, eeds, Mignon Gallery, Bath, Bluecoat Gallery, Liverpool, Ashgate Gallery, arnham, Abbot Hall, Kendal, A.I.A. Gallery, London; Leeds, Birmingham, ull and Lancaster Universities, Castlegate Gallery, Cockermouth. *Work in ollections:* Abbot Hall Gallery, Wakefield City A.G., Lincolnshire Arts ssoc., John Player Collection, Leeds Educ. Authority, Kettle's Yard, Univ. of ambridge and Northern Arts Assoc. *Signs work:* "Bennett" and date. *Address:* he Hollies, Port Carlisle, Cumbria CA5 5BU.

**BENNETT, Terence,** N.D.D., F.R.S.A., Yorkshire Television Fine Art ellowship (1973-74); painter in oil on canvas and water-colour, teacher; Head f Fine Art, Thomas Rotherham College, Rotherham (1976-91); *b* Doncaster, 7 ov., 1935. *Studied:* Doncaster School of Art (Eric Platt, T.A. Anderson). xhib: R.A., R.O.I., N.E.A.C., Drian Gallery, Travelling exhbn. Yorkshire, incolnshire, N.S., British Painting, Mall Galleries. *Work in collections:* uffield Foundation, Bank of England, Yorkshire Television, Yorkshire Arts ssoc., Leeds Educ. Authority, Halifax Bldg. Soc., Sheffield University, ambridge University, Doncaster Borough Council, I.C.I. Ltd. Prizes: Singer d Friedlander, Sunday Times Water-colour competition. *Signs work:* erence Bennett." *Address:* Rambler Cottage, 43 Main St., Sprotbrough, oncaster, S. Yorks. DN5 7RH.

**BENNETT, William,** R.M.S.; freelance artist of miniature portraits, still life d marine paintings in water-colour and oil; Council mem. R.M.S.; *b* London, 1 June, 1917. *m* Isabel Weaver. one *s.* one *d. Educ:* Heritage School. *Studied:* ir John Cass College, London. *Exhib:* R.A., F.B.A. Gallery. *Work in collec- ons:* H.M. The Queen Elizabeth II Collection, Balmoral Galleries, Geelong, ustralia, Manyung Gallery, Mt. Eliza, Victoria, Australia. *Signs work:* mono-

gram of initials - see appendix and "Wm. Bennett." *Address:* 4 Buttery C
Honiton, Devon EX14 8FB; and Route d'Hennebont, St. Yves 56310 Bubr
Morbihan, France.

**BENNEY, Prof. Adrian Gerald Sallis,** C.B.E., R.D.I. (1971), Hon. M./
(Leics., 1963), Des. R.C.A. (1954); goldsmith and silversmith; Professor
Silversmithing and Jewellery at Royal College of Art (1974-83); *b* Hull, 2
Apr., 1930. *m* Janet Edwards. three *s.* one *d. Educ:* Brighton Grammar Schoc
*Studied:* Brighton College of Art (1946-50); Royal College of Art (1951-5
under Prof. Robert Goodden, R.D.I. Royal Warrants of Appointment to H.M
The Queen (1974), Queen Elizabeth, The Queen Mother (1975), H.R.H. Tl
Duke of Edinburgh (1975) and H.R.H. The Prince of Wales.(1980). *Sig*
*work:* "Gerald Benney." *Address:* Beenham House, Beenham, nr. Readin
Berks. RG7 5LJ.

**BENSON, Rosemary,** R.E. (1997); artist in engraving, water-colour and o
*b* Malawi, 1948. *m* Mark Burgess, author and illustrator. *Educ:* Livingstor
High School, Zambia; Cambridge High School for Girls. *Studied:* Cambridξ
College of Arts and Technology (1966-67), Michaelis School of Fine A ι
University of Cape Town (1973-75), Slade School of Fine Art (1977-79
*Exhib:* R.A., R.E., R.W.S. *Address:* Stoke Cottage, Stoke St. Mary, Taunt
TA3 5BZ.

**BENSUSAN-BUTT, John Gordon,** landscape painter in water-colour;
Colchester, 6 June, 1911. *Educ:* Gresham's School, Holt; Magdalen Colleg
Oxford. *Studied:* as pupil of Lucien Pissarro (1935-39), and at R.C.A., etchir
(1935), Central School of Art and Crafts, lithography (1939). *Exhib:* R.A
N.E.A.C., R.B.A., Leicester Galleries, Redfern, etc. One-man shows at Frenc
Gallery (1937), Kensington A.G. (1949), Leicester Galleries (1957), Minorie
Colchester (1962, 1964, 1975), Ashmolean (Eldon Gallery) Oxford (1986
*Publications:* On Naturalness in Art (1981), Thomas Gainsborough in h
Twenties (1993). *Signs work:* see appendix. *Address:* 31b Lexden Rc
Colchester CO3 3PX.

**BENT, Medora Heather,** F.I.A.L.; painter in oil, water-colour; from 196
has taken up pottery; *b* North Kilworth, family home and chief influenc
Connemara. *m* Roger Bent. one *s. Educ:* The Laurels, Rugby, and Upper Chin
I.O.W. *Studied:* Slade School (1930-33), Diploma under Professor Schwab
Central School of Arts and Crafts: stained glass, pottery and modelling; worke
in Ireland, France, Hungary, Sark and Belgium. *Exhib:* N.E.A.C., Londc
Group, S.G.A., S.W.A., Nat. Soc. *Publications:* Paintings of Historical Housε
of Purbeck (1958). *Signs work:* "M. H. Bent." *Address:* 10 East St., Warehan
Dorset.

**BENTON, Graham,** N.D.D. (1964), A.R.B.S.A. (1986); abstra
painter/illustrator in oil, gouache, collage, charcoal, pastel; part-time art tuto
Former Sec. and Chairman Walsall Arts Council; Sec. Walsall Soc. of Artist
Associate mem. Penwith Soc. of Arts; Mem. N.S.E.A.D.; *b* Birmingham, 2

ıct., 1934. *Studied:* Walsall School of Art (1952-56, George Willott, Angus lacauley), Wolverhampton College of Art (1962-64, John Finnie, Bernard rett). *Exhib:* Stafford A.G., Lichfield A.G., Walsall A.G., Letchworth A.G., 73 Gallery, London, Keele University, Salthouse Gallery, St. Ives, Penlee louse, Penzance, R.B.S.A. Galleries, Wednesbury A.G., Camborne School of lines, Solihull A.G., Mid-art, Dudley, Staffordshire Open. *Signs work:* (Graham) Benton" - see appendix. *Address:* 17 Clarendon St., Bloxwich, /alsall, W. Midlands WS3 2HT.

**BERESFORD-WILLIAMS, Mary E.,** B.A.Hons. Fine Art, Reading (1953 lass 1); Cert. Educ. (1954); painter, printmaker and photographer; Mem. lewlyn Society of Artists; mem. Devon Guild of Craftsmen. South-West Arts lajor Award (1978). Photographer in Residence, Television South-West ı986-87); *b* London, 30 Apr., 1931. *m* David Beresford-Williams. one *s. Educ:* /atford Grammar School. *Studied:* painting: Reading University under Prof. J. ı. Betts. *Exhib:* Galleries in London and the South-west. *Work in collections:* aintings, photographs and prints in public and private collections. *ublications:* Since 1970 made many screen prints, sold in limited editions. ǃ988 book of photographs: A Portrait of TSW. *Signs work:* "M. Beresford-Villiams" or "MBW." *Address:* 11 Langdon Lane, Galmpton, nr. Brixham, S. ǃevon TQ5 0PQ.

**BERG, Adrian,** R.A.; Gold medal, Florence Biennale (1973), major prize, ʹolly Cobbold (1981), third prize, John Moores (1982); painter; *b* London, ǃ929. *Educ:* Charterhouse; Caius College, Cambridge (M.A.); Trinity College, ǃublin (H.Dip.Ed.). *Studied:* St. Martin's (1955-56), Chelsea (1956-58), ǃ.C.A. (1958-61). *Exhib:* 5, Tooth's (1964-75); 3, Waddington Galleries (1978-3), Waddington Galleries, Montreal, Toronto (1979), Rochdale A.G. (1980), , Piccadilly Gallery (1985-93), Serpentine Gallery, Walker A.G. (1986), ǃarbican Touring Exhbn. (1993-94). *Work in collections:* Arts Council, British ʹouncil, B.M., European Parliament, Govt. Picture Coll., Hiroshima City ǃuseum of Contemporary Art, Tate Gallery, Tokyo Metropolitan Art Museum. *ıgns work:* "Adrian Berg." *Address:* c/o Piccadilly Gallery, 16 Cork St., ,ondon W1X 1PF.

**BERLIN, Sven,** sculptor in stone, painter and writer; *b* 14 Sept., 1911. two *s.* ne *d. Educ:* St. Winifred's, Kenley. *Studied:* Redruth, Cornwall, under A. C. ǃambly. *Exhib:* Lefevre, Tooth's, London, Houston, Texas, New York, Tate ,ondon, Tate St. Ives, etc. *Work in collections:* Tate Gallery, V. & A., B.M., ǃusee de la Bataille de Normandie (1944), Nat. Library of Scotland, Musee ʹArt, Ovar, Portugal, Imperial War Museum, I.S.R., Fawley, Poole Technical ʹollege, Lord Weymouth, Longleat. *Publications:* Alfred Wallis; Primitive Nicholson & Watson, 1948), I Am Lazarus (Dent, 1961), Dark Monarch ǃent, 1962), Jonah's Dream (Dent, 1964), Dromengro (Collins, 1971), Pride of ǃe Peacock (Collins, 1972), Amergin (David and Charles, 1978), Coat of ǃany Colours (Redcliffe Press, 1994), Virgo in Exile (1996). *Signs work:* see appendix. *Address:* Old Keeper's Cottage, Gaunts, Wimborne, Dorset BH2 4JS.

**BERNARD, Mike,** B.A. (Hons.) (1978), R.A.S.Dip. (1981), R.I. (1997 painter in mixed media, acrylics, oil, tutor; demonstrator of painting technique to art societies;*b* Dover, 2 Aug., 1957. *m* Susan. one *s.* one *d. Studied:* Wes Surrey College of Art and Design (1975-78), R.A. Schools (1978-81). *Exhib* R.A., N.E.A.C., R.I., numerous one-man and group exhbns. *Commissions:* sev eral mural and large scale works. *Publications:* work repro.: writer for art mag azine. *Address:* Old House Farm, Nursted, Petersfield, Hants. GU31 5RD.

**BERRISFORD, Peter,** N.D.D., A.T.D., F.R.S.A.; painter (oils, water colours), lecturer, (Arts Council, National Trust, National Association o Decorative and Fine Art Societies, Swans (Hellenic); *b* Northampton, 11 Feb 1932. *m* Jacqueline. one *s. Studied:* Northampton, Chelsea, Bournemouth A Colleges (Travelling Scholarship 1953). *Exhib:* Bear Lane, Wildensteins Piccadilly, Trafford Galleries, London, R.B.A., R.A., John Moore's, regularl at Melitensia Gallery, Malta. *Work in collections:* Hertfordshire, Hull, Surrey Leicester, Sheffield, Northampton, Wales University, East Sussex C.C Lithographs: New York Book of Month Club, Curwen Studios. Paintings fo B.B.C.'s 'The Clothes in the Wardrobe' and 'The House of Eliott' (filmed 199 and 1993). *Signs work:* oils "Berrisford," water-colours "Peter Berrisford. *Address:* 73 Woodgate Rd., Eastbourne BN22 8PD.

**BERRY, John,** A.I.C.A., Soc. of Portrait Artists, U.S.; Portrait artist U.S Gallery of Presidents; artist in oil and pastel; *b* London, 9 June, 1920. *m* Jessie three *s.* two *d. Studied:* Hammersmith Art College; Royal Academy of Ar *Exhib:* Weighhouse one-man show; Patterson Gallery; Driffold Gallery. *Wor in collections:* Imperial War Museum, Regimental H.Q. Tidsworth, Hants *Publications:* work repro.: Esso Tiger, Ladybird Books, covers for Corgi, Fou Square, Panther, Penguin and Readers Digest. U.S. Contact: Bob Mallenfan Southwest Gallery, 4500 Sigma, Dallas, Texas. 75244 U.S.A. *Signs work:* "1 Berry 98." *Address:* Dove Cottage, 1 Scropton Old Rd., Hatton, Derbyshir DE65 5DX.

**BERRY, June,** D.F.A.Lond. (1948), R.E. (1986), R.W.S. (1993), N.E.A.C (1990), R.W.A. (1993); artist in etching, oil and water-colour; *b* Melbourne Derbyshire. *m* John Berry. one *s.* two *d. Educ:* Boston Lincs. *Studied:* Slad School of Fine Art (1941-42, 1946-49). *Exhib:* R.A., R.E., R.W.S., and i Germany and U.S.A. *Work in collections:* Ashmolean Museum Oxford, Roya West of England Academy, Graphotek, Berlin, National Museum of Wales Kettering A.G., Oldham A.G. *Publications:* Limited Edn. Livre d'Artist 'Passing Days' (1984). *Signs work:* "June Berry." *Address:* 45 Chancery La. Beckenham, Kent BR3 6NR.

**BERRY-HART, David James,** M.A.; painter and sculptor; *b* Trinidad 1940. *Studied:* St. Martin's School of Art (1959-1961), City of Birmingham Polytechnic (1981-83). *Exhib:* one-man shows: A.I.A. Gallery, London (1969)

Herbert A.G. Coventry (1970), Camden Arts Centre (1975), University of Warwick (1977), Imperial College (1979), Royal National College for the Blind (1979), Cannon Hill Park (1979), Whitefriars Coventry (1988), mid-Warwickshire College Gallery (1990), Worcester City A.G. (1991), Quaker Gallery, London (1994), Nuneaton A.G. (1996); group: Spectrum Central (1971), Art in Steel (1972), Gawthorpe Festival (1974), On the Town sculpture (1987), Cultural Connections (1995), Nottingham Trent University; with "The Firm" exhib. Hampshire (Touring) (1983-4), Carlisle A.G. (1984), Liverpool University (1985), Williamson A.G. (1986), Beecroft A.G. (1987), Chelmsford A.G. (1987). *Work in collections:* R.N.C.B., Imperial College. *Publications:* work reproMidlands Arts Magazine, Spectrum Central Catalogue. Awards: Arts Council (1975), West Midlands Arts Association (1978). *Address:* 13 Tennant St., Nuneaton, Warwickshire CV11 4NT.

**BERRYMAN, Derek James,** N.D.D. (1951), A.T.D. (1955), B.Ed.(Hons.) (1977), F.R.S.A. (1960); artist in oil, water-colour, etching, lithography; lecturer (retd.): London Guildhall Univ.Sir John Cass College, Leeds College of Art, Buckinghamshire C.H.E., Weston-super-Mare School of Art; *b* Chingford, Essex, 1926. *m* Irene Metzger. one *s.* one *d. Educ:* Normanhurst School, Chingford, St Aubyn's School, Woodford, S.W. Essex Technical College, University of Bristol. *Studied:* St. Martin's School of Art; Sir John Cass College; King's College, University of Durham; also English Speaking Union Scholarship to Syracuse University, U.S.A. *Exhib:* R.A., R.B.A., R.O.I., R.W.A., Scotland, Germany, U.S.A., and provincial galleries in England. *Work in collections:* Various U.S.A. Germany and Britain. War service: 1944-48 initially R.A.F.V.R. Air Crew cadet; Gordon Highlanders and Indian Army. *Signs work:* "Berryman" or initial "B" with date. *Address:* The Mill House, Wester Tillyrie, by Milnathort, Kinross-shire KY13 7RW, Scotland.

**BERTHOLD:** see DUNNE, Berthold.

**BEST, Ronald O'Neal,** R.C.A., Dip.F.A., Post, Dip.; teaches litho at Heatherly School of Fine Art, London; painter and printmaker; *b* London, 25 May, 1957. *Educ:* Sladebrook High School, London. *Studied:* Byam Shaw School of Art; Croydon College of Art; R.C.A. London; Asst. to Winston Branch, painter. *Exhib:* R.O.I., N.E.A.C., P.S., S.G.A., Salon des National, Paris, Lynn Stern Young Artists, London, Eva Jekel Gallery, Twentieth Century British Art Fair, R.C.A. London, 1492-1992 Un Nouveau Regard sur les Caraibes, Paris, Art House, Amsterdam, President Portobello Group, Pall Mall Deposit Gallery, the Portobello Group. *Work in collections:* R.C.A., Croydon College, Grange Museum, London. *Commissions:* London Art Forms. *Clubs:* Portobello Group. *Signs work:* "Ronald Best." *Address:* 51 Exton Cres., Stonebridge, London NW10 8DA.

**BETHEL, David,** C.B.E., LL.D.(Leic.), D.Litt. (Lough), R.W.A., F.R.S.A., N.D.D., A.T.D., F.S.A.E., F.C.S.D.; graphic and typographic designer; Director, Leicester Polytechnic (1973-87); Chairman, CNAA Committee for

Art and Design (1974-80); mem. Design Council (1980-88); Chairman, Design Council Educ. Advisory Com. (1981-88); Hong Kong University and Polytechnic Grants Com. (1982-92); Chairman, Hong Kong Council for Academic Accreditation (1990-92); Chairman, Education and Training Committee, Chartered Society of Designers (1987-90); Senior Vice-President, R.W.A. (1997); Chairman, Bursary Awards Com. Worshipful Company Framework Knitters (1994); *b* Bath, 7 Dec., 1923. *m* Margaret. one *s.* one *d. Educ:* King Edward's School, Bath. *Studied:* Gloucester College of Art (1946-48), West of England College of Art (1948-51). *Work in collections:* Gloucester and Stafford Art Galleries, R.W.A., and private collections in U.S.A. and Israel. *Signs work:* "David Bethel." *Address:* 48 Holmfield Rd., Stoneygate, Leicester LE2 1SA.

**BETHEL, Marion Ross,** illuminator and letterer in water-colour, gold leaf, ink, parchment in illuminated books; *b* Wiesbaden, Germany, 19 Mar., 1929. *Educ:* P.N.E.U. correspondence course. *Studied:* with Gladys Best, R.W.A., and Daisy Alcock, A.R.C.A., F.R.S.A. *Exhib:* Salon de Soc. des Artistes Français. *Publications:* in Revue Moderne. *Signs work:* "M.R.B." or "Marion Ross Bethel." *Address:* 17 Strand, Topsham, Devon.

**BEVAN, Daniel Vaughan Gwillim,** R.I., W.C.S.W.; artist in water-colour; *b* Cardiff, 8 June, 1921. *m* Betty Eileen, divorced. one *d. Educ:* Willesden and Hendon Technical Colleges. *Signs work:* "Vaughan Bevan." *Address:* Bryn Glas, Garndolbenmaen, Gwynedd, LL51 9UX.

**BEVAN, Oliver,** A.R.C.A. (1964); painter in oil, pastel, monoprint; *b* Peterborough, 28 Mar., 1941. *Educ:* Eton. *Studied:* R.C.A. (Carel Weight, Colin Hayes, Leonard Rosoman). *Exhib:* Angela Flowers (1981), Odette Gilbert (1984), Gallery 10 (1991), "City/Two Views", Barbican (1986); exhib. in and curated "The Subjective City" touring exhbn. (1990-91), "Witnesses and Dreamers" touring (1993-94), "The Motor Show" touring (1996-97); solo "Urban Mirror" National Theatre (1997). *Work in collections:* Contemporary Art Soc., Museum of London, Cleveland Gallery, Unilever, Sainsbury, Guildhall A.G. *Commissions:* four ptgs for B.A.A. Gatwick (1990), Art on the Underground (1993). *Publications:* "London in Paint" Mus. of London. *Signs work:* signed on back "Oliver Bevan" - elongated vertical in "B"; works on paper "OB'87", etc. *Address:* 130 Percy Rd., London W12 9QL.

**BEVAN, Tony,** Dip.A.D. (1974), H.D.F.A. (1976); painter in acrylic and oil; *b* Bradford, 1951; partner Glenys Johnson. one *d. Studied:* Bradford College of Art (1968-71), Goldsmiths' College (1971-74), Slade School of Fine Art (1974-76). *Exhib:* I.C.A. London touring Britain (1980-87), Haus der Kunst Munich (1989), Kunsthalle Kiel (1988), Whitechapel A.G. (1993). *Work in collections:* Staats Galerie Moderner Kunst Munich, Kunsthalle Kiel, Metropolitan Museum of Art N.Y., Yale University, B.M., Theo Wormland Foundation Munich, British Council, Arts Council, M.O.M.A. (N.Y.), Toledo Museum, Ohio, Wolverhampton A.G. *Signs work:* "Bevan." *Address:* Studio 2, Acme

Studios, 165 Childers St., London SE8 5JR.

**BEVIS, Michael John Vaughan,** Cert Ed., A.I.E., A.R.P.S., F.R.S.A., M.F.P.S., M.CollP., D.F.A. (Painting); Head of Art and Design Dept., St. Peter's High School, Burnham-on-Crouch; artist in oil, photographer; *b* London, 11 Oct., 1948. *m* Marie Janice Gair. two *d*. *Educ:* Clarks College (1960-65). *Studied:* Hornsey College of Art (Foundation, 1966-67), Walthamforest Technical College and School of Art (1967-70), Barking N.E.L.P. (1970-72), London University Inst. of Educ. (Associateship, 1980-81). *Exhib:* one-man: Loggia Gallery, London (1980); group: Mall Gallery, London. *Publications:* associateship report 'Some Art activities in Prison'. *Signs work:* "M.J.V. BEVIS." *Address:* 2 Bergen Ct., Maldon, Essex CM9 6UH.

**BEWICK, Pauline,** R.H.A., Áosdana; awards: Soroptimist Painting (1975), U.N. Yasushi Akashi Poster (1981), Irish Life Arts (1990); artist in water-colour, tapestry, sculpture, oil, etching, etc.; *b* Northumberland, 1935. *m* Dr. Patrick Melia, psychiatrist. two *d*. *Studied:* N.C.A.D., Dublin. *Exhib:* Taylor Gallery Dublin, Catto Gallery, Odette Gilbert Gallery London, Guinness Hop Store Dublin, Frank Lewis Kerry, etc. *Work in collections:* in many public and private collections worldwide. *Publications:* subject of Painting a Life by James White (1985); author and illustrator, Ireland: An Artist's Year (Methuen, 1990); A Boy and a Dolphin (Granada, 1983); illustrated, Irish Tales and Sagas (1994); author and illustrator: The South Seas and a Box of Paints (Art Books Int. London, 1996); The Yellow Man (1996). Documentary: A Painted Diary by David Shaw-Smith, R.T.E., Channel 4, Pompidou Centre Paris, also Los Angeles and Chicago film festivals (1994). Two years spent painting and writing in Polynesia. *Clubs:* Chelsea Arts. *Signs work:* see appendix. *Address:* Treanmanagh, Glenbeigh, Co. Kerry, Ireland.

**BICKNELL, John,** B.A.(Hons.) (1980), H.Dip.F.A.(Lond.) (1983), Slade prize (1983), Boise Scholarship (1983), Greater London Arts award (1986), John Moores prize (1987), Henry Moore Fellow, Leeds Polytechnic (1989-90); painter; *b* Surrey, 1958. *m* Christina Dorees. one *d*. *Educ:* Ottershaw School. *Studied:* W.S.C.A.D. (1975-77), N.E. London Polytechnic (1977-80), Slade School of Fine Art (1981-83). *Exhib:* numerous group shows, including John Moores, Whitechapel Open, Christie's, New Contemporaries, R.C.A., Contemporary Art Soc., London Contemporary Art Fair, Miro Foundation, Barcelona, Monjuic, Girona, Cleveland International Drawing Biennale; one-man shows: Pomeroy Purdy Gallery, London, Eleni Koronaiou Gallery, Athens. *Work in collections:* Slade, Boise Scholarship, Leics. C.C., Nat. West, Reed International, Texaco. *Signs work:* "John Bicknell." *Address:* 44 Chertsey Rd., Chobham, Surrey GU24 8PJ; 19 Tinou St., Kipseli 11257, Athens.

**BICKNELL, Les,** B.A. (Hons.); book artist, printmaking/sculpture; visiting lecturer, Camberwell College of Art; *b* Coventry, 4 Mar., 1963. *m* Jayne Knight. two *s*. *Educ:* Binley Park Comprehensive. *Studied:* London College of

Printing (1982-85). *Exhib:* over 20 one-man shows since 1985 including Maison du L.A.C., Domart-en-Pontenthieu, V. & A., Nigel Greenwoods. *Work in collections:* Tate Gallery, V. & A., Rijkmuseum, Bodleian Library, M.O.M.A., N.Y. Public Library. *Commissions:* Many bookworks, including Eastern Arts Board and Birmingham Libraries. *Publications:* edited: Mapping Knowledge, The Book as Art, Beyond Reading. *Address:* Eva's Place, Sibton Green, Saxmundham, Suffolk IP17 2JX.

**BIDDULPH, Elizabeth Mary,** R.O.I. (1952), Hon. senior mem. R.O.I. (1982), N.D.D. (1947), Hon.Cert.R.D.S. (1942); painter chiefly in oils, portraits, landscapes, still-life, flowers; *b* Port Elizabeth, S.A., 17 June, 1927. *m* Nicholas Osborne John Biddulph. one *s*. *Educ:* Hamilton House School, Tunbridge Wells. *Studied:* Wimbledon School of Art (1944-47) under Gerald Cooper, A.R.C.A., Slade School of Fine Art (1949-51). *Exhib:* yearly at R.O.I.; one-man shows, Hornsey Library (1971), Barclays Bank, Egham (1977), Egham Library (1985), murals in shop, Virginia Water (1984). *Commissions:* Repainted and designed ceiling panels for writer Ralph Dutton's home 1961-62 (original ones destroyed by fire). *Publications:* articles for Leisure Painter Magazine (1980-81, 1987). Judging panel, John Laing Painting Competition (1988). *Signs work:* "E. Biddulph." *Address:* 74 Clarence St., Egham, Surrey TW20 9QY.

**BINNS, David,** N.D.D. (1956), S.WL.A. (1968); R.S.P.B. Fine Art Award (1990, 1992, 1993, 1994); freelance artist in water-colour, lino, scraperboard; teacher SP courses; with wife runs own Brent Gallery; *b* Sutton-in-Craven, 30 Sept., 1935. *m* Molly. one *s*. two *d*. *Educ:* Ermysted's Grammar School, Skipton. *Studied:* Skipton Art School (Dan Binns, J. C. Midgley), Leeds College of Art and Pulée. *Exhib:* S.WL.A., R.I., H.C. Dickens, Bloxham, Oxfordshire, Manor House, Ilkley, Aquarious Gallery, Harrogate, Leigh Yawkey Woodson Museum, Wisconsin, U.S.A. *Publications:* work repro.: Dalesman, childrens animal books, circular jigsaws, print by Soloman & Whitehead, Medici cards, R.S.P.B. calendar and cards, Yorkshire Journal. *Clubs:* S.WL.A., B.W.S., Y.W.S., F.I.G.A. *Signs work:* "David Binns." *Address:* Holmestead, 9 Boundary Ave., Sutton-in-Craven, Keighley, Yorks. BD20 8BL.

**BINNS, Lorna,** A.R.C.A. (1938), R.W.S. (1977); painter in water-colour; *b* Sheffield, 23 Oct., 1914. *m* John Dawson Binns (decd.). two *d*. *Educ:* Abbeydale Girls' Grammar School, Sheffield. *Studied:* Sheffield College of Art (1930-35) under Maurice Wheatley, R.C.A. (1935-39) under Prof. Tristram. *Exhib:* R.A., F.B.A. Gallery, The Guildhall, R.W.S. Gallery. *Signs work:* "Lorna Binns." *Address:* 7 Egmont Ave., Surbiton, Surrey KT6 7AU.

**BIRCH, David William,** painter/printmaker in water-colour and wood engraving; *b* 28 Jan., 1945. *m* Annabel Carey (artist and art tutor). one *s*. *Educ:* Wellesbourne School, Birmingham. *Studied:* mentors: water-colour - Kay Kinsman, wood engraving - William T. Rawlinson. *Exhib:* R.A., R.I., R.W.S.,

R.E., S.W.E., R.W.A.; one-man shows: Birmingham and Midland Inst., John Noott Gallery, Broadway, Ombersley Gallery, Worcester, twice yearly at his studio, Confederation Life, Bristol. *Work in collections:* University of Bristol, Confederation Life Insurance Co. *Publications:* illustrated, Spinning Wheels at Snowshill Manor (National Trust). *Signs work:* "David W. Birch." *Address:* Croftsbrook, Blind La., Chipping Campden, Glos. GL55 6ED.

**BIRD, Henry,** A.R.C.A. (1933), Art Workers Guild, Peterborough Diocesan Advisory Com., Civil List for Services to Art; figure draughtsman, mural decorator; *b* Northampton, 1909. *m* Freda Jackson (decd.), actress. one *s. Educ:* Northampton. *Studied:* Northampton and R.C.A. *Exhib:* many exhbns. in public and private galleries. *Work in collections:* University & Nat. Library, Wales; Carlisle; Brighton; Northampton; Theatre Museum, Covent Gdn., Drottningholm Theatre Museum, Sweden. Mural paintings in Conference Centre, Ecton, Northants.; Earls Barton Church; University Commonwealth Studies, London; Royal Theatre, Northampton; Ashcroft-Fairfield, Croydon; Drottningholm Theatre Museum, Sweden. Total decorative schemes, St. Crispin Hospital Chapel, Northants.; Daventry Hospital Chapel; Denton Church, Northants; Charwelton Village Chapel, Northants. *Signs work:* "H. Bird." *Address:* Hardingstone House, Northants NN4 7BU.

**BIRNE, Max Sidney,** F.F.P.S.; landscape and abstract painter in oil, watercolour and gouache; *b* London, 12 Jan., 1927. *m* Rosemarie Kesselman. one *s. Studied:* City Literary Inst., London; Harrow School of Art. *Exhib:* one-man shows: Burgh House, Hampstead, Lauderdale House Highgate, Mandel's Gallery Goodmayes, Margaret Fisher Gallery London, Tricycle Theatre London; group shows: Loggia Gallery, Chenil Gallery, Alpine Gallery, Mall Galleries, Barbican Arts Centre, Bloomsbury Gallery, Usher Museum Lincoln, Brighton Polytechnic A.G. *Work in collections:* R.S.B.A.G. Birmingham, Boxfield Gallery, Stevenage. *Signs work:* "BIRNE." *Address:* 82 Preston Rd., Wembley, Middx. HA9 8LA.

**BIRO, Val (B. S.),** freelance illustrator, painter, author; assistant production manager, Sylvan Press (1945-46), production manager and art director, C. & J. Temple (1946-48), John Lehmann, Ltd. (1948-53); *b* Budapest, Hungary, 6 Oct., 1921. *m* (1) Vivien Woolley one *d* (2) Marie-Louise Ellaway. one *s-s* . one *s-d* . *Educ:* School of the Cistercian Monks, Budapest. *Studied:* Central School of Arts and Crafts, London. *Exhib:* Budapest, London. *Work in collections:* V. & A. Museum, British Museum. *Publications:* Author of the Gumdrop Series; Hungarian Folk Tales, Rub-a-Dub-Dub and other books for children; illustrated some 400 books, incl. My Oxford Picture Word Book, The Father Brown Stories, American Start with English. Lecturer on Art and storytelling. *Clubs:* Vintage Sports Car. *Signs work:* "Biro" or "Val Biro." *Address:* Bridge Cottage, Brook Ave., Bosham, W. Sussex PO18 8LQ.

**BISHOP, William Henry,** self taught artist in water-colour and oil of seascapes and landscapes; *b* Liss, Hants., 21 June, 1942. *m* Helen Dunkerley.

three *s. Educ:* King's School, Canterbury. *Exhib:* R.S.M.A., Armed Forces, Southampton Maritime Year; one-man show: Royal Exchange Gallery, London (1991). *Work in collections:* U.S.A., Australia, New Zealand, Oman, Singapore, Hong Kong, Falkland Islands, U.K., Gibraltar, Germany. *Commissions:* R.N. Museum, Portsmouth, and Mary Rose Museum, Portsmouth; HMS. Warrior Museum, The Mathew Project, City of Bristol. *Publications:* Dictionary of Sea Painters (E.H.H. Archibald). Represented in America by: Quester Gallery, Stonington, Connecticut 06378. *Signs work:* "W. H. Bishop." *Address:* West Mill, Mill Lane, Langstone, Havant, Hants. PO9 1RX.

**BIZON, Edna,** S.W.A. (1987); artist in oil; *b* 13 Aug., 1929. *m* Ken Bizon. *Educ:* Honor Oak School. *Studied:* St.Martin's School of Art (1943-44), Camberwell School of Art (1944-46, Lawrence Gowing, John Minton). *Exhib:* R.A.; one-man shows: Thorndike, Leatherhead (1970, 1977), Augustine, Holt (1973), Munich, W.Germany (1982), O'Nians King St.Galleries (1987), Look of Helmsley (1988), King St. Galleries (1990), Llewellyn Alexander (1991, 1993, 1995, 1997). *Signs work:* "Edna Bizon." *Address:* Drove End, West St., North Creake, Norfolk NR21 9LQ.

**BLACK, Ian,** Art Teaching Diploma, Bristol University (1956), R.W.A. (1978); art teacher and artist in oil, acrylic, pen and ink; Head of Art, Bristol Cathedral School; Hon. Sec. R.W.A.; *b* Bury St. Edmunds, 31 May, 1929. *m* Judith Rhiannon. *Educ:* Culford School, Bury St. Edmunds. *Studied:* Southampton College of Art (1949), Bath Academy of Art (1952-56) under William Scott, Martin Froy, Jack Smith, Terry Frost, Peter Lanyon. *Exhib:* five one-man shows, R.W.A., R.A., travelling exhibs. *Work in collections:* R.W.A., Walsall Educ. Centre, Bath University, N.Z. Government, St. Catherine's College, Oxford, Wadham College, Oxford, Oxford Corp., Clifton High School, Redland School, Dorset House, Oxford. *Signs work:* "IB" or "Ian Black." *Address:* Blakes Farm, Englishcombe, Bath BA2 9DT.

**BLACKBURN, Keith,** full time artist in oil and mixed media, and writer; *b* Wakefield, Yorks., 2 Apr., 1943. *Exhib:* Cornwall; one-man shows: Holland. *Publications:* Between September (Book Guild, 1994), Lamentations of a Young Pig (Book Guild, 1997), Changes in a Landscape (Minerva, 1998); designed own covers. *Clubs:* St. Ives Soc. of Artists. *Address:* c/o A.G Hoegen, Keizersgracht 42E, 1015 CR Amsterdam, Holland.

**BLACKBURN, Mavis,** N.D.D. (Painting), A.T.D. (1948), R.C.A. (1952), B.A. (1979); artist in oil, polymer and gouache; *b* Wallasey, Ches., 29 Oct., 1923. *Educ:* Upton Hall Convent School. *Studied:* Liverpool College of Art (1942-48, Alfred Wiffen, R.C.A., Will C. Penn, R.O.I., R.S.P. R.C.A., Martin Bell, A.R.C.A.). *Exhib:* Royal Cambrian Academy, Wirral Soc. of Art, Deeside Art Group, Atkinson Gallery, Southport, Glasgow Inst. of Fine Arts, R.B.A., R.A., etc.; one-man shows, Liverpool, R.C.A., Williamson Gallery, Birkenhead. *Work in collections:* Williamson A.G., Birkenhead, Senate House,

Liverpool University. *Signs work:* "Mavis Blackburn." *Address:* The Bend, Village Rd., West Kirby, Wirral, Merseyside L48 7EL.

**BLACKLOCK, George,** Dip.A.D. (1974), M.F.A. (1976); painter in oil and wax on canvas; Senior lecturer in painting, Wimbledon School of Art; *b* Durham, 11 Apr., 1952. one *s*. *Studied:* Stourbridge College of Art (1971-74, Barrie Cook), Reading University (1974-76, Terry Frost). *Work in collections:* A.C.G.B. *Signs work:* "George Blacklock." *Address:* 11-31 Oarsmen Rd., London N1.

**BLACKMORE, Clive David,** painter; *b* Kingston-on-Thames, 1940. *Studied:* Twickenham and Kingston Schools of Art. *Exhib:* regularly in the west country and New Academy, London. *Signs work:* "Clive Blackmore." *Address:* Eastcliff Farm, Rinsey, Ashton, Helston, Cornwall TR13 9TS.

**BLACKWOOD, Simon Anthony James,** Dip.Ad. (1970); artist in oil; *b* Chelmsford, 17 May, 1948. *m* Laura C.M. Blackwood. one *d*. *Educ:* Gilberd School, Colchester. *Studied:* Colchester School of Art, Coventry School of Art (Anthony Atkinson, Don Foster). *Exhib:* Art and Mysticism (1975) I.C.A. London; one-man shows: Dundas Gallery 'Bus Stop' Series (1985), Netherbon Arts Centre 'Aquatic Light' Series (1986), Anthony Mould Ltd. London (1989), Michael Parkin Fine Art (1991, 1995), William Hardie Gallery Glasgow (1992), Brian Sinfield Gallery Burford (1992, 1994), Kusav, Istanbul (1994, 1995), Cynthia Bourne, London (1996). *Signs work:* "S.A.J.B." or "S.B." *Address:* Breyberry Ltd., Kingham House, Kingham, Oxon. OX7 6YA.

**BLAKE, Frederick Donald,** R.I., R.S.M.A.; artist in oil, water-colour, pen and ink; *b* 7 June, 1908. *Educ:* Camberwell School of Arts and Crafts; Goldsmiths' College; Brixton School of Building. *Exhib:* R.A., R.O.I., R.I., R.B.A. *Publications:* work repro.: newspaper maps, war illustrations, railway posters, advertising drawings. *Clubs:* London Sketch, Chelsea Arts. *Signs work:* "F. Donald Blake." *Address:* The Wimbledon Beaumont, 35 Arterberry Rd., Wimbledon, London SW20 8AG.

**BLAKE, Jane,** R.M.S (1987), M.A.A. (1987); portrait painter, speciality: miniatures on ivory and vellum; sculptor, stained glass artist, writer, lecturer; *b* N.C., 1933. three *s*. *Educ:* Central Wesleyan College, S.C. *Studied:* privately (1947-85). *Exhib:* international miniature shows R.M.S. England, Ireland, Canada, Florida, N.J., D.C., Tampa Museum (1989). *Work in collections:* Governor's Mansions, Florida and S.C., U.S.A. hospitals and state bldgs. *Signs work:* miniatures: "Jane Blake, R.M.S., M.A.A." *Address:* 11148 Freedom Way, Seminole, Florida 34642, U.S.A.

**BLAKE, Marie Dora,** N.D.D. (1958), A.T.C. (1959), S.W.A. (1987); artist in oil and water-colour; tutor and organiser, Lyme Regis Painting Workshops; *b* London, 12 Mar., 1938. *m* Charles Calcutt Smith. two *s*. one *d*. *Educ:* Richmond and E.Sheen Grammar School. *Studied:* Kingston-on-Thames School of Art (1954-58), London University Inst. of Educ. (1959). *Exhib:* N.E.A.C., R.O.I., R.S.M.A., S.W.A. *Publications:* regular contributor to

Leisure Painter magazine. *Signs work:* "Marie Blake." *Address:* Long Close, Clappentail La., Lyme Regis, Dorset.

**BLAKE, Naomi,** F.R.B.S.; sculptor in bronze; *b* Czechoslovakia, 1924. one *s.* one *d. Studied:* Hornsey School of Art (1955-60). *Exhib:* Salon de Paris, R.B.S., City of Leicester Museum, R.A. International Art Fair, St. Paul's Cathedral, Barbican London, Exhbn. Gallery Swansea University. *Work in collections:* Leicester Arts Council, North London Collegiate, Oxford Synagogue, Jews College Hendon, Fitzroy Sq. London, Bristol Cathedral, Hebrew University Jerusalem, Leo Baeck College London, Tel Aviv University Israel, Yarnton Manor Oxford, Norwich Cathedral, Duai Abbey Reading, St. Botolph's Church Aldgate, St. Anthony's College, Oxford. *Publications:* contributor, Anthologies, Each in his Prison, The Bridge is Love, London Statues, The A.A. Book of London, Open Air Sculpture in Britain. *Signs work:* "N.B." *Address:* 41 Woodside Ave., London N10 3HY.

**BLAKE, Pippa Jane,** B.A. Hons. (1976); painter in oil and gouache; *b* Portsmouth, 6 Apr., 1954. *m* Sir Peter Blake. one *s.* one *d. Educ:* Downe House School, Berks. *Studied:* Camberwell School of Art (1972-76). *Exhib:* one-man shows: Sussex; mixed shows: Sussex, Hampshire and London. *Work in collections:* Gt. Britain, France and New Zealand. *Signs work:* "P. Blake" or P.B." *Address:* Longshore, 3 Western Parade, Emsworth, Hants. PO10 7HS.

**BLAKE, Quentin,** O.B.E., R.D.I., M.A., F.C.S.D.; illustrator and teacher; Head of Dept. of Illustration, Royal College of Art (1978-85), Visiting Professor (1988-); *b* Sidcup, Kent, 16 Dec., 1932. *Educ:* Downing College, Cambridge. *Studied:* part-time, Chelsea School of Art. *Exhib:* one-man shows, Workshop Gallery, Illustrators A.G.; retrospective of illustration work, National Theatre (1983); Chris Beetles' Gallery (1994, 1996). *Commissions:* All Join In (Maschler Prize 1991); Clown (Bologna Ragazzi Prize 1996). *Publications:* illustrated over two hundred children's books, also books for adults; Mr. Magnolia (Kate Greenaway medal 1981). *Signs work:* "Quentin Blake." *Address:* 30 Bramham Gdns., London SW5 0HF.

**BLAKER, Michael,** R.E. (1975); painter, etcher, writer; *b* Hove, 19 Jan., 1928. *Educ:* Brighton Grammar School, Heversham School. *Studied:* Brighton College of Art. *Exhib:* R.A., R.E., R.W.A., R.P., etc. *Work in collections:* Tate Gallery, V. & A., Ashmolean, etc. *Publications:* The Autobiography of a Painter-Etcher (1986); M.B. Etchings (1985); M.B. Paintings (1986); A Beginner's Guide to Oil Painting (1994). Editor, Printmaker's Journal (1983-93). Contributor to Printmaking Today. Work purchased: Barclays Bank, Lloyds of London, Bank of Vienna, etc. *Signs work:* see appendix. *Address:* 122 Grange Rd., Ramsgate, Kent CT11 9PT.

**BLAMEY, Norman Charles,** R.O.I. (1952), A.R.A. (1970), R.A. (1975); painter in oil; *b* London, 16 Dec., 1914. *m* Margaret Kelly. one *s. Educ:* Holloway School, London. *Studied:* The Polytechnic School of Art, Regent St. (1931-37). *Exhib:* R.A., R.H.A., R.O.I., R.B.A., N.E.A.C. and provincial galeries. Work in permanent and private collections. *Address:* 39 Lyncroft Gdns., London NW6 1LB.

**BLANDINO, Betty,** Dip. A.E. (London); potter in clay (stoneware/porcelain); *b* London, 12 Sept., 1927. *m* Dr. G.O. Jones C.B.E. *Studied:* Goldsmiths' College, London (painting/pottery). *Exhib:* Over 20 solo pottery exhbns. since 1973 and many group exhbns. *Work in collections:* Fitzwilliam Museum, Cambridge; Welsh Arts Council; National Museum of Wales; many city and county museums in U.K. and Europe. *Publications:* Coiled Pottery - Traditional and Contemporary Ways (Black/Chilton 1984); Revised edn. 1997). On Crafts Council Selected Index; President, Oxfordshire Craft Guild 1989-93); mem. Gloucestershire Guild of Craftsmen. *Signs work:* "Betty Blandino." *Address:* 12 Squitchey Lane, Summertown, Oxford OX2 7LB.

**BLASZKOWSKI, Martin,** Bronze Medal, Brussels (1958), Grand Prize, Buenos Aires (1960), First Prize, Competition: "Homage to Peace" of the City of Buenos Aires (1986); painter in oil, sculptor in wood; lecturer at Tulane University, New Orleans, U.S.A. (1976); *b* Berlin, 1920 (Argentine citizenship since 1958). *Exhib:* Brussels, Biennale Venecia, Argentine, Chile, Tate Gallery, London, Bienale de São Paulo, Brazil. *Publications:* Leonardo, 2.223 1969) Oxford, Sculpture International 2.26 (1968) Oxford, Sculpture International 3.28 (1970) London, Sculpture of this Century, Editions du Griffon, Neuchatel, Switzerland (1959), Dictionnaire de la Sculpture Moderne, Fernand Hazan, Paris (1970). *Signs work:* "BLASZKO." *Address:* Santa Fé 3786-11-A, Buenos Aires, Argentine.

**BLESKY, Wiltold John,** sculptor in stainless steel, resin, ceramic, mixed media; painter in oil and acrylic paints; *b* Poland, 26 July, 1934 (U.S.A. Nationality); married. two *s.* two *d. Educ:* Poland; U.S.A.; U.K. *Exhib:* Le Salon, Paris, Marjorie Parr Galleries, London Hilton Galleries, Loggia Gallery, Mall Galleries, Round House Gallery, New Metropole, Folkestone, Slater Gallery, Canterbury, Birmingham U. open-air exhbn. and other London and provincial galleries and open-air exhbns. *Clubs:* F.P.S., The Artists' League of Great Britain, I.C.A., Association Internationale des Arts Plastiques-UNESCO. *Signs work:* "W. John Blesky." *Address:* 13 Marlow Copse, Walderslade, Kent ME5 9DP.

**BLIK, Maurice,** A.T.C. (1968), P.P.R.B.S. (1997); sculptor in bronze; *b* Amsterdam, 21 Apr., 1939. one *s.* one *d. Educ:* Downer Grammar School. *Studied:* Hornsey College of Art (1956-60), University of London (1968-69). *Exhib:* Mall Galleries, Ben-Uri Gallery, Royal Academy, Art for Offices London, U.K.), Cavalier Galleries (Conn., U.S.A.), Museum Masters (New York), Irving Gallery (Palm Beach, U.S.A.), Blains Fine Art (London). Work in private and public collections. *Commissions:* East India Dock, London; J.P. Morgan, London; Donnington Valley, Newbury, U.K.; Middlesex University, London. *Clubs:* Chelsea Arts. *Signs work:* see appendix. *Address:* c/o Blains Fine Art, 23 Bruton St., Mayfair, London W1X 7DA.

**BLISS, Ian Reynolds,** N.D.D. (1954), A.T.D. (1955), R.I. (1992); artist in water-colour and wood engraving; social worker; *b* Derby, 2 Apr., 1930. *m* Jill Michelle Cheney. one *s*. three *d*. *Educ:* Repton. *Studied:* Leicester (1950-55). *Exhib:* R.A., R.I., Piccadilly Gallery, Nevill Gallery Canterbury. *Signs work* "IAN BLISS." *Address:* 10 Vicarage Lane, Wing, Leighton-Buzzard LU7 0NV.

**BLOCH, Gunther,** F.R.A.I.; 1st prize winner of first National Craft Competition (1948); art master of L.C.C. schools since 1948; sculptor in wood, stone, clay and ivory; *b* Dt. Krone, Germany, 24 Aug., 1916; married. one *s*. *Educ:* German Colleges; Leeds College of Art (John Frank Kavanagh); Regent St. Polytechnic; and in Germany under Gerhard Priedigkeit. *Exhib:* Berkeley Galleries, Cooling Galleries, Ben Uri Galleries, Leeds Art Gallery, Britain Can Make It. *Work in collections:* Denmark, France, Australia, New Zealand. *Sign work:* "Gunther Bloch" or "G. Bloch." *Address:* 88 Camden Mews, London NW1 9BX.

**BLOXHAM, Judith Ann,** B.Ed.Hons. (1985); artist, specialist in painting detailed silks, mainly ties; *b* Workington, Cumbria, 28 Jan., 1961. *m* David Gerald Bloxham. one *s*. one *d*. *Educ:* Whitehaven Grammar School. *Studied:* Cumbria College of Art and Design, Carlisle, St. Martin's College, Lancaster. *Exhib:* R.S.M.A. 4th International Miniatures Exhbn., Toronto, Fitz Park Museum, Keswick, St. Martin's, Lancaster, Cumberland Pencil Museum Keswick, Wild ties V. & A., Whale tail Nairobi. Work in private collections. *Commissions:* Mural commissions in Carlisle City. Specialist tie commissions including B.P. and Akito Racing. *Signs work:* "J.A.B." or "J.A. Bloxham." *Address:* 3 Boston Ave., Carlisle, Cumbria CA2 4DR.

**BOCKING, Helen,** Harrow Dip. in Illustration (1976); artist in water-colour of wildlife, country sports, animal and equestrian portraits; *b* Gillingham, 4 June, 1954. *Educ:* Fort Pitt School, Kent. *Studied:* Goldsmiths' College (1972), Harrow School of Art (1973-76, Sam Marshall, Brian Liddel). *Exhib:* S.WL.A. R.S.P.B., B.F.S.S., Game Conservancy; various one-man shows. *Work in collections:* S. London A.G., and many private collections. *Signs work:* "H Bocking." *Address:* 30 Town Dam Lane, Donington, nr. Spalding, Lincs. PE11 4TP.

**BODEN, Leonard,** R.P., F.R.S.A.; portrait painter; *b* Greenock, Scotland, 1911. *m* Margaret Tulloch. one *d*. *Educ:* Sedbergh. *Studied:* School of Art Glasgow; Heatherley School of Art, London. *Exhib:* R.P., R.S.A. *Work in collections:* Official portraits: Her Majesty Queen Elizabeth II, H.R.H. The Prince Philip, Duke of Edinburgh, K.G., K.T., G.B.E., His Holiness Pope Pius XII, Field-Marshal Lord Milne, G.C.B., G.C.M.G., D.S.O. *Publications:* work repro.: The Connoisseur; The Artist: many periodicals in this country and abroad; and as Fine Art Prints. *Clubs:* Savage, Chelsea Arts. *Signs work:* "LEONARD BODEN." *Address:* 36 Arden Rd., London N3 3AN.

**BODEN, Margaret,** P.S., S.W.A., U.A., F.R.S.A.; portrait painter; *b*

Ecclesmachen, Scotland. *m* Leonard Boden. one *d. Educ:* Dowanhill. *Studied:* School of Art, Glasgow; Heatherley School of Art, London. *Exhib:* R.P., R.O.I., Royal Inst. of Fine Arts, Glasgow; National Soc.; Summer Salon; Royal B'ham Soc. of Artists; City of Bradford A.G., etc. Honourable Mention, Paris Salon. *Publications:* work repro.: The Times, The Artist, many magazines and periodicals, etc. *Signs work:* "MARGARET BODEN." *Address:* 36 Arden Rd., London N3 3AN.

**BOLAN, Sean Edward,** G.R.A.; artist in ink and water-colour of landscapes, architecture, historical transport and military subjects; *b* Rowlands Castle, Hants., 25 May, 1948. *m* Margaret Janina. two *d. Educ:* Warblington Secondary Modern School, Havant, Hants. *Studied:* Portsmouth College of Art (1965-68). *Work in collections:* private, municipal, Science Museum, S. Kensington and Guards Museum. Plays cornet, leader 'The Charleston Chasers'. *Clubs: Signs work:* "Sean Bolan." *Address:* 8 Dunstall House, Stow Rd., Moreton in Marsh, Glos. GL56 0DR.

**BOLTON, Janet Mary,** Dip.A.D. (1970), A.T.D., S.B.A. (1992), R.H.S. Gold medallist (1994); teacher, artist in pastel and pencil specializing in botanical subjects; art teacher, Kingsmead School, Hednesford, Staffs., tutor, Lichfield College; *b* 26 Sept., 1947. *Educ:* Gravesend Girls' Grammar School. *Studied:* Bath Academy of Art (1968-70), Bristol University (1972). *Exhib:* R.H.S., S.B.A., Oxford University and numerous shows in Midlands. *Work in collections:* Oxford University and private collections worldwide. *Publications:* 'Fruits' design for Aynsley china 'Grande Tasse' range (1993). *Signs work:* "Janet M. Bolton," "J.M. Bolton" or "J.M.B." *Address:* 7 Raven Cl., Hednesford, Staffs. WS12 5LS.

**BOLTON, Richard Marston,** artist in water-colour; *b* Aberdeen, 28 June, 1950. *m* Margaret. two *s. Studied:* Shrewsbury School of Art. *Exhib:* Linda Blackstone Gallery, Pinner. *Work in collections:* St. Ives Museum. *Commissions:* Views of China and Tibet by Taiwanese Collector. *Publications:* written and illustrated: Weathered Textures in Water-colour, and Weathered Textures, Workshop (Watson & Guptil), Texture and Detail in Water-colour, and Creative Drawing and Sketching (Batsford). *Signs work:* "R.M. Bolton." *Address:* Granville House, 27 London Rd., St. Ives, Huntingdon, Cambs. PE17 4ES.

**BONADA, Cinzia,** R.B.A.; painter in oil and pencil; *b* Jersey, C.I., 22 Apr., 1938. *m* Johnny Bonada. one *s.* two *d. Educ:* Jersey Ladies College, Bush-Davies, Royal Ballet School. *Studied:* Richmond Adult College (1975-79, Charles Fowler) and with Peter Garrard (1982-87). *Exhib:* R.A., R.B.A., R.P., N.E.A.C., etc. Founder member of Small Paintings Group. *Work in collections:* Drapers' Hall, A.W.G., Japan, New Zealand, Europe, U.S.A., Egypt, Russia, Australia. *Commissions:* Trevor Eldrid Past Master/Drapers' Hall. Awarded first prize for artistic excellence by Kensington/Chelsea Arts Council. *Signs work:* "Cinzia." *Address:* 9 Alexandra Rd., E. Twickenham, Middx. TW1 2HE.

# WHO'S WHO IN ART

**BOND, Jane,** R.P., N.E.A.C., City & Guilds School of Art, (Roger de Grey, Dip. F.A. 1981), R.A. Schools (Peter Greenham, Post Grad Dip. F.A. 1984); *b* Zimbabwe, 1 Apr., 1939. artist in oil, charcoal and pencil of portraits, still lives, interiors. Formerly theatre, film and T.V. designer.; *Exhib:* R.A., N.E.A.C., Hayward Gall., National Theatre, Glyndebourne Opera House, etc. *Work in collections:* private: England, Europe and U.S.A. *Clubs:* Two Brydges. *Signs work:* see appendix. *Address:* 8 Ceylon Rd., London W14 0PY.

**BOND, Marj,** D.A. (Glas.), S.S.W.A. (1974), R.S.W. (1989), S.S.A. (1989); artist in oil, acrylic, etching; Vice-Pres., Scottish Artist Artist Craftsmen; *b* Paisley, Scotland, 23 May, 1939. *m* James Agray, architect. one *s.* two *d. Educ:* Paisley Grammar School. *Studied:* Glasgow School of Art (1956-60, David Donaldson, Mary Armour, Benno Schotz). *Exhib:* many one-man shows, R.S.A., S.S.A., R.S.W., Scottish Soc. of Woman Artists now Scottish Artist Artist Craftsmen, R.S.I. *Work in collections:* Arts in Fife, Edinburgh University. *Signs work:* "Marj." *Address:* Eden Cottage, Old Town, Gateside, Fife KY14 5SL.

**BONE, Charles,** P.P.R.I., A.R.C.A., Hon F.C.A. (Canada); F.B.I. Award for Design; painter and designer; former Governor, Federation of British Artists (Mall Galleries); Past President, Royal Institute of Painters in Water-colour; artist in water-colour, oil, variety of mediums including ceramic for murals; *b* Farnham, Surrey, 15 Sept., 1926. *m* Sheila Mitchell, F.R.B.S., A.R.C.A., sculptor. two *s. Studied:* Farnham School of Art; Royal College of Art. *Exhib:* 37 one-man, Spain, Holland, U.S.A. *Work in collections:* many mural paintings in public buildings and water-colours and oils in private collections. *Publications:* author, Charles Bone's Waverley, Foreword by H.R.H. Prince of Wales. Awarded Hunting Group prize of £5000 for a British water-colour (1984). *Signs work:* "BONE." *Address:* Winters Farm, Puttenham, nr. Guildford, Surrey GU3 1AR.

**BONE, Ronald,** Dip.A.D. (1972), M.A.(R.C.A.) (1976); painter and designer in acrylic and water-colour; *b* Consett, Co. Durham, 22 June, 1950; married. one *s.* one *d. Educ:* Consett Grammar School. *Studied:* Bath Academy of Art (1968-72), R.C.A. (1973-76). *Exhib:* R.A., R.W.A., C.C.A. Galleries, Linfield Galleries, John Noott, Broadway, Llewellyn Alexander. *Work in collections:* U.K., Europe and America. *Publications:* work repro.: illustrations in various books from London publishing houses. Many T.V. programmes. *Signs work:* "BONE." *Address:* Manor Farm Cottage, Pump La., Bathford, Bath, Avon BA1 7RT.

**BOOTH, Rosa-Maria,** A.R.M.S., H.S.F., M.P.S.G., Dip. Fashion (1970); painter and miniaturist in oil, acrylic, water-colour; *b* Olot, Spain, 9 Nov., 1947. *m* Peter Booth. *Educ:* Sagrado Corazón de Maria, Olot; Inst. Marti, Barcelona. *Studied:* privately and in Paris under Madeleine Scali; L'Escola Olotina, Spain (Emilio Parejo, J.M. Agusti); Thurrock Technical College (M. Martin). *Exhib:* R.A., R.M.S., Mall Galleries, Barbican, Westminster Gallery, Llewellyn

Alexander, N. Ireland, Spain, France, Sweden, Canada, U.S.A. *Work in collec-tions:* Some Private *Publications:* 100 Years of Miniatures by S. Lucas. Awards: 16 including 1st place I.M.A.S. Florida (drawing and pastel 1982; abstract 1984, 1988), Best in Mixed Media-Allegheny I.A.E. W. Virginia (1985). *Clubs:* Founder mem. H.S., M.P.S.G., A.R.M.S., M.A.S.-F. *Signs work:* "ROSMAR." *Address:* 36 Windsor Ave., Grays, Essex RM16 2UB.

**BORCHARDT, Karolina,** M.F.P.S., A.P.A., Mem. International Professional Artist (UNESCO); *b* Minsk, Lit, 26 July, 1913. *m* Karol. one *d.* *Educ:* Krakow, Poland. *Studied:* University of Stephen Batory in London. Diploma di Merito at Universita Delle Arti, Italy. *Exhib:* one-man shows, English Painters Art Group, London, Gallerie Internationale, New York, Richmond Gallery and Barrett Gallery, London; group shows, Barbican A.G., Bloomsbury Galleries, Mall Gallery, Weighouse Gallery, London, Salon des Nations, Paris, London Cassel Gallery, Loggia Gallery, New Vision Gallery, Centaur Gallery, and POSK Gallery, Germany Gallery P.R.O. Stuttgart, and many others. *Work in collections:* U.S.A., Poland, England, Spain and France. *Publications:* Karolina Borchardt, Introduction by Pierre Rouve, V.P. of World Art Critics Assoc. Now a British subject and lives in London. First Polish woman air pilot. *Clubs:* F.P.S. *Signs work:* "K. Borchardt." *Address:* 4 Somerset House, Somerset Rd., Wimbledon, London SW19.

**BORKOWSKI, Elizabeth Irena,** Dip.A.D., Prix de Rome, Feodora Gleichen award (1971) Sculpture; sculptor/painter in clay, bronze, water-colour, charcoal, pencil, art teacher; *b* Redhill, 7 May, 1949. *Educ:* Ursuline High School, Brentwood. *Studied:* Camberwell School of Art and Crafts, British School at Rome (Brian Taylor, Paul de Moncheaux). *Exhib:* R.A. Summer Show (1973), Palazzo Barberini National Museum of Rome (1973), Chelsea School of Art Rome Scholars (1986), Chelsea Harbour (1993). Elected A.R.B.S. (1992). *Signs work:* "Lissa Borkowski." *Address:* 3 High Trees Rd., Reigate, Surrey RH2 7EH.

**BORRIE:** see HOPE HENDERSON, Eleanor.

**BOSTOCK, James Edward,** R.E. (1961), A.R.C.A. (Lond.) 1939; illustrator, wood engraver, painter; formerly Academic Development Officer, Bristol Polytechnic; *b* Hanley, Staffs, 11 June, 1917; married. three *s. Educ:* Borden Grammar School, Sittingbourne, Kent. *Studied:* Medway School of Art, Rochester (1933-36), Royal College of Art (1936-39). *Exhib:* R.A., R.B.A., N.E.A.C., Crafts Centre of Great Britain, V. & A. Museum, many provincial galleries, travelling exhbns. to Poland, Czechoslovakia, S. Africa, New Zealand and the Far East. *Work in collections:* V. & A. Museum, Ashmolean Museum, British Museum, Wakefield Collection, Hunt Botanical Library, Pittsburgh, U.S.A., Hereford Museum. *Publications:* Roman Lettering for Students (Studio), 1959; wood engravings for Poems of Edward Thomas published by Folio Soc. (1988); articles in The Studio, The Artist, Guardian, Staffordshire Sentinel, Times Ed. Supp. *Clubs:* mem. Soc. Wood Engravers, East Kent Art

Society. *Address:* White Lodge, 80 Lindenthorpe Rd., Broadstairs, Kent CT10 1DB.

**BOSWELL, William Aubrey,** R.C.A., F.R.S.A.; artist; Principal Design Officer, County Planning Clwyd (Rtd.), Academician, Royal Cambrian Academy; *b* Nottingham, 30 May, 1926. *m* Jessie. one *s.* two *d. Studied:* Nottingham College of Arts and Crafts (1942). *Exhib:* Annual Summer Exhbns., Royal Cambrian Academy of Art. *Publications:* writer and illustrator of town trails: Denbigh, Corwen, Llangollen, Carrog, Wrexham, etc. *Signs work:* "William A. Boswell." *Address:* 24 Hilltop View Rd., Borras Park, Wrexham, Clwyd LL12 7SF.

**BOSZIN, Endre,** founded, Taurus Artists (1961), London; painter in oil and water-colour, sculptor in bronze; President, Sculptors Society of Canada (1971-73), (1979-83); *b* Hungary, 1923. *m* Charlotte de Sarlay. one *s.* one *d. Studied:* Budapest, R.C.A. *Exhib:* London Group; Festival of Visual Art at Harrogate, Edinburgh Festival; Grabovsky, Crane Kalman, Chiltern, Woodstock; Piccadilly Galleries, London, Gallery Raymond Creuze, Paris; International Medal Exhbns.: Madrid, Cologne, Helsinki, Prague; Sculpture Biennale: Dante Centre, Ravenna; Palace of Art, Budapest. *Work in collections:* Budapest, National Museum of Hungarian Art, Ujpest, City Collection, B.M., Pennsylvania Univ. *Clubs:* Sculptors Soc. of Canada. *Address:* 39 Gilgorm Rd., Toronto, M5N 2M4, Canada.

**BOTHWELL, Dorr,** painter, printmaker and teacher in oil, gouache, and serigraphic printing and collage; Mendocino Art Centre; *b* San Francisco, 3 May, 1902. *Educ:* Russ High School, San Diego; Univ of Oregon. *Studied:* Calif. School of Fine Arts and Rudolph Schaeffer School of Design, San Francisco. *Work in collections:* Metropolitan Museum, Museum of Modern Art and Brooklyn Museum, N.Y.; Achenbach Foundation of Graphic Art, San Francisco; Bibliotheque Nationale, Paris; V. & A.; Fogg Museum, Cambridge, Mass.; Whitney Museum, N.Y.; San Francisco Museum of Art; Oakland Museum, Oakland, Calif. *Signs work:* "Bothwell." *Address:* 925 N. Plaza Dr., Sp. 93 Apache Jct., Az. 85220, U.S.A.

**BOTT, Dennis Adrian Roxby,** Dip.A.D. (1972), Cert.Ed. (1973), A.R.W.S. (1981), R.W.S. (1983), A.W.G. (1989); painter in water-colour and oil; *b* Chingford, 29 Apr., 1948. *Educ:* Forest School, nr. Snaresbrook, London E17. *Studied:* Colchester School of Art (1967-69), Norwich School of Art (1969-72). *Exhib:* one-man shows, Ogle Gallery, Eastbourne, Gallery 33, Billingshurst, The Grange, Rottingdean, Ogle Gallery, Cheltenham, Bourne Gallery, Reigate, Worthing Museum and A.G., Canon Gallery, Chichester, Ebury Galleries. *Work in collections:* National Trust, Towner A.G., Eastbourne, Hove Museum, Brighton Museum. *Clubs:* Arts. *Signs work:* "Roxby Bott." *Address:* Maplewood, Cherry Tree Rd., Milford, Surrey GU8 5AX.

**BOTTOMLEY, Eric,** G.R.A. (1985); artist/illustrator in oil and gouache; *b* Oldham, 14 July, 1948. *m* Jeanette. *Educ:* N. Chadderton Secondary Modern.

*Studied:* Oldham School of Art and Crafts. *Exhib:* Omell Gallery, Shell House Gallery, Ledbury. *Work in collections:* National Museum of Wales (Industrial and Maritime Museum). *Publications:* illustrated three books, Limited Edn. prints, calendars, greetings cards, magazines and posters. *Signs work:* "Eric Bottomley." *Address:* The Old Coach House, Much Marcle, Ledbury, Herefordshire HR8 2NL.

**BOULTON, Janet,** painter, water-colour and paper relief, specialising in still life and landscape gardens; *b* Wiltshire, 14 Sept., 1936. *m* Keith Baines, poet and translator. one *d. Studied:* Swindon and Camberwell Schools of Art (1953-58). *Exhib:* widely in mixed shows including Belfast Arts Council Open, Chichester National, London Group, R.A. Summer Exhbns., etc; one-person shows: Mercury Gallery, 26 Cork St. W1. (1988, 1991, 1994, 1997). *Work in collections:* Southern Arts, Radcliffe Infirmary, John Radcliffe Hospital, I.O.W. Area Health Authority, National Gallery, Ottawa. *Publications:* edited and transcribed, Paul Nash Letters to Mercia Oakley 1909-1918 (Fleece Press, 1991), Monograph, Mercury Graphics (1985-91). Residencies: Lankmead Comprehensive, Abingdon (1980), Radcliffe Infirmary, Oxford (1986). *Address:* 64 Spring Rd., Abingdon OX14 1AN.

**BOURDON SMITH, Diana,** R.W.A. (1990); painter in oil; *b* 16 Dec., 1933. *Studied:* Kingston Art School. *Exhib:* R.A., N.E.A.C., R.W.A. *Work in collections:* Royal West of England Academy. *Signs work:* "D.M.B.S." *Address:* 19 Crescent La., Bath BA1 2PX.

**BOURGUIGNON, Doris (née Blair),** A.R.C.A.; painter in acrylic, oil, water-colour and gouache. *Studied:* College of Art, Belfast; R.C.A., London; Wallace Harrison, N.Y.; Fernand Leger, Paris; Andre Lhote, Paris. *Exhib:* one-man and group shows: Belfast, Galerie l'Angle Aigu, Brussels; Museum and A.G., Belfast. *Work in collections:* Museum and A.G., Belfast. *Publications:* illustrated Various Verses by John O'The North. *Signs work:* "Doris Bourguignon." *Address:* 8a Gunter Grove, London SW10 0UJ.

**BOURNE, D. Peter,** D.A. (Glasgow), R.S.W. (1982); painter in oil, gouache, water-colour; *b* Madras, India, 1 Nov., 1931. *m* Marjorie. two *s.* two *d. Educ:* Glasgow. *Studied:* Glasgow School of Art (1950-54, David Donaldson). *Exhib:* R.S.A. Edinburgh, R.G.I. Glasgow, R.S.W. Edinburgh. *Work in collections:* City Art (Edinburgh), Pictures for Schools (Edinburgh), Paintings in Hospitals. *Publications:* Dictionary of Scottish Painters - Paul Harris and Julian Halsby (Cannongate Publishing). *Signs work:* "Bourne." *Address:* Tressour Wood, Weem, Aberfeldy, Perthshire PH15 2LD.

**BOURNE, Jean Susan,** B.A.Hons. (1971), Dip.Mus.Stud. (1972), A.M.A. (1974), F.M.A. (1992); Museum curator; Curator, Towneley Hall Art Gallery and Museum, Burnley; President, North West Federation of Museums and Art Galleries (1993-94); *b* Rochdale, 23 Feb., 1950. *Educ:* Queen Margaret's School, Escrick, Lancaster University, Manchester University. *Publications:* museum guides, exhbn. catalogues, articles on oak furniture. *Address:* 94

Higham Hall Rd., Higham, Lancs.

**BOWEN, Denis,** A.R.C.A. (1949), Mem. A.I.C.A.; painter; directed The New Vision Centre (1956-66); Premio Internationale Europa Arte (1964) Silver Star with Antonioni Pasolini; visiting Associate Prof., University of Victoria, B.C., Canada (1969-71); elected 1994 to The Royal Cambrian Academy; *b* Kimberley, 5 Apr., 1921. *Studied:* King James I Grammar School, Almondbury; Huddersfield School of Art (1938-40); Royal College of Art (1946-49). *Exhib:* First Retrospective Bede 1300 Festival, Bede Gallery, Jarrow (1973); '50 years on', Second Retrospective Exhbn., Huddersfield A.G. (1989) and Ljubljana Municipal A.G., Slovenia (1992). Exhib. The Sixties Art Scene London, Barbican A.G. London, and internationally. Lecture tour Australia (1993). *Publications:* illustrated, A Concise History of English Painting by William Gaunt (Thames & Hudson, 1964), Dream of Icarus by Kenneth Coutts-Smith (Hutchinson, 1969), Etching and Engraving by John Brunsdon (Batsford, 1969), Art since 1945 by Herbert Read, Les Peintres Célèbres III Angleterre et Irlande, Alan Bowness (Mazenod, Paris 1964), L'Art Abstrait, Maeght Vols. 3.4. Michel Seuphor/Michel Ragon; critical writings in Art International Lugano, Vie des Arts, Art and Artists, D'Ars Milano, Arts Canada Toronto, R.S.A. Journal and Arts Review, London. Founder mem., Celtic Vision, co-ordinating Ireland, Wales, Scotland, Cornwall, Brittany and Galicia. Mem., Celtic League. *Address:* 4a Seymour Pl., London W1H 5WF.

**BOWETT, Druie,** artist in oils, and mixed media; *b* Ripon, Yorks., 1924. *m* John Bowett, M.R.C.V.S. three *s. Educ:* Queen Margaret's School, Harrogate College of Art (pupil of Jean-Georges Simon). *Exhib:* one-man shows Austin Hayes, York (1958, 1961), Wakefield, Midland Group Nottingham (1961, 1963, 1969), Sheffield University, Abbot Hall Kendal, Vaccarino Arte Contemporanea Florence, 359 Gallery Nottingham, T.S.B. Lincoln, Retrospective Exhbn. Worksop Notts. C.C., Drian Gallery London, Rufford Notts. C.C., Pierrepont Gallery, Cartwright Hall Bradford (1995), Angel Row Gallery Nottingham (1996); mixed exhbns. include Hart Gallery, A.I.A., I.P.G., R.A., Paris Salon, R.S.A., London Group, R.P., W.I.A.A. *Work in collections:* H.R.H. The Duke of Edinburgh, D. & C.C.'s of Bassetlaw, Rochdale, Nottinghamshire, Leicestershire, Sussex, Wakefield, Kendal, Derbyshire, John Players, Boots plc, Tetley Brewery, Landau Forte College Derby and others. B.B.C. Television and B.B.C. Radio. *Publications:* Painters Poetry (Ryton Books, 1986). *Clubs:* Lansdowne, A.I.A.P., I.A.A. *Signs work:* "Bowett." *Address:* Wilton Lodge, Blyth, Worksop, Notts. S81 8EH.

**BOWEY, Olwyn,** A.R.C.A., R.A., painter in oil and gouache.; *b* Stockton-on-Tees, Cleveland, 10 Feb. 1936. *Studied:* West Hartlepool School of Art, Royal College of Art. *Signs work:* "Olwyn Bowey". *Address:* 4 Peace Lane, Heyshott, Midhurst, Sussex GU29 0DF

**BOWNESS, Sir Alan,** C.B.E., M.A.; art historian; formerly Director, Henry Moore Foundation, Director of the Tate Gallery, and Professor of History of

Art and Deputy Director, Courtauld Inst. of Art, University of London; *b* London, 11 Jan., 1928. *m* Sarah Hepworth Nicholson. one *s*. one *d. Educ:* University College School, Downing College, Cambridge, and Courtauld Inst. of Art. *Publications:* William Scott: Paintings (Lund Humphries, 1964); Modern Sculpture (Studio Vista, 1965); Henry Moore: Complete Sculpture 1949-1986 (Five vols. Lund Humphries, 1965-1988); Alan Davie (Lund Humphries, 1968); Gauguin (Phaidon, 1971); Complete Sculpture of Barbara Hepworth 1960-69 (Lund Humphries, 1971); Modern European Art (Thames & Hudson, 1972); Ivon Hitchens (Lund Humphries, 1973); The Conditions of Success (Thames & Hudson, 1989); Bernard Meadows (Lund Humphries, 1994). *Address:* 91 Castelnau, London SW13 9EL.

**BOWYER, Francis David,** B.A. Hons. (1974), R.W.S. (1991); artist in water-colour and oil; part time teacher; *b* London, 20 May, 1952. *m* Glynis Porter. one *s*. one *d. Educ:* St. Mark's School, London SW6. *Studied:* St. Martin's School of Art (1971-75, Ken Roberts, Ken Bale), Hammersmith School of Art (1976-77, Ruskin Spear). *Exhib:* R.A. Summer Exhbn., N.E.A.C., R.W.S. *Work in collections:* Bankside Gallery. *Signs work:* "Francis Bowyer." *Address:* 12 Gainsborough Rd., Chiswick, London W4 1NJ.

**BOWYER, Jason Richard,** M.A., N.E.A.C.; Greenshield Foundation (1983), Daler-Rowney award R.A. Summer Exhbn. (1986), William Townesend scholarship (1987); British Council visit, Bulgaria (1991); painter in oil and pastel, draughtsman; part-time lecturer, University of Westminster; Founder, New English School of Drawing (1993); *b* Chiswick, London, 4 Mar., 1957. *Educ:* Chiswick School. *Studied:* Camberwell School of Art (1975-79), R.A. Schools (1979-82). *Exhib:* R.A. (1980-85, 1992-93); one-man show New Grafton (1991). *Publications:* Starting Drawing (Bloomsbury Press, 1988). *Clubs:* Arts, Dover St. *Signs work:* "J.R. Bowyer." *Address:* 35 Clifden Rd., Brentford, Middx. TW8 0PB.

**BOWYER, William,** R.A. (1981), R.W.S., N.E.A.C., R.P.; artist in oil paint, water-colour; Head of Fine Art, Maidstone College of Art (1970-81); Hon. sec. N.E.A.C.; *b* Leek, Staffs., 25 May, 1926. *m* Vera Mary. two *s*. one *d. Educ:* Burslem School of Art. *Studied:* R.C.A. (Carel Weight, Ruskin Spear). *Exhib:* R.A., N.E.A.C., R.W.S., many galleries London and provinces. *Work in collections:* R.A., R.W.S., N.P.G., Sheffield City A.G., City of Stoke-on-Trent, many provincial, and private collections home and abroad. *Clubs:* Arts, Dover St. *Signs work:* "William Bowyer." *Address:* 12 Cleveland Ave., Chiswick, London W4.

**BOYD, Arthur Merric Bloomfield,** painter in oil, graphics, ceramic; *b* Murrumbeena, Australia, 1920. *m* married. one *s*. two *d. Educ:* State School, Murrumbeena, Victoria, Australia. *Studied:* with parents. *Work in collections:* Australian National collections, V. & A., B.M. *Publications:* Monograph by Franz Phillipp (1967), illustrated St. Francis by T. S. R. Boase, Lysistrata (1970), Nebucadnezzar, intro. T. S. R. Boase (Thames & Hudson), Arthur Boyd

Drawings (Secker & Warburg, 1973), The Artist and the River (Bay Books 1982), The Art of Arthur Boyd by Ursula Hoff (Andre Deutsch). *Address:* P.O. Box 3343, Nowra North, N.S.W., Australia 2541.

**BOYD, G.,** A.T.D. (1951); Head of Painting, University of Hertfordshire (1976-93); *b* Bristol, 1928. *m* Pauline Lilian. one *s.* one *d. Educ:* Watford Grammar School. *Studied:* Watford School of Art and London University. *Exhib:* include London Group, R.A., John Moores, Belfast 68, Triangle Artists, N.Y., London and Barcelona, Atlantic Fusion: Lisbon, Madrid, London Docklands; one-man shows: A.I.A. (1962, 1967), Molton Gallery (1963), Oxford Gallery (1969, 1971, 1982), University of Hertfordshire (1980, 1988, 1994-95), Spacex 1983, Sandra Higgins Fine Arts (1991), Harriet Green (1997). *Work in collections:* Walker Gallery, Trinity College, Oxford, City of Barcelona, Azores, University of Hertfordshire. *Signs work:* "Graham Boyd" or "G. BOYD." *Address:* Blackapple, 54 Scatterdells Lane, Chipperfield, Herts. WD4 9EX.

**BOYD, James Davidson,** O.B.E., D.A. (Glas.), F.M.A., F.S.A.Scot., F.R.S.A., M.I.L.G.A.; director Dundee Art Galleries and Museums (1949-82); curator on staff of Glasgow Art Galleries and Museums under Dr. T. J. Honeyman (1946-49); artist in oil and water-colour; enamellist; *b* Glasgow, 10 Aug., 1917. *m* Elizabeth A. Ogilvie, D.A. (Glas.). *Educ:* Falkirk High and Technical Schools. *Studied:* Glasgow School of Art (1936-40). *Publications:* articles on art and history in various publications. *Address:* 16 Strips of Craigie Rd., Dundee DD4 7PZ.

**BOYD, John G.,** R.P., R.G.I.; painter; *b* Stonehaven, Kincardineshire, 7 Apr., 1940. two *s. Educ:* Mackie Academy, Stonehaven. *Studied:* Gray's School of Art, Aberdeen (1958-62) under R. H. Blyth; Hospitalfield College of Art (summer 1961) under James Cumming. *Exhib:* Everard Read Gallery, Johannesburg (1997), Contemporary Fine Art, Eton (1996), Portland Gallery, London, Bourne Fine Art (1995), Wm. Hardie, Glasgow (1994), Graeme Mundy Fine Art (1991), Open Eye Gallery (1989), Present Gallery, Lanark (1975), Armstrong Gallery, Glasgow (1970), New 57 Gallery, Edinburgh (1967), R.S.A., R.G.I., R.P. *Work in collections:* Jose Berardo Collection, Portugal; Paisley; Milngavie; People's Palace, Glagow. *Clubs:* Glasgow Art. *Signs work:* "Boyd." *Address:* Garden Flat, 3 Beaconsfield Rd., Glasgow G12 0PJ.

**BOYD-BRENT, James,** A.R.E. (1988), B.A.(Hons.) (1988), M.F.A. Univ. of Minnesota (1994); artist/printmaker in etching, woodcut, water-colour; lecturer, Minneapolis College of Art and Design, Minn. U.S.A.; *b* Solihull, England, 10 Aug., 1954. *m* Mary. one *s. Educ:* Selborne College. *Studied:* Anglia Polytechnic (1984, Walter Hoyle), Central/St. Martin's School of Art (1985-88, Norman Ackroyd, Bernard Cheese, David Gluck), University of Minnesota (1991-94, Malcolm Myers). *Exhib:* U.K. and U.S.A. *Work in collections:* U.K. and U.S.A *Clubs:* A.R.E., Mem. Southern Graphic Council,

U.S.A. *Signs work:* "James Boyd-Brent." *Address:* 1241 Fifield Ave., St. Paul, Minn. 55108, U.S.A.; 46 Shelly Gdns., Cambridge CB3 0BX.

**BOYDEN, Ann,** S.W.A.; portrait painter in oil, water-colour, pastel, teacher; art teacher for Adult Educ.; *b* London, 1 June, 1931. *m* Alan Boyden. three *s.* *Educ:* Godolphin School, Salisbury. *Studied:* Southern College of Art, Bournemouth (1948-52). *Exhib:* S.W.A., Nottingham Castle Gallery, Dillington House; solo shows: Ancaster Gallery, British Council, Brussels. *Clubs:* Dillington Water-colour Soc. *Signs work:* "Ann F. Boyden." *Address:* Russets, Lopen Rd., Hinton St. George, Som. TA17 8SF.

**BOYDEN, John,** B.A.(Lond.), Dip.A.G.M.S.(Manc.), A.M.A.; sculptor in wood and stone; Curator, Hove Museum of Art, Sussex (1973-86); *b* Tunbridge Wells, 1942. *m* Christine Portsmouth. two *s.* *Studied:* Ruskin School of Drawing. *Publications:* illustrations for The Farthing Press, Museum catalogues. *Address:* 3 Rosslyn Rd., Shoreham-by-Sea, W. Sussex BN43 6WL.

**BOYES, Judy Virginia,** S.W.A. (1984), B.W.S. (1985); self taught landscape painter in water-colour; *b* Alton, Hants., 1 July, 1943. *m* John Boyes. two *d. Educ:* Eggars Grammar School, Alton. *Exhib:* R.I., Mall Galleries, S.W.A., Westminster Gallery; one-man shows: Liverpool University, Atkinson A.G., Southport, Guildford House A.G., Forest Gallery, Guildford. *Publications:* front cover of Artist Magazine, features and articles on water-colour technique in Artist. *Signs work:* "Judy Boyes." *Address:* Town Foot, Troutbeck, nr. Windermere, Cumbria LA23 1LB.

**BOYT, Judy,** M.A., A.R.B.S., S.E.A.; awarded R.B.S. Silver medal for Rebellion (1993); sculptor in bronze, resins, gold and silver; *b* Wales, 7 June, 1954. *Educ:* Oxford High School, West Oxon. Tech. College, Henry Box, Witney. *Studied:* Oxford (Len McComb), Wolverhampton and North Staffs. Polytechnics. *Exhib:* U.K., U.S.A., Jersey, Switzerland, France. *Work in collections:* Polo - Horse Museum, Japan; Rebellion - East India House, London; Nashwan - The National Racing Museum, Newmarket; Golden Miller - Cheltenham Racecourse and National Racing Museum, Newmarket. *Commissions:* 'Rebellion' - Standard Life; Mitsubishi Motors Trophy, Badminton Horsetrials; JCB - Sir Anthony Bamford, DL. *Signs work:* "Judy Boyt." *Address:* Westwood, Easterton Sands, Devizes, Wilts. SN10 4PY.

**BRADSHAW, Bronwen,** B.A.(Hons.) (1966), R.W.A. (1988); artist in etching, silkscreen, oil, tempera, musician; *b* London, 7 Sept., 1945; divorced. one *d. Educ:* Sutton High School G.P.D.S.T. *Exhib:* R.A., R.W.A., R.E., New Munich Gallery, many group shows in the South-West. *Work in collections:* R.W.A. *Signs work:* "Bronwen Bradshaw," "Bradshaw" or "B.B." *Address:* The Dove, Butleigh, Glastonbury, Som. BA6 8TL.

**BRADSHAW, Peter,** freelance artist in oils and gouache; *b* London, 23 Oct., 1931; divorced. one *d. Educ:* Kingsthorpe Grove, Bective. *Studied:* Northampton School of Art (1945-47) under F. Courtney, E. Goodson. *Exhib:* United Artists, R.O.I., Northampton Town and County and local exhbns.

*Publications:* Railway Art. *Signs work:* "P. Bradshaw" (cat and robin featured in work). *Address:* 4 Bective Rd., Northampton NN2 7TD.

**BRADSHAW, Raymond Henry,** A.T.D.; draughtsman, portrait and figure artist in oil, crayon and ink; formerly Head of Art Dept. and Housemaster, Bancroft's School; vice-president, Hesketh Hubbard Art Soc. (Federation of British Artists); *b* 9 Jan., 1918. *m* Marjorie Bayliss. two *d. Educ:* Bancroft's School. *Studied:* West Ham School of Art (1935-36); Westminster School of Art (1936-38) under Mark Gertler, Bernard Meninsky, Mervyn Peake and Adrian Hill; Hornsey School of Art (1938-39). *Exhib:* R.B.A., R.A., R.P., etc. Work in private ownership in England, France, Switzerland, Sweden, America and Australia. *Publications:* illustrated, Introducing Local Studies (Dent.) *Signs work:* "Raymond H. Bradshaw." *Address:* Little Monkwood Lodge, Baldwins Hill, Loughton, Essex IG10 1SF.

**BRAND, Margaret,** A.I.M.B.I. (1968),M.M.A.A. (1969) ; medical artist, figurative and expressionist painter in oil, water-colour and mixed media; *b* London, 1938. *Educ:* Stella Maris Convent, Devon. *Studied:* Reigate and Redhill School of Art (1957-60); Post-grad. diploma in medical illustration, Guy's Hospital Medical School (1961); Deputy Head of Dept. of Medical Illustration, Guy's Hospital (1963-69). Private commissions. *Exhib:* R.A., R.M.S., London and provincial societies and galleries. *Publications:* work repro.: illustrations in medical scientific books and journals. *Signs work:* "M. Brand" or "M.B." *Address:* 51 Doctors Lane, Chaldon, Surrey CR3 5AF.

**BRANDEBOURG, Margaret,** (previously listed as M. E. Winter); part-time teacher in adult educ. for I.L.E.A.; *b* Surbiton, Surrey, 28 Apr., 1926. *m* Deryck Winter. *Educ:* Tiffin Girls' School. *Studied:* Kingston Art School and R.A. Schools. Since 1976 has worked in textiles. *Exhib:* British Crafts Centre, Seven Dials Gallery, etc. *Commissions:* in Portsmouth Museum. *Publications:* book on Seminole Patchwork (Batsford, 1987). Lectures and demonstrates on this subject. *Clubs:* Quilter's Guild (founder mem.). *Address:* 3 Cedars Rd., Hampton Wick KT1 4BG.

**BRANNAN, Noel Rowston,** A.T.D. (1952); painter; *b* Tynemouth, 25 Dec., 1921. *m* Mavis Annie (née Leitch). one *s.* one *d. Educ:* Humberstone Foundation School, Clee, Lincs. *Studied:* School of Art, Lincoln (1947-51), College of Art, Leicester (1951-52). *Exhib:* one-man: Willoughby Gallery, Corby Glen, Lincs. (1985); R.A., R.B.A., New English, A.I.A., etc. *Work in collections:* Usher Gallery, Lincoln, Riversley A.G. Nuneaton. *Clubs:* Lincolnshire Artists' Soc. *Signs work:* "Noel Brannan." *Address:* Athelstan, Hinckley Rd., Burbage, Leics. LE10 2AG.

**BRANSBURY, Allan Harry,** F.R.B.S., F.I.P.D., M.I.Mgt., N.D.D., A.T.C. (Lond.); artist, designer, educationalist; *b* Jersey, 1942; married. two *s. Educ:* Victoria College. *Studied:* West of England College of Art, Bristol, and the University of London Inst. of Educ., followed by study-travel in Canada and U.S.A. *Exhib:* various galleries including Royal Scottish Academy (1990 and

1992). *Commissions:* in Jersey and England. Artist in Residence, University of Sussex (1976). Principal of the London Borough of Bromley Centre for Arts and Crafts (1977-80). Resident in Scotland since 1980. *Signs work:* see appendix. *Address:* Burnside, Kilmuir, North Kessock, Inverness IV1 1XG.

**BRANSCOMBE, Dianne Lois,** R.M.S. (1996), A.R.M.S. (1993), S.W.A. (1994), H.S. (1991); artist in water-colour and oil, teacher; *b* Norwich, 1 Oct., 1949. *m* Robert. two *d. Educ:* Norwich City College. *Studied:* Goldsmiths' College (1969-72). *Exhib:* R.M.S., S.W.A., H.S., R.A. Summer show, Mandell's Gallery Norwich, Llewellyn Alexander Gallery London, and many mixed shows. *Signs work:* "D.L. Branscombe." *Address:* Bangala, The Green, Surlingham, Norwich, Norfolk NR14 7AG.

**BRASIER, Jenny,** R.H.S. Gold medals: for pencil drawing (1982, 1989), for paintings in water-colour on vellum (1988, 1994); botanical artist and illustrator in water-colour on vellum, pencil; *b* Worcs., 9 Aug., 1936. *m* John Brasier. two *s. Educ:* Sir James Smith's Grammar School, Camelford; University of Nottingham, School of Agriculture. *Exhib:* R.B.G. Kew, R.H.S., S.B.A., V. & A., Natural History Museum, Hunt Inst. Pittsburgh, Smithsonian Inst. Washington. *Work in collections:* V. & A., Natural History Museum, Nature in Art (Gloucester), Hunt Inst. for Botanical Documentation, Carnegie-Mellon University Pittsburgh. *Publications:* illustrated: Hosta, the Flowering Foliage Plant, Diana Grenfell; The Cyclamen Soc. Journals; illustrations included in: The Art of Botanical Illustration, Blunt and Stearn; The R.H.S. Dictionary of Gardening; An Approach to Botanical Painting, Evans and Evans; Treasures of the Lindley Library, Brent Elliott; Picturing Plants, Gill Saunders (V. & A.). *Signs work:* see appendix. *Address:* Sparrows, 11 Hazel Cl., Newton Poppleford, Sidmouth, Devon EX10 0DJ.

**BRASON, Paul,** R.P. (1994); portrait painter in oil; *b* London, 17 June, 1952. *m* Judy. two *s.* one *d. Educ:* King James I Grammar School, I.O.W. *Studied:* Camberwell College of Art (1970-74). *Work in collections:* N.P.G., Royal Collection Windsor Castle, Government Art Collection, Eton College, Trinity and Balliol Colleges, Oxford. *Clubs:* Arts. *Signs work:* "P.B." or "BRASON" and date. *Address:* Hinton House, 140 High St., Marshfield, Wilts. SN14 8LU.

**BRAYER, Yves,** painter; Member of Académie des Beaux-Arts, Paris; Officer Légion d'Honneur; Director, Marmottan Museum, Paris; *b* Versailles, France, 18 Nov., 1907. One of the best-known French figurative painters of his generation. He studied art in Montparnasse academies, then in the National School of Arts. He was deeply impressed by Spain and Italy (Prix de Rome 1930). Since 1945 he worked mainly in Provence, Camargue and travelled in many foreign countries. He has designed sets and costumes for ballets and lyrique theatre. He illustrated luxury editions including texts from Monthertant, Gide, Hemingway and Claudel. Many museums and collectors have bought his works. *Signs work:* "Yves Brayer." *Address:* 22 rue Monsieur le Prince, 75006

Paris.

**BRAZDA, Jan,** abstract painter, sculptor, stained glass artist and stage designer; *b* Rome, Vatican, 1917. *Studied:* Academy of Fine Arts, Prague, Prix de Rome, 1st Prize Triennale Milan, Gran Premio, Venice. *Exhib:* National Museum, Leonardo da Vinci Stockholm (1982), Centre International du Vitrail Chartres (1995); retrospective: Samlaren, stained glass (1977), Prins Eugen Waldemarsudde, Stockholm (1981). *Work in collections:* National Museum, Moderne Museet, Prins Eugen Waldemarsudde Stockholm, Röhsska Konstslöjdmuseum, Konstmuseum Gothenburg, Skissernas Museum Lund University. *Commissions:* designed Thermal Bath Giardini Poseidon, Ischia Bay of Naples; executed monument, stained glass windows, mosaics and bronzes Växjö Cathedral, Sankt Andreas Malmö, and other churches etc.; scenery: Covent Gdn. London, Lyric Opera Chicago, Bayer Staatsoper Munich, Royal Opera Stockholm, Bolshoi Moscow. Member of National Organisation of Swedish Artists (K.R.O), Swedish Actors Equity Assoc. *Address:* Rindögatan 44, S115 58 Stockholm, Sweden.

**BRAZIER, Connie,** S.W.A. (1980); artist in water-colour, and engraved glass; Glass Engraving Tutor (retd.), Sutton College of Liberal Arts; *b* Croydon. *m* Desmond Brazier. two *s. Educ:* Stamford High School for Girls, Lincs. *Studied:* Croydon School of Art (Reginald Marlow, Frederick Hinchliffe, Michael Cadman). *Exhib:* Europa Gallery, Sutton (1977, 1979, 1981, 1983, 1984), Whitehall, Cheam (1986), Fairfield Halls (shared) (1987), Civic Centre A.G., Tunbridge Wells (1987), Playhouse, Epsom (1991), R.I., R.M.S., S.B.A. *Clubs:* Lewes Art. *Signs work:* see appendix. *Address:* 27 Sadlers Way, Ringmer, Lewes, East Sussex BN8 5HG.

**BRECKMAN, Barbara Rosamund,** City and Guilds Fine Arts Dip. (1971), P.G.Dip.Art Therapy (1994); music and movement, figure (nude) artist in oil, pen and ink, pastel; *b* London, 19 Mar., 1947. *Studied:* City and Guilds of London Art School. *Exhib:* City of London Festival at Royal Exchange (1969,1970), Arthouse Gallery, Jerusalem (1972), Chelsea (March 1990), Staircase Gallery, Kew (1990), Drey Gallery, Chelsea (1991), Fulham Arts Soc. (1994), Crypt Gallery W.I. (1997). *Signs work:* "Barbara Breckman" or "B. BRECKMAN." *Address:* 22 Foyes Ct., 250 Shirley Rd., Southampton SO15 3SJ.

**BREEZE, George,** M.A., F.R.S.A., F.M.A.; museum curator; Head of Art Gallery and Museums, Cheltenham Borough Council; *b* Wilmslow, Ches., 12 Mar., 1947. *m* Rachel M. Breeze. two *s. Educ:* University of Manchester (B.A.), Barber Inst. of Fine Arts, University of B'ham (M.A.). *Publications:* include: Edith Payne (1978); Joseph Southall (1980); Arthur and Georgie Gaskin (1981) (cô-author); Margaret Gere (1984) (co-author). *Address:* c/o Cheltenham Art Gallery and Museums, Clarence St., Cheltenham, Glos. GL50 3JT.

**BRENNAND, Catherine,** B.Ed. Art and Design, R.I.; artist in water-colour, water-colour with wax resist, line and wash; specialises in paintings of buildings; *b* Woking, 11 Oct., 1961. *m* Mark Brennand. *Educ:* Dover Grammar School. *Studied:* Bishop Otter College, Chichester (1980-83, Geoff Lowe, Malcolm Norman, Alan Saunders). *Exhib:* Linda Blackstone Gallery Pinner, Stafford A.G., David Curzon Gallery, Wimbledon Village, Shell House Gallery, Ledbury, Broad Street Gallery, Wolverhampton. *Commissions:* The Crown Estate; Goodyear Plc; Stafford C.C.; Tarmac Building Materials Ltd.; Eldridge Pope & Co. Ltd.; Ivory Gate Plc. *Clubs:* Wolverhampton Art Soc. *Signs work:* "Brennand." *Address:* 27 Severn Drive, Perton, Wolverhampton WV6 7QU.

**BRENT, Isabelle,** painter/illustrator in water-colour and gold leaf; painter of commissioned portraits of animals throughout the world; *b* Caversham, 17 Mar., 1961. *Studied:* Loughborough College of Art and Design; further studies in France and Italy; research studies in the Dept. of Decorative Arts, Leicester Museum. *Exhib:* R.A., London and provincial galleries. *Work in collections:* throughout the world. *Publications:* written and illustrated: The Christmas Story, Cameo Cats, The Well-travelled Cat, A Cat for all Seasons, Noah's Ark*Signs work:* see appendix. *Address:* 5 Bouverie Ct., Whissendine, nr. Oakham, Rutland LE15 7HA.

**BRETT, Simon,** S.W.E., A.R.E. (1986); wood engraver; Chairman, S.W.E. (1986-92); *b* Windsor, 27 May, 1943. *m* Juliet Wood. one *d. Educ:* Ampleforth College. *Studied:* St. Martin's School of Art (1960-64, as a painter; learned engraving from Clifford Webb). *Exhib:* S.W.E., R.E., R.A., and occasional one-man shows. *Publications:* for own Paulinus Press (Francis Williams Award 1982 for 'The Animals of Saint Gregory'); Readers Digest Bible (1990), 'Clarissa', 'Jane Eyre', 'Confessions of St. Augustine', 'Amelia', 'The Folio Golden Treasury' (picture ed.), 'Fifty Love Poems' (Folio Soc.), edited 'Engravers' (1987, 1992); 'Wood Engraving-How to do it' (1994). *Signs work:* "Simon Brett." *Address:* 12 Blowhorn St., Marlborough, Wilts. SN8 1BT.

**BRETTINGHAM, Walter David,** N.D.D. (1953), A.T.D. (1954); painter in oil; *b* London, 1924. *Educ:* Marley School and Royal Navy. *Studied:* Sir John Cass College, London (1948-51), St. Martin's School of Art (1951-53), Bournemouth College of Art (1953-54). *Exhib:* one-man shows, Berystede Hotel, Ascot (1972), 3 Households Gallery, Chalfont (1973), Upper St. Gallery, Richmond (1974), Century Gallery, Henley (1979), Guildford House, Guildford (1981), Holkham Gallery, Norfolk (1982), Bloomsbury Gallery, London (1984). *Work in collections:* Deanery, Westminster Abbey, London University Educ. Inst. *Publications:* colour supplements, 'Pictorial Education' (1963-69); 'De Brethenham and Brettingham' (1971), 'Godless Waters' novel (1996). *Signs work:* "Brettingham." *Address:* 25 Cabrera Ave., Virginia Water, Surrey GU25 4EZ.

**BREWSTER, Martyn Robert,** B.A. (1974), Post. Grad. Dip. in Printmaking (1975), A.T.C. (1978); Eastern Arts award (1977), British Council

Award (1991); painter in oil and acrylic, drawings, printmaking; *b* Oxford, 24 Jan., 1952. *Educ:* Watford Boys' Grammar School. *Studied:* Herts. College of Art (1970-71), Brighton Polytechnic (1971-75), Brighton Art Teachers' Centre (1977-78). *Exhib:* one-man shows: Jill George Gallery London since 1988. *Work in collections:* Russel-Cotes A.G. and Museum, Dorset. Many public and private collections U.K. and abroad. *Publications:* Monograph on artist by Simon Olding (Scolar Press, 1997). *Signs work:* "Brewster" either on front or back of work with date. *Address:* 15 West Rd., Boscombe, Bournemouth, Dorset BH5 2AN.

**BRIDGE, Muriel Elisabeth Emily (Mrs. Millie Taylor),** N.D.D.; artist in mixed media, oils and paper collage and water-colour; *b* Rome, 1934. *m* John R. Taylor. one *s.* two *d. Studied:* (graphic design) at St. Martin's School of Art. *Exhib:* regularly with S.W.A. (collages); Bishops Kitchen, Chichester, Havant Art Centre, Chichester Centre of Arts and Bishops Palace in the Chi Festivities and R.I. exhbn. at the Mall Galleries. Paintings in private collections worldwide. *Commissions:* 8 ft. mural for office in Regents St. Winner of national art prize 1996. Is now painting host with Saga Holidays. *Clubs:* Mem. New Park Artists. *Signs work:* "M. Bridge." *Address:* The Mews, 22 Victoria Rd., Chichester, W. Sussex PO19 4HY.

**BRIDGEMAN, John,** A.R.C.A. (1949), F.R.B.S. (1960); sculptor; *b* Felixstowe, Suffolk. *m* Irene Dancyger, journalist. one *s.* one *d. Studied:* Colchester School of Art; Royal College of Art. Exhibited widely.*Work in collections:* sculptures at St. Helen's, Birmingham, Queen Elizabeth Hospital, Dudley Road Hospital, Keighley, Coventry Cathedral; 8ft. bronze group, St. Bartholomew's, Barking Rd., London; Mother and Child (Relief), West Bromwich; public gardens, Coventry, private gardens, private collections; font, Hillmorton Church, Rugby etc. *Signs work:* see appendix. *Address:* 27 Hyde Pl., Leamington, Warwickshire CV32 5BT.

**BRIERTON, Irene Annette,** S.W.A. (1988), H.S. (1997); painter of wildlife in water-colour; *b* Belper, 10 Dec., 1948. *m* Robert Brierton. one *s.* one *d. Educ:* Burnham Grammar School, Bucks. *Exhib:* R.I. (1985-88), S.WL.A. (1985), S.W.A., Llewellyn Alexander (Fine Paintings) Ltd., London, R.M.S. (1996). *Publications:* work repro.: paintings by W.W.F. as cards. *Signs work:* "Irene Brierton." *Address:* 17 St. Michael's Cl., Crich, Derbyshire DE4 5DN.

**BRIGHT, Madge,** A.R.O.I. (1990); winner, R.O.I. award Cornellissen prize; self taught artist in oil and mixed media; *b* S. Africa, 15 Feb., 1939. *m* P.S. Johnson. three *s. Educ:* Chaplin Gwelo, Rhodesia. *Exhib:* R.O.I. Mall Galleries, S.B.A., Britain's Painters, Hertford-Century Gallery Henley-on-Thames, Iwano Gallery Osaka Japan, Noor Gallery Bahrein, Look Out Gallery Plettenberg Bay S. Africa, Llewellyn Alexander Fine Art. *Work in collections:* National Gallery Zimbabwe. *Clubs:* S.B.A., Hertford Art Soc., Five Women Artists Plus. *Signs work:* "Madge Bright." *Address:* 1 Great Ash, Lubbock Rd., Chislehurst, Kent BR7 5JZ.

**BRIGSTOCK, Jane Lena,** A.R.E., B.A. Hons. (Painting) (1979), M.A. (Printmaking) (1980), British Institution Fund Printmakers award (1981); guest artist, California College of Art and Crafts (1981-82); painter in pastel, water-colour, printmaker; lecturer, Nene College, Northampton; Maidstone School of Art; Chelsea School of Art; *b* 28 Mar., 1957. *m* Michael John Addison. *Educ:* Wellingborough County High School for Girls. *Studied:* Maidstone School of Art, and Chelsea School of Art. *Exhib:* R.A., Cleveland Drawing Bienale, Royal Overseas League, Drew Gallery, Canterbury. *Work in collections:* Northampton C.C. Mem. Soc. of Painter-Printmakers. *Signs work:* "J.L. Brigstock." *Address:* 76 West Hill Rd., St. Leonards on Sea, E. Sussex.

**BRINDLEY, Donald,** A.R.C.A. Sculpture (1951), F.R.B.S. (1973); sculptor in clay, bronze, ceramics of portraiture, equestrian subjects; Consultant to Josiah Wedgwood & Sons, Royal Worcester Porcelain Co., and continental and American businessses; *b* Penkhull, Stoke-on-Trent, 22 Feb., 1928. one *s*. one *d*. *Educ:* Junior Art Dept. Burslem College of Art. *Studied:* R.C.A. (1948-51, Profs. Frank Dobson and John Skeaping, R.A.). *Work in collections:* H.M. The Queen, the late Lord Mountbatten. *Signs work:* "D. BRINDLEY" and see appendix. *Address:* Fernlea, Leek Rd., Stockton Brook, Staffordshire Moorlands ST9 9NH.

**BRINDLEY, Robert Edward,** A.R.S.M.A. (1996), Y.W.S. (1992); painter in water-colour, oil, pastel; *b* Burton on Trent, Staffs., 11 Feb. 1949., *m* Elizabeth Brindley (née Brooke). one *s*. one *d*. *Exhib:* Mall Galleries (R.S.M.A. and R.O.I.); Ferens Hull; Carrisbrooke Gallery; Mercer Gallery, Harrogate; Houses of Parliament. *Work in collections:* Royal Inst. of Naval Architects. *Commissions:* paintings for "Allied Breweries U.K. Ltd." Burton on Trent. *Publications:* illustrations for "Minewinding and Transport" (1988). Runs painting courses from home studio. *Signs work:* "Robert Brindley." *Address:* Holmesgrove Studio, Sandsend, Whitby, N. Yorks. YO21 3SX.

**BRINE, John Nicholas,** R.B.A., A.R.C.A. (1949); artist in oils and acrylic; Curator and Master of Painting and Drawing, Royal Academy Schools (Sept. 1955-Dec. 1960); Head of School of Fine Art, Ravensbourne College of Art and Design, Chislehurst; *b* 25 June, 1920. *m* Janet Pace, Cert. R.A.S. (1964). two *d*. *Studied:* Clapham School of Art (1935-39), R.C.A. (1946-49). *Signs work:* "BRINE." *Address:* 1 Herne Cottages, Walshes Rd., Crowborough, E. Sussex TN6 3RA.

**BRISCOE, Michael J.,** B.A. (Hons.); artist in oil and acrylic on canvas; *b* Colwyn Bay, 11 May, 1960. three *s*. one *d*. *Educ:* Eirias High School. *Studied:* Wrexham College of Art (1978-79, David Cooper), Sheffield City Polytechnic (1979-82, Brian Peacock, Terry Lee). *Exhib:* Sheffield National (1980), Stowells Trophy (prize winner), Wales '83 Travelling Exhbn., R.A. Summer Exhbn. (1983-85), Through Artists Eyes Mostyn A.G., Paris Salon des Nations (1984); mixed shows, Piccadilly Gallery (1984-85). Produces illustrations for advertising since 1988. Selling paintings in Holland, Germany in 1995. *Signs* *work:* "Mike Briscoe." *Address:* 81 Coed Coch Rd., Colwyn Bay, Clwyd LL29 9UW.

**BROAD, Ronald Arthur,** freelance artist in oil and water-colour specialising in winter landscape and line drawing; *b* Crookham, Berks., 2 Sept., 1930. *Educ:* Newbury Grammar School, St. Aidan's College (C. of E.), Birkenhead. *Studied:* tutored by George Bissill. *Exhib:* regularly at R.A. *Clubs:* Hockley Golf. *Signs work:* "Ronald A. Broad." *Address:* Belmont, Orchard Rd., S Wonston, Winchester, Hants. SO21 3EX.

**BROCKWAY, Michael Gordon,** N.E.A.C.; artist in oil and water-colour; *b* 11 Apr., 1919. *m* Margaret. two *s. Educ:* Stowe and Peterhouse, Cambridge. *Studied:* Farnham School of Art (1946-50), Cheltenham School of Art (1950), and Ruskin School of Drawing, Oxford (1951-54). *Exhib:* R.A., R.I., R.B.A., N.E.A.C. *Publications:* Charles Knight, R.W.S., R.O.I., 1952. *Signs work:* "MICHAEL BROCKWAY." *Address:* 1 Swan Lane Cl., Burford OX18 4SP.

**BRODERICK, Laurence John,** A.R.B.S., N.D.D. (1965); sculptor in figurative art - bronze and stone, well known for otter carvings and portrait heads; *b* Bristol, 18 June, 1935. *m* Ingrid. three *s. Educ:* St. Nichol's, Clifton, Bristol; Bembridge School, I.O.W. *Studied:* Regent St. Polytechnic (1952-57), Hammersmith School of Art (1964-65). *Exhib:* Century Galleries, Henley-on-Thames; Park St. Gallery, Bristol; Belgrave Gallery, London; Gallery 1667, Halifax, Canada; City of London Festival; Rue Paradis, Monte Carlo, Monaco; Manor Gallery, Royston; Printmakers Gallery, Inverness; Malcolm Innes Gallery, Edinburgh; Phoenix Gallery, Lavenham; Chester Arts Festival; Warrington Museum A.G.; since 1980 annual sculpture exhbn. Isle of Skye; mixed shows: Keats House, Hampstead; C.P.S., London; R.W.A., Bristol; R.A., London; R.B.A., London; Art London '91; Broxbourne Festival. *Work in collections:* Crucifix, Christchurch, Hants.; Madonna of the Magnificat, Priory, Dunstable, Beds.; St. George, Haberdashers' Aske's School, Elstree, Herts.; Elation, Mother and Child, The Otter, Cherrybank Gdns., Perth (Bell's); Teko - The Swimming Otter, The Otter Trust, Earsham, Suffolk; Leaping Salmon, Chester Business Park; Head of Philippe Chatrier (Pres. ITF), Queen's Club, London and Roland Gaross, Paris; Turtle, Prudential, London; Mother and Child, Leicester Royal Infirmary; Family of Otters, Powergen, Coventry. *Publications:* Life of Purcell (Chatto & Windus), Uncle Matts Mountain (Macmillan), Village life through the Ages (Evans), Soapstone Carving (Alec Tiranti). *Signs work:* "Laurence Broderick." *Address:* Thane Studios, 10 Vicarage Rd., Waresley, Sandy, Beds. SG19 3DA.

**BRODY, Frederick J.,** A.V.C.M. (1931), A.R.C.A. (1937), M.S.I.A. (1946), F.I.A.L. (1952), F.R.S.A. (1960); lecturer in art, interior designer, silversmith, cabinet-maker, painter in tempera; silverware at Sheffield and London, furniture in own furniture factory; *b* Sheffield, 31 May, 1914. *Studied:* Sheffield College of Art (1929-34); R.C.A. (1934-37) under Prof. Tristram, Sir William Rothenstein, John Nash, Bawden, Ravilious, Spencer, Barnett

Freedman. *Exhib:* London, provinces, International Exhbn. (Paris, 1937), B.I.F. exhbns., Britain Can Make It exhbn. Festival of Britain (1951) and U.S.A. *Signs work:* see appendix. *Address:* 15 Cherry Tree Drive, Sheffield S11 9AE.

**BROGAN, Honor,** B.A. (English and French), Dip.Ed. (1967 and 1968, Cardiff); artist in charcoal, oil, water-colour, clay; *b* Welshpool, 26 Jan. 1946. *m* Diarmuid Brogan (decd.). one *s. Educ:* Welshpool High School. *Studied:* Morley College (Peter Richmodd and Alan Thornhill). *Exhib:* Artist in Residence, Lichfield Festival (1996); Celtic/Uzbek Exchange at Tashkent Artists Union (1995); R.A. Summer (1997); Belgravehall Painters at Pump House, Battersea Park; B.A.C.F.; Chelsea Arts Soc.; Sculpture for Rumania; G.L.C. Peace Exhbn.; Not the Royal Academy. *Signs work:* "Honor Brogan." *Address:* 12 Westover Rd., London SW18 2RG.

**BRONDUM-NIELSEN, Birgitte,** R.I., S.S.W.A.; Diplome d'Honneur, Vichy (1964); artist in water-colours; illustrator; *b* Copenhagen, 1917. *m* H. Brondum-Nielsen. *Educ:* Copenhagen. *Studied:* College of Arts and Crafts, Copenhagen. *Exhib:* group shows: R.A., R.S.A., S.S.A., R.S.W., Pitlochry Festival Theatre, Charlottenborg (Copenhagen), Salon International de Vichy, Brighton Art Gallery, Royal Glasgow Institute of Fine Arts, English-Speaking Union Galleries (Edinburgh), The Danish Cultural Inst. (Edinburgh), The Mall Galleries, London; one-man shows: Bristol, Stirling, Edinburgh (seven), Roskilde (Denmark), Edinburgh Festival, Copenhagen. *Work in collections:* Glasgow Art Gallery, the private collection of H.R.H. The Duke of Edinburgh. *Publications:* illustrations for songbooks for children (Danish), De Smaa Synger, (Bestseller of Danish Childrens' songbooks, publ. 1948); Fairytales from many Lands; Switzerland, etc. *Signs work:* "BITTE B-N." *Address:* Tuborgvej 15 S. 3, 2900 Hellerup, Denmark.

**BROOK, Peter,** R.B.A.; painter in oil; *b* Holmfirth, Yorks., 6 Dec., 1927. *m* Margaret Thornsby. two *d. Studied:* Goldsmiths' College, London University. *Work in collections:* many public and private collections in this country, Switzerland, U.S.A., South Africa and Australia. *Publications:* 'Peter Brook - The Pennine Landscape Painter' and 'Peter Brook in the Pennines with Mary Sara'. Painted: West Riding; Pennine Landscapes; Oxford Almanak, 1974; Cornwall, 1974; Hannah Hauxwell (40 pictures) 1979-81; Scotland 1981-88; Bowland 1987-88; Sheepfarms 1988; Jim Cropper (One Man and His Dog winner) 15 paintings 1989-90. *Signs work:* "PETER BROOK." *Address:* 119 Woodhouse La., Brighouse, W. Yorks. HD6 3TP.

**BROOKE, Anne Isabella,** A.T.D.; landscape painter in oil and former art teacher; *b* nr. Huddersfield, 1916. *Educ:* Downe House, Newbury. *Studied:* The Byam Shaw, Chelsea and Huddersfield Schools of Art and London University Institute of Educ. *Exhib:* R.A., R. Scottish A., N.E.A.C., Paris Salon, R.B.A., R. Cambrian A., R.O.I., W.I.A.C., R.I. Salon, United Artists, National Soc. and many provincial exhbns. *Work in collections:* Official purchases: Harrogate A.G., Wakefield A.G., Keighley A.G., The Beecroft A.G., Southend-on-Sea, the former Herts., Lincs., Bristol and Northumberland Educ. Coms. *Signs work:* "A. Brooke." *Address:* 3 Oak Terr., Harrogate HG2 0EN.

**BROOKE, David,** B.A.Hons. (1978), S.G.F.A. (1993), U.A. (1994); artist in oil, acrylic, pen and ink; Hon. Treasurer, Soc. of Graphic Fine Art; *b* Yeovil, 24 Nov., 1956. *Studied:* Yeovil School of Art (1972-75), Hull College of Art (1975-78). *Exhib:* R.O.I., U.A., S.G.F.A., R.W.A., N.A.P.A., plus nine one-man shows and many mixed exhbns. in England. *Clubs:* S.G.F.A., U.A., N.A.P.A., *Signs work:* "D. Brooke" or "David Brooke." *Address:* 18 Stiby Rd., Yeovil, Som. BA21 3EF.

**BROOKE, Geoffrey Arthur George,** D.S.C., R.N. (retd.); oil painter; *b* Bath, 25 Apr., 1920. *m* V.M. Brooke. three *d. Educ:* R.N. College, Dartmouth. *Studied:* under Miss Sonia Mervyn, 28 Roland Gdns., SW7 (1949-50). *Exhib:* Army Art Soc. exhbns. *Signs work:* "G.A.G.B." *Address:* Beech House, Balcombe, Sussex RH17 6PS.

**BROOKES, Malcolm John,** A.T.D. (1964), R.B.S.A. (1974), R.Cam.A (1995); teacher, painter in gouache and oil; *b* Birmingham, 11 July, 1943. *m* Norma Turner. one *s.* one *d. Educ:* Moseley School of Art. *Studied:* Birmingham College of Art and Crafts (1959-64, Gilbert Mason). *Exhib:* R.B.S.A., Worcester A.G., Lichfield, Malvern, Stoke-on-Trent A.G., Dudley A.G., Icon Gallery, Birmingham, Royal West of England Academy, Mall Galleries, Royal Cambrian Academy. *Clubs:* R.B.S.A., R.Cam.A., Malvern Festival Artists. *Signs work:* "M.J. Brookes." *Address:* 3 Clive Rd., Bromsgrove, Worcs. B60 2AY.

**BROTHERSTON, Daphne,** F.S.B.A.; R.H.S. Grenfell silver gilt medal (1996); artist specializing in flower drawing with water-colour tint, and botanical painting; *b* 19 Apr., 1920. *m* Peter Brotherston, engineer. one *s.* one *d. Educ:* Sutton High School, G.P.D.S.T. *Studied:* Epsom A.E.C. *Exhib:* S.B.A. Westminster Hall, S.G.F.A. Knapp Gallery; three-man shows: Fairfield Halls, Hampton Court International Flower Show. *Publications:* work repro.: wedding cards/Christmas cards (C.C.A. Stationery Ltd.). *Clubs:* S.B.A. *Signs work:* "Daphne Brotherston." *Address:* 8 Bushby Ave., Rustington, W. Sussex BN16 2BZ.

**BROUGHTON, Aya,** F.R.S.A. (1994), N.S., M.F.P.S., W.I.A.C., S.W.A.; artist in water-colour and oil, mural painter; Associate, Société des Artistes Français; Paris Salon silver medal (1972, 1995); Lecturer for the Embassy of Japan; *b* Kyoto, Japan. *m* B. L. Broughton, M.A. (Oxon). *Educ:* Kyoto Furitsu Daiichi High School and the College, Kyoto, Japan. *Studied:* Newton Abbot School of Art and Dartington Adult Centre. *Exhib:* R.A. (1958), W.I.A.C., N.S., R.B.A., R.I., R.O.I., London Group, Paris Salon, United Soc., R.W.S. Exhbn. Flower Painting, Festival of Women, Wembley, London Exhbn. of Living British Women Artists, Flower Painters of the World (1971). *Work in collections:* in U.K., Japan, Switzerland, America, New Zealand. *Publications:* work repro.: La Revue Moderne, Western Morning News, Herald Express and

orquay Times, TV BBC 1 Peninsula. Article on Buddhism and Japanese Art
[he Mahabodhi Journal). *Signs work:* "AYA"; see appendix. *Address:*
reylands, 14 Cleveland Rd., Torquay, Devon.

**BROUGHTON, Neville,** M.B., Ch.B.Liverpool (1943), D.C.H., R.C.S.
953); past Flight Lieutenant R.A.F.V.R. (medical branch) service in U.K.,
aly, Austria, Middle East, Aden; retd. medical practitioner; self taught painter
 acrylic, water-colour and oil since 1970; *b* Lincoln, 11 Sept., 1919. *m*
orothy Mary Cunliffe. two *d. Educ:* Baines Grammar School, University of
iverpool. *Exhib:* R.A. (1983, 1984, 1988, 1991), Chenil Galleries London,
raves Gallery Sheffield, Usher Gallery Lincoln, Stockport Gallery, galleries
 U.S.A., Grantham A.G. Lincs. *Signs work:* "N. Broughton" or "Neville
roughton." *Address:* Long Acre, Laneham Rd., Rampton, Retford, Notts.
N22 0JX.

**BROWN, Deborah,** sculptor in glass fibre, papier mache and bronze; *b*
elfast, 1927. *Studied:* in Belfast, Dublin, Paris. *Exhib:* one-man shows and
ajor group exhbns. in Ireland, Gt. Britain, France, Germany, Scandinavia,
.S.A. and Canada. *Work in collections:* in Ireland, Gt. Britain and U.S.A.
*ommissions:* 1965, by Ferranti Ltd., panels for their building at Hollinwood,
lanchester; 1989 and 1991, major commissions in bronze. Prizes: 1970 First
rize Carroll Open Award, Irish Exhibition of Living Art, Dublin; 1970 Prize
pen Painting Arts Council of N. Ireland; 1980 Sculpture Prize Eva Limerick.
cluded in ROSC Dublin 1984. *Address:* 115 Marlborough Pk. Sth., Belfast
T9 6HW.

**BROWN, Doris,** S.W.A. (1987); freelance landscape artist in water-colour
nd ink, tutor and lecturer; *b* Newcastle under Lyme, Staffs., 17 Apr., 1933.
*duc:* Burslem College of Art, Stoke-on-Trent. *Studied:* Burslem and Stoke
chools of Art and privately under Reginald G. Haggar, R.I., F.R.C.A. *Exhib:*
.I., B.W.S., S.W.A., and numerous one-man shows. *Work in collections:*
lanley Museum, Stoke-on-Trent and Newcastle Fine A.G., University of
eele; paintings in private collections in England, America, Italy, S. Africa.
*lubs:* President and tutor to: Newcastle Water-colour Soc., Blythe Bridge
Vater-colour Soc., Oulton Water-colour Soc. *Signs work:* "Doris Brown."
ddress: 86 Dunbrobin St., Longton, Stoke-on-Trent, Staffs. ST3 4LL.

**BROWN, John Robert,** A.R.B.S.; sculptor in bronze and stone; formerly
lead of Art, Hampstead Garden Suburb Inst.; *b* London, 7 July, 1931. *m*
auline Brown. one *s.* one *d. Educ:* Queen Elizabeth's, Barnet. *Studied:*
lornsey School of Art, Hampstead Garden Suburb Inst. (Howard Bate, R.A.).
*igns work:* "J.R. Brown." *Address:* The Bow House, 35 Wood St., Barnet EN5
BE.

**BROWN, Julian Seymour,** A.T.D., N.D.D.; painter and graphic designer in
ater-colour, acrylic and oil; *b* Swansea, 3 July, 1934. *m* Gillian Thomas. two
two *d. Educ:* Swansea Grammar School. *Studied:* Swansea College of Art
950-55, Howard Martin), University College of Wales (1955-56). *Exhib:*

one-man shows: W.W.A.A. Gallery, Henry Thomas Gallery, Trapp Art Centi (1989, 1990, 1991); work exhib. throughout the Principality. *Work in colle tions:* Dyfed C.C. *Signs work:* "Julian Brown." *Address:* Penyrallt, Alltycna Johnstown, Carmarthen, Dyfed SA31 3QY.

**BROWN, Lucy,** M.A.(Hons.) Fine Art (1991); tutor; artist in mixed med installations; *b* Herts., 4 Aug., 1967. *Educ:* Haberdashers' Aske's School f Girls, Elstree. *Studied:* Edinburgh University and Edinburgh College of A (1986-91). *Exhib:* S.S.A., group and solo shows in Scotland. *Work in colle tions:* Edinburgh City Arts Centre, Glasgow Museums and Galleries. *Sig work:* "Lucy Brown" or not at all. *Address:* 48 Montrose Terr., Edinburgh EF 5DL.

**BROWN, Mary Rachel:** see MARAIS.

**BROWN, Neil Dallas,** D.A. (Drawing and Painting, 1958); major prizewi ner, Arts Council of N. Ireland Open Painting Exhibition (1970); painter in oi lecturer in painting studios, Glasgow School of Art; *b* Elgin, 10 Aug., 193 divorced. two *d. Educ:* Bell Baxter High School, Cupar, Fife. *Studied:* Dunde College of Art (1954-59, Alberto Morrocco), Royal Academy Schools (196( 61, Peter Greenham). *Work in collections:* Scottish Arts Council, Dundee Cit Museum, Skopje Museum, Yugoslavia, Nottingham City Art Galler Scunthorpe Education Committee, Hertfordshire County Council, Schoo Collection, Walker Art Gallery, Liverpool, Kingsway Technical Colleg Dundee. *Signs work:* see appendix. *Address:* 65 John St., Cellardyk Anstruther, Fife KY10 3BA.

**BROWN, Philip,** A.M.G.P., former V.P.S.I.A.C., former V.P.S.C.A painter, stained glass artist, lecturer, author and publisher; *b* London, 4 Nov 1925. *m* Gounil Hallin. five *d. Educ:* St. Paul's School, London. *Studied:* Slad School of Fine Art, Ateliers d'Art Sacré, Paris. *Exhib:* one-man shows: Londo Brighton, Oxford, Paris, Carmargue, Madrid, Malaga, Alicante, Swede Japan. *Work in collections:* stained glass in St. John's Cathedral, Umtata, S.A and many churches in England. *Publications:* The Essentials of Drawing an Painting; Picture Making; Still-Life and Plant Drawing; Working Outside; Wife Unravelled; A Painter in Spain (1996); Never Mind Piasso, Create Yo Own World (1997); Pen Drawing and Art of Hatching; Life Through Eyes c the Masters (all Icon Press). *Signs work:* "Philip Brown." *Address:* 1 Hugget La., Lower Willingdon, Eastbourne, E. Sussex BN22 0LZ.

**BROWN, Ralph,** R.A. (1972), F.R.B.S., (1992); sculptor in bronze draughtsman; *b* Leeds, 24 Apr., 1928. *m* Caroline Ann Clifton. two *s.* one *Educ:* Leeds Grammar School. *Studied:* Leeds College of Art, R.C.A. and i Paris, Italy and Greece. *Exhib:* frequent one man and group exhbns. in th country and abroad, since 1954. *Work in collections:* Tate Galler Rijksmuseum Kroller-Muller, Arts Council, Gallery of N.S.W., Sydne Stuyvesant Foundation, S.A., Contemporary Art Soc., Leeds City A.G., an many other provincial and foreign museums. *Commissions:* Harlow Nev own, Jersey Zoo. *Publications:* Motif 8. *Clubs:* Arts, Dover St. *Signs work:* e appendix. *Address:* The Old House, Frampton-on-Severn, Glos. GL2 7DY.

**BROWN, Stephen Edward,** A.R.B.A. (1996); artist in oil; *b* Chard, 20 Dec., 947. *m* Kathleen Irene. one *s.* one *d. Studied:* Somerset College of Art (1969-1), and privately with Patrick Larking, R.P., R.O.I. *Exhib:* R.W.A., R.B.A., .O.I., R.A. Summer Exhbn.; one exhbn.: Thompson's Gallery, Ainscough, Contemporary Art, Richmond Hill Gallery, all in London, Clifton Gallery, Bristol. *Signs work:* "S.B." *Address:* 92 King Cuthred Cl., Grange Park, Chard, om. TA20 2JD.

**BROWN, William McClure,** artist in painting, printmaking and sculpture; *b* unnyside, Toronto, Canada, 11 Dec., 1953. *Exhib:* ubiquitous. *Work in collecons:* National Maritime Museum Greenwich, Plymouth City Museum, Peel leritage Gallery Ontario, etc. *Publications:* written and illustrated: Contemporary Printmaking in Wales, Someone Stole a Bloater, Five Schools: mage and Word; The New Bestiary (Suel Publications, France), etc. *Signs ork:* "Wm. Brown." *Address:* (studio) 31 Newcastle Hill, Bridgend, Mid ilamorgan CF31 4EY.

**BROWNING, Mary Helena,** N.D.D. (1956), A.T.D. (1957), S.Eq.A. 1988); animal artist in pastel specializing in horses and dogs; *b* Watford, 15 Mar., 1935. *Educ:* East Haddon Hall School, Northants. *Studied:* Southampton College of Art (1953-56), Leicester College of Art (1956-57). *Exhib:* S.Eq.A. annually since 1985). *Publications:* Coursing - The Pursuit of Game with iazehounds (Standfast Press, 1976), Rebecca, the Lurcher. *Signs work:* MARY BROWNING." *Address:* Parish House, Greatworth, Banbury, Oxon. OX17 2DX.

**BROWSE, Lillian,** founder partner of Roland, Browse & Delbanco, 19 Cork t. W1; editor and writer of books on art; Hon. Fellow, Courtauld Inst. of Art 1986); former ballet critic, Spectator; organized wartime loan exhbns. at National Gallery, London (1940-45); also exhbns. for C.E.M.A. and British nst. of Adult Education. *Publications:* Augustus John Drawings (Faber & aber, 1941); Sickert (Faber & Faber, 1943); Degas Dancers (Faber & Faber 949); general editor of Ariel Books on the Arts, published for the Shenval ress by Faber & Faber; William Nicholson (Rupert Hart-Davis, 1955); Sickert Rupert Hart-Davis, May 1960); Forain - the Painter (Elek, 1978); contributed rticles to Apollo and Burlington Magazines; Sunday Times and Country Life. ddress: 19 Cork St., London W1.

**BRUCE, George J. D.,** elected R.P. (1959), Hon. Sec. (1970-84), Vice 'resident (1985-90), President (1991-94); portrait painter and painter of land-capes, still life, flowers etc. in oil; *b* London, 28 Mar., 1930. *Educ:* Vestminster. *Studied:* Byam Shaw School of Drawing and Painting (Brian D. .. Thomas, O.B.E., Patrick Phillips, R.P., Peter Greenham, R.A.). *Clubs:* Athenæum. *Signs work:* see appendix. *Address:* 6 Pembroke Walk, Kensington, London W8 6PQ.

WHO'S WHO IN ART

**BRUCE, Matt,** D.A. (Edin.), R.I.; teacher of painting and crafts, artist in all media, teacher at Victoria College, Jersey, Varndean School for Boys, Brighton, and Brighton College of Art evening classes (now retd.); *b* Shanghai, China, 17 Nov., 1915. *m* M. F. Bruce. one *s*. *Educ:* Dollar Academy, Scotland. *Studied:* Edinburgh College of Art (1932-39) under W. Gillies and J. Maxwell. *Exhib:* R.A., R.I., R.B.A., Brighton. *Signs work:* "Matt Bruce." *Address:* The Coach House, Old London Rd., Brighton BN1 8XQ.

**BRUNSDON, John Reginald,** A.R.C.A. (1958), R.E. (1995); full time artist in etching; *b* Cheltenham, 1933. *m* Ibby. ons *s*. four *s-s*. one *s-d Educ:* Cheltenham Grammar School. *Studied:* Cheltenham College of Art (1949-53), R.S.G. Dent, K. Oliver), R.C.A. (Julian Trevelyan, Alastair Grant, Edwin Ladell). *Exhib:* one-man shows, England, U.S.A., Canada, Australia, Sweden, Belgium. *Work in collections:* Arts Council, Tate Gallery, British Council, V & A. *Publications:* Technique of Etching and Engraving (Batsford, 1964). *Signs work:* "John Brunsdon." *Address:* Old Fire Station, Church St., Stradbroke, nr. Eye, Suffolk IP21 5HG.

**BRUNSKILL, Ann,** Assoc. of Royal Society of Painter Etchers (1969), painter and printmaker; *b* London, 5 July, 1923. *m* John Brunskill. three *s*. one *d*. *Educ:* Langford Grove School. *Studied:* Central School of Arts and Crafts, Chelsea College of Art. *Work in collections:* V. & A., Bibliothèque Nationale, University College, Oxford, South London Collection of Original Prints, Lib. of Congress, Washington, U.S.A., J. Lessing Rosenwald Alverthorpe Coll. U.S.A., Universities of Princeton, Yale, U.S.A., National Library of Australia, Canberra. *Signs work:* "Ann Brunskill" and "AB" with date on paintings. *Address:* Star & Garter Cottage, Egerton, Ashford, Kent TN27 9BE.

**BRYANT, Dena (née Bond),** artist in oils, scraper-board, water-colour, gallery owner and restorer; *b* Gloucester, 19 Mar., 1930. three *s*. *Educ:* Red Maids' School, Westbury-on-Trym, Bristol. *Studied:* Royal West of England Academy of Art. *Exhib:* St. Albans Gallery (1975), St. Albans Museum (1970), Paris, Salon de Nations (Jan. 1983), R.H.S. International Exhbn. (Mall Galleries, 1984), St. Albans Gallery (1987), Paris (1987), Galerie Salammbo, Paris (1988), St. Albans Abbey (1991), Luton Hoo Station House (1996), etc. *Work in collections:* St. Albans Gallery, South Africa, Canada, America. *Sign work:* "D.B.", "Dena" or a snail. *Address:* Luton Hoo Station House, New Mill End, East Hyde, Luton, Beds. LU1 3TR.

**BUCHANAN, Elspeth,** D.A. (Edin.); painter in oil; mem. of Council of S.S.W.A. (1956-59), S.S.A.; *b* Bridge of Weir, 29 Nov., 1915. *Educ:* St George's School for Girls, Murrayfield, Edinburgh. *Studied:* Edinburgh College of Art (1933-38) under Wellington. *Exhib:* R.A., R.Scot.A., S.S.A., S.S.W.A., G.I., N.E.A.C.; first one-man show, Great King St. Gallery; by invitation Alton Gallery, London SW13 (1990-95), R.S.A. Gallery. *Publications:* illustrated Land Air Ocean (Duckworth). *Clubs:* Soroptomist, Edinburgh. *Signs work:* "Elspeth Buchanan." *Address:* Viewpoint Residential Club, 7 Inverleith Terr., Edinburgh EH3.

**BUCK, Jon,** M.A., R.W.A., A.R.B.S.; sculptor in bronze; *b* Bristol, 8 Sept., 1951. *Studied:* Trent Polytechnic (1976-79), Manchester Polytechnic (1979-80), Fellow at Cheltenham College of Art and Design (1980-81). *Commissions:* 1995: John St., Porthcawl 'Street Beacon'; New Plaza, Harlesden 'On Our Heads'; 1996: British Consulate General, Hong Kong 'New Age'; 1997: Merthyr Tydfil Library, Merthyr Tydfil 'Common Knowledge'; 1998: Deal Pier, Deal, Kent 'Embracing the Sea'. *Signs work:* see appendix. *Address:* 8 Denmark Rd., Bath, Avon BA2 3RE.

**BUCKMASTER, Ann Devereaux,** M.S.I.A. (1951-80); freelance artist in pen; *b* London, 27 Mar., 1924. *m* the late Anthony Gilbert. *Educ:* Bromley High School. *Studied:* Beckenham School of Art, Bromley College of Art. Illustration and fashion drawing for magazines and advertising. *Address:* Kimbell House, Charlbury, Oxon. OX7 3QD.

**BUDD, Oliver Richard,** B.A. (Hons.) (1983); mural designer; *b* Farnborough, Kent, 10 Sept., 1960. *m* Fiona Campbell Graves. one *s*. *Studied:* Cheltenham College of Art (1980-83), apprenticed as mosaic artist/craftsman under Kenneth Budd (1983-85). *Commissions:* Murals include Abertillery Gwent, Local Life 1890-1900 (four mosaics); Gravesend, Waterman's Riot mosaic; Newport, Gwent, Shop Windows and Campbell's Steamers mosaics; Swanley, History of Bowls mosaic; Pontypool, Gwent, Pont Poell mosaic and 125th Anniversary of Pontypool Rugby Club mosaic; Warlingham, 125th Anniversary of Sainsbury mosaic; Biggleswade, R.S.P.B. mosaic (Sainsbury); Merthyr Tydfil, mid-Glamorgan, Transportation mosaic mural; Crumlin, Islwyn, Mines Rescue mosaic, and Crumlin Viaduct mosaic. *Clubs:* A.W.G. *Signs work:* As father, but reversed since his death - see appendix. *Address:* The Old Barn, Betsoms Farm, Pilgrims Way, Westerham, Kent TN16 2DS.

**BUDD, Rachel,** R.C.A., B.F.A. (Hons.), M.F.A. (Hons.); painter in oil on canvas; part-time lecturer, Cheltenham College of Art and Design, and Central St. Martin's School of Art; *b* Norwich, 6 Mar., 1960. *Studied:* University of Newcastle upon Tyne (1978-82, Prof. Rowntree), R.C.A. (1983-86, Peter de Francia). *Exhib:* one-man shows: Purdy Hicks (1991), '3 Ways' British Council travelling show, Hungary, Poland, Czechoslovakia (1990), Athena Art Awards (1987), London Group (1987), Lloyds Bldg. Art for the City (1987), R.A. Summer Exhbn. (1987), Contemporary Arts Soc. Market, Covent Gdn. (1987). *Work in collections:* County Nat.West. London, I.B.M., Contemporary Art Soc., Lloyds of London, Arthur Anderson Collection, I.C.I. *Signs work:* see appendix. *Address:* 67-71 Columbia Rd., London E2 7RG.

**BUFFET, Bernard,** *b* Paris, 10 July, 1928. Ecole des Beaux-Arts de Paris (1943); Prix de la Critique (1948); Chevalier de la Légion d'Honneur (1971). Elected at Académie des Beaux-Arts (1974). Has his own private Museum in Japan. The paintings of his chapel in Château l'Arc permanently shown in the Vatican.; *Exhib:* Main exhibits in Paris: La Passion, Horreur de la guerre, le Cirque, Jeanne d'Arc, les Oiseaux, la Corrida, l'Enfer de Dante, la Révolution

WHO'S WHO IN ART

Française. *Publications:* Main publications: Bernard Buffet by Pierre Bergé (1958), by Maurice Druon (1964), by Yann le Pichon (1986). *Address:* c/o Maurice Garnier, 6 avenue Matignon, Paris, 8.

**BUHLER, Michael Robert,** A.R.C.A.; artist in oil and acrylic; *b* London, 13 June, 1940. one *s.* one *d. Educ:* Bryanston School. *Studied:* Royal College of Art (1960-63, Carel Weight, Roger de Grey, Ruskin Spear, Colin Hayes) *Exhib:* Galeria Boitata, Porto Alegre, Brazil, Museo do Estado da Bahia, Brazil Eastern Arts Assoc., New Art Centre, R.A. *Work in collections:* Liverpool University, Carlisle City A.G., B.M., Arts Council, R.A., D.O.E. *Commissions:* Posters for British Museum (1979). *Publications:* Tin Toys 1945-1975 (Bergstrom and Boyle). "Abductees" animated film (1994). *Clubs:* Chelsea Arts. *Signs work:* "Michael Buhler." *Address:* 6 Cavell St., London E1 2HP.

**BULGIN, Sally,** B.A.(Hons.), M.A., Ph.D. (History of Art); painter in acrylic; Editor, The Artist magazine; *b* Ashford, Kent, 8 Nov., 1957. *Educ:* Highworth School for Girls, Ashford. *Studied:* Reading University (1977-81, Martin Froy, Terry Frost), Courtauld Inst., London (1981-91). *Exhib:* R.A. Dip Galleries, N.A.P.A. Annual, Clare College, Cambridge. Work in private collections. *Publications:* author of Acrylics Masterclass (1994); Oils Masterclass (1996) and Lucy Willis: Light in Watercolour (1997), (all Harper Collins). *Clubs:* Patron, National Assoc. of Painters in Acrylics; Hon. Vice-Pres., Royal Birmingham Soc. of Artists; Patron, Birmingham Pastel Society. *Signs work:* "Sally Bulgin." *Address:* 16 Blackwall Rd. North, Willesborough, Ashford, Kent TN24 0NU.

**BULLIVANT, Tina,** B.A.Hons.; artist in water-colour; *b* Brighton, 25 May, 1958. *m* Clive Bullivant. one *s. Educ:* Lourdes Convent. *Studied:* Brighton University (1976-80, Luther Roberts, Robert Birch). *Exhib:* S.W.A Sussex Open, Guild of Sussex Artists Open Exhbn., many mixed exhbns. *Work in collections:* Crawley Arts Council. *Clubs:* S.W.A., Guild of Sussex Artists (Life mem.). *Signs work:* "T. Bullivant, s.w.a" *Address:* 110 Streatfield Rd., Uckfield, E. Sussex TN22 2BQ.

**BULLOCK, Hazel,** M.F.P.S. (1970); painter in oil and acrylic; *Studied:* Sir John Cass School of Art (1962) under R. V. Pitchforth, Percy Horton, David Graham. *Exhib:* R.B.A., F.P.S., H.A.C., Browse and Darby, Whitechapel; one-man shows, Loggia Gallery (1973), Judd St. Gallery (1985), Phoenix Gallery, Highgate (1989), Phoenix Gallery, Lavenham (1989). *Work in collections:* private collections in England and Spain. *Clubs:* Arts. *Signs work:* "H. Bullock." *Address:* 32 Devonshire Pl., London W1.

**BULLOCK, Jean,** S.P.S. (1964); sculptor in clay cast in foundry bronze and polyester resins, occasionally wood and stone, printmaker; *b* Bristol, 27 Apr., 1923. *Educ:* Bishopshalt, Haberdasher Askes, George Watsons Ladies College, Edinburgh. *Studied:* Watford School of Art (Guido Belmonte), Camberwell School of Art (Dr. Karl Vogel). *Exhib:* R.A., S.P.S., Singapore Art Soc., Art Exhbns. Bureau Travelling Exhbns., Zillah Bell Gallery Thirsk, etc. *Work in*

# WHO'S WHO IN ART

*collections:* M. of D., Central Institute, NW1, South Norwood School, Tulse Hill; stained glass window, St. Giles, Lockton. *Signs work:* "JEAN BULLOCK." *Address:* Fern Cottage, Lockton, Pickering, N.Yorks.

**BUMPHREY, Nigel,** schoolmaster, gold and silversmith, and furniture maker; Diocesan adviser to Diocese of Norwich for Church Plate; *b* Norwich, 22 Feb., 1928. *m* Eileen. *Educ:* The City of Norwich School and Loughborough College. *Studied:* Central School of Arts and Crafts and Norwich Art School. *Exhib:* Norfolk Contemporary Crafts Soc., and others. Works mainly on commissions. *Work in collections:* Norwich City Collection. *Commissions:* Badges of office for various societies - British Association of Occupational Therapists, Travelling Club of Surgeons of Gt. Britain et al. *Signs work:* see appendix. *Address:* 28g Jessopp Rd., Norwich NR2 3QB.

**BUNTING, John Joseph,** F.R.B.S. (1972), A.R.C.A. (1954); sculptor in wood, stone and bronze; *b* 3 Aug., 1927. two *s.* three *d. Educ:* Ampleforth College, Oriel College, Oxford. *Studied:* St. Martin's School of Art (1949-51); R.C.A. (1951-54). *Exhib:* One-man shows at Paris (1965), Billingham (1972). *Work in collections:* Churches: St. Michael and All Angels (Oxford), War Memorial Chapel (Hambledon), St. Aidan's Church (Oswaldkirk); schools: St. Wilfrid's (Featherstone), St. Thomas à Becket (Wakefield), St. Bernard's (Rotherham). *Publications:* Monthly Report (1958-60), illustrations to Partage de Midi Paul Claudel (1963), Stages of the Cross (1972), John Bunting, sculptor (Paris, 1966), Sculptor's Luck (1993), On Making Saints (1994), Stone Crosses (1995), Sculptors Log (1997). *Address:* Nunnington, York YO6 5UP.

**BURDEN, Daniel,** A.R.C.A. (1955), R.W.A.; painter in oil, pastel, chalks, lino, collage; *b* Paris, 20 Jan., 1928. *m* Sallie Turner. two *d. Educ:* Kilburn Grammar School, London. *Studied:* Willesden Art School (1949-52, Ivor Fox, James Neal, Francis Gower), R.C.A. (1952-55, John Minton, Rodrigo Moynihan, Ruskin Spear, Colin Hayes). *Exhib:* R.A., R.W.A., A.I.A., R.B.A., Drian Gallery, Mignon Gallery, David Durrant Gallery, London Group, N.E.A.C., Salon des Independants Bordeaux. *Work in collections:* Leicester University, Southend Museum, Walsall Educ. Development Centre, Avon Art and Design Loan Service, R.W.A. Collection. *Clubs:* R.W.A. *Signs work:* "Burden." *Address:* Atelier Moulin A Vent, 47800 Moustier, Miramont de Guyenne, Lot et Garonne, France.

**BURDETT-SOMERS, Wilhelmina Maria,** A.R.M.S. (1983), H.S.F. (1983), M.A.S.-F. (1980), M.A.S.-N.J. (1985), M.A.S.-W. (1983), Mem. Min. Art of America (1990); Grumbacher Art award Gold Medal (1986); artist in miniature oil painting on copper, larger painting on canvas and board, founder mem. Hilliard Soc.; *b* The Hague, Netherlands, 23 July, 1923. *m* John Richard Burdett. *Educ:* Convent School, The Hague. *Studied:* Netherlands Royal Academie of Art. *Exhib:* all socs. annually to date, solo show: Queen's Gate, London (1981); R.A. Summer Show (1984). *Publications:* St. Pete, "Beach C/ abber. U.S.A. " (1997). *Signs work:* "W. Burdett-Somers, A.R.M.S., M.A.A."

*Address:* 18 Hunter Pl., Louth, Lincs. LN11 9LG.

**BURGESS, Peter,** painter in oil; *b* 1952. *Studied:* Wimbledon School of Art (1972-74), R.A. Schools (1974-77). *Exhib:* R.A., etc.; one-man shows: Thackeray Gallery, etc. *Work in collections:* Contemporary Art Soc., Derby City A.G., The Harborough Museum, Nottingham City Council, Leics. Educ. Authority, S. Derbyshire Health Authority, S. Nottingham College, Adam and Co., The Boots Co. plc.; many private collections in Britain, U.S.A. and Europe. *Signs work:* "Peter Burgess" on reverse of painting. *Address:* 43 Lees Hill St., Nottingham NG2 4JW.

**BURKE, Peter,** sculptor using reclaimed materials; *b* London, 29 Feb., 1944. *m* Wendy. two *d*. *Educ:* Bristol Technical School and Rolls Royce Bristol. *Studied:* Bristol Polytechnic (1972). *Exhib:* one-man shows: Festival Gallery, and Cleveland Bridge Gallery Bath, New Art Centre London (1992), New Art Centre Rochecourt (1993); mixed shows: London, Chicago, New Mexico, Berlin, Basel, Miami, Madrid, Zurich. *Work in collections:* Contemporary Art Soc. *Commissions:* Installation: Hat Hill Sculpture Foundation, Goodwood. *Publications:* Internet entry for sculpture at Goodwood: www.sculpture.org.uk. *Signs work:* "P. Burke," "PB." or not at all. *Address:* 9 Woolley Green, Bradford on Avon, Wilts. BA15 1TZ.

**BURLEIGH, Veronica,** Slade Scholarship (1927); portrait and landscape painter in oils and water-colour; *b* Hove, 17 Apr., 1909. *Educ:* Hoove Lea, Hove. *Studied:* Brighton School of Art (1926-27), Scholarship to Slade School (1927-30). *Exhib:* 31 one-man shows in England, Rhodesia and Zambia. *Work in collections:* Worthing. *Clubs:* S.W.A., Sussex Water-colour Soc., Sussex Painters. *Signs work:* "Veronica Burleigh." *Address:* 2 Corner Cottages, Blackstone, Henfield, Sussex.

**BURMAN, Chila Kumari,** B.F.A.(Hons.) (1980), M.F.A. (1982); mixed media artist, printmaker, photographer; *b* Liverpool, 17 Jan., 1957. *Studied:* Southport College of Art, Leeds Polytechnic, and Slade School of Fine Art (Phil Redmond, Barto dos Santos, Stanley Jones). *Exhib:* widely in Britain, recently in Canada. Work in private collections. *Publications:* contributed to Framing Feminism, and Visibly Female. *Signs work:* "C.K. Burman." *Address:* 20 Woodview Cl., Hermitage Rd., London N4 1DG.

**BURN, Hilary,** B.Sc.Hons. (Zoology) (1967), S.WL.A. (1983); freelance wildlife artist/illustrator in gouache, specialising in birds; *b* Macclesfield, Ches., 8 Apr., 1946. *Educ:* Macclesfield High School, and University of Leeds. *Exhib:* S.WL.A. Annual, regularly with R.S.P.B., Wildfowl Trust, Wildlife Originals Gallery, Nottingham, Wildlife A.G., Lavenham, Nature in Art, Glos. *Publications:* illustrated, R.S.P.B. Book of British Birds (1982); Wildfowl: An Identification Guide to the Ducks, Geese and Swans of the World (1987); Crows and Jays: An Identification Guide (1993); Handbook of the Birds of the World. *Clubs:* S.WL.A. *Signs work:* "Hilary Burn." *Address:* Huish Cleeve, Huish Champflower, Taunton, Som. TA4 2HA.

**BURNS, William,** R.I.B.A., F.S.A.I., F.R.S.A.; artist in oil; *b* Sheffield, 1923. *m* Betty. *Studied:* Sheffield Art School and architecture at Sheffield University. *Exhib:* R.O.I.; Medici Galleries, Bond Street; John Campbell Galleries, Kensington; Walker Galleries, Harrogate. *Work in collections:* John Campbell Gallery London, Walker Galleries Harrogate, Yorks. *Publications:* assisted with illustrating The Official War Diaries 1942-45. *Signs work:* "William Burns." *Address:* 29 Newfield Cres., Dore, Sheffield S17 3GE.

**BURNS McKEON, Katherine Balfour Kinnear,** D.A.(Edin.) 1950; Hong Kong Urban Council painting prize (1979), 1st prize (Painting) R.S.A., W.R.N.S. Art Competition (1945); artist in oil on canvas, muralist in mosaic, fresco; *b* Edinburgh, 10 Oct., 1925. *m* Leonard J. McKeon. two *s.* one *d. Educ:* Trinity Academy, Edinburgh. *Studied:* Edinburgh College of Art (1946-50, William Gillies, Leonard Rosoman). *Exhib:* Arts Council, S.S.A., Edinburgh, East Africa, Aden, Fiji, Hong Kong, London, France, Australia. *Work in collections:* Museums: Imperial War London, Nairobi, Hong Kong, Macau, Grimaud. *Commissions:* High Court, Dar es Salaam; murals: City Bank, Fiji; Hong Kong Bank, Paris; mosaic: Queen Elizabeth Stadium, Hong Kong and Mosque Social Centre. *Publications:* Hong Kong Art 1970-80; Fus Art, France 1996. 1st Prize, St. Raphael International Exhbn. (1990) and Grimaud (1994). *Signs work:* "Kitty Burns." *Address:* Hameau de Sauve Clare, Flayosc 83780, France.

**BURROUGH, Helen Mary (Mrs.),** R.W.A.; artist in oil, water-colour, sepia and wash; *b* Ceylon, 17 Feb., 1917. *m* T. H. B. Burrough. two *s. Educ:* St. George's Ascot. *Studied:* Miss McMuns Studio, Park Walk, Chelsea (1937), Prof. Otte Skölds' Ateljé, Stockholm (1938-39). *Clubs:* Royal Commonwealth Society. *Signs work:* "Helen." *Address:* The Old House, Frenchay, nr. Bristol BS16 1ND.

**BURROUGH, Thomas Hedley Bruce,** T.D., R.W.A., F.R.I.B.A.; chartered architect, artist in drawing and water-colour; Special Lecturer (Architecture), University of Bristol; Ex-Pres. Bristol Society of Architects; *b* Newport, Mon., 30 Apr., 1910. *m* Helen Mary Dickson, R.W.A. two *s. Educ:* Clifton College. *Studied:* R.W.A. School of Architecture (1928-32) (G. D. Gordon-Hake). *Work in collections:* R.W.A., Bristol City Art Gallery, Red Lodge. *Publications:* An Approach to Planning (Pitman), South German Baroque (Tiranti), Bristol Buildings (Studio Vista); contributor to The Banister Fletcher History of Architecture, XVIII Edition (Athlone) and Who's Who in Architecture (Weidenfeld and Nicholson). *Clubs:* Royal Empire Soc., Bristol Savages. *Signs work:* see appendix. *Address:* The Old House, Frenchay, nr. Bristol BS16 1ND.

**BURROWS, Geoffrey Norman,** painter in oil and water-colour; *b* St. Faiths, Norfolk, 16 May, 1934. *Educ:* The Paston Grammar School, N. Walsham, Norfolk. *Exhib:* R.A., R.W.A., R.B.A., R.O.I., R.M.S.A., N.E.A.C., R.I., Paris Salon, various mixed exhbns. at home and on the continent. *Work in collections:* Atkinson A.G., Southport, Norfolk C.C., Norwich Union Insurance

Co. *Clubs:* Norfolk and Norwich Art Circle. *Signs work:* "Geoffrey Burrows." *Address:* 84 Crostwick La., Spixworth, Norwich NR10 3AF.

**BURTON, Andrew Gerard Crossley,** M.F.A.; 1st prize, McGrigor Donald Sculpture Prize (1990); tutor/sculptor in clay, metal, rubber, stone; *b* 22 May 1961. *Educ:* Sevenoaks School. *Studied:* University of Newcastle-upon-Tyne (Derwent Wise, Norman Adams). *Exhib:* R.A., Laing Gallery, Hatton Gallery, Middlesbrough Gallery, etc. *Work in collections:* Newcastle University, Northern Arts Educ. Authority, Leicester Educ. Authority. *Signs work:* "Andrew Burton." *Address:* 65 Sidney Grove, Fenham, Newcastle-upon-Tyne NE4 5PD.

**BURTONSHAW, Keith,** B.W.S., U.A., N.S.; artist, teacher and demonstrator in water-colour and oils; *b* Beckenham, 25 Sept., 1930. *Educ:* Beckenham and Penge County School. *Studied:* Beckenham School of Art. *Exhib:* R.I., R.S.M.A. *Clubs:* London Sketch Club, Armed Forces Art Soc., Croydon Art Soc., Cantium Group of Artists, West Wickham Arts Assoc., Lewisham Soc. of Art. *Signs work:* "Keith Burtonshaw." *Address:* 150 Beckenham Rd., Beckenham, Kent BR3 4RJ.

**BUSBY, George Cecil,** M.S.I.A.D. (1970), R.B.S.A. (1971), S.G.A. (1979), F.R.S.A. (1970), G.R.A. (1987); painter and illustrator in water-colour, gouache, ink, acrylic; *b* Birmingham, 2 Feb., 1926. *m* Dora Snape. three *s.* one *d. Educ:* Montpelier College, Brighton. *Studied:* Birmingham College of Art (part time). *Exhib:* R.I., S.G.A., R.B.S.A., Kingsmead Gallery, Beckstone's Gallery, Cumbria, Tegfryn Gallery, Anglesey, and several Midland galleries. *Work in collections:* Warwick Castle, National Library of Wales; illustrations commissioned by: Courage Breweries, Abbey National Bldg. Soc., Amoco Oil Co., British Waterways, British Gas. *Publications:* work repro.: illustrator for Christmas cards, also included in books "To the Seaside" and "A Century of Railways." *Signs work:* "George Busby." *Address:* 377 Lugtrout La., Solihull, W. Midlands B91 2TN.

**BUSBY, John P.,** A.R.S.A., R.S.W., S.WL.A.; lecturer, Edinburgh College of Art (1956-88); *b* Bradford, 2 Feb., 1928. *m* Joan. one *s.* two *d. Educ:* Ilkley Grammar School. *Studied:* Leeds Art College (1948-52), Edinburgh Art College (1952-54); Post Grad. (1954-55), major travel scholarship (1955-56). *Work in collections:* S.A.C., Flemmings Bank, Bradford, Glasgow and Wakefield A.G's., Yorks Arts Assoc.; many private collections including H.R.H. The Duke of Edinburgh. *Publications:* The Living Birds of Eric Ennion (Gollancz), Drawing Birds (R.S.P.B.), Birds in Mallorca (Helm), Nature Drawings (Arlequin), many illustrated books. *Signs work:* "John Busby." *Address:* Easter Haining, Ormiston Hall, E. Lothian EH35 5NJ.

**BUSHE, Frederick,** O.B.E. (1994); sculptor; *b* Coatbridge, Scotland, 1931. *Studied:* Glasgow School of Art (1949-53), University of Birmingham (1966-67). Elected R.S.A. (1986); Scottish Arts Council Awards (1971, 1973) and S.A.C. Major Bursary (1977-78). Established Scottish Sculpture Workshop

(1980) and Scottish Sculpture Open Exhbn. (1981). *Address:* Scottish Sculpture Workshop, 1 Main St., Lumsden, Aberdeenshire AB54 4JN.

**BUSHELL, Dorothy,** R.M.S., S.W.A., Mundy Sovereign award (1983); miniature portrait painter in water-colour; *b* Halifax, Yorks., 3 Feb., 1922. *m* Philip Bushell. two *s*. one *d*. *Studied:* Halifax School of Art. *Exhib:* R.A. (1974, 1983, 1984, 1989, 1990, 1991, 1997), S.W.A. (1986, 1987), Mall Galleries, Westminster Gallery, R.M.S. (1982-97). *Work in collections:* Comte et Comtesse de Martigny, Soc. of Apothecaries, London, The Royal Anglian Regiment. *Signs work:* "D. Bushell, 98" *Address:* 90 Fairdene Rd., Coulsdon, Surrey CR5 1RF.

**BUTCHER, Sue,** U.E.I. Cert. A.D. (1979); artist in acrylic and plant fibres; *m* Edward Butcher. two *s*. *Educ:* Penarth Grammar School. *Studied:* Hereford College of Art (1977-80). *Exhib:* regular exhibitor R.A. and West of England, winner, Sainsbury's National Touring Exhib. (1982-83), Japan (1987, 1993), S.W.A. (1987), various mixed and one-man shows. *Work in collections:* Tayor Gallery, London, Hereford City A.G., Hereford Council Offices. B.B.C. and I.T.V. television programmes (1990), radio broadcasts to U.S.A. and Canada. *Signs work:* "S. Butcher." *Address:* Litley Orchard, Gorsty La., Hereford HR1 1UN.

**BUTLER, Anthony,** R.C.A. (Cambrian, 1960), A.T.D. (1950); schoolmaster; artist in oil and gouache; head of art, Birkenhead School (retd.); *b* Liverpool, 1927. *m* Jean. two *s*. one *d*. *Educ:* Liverpool Institute. *Studied:* Liverpool School of Art (1944-45, 1948-50) under Martin Bell, Alfred Wiffin, Alan Tankard. *Exhib:* R.A., New Burlington, Agnews, Northern Young Contemporaries. *Work in collections:* Walker Art Gallery, Liverpool; Whitworth Art Gallery, Manchester; Williamson Art Gallery, Birkenhead; and various county educational collections. *Commissions:* ceramic decoration commissioned by Dudley C.C. for new shopping precinct. *Signs work:* "BUTLER." *Address:* Otthon, Tan Yr Eglwys, Henllan, nr. Denbigh, Clwyd, Denbighshire LL16 5BD.

**BUTLER, Auriol,** F.R.S.A., Fellow, International Institute of Art, Associate, Société des Artistes Français; Gold and Silver medallist, Academia Internazionale, Rome; Life Fellow of the Royal Society of Arts; Gold medal and diploma from the Academia Italia (1981); artist in oil, pastel, water-colour; *b* Pitney, Somerset. *m* Richard Butler. one *s*. one *d*. *Studied:* Byam Shaw School, London, under Ernest Jackson, and at Slade School, pastel with Mlle. Landau in Paris. *Exhib:* Pastel Soc., London, R.B.A., S.W.A., London Group, Paris Salon, United Society, and in the U.S.A. *Publications:* work repro.: La Revue Moderne. Works include portraits of the Princess Royal, General Sir Michael Rose, etc. *Signs work:* "A. Butler." *Address:* Glebe Studio, Longham, Cornwood, Ivybridge, Devon PL21 9QZ.

**BUTLER, George,** R.W.S., R.B.A., N.E.A.C.; painter in oil and water-colour; *b* Sheffield, 17 Oct., 1904. *m* Kcenia (decd.). one *s*. one *d*. *Educ:* King

Edward VII School, Sheffield. *Studied:* Sheffield College of Art (1922-23), Central School of Arts and Crafts (1923-26). *Exhib:* annually in London, formerly in Aix en Provence. *Work in collections:* Graves Art Gallery, Mappin Art Gallery. *Commissions:* Portraits, houses. *Clubs:* Arts. *Signs work:* "George Butler." *Address:* Riversdale, Bakewell, Derbyshire DE45 1DU.

**BUTLER, James,** R.A. (1972), R.W.A. (1980), F.R.B.S. (1981); sculptor in bronze and stone; *b* Deptford, 25 July, 1931. *m* Angela Berry. five *d. Educ:* Maidstone Grammar School. *Studied:* Maidstone School of Art (1948-50); St. Martin's School of Art (1950-52). *Commissions:* Major commissions: portrait statue of President Kenyatta of Kenya, Nairobi; monument to Freedom Fighters of Zambia, Lusaka, Zambia; sculpture of The Burton Cooper, Burton-upon-Trent; memorial statue of Richard III, Castle Gardens, Leicester; statue of Field Marshal Earl Alexander of Tunis, Wellington Barracks, London; Dolphin fountain, Dolphin Sq., London; statue of John Wilkes, New Fetter La., London; bronze sculpture of the Leicester Seamstress, Hotel St., Leicester; statue of Thomas Cook, London Rd. Leicester; memorial statue to Reg Harris, N.C.C. Manchester; statue of Billy Wright, Wolverhampton; statue, James Greathead, Cornhill, London; D-Day Memorial and Green Howards, Crépon, Normandy. *Clubs:* Arts. *Signs work:* surname and year. *Address:* Valley Farm, Radway, Warwicks. CV35 0UJ.

**BUTLER, Richard Gerald Ernest,** painter, graphic designer; *b* Essex, 31 Dec., 1921. *m* Mary Driscoll; three children. *Studied:* Salisbury School of Art. *Exhib:* R.A., Arts Council Touring Exhbns., etc., one-man shows: Walker Galleries. *Publications:* work repro.: book illustration (Macmillan Educ.), mural designs (Fitzroy Robinson & Partners). *Signs work:* "Richard Butler." *Address:* 32 Denne Rd., Horsham, Sussex.

**BUTLER, Vincent,** sculptor, figurative, bronzes; mem. Royal Scottish Academy, Royal Glasgow Inst.; *b* Manchester, 1933. *Exhib:* numerous one-man shows in various parts of the country. *Work in collections:* private collections in Britain, U.S.A., Germany, Italy, Israel, etc. *Signs work:* see appendix. *Address:* 17 Dean Park Cres., Edinburgh EH4 1PH.

**BUTT, Anna Theresa,** (until 1985 Anna Adams); N.D.D. Painting (1945), N.D.D. Sculpture (1950); artist in water-colour, terracotta; *b* Richmond, Surrey, 9 Mar., 1926. *m* Norman Adams. two *s. Educ:* St. Michael's Modern School, Eastcote. *Studied:* Harrow School of Art (1939-46), Hornsey College of Art (1948-50). *Exhib:* widely in north of England as Anna Adams; R.A. Summer Show (1986, 1987, 1988, 1989, 1990, 1991). *Work in collections:* terracottas in Abbot Hall, Kendal, W. Yorks. Educ. Com., Moorside Mills Museum, Rochdale Museum. *Commissions:* Two angels for Habergham Parish Church, near Gawthorpe; Madonna, font panel and tabernacle panel for Our Lady of Lourdes, Milton Keynes (1975). *Publications:* several collections of poems under name of Adams; R. Wren's "Animal Forms" Batsford Book on Pottery (1977). *Signs work:* "Anna Butt" and see appendix. *Address:* Butts Hill,

Horton in Ribblesdale, Settle, N. Yorks. BD24 0HD.

**BUTTERFIELD, Sarah Harriet Anne,** B.Soc.Sci. Architecture Edin. (1975) 'Magna cum Laude', Cert. Fine Art Ruskin School of Fine Art, Oxford (1978), Distinction; qualified as architect 1983; self employed as artist since 1986; *b* London, 28 Aug., 1953. *Exhib:* Judd St. Gallery, London (1987), Agnew's Young Contemporaries (1988), Richmond Gallery, Cork St. (1990), Roy Miles Gallery (1991); one-man show: Cadogan Contemporary (1991, 1994, 1997). *Work in collections:* British Airways: Terminal 4 Departure Lounge, Gatwick Airport; Jerry's Home Store, Chelsea, London; David Lloyd Slazenger Racquet Club; Trusthouse Forte Hotels in Yorkshire and Exeter; Wimbledon Lawn Tennis Museum; 'Davies', Gt. Newport St., London; State St. Bank, London. Awards: Egerton Coghill Landscape prize (1977), Winsor and Newton award, Hunting Group Competition finalist, commendation Spectator Magazine Three Cities Competition. *Address:* 21 Ashchurch Grove, London W12 9BT.

**BUTTERWORTH, John Malcolm,** M.A.(Ed.), F.R.S.A., N.D.D., A.T.D.; artist in oils, water-colour, etching, silkscreen and lithography, paper; Fine Art Degree Course Leader, Design Faculty, Southampton I.H.E.; *b* Lancs., 16 July, 1945. *m* Lesley G. Arkless, B.A.Hons. two *s.* one *d. Educ:* Rochdale Technical School for Boys. *Studied:* Rochdale College of Art (1961-63), Newport College of Art (1965-66), Cardiff College of Art (1965-66), David Murray Scholarship (R.A.) 1965. *Exhib:* Wills Lane Gallery, St. Ives, University of Surrey, Southampton Civic A.G. (one-man shows), Pictures for Schools Exhbn., National Museum of Wales, Cardiff, Midsommergarten Gallery, Stockholm, Cleveland, Drawing Biennale, International Print Biennale, Monaco, "Outpost" Venice Biennale (1995). *Work in collections:* Bristol Educ. Authority, Kent Educ. Authority, Surrey University, Hampshire C.C. *Signs work:* normal signature for prints, "J.M.B." monogram for paintings. *Address:* 2 Nuns Walk, Winchester, Hants. SO23 7EE.

**BUXTON, Jennifer,** H.R.M.S. (retd.), Hon. Sec. R.M.S. (1980-87), Hilliard Soc.; portrait, animal and landscape painter in water-colour, silverpoint, pastel, oil, gouache and acrylic; first winner of R.M.S. Gold Memorial Bowl Award for best miniature (1985); *b* Hornsey, 12 Apr., 1937. *m* Captain Vic (R.N.). two *s. Educ:* Northfield School, Watford. *Studied:* Frobisher School of Animal Painting (1948-53, Marguerite Frobisher), Byam Shaw School of Art (1954-57, Dunstan, Phillips, Mahoney). *Exhib:* Watford, Manchester, Bath, Wells, Paris Salon, Kendal, Ulverston, Ilkley, Toronto, annually R.M.S. London. *Signs work:* "jb" or "J. Buxton." *Address:* Windy Ash, Ulverston, Cumbria LA12 7PB.

**BUYERS, Donald Morison,** D.A.(Aberdeen), R.S.W.; artist in oil and water-colour; lecturer retired; *b* Aberdeen, 1930. *m* Margaret. one *s.* one *d. Educ:* Aberdeen Grammar School. *Studied:* Gray's School of Art, Aberdeen, (1948-52). *Exhib:* Arts Council, Young Scottish Contemporaries,

Contemporary Art in Scotland, Painting 70, Edinburgh Open 100, Glasgow
Group, etc. *Work in collections:* Arts Council, I.B.M., Aberdeen A.G.
Universities of Colorado, U.S.A., Boston, U.S.A. and Aberdeen
Dunbartonshire Educ. Trust, Schools Pictures Leeds and Midlothian, Rober
Flemming, London, H.R.H. The Duke of Edinburgh, etc. *Signs work:* "Buyers."
*Address:* 96 Gray St., Aberdeen AB10 6JU.

# C

**CADENHEAD, William Collie Milne,** D.A., cert.R.A.S., Bronze Medal
R.A. Schools (1957), David Murray Landscape Scholarship (1957), elected
prof. member S.S.A. (1969); painter in oil and water-colour; lecturer in draw-
ing and painting, Duncan of Jordanstone College of Art, Dundee; *b* Aberdeen
8 Oct., 1934; married. *Educ:* Aberdeen Grammar School; Forfar Academy
*Studied:* Dundee College of Art (1951-55); travelled Europe (1956)
Hospitalfield Art College, Arbroath; R.A. Schools, London (1957-61). *Exhib.*
R.S.A., S.S.A., R.S.W., Savage Gallery, Compass Gallery, Royal Oversea
League, Edinburgh Festival (1968), etc., one-man shows, Woodstock Gallery
(1980), The Scottish Gallery (1981, 1983), Retrospective, Meffan Inst. (1992)
Texas Touring Exhbn. (1996-97). *Work in collections:* H.M. Queen Elizabeth
The Queen Mother, Scottish Arts Council, (Stations of the Cross), St. Fergus
Forfar: Meffan Institute, Forfar; Steel Company of Wales, Dundee A.G., and
private collections in U.K., Europe and U.S.A. *Signs work:* "Cadenhead.'
*Address:* The Rowans, Muir of Lownie, Forfar, Angus DD8 2LJ.

**CADMAN, Michael Lawrence,** R.I. (1970), A.R.C.A.; painter in water-
colour, acrylic, oil and pastel; Instructor Epsom School of Art (1945-68),
Croydon College of Art (1945-53); *b* Epsom, 1920. *Educ:* Glyn Grammar
School, Epsom, Surrey. *Studied:* Wimbledon School of Art (1937-41), R.C.A
(1941-44, Gilbert Spencer). *Exhib:* R.A., R.W.S., R.B.A., R.O.I., eight one-
man shows. *Commissions:* Protexulate Ltd. (large mural) Esher: Plant illustrations. *Publications:* Orange Cap - Red Cap (Paul Hamlyn, 1968); four fine art
prints (Cornish Harbours and Hedgerow themes, 1981). B.B.C. TV
(1947,1964). *Clubs:* R.I., St. Ives Soc. of Artists. *Signs work:* "Michael
Cadman." *Address:* Ballard Glebe, The Glebe, Studland, Dorset BH19 3AS.

**CAINE, Osmund,** B.A.(Hons.), M.D.C.S., A.S.M.G.P., M.S.I.A.; teacher,
painter in oil, water-colour, illustrator, lithographer, artist in stained glass and
mosaic; Principal Lecturer, Graphic Design, Twickenham College of
Technology (1962); *b* Manchester. *Studied:* Birmingham College of Art (1930-
37) and in Italy (1938). *Exhib:* R.A., N.E.A.C., R.B.A., R.B.S.A., V. & A.
Craft Centre, Lambeth Palace, Guildhall, and Walker, Adams, Piccadilly
Galleries, Leicester, Whitworth Gallery, R.I.B.A., Southwell-Brown Gallery

Richmond, Hampton-Hill & Ashbarn Gallery, Petersfield, and Garden Gallery, Kew, London; one-man exhbns.: Walker's Gallery; Richmond Hill Gallery (1961); Foyles A.G. (1966); Canaletto Gallery (1966, 1969); Open Studio, Kingston-on-Thames (1980); Old Bell Gallery, Chepstow (1981); Century Display Gallery, Surbiton (1982); Southwell-Brown Gallery, Richmond (1984); Garden Gallery, Kew; Merlin Theatre, Frome (1985); Duncan Campbell Fine Art, London (1986); Galerie Salammbo, Paris (1987); Questra Gallery, Kingston-on-Thames, Gallery Upstairs, Henley-in-Arden (1996). *Work in collections:* Ministry of Transport; Nottingham Castle A.G.; University of London; Dorset House, London; Borough of Richmond-on-Thames; Borough of Kingston-on-Thames; Melbourne A.G.; Erdington Abbey, B'ham; V. & A.; B'ham A.G. Stained glass: St. Gabriel's Church, Cricklewood, London (N. Aisle window); St. Paul's Church, Kingston (Porch window); St. Augustine's Church, Edgbaston, B'ham (Lady Chapel); St. Cuthbert's Church, Copnor, Portsmouth (E. window); St. Luke's Church, Wadestown, N.Z. (S. Aisle window); St. Keyne's Church, St. Keyne, Liskeard (N. Aisle window); All Saint's Church, Stechford, B'ham (S. Aisle window); All Saint's Church, Four Oaks, B'ham (N. & four S. Aisle windows); Private Chapel, Chile, S. America (E. window); Mortuary Chapel, Erdington Infirmary, B'ham (E. window); Old Church, Smethwick (S. Aisle windows); Fourteen Stations of the Cross, St. Mary's, Hong Kong; Private House, N. Wales (Memorial window); Private House, Knowle, B'ham (Geometric window). *Publications:* The Studio, The Artist, L'Art Moderne, Careers in Art, The School Leaver, etc. Films: The Glastonbury Giants (in conjunction with Mary Caine), (1966); The Ruskin Country (1966). *Signs work:* see appendix. *Address:* 25 Kingston Hill, Kingston-on-Thames, Surrey KT2 7PW.

**CAINS, F. Blanche,** S.W.A., A.T.D. (1927); artist in water-colour, mixed media, fabric collage, embroidery; art teacher, Head of Dept. Grammar School (mixed); *b* Bristol, 1905. *Educ:* St. George Grammar School, Bristol. *Studied:* West of England College of Art (1922-27) Princ. R. E. J. Bush, R.E. *Exhib:* R.A., R.I., R.W.A., S.W.A., various other galleries in London, Brighton, Bristol, etc. *Signs work:* "F.B. Cains." *Address:* 99 Summerhill Rd., St. George, Bristol BS5 8JT.

**CAINS, Gerald Albert,** N.D.D. (Painting S.L. 1953), A.T.D. (1957), A.R.W.A. (1971), elected R.W.A. (1978), A.D.A.E. (University of Wales, 1975); painter in oil and water-colour; *b* Stubbington, Hants., 11 May, 1932. *m* Ruth Lillian Blackburn. one *s.* one *d. Educ:* Gosport County Grammar School. *Studied:* Southern College of Art, Portsmouth (1949-53). *Exhib:* mixed: R.A.; R.W.A.; R.O.I.; R.B.A.; Football and Fine Arts, London 53: Pics for Schools (Cardiff); Euro '96 London; Wessex Artists, Southampton 78 (2nd prize). Selected for Touring Exhbn. A.C.G.B., Art Federations Bureau, R.W.A. *Work in collections:* Lancashire Museum Service, R.W.A., Walsall Museum Service, Wessex Longleat House. *Commissions:* mural: Southmead Hospital, Bristol. *Clubs:* R.W.A., Bath Soc. of Artists. *Signs work:* "G. A. CAINS." *Address:* 1

Broadway Cottages, Broadway Lane, Clandown, nr. Bath, Somerset BA3 2XP.

**CALDICOTT, Glenys Rita,** C. & G. (1982), A.R.M.S. (1990), S.W.A. (1991), S.M. (1991); Margaret Ryder award, R.M.S. (1989), Dartington Rose Bowl, S.M. (1991), Llewellyn Alexander award, R.M.S. (1992); miniaturist, specialising in animal portraits in gouache on card and vellum; *b* Nottingham, 20 Aug., 1941. *m* Harvey C. Caldicott. one *s. Educ:* Mablethorpe, Highfield College, Grimsby. *Studied:* Grimsby School of Art (1958-60, Peter Todd), Bourneville College of Art (1979-82, Alex Jackson). *Exhib:* R.M.S., S.W.A., S.M. Work in private collections. *Signs work:* "G.R. Caldicott." *Address:* Rose Cottage, 16 Flaxley Rd., Stechford, B'ham B33 9AS.

**CALLMAN, Jutta Gabrielle:** see SAUNDERS, Jutta Gabrielle.

**CALVERT, Diana,** N.E.A.C. (1979); artist in oil; *b* Capel, Surrey, 7 Oct., 1941. *m* Richard Martineau. *Educ:* Benenden School, Cranbrook, Kent. *Studied:* Byam Shaw (1959-63, Charles Mahoney). *Exhib:* R.A., R.P., R.B.A., N.E.A.C. *Signs work:* "D.C." *Address:* The Lawn, Walsham-le-Willows, Bury St. Edmunds, Suffolk IP31 3AW.

**CALVOCORESSI, Richard,** B.A., M.A.; Keeper, Scottish National Gallery of Modern Art, Edinburgh (since 1987); research asst., Scottish National Gallery of Modern Art (1977-79); research asst., Modern Collection, Tate Gallery (1979-82), asst. keeper (1982-87); *b* 1951. *m* Francesca Temple Roberts. one *s.* two *d. Educ:* Magdalen College, Oxford; Courtauld Inst. of Art, University of London. *Publications:* author, Magritte (1979, 1984, 1990, 1994); exhbn. catalogues: Tinguely (1982), Reg Butler (1983), Cross Currents in Swiss Art (1985), Oskar Kokoschka 1886-1980 (1986), and catalogue essays on Miró, Penck, Baselitz, Lüpertz, von Motesiczky, Gormley, Picabia, etc.; various articles and reviews. *Address:* Scottish National Gallery of Modern Art, Belford Rd., Edinburgh EH4 3DR.

**CAMBRON, Ghislaine,** Officier de l'Ordre de Léopold II (1990); artist, painter, ceramist; Directrice de L'Académie des Beaux-Arts de Molenbeek Saint-Jean (Brussels); Academie de Molenbeek, Brussels; Grand Prix de Belgique (1954), Grand Prix de Decoration (1955), Grand Prix de Belgique (1956), Prix de l'État Belge (1942), Distinction-Prix Europe Peinture (1962); *b* St. Amand-les-Eaux, 6 July, 1923. *m* Mariee. *Studied:* Académie de Bruxelles. *Work in collections:* Musée Art Moderne, Brussels, Centre Culturel, Uccle, Musée de Molenbeek, Timbres-Poste du Congo (Serie Masques). *Signs work:* "Cambron, Ghislaine." *Address:* Dréve Angevine, Domaine de la Motte, Bousval 1470, Brabant, Belgique.

**CAMERON, Ronald,** N.D.D. (1951); sculptor in bronze, terracotta, pewter and silver; *b* London, 8 Oct., 1930. *m* Dorothy. two *d. Educ:* Wilson's Grammar School. *Studied:* Camberwell School of Art (1947-51). *Exhib:* bronzes at Bruton Street Gallery, Mayfair, London; also galleries in Europe and N. America. *Signs work:* "R. Cameron." *Address:* 9 Morecambe St., London SE17 1DX.

**CAMP, Ann,** A.R.C.A. (1946), F.S.S.I.; freelance calligrapher and lettering designer; lecturer at Digby Stuart College, Roehampton Institute; retd. from teaching (1990); *b* London, 1924. *Studied:* Hampstead Garden Suburb Inst. and R.C.A. *Work in collections:* loan collections of V. & A., L.C.C. and National Museum of Wales; Book 4, R.A.F. Book of Remembrance in St. Clement Dane's Church; lettering on stamps, murals, etc. *Publications:* Pen Lettering (first published 1958 by Dryad Press; republished by A. & C. Black, 1984). *Clubs:* Soc. of Scribes and Illuminators. *Signs work:* "Ann Camp." *Address:* 115 Bridge La., London NW11 9JT.

**CAMP, Jeffery,** R.A. (1984); artist; lecturer, Slade School. *Educ:* Edinburgh College of Art, D.A. (Edin.). *Exhib:* one-man, Galerie de Seine (1958), Beaux Arts Gallery (1959, 1961, 1963), New Art Centre (1968), Serpentine Gallery (1973), S. London A.G. (retrospective, 1973), Bradford City A.G. (1979), Browse and Darby (1984, 1993), Nigel Greenwood Gallery (1986, 1990); retrospective, Royal Albert Memorial Museum, Exeter, Royal Academy of Arts, London, Manchester City A.G., Laing A.G., Newcastle (1988-89); group shows: Hayward Annuals (1974, 1982, 1985), British Council Touring Exhbns. to China and Edinburgh (1982) and to India (1985), Chantrey Bicentenary, Tate Gallery (1981), Narrative Painting I.C.A., London Arts Council Touring, The Hard Won Image Tate Gallery (1984); Twining Gallery, N.Y. (selected by William Feaver 1985), Peter Moores Liverpool Exhbn. (selected by William Feaver 1986); Athena Art Awards, Barbican Centre, London (1987), Land: Sea: Air, Herbert Read Gallery, Canterbury and tour (1987), `The Self Portrait' Artsite Gallery, Bath and tour (1987). *Publications:* Draw (1981). *Signs work:* see appendix. *Address:* 27 Stirling Rd., London SW9 9EF.

**CAMPBELL, Alexander Buchanan,** P.P.R.I.A.S. (1979), A.R.S.A. (1972), B.Arch. (1937), F.R.I.B.A. (1955); architect; *b* Findochty, 14 June, 1914. *m* Sheila Smith. one *s.* one *d.* *Studied:* architecture: Glasgow School of Architecture (Strathclyde University) (1930-37) under Prof. T. Harold Hughes, Dr. J. A. Coia. *Clubs:* Glasgow Art. *Signs work:* "A. Buchanan Campbell." *Address:* 19 Lochan Ave., Kirn, Dunoon, Argyll PL23 8HT.

**CAMPBELL, Joan Betty,** R.M.S. (1980), H.R.S.W.A. (1975); artist in water-colour, oil and acrylic; teacher of miniature painting, private tuition; *b* London, 4 May, 1923. *m* Archie Campbell. one *d.* *Educ:* Loughton County High School for Girls, Essex. *Studied:* Ilford Evening Institute (mostly self-taught). *Exhib:* Westminster Galleries, Llewellyn Alexander Gallery, M.A.S.-F., Paris Salon (1973, 1974), Bilan l'Art Contemporain of Paris (1978). *Publications:* Art Editor, Hillingdon Writer. *Signs work:* miniatures "J.B.C." or "JC" entwined; larger works "Joan Campbell." *Address:* 3 Fineshade Cl., Barton Seagrave, Northants NN15 6SL.

**CAMPBELL, Lee,** B.A. (Hons.) Fine Art (1991), M.A. History and Theory of Art (1993); professional artist and lecturer, painter in oil, drawings in charcoal; Artist-in-Residence, St. Saviour's Church, Pimlico. ; first Artist-in-Residence, King's School, Canterbury (1994-95),*b* New Zealand, 25 Feb. 1951. *Studied:* Chelsea School of Art, Canterbury College of Art, University of Kent. *Exhib:* Solo show: Fairfax Gallery, Tunbridge Wells (1997); Albemarle Gallery, London (1997 gallery artist). *Work in collections:* U.S.A., Scandinavia, Australia. *Commissions:* mural: Space Science Dept., University of Kent. Winner of Worshipful Co. of Painters Stainers award (1993). *Clubs:* F.P.S. (Hon. Sec.). *Signs work:* "Lee Campbell." *Address:* 212 Hood House, Dolphin Sq., London SW1V 3NQ.

**CAMPBELL, Raymond,** self taught artist in oil and acrylic, known for still life subjects; *b* Morden, Surrey, 2 Apr., 1956. *Educ:* Garth High, Morden. *Exhib:* R.A., etc. *Work in collections:* England, Germany, Austria, Australia. *Publications:* work repro.: limited edn. prints. *Signs work:* "Raymond Campbell." *Address:* 63 Courtnay Rd., Woking, Surrey GU21 5HG.

**CANNELL, Edward Ashton,** R.S.M.A., B.W.S., N.D.D., A.T.D.; painter and illustrator; *b* Isle of Man, 12 Sept., 1927. *Educ:* King William's College. *Studied:* Isle of Man School of Art, Liverpool College of Art. *Exhib:* R.A., R.I., R.B.A., R.S.M.A., Paris Salon (Silver Medal 1973, Gold Medal 1975), Bankside Gallery, Davy's of London Award (1983), Royal Exchange A.G., Francis Iles Gallery, Oliver Swann Gallery, Bourne Gallery, Clairmonte Galleries, Linda Blackstone Gallery. *Work in collections:* U.S.A., Canada, South Africa, Japan, Saudi Arabia and most European countries. *Publications:* freelance work for various publications, Foyle's, Cassells, Bass International, British Petroleum. *Clubs:* London Sketch, Wapping Group. *Signs work:* "Ashton Cannell." *Address:* Studio House, 52 Dyne Rd., London NW6 7DS.

**CANNING, Neil,** A.R.B.A. (1983); Paris Salon (1994) bronze medal; artist in mixed media and oils; *b* Enstone, Oxon., 28 Apr., 1960. *Educ:* Spendlove School, Charlbury, and Chipping Norton School. *Studied:* privately with Betty Bowman (1979-82). *Exhib:* R.A. (1981, 1982, 1984), John Player Portrait award N.P.G. (R.B.A.). *Work in collections:* University of Wales, National Westminster Bank, London Insurance Investment Trust, I.C.I., and paintings in hospitals. *Publications:* illustrated Skylighters (Methuen). *Clubs:* Oxford Art Soc. *Signs work:* "CANNING." *Address:* The Post Office House, Ffarmers, Llanwrda, Dyfed SA19 8LQ.

**CANTER, Jean Mary,** S.G.F.A. (1977); painter in gouache, water-colour, pencil and scraperboard; lecturer; tutor, Mid-Surrey Adult Educ.; President S.G.F.A.; *b* Epsom, 18 Mar., 1943. *Educ:* Convent of the Sacred Heart, Epsom. *Studied:* Epsom School of Art (1956-61); Wimbledon School of Art (1961-63). *Exhib:* S.G.F.A., R.W.S., S.B.A., R.I., R.M.S., Medici Gallery etc., S.G.F.A. Prizes: Frisk (1983, 1985); Rexel (1984); Daler-Rowney (1990); Liquitex (1993); Winsor and Newton (1996); Acco-Rexel (1996). *Work in collections:* Museum Collection, Ewell. *Publications:* work repro.: Demonstrations for many art books (Quarto); articles for "Artist's and Illustrator's" Magazine;

greeting cards etc. *Clubs:* S.G.F.A. *Signs work:* "JEAN CANTER." *Address:* 7 Cox Lane, Ewell, Epsom, Surrey KT19 9LR.

**CAPRARA, Julia Rosemary,** N.D.D., A.T.C. Lond. (1961), M.S.D.C., mem. 62 Group (1970); designer in embroidery, textile artist; *b* London, 27 Feb., 1939. *m* Alex. Caprara. one *s. Educ:* Perse School for Girls, Cambridge; Henrietta Barnett School, Hampstead. *Studied:* Hornsey College of Art (1955-61). *Exhib:* one-man show of Embroidery at Commonwealth Institute A.G.; 62 Group shows: Guildford House, National Museum of Wales, Congress House, Foyle's A.G. Australia, U.S.A., Japan. *Work in collections:* National Museum of Wales, Cardiff, Holocaust Museum, Israel; private collections. *Signs work:* "Julia Caprara." *Address:* 20 Crown St., Harrow-on-the-Hill, Middx.

**CARLETON, Elyn,** R.A.A., R.A.S., F.F.P.S.; creative artist, teacher and founder, Creator's A.G. (1980), Innovators (1988); Council and Publicity Officer, Ridley Art Soc. (1987-89); Council Mem. and Executive Officer, N.C.A.C. (1993-97); F.S.C.C.A.G. (1993, N.S.W.); *b* Palmyra, W.A. *m* Laurence E. Carleton. one *s.* two *d. Educ:* Australia. *Studied:* privately with Wesley Penberthy, Melbourne (1968-69); Victoria University, Wellington, N.Z. (Paul Olds, 1970-74); Dr. Desiderius Orban, O.B.E., Sydney (1975-79). *Exhib:* N.Z. Academy, Wellington, N.Z. (1973), Victoria University (1973), (In Mind) Eight Wellington Artists, N.Z. Academy, Wellington (1974), other galleries in N.Z. and Australia; U.K.: Mall Galleries, R.O.I., H.A.C., C.P.S., R.A.S., U.A., F.P.S., C.W.A.C., N.C.A.C., Bloomsbury Intaglio Crafts (Creative Images 1987), Richmond Antiquary (Two Hemispheres 1988), Chertsey Hall (Australian Paintings 1988-89), Bourne Hall (1989-97), Queensland House London (1990), Loggia (1991), Edith Grove (1993), Boxfield Stevenage (1994). *Work in collections:* B.H.P. H.Q. Sydney, N.C.R. World H.Q. Dayton, Ohio, Queensland House London, Stevenage Council; private collections in U.K., Europe, U.S.A., Singapore, N.Z., Australia. *Commissions:* B.H.P. H.Q. Sydney, others private. *Publications:* Creative Images, Art Yesterday, Today and Tomorrow, Art Appreciation, Hanging an Exhibition, Constructive Criticism, Abstract Art, Developed Unique Creative Art Teaching Method (1980). *Signs work:* "Elyn Carleton." *Address:* 12 Southcroft Pl., Englefield Green, Surrey TW20 0QG.

**CARLINE, Nancy Mona,** N.E.A.C.; artist in oil; *b* London, 30 Nov., 1909. *m* Richard Carline (decd.). one *s.* one *d. Educ:* Wycombe Abbey School. *Studied:* Slade School (1928-32, Prof. Henry Tonks, 1933-35, Vladimir Polunin). *Exhib:* R.A., N.E.A.C., London Group, Leicester Gallery, retrospective Camden Arts Centre (1985). *Work in collections:* Tate Gallery, Manchester City A.G. *Signs work:* "N.C."; early work "Nancy Carline." *Address:* 168 Oxford Rd., Cowley, Oxford OX4 2LA.

**CARNIE, Andrew John,** B.A. (1982), R.C.A. (1986); painter/sculptor in mixed medium; *b* 8 Jan., 1957. *m* Judith Mary Wallas. one *s.* one *d. Educ:* Lakes School, Windermere. *Studied:* Goldsmiths' School of Art, Royal College

# WHO'S WHO IN ART

of Art. *Exhib:* many mixed person shows and one-man shows, including Girray Gallery London, Winchester Gallery, Bracknell Gallery, Plymouth Art Centre, Tram Gallery, Columbus Gallery, Georgia, U.S.A. *Work in collections:* Unilever London, Chase Manhattan Bank London, Coopers and Lybrand London, Kaempher Corp., Washington, U.S.A. *Commissions:* D.C. Dance Company. *Publications:* Andrew Carnie (Winchester Gallery). *Signs work:* "ANDREW CARNIE" or not at all. *Address:* 5 Powell Rd., London E5 8DJ.

**CARO, Sir Anthony,** Kt. (1987), C.B.E., D.Litt.; Hon. Degree, Yale University (1989), awarded: Nobutaka Shikamai Memorial Prize, Tokyo (1990), Praemium Imperiale by Japan Art Assoc.; sculptor; part-time teacher of sculpture, St. Martin's School of Art (1953-79); Trustee, Tate Gallery (1982-); initiated with Robert Loder Triangle Summer Workshop, Pine Plains, N.Y. (1982); *b* London, 8 Mar., 1924. *m* Sheila Girling. two *s. Educ:* Charterhouse School and Christ's College, Cambridge. *Studied:* Regent St. Polytechnic and R.A. Schools. *Exhib:* numerous one-man shows worldwide including Galleria del Naviglio, Milan (1956), Andre Emmerich Gallery, N.Y. (1964, 1966, 1968, 1970, 1972-74, 1977-79, 1982, 1984, 1986, 1988, 1989, 1991), Washington Gallery of Modern Art (1965), Kasmin Gallery, London (1965, 1967, 1971, 1972), Mirvish Gallery, Toronto (1966, 1971, 1974), Kroller-Muller Museum, Holland (1967), Richard Gray Gallery, Chicago (1976, 1978, 1986, 1989), Knoedler Gallery, London (1978, 1982-84, 1986, 1989, 1991), Tate Gallery (1991), etc.; retrospective 1975: Museum of Modern Art, N.Y., Walker Art Center, Minneapolis, Museum of Fine Arts, Houston; 1976: Museum of Fine Arts, Boston; 1977: Tel Aviv Museum - retrospective of Table Pieces; exhbn. organised by British Council travels to N.Z. and Australia; 1992: Trajan Markets, Rome. *Commissions:* The Ledge Piece, National Gallery of Art, East Wing Building opened June, 1978, Washington D.C. Presented with the keys to New York City by Mayor Beame, March, 1976. *Address:* 111 Frognal, Hampstead, London NW3.

**CARPANINI, Prof. David Lawrence,** P.R.E. (1995), Dip.A.D., M.A. (R.C.A.), A.T.C., R.B.A., R.C.A., R.W.A., R.E., N.E.A.C.; painter, printmaker; British Inst. Awards Committee Sch. Engraving (1969); *b* Abergwynfi, Glam., 1946. *m* Jane Allen. one *s. Educ:* Glan Afan Grammar School, Port Talbot. *Studied:* Gloucestershire College of Art (1964-68), Royal College of Art (1968-71), University of Reading (1971-72). *Exhib:* R.A., R.B.A., R.W.A., R.E., N.E.A.C., Bankside Gallery, New Academy Gallery, Agnews, Piccadilly Gallery, Tegfryn, Albany, Mostyn, Fosse and Brandler Galleries, Welsh Arts Council, etc. *Work in collections:* National Library and National Museum of Wales, Contemporary Art Society for Wales, Newport A.G., Glynn Vivian A.G., Dept. Environment, R.W.A., N.C.B., A.S.T.M.S., Glam., Glos., Clwyd., Avon, Yorks. Educ. Authorities, and private collections in U.K., U.S.A., Canada, Europe Australia, etc. Television Films: C4 (1984), H.T.V. (1987). *Publications:* regular contributor to art periodicals. *Signs work:* "David L. Carpanini." *Address:* Fernlea, 145 Rugby Rd., Milverton, Leamington Spa, Warwickshire CV32 6DJ.

# WHO'S WHO IN ART

**CARPANINI, Jane,** Dip.A.D., A.T.C., R.B.A., R.W.A., R.W.S., R.C.A.; artist in water-colour and pencil; *b* Luton, 1949. *m* David L. Carpanini. one *s.* *Educ:* Bedford High School. *Studied:* Luton College of Art (1967-68), Brighton Polytechnic (1968-71), University of Reading (1971-72). *Exhib:* R.A., R.W.A., R.B.A., R.W.S., Bankside Gallery, Tegfryn, New Academy Gallery, Fosse and Brandler Galleries, Welsh Arts Council, Mostyn, Albany, etc. Winner of Hunting Group prize Watercolour of the Year (1983). *Work in collections:* National Library and National Museum of Wales, Burnley Building Soc., etc., and private collections in U.K., U.S.A., Europe. *Publications:* regular contributor to art periodicals, reproductions; cards, prints, calendars, catalogues, etc. *Signs work:* "Jane Carpanini." *Address:* Fernlea, 145 Rugby Rd., Milverton, Leamington Spa, Warwickshire CV32 6DJ.

**CARR, Thomas James,** O.B.E., D.Litt., R.U.A., A.R.H.A., N.E.A.C., R.W.S.; painter in oil and water-colour; *b* Belfast, 21 Sept., 1909. *m* Stella Vincent (decd.). three *d. Educ:* Oundle. *Studied:* Slade School (Prof. Henry Tonks). Numerous exhbns. and work in collections. *Publications:* T. Carr by Eamonn Malley. *Signs work:* "T. Carr." *Address:* Manor House, Itteringham, Norwich NR11 7AF.

**CARRICK, Desmond,** R.H.A.; artist in sculpture, oil, water-colour and tempera, lithography, stained glass and ceramics; secretary, Royal Hibernian Academy of Arts (1971-1982 resigned); *b* Dublin, 18 Dec., 1928. *m* Deirdre Mellett. *Educ:* Synge St. School. *Studied:* Dublin National College of Art. *Exhib:* R.H.A., Oireachtas, Waterford, Dublin Painters, Water-colour Soc. of Ireland, Living Art, Irish Contemporary Painters organized by the Cultural Relations Com. of Ireland, English and Canadian Contemporary Painters; one-man shows: Dublin (15) 1953-1992, England (1) 1989. *Commissions:* Murals in Guinness Visitors' Waiting Room (Dublin). *Signs work:* see appendix. *Address:* "Studio, " Woodtown, Rathfarnham, Co. Dublin 16.

**CARRINGTON-KERSLAKE, Lynette,** Dip.A.D., S.B.A., S.M., S.L.M. (R.H.S.); water-colour artist, illustrator and tutor; *b* Bath, 9 Oct., 1946. one *s.* one *d. Educ:* Wycliffe School, Avon. *Studied:* West of England College of Art (textiles). *Exhib:* Westminster Hall (S.B.A.), Northamptonshire, U.S.A. and France. *Publications:* currently working on Rare Flora of Mt. Kinabalu, N. Borneo (Sabah); illustrator of greetings cards. *Clubs:* S.B.A. *Signs work:* "L.C.K." or "Lynette Carrington-Kerslake" and see appendix. *Address:* 35 Nightingale Drive, Towcester, Northamptonshire NN12 6RA.

**CARRUTHERS, Derek William, Prof.,** (Emeritus), B.A., A.R.B.S.; artist in various media, mainly oil painting; *b* Penrith, Cumbria, 1935. *m* Eileen. one *s.* one *d. Educ:* Royal Grammar School, Lancaster. *Studied:* Durham University, King's College (now Newcastle University) (Victor Pasmore, Richard Hamilton, Lawrence Gowing). *Exhib:* John Moores Liverpool, 'Structure' Bradford Arts Festival, Midland View, Open Drawing Show, Cheltenham, etc. *Work in collections:* Northern Arts, Leics. Educ. Authority,

93

Bradford A.G., Abbot Hall Gallery Kendal, Leicester University, etc. *Commissions:* Relief for Attenborough Building, Leicester University. *Publications:* Artisan (1979), Haunting Monuments (1985), Recent Paintings (1985-88). *Signs work:* "CARRUTHERS" and "Derek Carruthers." *Address:* The School House, Harston, nr. Grantham NG32 1PS.

**CARSWELL, Fiona Charis,** B.A. Hons. (1983); artist in water-colour, mixed media and book binding; *b* Scotland, 10 Mar., 1960. *m* Richard Hackett. one *s.* two *d. Educ:* Rugby High School. *Studied:* Oxford Polytechnic (1980-83, Ivor Robinson). *Exhib:* various exhbns. showing book work and paintings in London, Brussels, Oxford and U.S.A. *Signs work:* "Fiona Charis Carswell" or "F.C.C." *Address:* Windrush Cottage, Fulbrook, Oxon. OX18 4BL.

**CARTER, Albert Henry,** B.Ed.(Hons., 1977), R.B.A. (1983); artist in water-colour, acrylic, etc.; Vice Pres., R.B.A.; former Director of Art, Oundle School; *b* Trowbridge, Wilts., 22 Feb., 1928. *m* Eunice Enfield. one *s.* three *d. Educ:* Trowbridge Boys' High School. *Studied:* St. Paul's College, Cheltenham (1973-77, Harold W. Sayer, A.,R.C.A.). *Exhib:* R.B.A., R.W.S., R.W.A., and provincial galleries. *Work in collections:* American Embassy, and many private collections in U.K., Canada, U.S.A., Russia, Germany, Hong Kong, Australia and France. *Signs work:* "A. H. Carter." *Address:* Haydn Studio, 27 South Rd., Oundle, nr. Peterborough PE8 4BU.

**CARTER, Bernard Thomas,** Hon.R.E. (1975), N.D.D. (1950), A.T.D. (1951); artist in oil; former keeper in charge of Pictures and Conservation, National Maritime Museum, Greenwich (retd. 1977); *b* London, 6 Apr., 1920. *m* Eugenie Alexander, artist (decd.). one *s. Educ:* Haberdasher Aske's. *Studied:* Goldsmiths' College of Art. *Exhib:* one-man shows, Arthur Jeffress (1955), Portal Gallery (twelve); mixed, R.A., Arts Council, British Council, galleries in Europe and U.S.A. *Commissions:* numerous. *Publications:* Art for Young People (with Eugenie Alexander). Work shown on television (BBC and ITV). *Signs work:* "Carter." *Address:* 56 King George St., Greenwich, London SE10 8QD.

**CARTER, Joan Patricia,** R.M.S. (1986), S.W.A. (1985); Gold medallist Paris Salon (1974), finalist Hunting Group prizes (1980), Hon. men. Gold Bowl R.M.S.; freelance portrait painter, book illuminator, illustrator and calligrapher in water-colour, pastel, acrylic and silverpoint; writer; *b* Vancouver, B.C., Canada, 11 Mar., 1923. *m* Alan Henry Carter. two *s. Educ:* Lord Selkerk School, Vancouver, Canada; C.F.E., Longbridge Rd., Ilford; Havering C.F.E., Hornchurch. *Studied:* `A' level art and Art History. *Exhib:* Schweinfurt, Germany, Paris Salon, R.A., numerous one-man shows etc., M.A.S.-F. *Work in collections:* miniature portrait (1.5" x 1") of Mrs. S. Lucas on gold bowl, R.M.S. (1985). *Publications:* Uncle Bill and Aunt Ethel, Allergy Cooking (Ian Henry Pub.), Solo Cooking on a Shoe String (Ian Henry Pub.), Illuminated Calligraphy (Search Press), Illuminated Alphabet (Search Press), Illuminated Design (Search Press), Silverpoint (Search Press), numerous Remembrance books - thirteen in England, one Normandy, France, one Tristan da Cunha, various talks and broadcasts, and articles; art work for book cover (Fowler Wright). *Signs work:* art books: "Patricia Carter"; other books: "J.P. Carter"; and see appendix. *Address:* 4 Osprey close Hoveton Norwich, Norfolk NR12 8DR.

**CARTER, Kenneth,** N.D.D. (Sculpture), A.T.D. (1955), F.R.B.S. (1970), R.W.A. (1995); sculptor in bronze and synthetic resins; *b* Hull, 16 June, 1928. *m* Brenda Hubbard. two *s.* two *d. Educ:* Kingston High School, Hull. *Studied:* Hull and Leicester Colleges of Art (1944-46, 1948-50, 1954-55). *Exhib:* Woodstock Gallery, London; various mixed exhbns. London and provinces. *Work in collections:* Exeter Cathedral Chapter House: 15 life-size niches; Ferens A.G., Hull. *Signs work:* "K. Carter." *Address:* Figgins Gallery, Church Rd., Lympstone, Devon EX8 5JT.

**CARTER, Mary,** painter in oil, egg tempera, gouache, water-colour; *b* Hartsdale, N.Y., 12 Apr., 1931. *m* Peter Gould, decd. one *s. Studied:* Art Students League of N.Y. (1951-55, Reginald Marsh, R.B. Hale). *Exhib:* Audubon Artists Annual N.Y. (1954, 1972), National Academy Design, N.Y. (1955, 1972), Hartford Athaneum, Conn. (1955), National Competition, Springfield Art Museum, Missouri (1966), Annual Drawings and Sculpture Show, Del Mar College, Corpus Christi, Tex. (1967), Hudson Guild Invitationals, N.Y. (1975-present), Krasdale Foods Gallery (1994). *Address:* 253 W. 16 St. New York, N.Y. 10011.

**CARTER, Mary Elizabeth,** M.A., A.R.C.A.; painter in oil of miniatures, portraits, rural and domestic scenes; *b* London, 1947. *m* J. B. Hiscock, painter. two *s.* one *d. Educ:* Ursuline Convent, Wimbledon. *Studied:* Kingston School of Art, Royal College of Art (Carel Weight, Roger de Grey). *Exhib:* Zaydler Gallery, Patricia Wells Gallery, R.W.A., Linfield Galleries, Bradford-on-Avon, Miniaturist for New Grafton Gallery, R.A. Summer Exhbn. since 1968. *Work in collections:* Southend-on-Sea Library, R.A., Camden Council. *Publications:* The Dog Who Knew Too Much. *Signs work:* "Mary E. Carter." *Address:* 2 Hodges Cottages, Hemyock, Cullompton, Devon EX15 3RW.

**CARUANA, Gabriel,** sculptor, painter, ceramist; *b* Malta, 7 Apr., 1929. *m* 1980 Mary Rose Buttigieg. two *d. Exhib:* one-man shows: Malta, England, Italy, Switzerland, Germany, Holland; participated in International Exhbn. of Ceramic Art (Faenza), Lincoln Centers, New York, World Bank, Washington D.C., U.S.A., Foresteria, Venice Bn. (1995). *Work in collections:* Museum of Fine Arts, Valletta, Malta; Whitworth A.G., Manchester; City of Manchester A.G.; Museum of Ceramics, Faenza, Italy; Albert Einstein (1879-1955) International Academy Foundation, Delaware, U.S.A., Malta University Campus, Museum of Ceramics, Deruta and Cervara di Roma, Italy; also several private collections. Artist of the Year, Malta (1985-86); 1988, town of Faenza hosts one-man show to honour 25 Years of Artistic Activity within the City. Founder and Hon. Director, Culture and Crafts Centre, The Old Mill,

B'kara, Malta. Artistically active since 1953. Studio: 37, Balzan Valley, Balzan, Malta; c/o Scultore Bianco Donato, Via Kafka 5, 00143, Roma, Italia. *Signs work:* "Gabriel Caruana." *Address:* Dr. Zammit St., Balzan, Malta, and 30 Carmel St., B'kara, BKR05, Malta. *Email:*http://www.zorin.com/gabriel/

**CARVER, Margaret,** R.M.S. (1995), S.W.A. (1997); artist in oil, pastel, water-colour, pencil; Chairperson, Gt.Yarmouth Soc. of Artists; *b* Caister-on-Sea, 10 Sept., 1941. *m* Richard Carver. two *s. Educ:* Caister High School; Gt. Yarmouth C.F.E. *Studied:* evening classes and part-time courses. *Exhib:* Westminster Galleries with S.W.A. and R.M.S., Norwich, Gt. Yarmouth. *Work in collections:* Gt. Yarmouth and District. *Signs work:* "M. CARVER." *Address:* 3 Orchard Cl., Caister-on-Sea, Gt. Yarmouth, Norfolk NR30 5DS.

**CARY, Caroline Anne,** F.P.S.; painter in acrylic and mixed media; *b* 28 July, 1940. *m* Lucius Cary. (divorced) one *s.* three *d* (one decd). *Studied:* Camberwell and Chelsea Colleges of Art under Lawrence Gowing. *Exhib:* mixed shows: Clarges Gallery, Jonathon Poole, Clark Fine Art, Gallery Zol, Bruton St. Gallery, Austin Desmond Fine Art, William Desmond Fine Art, Devon, etc.; solo shows: London: Loggia Gallery, Langton Gallery, Lord Leighton's Studio, Leighton House, Sue Rankin Gallery; Watatu Gallery, Nairobi, Century Gallery Henley, Galerie Souham, Paris, Z Gallery, N.Y. *Clubs:* Chelsea Arts. *Signs work:* "C.A.C." *Address:* The Studio, 14 Gunter Grove, London SW10 0UJ.

**CASE, David Charles,** M.A. (1966), Hon. R.E.; publisher; *b* 18 Oct., 1943. *m* Anthea. two *d. Educ:* Oakham School, Oxford University. *Address:* Marlborough Graphics, 6 Albemarle St., London W1X 4BY.

**CASSELDINE, Nigel,** A.R.W.A. (1985), R.W.A. (1991), Brandler Painting prize (1988); artist/painter in oil on gesso/drawing; Council mem. R.W.A. (1990-93); *b* Havering, Essex, 1947. *m* Jenny Partridge. one *s.* one *d. Educ:* N. Romford Comprehensive School. *Studied:* Camberwell and Sir John Cass Schools of Art (1966-68, part-time); studio assistant to F.V. Magrath (1969-72). *Exhib:* R.A., R.W.A., Bath Festival, Edinburgh Festival, Medici Gallery, Gloucester A.G. and Museum, etc. *Work in collections:* R.W.A., Cheltenham and Gloucester. *Publications:* 20th Century Painters and Sculptors by F. Spalding; Light by L. Willis. *Signs work:* "CASSELDINE" in red. *Address:* Mount Cottage, St. Marys, Chalford, nr. Stroud, Gloucs. GL6 8PU.

**CASSON, Sir Hugh Maxwell,** C.H., K.C.V.O., M.A., P.P.R.A., R.D.I., F.R.I.B.A., F.S.I.A.: Hon. Dr. R.C.A. (1975); architect; President, Royal Academy (1976-1985); director of architecture, Festival of Britain (1951); Prof. Environmental Design, R.C.A. (1953-75); *b* London, 23 May, 1910. *m* Margaret Macdonald, A.R.I.B.A. three *d. Educ:* Eastbourne College; St. John's College, Cambridge. *Studied:* architecture: Cambridge, British School at Athens, Bartlett School, University College, London; Regular contributor as author and illustrator to lay and technical press. Albert Medal R.S.A. (1984): Italian Order of Merit (1980).*Publications:* Homes by the Million, Victorian

Architecture, New Sights of London, Nanny Says, Diary, Hugh Casson's London, Hugh Casson's Oxford, Hugh Casson's Cambridge, Japan Observed, The Tower of London. *Address*: 6 Hereford Mans., Hereford Rd., London W2 5BA.

**CASSON, Simon John,** A.R.E. (1992), R.A.S.(M.A.) (1994), Central Printmaking Dip. (1990), B.A.(Hons.) Fine Art (1988); painter in oil, printmaker in etching; *b* York, 17 May, 1965. *Educ:* Rose Avenue School, Zambia, Cumbria, Penistone Grammar School, Sheffield. *Studied:* Barnsley College of Art (1985), Exeter College of Art and Design (1985-87), Central St. Martin's (1988-90, Norman Ackroyd), Royal Academy of Arts (1991-94, Prof. Norman Adams). *Exhib:* Regular solo shows at Long & Ryle Gallery, London. Private collections home and abroad. *Address:* 87a Albion Rd., Stoke Newington, London N16 9PL.

**CASTLE, Roger Bernard,** U.A. (1988); landscape marine artist in oil; council mem. U.A.; *b* Dartford, 30 Apr., 1945. *m* Brenda. two *s*. one *d*. *Educ:* Dartford. *Studied:* under the late William Walden, R.B.A. *Exhib:* R.A., R.O.I., N.E.A.C., R.B.A., U.A.; gallery artist at Century Gallery Henley, Roger Freen Fine A.G. Kent, Blackheath Gallery, F. Illes, Rochester. *Work in collections:* K.C.C. Ashford. *Signs work:* "R.B. CASTLE." *Address:* 26 Harper Rd., Ashford, Kent; studio: Hales Pl., High Halden, Kent.

**CATCHPOLE, Heather O.,** R.M.S., H.S.F., M.A.S.S.A.; National Dip. in commercial and Applied Art (1962); portrait artist in water-colour on ivorine, pastel; *b* Winnipeg, Canada, 26 Aug., 1942. *m* Brian E. Catchpole, L.D.S. *Educ:* Durban Girls' High School. *Studied:* Natal School of Arts and Craft. *Exhib:* R.M.S., R.A., Hilliard Soc. M.A.S-F. *Work in collections:* M.A.S.S.A. *Publications:* author/illustrator 'Heidi, Holly and other dogs'. In various books on techniques of miniature painting. *Signs work:* "Heather O. Catchpole," miniatures: the letter O with H inside with the year underneath it. *Address:* Heelers, Fitzhead, Taunton, Som. TA4 3JW.

**CATTRELL, Annie Katherine,** B.A.(Hons.) Fine Art (1984), M.A. Fine Art (1985); artist in glass, paper and mixed media; lecturer, Sculpture Dept., Cheltenham School of Art; *b* 15 Feb., 1962. *Studied:* Glasgow School of Art (1980-84, Sam Ainsley), University of Ulster (1984-85, Alistair MacLennan). *Exhib:* Collins Gallery Strathclyde University (1989), 369 Gallery 'Artist's Choice' (1990), Artist in Residence, Chessel Gallery (1991), Paperworks, Seagate Gallery (1992). *Work in collections:* S.A.C., MacManus A.G. and Museum Dundee, City Art Centre Edinburgh. *Publications:* reviews, Edinburgh Medicine vol.65, Alba (1991) Mar./Apr., etc. *Clubs:* Collective Gallery, Edinburgh. *Signs work:* "Annie Cattrell." *Address:* 10a Greenhill Park, Churchill, Edinburgh EH10 4DW.

**CAUDWELL, Celia,** N.D.D. (1995), S.W.A. (1993), S.B.A. (1994), A.U.A. (1994); artist in water-colour, oil, pen and ink, pottery/ceramics; gallery owner, mem. F.A.T.G.; *b* Ewell, Surrey, 11 July, 1943. *m* John Caudwell. two *s*. *Educ:*

Upper Chine School, Shanklin, I.O.W. *Studied:* Winchester School of Art (1961-64), Goldsmiths' College School of Art (1964-65). *Exhib:* Ryde Library/Gallery I.O.W., Boldrewood Gallery, Southampton University, Seely Gallery, Newport I.O.W., Westminster Gallery, Mall Galleries, Omell Gallery, Laing Art Competition Winchester. *Publications:* A Brief History of Winkle Street I.O.W. *Signs work:* "Celia Caudwell." *Address:* Brookside Cottage, Winkle St., Calbourne, I.O.W. PO30 4JF; The Afton Gallery, The Broadway, Totland Bay, I.O.W. PO39 0BW.

**CAULKIN, Martin,** R.I. (1983), R.B.S.A. (1983); artist in water-colour and ink; *b* B'ham, 12 Feb., 1945. *m* Anne Cherry, S.W.A. one *d. Educ:* Great Barr Comprehensive. *Studied:* B'ham College of Art (1962-65, Glyn Griffiths). *Exhib:* R.W.S., R.B.S.A., R.I., R.A. Summer Show, Singer and Friedlander water-colour exhbn., Shell House Gallery, Ledbury, Ombersley Galleries, Worcs., Montpellier Gallery, Cheltenham, Manor House Gallery, Chipping Norton, Bill Toop Gallery, Salisbury. *Publications:* Landscape in Watercolours (Studio Vista); Paintings from Photographs (Harper Collins). *Signs work:* "Martin Caulkin." *Address:* September Cottage, Naunton, Upton upon Severn, Worcester WR8 0PY.

**CAVANAGH, John Bryan,** couturier (retd. Sept. 1974); *b* Belmullet, 28 Sept., 1914. *Educ:* St. Paul's School.Trained with Molyneux and Balmain in Paris. *Exhib:* Munich, 1954 (Gold Medal); designed Wedding Dress for H.R.H. Duchess of Kent (June, 1961); designed Wedding Dress for H.R.H. Princess Alexandra (April, 1963). *Work in collections:* V. & A., Museum of Costume, Bath.*Signs work:* "JOHN CAVANAGH." *Address:* 10 Birchlands Ave., London SW12 8ND.

**CECIL, Roger,** artist in oil and oil pastel; David Murray Award (1966); *b* Abertillery, 18 July, 1942. *Studied:* Newport College of Art. *Exhib:* Howard Roberts Gallery, Cardiff (1966), R.A. Summer Exhbn. (1987, 1989); one-man shows, New Academy Gallery, London (1988, 1989, 1991, 1993, 1995-97), Cleveland Drawing Biennale (1989). *Publications:* B.B.C. documentary The Gentle Rebel. *Signs work:* "Roger Cecil." *Address:* c/o The New Academy Gallery, 34 Windmill St., London W1P 1HH.

**CERCI, Sharon L.,** F.M.A.S., A.R.M.S. (1983); scrimshander scribing on ivory with ink, lecturer; heraldic artist and designer; *b* Providence, R.I., U.S.A., 4 July, 1942. two *s.* one *d. Educ:* Brockton High School. *Studied:* B.H.P. Art School (1963). *Exhib:* I.F.M.A.S., R.M.S., International Circle of Miniature Artists, Spencer Gallery, Dunedin Fine Art Center. *Commissions:* Coat-of-Arms design: USCG cutter, Durable (1991), Dunedin Highland Games (1994), Ocala Scottish Games and Irish Feis (1996), Ye Mystic Krewe of Neptune, St. Petersburg, Fla. (1991), Neptunus Rex XIII, XIV, XV, XVI, XVII and XVIII (1991-97), Coat -of-Arms design with Expository entitled: The Trinity Arms d.b.a. the King's Crest (1993). *Publications:* author of 'Penning Generation Around theWorld'. *Signs work:* S within a C, "S.Cerci," "Sharon Cerci,"

"Cerci." *Address:* 1358 N. Lotus Drive, Dunedin, Florida, U.S.A.

**CHADWICK, Lynn,** C.B.E., 1st Prize, Venice Biennale (1956); sculptor, chiefly in iron and bronze; *b* London, 24 Nov., 1914. *m* Eva Reiner. two *s.* two *d. Educ:* Merchant Taylors. *Exhib:* Stedelijk Museum (Amsterdam, 1957), Palais des Beaux Arts, Bruxelles (1957), Arts Council of G.B. (London, 1957). *Work in collections:* Tate, Museum of Modern Art (N.Y.), Allbright Art Gallery (Buffalo), The Kroller-Müler Museum (Otterlo). *Publications:* Contemporary British Art (Herbert Read), Sir Herbert Read, Lynn Chadwick (Bodensee Verlag, Amriswill, Swiss), Pelican, Lynn Chadwick (Dr. J. P. Hodin, Zwemmer), Lynn Chadwick (Alan Bowness, Methuen), Dennis Farr and Eva Chadwick, Lynn Chadwick (O.U.P.). *Address:* Lypiatt Pk., Stroud Glos. GL6 7LL.

**CHALKER, Jack Bridger-,** A.R.C.A., R.W.A., A.S.I.A., Hon. F.M.A.A.; painter, illustrator, medical/surgical artist, illustrator in oil, gouache, pen and wash etc.; Consultant, Birmingham University (art and design); War artist with Australian Army, Bangkok (1945); *b* 10 Oct., 1918. *m* Hélène. three *s.* one *d. Educ:* Alleyn's School, Dulwich. *Studied:* Goldsmiths' College (1936-39), R.C.A. (1946-49). *Exhib:* R.B.A., R.W.A., R.P., London galleries; mixed shows: London, Cheltenham; one-man shows: Dixon Gallery London, R.W.A., etc. *Work in collections:* Cheltenham, Imperial War Museum London, War Memorial Canberra, Australia. *Publications:* author and illustrator: Burma Railway Artist (Leo Cooper, 1944, and Viking O'Neil Australia); wide range of surgical/medical publications. *Clubs:* Arts, Lansdowne. *Signs work:* "Chalker." *Address:* Bleadney Mill, Bleadney, nr. Wells, Som. BA5 1PF.

**CHAMBERLAIN, Trevor,** R.O.I. (1972), R.S.M.A. (1970); Bourlet Prize Winner at 1980 R.O.I. Exhbn.; marine, town and landscape painter in oil and water-colour; *b* Hertford, 13 Dec., 1933. *m* Elaine Waterfield. one *s. Educ:* Ware Central School. *Work in collections:* Guildhall A.G., London, Ferens A.G., Hull, Hertford Museum. *Publications:* The Connoisseur, Studio International, Dictionary of Sea Painters, 20th Century Marine Painting, Water-colour Impressionists; Co-author of 'Oil-Painting, - Pure and Simple', 'Oils'. *Signs work:* "T. Chamberlain." *Address:* Braeside, Goldings La., Waterford, Hertford, Herts. SG14 2PT.

**CHAMBERS, Stephen Lyon,** B.A.Hons., M.A., Rome Scholarship; painter in oil on canvas; *b* London, 20 July, 1960. *m* Denise de Coruova. two *s. Educ:* Holland Park Comprehensive. *Studied:* Winchester School of Art (1978-79), St. Martin's School of Art (1979-82), Chelsea School of Art (1982-83). *Exhib:* widely in Europe, U.S.A. and U.K. Represented by Flowers East, London. *Publications:* Strange Smoke by John Gillett; Paintings 1988-89 by Gerard Wilson; Felonies and Errors by Isabella Oulton. *Signs work:* paintings on canvas only signed on reverse. *Address:* 129 Offord Rd., London N1 1PH.

**CHANDLER, Cynthia Ann,** landscape and coastal scene painter in water-colour and oil and portrait painter in oil, pastel and water-colour; *b* Isleworth,

Middx., 1 Jan., 1937. *m* Frank Chandler. two *s.* one *d. Educ:* Hampton High School. *Studied:* Twickenham School of Art (Mr. Duffy, Mr. Kane, Miss Palby). *Exhib:* U.A., P.S., and several Midland exhbns. *Work in collections:* Nuneaton Art Gallery (3). *Clubs:* President, Rugby and District Art Soc., Coventry and Warwickshire Soc. of Artists, Banbury and District Art Soc. *Signs work:* "Cynthia Chandler," "CYNTHIA CHANDLER." *Address:* 36 Dunsmore Ave., Rugby, Warwickshire CV22 5HD.

**CHANEY, Judith Hilary Desforges,** B.Soc.Sc., M.Soc.Sc.; Director of Quality Control, The London Inst.; *b* 31 May, 1944. *Educ:* Nottingham High School for Girls, G.P.D.S.T., University of Birmingham. Taught at University of Leicester, University of Hong Kong, Sunderland Polytechnic. Registrar, Art and Design, C.N.A.A. (1985-91). *Address:* c/o The London Inst., Davies St., London W1.

**CHANG, Chien-Ying,** B.A. (1935); artist in water-colour; mem. of R.I., R.W.A. and Soc. of Woman Artists; *b* 27 June, 1915. *m* Cheng-Wu Fei, artist. *Educ:* National Central University, China, and Slade School of Fine Art. *Exhib:* R.A., R.I., R.B.A.; one-man shows at Leicester Gallery (1951, 1955, 1960). *Work in collections:* London University; St. John's College, Oxford; R.W.A.; Bristol; Grave's Gallery, Sheffield; Derby Art Gallery. *Publications:* work repro.: Studio, Art News and Review, Future, Picture Post, La Revue Moderne, Kunst, etc. *Signs work:* see appendix. *Address:* 27 The Fountains, Ballards Lane, London N3 1NL.

**CHANNING, Leslie Thomas,** A.R.I.B.A. (1941), U.A. (1973), A.N.S.P.S. (1975); artist in water-colour; architect (retd.); *b* Weymouth, 24 Apr., 1916. *m* (1st) Florence Helen (decd.); (2nd) Audrey Joan. one *s.* one *d. Educ:* The Wandsworth School and Regent St. Polytechnic Evening Inst. School of Architecture (1934-39). *Exhib:* R.I., U.A., N.S.P.S., Thames Valley Arts Club, Richmond Art Soc. *Clubs:* U.A., N.S.P.S., Thames Valley Arts, Richmond Art Soc. *Signs work:* "L. T. Channing." *Address:* 6 Spinnaker Ct., Becketts Pl., Hampton Wick KT1 4EW.

**CHAO, Shao-an,** M.B.E. (1980); Prof. in Art (Canton University, 1948); painter in ink and water-colour;*b* Canton, China, 6 Mar., 1905. *Studied:* painting at 15 under Kao Chi-feng, a key figure in the early development of `Lingnan Painting'. founded 'Lingnan School of Art' in Canton (1930); Conferred the honorary degree of Doctor of Letters by University of Hong Kong (1994) in recognition of services to the Arts.;*Exhib:* repeated one-man shows in major cities in China: Nanking, Shanghai, Canton, Chungking, etc. (1929-48); one man shows, in major universities and art museums and galleries in U.S.A., England, Japan, France, W. Germany, Switzerland, Italy, Canada, Australia, New Zealand, Singapore and Malaysia (1951-78); Urban Council Hong Kong Museum of Art (1979), National Museum of History, Taiwan (1980). *Work in collections:* Boston Museum of Fine Art, Washington County Museum, Nanyang University Museum, Singapore, Hong Kong Museum of Art and

National Museum of History, Taiwan, Museum für Kunsthandwerk, Übersee-Museum, Romer-Museum, Museum der Stadt Ettlingen, W. Germany (1989). *Publications:* Charming Cicadas Collection (1 vol.), Shao-an's Paintings (1 vol.), Recent Paintings by Prof. Chao Shao-an (3 vols.), Collection of Shao-an's Paintings (20 vols.), The Art of Chao Shao-an (1 vol.), The Paintings of Chao Shao-an (1 vol.). Awarded International Art Gold Medal by the Belgium Centenary Independence World Fair, Brussels; moved to Hong Kong in 1948 and re-established `Lingnan School of Art' there. To date, he has students in many parts of the world. Lectures: at a number of universities including University of Leeds, U.K. (1954), Harvard University and Berkeley University, U.S.A. (1960). *Signs work:* "CHAO Shao-An" and see appendix. *Address:* 295A Prince Edward Rd., (2nd Floor), Kowloon, Hongkong.

**CHAPLIN, Michael James,** N.D.D., R.E., R.W.S.; printmaker, water-colourist; Past Vice-Pres. Royal Soc. of Painter-Printmakers; *b* St. Neots, 19 Sept., 1943. *m* Gay Lloyd. one *s*. one *d*. *Educ:* St. Albans Boys' Grammar School. *Studied:* Watford College of Art (1961-64), Brighton College of Art (1966-67), post-graduate. *Exhib:* R.E. Annual, R.W.S. Open (Prizewinner 1989), R.A. Summer Shows. *Work in collections:* Ashmolean and Fitzwilliam museums; public and private collections worldwide, Royal Collections. *Commissions:* mural for Express Newspaper's boardroom. *Publications:* included in Encyclopedia of Water-colour Techniques; regular contributor to Artist Magazine. *Signs work:* "Michael Chaplin, R.E.R.W.S" *Address:* Suffield, Orchard Drive, Weavering, Maidstone, Kent ME14 5JG.

**CHAPMAN, John Lewis,** artist in water-colour, gouache, oil; *b* Blackburn, 11 Sept., 1946. *Studied:* Blackburn Art College (James Dolby). *Exhib:* R.A. Summer Exhbn., Patersons, London, Lewis Textile, Blackburn, Haworth A.G., Accrington, Jersey, Birmingham, Warrington, Newcastle, Harrods, London. *Work in collections:* Blackburn A.G. *Publications:* 22 signed Limited Editions (published by Miss Carter Publications, Bolton). *Signs work:* "J.L. CHAP-MAN." *Address:* 25 Silverwell St., Bolton BL1 1PP.

**CHAPMAN, June Dianne,** painter in oil; *b* Ruislip, 12 June, 1939. *Educ:* St. Joan of Arc's Convent School, Rickmansworth. *Studied:* Camberwell School of Art (1955-56). *Exhib:* R.A., R.B.A., R.O.I., U.A., Blackheath Gallery, Edwin Pollard Gallery, Foyles A.G.; group show: Kingsmead Gallery. *Signs work:* "J. Chapman" or "June Chapman." *Address:* 99f Mycenae Rd., Blackheath, London SE3 7SE.

**CHAPMAN, Mark,** B.A. (Hons.) Fine Art: 1st Class (1982), M.A. Fine Art (1983); artist in water-colour, metal and wood construction; Lecturer in Art and Design, School of Art, Weymouth College; *b* Cuckfield, Sussex, 30 Jan., 1958. *Studied:* Sunderland (1979-82), Birmingham (1982-83). *Exhib:* Leicestershire Schools Exhbn. (1983-90); Sculpture in the Garden, Deans Court, Wimborne (1991, 1993, 1995). *Signs work:* "M. Chapman." *Address:* Marnel Cottage, Church Lane, Osmington Dorset DT3 9EW.

# WHO'S WHO IN ART

**CHART, Helga,** R.S.W. (1994), S.A.A.C. (1996), D.A. (Edin.) Post Grad.; artist in oil and mixed media; lecturer in art and design, Edinburgh's Telford College; *b* Edinburgh, 31 Aug., 1944. *m* H. Robertson. one *s. Educ:* Edinburgh. *Studied:* Edinburgh College of Art (1962-66, Sir Robin Philipson, David Michie, John Houston). *Exhib:* mixed shows 1968-95; three solo shows Edinburgh; R.S.A., R.S.W., S.A.A.C., S.S.A. *Work in collections:* British Rail, IBM, Edinburgh schools, Pictures in Hospitals (Scotland). *Signs work:* "Helga Chart." *Address:* 19 Dalrymple Cres., Edinburgh EH9 2NX.

**CHATTEN, Geoffrey,** A.R.B.A. (1988); self taught painter of E. Anglian life and landscape, figures and marine subjects in oil; *b* Gorleston, Norfolk, 20 Sept., 1938. *Exhib:* R.A., R.B.A., R.O.I., Southwell Brown Gallery, Richmond, Surrey, John Noott Gallery, Broadway, Fosse Gallery, Fosse on the Wold, Waterman Gallery, London, Dassin Gallery, Los Angeles, Gt. Yarmouth Galleries. *Work in collections:* Maritime Trust, many private collections throughout Britain and overseas. *Publications:* Lydia Eva (Maritime Trust). *Signs work:* "Chatten." *Address:* 82 Suffield Rd., Gorleston, Norfolk NR31 7AL.

**CHATTERTON, George Edward,** F.I.A.L.; Accademia Italia Gold Medal (1979), Prize of Italy Distinction (1980); artist, cartoonist and photographer; *b* Kidderminster, 15 July, 1911. *m* Iris Betty Wilce. two *s. Educ:* Toronto. *Studied:* Kidderminster School of Art; photography at School of Photography, Farnborough. *Publications:* work repro.: since 1932 in leading London and Dundee illustrated journals, including London Opinion, Daily Mirror, Daily Sketch, Weekly News, etc. R.A.F. Artist/Photographer (1938-50). Cartoon creations include "Chad" of "Wot, No-?" fame (1938), "Sheriff Shucks" (1948), "Leo CV" mascot of Lions Clubs, G.B. (1969), etc. *Signs work:* see appendix. *Address:* Canal Cottage, Ryeford, Stonehouse, Glos. GL10 2LG.

**CHAUVIN, Enid,** Board of Educ. art dip. (1934), elected M.A.I.A. (1948), Hon. S.G.A. (1969); artist in oils, lithography and water-colour; art teacher; awarded Medal and Diploma of Merit, Annuale Italiana d'Arte Grafica (1968), Medal and Honourable Mention, Biennale degli Regioni, Ancona (1968); Diplome Palme d'Or des Beaux Arts (1969); Grand Prix de Bastia (1976); Mention International (1977); Fondation Michel Ange; Mention Speciale "Arts Inter" (Avignon) 1978; elected Conseiller Culturel of International Arts Guild (1969); Diplome d'Honneur I.A.G. (1984); Hon. Vice-President L'Internazionale de Centro Studi e Scambi Internazionali (1972); *b* Blackheath, 21 June, 1910. *m* Victor Patrick Law. one *s. Educ:* Blackheath High School. *Studied:* Blackheath School of Art and Goldsmiths' College. *Exhib:* R.A., R.B.A., R.O.I., A.I.A., United Artists, S.W.A., R.P., N.S., Senefelder Group, Redfern, Kensington, Mercury, Piccadilly, Curwen, and Furneau Galleries, Ganymed Editions, Exhbn. Grand Prix International de la Corse Porto Vecchio (1993); one-man exhbn. Heal's Gallery, Maison de la Culture, Ajaccio (1971, 1976, 1978, 1981), Bastia (1972, 1975, 1976), Calvi (1972, 1973, 1974), île

Rousse (1978, 1979, 1980, 1986), Geneva (1980), Monaco (1985), Marseille (1986), in artist's studio Santa Reparata-di-Balagna (1987-1996). Work purchased by Southampton Education Authority and Maison de la Culture. *Publications:* Circus Horses in Children's Oxford Ency., biography and reproduction in La Femme dans L'Art Contemporain (1972), Dix Ans d'Arts Graphiques et Plastiques (1970-80), Artistes et Modeles (1982) and Repertorium Artis (1984). *Signs work:* see appendix. *Address:* Place de L'Ormeau, Santa Reparata-di-Balagna, 20220 Ile-Rousse, Corsica.

**CHEEK, Carl F.,** A.R.C.A.; portrait painter in oil, pastel and conté; *b* Karlshamn, Sweden, 7 Mar., 1927;. divorced. one *s.* two *d. Educ:* Clifton College. *Studied:* Chelsea School of Art, Royal College of Art. *Exhib:* one-man shows: London (2), Manchester (1). *Commissions:* Sir Clough William Ellis, Lord Eden, Lord Butterfield, Field Marshal Sir Nigel Bagnall, etc. Taught at several art schools: Heatherleys, Berkshire College of Art, Croydon College of Art, S.E. Essex School of Art. *Signs work:* "Carl Cheek." *Address:* The Orangery, The Manor House, Norton sub Hamdon, Stoke sub Hamdon, Som. TA14 6SJ.

**CHEESE, Bernard,** R.E. (1988), A.R.C.A. (1950); printmaker in lithography and water-colour; *b* London, 1925. one *s.* three *d. Educ:* Beckenham Grammar School. *Studied:* Beckenham School of Art (Wolf Kassemoff), R.C.A. (Edwin Ladell). *Exhib:* Bankside Gallery, Zwemmer Gallery (1965), R.A., John Russell Gallery, Ipswich, St. John's Gallery, Bury St. Edmunds. *Work in collections:* Library of Congress, Washington, Cincinnati Museum, N.Y. Public Library, Leeds Library, V. & A. (Print Room). *Publications:* illustrated many music books for A. & C. Black. *Signs work:* "Bernard Cheese." *Address:* 2 High St., Nayland, Colchester CO6 4JE.

**CHEN, Chi,** painter-artist; *b* Wusih, China, 2 May, 1912. *Studied:* in China; 1940-46 art instructor St. John's University. *Exhib:* first one-man show Shanghai (1940). In 1947 invited to come to U.S.A.; one-man shows at universities, museums, galleries in New York, Boston, Philadelphia, Washington, D.C., Chicago, New Orleans, Houston, Dallas, Fort Worth, San Antonio, Denver, Seattle, San Francisco, Los Angeles, San Diego, etc. Recipient numerous gold medals: 1955 A.W.S. Spl. $1000 Award for Water-colour of the Year, 1960 Nat. Inst. Arts and Letters $1500 Grant, 1961 Nat. Academy Samuel Finley Breese Morse Medal, 1969 Nat. Academy Saltus Gold Medal of Merit, 1976 A.W.S. Bicentennial Gold Medal and many others. *Publications:* Aquarelles de Chen Chi (Shanghai 1942), A Portfolio of Chen Chi Paintings, Limited Edition (Switzerland 1965), Sketchbooks of Chen Chi (New York 1969), China from Sketchbooks of Chen Chi (New York 1974), Chen Chi Watercolours, Drawings, Sketches (New York 1980), Chen Chi Watercolour (Shanghai, The People's Republic of China 1981), Heaven and Water, Chen Chi (New York 1983), Heart & Chance (New York 1993). *Clubs:* Nat. Academy of Design, American Watercolour Society, Nat. Arts Club, Century

Club, Dutch Treat Club and others. *Signs work:* "Chen Chi." *Address:* 23 Washington Sq. North, New York, N.Y. 10011; Studio: 15 Gramercy Park, New York, N.Y. 10003, U.S.A.

**CHERRY, Anne,** M.A. (R.C.A.) (1973), S.W.A. (1987), A.R.B.S.A. (1990); artist in water-colour; *b* Isle of Sheppey, 16 Oct., 1948. *m* Martin Caulkin, R.I., R.B.S.A. one *d. Educ:* John Willmott Grammar School. *Studied:* Sutton Art College (1967-68), B'ham College of Art (1968-71), R.C.A. (1971-73, Joanne Brogden, Zandra Rhodes). *Exhib:* R.B.S.A. Galleries, R.W.S., R.I., Shell House Gallery, Ledbury, Ombersley Galleries, Worcs., Montpellier Gallery, Cheltenham, Manor House Gallery, Chipping Norton. *Publications:* "Landscape in Watercolour", Patricia Monahan, (Studio Vista), Beginner's Guides. *Signs work:* "Anne Cherry." *Address:* September Cottage, Naunton, Upton upon Severn, Worcester WR8 0PY.

**CHERRY, Norman,** D.A., M.C.S.D., F.R.S.A.; designer - jeweller and silversmith, precious and non-precious metals; academic; Head, School of Jewellery, U.C.E. ; *b* Airdrie, Lanarkshire, 2 Aug., 1949. *m* Kate Cherry, H.M.I. one *s. Studied:* Glasgow School of Art (1966-70, J. Leslie Auld). *Exhib:* various inc. Dundee Museums and A.G.'s. *Work in collections:* Tennessee Technological Univ., U.S.A. and Royal Museum of Scotland. *Commissions:* numerous*Publications:* Textile Techniques for Jewellers" by Arline Fisch (Lark Books). Churchill Fellow (1983). Although work is undertaken in various areas of jewellery and metalwork, a major preoccupation in recent years has been the weaving of metals. *Signs work:* Sponsors mark: N.C. inside lozenge struck on all precious metalwork and assayed and hallmarked @ Edinburgh. *Address:* School of Jewellery, Vittoria St., Birmingham B1 3PA.

**CHESSER, Sheila,** prize-winner, Festival of the Church and the Arts, Nottingham; painter in acrylic; *b* Cheshire, 21 Feb., 1915. *m* Dr. Eustace Chesser. *Educ:* Howells School, Denbigh. *Studied:* no formal art training. *Exhib:* Leicester Gallery, Redfern Gallery, Whitechapel Gallery, W.I.A.C., Art Council, Northern Ireland, Municipal Gallery, Modern Art, Dublin, Bradford City Art Gallery, Royal Scottish Academy; one-man shows: Midland Group Gallery, Nottingham, Thames Gallery, Eton, Greenwich Theatre Gallery. *Work in collections:* Leicester University. *Publications:* Through a Glass. *Clubs:* W.I.A.C., H.A.C., F.P.S. *Signs work:* see appendix. *Address:* 17 Wimpole St., London W1M 7AD.

**CHEVINS, Hugh Terry,** M.S.I.A.; artist, oil, gouache, pen and ink, commercial and book illustrator, landscape, mural painter, portrait painter; R.A. Bronze Medal (1953), Paris Salon Medaille d'Argent (1955, 1956); *b* Retford, 2 July, 1931. *Educ:* Gunnersbury Grammar School. *Studied:* Twickenham School of Art, Paris, R.A. Schools. *Exhib:* R.A., R.B.A., United Artists, Glasgow Academy, Paris, Piccadilly Gallery, Brighton Art Gallery, Bournemouth, Kingsmead Gallery. *Work in collections:* Rijksmuseum, Amsterdam, Science Museum, London. *Publications:* work repro.: Imperial hemical Industries, Reed Paper Group, Shell, John Laing, John Mowlem. *igns work:* "HUGH CHEVINS." *Address:* 2 Gaston Way, Shepperton, Middx. W17 8EX.

**CHILD, Josephine, Heather,** M.B.E.; painter in pen and ink, water-colour, alligrapher; chairman, Federation of British Crafts Societies (1973-76); author nd editor of calligraphy books; *b* Winchester, 1911. *Educ:* St. Swithun's chool, Winchester. *Studied:* Chelsea College of Art (exhbn. to R.C.A.). *Exhib:* a all the S.S.I. exhbns. and many others showing calligraphy. *Work in collec-ons:* V. & A., Harvard University Library, Boston Public Library, U.S.A., rafts Study Centre Bath, Ditchling Museum Sussex. *Commissions:* many pri-ate in U.K. and U.S.A. *Publications:* Decorative Maps (Studio Ltd., 1956), he Armorial Bearings of the Guilds of London (Warne, 1960), Calligraphy oday (Studio Vista Books, 1963), Heraldic Design (G. Bell & Sons, 1969), ormal Penmanship (Lund Humphries, 1971), Christian Symbols (G. Bell & ons, 1971), editor: The Calligraphers Handbook (A. & C. Black 1985). *Clubs:* oc. of Designer Craftsmen, Soc. of Scribes and Illuminators, Art Workers' uild. Now retired. *Address:* 70 Heath Rd., Petersfield, Hants. GU31 4EJ.

**CHILTON, Elizabeth,** Ruskin Cert. Fine Art and Design (1964-67); artist in il, some etching and sculpture; *b* Darlington, 1 Mar., 1945. *m* R. G. Denning. vo *s. Educ:* Headington School for Girls, Oxford. *Studied:* Ruskin School, xford University, University of Illinois, U.S.A., Mem. of the Italian cademy. *Exhib:* R.A., Paris Salon, Oxford University Colleges, N.E.A.C., .O.I., Southwark Cathedral. *Commissions:* mostly private. *Signs work:* Chilton." *Address:* Purlin House, Toot Baldon, Oxford OX44 9NE.

**CHRISTIE, Janet Mary,** D.A. (Edin.) (1961), F.S.B.A. (1986 resigned 997); R.H.S. Silver medal (1982), Grenfell medal (1985); former founder em. Soc. of Botanical Artists; painter in water-colour; *b* Kampala, Uganda, 12 lar., 1939. two *s.* one *d. Educ:* Cranley, Edinburgh. *Studied:* Edinburgh ollege of Art (1957-61, Robin Philipson, Gillies, John Maxwell, John louston). *Exhib:* R.S.S.W., S.A.A.C., R.H.S., also various mixed exhbns.; solo ows: Norwich, London, and Edinburgh area. *Signs work:* "J.M.C." *Address:* larbert, Springhill Rd., Peebles EH45 9ER.

**CHRISTIE, Talbot Patterson Wescott,** Dip.A.D. (Lond.) (1969), Byam haw Dip. A.D. (1969), R.A. Cert. A.D. (1973), Byam Shaw drawing prize; rtist in acrylic and oil; *b* Montreal, Canada, 22 Aug., 1946. *m* Foller Earnshan. ne *s.* one *d. Educ:* Canada, Libya, Switzerland, France. *Studied:* Byam Shaw chool of Art (1966-70, Maurice de Sausmarez); R.A. Schools (1970-73). xhib: Fine Art and Market Print Gallery, Exeter, Market Place Gallery, olyton, Heim Gallery, London, Museum of Wales, Cardiff, Grand Palais, aris. *Signs work:* "T.P. Christie." *Address:* 57 Bainton Rd., Oxford OX2 7AG.

**CHRISTOPHER, Ann,** R.A., F.R.B.S., R.W.A., B.A.; sculptor in bronze; *b* Vatford, Herts., 4 Dec., 1947. *m* K. Cook. *Educ:* Watford Girls' Grammar chool. *Studied:* Harrow School of Art (1965-66), West of England College of

Art (1966-69). *Exhib:* Redfern Gallery, London, Adelson Galleries Inc., Ne
York, R.A. *Work in collections:* Bristol City A.G., Contemporary Arts Soc
Chantrey Collection, London, Glynn Vivian A.G. *Commissions:* 1996 Mars
Mills, Plymouth, 1997 Linklaters & Paines, London. *Publications:* An
Christopher 'Sculpture 1969 - 89', also 'Sculpture 1989-94. *Signs work:* "AC
*Address:* The Stable Block, Hay St., Marshfield, nr Chippenham SN14 8PF.

**CHUGG, Brian J.,** N.D.D., A.T.D. (1951); painter in oil, etc., author; le
turer, North Devon College (1953-79); *b* Braunton, Devon, 3 Nov., 1926.
Mary Bryan Cooper. *Educ:* Challoners School. *Studied:* architecture: und
B.W. Oliver F.R.I.B.A. (1944-46); art: Bideford Art School (1946-49
Camberwell Art School under M. Bloch and K. Vogel (1949-50). *Exhil*
Westward Ho! Art Soc., one-man exhbns., Barnstaple (1953, 1958, 1994
*Publications:* author, Devon a Thematic Study; Victorian and Edwardia
Devon from Old Photographs, etc. *Signs work:* "BRIAN CHUGG" (plus date
*Address:* Crossley House, Bishops Tawton, Devon EX32 0BS.

**CHUHAN, Jagjit (Ms.),** D.F.A.(Lond.) (1977); artist in oil on canvas; par
time lecturer, Liverpool John Moores University; *b* India, 10 Jan., 195
*Studied:* Slade School of Fine Art (1973-77). *Exhib:* solo shows: Ikon Galler
B'ham (1987), Commonwealth Inst., London (1987), Horizon Gallery, Londc
(1987); mixed shows: Barbican Centre, London (1988), Horizon Galler
London (1990), Tate Gallery, Liverpool (1990-91), Galeria Civica, Marsal
Sicily (1991), Arnolfini, Bristol (1991). *Work in collections:* Oldham A.G
Leics. Schools Coll., Horizon Gallery, London (Indian Arts Council in th
U.K.), Arthur Anderson & Co. *Address:* 296 Brantingham Rd., Chorltor
Manchester M21 0QU.

**CINZIA:** see BONADA, Cinzia.

**CIPRIANI-BOND, Douglas,** (exhibits: Doug Cipriani), A.R.D.S
L.S.I.A.D., F.F.P.S; painter in various media, designer and design consulta
own practice in London; U.K. National Art Comm. for UNESCO (Internation
Association of Art); *b* London, 12 June, 1928. *m* Hilery Jane Gale-Smith. one
one *d*. *Educ:* Collegiate and St. Martha's College, Feltham. *Studiec*
Twickenham College of Art (1942-46) under F. Coulson-Davies. Also priva
tuition under E. Manning (1944-46) *Exhib:* one-man shows: Sussex Universit
Worthing Museum and A.G.; group shows: 'Invasion Artistique' exchang
exhbns - France/Britain; Pittsburgh, U.S.A.; New Burlington; U.A.; Loggi
Gallery; International Arts Centre; Cambridge, Surrey, Southampton an
London Universities; 'Today's Art' Brighton A.G.; 'Modern Art', Victoria A.C
(Bath Festival); transferred to Bristol City A.G.; Towner Gallery; 'Paintin
South East 1975' (touring art colleges and galleries); Royal Soc. of Art, B'har
*Work in collections:* Feltham Council and private collections in Canad
Holland and Britain. *Publications:* Studio Vista, Graphis Internation
(Zurich), Who's Who in Western Europe, Dic. of International Biographie
Men of Achievement, British Contemporary Art (1993). Designs and illustr

ons for BBC Publications 'Time & Tune', Radio Times, etc., and for BBC in onjunction with Sadler's Wells Ballet. Artist to United States Third Air Force 1958-59). Designed Thanksgiving display Coventry Cathedral (1978). *Clubs:* .D.S., I.A.A., S.I.A.D., F.P.S., Forum Soc. *Signs work:* "Cipriani." *Address:* )elroy House, 14 Melville Rd., Hove, Sussex BN3 1TH.

**CLAESSEN, George,** artist in oil and graphic media; *b* Colombo, Ceylon, 5 1ay, 1909. *m* Inez De Kretser. one *s.* one *d.* *Educ:* St. Joseph's College, :olombo. *Studied:* self-taught. *Exhib:* R.B.A., London, Kensington Gallery, ondon, Utd. Soc. of Artists, London, Imperial Inst., London, Hampstead Arts :ouncil, Petit Palais (Paris), S.G.A., A.I.A., New Vision Gallery (London), "enice Bienale (1956), hon. mention (plaque) V Biennial, São Paulo, Brazil 1959). *Work in collections:* Lionel Wendt Coll., Ceylon; The Sapumal 'oundation (Sri Lanka). *Publications:* Book of drawings (1946), Poems of a 'ainter (Mitre Press, London, 1967), Poems about Nothing (Arthur H. :tockwell Ltd., Devon, 1981), Collected Poems (Avon Books, London 1995). *igns work:* "Claessen" and "G.C." *Address:* 5 Spencer Rise, London NW5 AR.

**CLARK, Bruce Michael,** M.A., D.A.E., Cert. Ed.; painter in oil; *b* Bedfont, 7 July, 1937. *m* Jill Clark. two *s.* *Educ:* Strodes School. *Studied:* Bath \cademy of Art, Corsham (1958-60) under Howard Hodgkin, Gwyther Irwin, Villiam Crozier. *Exhib:* nine one-man shows including Chiltern Gallery, .ondon; Compendium Galleries, Birmingham; Worcester City A.G.; One Off jallery, Dover; Tabor Gallery, Canterbury; numerous group shows including Valker's Gallery, Woodstock Gallery, Kootenay Gallery, Canada, Festival de 'rovence, France, Minotaur Gallery, Toronto, Royal Academy, Rowley jallery, London. *Signs work:* "Clark." *Address:* Mingladon, Manns Hill, lossingham, Canterbury, Kent CT4 6ED.

**CLARK, Jean Manson,** R.W.S. (1972), hon. mem. N.E.A.C. (1981); artist n water-colour and oil; *b* Sidcup, Kent, 6 Aug., 1902. *m* Cosmo Clark, R.A. decd.). one *d.* *Educ:* Merton Court School, Sidcup. *Studied:* Sidcup School of \rt, R.A. Schools. *Exhib:* R.A.; retrospective exhbn. Bankside Gallery (June 983) including work by the late Cosmo Clark. Water-colours and oils in pri- ate collections. *Commissions:* ceiling painting: Woodford Green United Free :hurch; murals: Hadfield Hall, Cutlers' Hall, Sheffield (1954), Bankers' :learing House, Carpenters' Hall, London; three murals for Corpus Christi :hurch, Weston-super-Mare (1967). *Signs work:* "Jean Clark." *Address:* :hurch Lane Cottage, Shottisham, Woodbridge, Suffolk IP12 3HH.

**CLARK, John M'Kenzie,** D.A. (Dundee, 1950); N.D.D. (Painting) St. 1artin's (1956); artist in oil, water-colour, ink; winner of Punch scholarship; *b* )undee, 29 Nov., 1928. *Educ:* Harris Academy, Dundee. *Studied:* Dundee :ollege of Art (1945-50), Norwich Art College (1950-51), Hospitalfield Art :chool (1953), St. Martin's Art School (1955-56). *Exhib:* R.A., R.S.A., R.S.W., .S.A., R.G.I., United Soc. of Artists, one-man shows at Dundee, Edinburgh

# WHO'S WHO IN ART

(1960). Mem. Royal Glasgow Institute of Fine Art. *Work in collections:* City o
Dundee Permanent Collection (1961). *Publications:* work repro.: in Glad Mag
*Signs work:* "J. M'KENZIE CLARK." *Address:* 2 Birchwood Pl., Dundee DD
2AT.

**CLARK, Kenneth Inman Carr,** M.B.E. (1990), D.F.A. (Lond. 1948); artis
in ceramics; partner with Ann Clark, Kenneth Clark Pottery, Lewes; *b* 31 July
1922. *m* Ann Clark. one *s.* one *d. Educ:* Nelson College, N.Z. *Studied:* Slad
School of Fine Art (1945-48) painting, Central School of Art and Design (1949
under Dora Billington, ceramics, and G. Friend, engraving. *Exhib:* one-ma
shows, Piccadilly Gallery, Zwemmer Gallery, and many group shows i
England. *Work in collections:* Wellington, N.Z., Auckland, N.Z., Japan
*Publications:* Practical Pottery and Ceramics, Throwing for Beginners, Th
Potters Manual. *Signs work:* see appendix. *Address:* Merton House, Vicarag
Way, Ringmer, Lewes, E. Sussex BN8 5LA.

**CLARK, Norman Alexander,** R.W.S.; Royal Academy Schools Gol
Medallist and Edward Stott Scholar in Historical Painting (1931), Armitag
Bronze Medallist in Pictorial Design (1931), Landseer prize-winner in Mura
Decoration (1932), Leverhulme Scholar (1935); painter in oil and water-colour
*b* Ilford, Essex, 17 Feb., 1913. *m* Constance Josephine Barnard. one *d. Educ*
Bancroft's School, Woodford. *Studied:* Central School, London (1929), R.A
Schools (1930-35). *Exhib:* R.A., R.W.S. *Work in collections:* Harris Museum
and Art Gallery, Preston, Lancs., Imperial War Museum, and in private collec
tions. *Signs work:* "Norman Clark." *Address:* Mountfield, Brighton Rd
Hurstpierpoint, Sussex.

**CLARK, Peter Christian,** Oxford University Certificate of Fine Art; pro
fessional painter; *b* Bradford, Yorks., 19 Apr., 1950. *Educ:* Clifton Hous
School, Harrogate, H.M.S. Conway, Anglesey, N. Wales. *Studied:* Ruski
School of Drawing and Fine Art under Richard Naish, M.A. *Signs work:* "Pete
Clark" and "Christian Clark." *Address:* 40 Delancey St., London NW1.

**CLARK, Thomas Humphrey,** A.C.P., A.R.D.S.; artist in black and white
water-colour; *b* Manchester, 30 Jan., 1921. *m* Betty Whitley Clark. two *s. Educ*
Leeds Grammar School. *Studied:* Bradford Regional College of Art unde
Frank Lyle, A.T.D., Fred C. Jones, A.T.D., R.B.A. *Exhib:* Royal Cambria
Adademy. *Signs work:* "T. H. Clark." *Address:* Woodland Rise, Beemire
Windermere, Cumbria LA23 1DW.

**CLARKE, Edward,** M.A., R.A.S. (Cert.), B.A. (Hons.); figurative portrai
and landscape artist painting in oils and drawing in charcoal; *b* Hartlepool
1962. *Educ:* Manor Comprehensive School, Hartlepool. *Studied:* Clevelan
College of Art (1980-81), Sheffield Hallam University (1982-85), R.A. School
(1985-88). *Exhib:* R.A. Summer Exhbn. and R.A. Dip. Galleries, Londo
(1986, 1987, 1988), N.P.G., London (1988, 1991), Agnews, London (1990)
Gray A.G., Hartlepool (1994), Middlesbrough A.G. (1995). *Work in collec
tions:* various, including National Trust's Foundation for Art. *Signs work*

Edward Clarke." *Address:* 304 Catcote Rd., Hartlepool, Cleveland TS25 3EF.

**CLARKE, Geoffrey,** R.A., A.R.C.A.; artist and sculptor; *b* 28 Nov., 1924. *m* 947, Ethelwynne Tyrer. two *s. Educ:* Royal College of Art (Hons.). *Exhib:* ne-man shows: Gimpel, Redfern, Taranman, Yorkshire Sculpture Park and 'ravelling Retrospective. *Work in collections:* (stained glass) Coventry and .incoln Cathedrals, Taunton, Ipswich, Crownhill Plymouth; (sculpture) !oventry and Chichester Cathedrals; Cambridge (Churchill, Homerton, √ewnham), Exeter, Liverpool, Newcastle, Manchester and Lancaster Jniversities; Bedford, Chichester and Winchester Colleges. Other Principal ∕ork: Castrol House, Thorn Electric, Newcastle Civic Centre, Nottingham ºlayhouse, Culham Atomic Energy, Guard's Chapel, Birdcage Walk, Aldershot .andscape, St. Paul Minnesota, Majlis Abu Dhabi, York House, Warwick Jniversity. *Publications:* Symbols for Man by Peter Black. *Address:* Stowe Iill, Hartest, Bury St. Edmunds, Suffolk IP29 4EQ.

**CLARKE, Granville Daniel,** F.R.S.A.; City & Guilds 1st Class Hons. 1957), Full Tech. Cert. (1959); professional artist in water-colour and pencil; ∕Ieadowlands Trust - Scarlet Songs Publishing, Director; mem. Yorkshire ∕Vater-colour Soc.; environmental artist for: Sight Savers, Whale and Dolphin, ∕Vild Flower Conservation; multi-media lecturer, performer - Environmental ducation through The Arts, Kirklees (1992-97); *b* Keighley, Yorks., 26 Oct., 940. *Studied:* Barnsley College of Art (1955-60). Professional musician, Foggy Dew-O' (1965-76). *Exhib:* numerous one-man exhbns. since 1977, Iouse of Commons, London, major northern galleries, own Studio-Gallery, .aing at Mall Galleries since 1980, 'Barnsley to Bombay' - Round the World ∃xhbn. Work in collections worldwide. *Commissions:* English Nature, P.&O. !ruise Lines, various Fine Art publishers, TV art projects. *Publications:* ;ketches and Expressions (1991). *Address:* Huskar Cottage Studio, Silkstone !ommon, nr. Barsley, S.Yorks. S75 4RJ.

**CLARKE, Hilda Margery,** B.A. (Hons.), F.R.S.A.; artist in oils and other nedia; Director of 'The First Gallery'; *b* Manchester, 10 June, 1926. *m* ;eoffrey Clarke. two *s. Educ:* Eccles Secondary School. *Studied:* privately in ∕Ianchester (Master: L. S. Lowry) and Hamburg; Southampton College of Art 1960-65); Ruskin School Print Workshop, Oxford (1975); B.A. Southampton. ∃xhib: Tibb Lane, Manchester, Bettles Gallery, Ringwood; London Galleries: !amden Town, F.P.S., Buckingham Gate; Southampton City A.G., Hiscock ;allery, Southsea, New Ashgate, Farnham; one-man shows, Hamwic, ;outhampton, Westgate Gallery, Winchester, Southampton University; The ∃irst Gallery, Southampton, Turner Sims Concert Hall, Soton. *Work in collec-ions:* Southampton University of Southern Arts. *Publications:* catalogues for 'Two Memorable Men' (Crispin Eurich and L.S. Lowry); *touring exhbns:* 'Architect at Leisure" (Arthur Mattinson); "The Animated Eye" (Peter ∕Iarkey). *Signs work:* "H.M. Clarke." *Address:* The First Gallery, 1 Burnham !hase, Bitterne, Southampton SO18 5DG.

**CLARKE, Jeff,** A.R.E., N.D.D., Rome Scholarship (1956 - 58), British Inst Fund Scholarship; Visiting Tutor, R.A. Schools, Sunningwell Art School Oxford; painter and etcher; *b* Brighton, 1935. *Studied:* Brighton College of Ar (1952-56). *Exhib:* Oxford Bear Lane Gallery, Oxford Gallery, Museum o Modern Art Oxford, Christ Church Picture Gallery, R.E., R.A. Summer shows *Work in collections:* Ashmolean Museum, Oxford, Cambridge andReading Universities. Many private collections in Europe and U.S.A. *Signs work:* "Jeff Clarke". *Address:* 17 Newton Rd., Oxford OX1 4PT.

**CLARKE, Pat,** N.S., M.F.P.S., Surrey Dip. (1969); artist in water-colour oil, pastel; printmaker; Adult Education teacher, and special needs teacher (1970-80); *b* Banstead. *m* Peter Elliott. *Educ:* Reigate County School, Surrey and Hull University. *Studied:* Reigate Art School (1966-69). *Exhib:* Loggia Gallery, Gallery of Modern Art, London, Hereford City A.G., Rhyl Arts Centre etc; 35 one-woman shows, through Wales and England. Since 1984, join owner with husband of art gallery, Oriel y Odraig, Blaenau Ffestiniog, N Wales. *Publications:* To the Mountain (1994). *Clubs:* N.S., F.P.S. *Signs work* "Pat Clarke." *Address:* 4 Bryn Dinas, Rhiwbryfdir, Blaenau Ffestiniog Gwynedd LL41 4HD.

**CLARKE, Richard Cambridge,** B.A.(Hons.) (Open Univ.); water-colour artist; *b* Ilford, Essex, 1909. *m* 1939 Titia Faber (decd.). one *d. m* 1955 Ursula Davies (decd.). *m* 1987 Josephine Cox. *Educ:* Bishop's Stortford College (1921-26), Regent St. Polytechnic (part-time: 1937-38). *Exhib:* regularly at R.I (1951-67). *Publications:* various books illustrated for Longman, Heinemann etc.; 1993 book published by me of drawings, etchings and water-colours enti tled In Praise of Bishop's Stortford & Herts./Essex Border Country 1930-1980 Hon. Life-Mem. of Bishop's Stortford Art Soc. *Signs work:* "Richard C Clarke." *Address:* Saffron Cottage, 107 Ashdon Rd., Saffron Walden, Essex CB10 2AJ.

**CLARKSON, Jeff,** B.A., M.A.; landscape painter in oil and etching; *b* Cleethorpes, 26 June, 1949. *Studied:* Camberwell School of Art (1969-72) Hull Polytechnic (1988-90). *Exhib:* one-man shows: Colchester (1994), Hull (1991), Scarborough (1990), Bradford (1987); mixed shows: Halifax (1990) London (1973, 1974, 1980). *Work in collections:* Bradford University. *Signs work:* "J. CLARKSON." *Address:* Orchard Cottages, Hainton, Lincoln LN3 6LU.

**CLARYSSE, Maggy,** Dip. Brussels Academy of Art (1956); painter in oil water-colour, pastels, silk-screen printing; *b* Brussels, 21 Oct., 1937; married one *s. Educ:* Convent Sacre Coeur, Brussels. *Studied:* Brussels Academy of Art. *Exhib:* numerous exhbns. in U.K., France, Belgium. *Work in collections.* Bourne Gallery Reigate; private collections in U.S.A., Japan, Australia, S America. *Publications:* The Graphic Artist (1980). *Signs work:* "M. Clarysse." *Address:* 13 The Elms, Vine Rd., London SW13 0NF.

**CLATWORTHY, Robert,** R.A. (1973); sculptor; mem. Fine Art Panel o

National Council for Diplomas in Art and Design (1961-71); head of Fine Art, Central School of Art and Design (1970-75); *b* 1 Jan., 1928. *Studied:* West of England College of Art, Chelsea School of Art, The Slade. *Exhib:* Hanover Gallery (1954, 1956), Waddington Galls. (1965), Holland Park Open Air Sculpture (1957), Battersea Park Open Air Sculpture (1960, 1963), Tate Gallery British Sculpture in the Sixties (1965), Basil Jacobs Gallery (1972), British Sculpture '72, Burlington House, Diploma Galleries R.A. (1977), Photographer's Gallery (1981). *Work in collections:* Arts Council, Contemporary Art Society, Tate Gallery, V. & A., G.L.C.; Monumental Horse and Rider installed at 1 Finsbury Ave., EC2. (1984); portrait of Dame Elisabeth Frink purchased by N.P.G. (1985). *Address:* 1a Park St., London SE1.

**CLAUGHTON, Richard Bentley,** F.R.B.S.; sculptor; *b* London, 1917; married. one *s. Educ:* Woodford House School, Kent. *Studied:* Slade School (1946-49). Public commissions in London and provinces; Australia; Nigeria. *Exhib:* in galleries and open-air exhbns. in London and provinces; Holland and Lisbon. *Work in collections:* in Britain; Canada; Iraq and U.S.A. Former Director of Sculpture Studies, Slade School, University College, London. *Address:* Telham Lodge, Telham Lane, Battle, E. Sussex TN33 0SN.

**CLEMENT SMITH, Winifred May,** final diplomas in art subjects; artist in oil, water-colour and pastel; V.P. of Tunbridge Wells Art Club; *b* Tunbridge Wells, 26 Nov., 1904. *m* Clement Smith, architect. *Educ:* Tunbridge Wells. *Studied:* Regent St. Polytechnic, London. *Exhib:* S.W.A., R.I., R.O.I., R.P.S., and P.S., and provincial galleries. *Address:* The Priory, Tunbridge Wells, Kent TN1 1JJ.

**CLEMENTS, Jeff,** N.D.D. (1955), Fellow Designer Bookbinders; artist in acrylic, fine bookbinder; partner with Katinka Keus, Binderij Meridiaan, Amsterdam; formerly Dean, Faculty of Art and Design, University of theWest of England (to 1988); *b* Plymouth, 23 Feb., 1934. two *s. Educ:* Devonport High School for Boys. *Studied:* Plymouth College of Art (1950-55), Central School of Arts and Crafts (1956-57). *Exhib:* from 1955 Daily Express Young Artists to recent ones in the Netherlands. *Work in collections:* fine bindings in: Royal Library, V. & A., London; Royal Library, The Hague; The Museum of the Book, The Hague; Texas University; University of Indiana; Röhsska Museum, Sweden; The Keatley Trust; The John Paul Getty jr. Trust, etc.; paintings in private collections: Nice, London, Birmingham, Bristol, Exeter, Oxford, York, The Hague, Amsterdam, Washington D.C., etc. *Publications:* Book Binding (Arco, 1963), Ambachtelijk Boekbinden (Gaade, 1991). *Signs work:* see appendix. *Address:* Jan Luijkenstraat 38II, 1071 CR Amsterdam, Netherlands.

**CLEMENTS, Keith,** N.D.D., A.T.D., D.A.E., Ph.D.; painter, illustrator; designer, author, lecturer; *b* Brighton, 9 May, 1931. *m* Jackie Sinclair. one *s.* one *d. Educ:* Varndean Grammar School, Brighton. *Studied:* Brighton College of Art (1947-53), Birmingham School of Art Education (1964-65). *Exhib:* Alwin Gallery, Bloomsbury Workshop, R.A., R.E., Young Contemporaries,

Arts Council tours. *Work in collections:* Brighton Museum, University of Sussex. *Publications:* Henry Lamb: The Artist and his Friends (1985). *Signs work:* "Keith Clements." *Address:* 29 Meeching Rd., Newhaven, E. Sussex BN9 9RL.

**CLIFTON, David James,** A.R.C.A., M.A.; professor fine art; exhbn. artist, painter in water-colour and oil, mixed media; *b* Derby, 10 July, 1938. *Educ:* at private and public schools; sometime placed Truro's (Eton). *Studied:* Bournville School of Art (Ruskin Hall), Birmingham College of Art (1956-58), Royal College of Art (1958-61). *Publications:* Contemporary Situation; New Wave Writing; Poetry; Serious Matters; Existential Surreal Metaphysical Metaphor Ethic Image and Criterion. *Signs work:* "D. J. Clifton." Ref: no third party agent. *Address:* Flat 8, 63 Fountain Rd., Edgbaston, Birmingham B17 8NP.

**CLOUGH, Carolyn Stafford:** see STAFFORD, C. Carolyn.

**CLOUGH, Pauline Susan,** P.S. (1982); artist in pastel, acrylic and oil; *b* 16 Oct., 1943. *m* Peter Clough. one *s.* one *d. Educ:* Sharmans Cross High School. *Studied:* Bourneville School of Art, Birmingham (Phyllis Devey). *Exhib:* R.A., R.I., P.S., S.W.A., R.B.S.A. and many provincial galleries. *Work in collections:* Worthing Museum. *Clubs:* Council mem. Pastel Soc. *Signs work:* "P.S. Clough" and "Clough." *Address:* Sundown, 103 Allington Rd., Newick, Lewes, E. Sussex BN8 4NH.

**CLUTTERBUCK, Jan,** painter in water-colours; teacher of painting, Cassio College, Watford; Chairman, Women's International Art Club (1973-76); *b* Newton, Mass., 16 July, 1919. *m* Jeremy R. H. Clutterbuck. one *s.* one *d. Educ:* Greenbrier College, West Virginia. *Studied:* self-taught; studied printmaking at Harrow School of Art. *Exhib:* R.A., N.S., American Embassy. *Work in collections:* Gloucester Education Committee, Coventry Education Committee. *Clubs:* W.I.A.C. *Signs work:* "Jan Clutterbuck." *Address:* Penthands House, Sarratt, Herts. WD3 6BL.

**CLYNE, Henry Horne,** D.A.(Edin.); sculptor; Principal Lecturer i/c Sculpture Dept. (retd.); *b* Caithness, Scotland, 5 Mar., 1930. *m* Elaine Dunnett. one *s. Educ:* Edinburgh College of Art (1948-54); Harkness Fellow, U.S.A. (1959-61); IWCAT Tokoname, Japan (1986). *Exhib:* generally group shows and major Festivals (1954-66), and several one-man shows. *Work in collections:* University of Stirling (S.A.C.); University of East Anglia and Sainsbury Collection; IWCAT permanent collection (Japan); and many private collections in U.K., U.S.A., Europe and Japan. Awarded bronze medals, Bicentenaire, Haute Garonne; 1990 started "Sheepshapes", ceramic sheep individually hand-made. *Signs work:* "Henry H. Clyne" and see appendix. *Address:* Sunnymede, Horsebridge Rd., Kings Somborne, Stockbridge, Hants. SO20 6PT.

**CLYNE, Thora,** M.A.Hons. in Fine Art (1960); Special Prize (S.S.W.A., 1984); Anne Redpath Award (S.S.W.A., 1979); Andrew Grant postgrad. Scholarship and Travel Fellowship (1960-61); artist in oil, water-colour, pastel, pen and ink, lithography; *b* Wick, Caithness, 10 Nov., 1937. *m* G. Clemson, composer. *Educ:* Edinburgh University; Edinburgh College of Art (1955-61). *Exhib:* Lybster Gallery, Caithness (1993, 1995); group shows: Morrison Portrait Competition, Royal Scottish Academy (1991, 1995); Laing Landscape Competition (1991); Scotland's Gardens, Inverleith House, Edinburgh (1996); Braveart, Smith Gallery, Stirling (1996); 'Homage to Senefelder', Edinburgh Printmakers Workshop (1996); Society of Feline Artists, Patchings, Nottingham (1997); London Print Fair, Air Gallery (1997); S.O.F.A., Llewellyn Alexander, London (1997). *Work in collections:* Edinburgh Corporation Schools, Ross & Cromarty Educ. Authority, First Scottish-American Trust Co., Ltd., Gillies Bequest, R.S.A. *Commissions:* Portraits of cats. *Signs work:* "Thora Clyne." *Address:* Tillywhally Cottage, Milnathort, Kinross-shire KY13 7RN.

**COATE, Peter,** R.W.A., A.T.D., Chelsea Dip. (1950); painter in oil, water-colour, and teacher; Director, Mendip Painting Centre (1974-86); *b* Nailsea, Som., 9 Mar., 1926. *m* Margaret Bickerton (died 1978), one *s.* one *d. m* Pamela Somerville 1980. *Educ:* Sherborne. *Studied:* Chelsea under Robert Medley. *Exhib:* London Group, R.A., S.WL.A., R.W.A., R.O.I., many exhbns. in the west country, specialising in landscape, churches and other buildings in Somerset. *Work in collections:* R.W.A., Hertfordshire and Cumberland County Councils, Nuffield Foundation. *Signs work:* "Peter Coate." *Address:* The Manor Farm, Stone Allerton, nr. Axbridge, Somerset BS26 2NN.

**COATES, Thomas J.,** P.R.B.A., N.E.A.C., R.W.S., R.P.; awarded De Lazlo Medal, 1st and 3rd prizes in Sunday Times Water-colour Exhbns. (1988, 1989); painter of landscapes, townscapes and portraits in oil and water-colour; *b* 1941. *Studied:* Bournville and Birmingham Colleges of Art (1956-61), R.A. Schools (1961-64). *Exhib:* R.A., R.B.A., and many one-man shows including New Grafton Gallery. *Address:* Bladon Studio, Hurstbourne Tarrant, Hants. SP11 0AH.

**COBB, David,** P.P.R.S.M.A., R.O.I.; *m* Jean Main, Associate Fellow, Guild of Glass Engravers. *Signs work:* "DAVID COBB." *Address:* Woodis, Setley, Brockenhurst, Hants. SO42 7UH.

**COBURN, Ivor Basil,** D.A. (1955), N.D.D. (1956), A.R.U.A., F.S.B.A.; R.H.S. six Gold medals, two Grenfell; artist in water-colour and oil; *b* Belfast, 10 Apr., 1934. *m* Patricia. one *s.* three *d. Educ:* Grosvenor High School, Belfast. *Studied:* Belfast College of Art, Leeds College of Art, and University. *Exhib:* one-man shows: Belfast, Dublin, Newcastle, Londonderry, Glasgow, London, Belgium, France; group shows: London, Belfast, Brussels, Paris. *Work in collections:* U.S.A., Canada, France, Belgium, Holland, Australia, New Zealand, Israel, Sweden, England, Ireland, Scotland, Wales. *Clubs:* S.B.A. (Founder mem.). *Signs work:* "Ivor B. Coburn." *Address:* The Springs, 50 Megargy Rd., Magherafelt, Co. Londonderry BT45 5HP, N. Ireland.

**COCHRAN, Margi,** C.L.W.A.C. (1976), R.M.S. (1987), M.A.A. (1989);

artist in oil, pastel, water-colour and colour pencil; *b* Philadelphia, Pa., 30 Aug. 1925. *m* Arthur Oschwald, Jr. one *s*. one *d*. *Studied:* Philadelphia Museum School of Art (1945-47), Montclair Art Museum (1974-79). Teacher - private groups (1973-83). *Exhib:* 16 solo shows; many group shows; many juried shows, many awards, N.J., N.Y.C., Fla., Ga., Wash. D.C. International solo exhbn. (1995), Kirkleatham Old Hall Museum, Redcar, England. *Work in collections:* M.A.S.-F., Kirkleatham Old Hall Museum, Redcar. *Clubs:* C.L.W.A.C., R.M.S., M.A.A., M.A.S.-F., M.P.S.F.S. (Washington D.C.), G.M.A.S. *Signs work:* see appendix. *Address:* Box 483, Bernardsville, New Jersey 07924-0483, U.S.A.

**COCKER, Doug,** D.A., A.R.S.A., F.R.B.S.; sculptor; *b* Alyth, Perthshire, 1945. *m* Elizabeth. two *s*. one *d*. *Educ:* Blairgowrie High School. *Studied:* Duncan of Jordanstone, Dundee (1963-68). *Exhib:* R.S.A., Yorkshire Sculpture Pk., The British Art Show, Air Gallery London, Serpentine Gallery London, Fruitmarket Gallery, Edinburgh, Third Eye Centre, Glasgow. *Work in collections:* Arts Council, Scottish Arts Council, Contemporary Art Soc., Kelvingrove A.G., Glasgow, Peterborough A.G., Greenshields Foundation, Montreal, Leicester University, Hunterian A.G., Glasgow, Essex C.C., Staffs. C.C., M.M.A. Sarajevo. *Signs work:* "DOUG COCKER." *Address:* Lundie Mill, Lundie, Angus DD2 5NW.

**COCKRILL, Maurice,** artist in oil on canvas; *b* England, 1936; partner Helen Moslin. three *s*. *Studied:* Wrexham School of Art and University of Reading (1960-64). *Exhib:* one-man shows: Edward Totah Gallery (1984, 1985), Kunstmuseum, Düsseldorf (1985), Bernard Jacobson Gallery (1987, 1988, 1990, 1992, 1994, 1995), Retrospective '1974-94' Walker A.G. (1995) (illus. cat.), Galerie Clivage, Paris (1995), Annandale Galleries, Sydney (1995), Galerie Clivage, Paris (1997), Galerie Helmut Pabst, Frankfurt (1997), Royal West of England Academy (1998). *Work in collections:* A.C.G.B., Walker A.G., Unilever, B.M., Contemporary Art Soc., Centro Cultural Arte Contemporaneo, Polanco, Mexico, Kunstmuseum, Düsseldorf. *Signs work:* full signature on back. *Address:* 78b Park Hall Rd., London SE21 8BW.

**CODNER, Stephen Milton,** painter in oil, pastel, portrait, landscape, still life, etcher; *b* Clevedon, Som., 1952. *m* Carolyn Hamilton. three *d*. *Educ:* Bryanston School Dorset, Camberwell School of Art and Crafts, City and Guilds Art School. *Exhib:* R.A., R.P., R.W.A. *Signs work:* "S. M. CODNER" or "STEPHEN CODNER." *Address:* 23 Maplestead Rd., London SW2 3LY.

**COHEN, Bernard,** Slade Dip.; professional artist in painting and printmaking; Slade Professor and University of London Chair in Fine Art; Director of Slade School, U.C.L.; *b* London, 28 July, 1933. *m* Jean. one *s*. one *d*. *Studied:* Slade School of Fine Art (1951-54, Sir William Coldstream). *Exhib:* Gimpel Fils (1958, 1960), Hayward Gallery (1972 touring), Waddington Galleries (1972, 1974, 1977, 1979, 1981, 1990), Tate Gallery (1976), drawing retrospective Ben Uri (1994), 'Artist in focus', Tate Gallery (1995), and major group exhbns. worldwide. *Work in collections:* Arts Council, M.O.M.A. (N.Y.), Tate Gallery, V. & A., etc. *Signs work:* "Bernard Cohen" on works on paper only. *Address:* 80 Camberwell Grove, London SE5 8RF.

**COHEN, Mary,** artist in oil, pen and wash, water-colour; *b* London, 21 Nov., 1910. *m* Cdr. Kenneth Cohen, C.B., C.M.G., R.N. one *s.* one *d. Studied:* Florence, Slade under Prof. Tonks and Prof. Schwabe (1928-31), and Euston Road School. *Exhib:* Leicester Galleries Mixed Exhbns., R.A., R.B.A., N.E.A.C., London Group, Roland, Browse and Delbanco, New Grafton Gallery. *Work in collections:* National Trust, Whitworth, A.G. and private collections in Gt. Britain, France and U.S.A. *Signs work:* "Mary S. C." *Address:* 33 Bloomfield Terr., London SW1.

**COKER, Norman, Richard,** City & Guilds of London Inst. F.E.T.C. (1974), F.S.B.A. (1986); art teacher Adult Educ. Centres; artist in oil, lecturer; *b* Grays, Essex, 27 Jan., 1927. *m* Doreen Anne. *Educ:* Park Secondary School, Grays. *Studied:* Thurrock Tech. College. *Exhib:* Nairobi, Kenya (wild life), The McEwan Gallery, Scotland (British Flower Painters), The Veryan Gallery, Cornwall, Singapore, London, Amsterdam, The Frinton Gallery; one-man show at Beecroft Gallery, Westcliff-on-Sea (1991). *Work in collections:* many private collections worldwide including H.R.H. The Princess Anne, The Princess Royal, an equestrian portrait of H.R.H. with her horse Doublet. *Commissions:* James Last (orchestra leader) a painting of the Royal Albert Hall. *Publications:* work included in "The Encyclopedia of Flower Painting Techniques" by Sue Burton (Quarto, 1997); work in print with Rosentiel's, Chelsea, Medici, and Camden Graphics. Founder mem. S.B.A. *Signs work:* "Norman R. Coker." *Address:* "Tensing", Muckingford Rd., Linford, Stanford-le-Hope, Essex SS17 0RF.

**COLE, Sibylle (née Duijts),** R.B.S.A., F.R.S.A., L.F.A.C.; artist in oil, water-colour, etching, jewellery in silver and gold; *b* Amsterdam. *m* Boris N. Cole. two *s.* one *d. Studied:* art: Birmingham College of Art (B. Fleetwood-Walker, R.A.); jewellery and silversmithing: Jacob Kramer College (now Leeds College of Art). *Exhib:* R.A., and many art galleries; six solo shows. *Publications:* monograph on F.W. Elwell, R.A. *Signs work:* "Sibylle Cole (Duijts)." *Address:* 6 Wedgewood Grove, Roundhay, Leeds LS8 1EG.

**COLEBORN, Deanne,** A.R.C.A., R.E.; painter/etcher; *b* Worcs., 30 Dec., 1931. *m* Keith. six *d. Studied:* R.C.A. *Exhib:* R.A., R.E. *Signs work:* "DEANNE." *Address:* Downe Hall Farm, Downe, Kent.

**COLEBORN, Keith,** A.R.C.A., A.T.D., F.R.S.A.; until July 1976 principal, Ravensbourne College of Art and Crafts; regional art principal, N.W. Kent; principal, Bromley College of Art (1946-62); principal, Stourbridge School of Art (1937-40); principal, Wallasey School of Art (1940-46); *b* Portsmouth.*Address:* Downe Hall Farm, Downe, Kent.

**COLEMAN, Alan,** F.R.B.S. (1961), R.B.A. (1952), A.R.C.A. (1st Class, 1951); sculptor; *b* Croydon, Surrey, 1920. *m* Joan Bradley, M.B., C.H.B.,

M.R.C.Psych. D.P.M. three *s.* one *d. Studied:* Goldsmiths' College School of Art, R.C.A. *Address:* Derrysbourne, Wonersh, Guildford, Surrey GU5 0QZ.

**COLEMAN, Brian,** Mem. Pastel Soc.; painter in water-colour; Art Director/Graphic Designer, advertising; *b* Cheam, Surrey, 3 Sept., 1935. *m* Joan Coleman. *Educ:* Stoneleigh Secondary Modern. *Exhib:* Kingsmead Gallery, Bookham, Surrey. *Signs work:* "Brian Coleman." *Address:* 2 Sheraton Drive, West Hill, Epsom, Surrey KT19 8JL.

**COLEMAN, Christine,** A.N.S.P.S., A.B. (University of Chicago, 1946); sculptor in stone, wood and cement; *b* Joliet, Illinois, U.S.A., 22 Dec., 1925. *Educ:* Mary Ward Centre, London (1986-). *Exhib:* group shows in London. *Signs work:* "COLEMAN." *Address:* 24 Ladbrooke Gdns., London W11 2PY.

**COLLES, Dorothy Margaret Tyas,** Mem. Pastel Soc.;portrait painter in pastel and oil, drawings in pencil and chalk; *b* Cairo, 1917. *Educ:* Parsons Mead, Ashtead. *Studied:* Epsom Art School; Westminster Art School; St. Martin's School of Art. *Exhib:* P.S., R.P., R.A. Work in private collections. *Commissions:* mainly private families. *Publications:* Portraying Children; Christian Symbols Ancient and Modern with Heather Child. *Signs work:* "COLLES." *Address:* 70 Heath Rd., Petersfield, Hants. GU31 4EJ.

**COLLET, Ruth Isabelle,** artist in water-colour, mixed media, oil, linocut; *b* Royston, Herts., 15 June, 1909; married. three *d. Educ:* Bedales School, Petersfield, Hants. *Studied:* The Slade School of Fine Art (Prof. Henry Tonks, Wilson Steer), and later with Kathleen Brown and Marion Kratochurl. *Exhib:* one-man shows: Goupil Gallery, Gainsborough House, Suffolk, Ben Uri (2), English Speaking Gallery, Oxford, Annexe Gallery, Wimbledon, George Large Gallery, Redbourn, Sue Rankin Gallery, London; also many mixed exhbns. at Mall Gallery. *Work in collections:* Israel and Ben Uri, London. *Clubs:* Hesketh Hubbard Art Soc. *Signs work:* "Ruth Collet." *Address:* 13 Roy Rd., Northwood, Middx. HA6 1EQ.

**COLLETT, Paula,** B.A.(Hons.); public/community artist in textile/soft sculpture; workshop leader; *b* Wakefield, 16 July, 1969. *Educ:* Woodkirk High. *Studied:* Chelsea School of Art and Design (1989-92, Roger Hoare). *Exhib:* tree art: Oakwell Hall. *Work in collections:* Huddersfield Royal Infirmary, Airville Leisure Centre. *Signs work:* "P. Collett." *Address:* 11 Boldgrove St., Earlsheaton, Dewsbury, W. Yorks. WF12 8NA.

**COLLINGBOURNE, Stephen,** painter, sculptor; prize winner, R.S.A., and John Moores; teaches Edinburgh College of Art; *b* Dartington, 15 Aug., 1943. one *s.* one *d. Studied:* Dartington College of Art (1960-61); Bath Academy, Corsham (1961-64). *Exhib:* British Council, Malaya; Chapter, and Oriel, Cardiff; Camden Arts Centre, Zella 9, Fisher Gallery and Serpentine, London; Kettles Yard, Cambridge; MacRobert Arts Centre, Stirling; Third Eye Centre, Glasgow; City Art Centre, Edinburgh. *Work in collections:* Leicester A.G., Scottish and Welsh Arts Councils, Devon, Leicestershire and Hertford Educ. Authorities, City Art Centre, Edinburgh, Motherwell Council. *Commissions:*

Welsh Arts Council, Leicester University, Livingstone, Edinburgh. *Address:* Tofts, West Linton, Peeblesshire EH46 7AJ.

**COLLINGS, David,** Dip. (1969), A.T.D. (1972); artist in oil on board, canvas; teacher of mentally handicapped; *b* London, 1949. *Studied:* Redruth School of Art (1965-69), Berks. College of Education (1969-72). *Exhib:* widely in S.W. England, Brittany and Ireland. *Work in collections:* Contemporary Art Soc. *Clubs:* Newlyn Soc. of Artists. *Signs work:* "David Collings." *Address:* 3 Lyn Terr., Newlyn, Penzance, Cornwall.

**COLLINS, Michael,** Inter.Dip.A.C., N.D.D., A.T.D., S.G.F.A., F.S.A.I., F.R.S.A.; mixed media draughtsman/painter; schoolmaster; Head of Art Dept., Emanuel School, London (1974-95) (Assistant Art Master 1967-74); *b* New Malden, Surrey, 13 Mar., 1936. *Educ:* King's College School, Wimbledon. *Studied:* under E. M. Scales; and at Wimbledon School of Art (1962-65), Swansea College of Art (1965-66). *Exhib:* S.G.F.A., S.A.I. *Signs work:* see appendix. *Address:* 53 Lauderdale Drive, Petersham, Richmond, Surrey TW10 7BS.

**COLLINS, Peter Gerald,** A.R.C.A. (1950); artist in oil, water-colour, pen and ink; *b* London, 11 June, 1943. *m* Georgette Andreassi 1943. *Educ:* Willesden. *Studied:* Willesden School of Art, Hornsey School of Art, Royal College of Art. *Exhib:* by appointment in own studio. *Clubs:* Chelsea Arts. *Signs work:* "Peter Collins." *Address:* 7 Stanley Studios, Park Walk, Chelsea, London SW10 0AE.

**COMBES, Simon, Glenton,** S.WL.A. (1996); wildlife artist in oil; *b* Shaftesbury, Dorset, 20 June, 1940. *m* Susan Margaret Coutts. one *s.* one *d.* *Educ:* in Kenya .No formal art education. Took up painting after 14 year military career.; *Exhib:* three major exhbns. in U.S.A. *Work in collections:* Nature in Art. *Signs work:* "Simon Combes." *Address:* Laburnum Cottage, Bushley, Tewkesbury, Glos. GL20 6JB.

**CONLON, Elizabeth,** S.B.A.; self-taught part-time painter in oil, water-colour, egg tempera and embroidery;; *b* Dublin, 1938. *m* Norman Rogers. one *s.* one *d.* *Exhib:* anuually at S.B.A., R.S.M.A., R.O.I., etc. *Publications:* author and illustrator: Learn to Paint Flower Portraits in Water-colour. *Address:* 61 Orchard Ave., Poole, Dorset BH14 8AH.

**CONNER, Angela,** American Institute of Architects (Hons.) award, S.E.A. award; sculptor/painter in stone, bronze, water, light, wind; *b* London. *m* John Bulmer. one *d.* *Studied:* self taught; apprentice to Dame Barbara Hepworth. *Exhib:* solo shows: Lincoln Center, N.Y., Browse & Darby; mixed shows: Gimpel Fils Gallery, N.Y., Tryon Gallery, R.A. Summer Show, V. & A., Carnegie Museum of Modern Art, etc. *Work in collections:* Arts Council G.B., National Portrait Gallery, Museé de l'Armeé, Paris, Pittsburgh Museum of Modern Art, U.S.A., Jewish Museum, N.Y., Eton College, Chatsworth, House of Commons, etc.; private include Paul Mellon, Dr. Roy Strong, Lucien Freud, Lord Goodman, Crown Prince of Saudi Arabia, Princess Firyal of Jordan, Duke of Devonshire, Lord Sainsbury, Drue Heinz, Gunter Sachs, etc. Winner: competitions for Economist Plaza, St. James's London; Aston University; de Gaulle, Carlton Gardens London; Cambridge Market Sq., U.K.; Horsham Town Centrepiece, U.K.; Cosmic Cycle. *Signs work:* see appendix. *Address:* George and Dragon Hall, Mary Pl., London W11 4PL.

**CONNON, William John,** D.A. (1959), post-Dip. (1960); painter in oil, draughtsman; retd. lecturer in drawing and painting at Grays School of Art, Aberdeen; *b* Turriff, 11 Dec., 1929. *m* Margaret R. Mair. one *s.* one *d. Educ:* Turriff Academy. *Studied:* Grays School of Art under R. Henderson Blyth, R.S.A., Ian Fleming, R.S.A. *Exhib:* R.S.A., S.S.A., A.A.S., Aberdeen A.G., Artspace, Aberdeen. *Work in collections:* Aberdeen A.G., Scottish Arts Council, City of Edinburgh Art Centre, Royal Scottish Academy (Muirhead Bequest). *Signs work:* "wjconnon." *Address:* 8 Fonthill Rd., Aberdeen AB11 6UB.

**CONSTABLE, Richard Golding,** artist in gouache; *b* Lewes, 8 June, 1932. *m* Valerie Zelle. two *s.* four *d. Educ:* Marlborough College, Millfield School, Cambridge University. *Exhib:* London, Ipswich, Bath, Norwich, Lincoln, Woodbridge, Halesworth, Hereford, Spanish Biennale, Versailles, Singapore, W. Germany, Eire, Glasgow, New York, Cincinnati, Dubai, Al Ain, Abu Dhabi, Muscat. *Clubs:* Mem. Bath Soc. of Artists. *Signs work:* "R. Constable." *Address:* Courtfield, Norton sub Hamdon, Stoke sub Hamdon, Somerset TA14 6SG.

**CONTRACTOR, Dorab Dadiba,** N.S.; sculptor, artist, jeweller, designer; sculpture in wood, marble, stone, clay, plaster, school chalkstick, avocado stone, mango stone, tafua nut, betelnut and nutmeg. Also excels in pencil, pastel, pen and ink, water-colour and scraperboard; part-time instructor for creative art, sculpting in wood and stone, and modelling at several Adult Educ. Centres and technical colleges in the U.K. Employed by the Government of India in Archaeological Dept. to restore the famous rockcut sculptures of Ellora, Ajanta and Elephanta Caves; *b* Bombay, 13 Feb., 1929 into a Parsee Zoroastrian parents (naturalised British citizen). *Studied:* Sir J.J. School of Art, Bombay, and obtained Government of India Dip. in Modelling and Sculpture (1957). Won special awards for wood sculptures, Bombay State (1958-59). *Exhib:* group: Guggenheim Gallery, London (1970); joint: Central Library, Romford (1972), Euro Arts and Crafts, B'ham (1976), Mall Gallery, London (1978-81), Le Salon des Nations a Paris (1983); one-man shows: India House, London (1972), Woodstock Gallery, London (1975), Queen's Theatre, Hornchurch (1977), Central Library, Romford (1982), Kenneth More Theatre, Ilford (1988). *Work in collections:* H.R.H. Prince Philip, Duke of Edinburgh (Windsor Castle), H.M. The Queen (Buckingham Palace), H.M. The Queen Mother (Clarence House), the late Dame Barbara Hepworth (St. Ives, Cornwall), the late Henry Moore (in his collection). His works are very widely appreciated and regarded as collectors pieces for their uniqueness.They are in private collections of art connoisseurs throughout the world, and in public libraries, schools, hospitals and Town Hall, Romford. *Awards:* 'Premier Award' for the most outstanding work in miniature sculpture in school chalkstick, London (1969); 'Dennis Price Challenge Trophy' for the best wood sculpture, London (1970-78); silver medal for wood sculptures, London (1985-86). *Signs work:* "DORAB" or "D.C." *Address:* 10 Elizabeth House, Elvet Ave., Gidea Park, Essex RM2 6JU.

**CONWAY, Bryan,** S.Eq.A.; artist in oil and water-colour; *b* Derbyshire, 3 Jan., 1932; married. four *s. Educ:* Becket School, Nottingham. *Studied:* Arthur Spooner's studio and Nottingham College of Art. *Exhib:* Christie's of London annually, and many provincial galleries. *Publications:* work repro.: calendars British Coal, British Steel publications, numerous cards. *Signs work:* "Bryan Conway." *Address:* 14 Ellesmere Drive, Trowell, Nottingham NG9 3PH.

**CONWAY, Frances,** R.W.A.; painter in oil, conté, water-colour, collage; *b* Bristol. married. two *s.* two *d. Studied:* West of England College of Art, Bristol, under George Sweet, Robert Hurdle, Francis Hoyland, William Townsend. *Exhib:* England and France. *Work in collections:* Lord Bath's collection of Wessex Painters at Longleat; Royal West of England Academy. *Clubs:* R.W.A. *Address:* 37 Cornwallis Cres., Clifton, Bristol BS8 4PH.

**CONWAY, Jennifer Anne,** R.M.S. (1979), S.M. (1981), Dip.B.C.P.E. (1957); painter and miniaturist in water-colour and oils; *b* Brecon, Oct., 1935. *m* John F. Conway. one *s.* one *d. Educ:* Brecon Girls' Grammar School; Bedford College of Physical Education (1954-57). *Exhib:* R.A., Paris Salon, R.M.S., S.W.A., Mall Galleries, Westminster Gallery, Bankside Gallery, Woburn Abbey, Miniature Art Soc. Florida, Soc. of Miniature Painters, S and G, Washington, U.S.A.; one man shows: Brecknock Museum (1980, 1989), Lion House Gallery (1988), Hay (1991). *Work in collections:* Marchioness of Tavistock. *Publications:* work repro.: Welsh Crafts, Brecon 900 commemorative plate Royal Doulton, greetings cards, post cards, prints; illustrated book 'A Pocketful of Posies' by J. & J. Conway. *Signs work:* "J. Conway" and see appendix. *Address:* Copper Beech, Maescelyn, Brecon, Powys, Wales LD3 7NL.

**COOK, Christian Manuel,** N.D.D. (1965); artist in acrylic, gouache, pastel, charcoal, collage; lecturer in painting and drawing (Westminster Adult Educ. Service); *b* Grossenhain, Germany, 26 June, 1942. one *s. Educ:* Kent College, Canterbury. *Studied:* Camberwell School of Art (Robert Medley, Frank Auerbach, Frank Bowling, Patrick Proctor, Charles Howard). *Exhib:* Kingsgate Gallery, Hornsey Library (New Gallery), H.A.C. (Camden Arts Centre), City Literary Inst., Loggia Gallery. *Work in collections:* Westminster City Council. *Signs work:* "Christian Cook" or "C.M. Cook." *Address:* 77 Cumbrian Gdns., London NW2 1EH.

**COOK, David Albert,** wildlife artist in various media; paper sculptor; lecturer; has given workshops in Britain, America, Canada, Japan; Art Adviser to Historical Link Flanders-Kent; *b* Rochester, 18 Mar., 1940. *m* (1) Pauline Jean

# WHO'S WHO IN ART

Head (decd.). two *d*; (2) Anne Page. *Studied:* Medway College of Art and Regent St. Polytechnic. *Exhib:* S.WL.A., R.S.M.A. (Mall Galleries), Medici Gallery, and many one-man shows. works in numerous civic, corporate, educational and private collections. *Commissions:* through the Federation of British Artists or Medici Gallery. *Publications:* work repro.: greetings cards, prints, articles, techniques guides, instructional videos, books. Initiator and sponsor of the British Birds, Bird Illustrator of the Year P.J.C. Award for Individual Merit;*Signs work:* see appendix. *Address:* 85 Howdale Rd., Downham Market, Norfolk PE38 9AH.

**COOK, Ian David,** R.I., R.S.W. (1978); Post. Dip. Drawing and Painting (Glasgow 1973), Cargill Scholarship (1974); artist in gouache, oils, watercolour, teacher; *b* Paisley, 2 Mar., 1950. *m* Elaine. one *s. Educ:* Camphill High School, Paisley. *Studied:* Glasgow (1969-72, D. Ferguson, D. Donaldson). *Exhib:* R.G.I. since 1975, R.S.W. since 1978, Gallery 22 Dublin, Aitken and Dott (1980, 1981), Scottish Contemporary (1980), Herald Art Comp. (1981); one-man shows: Henderson's Gallery, Edinburgh (1981), Kelly Gallery, Glasgow (1979, 1981), Scottish Gallery (1984,1986): Scottish Arts Council award to Central Africa (1984). *Signs work:* "I.D. Cook." *Address:* Upper Flat, 3 Falside Rd., Paisley PA2 6JZ.

**COOK, Jennifer Martin,** N.D.D., A.T.D.; painter; *b* Preston, Lancs., 1942. *Educ:* Casterton School. *Studied:* Harris College, Preston (1960-65); Leicester College of Art (1965-66). *Exhib:* R.A. (1975, 1976, 1981, 1982, 1983); one-man shows: Mercury Gallery, London (1976, 1978), Leics. Museum and A.G. (1982); group shows: Yew Tree Gallery, Derbys., Oxford Gallery, Gallery on the Green, Lexington, Mass., U.S.A. *Work in collections:* Middlesbrough, Leic., Oxfordshire. *Publications:* work repro.: greetings cards for Aries Design and Medici Soc. *Signs work:* "Jenny Cook." *Address:* 17 Brookhouse Ave, Leicester LE2 0JE.

**COOK, Richard,** Dip.A.D. (Painting), M.A.(R.C.A.) Painting; artist; *b* Cheltenham, 31 Oct., 1947. one *s. Educ:* Salesian College, Oxford. *Studied:* St. Martin's School of Art (1966-70), R.C.A. (1970-73). *Exhib:* House Gallery, London (1981), Hayward Gallery, London (1976, 1980), Artists Market, London (1976-80), Serpentine Gallery, London (1987), Odette Gilbert Gallery, London (1989, 1991), Austin/Desmond (1995, 1997). *Work in collections:* B.M., Arts Council, Manchester City A.G. *Signs work:* "Richard Cook." *Address:* 13 North Corner, Newlyn, Penzance, Cornwall TR18 5JG.

**COOK, Richard Peter,** R.B.A., Dip.A.D. Maidstone (1971), Post Grad. Royal Academy Schools (1975), A.T.C. (1977), R.B.A. (1978), E.T. Greenshield Travelling Scholarship (1972), Richard Ford Spanish Scholarship (1981); landscape and portrait painter in oil, water-colour, gouache; *b* Grimsby, 27 Feb., 1949. *m* Christine. two *d. Educ:* Grimsby College of Art, Maidstone College of Art (1968-71), Royal Academy Schools (1972-75). *Exhib:* one-man show, R.A. Schools (1980); R.B.A. (1977-); R.A. Summer Shows (1975-81,

1983, 1993); Art in Action (1988-93); N.E.A.C.; Royal Portrait Soc.; N.P.G. in 1984 John Player Award Show; Singer & Friedlander Water-colour Exhbns. and commercial galleries. *Work in collections:* in U.K. and overseas. *Signs work:* "Richard P. Cook." *Address:* 17 Windlesham Gdns., Brighton BN1 3AJ.

**COOKE, Jean,** R.A., N.D.D., R.B.A.; painter; lecturer, Royal College (1965-74); *b* London, 18 Feb., 1927. *m* John Bratby. three *s.* one *d. Educ:* Blackheath High School. *Studied:* Central School of Arts and Crafts, Goldsmiths' College of Arts, Camberwell School of Art, City and Guilds, Royal College. *Exhib:* one-man show: Farnham (1962, 1964, 1973), Establishment (1963), Leicester Gallery (1964), Bear Lane, Bladon Gallery (1966), Phoenix (1970), New Grafton (1971); mixed show: R.A., Zwemmer, London Group, R.B.A., Arts Council, Young Contemporaries, Royal College of Art, Upper Grosvenor, Arundel, Furneaux (1968), Agnew (1974). *Work in collections:* R.A., R.C.A., Tate. *Signs work:* "Jean E. Cooke." *Address:* 7 Hardy Rd., Blackheath, London SE3.

**COOKE, Stanley,** artist in oil and water-colour; *b* Mansfield, Notts., 11 Jan., 1913. *m* Anne M. Clayton (decd.). one *s. Educ:* King Edward School, Mansfield. *Studied:* Mansfield School of Art (1924-32) and The Press Art School. *Exhib:* R.A., R.I., R.O.I., Britain in Water-colours exhbns., provinces; one-man shows at Drian Galleries, London and Mansfield Art Gallery. *Work in collections:* Quarry at Mansfield, Mansfield Art Gallery. *Publications:* work repro.: in Apollo, Arts Review and greetings cards. *Signs work:* see appendix. *Address:* Broadlands, Grasmere Cl., Guildford GU1 2TG.

**COOKSON, Dawn,** R.B.S.A. (1974); artist of portraiture, still-life, flower and landscape paintings in oil, tempera, pastel and water-colour; *b* B'ham, 11 June, 1925. *Educ:* Westonbirt School, Glos. *Studied:* Birmingham College of Art (1943-48, B. Fleetwood-Walker, R.A.), Accademia di Perugia, Italy (1954-56), Nerina Simi Studio, Florence (1955-58), and under Pietro Annigoni, Florence (1958-68). *Exhib:* R.P., P.S., R.B.S.A., B'ham Water-colour Soc., Fosseway Glos. bi-annually; one-man shows: Lygon Arms and Dormy House, Broadway, Worcs. (1972-82-85), Guildhouse, Stanton, Glos. (1976-79), Reade's Gallery, Aldeburgh, Suffolk (1977). *Work in collections:* throughout G.B., Europe and Overseas. *Clubs:* V.P. Birmingham Water-colour Soc. *Signs work:* "Dawn Cookson." *Address:* Quiet Place, Lifford Gdns., Broadway, Worcs. WR12 7DA.

**COOKSON, Delan,** F.S.D.C., Gold Medal (Vallauris, 1974), Churchill Fellow (1966); Senior Lecturer in ceramics at Buckinghamshire College of Higher Education; *b* Torquay, 13 Sept., 1937. *m* Judith. two *s. Educ:* Bournemouth School. *Studied:* Bournemouth College of Art, Central School of Arts and Crafts. *Exhib:* Oxford Gallery, British Crafts Centre, Craftsman Potters Assoc., Design Centre, Midland Group Gallery, Whitworth Art Gallery, New Craftsman, St. Ives; one-man shows: Salix, Windsor, Bohun Gallery, Henley and Galerie an Cross, St. Martin, Cologne. *Publications:* Ceramic

Review, Studio Porcelain and Studio Ceramics by Peter Lane. *Clubs:* Cornwall Crafts Assoc., C.A.C. Index Member. *Address:* Lissadell, St. Buryan, Penzance, Cornwall TR19 6HP.

**COOLIDGE, John,** A.B. (Harvard University, 1935), Ph.D. (New York University, 1948); director, Fogg Art Museum (1948-68); Prof. of Fine Arts, Harvard University (1955-85); *b* Cambridge, Mass., 16 Dec., 1913. *m* Mary Welch Coolidge. one *d. Educ:* Groton School, Harvard and New York Universities. *Publications:* Mill and Mansion (Columbia University Press, 1943); Patrons and Architects (University of Texas Press, 1990). *Address:* Fogg Art Museum, Quincy St. and Broadway, Cambridge, Mass.

**COOMBS, Jill,** F.S.B.A.; 3 Gold Medals (R.H.S.); botanical illustrator in water-colour; teacher, Chelsea Physic Garden - one course annually; *b* Horsham, 1935. *m* Bernard Coombs. one *s.* one *d. Educ:* High School for Girls, Horsham. *Studied:* West Sussex College of Art (1952-55), botanical illustration under Mary Grierson at Flatford (1976-79). *Exhib:* Kew Gdns. Gallery, National Theatre, R.H.S., Broughton Gallery, Arundel Festival, S.B.A. *Work in collections:* U.S.A., Australia, Japan, U.K. *Publications:* illustrated: Plant Portraits by Beth Chatto (J.M. Dent), Herbs for Cooking and Health by C. Grey Wilson (Collins); illustrated for: Country Life, Curtis Botanical Magazine, Flora of Iraq, Flora of Qatar, Flora of Egypt. *Signs work:* "Jill Coombs." *Address:* Weald House, Handford Way, Plummers Plain, Horsham, W. Sussex RH13 6PD.

**COOPER, Constance Mary,** S.W.A., F.R.S.A.; painter in oil; *b* Shoreham, Kent, 2 Nov., 1905. *m* D.G. Cooper. one *d. Educ:* privately. *Studied:* Croydon College of Art. *Exhib:* Mall Galleries, various London and provincial galleries, Australia, America. *Signs work:* "Constance Cooper." *Address:* 35 Shirley Pk. Rd., Croydon CR0 7EW.

**COOPER, Eileen,** artist in oil and works on paper, prints; *b* Glossop, 1953. *m* M. Southward. two *s. Studied:* Goldsmiths' College and R.C.A. (1971-77). *Exhib:* numerous solo and group shows. *Work in collections:* Arts Council, various museums. *Signs work:* "Eileen Cooper" on reverse. *Address:* c/o Jason Rhodes Gallery, 4 New Burlington Pl., London W1X 1SB.

**COOPER, Emmanuel,** potter stoneware and porcelain, writer and broadcaster; co-editor Ceramic Review; *b* Derbyshire, 12 Dec., 1938. *Educ:* Tupton Hall Grammar School, Derbyshire. *Exhib:* Contemporary Applied Arts, London, many other one-man and mixed exhbns. here and abroad. *Work in collections:* V. & A. *Publications:* A Handbook of Pottery, A History of Pottery (Longman); Taking up Pottery (Arthur Barker); New Ceramics (with E. Lewenstein); Pottery (Macdonalds); A Potters Book of Glaze Recipes (1979); A History of World Pottery (Batsford, 1980). Contributes art criticism to Time Out, Tribune, etc. *Signs work:* see appendix. *Address:* 38 Chalcot Rd., London NW1 8LP.

**COOPER, Josephine Mary,** S.M. (1974), R.M.S. (1983), U.A. (1975),

S.W.A.(1988); Silver Medallist, Paris Salon (1974), Prix Rowland (1977); artist in oil and water-colour, also drypoint engravings and monotypes; *b* Brighton, 8 Aug., 1932. *m* Tom Cooper. one *s*. one *d*. *Studied:* St. Albans School of Art under Kathleen Pargiter; Mid-Herts. College of Further Education under Kenneth Haw; Hertfordshire College of Art and Design under Peter Jacques; Will Raymont, privately. *Exhib:* R.M.S., U.A., S.M., R.I., R.S.M.A., R.B.A., Laing, S.G.A., Britain in Water-colour, Bilan de l'Art Paris and Quebec, Liberty of London, Medici Gallery, R.A. Summer Exhbn. (1980-85); one-man shows throughout mid-Herts area, also Liberty of London. *Publications:* included in 20th Century Marine Paintings. *Clubs:* Welwyn Garden City Art, Hertford Art Soc. *Signs work:* "Jo Cooper" and "JMC" (miniatures dated). *Address:* 27 Parkfields, Welwyn Garden City, Herts. AL8 6EE.

**COOPER, Julian,** B.A.(Hons.) Fine Art; painter in oil, water-colour, pastel; *b* Grasmere, 10 June, 1947. *m* Linda. *Educ:* Heversham Grammar School. *Studied:* Lancaster Art College (1963-64), Goldsmiths' College (1964-69), Boise Travelling Scholarship (1969-70). *Exhib:* London Group, Serpentine Gallery, J.P.L. Fine Art, Paton Gallery, V. & A., Laing A.G., University of Durham. *Work in collections:* A.C.G.B., Laing A.G., Bolton A.G., Lancaster University, Northern Arts, I.L.E.A., Abbot Hall A.G., Reuters, Unilever, Pentagram, Davy Offshore Modules, Ferguson Industrial Holdings. *Publications:* work repro.: book cover for Fleur Adcock's Under Loughrigg. *Signs work:* "Julian Cooper." *Address:* 100 Lake Rd., Ambleside, Cumbria LA22 0DB.

**COOPER, Paul Anthony,** N.D.D. (1951), F.R.B.S.; sculptor in all traditional and modern materials including precious metals and stones; *b* Wool, Dorset, 23 May, 1923. *m* Audrey Beryl Carnaby, A.R.C.A. one *d*. *Studied:* Poole College of Art (1939-41), Goldsmiths' College, London (1948-51), Lincoln College (1958). *Exhib:* R.A., Covent Garden London, Scone Palace Perth, R.I.B.A. *Work in collections:* Oxford City Educ. Authority, Lincoln Educ. Authority, and places open to the public at Bond St., Westminster, City of London, Thorpe Tilney, Lincoln and Denton, Grantham; private collections in this country and in Holland, Israel, U.S.S.R.; ecclesiastical work in churches in England, Westminster Abbey, Wales and the Falkland Islands. *Signs work:* "Paul Cooper." *Address:* Quarr Hill Cottage, Wool, Dorset.

**COOPER, William Alwin,** R.W.A.(1973), Artist Chairman (1993-96), Sherborne School (1952-83), Lecturer, Bristol University Extra Mural Dept. (1983-86); artist in oil and collage; *b* Merthyr Tydfil, 2 June, 1923. *m* Dorothy Tustain, G.R.S.M. one *s*. two *d*. *Educ:* Westminster School, Corpus Christi College, Cambridge. *Exhib:* one-man shows: Drian Gallery (1971), Albany Gallery, Cardiff (1972), Hambledon Gallery, Blandford, Pentagon Gallery, Stoke on Trent (1977), St. John's, Smith Sq. (1986), Rona Gallery, R.W.A.(1988), Bloomsbury Workshop Gallery (1994); group shows include:

R.A., N.E.A.C., UNESCO, New York; Westward TV Open (Prizewinner), South West Open (Prizewinner) 1991. *Work in collections:* Royal West of England Academy, Bryanston School, Staffordshire Educ. Com., Welsh Development Corporation, Sherborne School and various public and private collections. *Publications:* illustration in History of Corpus Christi College, Cambridge. *Signs work:* "Cooper." *Address:* Elizabeth House, Long St., Sherborne, Dorset DT9 3BZ.

**COOTE, Michael Arnold,** painter in oils, water-colour, acrylic, oil and soft pastel, charcoal, pencil; Company Director - Lithographers; Freeman of the City of London (1977); *b* London, 1939. *m* Anita Davies. two *s.* one *d. Studied:* mainly self-taught; Sir John Cass (sculpture and life class). *Exhib:* P.S., R.O.I., Mall Galleries, Alpine Gallery, many provincial galleries including John Noott Gallery. *Work in collections:* London, Bath, America, Germany, Italy. *Signs work:* see appendix. *Address:* 1 Tadlows Cl., Upminster, Essex RM14 2BD.

**COPELAND, Lawrence Gill,** Cranbrook Medal, U.S. State Dept. Purchase Award, Y.S.C. First Prize, National Merit Award, Craftsmen, U.S.A.; designer in metal; prof., Art Dept., City College of City University of New York (retd.); *b* Pittsburgh, Pa., U.S.A., 12 Apr., 1922. *m* Mary Cuteri. two *s.* one *d. Educ:* Ohio State Univ., Cranbrook Academy of Art, Univ. of Stockholm, Univ. of Paris. *Studied:* Stockholm (1947-48, Baron Erik Fleming), Paris (1948-49, Emeric Gomery). *Work in collections:* National Gallery, Washington, D.C. *Address:* 5 Peach Tree La., Warwick, N.Y. 10990, U.S.A.

**COPNALL, John,** painter in acrylics and oils; *b* Slinfold, Sussex, 16 Feb., 1928. *Studied:* R.A. Schools (1950-55). *Exhib:* one-man shows: Piccadilly Gallery, Bear Lane (Oxford), Stone Gallery (Newcastle), I.C.A. (London), Ikon (Birmingham), Sala Vayreda (Barcelona), Wolfgang Gurlitt (Munich), Boisserée (Cologne), Universa-haus (Nüremberg), Institut für Auslandsbeziehungen (Stuttgart), Aberdeen Museum, Demarco (Edinburgh), Galeri Mörner (Stockholm), Oxford Gallery, Oxford, Windsor Art Centre, Austin/Desmond (London), Reeds Wharf London, De La Warr Pavilion Bexhill; mixed shows: John Moores of Liverpool, R.A., Art Spectrum, London, Wildenstein, Hayward 72, Whitechapel Open. *Work in collections:* Bristol and York Universities, A.C.G.B., Aberdeen Museum, Ateneum Museum, Helsinki, Sara Hildred Museum, Tampere, Finland. *Publications:* work repro.: Studio International, Artist, Arts Review. *Signs work:* "john copnall" or "copnall." *Address:* 9 Fawe St. Studios, London E14 6PA.

**COPPINGER, Sioban,** B.A.Hons. (1977), A.R.B.S. (1991); sculptor in bronze, concrete and re-constituted stone; *b* 20 May, 1955. *Educ:* New Hall School, Boreham, Essex. *Studied:* Bath Academy of Art (1975-77). *Exhib:* 1993: The Bronze Bird, Gallery Pangolin, Glos.; R.B.S. Gallery, Chelsea Harbour Sculpture '93, London; 1st Royal West of England Academy Open Sculpture Exhbn. Bristol. Work in public places: Man and Sheep on a Park Bench, Rufford Country Park, Nottingham; The Gardener and the Truant Lion

(Chelsea Flower Show 1986); Stoke Mandeville Station, Bucks.; Sundial (Gateshead Garden Festival 1990); Templecombe Station, Somerset; The Birmingham Man, Chamberlain Sq., Birmingham. *Signs work:* "S. Coppinger." *Address:* Riverside Works, West Mills, Newbury, Berks. RG14 5HY.

**CORBETT, Peter George,** B.A. Hons. (1974); artist in oil on canvas, pencil; *b* Rossett, N. Wales, 13 Apr., 1952. *Educ:* Liverpool College. *Studied:* Liverpool College of Art and Design (1970-71, Maurice Cockrill), Manchester Regional College of Art and Design (1971-74, Brendan Neiland, Keith Godwin). *Exhib:* Centre Gallery (1979), Acorn Gallery, Liverpool (1985, 1988), Major Merseyside Artists, Liverpool (1988), Marie Curie Art (Open), Albert Dock, Liverpool (1988), Surreal Objects Exhbn. Tate Gallery, Liverpool (1989), Merkmal Gallery "Alternative 17" Liverpool (1991), Manchester Academy 136th Exhbn. (Open) 1995, The Three Month Gallery, Liverpool (1996), Academy of Arts, Liverpool (1997); one-man shows: Southport Arts Centre (1980), Liverpool Playhouse (1982), Pilgrim Gallery, Liverpool (1984), Royal Institution, Liverpool (1986), Church Gallery, London (1988), Anglican Cathedral (1988), Senate House Gallery, Liverpool University (1993), Atkinson Gallery, Southport (1995); two-man shows: Liverpool University (1983, 1990), Acorn Gallery, Liverpool (1985), Royal Liver Bldg., Pier Head, Liverpool (1991). *Work in collections:* Liverpool, London, Manchester, America and Australia. Founder Mem. Chair, Merseyside Visual Arts Festival (1989-90). *Signs work:* see appendix. *Address:* Flat 4, 7 Gambier Terr., Hope St., Liverpool L1 7BG.

**CORETH, Mark Rudolf,** sculptor in bronze (wildlife); *b* London, 5 Sept., 1958. *m* Seonaid. one *s.* two *d. Educ:* Ampleforth College. *Exhib:* Sladmore Gallery, London W1. (1986, 1990, 1992,1994,1996), Galerie la Cymaise, Paris (1993, 1995,1997), Sydney (1996), Geneva (1997). *Commissions:* life-size Cheetah Group, Dubai; Drinking Fountains at Globe Theatre and National History Museum. *Clubs:* Cavalry and Guards.*Address:* Stowell House, Stowell,Sherborne, Dorset DT9 4PE.

**CORNELL, David,** F.R.S.A. (1970), F.R.B.S. (1971), V.P.S.P.S. (1977), P.S.S.M.C.E. (1995); sculptor in bronze; *b* Enfield, 18 Sept., 1935. *m* Geraldine. four *s. Educ:* Essendene. *Studied:* Central School of Art, London and Harrow School of Art (1952-62, Friend, Fryer and Philip Turner) Engraving and Sculpture; Academy of Fine Art, University of Pennsylvania (1968-70, Robert Beverley Hale) Anatomy. *Exhib:* London: R.A., Mall Galleries, Guildhall, R.B.S. Hall Place, Pavlova Soc., Park Walk Galleries, Plazzotta Studio, Edith Grove Gallery, Harrods; Iberian Bronze Gallery, London and Dublin, Newmarket Gallery, Newmarket, Royal Fine Art, Tunbridge Wells, Armstrong-Davis Gallery, Arundel, Scone Palace Scotland, English Gallery, Beverly Hills, U.S.A., L.C.A. Chelsea, Royal West of England Academy, Bristol, Alwin Gallery, Tunbridge Wells. *Work in collections:* Wellcome Foundation, London. Recent works include portrait of Princess

Diana and Queen Mother. *Commissions:* Life-size: Sir Arthur Conan-Doyle, numerous coins for world mints. *Signs work:* "David Cornell." *Address:* Barcombe Manor, Innhams Wood, Crowborough, E. Sussex TN6 1TE.

**CORNWELL, Arthur Bruce,** S.G.F.A.dip.(1947); illustrator in gouache, oil, water-colour, indian ink; *b* Vancouver, B.C., 11 Feb., 1920. *m* Peggy Brenda Huggins. one *s. Educ:* Palms Public School, and Page Military Academy, California. *Studied:* Art Centre School, Los Angeles, Regent St. Polytechnic, London, Heatherly's, London, Academy Julien, Paris. *Exhib:* R.A., N.E.A.C., S.M.A., S.G.F.A., Sunderland Gallery, Bolton Gallery. *Work in collections:* Diploma Gallery, R.A. Stott Bequest, R.A., The Coaster. *Publications:* The Ship's Crew; work repro.: Yachting Monthly, Macmillan teach-visuals. *Signs work:* see appendix. *Address:* Westways, 132 Eastcote Rd., Ruislip, Middx. HA4 8DU.

**CORSELLIS, Jane,** N.E.A.C., R.W.A., R.W.S.; artist in oil, water-colour, etching, lithography; *b* Oxford, 1940. two *s. Studied:* Byam Shaw School of Art (Maurice de Sausmarez, Bernard Dunstan, R.A., Peter Greenham, R.A.). *Exhib:* R.A., R.B.A., N.E.A.C., R.W.A., R.W.S.; one-man shows: Hong Kong, Ottawa, Kuala Lumpur, Upstairs Gallery, R.A. London (1985, 1986), New Academy Gallery, London (1988, 1990, 1992, 1994). *Work in collections:* Canada, U.S.A., Italy, France, Malaysia, Singapore and U.K. *Commissions:* Freshfields. *Publications:* Painting Figures in Light (Phaidon and Watson Guptil, N.Y.). *Clubs:* Chelsea Arts; Arts Club, Dover St. *Signs work:* "Corsellis." *Address:* 8 Horbury Mews, London W11 3NL; Cwm-yr-Eglwys, Pembrokeshire, Wales.

**COSMAN, Milein,** Slade Diploma Fine Art; painter, graphic artist; *b* Gotha. *m* Hans Keller. *Educ:* Düsseldorf; International School, Geneva. *Studied:* Slade School. *Exhib:* one man shows: Berkeley Galleries, Matthiesen, Molton Gallery, City of London Festival, Camden Arts Centre, Aldeburgh Festival, Stadtmuseum, Düsseldorf. *Work in collections:* e.g. N.P.G., R.C.M., V. & A., British Academy, Cardiff University. *Publications:* Musical Sketchbook (Bruno Cassirer, Faber & Faber, 1957), Stravinsky at Rehearsal (Dobson, 1962), Strawinsky Dirigiert (Ullstein, 1962), Stravinsky Seen and Heard (Toccata Press, 1982); books illustrated: Penguin Music Magazine, A Composer's Eleven (Cardus, Cape, 1975), etc; work repro.: Radio Times and other national and foreign press, art and musical magazines. Series of Educational Programmes on Drawing for ITV. *Address:* 3 Frognal Gdns., Hampstead, London NW3.

**COTTINGHAM, Grenville George,** R.S.M.A.(1988), R.B.A.(1989); painter in oil, water-colour, acrylic; *b* Exeter, 16 Apr., 1943. *m* Lucy June. *Educ:* Exeter School. *Studied:* Exeter College of Art (1960-63), Liverpool College of Art (1963-64). *Exhib:* R.A, R.S.M.A., R.B.A., R.I., Bonhams; one-man shows, Hallam Gallery, SW14 (1989), Bruton St. Gallery (1994), Barnes Gallery (1996). *Work in collections:* P. & O., Marine Soc., 2nd Batt. Royal

Fusiliers, R.N. Reserve (London Division), Royal Artillery, Woolwich, London Mutual Insurance, Securities Investment Board. *Publications:* Seafarers' Sketchbook (Bartholomew Press), You Can Paint; work repro.: various ships of the P. & O. passenger fleet. *Clubs:* Wapping Group of Artists. *Signs work:* "Grenville Cottingham." *Address:* 83 Kidbrooke Grove, London SE3 0LQ.

**COTTON, Alan,** N.D.D., A.T.D.(B'ham), F.R.S.A., M.Ed.; painter in oil, water-colour and pastel; works on art films for television; Director, Devon and Exeter Art Centre, Executive Com., Devon Arts Forum, Arts Advisory Com., University of Exeter; *b* Redditch, 8 Oct., 1937. *m* Patricia Esme. two *s.* two *d. Educ:* Redditch County High School. *Studied:* Redditch School of Art, Bournville College of Art, B'ham College of Art, Universities of B'ham and Exeter (Research Fellow). *Exhib:* over 40 one-man shows in U.K., Canada, France and the U.S.A. including Hammer Galleries N.Y. (1993). *Work in collections:* City of Exeter A.G., City of Plymouth A.G., West Country Television, Royal Marines, Lympstone, Universities of Southampton and Exeter, etc. *Publications:* Learning and Teaching through Art and Crafts (Batsford). Represented by: David Messum Galleries since 1983. *Clubs:* Dover St. Arts, University of Exeter Staff Club. *Signs work:* "Alan Cotton." *Address:* Brockhill Studio, Colaton Raleigh, nr. Sidmouth, Devon EX10 0LH.

**COULING, Paula,** S.W.A. (1993); landscape painter in acrylic;*b* Birmingham. *m* Robert H. Couling. two *s.* No formal art training. *Exhib:* S.W.A. Westminster Gallery; solo shows: Christchurch. *Publications:* greetings cards by the Medici Soc. *Clubs:* Romsey Art Group, Hengist Group of Artists. *Signs work:* "Paula Couling." *Address:* 201 Salisbury Rd., Burton, Christchurch, Dorset BH23 7JT.

**COULOURIS, Mary Louise,** A.R.E. (1973); Dip. A.D. (London) (1961); Post Grad. Scholarship, Slade School (1962); French Government Scholarship (1963); Churchill Fellowship in U.S.A. and Mexico (1993); Mem. Printmakers Council; artist and printmaker; *b* New York, 17 July, 1939. *m* Gordon Wallace. one *s.* one *d. Educ:* Parliament Hill School. *Studied:* Slade School, London University (1958-62) under Antony Gross; Ecole des Beaux Arts, Paris (1963-64); Atelier 17, Paris (1963-64) under William Hayter. *Exhib:* R.A. (1966, 1971, 1972, 1973); one-man shows: London, Oxford, Paris, Aberdeen, Glasgow, Athens. Artists Exchange: Athens for Glasgow Year of Culture (1990). Sainsbury Wine Label Competition Winner (1997). *Work in collections:* Bibliotheque Nationale, Paris, New York Public Library, Nuffield Trust, Trinity College, Oxford, Bank of Scotland, Edinburgh District Council, Hambros Bank, Sainsbury PLC. *Commissions:* New Scottish Poetry Library; mural: British Rail (1985); print: British Healthcare Arts (1993). *Signs work:* "Mary Louise Coulouris." *Address:* 5 Strawberry Bank, Linlithgow, West Lothian EH49 6BJ.

**COULSON, Nancy Diana,** sculptor stone, marble, clay, wood, bronze; subjects: animals, portrait heads in terracotta, clay for bronze; *b* Kenilworth, 1926.

*m* Robert Coulson. two *s.* one *d. Educ:* Kingsley School. *Studied:* Leamington Spa, Chelsea Art School (1946-48), Chelmsford (Ivor Livi). *Exhib:* R.A., F.P.S., S.C.A., Vaughan College Leicester, Bury St. Edmunds, Aldeburgh, Chelmsford, Westcliff-on-Sea. *Work in collections:* Guy Harlings and Chapter House, Chelmsford; Mansion House, London; Broomfield Hospital; Lord St. John of Fawsley; Abe Lerner, N.Y.; Peter Rippon; Sir Alastair Stewart, Bt.; Baroness Platt of Writtle; Daniela Landschuetz Munich; and others, St. John Baptist Church Loughton; St. Barnabas Church Woodford. *Commissions:* church sculpture: Madonna (St. Barnabas). *Signs work:* "N.C." *Address:* Medlars, Mounthill Ave., Chelmsford CM2 6DB.

**COUSENS, Ruth Margaret,** F.S.A.I.; Medaille d'Or, Paris Salon (Tricentenaire 1973) T.C., Women of the Year Luncheon; artist in water-colour; art teacher of history, architecture and painting: St. George's Ramsgate, Maidstone Technical High, Sittingbourne Girls' Grammar, pupils of Wilmington Grammar Schools; Founder-Project Director, Castle Trust Arts Centre, Ramsgate; *b* London, 1930. *m* Stanley G. Cousens. one *s. Educ:* St. George's Ramsgate, and Clarendon Malvern. *Studied:* Rolle College, Exeter (1948-50, E.T. Arnold). *Exhib:* Paris Salon, R.A., R.I., R.I.B.A., etc.; one-man shows, 'Regency Ramsgate', Townley House, Ramsgate (1973), Royal Museum, Canterbury (1978), Geneva (1985), Westend, London (1986); by invitation: 'La Femme Creatrice d'Art', Monte Carlo (1976) (Brit. rep.), 'British Artists', Paris (1979), Expo Quebec, Canada (1980). *Work in collections:* Thanet Council, Ramsgate Charter Trustees; private: Sir Robert Bellinger, Rt. Hon. Edward Heath, M.P. *Publications:* work repro.: book jackets, retail postcards; booklet 'Regency Ramsgate'. *Signs work:* "R.M. COUSENS." *Address:* 17 Spencer Sq., Ramsgate, Kent.

**COUTU, Jack,** A.R.E., A.R.C.A.; printmaker and sculptor; etching and engraving on copper, miniature carving in boxwood and ivory; *b* Farnham, Surrey, 1924. *Educ:* Farnham Grammar School. *Studied:* Farnham School of Art (1947-51), R.C.A. (1951-54). *Work in collections:* King Gustave of Sweden, Museum of Fine Art, Boston, Mass., Bradford City Art Gallery, V. & A., Arts Council of Great Britain. *Publications:* articles in "International Netsuke Society Journal" (1996). *Signs work:* "Coutu" and see appendix. *Address:* Bramblings, 22 Quennells Hill, Wrecclesham, Farnham, Surrey GU10 4NE.

**COWAN, Judith,** B.A. (Hons.) Sculpture, 1st class, (1977), M.A. (1978), Gulbenkian Rome Scholarship, British School at Rome (1979); sculptor; *b* London, 8 Dec., 1954. *Studied:* Sheffield Polytechnic (1974-77); M.A. at Chelsea School of Art (1977-78). *Exib:* group exhbns in England and abroad; solo exhbns. include: Kettles Yard (1996), Stefania Miscetti, Rome (1995), Camden Arts Centre (1993), Yorkshire Sculpture Park (1992), Oriel Moystyn, Llandudno (1989-90) ou ing. *Work in collections:* A.C.G.B., London Borough of Tower hamlets, Leics. Educ, Authority. *Address:* 2a Culford Mews, London N1 4DX.

# WHO'S WHO IN ART

**COWAN, Ralph Wolfe,** A.P.S., A.A.A., A.S.A., P.I.; Royal Portrait Painter to: Sultan of Brunei (1984-), Monaco (1956, 1981), Morocco (1983), Malacanang Palace, Philippines (1982, 1983); portrait painter in oil; *b* Phoebus, Va., 16 Dec., 1931. *m* Judith Page. two *s. Studied:* Art Students League (1949-50, Bouché and Frank Reilly). *Work in collections:* Royal Palace Brunei, Palace Monaco, Royal Palace Morocco, Malacanang Palace Philippines, Carter Presidential Center, Atlanta, Reagan Private Coll., Los Angeles, Graceland Coll., Memphis, Portsmouth Museum, Portsmouth Va., N.P.G. Wash. D.C. *Publications:* seven Johnny Mathis album covers; first book "A Personal Vision" collector plate of His Holiness Pope John Paul II. *Signs work:* "Ralph Wolfe Cowan." *Address:* 243 29th St. West, Palm Beach, Fl.33407 U.S.A.

**COX, Stephen B.,** B.A.Hons., British Council Research Scholar, P.G.C.E. (Merit); artist, interior designer, teacher; director, 'Club Anglia' international summer school; taught art: Wellington College, Reading Grammar, Langley College; arts organiser, Hexagon Reading; founder, Regional Secretary Artists Union; production manager independent British films (1977-80); promoter pop groups/artists; fashion model photographer; sponsor, Manpower Services Commission YTS. *Educ:* Grange and Kingwood Grammar Schools. *Studied:* Reading University. Researched: Bucharest Fine Arts University. *Exhib:* now average four one-man shows and group shows annually U.K. and Europe. *Work in collections:* U.K., Europe, U.S.A. *Commissions:* painting/sculpture England. *Publications:* work repro.: many catalogues, radio, TV interviews U.K. and Europe. Council mem./Head of Westminster lobby: Design and Artists Copyright Soc. Events: produced/performed (as Nevetz) Germany, France, U.K., Romania. *Signs work:* "STEPHEN" and see appendix. *Address:* 60 Elmhurst Rd., Reading RG1 5HY; (studio) Chalkpit Farm, Englefield, Berks.

**COX, Vicky,** M.A. (1969), Dip.A.D. (1968); R.H.S. Silver medallist (1995); artist in coloured pencil, charcoal, oil; *b* Yorkshire, 13 Apr., 1943. *m* Robin Cox (divorced). one *d. Educ:* Doncaster Technical High School for Girls. *Studied:* Maidstone College of Art (1964-68, Gerry de Rose, Alex Koolman), Birmingham College of Art (1968-69). *Exhib:* six solo shows; more than 40 mixed shows: New York, Belgium, Poland, Channel Islands, Australia, Denmark, U.K. Many works in private collections in U.K and abroad. *Clubs:* Founder mem. S.B.A. *Signs work:* "Vicky Cox." *Address:* 39 Rosedale Rd., Richmond, Surrey TW9 2SX.

**COYNE, Douglas,** Hon. F.R.C.A., N.D.D. (Illustration) (1950); painter in oil and water-colour; *b* Newark-on-Trent, 6 June, 1930. *m* Dinah Wood. *Studied:* Newark School of Art (1944-48), Nottingham College of Art (1948-50). *Exhib:* one man shows: Chipping Campden (1988, 1990, 1993); mixed shows: with Oxford Art Soc. and Blockley Art Soc. *Work in collections:* Newark Museum. *Signs work:* "COYNE" (oils), "DOUGLAS COYNE" (water-colours). *Address:* Mill Cottage, Calf Lane, Chipping Campden, Glos. GL55 6JQ.

**CRABBE, Richard Markham,** A.R.C.A. (1951); painter; principal lecturer, Portsmouth Polytechnic Dept. of Fine Art (retd.); *b* Horley, Surrey, 1927. *m* Peggy Crabbe. two *s*. one *d*. *Studied:* Croydon School of Art and Royal College of Art. *Exhib:* Drum Croon, Wigan (1982), Galleri 17, Stockholm (1984), Portsmouth Museum (1995), Aspex Gallery, Portsmouth (1997). *Work in collections:* Portsmouth Museum, Wigan Educ. Com.,Koenig Braures, Duisburg, Germany, Southern Arts Assoc., S.W. Handelsbanken, Artothek, Düsseldorf, Germany, Hampshire C.C., Russell Cotes Museum Bournemouth. *Commissions:* Portsmouth City Arts and Social Services, residency, community centres (1995). *Clubs:* Art Space Portsmouth. *Signs work:* "R. Crabbe." *Address:* 22 Andover Rd., Southsea PO4 9QG.

**CRABTREE, Pamelam Ann,** B.A. Hons. (1983); painter in oil; *b* Preston, Lancs., 15 Sept., 1942. *m* Dennis Crabtree. two *s*. *Studied:* Harris School of Art, Preston (1958), Edge Hill College, Liverpool (1983). *Exhib:* one-man shows: Howarth A.G., Accrington, Lancaster Museum and A.G., 'Brantwood' (Ruskins House) Coniston, Univ. Central Lancs., Harris A.G., Preston, Grundy Municipal A.G., Blackpool, Recklinghausen, Germany, Stonyhurst College, Longridge. Writes poetry, collects antiquarian art and first edition books. *Clubs:* Salford Art, Preston Art Soc., Lytham Art Soc., New Longton Artists. *Signs work:* "Crabtree" (and date). *Address:* 'Highgate', 8 Birchwood Ave., Hutton, nr. Preston, Lancs. PR4 5EE.

**CRAIG-MARTIN, Michael,** B.A. (1963); M.F.A. (1966); artist; Trustee, Tate Gallery; *b* 28 Aug., 1941. one *d*. *Studied:* Yale University (1961-63, 1964-66). *Signs work:* "Michael Craig-Martin." *Address:* c/o Waddington Galleries, 11 Cork St., London W1X 1PD.

**CRAIGMILE, Heather,** U.A.; Mem. Chelsea Art Soc.; artist in oil and crayon; *b* Birkenhead, 13 Sept., 1925. *Educ:* Downe House, Cold Ash, Newbury, Berks. *Studied:* privately under Arnold Mason, R.A., Harold Workman, R.B.A., R.C.A., also at Chester Art School. *Exhib:* R.B.A., R.C.A., U.A., Chelsea Art Soc., one man show every two or three years at Beddgelert in Snowdonia and more recently in Isle of Anglesey. *Signs work:* "Heather Craigmile." *Address:* Trem-y-Dyffryn, Llanbedr, Conwy, Gwynedd LL32 8UN.

**CRAMP, Jonathan David,** A.T.D., R.W.S., F.R.S.A.; painter; Head of Art Dept., Fishguard C.S. School (1954-81); *b* Ninfield, Sussex, 29 Jan., 1930. *m* Elizabeth (painter). one *d*. *Educ:* Huish Grammar School, Taunton, Bexhill Grammar School. *Studied:* Hastings School of Art (1946-51) (Vincent Lines). *Work in collections:* Welsh Arts Council, Contemporary Art Society for Wales, Pembrokeshire County Museum, Schools Service, National Museum of Wales, Shell Oil (U.K.) Ltd., National Grid Co., Cartrefle and Caerleon Colleges of Education, various education authorities, the Government Art Collection, Providence Museum, Rhode Island, U.S.A. *Commissions:* Shell Oil (U.K.) Ltd., National Grid Co. *Signs work:* see appendix. *Address:* Heatherdene,

Windy-Hall, Fishguard, Pembs. SA65 9DU.

**CRAMPTON, Seán,** M.C. (1943), G.M. (1944), T.D. (1948), P.R.B.S. (1966-71), Master, A.W.G. (1978); sculptor; Professeur de sculpture, Anglo-French Art Centre (1946-50); Chairman of College Council, Camberwell School of Art (1988-90); Governor, London Institute (1989-90); Civic Trust Award (1984); R.B.S. Silver Medal (1965), R.B.S. Bronze Medal (1985), Civic Trust Award (1983); *b* Manchester, 15 Mar., 1918; married; five children. *Studied:* Vittoria Junior School of Art, and Central School of Art, Birmingham; Paris. *Exhib:* R.A., R.S.A., R.I. and R.I.B.A. Galleries, S.P.S.; 15 one-man shows in West End, etc. *Work in collections:* Sculpture in many churches throughout England and Scotland, and private collections. *Clubs:* Chelsea Arts, Athenæum. *Signs work:* "Seán Crampton" or "SC" within circle. *Address:* Rookery Farm House, Calne, Wilts. SN11 0LH.

**CRAWFORD, Alistair,** D.A. (1966), A.T.C. (1968), M.C.S.D. (1973-86), M.S.T.D. (1977-97), Fellow, Printmakers Council (1978), Churchill Fellow (1982), F.R.P.S. (1991), R.C.A. (1994); painter, printmaker, photographer, art historian; Research Professor of Art, University of Wales, School of Art, Aberystwyth; *b* Fraserburgh, 1945. *Studied:* Glasgow School of Art (1962-66). *Exhib:* over 30 one-man, over 100 group shows throughout Britain and abroad. Work in permanent collections throughout Britain and U.S.A. Various awards including Welsh Arts Council, British Council, British Academy, Gold Medal Fine Art, Royal National Eisteddfod of Wales (1985), Kraszna Krausz Award (1992), Balsdon Senior Fellow, British School at Rome (1995-96). *Publications:* John Thomas 1838-1905 photographer (Wales); Mario Giacomelli (Paris); Elio Ciol, Italia Black and White (Milan); Carlo Bevilacqua (Wales); Elio Ciol, Assisi (Milan, Paris, Munich). Numerous articles in U.K. and abroad. *Signs work:* "Crawford." *Address:* Brynawel, Comins Coch, Dyfed SY23 3BD.

**CRAWFORD, John Gardiner,** D.A., Post Dip., R.S.W., R.B.A., R.I.; painter in water-colour, acrylic; *b* Fraserburgh, 1941. *m* Elspeth Younger. one *s.* one *d. Educ:* Fraserburgh Academy. *Studied:* Gray's School of Art, Aberdeen. *Exhib:* Internationally. *Work in collections:* Worldwide. Awards: Gray's School of Art, First Prize for Painting (1962); Governor's Award for Painting, Hospitalfield College of Art (1963); Royal Scottish Academy, Bursary Award (1964); First Prize, Scottish Arts Council Open Exhbn. (1969); Scottish Arts Council, Bursary Award (1981); Hunting Award, First Prize for Water-colour (1982); R.I. Medal (1983); Hunting Award, Second Prize (1984). *Signs work:* "CRAWFORD." *Address:* 34 Strachan St., Arbroath, Angus DD11 1UA,

**CRAWFORD, Susan L.,** equestrian artist and portrait painter in oil; *b* Scotland, 11 May, 1941. *m* Jeremy Phipps. one *s.* one *d. Educ:* Priors Field, Godalming. *Studied:* Studio Simi, Florence (1968-70). *Exhib:* solo show at Tryon Gallery; part of large shows at N.P.G., Royal Scottish Academy, Queen's

Gallery, V. & A., R.A., National Gallery of Penang, R.P. *Commissions:* 19 Derby winners; Royal portraits. *Publications:* included in Stella Walker's 'Sporting Artist of the 20th Century', '100 Years of British Farming Livestock'; etc. *Signs work:* "S.L. Crawford." *Address:* Hillstreet Farmhouse, Tisbury, Salisbury, Wilts. SP3 6PU.

**CRAWSHAW, Alwyn,** S.E.A., B.W.S., P.N.A.P.A., F.R.S.A. (1978); artist in acrylic, water-colour and oil; director (partner), Russell Artists Merchandising Ltd., Kingston-upon-Thames, Surrey (1957-80); Lecturer and demonstrator on acrylic, oil and water-colour painting for Daler-Rowney & Co., Ltd. Bracknell Berks.; President, National Acrylic Painters Assoc.; elected Top Ten Art Video Teachers in America (1991); Founder/President, Soc. of Amateur Artists (1992); *b* Mirfield, Yorks., 20 Sept., 1934. *m* June Crawshaw. one *s.* two *d. Educ:* Hastings Grammar School for Boys. *Studied:* Hastings School of Art (1949-51) under Vincent Lines. *Exhib:* R.B.A.; one-man shows: Harrods, St. Paul's Gallery, London, Marina Gallery, Weybridge, Barclay A.G., Chester, Guildford Galleries, Guildford, Mensing Gallery, Germany; joint exhbn. with June Crawshaw, St. Helier Gallery, Jersey, C.I. (1992), and the Patricia Wells Gallery, Bristol (1989). *Publications:* Pub. by Harper Collins: Alwyn Crawshaw's Oil Painting Course (1992), A Brush with Art (1991), Alwyn Crawshaw Paints Oils (1992), Alwyn Crawshaw Paints on Holiday (1992), Alwyn Crawshaw's Acrylic Painting Course (1993), Alwyn Crawshaw's Watercolour Painting Course (1991), Crawshaw Paints Acrylics (1994), Crawshaw's Sketching and Drawing Course (1995), Crawshaw Paints Constable Country (1996), Alwyn and June Crawshaw's Outdoor Painting Course (1997); Learn to paint with Acrylic Colours (Collins); Learn to paint with Watercolours (Collins); Learn to paint landscapes (Collins); Learn to paint boats and harbours (Collins); Learn to Sketch (Collins); Learn to Paint Still Life (Collins); Learn to Paint Outdoors in Watercolour (Collins); Learn to Paint in Oils for the Beginner (Collins); The Artist at Work - Alwyn Crawshaw (Collins); Sketching with Alwyn Crawshaw (Collins); The Half-Hour Painter (Collins). Guest on BBC Radio, BBC T.V., Independent Radio, discussing painting techniques; guest on the 'Gay Byrne Radio Show' R.T.E. Ireland (Mar. 1991), T.S.W. television series 'A Brush with Art' by Alwyn Crawshaw, 12 half hour programmes, 'Crawshaw Paints in Oils', 8 half hour programmes, 'Crawshaw Paints on Holiday', 6 half hour programmes (1992), 'Crawshaw's Watercolour Studio' 8 half hour programmes (1993), Crawshaw Paints Acrylics, 8 half hour programmes (1994), Crawshaw's Sketching and Drawing Course, 10 half hour programmes (1995), "Crawshaw Paints Constable Country" T.V. for Anglia and Channel 4, 6 half hour programmes. All TV series screened network by Channel 4, and screened by P.B.S. America from April 1993, and Japan. *Signs work:* "ALWYN CRAWSHAW." *Address:* The Hollies, Stubb Rd., Hickling, Norwich NR12 OYS.

**CRAWSHAW, Donna,** S.W.A., S.E.A.; animals and landscape painter in acrylic and water-colour; *b* Woking, Surrey, 1960. *m* Andrew G.L. Goolding

(Fine Art Dealer). *Studied:* West Surrey College of Art and Design. *Exhib:* Omell Galleries Windsor, London, Ascot, Harrods London, John Magee Belfast, Forest Gallery Guildford, Godalming Galleries, Gallery at Trapp, Dyfed, Mall Galleries and Westminster Hall (various). *Publications:* work repro.: Country Fine Arts and Solomon & Whitebread - Fine Art Prints; Royal Worcester Porcelain by Bradford Exchange; greetings cards by various. *Signs work:* "Donna Crawshaw." *Address:* Rhiwe Farm, Llanddeusant, Llangadog, Dyfed SA19 9SS.

**CRAWSHAW, June,** B.W.S. (1987), S.W.A. (1988), N.A.P.A. (1997); artist in water-colour, oil and acrylics, potter in ceramics, porcelain; Director, Teaching Art Ltd., Newark, Notts.;*b* Woking, Surrey, 20 June, 1936. *m* Alwyn Crawshaw. one *s.* two *d. Educ:* Kingfield Secondary School, Woking. *Studied:* painting under Alwyn Crawshaw, S.E.A., B.W.S., P.N.A.P.A., F.R.S.A. (1970-87); ceramics at Danefield College, Woking (1975-80, June Duckworth). *Exhib:* joint exhbns. with Alwyn Crawshaw, Donna Crawshaw, S.W.A., Godalming Galleries (1985), Yorkshire Artists (1987), Sidmouth Visual Arts Festival (1981-87), B.W.S. (1987), joint exhbn. with Alwyn Crawshaw Harrods (1986), S.W.A. Annual Exhbn., B.W.S. Annual Exhbn., joint exhbn. with Alwyn Crawshaw at The Patricia Wells Gallery, Bristol (1989), and St. Helier Gallery, Jersey, C.I. (1992). Teaches with Alwyn Crawshaw on painting courses every year since 1982. *Publications:* Watercolour Made Easy (Harper Collins, 1995); Alwyn and June Crawshaw's Outdoor Painting Course (1997). Featured in TV series: 'Crawshaw Paints on Holiday' Channel 4 (1992) and P.B.S. America (1993) and book of series; 'Crawshaw Paints Acrylics' Channel 4 (1994) P.B.S. America (1994) and book of series; 'Crawshaw's Sketching and Drawing Course' Channel 4 (1995) P.B.S. America and book of series. All three series in Japan. *Signs work:* "June Crawshaw" (paintings), and see appendix. *Address:* The Hollies, Stubb Rd., Hickling, Norwich NR12 OYS.

**CRAXTON, John,** R.A.; artist in oil, tempera, conté crayon; *b* London, 3 Oct., 1922. *Educ:* various private schools. *Studied:* Goldsmiths' College and Academie Julian. *Exhib:* Leicester Galleries, London Gallery, Galerie Gasser, Zürich, British Council, Athens, Retrospective, Whitechapel (1967). *Work in collections:* Tate Gallery, City Art Gallery, Bristol, Manchester and Birmingham A.G., Melbourne A.G., British Council, Arts Council, Victoria and Albert Museum, Ministry of Works, British Museum. *Publications:* John Craxton, by Geoffrey Grigson, Horizon (1948), The Poet's Eye (1944: 16 lithographs), sets and costumes for Royal Ballet, Daphnis and Chlöe (1951), Apollo (1966). *Signs work:* "Craxton." *Address:* Moschon 1, Hania, Crete.

**CREBER, Frank,** B.F.A. (1981), M.F.A. (1987); artist in oil on canvas, water-colour, pen and ink; *b* Amersham, Bucks., 12 Jan., 1959. *m* Marguerite. two *s. Studied:* Newcastle University (Roy Kitchen), Chelsea School of Art (Ian Stephenson). *Exhib:* Sue Williams, Portobello Rd. (1988, 1989, 1991), Barclays Bank Young Painters £10,000 competition, Henry Moore Gallery,

R.C.A. London (awarded joint winner 1987), Paton Gallery, London (1990), Artist of the Day, Flowers East, London (1989). *Work in collections:* Unilever, Arthur Andersen & Co., Art for Hospitals, Leics. Schools Coll., Stanhope Construction Ltd. *Signs work:* see appendix. *Address:* 43 Jennings Rd., E. Dulwich, London SE22 9JU.

**CREE, Alexander,** D.A.(Edin.) 1950; painter in oil, pastel and water-colour; *b* 24 Feb., 1929. *Educ:* Dunfermline High School. *Studied:* Edinburgh College of Art (1946-52), Post Graduate Scholarship (1950), Travelling Scholarship (1951). *Exhib:* Scottish Lyceum Club (1957), Demarco Gallery (1968, 1976), Loomshop Gallery (1969), Shed 50 (1974), Macaulay Gallery (1990), Solstice Gallery (1991), Westgate Gallery (1991), Open Eye Gallery (1993), Ewan Mundy Gallery, Broughton Gallery, Kingfisher Gallery, Gallery 41. *Work in collections:* Scottish Arts Council, Nuffield Foundation. *Signs work:* "A. Cree." *Address:* Braeheads, E. Linton, E. Lothian EH40 3DH, Scotland.

**CREFFIELD, Dennis,** *b* London, 29 Jan., 1931. *Educ:* Colfes Grammar School. *Studied:* Borough Polytechnic with David Bomberg (1948-51), Slade School (1957-61); Gregory Fellow in Painting at the University of Leeds (1964-67). *Exhib:* many mixed and one-man exhbns. *Work in collections:* include, Tate Gallery, Contemporary Art Soc., National Trust Foundation for Art, House of Commons, Arts Council of Gt. Britain, Government Art Collection, Imperial War Museum. *Signs work:* "Dennis Creffield." *Address:* 45 Marine Parade, Brighton BN2 1PE.

**CREME, Benjamin,** artist in oil; *b* Glasgow, 1922. *m* Phyllis Power. two *s.* one *d. Educ:* Queens Park, Glasgow. *Studied:* with Jankel Adler. *Exhib:* A.I.A., London Group, Carnegie International (1952), Whitechapel (1954), Arts Council (1974), I.C.A. (1979); one-man shows: Gallery Apollinaire (1952), St. George's Gallery (1955), Bryant M. Hale Gallery (1964), Dartington New Gallery (1977), Themes and Variations Gallery (1985), England & Co. (1988); group shows: South Molton Gallery, Gimpel Fils, Redfern, Roland Browse and Delbanco, Leger Gallery, Reid and LeFevre. *Work in collections:* Pembroke College, Oxford, V. & A., B.M. *Publications:* Cage Without Grievance (W.S. Graham, Parton Press, 1942). *Signs work:* "Creme." *Address:* P.O. Box 3677, London NW5 1RU.

**CRESWELL, Alexander Charles Justin,** artist in water-colour, author; tutor, Prince of Wales Inst. of Architecture; *b* Helsinki, 14 Feb., 1957. *m* Mary Curtis Green. *Educ:* Winchester College. *Studied:* Byam Shaw School of Art (1976), W. Surrey College (1976-78). *Exhib:* Spink & Son, Cadogan Gallery, New Academy, also Europe, Hong Kong and S. Africa. *Work in collections:* Palace of Westminster, The Royal Collection. *Publications:* The Silent Houses of Britain (1991). *Clubs:* Architecture, A.W.G. *Signs work:* "Alexander Creswell." *Address:* Copse Hill, Ewhurst, Surrey GU6 7NN.

**CREW, Rowan Alexander,** A.R.B.A. (1987), R.B.A. (1988); self taught artist in water-colour, acrylic and oil; *b* Woodchurch, Kent, 31 Dec., 1952. *m*

Linda Bannister. two *d. Educ:* Homewood Secondary Modern. *Exhib:* R.I., R.B.A. *Work in collections:* K.C.C., and private collections. *Signs work:* "Rowan Crew." *Address:* Brookfarm House, Brook St., Woodchurch, Ashford, Kent TN26 3SR.

**CRISFIELD CHAPMAN, June,** D.A. (Glasgow) (1955); wood engraver, portrait painter (oil), illustrator (literary, theatre, plant themes in engraving, gouache); *b* Kent, 4 June, 1934. *m* William Woodside Chapman, D.A. two *s. Educ:* Kilmarnock Academy. *Studied:* Glasgow School of Art. *Exhib:* solo shows: Royal National Theatre London, International Shakespeare Globe Centre London, Edinburgh College of Art, Royal Scottish Academy of Music and Drama Glasgow, Glasgow City A.G. Kelvingrove, etc.; group shows: Edinburgh International Festival, Royal Scottish Academy, Royal Society of Painter Printers' Open, Chaucer/Caxton, Westminster Abbey, etc. *Work in collections:* engravings in Glasgow and Edinburgh City, and Ashmolean, Oxford Collections, paintings in theatres including 'Tribute to Scottish Theatre' in Glasgow. *Commissions:* portraits, engraving, theatre gouaches. *Publications:* engravings in Folio Book Society's Shakespeare (1988), 'The Countryman' regular series, etc. *Signs work:* "CRISFIELD/CRISFIELD CHAPMAN" or "CRISFIELD CHAPMAN." *Address:* 23 Smythe Rd., Billericay, Essex CM11 1SE.

**CROFT, Ivor John,** C.B.E., M.A. (Oxon. and Lond.); painter and former civil servant; *b* 6 Jan., 1923. *Educ:* Westminster School; Christ Church, Oxford; Institute of Education, University of London; London School of Economics and Political Science. *Exhib:* group shows: various, 1958 onwards including Camden Arts Centre (Survey of Abstract Painters, 1967); John Player Open Exhbn. (1968, 1969); Covent Garden Gallery (Critical Discoveries, 1973); Lorient, Brittany (Festival Interceltique, 1993); one-man shows: Gardner Centre for the Arts, University of Sussex (1970); University of Warwick (1971). *Publications:* work repro.: Art and Artists, postcard. *Clubs:* Reform. *Signs work:* "John Croft" on back. *Address:* 15 Circus Mews, Bath BA1 2PW.

**CROKER, Valerie,** S.B.A. (1987), H.S. (1994); artist in water-colour, pen and ink; *b* Cardiff, 19 Aug., 1931. one *s.* one *d. Educ:* Abbey School, Reading. *Studied:* Maidenhead Art School (1950), Reading University (1951-53, Prof. Betts). *Exhib:* S.WL.A., U.A.; solo shows: Henley, Bath, Wells, Winchester; and many other mixed shows in U.K. and abroad. *Publications:* illustrated: People and Places by J. H. B. Peel, Old Wives Tales by Eric Maple, The Secret Lore of Plants and Flowers by Eric Maple, Still Waters by Margaret Cornish. *Signs work:* "Valerie Croker" or "V.C." *Address:* Poacher's Croft, 12 Compton Bassett, Calne, Wilts. SN11 8RE.

**CROOK, P. J.,** R.W.A. (1993); painter; *b* Cheltenham, 28 June, 1945. *m* Richard Parker Crook, painter. one *s.* one *d. Studied:* Gloucestershire College of Art (1960-65). *Exhib:* One Woman Show: Montpelier Sandelson, London

(1994-96), Galerie Alain Blondel, Paris (1991, 1993, 1995, 1997), Royal West of England Academy (1997), Brian Sinfeld, Compton Cassey (1997), Portal Gallery, London (1980-94), 112 Greene Street, New York (1989), Cheltenham A.G. and Museums (1986); retrospective (1980-96): Cheltenham A.G. and Museums; Oriel Gallery, Theatre Clwyd, Mold; Musée Paul Valery, séte; Rye A.G.; group shows: Royal Academy of Arts (1978-83 1985, 1987, 1988, 1990.1991, 1994, 1995), Royal West of England Academy (since 1978) (First prize 1984; A.R.W.A. 1988, R.W.A. 1093), Royal Bath and West Open (First prize 1978), World Newspapers, Sotherby's, R.A. Prizewinner (1982), Cheltenham Group, Purchase prize (1983), First prize (1990), Tolly Cobbold/Eastern Arts Open (1985), Athena Internatinal Arts Awards Open (1985,1987), Five Gloucestershire Artists, Cheltenham Festival (1985), John Player Portrait Award Exhbn., National Portrait Gallery (1986), small Pictures, Salisbury, Prizewinner (1986), British Figurative Painting since 1945, British Council tourr of the far east (1988-89), Friends of Carel Weight, London (1991), South West Open, Special Commendation (1992). Contemporary Icons, Royal Albert Memorial Museum, Exeter (1992), The Gift of Life, London, Prizewinner (1993), Manchester Academy of Fine Arts (since 1993), Dept of Transport Exhbn., London, Purchase prize (1993), Reclaiming the Madonna, lincoln Museum and A.G. tour (1993-94), Murs Peints, Marie de Paris (1995), Salon des Independants, Paris (1995), Die Kraft der Bilder, Realismus der Gegenwart, Berlin (1996), Contemporary British Painting, Toronto (1996).*Work in collections:* Imperial War Museum; Dept. of Transport; Cheltenham A.G. and Museum; Allied Domecq plc; J.P. Morgan Inc; Ralli Institute, Geneva; University of Pennsylvania; London Business School; Cheltenham Racecourse; City of Paris. *Publications:* P.J. Crook: Peintures (Editions Ramsay, Paris, 1993); P.J. Crook: A Retrospective (Cheltenham A.G and Museums, 1996). *Clubs:* Arts, London. *Signs work:* "P.J. Crook." *Address:* The Old Police Station, 39 Priory La., Bishop's Cleeve, Cheltenham GL52 4JL.

**CROSBIE, William,** B.A. (1935), R.S.A. (1975), R.G.I. (1980), Hon. F.G.S.A. (1996); painter in oil, water-colour, pastel; *b* Hankow, Hupeh, China. *m* Anne Roger. two *d. Educ:* Glasgow Academy. *Studied:* Glasgow School of Art (1930-36); Ecole de la Grand Chaumière; Studio of Fernand Leger (1936-39, Aristide Malol). *Exhib:* Sydney State Gallery, Wellington State Gallery. *Work in collections:* Kelvingrove Gallery Glasgow, Aberdeen, Bradford Gallery, London War Museums, National Portrait Gallery of Scotland, Scottish National Gallery of Modern Art. *Publications:* Childrens readers, poetry books. *Clubs:* Glasgow Art. *Signs work:* "Crosbie" followed by year in roman numerals. *Address:* Rushes House, 10 Winchester Rd., Petersfield, Hants. GU32 3BY.

**CROSS, Roy,** R.S.M.A. (1977), S.A.A. (1952); historical marine and aviation painter in gouache and oils; *b* London 1924. *m* Rita May (decd.). one *s. Exhib:* Malcolm Henderson Gallery, St. James's, (1973); one-man shows: Börjessons Gallery, Gothenborg, Sweden, (1975 and 1977); Marine Arts allery, Salem, Massachusetts (1976 and 1989). *Publications:* twelve limited dition prints of marine pictures signed and numbered by the artist (1977-1989) ublished in Sweden (2), U.S.A. (7) and Britain (3), plus art prints by Franklin Mint, Rosenstiel's, plates by Hamilton Collection, etc. *Signs work:* "Roy Cross )" and usually dated. *Address:* Squirrels, Hither Chantlers, Langton Green, 'unbridge Wells, Kent TN3 0BJ.

**CROSS, Tom,** N.D.D.(1953), Dip.(Lond.)(1956); painter in oil and ouache; Principal, Falmouth School of Art (1976-87); mem. London Group; Chairman, Penwith Soc. of Artists (1982-84); *b* Manchester, 1931. *m* Patricia. ne *s. Studied:* The Slade School, Abbey Minor Scholarship, Rome, French iovt. Scholarship. *Exhib:* one-man shows, Penwith Galleries, Montpelier tudio, Charleston, S.C. *Work in collections:* Welsh Arts Council, Contemporary Art Soc. for Wales, Leicester and Glamorgan Educ. Authorities. *ublications:* The Shining Sands, Artists in Newlyn and St. Ives 1880-1930; 'ainting the Warmth of the Sun, St. Ives Artists 1939-75. *Clubs:* Chelsea Arts. *igns work:* "Tom Cross." *Address:* Dinyan, Port Navas, Constantine, Cornwall.

**CROSSLEY, Bob,** painter, printmaker; *b* Northwich, 1912. *m* Marjorie. one two *d. Educ:* Heybrook School, Rochdale. *Exhib:* 9 one-man shows: Crane Gallery, Manchester (1959), Reid Gallery, London (1960, 1964), Gallery Bique, Madrid (1965), Reid Gallery, Guildford (1966), Curwen Gallery, London (1972), Singers Fridden Division, Stevenage (1972), John Player & Sons, Nottingham (1972), Bristol Arts Centre (1980), Penwith Galleries, St.Ives (1987). *Work in collections:* Contemporary Art Society, Rochdale A.G., Durban, A.G., S.A., Winnipeg A.G., College of Advanced Education, Port Elizabeth, S.A., Hereford A.G., Open University, Sommerfield College. *Signs work:* "Crossley." *Address:* Studio Annexe, Porthgwidden, St. Ives, Cornwall TR26 1PL.

**CROSSLEY, Gordon,** painter in oil; Senior lecturer in Art and Design, Barking College of Technology; *b* Surrey, 6 Dec., 1929. *m* Jo Glosby. one *s.* three *d. Educ:* Rutlish School, Merton. *Studied:* Wimbledon School of Art. *Exhib:* R.A., R.B.A., N.E.A.C., P.S., N.S., Madden Gallery; one-man shows, Phoenix Gallery (1984), Gainsborough Gallery, Beecroft Gallery. *Work in collections:* Essex Museum. *Signs work:* see appendix. *Address:* The Sanctuary, Sheering, nr. Bishop's Stortford, Herts. CM22 7LN.

**CROW, Barbara Joan (née Walmsley),** R.C.A.; wood engraver and illustrator; teacher; *b* Liverpool, 1942. two *d. Educ:* Merchant Taylors' School for Girls, Liverpool. *Studied:* Slade School (1959-62, Sir William Coldstream), Bristol Polytechnic (1982-84) postgraduate printmaking. *Exhib:* R.W.A., R.C.A., S.W. Arts 'Artists in Schools', Arnolfini (1983), S.W.E. *Clubs:* A.A.D.W., Assoc. of Illustrators. *Signs work:* "Barbara Crow." *Address:* Manor Lodge, Llangattock-vibon-Avel, Monmouth, Gwent.

**CROW, Kathleen Mary,** R.O.I. (1988), N.S. (1983); painter in oil and water-colour; *b* Oxton, Notts., 4 June, 1920. *m* John Richard Crow. one *s*. on *d*. *Educ:* Ackworth; Basel, Switzerland. *Studied:* Nottingham Polytechni (1964-76 part-time, Ronald Thursby), Leicester (1976-82 part-time, Lesli Goodwin). *Exhib:* R.A. Summer Exhbns., R.W.A., R.O.I., R.I., N.S Nottingham, Rufford, Leicester, Oakham. *Clubs:* Nottingham Soc. of Artist: *Signs work:* see appendix. *Address:* 2 Blind La., Oxton, Southwell, Nott: NG25 0SS.

**CROWE, Barbara,** R.I., S.W.A., S.B.A.; painter in water-colour and oi teacher, demonstrator; *b* Wirral, Ches. *m* Ronald Crowe. one *s*. three *d*. *Studiea* Bolt Court, Croydon Art School, Epsom Art School, but mostly self-taugh *Exhib:* R.I., S.W.A., S.B.A., Mall Galleries, Westminster Gallery, Londor *Publications:* contributor to Artist and Leisure Painter, alsoWater-Colou Impressionists by Ron Ransan. *Clubs:* Dorking, Guildford and Sussex Art Soc *Signs work:* "Barbara Crowe." *Address:* Dormers, Hammerfield, Abinge Hammer, nr. Dorking, Surrey RH5 6QY.

**CROWE, Maida,** F.F.P.S.; sculptor in wood and stone; *b* Axminster, 1915 *m* Jim Crowe. *Educ:* privately. *Studied:* City and Guilds of London (1957-62) *Exhib:* R.B.A., F.P.S., A.I.R., Barbican, Surrey, Birmingham, Southampto and London Universities, etc.; open air, Berkeley Sq., and Brixton; one-ma shows, Loggia Gallery, Cockpit Gallery, I.A.C., Bridport and Southwar Cathedral. *Publications:* First and Last - a Search for Meaning (Purzebrool Press, 1994). *Clubs:* F.P.S., I.C.A., N.F.T. *Signs work:* "MAIDA." *Address* 906 Keyes House, Dolphin Sq., London SW1V 3NB.

**CROWE, Victoria Elizabeth,** N.D.D. (1965), M.A. (R.C.A.) (1968) R.S.W. (1983), A.R.S.A. (1987); artist in oil and water-colour; part-time lec turer, Edinburgh College of Art; *b* 1945. *Studied:* Kingston College of Ar (1961-65), R.C.A. (1965-68). *Exhib:* R.A., R.S.A.; one-man shows, Scottis! Gallery, Edinburgh (1970, 1974, 1977, 1982), Thackeray, London (1983, 1985 1987, 1989, 1991, 1994), Mercury Gallery, Edinburgh (1986). *Work in collec tions:* R.A., R.C.A., Scottish National Gallery of Modern Art, Scottish Art: Council, N.P.G. London, Scottish N.P.G., I.L.E.A., Edinburgh Educ Authority. *Signs work:* "Victoria Crowe." *Address:* The Bank House, Main St. W. Linton, Peeblesshire EH46 7EE.

**CROWTHER, Hugh Melvill,** artist in oil, pastel; *b* Newby, nr Scarborough, Yorks., 25 June, 1914. *m* Margaret Steele Wainey. *Educ:* St John's, Tutshill, Chepstow. *Studied:* Newport Technical College, Gwent *Exhib:* Royal Glasgow Institute of Fine Arts, Cardiff, Newport, Monmouth Hereford, Gloucester, London. *Work in collections:* Newport Museum, Gwent *Publications:* work repro.: Chepstow Castle, Village Smithy, Naturalist': Collection, all in La Revue Moderne. *Clubs:* West Gloucestershire Art Soc. Wye Valley Art Soc., Gloucestershire Soc. of Artists. *Signs work:* see appen dix. *Address:* Meadow End, Tidenham, Chepstow, Gwent NP6 7JG.

**CROWTHER, Stephen,** A.R.C.A., R.B.A. (1958); artist in oil, charcoal onté, pastel; lecturer, drawing and painting, College of Art, Hartlepool (1950-987); *b* Sheffield, 23 Aug., 1922. *m* Sheila Maria Higgins. two *s*. one *d*. *Educ:* De la Salle College, Sheffield. *Studied:* Sheffield College of Art; Royal cholarship to Royal College of Art (1941); war service (1941-46); R.C.A. 1946-49). *Exhib:* R.A., R.B.A., R.P., Llewellyn Alexander Gallery, London, nd many provincial galleries; one-man shows: Gray A.G., Hartlepool; Billingham A.G.; Zaydler Gallery, London; Green Dragon Yard A.G., Stockton; Abbot Hall A.G., Kendal; Middlesbrough A.G. *Work in collections:* Gray A.G.; Derbyshire and Hartlepool Education Committees; Abbot Hall A.G., Kendal; Hartlepool, South Tees, Cleveland; Bradford General Hospitals; Yarm School, Yarm, Cleveland; Higgs and Hill; The Sultan of Oman. *Commissions:* Port Solent Marina, Portsmouth, for Higgs and Hill (1989); three oils for the Sultan of Oman, (1992); a large portrait, three-quarter length, of a Mother and Two Daughters, (1995). *Publications:* in The Complete Portrait Painting Course including front cover; and Perspective for Artists, both by Angela Gair (Mitchell Beazley, 1990); The Oil Painter's Question and Answer Book by Hazel Harrison (Quarto Publishing), and many other books. *Clubs:* President and Hon. Mem. Hartlepool Art Club. *Signs work:* see appendix. *Address:* 5 The Cliff, Seaton Carew, Hartlepool, TS25 1AB.

**CRYAN, Clare,** A.T.C., D.A.; artist specializing in water-colour; Tutor-in-Charge, The Blue Door Studio; *b* Dublin, 1935. *Educ:* Dominican Convent, Sion Hill. *Studied:* National College of Art, Dublin; Ulster College of Art, Belfast and with Kenneth Webb in The Irish School of Landscape Painting. *Exhib:* R.H.A., R.U.A., N.S., Salon d'Automne, Festival International Paris, Osaka, Brussels, Luxembourg, Hong Kong. *Work in collections:* Killiney Castle, Dublin, H.M. Queen Beatrix of the Netherlands. *Clubs:* European Inst. of Water-colours. *Signs work:* "Clare Cryan." *Address:* The Blue Door Studio, 16 Prince of Wales Terr., Dublin 4.

**CRYER, Ian David,** painter in oils; *b* Bristol, 1959. *m* Wendy Patricia. *Educ:* Ridings High School, Bristol. *Studied:* part-time Bristol Polytechnic (1978-82); and in Kensington under Leonard Boden, R.P. (1978-81). *Exhib:* Bristol Art Centre (1976), P. Wells Gallery (1983), Linfield Galleries (1984, 1985), R.A., R.B.A., R.W.A., N.E.A.C., Hunting Group finalist (1990), Discerning Eye (1991), Cooling Gallery (1992), 1st International Art Biennial, Malta (1995). *Work in collections:* many private collections including Price Waterhouse, Longleat House and Bass Museum, Burton-on-Trent. *Signs work:* 'Ian Cryer." *Address:* 93 Bath Rd., Willsbridge, Bristol BS15 6ED.

**CUBA, Ivan,** D.Litt.; professor extraordinary of art, proclaimed for distinguished service, Dictionary of International Biography, Vol. V (1968); elected The Temple of Arts, U.S.A. (1970); elected Fellow, Academy Leonardo da Vinci and Poet Laureate Award (1979); President, Temple of Art Academy, N.Z.; developed educational composite painting, segment painting and aluminium engravure, discovered colour-balancing by mathematics and weight changes in matter; decorations include 14 diplomas, four sets of other letters and two gold medals, ten other. Awarded, International Poet Laureate (1995) India; International Man of Year (1995-97). *Studied:* University of Auckland N.Z. *Exhib:* U.K., U.S.A., N.Z. Author of books. *Address:* P.O. Box 5199 Wellesley St., Auckland, N.Z.

**CULLINAN, Edward,** C.B.E., R.A.; architect, artist; has taught and lectured in Canada, U.S.A., Australia, N.Z., Norway, Malta, Japan, Eire, etc. and many places in England, Wales and Scotland; Founder and principal architect Edward Cullinan Architects, authors of many modern bldgs. and receivers of many awards; *b* London, 17 July, 1931. *m* Rosalind. one *s.* two *d. Studied:* architecture: Architectural Assoc., Cambridge and Berkeley, Calif. *Publications:* Edward Cullinan Architects by Kenneth Powell (Academy Editions, 1995). *Signs work:* "E.C." or "Edward Cullinan Architects." *Address:* The Wharf, Baldwin Terr., London N17RU.

**CUMBERLAND-BROWN, James Francis,** M.R.S.H., A.R.M.S., H.S.; self taught miniature marine artist in scrimshaw (engraving) and pencil; *b* Finsbury, 12 Apr., 1934. *m* Tamara Robertson Provis. two *d. Educ:* Kingham Hill, Oxon. *Exhib:* R.M.S., H.S., Montelimar, France, and numerous private galleries throughout Australia. *Work in collections:* National Maritime Museum, Australia; W.A. Maritime Museum; Murdock University; Museum of Fine Art, Geneva; McKenzie Gallery, Perth. *Signs work:* "J.F.C." *Address:* Foxham, 146 Preston Point Rd., East Fremantle, W.A. 6158.

**CUMMINGS, Albert Arratoon Runciman,** U.A. (1973), F.S.A. (Scot.)(1973); painter in tempera, oil and water-colour, book illustrator, picture restorer; *b* Edinburgh, 20 Aug., 1936. *m* Marjorie Laidlaw. one *s.* one *d. Educ:* Edinburgh. *Studied:* apprentice stage designer under William Grason, Edward Bowers, painting under Charles Napier, Robert Jardine. *Exhib:* U.A., Scottish Gallery, Fine Art Soc., Edinburgh Gallery, Open Eye Gallery. *Work in collections:* Leeds Educ. authorities, Edinburgh Hospital Board. *Publications:* Dictionary of Scottish Art and Arch (Pub. Antique Collectors Club). *Clubs:* Scottish Arts. *Signs work:* "A. Runciman, pinx," and see appendix. *Address:* 4 School Rd., Aberlady, E. Lothian.

**CUMMINGS, Ann,** painter in oil, pastel and egg tempera; *b* Edinburgh, 12 Dec., 1945. *m* Dr. Laurie Jacobs, B.Sc., M.B.Ch.B. three *s. Educ:* Stamford College (1989-91), and under Albert A.R. Cummings (1991-94). *Exhib:* Edinburgh, Glasgow, Dunkeld, Stamford and Peterborough. *Clubs:* Welland Art Soc. *Signs work:* "A.C." *Address:* Hollywell, 38 Church St., Werrington, Peterborough, Cambs. PE4 6QE.

**CUMMINGS, George Reid,** L. Bryne Waterman Award (1995) Boston, U.S.A. for work in preserving the history of the modern whaling industry, Lay Mem., Royal Soc. Marine Artists; artist in oil; *b* Edinburgh, 11 May, 1932. *m* Mabel A. one *s.* one *d. Studied:* Carrickvale Academy; studied the use of oil painting by Joan Renton, R.S.A. Edinburgh (1985). *Exhib:* R.S.M.A. (1988);

ermanent exhbns.: Kendall Whaling Museum, Sharon Boston, U.S.A.; andefjord Whaling Museum, Sandefjord, Norway; Grytviken Whaling Iuseum, South Georgia, Falkland Islands; also at Tonsberg Maritime Iuseum, Tonsberg, Norway and Chr. Salvesen plc. Edinburgh. *Commissions:* :om Sir Gerald Elliott, Past Chairman Chr. Salvesen plc., Sir Maxwell Harper ;ow, and numerous private individuals worldwide. Specializes in recording ccurate details of the modern whaling industry ships and general maritime art. aintings are technically correct giving very accurate detail of the vessel paint- d for historic purposes. *Signs work:* "Goerge R. Cummings, Edinburgh" and ear completed, *Address:* 19 Blackford Hill View, Edinburgh EH9 3HD.

**CUMMINS, Gus,** N.D.D. (1963), M.A. (R.C.A.)(1997), R.A. (1992); ainter in oil, gouache, water-colour, etc.; *b* London, 28 Jan., 1943. *m* Angela ;raven, painter. two *s.* one *d. Educ:* Sutton and Wimbledon Art Schools, and .C.A. *Exhib:* extensively, six solo shows since 1990. *Work in collections:* .A., R.C.A., Contemporary Art Soc., Towner Coll., Hastings Museum. Coll., Iastings Library, Freshfields plc., F.T. Coll. *Clubs:* Chelsea Arts. *Signs work:* Gus Cummins." *Address:* Harpsichord House, Cobourg Pl., Hastings, Sussex 'N34 3HY.

**CURMANO, Billy,** M.S. (1977), B.F.A. (1973); intermedia artist; *b* U.S.A., 949. *Educ:* Art Students League, N.Y.C.; University of Wisconsin; former lirector, Broadway Galleries. *Exhib:* solo shows: Chapel Hill, Minneapolis, Ailwaukee, La Crosse, Winona, St. Joseph; group shows: Vienna iraphikbiennale, Austria (1977), International Miniprint, Ourense, Spain 1992-93), Franklin Furnace, N.Y.C. (1987), Small Works, N.Y.C. (1986), 'ublic Works, N.Y.C. (1984), Metronom, Barcelona, Spain (1981), :hautauqua National, N.Y. (1980), Art in the Mail, N.Z. (1976), # 18, N.Y.C. 1972), Paula Insel Annual, N.Y.C. (1972), Tyler National, Texas (1972), iraphics U.S.A., Chicago (1971). *Signs work:* "Billy Curmano." *Address:* Route # 1, Rushford, Mn. 55971, U.S.A.

**CURRY, Denis Victor,** Dip.F.A. (Slade) painting (1950) sculpture (1951), R.C.A. (1992); artist/scientist in oil, water-colour, bronze, stone, kinetic; *b* Jewcastle-on-Tyne, 11 Nov., 1918. *m* Jennifer Coram. *Educ:* Durham Johnson ;chool. *Studied:* Durham (Kremer), Slade School of Fine Art (Schwabe, :oldstream). *Exhib:* London Group, R.A., R.W.A., Slade Bi-Centenary, Oriel, :ardiff, W. Wales Arts Centre, Fishguard, Residency - sculpture, St. David's 1991), R.Cam.A., Sculpture at Margam, National Eisteddfod (1994); many ;roup and one-man shows U.K. and abroad. *Work in collections:* 'embrokeshire Museum and A.G., Tunnicliffe Museum, Anglesey, Chatsworth Iouse. *Commissions:* Numerous. Currently large-scale bronzes (Mrs. Sulivan, 3enton Castle). *Publications:* Poetry Wales, This Land is Our Land (B.M. Jat.Hist. 1989), Laying Out the Body (Seren 1992), R.Ae.Soc. Symposium - Aan-powered Aircraft Group (1975), own publication: Denis Curry Painting ;culpture Images (1985). *Signs work:* "Denis Curry," "D. Curry" or "D.C."

*Address:* Fron, Llanycefn, Clynderwen, Dyfed SA66 7XT.

**CURSHAM, Juliet,** S.Eq.A.; self taught sculptor in bronze of equestria subjects, animals and figures; *b* Nottingham, 23 Aug., 1960; divorced. one *s Educ:* Ockbrook Girls' School, Derbyshire, Nottingham High Schoo Winkfield Place, Berks. *Exhib:* Les Hirondelles Gallery, Geneva; Van Del Gallery, Palm Beach, Florida; Osbourne Gallery, London; Tryon Gallery London; Compton Cassey Gallery, Gloucestershire; Osbourne Studio Gallery Royal Hong Kong Jockey Club. *Work in collections:* Life size horse and jock ey for the Hong Kong Jockey Club at Happy Valley. *Signs work:* "Julie Cursham." *Address:* Prestwod Hall, Loughborough, Leics. LE12 5SQ.

**CURTIS, Anthony Ewart,** Dip.A.E.(Lond.), R.W.A.; experimental an landscape artist; *b* Wakefield, 7 July, 1928. *m* Joyce Isabel Yates. three *s*. one Served R.N., (1946-48) *Educ:* Kingswood Grammar School, Loughboroug (1948-50); London (1974-76). *Studied:* Bath Academy, Corsham (1950-51 Peter Potworowski, William Scott, Ken Armitage, Peter Lanyon, Brya Wynter). *Exhib:* (1952-): Redfern, Zwemmers, Daily Express Young Painters London Group, R.W.A. (1952 to date), Arts Council Modern Stained Glas (1960-61), R.I. (1983), R.W.S. (1984), 'Migraine Images' at St. Martin-in-the Fields (1993). One-man shows include Bear Lane, Oxford (1959), Readin (1961), Cookham (1964), R.W.A. (1995); ceramic sculpture: Scopas, Henle (1975), Century, Henley (1980), Recent and Retrospective Work, Bloomsbur Gallery, University of London (1987), Retrospective shows 'Recollections' Wooburn Festival (1992), Australian Works, Methuen Gallery, R.W.A. (1995) *Work in collections:* R.W.A., Bristol Educ. Com., sand-blasted screen St.Andrew's, High Wycombe. *Publications:* work repro.: Young Artists o Promise (1957). Five-month working visit to Australia (1988-89); working vis its to Oregon, U.S.A. (1990-93). *Signs work:* "Anthony Curtis," or see appen dix (on small works). *Address:* Oak Tree House, 143 Heath End Rd., Flackwe Heath, High Wycombe, Bucks. HP10 9ES.

**CURTIS, David Jan Gardiner,** R.O.I. (1988), R.S.M.A. (1983); artist in o and water-colour, designer; *b* Doncaster, 15 June, 1948. *Educ:* Doncaste Grammar School. *Exhib:* R.A., R.S.M.A., R.I., R.W.S., R.B.A., N.E.A.C Singer Friedlander/Sunday Times water-colour competition 1st prizewinne (1992). *Work in collections:* Doncaster Museum and A.G., Ferens Gallery Hull. *Publications:* author, A Light Touch - The Landscape in Oils and Th Landscape in Water-colour - a Personal View and films of the same titles *Clubs:* R.O.I., R.S.M.A. *Signs work:* "D.J. Curtis." *Address:* The Cottage Slaynes La., Misson, Doncaster, S. Yorks. DN10 6DY.

**CURTIS, Joyce,** Dip.A.E.(Lond.); artist and children's book illustrator i water-colour, gouache, oil, pencil; former Organiser (S.Bucks.), Bucks. Ar Week Visual Images Group; *b* Sulhamstead, 5 Aug., 1934. *m* Anthony Curtis three *s*. one *d*. *Educ:* Faringdon Grammar School; Post-grad. Dip., Londo (1985-86). *Studied:* Bath Academy of Art, Corsham (1952-54, Potworowski

Litz Pisk, Frost, Meadows, Armitage, Ellis). *Exhib:* solo shows, Dixon Gallery, University of London (1986), Corsham (1990), High Wycombe Museum (1993); three joint exhbns. with husband; mixed shows including R.W.A. *Signs work:* "Joyce Curtis." *Address:* Oak Tree House, 143 Heath End Rd., Flackwell Heath, High Wycombe, Bucks. HP10 9ES.

**CZERWINKE, Tadeusz.,** N.D.D. (1957), A.T.C. (1973), S.P.S. (1976), D.A.E. (1981); sculptor, carver, modeller and potter in stone, wood, perspex, bronze and terracotta; Head of Arts and Crafts Dept., Shoeburyness Comprehensive School; *b* Poland, 19 May, 1936. *m* Ewa. one *s*. one *d*. *Educ:* St. Peter's Winchester. *Studied:* Winchester School of Arts and Crafts (1957, Norman Pierce, F.R.B.S.). *Exhib:* regularly at S.P.S., Mall Galleries, Federation of British Artists, A.P.A. in G.B., Salon des Nations, Paris; one-man portrait sculpture exhbn. Posk Gallery (1987) and at the Polish Hearth, London. *Work in collections:* Church of Czestochowa, Huddersfield; Kosciuszko Museum, Rappersville, Switzerland; St. Peter's Hinkley, Leics.; Les Laurents, Dordogne, France; St. Catherine's Dock, London; Our Lady of Lourdes Convent, Kent; Town Hall, Monte Cassino, Italy; Parish Church, Devonia Rd., London; St. Sebastian & John the Baptist, Preston; Andrzej Bobola Church, London; Memorial, Eaton Pl., London; General Sikorski Museum, London; Memorial, Marshal J. Pilsudzki Inst., London; Posk (Centre of Polish Culture, London); Dom Narodowca, London; S. Michalowski, Shute House, nr. Honiton; sculptures and portraits in private collections in U.K. and overseas. *Signs work:* "Tad. Czerwinke." *Address:* 20 Whitehouse Way, Southgate, London N14 7LT.

**CZIMBALMOS, Magdolna Paal,** S.I. Museum, N.Y., Gold Med. (1958, 1960, 1962, 1963, 1966); personal letter from President J. F. Kennedy for portrait of Jacqueline Kennedy (1961); Italian Culture Award, N.Y. (1967); Szinyei Merse Gold Med., N.Y. (1971); several Silver Med. and Hon. Men.; artist in oil; *b* Esztergom, Hungary. *m* Kalman Sz. Czimbalmos. one *d*. *Studied:* under Prof. A. Bayor pr. Art Sch. Esztergom, Hung., Radatz pr. Art Sch. Germ. *Exhib:* Paris, Germany, Monaco, Canada, U.S.A., Budapest (1982), Esztergom, Hungary (1985); several one-man and group shows. *Work in collections:* S.I. Museum, N.Y., International Inst., Detroit, Carnegie International Cent., N.Y., Bergstrom Art Cent., Ill., City Museum, Esztergom and Budapest, Hungary. *Clubs:* S.I. Museum, N.Y., World Fed. of Hung. Artists, International Soc. of Fine Artists, U.S.A. *Signs work:* "Magdolna Paal Czimbalmos" and see appendix. *Address:* 31 Bayview Pl., Ward Hill, Staten Island, New York, 10304.

**CZIMBALMOS, Szabo Kalman,** Hung. Roy. Acad. Pr. (1933), S.I. Museum, N.Y., Pr. Gold Med. (1950, 1956, 1962, 1963, 1967), St. Stephen Gold Medal, N.Y. (1971), several Silver Med. and Hon. Men.; M.F.A., painter-educator, Dir. Czimbalmos Pvt. Art Sch., N.Y.; owner, Czimbalmos Fine Art Studio, S.I., N.Y.; artist in oil, water-colour, tempera; *b* Esztergom, Hungary, 1914. *m* Magdolna Paal Bohatka. one *d*. *Studied:* Royal Academy of Fine Art,

Budapest (1936) under Prof. J. Harahghy, E. Domanowsky; postgrad. Vienna, Munich, Paris, Rome. *Exhib:* Munchen, Paris, Monaco, Canada, U.S.A., Budapest (1982), Esztergom, Hungary (1985); several one-man and group shows. *Work in collections:* S.I. Museum, N.Y., S.I. Com. Coll. N.Y., Bergstrom Art Center, Ill., City Museum, Esztergom, Hung., etc.; murals in churches, convents and private inst., U.S.A. *Clubs:* Bavaryan Fine Art Soc., S.I. Museum, N.Y., World Fed. of Hung. Artists, International Soc. of Fine Artists, U.S.A. *Signs work:* "K. Sz. Czimbalmos" and see appendix. *Address:* 31 Bayview Pl., Ward Hill, Staten Island, New York, 10304.

# D

**DACK, Tom,** artist in water-colour; oils, gauche and line, specialises in marine, aviation and landscape;*b* Newcastle Upon Tyne, 26 May, 1933. *m* Catherine;. one *s.* one *d. Educ:* Newcastle College of Art. *Exhib:* Four solo shows. *Signs work:* See appendix. *Address:* 13 Selwyn Ave., Whitley Bay, Tyne & Wear NE25 9DH.

**D'AGUILAR, Michael,** gold, silver and bronze medals, Royal Drawing Soc., Armitage and silver medal, R.A. (1949); artist in oil and pastels; *b* London, 11 May, 1922. *Educ:* privately and in Spain, Italy and France. *Studied:* R.A. Schools under Henry Rushbury, R.A., Fleetwood-Walker, A.R.A., William Dring, R.A. (1948-53). *Exhib:* R.A., R.B.A., N.E.A.C., Irving Galleries, Gimpel Fils, Leicester Galleries, Young Contemporaries; one-man shows, Gimpel Fils, Irving Galleries, New Grafton Gallery, Bruton St. Gallery, Redfern Gallery. *Publications:* work repro.: Artist, Studio, La Revue Moderne des Arts; articles in Diario de Tarragona. *Clubs:* Chelsea Arts. *Signs work:* "M. D'Aguilar." *Address:* Studio 4, Chelsea Farm House, Milmans St., London SW10.

**D'AGUILAR, Paul,** artist in oil, water-colour; 1st prize for drawing at R.A. Schools (1949); gold, silver and bronze medals, R.D.S.; *b* London, 9 Sept., 1927. *Educ:* privately in Spain, Italy and France. *Studied:* R.A. Schools (1948-53) and with Prof. Barblain (Siena). *Exhib:* R.A., Redfern, Young Contemporaries, Leicester Galleries, Daily Express Young Artists, R.B.A., N.E.A.C., Sindicato de Iniciativa (Spain), Irving Gallery (1952), Temple Gallery (1960), New Grafton, Canaletto (1971), Southwell Brown Gallery (1974), Langton Gallery (1973, 1976). *Work in collections:* Lord Rothermere. *Publications:* work repro.: Artist, Studio, Collins Magazine, La Revue Moderne, Drawing Nudes (Studio Vista). *Signs work:* "P. D'Aguilar." *Address:* 11 Sheen Gate Gdns., London SW14.

**DAINES, Deirdre,** R.A. Silver medal, bronze medal and Greenshields Award, R.A. Cert., Eric Kennington prize for drawing, Winsor and Newton prize; painter in oil drawing and pastel, mainly figure paintings; teacher; *b* Ware, 2 May, 1950. *Educ:* Tottenham High Grammar School. *Studied:* R.A. Schools (1970-73, Peter Greenham). *Exhib:* New Grafton, R.A. Summer Exhbn., R.P., Agnew's, Watermans; one-man shows, Thomas Agnew (1988), Cale Art (1982). *Work in collections:* Guinness, Nuffield Trust, Pole Careen, Bonham Carter. *Clubs:* N.E.A.C., Dover St. Art. *Signs work:* "Daines." *Address:* 34a Eardley Cres., London SW5 9JZ.

**DAKEYNE, Gabriel,** Membre Associé des Artistes Français; artist in colage, pen and ink, water-colour; *b* Marske-by-the-sea, Yorkshire, 23 Feb., 1916. *n* Wing-Cdr. Jack Brain, Retd. two *d. Educ:* home. *Studied:* Swindon Art School, Press Art School, The Hague Holland. *Exhib:* R.A., Royal West of England Academy, Paris Salon, S.W.A., Graphic Artists, Flower Paintings, 9th Grand Prix de la Côte d'Azure Cannes, one-man show: St. Aldates, Oxford. *Publications:* work repro.: La Revue Moderne. *Signs work:* see appendix. *Address:* Sadlers Cottage, Sadlers End, Sindlesham, Wokingham RG41 5AL.

**DALBY, Claire,** R.W.S., R.E.; Vice-Pres. R.W.S. (1994); artist in water-colour drawing, wood-engraving and botanical illustration; *b* St. Andrews, 1944. *m* D. H. Dalby, Ph.D. *Studied:* City and Guilds of London Art School (1964-67). *Exhib:* R.A., R.W.S., R.E.; one-man shows: Consort Gallery, Imperial College, London (1981, 1988), Shetland Museum, Lerwick (1988, 1991, 1995). *Publications:* "Claire Dalby's Picture Book" (Carr, Kettering 1989); Designed and illustrated two wallcharts on Lichens (Natural History Museum 1981, 1987). *Signs work:* see appendix. *Address:* 132 Gordon Rd., Camberley, Surrey GU15 2JQ.

**DALE, William Scott Abell,** M.A. (Toronto, 1946), Ph.D. (Harvard, 1955); Prof. Emeritus; Professor of Art History, University of Western Ontario (1967-87); Deputy Director, National Gallery of Canada (1961-67); director, Vancouver Art Gallery (1959-61); curator, Art Gallery of Toronto (1957-59); research curator, Nat. Gallery of Canada (1951-57); mem. College Art Assoc. of America, Medieval Academy of America, R.S.A.; research fellow, Dumbarton Oaks, Washington (1956-57); *b* Toronto, 18 Sept., 1921. *m* Jane Gordon Laidlaw. three *s. Educ:* University of Toronto Schools; Trinity College, Toronto; Harvard University. *Address:* 1517 Gloucester Rd., London, Ont., N6G 2S5, Canada.

**DAMINATO, Vanda,** Accademico Accademia Arti Incisione, Pisa; Mem. Galerie Internationale, N.Y.; M.D. Fine Art, Milano; Dumont-Landis Fine Art, N.J.; La Permanente, Milano; painter in oil, constructions, collages, prints, image inventor for industrial Groups like: "Sirti - Pirelli", "Goglio Luigi"; *b* Mezzolombardo, 1951. *Exhib:* Palazzo Grassi, Venezia; Galerie Internationale, N.Y.; Wallace Gallery, Miami; Museo Leonardo da Vinci, Milano; Palazzo Gran Guardia, Verona; Villa Olmo, Como; Museo D'Annunzio, Pescara; Museo d'Arte Moderna, Malta. Creator of Maristel - Sirti - Pirelli's image "Telecom" exhbn. Geneve (1991). *Signs work:* "DAMINATO." *Address:*

Corso XXII Marzo 28, 20135 Milano, Italy.

**DANIEL, Brigitte M.,** S.B.A., C.B.M. (1997), R.H.S. Silver Grenfell Medal (1997); artist in water-colour/clay; *b* Bucks., 30 Oct., 1959. *m* Dr. R.W. Daniel. *Educ:* U.C.L. (Botany). *Signs work:* see appendix. *Address:* 'Lodeleigh', East End, Northleigh, Witney, Oxford OX8 6PX.

**DANIELS, Alfred,** R.W.S., R.B.A., A.R.C.A.; painter in oil, alkyd and acrylic; part-time tutor Middx. Poly, Sir John Cass, R.C.A.; *b* London, 1924. *m* Margot Hamilton Hill. *Educ:* George Greens School. *Studied:* Woolwich Polytechnic, R.C.A. *Exhib:* R.A., Rona Gallery, Mall Gallery, Bankside Gallery. *Work in collections:* G.L.C., Cambridgeshire Educ. Com., Leicester Educ. Com., Sheffield A.G., Leeds University, Bezalel Museum, Israel. I.L.E.A., Hammersmith Town Hall, British Rail, O.U.P., St. Fergus Gas Terminal. *Publications:* Drawing and Painting (1961), Drawing Made Simple (1963), Enjoying Acrylics (1975), Painting with Acrylics (1988);work in repro.: Studio International, The Artist, Art and Artists, R.A. Illustrated, Arts Review. *Signs work:* "Alfred Daniels." *Address:* 24 Esmond Rd., London W4 1JQ.

**DANIELS, Harvey,** artist in all paints and inks; *b* London, 17 June, 1936. *m* Judy Stapleton. two *d. Studied:* Willesden School of Art; Slade School of Fine Art (Ceri Richards). *Exhib:* London, U.S.A., Scandinavia. *Work in collections:* Museum of Modern Art, N.Y., V. & A., Towner A.G., Metropolitan Museum, N.Y., Bergens Kunstforening, Norway. *Publications:* article for catalogue of Peacock Printmakers, 'The Day Book: 378 British Artists', edited by Andrew Jones, exhbn. by Harvey Daniels. *Signs work:* "H. Daniels." *Address:* 70 Southdown Ave., Brighton BN1 6EH.

**DANNATT, George,** F.R.I.C.S.; painter and constructivist; music critic; *b* Blackheath, 1915. *m* Ann Doncaster. *Educ:* Colfe's School and College of Estate Management; self-taught as a painter. *Exhib:* one-man shows: Newlyn-Orion, retrospective (1960-81); Galerie Schreiner, Basel, Switzerland (1981); Galerie Artica, Cuxhaven, Germany (1984, 1990); Michael Parkin, London (1988); New Ashgate, Farnham (1992); Dorset County Museum (1993); Chesil Gallery, Portland (1994); Reed's Wharf Gallery, London (1994); The Book Gallery, St. Ives, Cornwall (1995, 1997); Town Mill Gallery, Lyme Regis (1997); Dorset County Museum (1997); Russel-Cotes Gallery, Bournemouth (1997); mixed shows: Newlyn-Orion and Penwith Galleries, Cornwall; Gordon Hepworth, Exeter; Parkin, Redfern, Austin-Desmond Galleries, London; Galerie Artica, Germany; Basel Arts Fair 1997 (New Art Centre). *Work in collections:* Dorchester County Museum. *Publications:* "One Way of Seeing", an anthology in English and German with reproductions of his work in painting and photography. Introductions to several catalogues of the sculpture of Denis Mitchell. Music criticism for the News Chronicle (1945-56), Penguin Music Magazine (1946-49). On the life and work of Arthur Bliss (Novello complete catalogue, 1982) and the D.N.B. entry upon this composer, 1971-80 Edn.

# WHO'S WHO IN ART

Concert and record-sleeve programme notes. Established: The George Dannatt Charitable Trust (1986). Mem. Newlyn Society of Artists; Hon. Mem. Critics' Circle (Music Section). *Clubs:* Garrick, Savage. *Address:* East Hatch, Tisbury, Wilts. SP3 6PH.

**DANVERS, Joan,** I.A.A.; painter in oils, potter, calligrapher; *b* Diss, Norfolk, 4 Feb., 1919; married. one *s. Educ:* Diss Grammar School; Norfolk and Norwich Hospital, S.R.N. (1940). *Studied:* Chelmsford School of Art under Clifford Smith; Belstead House, Ipswich under Cavendish Morton, R.O.I., R.I.; calligraphy at Wensom Lodge under Mr. Webster, and at Belstead House with Gerald Mynott. Silver Palette award (1966) International Amateur Art Exhbn. *Clubs:* Writtle Art Group (until 1976), Norfolk and Norwich Art Circle. *Signs work:* "Joan Danvers" and see appendix. *Address:* Little Haven, Cromer Rd., W. Runton, Cromer, Norfolk.

**d'ARBELOFF, Natalie,** painter, printmaker, book-artist; *b* Paris, 7 Aug., 1929. *Educ:* Marymount School, N.Y. *Studied:* Art Students' League, N.Y., Central School of Art, London. *Exhib:* numerous group shows; solo shows include: Museum Fine Arts, Colorado Springs, Camden Arts Centre, Victoria & Albert Museum, Rijksmuseum, Meermano-Westreenianum, The Hague. *Work in collections:* V. & A., Manchester Polytechnic Library, Library of Congress, Washington D.C., N.Y. Public Library, Harvard, Princeton, Newberry Library, Humanities Research Center, Austin, National Library, Australia, etc. *Commissions:* murals: Asuncion, Paraguay and London. *Publications:* Creating in Collage (Studio Vista), An Artist's Workbook (Studio Vista), Designing with Natural Forms (Batsford), Livres d'Artiste (own NdA Press), Augustine's True Confession, The Augustine Adventures. *Signs work:* see appendix. *Address:* c/o Society of Design Craftsmen, 24 Rivington St., London EC2A 3DU.

**DARBISHIRE, Stephen John,** B.Ed. (1971), R.B.A. (1983); painter in oil, water-colour, pastel; *b* Greenodd, Cumbria, 9 Dec., 1940. *m* Kerry Delius. two *d. Educ:* Ulverston Grammar School, Cumbria. *Studied:* Byam Shaw School of Art (1958-59). *Exhib:* R.A., R.B.A., R.P., R.I.O., N.E.A.C. *Signs work:* "Stephen J. Darbishire." *Address:* Agnes Gill, Whinfell, Kendal, Cumbria LA8 9EJ.

**DARBY, Philip,** self taught artist in oil; *b* Birmingham, 14 June, 1938. *m* Susan. two *s. Exhib:* Newlyn Orion, Penwith Soc., Galerie Artica, Cuxhaven, Germany, R.W.A. *Work in collections:* Open University. *Signs work:* "Phil Darby." *Address:* Prospect House, Trevegean, St. Just, Penzance, Cornwall TR19 7NX.

**DARTON WATKINS, Christopher,** M.A.(Oxon.) (1951); painter in oil, wax, collage and mixed media; *b* Hants., 1928. *m* Torun. one *s. Educ:* Ampleforth College and Oxford. *Studied:* Ruskin School of Art, and privately. *Exhib:* Bear Lane Gallery, Oxford, Arnolfini Gallery, Bristol, Gallery Aix, Stockholm, Seifert-Binder Gallery, Munich, Alwin Gallery, London, Indar

147

# WHO'S WHO IN ART

Pasricha Fine Art, Anthony Dawson Fine Art, Edwin Pollard Gallery, David Curzon Gallery, Gerard Peters Gallery, Santa Fe, Original A.G., Båstad, Sweden. *Work in collections:* Linacre and Hertford Colleges, Oxford, Liverpool University, Royal Hospital, Chelsea, S.N.E.E., Lisbon, Soc. of Apothecaries, Stockholm, Svenska Handsbanken, Stockholm, Charterhouse Bank, London. *Clubs:* Chelsea Arts. *Signs work:* "Darton Watkins." *Address:* 7 Parkstead Rd., London SW15 5HW.

**DARWIN, Thomas Gerard,** F.R.B.S. (1976), B.Ed. (1976); sculptor in resins and metal powders; *b* Standish, Lancs., 10 June, 1928. *m* Marie Agnes (decd.); three *s.* two *d.* remarried Bridget. *Educ:* St. Peter's College, Freshfield. *Studied:* St. Mary's College, Strawberry Hill (1951-53, L. de C. Bucher, K.S.S., A.R.C.A.), Wigan School of Art (1955-57, Woffenden). *Exhib:* one-man show: Rural and Industries Bank, Perth, W.A.; numerous joint shows. *Work in collections:* Monument (Warrior and Maiden) Manzini, Swaziland; several religious works in churches and schools in England and Australia, busts in private collections and public places in Swaziland and Australia. *Signs work:* "G. Darwin." *Address:* Ezulwini, 34 Croyden Rd., Roleystone, W.A. 6111.

**DAS, Jatin,** artist in oil on canvas, pen and ink on paper and graphics; was Mem. General Council, LKA - National Academy of Art; *b* Orissa, India, 2 Dec., 1941; divorced. one *s.* one *d. Studied:* Sir J. J. School of Arts, Bombay. *Exhib:* Paris Biennale (1971), Venice Biennale (1978), Commonwealth Institute, Triennale, India 2nd., 3rd., 4th., London (1978), Birmingham City Museum (1975), Kassel (1975), and many exhbns. in India. *Work in collections:* National Gallery of Modern Art, New Delhi, Dalhem Museum, Berlin, Lalit Kala Academy, New Delhi, Smithsonian Inst., Washington, Grey Foundation, U.S.A. *Publications:* Book of Poems (1972). *Signs work:* see appendix. *Address:* C.12 Nizamuddin East, New Delhi 13, India; Studio: 134 Asian Games Village, Siri Fort, New Delhi-49.

**DAVIDSON, Anne,** D.A. (1959), A.R.B.S. (1988); sculptor in bronze, resin bronze, fibreglass; *b* Glasgow, 3 Feb., 1937. *m* James G. Davidson. one *s.* three *d. Educ:* Convent of the Sacred Heart, Aberdeen. *Studied:* Gray's School of Art (1955-59, Leo Clegg). *Exhib:* Aberdeen Artists Soc., Institut Français, London, Posk Gallery, London, Coventry Cathedral, Dundee A.G., etc. *Work in collections:* St. Mary's Cathedral, Aberdeen, St. Mary's, Inverness, and other churches, schools, etc.; public works in Edinburgh, Aberdeen and New York; portraits etc. in private collections. *Signs work:* "Anne Davidson." *Address:* 15 Redmoss Pk., Aberdeen AB12 3JF.

**DAVIDSON DAVIS, Philomena,** P.P.R.B.S., R.W.A., F.R.S.A.; sculptor; *b* Westminster, 1949. *m* Michael Davis, sculptor/founder. two *d. Educ:* Convent of Jesus and Mary, Willesden. *Studied:* sculpture: City and Guilds, London (1967-70, James Butler, R.A.), R.A. Schools (1970-73, Willi Soukop, R.A.). *Exhib:* R.A. Summer Show, R.W.A. Bristol, sculpture at Margam, Chelsea Harbour Sculpture (1993, 1996). April 1990 elected first woman President

148

Royal Society of British Sculptors (1990-96), Managing Director, The Sculpture Company (1995-present day). *Work in collections:* life-size bronzes Queens Ct., Milton Keynes Shopping Centre; Lady Henry Somerset Memorial, Victoria Embankment Gdns., London; "Fairway" a large outdoor sculpture for Donnington Valley. Hotel and Golf Course, Newbury, Berks. *Clubs:* Chelsea Arts. *Signs work:* see appendix. *Address:* The Mike Davis, Bronze Foundry, St James St., New Bradwell, Milton Keynes, Bucks.

**DAVIES, Anthony John,** R.E. (1994); artist/printmaker in etching and lithography; currently, Visiting Prof., Florida State University, U.S.A.; *b* Andover, Hants., 14 Jan., 1947. *Educ:* Andover Grammar School. *Studied:* Winchester School of Art (1966-70), R.C.A. (1970-73), Prix de Rome, engraving (1973-75). John Brinkley Fellow (1990-91). *Exhib:* over 57 one-man shows: U.K., U.S.A., S. Africa, N.Z. Represented U.K. at numerous overseas print biennales. *Work in collections:* U.S.A., Japan, Norway, Hungary, Poland, Russia. *Publications:* numerous exhbn. catalogues, articles and reviews. *Signs work:* "A.J. Davies." *Address:* c/o 421 Dean St., Grey Lynn, Auckland, N.Z.

**DAVIES, Gareth,** Hon. S.G.F.A.; artist in pencil, black ink, coloured pens; *b* St. Asaph, N. Wales, 10 Feb., 1972. *Educ:* Gogarth School/TVEI Centre Gogarth. *Exhib:* S.G.F.A., Botanical Fine Art Soc. *Publications:* Heroes All: The Story of the R.N.L.I. by Alec Beilby. *Signs work:* "G.P. Davies." *Address:* Bryn Awelon, Pentywyn Rd., Deganwy, Gwynedd LL31 9TL.

**DAVIES, Gordon Lionel,** A.R.C.A.; artist; *b* 14 Apr., 1926. *Educ:* Sevenoaks School. *Studied:* Camberwell School of Art (1949-50), R.C.A. (1950-53). *Exhib:* R.A. Summer Exhbns. (1953-91); one-man shows: Wye College, Kent (1964, 1967), King St.Galleries (1973, 1975, 1977, 1979, 1983, 1985); retrospective at The Royal Museum and A.G., Canterbury, Sally Hunter Fine Art (1993, 1994,1997). *Work in collections:* mural decorations at Wolfson College, Cambridge, Wye College, Kent, Braxted Park, Essex, Clerical and Medical Assurance Bldg., Bristol; shellwork decoration at Basildon House, Pangbourne for National Trust. *Publications:* botanical illustrations for House and Garden magazine (1949-70); Working with Acrylics (Search Press). *Signs work:* "Gordon Davies." *Address:* South View, Hastingleigh, Ashford, Kent TN25 5HU.

**DAVIES, Iris Mary,** F.S.B.A. (1986), B.Sc. (1949), Cambs. Cert. in Teaching (1950); artist in water-colour; retd. from teaching (1979); *b* Shotley, Ipswich, 4 Oct., 1919. *m* David Maldwyn Davies, B.Sc. one *d*. *Educ:* University College of Wales, Aberystwyth, Cambridge University. *Studied:* Cambridge University and privately. *Exhib:* R.I. (1982-89), S.B.A. (1986-95), S.W.A. (1987-93). *Signs work:* "Mary Davies." *Address:* High Trees, Minstead, Lyndhurst, Hants. SO43 7FX.

**DAVIES, Ivor,** N.D.D. (1956), A.T.D. (1957), Ph.D. (Edin.) (1975), V.P.R.C.A. (1993); artist/painter in oil, tempera, water-colour, gouache, crayon; *b* Wales, 9 Nov., 1935. *Studied:* Cardiff (1952-56) and Swansea (1956-57)

Colleges of Art, Lausanne University, Edinburgh University. *Exhib:* over 20 one-man shows worldwide since 1963, also Multi-media Destruction in Art 1960's. *Work in collections:* Deal Coll. Dallas, A.C.G.B., W.A.C., National Museum of Wales, etc. *Publications:* articles on Modern Art History, others in Welsh language journals; illustrations: Spirit (1971), Rubaiyat (1981), Science and Art (1981). *Signs work:* "Ivor Davies." *Address:* 99 Windsor Rd., Penarth CF6 1JF.

**DAVIS, Cynthia,** self taught artist in oil; *b* Allahabad, India. *m* Eric Bernard Davis. *Exhib:* St Ives Soc. of Artists, Mariners Gallery, Penwith Gallery. *Signs work:* "Cynthia Davis." *Address:* 1 Bay Villas, St. Ives Rd., Carbis Bay, St. Ives, Cornwall TR26 2SX.

**DAVIS, Derek Maynard,** F.C.P.A.; Artist in Residence, University of Sussex (1967); painter, potter; Hon. Mem. International Academy of Ceramics; *b* London, 1926. *m* Ruth. one *s. Educ:* Emanuel School, Wandsworth. *Studied:* painting: Central School of Arts and Crafts, London, under Keith Vaughan, Robert Buhler. *Exhib:* Istanbul, Munich, Toronto, Zurich, Tokyo, Paris, Primavera (London and Cambridge). *Work in collections:* Paisley Museum, V. & A., Portsmouth Museum, Southampton Museum, Keramion, Frechen, Germany, University of Sussex, Bradford Museum, Garth Clark Collection, U.S.A., Contemporary Art Soc., Musee Ariana, Geneva, Switzerland. *Signs work:* "D.M. Davis." *Address:* Duff House, Maltravers St., Arundel, Sussex BN18 9AP.

**DAVIS, James,** L.I.F.A.; Freeman the Worshipful Company Painter-Stainers (1972); Freeman of the City of London (1973); sculptor, carver and restorer in stone, marble; *b* London, 16 July, 1926. *m* Joan Davis. *Educ:* Eastbrook Boys School, Dagenham, Essex. *Studied:* Sir John Cass School of Art (1949-53) under Bainbridge Copnal. *Exhib:* Guildhall; Leighton House, Royal Exchange, Mall Galleries. *Work in collections:* Painters Hall, Chelsea and Kensington Town Hall, Community Centre, Shoeburyness, Barclay International, Gracechurch St., St. Nicholas Church, Elm Park, Essex, St. Nicholas Church, Canewdon, Essex, Hyde Park Corner, London W1. *Signs work:* "J. Davis." *Address:* Studio Workshop, 39a West Rd., Shoeburyness, Essex, SS3 9DR.

**DAVIS, John Warren,** M.C., A.T.D.; sculptor in wood, stone and metal; *b* Christchurch, 24 Feb., 1919. *m* Evelyn Ann. three *s.* one *d. Educ:* Bedford School. *Studied:* Westminster School of Art (1937-39), under Bernard Meninsky and Mark Gertler; Brighton College of Art (1948-52), under James Woodford, R.A. *Work in collections:* Cardiff, Leeds, Southampton, New York, Arts Council, Contemporary Art Soc., London, Houston, Texas, Fogg Art Musem, Mass., U.S.A. *Address:* Northfields Farm, Eastergate, Chichester, Sussex PO20 6RX.

**DAVIS, Kate,** B.A. (1982), H.Dip. (1986), M.A. (Status) Oxon. (1992), Stanley Picker Fellow (1986-87), Whitechapel Young Artist of Year (1988);

sculptor/lecturer object-based, using video, photography, drawing; Tutor of Fine Art, Ruskin School of Drawing, Oxford; *b* Chesham, Bucks., 23 Feb., 1960. *m* A. Ruethi. one *d. Educ:* Loreto College, St. Albans. *Studied:* Herts. College of Art and Design (1978-79), Falmouth School of Art (1979-82), Slade School of Fine Art (1983-85). *Exhib:* solo shows: Milch, London, Newlyn A.G., Penzance, South Hill Art Centre, Bracknell, Whitechapel A.G., and numerous group shows in Britain and abroad. *Work in collections:* "Little Red" National Sculpture Centre, Oronsko, Poland. *Publications:* Kate Davis (Milch Gallery, 1997). *Signs work:* "K.A. DAVIS," "KAD" or not at all. *Address:* 56 Nelson Rd., London N8 9RT.

**DAVIS, Michael Robert,** N.D.D., M.A. (R.C.A.); artist in charcoal conté (drawing), lecturer; Principal Lecturer (Painting), Kent Inst. of Art and Design; *b* Birmingham, 11 Sept., 1943. *m* Susan Davis. one *d. Educ:* Birmingham College of Art (1959-64), Royal College of Art (1964-67). *Exhib:* R.A. Summer Exhbn. since 1986, Hayward Annual (1982), 15 British Painters, British Council, Barcelona, 5 British Artists - de Grey, Davis, Hockney, Freud, Weight, Alabama U.S.A., Mike Davis (drawings El Palau Valencia), Cassian de Vere Cole, London. *Work in collections:* Arts Council, and private. *Publications:* Guardian Arts Review, Contemporary Arts Review Guardian, Times Arts Review, 5 British Artists Honouring England, Alabama Times, Panning for Gold - George Melly (1993), Andrew Lambirth review or show at Cassian de Vere Cole (1996). *Signs work:* see appendix. *Address:* 5 Elmers End Rd., London SE20 7ST.

**DAVIS, Pamela,** V.P.R.M.S. (1979), F.S.B.A. (1985), S.W.A. (1977), S.G.F.A. (1992), H.S.F. (1983); miniaturist and flower painter in water-colour, acrylic, gouache; Vice-Pres. R.M.S.; *b* Molesey, 27 Aug., 1927. *m* Ronald. two *s. Educ:* Ashford County School. *Studied:* Twickenham School of Art (1942-45, Dorothy Parlbey). *Exhib:* Westminster Gallery, London: R.M.S., S.W.A., S.B.A.; Llewellyn Alexander Gallery, London; Linda Blackstone Gallery, Pinner. *Signs work:* "Pamela Davis." *Address:* 4 Broomfield, Sunbury-on-Thames, Middx. TW16 6SW.

**DAVIS, Robin,** self-taught painter in oil; *b* Bournemouth, 28 Feb., 1925. one *s.* one *d. Educ:* St. Catherine's College, Oxford; Birkbeck College, London. *Exhib:* one-man shows: Woodstock Gallery, London (1960), New Vision Centre, London (1964), Aston University, B`ham (1965), Horizon Gallery, London (1988), Belgrave Gallery, London (1995), Bakehouse Gallery, Penzance (1996). *Signs work:* "Robin Davis." *Address:* 45 Trelissick Rd., Hayle, Penzance, Cornwall TR27 4HY.

**DAWSON, Patricia Vaughan,** printmaker, sculptor and writer; *b* Liverpool, 23 Jan., 1925. *m* James N. Dawson. one *s.* two *d. Educ:* Croham Hurst School. *Studied:* Croydon School of Art (1941-45) under Reginald Marlow and Ruskin Spear. *Exhib:* Bear Lane Gallery, R.A., London Group, Pastel Soc., R.S.P.A. *Work in collections:* B.M., Bibliothèque Nationale. *Publications:* The Artist

Looks at Life (a series of books and slides published by Visual Publications introducing art to children). *Address:* Flat 1, 3 Albion Villas Rd., London SE26 4DB.

**DAWSON, Peter,** R.I., B.Ed.; painter in water-colour, oil; teacher; Adviser for Art and Design, Hertfordshire; *b* Leeds, 19 Mar., 1947. *m* (1) Andrea Dixon, (2) Sarah Harrison. *Educ:* Roundhay School, Leeds. *Studied:* Bingley College of Educ. (1967-71). *Exhib:* R.I., Yorkshire Artists, Hitchin Museum, Luton A.G., October Gallery, San Francisco, Federation of Canadian Artists Gallery, Vancouver, Fry Art Museum, Seattle, Shell House Gallery, Attendi Gallery. *Work in collections:* Herts. Educ. Authority, Luton A.G. *Publications:* Co-author, Albania - A Guide and Illustrated Journal; prints and limited editions. *Signs work:* "P. Dawson" or "Peter Dawson." *Address:* Little Cokenach, Nuthampstead, Royston, Herts. SG8 8LS.

**DAY, D.P.A.,** Prof., A.G.P.P. (1979), S.G.F.A. (1986); archivist for S.G.F.A.; artist in oil and water-colour; *Exhib:* Mall Galleries, Knapp Gallery, Art Connoisseur Gallery and Westminster Gallery. *Signs work:* "Daphne Day." *Address:* 20 The Avenue, Bedford Pk., Chiswick, London W4 1HT.

**DAY, Jane,** B.Ed.(Hons.) (1989); ceramist in T-material; Subject Leader (ceramics), City of Bath College; *b* Cambridge, 18 June, 1966. *Educ:* Bath College of Higher Educ., but largely self taught. *Commissions:* Selfridges, London (Smokefired Vessel Forms). *Signs work:* see appendix. *Address:* 2 West Barnes, Shepreth Rd., Barrington, Cambridge.

**DAY, Lucienne,** R.D.I., A.R.C.A. (1940), F.C.S.D.; textile designer; Royal Designer for Industry (1962), (Master 1987-89); Hon. Doctor of Design, Southampton University (1995); *b* Coulsdon, Surrey, 1917. *m* Robin Day. one *d. Educ:* Convent of Notre Dame di Sion, Worthing. *Studied:* Croydon School of Art (1934-37), R.C.A. (1937-40). *Exhib:* London, Manchester, Zürich, Milan, Oslo, Toronto, New York, Tokyo, Kyoto, Gothenberg. *Work in collections:* V. & A., Whitworth A.G., University of Manchester, museums of Cranbrook, Michigan, Museum of Industrial Design Trondheim, Norway, Röhsska Konstslöjd Museum, Gothenburg, Sweden, Musee des Arts Decoratifs, Montreal, and Art Inst. of Chicago. *Signs work:* silk mosaic tapestries: "L." *Address:* 49 Cheyne Walk, Chelsea, London SW3 5LP.

**DAY, Robin,** O.B.E., A.R.C.A., F.C.S.D., R.D.I.; designer; *b* High Wycombe, Bucks., 1915. *Studied:* High Wycombe School of Art and R.C.A. *Exhib:* Museum of Modern Art, New York, I.C.A., Triennale, Milan (1951), Copenhagen, Oslo, Stavanger, Bergen, Zürich, Canada. *Work in collections:* Museum of Modern Art, New York, Trondheim Industrial Art Museum, V. & A. *Publications:* work repro.: many architectural and design publications here and abroad. *Clubs:* Alpine, Eagles Ski. *Address:* 49 Cheyne Walk, Chelsea, London SW3 5LP.

**DAYKIN, Michael,** M.A. (R.C.A.); artist, curator; *b* Yorkshire, 1947. *Studied:* Watford School of Art (1970-71), St. Martin's School of Art (1971-

74), R.C.A. (1974-77). *Exhib:* City University Gallery, Cleveland College of Art Gallery, XO Gallery, The Figure of Eight Gallery. *Work in collections:* Northern Arts, Brown and Wood, Benchmark Holdings (commission), Quaglino's (commission). *Signs work:* "Daykin." *Address:* 9 Lowder House, Wapping Lane, London E1 9RJ.

**DEAKIN, Liz (née Boatswain),** S.W.A.; artist in water-colour, gouache and acrylics of landscapes, flower painting, interiors, silk painting and murals; runs painting courses and gives demonstrations to societies; *b* Dorchester, 1929; marriage dissolved; two children. *Studied:* Poole School of Art, and with Edward Wessen. *Work in collections:* many private collections throughout the world, including the Royal Family. *Publications:* "Deakin's Dorset"; designs hotel brochures. *Signs work:* "Liz Deakin." *Address:* 3 Hunters Mead, Motcombe, Shaftesbury SP7 9QG.

**DEAKINS, Cyril Edward,** A.R.E. (1948), A.T.D. (1947); painter in oil, tempera and water-colour, wood-engraver; *b* Bearwood, nr. Birmingham, 5 Oct 1916 married. one *s.* one *d. Educ:* Christ's College, Finchley. *Studied:* under J. C. Moody, Norman Janes, at Hornsey School of Art. *Exhib:* R.A., N.E.A.C., R.E., R.B.A., R.I. *Work in collections:* Print Collectors' Club, presentation print, Ellingham Mill E. Anglian Artists Exhbn. (1977), Beecroft A. G., Westcliff (1986). *Publications:* work repro.: four postage stamp designs for Govt. of Bermuda, 1953, book and magazine illustrations; articles on water-colour, Leisure Painter since 1977. *Signs work:* "C.D." or "Cyril Deakins." *Address:* 1 Mill Lane, Dunmow, Essex CM6 1BG.

**DEAKINS, Sylvia,** A.T.D. (1946), S.G.F.A. (1986), C.D.S. (1987); painter and illustrator in oil, gouache, pastel, ink, collage; Vice-Pres. Cambridge Drawing Soc. (1997); *b* Eccleshill, W. Yorks., 18 Oct., 1924. *m* C.E. Deakins. one *s.* one *d. Educ:* Hendon County Grammar. *Studied:* Hornsey College of Art (1941-46, Douglas Percy Bliss, Russell Reeve, Francis Winter). *Exhib:* R.A., R.B.A., N.E.A.C., and numerous galleries in E. Anglia. *Publications:* illustrated many for O.U.P. Longmans, Ward Lock, including A Beginner's Bible (1958), and Listening to Children Talking (1976). *Signs work:* "Sylvia Deakins." *Address:* 1 Mill La., Gt. Dunmow, Essex CM6 1BG.

**DEAKINS, Thomas William (Tom),** B.A. (Hons.) (1980), A.T.C. (1982), Charles Spence Memorial prize (1977); painter in oil, drawing media; *b* Barnet, 8 Dec., 1957. *m* Ann Logan. one *s. Educ:* Newport Grammar School, Essex. *Studied:* University of Newcastle upon Tyne (1976-80, Kenneth Rowntree, Derwent Wise). *Exhib:* R.A. Summer Shows since 1983, Medici Gallery (1989), William Hardy Glasgow (1991), Chappel Gallery, Colchester (1995), Art Dot Com (Internet) 1997. *Work in collections:* Hatton Gallery, University of Newcastle, Epping Forest District Museum, Beecroft A.G. Westcliff on Sea. *Signs work:* "T. Deakins" or "T.D." *Address:* Clock House Cottage, 79a The Causeway, Gt. Dunmow, Essex CM6 2AB.

**DEAN, Beryl,** M.B.E. (1975), A.R.C.A. (1937), F.S.D.C. (1970); freelance designer, author, lecturer, embroiderer; *b* Bromley, 1911. *m* W. M. Phillips; two stepsons. *Educ:* Bromley High School, G.P.D.S.T. *Studied:* Bromley School of Art (1932), Royal School of Needlework (1929), Royal College of Art (1935). *Exhib:* solo shows, Ecclesiastical Embroidery: St. Paul's Cathedral, etc., and abroad. *Work in collections:* V. & A., Collection of the Embroiderers Guild, London, etc. *Commissions:* Cathedrals, Churches G.B., U.S.A., etc. *Publications:* Ecclesiastical Embroidery, Ideas for Church Embroidery, Church Needlework, Creative appliqué, Embroidery in Religion and Ceremonial, Church Embroidery, Designing Stitched Textiles for the Church. *Address:* 59 Thornhill Sq., London N1 1BE.

**DEAN, Dorothy,** S.W.A.; artist in gouache, oil, pastel; *b* 14 May 1920. *m* K.W. Howard. one *s. Educ:* Bromley County School, Kent. *Studied:* Goldsmiths' School of Art (1936-39), Eastbourne Art School, Guildford (part-time post war). *Exhib:* R.I., R.O.I., R.B.A., R.P.S., P.S., numerous solo and shared exhbns. in S. England. *Signs work:* "Dorothy Dean" and "D. Dean." *Address:* Ashley Cottage, Bentworth, Alton, Hants. GU34 5RH.

**DEAN, John H. W.,** R.M.S., S.M., F.R.S.A., F.S.O.A.; Fellow British Soc. of Painters; Founder Mem. and Pres., Upper-Wharfedale Museum Soc.; self taught artist in oil of large river landscapes, miniatures on ivory in oil; *b* Grassington, N. Yorks., 25 Mar., 1930. *m* Dorothy. *Educ:* Grassington C. of E. School. *Exhib:* R.M.S., U.A., S.M., Yorkshire Artists, International Art Fair, Olympia, Salon des Nation, Paris. *Work in collections:* Shell Oil International, A.E. Auto Parts, John Ward Textiles, Lord Harewood, The Earl of Burlington, etc.; and in most countries of the world. *Publications:* work repro.: Limited Edition prints by Delta Prints, Guernsey, self and Medici. *Signs work:* "John Dean, R.M.S." in black on oils, "J. Dean" in black on miniatures. *Address:* Norwood, 13 Southwood La., Grassington, Skipton, N. Yorks. BD23 5NA.

**DEAN, Pauline Margaret,** R.H.S. Gold medals (5); freelance botanical illustrator in water-colour, inks, pencil; nurse (retd.); tutor of Botanical Art Courses, R.H.S. Gdn. Wisley, Surrey; *b* Brighton, 20 Aug., 1943. *m* George. three *s.* one *d. Educ:* Brighton and Hove High School; no formal art training. *Exhib:* Kew Gdns. Gallery, Library, R.H.S. London, annually R.H.S. shows Vincent Sq. London, Linnean Soc., London, Guildford House Gallery, Guildford. *Work in collections:* Hunt Inst. for Botanical Illustration, Pittsburgh, U.S.A.; Linnean Soc. London; Lindley Library R.H.S. London. *Publications:* with other artists: various inc. Curtis' Botanical Magazine, R.H.S. New Dictionary of Gardening, The New Plantsman. *Signs work:* "P.M. Dean." *Address:* 27 Poltimore Rd., Guildford GU2 5PR.

**DEAN, Ronald Herbert,** R.S.M.A. (1970), F.C.I.I. (1965); self-taught painter in water-colour and oil; Insurance broker; *b* Farnborough, Hants., 1929. *m* Audrey Grace Payne. two *d. Educ:* Farnborough Grammar School. *Exhib:* R.S.M.A., R.I., R.B.A., Biarritz, Salem Or., U.S.A., National Maritime Museum. *Clubs:* Tonbridge Art Group. *Signs work:* "RONALD DEAN" print-

# WHO'S WHO IN ART

ed. *Address:* 8 Glebelands, Bidborough, Tunbridge Wells, Kent.

**DEANE, Frederick,** R.P. (1972); painter in oil, gouache, pastel; *b* Manchester, 1924. *m* Audrey Craig. two *s*. one *d. Studied:* Manchester College of Art (1940-43), R.A. Schools (1946-51, Philip Connard). Served with Para Regt. 1st Airborne Div. (1943-45). Visiting tutor: Manchester College of Art (1952-60), City of London Polytechnic (1970-82). *Exhib:* R.A., R.P. *Work in collections:* Chatsworth; Oxford, Cambridge, Manchester, Rhodes, McGill and Kent Universities; Manchester City A.G. *Clubs:* Chelsea Arts. *Signs work:* "Deane." *Address:* Penrallt Goch, Llan Ffestiniog, Gwynedd LL41 4NS.

**DEANE, Jasper,** Cert.F.A. (Oxon.) (1971), Dip.F.A. (1974), M.A. (1978); artist in water-colour and oil; *b* Ches., 15 July, 1952. *Educ:* Bryanston School, Blandford. *Studied:* Ruskin School of Drawing (1969-71), Ealing School of Art (1972-74), R.C.A. (1975-78). *Exhib:* Ruskin R8 Show, Oxford Graduate Centre (1970), Folio Soc. (1976, 1977, 1978), Valentine Show, Illustrators Gallery (1977), The Animal in Art, R.C.A. (1977), Spirit of London, Royal Festival Hall (1978), 'Well Travelled', Gardiner Centre, University of Sussex (1987), 'Maginot Line' drawings for an opera, Riverside Studios (1988), 'Breakthrough' 25 years of illustration at the R.C.A. (1988); one-man shows: Cale Art (1985), Stephen Bartley Gallery (1986, 1987), Friends of the Arts, London (1990), 'Artistes 93 avec Stop à la Destruction du Monde', Paris (1993), Pimlico (1996). *Publications:* A Duck Flies Up (Ealing, 1974), Cornish Travel Sketches (R.C.A., 1978), The Pillow Book of Siesho-Nagon (Folio Soc., 1979), Ink Flamingoes (1981), Renditions Magazine (University of Hong Kong, 1982), Field Magazine, Sporting Horse. *Clubs:* Old Students Assoc. R.C.A., Chelsea Arts. *Signs work:* "J.D." or "Jasper Deane." *Address:* 13c St. Stephens Ave., London W12 8JB.

**de BURGH, Lydia,** R.U.A. (Hon.), U.W.S., U.W.A., Dip.Mem. Chelsea Art Soc. (1958-65); portrait and landscape painter in oil and water-colour; lecturer; *b* London, 3 July, 1923. *Educ:* privately. *Studied:* under Sonya Mervyn, R. P. (1948-51), Byam Shaw School of Art (1952), Edward Wesson, R.I. *Exhib:* London, N. Ireland Office (1955), Boston, Vose Gallery (1957), R.P., R.B.A., R.G.I., R.U.A., Royal Birmingham, Wildlife Artists, etc.; retrospective exhbns. 1993 Down Museum, Belfast for 6 weeks. *Work in collections:* (personal sittings) of H.M. The Queen and the Royal Family; numerous works in public and private collections. *Commissions:* portraits and landscape. *Publications:* autobiography, "Lydia's Story" (1991), further autobiog. "Another Way of Life" (to be published 1998). *Signs work:* "L. de Burgh, R.U.A." (or earlier works A.R.U.A.). *Address:* 4 Church Ct., Clough, Downpatrick, Co. Down, N. Ireland BT30 8QX.

**de FRANCIA, Peter,** painter in oil, author; Principal, DFA, School of Art, Goldsmiths, College, University of London; Professor, School of Painting, R.C.A. London (1972-87); *b* Beaulieu, Alpes Maritimes, France, 25 Jan., 1921. *Studied:* Academy of Brussels, Slade School. *Work in collections:* Museum of

155

Modern Art, N.Y., Arts Council of Gt. Britain, Tate Gallery, V. & A., British Museum, National Gallery of Modern Art, Prague, Imperial War Museum; private collections in U.K., and U.S.A. *Publications:* Fernand Léger (Cassells, 1968-69); Fernand Léger (Yale University Press, London, Sept. 1983); "Untitled" 49 drawings (Brondums Forlag, Copenhagen 1989). *Signs work:* see appendix. *Address:* 44 Surrey Sq., London SE17 2JX.

**DE GOEDE, Julien Maximilien,** painter in mixed media; *b* Rotterdam, Holland, 20 May, 1937. *Educ:* High School, Nijmegen. *Studied:* Academie voor Beeldende Kunsten en Kunstnijverheid, Arnhem (1953-55), Eindhoven School of Art (1955-56), Julian Ashton School of Art, Sydney (1957-58). *Exhib:* Three one-man shows, Canberra, four one-man shows, Grabowski, London, two House, London, one Riverside Studios, London. *Work in collections:* Australian National University, Leicestershire Educ. Com., Contemporary Art Society, Eastern Arts Assoc., Laing A.G., Newcastle upon Tyne, Museum Sztuki, Lodz, Poland, Arts Council of Gt. Britain, Bedfordshire Educ. Service, City Art Gallery, Bristol, Deutsche Bank, Unilever, Jhonson & Jhonson. *Signs work:* "Jules de Goede." *Address:* 71 Stepney Green, London E1 3LE.

**DE LA FOUGÈRE, Lucette,** R.B.A., R.O.I., N.S.; painter in oil, watercolour, gouache, and sculptor in ceramics; *b* London. *Educ:* both in Touraine, France, and London. *Studied:* under Leopold Pascal and Krome Barratt, P.P.R.O.I., R.B.A. *Exhib:* R.A., Royal Society of British Artists, Royal Institute of Oil Painters, National Soc. of Painters, Printers and Engravers; one-man show: Mall Galleries; works permanently on tour in Great Britain and U.S.A. *Work in collections:* The National Museum of Wales, Cardiff. *Clubs:* Chelsea Arts. *Signs work:* "FOUGÈRE." *Address:* The Studio, 20 Lower Common South, Putney, London SW15.

**DELHANTY, Denys,** A.T.D. (1949), R.W.A. (1963); artist in collage, oil, water-colour, gouache; past Hon. Sec. and council mem. R.W.A.; Head of Art, Cheltenham Ladies College (1951-64), Senior Lecturer, Rolle College, Exmouth and Gloucester (1964-81); *b* Cardiff, 13 Oct., 1925. *m* Kate Ormrod. three *s.* one *d. Educ:* St. Illtyd's College, Cardiff. *Studied:* Cardiff College of Art (1942-44, 1947-50, Ceri Richards). *Exhib:* R.W.A., etc. *Work in collections:* R.W.A., Welsh Arts Council, Cheltenham A.G. *Signs work:* "Denys Delhanty." *Address:* Combe House, Sheepscombe, Stroud, Glos. GL6 7RG.

**DELHANTY, Kate Elizabeth,** D.F.A. (Slade); artist in oil; artist mem. R.W.A.; taught art at Cheltenham Ladies College (1953-60); *b* London, 8 Nov., 1928. *m* Denys Delhanty. three *s.* one *d. Educ:* Downe House, Newbury, Berks. *Studied:* Reading University, Slade School of Fine Art (1950-53, Prof. Coldstream). *Exhib:* R.A., Bristol (R.W.A.), Cheltenham A.G., Bristol Guild, etc. *Work in collections:* R.W.A., Cheltenham A.G. *Publications:* articles in Leisure Painter Magazine. *Signs work:* "Kate Delhanty." *Address:* Combe House, Sheepscombe, Stroud, Glos. GL6 7RG.

**DEMARCO, Richard,** O.B.E., l'Ordre des Arts et Lettres de France, Cavaliere de la Reppublica d'Italia, Gold Order of Merit Republic of Poland, Hon. F.R.I.A.S., Hon.D.F.A. (A.C.A.), R.S.W., S.S.A.; water-colourist/printmaker in water-colour, gouache, pen and ink, screen printing, etching; Prof. of European Cultural Studies, Kingston University; Artistic Director, Demarco European Art Foundation; *b* Edinburgh, 9 July, 1930. *m* Anne Muckle. *Educ:* Holy Cross Academy, Edinburgh. *Studied:* Edinburgh College of Art (1949-54, Sir William Gillies, Leonard Rosoman). *Exhib:* over sixty one-man shows including Third Eye Centre, Aberdeen Artspace, Editions Alecto Gallery. *Work in collections:* S.N.G.M.A., Dundee City A.G., V. & A., Aberdeen A.G., Hunterian Museum Glasgow, S.A.C., Edinburgh City A.G., Citibank, Chemical Bank, Bank of Scotland, Royal Bank of Scotland, Clydesdale Bank, H.R.H. Prince Philip, H.R.H. Prince Charles. *Publications:* The Road to Meikle Seggie The Artist as Explorer. *Clubs:* Scottish Arts. *Signs work:* "Richard Demarco." *Address:* (home) 23a Lennox St., Edinburgh EH4 1PY; (office) Kingston University, Millenium House, 21 Eden St., Kingston-on-Thames, Surrey.

**DEMEL, Richard,** Ph.D. (1981), Art Diploma (1948), F.I.L.Incorp. Linguist, F.R.S.A.; retd. art master, writer; lecturer: Univ. of Padova and Venice; stained glass artist (transparent mosaic method inventor), painter, engraver; *b* Ustron, Poland, 21 Dec., 1921. *m* Anna Parisi. one *s.* one *d. Educ:* Andrychow and Biala-Bielsko. *Studied:* Accad. d. Belle Arti (1945-47), Rome, Polish Accad. Art Centre, Rome, London (1945-49); London University Slade School (1949); LCC Central School of Art (1949-51) B.A. Lang, Venice University; M.A. Lang, Polish University, London; asst. to J. Nuttgens (St. Etheldreda's Church windows); asst. lecturer to Prof. M. Bohusz-Szyszko. *Exhib:* 22 one-man and 120 collective; ITV film (1961), BBC TV on pupils' work (with Miró 1962); Polish TV Documentary (1992); designed and exec; H.C. Comu. S.Leonards O.S. (4); Rome (1); 3 mosaic windows: Cathedral, Padua; Duomo Cittadella (4); Codevigo Church (2) Italy. *Publications:* in 60 art encyclopaedias and art publications. Biographer of Sergiusz Piasecki. *Signs work:* see appendix. *Address:* Via S. Domenico 21-35030 Tencarola, Padova, Italy.

**de MEO, P. (Pamela Synge),** artist in oil and water-colour; *b* London, 2 Sept., 1920. *m* Major Brian Synge. three *s. Educ:* Cheltenham Ladies' College. *Studied:* St. Martin's College of Art, Chelsea School of Art, Heatherleys (1953). *Exhib:* R.A. (1988), Paris Salon, R.B.A. Galleries, Chelsea Artists, Bankside Gallery (G.B., U.S.S.R. Assoc., 1985), Mall Galleries, Bowmore Gallery, Halkin St., W1 (1989), Charity Exhbn. for Red Cross (1991), Gagliardi Gallery, Chelsea (1993), Patterson Gallery, Albemarle St. (1994), Chelsea Arts Soc. (1993, 1994), Britain-Russian Assoc. (1995); one-man show: Tradescant Trust Museum (1988). *Clubs:* Dover St. Arts, Chelsea Arts. *Signs work:* "P. de Meo." *Address:* 4 Pembroke Cl., Grosvenor Cres., London SW1X 7ET.

**de MERIC, Rosalie,** F.F.P.S., B.A. (Fine Art) Norwich; painter; *b* 1916. *m* Thomas Blackburn, 1945. one *d*. *Educ:* Private boarding school. *Studied:* Medway, St. Martin's and Norwich. *Exhib:* widely in U.K. and abroad. *Signs work:* "de Meric." *Address:* Lavender Cottage, Westleton, Saxmundham, Suffolk IP17 3AG.

**DENAHY, John Albert,** N.E.A.C. (1980); painter in oil, water-colour and pastel; *b* London, 1922. *m* Judith Eveline Partington. two *d*. *Educ:* St. Joseph's, Deptford. *Studied:* Eltham Art Centre. *Exhib:* R.A., N.E.A.C., R.B.A., R.W.E., W.H. Pattersons (N.E.A.C.); one-man show Anna-Mei Chadwick Gallery (1989, 1991, 1993); mixed exhbns.: Moya Bucknall Fine Art, Woodlands A.G., Greenwich Theatre, Tudor Barn, Eltham. Prize winner N.E.A.C. Centenary Exhbn. (1986), Daler Rowney 1st prize R.B.A. (1987), prize winner Ass. Artistique de la Banque de France (1986). *Work in collections:* B.P. International, Bank of England Services Ltd., I.B.M. *Publications:* Leisure Artist magazine. *Signs work:* "J.D." or "J. Denahy." *Address:* 117 Church Rd., Hatfield Peverel, Essex CM3 2LB.

**DENISON, David,** surrealist artist in acrylic and oil; tutor, Prison Staff College, Wakefield; *b* Wakefield, 21 May, 1939. *m* Linda. one *s*. two *d*. *Educ:* Snapethorpe Secondary Modern School, Wakefield. *Studied:* Doncaster College of Art (1972). *Exhib:* Wakefield, Skipton, London, Keighley, Bradford, Camden Arts Centre; one-man shows: Manor House Public A.G., Ilkley (1970, 1977), Goole Museum and A.G. (1971), Wakefield Museum and A.G. (1972, 1974), Leeds City Gallery (1973), Doncaster A.G. (1973), Arthur Koestler Exhbn. London (1977), Bradford Cartwright Hall (1980), Angela Flowers Gallery, Arts Council of Gt. Britain. *Work in collections:* Brighton Museum and A.G., Sir Roland Penrose Collection. *Publications:* illustrated The Battle of Wilderness Wood by R. Adams. *Signs work:* "D. Denison." *Address:* 58 Station Rd., Burley in Wharfedale, W. Yorks.

**DENLEY-HILL, William George,** A.R.C.A. (1929); artist in water-colour and oil; H.M. Inspector Art Schools (1949-72); Principal, Newton Abbott School of Art (1939-45), Bournville School of Art (1945-49); *b* London, 27 June, 1906. *m* G.M. Denley-Hill, A.R.C.A. two *s*. *Studied:* R.C.A. (1926-29, Sir William Rothenstein). *Exhib:* Manor House Fine Arts, Cardiff, York City A.G. *Work in collections:* B'ham City A.G., Newport A.G. *Publications:* illustrated numerous children's books for Blackwell of Oxford. *Signs work:* "W.G.D. Hill." *Address:* 19 Lower St., Merriott, nr. Crewkerne, Somerset TA16 5NL.

**DENTON, Kenneth Raymond,** R.S.M.A., F.C.S.D., F.R.S.A., I.S.M.P.; landscape and marine artist in oil; *b* Chatham, 20 Aug., 1932. *m* Margaret Denton. three *s*. *Educ:* Troy Town School, Rochester. *Studied:* Rochester School of Art and Technical School, Medway College of Art for decorative design and painting, landscape painting with David Mead. *Exhib:* York, Rochester, London, Eastbourne, Thames Ditton, Stratford-on-Avon, Norwich,

Los Angeles, Mystic, Vancouver, San Francisco, Pennsylvania, Washington D.C., Tunbridge Wells; 40 one-man shows, R.O.I., R.B.A., etc. *Publications:* work repro.: Medici Soc., Royles, Artists Britain, Yachting Monthly, Yachting World, Connoisseur, Guild Prints. *Clubs:* R.S.M.A. *Signs work:* "Kenneth Denton." *Address:* Priory Farm Lodge, Sporle, Kings Lynn, Norfolk PE32 2DS.

**de QUIN, Robert,** N.D.D. (1950); sculptor working in welded metals mainly in abstact style; retd. art teacher; *b* Namur, Belgium, 6 July, 1927. *m* Diana. two *d. Educ:* Belgium and U.K. *Studied:* Hornsey School of Art (1945-50). *Exhib:* several one-man shows including Mall Galleries (1972); numerous group shows including Berkeley Sq., London (1972), B.P. Oil sculpture, Festival Hall, London (1990), Dolphin Sq. sculpture, London (1993), Loggia Gallery, London. *Work in collections:* Britain, Belgium, S. Africa, U.S.A.; several commissioned works. *Clubs:* Fellow and Chairman, F.P.S. and Loggia Gallery, London. *Signs work:* "Robert de Quin." *Address:* 95 Fortis Green, London N2 9HU.

**DERRY, Pamela Mary,** N.S.; artist in oil; *b* Welwyn Garden City, 13 Apr., 1932; married. two *s.* two *d. Educ:* Bedford High School. *Exhib:* Mermaid Theatre, London, New Ashgate Gallery, Farnham, Century Gallery, Henley, Bladon Gallery, Andover, Fortescue Swann Gallery, London. *Work in collections:* Chelmsford Council, Russell Cotes Museum and Gallery, Bournemouth. *Publications:* work repro.: Leisure Painter. *Clubs:* N.S. *Signs work:* "Pamela Derry." *Address:* Whitemoor Farm, Whitemoor, Holt, Wimborne, Dorset BH21 7DA.

**de SAULLES, Mary,** A.R.I.B.A., (1948), A.A.dip (1947), F.C.S.D. (1959), F.R.S.A. (1981); architect and designer, interior, exhbn., display; deputy to chief officer of specialized design section, L.C.C. Architects' Dept. (1950-52); partnership with John Lunn, F.S.I.A. (1951-55); Industrial Designer, B.E.A. (1959); private practice (1960), interiors, exhbns., housing, etc. Conservation consultant.; *b* Westcliff-on-Sea, 1925. *m* Patrick de Saulles, A.A.dip. (d. 1997). two *s. Studied:* architecture: Architectural Assoc. School of Architecture. *Publications:* The Book of Shrewsbury (Barracuda Books Ltd.). Designers in Britain, Nos. 4 and 5, Architectural Review. *Clubs:* Architectural Assoc. *Signs work:* "Mary de Saulles." *Address:* Watergate House, St Mary's Water Lane, Shrewsbury SY1 2BX.

**DESMET, Anne,** M.A.(Oxon.) (1986), R.E. (1991), Dip. (Advanced Printmaking) (1988), Rome Scholar in Printmaking (1989-90); artist in wood engraving and collage; *b* Liverpool, 14 June, 1964. *Educ:* Sacred Heart High School, Liverpool. *Studied:* Ruskin School of Art (1983-86), Central School of Art (1987-88). *Exhib:* group shows: worldwide; solo shows U.K.: Duncan Campbell Gallery, Royal Overseas League, Godfrey & Twatt Gallery; and Ex Libris Museum Moscow, Russia. *Work in collections:* Ashmolean Museum, V. & A., National Art Library. *Commissions:* Sotheby's, British Museum.

*Publications:* Engravers Two (Silent Books), The Times, O.U.P. *Signs work:* "ANNE DESMET" or "A.J.D." *Address:* c/o Duncan Campbell Contemporary Art, 15 Thackeray St., London W8 5ET.

**DE VASCONCELLOS, Josefina,** M.B.E., F.R.B.S., Hon. D.Litt.; sculptor in stone, bronze, wood, perspex, lead; *b* Molesey-on-Thames. *m* the late Delmar Banner. *Educ:* Bournemouth High School. *Studied:* Regent St. Polytechnic; Florence; Paris. *Exhib:* R.A., Salon. *Work in collections:* National Gallery, Rio de Janeiro; Glasgow A.G.; Southampton A.G.; Sheffield A.G.; Gloucester Cathedral; Liverpool Cathedral; National Memorial to the Battle of Britain, Aldershot; Mary and Child, St. Paul's Cathedral. *Clubs:* Royal Overseas, Reynolds. *Signs work:* see appendix. *Address:* Prince Charlies House, 95 Strickland Gate, Kendal, Cumbria LA9 4RA.

**de VERE COLE, Cassian,** art dealer; Director, Cassian de Vere Cole Fine Art (since 1993) specialist in twentieth century British and contemporary art; previously: Christie's, London (1990-92), freelance New York, Chicago (1989-90), Parkin Gallery, London (1986-88); *b* London, 17 Nov., 1966. *Clubs:* Chelsea Arts. *Address:* c/o Cassian de Vere Cole Fine, Art 50 Elgin Cres., London W11 2JJ.

**DEVLIN, George,** R.S.W. (1964); painter in oil, water-colour, etching and ceramics; *b* Glasgow, 8 Sept., 1937. *Studied:* Glasgow School of Art (1955-60). *Exhib:* many one-man shows; Belfast Open 100, 2nd British Biennale of Drawing, Contemporary Scottish Painting (Arts Council), etc. *Work in collections:* H.M. The Queen, Scottish National Gallery of Modern Art, Arts Council, Aberdeen A.G., Essex County Council, Leicester and Strathclyde Universities, Edinburgh City Collection, Argyle County Council. *Publications:* illustrations for Scotsman and Maclellan Publishers. Designed set and costumes for new ballet by Walter Gore (1973) and presented by Scottish Ballet. *Signs work:* "Devlin." *Address:* 6 Falcon Terr. Lane, Glasgow G20 0AG.

**DEWSBURY, Gerald,** B.A.; landscape, architecture and natural history painter in oil and water-colour; *b* Dartford, 11 Jan., 1957. *m* Kim Rolling. one *s.* one *d. Educ:* King Edward VI Grammar School, Retford. *Studied:* Falmouth School of Art (1977-80). *Exhib:* R.A., London; John Noott Gallery, Broadway; St. David's Hall, Cardiff; Theatr Clwyd, Mold; Alderley Gallery, Alderley Edge; plus numerous others. *Work in collections:* Stowells of Chelsea; Grosvenor Museum, Chester; Soc. for Contemporary Art in Wales; plus numerous private collections. *Signs work:* "Gerald Dewsbury" or "G.D." *Address:* Tyn-Y-Ffridd, Llangwm, nr. Corwen, Clwyd LL21 0RW.

**DEXTER, James Henry,** designer; *b* 23 July, 1912. *m* Marjorie Ellen Gurr. *Educ:* Leicester College of Art. *Exhib:* N.E.A.C., R.A., London Group, various provincial galleries. *Work in collections:* Corporation of Leicester. *Signs work:* "James Dexter." *Address:* 52 Scraptoft Lane, Leicester LE5 1HU.

**DICK, Colin,** N.D.D. (1951); figurative painter in oil, water-colour, stoneware sculpture, retd. teacher; former Head of Art, Campion School, Royal

Leamington Spa; *b* Epsom, Surrey, 28 Feb., 1929. *m* Delia D., M.A. one *s*. two *d. Educ:* Wennington School, and Leighton Park. *Studied:* St. Martin's (1947-51, Frederick Gore, R.A., R.V. Pitchforth, R.A.). *Exhib:* 'Romanies, Fairs and Local Customs' Nuneaton Riversley Gallery (1995), Herbert A.G. Retrospective, Christchurch J.C.R. Oxford, Musée Boulogne sur Mer, Biarritz Galerie Municipal, 'Coventry between Bombing and Reconstruction' Herbert A.G. (1997), R.A. Summer Exhbns. (seven oil paintings). *Work in collections:* Herbert A.G. and Museum, Coventry (35 paintings). *Clubs:* Umbrella for the Arts, Coventry. *Signs work:* "Colin Dick." *Address:* Stoke Green Studio, 98 Binley Rd., Stoke, Coventry CV3 1FR.

**DICKENS, Alison Margaret,** company director; painter in oil; *b* London, 1917. *m* G.E.J. Dickens (decd.). one *s*. one *d. Educ:* Haberdasher Aske's Girls' School. *Studied:* Ealing Art School (Kenneth Procter). *Exhib:* R.A., N.S., R.P., S.W.A.; numerous one-man shows at own studio, E. Horsley, and Thorndike Theatre, Leatherhead. *Work in collections:* Japan. *Publications:* dust cover for Foyles. *Signs work:* "Alison M. Dickens" and see appendix. *Address:* Norrels Lodge North, Norrels Drive, E. Horsley, Surrey KT24 5DL.

**DICKER, Molly,** S.W.A.; Fellow, Printmakers Council, award, Salons de Nations, Paris; painter/printmaker in oil, oil pastel, pencil, etching materials, etc.; retd. teacher; *b* Kent, 1924. *m* Basil H. Dicker. one *s*. one *d. Educ:* Gads Hill Place. *Studied:* Medway College of Art (Dip.), Southampton College of Art. *Exhib:* R.A., R.B.A., R.O.I., U.A., R.W.A., P.S., Federation of British Artists, S.W.A., Wessex Artists, private galleries, three solo shows, other mixed exhbns. Work in private collections. *Signs work:* "Molly Dicker." *Address:* Garston House, East Meon, Petersfield, Hants.

**DICKERSON, John,** M.F.A., (1968), Dr.R.C.A. (1974); artist and lecturer in painting, ceramics, mixed media sculpture, drawing; subject leader for studio art, Richmond College, London; *b* Swaffham, Norfolk, 11 Oct., 1939. *Educ:* Hammond's School, Swaffham. *Studied:* Goldsmiths' College, Art Students' League, N.Y., Pratt Inst., N.Y. (1966-68), R.C.A. (1971-74). *Work in collections:* Japan, U.S.A., U.K., Taiwan, Malaysia, Sweden, Australia, Yugoslavia, Hong Kong, Spain. *Publications:* author: Raku Handbook; Pottery Making - A Complete Guide; Aspects of Raku Ware; Pottery. *Signs work:* some ceramics and sculpture carry "JD" monogram; works on paper "John Dickerson." *Address:* 47 Creffield Rd., London W5 3RR.

**DICKS, Margo,** S.G.F.A.; R.H.S. medallist for Botanical Painting (1989, 1991, 1994); sculptor, potter and painter in water-colour; *b* Coventry, 1925. *m* Dr. David Dicks. two *d. Educ:* Clarence House School, Coventry, Italia Conti School, London. *Studied:* pottery with Cecil Baugh, Jamaica (1954-56), recently, sculpture with Nigel Konstam, Italy. *Exhib:* Mall and Westminster Galleries. *Clubs:* Arts. *Signs work:* "Margo Dicks" or "M.D." *Address:* Bradstones, Hewshott Lane, Liphook, Hants. GU30 7SU.

**DICKSON, Evangeline Mary Lambart,** B.W.S.; artist in water-colour and other media; *b* 31 Aug., 1922. *m* John Wanless Dickson, F.R.C.S. one *s*. two *d*. *Educ:* Stover, Newton Abbot. *Studied:* under Anna Airy, R.I., R.O.I., R.E. *Exhib:* solo shows: E. Anglia, London, Ipswich B.C. Museums and Galleries, Salisbury and S. Wiltshire Museum, English Heritage (Framlingham Castle); group shows include Cambridge, Hertfordshire, Yorkshire, Scotland, Paris Salon, R.W.S. Open and R.I. exhbns. (London), Ipswich B.C. Museums and Galleries, Gainsborough's House, Sudbury, Suffolk. *Work in collections:* Sheffield City A.G's (Picture lending scheme, Graves A.G.), Ipswich B.C. Museums and Galleries. *Publications:* illustrations "In Search of Heathland", Lee Chadwick (Dobson Books Ltd.) and for Collins publishers. *Clubs:* B.W.S., Yorks., Ipswich Art Soc., Eight Plus One Group. *Signs work:* "E.M. Dickson" and see appendix. *Address:* Stow House, Westerfield, Ipswich, Suffolk IP6 9AJ.

**DICKSON, James Marshall,** D.A. (Edin., 1964), R.S.W. (1972); artist in ink, gouache, P.V.A.; Head of Art, Lochgelly Centre; *b* Kirkcaldy, 31 July, 1942. *Educ:* Beath High School. *Studied:* Edinburgh College of Art (1960-64, Stuart Barrie). *Exhib:* R.S.W. (Edin.), R.G.I. (Glasgow), Kirkcaldy A.G., Perth A.G., Loomshop Gallery. *Work in collections:* Banff County, Angus County, Aberdeen, Tayside, Leeds Educ. *Signs work:* "James Marshall Dickson, R.S.W." *Address:* 44 Main St., Lochgelly, Fife.

**DICKSON, Jennifer,** R.A., R.E., LL.D. (1988), C.M. (1995); printmaker and photographer; *b* Piet Retief, S. Africa, 17 Sept., 1936. *Studied:* Goldsmiths' College School of Art (University of London, 1954-59) and Atelier 17, Paris, under S. W. Hayter. *Work in collections:* V. & A.; National Gallery of Canada; Hermitage, Leningrad; Cleveland Art Institute, etc. *Publications:* 30 major suites of original prints. *Address:* 20 Osborne St., Ottawa, Ontario K1S 4Z9, Canada.

**DIGGLE, Philip,** painter in oil on canvas; *b* 30 Dec., 1956. *Educ:* Ancoats Manchester Grammar; Trinity College, Oxford. *Exhib:* Bede Gallery, Jarrow, Warwick Arts Trust (1985), Angela Flowers Gallery (1986, 1987), Art Now, London (1986, 1987, 1988), Festival of the 10th Summer, Manchester (1986), Barcelona Workshop (1988), Flowers East (1989, 1991); one-man shows: Rochdale A.G. (1985), Angela Flowers Gallery (1985), Warwick Arts Trust (1985), Some Bizarre Gallery (1988, 1989), Barbizon Gallery, Glasgow (1989, 1990, 1991), Barcelona Workshop (1989), Flowers East (1991); Granada/LWT (1988), B.B.C. Playbus (1990). *Work in collections:* Chase Manhattan Bank, N.Y., Rockefeller Center. *Address:* 498 Archway Rd., London N6 4NA.

**DI GIROLAMO, Megan Ann,** M.A. Ceramics (1987), A.T.C. (Lond.) (1963), N.D.D. Pottery (Main) Terracotta (A.D.D.) (1962); ceramist in ceramics, stoneware and raku; lecturer; *b* New Delhi, 13 Jan., 1942. *m* Romeo di Girolamo. two *d*. *Educ:* Aylesbury Grammar School. *Studied:* High Wycombe College F.E.; Hornsey School of Art; S. Glamorgan Inst. of Higher Educ. *Exhib:* Grosvenor Sq., London (1985), The Mall, London (1987), Brighton

Polytechnic (1987), N.C.A. Dublin (1987). Work in private collections. *Publications:* illustrated, The Crab and its Relatives, Animal Weapons, Animal Defenses. *Signs work:* see appendix. *Address:* Bridge Bend, Nash Lee Rd., Wendover, Bucks.

**DI GIROLAMO, Romeo,** R.B.A., N.D.D.; artist in oil; Bcks Architectural Competition (1953, 1954); Bucks Art Scholarship (1954-59); Granada Theatre National Painting Prize (1957); David Murray Travelling Scholarship awarded by R.A. (1959); formerly Head of Art Depts., Gt. Marlow Secondary, Slough Grammar for Boys, The Radcliffe Comprehensive; at present Head of Painting Dept., Amersham College of Further Education and School of Art (formerly High Wycombe School of Art); mem. of the Academic Board and Governor of the College; *b* Civitella Casanova, Italy, 1939. *m* Megan, A.T.C. *Educ:* Quainton and Waddesdon secondary schools. *Studied:* High Wycombe School of Art (1954-59). *Exhib:* R.A., R.B.A., Art Bureau Travelling exhbns. and many one-man shows. *Work in collections:* private collections in many countries. *Signs work:* "Romeo di Girolamo." *Address:* Bridge Bend, Nash Lee Rd., Wendover, Bucks.

**DINKEL KEET, Emmy Gerarda Mary,** A.R.C.A. (1933), R.W.A. (1987); artist in water-colour brush drawings; former teacher of art and crafts, Sherborne School for Girls; Principal Asst., Malvern College of Art; and part-time in schools in Scotland; *b* 5 Sept., 1908. *m* E. Michael Dinkel, R.W.S., R.W.A., F.S.G.E., A.R.C.A. two *s.* two *s-d. Studied:* Southend College of Art (1927-30), R.C.A. (1930-33, Sir William Rothenstein, Prof. Tristram, Prof. Osborne, Robert Austin, Edward Johnston, Eric Ravilious); studied peasant art and design in Hungary. *Exhib:* R.A., R.W.A., R.S.A., Laing A.G., Brighton A.G., many provincial art galleries. *Publications:* "Dream Children", collected works of Emmy Dinkel-Keet, recently published. *Signs work:* "E.G.M. Dinkel-Keet." *Address:* 1 The Mead, Cirencester, Glos. GL7 2BB.

**DINN, Catherine Margaret,** B.A. (1979), M.A. (1980), Dip. Art Gallery and Museum Studies (1981); Curator, Falmouth Art Gallery (1981-92); free-lance writer and lecturer; *b* Norfolk, 4 Sept., 1957. *m* Michael E. Richards. one *d. Educ:* Walthamstow Hall, Sevenoaks. *Studied:* History of Art and English, University of Nottingham (1976-79), Courtauld Inst. of Art (1979-80), University of Manchester (1980-81). *Publications:* Co-author (with David Wainwright) of biography of Henry Scott Tuke, R.A. (Sarema Press, 1989; reprinted 1991). *Address:* Boscolla, Florence Pl., Falmouth, Cornwall TR11 3NJ.

**DI STEFANO, Arturo,** M.A. Fine Art (1981); painter in oil on linen, wood-cuts, etchings; *b* England, 25 Feb., 1955. *m* Jan Di Stefano. one *s. Studied:* Goldsmiths' College, University of London (1974-77, Jon Thompson), R.C.A. (1978-81, Peter de Francia). *Exhib:* Kettle's Yard, Cambridge (1988), Serpentine Gallery (1989), John Hansard Gallery (1989); one-man shows, Oxford O4 Gallery, Pomeroy Gallery, London (1987), Woodlands Gallery

(1987), Fasolino Gallery, Turin (1987), Pomeroy Purdy Gallery, London (1989), Purdy Hicks (1991,1993,1996), Walker A.G. (1993). *Work in collections:* Unilever, Arthur Andersen, Museum of London, N.P.G. London, Government Art Collection, Walker A.G., L'pool, Barclays Bank, Leicester Museum, Harris Museum, Preston. *Commissions:* Portrait of Sir Richard Doll for National Portrait Gallery, London. *Publications:* The School of London: A Resurgence in Contemporary Painting (Alistair Hicks, Phaidon 1989); four catalogues: 1989, 1991, 1993, 1995. *Signs work:* "A. Di Stefano." *Address:* 92 Fairfoot Rd., Bow, London E3 4EH.

**DOBSON, Mary:** see THORNBERY, Mary.

**DOCHERTY, Michael,** D.A. (Edin.) (1968), Post-Grad. Dip. (1969), A.R.S.A. (1984); artist in oil/acrylic on canvas/wood, ink/graphite on paper/card; lecturer, Edinburgh College of Art; *b* Alloa, 28 Dec., 1947. *m* Odette Dominique Vitse. one *s.* one *d. Educ:* St. Modan's High School, Stirling. *Studied:* Edinburgh College of Art (1964-68, 1968-69). *Exhib:* Richard Demarco Gallery, New 57 Gallery, Fruitmarket Gallery, French Inst., National Gallery of Modern Art, Freemantle Art Centre, Western Australia, Canabias, France, R.S.A., R.S.W., Air, London, Fine Art Soc. *Work in collections:* Contemporary Art Soc., Scottish National Gallery of Modern Art, Scottish Arts Council, Edinburgh College of Art. *Signs work:* "Michael Docherty" on reverse. *Address:* 20 Howard Pl., Edinburgh EH3 5JY.

**DODD, Alan,** Cert. R.A.S. (1966); painter, interior designer, muralist; *b* Kennington, Ashford, Kent, 23 Nov., 1942. *Studied:* Maidstone College of Art, Royal Academy Schools. *Exhib:* R.A. Bicentenary Exhibition (1968); one-man shows: New Grafton Gallery (July, 1969, Nov., 1970, Oct. 1972), 'Four English Painters' Galleria Estudio Cid, Madrid (Nov., 1970). *Work in collections:* V. & A., Sir John Soane's Museum; also in private collections in England, U.S.A., Australia, Spain, Portugal. *Signs work:* "Dodd" with date. *Address:* 295 Caledonian Rd., London N1 1EG; High Hall, Weston, Beccles, Suffolk NR34 8TF.

**DODDS, Andrew,** F.C.S.D., N.D.D.; freelance illustrator and painter; Principal Lecturer, Suffolk College, School of Art and Design (retd. 1991); *b* Gullane, Scotland, 5 May, 1927. *Studied:* Colchester School of Art (1942-45), L.C.C. Central School of Arts and Crafts (1947-50). *Exhib:* R.A.; one-man exhbns.: Drawn from London, Mermaid Theatre (1961), Minories, Colchester (1968). *Publications:* Designers in Britain, Radio Times and other national publications. Has illustrated 35 books including own books 'East Anglia Drawn' (1987) and 'London Then' (1994). *Signs work:* "Andrew Dodds." *Address:* The Round House, Lower Raydon, Ipswich, Suffolk IP7 5QN.

**DODDS, James,** Shipwright (1976), B.A. (1980), M.A. (1984); artist in oil and linocut; *b* Brightlingsea, 3 May, 1957. *m* Catherine. one *s.* one *d. Studied:* Colchester School of Art (1976-77), Chelsea School of Art (1977-80), R.C.A. (1981-84). *Exhib:* Sue Rankin Gallery (1992), Aldeburgh Festival (1984, 1990,

1995), Bircham Gallery, Norfolk (1988, 1989, 1992), Printworks, Colchester (1989, 1990, 1992), Chappel Galleries, Colchester (1989, 1990, 1994), Simbouras Gallery, Athens (1995), Union of Artists, St. Petersburg (1997), Hitzacker, Germany (1997). *Work in collections:* Britten-Pears Library, Ipswich and Horniman Museums. *Commissions:* Nationl Trust, Lloyds Register. *Publications:* Peter Grimes, The Wanderer, The Shipwright Trade, Wild Man of Orford. *Signs work:* "James Dodds" or "J.D." *Address:* Barnacle House, 20 St. John's Rd., Wivenhoe, Colchester, Essex CO7 9DR.

**DOGGETT, Susan Marguerite,** B.A. (Hons.); W.C.C. award for Contemporary Craft (1994); book artist and bookbinder in mixed media; Lecturer in book arts, Croydon College; *b* Reading, 24 Sept., 1960. *Educ:* Waingel's Copse School, Woodley, Reading. *Studied:* Oxford Brookes University and Brighton University. *Exhib:* Red Herring Brighton, Festival Hall London, Royal Library Copenhagen, Angel Row Gallery Nottingham, Economist Bldg. London, Pavilion Gallery Brighton, Crafts Council, London. *Clubs:* Fellow of. Designer Bookbinders. *Signs work:* "S.D." or "Sue Doggett." *Address:* 11 Hollingbourne Rd., Herne Hill, London SE24 9NB.

**DONALD, George M.,** D.A. (1967), A.T.C. (1969), M.Ed. (1980), R.S.A. (1993), R.S.W. (1976); artist in printmaking, papermaking; lecturer in drawing and painting, Edinburgh College of Art; *b* Ootacamund, S. India, 12 Sept., 1943. one *s.* one *d. Educ:* Aberdeen Academy. *Studied:* Edinburgh College of Art and Hornsey College of Art; Edinburgh University. *Work in collections:* V. & A., R.S.A., S.A.C., Aberdeen A.G., S.N.G.M.A., Hunterian Museum; and in public and private collections in U.K., U.S.A., Europe, Far East. *Signs work:* "George Donald." *Address:* Bankhead, By Duns, Berwickshire TD11 3QJ.

**DONNE, Leonard David,** N.D.D., A.T.D. (1951); artist in oil, water-colour and etching; Head of Art, Cheshunt School; *b* Leicester, 19 June, 1926. *m* Elizabeth Donne. one *s.* two *d. Educ:* Wyggeston School, Leicester. *Studied:* Leicester College of Art under D. P. Carrington. *Exhib:* one-man shows: Gordon Maynard Gallery (1974), Loggia Gallery (1973), Countesthorpe College (1976), Hitchin Museum (1977), Loggia Gallery (1984), Birmingham University (1992), and various provincial and London galleries. *Clubs:* F.P.S. *Signs work:* "D.D." *Address:* 15 Church St., Leintwardine, Herefordshire SY7 0LD.

**DOREY, Russell Peter,** B.A. Hons. (Painting), Post.Grad.Dip. R.A. Schools; artist in oil on canvas, pencil drawing; *b* Chelmsford, Essex, 26 Mar., 1961. *Educ:* Felsted School, Essex. *Studied:* Maidstone College of Art (1979-82, John Titchell, A.R.A.), R.A. School (1983-86, Norman Blamey, R.A.). *Exhib:* R.A. Summer Exhbns. (1985-86), Agnews Young Contemporaries (1988). *Signs work:* "Russell Dorey." *Address:* 29 Norland Sq., Holland Pk., London W11 4PU.

**DORMENT, Richard,** B.A. (1968), M.A. (1969), M. Phil. (1975), Ph.D. (1975); art critic, Daily Telegraph; *b* U.S.A., 15 Nov., 1946. *m* Harriet Waugh.

one *d* (by a previous marriage). one *s. Studied:* Princeton University (1964-68), Columbia University (1969-75). *Publications:* Alfred Gilbert (1985); Alfred Gilbert, Sculptor and Goldsmith (exhbn. catalogue, R.A. London, 1986); British Painting in the Philadelphia Museum of Art, From the Seventeenth through the Nineteenth Century (1986). *Address:* 181 Marsh Wall, London E14 9SR.

**DOUBLEDAY, John,** sculptor; *b* Langford, Essex, 1947. *m* Isobel J. C. Durie. *Educ:* Stowe. *Studied:* Goldsmiths' College (1965-68). *Exhib:* one-man shows in London, New York, Amsterdam, Cologne. *Work in collections:* public works: include Mary and Child Christ (1980) Rochester Cathedral; Charlie Chaplin (1981) Leicester Square; Isambard Kingdom Brunel (1982) Bristol and Paddington; The Beatles (1984) Liverpool; Commando Memorial C.T.C.R.M. (1986); Sherlock Holmes (1991) Switzerland; Graham Gooch (1992) Chelmsford; J.B. Pflug (1994) Braith Mali Museum, Biberach; Nelson Mandela (1997) U.W.C. in Italy, U.K., U.S.A.,Singapore and Swaziland; public collections: Ashmolean Museum, B.M., V. & A., and Tate. *Address:* Goat Lodge Farm, Great Totham, Maldon, Essex CM9 8BX.

**DOUGLAS, Jean Mary,** Dip.A.E. (1979), S.B.A. (1991); artist in pastel, school teacher (retd.); *b* London, 26 Sept., 1927. *m* Frank Douglas. two *d. Educ:* Loughton County High School and Teacher Training College, Portsmouth. *Studied:* London University Art Diploma (1976-79). *Exhib:* Royal Exchange, Guildhall, Mall Galleries, Central Hall Westminster. *Publications:* Reproduction rights of paintings sold to Royle and Medici. *Signs work:* "J.M.D." *Address:* Park House, Liston, Sudbury, Suffolk CO10 7HT.

**DOUGLAS, Jon,** F.R.B.S., F.R.S.A.; sculptor in foundered bronze and resin bonded bronze, decorative art designer; *b* London, 7 Mar., 1911. *m* Doris Helen. two *s.* one *d. Educ:* University College School, Frognal, Hampstead; Bethany College, Goudhurst, Kent. *Studied:* Institute Quinche, Lausanne (1928-31). *Exhib:* Mall Galleries, Camden Art Centre, R.B.S. Work in permanent collections worldwide. *Signs work:* "Jon Douglas." *Address:* 47 Finchley La., Hendon, London NW4 1BY.

**DOUGLAS-DOMMEN, Marguerite France,** C.I.A.L.; artist in oil and water-colour; *b* 12 July, 1918. *m* John Haig Douglas. one *s.* three *d. Educ:* Cheltenham Ladies' College. *Studied:* Derby, Lausanne (1935) and R.A. Schools under Russell and Monnington (1936-39). *Exhib:* S.S.A., R.S.W., Ancona. *Publications:* work repro.: illustrated three books of James Hogg's poetry. *Clubs:* Reynolds. *Signs work:* "M.F.D." *Address:* Craigsford, Earlston, Berwickshire TD4 6DJ.

**DOVER, Peter Charles,** B.A. (Hons.) Graphic Design (1984), M.A. (R.C.A.) Fine Art (1988), A.R.E. (1995); printmaker painter maker in relief printmaking on paper, found objects and materials; also musician - latest project 'Feeler' since 1996; *b* Merseyside, 10 Apr., 1954. *Educ:* Wallasey Gramar School. *Studied:* Wallasey College of Art (1980-81), Leeds Metropolitan

University (1981-84), R.C.A. (1986-88, under the late Alistair Grant). *Work in collections:* Tate Gallery, Ashmolean, Dudley Museum, Plymouth Museum, London Hospital, St.Thomas's, Estonia National Museum. *Commissions:* I.T.U. Floor of Gt. Ormond Street Hospital for Sick Children, silkscreen mural 'The Sea' (1990-91). *Signs work:* "P.C. Dover" usually verso. *Address:* 8 Betts House, Betts St., London E1 8HN.

**DOWLING, Jane,** B.A. (Oxon.) Hons. (1946), M.A. (Oxon.) (1977); painter, etcher, engraver; tutor, Royal Academy Schools, and Ruskin School, Oxford; *b* 1925. *m* Peter Greenham, (decd.). one *s.* one *d. Educ:* St. Anne's College, Oxford. *Studied:* Slade and Ruskin; Byam Shaw; Central School (Gert Hermes). *Exhib:* New Grafton Gallery, R.A. Summer Exhbn. since 1954; many mixed exhbns., Travelling Arts Council exhbn. with Peter Greenham (1984), 'The Glass of Vision' at Chichester Cathedral, 'The Long Perspective' Agnews (1987), 'A Personal Choice' Kings Lynn (1988), 'Art in Churches' Tewkesbury and Worcester (1991), small retrospective, Mompesson House, Salisbury (1992). *Work in collections:* Farringdon Trust Buscot House, Southampton City A.G., John Radcliffe Hospital, Oxford, Ashmolean Museum and Churchill Hospital. *Commissions:* small mural: Edwin Abby Mural Fund for the Oxford Oratory Church (1995). *Publications:* various articles. *Clubs:* Oxford Union. *Signs work:* "J.D." and see appendix. *Address:* The Old Dairy, Charlton-on-Otmoor, nr. Islip, Oxon. OX5 2UQ.

**DOWLING, Tom,** artist in oil; *b* Dublin, 23 June, 1924. *Educ:* Royal Naval College, Dartmouth. *Studied:* City & Guilds of London Art School (1963-67, Gilbert Spencer, Rodney Burn, Bernard Dunstan). *Exhib:* R.A., R.B.A., N.E.A.C., R.O.I., R.P., R.E., Richard Allen Gallery, New Grafton Gallery, Pictures for Schools exhbn. *Clubs:* Emsworth Sailing. *Signs work:* "TOM DOWLING" or "T.B.D." (on small paintings). *Address:* 31 Slipper Rd., Emsworth, Hants. PO10 8BS.

**DOWNIE, Kate,** D.A., Post Dip.F.A.; artist/lecturer in acrylic, collage, printmaking, photography; part-time tutor, Fine Art Dept., Edinburgh College of Art; *b* N. Carolina, U.S.A., 7 June, 1958. *m* Peter Clerke. one *d. Educ:* Ellon Academy, Aberdeenshire. *Studied:* Gray's School of Art, Aberdeen (1975-80, Alexander Fraser, Francis Walker). *Exhib:* Collins Gallery, Glasgow (1991), Talbot-Rice Gallery, University of Edinburgh (1992), Amsterdam, Brussels, Utrecht, Cardiff, Aberdeen. *Work in collections:* Aberdeen A.G., Aberdeen University, Edinburgh University, Kelvingrove A.G., Peoples Palace Glasgow, Allied Breweries, Cleveland A.G., S.A.C., B.B.C. Scotland. *Clubs:* Scottish Arts, Edinburgh. *Signs work:* "Kate Downie." *Address:* 12 Iona St., Edinburgh EH6 8SF.

**DOWSON, Sir Philip Manning,** C.B.E., P.R.A., M.A., A.A.Dip., R.I.B.A., F.C.S.D., Hon. F.A.I.A., Hon. F.R.C.A.; architect; Founder architectural partner, Arup Associates, and a senior partner, Ove Arup Partnership (1969-90), Consultant (1990-); *b* Johannesburg, 16 Aug., 1924. *m* Sarah. one *s.* two *d.*

*Educ:* Gresham's School, University College, Oxford University (1942-43), Clare College, Cambridge University (1947-50). *Studied:* Architectural Assoc. (1950-53, Arthur Korn, Ernesto Rogers, Edwardo Catalano). *Exhib:* Arup Associates: R.A. Summer Exhbns., R.I.B.A. Anthology of British Architecture (1981), Venice Biennale (1982), R.I.B.A. Architecture Now (1983), R.I.B.A. The Art of the Architect (1984). *Clubs:* Garrick. *Signs work:* "Philip Dowson." *Address:* President's Office, Royal Academy of Arts, Piccadilly, London W1V 0DS.

**DOYLE, John,** M.B.E. (1994), R.W.S.; 3rd prize Singer & Friedlander; artist in water-colour and aquatint; President, Royal Water-colour Soc. (1996-); *b* London, 15 Feb., 1928. *m* Elizabeth. two *s.* two *d. Educ:* Sherborne School. *Exhib:* Canterbury Cathedral (1973, 1976), R.A., R.W.S., Spinks (1981, 1983, 1990), Catto Gallery, Hampstead (1989), numerous local exhbns. *Work in collections:* The Vatican. *Publications:* An Artist's Journey down the Thames (Pavilion Books, 1989), Canterbury Cathedral 'An Artist's Pilgrimage' (1997). *Clubs:* Garrick. *Signs work:* "J.D." on small works, "John Doyle" on large works either pencil or water-colour. *Address:* Church Farm, Warehorne, Ashford, Kent TN26 2LP.

**DRAGER, Bertha,** artist in water-colour and oil; teacher of art, Washington Junior High School, Honolulu (1930-33); fashion: Okla. City University (1940), Cornell Extension, N.Y. (1962); *b* Moorefield, W.Va., U.S.A., 29 Dec., 1905. *m* John C. Drager. *Educ:* B.F.A. University, Okla. (1930), Art Students' League, N.Y. (1940), Traphagen School of Fashion, N.Y. (1941), Kokoschka's School, Salzburg (1960). *Exhib:* National, Manila, Philippines, Okla. Museum of Art, Crespi A.G., N.Y.C. (1960), Art's Place II Okla. City A.G. *Work in collections:* University of Okla. Museum of Art. *Publications:* author and illustrator, Hat Tactics (and film 'Hat Tactics'). *Signs work:* "BRETT DRAGER." *Address:* Quail Plaza Apts., Apt. 112, 11002 N.May Ave., Oklahoma City 73120, U.S.A.

**DRAGER, Brett:** see DRAGER, Bertha.

**DRAPER, Kenneth,** M.A. (1969), R.A. (1992); artist/sculptor and painter in resins, pigments for sculpture and paintings, and pastel on paper; *b* Killamarsh, Sheffield, 19 Feb., 1944. *m* Jean Macalpine (common law). one *s. Educ:* Killamarsh Secondary Modern. *Studied:* Kingston College of Art and R.C.A. (Profs. Bernard Meadows, Bryan Kneale, Ralph Brown, Elizabeth Frink). *Exhib:* one-man shows: Redfern Gallery, Royal Academy, Hart Gallery, Islington, Peter Bartlow Gallery, Chicago, Adelson Gallery, N.Y. *Work in collections:* A.C.G.B., Contemporary Arts Soc., Fitzwilliam Museum, Ashmolean Museum, Courtauld Inst. *Publications:* The Life and Art of Kenneth Draper by Roger Bertoud. *Signs work:* "Kenneth Draper." *Address:* Hart Gallery, 113 Upper St., Islington, London N1 1QN.

**DREISER, Peter,** glass designer and engraver; copper-wheel technique; Founder Mem. and Fellow, Guild of Glass Engravers, Fellow, Soc. of Designer

# WHO'S WHO IN ART

Craftsmen, Vice President, Royal Miniature Soc.; teacher of glass engraving at Morley College, London; *b* Cologne, 11 June, 1936. *Studied:* School for Art Glass, Rheinbach, Bonn (1951-54, Prof. A. Dorn, Prof. O. Pietsch, Prof. O. Lippert). *Work in collections:* City of Portsmouth Museum, Northampton Museum, V. & A., Corning Museum of Glass, Fitzwilliam Museum Cambridge, Ulster Museum Belfast. *Publications:* Engraving and Decorating Glass by Barbara Norman; Modern Glass by R. Stennett-Wilson; International Modern Glass by Geoffrey Beard; Glass Engraving: Lettering and Design by David Peace; co-author of The Techniques of Glass Engraving. *Signs work:* "P. Dreiser." *Address:* 18 Rowland Ave., Kenton, Harrow, Middx. HA3 9AF.

**DREW, Joanna Marie,** C.B.E. (1985), Officier, l'Ordre des Arts et Lettres, 1988 (Chevalier, 1979); Director, Hayward and Regional Exhbns., South Bank Centre, (1987-92); *b* Naini Tal, India, 28 Sept., 1929. *Educ:* Dartington Hall; Edinburgh University (M.A.Hons. Fine Art); Edinburgh College of Art (D.A.). Arts Council of G.B. 1952-88: Asst. Director of Exhbns. (1970), Director of Exhbns. (1975), Director of Art (1978-86), Mem. Council, R.C.A. (1979-82). *Address:* Lloyds Bank, Wallingford, Oxon.

**DRING, Lilian M.,** A.R.C.A. (1929); F. Soc. Designer-craftsmen; designer-embroiderer, specialist in hand-machine stitched applique; *b* Surbiton, 15 Mar., 1908. *m* James Dring (divorced 1946). one *s. Studied:* Kingston School of Art under A. J. Collister (1922-26), R.C.A. under Profs. Tristram and Reco Capey 1926-29). Retro-exhbn. (July 1987), Kingston Heritage Centre 60 years work early graphics, needlework, water-colours Courtesy Kingston on Thames Polytechnic (graphics) for student of original School of Art, 1922-26; 2nd Retro exhbn. (Aug. 1989), Orleans Gallery Riverside, Twickenham; (B.B.C.) "Kaleidoscope" (3/5/91); R.E. "Patchwork of Century" 40th Anniv.: Royal Festival Hall. *Work in collections:* V. & A., Royal Festival Hall, National Film Inst., London Transport Museum, National Trust. Official purchases: Modern Church Embroidery (Council for Care of Churches), includes sets of vestments for Gloucester Cathedral, cope for Kew Church, etc. Specializes in fabric house-portraits (including Hovingham Hall, etc.), two works, Royal Scottish Museum Edinburgh, one, Dundee College of Art. Recent work: Needlework 'Tribute" to the late Lord Reilly. *Signs work:* see appendix. *Address:* 6 Devoncroft Gdns., Twickenham, Middx.

**DRING, Melissa Jane,** B.Sc. (Hons.) (1989), I.A.I., P.S., F.B.I.Dip. (1988); police forensic artist, portrait painter in pastel and oil, freelance courtroom artist; *b* Winchester, 1 Apr., 1944. *m* Michael Little. two *s. Educ:* St. Swithun's, Winchester. *Studied:* Winchester School of Art, R.A. Schools. *Exhib:* R.A., R.P., R.B.A., P.S. *Work in collections:* Northampton Central Museum and A.G. *Publications:* articles on forensic artwork in Police Review, and The Journal of Audiovisual Media in Medicine. *Signs work:* "Melissa Dring." *Address:* 10 St. George's Pl., Northampton NN2 6EP.

**DRLJACHA, Zorica,** A.R.B.S.; awarded First Prize British Institute in

Sculpture (1961), anatomy drawing competition (1962). Landseer Scholarship, first prize and silver medal (1963), Catherine Adeline Sparkes prize; sculptress in bronze, aluminium, resin, ciment fondu; *b* Yugoslavia, 14 July, 1942. *n* Mladen. two *d*. *Educ:* Grammar school (Yugoslavia), Luton College of Technology. *Studied:* Goldsmiths' College under H. W. Parker, F.R.B.S., R Jones, R.A.; R.A. Schools under C. Mahoney, R.A., Sir Arnold Machin O.B.E., R.A., Sir Henry Rushbury, K.C.V.O., C.B.E. *Exhib:* R.A. summer exhbns., R.B.S., Alwyn, Chelsea, Forty Hall, Portrait Society, open-air Holland Park, Davies St., Ealing, Chiswick, etc. *Work in collections:* England, U.S.A. Yugoslavia, Germany, Italy, France. *Commissions:* figures for "Battle of Trafalgar" at Madame Tussauds (1966), Expo '67 (Canada). *Address:* 152 Sutton Ct. Rd., Chiswick, London W43HT.

**DRUMMOND, V. H.,** artist and author of children's books; water-colour painter; *b* London, 1911. *m* A. C. Swetenham. *Studied:* St. Martin's (1930) *Exhib:* Oliver Swann Gallery. *Publications:* Library Association's award (1957) best illustrated children's book, Mrs. Easter and the Storks, Mr. Finch's Pet Shop, Mrs. Easter and the Golden Bounder, Lady Talavera, Tidgies Innings Little Laura, Mrs. Easter's Parasol (Faber), The Flying Postman, I'll Never be Asked Again (Debrett, 1979). Drawings for B.B.C. animated film Little Laura *Signs work:* "V. H. Drummond." *Address:* 24 Norfolk Rd., St. John's Wood London NW8.

**DRURY, Christopher,** Dip.A.D. (1970); sculptor, land artist in objects and materials from nature, photography; *b* Colombo, Ceylon, 1948. two *d*. *Educ:* Canford School. *Studied:* Camberwell School of Art (1966-70, Paul de Moncheaux, Brian Taylor). *Exhib:* one-man shows: London, Los Angeles Leeds, Dublin, Edinburgh; mixed shows: Europe, America and Japan. *Work in collections:* C.A.S., Leeds City A.G., Towner A.G. Eastbourne, Cheltenham A.G. *Commissions:* Site specific works and loop chambers in Britain, Europe America and Japan. *Publications:* The Unpainted Landscape, Medicine Wheel Shelters and Baskets, Amanita Muscaria, Stones and Bundles, Vessel. *Signs work:* "Chris Drury." *Address:* 18 Eastport La., Lewes, E. Sussex BN7 1TL.

**DUBERY, Fred,** A.R.C.A.; painter in oil, illustrator; Prof. of Perspective Royal Academy; *b* Croydon, 12 May, 1926. *m* Joanne Brogden. *Educ:* Whitgift School, Croydon. *Studied:* Croydon School of Art, and R.C.A. *Exhib:* Leicester Gallery, Rowland, Browse and Delbanco. R.A., N.E.A.C., New Grafton Gallery, Trafford Gallery, Markswood Gallery, Patterson Fine Arts, Waterman Fine Art, Alresford Gallery. *Work in collections:* Brighton City A.G. Huddersfield City A.G., Nuffield Foundation, Arts Club Dover St., Worcester College, Oxford. *Publications:* Drawing Systems, Dubery and Willats (Studio Vista); Perspective and other Drawing Systems, Dubery and Willats (Herbert Press). *Clubs:* N.E.A.C. *Signs work:* "Fred Dubery." *Address:* Buxhall Lodge Gt. Finborough, Stowmarket, Suffolk IP14 3AU.

**DUCHIN, Edgar,** M.A. (Oxon.), B.A. (O.U.); artist in oil and gouache; conultant solicitor; founder chairman, Solicitors Art Group; *b* 3 Sept., 1909. *m* Betty Margaret Bates. two *s*. two *d. Educ:* St. Paul's School; Brasenose College, Oxford. *Exhib:* Margaret Fisher Gallery, Hesketh Hubbard Art Soc. (prize winner). *Work in collections:* Prof. Dr. Paul Hodin, Dr. M. Altmann, Mr Nigel Wray, Mrs Alice Schwab. *Clubs:* Savile. *Signs work:* "Edgar Duchin." *Address:* 16 West Heath Drive, London NW11 7QH.

**DUCKER, Catherine,** B.A. (Hons.) Fine Art, A.R.W.S.; painter in water-based and oil paints: subject focus is colour and abstracted forms from flowers and the natural landscape; *b* Wallingford, 24 Apr., 1973. *Studied:* Central St. Martin's (1990-91, 1992-96). *Exhib:* Contemporary Art Soc. (1996), Royal Water-colour Soc. (1997), Henley Festival (1997), Reading Gallery, etc. *Commissions:* Henley Festival, and various private garden commissions. *Address:* Littlestoke Farm, Littlestoke, Wallingford, Oxon.

**DUCKETT, Ernest John,** P.S. (1951); portrait and landscape painter in oil, pastel and water-colour; *b* Much Wenlock, Shropshire. *m* A. P. J. Wyse. *Educ:* Much Wenlock and Birmingham. *Studied:* Shrewsbury Art School under M. S. A. Daynes and at Stoke-on-Trent. *Exhib:* R.A., Paris Salon, R.P., R.O.I., R.B.A., N.S., and provincial galleries. *Clubs:* Imperial Arts League, Chelsea Arts. *Signs work:* "E. John Duckett." *Address:* The Orchard, London Rd., Southborough, Tunbridge Wells, Kent TN4 0RJ.

**DUCKWORTH, Barbara,** F.M.A.A., A.I.M.B.I., S.R.N.; medical artist, artist in water-colour, conté, black and white, oil and pastel; *b* Wallasey, Ches., 11 Oct., 1913. *Educ:* Sandford Private School, Blundellsands. *Studied:* Liverpool College of Art (1934-38). *Exhib:* Walker Art Gallery, Liverpool; Liver Sketching Club; medical work at B.M.A. House, London, and Med. Institution, Liverpool. *Work in collections:* Fundus and eye paintings, St. Paul's Eye Hospital, Liverpool. *Publications:* many illustrations in medical journals; medical text-books. *Signs work:* "Barbara Duckworth." *Address:* 131 Milner Rd., Heswall, Wirral, Ches. L60 5RX.

**DUDLEY NEILL, Anna,** D.F.A. (Lond., 1957), R.I. (1980); artist in water-colour and oil; *b* Merton, London, 26 July, 1935. *m* Michael A. Neill. two *s. Educ:* Tolworth Secondary School. *Studied:* Winchester School of Art (1950-54), Slade School of Fine Art (1954-57). *Exhib:* Deist, Belgium (1977, 1979), R.I., R.B.A., etc. *Clubs:* R.I. *Signs work:* "Anna Dudley." *Address:* 15 Putney Heath La., London SW15; 4 Cossack Lane House, Lower Brook St., Winchester, Hants SW15 3JG.

**DUFFIN, Stuart,** R.E., A.R.S.A.; artist in etching and mezzotint; Studio Manager, Glasgow Print Studio; active musician; *b* Windsor, 13 June, 1959. *m* Elspeth Roberts, painter. one *s*. one *d. Studied:* Gray's School of Art, Aberdeen Dip.Fine Art Printmaking). *Work in collections:* Scottish Arts Council, Jerusalem Foundation, Glasgow City Council, Kharkov Museum. Artist and writer with 'The Moors' multi-media projects. *Address:* 40 Cromarty Ave., Glasgow GU3 2HG.

WHO'S WHO IN ART

**DUFFY, Stephen James,** artist, potter, printmaker in linocuts, screen-print
lithography, water-colour, ceramics; *b* Winchelsea Beach, E. Sussex, 5 Feb.
1962. *Educ:* Rye Comprehensive. *Exhib:* Rye Soc. of Artists, Fremantle Print
Biennial, W.A., Farnham Maltings Gallery, Modern Print Gallery, Wirksworth
Ormond Rd. Printmakers, Grundy A.G., Blackpool, Rye A.G. Easton Rooms
U.A., various mixed exhbns. *Publications:* Rye Nature Reserve, Irish Folk
Tales (to be published). *Clubs:* Printmakers Council, U.A., Rye Fishheads.
*Signs work:* see appendix. *Address:* 88 New Winchelsea Rd., Rye, E. Sussex
TN31 7TA.

**DUFFY, Terry,** B.A.Hons.; painter in oils on canvas/paper; Chair: British
Art and Design Assoc. (1986-95); Founder: Arena Studios, Liverpool (1984);
Mem.: N.W.A.B. (1992-95); Dean/Head of Faculty Art & Design, Liverpool
(1986-91); Mem.: Manchester Academy of Fine Art (1995); 1992 British
Council visiting Professor of Fine Art: Hungarian Academy, Budapest; *b*
Liverpool, 25 Mar., 1948. *m* Angela. one *s.* one *d. Studied:* Liverpool Art
College (1972-75). *Exhib:* one-man shows: Acme London (1976), Air London
(1981), Harris Preston (1984), Blom & Dorn, N.Y. (1984), Laing Newcastle
(1989), Merkmal Liverpool (1993); group shows: New Contemporaries (1976),
Sotheby's Fine Art prize Chester (1980), European Artists Stuttgart (1981),
I.C.A. London (1982), Contemporary Arts Soc. London (1991-93), John
Moores Liverpool (1991), ART (1991-94), and many others. *Work in collec-
tions:* many corporate and private collections in Europe and U.S.A., including
Sainsbury, Bosch, Liverpool University, Maxwell U.S.A., etc. *Publications:*
"Her Revealing Dress" Quartet London (1986), cover for Collins "Chopin'
concertos (1992), cover for Edmund White's "States of Desire" (Penguin 1984).
Reviews: Studio International (1975), Guardian (1979, 1983, 1993), Time Out
(1980), Art Scene U.S.A. (1980), B.B.C. World News (1980), Art Review
(1984), Art World U.S.A. (1986), The TUBE (1985), Independent (1990).
*Signs work:* see appendix. *Address:* Studio: 136 Grove Rd., Wallasey L45 0JF.

**DUFORT, Antony,** M.A. (1975), Dip.A.D. (1974) Chelsea School of Art;
painter, sculptor and portrait painter; *b* Belfast, 12 June, 1948. *Educ:*
Ampleforth College, New College Oxford. *Studied:* Central School of Art
(1971, Norman Ackroyd), Winchester School of Art (1971, John Bellany),
Chelsea School of Art (1972-74, Norman Blamey, painting; 1974-75, Dick
Hart, printmaking). *Exhib:* R.A., N.E.A.C., R.W.S., R.O.I., R.B.A., R.P., Maas
Gallery, Milne and Moller, 20th Century British Art Fair, World of Water-
colours, Art 91 (Olympia), Gallery Seiho, Tokyo, Leaving portraits from Eton
College, Dulwich Picture Gallery (1991), Dept. of Transport (1992), The
Discerning Eye (1992), St. James's Art Group (1993); one-man shows: St.
Catherine's College, Oxford (1971), Artist's Market Gallery: Portraits and
Paintings (1973), Arts Theatre, London (1981), Leighton House Museum
(1988), Maas Gallery (1990), Artbank Gallery, Glasgow (1993), Knöll Gallery
Basel (1994). *Work in collections:* Eton College, Brooks' Club, Hard Rock
Cafe, Los Angeles, M.V.E.E. Chobham, Oriel College, Oxford, London

Oratory School (bronze Virgin and Child) 1995. *Publications:* wrote and illustrated: Ballet Steps, Practice to Performance (Clarkson N. Potter, N.Y. 1985), paper back edition, Hodder & Stoughton (1993). *Signs work:* "Antony Dufort" or "Dufort." *Address:* 126 Branksome Rd., London SW2 5JA.

**DUGDALE, Mary,** Distinction Adv. Art (Leeds), Dip. U.S.W.A., U.W.S.; painter in pastel, oil, water-colour; art teacher, Girls' Schools, Burnley; Past President, U.S.W.A., Com., U.W.S.; *b* Burnley, Lancs., 15 July, 1921. *m* Dr. N. Dugdale (decd.). *Educ:* Burnley High School for Girls. *Studied:* Burnley College of Art, Belfast College of Art, City of Leeds Training College. *Exhib:* five solo exhbns., many group shows. *Commissions:* portraits of many public figures, including Lord Eames, Archbishop of Armagh. *Publications:* book cover for husband's last book (1997). *Clubs:* local art. *Address:* 16 Massey Park, Belfast BT4 2JX.

**DUNBAR, Lennox,** A.R.S.A. (1990); artist in drawing, painting and printmaking (etching); Lecturer in Charge of Printmaking, Grays School of Art, Aberdeen; *b* Aberdeen, 17 May, 1952. *m* Jan Storie. two *s.* one *d. Educ:* Aberdeen Grammar School. *Studied:* Grays School of Art, Aberdeen (1969-74). *Exhib:* New Scottish Prints (1983, N.Y. and touring U.S.A.), Bradford Print Biennale (1984), Cleveland Drawing Biennale (1989), Intergrafik, Berlin 1990), and many group exhbns. national and international. *Work in collections:* Aberdeen, Paisley, Middlesbrough A.Gs., Portland Museum, Oregon, U.S.A., B.B.C., Mobil Oil, Royal Scottish Academy, Contemporary Art Soc., etc. *Signs work:* "Dunbar" or "L.R. Dunbar." *Address:* West Denmore, Auchnagatt, Ellon, Grampian AB41 8TP.

**DUNCAN, Clive Leigh,** F.R.B.S. (1983), R.B.A. (1984), N.D.D. (1966); sculptor; Principal lecturer and Head of Sculpture, London Guildhall University, Sir John Cass Faculty of Arts, Design & Manufacture (1973-93); President, Thomas Heatherly Educational Trust (1974-94); *b* London, 1944. *m* Janet McQueen, painter. one *s.* one *d. Educ:* John Colet School, Wendover. *Studied:* High Wycombe College of Art (1961-64), Camberwell School of Art 1964-66 under Sidney Sheppard), City and Guilds School of Art (1966-68 under James Butler, R.A.). *Exhib:* R.A., R.B.A., Guildhall, London, G.I., Nicholas Treadwell, Portland Sculpture Pk., Playhouse Gallery, Harlow. *Signs work:* "DUNCAN." *Address:* Holme Cottage, Shiplake, Henley on Thames, Oxon. RG9 3JS.

**DUNCAN, Terence Edward,** picture framer and artist in oil and water-colour; mem. Guild of Master Craftsmen (1980); *b* Herts., 17 Aug., 1947. *Educ:* Manland Secondary Modern, Harpenden. *Studied:* St. Albans School of Art; Harpenden Art Centre. *Exhib:* St. Albans Gallery (1971), Amateur Artists' Exhbn., London (1967), Batchwood Hall, St. Albans. *Publications:* article, Hertfordshire Countryside; woodwork projects Guild of Mastercraftsmen; Traditional Woodworking Tools (Eddington Press, 1989). Lecturing on: woodwork, Oaklands College, Harpenden (1993), picture framing, Oaklands College

Hatfield Campus (1996, 1997), antique furniture restoration, Stanmore College, Middx. (1996, 1997). *Signs work:* "Terry" with date. *Address:* Luton Hoo Station House, New Mill End, E. Hyde, Luton, Beds. LU1 3TR.

**DUNHAM, Peter Browning,** Dip., architecture, London (1933), Donaldson medallist (1933), F.R.I.B.A.; architect and painter in oil and water-colour; *b* Luton, 9 Oct., 1911. *m* Constance Young. one *s*. one *d*. *Educ:* Malvern College. *Studied:* Bartlett School of Architecture. *Exhib:* R.A. (oils, water-colour and architecture). Principal architectural works: Luton and Dunstable Hospital; schools in Hertfordshire and Bedfordshire; Housing. Winner of several awards in open architectural competitions, housing medals and Civic Trust awards.*Publications:* work repro.: illustrated in technical press. *Signs work:* "PETER DUNHAM." *Address:* 5 Wherry Quayside, Coltishall, Norwich NR12 7AQ.

**DUNHAM, Susan,** Curator, Doll Museum of Oregon, Mem. U.F.D.C., Mem. O.D.A.C.A.; artist, designer and doll maker in porcelain buisque; Owner, Dunham Arts, designer of artist original dolls; *b* Portland, Oregon, 6 Aug., 1943. *m* Jack Dunham, Jr., D.M.D. two *s*. *Educ:* Grants Pass, Oregon High School. *Studied:* University of Oregon (1983-85, Paul Buckner). *Exhib:* U.F.D.C. National Doll Convention (1983), Convention of Dolls, Victoria, Australia (1985). *Work in collections:* Ruth Doll Museum, China; Favel Museum, Klamath Falls, Oregon; Doll Castle Museum, N.J.; Jimmy Carter Library Collection, Ga.; Yokohama Doll Museum, Japan. *Clubs:* Eugene Doll, O.D.A.C.A. *Signs work:* "SUSAN Dunham" hand printed. *Address:* 36429 Row River Rd., Cottage Grove, Oregon 97424.

**DUNLOP, Alison M.,** B.A.(Hons.) (1980), R.S.W. (1990); Greenshield Foundation award (1982, 1986); painter in water-colour, oil; President, S.A.A.C.; *b* Chatham, Ontario, Canada, 24 Mar., 1958. *m* R.F. Hood. *Studied:* University of Western Ontario, London (1976-78), L'Ecole des Beaux-Arts, Besançon, France (1978-79), University of Guelph, Canada (1979-80), Edinburgh College of Art (1982-83). *Exhib:* Canadian Soc. of Painters in Water-colours, Gallerie Rochon, Toronto, R.S.W., S.A.A.C., Scottish Gallery, Thackeray Gallery, Kingfisher Gallery, Bruton Gallery. *Work in collections:* Canada, U.S.A., G.B. *Signs work:* "DUNLOP" and year. *Address:* Croft Cottage, Crichton, By Pathhead, Midlothian EH37 5UZ.

**DUNLOP, Jim,** artist in oil, water-colour, pen and ink, damask designer; *b* 15 Oct., 1929. *Educ:* Brownlee School, Lisburn. *Studied:* privately with Sidney Smith at his studio in Belfast. *Exhib:* Ulster, Australia, Germany. *Work in collections:* Ulster Bank Head Office, Zoltan Frankl, and various military collections in Gt. Britain and Germany. *Commissions:* limited editions, signed prints of N. Ireland street scenes (Shelden Fine Art); Ulster Bank: water-colours of their premises of architectural merit in the Republic of Ireland and Northern Ireland. *Signs work:* see appendix. *Address:* 20 Ashgrove Pk., Belfast 14.

**DUNN, Alfred,** A.R.C.A. (1961); artist; *b* Wombwell, Yorks, 4 Oct., 1937.

*Educ:* Wath-upon-Dearne Grammar School. *Studied:* Royal College of Art (1959-61). *Exhib:* Galerie Buchhandlung Claus Lincke, Dusseldorf (1976), Monika Beck Gallery, Hamburg (1976, 1993), Redfern Gallery, London (1965, 1966, 1969, 1971, 1975, 1978, 1983, 1993), L'Umo del Arte, Milan (1971), Atlantis Gallery (1982), Galarie Julia Philippi, Heidelberg (1994); Das Druckgraphisce work retrospective 70er bis 90er Jahre (1944). *Work in collections:* Manchester City A.G., Cadillac Co., Houston, General Hardware Manufacturing Co., New York, Monika Beck Gallery, Germany, L'Umo del Arte, Milan, Yorkshire Sculpture Park, V. & A., Arts Council, London. *Commissions:* Concourse - Macau Ferry Terminal, Hong Kong; Hotel Victoria, Hong Kong; 57 4nd Dorothy Weinstein, New York, U.S.A. *Signs work:* "Alf Dunn." *Address:* Little Moss Farm, Trawden, nr. Colne, Lancs. BB8 8PR.

**DUNN, Anne,** painter, all mediums; *b* London, 4 Sept., 1929. *m* (1) Michael Wishart, 1950;one *s* (2) Rodrigo Moynihan, 1960. one *s*. *Studied:* Chelsea, Academie Julian, Paris. *Exhib:* one-man shows, Leicester Galleries (8); Redfern Gallery, London; Fischbach Gallery, N.Y.(8); Philadelphia; Ville de Paris (2); Gallery 78, Federicton, Canada (2); many group shows worldwide, R.A. (1978-93). *Work in collections:* Arts Council, M. of W., Carlisle City A. G., Columbus Gallery of Fine Arts, U.S., Beaverbrook A.G., N.B., Financial Times Inc. G.B., Commerce Bankshares, Kansas City, Mo., Amerada Hess Corp. N.Y., Xerox Corp. N.Y., Chemical Bank N.Y., Bank of Nova Scotia, Canada, New Brunswick Provincial Art Bank, Canada, The Art Centre, University of New Brunswick, Canada. *Publications:* Editor, Art and Literature (1964-68). *Clubs:* W.I.A.C. *Signs work:* "Anne Dunn." *Address:* Domaine de St. Esteve, Lambesc, B.D.R. 13410, France.

**DUNN, Philip,** Dip.A.D. (Fine Art) (1968), A.T.C. (1969); painter/print-maker in acrylic, oil, gouache, screenprinting; Mem. Fiveways Artists' Open House since 1990; *b* London, 26 May, 1945. *m* Carole-Anne White. *Educ:* Chiswick Grammar School, London. *Studied:* Twickenham College of Technology (1964), Hornsey College of Art (1964-68), Brighton College of Art (1968-69). *Exhib:* many including London, N.Y., Brighton, Bath, Cheltenham, also twenty solo exhbns. since 1968. Exhib. exclusively through Window Gallery, Brighton since 1982. *Work in collections:* Brighton Centre. *Clubs:* Sussex Arts. *Signs work:* "Philip Dunn." *Address:* c/o Window Gallery, 59 Ship St., Brighton, E. Sussex BN1 1AE.

**DUNNE, Berthold,** Mem. Water-colour Soc. of Ireland (1951); artist in water-colour; *b* Dublin, 21 Sept., 1924. *m* Barbara Kelly. two *d*. *Educ:* Christian Brothers Schools, Synge Street. *Studied:* National College of Art, Dublin, under John Keating, P.R.H.A., and Maurice MacGonigal, R.H.A. (1946-51). *Exhib:* R.H.A., Oireachtas Art Exhbn., Water-colour Soc. of Ireland. *Work in collections:* Self-portrait in the National Self-Portrait Collection; one painting in Water-colour Soc. of Ireland Coll.; University of Limerick. *Signs work:* "Berthold," see appendix. *Address:* Goa, Shrewsbury

Rd., Shankill, Co. Dublin, Ireland.

**DUNSTAN, Bernard,** A.R.A. (1959), R.A. (1968), N.E.A.C., R.W.A. (past president, 1980-84); painter in oil and pastel; Trustee, R.A. (1990-95); *b* 19 Jan., 1920. *m* Diana Armfield, R.A. three *s. Educ:* St. Paul's School. *Studied:* Byam Shaw School (Ernest Jackson), Slade School of Fine Art. *Exhib:* R.A., etc., one-man exhbns. at Agnew's, etc. *Work in collections:* Bristol, Rochdale, Coventry, National Gallery of New Zealand, London Museum, National Portrait Gallery, Royal Collection, Contemporary Art Soc., Arts Council, etc. *Publications:* Painting Methods of the Impressionists, The Paintings of Bernard Dunstan (1993), ed. Ruskin's Elements of Drawing. *Clubs:* Arts. *Signs work:* "B.D." *Address:* 10 High Pk. Rd., Kew, Surrey TW9 4BH.

**DURANTY, Charles Henry,** artist in water-colour; *b* Romford, Essex, Feb., 1918. *m* Vivian Marguerite. *Educ:* St. Lawrence College, Ramsgate Kent. *Exhib:* Leicester Galleries, Roland, Browse & Delbanco, New Grafton, Mercury, Heal's, Zwemmers, Medici, Thackeray Gallery, London; outside London: Ashgate, Farnham, Rye Art Gallery, Sussex, Brighton Art Gallery, Sussex, Guildford House and Reid's Gallery, Guildford, Westgate Gallery, Winchester, Phoenix Gallery, Lavenham, Blakesley Gallery, Northamptonshire; abroad: Johannesburg, S.A., Galerie Racines, Brussels. *Publications:* Audition (poetry). *Signs work:* "Charles Duranty." *Address:* Blue Horses, Levylsdene, Merrow, Guildford, Surrey GU1 2RT.

**DURBIN, Eleanor Mary,** B.A. (Hons.) (1972), M.Phil. (1984); artist/teacher in painting in acrylic, gouache, water-colour, printmaking: etching, woodcut; Head of Art Dept., Guildford High School; *b* London, 11 June, 1949. *m* Martin Henley. one *s.* one *d. Educ:* Twickenham County School, Middx. *Studied:* Hornsey College of Art (1967-68), Leeds University (1968-74, Prof. Sir Lawrence Gowing). *Exhib:* Cleveland Drawing Biennale (1975, 1977); Chenil Galleries, Young British Printmakers (1978); Printmakers Council National Touring exhbn. (1979); R.W.S., Bankside Gallery, Contemporary Water-colours (1983); Tradescant Museum of Garden History (1986). *Signs work:* "Eleanor Durbin." *Address:* 89 Park Rd., Teddington, Middx. TW11 0AW.

**DURBIN, Leslie,** C.B.E. (1976), L.V.O. (1943), Hon. LL.D. (Cambridge) 1963; silversmith; liveryman of Worshipful Company of Goldsmiths (1943); *b* Fulham, London, 21 Feb., 1913. *m* Phyllis Ginger, R.W.S. one *s.* one *d. Commissions:* Altar plate for Guildford Cathedral (1938); principal part in making Stalingrad Sword to Prof. R.M. Gleadowe's design (1943); R.A.F. (1941-1945); Regional variants of £ coin design (1983); Coventry Cathedral; Smithsonian Institution, Washington D.C.; St. George's Chapel, Windsor. Apprenticeship and journeyman with late Omar Ramsden (1929-1938). *Address:* 298 Kew Rd., Richmond, Surrey TW9 3DU.

**DURRANT, Roy Turner,** N.D.D. (1952), F.R.S.A. (1953), F.F.P.S., N.E.A.C. (1985); painter; *b* Lavenham, Suffolk, 4 Oct., 1925. *m* Jean, née

Lyell. four *s. Educ:* Camberwell School of Art (1948-52); served in Suffolk Regt. (1944-47). *Exhib:* R.A., Artists of Fame and Promise (Leicester Galleries), London Group, N.E.A.C., etc.; about thirty one-man exhbns. in London and provinces including: Beaux Arts Gallery (1950), Artists' International Assoc. Gallery (1953, 1957, 1969), Roland, Browse and Delbanco (1954), Grabowski Gallery (1959), Loggia Gallery (1973, 1975, 1981, 1984), Galerie of M.A. Lausanne (1988), Belgrave Gallery, London (retrospective) 1991. *Work in collections:* Impington Village College, Cambs.; Sirrell Collection, C.W.A.C.; City Museum and A.G., Gloucester; Leeds University; Linton Village College, Cambs.; Leicester Educ. Dept., Grammar School, Ashby-de-la-Zouch; Tate Gallery, London; Museum and A.G., Luton; Graves A.G., Sheffield; Dept. of Biochemistry, Cambridge University; British Rail (Sealink); Usher Gallery, Lincoln; Imperial War Museum, London; Bury St. Edmunds Town Council; City of Bradford A.G.; Southampton A.G.; Carlisle A.G.; Kettles Yard Collection, Cambridge University; Holywell Manor, Oxford; Bertrand Russell Foundation, Nottingham; Castle Museum, Norwich; University of Adelaide, Australia; Western Australia A.G., Perth; University of Mass., Amherst, U.S.A.; Beecroft A.G., Westcliff-on-Sea, Essex; G.M.A., Rio de Janeiro; Worthing A.G.; Museum of Art, Hove; R.A.F. Museum, Hendon; 8th Air Force Museum, Barkside, Louisiana, U.S.A. Work in many private collections. *Publications:* A Rag Book of Love, poems (Scorpion Press, 1960). *Signs work:* see appendix. *Address:* 38 Hurst Pk. Ave., Cambridge CB4 2AE.

**DUVAL, Dorothy Zinaida,** mem. U.A. (1962), F.B.A. (1963-78); gold medal, Accademia Italia (1980); silver medal, Paris Salon (1959), art merit, Stock Exchange Art Soc., (1969, 1973, 1981, 1986); oil painter, teacher of art; *b* Ipplepen, Newton Abbot, Devon, 26 Sept., 1917. *Educ:* Bedford Park High School. *Studied:* Slade School. *Exhib:* R.A., R.P., N.E.A.C., R.B.A., R.O.I., R.Scot.A., U.A., R.S.M.A. (1987, 1990), Paris Salon, Galerie Vallombreuse, Biarritz (1976) awarded Dip. of Merit (1986); one-man shows: Saffron Gallery, Saffron Waldon, Broadstairs Library (1978), Margate Library (1979), Westminster Gallery U.A. exhbn. annually (1962-97). *Work in collections:* Grenadier Guards, H.Q., (Harry Nicholls, V.C.). *Signs work:* "D. Z. Duval." *Address:* 166 Percy Ave., Kingsgate, Broadstairs, Kent CT10 3LF.

**DYNEVOR, Lucy (née Rothenstein),** painter and formally conservator of works of art; *b* Sheffield, 1934. *m* Lord Dynevor; (divorced). one *s.* three *d. Educ:* The Old Palace, Mayfield, Sussex. *Studied:* Ruskin School of Fine Art in Oxford and conservation of art with Dr. Helmuth Ruhemann. *Exhib:* one-man shows: University College of Swansea, New Grafton Gallery, London (1991); mixed shows include Crane Kalman Gallery (1995). *Signs work:* "L.D." or "Lucy Dynevor." *Address:* 4 Magnolia Wharf, Strand-on-the-Green, London W4 3NY.

**DYRENFORTH, Noel,** artist in batik; *b* London, 17 June, 1936. one *s. Educ:* St. Clement Danes, London; C.A.C. Bursary (1977); Craftsmen-in-residence Arts Victoria '78, Toorak State College; study/travel in U.S.A. Indonesia, India, China. *Studied:* Goldsmiths' College of Art, University o London, Central School of Art, London. *Exhib:* one-man shows: 1965-90 Cambridge, London, Coventry, Bradford, Loughborough, Oxford, Nottingham L.A. (U.S.A.), Lincoln, Hull, Halifax, Melbourne (Australia), Bremen and Cologne (Germany), Banbury, Tokyo (Japan), Indonesia, Guizhou University China (1990), over 100 mixed exhbns. *Work in collections:* V. & A., and six others. *Publications:* Batik with Noel Dyrenforth by J. Houston (Orbis Publications, London); The Technique of Batik by Noel Dyrenforth (Batsford Publishing Co. 1988), new paperback issue (1997). *Address:* 11 Shepherds Hill Highgate, London N6 5QJ.

**DYSON, Douglas Kerr,** A.R.C.A. (1949); painter and draughtsman; lecturer (retd.), Department of Visual Studies, Faculty of Art and Design, Manchester Polytechnic; *b* Halifax, 11 Dec., 1918. *m* Sylvia Varley. one *s. Educ:* Royds Hall Grammar School, Huddersfield. *Studied:* Huddersfield School of Art (1935-39), R.C.A. under Gilbert Spencer and Rodrigo Moynihan (1946-49). *Exhib:* R.A., Manchester Academy. *Work in collections:* Manchester Education Committee, Manchester City Art Gallery; Co-operative Insurance Society; private collections. *Signs work:* "Dyson." *Address:* 32 Broomfield La., Hale, Cheshire WA15 9AU.

# E

**EAMES, Angela,** B.A.Hons., H.D.F.A., M.A.(Computing in Art and Design); artist/lecturer in drawing/electronic media; *b* Malmesbury, Wilts., 28 May, 1951. *m* Bill Watson. *Educ:* Woking County Grammar School. *Studied:* Bath Academy of Art (1971-74, Michael Kidner), Slade School of Art (1974-76, Tess Jaray, Noel Forster), Middlesex University (1991-92, John Lansdown). *Exhib:* widely, including London, Berlin, Linz, Bratislava and the U.S.A. Work commissioned and in private collections. Lectures: Associate Senior Lecturer in Computer Aided Studies, University of Wolverhampton. *Signs work:* "A. Eames." *Address:* 15 Chapter Rd., Kennington, London SE17 3ES.

**EARDLEY, Enid Mary,** N.S., Hon. Paris Salon (1976); portrait painter in oil and water-colour; *m* Edward Derek Eardley. one *s. Educ:* Northwood College. *Studied:* Central School (1939) and under Steven Spurrier and Stanley Grimm (1964). *Exhib:* one-man shows, Cooling Galleries (1968), Marlow Gallery (1970), Alpine Gallery (1981), R.P., R.O.I., N.S. *Signs work:* "E. EARDLEY." *Address:* Stable Cottage, Old Amersham, Bucks. HP7 0HJ.

**EARLE, Donald Maurice,** A.T.D., D.A.E., M.Phil., Ph.D., F.R.S.A.; artist; taught art in variety of secondary schools (1951-88); *b* Melksham, Wilts., 15 Aug., 1928. *m* Jennifer Mary Isaac. *Educ:* Trowbridge (Wilts.) Boys' High School. *Studied:* W. of England College of Art, Bristol (1944-47, 1949-51).

*Exhib:* N.E.A.C., R.W.S., R.W.A., R.B.S.A. and one-man shows in public galleries. Work in private and public collections. *Signs work:* "D. M. Earle." *Address:* 50 Maltese Rd., Chelmsford, Essex CM1 2PA.

**EASTON, Arthur Frederick,** Surrey Dip. (1964), R.O.I. (1979), N.S. (1980); Dip. of Merit for Painting, University of Arts, Italy (1982); Pres. Reigate Soc. of Artists; artist in oil and water-colour, art teacher; *b* Horley, Surrey, 9 Feb., 1939. *m* Carolle. three *d*. *Studied:* Reigate School of Art and Design (1961-64). *Exhib:* R.A., R.O.I., R.B.A., N.S., R.P., N.E.A.C.; 17 one-man shows; 14 shared shows; 32 mixed shows. Prize winner Upper St. Gallery (1973), Hunting Art Prize exhbn. (1990), International Arts Fair, Olympia (1991). *Work in collections:* Museum of British Labour. *Publications:* work repro.: The Artist, Quarto Publishing, Leisure Painter; posters, Ikea of Sweden; greetings cards, Les Editions Arts et Images du Monde. *Clubs:* Reigate Soc. of Artists. *Signs work:* "A. Easton." *Address:* 4 Winfield Grove, Newdigate, Surrey RH5 5AZ.

**EASTON, David William,** R.I. (1985), N.D.D. (1956), B.Ed.(1976); painter in water-colour, pastel, oil, gouache; *b* Leicester, 29 Aug., 1935. *m* Shirley. two *s*. one *d*. *Educ:* Wyggeston School, Leicester. *Studied:* Leicester College of Art (1952-56). *Exhib:* R.A., P.S., R.I., and many galleries throughout the U.K. *Publications:* Watercolour Flowers (Batsford, 1993), and Watercolour Inspirations (Batsford, 1997). *Signs work:* "David Easton." *Address:* 9 Evington La., Leicester LE5 5PQ.

**EASTON, Frances,** 1st Class Dip. (Florence, 1960); painter of landscapes, nudes and still life in oil; *b* Kenya. *m* Keith Stainton. three *s*- *s*. three *s*- *d*. *Educ:* Wycombe Abbey. *Studied:* Accademia di Belle Arti, Florence (1957-60, Prof. Giovanni Colacicchi). *Exhib:* one-man shows: London, Paris, Rome, most F.B.A. socs., Paris Salon (1977), Laing Competition (1986), Venice - Treviso (award). *Work in collections:* U.K., France, Canada. *Commissions:* Kennedy Inst., London (Founder's portrait); Suffolk/W. Germany 'Twinning' landscape of Gainsborough's birthplace. *Clubs:* Hesketh Hubbard Art, Hurlingham, The Arts. *Signs work:* "Frances Easton (Stainton)." *Address:* 5 Chelsea Studios, 410 Fulham Rd., London SW6.

**EASTON, Isabella,** B.A. (Hons.) (1993), Fine Art painting; B.Tec. Nat. Dip. (1990); painter and printmaker, painting in oil and water-colour, print in etching; *b* Epsom, Surrey, 28 Dec, 1971. *m* Daniel Wray. two *s*. *Studied:* Suffolk C.F.E. (1988-90), Winchester School of Art (1990-93), R.A. Schools. *Exhib:* Sackville Gallery (1996), Langham Fine Art (1996), Belgrave Gallery, London (1996, 1997), N.E.A.C., Mall Galleries, London (1996), Open Studios, Suffolk (1997), etc. *Publications:* Alphabet book entitled 'Alf & Betty', illustrated and created in 1996; Images in chine colle etching, presently limited edition of 20 - to be published. *Signs work:* "Bella Easton." *Address:* 54 Theatre St., Battersea, London SW11 5NF.

**EASTON, Shirley,** S.W.A. (1988-92), N.D.D. (1956), A.T.D. (1957);

painter in water-colour and acrylic, painting tutor; *b* Leicester, 28 Apr., 1935. *m* David Easton, R.I. two *s*. one *d*. *Educ:* Gateway Girls' School, Leicester. *Studied:* Leicester College of Art (1952-57, D.P. Carrington). *Exhib:* R.A. (1986), R.I. (1985-96), S.W.A. (1988, 1990, 1991). *Work in collections:* Leicester University. *Signs work:* "Shirley Easton." *Address:* 9 Evington La., Leicester LE5 5PQ.

**EASTON, Timothy,** Heatherley's Scholarship, London (1966), Elizabeth Greenshields Memorial Award, Montreal (1973); painter in oil on canvas, sculptor in bronze; *b* 26 Aug., 1943. *m* Christine Darling. two *d*. *Educ:* Cranleigh, Mowdon and Christ College. *Studied:* Kingston School of Art (1960-64), Heatherley School of Art (1966-67). *Exhib:* Chicago, Kansas, Los Angeles, Washington, New York and various Art Expos in America between 1968 and 1987; London and provinces from 1970 onwards; Germany, Luxembourg and Jersey 1984-1987. *Work in collections:* Hereford City A.G. *Publications:* John Hedgecoe's Nude Photography (Ebury Press, 1984). *Signs work:* "Timothy Easton" or "Easton." *Address:* Bedfield Hall, Bedfield, Woodbridge, Suffolk.

**EASTOP, Geoffrey Frank,** N.D.D. (1951), A.T.D. (1952), F.S.D.C. (1979); lecturer, potter; *b* London, 16 Jan., 1921. *m* Patricia Haynes. three *s*. one *d*. *Educ:* St. Olave's Grammar School. *Studied:* Goldsmiths' College (1949-52); Academie Ranson, Paris (1952-53). *Exhib:* V. & A., London (1983-95), Stuttgart (1982), Cologne (1983), International Ceramics, Holland (1990), Contemporary Ceramics, London (1991) (solo); Touring retrospective: Portsmouth City Museum, Newbury Museum, Holburne Museum, Bath (1992-93), Berkeley Sq. Gallery, London (1995). *Work in collections:* V. & A., National Museum of Wales, Fitzwilliam Museum, Cambridge, Southampton Museum A.G., Reading Museum, B'ham City Museum, Portsmouth City Museum. *Publications:* 'The Hollow Vessel' (1980), 'Forty years of change in Studio Pottery' (1993). *Clubs:* Craft Potters' Assoc. of Gt. Britain, S.D.C. *Signs work:* see appendix. *Address:* The Pottery Ecchinswell, Newbury, Berks. RG20 4TT.

**EAVES, John,** A.T.C. (1952); *b* Bristol, 10 Nov., 1929. *m* Cecily Edith. two *s*. two *d*. *Educ:* Bembridge School, Bembridge, I.O.W. *Studied:* Bath Academy of Art, James Tower (ceramics), William Scott (painting) (1949-52). *Exhib:* throughout G.B., Germany and U.S.A. *Work in collections:* Arts Council of G.B.; City A.G., Bristol; Royal West of England Academy; South West Arts; Victoria A.G., Bath; University of Bath; Prediger, Schwäbisch Gmünd, G.; City of Braunschweig, G. *Publications:* in Henry Cliffe's Lithography (Studio Vista, 1965). Awarded Winston Churchill Travelling Fellowship to U.S.A. (1966), Print and Water-colour Prizes, Westward T.V. Open Competition (1973, 1975), Leverhulme Emeritus Fellowship (1986) to study painter Emil Nolde. *Signs work:* "Eaves '98." *Address:* 2 Belgrave Pl., Bath, Avon BA1 5JL.

**ECCLESTON, Harry Norman,** O.B.E., P.P.R.E. (1975-89), Hon. R.B.S.A.

(1989), R.W.A. (1991), P.R.E. (1975), R.W.S. (1975), R.E. (1961), A.R.E. (1948), A.R.C.A. (1950), A.T.D. (1947), A.R.W.S. (1964), Hon. N.E.A.C. (1996); engraver in all processes; artist in oil and water-colour; artist designer at the Bank of England Printing Works (1958-83); *b* Bilston, Staffs., 21 Jan., 1923. widower. two *d*. *Educ:* Wednesbury County Commercial College. *Studied:* Birmingham College of Art (1939-42) and R.C.A. (1947-51). *Exhib:* R.A., R.E., R.W.S., etc. *Clubs:* Arts. *Signs work:* "H. N. Eccleston." *Address:* 110 Priory Rd., Harold Hill, Romford, Essex RM3 9AL.

**EDEN, Max Nigel Byron,** N.D.D. (1950), A.T.D. (1951); painter in oil, acrylic, water-colour; *b* St. Helens, Lancs., 12 Nov., 1923. *m* Valerie Currie. one *s*. one *d*. *Educ:* Cowley School, St. Helens (1928-41), Borough Rd. College, London (1942-43, 1947-48), R.A.F. (1943-47). *Studied:* Liverpool College of Art (1948-51, Martin Bell), Ecole des Beaux Arts de Paris (1951-52, Prof. Souverbie), Copenhagen Academy of Art (1954-55, Prof. Scharff). *Exhib:* from 1952 in France, Denmark, England, U.S.A., Canada and Spain. Recent, "Orsini" London (1991), "Academy" Liverpool (1996), Gallery "Arabal", Callosa, Spain. *Work in collections:* Southport Atkinson Gallery; private collections: Leo and Jilly Cooper, also in Europe, U.K., U.S.A., and Canada. *Signs work:* "Eden." *Address:* 36 Ash St., Southport, Merseyside PR8 6JE.

**EDGERTON, Charmian,** B.A. (Hons.) (Graphic Design), S.B.A., S.W.A.; painter in pastel; *b* 16 Sept., 1944. *m* Nick Edgerton, psychologist. one *d*. *Educ:* Hillcourt School, Dublin. *Studied:* Zurich Kunstgeverbe Schule (1961), Dublin (1962, K. McGonigal), Stoke-on-Trent Polytechnic (1967, graphic design/illustration). *Exhib:* Medici (1991), Alresford Gallery (1993), Gallery Artist of John Thompson Gallery and Alresford Gallery, Aldburgh and Albemarle St., assorted Opens, Barry Keene Gallery, Henley, Blackheath Gallery SE3, John Noott Gallery, Broadway, Pheasantry Fine Arts, Headcorn, Kent, 20th Century Gallery, Windsor, John Falle, Jersey. *Publications:* Pastel Painting, and Flowers and Plants Ed. Jenny Rodwell (Cassell, 1993); author, Learn to Draw Flowers (Harper Collins). Regular contributor to Leisure Painter magazine, and demonstrator for Rowney's Pastels. *Signs work:* "Charmian" and "C.P.E." *Address:* 13 Camden Row, London SE3 0QA.

**EDWARDS, Alan C.L.,** B.A. (Hons.) (1982), P.G.C.E. (1983), A.T.D. (1983), M.Ed. (1990); painter/teacher; Director (media) N.A.P.A.; *b* 1947. *m* Carmel Wood. two *s*. two *d*. *Studied:* Laird School of Art (1965-67), Liverpool Polytechnic (1979-83), Liverpool University (1986-90). *Exhib:* Five Artists, Unity Theatre, Liverpool (1981), School of Architecture, Liverpool (1982), Stowells Trophy, R.A. Galleries London (1982), Artists of Wirral, Williamson A.G., Birkenhead (1984), Merseyside Artists 3, Touring Exhbn. (1986-87), N.A.P.A. Annual Exhbn. (1988-97), Theatre Clwyd (1995). *Work in collections:* England, N.Z. and Ireland. *Publications:* Visual Resource Packs for Teachers. *Signs work:* "Alan Edwards." *Address:* 6 Berwyn Boulevard, Bebington, Wirral, Merseyside L63 5LR.

**EDWARDS, Benjamin Ralph,** C. & G. Dip. (1972), R.A.S. Cert. (1977), A.T.C. P/G Goldsmiths' College (1978); painter/etcher in black and white etching, drawing, charcoal and pencil, lecturer; painting tutor P/T City and Guilds Art School, London; *b* London, 11 Dec., 1950. *m* Ylva. one *s. Educ:* St. Christopher School, Letchworth, Herts. *Studied:* pre college with Capt. P.J. Norton, D.S.O., R.N.; City and Guilds Art School (1968-72, Eric Morby), Atelier 17, Paris (1972-73, S.W. Hayter), R.A. Schools (1973-77, Roderick Barret). *Exhib:* R.A. Summer Exhbn. (1977 onwards), Kanagawa Prints, Okohama, Japan (1982-84), R.E. (1969-75). *Work in collections:* V. & A., Wellesley College Library, Mass., Newberry Library, Chicago, Bridwell Library, Dallas, Texas. *Publications:* illustrated, The Four Seasons at Parkgate Cottages (Parkgate Press), A Fox under my Bed (Macmillan). *Signs work:* see appendix. *Address:* The Parkgate Press, 7 Argyle Rd., N. Finchley, London N12 7NU.

**EDWARDS, Brigid,** B.Sc. (1975); artist in water-colour on vellum; *b* London, 16 Feb., 1940. *m* R.J. Edwards. *Educ:* Our Lady of Sion, London, University College, London. *Studied:* Central School of Art (1960-63). *Exhib:* R.H.S., R.B.G. Kew, R.A. *Work in collections:* Hunt Inst., Carnegie Mellon University, Penn., R.B.G. Kew. *Publications:* illustrated, 'Primula' monograph (Batsford). *Signs work:* "Brigid Edwards" or not at all. *Address:* c/o Thomas Gibson Fine Art Ltd., 44 Old Bond St., London W1X 4HQ.

**EDWARDS, John Colin,** R.P., Cert. R.A. Schools; portrait, nude and wildlife painter in oil, pencil, chalk, etc.; *b* Kidderminster, 23 Aug., 1940. *m* Patricia Rose, M.Sc. two *d. Studied:* Pietro Annigoni in Florence; R.A. Schools; E.T. Greenshields Foundation award, Canada (1970, 1972); Silver and Bronze Medallist R.A. Schools; W.W.F. Art Award (1986). *Exhib:* Tate Gallery, N.P.G., R.A., R.P., Windsor Castle. *Work in collections:* H.M. The Queen; Baroness Thatcher, O.M.; Royal Collection, Windsor; H.M. The Queen Adjutant General's Corps; Royal College of Radiologists; The Law Society; Carpenters Company; Cambridge, Oxford, Birmingham (Aston), Leicester universities, etc. *Publications:* Tate Gallery Publications, Mitchell Beazley and Collins Publishers, etc. *Signs work:* "John Edwards" and "Edwards." *Address:* Chesterville Gallery and Studio, Chester Rd. North, Kidderminster, Worcs. DY10 1TP.

**EDWARDS, Sylvia,** artist, printmaker, painter in water-colour, oil, acrylic; *b* Boston, Mass. *m* Sadredin Golestaneh. one *s.* two *d. Educ:* Boston public schools. *Studied:* fine art at Massachusetts College of Art, Boston, Mass. (1956-60, Prof. Lawrence Kupferman), Boston Museum of Fine Arts. *Exhib:* consistently in one-woman and mixed shows and international art expositions; London: Berkeley Sq. Gallery, C.C.A. Gallery and Christopher Hull Gallery; Tokyo, Bankamura, Mitsukoshi Mihonbashi Branch; Osaka, Nii Gallery (1989); Alexandria, Egypt, Alexandria Museum of Fine Arts (1980); Mediterranean Biennale (1980); Munson Gallery, Chatham, Mass. (1992);

Morehead Planetarium, Chapel Hill, N.C.; Natalie Knight Gallery, Johannesburg, S.A. (1991); Singapore, Art Base Gallery (sponsored by Citibank, 1989); Bankamura, Tokyo (1991); C.C.A. Gallery Oxford (1996). *Work in collections:* Tate Gallery, London; National Museum of Women in the Arts, Washington, D.C.; Alexandria Museum of Women in the Arts; Alexandria Governorate, Egypt; Cape Museum of Fine Arts, Dennis, Mass.; Midwest Museum of American Art, Elkhart, Indiana. *Publications:* 'The Nucleus' narrative book of drawings; 'The Undoing of the Square', Sylvia Edwards 'Works on Hand Cast Paper'; work widely published by U.N.I.C.E.F., Coriander Studios and C.C.A. Galleries, London for limited editions in silk-screen, and the London Art Group for prints; numerous gallery handbooks and catalogues; articles and television talks 'Sylvia Edwards Talks with Mel Gooding' The Bernice Speen Show. *Signs work:* "Sylvia Edwards." *Address:* 14 Cadogan Sq., London SW1X 0JU.

**EICHLER, Richard W.,** Professor, holder of "Schiller-Preis" (1969); art writer and critic; *b* Liebenau, Bohemia, 8 Aug., 1921. *m* Elisabeth Eichler (née Mojr). one *s.* six *d. Educ:* Gymnasium at Reichenberg. *Studied:* Vienna, Munich (history of art). *Publications:* Könner-Künstler-Scharlatane (Munich, 1960; 7th ed., 1970), Künstler und Werke (Munich, 1962; 3rd ed., 1968), Der gesteuerte Kunstverfall (Munich, 1965; 3rd ed., 1968), Verhexte Muttersprache (1974), Wiederkehr des Schönen (Tübingen, 1984; 2nd ed. 1985), Unser Geistiges Erbe (1995), and many papers. *Address:* Steinkirchner Strasse 16, D81475 München, Bundesrepublik Deutschland.

**EISELIN, Rolf,** Architect SIA dipl.EPFZ, reg. arch. State of Illinois, U.S.A. and Switzerland; *b* Zürich, 6 Nov., 1925. Architect with Skidmore, Owings & Merrill, Chicago (in team for U.S. Air Force Academy design), and other firms in New York, Boston, Paris. *Exhib:* individual show, prints: San Francisco Museum of Modern Art; group shows: architecture: Univ. Zürich; sculpture: Oakland Art Museum; painting: Univ. California; prints: U.S. National Museum, Washington; photography: Musée d'histoire naturelle, Fribourg; Honour Medal, Nat. Exhbn., Jersey City Museum; hon.mention, Photography USA 88, 89. *Work in collections:* San Francisco Museum of Modern Art, Graphik-Sammlung ETH Zürich. *Address:* Rés. La Côte 60, 1110 Morges, Switzerland.

**ELDRIDGE, Harold Percy,** A.R.C.A. (1950), artist in oil, mural painter ; *b* London, 8 June, 1923. *m* Sheila May Smith. one *s.* two *d. Studied:* Camberwell School of Arts and Crafts and R.C.A. *Exhib:* R.A., R.B.A., London Group. Murals at European Patisserie (S. Kensington), Mortlake Primary School (Surrey). *Publications:* work repro.: in The Sketch. Also illustrations, scale models and historical reconstructions for Schools Television Programmes. Taught art at school in Coventry, but now retired. Now makes harpsichords and restores early pianos. *Address:* 42 Beechwood Ave., Coventry.

**ELIAS, Harold,** B.F.A., M.F.A., Ph.D.(honoris causa); teacher at various colleges (1952-80); served with U.S. Air Force (1941-45); *b* 3 Mar., 1920; married. two children. *Exhib:* over 90 juried regional and national exhbns. including "American Art Today", Metropolitan Museum of Art; Pennsylvania Academy of Fine Arts; Detroit Inst. of Art; Chicago Art Inst.; Creative Gallery, N.Y.; Denver Art Museum, etc.; over 200 one-man shows throughout the United States; American Federation of Arts and the Smithsonian Inst. Travelling shows; International Sculpture Competition, Brussels. *Work in collections:* University of Idaho, Illinois State Museum, University of Illinois, Massillon Museum, Massillon, Ohio; private collections in the East, Midwest, South and Western states. *Address:* 2612 High Oak Drive, Arlington, Texas 760012-3544 U.S.A.

**ELLIOTT, J.:** see BATES, Joan.

**ELLIOTT, Mary E.:** see BERESFORD-WILLIAMS, Mary E.

**ELLIOTT, Walter Albert,** F.B.I.S., L.F.I.B.A., S.G.F.A., P.S., U.A.; artist in pastel, oil, water-colour, acrylic; mem. Academy of Italy, Pres. Ilfracombe Art Soc., mem. International Assoc. of Art; *b* Wembley, 24 Oct., 1936. *m* Beryl Jean. one *s.* one *d. Educ:* Pinner Grammar School; de Havilland Aero College. *Studied:* Hammersmith Polytechnic, Harrow College of Art. *Exhib:* annually: P.S., S.G.F.A., U.A. (Mall Galleries), Pilton Arts Exhbn., Ilfracombe Art Soc.; Burton Gallery, Bideford (1976), Salon de Paris (1984), Torbay Guild of Artists. Permanent exhbn. of artwork at the Elliott Gallery, Hillsview, Braunton, N. Devon. EX34 9NZ. *Work in collections:* 'The Ascent of Man' (N. Devon Atheneaum 1970-81); Europe, Geneva, Canada, Australia, U.S.A. *Publications:* articles, Spaceflight, British Interplanetary Soc. *Signs work:* "Walter A. Elliott." *Address:* Sollake Studio, Warfield Villas, Ilfracombe, N. Devon EX34 9NZ.

**ELLIS, Christine Elizabeth,** A.D.B. (1960), A.O.I (1990); landscape and portrait artist in pencil, ink, water-colour, acrylic and oil; illustrator; writer; *b* London, 10 Sept., 1939. *Educ:* Sacred Heart High School. *Studied:* Maria Assumpta College, Kensington (1957-59), Theatre Arts at Rose Bruford College, Kent (1959-60), part-time at Regent St. Polytechnic, Richmond and Putney Schools of Art. *Exhib:* in mixed gallery exhbns. including I.L.E.A; S.W.A at Westminster; Fraser Carver; Knapp; A.O.I and Figerative Arts. *Work in collections:* life-size, paper based, illustrative sculpture at Bursledon Brickwork's Museum. *Commissions:* Cover illustrations 1997 Egon Ronay Guides. Landscapes and portraits: Martina Navratilova; All England Club, Wimbledon; Equitable Life, and for private individuals in many countries. Illustrations: St. George's; La Prairie; Keymer Tiles; Wates; Squires. *Publications:* B.B.C. short stories for children broadcast (1979-82). Limited edition prints: National Trust Enterprises Chartwell. *Clubs:* mem. F.B.A. *Signs work:* "C.E. Ellis." *Address:* North Cottage, 6b High St., Hampton on Thames, Middx. TW12 2SJ.

**ELLIS, E.N.,** R.E. (1987), S.W.E. (1984); wood engraver; *b* Sydney,

Australia, 14 May, 1946. *m* P.J.N. Ellis. *Educ:* Manly Girls, Sydney. *Studied:* John Ogburn, and National Art School, Sydney. *Exhib:* R.A., R.E., Duncan Campbell (1988, 1990, 1993, 1996), Southern Arts touring (1991-92), Godfrey and Twatt (1987-97), N.S.W. State Library, Australia, Fine Art Soc., London. *Work in collections:* V. & A., University Library of California, Australian National Library Canberra, Ashmolean Museum Oxford, Fitzwilliam Museum Cambridge, Art Gallery of N.S.W. Australia, London Transport Museum, Museum of London. *Commissions:* London Transport: 'Art on London Transport' poster (1996). *Publications:* Prigs Seven Virtuous Lady Gardeners (Smith Settle, 1997). *Clubs:* Chelsea Arts. *Signs work:* "E.N. Ellis." *Address:* Rhyd Goch, Ystrad Meurig, Ceredigion SY25 6AJ.

**ELLIS, Harold,** draughtsman and artist in oil, water-colour, line; *b* Baildon, 10 Apr., 1917. *m* Margaret Lovatt. one *s.* one *d. Educ:* Bradford Grammar School. *Studied:* as apprentice in commercial art studio, Messrs. Field, Sons & Co., Lidget Green, Bradford (1933-39). *Exhib:* Bradford City A.G. *Publications:* work repro.: cartoons, general anonymous commercial work. *Signs work:* "H. Ellis" or "ELLIS." *Address:* 5 Whitelands Cres., Baildon, Shipley, Yorks. BD17 6NN.

**ELLIS, John Colin,** U.A. (1988), M.B.I.A.T. (1971), M.I.P.D. (1973); artist/architectural illustrator in water-colour, oil, acrylic; artist working mainly on architectural subjects, plus land and town scapes developing into abstract art; designer/illustrator within retail commercial and residential sectors; *b* Fleetwood, Lancs., 1945. *m* Penny. one *s.* one *d. Educ:* Bailey Secondary, Fleetwood. *Studied:* Blackpool School of Art (1961-67). *Exhib:* one-man shows: N.Wales, Stamford, Peterborough, London. *Publications:* work repro.: housing sale illustration and brochure design. *Clubs:* U.A. *Signs work:* "John C. Ellis." *Address:* The Gallery, Braceborough, Stamford, Lincs. PE9 4NT.

**ELLIS, Noel,** A.R.C.A. (1948); painter and printmaker; *b* Plymouth, 25 Dec., 1917. *m* Linda Zinger. *Educ:* Sutton High School, Plymouth. *Studied:* Plymouth School of Art, R.C.A. *Exhib:* R.A., R.O.I., R.B.A., N.E.A.C., London Group, Grundy A.G., Blackpool, Plymouth A.G., Works in public and private collections. *Signs work:* "Noel Ellis" (cursive script). *Address:* 95 Bennerley Rd., Battersea, London SW11 6DT.

**ELLIS, Robert,** A.R.C.A., R.B.A., F.R.S.A., M.D.I.N.Z., M.F.I.M.; Professor Emeritus, Auckland University, N.Z.; *b* Northampton, 2 Apr., 1929. *m* Elizabeth. two *d. Educ:* Kingsthorpe C. of E. School, Northampton. *Studied:* Northampton School of Art (1943-47), R.C.A. (1949-52). *Exhib:* 50 one-man shows in N.Z., Australia and U.S.A.; group shows in Australia, Canada, Malaysia, India, Japan, England, U.S.A. *Work in collections:* all major N.Z. public collections, National Gallery of S. Australia, British Foreign Office, N.Z. Arts Council, etc. *Signs work:* "Robert Ellis." *Address:* 23 Berne Pl., Auckland 10, N.Z.

**ELLIS, William John,** F.R.S.A.; artist in oil, water-colour, crayon;

author/artist; *b* Rhyl, 21 Sept., 1944. *m* Gaynor Ellis. one *s.* one *d. Educ:* Glyndwr Secondary Modern, Rhyl. *Studied:* Glyndwr Secondary and later under Robert Evans Hughes. *Exhib:* Rhyl Town Hall and Holywell Library. *Publications:* author of Seaside Entertainments 100 Years of Nostalgia; Rhyl in old Picture Postcards; Entertainment in Rhyl and N. Wales (published July 1997). *Clubs:* Clwydian Art Society, Clwyd Assoc. for the Visual Arts, Mem. of Rhyl Liberty Players, Abergele Players, British Music Hall Soc., Manchester Music Hall Soc., Derbys. and Notts. Music Hall Soc. *Signs work:* "B. Ellis." *Address:* 2a Carlisle Ave., Rhyl, Clwyd LL18 3DU.

**ELMORE, Pat,** R.B.A. (1996); sculptress in stone and wood, also portraits and ceramics; *b* Rugby, 10 Sept., 1937. four *s.* two *d. Exhib:* solo shows, Bampton Arts Centre, Bedford Central Library, Swindon Links Library, Wantage Museum, The Stable Gallery at Green College Oxford; group shows: R.B.A., Mall Galleries, R.W.A., Cheltenham Art Soc., Syon Lodge London, Salammbo Galerie Paris, Gloucester Museum, Jersey (Village Gallery). *Work in collections:* Thamesdown Arts, Abingdon Town Council, The Church Army Exeter, Magdalen College Oxford. Permanent sculpture garden and gallery, and ongoing sculpture tuition at Nutford Lodge. *Address:* Nutford Lodge, Longcot, nr. Faringdon, Oxon. SN7 7TL.

**ELPIDA, née Georgiou,** B.A.Hons. (1986), M.A. (1990); artist in oil on canvas; *b* London, 23 Sept., 1958. *Educ:* St Marylebone School for Girls. *Studied:* St Martin's School of Art (1983-86), R.A. Schools (1987-90). *Exhib:* R.O.I. at Lloyd's, Royal Overseas League (prizewinner), 'New Generation' Bonham's, R.A. Summer Show (1991) (prizewinner, Guinness award), R.A. Premium Show (Winsor and Newton award), Berlin Academy of Art; one-man shows: Christopher Hull Gallery, Lynne Sterne Gallery, 'The Leicestershire Collection', Leicester, 'East End Open Studios', Acme Studios, London, Whitechapel Open. *Work in collections:* Unilever plc, Guinness Collection. *Signs work:* "Elpida." *Address:* 65 Ellesmere Rd., Chiswick, London W4 3EA.

**ELSTEIN, Cecile,** sculptor, printmaker, environmental artist; N. W. Arts Bursary Award (1983), Sericol colour prize, 9th British International Print Biennale, Bradford (1986), M.A. Art as Environment (1996); *b* 8 Feb., 1938. *m* Max Elstein. one *s.* one *d. Educ:* Cape Town, S. Africa. *Studied:* Michaelis School of Art (part time), studied ceramics and influenced by Catherine Yarrow, London (1965-69), sculpture and printmaking at West Surrey College of Art and Design (1975-76), Manchester Metropolitan University (1996). *Exhib:* U.K. and abroad since 1974 including S.P.S. London, Manchester Academy of Fine Art, Mini Print International, Cadaques, Spain (1983, 1984, 1987), Mini Print Travelling Show (1987), II Carbo Frio International Print Biennale, Brazil (1984, 1985), accepted R.A. London (1985), Singapore Festival of Arts (1986), Seoul International Print Biennale (1986), International Art Focus, Cambridge (1987), Clare Hall, University of Cambridge (1988), Casabella Gallery, Manchester (1988), Whitworth A.G. (1991), Ucheldre

Centre, Holyhead (1993), Art House Gallery, Manchester (1994-95), National Trust Wimpole Hall, Cambs., Summer Sculpture Exhbn. (1997). *Work in collections:* Tuft's Collection of Fine Prints Alsager/Massachusetts, Suffolk C.C., Whitworth A.G., etc. *Publications:* Design for Physical Variety EcoDesign, Spirit and Healing in Design Vol. III, No. 3; Empathy serves Place and Identity, Streetwise (1997). *Clubs:* M.A.F.A., M.P.C., F.I.B.A., F.P.S., P.M.S.A., F.R.S.A. *Signs work:* see appendix. *Address:* 25 Spath Rd., Didsbury, Manchester M20 2QT.

**ELVIN, Keith (The Revd.),** B.Sc.(Hons.) (1952), S.B.A. (1993), U.A. (1995); painter in oil and water-colour; retd. priest/schoolmaster; *b* London, 5 Apr., 1924. *m* Jill Rockley. one *s.* two *d. Educ:* St. Dunstan's College, University of Bristol. *Studied:* with private tutor in Cornwall (1977-87). *Exhib:* S.B.A., U.A., 'Not the R.A.', R.O.I., R.H.S., many mixed and one-man shows including Patricia Wells, Thornbury; Carousel, Chipping Sodbury; Rooksmoor, Bath; Portscatho, Cornwall; Clifton, Bristol. *Work in collections:* Bristol University S.C.R., Wills Hall Conference Centre. *Publications:* work repro.: Medici: numerous paintings and complete calendar. *Signs work:* "Keith Elvin." *Address:* 26 Westfield House, Cote Lane, Westbury-on-Trym, Bristol BS9 3UN.

**ELWES, Helen,** B.F.A. (Oxon), Post-Grad.Dip. R.A. Schools; painter in oil and tempera; *b* London, 5 Apr., 1958. *Studied:* West Surrey College of Art and Design (1976-77), Ruskin School of Drawing and Fine Art, Oxford (1979-82), R.A. Schools (1983-86, Peter Greenham, R.A.). *Exhib:* R.A., R.P., N.E.A.C., Agnews, New Grafton Gallery; one-man shows: Oxford Arts Centre (1982). *Commissions:* The Archbishop of Liverpool - Rev. Derek Worlock (1989), and work for: The National Trust, and Sir Brinsley Ford (1988). *Publications:* 'Art School' (Macmillan). Awards: Landseer Scholarship (1984), Richard Ford Award (1986). *Signs work:* "H.E." joined. *Address:* 24 Cheyne Row, London SW3 5HL.

**ELWYN, John,** A.R.C.A., R.I., A.R.Cam.A., (Hon); artist in oil, acrylic and water-colour; lecturer, Portsmouth College of Art (1948-53); lecturer, Winchester School of Art (1953-77); *b* Newcastle Emlyn, Dyfed, 20 Nov., 1916. *m* Gillian Butterworth, pianist. *Educ:* Llandyssul Grammar School. *Studied:* Carmarthen Art School (1935-38), West of England College of Art, Bristol (1937-38), Royal College Art (1938-40, 1946-47). *Work in collections:* Welsh Arts Council; Southampton University; Cardiff University; Ministry of Public Buildings, Whitehall; Aberystwyth University; Pembroke College, Cambridge; Steel Company of Wales; Glynn-Vivian Gallery, Swansea; National Library of Wales; Gregynog Collection; Contemporary Art Soc. for Wales; Newport Art Gallery; Leeds University; North Wales Assoc. of Arts; Nuffield Foundation; Exeter University; and 15 other education authorities; National Eisteddfod Gold Medal (1956). *Commissions:* Shell, G.P.O., Radio Times, Glaxo Laboratories, Midland Bank Ltd., etc. *Signs work:* "JOHN

ELWYN." *Address:* 5 Compton Rd., Winchester SO23 9SL.

**EMERY, Edwina,** A.R.B.S. (1984); Freeman of Worshipful Company of Goldsmiths (1986); sculptor and designer in chalk, oil and acrylic; retained exclusively by Garrard, the Crown Jewellers, animalier, portrait and design since 1982; *b* Huntingdonshire, 10 May, 1942 divorced. two *s.* two *d. Educ:* Grammar School and privately. *Exhib:* permanently at Garrard, Regent St., Oscar and Peter Johnson Gallery. Work collected by Royalty and Heads of State worldwide, also private collectors. *Commissions:* include prestigious confidential commissions, also racing, polo, portraits Lester Piggott and Willie Shoemaker, many for industry and commerce. *Publications:* Commercial Art in Youth. *Clubs:* The Farmers, Whitehall Court. *Signs work:* see appendix. *Address:* Little Manor, Ibberton, Dorset DT11 0EN.

**EMMERICH, Anita Jane (née MOSSIE POLLOK),** International member and exhibitor: R.M.S., S.W.A., M.A.S.-F., G.M.A.S., W.F.M.; miniature painter specializing in portrait silhouettes in oil on vellum or old ivory; ink on board and fine modern oil canvases; several major awards, U.K. and U.S.A.; *b* London, 3 Feb., 1938. *m* W. M. Ernst. two *s. Educ:* Sydenham High School for Girls (G.P.D.S.T.). *Studied:* self taught artist. *Exhib:* England, N. Ireland, France, U.S.A., Australia. Lannards Gallery, Billingshurst, West Sussex.*Work in collections:* R.M.S. Diploma collection, Llewellyn Alexander Gallery, London, Work in private collection. 1993 Contemporary Art Consultant, Diocese of Rochester Kent. Previously mem. of S.M., S.Lm., H.S.F., A.S.M.A. (Q), (T), (N.S.W.). *Signs work:* see appendix. *Address:* Wychling Over, Pilgrims Way, Westwell, nr. Ashford, Kent TN25 4NQ.

**EMSLEY, Kenneth,** M.A. (Cantab.), LL.M. (Newcastle), A.C.I.S., F.R.Hist.S., F.R.S.A.; artist in water-colour, pen and ink, author, retd. lecturer; President, Soc. of Miniaturists, President, British Water-colour Soc.; former chairman, Bradford Arts Club; *b* Shipley, 7 Dec., 1921. *m* Nancy Audrey Slee, B.Sc., Dip.Ed. *Educ:* Loughborough College, St. John's College, Cambridge. *Studied:* various schools under Edward Wesson, Arnold Dransfield. *Exhib:* Mall and Bankside galleries, London, Florida, U.S.A., Cartwright Hall, Bradford. *Publications:* Northumbria, Tyneside, Historic Haworth Today, etc. *Clubs:* Leeds Fine Art. *Signs work:* "K.E." or "K. EMSLEY." *Address:* 34 Nab Wood Drive, Shipley, W. Yorks. BD18 4EL.

**ENGLAND, Frederick John,** N.D.D., A.T.C. (Lond.), I.A.G., M.F.P.S., Norwegian Scholarship (1960), Medaille d'Argent, Paris Salon (Gold Medal, 1975), Diploma d'Honneur, International Arts Guild, Monte Carlo; painter in oil, lithograph, etching, water-colour; ex-lecturer in painting and design at Leek School of Art; Pres. Soc. of Staffordshire Artists; director, England's Gallery, Leek; *b* Fulham, London, 5 Mar., 1939. *m* Sheelagh Jane. *Educ:* Deacons School. *Studied:* Brighton College of Art and Crafts (1956) under Sallis Bonney, R.O.I., R.W.S., Charles Knight, R.O.I., R.W.S., R.T. Cowen, Principal; Hardanger Folkschule, Norway (1960) under Oddmund J. Aarhus;

London University (1961) under Ronald Horton. *Exhib:* Paris Salon, Arts Council of N. Ireland, R.B.A., R.I. Summer and Winter Salon, R.B.S.A., Manchester Academy, Bradford Open Exhibition, Trends Free Painters and Sculptors, R.W.A., S.I.A. (travelling shows included). Open Exhibition Stafford, Society of Staffordshire Artists; one-man shows: Galerie Helian, Montreux, England's Gallery, Burlington Gallery, Buxton Schaffer Gallery, Market Drayton, Galerie für Zeitgenössische Kunst, Hamburg, Galerie Bernheim-Jeune, Paris, I.A.G. Monte Carlo, Zilina, Czechoslovakia, Octagon Gallery, Bolton, University of Keele, Gallerie Helion, Montreux. *Work in collections:* Nicholson Institute, Goritz Coll., Fenning Coll., Geneva, City of Stoke-on-Trent Art Gallery. Reviewed work in La Revue Moderne, Les Journal des Jeunes, Boomerang (Paris Salon Edition of One Hundred Young European painters), Dictionnaire des Artists, Repertorium Artis, Dictionnaire International d'Art Contemporain. *Signs work:* "England." *Address:* Ball Haye House, 1 Ball Haye Terr., Leek ST13 6AP Staffs.

**EUSTACE, Eric George,** H.S. (1991), A.R.M.S. (1993); painter in watercolour and acrylic; *b* Dunstable, 14 Jan., 1925. *m* Edna Roberts. *Studied:* art at Luton College (1953-55). *Signs work:* "Eric G. Eustace." *Address:* 28 Buttercup Close, Dunstable, Beds. LU6 3LA.

**EVANS, Bernard,** N.D.D. (1954), A.T.D. (1955); artist in oil, water-colour, pastel; Tutor/Director, Mounts Bay Art Centre, Newlyn, Penzance; Com. Mem., Newlyn Soc. of Artists; *b* Liverpool, 6 July, 1929. *m* Audrey M. Evans. three *s.* two *d. Educ:* St. Francis Xavier's Grammar School, Liverpool. *Studied:* Liverpool College of Art, Camberwell School of Arts and Crafts (Martin Bloch, Richard Eurich, R.A.). *Exhib:* Darlington Nottingham, Lincoln, Newlyn, Penzance. *Signs work:* "Bernard Evans" or "B. Evans" or "B.E." *Address:* Trevatha, Faugan La., Newlyn, Penzance, Cornwall TR18 5DJ.

**EVANS, Brenda Jean,** B.A.Hons. (1976), R.A.S. (1979), S.W.A. (1986); artist in water-colour; *b* Birmingham, 6 June, 1954. *Educ:* Aldridge Grammar School. *Studied:* Sutton Coldfield School of Art, Loughborough College of Art, R.A. Schools. *Exhib:* R.A. Summer Shows, Highgate Gallery, Tenterden, S.W.A., Grape Lane Gallery, York, Edinburgh, New Grafton Gallery, Business Art Galleries. *Work in collections:* H.R.H. Princess Michael of Kent, Mr. and Mrs. Ronnie Corbett. *Signs work:* "Brenda Evans." *Address:* 61a Beulah Rd., Walthamstow, London E17 9LD.

**EVANS, David Pugh,** A.R.C.A. (1965), R.S.W. (1975), R.S.A. (1989); artist/lecturer in oil and acrylic; lecturer, Edinburgh College of Art; Mem. of Council, Royal Scottish Academy; *b* Abercarn, Gwent. *Educ:* Newbridge Grammar School, Gwent. *Studied:* Newport College of Art (1959-62, Thomas Rathmell), R.C.A. (1962-65, Prof. Carel Weight). *Exhib:* Fruit Market Gallery, Edinburgh, University of York, Mercury Gallery, London. *Work in collections:* Carlisle A.G., S.A.C., Hunterian Museum, Glasgow, Glasgow A.G., Royal Scottish Academy, R.A., City A.G., Edinburgh, Aberdeen A.G., Scottish

Television. *Signs work:* "D.P. Evans." *Address:* 17 Inverleith Gdns., Edinburgh EH3 5PS.

**EVANS, Eurgain,** N.D.D. (1958), R.A. Schools Cert. (1961); painter in oil and water-colour; retd. lecturer, Faculty of Art and Design, W. Glamorgan Inst. of Higher Educ., Swansea; *b* Betws y Coed, Gwynedd, 28 Mar., 1936. *Educ:* Llanrwst Grammar School. *Studied:* Wrexham College of Art; R.A. Schools. *Exhib:* Pritchard Jones Hall, Bangor University Wales, London Welsh Assoc. Young Contemporaries, R.A., F.P.S., etc. *Work in collections:* National Museum of Wales, Aberystwyth, and many private collections. *Signs work:* "Eurgain." *Address:* 14 Valley View, Sketty, Swansea SA2 8BG, S. Wales.

**EVANS, Garth,** sculptor and draughtsman; *b* Cheadle, Ches., 23 Nov., 1934. *m* Leila Philip. one *s. Studied:* Regional College of Art, Manchester, and Slade School. *Work in collections:* Metropolitan Museum, N.Y.; Museum of Modern Art, N.Y.; Tate Gallery; V. & A.; Power Gallery of Contemporary Art, Sydney; Manchester City A.G.; Portsmouth City A.G.; Bristol City A.G.; Contemporary Arts Soc. of G.B. Lives and works in both London and New York. *Signs work:* " Garth Evans." *Address:* 106 North 6th St., Brooklyn, N.Y.11211.

**EVANS, Margaret Fleming,** D.A., A.T.C., U.A.; portrait painter in oils and pastels, art tutor; teacher in adult education in Kent; *b* Glasgow, 9 Apr., 1952. *m* Malcolm William Evans. one *s.* one *d. Educ:* Whitehill Senior Secondary School, Glasgow. *Studied:* Glasgow School of Art (1970-74, Dr. David Donaldson, R.P., A. Goudie, R.P., L. Morocco, J. Robertson, A.R.S.A.). *Exhib:* London and S.E. England. *Signs work:* see appendix. *Address:* Larasset, High Halden, Ashford, Kent. TN26 3TY.

**EVANS, Marlene Elizabeth,** S.W.A. (1990), A.B.W.S. (1987), A.Y.A. (1989); artist of botanical studies and landscapes in water-colour, ink, mixed media; *b* Barking, Essex, 17 Feb., 1937. *m* Lyn Evans (decd.). one *s.* one *d. Educ:* Racecommon Rd. School, Barnsley. *Studied:* Barnsley School of Art (textile design, L.H.H. Glover, A.R.C.A., A.T.D., R. Skinner, A.T.D.). *Exhib:* one-man shows: Cawthorne S.Y. (1990), Ossett, W. Yorks. (1991), annually S.W.A. and B.W.S., also various mixed exhbns. *Signs work:* "M.E. Evans." *Address:* 14 Spencer St., Barnsley, S. Yorks. S70 1QX.

**EVANS, Nicholas,** R.C.A. (1981); Welsh Arts Council award; self-taught artist in oil on board and canvas, and water-colour, sculptor and lecturer; *b* Aberdare, S.Wales. *m* Annie Maud Lambert. two *s.* one *d. Educ:* Junior and Secondary schools. *Exhib:* R.A.; R.C.A.; National Eisteddfodau; N.E.A.C.; Oriel, Cardiff; Browse & Darby; Herbert, Coventry; National Gallery, Bulgaria; Rechlingshausen, Germany; Turner Gallery, Penarth; Bury St. Edmunds; Swansea University; Glynn Vivian, Swansea; York University; Barbican; Chapter Arts; Doncaster A.G. (purchased by Contemporary Art Soc., Tate); MacRoberts Arts Centre; Hayward Gallery; Bede, Jarrow; R.W.A. *Work in collections:* National Museum of Wales, Arts Council of G.B., Welsh Arts Council, Sir Richard Hyde-Parker, Duke of Devonshire, Dept. of Environment,

Contemporary Art Soc., National Library of Wales, Aberystwyth, West Wales Assoc. for Arts, New York, California, Alberta. *Publications:* Symphonies in Black (Y Lolfa, Wales, 1987). *Signs work:* "NICK EVANS." *Address:* Shalom, 16 College St., Abernant, Aberdare, Rhondda Cynon Taff CF44 ORN.

**EVANS, Ray,** R.I., F.S.A.I.; painter, writer and illustrator; *b* 1920. one *s.* one *d. Studied:* Manchester College of Art (1946-48), Heatherleys under Iain Macnab (1948-50). *Work in collections:* Gulbenkian Foundation; Nat. Library of Wales; Winchester Guildhall Gallery and many private collections in Europe, Britain, U.S.A. and Canada. *Publications:* Many books written and illustrated for John Murray, Consumers Assoc., Harper Collins and Batsford 'How to be a Successful Illustrator' (1993), 'Mastering Water-colour' (1994). Prints and calendars for Royles, I.O.D., B.P., Whitbreads, Co-op, Abbey National, Allan & Bertram etc. Specialises in architectural subjects. Entry in new 20th Century Painters and Sculptors, pub. by Antique Collectors Club. *Signs work:* see appendix. *Address:* New House, Eversglade, Devizes Rd., Salisbury, Wilts. SP2 7LU.

**EVELEIGH, John,** Dip. F.A. (Lond.) (1951), F.R.S.A. (1965), elected Fellow (W'ong) (1988), D.C.A. (W'ong) (1991), Aust. W.C.I. (1991), Professional Fellow James Cook (1991), M.W.L.A. (1995); practising artist in oil, water-colour, pastel, ink, etc.; Hon. Founder Arts Director, New Metropole Arts Centre, Kent; Hon. Founder Arts Director, The Long Gallery University of Wollongong, N.S.W.; *b* London, 15 Dec, 1926. *m* Margaret. three *s. Educ:* The Slade - London University (1948-52, Sir William Coldstream). *Exhib:* Camberwell, Herts and Kent County Councils, Welsh, Contemporary Arts Soc., Wollongong City A.G. *Work in collections:* Wollongong University, James Cook University, Metropole Arts Centre. *Commissions:* public and private, protrait and landscape. *Publications:* work repro.: many catalogues and articles. *Signs work:* " John Eveleigh." *Address:* 4 Broadfield Rd., Folkestone, Kent CT20 2JT.

**EVETTS, Leonard Charles,** M.A., M.Sc., D.Litt., A.R.C.A.; stained glass artist, letterer, water-colour painter; Master of Design, Department of Fine Art, University of Newcastle upon Tyne (retd.); *b* 12 Jan., 1909. *m* (1) Joan C. M. Macdonald; (2) Phyl Dobson. *Educ:* Royal College of Art (Prof. E. W. Tristram, Edward Johnston, 1930-33), student demonstrator under Edward Johnston. *Exhib:* R.A. *Publications:* Roman Lettering (Pitman, 1938); numerous articles on English stained glass and Roman inscriptions in periodicals and archæological journals. *Clubs:* Pen and Palette. *Signs work:* "L. C. Evetts" or "Leonard Evetts." *Address:* The Stead, Woolsington Bridge, Newcastle upon Tyne NE13 8BL.

**EYTON, Anthony,** R.A. (1986), R.W.S., R.W.A., R. Cam. A., Mem. London Group, N.D.D., Abbey Major Scholarship in Painting (1950); prize winner, John Moore's Exhbn. (1972), awarded Grocer's Co. Fellowship (1973), 1st prize, Second British International Drawing Biennale, Middlesbrough

(1975), Charles Wollaston Award, R.A. (1981), British Painting 1952-77, R.A. (1977); artist in oil, teaches at Royal Academy Schools; *b* Teddington, 17 May, 1923. *Educ:* Twyford School (1932-37), Canford School (1937-41). *Studied:* Reading University (1941); Camberwell School of Arts and Crafts (1947-50). *Exhib:* London Group, R.A.; one-man shows: Browse and Darby (1981, 1985, 1987, 1990, 1993, 1996); Retrospective: South London A.G. (1980). *Work in collections:* Arts Council, Tate Gallery, Imperial War Museum, Govt. Picture Collection, Plymouth A.G. *Address:* 166 Brixton Rd., London SW9 6AU.

# F

**FABER, Rodney George,** S.G.F.A. (1987); self taught artist in water-colour and pen and ink drawing; *b* Liverpool, 8 June, 1935. *m* Asne Wainer. *Educ:* Hasmonean Grammar School. *Exhib:* S.G.F.A. Annual exhbns. and mixed exhbns. in various galleries in London and the Home Counties. Commission and other works in numerous private collections both in U.K. and abroad. Rexel prizewinner S.G.F.A. (1992). *Signs work:* "FABER." *Address:* Studio: 37 Darwin Ct., Gloucester Ave., London NW1 7BG.

**FADE, Lynn,** M.A.; Curator, Grundy Art Gallery, Blackpool; *b* London, 22 Mar., 1969. *m* J.S.C. Barnes, M.A. *Educ:* Leicester Polytechnic, University of Leicester. *Address:* Grundy Art Gallery, Queen St., Blackpool FY1 1PX.

**FAILES, Colin Michael,** City & Guilds Dip. (Sculpture) (1972), Beckworth travel scholarship to Egypt (1972), Postgrad. (Sculpture) Cert. R.A. Schools, Silver medal (Sculpture) (1975), bronze medal (Sculpture) (1976); mural artist and sculptor in acrylic, wax modelling; *b* Farnborough, Kent, 2 Oct., 1948. *Educ:* Arle School, Cheltenham. *Studied:* City & Guilds of London Art School (1969-72, James Butler, R.A.), R.A. Schools (1973-76, Willi Soukop, R.A.). *Exhib:* R.A. Summer Exhbns. (1976, 1980, 1987, 1988). *Work in collections:* London, Monaco, Luxembourg. *Commissions:* murals: "Oriana" P.&O.; Vintners' Hall, City of London; Bridge Housing Assoc., London. *Publications:* work repro.: in "Painting Murals" (MacDonald Orbis), and "Murals" (New Holland). *Clubs:* Reynolds. *Signs work:* "COLIN FAILES" or "C.M. Failes." *Address:* 6 Elfindale Rd., London SE24 9NW.

**FAIRCLOUGH, Bernard Peake,** A.T.D., D.A., Manc., F.R.S.A., Head of School of Art, Darlington, until 1975; artist in oil, gouache, acrylic; *b* Glossop, Derbyshire, 5 Dec., 1915. *m* Patricia Mary Poulton. one *s.* one *d. Educ:* Glossop Grammar School. *Studied:* Manchester School of Art, principal, R. C. Dawson, A.R.C.A., painting, L. R. Baxter. *Exhib:* Manchester, Salford, Birmingham, Derby municipal galleries, Whitechapel A.G., private galleries in London, Arts Council Travelling exhbn., R.S.A. *Work in collections:* Manchester Educ. Com. Schools Collection. *Signs work:* "Fairclough." *Address:* Newholme, Newbiggin, Barnard Castle DL12 0TY.

**FAIRCLOUGH, Michael,** R.E. (1964), Rome Scholar in Engraving (1964-66), N.E.A.C. (1995); painter and printmaker; lecturer, Belfast College of Art (1962-64); West Surrey College of Art (1967-79); *b* Blackburn, 16 Sept., 1940. *m* Mary Malenoir. two *d*. *Studied:* Kingston School of Art (1957-61); British School at Rome, (1964-67); Atelier 17, Paris (1967). *Exhib:* one-man shows Henley-on-Thames, Farnham, London, Toronto, Auckland, N.Z., etc. *Work in collections:* V. & A., Ashmolean, Usher Gallery, Bowes Museum, Royal Albert Museum, New York Public Library, etc. *Commissions:* mural, Farnham Post Office (1970), Post Office 'National Trust' issue of five stamps (1981), Avebury Press (1995). *Signs work:* "Michael Fairclough." *Address:* Tilford Green Cottages, Tilford, Farnham, Surrey GU10 2BU.

**FAIRFAX-LUCY, Edmund,** N.E.A.C.; painter of interiors, still-life and landscapes in oil; *b* 1945. *Studied:* City & Guilds of London Art School, and R.A. Schools (1967-70) winning David Murray Travelling Scholarship (1966, 1967, 1969). *Exhib:* R.A. since 1967, New Grafton Gallery since 1971. *Work in collections:* Brinsley Ford. *Address:* Charlecote Park, Warwick.

**FAIRGRIEVE, James Hanratty,** D.A. (Edin.), R.S.W., A.R.S.A.; Gillies award, R.S.W. (1987); full time lecturer, painter in acrylic; *b* Prestonpans, E. Lothian, 17 June, 1944. *m* Margaret Fairgrieve. two *s*. one *d*. *Educ:* Preston Lodge Senior Secondary School. *Studied:* Edinburgh College of Art. *Exhib:* Hawarth A.G. (1974), Triad Arts Centre (1974), Scottish Gallery (1974), Scottish Arts Club (1973), New 57 Gallery (1969, 1971); one-man shows: Edinburgh University (1975), Scottish Gallery (1978), Mercury Gallery, London (1980, 1982, 1987), Macauley Gallery (1983), Mercury Gallery, Edinburgh (1984), Stichell Gallery (1990). *Work in collections:* Edinburgh Corp., Scottish Arts Council, National Bank of Chicago, Milngavie A.G., H.R.H. The Duke of Edinburgh, Argyll Schools, R.C.P., Perth A.G., Lord Moray, Leeds Schools. *Signs work:* "James H. Fairgrieve." *Address:* Burnbrae., Gordon, Berwickshire, Scotland TD3 6JU.

**FAIRMAN, Sheila,** R.M.S., S.W.A., F.S.B.A., H.S.F.; awarded R.M.S. Gold Bowl (1989), Hunting Group art prize, runner up (1982); painter in oil and water-colour and miniaturist; *b* Benfleet, Essex, 18 Aug., 1924. *m* Bernard Fairman, F.A.P.S.A. one *s*. *Studied:* Southend-on-Sea College of Art (1938-41). *Exhib:* R.A., R.M.S., R.S.M.A., R.P., R.I., R.O.I., S.W.A., S.B.A. *Work in collections:* Beecroft A.G., Southend-on-Sea. *Signs work:* "SHEILA FAIRMAN" or "S.F." *Address:* 39 Burnham Rd., Leigh-on-Sea, Essex SS9 2JT.

**FAIRS, Tom,** N.D.D. (1950), A.R.C.A. (1953); painter in oil paint, oil pastel, stained glass designer; Senior lecturer, Theatre Dept. Central School of Art and Design (retd.); *b* London, 3 Oct., 1925. *m* Elisabeth Russell Taylor, author/academic. *Studied:* Hornsey School of Art (1948-50), R.C.A. (1950-54). *Exhib:* Arts Council Travelling Exhbns., Beaford Centre, Dartington Hall, Covent Garden Gallery, Roland, Browse & Delbanco, Hambledon Gallery, Illustrators Art, Rooksmoor Gallery, Leeds Playhouse, Stables Folkestone, The

Thackeray Gallery, Ombersley Gallery, R.A. Summer Exhbns. *Commissions:* stained glass in Britain and Bahrain. *Signs work:* "FAIRS." *Address:* 21 Steeles Rd., London NW3 4SH.

**FAIRWEATHER, Dorothy,** painter/etcher; *b* 4 Aug., 1915, married. one *s. Educ:* privately. *Studied:* Folkestone School of Art (1930-34), Liverpool School of Art (1942-44). *Exhib:* leading London galleries including R.A., Barbican, Paris (1983-84), Germany (1989). *Work in collections:* Britain and abroad. President Soroptimist Club of Sevenoaks (1973-74, 1984-85). *Address:* Lanterns, 4 Cade La., Sevenoaks, Kent TN13 1QX.

**FAKHOURY, Bushra,** B.A., M.A., Ph.D. (Lond.); sculptor in bronze, stone; *b* Beirut, 1 Apr., 1942. two *s. Educ:* St. Paul's, Wimbledon School of Art and Emanuel. *Studied:* Beirut University College, American University of Beirut, University of London. *Exhib:* Bloomsbury Galleries (1986), Mall Galleries (1986), Jablonski Gallery (1987), Ashdown Gallery (1988), Kufa Gallery (1989). *Publications:* Art Education in Lebanon. *Signs work:* see appendix. *Address:* 57 Madrid Rd., Barnes, London SW13 9PQ.

**FALCONBRIDGE, Brian,** Dip. A.D. (Fine Art) (1973), H.D.F.A. (Slade) (1975), elected F.R.B.S. (1997); Head of Visual Arts Dept., Goldsmiths'; sculptor in bronze; *b* Fakenham, 1 May, 1950. one *s.* one *d. Educ:* Fakenham Grammar School. .*Studied:* Canterbury College of Art (1968-69), Goldsmiths' College School of Art (1970-73), Slade School of Fine Art (1973-75). *Exhib:* numerous mixed and solo exhbns. in Europe and Far East. *Work in collections:* A.C.G.B., Contemporary Art Soc., University of East Anglia, British Council and numerous private collections in U.K. and abroad. *Signs work:* "Brian Falconbridge." *Address:* c/o Visual Arts Dept., Goldsmiths' University of London, New Cross, London SE14 6NW.

**FALLA, Kathleen M.,** F.F.P.S (1985); painter in water-colour and pastel, relief printmaker and sculptor in wood; *b* Guernsey, C.I., 25 Jan., 1924. *m* Kenneth R. Masters. one *s.* one *d. Educ:* Ladies College, Guernsey. *Studied:* Guildford School of Art and Morley College, London. *Exhib:* solo shows: Lauragais, France, University of Surrey, Godalming Museum; shared shows: Loggia Gallery, Farnham Maltings; group shows: Barbican, West of England Academy, Brighton Polytechnic Gallery, Bloomsbury Galleries, etc. *Signs work:* "Kit Falla." *Address:* Old Barn Cottage Church La., Witley, Surrey GU8 5PW.

**FALLSHAW, Keith George,** N.S. (1979); artist in oil, pastel and pencil, graphic designer, sculptor in clay, plaster, Perspex, wood, brass, and bronze; former council mem. N.S.; M.D. of Creative Media Communications Ltd., design and advert. consultants; *b* London, 17 Nov., 1946. *Educ:* Broxhill School, Romford and privately. *Studied:* art privately with Leonared Boden, F.R.S.A.; sculpture privately with Edmund Holmes; graphic design at the London College of Printing (Leonard Cusdens and Don Smith). *Exhib:* Mall Galleries, N.S., U.A., Deben Gallery; various London and U.K. *Signs work:*

"Fallshaw" or in sculpture "KF." *Address:* Bay Tree Cottage, No. 1 Crown Terr., Bishop's Stortford, Herts. CM23 2DP.

**FARLEY, James Osmer,** A.R.B.S. (1990), A.N.S.S. (1985); portrait and architectural sculptor in clay, wax, direct metal, steels, bronze, copper; *b* Cleveland, Ohio, 10 Apr., 1935. *m* Gillian Lewin. one *d. Studied:* Pennsylvania Academy of Fine Art (1952-56, Walker Hancock, Harry Rosin, Andrew Wyeth), Chicago Art Inst. (1957-59, Edvard Chaisang). *Exhib:* Art and the Corporate Image (1981). *Work in collections:* Arizona: Bell Center, Sun City; City Hall, Glendale; Centennial Hall, Mesa; St. Luke's Hospital, Phoenix; Hanna Boys Center, Sonoma, Calif. *Clubs:* F. & A. Masonic Lodge. *Signs work:* "James Farley." *Address:* 150 Scott Ellis Gdns., St. John's Wood, London NW8 9HG; 4718 E. Portland, Phoenix, AZ. 85008, U.S.A.

**FARQUHARSON, Alex,** M.A. (Dist.) Arts Critic, B.A. English/Art Comb. Hons.; curator; Exhbn. Officer, Spacex Gallery, Exeter; *b* Chalfont St. Giles, 26 Sept., 1969. *Educ:* Exeter University, City University, London. *Studied:* Exeter College of Art and Design (now Plymouth University) (1988-91). *Publications:* numerous catalogue texts. *Address:* c/o Spacex Gallery, 45 Preston St., Exeter EX1 1DF.

**FARQUHARSON, Andrew Charles,** artist in water-colour; *b* Johannesburg, S. Africa, 14 Dec., 1959. *Educ:* St. John's College, Johannesburg. *Studied:* under his mother. *Exhib:* group show Johannesburg. Lectured: University of Wales, Anglo Spanish Soc., Inst. of Spain. *Signs work:* "A.C. Farquharson." *Address:* 80b Naylor Rd., Peckham, London SE15.

**FARR, Dennis Larry Ashwell,** C.B.E., M.A., Hon.D.Litt., F.R.S.A., F.M.A.; Director, Courtauld Institute Galleries (1980-93); Director, Birmingham Museums and Art Gallery (1969-80); Senior Lecturer in Fine Art, University of Glasgow (1967-69); Curator, Paul Mellon Collection, Washington, D.C. (1964-66); Asst. Keeper, Tate Gallery, London (1954-64); *b* 3 Apr., 1929. *m* Diana Pullein-Thompson, writer. one *s.* one *d. Educ:* Luton Grammar School. *Studied:* Courtauld Inst. of Art, University of London (1947-50). *Publications:* William Etty (1958), Catalogue of the Modern British School in the Tate Gallery (with M. Chamot and M. Butlin, 1964-65), English Art 1870-1940 (1978), Lynn Chadwick, Sculptor (with Eva Chadwick, 1990), etc. *Address:* Orchard Hill, Swan Barn Rd., Haslemere, Surrey GU27 2HY.

**FARRELL, Alan Richard,** A.R.M.S. (1984), R.M.S. (1995); painter in water-colour and oil, dealer in antiques and paintings, chartered electrical engineer (M.I.E.E.); *b* London, 17 May, 1932, married. two *d. Studied:* S.E. Essex Technical College and School of Art (1953-56). *Exhib:* R.M.S., R.I., R.S.M.A., R.B.A., U.A., Chelsea Art Soc., International Boat Show, Britain in Water-colours, Laing Exhbn., Armed Forces Art Soc. *Signs work:* "ALAN FAR-RELL" printed bottom right or left-hand corner; paintings dated on reverse; and see appendix. *Address:* The White House, Whitesmith, nr. Lewes, E. Sussex BN8 6JD.

# WHO'S WHO IN ART

**FARRELL, Anthony,** N.D.D. (1965), R.A.Dip. (1968); artist in oil, etching; *b* Epsom, 28 Mar., 1945. *m* Sarah. one *s.* three *d. Educ:* Belfairs High School. *Studied:* Camberwell School of Art (1963-65), R.A. Schools (1965-68). *Exhib:* R.A. Common Room, Minories, Colchester, R.A. Summer Exhbns., Serpentine Gallery, Christchurch Mansions, Ipswich. *Work in collections:* A.C.G.B., The Minories, Colchester, Epping Forest Museum, Manchester City A.G., Beecroft A.G., Westcliff-on-Sea, Borough of St. Edmundsbury and Suffolk C.C., Essex Health Authority, Ipswich Borough Council. *Signs work:* "Anthony Farrell." *Address:* 6 Avenue Rd., Leigh-on-Sea, Essex SS9 1AX.

**FARRELL, Don,** R.I. (1984), R.B.A. (1985), F.C.A.; bronze medal R.I. (1984); Daler Rowney award R.B.A. Exhbn. (1992); painter in water-colour; *b* Vancouver, B.C., 3 Oct., 1942. *m* Margaret. two *s. Exhib:* annually at R.I. (1984-91), R.B.A. (1983-91). *Work in collections:* H.R.H. The Prince of Wales; private and corporate collections: Britain, Canada, U.S.A. and Europe. *Signs work:* "Don Farrell." *Address:* 6461 McKenzie Drive, Delta, B.C., Canada V4E 1N8.

**FASTNEDGE, Ralph William,** D.F.C., B.A.; formerly curator, The Lady Lever Art Gallery, Port Sunlight, Merseyside; *b* London, 16 Apr., 1913. *Educ:* University College School; Worcester College, Oxford; Courtauld Inst. of Art. *Publications:* English Furniture Styles (1500-1830), Penguin Books, 1955; Sheraton Furniture, Faber; Shearer Furniture Designs, Tiranti; Regency Furniture (revision), Country Life. *Address:* Glannant, Llanfechain, Powys SY22 6XE.

**FAULDS, James Alexander,** D.A.; artist in water-colour and oil; art teacher; *b* Glasgow, 15 Jan., 1949. *Educ:* Knightswood Secondary School. *Studied:* Dundee College of Art (1968-72). *Exhib:* Dundee under 30's, R.S.A., S.S.A., Colquhoun Memorial, Group 81, Glasgow, Eden Court Gallery, Contemporary British Water-colours, Festival Theatre, Pitlochry, R.S.W., John Laing, London, Nürnberg, Germany. *Clubs:* Glasgow Art; founder mem., Group 81, Glasgow. *Signs work:* see appendix. *Address:* 3 Camphill Ave., Glasgow G41 3AV.

**FAULKNER, Amanda,** B.F.A.(Hons.) (1982), M.F.A. (Printmaking) (1983); artist in charcoal and pastel on paper, acrylic on canvas, lithography and etching; Senior lecturer in Fine Art, Chelsea School of Art; *b* Poole, 5 Dec., 1953. one *s. Educ:* St. Anthony's, Leweston, Dorset, and Canford School, Dorset. *Studied:* Bournemouth College of Art (1978-79), Ravensbourne College of Art and Design (1979-82), Chelsea School of Art (1982-83). *Exhib:* regularly at Angela Flowers Gallery and Flowers East since 1983; and in U.K. and internationally. *Work in collections:* including A.C.G.B., Unilever plc, V. & A., Contemporary Art Soc., Whitworth A.G., Silkeborg Kunstmuseum, Denmark. *Clubs:* Chelsea Arts. *Signs work:* "Amanda Faulkner." *Address:* 131 Listria Pk., London N16 5SP.

**FAULKNER, Robert Trevor,** A.R.C.A. (1955), F.R.B.S.; figurative sculptures in bronze, terracotta, ciment-fondu and direct metal; specialist in poly-chrome metal wild-life subjects, designs for pewter holloware; *b* 17 Sept., 1929, married. one *d*. *Educ*: Penistone Grammar School. *Studied*: Sheffield School of Art (1946-50); R.C.A. (1952-55). *Exhib*: Moorland, Alwin (London). *Work in collections*: Ulster Museum, Derbys., Oxford, Lancs., and Sheffield Educ. Authorities. *Commissions*: medals for Virginia Air and Space Museum; trophy, Royal Aero Club; medals for B.M.F.A. *Publications*: Manual of Direct Metal Sculpture (Thames & Hudson, 1978). Gallery: John Noott, Broadway, Worcs. *Signs work*: "TREVOR FAULKNER" or "T.F." *Address*: 4 Birchitt Cl., Bradway, Sheffield S17 4QJ.

**FAUR, Aurel-Sebastian,** 1st prize for portrait sculpture (1939) School of Beaux Arts, Bucharest; painter on porcelain in water-colour and oil, portrait sculptor in clay (bronze casted), alabaster; *m* Yvonne-Constance. *Educ*: School of Beaux Arts, Bucharest. *Studied*: School of Beaux Arts, Bucharest (1934-37), School of Ceramics, Sèvres, France. Worked at Manufacture Nationale de Sèvres (Iser, Despiaux, Maillol). *Exhib*: Paris: Salon d'Automne, Salon des Indépendants, Salon des Tuileries, Grandes Galeries d'Art Contemporain; Bruxelles: Musée de Peinture Moderne, Wauxhall. *Work in collections*: Simu and Dona State Museums, Bucharest. *Signs work*: "Sebastian Faur" see appendix. *Address*: 91-41 71st. Road, Forest Hills, New York, N.Y.11375.

**FAUST, Pat,** artist in oil, water-colour, pastel, theatrical designs, murals; *b* Lancs. *Educ*: Culcheth Hall, Ches. *Studied*: Manchester Regional College of Art; Crescent Theatre, Birmingham. *Exhib*: R.G.I., Manchester Academy, Birmingham A.G., Sewerby Hall, Bridlington, Scarborough A.G. and Town Hall, Ferens A.G., Hull, Beverley, Cartwright Hall, Bradford, Pannett, Whitby, R.A., R.B.A., S.W.A., R.Cam.A., U.A.S., Leeds City A.G., Paris Salon, Gallery Vallombreuse Biarritz, Brye A.G., Glaisdale, City Gallery, Darlington, Francis Phillips Gallery, Sheffield, Northern Academy of Art, Harrogate A.G., Guildhall, York, Yorkshire Artist Biennal, City A.G. York, Yorkshire Pastel Soc., Haworth, Cliffe Castle Museum and A.G. Keighley, Yorks.; one-man shows: Marshalls, Scarborough, Hull University,Yorkshire Pastel Soc., Dewsbury A.G. and Museum. *Work in collections*: Scarborough A.G., Scarborough Town Hall, Menston Hospital and private collections. Official purchases: painting of Scarborough A.G. (hung R.A.) by Scarborough Corp. Winner shield best medium (1992) and award (1993, 1994) Sewerby Hall, Bridlington. *Clubs*: Leeds Fine Art, Scarborough Arts Soc. *Signs work*: "Pat Faust." *Address*: 25 Sea-Point, Flat Cliffs, nr. Filey, N.Yorks. YO14 9RD.

**FAWSSETT, Ann:** see ATKIN, Ann.

**FEASEY, Judith Mary,** Cert. R.A.S. (1976), A.T.C. (1977); painter/etcher in oil on canvas, water-colour, etching; *b* Southgate, 3 Sept., 1945. *Educ*: St. Maurs Convent, Weybridge, Surrey. *Studied*: Guildford School of Art (1965-69), R.A. Schools (1973-76) Turner gold medal for landscape painting. *Exhib*: R.A., G.L.C. Spirit of London; four-man show, Alfred East Gallery, Kettering,

Mall Galleries, London, etc. *Signs work:* "J. Feasey" or "J.M.F." *Address:* 90 Webster Rd., London SE16 4DF.

**FEDDEN, Mary,** R.A.; Slade Diploma of Fine Arts; teacher of painting at Royal Coll. of Art (1958-64); Yehudi Menuhin School (1965-70); President, Royal West of England Academy (1983-88); Hon. D.Litt. Bath Univ.; *b* Bristol, 14 Aug., 1915. *m* Julian Trevelyan (decd.). *Educ:* Badminton School, Bristol. *Studied:* Slade School of Art. *Exhib:* Leicester Gallery, Gimpel Fils, R.W.A., London Group; solo shows: Christopher Hull, Bohun Gallery (4), Redfern Gallery (6), New Grafton Gallery (6), Beaux Arts Gallery (3),R.W.A. and le Provincial galleries , *Work in collections:* H.M. The Queen, Prince Hassan of Jordan, Tate, Hull, Carlisle, Melbourne, National Gallery of N.Z., Bristol, Bath and Durham. Official purchases: murals, Charing Cross Hospital, Contemporary Arts Soc., Yorkshire C.C., Leicestershire C.C., Hertfordshire C.C., Min. of Works, Orient Line, Bristol Educ. Com., Barnet Hospital. *Signs work:* "Fedden." *Address:* Durham Wharf, Hammersmith Terr., London W6 9TS.

**FEENY, Patrick A.,** F.M.G.P.; ecclesiastical artist and watercolourist; *b* Harrow, Middx., 30 Nov., 1910. *Educ:* Stonyhurst College. *Signs work:* see appendix. *Address:* Enstone Cottage, High St., Feckenham, Worcs. B96 6HS.

**FEI, Cheng-Wu,** painter; Prof. (1941-46), College of Fine Art, National Central University, China; *b* China, 30 Dec., 1914. *m* Chien-Ying Chang, artist. *Studied:* National Central University, China (1930-34), Slade School of Fine Art (1947-50). *Exhib:* R.A., R.I., R.W.A., R.W.S., N.E.A.C.; one-man shows at Leicester Galleries. *Work in collections:* Royal West of England Academy, Universities' China Committee, Grave's Gallery, Sheffield, Derby A.G., etc. *Publications:* Brush Drawing in the Chinese Manner (Studio); work repro.: Studio, Art News & Review, La Revue Moderne, Kunst, etc. *Signs work:* see appendix. *Address:* 27 The Fountains, Ballards Lane, London N3 1NL.

**FEILER, Paul,** painter; *b* 30 Apr., 1918. *m* Catharine Armitage. three *s.* two *d. Educ:* Canford School, Dorset. *Studied:* Slade School of Fine Art. *Exhib:* one-man shows since 1953; Redfern Gallery, London, Grosvenor Gallery, Warwick Arts Trust, London, U.S.A. *Work in collections:* Tate Gallery, Arts Council, British Council, Liverpool, Manchester, Warwick, London, Oxford, Cambridge, Newcastle Universities; galleries in England, U.S.A., France, Austria, Canada and New Zealand. *Address:* Kerris, nr. Penzance, Cornwall.

**FELL, Michael Anthony,** F.S.D.C.; painter/printmaker in oil, etching, lithography; former Head of Foundation Studies, City & Guilds of London Art School; visiting tutor, Prince of Wales Inst., London; *b* London, 31 Jan., 1939. *m* Maureen. two *s. Educ:* St. George's, Weybridge. *Studied:* St. Martin's School of Art, City & Guilds of London Art School. *Exhib:* Jordan Gallery (1972-84), Halesworth Gallery (1972-85), Mall Galleries, Clementi House Gallery (1991), Gallery Renata, Chicago, Belanthi Gallery, New York, Chappel Galleries, Essex (1993), Comteroux Perpignan (1993), Flaran, France (1996), Grosvenor

Gallery, London (1996). *Work in collections:* B.M.; Arts Council; Victoria National Gallery and University of Melbourne, Australia; Churchill Library, Massachusetts. *Signs work:* "Michael Fell." *Address:* 17 Fonnereau Rd., Ipswich, Suffolk IP1 3JR; and Barrere, Vic Fezensac, 32190 France.

**FELLOWS, Elaine Helen,** B.A.(Hons.) (1981), H.S. (1987), S.W.A. (1988), R.M.S. (1992), U.S.M. (1990); professional painter of portraits and still life in miniature in water-colour on vellum or ivorine; *b* Walsall, 27 Nov., 1959. *Studied:* Walsall College of Art (1977), Wolverhampton Polytechnic (1978-81). *Exhib:* R.M.S. (Hon. mention 1989), S.W.A., Hilliard Soc. (Bell award 1990), Ulster Soc. of Miniaturists (Madam MacCarthy Mór memorial award 1991), Llewellyn Alexander Gallery, Medici Galleries, Limpsfield Water-colours, Riverside Gallery, Jane Marler Gallery, France, Hong-Kong, U.S.A., Linda Blackstone Gallery. *Work in collections:* G.B., U.S.A., France, Germany. *Publications:* The Techniques of Painting Minaitures; contributor to The Magic of Miniatures. *Signs work:* see appendix. *Address:* The Bwlch, Beguildy, Knighton, Powys LD7 1UG.

**FEREDAY, Joseph,** R.E.; Diploma in Fine Art, Slade School; *b* Dudley, 9 Feb., 1917. *Studied:* Wolverhampton and Birmingham College of Art, Slade School (1946-48). *Work in collections:* Portsmouth A.G., Southampton University, De Witt Gallery, Holland, Michigan, Plymouth A.G., Bilston A.G., St. Mary's College, Twickenham, Portsmouth Corp., Seely Library, Ryde, I.O.W., British Embassy, Helsinki, Galerie Alphonse Marré, Chartres; one-man shows: Woodstock Gallery, London, Hiscock Gallery, Portsmouth, Galerie de Vallombreuse Biarritz, Southampton University, Vectis Gallery, Bembridge. *Address:* Yarborough House, New Rd., Brading, I.O.W. PO36 0AG.

**FERGUSON, Malcolm Alastair Percy,** R.W.A., D.F.A.(Lond., 1950); religious landscape and portrait painter; visiting teacher; *b* Blackwater, Hants., 19 Dec., 1913. *m* Rosemary J.M. Holdsworth (decd.). one *s.* one *d. Educ:* Durham School, R.M.A., Sandhurst, (invalided shortly after). *Studied:* Portsmouth and Croydon Schools of Art (1935-38), Slade School (1939, 1948-51, under Schwabe, Coldstream Monnington). *Exhib:* R.A., N.E.A.C., R.P., R.W.A., R.B.A., Paris Salon, Nat. Gall. of Wales, Bradford City A.G., etc.; one-man shows: London, provinces and abroad. *Work in collections:* Plymouth City A.G., R.W.A., Talbot Bequest Bristol, Somerset Museum Service, high altar triptych 12C. St. Mark's, Lord Mayor's Chapel Bristol (1992). Official purchases: Sponsored by Anglo American and De Beers, to paint 'True Fresco' (1982, 1985), domed apse, St. Cuthbert's, Transkei. 1985-89, four altar panels and 30 ft. choir balustrade in egg tempera St. Augustine's Church, Penhalonga, Zimbabwe; various portraits, Chairman Cecil Whiley of George. M. Whiley Ltd. Gold Beaters Ltd., etc. *Publications:* work repro.: various magazines. *Signs work:* "Malcolm A.P. Ferguson." *Address:* 7 Mill St., North Petherton, Som. TA6 6LX.

**FERGUSON, Mary,** F.F.P.S.; painter in oil, charcoal, pen and wash; *b* 6

May, 1919. *m* E.A. Ferguson. two *s*. *Educ:* Friends School, Ackworth. *Studied:* The Gallery Schools, Melbourne, Australia (1953-55, Charles Bush), Reigate School of Art (1957-60, Denis Lucas, Walter Woodington). *Exhib:* one-man shows: London including Loggia Gallery, F.P.S.; mixed shows: London and provincial galleries. *Work in collections:* Australia, Canada, Mallorca, Hong Kong and U.K. *Clubs:* F.P.S., Reigate Soc. of Artists. *Signs work:* "Ferguson" or "MF" joined. *Address:* Bayhorne Lodge, 164 Balcombe Rd., Horley, Surrey RH6 9DS.

**FERGUSSON: see BATTERBURY, Helen Fiona**

**FERRIAN, Marie,** sculptor in wood, terracotta, stone; *b* Hummelstown, Pa., 1 Jan., 1927. *m* George Ferrian. one *s*. *Educ:* S.T.H.S. *Studied:* Corcoran School of Art (painting: 1945-47, Eugene Weisz; sculpture: 1963-65, Heinz Warneke). *Exhib:* St. Camillus, Women's National Bank, Firenze House, Corcoran Gallery, Art Barn (2). *Work in collections:* National Museum of Women in the Arts. *Publications:* three children's books; featured in American Craftsmen (1975). *Signs work:* "M.F." *Address:* 4230 Silverwood La., Beth, M.D. 20816, U.S.A.

**FERRY, David Dawson,** B.A. (Hons.) (1979), H.D.F.A. (Lond.) (1981); printmaker/painter/collagist; lecturer, Camberwell/Canterbury Art Schools; 1993, appointed Head of Printmaking, Winchester School of Art; 1996, appointed Head of Fine Art, University of Southampton; *b* Blackpool, 5 Feb., 1957. *Studied:* Blackpool College Tech. (1975-76), Camberwell School of Arts and Crafts (1976-79, Mario Dubsky, Agathe Sorell), Slade School of Fine Art (1979-81, Stanley Jones). *Exhib:* Contemporary Printmaking Air Gallery, R.A., S. London A.G., Ferens A.G., Hull, Offenbach, Germany, Paris 'Trace' Biennale; one-man shows, first and second International Contemporary Art Fairs at Barbican A.G., London Olympia, 5 Contemporary Printmakers, National Museum of Wales British Tour, The Star Chamber, Herbert Read Gallery, Canterbury, Kent University, Drew Gallery Canterbury, Boundry Gallery, London, Fachhochschule, Düsseldorf, Germany, Photomontage exhbn. in Dresden and Poland (1995). *Work in collections:* Grundy A.G., Blackpool, University College and St.Thomas Hospital, London, Maidstone A.G., Nuclear Electric, Marconi Instruments U.K. *Commissions:* G.E.C. U.K. (1997). *Publications:* author, Painting Without a Brush, U.K. (1991), U.S.A. (1992), France (1994). Recent work produced in photography, photomontage and video. Elected full mem. Graphic Fine Art Soc. Formed video production titled 'Lost Shoe Productions.' *Signs work:* "D.D. Ferry" or "D.D.F." *Address:* c/o Winchester School of Art, Hants. SO23 8DL.

**FESTING, Andrew Thomas,** R.P. (1992); portrait painter in oil; *b* Chalford, 30 Nov., 1941. *m* Virginia Fyffe. one *d*. *Educ:* Ampleforth College. *Exhib:* R.P. *Work in collections:* National Gallery Dublin, Royal Coll. *Signs work:* "A.T. Festing." *Address:* 3 Hillsleigh Rd., London W8.

**FIELD, Peter L.,** A.T.D., F.R.S.A.; artist, teacher and lecturer; Head of Faculty of Art and Design, City of Birmingham Polytechnic (retd. 1982); *b* Winson, Glos., 7 Feb., 1920. *m* Cynthia G. Barry. two *d. Educ:* Rendcomb College. *Studied:* Cheltenham School of Art (1937-39) under A. Seaton-White, Goldsmiths' College School of Art (1946-49) under Clive Gardner. *Exhib:* London and provincial exhbns. *Work in collections:* Swindon Art Gallery, Swindon Corporation. *Signs work:* "Peter L. Field." *Address:* 264 Mary Vale Rd., Bournville, Birmingham B30 1PJ.

**FINCH, Michael,** B.A.(Hons.) (1980), M.A.(R.C.A.) (1986); painter in mixed media; Senior tutor, Parsons School of Art, Paris; *b* London, 6 July, 1957. *m* Bridget Strevens. one *d. Studied:* Ravensbourne College of Art (1976-80, Brian Fielding), R.C.A. (1982-86, Peter de Francia). *Exhib:* one-man shows: City Museum, Peterborough (1983), Groucho Club (1987, 1988), Pomeroy Purdy (1990, 1992), Purdy Hicks (1994). *Work in collections:* Unilever, T.I. Group Coll., Deutsche Bank. *Publications:* Sodium Nights (1990), 'N17'. *Clubs:* Groucho. *Signs work:* see appendix. *Address:* 59 rue de Meaux, 60300 Senlis, France.

**FINCH, Patricia,** F.R.B.S., S.W.A., S.P.S., F.S.N.A.D., C.P.S., A.W.G., F.R.S.A.; sculptor; *b* London, 1921. two *d. Educ:* King's College, London, West London Hospital. International Grollo d'Oro Silver medal (1976), Silver cups (1981, 1983). *Exhib:* London, New York, Geneva, Glasgow, Venice, Malta, Le Touquet; mixed annual exhbns.: Mall Galleries, Westminster Galleries, R.A. Summer exhbn. (1979), FIDEM XIII British Museum, XXIV Budapest. Demonstrator, Tate Gallery Sculpture Course (1983). *Work in collections:* B.M. Coins and Medal Dept., Bank of England Museum: two busts, Royal Academy of Dancing, Musée Quentovic, Le Touquet, Museum of Fine Arts, Malta, Town Hall, Rhodes. Private collections: in U.K., various European countries, Canada, U.S.A., S. America, Japan, Australia, Nigeria. Over 130 portrait commissions carried out. Tutor, Hulton Studio for Visually Handicapped (1986-90). Demonstrator/lecturer portrait bust, Islington etc. Finalist L.D.D.C. (1988, 1989). Life-size figurative bronze Golders Hill Park unveiled 1991. *Commissions:* Goldsmiths' Hall London, Prime Warden Medal, silver (1996), Bronze bust Glenn Miller 1½ life-size for Corn Exchange, Bedford (1994). *Signs work:* "P. Finch." *Address:* 851 Finchley Rd., London NW11 8LY.

**FINCH, William Robert,** F.I.A.L. (1953), freelance journalist; artist various media, etcher; lecturer art country life; late head art dept. Beal Grammar School, Ilford; Chigwell School, Essex; founder-tutor, Over 40's Art Groups; lecturer Extra Mural Dept., Cambridge and London Universities; *b* Lowestoft, 5 Apr., 1905. *m* Peggy Doreen Hill. two *s. Educ:* Lowestoft Grammar School, College St. Mark and St. John, Chelsea. *Studied:* self taught. *Exhib:* R.A., East End Academy, Reading Art Guild, Assembly Rooms, Norwich, Southwold and Ilford, etc.; one-man show, Starston Gallery, Norfolk. *Work in collections:*

Bury St. Edmund's Cathedral; Mrs. Lewis L. Douglas, New York; R. Hone, Esq.; Chigwell School, private Germany, France, Canada, Australia, U.S.A., Italy, etc. Official purchases: Ilford Libraries, Boy Scouts' Assoc., Westminster Bank, "Snowdrift" Lubricants. *Publications:* East Anglian Magazine, Review Assoc. Agriculture, Essex Countryside, Y.H.A. publications, etc. author/illustrator: Journeying into Essex, In and Around Folkestone, Introducing Essex to America, Country Buildings, 100 years of Snowdrift Lubricants, The Sea in My Blood. *Signs work:* "Finch." *Address:* Waveney Cottage, Weybread, Diss, Norfolk IP21 5UA.

**FINDLAY, Sheila Anne Macfarlane,** R.W.S., D.A.(Edin.), Post-Grad.(1950), Travelling Scholar (1951); artist and illustrator in water-colour and oil; *b* Auchlishie, Kirriemuir. *m* Alfred Hackney, A.R.W.S., A.R.E., D.A.(Edin.). two *d. Educ:* Webster's Seminary. *Studied:* Edinburgh College of Art (1945-51) under John Maxwell, Sir William MacTaggart, Leonard Rosoman. *Exhib:* R.A., R.W.S., Catto Gallery. *Work in collections:* private collections. *Publications:* children's books illustrated for Faber & Faber, Adprint, Harrap, Odhams, Medici Soc. *Signs work:* "Sheila Findlay." *Address:* Barnside, Lodge La., Cobham, nr. Gravesend, Kent DA12 3BS.

**FINEGOLD, Stephen M.,** B.A. (Hons.) 1st class Postgrad. (Dip.); artist in oil, acrylic, pastel, collage, print; Artistic Director, F.C.A. Gallery; *b* London, 17 June, 1959. *m* Josephine. two *s. Educ:* Beal Grammar School, Ilford. *Studied:* Bradford College, Croydon O.C.A. (1988). *Work in collections:* F.C.A. Gallery, U.K., Spain, France, Australia. *Signs work:* "Finegold." *Address:* Chantry House, Warley Town Lane, Warley, Halifax, W. Yorks. HX2 7SA.

**FINER, Stephen,** artist in oil on canvas; *b* London, 1949. *Studied:* Ravensbourne College of Art (1966-70). *Exhib:* one-man shows: Four Vine Lane, London (1981, 1982, 1985), Anthony Reynolds Gallery (1986, 1988), Berkeley Sq. Gallery (1989), Bernard Jacobson Gallery (1992, 1995), Woodlands A.G. (1994), Agnew's (1998); mixed shows: British Art 1940-1980, from the Arts Council Coll., Hayward Gallery (1980), Collazione Ingleze 2, Venice Biennale (1984), The Portrait Now, N.P.G. (1993), Men on Women (1997-98), etc. *Work in collections:* A.C.G.B., British Council, Contemporary Arts Soc., Southport A.G., N.P.G. *Signs work:* "S.A. Finer" on reverse. *Address:* 20 Kipling St., London SE1 3RU.

**FINLAY, Ian,** C.B.E., M.A. (Hons.), H.R.S.A.; Liveryman, Worshipful Company of Goldsmiths, London; Professor of Antiquities to Royal Scottish Academy; formerly Director, Royal Scottish Museum and Secy. Royal Fine Art Commission, Scotland; *b* Auckland, N.Z. *m* Mary Scott Pringle. two *s.* one *d. Educ:* Edinburgh Academy, University of Edinburgh. *Publications:* Scotland (O.U.P.), Art in Scotland (O.U.P.), Scottish Crafts (Harrap), History of Scottish Gold and Silver Work (Chatto), The Lothians (Collins), The Highlands (Batsford), The Lowlands (Batsford), Celtic Art (Faber), Priceless Heritage: the

Future of Museums (Faber), Columba (Gollancz). *Address:* Currie Riggs, Balerno, Midlothian EH14 5AG.

**FIRMSTONE, David James,** M.B.E. (1996), N.D.D., A.T.D.; artist in tempera, oils and water-colour; Senior Art Adviser, Cheshire; Director, Woodford Visual Art Centre; *b* Middlesbrough, 28 Apr., 1943. *m* Jean Gilbert-Firmstone. one *s. Studied:* Middlesbrough College of Art, Birmingham University. *Exhib:* R.A. (1995-97), Hunting Prize (1994-95), Piccadilly Gallery; mixed shows: Manchester Academy (prizewinner), San Giovanni valdarno, Italy. *Commissions:* Est, est, est Restaurants, Ductile Steel. *Publications:* Cheshire in Tuscany. *Signs work:* "David J. Firmstone." *Address:* Larkton Hall Cottage, Goldford Lane, Bickerton Malpas, Ches.SY14 8LL.

**FIRTH, Annette Rose,** N.D.D., F.S.B.A.; botanical artist and china decorator in water-colour and on-glaze colours; Tutor at The Niccol Centre, Cirencester, Flatford Mill and Missenden Abbey; *b* Portsmouth, 21 May, 1921, widow. two *d. Educ:* home and Lewes, Sussex. *Studied:* in Florence (1938-39, Aubrey Waterfield), Central School, London, Whiteland College, Putney Mary Yules). *Exhib:* S.B.A. and S.W.A., Central Hall Westminster, R.H.S., Fossewerg Artists, Glos. Soc. of Botanical Illustrators. *Commissions:* various miniature portraits. *Publications:* The Alphabet of Roses, and Mary's Flowers. *Signs work:* "A.F." *Address:* 29 Coxwell St., Cirencester, Glos. GL7 2BQ.

**FIRTH, Sir Raymond William,** M.A. (N.Z.), Ph.D.(Lond.), F.B.A., Emeritus Prof. of Anthropology, University of London; field research in Solomon Islands, 1928-29, 1952, 1966; Malaya, 1939-40, 1963; *b* Auckland, N.Z., 25 Mar., 1901. *m* Rosemary Upcott. one *s. Educ:* Auckland University College, London School of Economics. *Publications:* Art and Life in New Guinea (Studio, 1938); The Social Framework of Primitive Art (ch. in Elements of Social Organization), (Watts, 1951), Tikopia Woodworking Ornament, Man 40, 27), Tikopia Art and Society in Primitive Art and Society (ed. A. Forge) O.U.P. (1972), Art and Anthropology in Anthropology Art and Aesthetics (ed. J. Coote & A. Shelton) Clarendon (1992). *Address:* 33 Southwood Ave., London N6 5SA.

**FISHER, Don Mulready,** M.S.I.A., M.F.P.S.; portrait and landscape painter in oil and gouache; TV film and theatre designer; writer; *b* Finchley, 27 Apr., 1923. *m* Lyliane Guelfand. one *s.* one *d. Educ:* Golders Hill School and Ravensfield College. *Studied:* Hampstead Garden Suburb Institute, Art Class 1940-41); St. Martin's School of Art under Ruskin Spear, R.A. (1943-46). *Exhib:* London Group, R.O.I., R.B.A., N.E.A.C., N.S., Berkeley Galleries, New Burlington Galleries, Piccadilly Gallery, Salon des Nations, Paris (1984), Trends (1984), Barbican Centre, Paris Salon (1985-87); one-man shows, Dowmunt Gallery (1980), Cork St. Fine Arts Gallery (1983). *Work in collections:* Britain, France, Sweden, Spain, Canada, U.S.A., Australia, Italy, Belgium. *Publications:* Designers in Britain Nos. 6 & 7. *Clubs:* Chelsea Arts. *Signs work:* see appendix. *Address:* 26 Rue Monsieur le Prince, 75006 Paris.

# WHO'S WHO IN ART

**FISHER, Isabelle Diane Mulready,** Diplomee Beaux Arts, Paris; stained glass artist; *b* Hampstead, 10 Dec., 1954. one *s. Educ:* Lycee Français de Londres. *Studied:* Sir John Cass College (1973-74), Wimbledon School of Art (1974-77), Beaux Arts, Paris (1978-82, Allain, Master of stained glass). *Exhib:* U.F.P.S. Luxembourg Museum, Paris (1981), Chartres Stained Glass Museum (1982), Sacred Art, le Salon des Nations (1984), Homage to Joan Miro Exhbn., Barcelona (1985). *Commissions:* window, 'Noah after the flood' l'Eglise de Ligny le-Ribaut, Loiret, France (1981); four windows, Hotel le Kern, Val d'Isere; six memorial windows for the St. Martin's Chapel (Benedictine Monastery) Monte Cassino, Italy (1989-91). *Address:* Rue de la Halle, Martel, Lot, 46.600 France; and 26 Rue Monsieur le Prince, 75006, France.

**FISHER, Myrta,** D.F.A.(Lond.) Slade School (1937-40); awarded Henriques Scholarship (1938); student of the British School at Athens (1954-55); works in acrylic; *b* Wimbledon, 28 Aug., 1917. *Exhib:* widely in London, Sussex and Suffolk, also with the Eastbourne Group. Work in many private collections, also purchased by American Express and the Towner A.G., Eastbourne. *Signs work:* "M.F." *Address:* Pennyhaven, Norton Rd., Newhaven, E.Sussex. BN9 0BP.

**FISHER, Reginald Stanley,** S.G.F.A. (1991); artist in oil, line and wash, pencil; retd. technical graphics illustrator and designer; Com. mem. S.G.F.A.; Assoc. mem. Armed Forces Art Soc.; *b* London, 9 Nov., 1926. *Studied:* weekend courses at Heatherley School S.E. Federation of Art Socs. (Carl Cheek, Patrick Larking, Alfred Noakes). *Exhib:* S.G.F.A., U.A., R.B.A., R.I. Summer Show, Wardour Gallery, S.E.F.A.S., Int. Amateur, Wembley Art Soc., Armed Forces Art Soc., Blickling Hall, Norfolk; two one-man shows, Wembley. *Commissions:* several private commissions. *Publications:* illustrated technical books for B.P. Oil. *Signs work:* see appendix. *Address:* 36 Aldbury Ave., Wembley, Middx. HA9 6EY.

**FITZGERALD, Susan Margaret,** B.A. (1978), M.A. (1988); full-time painter in water-colour and oil; *b* Linc., 8 Jan., 1946. *m* Edward Michael Fitzgerald. two *s. Educ:* Boston Girls' Grammar School. *Studied:* York School of Art (1962-64), Sunderland College of Art (1964-67). *Exhib:* Chris Beetles Ltd., London; The Catto Gallery, London; World of Drawings and Watercolours, London; Adam Gallery, Bath; Bourne Gallery, Reigate; Medici Gallery, London; Nevill Gallery, Canterbury. *Commissions:* Medici Gallery, London, Nevill Gallery, Canterbury. Much time spent painting in France in her studio nr. Montpellier. Has lived/worked in Middle East and Far East. *Signs work:* "Sue Fitzgerald." *Address:* Paragon House, 3 Stone Rd., Broadstairs, Kent CT10 1DY.

**FLEMING, James Hugh,** B.A.Hons. (1987); printmaker, painter, illustrator, lecturer, poet; *b* Barrow in Furness. *m* Norma. one *s.* one *d. Studied:* Open University, Liverpool Polytechnic. *Exhib:* Acorn Gallery, Bluecoat Gallery, Hanover Gallery, Davey Gallery, Williamson A.G., Dee Fine Arts, Marie Curie

Foundation, Merseyside Artists Touring Exhbn., Heffers, Oriel Mostyn, Cadaques Mini Print, Intaglio Mini Print, Manchester Academy, Humberside Printmaking Exhbn. Theatre Clwyd, Ruthin Craft Centre, Broekman A.G. *Clubs:* N.A.P.A., Wirral Soc. of Arts, A.B.W.S., Bluecoat Studio Print-makers' Group. *Signs work:* "Jim" and see appendix. *Address:* 19c Church Rd., West Kirby, Wirral, Merseyside L48 0RL.

**FLETCHER, Adelene,** N.D.D. (1960), S.B.A. (1989); artist in water-colour; *b* Stockport, 6 Aug., 1940. *m* A.J. Fletcher. one *s.* one *d. Educ:* Fylde Lodge High School. *Studied:* Stockport Art School (1956-58), Manchester Regional College of Art (1958-60). *Exhib:* R.I., R.W.S., S.B.A., and many mixed exhbns. *Signs work:* "A. Fletcher." *Address:* 20 Alexandra Rd., Warlingham, Surrey CR6 9DU.

**FLETCHER, Alistair Richard,** B.A.Hons. (1985), A.R.E. (1985), British Inst. award (1983), Commendation Stowells Trophy (1984), Garton and Cook award (1985); teacher, artist in etching, drawing and water-colour; *b* Gosforth, Northumberland, 25 Jan., 1963. *m* E.M. Fletcher. one *s.* two *d. Educ:* Henry Smith School, Hartlepool. *Studied:* Cleveland College of Art and Design (1981-82), Kingston Polytechnic (1982-85), Bretton Hall (1986-87). *Exhib:* R.E., Coach House Gallery, Guernsey, Darlington A.G. *Clubs:* R.E. *Signs work:* "Alistair R. Fletcher." *Address:* Wyndham School, Egremont, Cumbria.

**FLETCHER-WATSON, James,** R.I. (1952), R.B.A. (1957); painter in water-colour; *b* Coulsdon, Surrey, 25 July, 1913. *Educ:* Eastbourne College. *Studied:* R.A. School of Architecture (silver medal for design, 1936). *Exhib:* R.A., R.I., R.B.A., Paris Salon, Stockholm, Windrush Gallery (annually). *Publications:* British Railways carriage posters; written instruction book on watercolour painting (Batsford, 1982, second book 1985, third book 1988, fourth book 1993, fifth book 1997), third video painting instruction (1993). *Signs work:* "J. Fletcher-Watson." *Address:* Windrush House, Windrush, nr. Burford, Oxford.

**FLOWER, Rosina,** M.F.P.S., S.A.F.; painter; *b* London. one *s.* one *d. Educ:* London and Headley. *Studied:* 1971-75: P.D. Dennis Syrett, Bassetsbury Manor (Tom Coates), Burleighfield House (Anne Bruce). *Exhib:* R.B.A., R.O.I., P.S., Britains Painters, Medici Gallery, Roy Miles Gallery, Albemarle Gallery, Waldorf Hotel, London; solo shows: Loggia Gallery London, Henley Management College, Oxon., Boxfield Gallery, Stevenage, Talent Store London. Work in hospitals and private collections.*Publications:* work repro.: greetings cards. *Clubs:* Cookham Painters, F.P.S. *Signs work:* "Flower," "R. Flower" or "Rosie." *Address:* 132 Roberts Ride, Hazlemere, Bucks. HP15 7AN.

**FLUDGATE, Bob,** artist in oil, pen and ink, pastel; writer; *b* Islington, London, 18 Oct., 1950. one *d. Educ:* Highbury Grove Grammar School. *Work in collections:* Channel Islands and London. *Signs work:* "Bob Fludgate." *Address:* c/o Nevill Gallery, 43 St. Peter's St., Canterbury, Kent CT1 2BG.

**FLYNN, Mary Theresa,** R.S.W. (1969), D.A. (1951); landscape, figurative and still life freelance artist in water-colour, acrylic and oil; former principal teacher of art, John Paul Academy, Glasgow; *b* Selkirk, 30 Nov., 1923. *Educ:* Galashiels Academy. *Studied:* Edinburgh College of Art (1946-51, Sir Robin Philipson, P.P.R.S.A., R.A., R.S.W., Leonard Rosomon, O.B.E., R.A., R.S.W., Derek Clarke, A.R.S.A., R.S.W., J. Kingsley Cook). *Exhib:* R.S.W., R.S.A., R.G.I., S.S.W.A., S.A.A.C.; one-man shows: B.B.C. Club, Blythswood Gallery, R.S. Acad. of Music and Drama, Galashiels Scott Bi-centenary show, Gallery Paton, E.S.U. Gallery; numerous shared exhbns. *Work in collections:* Lillie A.G., S.A.C., Leeds Museum Service. *Signs work:* "Theresa Flynn." *Address:* 6 Rosebery Cres., Edinburgh EH12 5JP.

**FOLKES, Peter Leonard,** A.T.D., R.W.A., V.P.R.I., Hon. F.C.A.; painter in oil, water-colour and acrylic; Demonstrator and Lecturer; Tutor, Artscape Painting Holidays; *b* Beaminster, 3 Nov., 1923. *m* Muriel Giddings. two *s*. *Educ:* Sexey's School Bruton. *Studied:* West of England College of Art, Bristol (1940-42 and 1947-50). *Exhib:* R.A., R.W.A., R.I.; one-man shows: Crespi Gallery, New York (1965), University of Southampton (1965, 1973), Barzansky Gallery, New York (1967), Alwin Gallery, London (1970), Gainsboroughs' House Gallery, Sudbury (1977), R.W.A. Galleries, Bristol (1986). *Work in collections:* Arts Council of Great Britain, R.W.A. *Signs work:* "Folkes." *Address:* 61 Ethelburt Ave., Swaythling, Southampton SO16 3DF.

**FOLLAND, Ronald Norman,** self-taught artist in oil, acrylic and water-colour; *b* Portsmouth, 5 Dec., 1932. two *s*. *Educ:* Cowplain Boys' School, Hants. *Exhib:* one-man shows, Frost and Reed (Bristol, Worthing, London), To-Day Southern TV., Nationwide B.B.C. TV., Harrogate, Birmingham, St. Helier, Jersey, Bournemouth, etc. *Work in collections:* U.S.A., Canada, Australia, New Zealand, France, Ireland, Russia, Scandinavia, Germany and Israel. Rated in Top Ten Artists Poll yearly since 1965. *Clubs:* Fine Art Trade Guild. *Signs work:* see appendix. *Address:* 63 Milton Rd., Ickenham, Uxbridge, Middx. UB10 8NJ.

**FOOT, Victorine,** D.A.; artist in oil, mural painting; Directorate of Camouflage (1941-45); *b* Kent, 1 May, 1920. *m* Eric Schilsky, R.A., R.S.A. (decd.), sculptor. one *d*. *Educ:* Oakdene School. *Studied:* Central School of Arts and Crafts, Chelsea School of Art, Edinburgh College of Art. *Exhib:* R.A., R.S.A., S.S.A., N.E.A.C., London Group, etc., Scottish Gallery, Edinburgh (1969, 1979, 1984), LYC Gallery (1981), Kingfisher and Broughton (1993), Dunóas Street Gallery, Edinburgh (1996). *Work in collections:* Arts Council (Scottish Committee), Imperial War Museum, Aberdeen A.G., Scottish National Portrait Gallery. *Signs work:* "Victorine Foot," "V.F." *Address:* The Studio, 16a Meadow Pl., Edinburgh EH9 1JR.

**FORD, Jenifer,** V.P.N.S., F.R.S.A., Cert. Fine Art (University of Cape Town) (1953); portrait, landscape and still-life painter; *b* Cape Town, 25 June, 1934. *m* His Hon. Judge Peter Ford. one *d*. *Educ:* Rustenburg School, Cape

Town. *Studied:* Michaelis Art School and under Bernard Adams, R.P. *Exhib:* R.P., R.O.I., N.S., C.P.S., Arts Exhbn. Bureau, Painting South East (1975), Haus der Kunst, Munich (1988-89), Kunst in Giesing (1985-90), European Patent Office, Munich (1980-89), S.W.A.; solo shows in England and Germany. *Work in collections:* European Patent Office, Bayern Versicherung, Munich, Patents Appeal Court, Stockholm. *Signs work:* "Jenifer Ford." *Address:* 59 Lancaster Ave., Hadley Wood, Barnet EN4 0ER.

**FORD, Michael,** freelance artist in oils, water-colour, black and white; *b* 28 July, 1920. *Educ:* privately. *Studied:* London University; Goldsmiths' College Art School (Clive Gardiner, 1937-40). *Exhib:* R.A., R.P., N.E.A.C., R.B.A., United Soc., P.S., Paris Salon, Russell Cotes Gallery, Towner Art Gallery, also touring exhbns. on loan, etc. *Work in collections:* Three oil paintings by M. of I. (War Artists' Exhbn.). *Publications:* work repro.: Two paintings bought by M. of I.; portraits commissioned by magazines and newspapers. *Signs work:* "Michael Ford." *Address:* Studio Cottage, Winsor Rd., Winsor, Southampton SO40 2HP.

**FORD, Olga Gemes,** M.S.I.A. graduated in arch. (Techn. University, Berlin); lecturer, The City of Leicester Polytechnic and School of Architecture; traveller and freelance photographer, works for distinguished art publishers here and abroad (Photographic Illustrations); *m* Oliver E. Ford, B.Sc. (London), Ph.D. (Zürich), F.R.I.C. (decd.). *Educ:* Realschule, Vienna. *Studied:* architecture: Vienna, Dresden, Berlin, Paris; under Prof. Poelzig. *Exhib:* Britain Can Make It, Cotton Board, Manchester. *Publications:* work repro.: in Architectural Review, L'Architecture d'Aujourd'hui, La Construction Moderne, Design, 46 Designers in Britain 2 and 4, Decoration, etc. *Signs work:* "OLGA GEMES FORD" or "OLGA FORD." *Address:* 12 Highgate Spinney, Crescent Rd., London N8 8AR.

**FORTNUM, Peggy,** book illustrator and designer; *b* Harrow-on-the-Hill, 23 Dec., 1919. *m* Ralph Nuttall-Smith, painter and sculptor. two *s-s. Educ:* St. Margaret's, Harrow. *Studied:* Central School of Arts and Crafts. *Exhib:* V. & A., (children's books), Public Libraries (Britain and America), British Museum (children's book show), Regional Book Show, I.C.A., Minories Colchester. *Work in collections:* The Dromkeen Collection of Australian Children's Literature. *Publications:* textile designs, magazines, illustrations for eighty books, which include The Happy Prince and Other Stories (Oscar Wilde), The Reluctant Dragon (Kenneth Grahame), A Bear Called Paddington, 12 Books (Michael Bond), Thursday's Child (Noel Streatfield), Robin (Catherine Storr), Little Pete Stories (Leila Berg), A Few Fair Days (Jane Gardam), Running Wild (Autobiography) (Chatto & Windus); drawings for television: Playschool, Jackanory. *Signs work:* "PEGGY FORTNUM" or "P.F." *Address:* 10 Hall Barn, West Mersea, Essex CO5 8SD.

**FORWARD, Hubert W.F.,** N.D.D. (1951), A.T.D. (1952); artist in oil, water-colour, lithography, ceramics, calligraphy; art master, lecturer in ceramics; Head of Art, Hewett School, Norwich; Lecturer i/c Ceramics, Norwich School of Art (1953-82); *b* Tottenham, 1927. *m* Beryl Woodward. two *s*. *Educ:* Tottenham Grammar School. *Studied:* Hornsey College of Art (1945-52). *Exhib:* East Anglian Artists, R.I. (1969), British Artists, Los Angeles (1961) *Work in collections:* Guildhall, City of London (calligraphy), University of East Anglia (lithographs) and many private collections. *Publications:* work repro. by Studio Publications and New York Times. *Clubs:* S.G.F.A., Norwich Twenty Group. *Signs work:* "H. FORWARD" and see appendix. *Address:* 12 Mill Hill Rd., Norwich, Norfolk NR2 3DP.

**FOSTER, Judith,** N.D.D., A.R.C.A.: painter/printmaker in oil, watercolour, pastel, etching; *b* 19 Oct., 1937. *m* Richard Pinkney. *Educ:* Bath High School G.P.D.S.T. *Studied:* Ipswich School of Art (1955-59, Philip Fortin, Colin Moss), R.C.A. (1959-62, Carel Weight, Ruskin Spear, Ceri Richards), Abbey Minor Scholarship (1962). *Exhib:* one-man shows: Ipswich, Bath, Peterborough, Edinburgh, Northampton; group shows: U.K., Belgium, Finland, and R.A., R.C.A. *Work in collections:* local authority collections; private collections U.K., U.S.A., Europe. *Clubs:* Suffolk Group, Ipswich Art Soc. Bearing 0900. *Signs work:* "J. Foster" or initials on small works. *Address:* 10 The Street, Bramford, Ipswich, Suffolk IP8 4EA.

**FOSTER, Sir Norman Robert,** A.R.A., R.D.I. Dip.Arch. (Manc.), M.Arch. (Yale), R.I.B.A., F.C.S.D., Hon. F.A.I.A., Hon. B.D.A.; Chairman. Sir Norman Foster and Partners Ltd.; *b* Reddish, 1 June, 1935. *Educ:* Burnage Grammar School, Manchester. *Studied:* architecture: Manchester University School of Architecture and Dept. of Town and Country Planning, Yale University School of Architecture. *Exhib:* R.A., London, Paris, Bilbao, Barcelona, Seville, Tokyo, Florence, Nimes, Sainsbury Centre for Visual Arts, Manchester, Milan, New York, Zürich, München. *Work in collections:* Museum of Modern Art, N.Y., Centre Georges Pompidou, Paris. *Publications:* Norman Foster: Buildings and Projects Vols. 1, 2 & 3 (1990), Vol. 4 (1996). *Signs work:* see appendix. *Address:* Foster and Partners, Riverside Three, 22 Hester Rd., London SW11 4AN.

**FOSTER, Richard Francis,** R.P.; Lord Mayor's award for London Views (1972); painter in oil; *b* London, 6 June, 1945. *m* Sally Kay-Shuttleworth. one *s*. two *d*. *Educ:* Harrow and Trinity College, Oxford. *Studied:* Signorina Simi, Florence (1963-66), City and Guilds, London (1967-70). *Exhib:* R.A., R.P.; one-man shows, Jocelyn Feilding Gallery (1974), Spink & Son (1978, 1982, 1984, 1991, 1997). *Clubs:* A.W.G., Chelsea Arts. *Signs work:* "Richard Foster." *Address:* 5a Clareville Grove, London SW7 5AU.

**FOUNTAIN, Desmond Hale,** F.R.B.S. (1986), Pre-dip. (Stoke-on-Trent 1966), Dip.A.D. (Exeter), A.T.D./Cert.Ed. (Bristol 1970); sculptor, female nudes and life-size children, bronze editions of nine; *b* Bermuda, 29 Dec., 1946. divorced. one *s*. one *d*. *Educ:* Normanton College, Buxton, Derbys. *Exhib:* one-man shows (1980-96): Alwin Gallery, London; Coach House Gallery,

# WHO'S WHO IN ART

Guernsey; Sally le Gallais, Jersey; Windjammer Gallery, Bermuda; Renaissance Gallery, Conn., U.S.A.; Cavalier Galleries, Conn., U.S.A.; The Sculpture Gallery, Bermuda; Falle Fine Art, Jersey; Bermuda National Gallery. *Work in collections:* throughout U.S.A., Canada and Europe, numerous hotels, banks, public sites, corporations and Bermuda National Gallery. Founded the vehicle for Bermuda National Gallery (1982). *Signs work:* "Desmond Fountain" or "Fountain." *Address:* P.O. Box FL317, Flatts FLBX, Bermuda.

**FOWKES, David Reeve,** B.A.; *b* Eastbourne, 15 Dec., 1919. *m* Lorna Fowkes. one *s.* one *d. Educ:* Eastbourne Grammar School; Reading University (1938-40, 1946-48). *Exhib:* Scottish Gallery Edinburgh (1973, 1976, 1980), Aberdeen University (1974, 1983), Peter Potter, Haddington (1979), Manor House, Ilkley (1984), Stonegate Gallery, York (1984, 1985, 1988, 1990, 1993, 1995, 1997), Towner, Eastbourne (1985), York University (1987), Abbot Hall, Kendal (1989), Charlotte Lampard, London (1989). *Work in collections:* H.M. The Queen, Aberdeen A.G., Angus County, Towner, Eastbourne, N. of Scot. College of Agriculture, Rowett Inst., Rowntree, Scottish Arts Council. *Publications:* A Gunner's Journal (1990). *Signs work:* "FOWKES." *Address:* 75 Bishopthorpe Rd., York YO2 1NX.

**FOWLE, LeClerc,** R.O.I., R.W.A., F.R.S.A., Paris Salon gold and silver medallist; 1st prize Laing Comp. (1979); painter in oil, pen and pencil, and pastel; *b* Haslar, Hants. *m* Brigadier J. LeC. Fowle, C.B., C.I.E. (decd.). *Studied:* privately and at Slade School of Fine Art. *Exhib:* Extensively 'One Painter Exhbns.' Bond St., London, R.A., R.O.I., R.W.A., R.S.A., Leicester Galleries (Fame and Promise), N.E.A.C., R.B.A., and many galleries in London and all over England. *Work in collections:* America, Australia, Portugal, Switzerland, England. *Clubs:* Cavalry and Guards, Chelsea Arts. *Signs work:* "LeClerc Fowle." *Address:* 23 Casson House, Kramer Mews, London SW5 9JG.

**FOWLER, Ronald George Francis,** S.G.F.A. (1982); Mem. of Council (1985-94); printmaker in etching, aquatint, drypoint and wood engraving; *b* London, 15 Apr., 1916. *m* Elizabeth Jean Stewart. one *s.* two *d. Educ:* Strand School, London, and Birkbeck College, University of London. *Studied:* Glasgow School of Art, Warrington School of Art, and Chester C.F.E. *Exhib:* R.S.B.A., N.S.P.S., S.G.F.A., Mall Prints and numerous one-man shows in N.W. England. *Work in collections:* Buxton Museum and A.G., Derbyshire. *Signs work:* "FOWLER." *Address:* Yew Tree Cottage, Lower Whitley, Ches. WA4 4JD.

**FRAME, Roger Campbell Crosbie,** C.A. (1973); Secretary of: R.S.W.; Chartered Accountant; *b* Glasgow, 7 June, 1949. *Educ:* Glasgow Academy. *Clubs:* Glasgow Art. *Address:* 29 Waterloo St., Glasgow G2 6BZ.

**FRANCESCONI, Anselmo:** see ANSELMO (Anselmo Francesconi).

**FRANCIS, Audrey Frances,** R.I. (1994); artist in pencil, water-colour and gouache; *b* 5 Oct., 1931. *m* O.R. Francis. *Educ:* Girdlers School, Kent. *Studied:*

Wimbledon School of Art (1948-52), Central School of Arts and Crafts (1953) *Exhib:* R.I., R.W.S. Open, N.E.A.C., and mixed exhbns. *Signs work:* "F Francis." *Address:* Grove Cottage, Waldron, nr. Heathfield, E. Sussex TN2 0RB.

**FRANCYN, (Dehn Fuller),** F.F.P.S., W.I.A.C., N.S.; painter in oils an gouache; *b* Portsmouth. *m* Curt Dehn. one *s.* one *d. Educ:* at home. *Exhib:* one man shows: Paris, The Hague, Utrecht, Sydney, London; group shows: Fre Painters and Sculptors, W.I.A.C., Hampstead Artists, N.S., etc. *Work in collec tions:* Holland, Germany, U.S.A., Australia. *Publications:* Poems, Man' Moment (U.S.A.), portfolio of folk-songs, collection of poems. *Clubs:* I.C.A Hampstead Artist. *Signs work:* see appendix. *Address:* 6 Elsworthy Ct. Elsworthy Rd., London NW3.

**FRANKENTHALER, Helen,** First Prize, Paris Biennale (1959); painter i oils, acrylic, on unsized cotton-duck; *b* New York, 12 Dec., 1928. *Educ* Bennington College, Vermont, U.S.A. (B.A.). *Exhib:* retrospective: Museum o Modern Art, N.Y. (1989), Guggenheim Museum, N.Y. (1985), Sterling an Francine Clark Art Inst. (print retrospective), Williamstown, Ma. (1980) United States Information Agency Travelling Exhbn.; Japan, Australia Philippines, Singapore, Korea, Hong Kong, Mexico, Brazil, Venezuela Colombia (1978), Corcoran Gallery of Art, Washington, D.C. (1975), Whitne Museum of American Art, N.Y. (1969). *Work in collections:* New York City Solomon R. Guggenheim Museum, Museum of Modern Art, Whitne Museum, Met. Museum of Art; Washington D.C.: National Gallery of Art Corcoran Gallery of Art, Smithsonian Institution - Hirshhorn Museum an Sculpture Garden; Albright-Knox A.G., Buffalo; Art Institute, Chicago Cleveland Museum of Art; San Francisco Museum of Art. *Signs work:* se appendix. *Address:* 173 East 94th St., New York 10128.

**FRANKLAND, Eric Trevor,** A.R.W.S., R.E., A.R.B.A.; mem. of Th London Group, Leverhulme Fund award, Landseer Scholarship, R.A. Silve Medal for Drawing; painter and printmaker; visiting lecturer, Medway Colleg of Art, Hornsey College of Art and Middlesex University as an associate senio lecturer; Hon. Treasurer, Royal Soc. of Painter Printmakers; *b* Middlesbrough 1931. *m* Dorothy Southern, artist. *Studied:* Laird School of Art, Birkenhead R.A. Schools, London. *Exhib:* many solo shows, and most major group exhbns Work in public and private collections. *Signs work:* "Trevor Frankland" o prints, "FRANKLAND" on other works, sometimes "T.F." *Address:* 1 Spencer Rd., London SW18 2SP.

**FRANKLIN, Ellen,** F.P.S.; Mem. Ben Uri Gallery; painter in oil; *b* Berlin 18 Aug., 1919. *Studied:* Reiman School of Art, Berlin (1936-38), Morle College, London. *Exhib:* Gladstone Pk. Gables Gallery (1980, 1995, 1997) Loggia Gallery (1985, 1991), Trends (1987, 1989), Ben Uri (1988, 1992) Cardiff (1988), Morley Gallery (1991, 1993, 1994, 1995, 1996, 1997). Work i private collections. *Signs work:* "E. Franklin." *Address:* 44 Beechcroft Gdns.

Wembley, Middx. HA9 8EP.

**FRASER, Donald Hamilton,** R.A.; painter; *b* London, 30 July, 1929. *m* Judith Wentworth-Sheilds, 1954. one *d. Studied:* St. Martin's School of Art, London (1949-52) and in Paris (French Gov. Scholarship); Tutor, Royal College of Art (1958-84); Hon. Fellow R.C.A. (1984); Hon. Curator, Royal Academy (1992); Trustee, Royal Academy (1993); Vice-Pres. Royal Overseas League since 1986; Vice-Pres. Artist's General Benevolent Inst.; mem. since 1986 of Royal Fine Art Commission. *Exhib:* Over 70 individual exhbns. in Europe, N. America and Japan. *Work in public collections* throughout the world. *Publications:* 'Gauguin's Vision after the Sermon' (Cassell, 1968), 'Dancers' (Phaidon, 1988). *Clubs:* Arts. *Signs work:* see appendix. *Address:* c/o Royal Academy of Arts, London W1V 0DS.

**FRASER, Elizabeth Bertha,** Mem. Society of Portrait Sculptors; sculptor in wax, plaster, bronze, painter in oil; *b* Teddington, London, 1914. *m* Lindley Maughton Fraser. *Studied:* Birmingham School of Art, Central School of Art, London, Westminster School of Art, London, Edinburgh College of Art . *Exhib:* R.A.; one-man shows, London and Edinburgh, Tour of Britain Sculptors Society, Society of Portrait Sculptors Yearly Exhbn., Edinburgh Younger Academy. *Commissions:* portrait heads. *Publications:* work repro.: television talks, theatrical designs. *Clubs:* Chelsea Arts. *Signs work:* "Liz Fraser," "Elizabeth Scott-Fraser" or "Elizabeth Fraser." *Address:* The Studio, 7 Ridgway Gdns., London SW19 4SZ.

**FREDRICK, Waveney,** R.B.S.A. (1978), P.S. (1983); Feeney award, Birmingham (1977), Herring award, Pastel Soc. (1983), Pastel Soc. of Canada award (1989); painter in pastel, gouache, water-colour, oil; *b* Luton, 1911. *m* J.A. Fredrick. one *s. Educ:* King Edward VI School, Birmingham. *Studied:* East Anglian School of Painting (Sir Cedric Morris, Arthur Lett Haines). *Exhib:* P.S., R.B.S.A., Walsall A.G., Oxford, Keele and Birmingham universities, Gallery of Modern Art, Washington D.C. *Work in collections:* Herbert A.G., Coventry. *Signs work:* "Waveney Fredrick." *Address:* 4 Dinmore Ave., Birmingham B31 2BG.

**FREEMAN, Lily,** F.B.S., B.A. Hons. (1978); painter in oil and water-colour; lecturer on Modern Art, University of 3rd Age; *b* Vienna, 7 Feb., 1920, widow. one *d. Educ:* Realgymnasium, Vienna. *Studied:* Vienna, Arthur Segal School, Hampstead (A. Segal, Marianne Segal). *Exhib:* N.Y. Expo (1985), Barbican (1982), Orangery, Holland Pk. (1979, 1981-85), Alicante, Spain (1983), Loggia Gallery (1978, 1982, 1984), Cockpit Theatre, Odeon Marble Arch, Hampstead Town Hall, New Art Theatre, Alpine Club, Hampstead Art Centre, Ben Uri Gallery, Royal Overseas League, Guildhall, London, Tradescant Trust, Leighton House, Burgh House. *Work in collections:* Dr. Lansky, Vienna. *Address:* 65 Dunstan Rd., London NW11 8AE.

**FREER, Roy,** N.D.D., A.T.D., R.O.I., R.I.; artist in oil and water-colour; art course tutor and organiser, demonstrator, lectures on appreciation of painting and drawing. *Studied:* Bournville School of Art, Birmingham College of Art *Signs work:* "ROY FREER" dated. *Address:* 184 Maple Rd., Penge, Londor SE20 8JB.

**FREETH, Peter,** Dip. Fine Art, A.R.A. (1990), R.A. (1992), R.E. (1991) printmaker in etching, aquatint, water-colour, teacher; Tutor of Etching, R.A Schools, London; *b* B'ham, 15 Apr., 1938. *m* Mariolina. two *s. Educ:* K.E.G.S Aston, B'ham. *Studied:* Slade School of Fine Art (1956-60, Antony Gross William Coldstream). *Exhib:* R.A., R.E., Christopher Mendez, London SW1 *Work in collections:* V. & A., B.M., Arts Council, Fitzwilliam Cambs. Metropolitan Museum, N.Y., National Gallery, Washington, Ashmolean Oxford. *Signs work:* "P. Freeth." *Address:* 83 Muswell Hill Rd., London N1C 3HT.

**FRENKIEL, Stanislaw,** R.W.A.; painter; Emeritus Reader, University of London; Head of Dept. of Art and Design, Institute of Education (1973-83); h.c. Professor Cracow Academy of Fine Art; Mem. London Group; *b* Cracow. 1918. *m* Anna. one *s.* one *d. Studied:* Cracow Academy of Fine Art, Académie Libanaise des Beaux Arts, Beirut, Sir John Cass College and Courtauld Institute, London. *Exhib:* one-man shows: American University, Beirut (1947); Grabowski Gallery, London (1960-1974); Cracow Palace of Fine Art (1965 1981, 1992); Galerie Tamara Pfeiffer, Brussels (1973, 1978, 1980); Zacheta Retrospective, Warsaw (1981); Drian Gallery, London (1981); Bloomsbury Gallery (1983, 1987); R.W.A. Bristol (1985); Polish Cult. Inst., London (1990); Gallery "Zapiecek", Warsaw (1992); Kennedy Gallery, Key West, Flo. (1995); retrospective: Royal Academy, Bristol (1996), Queen Street Gallery, Sydney, N.S.W. (1997); mixed shows: London Group since 1977, R.W.A. Bristol since 1985, Jestesmy, Zacheta, Warsaw (1992), Erotic Art, National Museum, Warsaw (1994). *Work in collections:* Hampstead Memorial Hospital, University of London, R.W.E. Academy, Bristol, Penn State University, U.S.A., Stamford University, U.S.A., Kennedy Gallery, Flo.; National museums: Cracow, Warsaw, Lodz, Poznan, Gdansk, Poland. *Publications:* "Beirut Drawings" (1986), "Erotomachia" Edn. of 10 etchings (Black Star Press, 1994). *Signs work:* see appendix. *Address:* 6 Clement Rd., London SW19 7RJ.

**FREUNDLICH, Grace Ruth,** Travelling Fellowship, Scottish Arts Council (1979), Fellowship, Provincetown Workshop (1976); artist in acrylic, ink, oil, graphite; instructor; exhbn. com., Provincetown Art Assoc. and Museum; *b* New York, 6 May, 1939. *m* Jesse Freundlich Winch. one *s. Educ:* University of Wisconsin, Madison (1964). *Studied:* Hunter College Graduate School (Bob Swain), Provincetown Workshop (Leo Manso, Victor Candell). *Exhib:* Gallery Matrix, Provincetown (1994, 1995), Foundry Gallery, Washington, D.C. (1981), Demarco Gallery, Edinburgh (1980), Provincetown Workshop (1976), Provincetown Art Assoc. and Museum (1986-96); solo show, Roosevelt House of Hunter College, N.Y. (1975). *Work in collections:* University of Wisconsin, Hunter College, Histadrut, Israel, American Forum, National Press Bldg.,

Washington D.C. *Commissions:* The Land, The Sea, American Forum, Washington D.C. *Publications:* Précis, with Robert E. Miller on exhbns. at Gallery Matrix, Provincetown. *Clubs:* College Art Assoc., Women in the Arts, National Women's Museum, Washington, D.C. *Signs work:* "G.F." or "G. Freundlich." *Address:* 200 W. 93rd St., New York, N.Y. 10025, U.S.A.

**FRIEDEBERGER, Klaus,** painter; *b* Berlin, 1922. *m* Julie. *Educ:* Quakerschool Eerde, Holland. *Studied:* E. Sydney Tech. College. *Exhib:* one-man shows: Belfast (1963); London (1963, 1986, 1990, Retrospective 1992); group shows since 1944. Europe Prize, Ostende 1964 (Gold Medal), National Gallery of Australia: 'Surrealism' (1993), 'The Europeans' (1997). *Work in collections:* private: Australia, England, Europe, U.S.A. Official purchases: Mosman Art Prize 1949, National Gallery of Australia. *Publications:* Arts Review, Art and Australia, Twenty Five Years Annely Juda Fine Art (London 1985), Surrealism (Canberra 1993), The Dictionary of Art (Macmillan 1996), The Europeans (Canberra 1997), etc. *Signs work:* "Friedeberger." *Address:* 16 Coleraine Rd., London SE3 7PQ.

**FRIERS, Rowel Boyd,** M.B.E., Hon. M.A. Open University, R.U.A., U.W.S.; oil painter and cartoonist (Belfast Telegraph, Irish Times), stage designer, illustrator (TV. Graphics, B.B.C. & U.T.V.); President, Royal Ulster Academy (1993-97); *b* Belfast, 13 Apr., 1920. *m* Evelyn Maude Yvonne Henderson. two *s.* one *d. Educ:* Belfast. *Studied:* Belfast College of Art. *Exhib:* London, R.H.A., Royal Ulster Academy; many one-man shows, included in National Self Portrait Gallery (Limerick, Ireland), Kneafsey Gallery (1985). *Work in collections:* Haverty Trust for Irish National Collection, Belfast Art Gallery, C.E.M.A. (N.I.) and Haverty Trust, National Self Portrait Gallery (Ireland). *Publications:* Wholly Friers and Mainly Spanish, Riotous Living, Pig in the Parlour, Book of Friers and The Revolting Irish, On The Borderline, autobiography: Drawn from Life (Blackstaff); work repro.: in Dublin Opinion, Punch, London Opinion, Radio Times, Belfast Telegraph, Lines of Laughter, This is My Best Humour. Cartoonist for Irish Times and now drawing for Ulster News Letter. *Signs work:* see appendix. *Address:* Millbank House, Victoria Rd., Holywood, Co. Down BT18 9BD.

**FRÖHLICH-WIENER, Irene,** sculptress in bronze, stone, wood and fibre-glass; *b* Luzern, Switzerland, 26 Aug., 1947. *m* Josef Fröhlich. two *d. Educ:* Kantons-Schule, Luzern (Matura), Institut Maïeutique (Art-therapy). *Studied:* Centre de la gravure Contemporaine, Geneva (1969), Marylebone Inst. (1973-74, carving under E. Mehmet), H.G.S. Inst. (John Brown), Sir John Cass School of Art (Clive Duncan). *Exhib:* R.B.A., Royal Festival Hall, Camden Art Centre, Woodstock Gallery, Smee Gallery, Norfolk, Ben Uri Gallery, Mall Galleries, Old Bull Art Centre, Draycott Gallery, Blenheim Gallery, Cecilia Coleman Gallery, October Gallery. *Work in collections:* The Silver Gallery, Bury St. Edmunds, Helmut Stern Collection, Michigan, McHardy Sculpture Co., London. *Commissions:* Rank Xerox (1996) award. *Signs work:* "Irene."

*Address:* 53 Oakleigh Ave., London N20 9JE.

**FROST, Anthony,** D.F.A. (1973); artist in acrylic paint on canvas; *b* St. Ives, Cornwall, 4 May, 1951. *m* Linda Macleod. two *s. Educ:* North Oxon. Technical College and School of Art, Banbury. *Studied:* Cardiff College of Art (1970-73, Eric Malthouse, Terry Setch, Alan Wood). *Exhib:* Four Young Artists, Penwith Gallery, St. Ives; John Moores, Liverpool; Public Hanging, St. Ives; Dangerous Diamonds, Hull; Anthony Frost - on Colour, Newlyn Gallery; "Viva Blues" Newlyn Gallery (1996), touring Birmingham, Darlington and London (1997). *Work in collections:* Littlewoods Organisation, Liverpool, Nuffield Trust, Contemporary Arts Soc., Cornwall C.C. *Clubs:* Subbuteo Football, Petanque, Boule. *Signs work:* "Anthony Frost." *Address:* Rosemergy Cottage, Morvah, Penzance TR20 8YX.

**FROST, Terry,** R.A.; painter in oil, acrylic, collage; *b* Leamington Spa, 1915. *m* Kathleen. five *s.* one *d. Educ:* Central School, Leamington Spa. *Studied:* Stalag 383, Camberwell School of Art and St. Ives. *Exhib:* numerous one-man and mixed shows from 1944 to the present. *Work in collections:* Tate Gallery, B.M., V. & A., and many other public and private collections in Great Britain, U.S.A., Canada and Europe. *Commissions:* British Airways. *Publications:* 'Terry Frost' (Scolar Press, 1994). *Clubs:* Chelsea Arts. *Signs work:* "Terry Frost" on verso. *Address:* c/o The Royal Academy, Piccadilly, London W1V 0DS.

**FROY, Martin,** D.F.A. (1951); Emeritus Professor of Fine Art, Reading University; *b* London, 9 Feb., 1926. *Studied:* Slade School; Gregory Fellow in Painting, Leeds University (1951-54); Trustee, National Gallery (1972-79); Tate Gallery (1975-79); Fellow U.C.L. (1978). *Work in collections:* Tate Gallery, Museum of Modern Art, N.Y., Chicago Art Institute, Arts Council, Contemporary Art Society, Royal West of England Academy, Leeds University, Art Galleries of Bristol, Carlisle, Leeds, Reading, Southampton, Wakefield. *Commissions:* Artist Consultant for Arts Council to City Architect, Coventry (1953-58); mosaic decoration, Belgrade Theatre (1957-58); two murals in Concert Hall, Morley College (1958-59). *Address:* University of Reading, RG1 5AQ.

**FRUHMANN, Johann,** painter; *b* Weissenstein a.d. Drau Kärnten, Austria, 22 Apr., 1928. *m* Christa Hauer. *Studied:* Kunstgewerbeschule Graz with Prof. Silberbauer and Wickenburg (1943-48), Akademie der bildenden Künste Wien with Prof. Andersen and Prof. Gütersloh (1948-50). *Work in collections:* Graphische Sammlung Albertina, Wien, Neue Galerie, Graz, Sammlung der Stadt Wien, Bundesminsterium für Unterricht, Art Museum, Cincinnati, Museum des 20. Jhd., Wien (1965), Österr. Sraatspreis for Painting. *Signs work:* "JOH. FRUH." on back of painting. *Address:* 1a 3552 Schloss Lengenfeld, Lengenfeld dei Krems, Austria.

**FRY, Arthur Malcolm,** M.B.E., Hon. Rtd. R.W.S., Hon. Mem. American Watercolor Soc.; late director R.W.S. and R.E.; *b* 20 May, 1909, married. one *s.* one *d. Educ:* Latymer Upper School; Bournemouth School of Art (Geoffrey Baker, Leslie Ward, R.E.). *Exhib:* principal London galleries; one man shows, Bavaria, London, Bournemouth, Salisbury, Swindon. *Work in collections:* U.S.A., Canada, Denmark, Australia, Bournemouth Corp. *Clubs:* Athenaeum. *Signs work:* "Malcolm Fry." *Address:* 24 Goddington Chase, Orpington, Kent BR6 9EA.

**FRY, Minne,** B.A. (1953); painter and printmaker in oil, water-colour, etching; *b* Johannesburg, 20 Dec., 1933. *m* Lionel Fry. one *s.* two *d. Educ:* University of the Witwatersrand. *Studied:* Central School of Art (1955, Cecil Collins, Mervyn Peake). *Exhib:* New Vision Centre (1958), Camden Galleries (1989). *Work in collections:* C.A.S. *Signs work:* "Minne Fry." *Address:* 16 Caroline Pl., London W2.

**FRYER, Katherine Mary,** A.T.D. (1932); Princess of Wales Scholarship for wood engraving (1932), Hoffmann Wood (Leeds) gold medal for painting (1968); artist in oil and water-colour; 1937-47 taught at Bath School (later Academy) of Art Corsham; lecturer in School of Painting, B'ham College of Art (retd.); *b* Roundhay, Leeds, 26 Aug., 1910. *Educ:* Roundhay High School, Leeds. *Studied:* Leeds College of Art (1926-32, E. Owen Jennings). *Exhib:* R.A., R.B.S.A., etc. *Work in collections:* R.A., B'ham Register Office, etc. *Signs work:* "K.M. Fryer" or "K. FRYER." *Address:* 47 Moor Pool Ave., Harborne, Birmingham B17 9HL.

**FULLER, Peter Frederic,** R.A.I. (1976), A.A.H. (1976), F.P.S. (1991); Whatman prize; painter in water-colour; art historian; *b* Ramsgate, 10 Apr., 1929. *m* Rosemary Blaker. one *d. Educ:* John Hezlett School. *Studied:* Maidstone College of Art. *Exhib:* R.A., R.B.A., R.P.S., R.W.S. (Open), R.I., N.E.A.C., F.P.S., R.S.M.A., K.C.C. 'Kent Artists', Britain in Water-colours, Towner A.G., E. Stacey-Marks Gallery Eastbourne, Arts Centre Folkestone, Arune Arts Centre Arundel, Roger Green Fine Art High Halden, Bakehouse Gallery Sevenoaks, Cloisters Gallery Canterbury, Leeds Castle, etc. *Work in collections:* America, Australia, Canada, France, Germany. *Clubs:* Maidstone Art, Maidstone Archaeological Group. *Signs work:* "Peter Fuller." *Address:* 31 Sandling La., Penenden Heath, Maidstone, Kent ME14 2HS.

**FULLER, Violet,** F.F.P.S.; artist in water-colour, oil, pastel; *b* Tottenham, 26 July, 1920. *Studied:* Hornsey School of Art (1937-40) under Russell Reeve, R.B.A., A.R.E.; Stroud School of Art (1942-44) under Gwilym E. Jones, A.R.C.A. *Exhib:* Paris, R.A., R.I., R.B.A., N.E.A.C., W.I.A.C., Whitechapel A.G. (1967), 9 painters of East London, Bath Festival (1967), Brighton Festival (1988, 1989, 1991, 1993); one-man shows: Woodstock Gallery (1958, 1959, 1961, 1963, 1967, 1970), Old Bakehouse Gallery, Sevenoaks (1968, 1970), Hornsey Library (1968, 1973), New Gallery, Hornsey (1975), Forty Hall, Enfield (1974, 1984), Bruce Castle, Tottenham (1980), Loggia Gallery (1983, 1986, 1991). *Work in collections:* London Borough of Haringey, London Borough of Enfield. *Signs work:* "VIOLET FULLER." *Address:* 1 Helena Rd.,

Woodingdean, Brighton, Sussex BN2 6BS.

**FURNIVAL, John P.,** A.R.C.A.; artist in pen and ink and mixed media; lecturer, Bath Academy of Art; editor, Openings Press; *b* London, 29 May, 1933. *m* Astrid Furnival. two *s.* one *d. Studied:* Wimbledon College of Art; Royal College of Art. *Exhib:* Biennale des Jeunes, Paris; one-man show: Thumb Gallery, London; retrospective: Laing Gallery, Newcastle, Arnolfini, Bristol, plus various international exhbns. of visual and concrete poetry. *Work in collections:* Arts Council of Gt. Britain, Arnolfini Trust, Munich Pinakothek. *Publications:* The Bang Book (Jargon Press), The Lucidities (Turret Books). *Clubs:* Dorothy's Umbrellas Dining Society (DUDS). *Signs work:* "John Furnival." *Address:* Rooksmoor House, Woodchester, Glos. GL5 5NB.

# G

**GAGE, Anthea Dominique Juliet,** S.S.A., R.S.W.; art teacher, artist in gouache and water-colour; full time teacher, Royal High School, Edinburgh; *b* Edinburgh, 21 Mar., 1956. *Educ:* John Watsons School, Stevenson's College of Educ. *Studied:* Edinburgh College of Art (Dip. 1974-78, Post. Dip. 1978-79, David Michie, George Donald). *Exhib:* annually at S.S.A., R.S.W.; various mixed exhbns. *Signs work:* "Anthea D.J. Gage." *Address:* 16/8 Craighouse Gdns., Edinburgh EH10 5TX.

**GAGE, Edward Arthur,** M.B.E. (1992), R.S.W. (1963), D.A.(Edin.), Past President S.S.A.; painter in oil and water-colour, illustrator, journalist, broadcaster; art master, Fettes College (1952-68); Senior Lecturer, Napier University (1968-86); art critic, The Scotsman; *b* Gullane, 28 Mar., 1925. *m* Valerie Alexandra. one *s.* two *d. Educ:* Royal High School of Edinburgh. *Studied:* Edinburgh College of Art (1941-42, 1947-52) under Sir W. G. Gillies. *Work in collections:* Scottish National Gallery of Modern Art, Aberdeen A.G., University Galleries Aberdeen, Edinburgh, Glasgow, Edinburgh City Scottish Arts Council, Argyll C.C. *Publications:* The Eye in the Wind (Scottish Painting since 1945) Collins, 1977; *work repro:* Radio Times and B.B.C. Publications, illustrations in books for major publishing houses - Bodley Head, Dents, Longmans. *Signs work:* "Edward Gage." *Address:* 6 Hillview, Edinburgh EH4 2AB.

**GAINSFORD, Sylvia Petula,** N.D.D. (1964), A.T.D. (1965); artist and illustrator in acrylic, water-colour, ink; co-Proprietor, Gallery One, Fishguard, Pembrokeshire; *b* Tonbridge, Kent, 2 Sept., 1942. *m* Leon Olin. *Studied:* Royal Tunbridge Wells (1962, painting and wood engraving). *Exhib:* numerous permanent: Gallery One, Fishguard. *Work in collections:* Webber Coll. Ontario, Kallis Foundation, Beverly Hills. *Publications:* Food from the Countryside (Leon and Sylvia Olin); Just Like you and me by Johnny Morris; commissioned by A.G. Müller (Switzerland) to illustrate The Tarot of the Old Path (now worldwide publication and best seller) - originals with Sotheby's; Tarot of Northern Shadows (1997). *Signs work:* "Sylvia P. Gainsford." *Address:* Fron Haul, Rhos-y-Caerau, Goodwick, Pembrokeshire SA64 0LB.

**GALE, Raymond David George,** N.D.D. (1958), A.T.C. (Lond.1959); printmaker, teacher; *b* Hanwell, London 25 June, 1937. *Studied:* Ealing School of Art (1953-58), Hornsey College of Art (1958-59). *Clubs:* S.G.A. *Signs work:* "Ray Gale." *Address:* 283 Hounslow Rd., Hanworth, Middx.

**GALE, Richard John,** Dip. A.D. (1968), M.A. (R.C.A., 1973); artist in oil; *b* Bristol, 8 Feb., 1946. *m* Francis Joan. *Educ:* Weston-super-Mare Grammar School. *Studied:* Kingston upon Thames School of Art (1965-68), R.C.A. (1970-73). *Signs work:* "R. Gale." *Address:* 5 Hillside Rd., Clevedon, Avon.

**GALLAGHER, Brian,** artist in water-colour, pastel and pencil; Secretary and Council mem. Pastel Soc; tutor to painting courses; *b* Chester, 31 May, 1935. *m* Rosemary June Webb. one *s. Studied:* Portsmouth College of Art, privately under Herbert Green. *Exhib:* P.S., S.WL.A., Porthill Gallery London, Anna-Mei Chadwick Gallery, London, R.B.S.A. Galleries, Birmingham, John Nevill Gallery, Canterbury, Cowleigh Gallery, Malvern, and many provincial galleries. *Publications:* work repro.: contributor to art magazines. *Clubs:* London Sketch. *Signs work:* "Brian Gallagher." *Address:* 99 Gilmore Cres., Ashford, Middx. TW15 2DD.

**GALVANI, Patrick,** painter in water-colour and oil, journalist, author; *b* Bures, Suffolk, 11 Sept., 1922. *m* Madeleine. one *s. Educ:* University College School. *Studied:* U.C.S. and self-taught. *Exhib:* London, Florida and Mandell's Gallery, Norwich, various galleries in East Anglia. *Commissions:* various houses. *Clubs:* Ipswich Art. *Signs work:* "PATRICK GALVANI." *Address:* 5 Gracechurch St., Debenham, Suffolk IP14 6RA.

**GAMBLE, Tom,** R.W.S.; painter in oil and water-colour; Mem. A.W.G.; senior lecturer, Art and Design, Loughborough College of Art (1952-84); Freeman of City of London, and Liveryman of the Worshipful Company of Painter/Stainers; *b* Norton-on-Tees, 6 Feb., 1924, married. one *s. Studied:* Constantine College, Middlesbrough. *Exhib:* R.A., R.W.S., Bankside Gallery London, Royal Festival Hall, Mall Galleries, Brian Sinfield, Milne & Moller, Leicester A.G., Middlesbrough A.G., Exposicion International de Aquarda Barcelona, American and Canadian Water-colour Socs., and various provincial galleries. *Work in collections:* Lloyds of London, University of Loughborough, Notts. C.C., Leics. C.C., Crathorne Collection; private collections in Europe, U.S.A., Canada. *Clubs:* Arts. *Signs work:* "Tom Gamble." *Address:* 10 Blythe Green, East Perry, Huntingdon, Cambs.

**GAMLEN, Mary,** A.T.D. (Lond. 1936); Hon. U.A.; sculptor in wood and terracotta, painter in oil and water-colour; *b* London, 1913. *m* Alan Somerville Young. one *s.* two *d. Educ:* Student at Hornsey School of Art; on staff there (1937-1945). *Exhib:* R.A., R.B.A., N.E.A.C., R.W.S., Edinburgh R.A., Fermoy Gallery, Kings Lynn, Premises, Norwich, Mall Galleries. *Work in collections:*

Museum of the Royal Marines (Lying-in-State of Sir Winston Churchill), Belize Cathedral (reredos), Norfolk (village signs), Holt Church (carving of St. Andrew), Thorpe Market Church (restoration work). *Signs work:* "GAMLEN" or "Mary Gamlen" and see appendix. *Address:* Ham House Pottery, Southrepps, Norwich, Norfolk NR11 8AH.

**GANLY, Rosaleen Brigid,** A.R.H.A. (1928), R.H.A. (1935), H.R.H.A. (1983); artist in oil, water-colour, egg-tempera, pastels, pen and ink, etc.; *b* Dublin, 29 Jan., 1909. *m* Andrew Ganly. one *s*. one *d*. *Studied:* Dublin School of Art under Sean Keating, Patrick Tuohy, Oswald Reeves, Oliver Sheppard and George Atkinson, and at R.H.A. School under D. OBrien, Sean O'Sullivan, Richard Orpen, etc., Cubism under André L'hote, Paris. *Exhib:* R.H.A. (yearly since 1928), yearly with Water-colour Soc. of Ireland, Limerick, Galway, Cork, Berlin, America, Canada, Dublin Municipal Gallery of Modern Art, Royal Dublin Soc., Waterford, Blackrock (All Saints Church, murals in egg-tempera), murals in church, Ennis, Co. Clare; one-man shows, Dublin Painters Gallery (1936), Dawson Gallery (1965), Lincoln Gallery, Dublin (1980); two-man shows with B. M. Flegg, Wexford and Dunlaoghaire; retrospective exhbn. Gorry's Gallery, Dublin (1987). *Work in collections:* Haverty Trust, National Self Portrait Gallery, Limerick, Royal Dublin Soc. of Ireland. *Publications:* work repro.: numerous book illustrations and dust jackets. *Signs work:* Early work, up to 1936, two capital B's within a circle or "Brigid OBrien"; all works, from 1936 signed "RBG." *Address:* 6a Laurel Hill, Upper Glenageary Rd., Dunlaoghaire, Co. Dublin.

**GARDINER, Vanessa,** B.A. (Hons.) (1982); painter in acrylic, collage on board; *b* Oxford, 7 Apr., 1960. one *s*. *Studied:* Oxford Polytechnic (1978-79), Central School of Art and Design (1979-82, David Haughton). *Exhib:* solo shows: Duncan Campbell Contemporary Art, London (1991, 1992, 1996), Gordon Hepworth Gallery, Exeter (1993), Mill Lane Gallery, Lyme Regis, Dorset (1997). *Publications:* work repro.: Modern Painters Magazine, Summer 1996 – review by Elizabeth James. *Signs work:* "Vanessa Gardiner." *Address:* Lilac Cottage, Fernhill, Charmouth, Dorset DT6 6BX.

**GARDNER, Annette,** painter in oil; Principal and Teacher, Wood Tutorial College; Founder and Director, New End Gallery; *b* 11 June, 1920. *m* C. J. Wood, M.A., (decd.1972). one *s*. one *d*. *Studied:* Twickenham Art School (1952-54); Hampstead Garden Suburb Institute (1954-56) under Mr. Gower; St. Martin's (1960-63) under David Tindle; principal teacher Walter Nessler. *Exhib:* Numerous group shows and travelling exhbns.; finalist, Woman's Journal Painting of the Year (1961). *Work in collections:* Australia, England, U.S.A., Israel, Hungary. *Clubs:* F.P.S., Ben Uri. *Signs work:* "A. Gardner." *Address:* The Studio, 18 Canons Drive, Edgware, Middx. HA8 7QS.

**GARDNER, Derek George Montague,** V.R.D., R.S.M.A., Commander R.N.V.R.; Hon. vice-president for life R.S.M.A.; marine artist in oil and water-colour; Rudolph Schaefer award at International Exhbn. of Marine Art, Mystic,

U.S.A. (1984); *b* Gerrards Cross, Bucks, 13 Feb., 1914. *m* Mary née Dalton. one *s.* one *d. Educ:* Monkton Combe Junior School and Oundle School. *Exhib:* R.S.M.A., United Artists, Bermuda, IPG; one-man shows, Polak Gallery, London (1972, 1975, 1979, 1982, 1987, 1990, 1995). *Work in collections:* National Maritime Museum, Greenwich; Bermuda Maritime Museum; R.N. College, Dartmouth. Mentioned in Despatches, H.M.S. Broke (1942). *Clubs:* Naval Club. *Signs work:* "Derek G. M. over Gardner." *Address:* High Thatch, Corfe Mullen, Wimborne, Dorset BH21 3HJ.

**GARDNER, Peter Colville Horridge,** R.O.I. (1977), A.T.D. (1951), F.R.S.A. (1969); artist in oil; *b* London, 25 Oct., 1921. *m* Irene. *Educ:* St. Matthias C. of E. School, London SW5. *Studied:* Hammersmith School of Art (1935-38, 1946-50), London University Inst. of Educ. (1950-51). *Exhib:* R.A., R.B.A., R.O.I., N.E.A.C. *Work in collections:* Nuffield Foundation, York University. *Signs work:* "Peter Gardner." *Address:* 11 Pixmead Gdns., Shaftesbury, Dorset SP7 8BZ.

**GARFIT, William,** R.B.A.; I.L.E.A. Dip with hon., Byam Shaw School Cert. with Distinction, R.A.S. Cert.; artist in oils, specialising in River Landscapes and pen and wash illustration work; *b* Cambridge, 9 Oct., 1944. *m* Georgina Joseph. one *s.* two *d. Educ:* Bradfield College. *Studied:* Cambridge School of Art (1963), Byam Shaw (1964-67), R.A. Schools (1967-70). *Exhib:* one-man shows, Waterhouse Gallery (1970, 1972, 1974), Mall Galleries (1976), Stacey Marks, Eastbourne (1978), Tryon and Moorland Gallery, London (1981, 1983, 1985, 1988, 1991), Holland & Holland Gallery (1994). *Publications:* illustrated, Dudley worst dog in the World, Amateur Keeper, Your Shoot, The Woods Belong to Me, The Fox and the Orchid, Prue's Country Kitchen, Cley Marsh and its Birds, The Game Shot, How the Heron got Long Legs, The Woodpigeon, author of Will's Shoot (1993). *Signs work:* "William Garfit." *Address:* The Old Rectory, Harlton, Cambridge CB3 7ES.

**GARLICK, Kenneth John,** M.A., Ph.D., Hon. D. Litt., F.M.A., F.S.A.; art historian; Keeper of Western Art, The Ashmolean Museum, Oxford (1968-84); *b* Glastonbury, 1 Oct., 1916. *Educ:* Elmhurst Grammar School, Street, Balliol College, Oxford, Courtauld Institute of Art, University of London. *Publications:* Sir Thomas Lawrence: a Catalogue (Walpole Society, Vol.XXXIX, 1964); Sir Thomas Lawrence (Phaidon, 1989). *Clubs:* Reform. *Address:* 39 Hawkswell Hse., Hawkswell Gdns., Oxford OX2 7EX.

**GARMAN, Evelyn Daphne,** N.S. (1980), S.W.A. (1985); sculptor in clay, wax, bronze, resin bronze; *b* Beaconsfield, 6 Apr., 1913. *m* R. C. Garman, artist. three *d. Educ:* Convent of the Holy Child Jesus, Sussex. *Studied:* London studio of A. Acheson, A.R.A. privately (1933-38). *Exhib:* S.W.A., N.S., S.P.S., Winchester, Andover, and two private shows with husband. *Work in collections:* Heads of Founders in Winsor and Newton Museum, Wealdstone, Harrow. *Clubs:* Cheltenham and Cotswold. *Signs work:* "E.D.G." or "D. GARMAN." *Address:* Ashburnham, 8 Charnwood Cl., Cheltenham, Glos. GL53 0HL.

# WHO'S WHO IN ART

**GARRARD, Peter John,** P.P.R.B.A., R.P., N.E.A.C., R.W.A.; painter in oil; *b* 4 Jan., 1929. *m* Patricia Marmoy. one *s.* two *d. Educ:* Magdalen College School, Brackley. *Studied:* Byam Shaw School of Drawing and Painting. *Work in collections:* public and private collections in England, America, Australia, Canada, Germany, etc. *Signs work:* "P.J.G." *Address:* 340 Westbourne Park Rd., London W11 1EQ.

**GARRETT, Roger MacLean,** M.A.,Ph.D.; artist in oil; University Lecturer; Senior Lecturer, University of Bristol; *b* Nairn, Scotland, 10 Feb., 1942. *m* Bertha Garrett. one *s.* one *d. Exhib:* R.W.A. (1995), R.A. (1997), School House Gallery, Bath (1997). *Signs work:* "R.G." *Address:* 38 Holmes Grove, Henleaze, Bristol BS9 4EE.

**GATTEAUX, Marcel,** Canuelo award (1995); landscape and still-life artist in oil; *b* Mitcham, Surrey, 1 Oct., 1962. *Studied:* Camberwell School of Art (1980-81, Dick Lee, Sargy Mann); then studied restoration for a number of years before redirecting his attention to painting. *Exhib:* one-man show, Caelt Galley (1997); many mixed exhbns. *Work in collections:* Churchill Hotel, London; Cliveden and private collections in the U.K. and U.S.A. *Commissions:* Many commissions for the mediterranean landscapes; mainly Provence, Andalucia, Venice and the Greek Islands. *Signs work:* see appendix. *Address:* 182 Westbourne Grove, London W11 2RH.

**GEARY, Robert John,** F.C.S.D. (1980), F.R.S.A. (1981), Hon S.G.F.A. (1994); graphic artist and illustrator in ink and water-colour; Graphics Officer, Geological Museum S. Kensington (1971-85); *b* London, 15 Jan., 1931. *m* Hazel Mair Plant. one *d. Studied:* Hammersmith School of Arts and Crafts (1945-48) under Wm. Washington, D.V. Playfair and Ernest Fedarb. *Exhib:* S.G.A. *Work in collections:* University of Kent. *Publications:* work repro.: several childrens books, Radio Times, The Folio Soc., humorous illustrations for Punch, The Oldie, Daily Mail, The Sunday Telegraph and The Times Supplements. *Address:* 70 Felton Lea, Sidcup, Kent DA14 6BA.

**GEDDES, Stewart John,** M.A. Arts Criticism (1997), B.A. (Hons.) Fine Art (1983), R.W.A. (1996); landscape painter in oil, tutor; *b* Aylesford, Kent, 4 Mar., 1961. *m* Juliet Simmons. *Educ:* Maidstone School for Boys. *Studied:* Canterbury College of Art (1979-80, Eric Hurran), Bristol Polytechnic (1980-83, Alf Stockham), City University, London (1996-97, Dr. Eric Moody). *Exhib:* R.A., R.W.A., Waterman Gallery, Cadogan Contemporary, London. *Work in collections:* House Of Commons. *Signs work:* "S.J. Geddes" on back of work. *Address:* 49 Noyna Rd., Tooting Bec, London SW17 7PQ.

**GEE, Arthur,** S.WL.A. (1969), N.A.P.A. (1993); painter/printmaker including wildlife and landscape; Cert. of Merit, University of Art, Salsomaggiore, Italy (1982); Purchase prizewinner (1990), Mini-print International, Barcelona; Finalist, Laing Competition (1991, 1994), Manchester/London; Daler Rowney cryla award, N.A.P.A. Exhbn. B'ham (1993); Artists Newsletter Award, N.A.P.A. Exhbn. B'ham (1997); Invited Member, Sefton Guild of Artists

(1997); *b* Latchford, Warrington, 10 Jan., 1934. *m* Margaret Ray Robinson. one *s*. one *d*. *Educ:* Penketh and Sankey Sec. School, Warrington. *Studied:* St. Helen's College of Art and Design (1983-84). *Exhib:* throughout U.K. and abroad, S.WL.A. annually since 1965, Mall Galleries, London (F.B.A.). *Commissions:* F.B.A. and B.A.S.C., plus private commissions. *Publications:* Three poems illustrated in "Flights of Imagination" (Blandford Press, 1982). *Signs work:* "Arthur Gee." *Address:* 31 Karen Cl., Burtonwood, Warrington, Ches. WA5 4LL.

**GELDART, William,** artist/illustrator in pencil, pen and ink, scraperboard, pen and wash, gouache; *b* Marple, Ches., 21 Mar., 1936. *m* Anne Mary. one *s*. one *d*. *Educ:* Hyde Grammar School. *Studied:* Regional College, Manchester (1956-57). *Exhib:* R.A., Manchester Fine Arts, various others. *Work in collections:* Hallé Orchestra, Manchester International Airport, Ciba Geigy, I.C.I., Rolls Royce, C.J.S., I.C.L., Reynolds Chains, Manchester Grammar School, Chetham School of Music. *Publications:* written and illustrated: Geldart's Cheshire (The Whitethorn Press); illustrated: Fox at Drummer's Darkness (Joyce Stranger/Dents), Kym (Joyce Stranger/Michael Joseph), Ghostly Laughter (Barbara Reson/Beaver), Un Petit Soldat (Jack London/Editions Gallimard), La Forêt des Verts Lutins (Philippa Pearce/Editions Gallimard), Kes (Barry Hines/Editions Gallimard), Kit (Jane Gardam/Julia Macrae books), etc. *Address:* Geldart Gallery, Chelford Rd., Henbury, nr. Macclesfield, Ches. SK11 9PG.

**GELLER, William Jasper,** F.R.S.A., S.G.F.A.; artist in pen and ink, gouache, egg tempera; designer; Past Pres., Soc. of Graphic Fine Artists; *b* London, 21 Dec., 1930. *m* Olive. two *d*. *Educ:* Loughton School. *Studied:* City of London, Apprentice in Art, Central School, Regent Polytechnic (1947-52). *Exhib:* R.S.M.A. Annual show, S.G.F.A. Annual show, F.B.A. Touring Exhbn. *Work in collections:* Port of London Authority and private collections. *Publications:* 20th Century British Marine Painting. *Clubs:* Rotary International, R.Y.A. *Signs work:* "William Geller." *Address:* 17 Silver St., Maldon, Essex CM9 4QE.

**GENTLEMAN, David,** R.D.I. (1972); artist and designer: water-colour, lithography, wood engraving, etc.; *b* London, 11 Mar., 1930. *m* Susan Evans. one *s*. three *d*. *Educ:* Hertford Grammar School. *Studied:* St. Albans School of Art (1947-48), R.C.A. (1950-53, Edward Bawden, John Nash). *Exhib:* solo exhbns. at Mercury Gallery, London (1970-97). *Work in collections:* B.M., V. & A., Tate Gallery, National Maritime Museum, Murals at Charing Cross Underground Station. *Publications:* David Gentleman's Britain, - London, - Coastline, - Paris, - India, - Italy and many illustrated. *Signs work:* "David Gentleman." *Address:* 25 Gloucester Cres., London NW1 7DL.

**GEORGE, Grace Courtenay,** University of Oxford Secondary Teachers Art Cert.; artist in water-colour and lino and wood block; Head of Art Department, The Grammar School, Chipping Sodbury, Bristol (1939-69); art mistress, Hereward School, March, Cambs. (1934-38); exchange teacher, South High School, Lima, Ohio, U.S.A. (1948); Mem. National Society of Art Education; *b* Bristol, 9 Sept., 1909. *Educ:* Hillside House School and Duncan House School, Clifton, Bristol. *Studied:* W. of England College of Art, Bristol, principal, R. E. J. Bush. *Signs work:* "G. C. George." *Address:* Middle Thatched Cottage, Lower St., West Harnham, Salisbury, Wilts. SP2 8EY.

**GEORGE, Patrick,** artist; *b* Manchester, 1923. *m* 1st 1955 June Griffith (dissolved 1980); four *d*. 2nd 1981 Susan Ward. *Stidied:* Edinburgh College of Art, Camberwell School of Art; Taught, Slade School, University College London (1949-88); Prof. of Fine Art (1983); Slade Prof. (1985-88). *Exhib:* retrospective, Serpentive Gallery (1980). *Work in collections:* Arts Council, Tate Gallery, etc. Dealers: Browse and Darby. *Address:* 33 Moreton Terr., London SW1 2NS.

**GEORGIOU, Elpida:** see ELPIDA.

**GETHIN, Jackie,** C.I.C., S.B.A.; artist in water-colour; Council mem. Soc. of Botanical Artists; *b* Brikendon, Herts., 14 May, 1949. *m* Richard. three *d*. *Educ:* Effingham House School, Cooden, Sussex. *Studied:* Southampton College of Art, Bournemouth and Poole College of Art (Keith Rennison). *Exhib:* numerous mixed shows including S.B.A. *Work in collections:* Francis Iles, Rochester. *Signs work:* "Jackie Gethin." *Address:* Trotts Ash, Sole Street, nr. Gravesend, Kent DA12 3AY.

**GIARDELLI, Arthur,** M.B.E., M.A. (Oxon); Chairman, 56 Group Wales; painter and sculptor in mixed media (wood, brass, burlap, oil, etc.) for wall panels, water-colour, and lecturer; *b* London, 11 Apr., 1911, married. one *s*. one *d*. *Educ:* Alleyn's School, Dulwich, Hertford College, Oxford. *Studied:* Ruskin School of Art, Oxford. *Exhib:* Amsterdam, Paris, Chicago, Washington, Bologna, Bratislava, London, New York, Cardiff. *Work in collections:* Arts Council of Great Britain, Welsh Arts Council, National Museum of Wales, National Library of Wales, Museum of Modern Art, Dublin, National Gallery Slovakia, National Gallery Prague, Musée des Beaux Arts, Nantes, Estorick Collection, Grosvenor Gallery, London, Tate Gallery. *Commissions:* wall panel: Argus Newspaper; door: Grosvenor Gallery, and Brook St. Gallery. *Publications:* The Delight of Painting (University College, Swansea); work repro.:art magazines. *Signs work:* see appendix. *Address:* Golden Plover Art Gallery, Warren, Pembroke SA71 5HR.

**GIBB, Avril V.:** see WATSON STEWART, (Lady) Avril Veronica.

**GIBBONS, John,** B.A. Hons. (Sculpture); Head of Sculpture, Winchester School of Art; *b* Ireland, 1949. *Educ:* Ireland. *Studied:* sculpture: St. Martin's School of Art (1972-75, David Anneley, William Tucker). *Exhib:* one-man shows: International Arts Centre, London (1975), Project Gallery, Dublin (1979), Nicola Jacobs Gallery, London (1981), Triangle Center, N.Y.C. (1984), Serpentine Gallery (1986), John Hansard Gallery, Southampton University (1986), Galerie Wentzel, Köln (1987), Madeleine Carter Fine Art, Boston, Mass. (1988), Flowers East (1990, 1992, 1994, 1997), Flowers Graphics

(1996), Butler, The Castle, Kilkenny Ireland (1996), Whitworth A.G. Manchester (1997), Kettles Yard, Cambridge (1997). *Work in collections:* A.C.G.B., Syracuse University, N.Y., Edmonton A.G., Alberta, Gulbenkian Foundation, Comino Foundation, Museum of Contemporary Art, Barcelona, Tate Gallery; private collections: U.K., U.S.A., Germany, Ireland, Canada, Japan, France. *Publications:* Gonzalez: A Legacy; Introduction to catalogue, South Bank Centre, Whitechapel. *Signs work:* "J.G." welded on. *Address:* 14 Almond Rd., London SE16 3LR.

**GIBBONS-SMITH, Leo Illesley,** P.U.A.; Past Mem. of Executive Council, Federation of British Artists, Vice-Pres. Soc. of Graphic Fine Arts, Pres. United Society of Artists, Pres. Herts. Visual Arts Forum; painter in water-colour, pastel, acrylic, landscape, portrait, works of the imagination; Art Director in publishing and advertising, illustrator, typographer; latterly art editorial, Radio Times; *b* Cobham, Surrey. *m* Constance Hilda. one *d. Educ:* Kingston Grammar School. *Studied:* Hornsey College of Art (1945-49). *Exhib:* Mall Galleries, R.B.A., R.I., R.P., P.S., N.E.A.C., R.W.S.; several one-man shows. *Work in collections:* Ealing Educ. Com. *Signs work:* "Leo Gibbons-Smith" or "L.I.G.S." *Address:* 207 Sunnybank Rd., Potters Bar, Herts. EN6 2NH.

**GIBBS, Timothy Francis,** M.A. (Oxon., 1948), C.F.A. (Oxon, 1949); painter in oils, acrylic and water-colour; deputy Ruskin master (1974-79), Ruskin School; *b* Epping, Essex, 21 Aug., 1923. *m* Bridget Fry. one *s.* two *d. Educ:* Trinity College, Oxford. *Studied:* Ruskin School (1947-49). *Exhib:* one-man shows: Piccadilly Gallery (1955), Leicester Galleries (1962, 1963, 1966, 1969), Ashmolean Museum (1981), Rockefeller Art Collection, New York (1986), Clarendon Gallery (1987, 1990), Cadogan Contemporary (1993). *Work in collections:* Government Art Collection, Atkinson A.G., Southport, Financial Times, Royal College of Music, Nottingham, Hertfordshire Educ. Authority, mural Barclays Bank, Guildford. *Signs work:* "T. F. Gibbs." *Address:* 55 Hardinge Rd., London NW10 3PN.

**GIBSON, Jean,** awarded minor travelling scholarship to Italy; sculptor in hardboard, fibreglass, resin, herculite; *b* Staffs., 17 Dec., 1935. *m* Anthony Whishaw. two *d. Educ:* Abbots, Bromley. *Studied:* Royal College of Art. *Exhib:* Leicester Gallery, London (1968, 1969), Oxford Gallery (1974), Metropole A.G. and Centre, Folkestone (1973), Nicola Jacobs Gallery, London (1981). *Work in collections:* U.S.A., London, Israel, private collections. *Signs work:* "J. Gibson." *Address:* 7a Albert Pl., Victoria Rd., London W8.

**GIBSON, Veronica,** B.A. (Hons.); painter in oil, private teacher; *b* St. Albans, Herts., 15 Apr., 1954. *Educ:* Loreto College. *Studied:* Hertfordshire College of Art (1972-73), Canterbury College of Art (1978-81, Thomas Watt, D.A. Edin.). *Exhib:* R.A., N.E.A.C., R.O.I., R.W.A., Cardiff. *Work in collections:* S. Glamorgan; private: France and Sweden. *Signs work:* see appendix. *Address:* Ty Coed, Chapel St., Bedlinog, Mid Glamorgan, CF46 6TS.

**GIFFARD, Colin Carmichael,** M.A. Cantab., Dip.Arch. London

(A.R.I.B.A. 1947-57), R.W.A.; R.I.B.A. Schools Drawing Prize (1932), Rome finalist (Arch.) 1939; painter in oil, acrylic; lecturer, Bath Academy of Art, Sydney Place (1951-68); *b* London, 1915. *Educ:* Charterhouse, Clare College, Cambridge; University College, London. *Studied:* painting: Bath Academy of Art (1948-51). *Exhib:* R.A., R.W.A., London Group, Bristol City A.G., Salon des Nations, Paris; one-man shows, Woodstock Gallery, London (3). *Commissions:* murals in schools for Herts., Wigan Educ. Coms. Work purchased: R.W.A., Newton Park Coll., Bath, Bristol, Walsall Educ. Coms. *Address:* Little Mead, Freshford, Bath BA3 6DH.

**GIFFORD, Denis,** strip cartoonist, author, editor, cartoon historian, lecturer, collector; *b* 26 Dec., 1927. *m* Angela Kalagias (divorced). one *d. Educ:* Dulwich College. *Exhib:* "Aaargh" (I.C.A.), International Comic Festival (Lucca), S.S.I., B.D. 86 (Sierre). *Publications:* British Comic Catalogue (Mansell), Happy Days - 100 Years of Comics (Jupiter), Victorian Comics (Allen & Unwin), Discovering Comics (Shire), Stap Me the British Newspaper Strip (Shire), Stewpot's Fun Book (ITV), Morecambe and Wise Comicbook (Carousel), Eric and Ernie's TV Funbook (ITV), Two Ronnies Comicbook (Carousel), Comics of World War One, Penny Comics of the Thirties, Great Cartoon Stars (Jupiter), Best of Eagle (Joseph), Quick On The Draw (ITV), British Comics Price Guide (Ace), International Book of Comics (Dean), Complete Catalogue of British Comics (Webb & Bower), British Animated Films (McFarland), Encyclopedia of Comic Characters (Longman). *Clubs:* Assoc. of Comics Enthusiasts (founder), Soc. of Strip Illustration (founder-mem.), Cartoonists. *Address:* 80 Silverdale, Sydenham, London SE26.

**GILBERT, Christopher G.,** M.A., F.S.A.; Formerly Director, Leeds City Art Galleries; President, Chippendale Soc.; Chairman, Furniture History Soc; Vice-President, Regional Furniture Soc.; *b* Lancaster, 1936. *m* Mary Catriona. two *d. Educ:* St. George's School, Harpenden; Keele University; University of Durham. *Publications:* Thomas Chippendale (1978), Catalogue of the Leeds Furniture Collection (1978), English Vernacular Furniture (1991), John Channon and Brass-inlaid Furniture (1993), Pictorial Dictionary of Marked London Furniture (1996); numerous exhbn. catalogues and articles on historic furniture. *Address:* 8 North Park Grove, Leeds LS8 1JJ.

**GILBERT, Dennis,** N.E.A.C.; portrait and landscape painter; formerly senior lecturer, Chelsea School of Art; *b* London, 7 Jan., 1922. three *s.* one *d. Educ:* Weston-super-Mare. *Studied:* St. Martin's School of Art (1946-51). *Exhib:* R.A., Paris Salon, R.P., R.B.A., N.E.A.C., Soc. of Landscape Painters, Browse & Darby, Leicester Galleries, Redfern, W.H. Patterson Fine Art, Thompsons Gallery, Duncan Miller and Zwemmer Galleries, etc.; one-man shows: F.B.A. Gallery (1968), Langton Gallery (1982), Gill Drey Gallery (1989). *Clubs:* Arts, Chelsea Arts. *Signs work:* "Dennis Gilbert." *Address:* Top Studio, 11 Edith Gr., Chelsea, London SW10 0JZ.

**GILBERT, George,** R.S.W. (1973), D.A. (Glasgow) 1961, Post. Dip.

(1962); artist in water-colour, acrylic, pen and wash; *b* Glasgow, 12 Sept., 1939. *m* Lesley. three *s. Educ:* Glasgow. *Studied:* Glasgow School of Art (1957-61): Guthrie Book Prize (portraiture). *Exhib:* one-man shows: Kelly Gallery, Glasgow (1967), Byre Theatre, St. Andrews (1979), Loomshop Gallery, Lower Largo (1981, 1988, 1990), Torrance Gallery, Edinburgh (1991); several joint shows in Glasgow and Edinburgh; regular exhibitor at R.S.A., R.S.W., etc., also Commonwealth Arts Festival, Bath Art Fair, Cleveland International Drawing. *Work in collections:* Nuffield Foundation, Fife Regional Council; many private home and abroad. *Signs work:* "George Gilbert." *Address:* 44 Marketgate South, Crail, Fife KY10 3TL.

**GILBERT, Stephen,** Diploma, Slade School (1935); sculptor and painter; *b* Fife, Scotland, 1910. *m* Jocelyn Chewett. one *s.* one *d. Educ:* University College School, University College, London. *Exhib:* Galerie Nova Spectra, The Hague (1984), Galerie 1900-2000, Paris (1987), Art Fair, Bâle (1987), Galerie Jean-Paul Villain, Paris (1987), Belgrave Gallery, London (1992). *Work in collections:* Tate Gallery, Stedelijk Museum, Arts Council, British Council, Leicester Museum, Leicester University, Sheffield Museum, Norwich Museum, Alborg Museum, British Steel Corp., G.L.C. *Signs work:* "Stephen Gilbert." *Address:* 7 Impasse du Rouet, Paris, 14e.

**GILDEA, Paul Rudolph,** B.A. Hons. Fine Art; artist in oil on canvas; part time tutor, Fulham and Chelsea A.E.I.; *b* London, 3 Jan., 1956. *Educ:* Dulwich College. *Studied:* Camberwell School of Arts and Crafts (1975-76), Middlesex Polytechnic (1976-79). *Exhib:* Serpentine Summer Show (1982), Whitechapel Open (1987), Riverside Open (1987), R.A. Summer Show (1987). *Signs work:* "Gildea." *Address:* 41 Ballater Rd., Brixton, London SW2 5QS.

**GILES, A. Frank Lynton,** Médaille d'Argent, Paris Salon (1948), A.R.W.A. (1970), R.W.A. (1978); artist in oil, acrylic, water-colour, pastel and graphics, etc.; Finalist Sunday Times water-colour competition (1990), Mem. Advertising Association, Royal Soc. of Arts; *b* London. three *s. Studied:* Goldsmiths', St. Martin's. *Exhib:* R.A., and most other societies including R.S.A., R.Cam.A. (Eminent Artists Eastbourne), Bradford, R.P., R.B.A., R.I., R.W.S., N.E.A.C., Alresford Gallery, Bertrand Russell Centenary, Arts Council, C.E.M.A., Worthing A.G. (1996), Sheffield Open, Chesterfield, R.W.A. Sunday Times tours, toured by R.A. with C.E.M.A. in 1944, and Arts Council in 1949. *Work in collections:* Sheffield, Bristol, Worthing, Canada and private collections. *Commissions:* Portraits *Publications:* R.A. Illustrated, R.W.A. 150th Anniversary Illustrated, Sussex Arts Publications. *Signs work:* "FRANK LYNTON GILES" or "Lynton Giles." *Address:* 19 Browning Rd., Worthing, W. Sussex BN11 4NS.

**GILES, Peter Donovan,** N.D.D. (Special level Illustration) 1959, A.T.C. (Lond.) 1960, F.R.G.S.; painter, illustrator and sculptor; counter-tenor; teaches part-time, Manwood Grammar School, Sandwich; *b* Perivale, Middx., 15 Feb., 1939. *m* Elizabeth Ann Broom. one *s.* one *d. Educ:* Castlehill College, Ealing.

*Studied:* Ealing School of Art (1954-59), Hornsey College of Art (1959-60). *Exhib:* All Hallows on the Wall, EC2; provincial one-man shows; lecture tours, U.S.A. and Canada (1973, 1975, 1978,1996). *Work in collections:* Lichfield City A.G., War Memorial Ely Cathedral. *Publications:* novels, non-fiction, cartoon collection, board games. *Signs work:* "Peter Giles." *Address:* Filmer House, Bridge, Canterbury, Kent CT4 5NB.

**GILES, Phyllis Margaret,** M.A. (Cantab., 1928), Founder Fellow of Lucy Cavendish College, Cambridge, University of London School of Librarianship Diploma (1930); Librarian of Fitzwilliam Museum, Cambridge (1947-74); Asst. University of London Library (1933-43); Asst. Librarian, Min. of Town and Country Planning (1943-47); *b* London, 20 Jan., 1907. *Educ:* Clapham High School and Girton College, Cambs. *Clubs:* Cambridge Drawing Society. *Address:* 25 Mill Ct., Wells on Sea, Norfolk NR23 1HF.

**GILI, Katherine,** B.A. (1970); sculptor in steel; *b* Oxford, 6 Apr.,1948. *m* Robert Persey. one *s.* *Studied:* Bath Academy of Art (1966-70), St Martin's School of Art (1971-73). *Exhib:* Tate Gallery, Hayward Gallery, Serpentine Gallery, R.A., Conde Duque Centre Madrid, Salander / O'Reilly, N.Y. *Work in collections:* Arts Council of England, and private collections in Britain, Spain and U.S.A.; Cranfield Inst., Cartwright Hall, General electric H.Q. U.S.A.,City of Lugano Switzerland, Dumfries and Galloway. *Publications:* numerous exhbn. catalogues, reviews, articles. *Signs work:* see appendix. *Address:* 7 The Mall, Faversham, Kent ME13 8JL.

**GILL, Stanley Herbert,** A.R.C.A., A.T.D.; art teacher (retd.), painter in oil, water-colour, lithographer; painting instructor, York and Dewsbury Schools of Art (1936-41); Head of Dept., School of Fine Art and Graphic Design, Salisbury College of Art (1947-72); *b* Leeds, 21 May, 1912. *m* Lavinia P. Leader. one *s.* *Educ:* City of Leeds School. *Studied:* Leeds College of Art (1928-31), R.C.A. (1931-35) under Gilbert Spencer, Sir William Rothenstein. *Exhib:* R.A., British Art Centre, Leeds, Yorkshire Artists, Bradford, York, Wakefield, Preston, Brighton, Southampton, Salisbury. *Work in collections:* Bethnal Green Museum of Childhood. *Signs work:* "S. H. Gill." *Address:* 1 Hadrian's Cl., Salisbury SP2 9NN.

**GILLESPIE, Michael Norman,** A.R.B.S.; sculptor in bronze; *m* Lesley Todd. two *s.* one *d.* *Educ:* St. Paul's School. *Studied:* Hammersmith College of Art (1952-56). *Exhib:* nineteen plus mixed shows. *Publications:* Studio Bronze Casting (Batsford, 1969). *Signs work:* "M.N. Gillespie." *Address:* 53 Cottenham Rd., Histon, Cambridge CB4 4ES.

**GILLEY, Leonard Christopher,** freelance artist in oil and water-colour; *b* Camberwell, 28 May, 1915. *m* Eleanor Betty Shadbolt. *Educ:* Strand School, Tulse Hill. *Studied:* Camberwell School of Art. *Publications:* work repro.: in magazines, Press, posters, etc., for national advertisers at home and overseas, also art galleries and private collections. *Signs work:* see appendix. *Address:* Springfield House, Trellech, Monmouth, Gwent NP5 4PF.

**GILLISON TODD, Margaret,** M.C.S.P., Dip.Ed.Lond.; painter and illustrator; Keeper of Display, Grosvenor Museum, Chester (1966-77); *b* Warwick, 1916. *m* Hugh Michael Todd. *Educ:* Howell's School, Denbigh. *Exhib:* R.Cam.A., N. Wales Group, S. Wales Group, S.E.A. Pictures for Schools, National Eisteddfod, Royal Horticultural Soc. (Silver Gilt and Silver Medals), Alpine Garden Soc. (Gold Medal), etc. *Publications:* illustrations for "The Flora of Flintshire" by Goronwy Wynne (1993); A Histology of the Body Tissues, illustrated (E. & S. Livingston, Edinburgh); Louise Rayner (Grosvenor Museum, Chester); work repro.: medical and botanical publications, etc. *Signs work:* "MARGARET GILLISON," "MARGARET GILLISON TODD," or initials. *Address:* Pen-y-Llwyn, Llanarmon-yn-lâl, Mold, Flintshire CH7 4QW.

**GILLMOR, Robert,** N.D.D. (1958), A.T.D. (1959); freelance illustrator, designer, painter in water-colour, black and white, lino-cut prints; Director Art and Craft, Leighton Park School (1959-65); President, S.WL.A.(1984-94), President, Reading Guild of Artists (1969-84); *b* Reading, 6 July, 1936. *m* Susan Norman, painter. one *s.* one *d. Educ:* Leighton Pk. School, Reading. *Studied:* School of Fine Art, Reading University (1954-59, Prof. J.A. Betts, William McCance, Frank Ormrod, Hugh Finney). *Exhib:* S.WL.A. *Work in collections:* Ulster Museum and A.G., Belfast, Reading Museum and A.G. *Publications:* 100 books illustrated. *Signs work:* "R.G." or "Robert Gillmor." *Address:* 58 Northcourt Ave., Reading, Berks. RG2 7HQ.

**GILLMORE, Olwen Nina,** S.W.A.; sculptor in clay and bronze; *b* Zimbabwe, 12 Mar., 1936. *m* Charles Gillmore. two *s.* three *d. Educ:* U.S.A. (1980-82), London Karin Jonzen (1983-90). *Exhib:* Chelsea; S.W.A. London; Chichester Cathedral. *Commissions:* Several (private). *Signs work:* "Olwen." *Address:* Sarnesfield, Lurgashall, Petworth, W. Sussex GU28 9EZ.

**GILMORE, Sidney,** sculptor in steel, wood, stone and glassfibre; *b* London, 3 June, 1923. *Educ:* Willesden Grammar School. *Studied:* Willesden College of Technology. *Exhib:* R.A., F.P.S., Chicago British Fortnight, U.S.A., Bradford A.G., Heals, London, City of Westminster, etc. *Clubs:* F.P.S. *Signs work:* "Sidney Gilmore." *Address:* 111 Sudbury Ave., N. Wembley, Middx. HA0 3AW.

**GILMOUR, Albert Edward,** artist in oil, pen and ink; sec., Gateshead Art Club (1950-51); retd. B.R. train driver; *b* W. Hartlepool, 31 May, 1923. *m* Elaine Bolton. one *s.* one *d. Educ:* Heworth and Felling Elementary Schools. *Studied:* courses at Gateshead Technical College, King's College, Newcastle. *Exhib:* Federation of Northern Arts Socs. Exhbns., Artists of the Northern Counties Exhbns., Artists of Durham Exhbn., Gateshead Art Club Exhbns. *Publications:* Locomotive Express, British Railways Magazine, N.E. Region. *Clubs:* Park Rd., and West End Group, Newcastle; Gateshead Art. *Signs work:* "GILMOUR." *Address:* 11 Limewood Grove, Woodlands Pk., North Gosforth, Newcastle upon Tyne NE13 6PU.

**GILMOUR, Pat,** B.A.(Hons.), Hon.R.E.; Visiting Prof., History of Graphic

Art, E. London University; Founding Curator of Prints, Tate Gallery (1974-77) and National Gallery of Australia, Canberra (1982-89); *b* Woodford, Essex, 19 Mar., 1932. *m* Alexander Gilmour. two *d*. *Educ:* Glasgow Art School, Sidney Webb College, London University. *Publications:* author: Modern Prints (1970); Tate: Henry Moore, Graphics in the Making (1975), Artists at Curwen (1977); A.C.G.B.: The Mechanised Image (1978); B.B.C.: Artists in Print (1981); N.G.A.: Ken Tyler Master Printer (1985) and Lasting Impressions: Lithography as Art (ed.) (1988); Hayward Gallery: Shiko Munakata (1991); Rigler-Deutsch Foundation in assn. University of Washington Press, The Prints of June Wayne: A Catalogue raisonné (1997). *Address:* 25 Christchurch Sq., London E9 7HU.

**GINESI, Edna,** A.R.C.A.; figure draughtsman and painter in oil; Mem. London Group, Mem. Chiswick Group; *b* Leeds, 15 Feb., 1902. *m* Raymond Coxon. *Educ:* privately. *Studied:* Leeds College of Art, R.C.A. *Exhib:* London and provinces, Canada and U.S.A. *Work in collections:* Tate Gallery (2); Nat. Gallery of Wales, Leeds, Wakefield, Bradford and Manchester City Art Galleries. *Signs work:* "E. Ginesi" or "E. GINESI." *Address:* Rowfant Mill Studio, Old Hollow, Pound Hill, Crawley, W. Sussex RH10 4TB.

**GINGER, Phyllis Ethel,** R.W.S. (1958); freelance illustrator and water-colour artist; *b* London, 19 Oct., 1907. *m* Leslie Durbin. one *s*. one *d*. *Educ:* Tiffin's Girls' School, Kingston-on-Thames. *Studied:* Richmond School of Art (1932-35), Central School of Arts and Crafts (1937-39) (John Farleigh, William Robins, Clark Hutton). *Work in collections:* water-colours, Pilgrim Trust Recording Britain Scheme; drawings and lithographs in Washington State Library, Victoria and Albert Museum, London Museum, South London Art Gallery. *Publications:* Alexander the Circus Pony (Puffin Book); London and The Virgin of Aldermanbury, by Mrs. Robert Henrey. *Signs work:* "Phyllis Ginger." *Address:* 298 Kew Rd., Kew, Richmond, Surrey TW9 3DU.

**GIRUIN, Joy,** B.A. Hons. Fine Art (1984), Post Grad. Dip. in Painting (1987), artist in oils and pastels; Art Tutor; *b* Herts, 15 Nov., 1961. *Educ:* University of Northumberland (1984), Royal Academy Schools of Art (1987). *Exhib:* regularly at Cadogan Contemporary Gallery, London. *Work in collections:* Barings Bank, National Trust Foundation for Art , Paintings in Hospitals, London Weekend T.V., Manchester City A.G., Exeter Museum and A.G. *Commissions:* Gardens, Italian landscape. *Clubs:* A.C.G and Sailing. *Signs work:* " Joy Giruin." *Address:* 133a Friern Park, London N12 9LR.

**GLANVILLE, Christopher,** R.W.A.; David Murray Landscape Scholarship (1968, 1970); landscape painter in oil on canvas, oil on panel; Vice-President R.W.A. (1992-97); *b* London, 10 Aug., 1948. *m* Zelda Glanville, potter. one *s*. *Educ:* St. Clement Danes Grammar School, London. *Studied:* Heatherly School of Art (1965), Byam Shaw School of Art (1967-70, B. Dunstan, M. de Sausmarez), R.A. Schools (1970-73, P. Greenham). *Exhib:* R.A., R.W.A., Bruton Gallery, Kaplan Gallery, Woburn Abbey, Sandford

Gallery, National Museum of Wales., N.E.A.C., Alresford Gallery, Sinfield Gallery. *Work in collections:* R.W.A., Richmond Museum. *Signs work:* "GLANVILLE." *Address:* 8 Mill St., Kingston-upon-Thames, Surrey KT1 2RF.

**GLASS, Margaret,** Mem. Pastel Soc., Associate Société des Artistes Français, Membre Société des Pastellistes de France, F.R.S.A.; landscape and marine artist in pastel and oil; *b* Chesham, Bucks., 1950. *Signs work:* "M.R.G." *Address:* 48 The St., Melton, Woodbridge, Suffolk IP12 1PL.

**GLAZEBROOK, Christina Fay,** S.G.F.A. (1987); artist in pastel, water-colour; teacher of art for Herts. C.C., and Watford Borough Council; *b* Watford, 1 Apr., 1934. *m* Charles Michael Glazebrook. two *s. Educ:* Watford Technical College of Art. *Studied:* Cassio College, Watford (1976) and St. Alban's College of Art (1981). *Exhib:* P.S. (1980-81), Liberty's (1982), S.G.A. (1985, 1987), Herts. in the Making (1986-87), Mall Galleries, Knapp Gallery, London, and many one-man shows. *Signs work:* "Fay Glazebrook." *Address:* 10 Monkshood Cl., Highcliffe, Christchurch, Dorset BH23 4TS.

**GOAMAN, Michael & Sylvia,** banknote and stamp designers; *b* East Grinstead, 14 Feb., 1921. *m* Sylvia Priestley, b London, 30 Apr., 1924. three *d. Studied:* (Michael) at Reading University (1938-39); (Sylvia) at Slade (1940-41); (Michael and Sylvia) at London Central School of Arts and Crafts (1946-48). *Exhib:* similarly. *Publications:* work repro.: U.K. and widely overseas. *Signs work:* see appendix. *Address:* 91 Park Rd., Chiswick, London W4 3ER.

**GOBLE, Anthony Barton,** painter in oil; Director, Oriel Llanover, National Eisteddfod prize winner (1974); Artist in Residence, Llanover Hall, Cardiff (1979); W.A.C. grants/burseries, including award to visit artists/galleries, U.S.S.R. (1982); Oppenheim/John Downes award (1984); national chairman, A.A.D.W. (1985); president, Artists Benevolent Soc. (1986-87); *b* Oct., 1943. *m* Janice Anne Morgan. two *s.* two *d. Educ:* St. Mary's College, Rhos-on-Sea, Wrexham School of Art. Numerous exhbns. and permanent collections. *Commissions:* Church in Wales/W.A.C. mosaic commission (1985); St. Saviours, Cardiff High Altar reredos painting commission (1988). *Clubs:* R.Cam.A., Welsh Group, Penwith Soc. *Signs work:* "Goble." *Address:* 10 Cyril Cres., Cardiff CF2 1DQ.

**GOELL, Abby,** B.A., M.F.A.; painter in oil, acrylic, lithograph, assemblage; Sen. Mem., Amer. Soc. of Appraisers; *b* U.S.A. one *s. Educ:* Syracuse Univ.; Columbia Univ. (M.F.A. 1965); Art Students' League, N.Y. (Life Mem.). *Exhib:* Childe Hassam Purchase Exhbn. N.Y.C. (1977), Amer. Acad. and Inst. of Arts and Letters (1977), U.S. Dept. of State, Havana (1979-82). *Work in collections:* M.O.M.A. (N.Y.), Yale Univ. A.G., Grafisches Kabinet, Munich, Chase Manhatten Bank, N.Y., Atlantic-Richfield Oil Co., Sloane-Kettering Memorial Center, N.Y., N.Y. Public Library Print Coll., Neuberger Mus., Purchase N.Y. Smith College, Founder/Publisher Arcadia Press, N.Y. *Publications:* editor, English Silver 1675-1825 (Eusko & Wenham, rev. ed.

1980). *Clubs:* Dutch Treat, N.Y. *Signs work:* "Goell" and date. *Address:* 37 Washington Square W, New York, N.Y. 10011, U.S.A.

**GOLDBACHER, Fiona C.,** water-colourist, sculptress in marble; *b* London, 1935. *m* Rodolfo Goldbacher. one *s.* one *d. Educ:* Iona College, N.Z. *Studied:* under Ruth Liezman. *Exhib:* Chiba Museum,Tokyo; Tanja Flandria, Morocco; Blackheath, Bow House, Heiffer, Thompsons, Gagliardi Galleries, London; Turtle Gallery, Sussex. *Work in collections:* Sanyu Art Japan, Blackheath, Gagliardi, Thompsons Galleries, London, John Noott, Broadway, Cotswolds, Turtle Gallery, Sussex. *Publications:* work repro.: various cards and prints. *Signs work:* "Fiona C. Goldbacher." *Address:* 14 Edmunds Walk, London N2 0HU; and 43 via Borgo 2, Strettoia (Lucca), Tuscany.

**GOLPHIN, Janet,** R.W.S. (1992), R.B.A. (1993); artist in water-colour, oils, mixed media; *b* Pontefract, 7 Nov., 1950. one *s. Exhib:* Bankside Gallery, London, Medici Soc., London, Thompsons Gallery, London, Mall Galleries, Richmond Hill Gallery, Richmond, Surrey, R.A. Summer Exhbn. *Work in collections:* H.M. The Queen, Provident Financial, Brodsnorth Hall, nr. Doncaster. *Clubs:* R.W.A., R.B.A., Manchester Academy of Fine Art, Leeds Fine Art. *Signs work:* "Janet Golphin." *Address:* 23 Carleton Cres., Pontefract, W. Yorkshire WF8 2QP.

**GOMBRICH, Sir Ernst Hans,** O.M.(1988), Kt. (1972), C.B.E. (1966), Ph.D. (Vienna, 1933), F.B.A. (1960), F.S.A. (1961), Hon. degrees: Belfast (1963), Leeds, St. Andrews (1965), Oxford (1969), Cambridge (1970), Manchester (1974), Chicago (1975), Harvard (1976), London (1976), Philadelphia (1977), Essex (1977), Brandeis (1981), R.C.A. (1984), New York U.N. (1986), Emory (1991); Director, Warburg Institute and Prof., History of the Classical Tradition in the University of London 1959-76; *b* Vienna, 30 Mar., 1909. *m* Ilse Heller. one *s. Educ:* Theresianum and University, Vienna. *Publications:* Caricature (with E. Kris, 1940); The Story of Art (1950); Art and Illusion (1959); Meditations on a Hobby Horse (1963); Norm and Form (1966); Aby Warburg (1970), Symbolic Images (1972); The Heritage of Apelles (1976); The Sense of Order (1979); Ideals and Idols (1979); The Image and The Eye (1982); Tributes (1984); New Light on Old Masters (1986); Reflections on the History of Art (ed. R. Woodfield, 1987); articles in learned journals. *Address:* 19 Briardale Gdns., London NW3 7PN.

**GOODCHILD, Francis Philip,** A.R.C.A. (Des.) (1926), F.S.A.E. (1946), Royal Exhibitioner (1923); Princ., Tiverton School of Art (1934-47), Princ., Newton Abbot College of Art (1947-64); artist in water-colour; *b* Leyton, 12 Mar., 1904. *m* Emily Grace Muton. one *d. Studied:* High Wycombe School of Art under W. J. Stamps, A.R.C.A. (1919-23) and at R.C.A. under Sir William Rothenstein, Profs. Tristram and Bell (1923-26). *Exhib:* R.W.A., Devon Art Soc.; R.C.A. Old Students Arts Council of Gt. Britain Touring Collection and privately. *Signs work:* "FRANCIS, PHILIP, GOODCHILD." *Address:* Spindlewood, Churston Cl., Galmpton, Brixham, S. Devon TQ5 0LP.

**GOODE, Mervyn,** landscape painter known for his oil paintings of the English countryside; *b* 1948. *Educ:* Gloucestershire College of Art. *Exhib:* has exhib. widely through the U.K. and also in the U.S.A.; one-man exhbns.: Highton Gallery, EC4 (1970), Alpine Gallery, W1 (1970, 1971), King St. Galleries, SW1 (1974), Furneaux Gallery, SW19 (1975), Southwell Brown Gallery (1976, 1984), Fraser Carver Gallery (1977), Reid Gallery (1978, 1981, 1983, 1985, 1987, 1989, 1991, 1993), Windsor and Eton Fine Arts (1978, 1980), Century Gallery (1982, 1984, 1985), David Messum (1982, 1993), Medici Gallery, W1 (1983, 1985, 1990), H.C. Dickins, W1 (1987, 1989), Arun Art Centre (1987), Bennet Galleries, U.S.A. (1988), Bourne Gallery (1992); mixed exhbns.: Medici Gallery, W1; H.C. Dickins, W1; Mall Galleries (R.O.I.); Royal Academy Business Art Galleries, W1; Southampton A.G.; Bruton Gallery, Somerset; Southwell Brown Gallery, Richmond; Edwin Pollard Gallery, SW19; Bourne Gallery, Reigate; David Curzon Gallery, Thames Ditton; Century Galleries - Hartley Wintney and Henley-on-Thames; Nevill Gallery, Canterbury; Omell Galleries - Windsor and Beaconsfield; Kingsmead Gallery, Bookham; Wykeham Gallery, Stockbridge; Peter Hedley Gallery, Wareham; River Gallery, Arundel; H.C. Dickins, Bloxham; David Messum., Beaconsfield; Burlington Paintings, W1; John Noott, Broadway, Worcs. *Publications:* work repro.: by the Medici Soc., Kingsmead Publications, Bucentaur Gallery and Southwell Brown Gallery; in numerous periodicals and books; on I.T.V. and B.B.C. TV, etc. *Signs work:* "Mervyn Goode." *Address:* Lane Copse, Hawkley Hurst, Hampshire.

**GOODWIN, Leslie Albert,** R.I., R.O.I., R.W.A.; artist in oil, water-colour, pastel, book illustrator; Chairman, Leicester Soc. Artists; *b* Leicester, 13 June, 1929. *m* Elizabeth Whelband. *Studied:* Leicester College of Art (1949-55). *Exhib:* R.A., R.W.A., R.I., P.S.; six one-man shows, Vaughan College, Leicester University; mixed shows, Leicester A.G. *Work in collections:* English Electric - Nuclear Power Division; Bristol Old Vic Co.; Leicester Royal Infirmary; various public collection. N.H.S. Founder 'Asterisk' Soc. of Artists; broadcaster/art critic for B.B.C. *Publications:* work repro.: The Artist, Artist and Illustrators. *Signs work:* see appendix. *Address:* The Studio, 28 Lubbesthorpe Rd., Braunstone, Leics. LE3 2XD.

**GOOSEN, Frederik Johannes,** V.B.K.H'sum (1981), R.S.M.A. (1990), E.K.C. (1992), K.V. Gooi & Vechtstreek (1993); artist in oil and water-colour; *b* Hilversum, 13 Dec., 1943. *m* M.R. Bekenkamp. two *s.* *Exhib:* one-man shows: Netherlands: Wassenaar, s'-Hertogenbosch, Enschede, Alkmaar, Nieuwkoop; Bale, Geneva, New York, Washington D.C., Mystic and Westport U.S.A., London, Edinburgh, Mönchengladbach. *Work in collections:* Mystic Seaport Museum, C.T., and several public bldgs. in Holland. *Signs work:* "F.J. Goosen." *Address:* Waterschapslaan 14, Blaricum, Netherlands.

**GORALSKI, Waldemar Maria,** sculptor in silver and amber, jewellery designer, architect; *b* Lwow, 2 Jan., 1942. *m* Agnieszka, M.Sc. *Studied:* Faculty of Architecture and Dept. of Sculpture and Painting, Gdansk Polytechnic (1962-68). Artistic acknowledgement, Fachhochschule Köln, Dept. of Art and Design (1981). *Work in collections:* Arts Gallery Centre, University of London; Polish Culture Inst., London; Sac Freres, London; Museum Zamkowe, Malbork; Galerie Walinska, Arnhem; Galerie Konstrast, Nijmegen; Kunst-Treff Galerie, Worpswede; Old Warsaw Galleries, Alexandria, Virginia; Aleksander Galleries, St. Petersburg, Florida; Amber Gallery, Skodsborg, Copenhagen. *Signs work:* "W. Goralski" or "W.G." *Address:* Einigkeitstr. 34, D-45133 Essen.

**GORDON-LEE, Michael,** A.L.I. (1977); landscape architect and garden designer, works in pastel, pencil, oil, water-colour, and sculpts in wood; Environmental Action Manager, Cheshire C.C.; *b* Harrow, 1943. one *s.* one *d. Educ:* Whitehawk Boys School. *Studied:* Hammersmith College of Art and Building. *Exhib:* Manchester Academy, Pastel Soc. (Mall Galleries), R.W.A., Theatre Clwyd, Mold, Cheshire Artists, Finalist Look North TV painting competition (1984), Merseyside Artists. Work in public and private collections. *Clubs:* Grosvenor Art Soc. *Signs work:* "GORDON-LEE." *Address:* 2 Orchard Cottages, Eaton Rd., Tarporley, Cheshire CW6 0BP.

**GOURDIE, Thomas,** M.B.E., D.A.(Edin.); Soc. of Scribes and Illuminators; calligrapher and handwriting consultant; *b* Cowdenbeath, 18 May, 1913. *m* Lilias Taylor. one *s.* two *d. Studied:* Edinburgh College of Art. *Work in collections:* Imperial War Museum; Kirkaldy A.G. *Publications:* Puffin Book of Handwriting (Penguin Books); Handwriting For Today, Improve Your Handwriting and Calligraphy for the Beginner (A. & C. Black); Handwriting Made Easy (Taplinger, U.S.A.); Mastering Calligraphy (Pitman, Australia); Mastering Calligraphy (Search Press); The Simple Modern Hand (Blackie and Son); The Sonnets of Shakespeare (Cassell). *Address:* 3 Douglas St., Kirkcaldy, Scotland.

**GOW, Neil,** sculptor in wood; *b* Greenford, Middx., 22 Mar., 1940. *m* Jean Evans. one *s.* one *d. Educ:* Fitzgeorge, Malden, Kingston Technical College. *Exhib:* R.W.A., S.W.A., Amnesty International Sculptures (Bristol and London), Henry Brett Gallery, 5D Gallery, Kennys Galway, etc. *Clubs:* Glos. Soc. of Artists, Marlborough Artists. *Signs work:* see appendix. *Address:* Brownshill Cottage, Brownshill, Stroud, Glos. GL6 8AG.

**GRAA JENSEN, Lisa,** B.A. (Hons.) (1978), R.I. (1996), A.O.I. (1994); illustrator and painter in water-colour, pen and ink; *b* Copenhagen, Denmark, 2 Mar., 1953. *m* J.A. Hendrich, M.A. one *s.* one *d. sSudied:* Sir John Cass School of Art, (1974-75), Camberwell School of Art (1975-78, John Lawrence). *Exhib:* R.I., Mall Galleries mixed shows, C.C.A. Galleries, numerous exhbns. in South East, work available at Forest Gallery, Guildford. *Commissions:* Fine Art prints for Rosenstiels and C.C.A Galleries, cards for Royle, Paperhouse, Kingsmead, Royal Academy Enterprises. *Publications:* work repro.: Kestrel Books, Hamlyn, BBC Publications, Radio Times, Heinemann Macmillan. *Signs work:*

'Lisa Graa Jensen." *Address:* 45 Wodeland Ave., Guildford, Surrey GU2 5JZ.

**GRAHAM, David,** R.P., A.R.C.A.; painter in oil; *b* Hammersmith, 20 May, 926. *Educ:* Latymer Foundation School. *Studied:* Hammersmith School of \rt, St. Martin's School of Art, and Royal College of Art. *Exhib:* R.A., R.P., \rts Council, Leicester Galleries, Browse and Darby, Bruton St. A.G., Damkar 3urton, Ontario, Brighton A.G. Herbert A.G., and Museum, Coventry (retro-pective, 1987), etc. *Work in collections:* Guildhall A.G., I.L.E.A., Coca Cola .td., London Museum, Contemporary Art Soc., I.B.M., Belgrave House Art Coll., and private collections. *Publications:* Video, "A Painters View", 3uildhall University. *Clubs:* Chelsea Arts. *Signs work:* "David Graham." \ddress: 2 Curran Studios, Lucan Pl., London SW3.

**GRAHAM, Halina (Lady Graham),** B.A., M.A., B.Ed., F.S.A.; curator, Cecil Higgins Art Gallery, Bedford, since 1971; *m* Sir James Graham, Bt. Responsible for building of new wing (opened 1976), setting up of Victorian Mansion (1978 and 1984) and major purchases at dispersal of Handley-Read ollection (1972), and subsequently. *Publications:* Cecil Higgins, Collector Extraordinary; Guide to the Cecil Higgins Art Gallery (with husband), articles n Burlington Magazine, Apollo, Arts Review, Antique Collector, reviews and ·roadcast talks. *Address:* Cecil Higgins Art Gallery, Castle Cl., Bedford MK40 ·NY; Norton Conyers, nr. Ripon, N. Yorks. HG4 5EH.

**GRAHAM, Peter,** B.A. (1980); artist in oil; *b* Glasgow, 17 Feb., 1959. *Educ:* St. Aloysius College, Glasgow. *Studied:* Glasgow School of Art (1976-·0, John Cunningham, Barbara Rae). *Exhib:* Bourne Gallery Reigate, Catto 3allery London, many mixed shows including R.S.A., R.O.I. and R.S.M.A. *Work in collections:* British Council, Nan Yang Academy, Singapore, Lord Morton of Shuna, Lord Max Rayne, Lady Graham, Edinburgh, Lady Nairn, ·erth. *Commissions:* Western Baths Club, Glasgow *Publications:* work repro.: ·ine Art Prints, Modern Art Edition's New York. *Signs work:* "Peter Graham" ·r "Graham." *Address:* 57 Kirklee Rd., Glasgow G12 0SS, Scotland.

**GRANGER, Margaret I.,** S.B.A.; artist in water-colour, and embroidery ombined with water-colour; Counsellor in medical centre; *b* London, 21 Feb., ·939. *m* David Granger. one *s.* two *d. Educ:* Stoneleigh East School, Surrey. *Studied:* City & Guilds, embroidery and design at Surbiton College of Adult Educ. (1976); art at Epsom Adult Educ. College (1982). *Exhib:* Medici Gallery, Mall Galleries, Westminster Gallery, Old Chapel Gallery, Pembridge, Herefordshire, Hampton Court Flower Show, Outwood Gallery, Surrey, Epsom ·layhouse, Liberty's London. *Work in collections:* U.K., America, Australia, apan. *Publications:* work repro.: greetings cards and calendar for Medici Soc. *Signs work:* see appendix. *Address:* Holmbush House, 64 High St., Findon, W. 3ussex BN14 0SY.

**GRANGER-TAYLOR, Nicolas,** artist in oil; *b* London, 18 June, 1963. *Educ:* Latymer Upper School, Hammersmith. *Studied:* Kingston Polytechnic 1981-82), Bristol Polytechnic (1982-85), R.A. Schools (1987-90). *Exhib:*

Royal Festival Hall (1986, 1987, 1988), N.P.G. (1987, 1990), R.A. Summe Exhbn. (1987, 1989, 1992), Cadogan Contemporary (1989, 1990); one-mar shows Cadogan Contemporary (1988), Waterman Fine Art (1991, 1993). *Sign work:* "N. Granger-Taylor" or "N.G.T." *Address:* c/o Waterman Fine Art Ltd. 74a Jermyn St., London SW1Y 6NP.

**GRANT, Keith Frederick,** A.R.C.A.; landscape and portrait painter; *i* Liverpool, 10 Aug., 1930. one *s.* one *d. Educ:* Bootle Grammar School, Lancs *Studied:* Willesden School of Art, Royal College of Art. *Work in collections* Mural/mosaics, Charing Cross Hospital, London (1979), Gateshead Metro Station (1981/83), Beaverbrook Foundation, Peter Stuyvesant Coll., Art Council of G.B., Contemporary Art Soc., V. & A., Fitzwilliam Museum Cambridge, Manchester City A.G., National Gallery of N.Z. and other publi and private collections at home and abroad. Agents: Crane Kalman Gallery Cassian de Vere-Cole Fine Art, and Cadagon Contemporary Gallery. *Sign. work:* "Keith Grant" or "K. F. Grant." *Address:* Årnes Brygge, 3810 Guarv Norway.

**GRANT, Marianne,** N.S. (1977), F.R.S.A. (1975); painter in oil; *b* St Gallen, Switzerland, 1931, married. one *s.* one *d. Educ:* High School, Zürich *Studied:* Art Colleges in Zürich and Geneva. *Exhib:* one-man shows B. H Corner Gallery, Cooling Gallery, Century Galleries, Henley-on-Thames, Eas London Gallery, El Greco Gallery, Royal Northern College of Music Debenhams of Romford. *Work in collections:* Ernst Waespe (Zürich), Standar Telephone and Cables Ltd., Arts Centre Hornchurch. *Publications:* worl repro.: Fine Art Prints for 'Prints for Pleasure' and Peinture. *Clubs:* N.S., Esse Art. *Signs work:* "Marianne Grant." *Address:* Erlenwiesenstrasse 18, 815: Glattbrugg (Zürich), Switzerland.

**GRANVILLE,** artist in acrylic; *b* Liverpool, 12 July, 1945. *Studied* Norwich College of Art (1961-65), Southport College of Art (1980-82). *Exhib* Over fifty exhbns. in England and Spain since 1967. *Work in collections* Museo de la Real Academia de Bellas artes de San Fernando, Madrid *Publications:* work repro.: various exhbn. catalogues, articles and reviews Work inspired by Spain and all things Spanish. *Signs work:* see appendix *Address:* 14b Derwent Ct., Troutbeck Rd., Liverpool L18 3LF.

**GRAVETT, Guy Patrick,** photographer and painter; *b* Wye, Kent, 2 Nov. 1919. *Educ:* Lewes County Grammar School. *Studied:* Brighton College of Ar (1937-39) under Sallis Benney, Laurence Preston and Walter Bayes. *Exhib* various. *Clubs:* Royal Ocean Racing. *Signs work:* "Gravett" or "Guy Gravett" followed by year. *Address:* Hope Lodge, 41 Hassocks Rd., Hurstpierpoin Sussex BN6 9QL.

**GRAY, Elizabeth,** L.R.A.M.; self taught painter in water-colour; *i* Scarborough, Yorks, 1928. *m* Dr. David Trapnell. two *s. Educ:* Quee Margaret's School, Yorks. *Exhib:* one-man shows, Tryon Gallery, London Sportsmans Edge Gallery, N.Y.; Old Amersham, Bourton-on-the-Water, etc *'ork in collections:* Nature in Art, Gloucester; The Bank of England; Leigh awkey Woodson Art Museum, Wausau, Wisconsin, U.S.A. *Commissions:* 'ature in Art, Gloucester. *Publications:* The Wild and the Tame by H. Beamish 1957). *Signs work:* "Elizabeth Gray." *Address:* Dumbles Cottage, Awre, ewnham GL14 1EP.

**GRAY, Jane Campbell,** A.R.C.A., F.M.G.P.; stained glass artist; iveryman, Worshipful Company of Glaziers (1983); *b* Lincoln, 1931. *m* Kiril 'ray. two *d. Studied:* Kingston School of Art (1949-52); Royal College of Art 1952-55) under Lawrence Lee and assisted him with Coventry Cathedral nave indows (1955-58). Examples of work: Uxbridge - St. Margaret's; Civic 'entre entrance screen and Alphabet of Flowers in Marriage Room; Hillingdon lospital Chapel (26 panels); St. Peter's, Martindale, Cumbria (15 windows); itminster, Somerset (East window, 1989); Shrewsbury Abbey (1992); .pothecaries' Hall; Glaziers Hall, London Bridge. Over 150 lights in 58 hurches; coats-of-arms, domestic windows. *Signs work:* "Jane Gray," and see ppendix. *Address:* Ferry Cottage, Shrawardine, Shrewsbury SY4 1AJ.

**GRAY, Stuart Ian,** lithographer, painter in water-colour; water-colour offi- er, N.S.; *b* 19 Apr., 1925. *Educ:* Streatham Grammar School. *Exhib:* .S.M.A., R.I., Mall Galleries, Guildhall. *Publications:* work repro.: British 1arine Painting by Denys Brook-Hart. *Signs work:* "Stuart Gray." *Address:* )sborne Cottage, York Ave., E. Cowes, I.O.W. PO32 6BD.

**GREAVES, Derrick,** A.R.C.A. (1952): painter and printmaker; *b* Sheffield, June, 1927. *m* Mary Margaret (divorced 1991); two *s.* two *d.*; *m* Sally Butler 994. *Studied:* R.C.A. (Carel Weight, John Minton) and in Italy. *Exhib:* :ontemporary Art Soc., Venice Biennale, Pushkin Museum Moscow, John 1oores, Carnegie International Pittsburgh, R.A., Mall Galleries; one-man hows: Beaux Arts, Zwemmer, Inst. of Contemporary Arts, Bear Lane Oxford, ielfast and Dublin, Whitechapel Gallery, Cranfield Inst. of Technology, 1onika Kinley, City Gallery Milton Keynes, Hart Gallery London, Galerie )aniel Wahrenberger, Zurich. *Work in collections:* A.C.G.B.; Bank of Ireland, )ublin; N.Y. Public Library; Leeds, Reading, Sheffield, Southampton and Valker A.Gs.; Wesleyan University, Chicago; Tate Gallery; British Museum, tc. *Publications:* folios and books: Also (with Roy Fisher) 1971; Songs of iilitis (1977); Sanscrit Love Poems (1987). *Signs work:* "Derrick Greaves." .ddress: The School, Weston Longville, nr. Norwich, Norfolk NR9 5JU.

**GREAVES, Jack,** A.R.C.A., R.W.A., Rome Scholar; sculptor in bronze, ainter in pastel, oil; Visiting Prof. O.S.U.; *b* Leeds, 24 Sept., 1928. *m* Mildred 'lace. four *s. Studied:* Leeds College of Art, R.C.A. *Exhib:* Zwemmer, R.A., ).S.U. Gallery, Bruton Gallery, Vorpal, N.Y. and Francisco, Gallery 200, :olumbus, Ohio. *Work in collections:* Naiad Fountain, Capital Sq., Columbus, )hio; The Guardian, Police Memorial Gdn., Toledo; Christ Teaching, Cols., )hio; Family Planning Bldg., Tucson, Arizona; Coventry A.G.; Bristol A.G.; Irts Council; R.W.A.; National Revenue Corp., U.S.A.; Columbus Museum,

State Saving, U.S.A.; Sirak Collection, U.S.A. *Signs work:* "Greaves. *Address:* The Long House, Snainton, Scarborough, N.Yorks. YO13 9AP.

**GREEN, Alan,** A.R.C.A.; painter; *b* London, 22 Dec., 1932. *m* June Green two *d*. *Studied:* Royal College of Art (1955-58). *Exhib:* Documenta VI Kasse (1977), 'British Art Now' Guggenheim Museum, N.Y. (1979), 'Britis Contemporary Art' Japan (1982). *Work in collections:* includes Arts Council o Gt. Britain; British Council; Guggenheim Museum, N.Y.; McCrory Corp N.Y.; Tate Gallery, London; Kunstmuseum Hannover; National Museum o Art, Osaka, Japan; Power Gallery, Sydney, Australia; Kunsthalle Bielefeld Musee d'Ixelles, Brussels. Agents: Annely Juda Fine Art London. *Address:* c/ Annely Juda Fine Art, 23 Dering St., London W1R 9AA.

**GREEN, Alfred Rozelaar,** R.W.A. (1994); Mem. Paris Salon Comparaisons Nationale Beaux Arts; painter in oil, pastel, charcoal; *b* London 14 July, 1917. *m* Betty Marcus. three *s*. *Educ:* Uppingham, Cambridge (tw years engineering). *Studied:* Central School of Arts and Crafts (1937 Meninsky, Roberts); Academie Julian, Paris; Atelier Marcel Gromaire (1938 39). *Exhib:* London, Whibleys, Paris, Brussels, The Hague, Bale, Lyon Marseille, New York, Strasbourg, Cannes. *Work in collections:* Musee d'A Moderne, Paris, Strasbourg, Prefecture Vaucluse, Musee d'Orange *Publications:* 40 years of Painting (Ed. Dragger, 1988). Founded and directe Anglo-French Art Centre, St. John's Wood, London. In 1946 combined a school and 'Académie Libre' with gallery showing works of artists from Pari (André Lhote, Lurcat, Germaine Richier, Saint-Saens, Couturier, Domginuez etc.) who taught and lectured during their exhbns. Centre closed 1951. *Sign work:* "A. Rozelaar Green." *Address:* 11 Rue de Savies, 75020 Paris.

**GREEN, Anthony,** R.A. (1977), Dip.F.A. Slade (1960), Harkness Fello (1967-69); elected Fellow of University College, London (1991); painter in oi *b* London, 30 Sept., 1939. *m* Mary Cozens-Walker. two *d*. *Educ:* Highgat School, N.6. *Studied:* Slade School of Fine Art. *Exhib:* over fifty one-ma shows worldwide since 1962. *Work in collections:* Tate Gallery, Arts Council museums and art galleries in U.S.A., Japan, Brazil, etc. *Publications:* A Gree Part of the World (Thames and Hudson). *Signs work:* "Anthony Green," "A Green," "Anthony," "A.G." or not at all. *Address:* 40 High St., Little Eversden Cambs. CB3 7HE.

**GREEN, David John,** R.O.I., N.S.; landscape painter in water-colour an oil; *b* London, 23 Feb., 1935. *m* Eileen Ann. two *s*. *Educ:* Goldington Rd Secondary Modern, Bedford. *Exhib:* R.I., R.B.A., R.O.I.; one-man shows London, Cambridge, Bedford. *Work in collections:* Luton Museum, Bosto English Gallery. *Signs work:* "DAVID GREEN." *Address:* The Wilde Gallery, Wilden, Beds. MK44 2QH.

**GREEN, Richard,** Dip.A.D. (1968), M.A. (1970), F.R.S.A. (1988); Curator York City Art Gallery (since 1977); previously Keeper of Fine Art, Laing Ar Gallery, Newcastle upon Tyne (1971-77); *b* 12 Oct., 1946. *Educ:* Palmer' chool, Grays. *Studied:* S.W. Essex Technical College and School of Art; Bath Academy of Art; Goldsmiths' College School of Art (1964-68) studied history f art at University of London, Courtauld Inst. of Art (1968-70). *Publications:* umerous exhbn. catalogues, articles and reviews. *Address:* c/o York City Art Gallery, Exhibition Sq., York YO1 2EW.

**GREENBURY, Judith Pamela,** R.W.A. (1979); painter in oil, water-olour; *b* Bristol, 17 Feb., 1924. *m* C. L. Greenbury, M.D. three *s. Educ:* Badminton School, Westbury-on-Trym, Bristol. *Studied:* West of England College of Art (1943-46) under George Sweet, Slade School (1946-47) under Prof. Schwabe. *Exhib:* R.A., R.W.A., R.S.P.P., N.E.A.C., Bear Lane Gallery, Oxford, Mall Galleries, London. *Work in collections:* R.W.A. *Publications:* Spey Portrait: A Memoir of Fishing and Painting on the Spey 1974-1989." *Signs work:* "J.G." *Address:* Clarence House, 11 New St., Henley-on-Thames, Oxon. RG9 2BP.

**GREENHALF, Bette,** B.Sc. (Econ.) Hons. Lond.; Advanced Printmaking Central St. Martin's; Current B.A. Hons. Fine Art; M.A. Multimedia (comput-r); contemporary artist, writer; *b* London, 28 Dec., 1932. *m* Tom Greenhalf decd.). *Studied:* Camden Inst. and Central/St. Martin's, London. *Exhib:* R.A., Festival Hall, Mall Galleries, Camden Art Centre, Chaucer Festival, Barbican, Artists for Nuclear Disarmament. *Work in collections:* Nelson Mandela, the Prime Minister, Chaucer Heritage Trust, War Child Bosnia. *Publications:* Who's Who in International Art, British Contemporary Art (1993); artist's books: Venice Biennale 1895-1995 (a socio-political history); Etchings & poems: World War I, Tiananmen Square, Chaucer, Hampstead. *Signs work:* "Bette Greenhalf." *Address:* 91 Greenhill, Hampstead High St., London NW3 5TY.

**GREENHALF, Robert Ralph,** R.B.A. (1982), S.WL.A. (1981), Dip. A.D.(Graphics)(1971); artist in etching and water-colour; *b* Haywards Heath, 28 June, 1950. *m* Sally Grace. one *s. Educ:* Haywards Heath Secondary Modern School. *Studied:* Eastbourne School of Art (1966-68), Maidstone College of Art (1968-71). *Exhib:* R.A., R.B.A., S.WL.A., many mixed exhbns. and one-man shows London, England and Wales, Switzerland, Holland and U.S.A. *Work in collections:* South East Arts, Hastings Museum. *Publications:* Towards The Sea" (Arlequin Press, 1997). *Signs work:* "Robert R. Greenhalf." *Address:* Romney House, Saltbarn La., Playden, Rye, E. Sussex TN31 7PH.

**GREENMAN, Edwin,** A.R.C.A., R.P., F.R.S.A.; artist in oils; head of dept., drawing, painting and design, Guildford School of Art; head of Sir John Cass School of Art, London; elected to Royal Society of Portrait Painters (1968), Hon. sec. (1984-85), Hon. treasurer (1985-89); *b* Beckenham, Kent. *m* Freda Johns. one *s. Studied:* Beckenham School of Art (1926-29) under Henry Carr, R.A.; R.C.A. (1929-33) under Rothenstein, Spencer, Tristram and Malcolm Osbourne. *Exhib:* engravings at World's Fair, New York (1938), and at Prague; paintings at R.A. *Work in collections:* V. & A.; Contemporary Art Fund;

Travelling Art Exhbns., Bureau Collections. *Commissions:* Portrait commis
sions include Windsor Herald, Moderator of Church of Scotland, Lord
Northbrook, Dame Sheila Quinn, Sir Lynton White, Sir John Harvey Jones
Mrs André Previn. *Clubs:* Chelsea Arts. *Signs work:* "Greenman." *Address:*
Griffin Ct., Griffin Way, Great Bookham, Surrey KT23 4JQ.

**GREENSMITH, John Hiram,** N.D.D. (1955), A.T.D. (1956), A.R.W.S
(1976), N.E.A.C. (1978), R.W.S. (1983), A.R.Cam.A. (1986); painter in water
colour; former Head of Fine Art, All Saints School, Sheffield; *b* Sheffield, 2:
Apr., 1932. one *s.* one *d. Educ:* De la Salle College, Sheffield. *Studied*
Sheffield College of Art. *Exhib:* R.A., R.W.S., R.B.A., R.C.A., N.E.A.C.
M.A.F.A. *Signs work:* "John Greensmith." *Address:* 77 Whirlowdale Cres.
Sheffield S7 2ND.

**GREENWOOD, Eileen Constance,** A.R.C.A. (Design) 1935-38 F.B.I
award, Pedagogic Dip. (1939), R.E. (1938); artist, printmaker: etching/aquatint
draughtswoman: mixed media; Lecturer/Founder Principal, Sittingbourne
College of Educ. (retd.); *b* Middx., 26 May, 1915. *m* Ernest Greenwood
A.R.C.A., P.P.R.W.S. one *d. Educ:* Camden School for Girls, Frances Mary
Buss Foundation. *Studied:* R.C.A., Courtauld Inst., Goldsmiths' College
*Exhib:* R.A., Bankside, many London and provincial galleries; four solo shows
*Work in collections:* G.B., France, Germany, Japan, America, Australia. *Sign.*
*work:* "Eileen Greenwood" (all prints with 'cat' logo in margin). *Address*
Brushings Farm House, Broad St., nr. Hollingbourne, Kent ME17 1RB.

**GREENWOOD, Ernest,** P.P.R.W.S. (1976), A.R.C.A. (1931-35), F.R.S.A.
artist in oil and water-colour; Inspector of Art Educ. for K.E.C.; guest lecture:
for W.F. & R.K. Swan (Hellenic) Ltd.; since 1977 on "Art Appreciation", "The
Art and Architecture of Roman and Romanesque France"; *b* Welling, Kent, 1:
Feb., 1913. *m* Eileen C. Greenwood. one *d. Educ:* Gravesend Grammar School
*Exhib:* R.A., N.E.A.C., R.I., R.B.A., etc.; lectures and exhbns. given annually
since 1985 in U.S.A. Exhbns. with wife at Tubac Arts Centre, Arizona, by invitation of the Director; one-man show at Bankside Gallery, London (Sept.
1991). *Work in collections:* Preston, Southend, Tate Gallery, Middlesbrough
A.G., Lannards Gallery Billingshurst, Wenlock Fine Art; private collections
U.S.A., Municipal Galleries of Brighton, Hastings, Hull; "Holcaust" painting
now in Ben-Uri collection, London. *Commissions:* Decorations for Judges
chambers, Canterbury Crown Court. Guest at the feast of St. Catherine, St
Catherine's College, Oxford. *Signs work:* "Ernest Greenwood." *Address.*
Brushings Farm House, Broad St., nr. Hollingbourne, Kent ME17 1RB.

**GREENWOOD, Maurice Arthur,** R.C.A. (1996), Associats (1988); artist
in water-colour and oil; art tutor; part-time lecturer, Llandrillo Technical
College: Extra Mural Dept., University College, N. Wales since 1982; *t*
Rochdale, 12 Dec., 1930. *m* Joan. two *s. Studied:* part-time Rochdale Art
School (1946-48) ( Peter Burgess Shorrock, 1960-65). *Exhib:* R.Cam.A., and
many open and one-man shows. *Work in collections:* Gwynedd Library

Services; private collections in U.S.A., British Columbia, Australia, U.K. *Signs work:* "Maurice A. Greenwood, R.C.A." *Address:* Woodlands, 12 Shaftesbury Ave., Penrhyn Bay, Llandudno, N. Wales LL30 3EH.

**GREENWOOD, Philip John,** N.D.D. (1965), A.T.C. (1966), R.E. (1982); printmaker in etching and painter; *b* Dolgellau, N. Wales, 20 Nov., 1943. *m* Valery Ratcliff (decd.). four *s. Educ:* Dolgellau Grammar School. *Studied:* Harrow College of Art (1961-65), Hornsey Teachers Training College (1965-66). *Exhib:* R.A., R.E., Tate Gallery, R.G.I., 'Printmaking in Britain', Sydney; British Council Gallery, Athens; British Printmakers, Melbourne; Galerie Tendenz, Germany; J. One Fine Arts, Tokyo; Galerie Deux Tetes, Canada; 'Overseas Printmakers', Auckland, N.Z., Galerie Beumont, Brussels. *Work in collections:* Tate Gallery, Arts Council, British Council, Derby Museum, Greenwich Museum, Oldham A.G., Graves A.G., Warwick Museum and A.G., Lincoln A.G. and Museum, etc. *Clubs:* Arts. *Signs work:* "Greenwood." *Address:* 30 Leigh Hill Rd., Cobham, Surrey KT11 2HX.

**GREENWOOD, Sydney,** A.T.D., R.I., R.W.A., F.R.S.A.; work in lithography, etching, water-colour, oil; formerly Lecturer in Painting, Manchester College of Art, and Head of Fine Art and Design, and Vice Principal, Southampton College of Art; *b* Stalybridge, Ches., 11 Jan., 1913. *Studied:* under C. Hanney, later at Goldsmiths' College, London University and Croydon School of Art, and in France. *Exhib:* R.A., West of England Academy, Mall Galleries, Bruton St. Gallery, London, Arlesford Gallery, Winchester, Ben Uri Gallery, London, European Fed. of Artists, Brussels, Kronberg. Represented in private and public collections in G.B. and U.S.A. etc. *Signs work:* "Sydney Greenwood." *Address:* 9 Bingham Drive, Lymington, Hants. SO41 3PR.

**GREIG, Donald,** R.S.M.A. (1967), Gold Medal Paris Salon (1967); painter in water-colour and oil, printmaker; *b* London, 1916. *m* Rita Greig, R.W.A., R.O.I., N.E.A.C. one *s. Studied:* Southend College of Art (Charles Taylor, R.W.S). *Exhib:* R.A., R.W.A., R.B.A., N.E.A.C., R.I., R.S.M.A., and various one-man shows. *Work in collections:* National Maritime Museum, Greenwich, Municipal Gallery, Scunthorpe. *Signs work:* "DONALD GREIG." *Address:* Tor Brook Studio, Woodleigh, Kingsbridge, S. Devon TQ7 4DF.

**GREIG, Rita,** R.W.A. (1983), R.O.I. (1974), N.E.A.C. (1974), Silver Medal Paris Salon (1974); painter principally in oil, also water-colour and pastel, printmaker; *b* Norwich. *m* Donald Greig, R.S.M.A. one *s. Educ:* Selhurst Grammar School, Ware Grammar School. *Studied:* privately. *Exhib:* R.A., R.W.A., R.O.I., N.E.A.C., R.B.A., various one-man shows in Britain and abroad, also shared shows with husband, Donald Greig. *Work in collections:* Royal West of England Academy, Chase Manhattan Bank Collection, Bishop Otter College. *Signs work:* "R.G." *Address:* Tor Brook Studio, Woodleigh, Kingsbridge, S. Devon TQ7 4DF.

**GRESTY, Kenneth H.,** F.R.S.A. (1971), F.I.A.L. (1966), A.T.D. (1951), D.A., Manc. (1950), N.D.D., painting (1950); Head of Faculty, North Bolton

Sixth Form College; Mem. Manchester Academy (1954); *b* Manchester, 17 May, 1928. *m* Marjorie Ingred Smith. four *s. Educ:* Sale Grammar School. *Studied:* Manchester Regional College of Art under H. Williamson, R.W.A. (1944-46, 1948-51). *Exhib:* R.A., Manchester Academy of Fine Arts. *Work in collections:* Rutherston Collection. *Publications:* work repro.: in Cheshire Life, Lancashire Life, and local press. *Signs work:* "K. H. Gresty." *Address:* 5 Ivy Terr., Borth-Y-Gest, Porthmadog, Gwynedd LL49 9TS.

**GREY, Jenni,** B.A. (Hons.), M.A., Fellow, Designer Bookbinders; fine binder and book artist; part-time tutor, University of Brighton; *b* London, 3 July, 1950. *Educ:* Bexley Grammar School. *Studied:* Brighton Polytechnic. *Exhib:* regularly since 1982 in England, Europe and America. *Work in collections:* National Poetry Library (England), Koninklijke Bibliotheek (Holland), University of Georgia and Wellesley College (U.S.A.), Les Amis de la Reliure d'Art (France), Biblioteca Wittockiana (Belgium). *Address:* 26 Stafford Rd., Brighton BN1 5PF.

**GRIBBIN, Lancelot Benedict,** A.T.D. (1949); B.A. (Hons.) Hist. of Art (1953); painter in oil, photographer; lecturer, Victoria and Albert Museum; former principal lecturer, London College of Printing; visiting lecturer, Messrs. Sotheby's Educational Studies; International freelance lecturer in History of Architecture and Decorative Arts; *b* Gateshead-on-Tyne, 7 Nov., 1927. *m* Joanna Mary Satchell. two *s.* two *d. Educ:* Dartford Grammar School. *Studied:* Sidcup School of Art under Ruskin Spear, A.R.A., Robin Guthrie, William Clause; Courtauld Inst. of Art. *Exhib:* R.A., N.E.A.C., London Group, National Soc.; one-man shows, Artists' House, Manette St., etc. *Signs work:* "L. B. GRIBBIN" (written with brush). *Address:* 8 Mile House La., St. Albans, Herts. AL1 1TB.

**GRICE, Sarah,** P.S., S.Eq.A.; Hon. mention Paris Salon; artist in pastel and oil specializing in animals; *b* Bootle, Cumbria, 1913. *m* Richard Grice (decd.). *Educ:* private schools in Cumbria. *Studied:* in Paris with Roger Marx, animal sculptor (1927-29), in London (1934-37). *Exhib:* R.A., R.S.A., Paris Salon, and six solo shows. *Signs work:* "Sarah Grice." *Address:* Well Cottage, Cottesmore, Oakham, Rutland LE15 7DH.

**GRIERSON, Janet (Deaconess),** B.A. Hons. (Lond.) (1934), M.A. Lambeth (1982); painter in oil and water-colour; *b* Dublin, 10 Apr., 1913. *Educ:* Westfield College (1931-34), King's College, University of London (1934-36). *Studied:* (part time) at N. Worcs. College (1978-82), Malvern Hills College (1984-89). *Exhib:* galleries in Malvern, including one-man shows. *Signs work:* "Janet Grierson." *Address:* Flat 8 Parkview, Abbey Rd., Malvern, Worcs. WR14 3HG.

**GRIFFIN, Alison Mary,** B.A. Art and Design (1974); miniature painter, and landscape and interior artist in water-colour and acrylic; *b* Sutton Coldfield, 23 May, 1953. *m* Charles Griffin (divorced). one *s.* one *d. Educ:* Boldmere High School for Girls, Sutton Coldfield. *Studied:* Sutton College of Art (1969-71, H.

Muskett), Bath Academy of Art (1971-74, M.Flinn). *Exhib:* Francis Iles Gallery, Rochester, Westminster Gallery, London, Mall Galleries, London. Work in private collections. *Publications:* work repro.: Limited Editions Prints, Rosenstiels. *Signs work:* "Alison Griffin." *Address:* Wisteria House, 68 North St., Barming, Maidstone, Kent ME16 9HF.

**GRIFFIN, David Brian,** graphic designer painter in oil and water-colour, subject matter mainly nautical; Council mem. Chelsea Art Soc. since 1974, Vice-Pres. (1991-96); *b* Brighton, 15 Feb., 1927. *m* Kathleen Martin. one *s*. one *d*. *Educ:* Central School, Catford and Sayers Croft, Ewhurst. *Studied:* Camberwell, Northampton and St. Martin's Schools of Art (1940-43 under Roland Vivian Pitchforth, R.A., R.W.S.). *Exhib:* R.S.M.A., Armed Forces, Omell Galleries, Piccadilly. *Work in collections:* Europe, U.S.A., and Far East. Listed in "20th Century British Marine Painting". *Commissions:* include Eagle Star and British Petroleum. Served R.A.S.C. (maritime) and R.N.V.R. *Clubs:* Wapping Group of Artists, Chelsea Art Soc., Armed Forces Art Soc. *Signs work:* "David Griffin." *Address:* 19 Ross Rd., Wallington, Surrey SM6 8QN.

**GRIFFITH, David Lloyd,** R.Cam.A. (1995), Associate (1988); artist in oil, acrylic, gouache; former Tutor, life-drawing evening class at Conwy, sponsored by University of N. Wales (1992-96); *b* Colwyn Bay, 30 Mar., 1956. *Educ:* Ysgol Emrys Ap Iwan, Abergele, Clwyd. *Studied:* N.E. Wales Inst. (1975-76, N.D. Mackinson, R. Hore), Open College of the Arts (1989-93, E. Williams, H. Bowcott, N. Griffiths). *Exhib:* Theatr Clwyd (1980), Rhyl Arts Centre (1997); selected group shows Royal Cambrian Academy, including "Celtic Arts", Folkestone, Kent (1995), " I Know what I like, or do I?", Kings College, Cambridge (1997). *Signs work:* "D.L.G." *Address:* 35 Glan y Fedw, Betws Yn Rhos, Abergele, Clwyd LL22 8AP.

**GRIFFITHS, David,** D.F.A. (Slade); portrait painter in oils; *b* Liverpool, 1939. *Educ:* Pwllheli Grammar School (1951-57). *Studied:* Slade School of Fine Art (1957-61, Sir William Coldstream). *Exhib:* Royal National Eisteddfod. *Work in collections:* City Hall, Cardiff; Museum and A.G., Newport; Croydon Town Hall; House of Lords; Eton College; R.C.S.; National Library of Wales; University of Wales, Cardiff, Swansea and Aberystwyth; Llandovery College; Trinity College; Assoc. of Anaesthetists; Speaker's House, Westminster; H.T.V. Television; Waverley School; Liverpool University; Assoc. of Chartered Surveyors; University of Indianapolis; several public and private collections throughout the country. *Signs work:* "David Griffiths." *Address:* Westville House, 49 Westville Rd., Cardiff CF2 5DF.

**GRIFFITHS, Tom,** painter, designer and illuminator on vellum; Senior lecturer, Norwich School of Art (1942-49); chairman, Norfolk and Norwich Art Circle (1957, 1958, 1978), President (1983-). *Educ:* City of Norwich School. *Studied:* Norwich School of Art, Heatherleys' and The Grosvenor (London). *Exhib:* R.A., R.O.I., N.S., and provincial art galleries; one-man shows of townscapes (Norwich). *Work in collections:* many illuminated vellums include

Loyal Address (Norwich); Freedom Scrolls for H.M. Queen Elizabeth the Queen Mother, Sir John Barbirolli (King's Lynn); the Royal Air Force and Regimental presentations and the County War Memorial Book of Remembrance, Norwich Cathedral. *Signs work:* "Tom Griffiths." *Address:* 15 Essex St., Norwich.

**GRIGSBY, John Higham,** N.D.D., A.T.D., A.R.E. (1973), R.E. (1978); *b* Staffs., 18 Dec., 1940. *Studied:* Stoke and Leicester Colleges of Art. *Exhib.* Young Contemporaries, R.A., N.E.A.C., R.W.A., R.W.S. Galleries, Mall Galleries, F.B.A. Touring Exhbns., Woburn Abbey, Glasgow Institute, London Group, Buenos Aires Print Biennale; Exhbn. of etchings at Market Print Gallery, Exeter, Phoenix Gallery, Henley and Bedford School. *Work in collections:* Reading Museum; Whitgift Foundation; Graves Gallery, Sheffield; Open University; National Museum of Wales; Williamson Gallery, Birkenhead; Portland State University (U.S.A.); Camden and Greenwich Councils; Hertfordshire, mid-Glamorgan and Sheffield Education Authorities; Exeter University; Bedford School; Fylde Arts Assoc; Imperial College; Fitzwilliam Museum. *Commissions:* Two murals for Trust Houses (1962); Limited edition etching for Unistrut U.K. (1978) and the P.C.C. (1982). *Signs work:* "John Grigsby." *Address:* 152a Mackenzie Rd., Beckenham BR3 4SD.

**GRIMSDALE, Michael,** artist in oil, water-colour, pastels, charcoal, pencil and ink; *b* London, 1 Dec., 1936. *m* Trisha Lord, water-colourist. one *s. Educ:* Cheltenham College, R.M.A. Sandhurst. *Studied:* St. Martin's School of Art, London (1958-60). *Exhib:* R.A. Summer Show, S.Eq.A., Christie's, Osborne Studio Gallery, Equus Newmarket, Tanjah Flandria, Tangiers, Arden Gallery, Sydney. *Work in collections:* World Trade Club, Dubai, Apothecaries Hall, London, Museum of Music, Taiwan, Holocaust Museum, Chicago, Harlequin and Bath Rugby Clubs; private collections in Argentina, U.S.A., Australia, Mexico, U.K., Saudi Arabia, France, Morocco. *Signs work:* "Grimsdale." *Address:* 235 Upper Richmond Rd., Putney, London SW15 6SN.

**GROARKE, Michael,** M.A., M.C.S.D., chartered designer; B.E.D.A. Cert. (Registered European designer); wallpaper/textile/ceramics designer, painter in water-colour and oil; *b* Manchester, Oct., 1943. *m* Prudence J. Hyde. two *s. Educ:* Manchester High School of Art. *Studied:* Calico Printers Assoc. Design School, Manchester Polytechnic Faculty of Art and Design, Rochdale College of Art. *Exhib:* R.A., R.W.S., R.I., R.Cam.A.; design work/exhib. Britain, Europe and America. *Signs work:* "M.G." or "Michael Groarke." *Address:* Fourways, 2 Grosvenor Rd., Marple, Stockport SK6 6PR.

**GROSSMAN, Vera,** S.W.A. (1987), U.A. (1986); sculptor for portrait and ethnic characters in clay, artist in oil on canvas; *b* London. one *s. Educ:* Reading Bluecoat School. *Studied:* no formal training; private tuition for: portrait painting (1976-82, Leonard Boden, R.P.; 1983-85, Joyce Wyatt, R.M.S., P.S., U.A.); sculpture (1979-84, Alan Sly, R.A., A.R.B.S.). *Exhib:* Mall Galleries, Westminster Central Hall, Ben Uri Gallery, Alpine Gallery, Chelsea Manor St.

Gallery, "Smiths" Covent Gdn. *Signs work:* "Vera Grossman." *Address:* 16 Bedford Rd., Chiswick, London W4 1JH.

**GROSVENOR, Stella Athalie (Mrs.),** R.B.S., Slade Dip. Fine Art (1937); sculptor in bronze, resin, stone, wood, painter in oil; *b* Beaconsfield. *m* Hugh N. W. Grosvenor, A.R.I.B.A. *Educ:* St. Margaret's School, Hampstead. *Studied:* Slade School under Prof. Schwabe and Prof. Gerrard. *Exhib:* group shows, Society Portrait Sculptors, Hampstead Artists Council, R.A., Travers Gallery, Erica Bourne Gallery; one-man show, Foyles, London (1968). *Work in collections:* Dixons. *Publications:* Art Editor, National Trade Press; Illustrated, Caxton Publishing Co. *Clubs:* Hampstead Artists Council, R.B.S. *Signs work:* "A. Grosvenor." *Address:* 35 Flask Walk, London NW3 1HH.

**GROVES, John Michael,** R.S.M.A. (1977), N.D.D. (Illustration, 1957); artist in pastel, oil, pen and ink; *b* Lewisham, London, 9 Mar., 1937. *Educ:* Kilmorie Secondary School, London. *Studied:* Camberwell School of Arts and Crafts (1953-57). *Exhib:* R.S.M.A., Mall Galleries, London. *Commissions:* five (3'x5') historical oils for this country and abroad. *Signs work:* "J. Groves." *Address:* 114 Further Green Rd., Catford, London SE6 1JQ.

**GRUFFYDD, Pegi,** B.A. (Hons.) (1982), A.R.C.A. (1985), Dip.R.A. (1986); painter/printmaker in oil, water-colour, etching, lithography; *b* Pwllheli, N. Wales, 28 Apr., 1960. *Educ:* Ysgol Glan-y-Môr, Pwllheli. *Studied:* Manchester Polytechnic (1978-79), Wolverhampton Polytechnic (1979-82), R.A. Schools (1983-86). *Exhib:* R.A. Summer Exhbn. (1984-85), Royal National Eisteddfod of Wales (1980-88), Young Artists Forum, Cardiff University, Wales '83, the Welsh Group Touring Exhbn., Midwales Open, Aberystwyth, North Wales Open, Llandudno; one-man show, Theatre Gwynedd, Bangor; group show, Oriel, Bangor. Gallery: Oriel Glyn-y-Weddw, Llanbedrog. *Signs work:* "Pegi Gruffydd" or "P.G." *Address:* Llymgwyn Farm, Chwilog, Pwllheli, Gwynedd LL53 6HJ.

**GRÜNEWALD, Eleanor Mavis (née Wilson),** N.D.D. (Painting), A.T.D. (Leeds); artist in oil, acryl, aquarelle; teaches art at Kronberg Art School, Germany; *b* Stockton-on-Tees, 2 Mar., 1931. *m* Karl-Heinz Grünewald. one *s.* two *d. Educ:* Richard Hind School, Stockton. *Studied:* Middlesbrough School of Art, Leeds College of Art. *Exhib:* Frankfurt, Wiesbaden, Marburg, Paris, Le Salon, Grand Palais des Champs-Elysees, China: Peking, Shanghai; Egypt: Cairo, Alexandria, with the Frankfurt Union of Professional Artists. *Work in collections:* Cities of Frankfurt, Wiesbaden, Marburg, Middlesbrough. *Clubs:* Berufsverband Bildender Künstler. *Signs work:* "Mavis Wilson-Grünewald." *Address:* Fahrgasse 21, 60311 Frankfurt/Main.

**GUARNORI, (TRUELOVE), Jacky,** F.S.B.A. (1985), S.Lm. (1986); self taught flower painter in water-colour; *b* Surrey, 1943. *m* Peter Truelove. two *s* one *s-s.* two *s-d. Educ:* Grey Coat Hospital, London. *Exhib:* S.B.A. (London and regions); solo shows: Bromley (4), Croydon (2), Cranbrook (1), Francis Iles Fine Art, Sevenoaks Wildfowl Trust, Kent Painters Group, Soc. of

Limners, Samlesbury Hall. *Work in collections:* Orpington Library. *Publications:* work repro.: greetings cards and calendars. *Signs work:* "Jacky Guarnori" or "J.G." (miniatures). *Address:* Oak Bank, Hill Top, Windermere, Cumbria LA23 2HG.

**GUEST, Alan Sexty,** artist in oil; teacher, private tutor, lecturer, autodidact; teacher, Coventry City Council; *b* 11 Dec., 1920. *m* Kathleen Guest. two *s.* five *d. Educ:* Woodlands, nr. Doncaster. *Exhib:* Nuneaton A.G., Coventry, Chalk Farm; two paintings selected by BBC Search for an Artist; TV appearances. *Commissions:* by owner of L'escargot, now hanging in the Curragh. *Clubs:* Unicorn. *Signs work:* "A. Guest." *Address:* 19 Sharp Cl., Holbrooks, Coventry.

**GUISE, Christopher John,** M.A., R.M.S.; marine painter in oil on wood panels, miniaturist in oil on ivorine; formerly on staff, Hurstpierpoint College; *b* Darjeeling, India, 19 June, 1928. *m* Phyllis Gibson. one *s.* one *d. Educ:* Charterhouse and Brasenose College, Oxford. *Exhib:* R.M.S. since 1983, Brighton, Washington, N.Y., Boston, Toronto, Maritime and Sailing Centres. *Signs work:* "C.J. GUISE." *Address:* Carys, West Furlong La., Hurstpierpoint, W. Sussex BN6 9RH.

**GUMUCHIAN, Margaret,** D.A. (Manc.), A.T.D., F.R.S.A.; artist in oil, gouache and lithography; *b* Manchester, 8 June, 1927. *m* Ian MacDonald Grant. one *d. Studied:* Regional College of Art, Manchester. *Exhib:* R.A., R.B.A., M.A.F.A., S.M.P. regional galleries, Paris, and Biarritz. *Work in collections:* School Loans Collection, Salford; Salford Art Gallery, Rutherston Loans Collection, Manchester City A.G. and various private collections, Arctophile. *Signs work:* "Mgt. Gumuchian." *Address:* Barrachnie, Aldersgreen Ave., High Lane, Stockport, Cheshire SK6 8EB.

**GUNN, James Thomson,** F.I.A.L., A.I.P.D., D.A., R.I.Dipl; artist in oil, water-colour, gouache, mixed media and designer; Letter of Commendation from H.M. The Queen (R.A.F. 1957); Diploma of Merit conferred by University delle Arti (1982); Highland Society of London award, R.S.A. (1985); *b* Gorebridge, 9 Apr., 1932. *m* Mary Lang (née Linton). one *d. Educ:* Dalkeith High School. *Studied:* Edinburgh College of Art (1956), Diploma (Travelling Scholar). *Exhib:* R.S.A., R.S.W., R.I., S.S.A., R.G.I., City Art Centre (1983). *Work in collections:* Royal Collection, Argyll Educ. Com.; represented in private collections. *Clubs:* I.A.L., I.P.D. *Signs work:* see appendix. *Address:* 3 Park Cres., Easthouses, Dalkeith, Midlothian EH22 4EE, Scotland.

**GUNSTON, Irene,** B.A.(Hons.) (1982); sculptor in clay, bronze, plaster; *b* Aberkenfig, S. Wales, 19 Aug., 1960. *Studied:* Cardiff College of Art (1978-79), Canterbury College of Art (1979-82). *Work in collections:* B.M. Coins and Medals Dept. *Publications:* 1/50,000: poems by Elizabeth James (Vennell Press, 1992). *Signs work:* sculptures usually unsigned; drawings and prints "I.G." or "I. Gunston." *Address:* 86 Barchester St., London E14 6BE.

**GWYNNE-JONES, Emily,** A.R.C.A. (1970); Mem. Contemporary Portrait Soc.; painter in oil and water-colour; *b* 7 July, 1948. *m* M. Frank Beanland, painter. one *s.* two *d. Studied:* R.A. Schools, R.C.A. (1966-70), N.E. London Polytechnic (textiles), Central School (etching) (1977-78). *Exhib:* R.A. (1966-90), Mayor Gallery, New Grafton Gallery, Pigeon Hole Gallery, Brotherton Gallery, Discerning Eye, Mall Galleries (1991-92), N.E.A.C.; one-man show, Michael Parkin (1977). John Player Award N.P.G. (1987-88). *Work in collections:* R.A., Nuffield Trust, National Trust, Eton College, Paintings for Hospitals, B.S.I. *Publications:* illustrated, Pavane for a Dead Infanta by Hugh Ross Williamson. *Signs work:* "E.G.J." or "E. Gwynne-Jones." *Address:* Metfield Lane Farm, Fressingfield, Eye, Suffolk IP21 5SD.

**GYLES, Pauline Yvonne,** A.R.M.S. (1981), R.M.S. (1985), F.S.B.A. (1986); self taught miniature painter in water-colour; Hon. Sec., Royal Miniature Soc.; *b* Bournemouth, 31 Aug., 1931. *m* Brian Gyles. *Educ:* private schools England and Switzerland. *Exhib:* Medici, Liberty's, Llewellyn Alexander, London, Linda Blackstone, Pinner, Peter Hedley, Wareham, S.B.A., R.M.S. *Work in collections:* Russel Cotes A.G. and Museum, Bournemouth, Soc. of Apothecaries. *Signs work:* "Pauline Gyles." *Address:* Balcombe Cottage, 11 Wilderton Rd., Branksome Pk., Poole, Dorset BH13 6ED.

# H

**HABGOOD, Yvonne Veronica,** M.F.P.S. (1981); painter in oil and alkyd on canvas, pastel on paper; *b* Lincoln, 2 Oct., 1954, divorced. *Educ:* St. John's School, Episkopi, Cyprus. *Exhib:* Mall Galleries, F.P.S., Loggia Gallery, N.S.P.S. (1982), Manchester Academy, Commonwealth Inst.; one-man shows: Bagazzo Gallery Marlborough, Loggia Gallery, etc. *Work in collections:* Bath Rd. Gallery, Old Town, Swindon and numerous private collections including Jamaica and Canada. *Signs work:* "Habgood." *Address:* 15 Priors Hill, Wroughton, Swindon, Wilts. SN4 0RT.

**HACKNEY, Alfred,** R.W.S., A.R.E. (1951), D.A., Edin. (1950); artist in etching, engraving, pen and water-colour; senior lecturer, Medway College of Art, Rochester; freelance illustrator and designer; *b* Yorks., 18 May, 1926. *Educ:* Burslem School of Art, Stoke-on-Trent. *Studied:* Edinburgh College of Art and travelling scholarship to France and Italy. *Exhib:* R.A., London Group, Soc. of Staffordshire Artists, S.E.A., R.E., R.S.A., S.S.A. *Work in collections:* R.A., and numerous public and private collections. *Signs work:* "Alfred Hackney." *Address:* Barnside, Lodge La., Cobham, nr. Gravesend, Kent DA12 3BS.

**HACKNEY, Arthur,** V.P.R.W.S. (1973-76), R.E., A.R.C.A.; etcher; painter in oil and water-colour; Head of Dept., West Surrey College of Art and Design (retd. 1985); Mem. Fine Art Board, Council for National Academy Awards (1975-78), Hon. Ret. R.W.S. (1996), Hon. Ret. R.E. (1990); *b* Stainforth, Yorks., 13 Mar., 1925. *m* Mary Hackney. two *d. Educ:* Stoke-on-Trent.

*Studied:* Burslem School of Art and R.C.A. (travelling scholarship). *Exhib:* R.A., R.E., R.W.S. *Work in collections:* V. & A. Museum; Bradford City A.G.; Nottingham Castle A.G.; Keighley A.G.; Wakefield City A.G.; Graves A.G. (Sheffield); Wellington A.G. (N.Z.); Stoke-on-Trent A.G.; Ashmolean. *Publications:* in 20th Century Painters and Sculptors, Who's Who. *Clubs:* Chelsea Arts. *Signs work:* see appendix. *Address:* Woodhatches, Spoil Lane, Tongham, Surrey GU10 1BP.

**HACKNEY, Isla Katrina,** M.A. Hons. (Edin.) (1985), A.R.W.S. (1993); artist in water-colour, acrylic, oil, lecturer in art and design; *b* Wrotham, Kent, 6 June, 1962. *Educ:* Gads Hill Place School, Kent, and Gravesend Grammar School. *Studied:* Edinburgh College of Art (Elizabeth Ogilvie, Robert Callender, William Baillie), Edinburgh University (specialized in British art (Martin Hammer) and Scottish art (Duncan MacMillan)). *Exhib:* regularly at Bankside Gallery, London. *Publications:* author: 'Charles Rennie Mackintosh' and 'A History of Water-colour Painting'. *Signs work:* "Isla K. Hackney." *Address:* 5 Randolph Cres., Edinburgh EH3 7TH.

**HACKNEY, Mary,** A.R.C.A., P.S.; painter in oil, pastel, water-colour; teacher of life painting and portrait; *b* Coventry, 28 Nov., 1925. *m* Arthur. two *d. Educ:* Sacred Heart, Coventry. *Studied:* Birmingham College of Art, R.C.A. (1946-49). *Exhib:* R.A., P.S., Mall Galleries, New Ashgate, Farnham, and provinces. *Work in collections:* Leicester City (Pictures for Schools), many private collections. *Signs work:* "Mary Hackney." or "M.H." *Address:* Woodhatches, Spoil Lane, Tongham, Surrey GU10 1BP.

**HADDON, Joyce Critchley,** N.E.A.C., R.B.A.; genre painter of portraits in oil and water-colour; *b* Cambridge, 15 Aug., 1913. one *s.* two *d. Educ:* Perse High School, Cambridge. *Studied:* R.A. Schools. *Exhib:* R.A., N.E.A.C., R.B.A.; one-man show at Blackheath Gallery and others. *Address:* 46 High St., Sutton Courtenay, Abingdon, Oxon.

**HAENGGI, Fernand Francis,** art dealer and consultant; founder-director, Gallery 101, Johannesburg (1961-72), director/owner, Gallery 21, Johannesburg (1972-1993) and Gallery 21, London (1974-76), created The Haenggi Foundation Inc. (1978); *b* Dijon, France, 28 Jan., 1934 (Swiss nationality). *m* Caroline Nicholson. one *s.* two *d. Educ:* Basel and St. Gallen, Switzerland. *Publications:* Armando Baldinelli (1974), Lucas Sithole (1979), Zoltan Borbereki (1981). *Address:* Postfach 203, CH-3803 Beatenberg, Switzerland.

**HAGUE, Jonathan,** N.D.D., A.T.D., Netherland State Scholarship; *b* Llandudno, 18 Nov., 1938. *Studied:* Liverpool College of Art (1957-63), Royal Academy of Fine Art, The Hague (1964-66). *Exhib:* one-man shows: The Germeente Museum, The Hague; The Royal Institute Gallery, Piccadilly; sponsored John Lennon. *Signs work:* "HAGUE." *Address:* 2 Regent St., Leamington Spa, Warwicks. CV32 5HW.

**HAIG, George Douglas (The Earl Haig),** Associate Royal Scottish

Academy; painter in oil and water-colour; *b* London, 15 Mar., 1918. *m* (2nd) Donna Geroloma Lopez y Royo. one *s.* two by 1st. marriage *d. Educ:* Stowe and Christ Church, Oxford. *Studied:* Camberwell School of Art (1945-47) under Victor Pasmore, other members of Euston Rd. School and privately with Paul Maze. *Exhib:* Redfern Gallery, The Scottish Gallery and elsewhere. *Work in collections:* paintings: Arts Council and Scottish National Gallery of Modern Art. *Signs work:* "Haig." *Address:* Bemersyde, Melrose TD6 9DP.

**HAINARD, Robert,** Doctorat es sciences honoris causa de l'Université de Genève; Prix Ed. M. Sandoz d'art animalier de l'Academie Grammont, Paris; wildlife artist in colour woodcuts, stone, bronze and wood sculptures, field observer and nature conservationist; *b* 11 Sept., 1906. *m* Germaine. one *s.* one *d. Educ:* Ecole des Arts Industriels, Ecole des Beaux Arts, Genève. *Exhib:* numerous every year in Switzerland and abroad. *Work in collections:* Musée d'Art et d'Histoire, Genève. *Publications:* author, Et la nature ? (1943), Les Mammifères Sauvages d'Europe (1948-49, 1961-62, 1971-72, 1986-87), Défense de l'Image (1967), Expansion et Nature (1972), Le Monde sauvage de Robert Hainard (1988), etc., illustrator of more than fifty books. *Signs work:* "ROBERT HAINARD." *Address:* 51 chemin de Saule, CH 1233 Bernex-Genève, Switzerland.

**HAINAULT, June,** essentist painter/printer in oil, acrylic, water-colour; *m* H.J. Mundy (decd.). two *s. Studied:* Regent St. Polytechnic; Heatherley School of Art. *Exhib:* solo shows: The Gallery, Cork St., London (1994), Hanover Galleries, Liverpool (1986), Fitzroy Gallery, London (1980), Carnival '75, University of Manchester (1975), Loggia Gallery (1972, 1975), Upper St. Gallery, Islington (1972, 1975), Cockpit Theatre (1970), Old Bakehouse, Sevenoaks (1970), New Town Gallery, Uckfield (1969, 1976), Lightning Mark, Rye (1967), Il Traghetto Gallery, Venice (1966), St. Martin's Gallery, London (1965). *Clubs:* F.P.S. Eastbourne Group. *Signs work:* "Hainault." *Address:* The Oast House, Five Ashes, Horleigh Green, nr. Mayfield, E. Sussex TN20 6NL; and Kinkwall, Walls, Shetland ZE2 9PD.

**HAINSWORTH, George,** Slade Dip., Gulbenkian Scholar (Rome); artist in oil paint, variety of sculptural media: stone, bronze, etc.; Prof. in Fine Art, Leeds Metropolitan University; *b* Leeds, 15 Dec., 1937. *m* Lucy M. Rogers. one *s.* one *d. Studied:* Leeds College of Art (1955-60), Slade School of Fine Art (1960-62, William Coldstream), British School at Rome (1962-63). *Exhib:* one-man shows: Serpentine Gallery, Ikon Gallery B'ham, Spacex Gallery Exeter, Sue Rankin Gallery, Ainscough Contemporary Art, London; two-person (with Lucy): Cartwright Hall Bradford, York University, Bradford University, Dean Clough Halifax, Doncaster City A.G. *Work in collections:* Leeds University, Hammond Suddard, Baring Investors, Provident Financial Group plc, many private collections. *Clubs:* M.M. Arts Group, London, Yorkshire Sculptors Group, Leeds Fine Art. *Signs work:* "G. Hainsworth." *Address:* Otter House, Hunsingore, nr. Wetherby, W. Yorks. LS22 5HY.

**HALE, Elsie,** H.S., Paris Salon (Gold medal, 1978), Le Diploma de Societaire Bilan de Contemporain (Paris), Marie-Louise Jules Richard prize (Paris Salon, 1978); painter in oil on canvas, water-colour, (specialising in miniatures on ivorine); *b* Worcester, 5 May, 1913. *m* Arthur James Hale, A.I.A.C. one *d. Educ:* St. George's School, Worcester. *Studied:* Worcester College of Art (G. Williams). *Exhib:* Paris Salon (1978, 1979, 1980), Town Hall Paris (1978), R.A. (1980-86), London, Brighton and Yorkshire Galleries. *Work in collections:* U.K., America, Australia, Canada, New Zealand, Norway. *Signs work:* "Elsie Hale." *Address:* 19 Drovers End, Ancells Farm, Fleet, Hants. GU13 8XB.

**HALE, Helen Margaret,,** R.O.I., N.S., S.W.A., F.P.S.; painter and sculptor; *b* Harpenden, 18 Apr., 1936. *m* Horne Shepherd (decd.). *Educ:* St. George's School, Harpenden. *Studied:* St. Martin's School of Art and Sir John Cass School of Art. *Exhib:* group shows: London, Edinburgh, Paris, Munich. *Signs work:* "HALE." *Address:* Atheldene, Loxwood Rd., Rudgwick, Horsham, W. Sussex RH12 3DW.

**HALES, Gordon Hereward,** R.S.M.A. (1981), R.B.A., F.R.S.A., M.Cam.; painter in water-colour, pastel and oil; *b* Matlock, Derbys., 24 Feb., 1916. *m* Margaret Lily Adams. two *d. Educ:* Avenue Road School and The Gateway School, Leicester. *Studied:* Leicester College of Art, Northampton School of Art. *Exhib:* R.I., R.O.I., P.S. *Clubs:* Wapping Group of Artists (president), London Muster of Artists (founder), The Artists Soc., and Langham Sketching Club, Armed Forces Art Soc. *Signs work:* "GORDON HALES." *Address:* 11 Rosecroft Drive, Watford, Herts. WD1 3JG.

**HALL, Christopher Compton,** R.B.A. (1988), D.F.A. (1954); painter in oil; *b* Slaugham, Sussex, 25 Dec., 1930. *m* Maria Galassi. three *s. Educ:* Bedales School. *Studied:* Slade School of Fine Art (1950-54). *Exhib:* Portal Gallery, New Grafton Gallery, R.A., Waterman Fine Art, Lynne Stern Assoc. *Work in collections:* London Museum, National Library of Wales, Reading A.G., Arts Council, O.U.P. Elected R.B.A. (1987) and to R.Cam.A. (1994). *Signs work:* "C.C. Hall." *Address:* Catherine Villa, Station Rd., Newbury, Berks.

**HALL, Dennis Henry,** A.R.C.A. (1955); graphic designer and producer/publisher of Illustrated Limited Edition Books; *b* Caterham, 1927. *m* Sylvia Stokeld, A.R.C.A. *Educ:* Lancing College. *Studied:* Chelsea School of Art (Brian Robb), R.C.A. (John Lewis). Taught design: Norwich, Leeds and Oxford Schools of Art or Polytechnica. Founded and ran The Inky Parrot Press at Oxford Polytechnic (1981-87) and now runs the Previous Parrot Press. Books in: V. & A., Cambridge University Library, National Library of Scotland, Rijksmuseum, Columbia and Harvard Libraries, full set (44 vols.) in Brookes Oxford University Library. *Address:* The Foundry, Church Hanborough, nr. Witney, Oxon. OX8 8AB.

**HALL, Margaret MacLeod,** A.T.D. (1944), S.G.A. (1952), A.M.A. (Indian

Art) (1966); illustrator in pen and ink, water-colour, wood engraving, author and lecturer; *b* Hampstead, London, 1 Jan., 1922. *Studied:* Harrow School of Art (1938-43), Hornsey College of Art (1943-44). *Work in collections:* The Hall, W. Bridgford, Notts., Castle Museum, Nottingham. *Publications:* with John Irwin: Indian Painted and Printed Fabrics (Ahmedabad, 1971), Indian Embroideries (Ahmedabad, 1973); illustrations, The Sanchi Torso, V. & A. Year Book (1973); and in periodicals; now editing work of John Irwin. *Signs work:* "Margaret Hall" or "Margaret M. Hall." *Address:* 174 Portland Rd., London W11 4LU.

**HALL, Nigel John,** M.Art R.C.A.; sculptor; *b* Bristol, 30 Aug., 1943. *m* Manijeh (née Yadegar). *Educ:* Bristol Grammar School. *Studied:* West of England College of Art (1960-64), Royal College of Art (1964-67), Harkness Fellowship (1967-69). *Exhib:* one-man shows, Galerie Givaudan, Paris; Wilder Gallery, Los Angeles; Galerie Neuendorf, Hamburg and Cologne; Serpentine Gallery, London; Juda Rowan Gallery, London; Nishimura Gallery, Tokyo; Elkon Gallery, N.Y., Galerie Maeght, Paris. *Work in collections:* Tate Gallery, V. & A., Arts Council of Great Britain, National Galerie, Berlin, Dallas Museum of Fine Art, Tokyo Metropolitan Museum, Chicago Art Institute, Kunsthaus, Zurich, Museum of Modern Art, N.Y. *Signs work:* "NIGEL HALL." *Address:* 11 Kensington Pk. Gdns., London W11 3HD.

**HALL, Pauline Sophie,** B.Sc. (1938); artist in woodcut, wood engraving, linocut; ex-mem. S.WL.A.; *b* Birmingham, 23 June, 1918. *m* Prof. K. R. L. Hall (decd.). *Educ:* Birmingham University, Oxford University. *Studied:* Michaelis School of Art, Cape Town (1955-60). *Exhib:* R.E., S.WL.A. (Mall Galleries); one-man shows, Cape Town (1973), The Shakespeare Centre, Stratford-on-Avon (1984), Coleg, Harlech (1992). *Work in collections:* "SWAN", Wallsworth Hall, Glos. *Signs work:* "Pauline S. Hall." *Address:* Park View Flat, Church Rd., Snitterfield, Warwickshire CV37 0LE.

**HALLETT, Roger Michael,** D.F.A. (Slade) 1957; painter in oil, water-colour, tempera, sculptor; Director, Hallett's Panorama, and Bath Panorama Ltd.; *b* Bristol, 1 June, 1929. *m* Sylvia Craig. one *s.* two *d. Educ:* Bristol Cathedral School. *Studied:* Slade School of Fine Art (1954-57). *Exhib:* London, Paris, Edinburgh, Sydney, Melbourne, Newcastle, Bristol. *Work in collections:* Hallett's Panorama of Bath, Britain's largest oil painting (200 ft. x 20 ft.) hung in a circle, on permanent display at the Thames Barrier Visitors Centre. *Clubs:* London Sketch. *Signs work:* "Roger Hallett." *Address:* The Old Vicarage, Watery Lane, Twerton, Bath, Avon. BA2 1RL.

**HALLIDAY, Charlotte Mary Irvine,** R.W.S. (1976), N.E.A.C. (1961); topographical artist; Keeper, New English Art Club since 1989; *b* Kensington, 5 Sept., 1935. *Educ:* Wester Elchies, Francis Holland. *Studied:* R.A. Schools (1953-58). *Exhib:* R.W.S., R.B.A., N.E.A.C., etc. *Commissions:* Salisbury Cathedral, Selfidges, Lord's Pavilion, the Monument, London Clubs, City Banks and many private houses. *Publications:* Illustrations for Dictionary of

Edwardian Architecture by A. Stuart Gray (1985) and co-author, with him, of "Fanlights", a visual architectural history (1990). *Signs work:* "Charlotte Halliday" or "CMIH." *Address:* 36a Abercorn Pl., London NW8 9XP.

**HALLIDAY, Irene,** D.A. (1952), R.S.W. (1955); artist in gouache; *b* Kingsmuir, Angus, Scotland, 26 Sept., 1931. *Educ:* Arbroath High School. *Studied:* Dundee College of Art (1948-53, Alberto Morrocco, R.S.A., R.S.W.). *Exhib:* 35 one-man shows, Arbroath, Dundee, Edinburgh, Manchester, Salford, New York State. *Work in collections:* art galleries of Arbroath, Bolton, Dundee, Glasgow, Greenock, Salford; education authorities of Dundee, Dunbartonshire, Edinburgh, Fife, Manchester, Wigan; Granada TV., British National Oil Co., Shell Centre, London, Manchester Ship Canal Co. *Signs work:* "Halliday." *Address:* 46 Highfield Dene Rd., Didsbury, Manchester M20 2ST.

**HALLIDAY, Thomas Symington,** M.B.E., F.R.S.A., F.I.A.L.; European Banner of Arts (1984); World Culture Award (1984); Italian Oscar (1985); Gold Medal, Accademia Italia; Gold Medal, International Parliament, U.S.A.; Contemporary Art Soc., Milan; awarded Gold Medal, Artist of the Year (1988); Founder Mem. Guild of Aviation Artists; *b* Thornhill, Dumfriesshire, 1902. *Educ:* Ayr Academy. *Studied:* Glasgow. *Exhib:* R.A., Paris Salon, R.S.A., G.I., R.S.W., S.S.A., N.E.A.C., R.S.M.A. *Work in collections:* "Stag" sculpture, official presentation to H.M. The Queen; drawings "H.M.S. Duke of York" and "Valiant" purchased by H.R.H. Duke of Edinburgh; work in many public collections. *Commissions:* stained glass. *Publications:Scottish Sculpture;* work repro.: in Studio, Scots Magazine, Life and Work, Wood. *Signs work:* "T. S. HALLIDAY." *Address:* 9 Hill Cres., Wormit, Newport-on-Tay DD6 8PQ.

**HALSBY, Julian,** M.A. (Cantab.), R.B.A. (1994), F.R.S.A. (1997); painter in oil, art historian, critic; Mem. International Assoc. of Art Critics; *b* London, 1948. *m* Miranda Halsby, printmaker. one *s.* one *d.* *Studied:* Emmanuel College, Cambridge (art history). *Exhib:* R.A., R.B.A., N.E.A.C., many mixed exhbns. in the U.K. and France. *Publications:* Scottish Watercolours 1740-1940 (Batsford, 1986), Dictionary of Scottish Painters 1600-2000 (with Paul Harris) (Phaidon/Canongate, 1990), Venice: The Artists' Vision (Batsford, 1990), The Art of Diana Armfield, R.A. (David & Charles, 1995); plus many exhbn. catalogues and articles for "The Artist." *Signs work:* "HALSBY." *Address:* 44 Claremont Rd., Highgate, London N6 5BY.

**HAMBLING, Maggi,** Boise Travel award, N.Y. (1969), Arts Council award (1977), Artist in Residence, National Gallery (1980-81); artist in oil on canvas, water-colour, drawing, sculpture in bronze, printmaking; *b* Suffolk, 1945. *Studied:* Camberwell School of Art (1964-67), Slade School of Fine Art (1967-69); studied with Lett Haines and Cedric Morris (1960). *Exhib:* solo shows: National Gallery (1981), Serpentine Gallery (1987), Arnolfini Gallery, Bristol (1988), Bernard Jacobson Gallery (1990), Yale Center for British Art (1991), Northern Centre for Contemporary Art (1993), Marlborough Fine Art (1996), National Portrait Gallery (1997), Yorkshire Sculpture Park (1997). *Work in col-*

*lections:* Tate Gallery, Whitworth A.G., A.C.G.B., National Gallery, British Museum, N.P.G., Gulbenkian Foundation, Australian National Gallery. *Commissions:* Public statue for Oscar Wilde, London (1997). Jerwood Painting Prize (1995). *Clubs:* Green Street. *Signs work:* surname on back. *Address:* c/o Marlborough Fine Art, 6 Albemarle St., London W1X 4BY.

**HAMILTON, Katherine,** Dip. (Byam Shaw) (1974), Dip. Dance and Choreography (1977); painter in oil on canvas, pastel; married. two *s. Educ:* Dartington Hall School. *Studied:* Byam School of Art (1971-74, Diana Armfield); London School of Contemporary Dance (1974-77). *Exhib:* solo shows: Christopher Hull Gallery, Sue Rankin Gallery (1993), Thackeray Gallery (1994); mixed exhbns.: Piccadilly Gallery, New Academy Gallery (1996), Chappel Gallery (1997), R.A. Summer Show (1997). *Commissions:* fourteen portraits (1996-97). *Signs work:* "Katherine Hamilton." *Address:* Theale House, Frostenden Corner, nr. Beccles, Suffolk NR34 7JA.

**HAMILTON, Thomas Gottfried Louis,** B.A.Hons.(Arch.), R.I.B.A. (1956); architect, artist in pen, pencil and water-colour; *b* Berlin, 29 Mar., 1930. *m* Georgina Vera Craig. one *s.* one *d. Educ:* King's School, Canterbury; U.C.L. *Studied:* architecture: Bartlett School of Architecture (1949-55, Prof. A.E. Richardson). *Exhib:* private galleries. *Clubs:* The Arts, Dover St. *Signs work:* "Thomas Hamilton." *Address:* 55 Addison Ave., London W11 4QU.

**HAMMOND, Hermione,** Rome Scholar (Painting, 1938.; *Studied:* Chelsea Polytechnic, R.A. Schools (Dip.). *Exhib:* one-man exhbns.: Bishopsgate Institute (1956); Colnaghi's (1957); Arthur Jeffress (1961); All Hallows, London Wall (1965); New Grafton (1970); Great King St. Gallery, Edinburgh (1972); Six Portfolios, Chelsea (1973); Hartnoll & Eyre Iran & Cyprus (1978), Michael Parkin and University of Hull (1993). *Work in collections:* ceiling decoration, University of London, Guildhall collection, Museum of London, Fondation Custodia, Institut Néerlandais, Paris, Fitzwilliam Museum, Hunterian A.G., Glasgow, Brymor Jones Library, University of Hull. *Publications:* Oxford Almanack, Arts Review, R.I.B.A. Journal, Country Life. *Signs work:* "Hermione Hammond." *Address:* 2 Hans Studio, 43a Glebe Pl., London SW3 5JE.

**HAMPTON, F. Michael,** wildlife artist in water-colour, scraper-board and acrylic; S.WL.A.-W.W.F.N. Fine Art award (1988); *b* Croydon, 29 May, 1937. *m* Julie. one *s. Studied:* Croydon Art School. *Exhib:* R.S.P.B., Sandy, Arnhem Gallery, Croydon, Blackheath Gallery SE3, The Wildlife Gallery, Lavenham, Farnham, Surrey, Medici Gallery, London, Port Lympne Zoo Park, Hythe, Kent, Ringstead Gallery, Hunstanton, Cotswold Wildlife Gallery, Lechlade, Glos. *Commissions:* Mr. John Aspinall. *Publications:* work repro.: three jackets of 'British Birds', two jackets of R.S.P.B. 'Birds', (1980-1983), Calendar for Sussex Fine Arts, S.WL.A. Calendars (1987,1988), S.WL.A.-R.S.P.B. Calendar (1990, 1991, 1992), B.B.C. Wildlife Magazine (Aug. 1992). *Clubs:* S.WL.A., Croydon Art. *Signs work:* "M" and "H" with grebe's head, see appendix. *Address:* 13 Sandy Way, Shirley, Croydon, Surrey CR0 8QT.

**HANCERI, Dennis John,** R.S.M.A. (1970); graphic designer, water-colour and gouache; *b* London, 7 June, 1928. *m* Jill. one *s.* one *d. Studied:* St. Martin's School of Art. *Exhib:* one-man show, Denver, Colorado, U.S.A., Centaur Gallery, Dallas, Texas, Southport, Connecticut, U.S.A.; also shows at Mystic Seaport, Connecticut. *Clubs:* Wapping Group of Artists. *Signs work:* "Dennis John Hanceri." *Address:* 97 Horncastle Rd., London SE12.

**HANKEY, Christopher Alers,** O.B.E., M.A., B.Sc.; painter in oil; Mem. Armed Forces Art Soc.; retd. Civil Servant; *b* Oxted, Surrey, 27 Apr., 1911. *m* (1) Prudence Brodribb. one d. (2) Helen Cassavetti. one *s. Educ:* Rugby School, New College, Oxford, University College, London. *Exhib:* R.A., R.B.A., R.O.I., National Soc., R.A. Artists in Japan and other exhbns. in Japan, Anna-Mei Chadwick Gallery (Parsons Green), Nevill Gallery, Canterbury. *Clubs:* Ebury Court. *Signs work:* "Hankey" or "Christopher Hankey." *Address:* New Cottage, French Street, nr. Westerham, Kent TN16 1PW.

**HANLEY, Liam Powys,** self-taught painter in oil on canvas, water-colour, and gouache; *b* S. Kensington, 4 Apr., 1933. *m* Hilary Hanley. one *s.* one *d. Educ:* Wrekin College, Salop. *Exhib:* Stone Gallery, Newcastle, Mermaid Theatre, Thackeray Gallery, London, R.A., Abbot Hall A.G., Kendal, Phoenix Gallery, Lavenham, Suffolk, Beardsmore Gallery, London. *Publications:* The Face of Winter by James Hanley. *Signs work:* "Hanley, L." *Address:* 21 Woodsome Rd., London NW5 1RX.

**HANLY, Daithi Patrick,** B.Arch., F.R.I.A.I., F.R.I.B.A., F.R.T.P.I.; architect, planner, landscaper, sculptor in stone; former Dublin City Architect; Advisory consultant architect, National College of Art and Design; *b* Cavan, 11 Mar., 1917. *m* Joan Kennedy. one *s.* one *d. Studied:* National University, College of Art, Dublin. *Exhib:* R.H.A., Oireachtas, sculpture in stone, architectural drawings. Won competition Garden of Remembrance, Dublin (1966). Architect to Royal Dublin Society for Simmonscourt Pavilion large exhibition complex, seaside garden village in Blainroe, Wicklow with golf clubhouse, on 550 acres. Designed Basilica at Knock for 7,500 pilgrims. *Signs work:* "D. P. Hanly" or "D.P.H." *Address:* San Elmo, Vico Rd., Dalkey, Dublin, Ireland.

**HANN, Priscilla,** B.A., S.Eq.A.; sculptor; *b* Pattingham, nr. Wolverhampton, 11 Oct., 1943. *m* Patrick Kennedy. *Educ:* Downe House, Newbury. *Studied:* Wolverhampton College of Art (1961-65, Ron Dutton), Tyler School of Art, Philadelphia (Dean Le Clair). *Work in collections:* 'Natives of Furlong', Ringwood, Hants. *Clubs:* S.Eq.A., Friend of R.A., British Sporting Art Trust, Public Sculpture and Monuments Assoc. *Signs work:* "P. Hann." *Address:* Tetstill, Neen Sollars, Cleobury Mortimer, Worcs. DY14 9AH.

**HANSCOMB, Brian,** A.R.E. (1991); self taught artist in pastel, drawing and copperplate engraving; *b* Croxley Green, Herts., 23 Sept., 1944. *m* Jane Wilkins, née Hunt. two *d. Educ:* Rickmansworth Grammar School. *Exhib:* R.A., R.W.A., R.E., N.E.A.C., Clarges Gallery, Crane Kalman Gallery, Beaux

Arts Gallery; one-man shows: England and Germany. *Work in collections:* D.O.E., V. & A. National Art Library, Royal Cornwall Museum and A.G., Bodleian Library. *Publications:* On the Morning of Christ's Nativity (Folio Soc., 1987); Sun, Sea and Earth (Whittington Press, 1989); Cornwall - An Interior Vision (Whittington Press, 1992). *Signs work:* "B. Hanscomb" or "B.H." *Address:* Tor View, Limehead, St. Breward, Bodmin, Cornwall PL30 4LU.

**HARDAKER, Charles,** A.R.C.A. (1958), N.E.A.C. (1969), R.B.A. (1984); painter in oil and pastels; tutor in painting and drawing; *b* Oxford, 1 May, 1934. *m* Annick née Pouletaud. *Educ:* Wellesbourne School, B'ham. *Studied:* B'ham College of Arts and Crafts (1949-53), R.C.A. (1955-58). *Exhib:* R.A., N.E.A.C., R.B.A., R.P., five one-man shows, San Francisco (2), London (3). *Work in collections:* Tate Gallery (Chantrey Bequest), Guildhall of London, G.L.C., National Library of Wales, Northumbria Water, B.P., I.C.E. *Signs work:* "Hardaker." *Address:* Studio 1, St. Oswald's Studios, Sedlescombe Rd., Fulham, London SW6 1RH.

**HARDIE, Gwen,** Richard Ford award, R.A. (1982), Hons. Degree (1983), Daad Scholarship, W. Berlin (1984), Edward 7th British-German Foundation, W. Berlin (1986); painter in oil, sculptor in cement, plaster; *b* Newport, Scotland, 7 Jan., 1962. *Educ:* Inverurie Academy. *Studied:* Edinburgh College of Art (1979-84, John Houston), H.D.K., W. Berlin (1984-85, Baselitz). *Exhib:* solo shows: Fruitmarket Gallery, Edinburgh (1987), Fischer Fine Art, London (1989), S.N.G.M.A. (1990), Talbot Rice A.G., Edinburgh, Annely Juda, London (1994), Jason & Rhodes, London (1996), Peterborough Museum and Fine A.G. (1997); group shows: Vienna (1986), American tour (1989-92), Frankfurt (1993), Jason & Rhodes, New Artists: Hardie Colvin & Boyd (1995). *Work in collections:* S.N.G.M.A., Metropolitan Museum N.Y., Gulbenkian Museum Lisbon, Arts Council, etc. *Commissions:* Portrait of Jean Muir (1985). *Signs work:* "G. HARDIE" or "G.H." *Address:* c/o Jason and Rhodes, 4 New Burlington Place, London W1X 1FB.

**HARDING, Jane Mary,** S.W.A. (1982); artist in line and water-colour; *b* London. *m* David Harding. *Educ:* Haberdashers' Aske's Girls' School. *Studied:* Lytham St. Annes School of Art (1940-41). *Exhib:* S.W.A. annually, Britain in Water-colour, Ealing Art Group. *Work in collections:* London Borough of Ealing Central Library. *Publications:* editorial illustrations for Amalgamated Press, Odhams, Franey's London Diary, Grolier Press, Sunday Times, Ward Gallery. *Clubs:* Ealing Arts. *Signs work:* "Jane Harding." *Address:* Melvin House, 13 Hartington Rd., Ealing, London W13 8QL.

**HARDY HENRION, Daphne,** sculptor in clay for terracotta or bronze; *b* 20 Oct., 1917. *m* F.H.K. Henrion. two *s.* one *d. Educ:* The Hague, Holland. *Studied:* R.A. Schools (1934-38). *Exhib:* Beaux Arts Gallery (1946), A.I.A. Gallery (1966), Old Fire Engine House, Ely (1975, 1979), Bury St. Edmunds (1981), Churchill College (1993), Lynn Strover Gallery, Fen Ditton (1996). *Work in collections:* bust of Arthur Koestler at N.P.G., sculpture in relief on

Addenbrooke Hospital, Cambridge. *Signs work:* "Daphne Hardy Henrion," "Daphne Henrion," "D.H." or "D.H.H." *Address:* 13 Owlstone Rd., Cambridge CB3 9JH.

**HARGAN, Joseph R.,** D.A. (1974), P.P.A.I. (1989); elected Associate, Glasgow Group (1994), Stirling Smith award (1978), Cargill award (1980), Torrance award (1982), Meyer Oppenheim prize R.S.A. (1985), Hunting Group prizewinner, London (1988), Paisley Art Inst. award (1993); Founder Mem. and Chairman of Group 81; elected Pres. P.A.I. (1989), elected P.A.I. (1996); *b* Glasgow, 23 Jan., 1952. *m* Anne Louise Clarke. *Studied:* Glasgow School of Art (1970-74, Danny Ferguson, Drummond Bone, David Donaldson). *Exhib:* R.S.A., R.G.I., R.S.W., Art Club, Group 81, R.A., P.A.I., B.W.S. (1983), S.S.A., etc. *Clubs:* Glasgow Art. *Signs work:* "Hargan." *Address:* 40 Oakshaw St., Paisley PA1 2DR.

**HARLE, Dennis F.,** artist in oil and gouache, naturalist; nature reserve warden; *b* Sandwich, 26 May, 1920. *m* Heather Harle; three d. from first marriage. *Educ:* Sandwich; *Studied:* Ramsgate and Canterbury Schools of Art (Evening classes). *Exhib:* Reading Museum and A.G., S.WL.A.; one-man shows, Deal (1978), Maidstone (1963), Sandwich (1960). *Clubs:* S.WL.A. (founder mem.). *Signs work:* "Dennis F. Harle" or "D." *Address:* The Studio, No 72 Strand St., Sandwich, Kent CT13 9HX.

**HARRIGAN, Claire,** B.A. Hons. (1986), R.S.W. (1992); painter in watercolour, acrylic, gouache and pastel; *b* Kilmarnock, 8 Nov., 1964. *Educ:* Sacred Heart Academy, Girvan. *Studied:* Glasgow School of Art (1982-86, Peter Sumsion, Neil Dallas-Brown, Barbara Rae). *Exhib:* solo shows: Christopher Hull Gallery, London; Gatehouse Gallery, Glasgow; Open Eye Gallery, Edinburgh; Macaulay Gallery, Stenton. *Signs work:* "Claire Harrigan." *Address:* 53 King St., Crosshill, By Maybole, Ayrshire KA19 7RE.

**HARRIS, Geoffrey,** A.R.C.A. (1954); sculptor; Senior lecturer, Ravensbourne College of Art and Design (1960-86); Assistant to Leon Underwood (1954), Assistant to Henry Moore, O.M., C.H. (1957-60); *b* Nottingham, 1928. *m* Gillian Farr, M.S.I.A., textile designer. two *s. Educ:* Leeds Modern School. *Studied:* Leeds College of Art (1948-51), Royal College of Art (1951-54). *Exhib:* one-man shows: Leicester Galleries, London (1964), Queen Square Gallery, Leeds (1964). *Work in collections:* in Britain, Europe, U.S.A. *Commissions:* Baildon Primary School, Yorkshire, L.C.C. Maitland Park Housing Scheme, St. Pancras, Eurolink Industrial Centre, Sittingbourne, Kent. *Signs work:* "Harris." *Address:* 5 Queen's Rd., Faversham, Kent ME13 8RJ.

**HARRIS, Josephine,** R.W.S., N.E.A.C., F.G.E.; artist in water-colour, drawing and engraved glass; *Educ:* privately. *Studied:* Plymouth College of Art (1948-52) under William Mann, A.R.C.A., gained N.D.D. *Work in collections:* Plymouth A.G., Graves A.G., Sheffield, South London A.G., I.L.E.A., K.C.C. Work to commission for public companies and private individuals in engraved glass. *Signs work:* "Josephine Harris" or "J.H." *Address:* Workshop No. 2, 46-52 Church Rd., Barnes, London SW13 0DO.

**HARRIS, Lyndon Goodwin,** R.I., R.S.W., R.W.A., Dip. Fine Art (Lond.), A.T.D., Courtauld Certificate, Leverhulme, Pilkington, and Slade Scholar; Slade Anatomy Prizeman, Gold Medal Paris Salon (painting, 1956), Hon. Men. (painting, 1948) and Hon. Men. (etching, 1949); artist in oil, water-colour, stained glass; etcher; *b* Halesowen, Worcs., 25 July, 1928. *Educ:* Halesowen Grammar School. *Studied:* Birmingham College of Art, L.C.C. Central School of Art and Crafts, Courtauld Inst., Slade School (Profs. Randolph Schwabe and Sir William Coldstream) and University of London Institute of Education. *Exhib:* Paris Salon, R.A. (first exhib. at age of 13), R.S.A., R.I., N.E.A.C., R.B.A., R.S.W., R.G.I., R.W.A., Britain in Water-colour, Birmingham, Bradford, Wolverhampton, Bournemouth, Blackpool, Southport and other principal provincial galleries. *Work in collections:* University College, London; Min. of Works; Birmingham and Midland Inst.; City of Worcester; stained-glass window, Gorsty Hill Methodist Church, Halesowen. *Publications:* Masters of Water-colour and Their Techniques (The Artist), Young Artists of Promise, Souvenir Handbook of Halesowen, Birmingham Post, etc. *Signs work:* "Lyndon G. Harris." *Address:* c/o Lloyds Bank, 23 Hagley St., Halesowen, W. Midlands B63 3AY.

**HARRIS, Phyllis,** S.W.A., N.D.D., S.G.F.A.; artist in water-colour and pen, lithography, linocut, school teacher (retd.); *b* London, 3 Aug., 1925. *m* David Harris. one *s.* one *d. Educ:* Brondesbury High School, London and Abbey School, Reading. *Studied:* Reading University School of Art, Brighton and Camberwell, Harrow School of Art (lithography). *Exhib:* S.W.A., Brent and Harrow, S.G.F.A., London. *Clubs:* S.W.A., Wembley Art Soc., Harrow Art Soc., S.G.F.A. *Signs work:* "Phyl Harris." *Address:* 55 Slough Lane, Kingsbury, London NW9 8YB.

**HARRISON, Christopher David,** B.A. (Hons.), A.T.C.; artist in water-colour, collage, oils; Director, Bircham Art Gallery; *b* Gt. Yarmouth, 21 Oct., 1953. *m* Deborah Margaret. two *s. Educ:* Bromley Grammar School, Kent, Boston Grammar School, Lincs. *Studied:* Jacob Kramer College of Art, Leeds (1973-74), Reading University (1974-78), London University Inst. of Educ. (1978-79). *Exhib:* R.B.A., R.A., R.I., R.W.S.; many mixed exhbns. throughout England; regular one-man shows Norfolk. *Signs work:* "Christopher Harrison." *Address:* 49 Church La., Bircham, King's Lynn, Norfolk PE31 6QW.

**HARRISON, Claude,** R.P., A.R.C.A.; artist in oil, oil and tempera, pen and wash, etc.; primarily a painter of conversation pieces and imaginative landscapes; *b* Leyland, Lancs., 31 Mar., 1922. *m* Audrey Johnson, painter. one *s. Educ:* Hutton Grammar School, Lancs. *Studied:* Preston (1938-40), Liverpool (1940-41), R.C.A.(1947-49). *Exhib:* R.A., R.P., R.S.A., R.B.A., etc. *Work in collections:* Harris A.G., Preston, Abbott Hall, Kendal, Lancaster City Museum, Bournemouth A.G., etc. *Publications:* The Portrait Painters'

Handbook (Studio Vista, 1968); Book of Tobit (1970). *Signs work:* "CLAUDE HARRISON." *Address:* Barrow Wife, Cartmel Fell, Grange over Sands, LA11 6NZ, Cumbria.

**HARRISON, Margot,** artist in water-colour, oil; *b* 2 Jan., 1915. *m* George Francis Harrison, M.B.E. two *d*. *Educ:* Queen Anne's, Caversham. *Studied:* privately under Prescoe Holeman (1938), and Kingsley Sutton, F.R.S.A. (1965); Farnham School of Art, part-time (1966-69, John Wilkinson, A.R.C.A.). *Exhib:* Paris Salon (1972, 1973); one-man shows: Alpine Gallery (1975), Bradshaw Room F.B.A. (1978), Mall Galleries (1974), Bradshaw Room F.B.A. (1982), R.O.I., Britain in Watercolours, R.B.A. *Work in collections:* B.P. (1974), National Trust (1980). *Signs work:* "Margot Harrison." *Address:* Stoney Cottage, The Bury, Odiham, Hants. RG29 1LY.

**HARRISON, Marguerite Hazel,** National Froebel Foundation Diploma in Art; artist in oil, pen and wash, and pastels; *b* Llandudno, N. Wales, 7 Oct., 1927. *m* Michael Harrison. three *s*. two *d*. *Educ:* Royal Masonic School, Rickmansworth, Herts. *Studied:* mainly self-taught; tuition for a period under Kenneth A. Jameson. *Exhib:* R.A., R.Cam.A., Grosvenor Art Soc., Wirral Soc. of Art. *Signs work:* "Marguerite Harrison" and see appendix. *Address:* 2 The Courtyard, Poulton Hall, Bebington, Merseyside L63 9LN.

**HARRISON, Stephanie Miriam,** N.D.D., F.S.B.A., R.M.S.; painter, book illustrator, graphic designer; *b* Kings Lynn, 10 Dec., 1939. *m* John Harrison. *Studied:* Medway College of Art, Rochester (1955-60). *Exhib:* Westminster Gallery, Mall Galleries, Linda Blackstone Gallery and galleries throughout the U.K.; several one-man shows. *Work in collections:* Science Museum, B.M. (Natural History), and private collections. *Publications:* Wild Flowers of Britain, Marine Life, Handbook of British Mammals, Private Life of a Country House, greetings cards, stationery. *Signs work:* "Stephanie Harrison," "S. Harrison" or "S.M.H." *Address:* 1 Leydens Ct., Stick Hill, Edenbridge, Kent TN8 5NH.

**HART-DAVIES, Christine Ann,** B.A. Hons., R.M.S., F.S.B.A.; botanical artist and illustrator; *b* Shrewsbury, 1947. *Studied:* fine art, typography at Reading University (1966-70). 5 R.H.S. Gold medals. *Exhib:* Brisbane, London, R.B.G. Kew, U.S.A. *Work in collections:* Hunt Inst. Botanical Documentation, Pittsburgh, Shirley Shirwood Collection Contemp. Botanical Artists. *Signs work:* "CHRISTINE HART-DAVIES," "CH-D" (miniatures). *Address:* 31 Shaftesbury Rd., Poole, Dorset BH15 2LT.

**HARTAL, Paul,** Ph.D.; artist and theorist, originator of Lyrical Conceptualism (1975); founder of the Centre for Art, Science and Technology; oil and acrylic paintings, works on paper, concrete poetry, various writings (fiction and non-fiction); *b* Hungary, 1936. *Studied:* M.A. Thesis: Georg Lukacs: Aesthetics and History, Concordia University, Montreal; Doctoral Dissertation: The Interface Dynamics of Art and Science, Columbia Pacific University, California. *Exhib:* Musée du Luxembourg, Paris (1978), Véhicule, Montreal

(1980), Montreux Centre, University of Lausanne (1983), Seoul International Fine Art Centre (1987), OURS, Montreux (1990), Ward-Nasse Gallery, N.Y. (1992), Milan Art Centre, Italy (1993), Musée de la Poste, Paris (1994); Space Center, Houston (1994); Municipal Library, Saint-Laurent, Québec (1994); International Painting Exhibition, Seoul (1995); Centre Cultural d' Alcoi, Spain (1996), Galerie Michel-Ange, Montréal (1997). *Commissions:* Seoul Olympic Games; Orbitor U.S.A.; Book and record illustrations. *Publications:* Encyclopedia of Living Artists; Olympic Catalogue, Seoul; UNICEF Italia; Artists/USA, Phil. Black and White (1984), The Brush and the Compass (1988); The Kidnapping of the painter Miró (illustrated novel,1997); articles: Leonardo, Pulsar, Contemporary Philosophy, poetry. Awards include: Prix de Paris; Rubens; National Library of Poetry; International Poetry Hall of Fame (U.S.A.). *Signs work:* "Hartal." *Address:* Box 1012, St. Laurent, Quebec H4L 4W3, Canada.

**HARTILL, Brenda,** R.E., Dip.F.A. Hons. (1964); artist/printmaker in etching, collagraph, oil (previously theatre design); *b* London, 27 Feb., 1943. *m* Harold Moores. one *s.* one *d. Educ:* Kings School, Ottery St. Mary; Kelston High, Auckland, N.Z. *Studied:* Elam School Fine Art, N.Z.; Central School of Art (theatre design, Ralph Koltai). *Exhib:* R.A. Summer Show, R.E. Bankside Gallery, over 50 galleries worldwide; solo shows: New Academy Gallery and galleries in Australia, N.Z., U.S.A., Barbican Centre. *Clubs:* R.E. *Signs work:* "Brenda Hartill." *Address:* Globe Studios, 62a Southwark Bridge Rd., London SE1 0AS.

**HARVEY, Jake,** D.A. (1972), R.S.A. (1989); sculptor, carver of limestone/ granite, and forger of iron / steel; Head of Sculpture, Edinburgh College of Art; *b* Yetholm, Kelso, Roxburghshire, 3 June, 1948. *m* Penny Harvey. one *s.* two *d. Educ:* Kelso High School. *Studied:* sculpture: Edinburgh College of Art (1966-72) Postgraduate (1971-72), Travelling Scholarship to Greece (1971-72), William Gillies Bursary Research Travel in India (1989). *Exhib:* R.S.A., Talbot Rice A.G., City Art Centre (Edinburgh), Third Eye Gallery (Glasgow), Camden Arts Centre, Leinster Gallery, Houldsworth F.A., Art First (London), Pier Art Centre (Stromness), Aberdeen A.G., Seagate (Dundee), Maclaurin (Ayr), Stavanger (Norway), Lulea (Sweden), Kemi (Finland). *Work in collections:* Scottish Arts Council, Edinburgh Museums and Galleries, University of Edinburgh, Contemporary Art Soc., Aberdeen Art Gallery, Hunterian Museum, Kulturoget, Lulea, Sweden. *Commissions:* Hugh MacDiarmid Memorial, Langholm; Compaq Computers Commission, Glasgow; Newcraighall Mining Commission, Edinburgh; Poachers Tree, Maclay, Murray and Spens; Motherwell Heritage Centre; Hunterian A.G., Glasgow. *Signs work:* "Jake Harvey" and see appendix. *Address:* Maxton Cross, Maxton, St. Boswells, Roxburghshire.

**HARVEY, Michael Anthony,** N.D.D. (1957), F.R.S.A. (1972), Linton prize (1973); artist in oil, pastel; journalist and art critic; mem. S.G.F.A., Reigate

Soc. of Artists, life mem. I.A.A. (Unesco); *b* Kew; divorced. one *s. Educ:* Bryanston. *Studied:* Wimbledon School of Art (1955-57). *Exhib:* Whibley, Rutland, Fine Arts, Qantas and Connoisseur Galleries W1., Brighton Pavilion, Portsmouth Museum, and Melbourne, Oslo, Dortmund; fourteen one-man shows. *Work in collections:* Johns Hopkins University, Camden Council, E. Sussex Council. *Publications:* work repro.: B.B.C. TV, The Times, Standard, Artist. *Clubs:* Royal Society of Arts, London. *Signs work:* "Michael" or "Michael A. Harvey." *Address:* 15 Waterloo Sq., Bognor Regis, W. Sussex PO21 1TE.

**HARVEY, Pat:** see YALLUP, Pat.

**HAUGHTON, Wilfred James,** President and Founder, Ulster Watercolour Soc. (1977), F.R.S.A. (1960), A.R.U.A. (1951), R.U.A. (1956), vice-president, R.U.A. (1956), president R.U.A.(1964-70), elected Hon. A.R.U.A. (1996), mem. W.C.S.I.; artist in oil, water-colour and pastel; past managing director, Frazer & Haughton Ltd.; *b* Hillmount, 14 Dec., 1921. *m* Priscilla Elizabeth McLaughlin. three *s.* one *d. Educ:* Terra Nova School, Birkdale, Southport, Lancs.; Worksop College, Notts. *Studied:* self-taught. *Exhib:* R.H.A., R.U.A., Royal Scottish Water-Colour Soc., R.I., W.C.S.I. *Work in collections:* oil painting, C.E.M.A.; oil painting, Thomas Haverty Trust (Dublin). *Publications:* Author of "Brush Aside" and "Purely Watercolour". *Signs work:* see appendix. *Address:* 17 Dromona La., Cullybackey, Ballymena, Co. Antrim, N. Ireland BT42 1NT.

**HAWDON, Paul Douglas,** B.A. (Hons.) (1982), Dip. R.A. Schools, R.E.; painter/printmaker in oil, gouache, etching; *b* Manchester, 13 Oct., 1953. *m* Helena Earl. one *d. Educ:* Hyde County Grammar School. *Studied:* St. Martin's School of Art (1978-82), R.A. Schools (1982-85), Rome Scholar, British School (1988-89). *Exhib:* R.E., London Group, Twelve Contemporary Figurative Artists, R.A., Christie's Print prize (1985, 1990), 11th International Print Biennale, Bradford. *Work in collections:* Metropolitan Museum of Fine Art, N.Y. *Publications:* Printmaking Today Vol.4 No.2. *Clubs:* Chelsea Arts. *Signs work:* "Paul Hawdon" or "P.D.H." *Address:* 62 Marshall Rd., Cambridge, CB1 4TY.

**HAWES, Meredith William,** A.R.C.A., R.W.S., F.R.S.A., A.S.I.A.; Freeman of the City of London; artist in water-colour, oil, gouache; College of Art Principal (retd.); tutor (P.T.), Exeter University (Extra-mural Dept.); *b* Thornton Heath, Surrey, 17 Apr., 1905. *m* Margaret Charlotte. one *s.* six *d. Educ:* Selhurst Grammar School, Croydon. *Studied:* Croydon School of Art (1922-24), R.C.A. (1924-28). *Exhib:* R.A., R.W.S., N.E.A.C., Paris, U.S.A. and many provincial galleries. *Publications:* illustrations for John Murray, Jonathan Cape, V. & A. Museum, O.U.P. *Signs work:* "M.W. HAWES." *Address:* Emslake House, 2 Anderton Villas, Millbrook, Torpoint, Cornwall PL10 1DR.

**HAWKEN, Anthony Wellington John,** A.R.B.S. (1979), Cert. R.A.S. Sculpture (1971); sculptor in plastics and stone, etcher; *b* Erith, Kent, 4 July,

1948. *m* Deirdre Bew. two *s*. *Educ:* Northumberland Heath Secondary Modern School. *Studied:* Medway College of Art (1965-68, John Cobbett), R.A. Schools (1968-71, Willi Soukop). *Exhib:* Hammersmith Summer Exhbn., R.B.S., Chichester, Stratford upon Avon; one-man show, Blackheath Gallery. *Signs work:* "A. Hawken." *Address:* 1 Chevening Rd., Greenwich, London SE10 0LB.

**HAWKINS, Barbara,** ceramics painter and water-colourist; *b* Yorks., 18 Oct., 1952. *m* Michael Hawkins. two *d*. *Studied:* St. Albans and Bristol. *Exhib:* Open Eye, Edinburgh, Simon Drew Gallery, etc. Work in collections internationally. *Clubs:* Fellow, Craft Potters Assoc., Mem., Glos. Guild of Craftsmen. *Signs work:* " MBH." *Address:* Port Isaac Pottery, Roscarrock Hill, Port Isaac, Cornwall PL29 3RG.

**HAWKINS, Michael,** potter; *b* 2 Aug., 1950. *m* Barbara. two *d*. *Studied:* Cornwall. *Exhib:* London, Edinburgh, Bath, etc. Work in collections internationally. *Clubs:* Fellow, Craft Potters Assoc., Mem., Glos. Guild of Craftsmen. *Signs work:* " MBH." *Address:* Port Isaac Pottery, Roscarrock Hill, Port Isaac, Cornwall PL29 3RG.

**HAWKINS, Philip Dennis,** G.R.A.; artist in oil, pencil; *b* B'ham, 26 Sept., 1947. *m* Sonya. one *s*. one *d*. *Educ:* Lordswood Boys' Technical School, B'ham. *Studied:* B'ham College of Art (1964-68). *Exhib:* N.R.M. York, Science Museum, B'ham, Festival Hall London, regularly with G.R.A. *Work in collections:* B'ham Post and Mail Ltd., Bristol United Press, B.B.C., Docklands Light Railway, European Passenger Services, Railfreight, Freightliner, etc. *Publications:* Fine art prints, work featured in calendars, greetings cards, magazines, books, etc. Co-director, Quicksilver Publishing. *Clubs:* President, Guild of Railway Artists. *Signs work:* "Philip D. Hawkins." *Address:* 112 Chaffcombe Rd., Sheldon, Birmingham B26 3YD.

**HAY, Ian,** N.D.D. (1960), A.R.C.A. (Painting 1963); awarded the Andrew J. Lloyd prize for landscape painting; artist in pastel, water-colour, etching, art lecturer; Senior Lecturer in drawing, Colchester School of Art; *b* Harwich, 25 Jan., 1940. *m* Teresa Sliska. two *s*. *Educ:* Harwich School. *Studied:* Colchester School of Art (1955-60, Hugh Cronyn), R.C.A. (1960-63, Ruskin Spear). *Exhib:* Craftsman Gallery and Minories, Colchester, Sandford Gallery, London, Phoenix Gallery, Lavenham, Wivenhoe Arts Centre, Patisserie Valerie, London SW3. *Work in collections:* Doncaster City A.G., The Guildhall A.G., Graves A.G., Sheffield. *Commissions:* A series of paintings commissioned by Ernst & Young for their office space in Birmingham (1996). *Clubs:* Colchester Art Soc. *Signs work:* "Ian Hay." *Address:* 32 Tall Trees, Mile End, Colchester, Essex CO4 5DV.

**HAYES, Colin Graham Frederick,** R.A., M.A.(Oxon), Hon.A.R.C.A., Hon. F.R.C.A., President R.B.A (1993-); painter in oil and water-colour; reader, Royal College of Art (1949-84); *b* London, 17 Nov., 1919. *m* (1) Jean Westbrook Law (d. 1988); three d. (2) Marjorie L. M. Christensen. *Educ:*

Westminster School; Christ Church, Oxford. *Studied:* Bath School of Art; Ruskin School of Drawing. *Exhib:* Marlborough, Agnews, Search, New Grafton. *Work in collections:* Arts Council, British Council, Carlisle A.G. and others. *Publications:* Stanley Spencer, Renoir, Rembrandt, A Grammar of Drawing. *Clubs:* Arts, Chelsea Arts. *Signs work:* "Hayes." *Address:* 26 Cleveland Ave., London W4 1SN.

**HAYNES, Alexandra,** B.A.; artist in oil and water-colour; *b* 17 Mar., 1966. *Educ:* New Hall, Boreham, Chelmsford, Essex. *Studied:* Shrewsbury Foundation Course, Cheltenham Art College (Michael Hollands, Leslie Prothero). *Exhib:* Mail on Sunday, Dover St. (1988), Contemporary Fine Art Gallery, Eton; one-man shows: Soloman Gallery, London (1988), Mistral Gallery, London (1989, 1990, 1991), Flying Colours Gallery, Edinburgh (1990), Bruton Street Gallery (1992). *Publications:* A Life with Food, Peter Langan by Brian Sewell. *Signs work:* "A. Haynes." *Address:* Edgcote, Banbury, Oxon. OX17 1AG.

**HAYWARD-HARRIS, Martin John,** artist and sculptor of wildlife subjects in oil, water-colour, etchings, bronze; *b* Reading, 28 Oct., 1959. *Educ:* Maiden Erlegh Comprehensive. *Studied:* Berks. College of Art and Design (1978-84). *Exhib:* S.WL.A., B.T.O., R.S.P.B., W.T.N.C.; one man show: Phyllis Court Club, Henley-on-Thames (1990, 1993), East African Wildlife Soc. *Work in collections:* Natural History Museum London, Zoologisk Museum, Copenhagen. *Publications:* work repro.: etchings published by H.C. Dickins, auctioned at Sotheby's; Birding World; cover illustration 'In Search of Stones' M. Scott Peck, M.D. auctioned at Christie's. *Signs work:* "Martin Hayward-Harris." *Address:* 47 Clarendon Rd., Earley, Reading, Berks. RG6 1PB.

**HAZZARD, Charles Walker,** B.A. (Hons.) Fine Art (1987), Sir Henry Doulton School of Sculpture (1988-90), Postgrad. H.Dip. Sculpture (1991), A.R.B.S. Dip. (1992); Director and Trustee, Royal Soc. of British Sculptors; sculptor and fabricator in wood; Brother, Art Workers' Guild (1996); Henry Moore sponsored Sculpture Fellow, Loughborough College of Art and Design (1996-98); *b* B'ham, 5 Feb., 1964. *Studied:* Cheltenham University (1984-87, Roger Luxton), Sir Henry Doulton School of Sculpture (1988-90, Colin Melbourne), City and Guilds of London (1990-91, Alan Sly). *Exhib:* national shows. *Publications:* books illustrated: British Contemporary Art (1993), Encyclopedic Techniques of Sculpture (1995), British Artists since 1945. *Signs work:* "C.W.H." or not at all. *Address:* 19 Steward St., Spitalfields, London E1 6AJ.

**HEALER, George,** A.R.B.S. (1974); sculptor in clay, plaster, wood, cast aluminium, brass and bronze; *b* 25 Sept., 1936. *m* Brenda Maureen Healer. one *s.* two *d. Educ:* Bullion Lane School. *Studied:* Sunderland College of Art (1952-56) under Harry Thubron, A.R.C.A., and Robert Jewell, A.R.C.A. *Exhib:* R.A., R.G.I., Commonwealth Institute, Woolgate House, London,

D.L.I. Durham City, Gulbenkian Gallery, Newcastle-upon-Tyne. *Work in collections:* life-size figures of John and Josiphe Bowes, Bowes Museum, Barnard Castle, Co. Durham. *Publications:* article, Aluminium for Schools for the British Aluminium Federation. *Signs work:* "HEALER" hammered into metal with flat chisel. *Address:* 12 Melville St., Chester-le-Street, Co. Durham DH3 6JF.

**HEALER, Reuben John,** H.N.D. (1984); graphic designer/illustrator; *b* Gateshead, 17 Dec., 1963. *Educ:* Hermitage Comprehensive. *Studied:* graphic design: New College, Durham (N.D.A.D. 1980-82); Cumbria College of Art and Design (H.N.D. 1982-84). Graphic designer for: Newcastle Architecture Workshop (1984-85), Pendower Hall, E.D.C. (1985-88), By Design, Seaham, Co. Durham (1988). *Address:* 21 Bede Terr., Chester-le-Street, Co. Durham.

**HEARSON. Susan: see VOGEL,Suzi**

**HEAT, Ann Olivia,** artist in oil; *b* Esher, Surrey, 30 July, 1945. *m* Trevor Harvey Heat. *Educ:* Waynflete, Surrey. *Studied:* The Kathleen Browne School under Kathleen Browne and her Polish husband Marian Kratochwil. *Exhib:* R.A., R.B.A., R.P., R.O.I., N.E.A.C. *Clubs:* R.B.A. *Signs work:* "A.H." *Address:* Stumps Grove Farm, Whitehill La., Ockham, Ripley, Surrey GU23 6PB.

**HECHLE, Ann,** F.S.S.I.; calligrapher in vellum, water-colour, gold leaf; *b* 31 Dec., 1939. *Studied:* Central School of Art and Crafts (1957-60, Irene Wellington). *Exhib:* 'Lavenders Blue' Paperpoint (1988), other group exhbns. *Work in collections:* Minnesota Manuscript Initiative, U.S.A., V. & A., Crafts Study Centre, Bath. *Commissions:* 19 calligraphic panels for St. Mary's Hospital, Isle of Wight. *Publications:* co-author: More than Fine Writing (Life and work of Irene Wellington). Film: In the Making (B.B.C. 1979). *Address:* The Old School, Buckland Dinham, Frome, Somerset BA11 2QR.

**HEINDEL, Robert,** self taught artist; Director, The Obsession of Dance Co; *b* Toledo, Ohio, 1 Oct., 1938. *m* Rosalie. three *s. Educ:* St. Angus Grade School, Central Catholic High School. *Exhib:* Atlanta, Georgia; American Artists Gallery; Kansas City A.G.; Dallas, Texas - The Vineyard Gallery; San Francisco Gallery One; Royal Festival Hall, London; New London Theatre; Hotel de Paris, Monte Carlo. *Work in collections:* Smithsonian Inst., Washington D.C.; Caltex Corp., Dallas; Chrysler Corp., Detroit; Columbia Pictures, Los Angeles; Ford Motor Co., Detroit; Goodyear Rubber Co., Akron; The Grace Co., N.Y.; The Ladd Co., Los Angeles; Manufacturers Hanover Bank, N.Y.; Phillips Petroleum, Dallas; Quasar Oil Corp., N.Y.; Readers' Digest Inc., N.Y.; Time Inc., N.Y.; United Artists, Los Angeles; United Energy Resources Corp., Houston; Coca Cola; Champion Paper. *Publications:* illus. The Complete Phantom of the Opera (Pavilion Books); J. Steinbeck - The Grapes of Wrath; All the Kings Men. *Clubs:* Mortons, London. *Signs work:* "R. Heindel." *Address:* 140 Banks Rd., Easton, Connecticut 06612, U.S.A.

**HEINDORFF, Michael,** M.A. (1977), Fellow, R.C.A. (1988); painter in oil, water-colour, pencil, print; senior tutor, R.C.A.; *b* Braunschweig, Germany, 26

WHO'S WHO IN ART

June, 1949. *m* Monica Buferd. one *s*. one *d*. *Educ:* Wilhelm Gymnasium, Braunschweig. *Studied:* Braunschweig University (1970-75), R.C.A. (1975-77, Peter de Francia, Philip Rawson). *Exhib:* Bernard Jacobson Gallery, London, New York, Los Angeles since 1978, R.A. (1988-89), and others internationally. *Work in collections:* Herzog Anton Ulrich Museum, A.C.G.B., Museum of London, Imperial War Museum, Museum of Modern Art, N.Y. *Commissions:* Imperial War Museum (1986); Designers Guild (1992). *Publications:* CD-ROM (IBM Compatible PC) of drawings (1995). *Clubs:* Chelsea Arts. *Signs work:* "M. HEINDORFF." *Address:* 2 Shrubland Rd., London E8 4NN.

**HEINE, Harry,** R.S.MA., F.C.A., C.S.M.A., N.W.S.; self taught artist in water-colour; *b* Edmonton, Alberta, Canada, 24 July, 1928. *m* Teresa. one *s*. two *d*. *Exhib:* R.I., R.S.MA., F.C.A., Mystic International (U.S.A.), Northwest Marine exhbn. (U.S.A.), and one-man shows in Canada and U.S.A. *Work in collections:* U.S.A.: Washington State Arts Commission, Mystic Seaport Museum, Conn.; Canada: Legislative Bldgs., Victoria, Mendel Gallery, Saskatoon, Maritime Museum, Victoria, Government House, Victoria, Alberta Art Foundation; England: Capt. Cook Museum, Middlesbrough, National Maritime Museum, Greenwich. *Publications:* Pacific Salmon (Govt. of Canada, Dept. of Fisheries and Oceans). *Signs work:* "HEINE." *Address:* 7059 Brentwood Dr., Brentwood Bay, B.C. VO5 1AO, Canada.

**HELD, Julie,** B.A. (Hons.) (1981), R.A. Schools Postgrad. Dip. (1985); painter in oil on canvas and water-colour on paper; part-time curator and tutor/lecturer; *b* 25 Mar., 1958. *Educ:* J.F.S. Comprehensive School. *Studied:* Camberwell School of Art (1977-81, Philip Mathews), R.A. Schools (1982-85, Peter Greenham). *Exhib:* Piccadilly Gallery, Boundary Gallery, R.A., Waterman Gallery, Festival Hall, Hayward Gallery, Royal Overseas League, 5th International Cleveland Drawing Biennial, Ben Uri Art Soc., The Barbican, Brighton and Hove, Bosel Art Fair, Touring shows. *Work in collections:* Limerick, Keele University, Nuffield College, Oxford University, Ben Uri Art Soc., Museum of the Negev, Israel, Usher Gallery, Lincoln, Open University. *Signs work:* "J. HELD" or "J.H." on small works. *Address:* 98 Cecile Park, London N8 9AU.

**HELLEBERG, Berndt,** sculptor; *b* Stockholm, 17 Dec., 1920. *m* Margareta Kinberg. *Educ:* High School, Härnösand. *Studied:* Stockholm (1945-48), Konstfackskolan, Stockholm (1947-49), France (1950-52). Prize, The Unknown Political Prisoner, London (1953), first prize winner, competition of modern medals (Stockholm 1955), first prize winner 20,000 Sw. crowns, competition of underground station decoration (Stockholm 1960). *Exhib:* Tate Gallery, London, Stockholm, Paris, U.S.A., etc. *Work in collections:* The underground station, Hornstull, Stockholm; Cathedral Window, Baptist Church, Stockholm; several playground sculptures in Sweden; several sculptures in Stockholm and Sweden; Sculpture 9m high in Riyadh, Saudi Arabia (1981). *Signs work:* "Berndt Helleberg." *Address:* Saturnusu 7, 18450

Akersberga, Sweden.

**HEMBLEY, Stephen James,** S.G.F.A.; painter in oil, water-colour, pen and ink; Founder of Shire Studios; part-time tutor; *b* Bournemouth, 21 July, 1957. *m* Rachel Crawford. *Educ:* Winton School. *Studied:* under George Denham at Bournemouth. *Exhib:* one-man shows: London, Telford, Shrewsbury, N.E.C. Birmingham; numerous group shows. Work in private collections worldwide. *Publications:* books illustrated for Tamarisk. *Signs work:* "S.J. HEMBLEY." *Address:* c/o Shire Studios (Telford), 25 Bishopdale, Telford, Shropshire TF3 1SA.

**HEMMANT, Lynette,** N.D.D. (1958); landscape and still-life painter in oil, mixed media, black and white drawing, etching and general illustration; *b* London, 20 Sept., 1938. *m* Jüri Gabriel, literary agent. *Studied:* St. Martin's School of Art (1954-58, Roger Nicholson, Bernard Cheese, Vivian Pitchforth). *Exhib:* R.O.I., and various solo and mixed shows in London, Home Counties, Italy and Australia since 1984. *Publications:* work repro.: Heinemann Group, Hamish Hamilton, Random House, O.U.P. *Clubs:* S.G.F.A. *Signs work:* "HEMMANT." *Address:* 35 Camberwell Grove, London SE5 8JA.

**HEMPTON, Paul Andrew Keates,** M.A., R.C.A.; artist in oil paint, water-colour, and etching; assoc. lecturer, University of Wolverhampton; Fellow in Fine Art, University of Nottingham (1971-73); *b* Wakefield, Yorks., 3 Oct., 1946. *m* Margaret Helena. one *s.* two *d. Educ:* King's School, Chester. *Studied:* Goldsmiths' College School of Art (1964-68), R.C.A. (1968-71) under Prof. Carel Weight. *Work in collections:* Arts Council, British Council, V. & A., Contemporary Arts Soc., Arnolfini Trust, South West Arts, Leicester Educ. Authority, Nottingham University, Bury, A.G., Newport A.G., Wakefield A.G., Whitworth A.G., Nottingham Castle A.G., Wolverhampton A.G., Wiltshire C.C., Arthur Andersen, London. *Signs work:* "P.H." *Address:* 9 West End, Minchinhampton, Stroud, Glos. GL6 9JA.

**HEMS, Margaret,** F.S.B.A.; Royal Drawing Soc. (1940-43), Grenfell Medal R.H.S. (1984-86), Founder mem. F.S.B.A. (1985); botanical artist in water-colour and pencil; *b* Fyfield, Essex, 1 Jan., 1931. *m* John Hems. one *s.* one *d. Educ:* Clark's College, Ilford. *Studied:* a period of art classes at Minehead (1981, Sylvia Cave), botanical illustration under Mary Grierson at Flatford. *Exhib:* S.B.A., H.S., Westminster Gallery, Mall Galleries, galleries, West Country, East Anglia, and other mixed exhbns. in England and Wales. *Work in collections:* private: Britain, Europe, U.S.A., Australia. *Publications:* greetings cards for Medici and Parnassus Gallery, numerous exhbn. catalogues. *Signs work:* "M. Hems" or "M.H." joined. *Address:* The Old School House, Pebmarsh, Halstead, Essex CO9 2NH.

**HEMSLEY, George Philip,** R.A. Schools cert. (1958), N.D.D. (1954), British Institution award (1958), R.A. Silver medal, Landseer Scholarship, Leverhulme Scholarship, David Murray studentships; painter in oil and water-colour; teacher and lecturer; *b* Stocksbridge, Yorks, 9 Dec., 1933. *Educ:*

Surbiton Grammar School. *Studied:* Kingston School of Art, R.A. Schools (Henry Rushbury, Peter Greenham). *Exhib:* R.A., R.B.A, N.E.A.C., R.P., Redfern, Guildhall. *Work in collections:* Guildhall, London Boroughs of Camden, Hackney, Kingston-upon-Thames, Dept. of Educ. and Science, Leicester Educ. Authority. Work loaned to Inst. of Practitioners in Advertising. *Publications:* work repro.: T.E.S. *Signs work:* "Philip Hemsley." *Address:* 18 Ellis Farm Cl., Mayford, Woking, Surrey GU22 9QN.

**HEMSOLL, Eileen Mary,** A.T.D. (1946), R.B.S.A. (1978); artist in enamel on earthenware, oil, oil pastels, water-colour; retd. art teacher; *b* West Bromwich, 4 Feb., 1924. *m* Eric Hemsoll. one *s.* one *d. Educ:* Queen Mary's, Walsall. *Studied:* B'ham College of Art (1941-46, Eggison, Fleetwood Walker). *Exhib:* R.A., R.A. Travelling Exhbn., Local Artists, B'ham A.G., Artists for Art, R.B.S.A. Paint the City (1989), Mall Gallery Pastels Today (1994, 1995); one-man shows: Worcester College (1978), Flint Gallery, Walsall (1984), Summer Show Sally Hunters, Belgrave Sq. (1986). *Signs work:* "Eileen Hemsoll." *Address:* 18 Mead Rise, Edgbaston, Birmingham B15 3SD.

**HENOCQ, Ron,** Slade Dip. (1973), San Carlos Escuela del Arte M.A. (1976); artist, Gallery Director, Cafe Gallery since 1984; *b* 22 Mar., 1950. *Signs work:* "R.Henocq." *Address:* Cafe Gallery, Southwark Park, London SE16.

**HENRI, Adrian,** Hons. B.A. Fine Art (1955), Hon. D. Litt. (1990); artist in acrylic/canvas; author; President, Liverpool Academy of Arts (1972-81); *b* Birkenhead, 1932. *Studied:* Dept. of Fine Art, King's College, Newcastle. *Exhib:* one-man shows: Whitford Gallery, London (1997), Storey Inst., Lancaster (1994); Touring Retrospective (1986); Wolverhampton City A.G. (1976), Williamson A.G. (1975), Art Net, London (1975), I.C.A. (1968); other shows: John Moores Liverpool (1962, 1966, 1968, 1974, 1978, 1980, 1989), John Moores £2,000 Prize (1972), murals, Royal Liverpool Hospital (1980 and 1983). *Work in collections:* Walker A.G., Williamson A.G., and A.C.G.B. Collection. *Publications:* a number of books of poetry. *Clubs:* Chelsea Arts. *Signs work:* "Adrian Henri." *Address:* 21 Mount St., Liverpool L1 9HD.

**HENRY, Bruce Charles Reid,** B.D. (Lond.) (1943), S.WL.A. (1982); painter in water-colour, pastel, oil, retd. school teacher; *b* nr. Kandy, Sri Lanka, 22 July, 1918. *m* Joyce M. Henry. one *s.* one *d. Educ:* Colchester Royal Grammar School, Tettenhall College, Staffs. *Exhib:* Mall Galleries (annually), S.WL.A., Budleigh Salterton, Newport, I.O.W., Sladmore Gallery, London, Northern Exhbn. of Wildlife Art, Chester. *Work in collections:* Nature in Art, Gloucester. *Publications:* Author/illustrator, Highlight the Wild - The Art of the Reid Henrys (Palaquin Publishing, 1985). *Signs work:* "Bruce Henry." *Address:* 90 Broomfield Ave., Worthing, W. Sussex BN14 7SB.

**HENTALL, Maurice,** F.R.S.A. (1951), S.B.A. (1987); retd. 22 years Managing Director of London Studios; part-time Art Tutor, painter in water-colour, acrylic, oil; several years Easter tutorial at Pendley Manor; *b* Hornsey.

Nora Nelson. *Studied:* Hornsey College of Art. R.A.F.V.R. from 1940, injured March 1942. Whilst convalescent official War Publication artist: encouraged by R. Stanton, Sir Alfred Munnings, Sir James Gunn. *Exhib:* R.A., Mall Galleries, Westminster Central Hall - portraits, wildlife, botanical, including miniatures. *Commissions:* motif Golden Jubilee of Sperry Gyroscope Co. unveiled by Earl Mountbatten of Burma 1963). *Publications:* Royal Manor of Hanworth; repros. Gordon Fraser, Medici, etc. *Signs work:* "MAURICE HEN-'ALL." *Address:* 42 The Broadway, Gustard Wood, Wheathamstead, Herts. AL4 8LP.

**HENTHORNE, Yvonne,** Professor, N.D.D. (Painting 1965), A.T.C. (1966), '.R.S.A. (1967), Italian Government Bursary (1969), Brazilian Government scholarship (1971), W. German Research Grant (1974-75); constructed painting; Head of Foundation Studies Dept., Wimbledon School of Art; *b* Wetherby, Yorks., 1942. *m* Gary Crossley, Professor, Surrey Institute. one *d. Educ:* Grey Coat Hospital, Westminster. *Studied:* London University Goldsmiths' College of Art (1961-66, Patrick Millard, Albert Irwin, Andrew Forge). *Exhib:* open, Young Contemporaries, Tate, Birmingham Festival, Midland Group Gallery, Sheffield Open National, S.W.A., R.B.A.; one-man shows, Ikon Gallery, Birmingham; Belgrade, Coventry; Laing Gallery, Newcastle-on-Tyne. *Work in collections:* U.K., Europe, U.S.A. *Signs work:* "Yvonne Crossley." *Address:* The Chestnuts, Bishops Sutton, Hants. SO24 0AW.

**HENTY-CREER, Deirdre,** F.R.S.A.; Utd. Artists Council (1947-1955); F.C.I.A.D. (1945); Artists of Chelsea (1961); Com. Chelsea Art Soc.; Com. Armed Forces Art Soc.; artist in oil; *b* Sydney, Australia. *Educ:* privately. *Exhib:* R.A., R.O.I., R.B.A., N.E.A.C., N.S., U.A., many municipal galleries, Submarine Museum, Gosport, Victory Museum, Portsmouth, etc. One-man shows, Fine Art Soc., Frost & Reed, Cooling, and Qantas Galleries, Bond St., Upper Grosvenor Gallery, Harrods; Nice XIV Olympiad Sport in Art at V. & A., R.N. College, Greenwich. *Work in collections:* H.R.H. the Prince of Wales, Lord Rank, Lord Rootes, Ronald Vestey, Esq. *Publications:* work repro.: The Artist, Cover of Studio, Medici Soc., T.A.V.R. Mag., Royal Sussex Regt. Mag., Poster for Municipality of Monaco, The Sphere, Stanton Corp., N.Y., Chrysons of California, U.S.A., Gruehen of Innsbruck. Portraits include: H.R.H. Prince Michael of Kent; Governor-Gen. of Australia, Sir John Kerr; Mayor of Kensington, Sir Malby Crofton, Bt.; Prime Minister of Malta, Dr. Borg Olivier; First Sea Lord, Sir Henry Leach, etc. *Address:* 5 St. Georges Ct., Gloucester Rd., London SW7.

**HEPWORTH, Elizabeth Barbara,** painter in oil, water-colour, pastel; retd. teacher, until recently took summer school at Pendley Manor, Tring; *b* Walton on Thames, Surrey, 1904. *Educ:* Maybury House School, Woking, Convent of St. Mawr, Weybridge. *Studied:* Camberwell School of Art (William Coldstream, Victor Pasmore, Claude Rogers). *Exhib:* R.A., N.E.A.C., Leicester Gallery, and various one-man shows. *Signs work:* "E.B.H." *Address:* 21b

Regents Park Rd., London NW1 7TL.

**HERBERT, Albert,** A.R.C.A.; painter of mainly religious or symbolic sub jects in oil and etching; ex Princ. lecturer, St. Martin's School of Art; *b* London 10 Sept., 1925. *m* Jacqueline. three *d*. *Studied:* R.C.A. (1949-53), British School at Rome (1953-54). *Exhib:* R.A., Poetry Soc., University of California Westminster, Norwich, Winchester and St. Paul's Cathedrals, Castlefiel Gallery, England and Co., Lancaster University, etc. *Work in collections* Contemporary Art Soc., Coventry Training College, Methodist Educ. Com Shell, Stoke-on-Trent A.G., Glamorgan, Herts., Notts. and Somerset C.C's Agent: England and Co., London, W11. *Clubs:* Chelsea Arts. *Signs work* "Albert Herbert." *Address:* 4 Clifton Terr., Cliftonville, Dorking RH4 2JG.

**HERBERT, Barry,** artist/printmaker, drawings and prints; Head of Fine Ai Dept., University of Leeds (1985-92); *b* York, 19 Mar., 1937; married. one *s* one *d. Educ:* Archbishop Holgate's School, York. *Studied:* James Graham College. *Exhib:* 38 one-man shows include: Serpentine Gallery, London (1971); Mappin Gallery, Sheffield (1972), Galerie Brechbühl, Switzerlan (1972, 1976, 1979, 1982, 1984), Galerie Steinmetz, Bonn (1979, 1984, 1993) Karl-Marx-Universität, Leipzig, (1980), Gilbert Parr Gallery, London (1982) Richard Demarco Gallery (1992). *Publications:* 30 editions of prints publishe in Germany, Switzerland and England; "Barry Herbert - Künstler-Grafiker" (1979); "Barry Herbert" - Drawings and Etchings (1997). *Signs work:* "Barry Herbert." *Address:* 43 Weetwood Lane, Leeds LS16 5NW.

**HERIZ-SMITH, Bridget,** B.F.A. (Hons.), S.G.A. (1985); award with com mendation, History of Art (1977); sculptor in cast, cement and bronze; admin istrator, Clock House Studios (1979-86); *b* Hamburg, 13 Dec., 1949. *Educ* Framlingham Mills Grammar School. *Studied:* Goldsmiths' College Ravensbourne College (1974-77, Eric Peskett). *Exhib:* Sculpture in Anglia (1978, 1981, 1989), R.A. Summer Show (1988, 1992), Musée Lachelevici Belgium, Gallerie Alinna, Finland; groups: Young Blood, Suffolk Group Bearing 090°. *Work in collections:* Women's Art, New Hall, Cambridge. *Sign work:* "B.Heriz." *Address:* 1 Allums Yd., Low Rd., Badingham, Suffolk IP1 8JS.

**HERMAN, Josef,** O.B.E. (1981); Gold medal for services to art in Wales painter in oil, water-colour, drawing; *b* Warsaw, 3 Jan., 1911. *m* Eleanore. one *s*. one *d. Educ:* Warsaw. *Studied:* Warsaw School of Art and Decoration *Exhib:* Glasgow (1942), Edinburgh (1942), London (1943), Roland, Browse & Delbanco (1946-), British Council, Arts Council, retrospective Whitechape A.G. (1956), Camden Arts Centre (1980). *Work in collections:* Arts Counci British Council, B.M., National Museum Cardiff, Contemporary Art Soc. National Museum Bezalel, Jerusalem, Tate, V. & A., National Galleries of Johannesburg, Melbourne, Ottawa, Wellington, etc. *Publications* Ystradgynlais, a Welsh mining village; Related Twilights; Notes from a Welsh Diary. *Signs work:* all works signed on the back - see appendix. *Address:* 120

dith Rd., London W14 9AP.

**HERON, Patrick,** painter; *b* Leeds, 1920. *Exhib:* one-man shows: Waddington Galleries, Bertha Schaefer Gallery (N.Y.), Galerie Lienhard Zürich), São Paulo Bienal (1953 and 1965), Edinburgh, Oslo, Dublin, Rio de aneiro, B. Aires, Santiago, Lima, Caracas, Waddington Fine Art, Montreal, ydney, Melbourne, Toronto, etc. *Work in collections:* Tate Gallery; Gulbenkian Foundation; N.P.G.; Contemporary Art Society; V. & A.; B.M.; Arts Council; British Council; Stuyvesant Foundation; Wakefield; Manchester; Cardiff; Aberdeen; Belfast; Eastbourne; Exeter Univ.; Plymouth; Univ. of Warwick; Univ. of Stirling; Bedford; Oxford; Oldham; Leeds; Montreal; 'oronto; Vancouver; Toledo, Ohio; Smith College, Mass.; Brooklyn; Albright-Knox, Buffalo; Univ. of Michigan, Ann Arbor; Nat. Gall. of W. Australia, 'erth; Boymans Museum, Rotterdam; Power Collection, Sydney, etc. *Address:* Eagles Nest, Zennor, St. Ives, Cornwall; and 12 Editha Mans., Edith Grove, London SW10.

**HERON, Susanna,** B.A. (Hons.) (1971); sculptor; *b* England, 22 Sept., 949. *Exhib:* solo shows since 1985 include Whitechapel A.G., Camden Arts Centre, Newlyn A.G. *Work in collections:* Stedelijk Museum, Arts Council, V. & A., C.A.S., etc., museums in Europe and Australia. *Commissions:* Major commissions: 21m. x 2.5m. carved slate frieze, new building for Council of European Union, Brussels (1995), sole British representative; front new British Embassy, Dublin (1995); sunken courtyard for new Shoreditch Campus or Hackney Community College (1997); watercourse and woodland garden (2 acres) Fell Foot Park, Lake Windermere, National Trust (1997-98). *Publications:* photographs and text: Shima: Island and Garden (Abson, 1992); Stills from Sculpture (Abson, 1997). *Signs work:* see appendix. *Address:* 39 Norman Gr., London E3 5EG.

**HERRIOT, Alan B.,** artist/sculptor in cold cast GRP, painting in oil, acrylic and water-colour; Proprietor, Endeavour Art Studios, Edinburgh; *b* 20 Feb., 952. *Studied:* Duncan of Jordanstone, Dundee (1969-74, Scott Sutherland, ames Morrison). *Exhib:* Aros Centre Skye, Whisky Heritage Centre Edinburgh, Inverary Court House. *Work in collections:* Miner's Monument, Newtongrange, Horse and Figure, Loanhead; 51st Highland Division Liberation Monument, Schijndel (Holland) and Perth (Scotland). *Publications:* The Foundling; Christmas is Coming; Travellers Tales; Broonies, Silkies and Fairies; Quest for a Kelpie. *Signs work:* "Alan B. Herriot" and see appendix. *Address:* Endeavour Art Studios, 75 Trafalgar La., Leith, Edinburgh EH6 4DQ.

**HESELTINE, John Robert,** B. of E. Drawing (1941), B. of E. Pictorial Design T.D. (1941); artist in oil and water-colour, portrait artist; *b* Ilford, Essex, 4 Sept., 1923. *m* Pam Masco. one *s.* one *d. Studied:* S.E. Essex College of Art Francis Taylor, A.R.C.A., Allen Wellings, A.R.C.A.). *Exhib:* V. & A., R.W.S., R.P.S., Bourne Gallery, David Messum London, Priory Gallery Cheltenham, U.S.A. and Scandinavia. *Work in collections:* Dartmouth Naval College, Fleet

Air Arm, Yeovilton; private and corporate collections. *Publications:* illustrated 1949-88: Odhams Press, Fleetway, I.P.C., London Times, London Standard U.S.A. and Europe. *Clubs:* Wentworth. *Signs work:* "John Heseltine." *Address* East House, East St., Petworth, W. Sussex GU28 0AB.

**HEWISON, William,** N.D.D., painting (1949), A.T.D. (1950), M.S.I.A. (1954); illustrator in ink; line and line and wash, and colour; Art Editor, Punch (1960-1984); *b* South Shields, 15 May, 1925. *m* Elsie Hammond. one *s.* one *d.* *Educ:* South Shields High School; London University. *Studied:* South Shield Art School (1941-43), Regent St. Polytechnic Art School (1947-49). *Exhib:* Four one-man shows, National Theatre; drawings permanently in V. & A. and B.M. *Publications:* work repro.: illustrations and cartoons; Press advertise ments, Punch, The Times; book jackets; books, Types Behind the Print Mindfire, The Cartoon Connection, How to Draw and Sell Cartoons. *Signs work:* "Hewison" or "H." *Address:* 5 Southdown Drive, London SW20 8EZ.

**HEWLETT, Francis,** R.W.A. (1979), D.F.A. (1955), N.D.D. (1952) painter in oil paint, also worked in polychrome ceramic (1967-76); Painter in Residence: Gregynog Hall, Powys (1977), Newlyn Soc. of Artists; Head of Painting, Falmouth (1963-81); *b* Bristol, 26 Sept., 1930. *m* Liz Allen. one *s.* two *d.* *Educ:* Fairfield Grammar School, Bristol. *Studied:* West of England College of Art (1948-52, George Sweet), Ecole des Beaux Arts, Paris (1953, Ateliers o Legeult and Brianchon), Slade School (1953-54, W. Coldstream, C. Rogers) *Exhib:* shown since 1958, Newlyn, R.W.A., R.A., Dublin, Belfast, Browse and Darby, London (1993). *Work in collections:* Belfast, Plymouth, Leicester Portsmouth, Southampton, Aberystwyth, Gregynog Hall, Duisburg (Germany) *Signs work:* "Francis Hewlett" or "F.H." *Address:* 21 Penwerris Terr. Falmouth, Cornwall TR11 2PA.

**HEYWORTH, James Charles,** L.D.A.D. distinction University of London (1982); illustrator/painter in gouache, water-colour, pen and ink, airbrush; *b* London, 28 Feb., 1956. *Educ:* Wandsworth School. *Studied:* Putney School of Art (1975), Byam Shaw School of Drawing and Painting (1976, D. Nixon) Goldsmiths' College (1979-82, Bernard Cheese). *Exhib:* Battersea Arts Centre. Ripley Arts; one-man Bury Metro Arts Assoc. Work in private collections *Clubs:* Assoc. of Illustrators. *Signs work:* "James Heyworth." *Address:* 99 Sutton Common Rd., Sutton, Surrey SM1 3HP.

**HICKEY, Michael,** F.L.S. (1979), F.S.B.A. (1986), M.I.Hort. (1987), Silver Lindley Medal (1978), Silver Gilt Lindley medal (1980); artist in pen and Indian ink for scientific botanical illustration; part-time lecturer, author; Vice-Pres. Soc. of Botanical Artists (1988-97); Chairman, Glos. Soc. for Botanica Illustration; *b* Seaford, E. Sussex, 10 Mar., 1930. *m* Robin Florence Petersen two *d.* *Educ:* Eastbourne College; Plumpton Agricultural College; University of Botanic Gdn., Cambridge (qualified 1954). *Studied:* St. Paul's Teacher Training College (qualified as a teacher 1957). *Exhib:* Botanical Soc. of the British Isles, R.H.S., S.B.A. (Mall Galleries, Westminster Gallery)

Cheltenham and Glos. C.H.E., Linnean Soc., Glos. Soc. for Botanical Illustration. *Work in collections:* Hunt Inst. for Botanical Documentation, Carnegie Mellon University, Pittsburgh. *Publications:* over 20 books illustrated and some as author or co-author, including '100 Families of Flowering Plants' with Clive King (C.U.P. 1981), illustrated 'A New Key to Wild Flowers' by John Hayward (C.U.P. 1987), author/artist 'Drawing Plants in Pen and Ink' (Cedar 1994), co-author 'Common Families of Flowering Plants' by M.H. & C. King (C.U.P. 1997), co-artist 'The Shaping of Cambridge Botany' by Dr. S.M. Walters (C.U.P. 1981), co-artist 'Secondary Pollen Presentation' by P.F. Yeo (Berlin 1993), co-artist 'Wild and Garden Flowers' by Max Walters (Harper Collins 1993). *Signs work:* see appendix. *Address:* Hamlyn Cottage, France Lynch, Stroud, Glos. GL6 8LT.

**HICKLING, Edward Albert,** artist in oil and water-colour; retired; *b* Nottingham, 2 May, 1913. *Educ:* Nottingham. *Studied:* Nottingham College of Art (1927-39) under A. Spooner, R.B.A. *Exhib:* R.A., R.B.A., R.I., R.O.I., R.P., R.S.M.A. *Work in collections:* City of Derby Museums and A.G. *Clubs:* Nottingham Soc. of Artists. *Signs work:* "E. A. Hickling." *Address:* 25 Wilsthorpe Rd., Breaston, Derbys. DE72 3EA.

**HICKS, Anne,** R.W.A., Slade Dip.; artist in oil and gouache of portraits, murals, costume design, environmental design; Adult Education Avon and Visiting Lecturer, University Architects Dept., Bristol (1976-84); *b* London. *m* Jerry Hicks. one *s.* one *d. Educ:* Hampstead and Minehead. *Studied:* Slade School under Profs. Schwabe and Coldstream. *Exhib:* R.W.A., British Women Painters Musée de l'Art Moderne, Paris (1967); two-person shows with husband: Bristol, Cardiff, Dorchester, etc. (1954-90). *Work in collections:* England, France, America, New Zealand. *Signs work:* "Anne Hicks." *Address:* Goldrush, Gt. George St., Bristol BS1 5QT.

**HICKS, Jerry,** M.B.E., A.T.D., R.W.A., Slade Dip., Judo 7th Dan; painter including portraits, murals; environmentalist; *b* London, 12 June, 1927. *m* Anne Hayward, painter. one *s.* one *d. Educ:* Actors' Orphanage, Rishworth, Sandhurst. *Studied:* Slade under Coldstream, Freud and with Stanley Bird and Walter Bayes. *Exhib:* R.A., R.W.A., R.B.A., two-person shows with wife: Bristol, Cardiff, Dorchester, etc. (1954-90). Winner of Bristol 600 Competition (1973), Queen's Jubilee Award (British Achievement), Olympic Painting prize (1984). *Work in collections:* Britain, U.S.A., Canada, St. Lucia, Germany, Italy, France, Australia, Japan. *Signs work:* "Hicks." *Address:* Goldrush, Gt. George St., Bristol BS1 5QT.

**HICKS, June Rhodes,** B.A. (Hons.) (1956), M.A. (1960); printmaker in etching; former teacher; *b* Yorks., 5 June, 1935. *m* J. Michael Hicks. two *s.* one *d. Educ:* Universities: Leeds, Belfast. *Studied:* Penzance School of Art (Bouverie Hoyton, John Tunnard, Joan Whiteford). *Exhib:* solo shows in Cornwall. *Work in collections:* galleries in Cornwall and elswhere; and in private collections. *Clubs:* Founder mem. Penwith Printmakers, mem. St. Ives

Soc. of Artists, mem. Penzance Soc. of Artists. *Signs work:* "June Hicks." *Address:* Vingoe Cottage, Trevescan Sennen, nr. Penzance TR19 7AQ.

**HICKS, Nicola,** M.B.E., R.W.A., F.R.B.S., M.A., R.C.A.; sculptor in plaster and straw, bronze; *b* London, 1960. *m* Daniel Flowers. one *s*. one *d*. *Studied:* Chelsea School of Art (1978-82), Royal College of Art (1982-85). *Exhib.* numerous solo and mixed exhbns. in U.K. and abroad. *Commissions:* monument to The Brown Dog, Battersea Park, London. *Clubs:* "HICKS." *Address:* c/o Flowers East, 199-205 Richmond Rd., London E8 3NJ.

**HICKS, Philip,** Dip.R.A.S.; painter in oil, acrylic and water-colour. Chairman, A.G.B.I.; *b* England, 1928. *m* Jill. one *s*. one *d*. *Educ:* Winchester College. *Studied:* Chelsea School of Art and R.A. Schools. *Exhib:* one-man shows, Marjorie Parr, Robert Self, Hoya, New Art Centre Galleries, Gallery 10, London, Oxford Gallery, V.E.C.U. Antwerp, Engström Galleri, Stockholm; retrospective, Battersea Arts Centre, London, Bohun Gallery, Henley, 1977 British Council award, David Messum Fine Art, London. *Work in collections:* Tate Gallery, V. & A., Contemporary Art Soc., Imperial War Museum, Nuffield Foundation, R.C.M., De Beers, Mirror Group, Wates Ltd., Nat. West. Bank, B.P., APV Holdings, Chandris Shipping. *Commissions:* Wates Ltd., Control Data Corporation, Chandris Shipping. *Clubs:* Chelsea Arts and Arts Club. *Signs work:* "Philip Hicks" (often on reverse) or "HICKS." *Address:* Radcot House, Buckland Rd., Bampton, Oxon. OX18 2AA.

**HIGGINS, John,** self taught artist in water-colour and drawing; *b* Carshalton, 10 July, 1934. *m* Nicola. two *s*. *Exhib:* Higgins Gallery, St. Ives. Art tuition: private and residential. *Address:* 6 Richmond Pl., St.Ives, Cornwall TR26 1JN.

**HIGGINS, Nicola,** artist in water-colour; private water-colour tutor, tutoring on residential art holidays; *b* Rustington, Sussex, 1 Mar., 1943. *m* John. one *s*. *Exhib:* Higgins Gallery, Sloop Craft Market, St. Ives. *Signs work:* "Nicola." *Address:* 6 Ricmond Pl., St. Ives, Cornwall TR26 1JN.

**HIGSON, John,** M.F.P.S.; self taught sculptor in wood and ceramic, painter in water-colour and pastel; *b* 30 Oct., 1936. *Educ:* Malden West County Secondary. *Exhib:* one-man shows: Bourne Hall, Ewell, Russell Studio, Wimbledon, Malden Centre, New Malden. *Address:* 22 Croxton, Burritt Rd., Kingston upon Thames, Surrey KT1 3HS.

**HILL, Anthony,** artist, plastician and theorist: works in industrial materials; awarded Leverhulme Fellowship, Hon. Research Fellow, Dept. Mathematics, University College, London (1971-73); currently visiting research associate (Maths. Dept. UCL); *b* London, 23 Apr., 1930. *m* Yuriko Kaetsu, ceramist. *Educ:* Bryanston. *Studied:* St. Martin's (1947-49), Central School (1949-51). *Exhib:* Kasmin Gallery (1966, 1969, 1980); retrospective exhbn. Hayward Gallery (1983). *Work in collections:* Tate Gallery, V. & A., British Museum, provincial galleries; Museum of Modern Art, Grenoble, Tel Aviv and Santiago, Louisiana Museum Denmark, Gulbenkian Museum Lisbon. *Publications:* edited Data Directions in Art Theory and Aesthetics (Faber, 1986), Duchamp-Passim (Gordon and Breach 1995); articles and work repro.: in English, Continental and American publications since 1950. *Signs work:* "Anthony Hill." and see appendix. Since 1975 has made works signed "Rem Doxford", and "Redo." *Address:* 24 Charlotte St., London W1.

**HILL, Charles Douglas,** artist in oil; *b* Dewsbury, W. Yorks., 16 June, 1953. *m* Jennifer Haylett, singer. *Educ:* Dewsbury, England, and Squamish, Canada. *Exhib:* worldwide; and Longships Gallery, St. Ives. *Publications:* work repro.: book cover (Black Swan Pub.), articles 'Cornish World', 'Inside Cornwall." *Clubs:* St. Ives Soc. of Artists. *Address:* Longships Gallery, St.Andrew's St., St. Ives, Cornwall TR26 1AN.

**HILL, Derek,** C.B.E.; painter in oil on canvas or board, stage designer; director of Art, British School at Rome (1953-55 and 1957-59); organiser of Degas Exhbn. at Edinburgh Festival and Tate Gallery; *b* Southampton, 6 Dec., 1916. *Educ:* Marlborough College. *Studied:* Munich, Vienna, Paris, and theatre design in Russia, China and Japan. *Exhib:* Marlborough Gallery, London (1978), Leicester Galleries, Whitechapel Gallery (1961), Colnaghi Gallery. *Work in collections:* Tate Gallery, Belfast Art Gallery, Dublin Municipal Gallery, Arts Council, National Gallery of Canada, etc. *Publications:* co-author, Islamic Architecture:Its Decoration (Faber & Faber, 1964); co-author, Islamic Architecture in N. Africa (1976). *Signs work:* "D.H." in a circle when picture is signed. *Address:* St. Colomb's, Churchill (Letterkenny), Co. Donegal, Ireland.

**HILL, Francis,** Cert. Criminology (1959); self taught painter in oil; retd. police chief inspector; formerly Head of Security, National Gallery and N.P.G.; *b* Barnsley, 11 Sept., 1917. *m* Barbara Heward. two *s.* two *d. Educ:* Leeds University. *Exhib:* R.A. (1982, 1984, 1992, 1993), National Gallery (staff), Sotheby's, Royal Exchange London, Hertfordshire Artists. Work in private collections. *Publications:* chapter with illustration: A World of Their Own (Pelham); Royal Academy Exhibitors 1971-1989. *Signs work:* "Francis Hill." *Address:* Three Roses, 38 Brockswood La., Welwyn Garden City, Herts. AL8 7BG.

**HILL, Reginald H.,** S.G.F.A.; artist in oil, water-colour, pastel and pencil of portraits, landscapes, figure; President, Croydon Art Soc.; *b* London, 26 Feb., 1919. *m* Jean Hill (decd.). one *s.* one *d. Educ:* Vauxhall Central School, London. *Studied:* City & Guilds Art School (1969-72, Middleton Todd, R.A., Robin Guthrie, R.P.; 1972-75, Rodney Burn, R.A.). *Exhib:* R.A., R.S.P.P., N.E.A.C., S.G.F.A. Work in private collections worldwide. *Commissions:* Numerous. *Publications:* illustrated 'Scorched Earth' by 'Detonator' (Col. Brazier). *Clubs:* Chelsea Arts. *Signs work:* "Reg. Hill," "R. Hill" or "R.H.H." *Address:* "Raffaello", 54 Hermitage Rd., Kenley, Surrey CR8 5EB.

**HILL, Ronald James,** U.A., S.G.F.A., F.S.A.I.; freelance artist in oil, water-colour, pen and ink; tutor; *b* London, 19 Oct., 1933. *m* Betty Bunn (decd.).

*Educ:* Willesden Technical College. *Studied:* Heatherley's School of Art (1958-65, Jack Merriot, Patrick Larkin, Harry Riley). *Exhib:* Paris Salon (1966-69), R.B.A., U.A.; one man shows, Brent, Wantage. *Commissions:* Landscapes and architectural subjects in all media. *Signs work:* "RONN." *Address:* Orpheus Studio of Fine Art, Pound Cottage, Kingston Lisle, Wantage, Oxon. OX12 9QL.

**HILL, Sonia Geraldine,** painter in oil; *b* London, 26 Sept., 1939. *Educ:* Dorchester Abbey School, Oxon. *Studied:* Maidenhead Art College, Berks.; Zambia (pupil with Andrew Hayward). *Exhib:* R.A. (1993) (two), and two further works accepted by Selection Com. (1997). *Publications:* R.A. Illustrated (1993). *Signs work:* "S.G. Hill." *Address:* 6A Warfield Rd., Hampton, Middx. TW12 2AY.

**HILLHOUSE, David,** B.A. (1969), A.T.D. (1971), R.C.A. (1979), A.M.A. (1982); artist in water-colour and egg tempera; Principal Museum Officer, Wirral Museum Services, Birkenhead; *b* Irby, Wirral, 19 June, 1945. *m* Paula Lane. two *s. Educ:* Birkenhead Institute. *Studied:* Laird School of Art (1964-66), Liverpool College of Art (1966-69). *Exhib:* Merseyside, Wales and Bristol. *Clubs:* R.Cam.A., Wirral Soc. of Arts, Museums Assoc., Deeside Art Group. *Signs work:* "David Hillhouse." *Address:* 49 Cortsway, Greasby, Wirral L49 2NA.

**HILLI:** see THOMPSON, Hilli.

**HILLIER, Matthew,** S.WL.A., S.A.A. (U.S.A.); wildlife artist in acrylic, pastel and water-colour; Council mem. S.WL.A.; *b* Slough, 7 May, 1958. *Studied:* Dyfed College of Art. *Exhib:* Christie's Wildlife Auction (1994-97), Pacific Rim Wildlife Art Expo (1994, 1995) Tacoma, Vancouver, Soc. of Animal Artists (1995, 1996), Birds in Art, Wisconsin (1993, 1994, 1996), Florida Wildlife Art Expo (1997), South Eastern Wildlife Expo (1997), Friends of Washington Zoo Wildlife Art Show (1996, 1997). *Commissions:* Ambleside Studio, Michigan. *Publications:* Fine Art Limited Edition prints (Millpond Press, Florida); illustrated: The Rhinocerous, a Monograph (Basilisk Press Limited Edition Book). *Signs work:* "Matthew Hillier." *Address:* 166 Elmer Rd., Middleton-on-Sea, W. Sussex PO22 6JA.

**HILLS, Peter Faber,** N.D.D., R.A.Cert., F.R.B.S., Past Secretary of the 65 Group (Public School Art Masters); Churchill Fellow in Sculpture (1972); sculptor in clay, stone, wood; schoolmaster; Director of Art, Tonbridge School (1963-79), retd. from Tonbridge School (1988); *b* Bearsted, Kent, 4 Dec., 1925. *m* Ann-Mary Ewart (née Macdonald). two *s.* one *d. Educ:* Tonbridge School. *Studied:* Bromley College of Art (1948-50), R.A. Schools (1950-55); assistant to Maurice Lambert, R.A. (1955-60), and worked for Sir Henry Rushbury, R.A., Sir Albert Richardson, P.R.A. *Work in collections:* Lord Leighton Museum, Kensington, Skinner's Library, Tonbridge School. *Signs work:* "HILLS." *Address:* 33 Yardley Park Rd., Tonbridge, Kent.

**HINCHCLIFFE, Michael,** artist in water-colour, designer; *b* London, 25

Apr., 1937. *m* Gillian. two *d. Educ:* St. Marylebone Grammar School. *Studied:* St. Martin's School of Art. *Exhib:* R.I., U.A.; many one-man shows. *Work in collections:* Weybridge Museum. *Signs work:* see appendix. *Address:* 37 The Furrows, Walton on Thames, Surrey KT12 3JG.

**HIND, Margaret Madeleine,** S.Lm., M.A.S.-F., Froebel Cert.; miniaturist working mainly in water-colour with gold leaf on ivorine/vellum; *b* Minera, N. Wales, 1927. *m* Lt. Col. J.G. Hind, O.B.E. (retd.). three *d. Educ:* Woodford House School, Croydon, Coloma Froebel College (1945-48). *Studied:* art: privately under C.S. Spackman, R.B.A. (1943-45), Helen Gaudin (Washington D.C., 1976-78); started miniature painting (1986). *Exhib:* R.A., R.M.S., Llewellyn Alexander Gallery, Medici Gallery London, Hilliard Soc., Soc. of Limners, Miniature Soc. of Florida. Awarded Historical, Mythological prize M.A.S.-F. (1995). Paints stories from Chaucer/King Arthur, etc. in the medieval manner. *Signs work:* see appendix. *Address:* 27 Birch Cl., Send, nr. Woking, Surrey GU23 7BZ.

**HINKS, Thomas,** N.D.D. (1951), F.R.S.A. (1981); lecturer-demonstrator, artist in water-colour, oil, acrylic; demonstrator, Daler Rowney; visiting lecturer at res. colleges and art societies; *b* Newcastle, 26 Apr., 1930. *m* Vera. one *s.* one *d. Educ:* Newcastle School of Art, Stoke-on-Trent College of Art. *Studied:* under Arthur Berry. *Exhib:* 15 one-man shows in Midlands. *Work in collections:* Stoke-on-Trent City A.G., Newcastle Museum and A.G., Keele University, W.E.A. Centre; paintings in America, Canada, Spain, Greece, France, Norway, and many private U.K. collections. *Publications:* author of New Methods and Techniques in Art - for schools. *Clubs:* Chairman, Unit Ten Art Soc., N.A.P.A., Soc. of Staffs Artists. *Signs work:* "Tom Hinks." *Address:* Fairways, High St., Caverswall, Stoke-on-Trent, Staffs. ST11 9EF.

**HINWOOD, Kay,** P.S., U.A.; painter in oil, pastel, etc.; *b* Bromley, 26 Nov., 1920. *m* (1) the late George Hinwood, (2) the late Douglas Zeidler. one *s.* one *d. Educ:* Stratford House School, Bickley. *Studied:* first Paris, with Edouard MacAvoy, later privately with Sonia Mervyn; City and Guilds Art School, London; Kathleen Browne Studios, Chelsea under Marian Kratochwil and Kathleen Browne. *Exhib:* R.P., R.B.A., R.O.I., P.S., U.A., S.W.A., Mall Galleries. *Work in collections:* England, U.S.A., Canada, France, Spain, Australia, Holland. *Clubs:* Chelsea Arts. *Signs work:* "K. Hinwood." *Address:* 27 Edward Rd., Bromley, Kent BR1 3NG.

**HIPKISS, Percy Randolph,** R.B.S.A. (1971); freelance artist in oil, water-colour and pastel; jewellery designer; *b* Blackheath, Birmingham, 8 Aug., 1912. *m* Dorothy Alice Boraston. one *s.* one *d. Educ:* at Blackheath. *Work in collections:* Dudley A.G., and in private collections throughout U.K., America, Australia, Belgium. *Clubs:* past-president, Birmingham Water-colour Soc.; President, Dudley Society of Artists *Signs work:* "Hipkiss." *Address:* 18 Lewis Rd., Oldbury, Warley, W.Mid B68 0PW.

**HIRST, Barry Elliot,** N.D.D. Painting (1956), D.F.A. (Lond.) (1958),

F.R.S.A. (1989); painter; Emeritus Prof. of Fine Art, University of Sunderland. *b* Padstow, Cornwall, 11 June, 1934. *m* Sheila Mary. one *s.* two *d. Educ* Alleyns School, Dulwich. *Studied:* Camberwell School of Art (1950-52, 1954-56), Slade School (1956-58, Keith Vaughan, Claude Rogers). *Exhib:* over twelve one-man shows, London, Sydney, N.Y., Glasgow, Edinburgh, Newcastle upon Tyne, Riga. *Work in collections:* Contemporary Arts Soc. British Council, Sunday Times, Croydon Educ. Com., Northern Arts Assoc. Tyne & Wear Museums, University of Sunderland, Darlington Memorial Hospital, Olinda Museum Brazil, Derby Museum and A.G., H.R.H. Duchess of Kent, Latvian National Museum Riga, Latvian Academy of Art Riga, R.A.C. Sunderland and Portsmouth Newspapers, Sao Paulo Museum Brazil, B.P. *Publications:* 'From a Painting by Masaccio' with C. Day-Lewis, 'The Way of It' with R.S. Thomas, 'Waiting for the Barbarians' with Roy Fuller, 'An Ill-Governed Coast' with Roy Fuller, 'Kisses' with Alistair Eliot. *Clubs.* Sunderland Assoc. Football. *Signs work:* "BARRY HIRST" or "B.E. HIRST.' *Address:* c/o Mercury Gallery, 26 Cork St., London W1X 1HB.

**HIRST, Derek,** A.R.C.A.; artist; *b* Doncaster, 11 Apr., 1930. *Studied.* Doncaster School of Art (1946-48), R.C.A. (1948-51). *Exhib:* Drian Galleries (1961), Tooth's Gallery (1962-63), Stone Galleries, Newcastle upon Tyne (1962), University of Sussex (1966), Towner A.G. (1966), Angela Flowers Gallery (1970, 1972, 1975, 1979, 1984, 1987, 1989), Victorian Centre for the Arts, Melbourne, Australia (1980), Pallant House Gallery, Chichester (1987, 1991), Flowers East (1991, 1995), Flowers East at London Fields (1993). *Work in collections:* Tate Gallery, V. & A., National Gallery of Canada, A.C.G.B., Contemporary Art Soc., D.O.E., Fundaçao dos Museus Regionaise de Bahia, Brazil, Bank of Ireland, Dublin, Universities of Sussex and Southampton, Art Inst. of Detroit, Brooklyn Museum, N.Y., Arizona State University, Phoenix Art Museum, etc. *Signs work:* "Derek Hirst." *Address:* 3 The Terrace, Mill La. Sidlesham, Chichester, W. Sussex PO20 7NA.

**HISLOP, Helga,** Cert.A.D. (Dist.) (1962), Dip.A.D. (graphics) (1964), F.S.B.A. (1986), I.A.A.S.B.A. (1995); botanical artist in water-colour; *b* London, 18 Jan., 1941. one *d. Educ:* Willoughby H.S. High School, Sydney, Australia. *Studied:* Cardiff College of Art (1959-62, A.T. Kitson), Central School of Arts and Crafts (1962-64, P. Kitley). *Exhib:* mixed shows: Mall Galleries, Westminster Gallery, Linnean Soc., R.H.S., Hunt Inst. *Work in collections:* The Shirley Sherwood Collection of Contemporary Botanical Art. *Publications:* Botanicus Publishing Limited. *Signs work:* "Helga Hislop" hidden in work. *Address:* The Mill House, Little Sampford, nr. Saffron Walden, Essex CB10 2QT.

**HITCHCOCK, Harold Raymond,** F.R.S.A. (1972); Hon. Col. of State of Louisiana U.S.A. (1974); artist in water-colour and oil; *b* London, 23 May, 1914. *m* Rose Hitchcock. two *s.* one *d. Studied:* Working Mens College, Camden Town (1935-36) under Percy Horton, Barnett Freedman. *Exhib:* one-man shows: Hanson Gallery, New Orleans (1990), M.K. Vance Gallery, Chicago (1992), Campbell & Franks (Fine Art) Ltd. (1975), Pilkington Glass Museum (1973), Hilton Gallery (1970), Upper Grosvenor Gallery (1969), Woburn Abbey (1967), Walker Gallery (1956); retrospective shows: R.I. Galleries (1967), Philadelphia Art Alliance, U.S.A. (1982); touring exhbn. in U.S.A.: New Orleans, Huntsville, Atlanta City, Daytona Beach, Corpus Christi and Winston Salem (opened by the Duke of Bedford, 1972); R.S.A., London (1984), Gallery 106, Perrysberg, Ohio (1984), Clossons Gallery, Cincinnati (1985), Christopher Wood Gallery, London (1986). *Work in collections:* V. & A., Rowntree Memorial Trust, Hunterian A.G. of University of Glasgow, Lidice Memorial Museum, Czechoslovakia, Museum of Fine Art, N. Carolina, University of Louisiana, Hannema-de Stuers Foundation, Nijenhuis Castle, Netherlands, New Orleans Museum of Fine Art. *Publications:* Harold Hitchcock : A Romantic Symbol in Surrealism (1982) by Dr. Ian Williamson. *Signs work:* see appendix. *Address:* Meadow View, Ugborough, Ivybridge, Devon PL21 0NZ.

**HITCHCOCK, Malcolm John,** R.W.A.; painter in oil or oil over egg tempera of railway subjects, also nudes in mixed media; *b* Salisbury, 17 Apr., 1929. *m* Zaidee Lindsay, author. *Educ:* Andover Boys' School. *Studied:* Andover School of Art. *Exhib:* one-man shows, London and provinces; R.A., R.W.A., Paris Salon, Brussels and Dusseldorf. *Work in collections:* Reading Museum and A.G., Bristol R.W.A. *Publications:* work repro.: series of articles in The Artist. *Signs work:* "M.J. HITCHCOCK" and date. *Address:* Quint, Rectory Rd., Padworth Common, Reading, Berks. RG7 4JD.

**HITCHENS, John,** painter on canvas, also works in variety of three-dimensional materials; *b* Sussex, 1940; married. two *s. Educ:* Bedales School. *Studied:* Bath Academy of Art. *Exhib:* Regular London exhbns. since 1964. *Work in collections:* public and permanent collections U.K. and abroad. 1979: 52ft. mural, "A Landscape Symphony". *Signs work:* "John Hitchens." *Address:* The Old School, Byworth, Petworth, Sussex GU28 0HN.

**HO, Dr. Kok-Hoe,** D.Sc. (Hon.), P.B.M., M.S.I.A., F.R.A.I.A., F.R.I.B.A., A.P.A.M., A.R.A.S., A.R.P.S.; awarded St. Andrew's Gold (1935) and Bronze (1937); 2nd Inter-School Art gold medal (1939); architect; artist in oil and water-colour painting, pen and pencil drawing; art-photographer; president-director, Ho Kwong-Yew & Sons, Architects, Singapore; Chairman, Singapore Art Soc. (1953-70); *b* Singapore, 14 July, 1922. *Educ:* St. Andrew's School, Singapore. *Studied:* graduated N.S.W. College of Architecture, Sydney. *Exhib:* Sydney (1948-49); Singapore (1954-62); Kuala Lumpur (1960-62), etc. Photo salons: London (1957); La Coruna (1958); Hongkong (1958), etc. Architectural Work: National Museum, Kuala Lumpur, etc. *Publications:* Travel Sketches and Paintings, etc. *Clubs:* Royal Art Soc.; Royal Institute of Australian Architects; R.I.B.A.; Royal Photographic Soc. of Great Britain; Singapore Art Soc. *Signs work:* "Ho Kok-Hoe." *Address:* 9 Camden Park, Singapore 1129.

**HOARE, Diana C.,** B.A. Hons.; lettering designer, calligrapher, letter carver, carving on stone and slate, calligraphy; *b* London, 10 Feb., 1956. *m* William Taunton. one *s*. two *d*. *Educ:* Godolphin and Latymer; University of Kent, Canterbury. *Studied:* privately with Vernon Shearer, Ievan Rees, Heather Child, Sam Somerville. *Exhib:* solo exhbns. in Dorset, London and B'ham. *Work in collections:* two MS. books at University of Austin, Texas. *Publications:* Advanced Calligraphy Techniques (Cassells), Everybodys Wine Guide (Quarto). *Signs work:* see appendix. *Address:* Upper House Farm, Dilwyn, Hereford HR4 8JJ.

**HOBART, John,** B.Sc. (Lond.), R.C.A.; self taught artist in oil and watercolour; past Vice-Pres. Royal Cambrian Academy; Fellow, University College of N. Wales, Bangor; *b* London, 27 May, 1922. one *s*. two *d*. *Educ:* University College, London. *Exhib:* one-man, Theatre Gwynedd; group shows, Plas Mawr, Conway, Tegfryn Gallery, Cambrian Academy, R.I., N.Wales Group, Newlyn, Penwith, Kings College, Cambridge. *Work in collections:* University College of N.Wales, Bangor; private collections in U.S.A., Canada, Australia, G.B., Holland, Germany. *Signs work:* "J. Hobart." *Address:* Buswisnan, Ludgvan, Penzance, Cornwall TR20 8BN.

**HOBSON, Anthony Francis,** Ph.D., N.D.D., A.T.D., F.R.S.A., F.S.E.A.D., Hon.F.H.S.; painter, art historian; Hon. Research Fellow, Coventry University; *b* Leicester, 28 Feb., 1920. *m* June Lea. one *s*. one *d*. *Educ:* Wyggeston School, University of Leicester. *Studied:* Leicester College of Art (1936-38, 1946-51). *Exhib:* R.A., R.S.A., R.P., R.B.A., R.O.I., R.S.M.A., R.B.S.A., P.S., Aviation Artists, etc.; one-man shows: Leamington Spa (1971, 1975, 1980, 1985, 1986). *Work in collections:* Imperial War Museum; R.A.F. Museum; Leamington Spa A.G. *Publications:* J. W. Waterhouse, R.A. (Studio Vista, 1980; Phaidon, 1989, 1992). *Clubs:* Past President, Coventry and Warwickshire Soc. of Artists. *Signs work:* "Anthony Hobson." *Address:* Pear Tree Cottage, Ilmington, Warwickshire CV36 4LG.

**HOCKIN, Julie,** A.R.M.S. (1990), H.S. (1984), S.O.F.A. (1996); self taught professional artist specialising in miniatures and larger paintings, in watercolour, graphite and coloured pencils; specialising in wildlife and botanical subjects, also cats; Creative Director, Hockin and Roberts Ltd., St. Austell; *b* St. Austell, 3 Feb., 1937. one *d*. *Educ:* St. Austell Grammar School. *Exhib:* National Trust Cotehele, Marwell Zoological Pk. Winchester, Carlyon Bay Hotel, St. Austell, Llewellyn Alexander Gallery, London. *Signs work:* "Julie Hockin" or "JH" joined. *Address:* Cedar Lodge, Trevarth, Mevagissey, St. Austell, Cornwall PL26 6RX.

**HODGES, Cyril Walter,** Hon. D.Litt. (Sussex) 1979; author, mural painter, illustrator, stage designer; *b* Beckenham, 1909. *m* Greta Becker. two *s*. *Educ:* Dulwich College. *Studied:* Goldsmiths' College. *Publications:* work repro.: advertisements, books, magazine illustrations in England and U.S.A. Special subjects: Shakespearean Theatres. Designer of Mermaid Theatre (1951),

Lloyd's 1951 Exhbn. Mural painting U.K. Provident Inst. (1957). Retrospective exhbn. Folger Library, Washington D.C. (1988). Reconstructional designs Rose Theatre excavation (1989). Columbus Sails, The Globe Restored, The Namesake, The Marsh King, Shakespeare's Theatre, The Overland Launch, Shakespeare's Second Globe, Playhouse Tales, The Battlement Garden. Awarded Kate Greenaway Medal for Illustration (1964). *Signs work:* "C. Walter Hodges." *Address:* 36 Southover High St., Lewes, Sussex BN7 1HX.

**HODGES, Gillian Mary,** S.W.A. (1987), S.Lm. (1997); portrait painter in oil, pastel and water-colour; portraits in miniature, oils and water-colour; *b* Twickenham, Middx. *m* Peter Steer Hodges. two *s. Educ:* Richmond School of Art under Jack Fairhurst, A.R.C.A., Salisbury School of Art and Heatherley School of Art (part time). *Exhib:* S.W.A., various societies in S. and S.W. of England, Northern Ireland. *Work in collections:* 'The Pageant' in Farnham (Surrey) Public Library; Officers' Mess QARANC, Aldershot; Inst. of Aviation Medicine, Farnborough. *Signs work:* "G. M. Hodges." *Address:* 23 Coniston Drive, Folly Hill, Farnham, Surrey GU9 0DB.

**HODGKINS, Barbara,** sculptor in marble, bronze; *b* U.S.A. *Educ:* Wellesley College, Columbia University, U.S.A. *Studied:* Chelsea School of Art, London. *Work in collections:* Sculpture in corporate collections: Prudential, Bank of China, Bank of Denmark, B.P., Reynolds, Hewlett-Packer, Foote, Cone, Belding, MCL (Art and Work award 1987) and in private European, Asian and American collections. *Clubs:* Mem. Royal Soc. of British Sculptors. *Address:* 5 Hurlingham Ct., Ranelagh Gdns., London SW6 3SH; and C.P.200, Pietrasanta (Lucca) 55045, Italy.

**HODGSON, Carole,** F.R.B.S., H.D.F.A. (1964); sculptor in cement, bronze, wax, ceramics, lead; Senior lecturer, Kingston University; *b* London, 1940. *Studied:* Wimbledon School of Art (1957-62), Slade School of Fine Art (1962-64). *Exhib:* Angela Flowers Gallery, Flowers East, A.C.G.B., W.A.C., Wustum Museum, U.S.A., Whitefriars Museum, Coventry, New Ashgate, Farnham, Llanelli Festival, Christie's Fine Arts, Centro Cultural Recoleta Buenas Aires, Insitute Chileno-Britanica Santiago Chile. *Work in collections:* Welsh Contemporary Arts Soc., A.C.G.B., W.A.C., British Council, D.O.E., Contemporary Arts Soc., Unilever House, Universities of Wales, London, Wisconsin U.S.A., British Medal Soc., Manpower. *Publications:* From the Sea to the Wall (Kingston University Press). *Signs work:* "Carole Hodgson." *Address:* c/o Flowers East, 199-205 Richmond Rd., London E8 3NJ.

**HODGSON, Josanne,** S.B.A.; botanical artist/etcher in water-colour, pastel, etching; *b* Blundellsands, Liverpool, 26 May, 1932. *m* Barrie B. one *s.* two *d. Studied:* Southport School of Art. *Exhib:* two solo, many shared in London, the North-West, N.Wales and the North-East. *Publications:* work repro.: greetings cards. *Clubs:* S.B.A., N.Wales Soc. of Botanical and Fine Water-colour Artists. *Signs work:* "Josanne Hodgson." *Address:* 10 Aylesby Close, Knutsford, Ches. WA16 8AE.

**HODGSON, Kenneth Jonah,** B.A., G.O.E. Dip. S.W. C.Q.S.W., P.T.A.; artist in acrylic, oil and water-colour; Exec com. mem., Merseyside Arts (1985-87); Steering com. sec., Merseyside Contemporary Artists (1988-89); *b* Liverpool, 2 Aug., 1936. two *d. Educ:* Liverpool, Herts, Oak Hill College, London, The Open University, N.E.W.I. Wrexham Cymru. *Exhib:* R.Cam.A., Williamson A.G.,various Liverpool and Chester galleries; collective exhbns. in Newcastle-Staffs, Ludlow, Crosby and R.B.S.A. Gallery B'ham; individual exhbns. on Merseyside and Wirral. Daylight Group - a Tate Liverpool/Metropolitan Borough of Wirral S.S.D. Arts Project, Art Forum - M.B.W. - S.S.D. (1993). Paintings in private and public collections in U.K. and other countries. *Clubs:* Sec., Wirral Soc. of Arts (1983-87); Founder, National Acrylic Painters' Assoc. *Signs work:* "Kenneth J. Hodgson." *Address:* N.A.P.A., 134 Rake La., Wallasey, Merseyside L45 1JW.

**HODIN, Josef Paul,** L.L.D. (Prague), Ph.D. (Hon., Uppsala), D.S.M., 1st Class, Czech; Commander order of merit, Italian; St. Olav Medal, Norwegian; Grand Cross, order of merit, Austrian; Grand Cross, order of merit, German; Silver Cross of Merit, Vienna; Prof. Art History h.c.(Vienna); author, art historian, critic; press attaché to the Norwegian Govt. (1944-45); director of Studies, I.C.A. (1949-54); co-editor of Quandrum, Brussels; mem. executive comm. British Society of Aesthetics; hon. mem. Editorial Council J.A.A.C., Cleveland; awarded intern. 1st prize for art criticism, 1954 (Biennale, Venice); *b* Prague, 17 Aug., 1905. *m* Doris Pamela Simms. one *s.* one *d. Educ:* Realschule, Realgymnasium, and Charles University, Prague. *Studied:* Dresden, Berlin, Paris, Stockholm, and Courtauld Inst. of Art, London University. *Publications:* numerous. *Address:* 12 Eton Ave., London NW3 3FH.

**HODSON, John,** sculptor in stone and bronze; *b* Oxford, 19 Aug., 1945. *Educ:* Cardinal Hinsley School, London. *Studied:* Courtauld Inst. of Art, London. *Exhib:* one-man show London (1973), Paris Salon, Salon des Independants and other international exhbns. *Publications:* work repro.: Modern Art Revue, Courtauld Inst. of Art, London. *Signs work:* "Hodson." *Address:* 40 Clement Cl., London NW6 7AN.

**HOFER, Paul,** Dr.-phil. (1938), Privatdocent Univ. Bern (1948), ao. Prof. (1956); Prof. of Ecole polytechnique, Univ. Lausanne (1961); Prof. Eidg. Techn. Hochschule, Zürich (1964, o. Prof., 1967-80); historian of Art; *b* Bern, 8 Aug., 1909. *m* Gertrud Wild, Dr.-phil. *Educ:* Bern, Elementary School and Gymnasium. *Studied:* history at Univ. of Bern under Prof. Artur Weese and H. R. Hahnloser, Univ. of Munich under Prof. Wilhelm Pinder. *Publications:* Die Italienische Landschaft im 16. Th. (1946), Die Kunstdenkmäler des Kantons Bern, Vol. I, Basle (1952), Vol. II, Basle (1959), Vol. III, Basle (1947), Vol. V, Basle (1969); Die Wehrbauten Berns (1953), Flugbild der Schweizer Stadt (with Prof. Hans Boesch, Univ. of Zürich, 1963), Palladios Erstling (1968), Fundplätze, Bauplätze (1970), Die Frühzeit von Aarberg (1973), Die

Stadtanlage von Thun im 12 und 13 Jahr hundert (1981), Die Burg Nydegg in Bern (1991), Spätbarock in Bern (1992), Reisejournale 1959-1988 (1993). *Address:* Villettegässchen 32b, Muri near Bern.

**HOFFER, Francis Peter Bernard,** Dip.Arch., F.C.S.D., F.F.B.; architect/designer, painter; hon. sec., Society of Mural Painters (1948-51); *b* Berlin, 1924. *m* Maria Pilar Perez Vales, three children. *Educ:* Bunce Court School, Kent. *Studied:* St. Martin's School of Art, London, and Cambridge. *Exhib:* R.B.A., Leicester Gallery, Arts Council, Amsterdam, Milan. *Work in collections:* U.S. Theatre Library, Washington and private collections. *Publications:* work repro.: Das Kunstwerk, Gebrauchsgraphik, Designers in Britain, Studio, Domus, Architectural Review, Architectur und Wohnen, Abitare. *Signs work:* "F. P. Hoffer." *Address:* 16 Downshire Hill, London NW3.

**HOFFMANN, Edith,** Ph.D., Munich, 1934; art historian and critic; editorial asst. Burlington Magazine (1938-46); asst. editor of the Burlington Magazine (1946-50); Lecturer, Hebrew University of Jerusalem (1960-61); art editor of the Encyclopaedia Hebraica (Jerusalem, 1953-65); *m* Dr. E. Yapou. one *d.* *Educ:* in Berlin, Vienna, Munich. *Publications:* Kokoschka: Life and Work (1947); Chagall: Water-colours (1947); contributions to the Burlington Magazine, Apollo, Art News (New York), Phoebus (Basle), Studio, Manchester Guardian, Listener, New Statesman, Twentieth Century, Neue Zürcher Zeitung, etc. *Address:* Alfasi St. 27, 92 302 Jerusalem, Israel.

**HOFLEHNER, Rudolf,** skulpturen and painter; Professor an der Akademie der bildenden Künste, Stuttgart; skulpturen in Eisen, massiv; *b* Linz, 8 Aug., 1916. *m* Luise Schaffer. *Studied:* Akademie der bild. Künste, Vienna. *Signs work:* see appendix. *Address:* Italien, Val d'Elsa, Podere Pantaneto, Provincia Siena; and Ottensteinstrasse 62, 2344 Maria Enzersdorf-Südstadt, Österreich.

**HOGAN, Prof. Eileen,** M.A. (R.C.A.), R.W.S.; painter; *b* London, 1 Mar., 1946. *m* Ken Ersser. *Educ:* Streatham Hill and Clapham High School. *Studied:* Camberwell School of Art and Crafts (1964-67), British School of Archaeology at Athens, Royal College of Art (1971-74, Carel Weight). *Exhib:* regularly at the Fine Art Soc., numerous one-man shows in Europe and America. *Work in collections:* V. & A., Imperial War Museum, R.A., and overseas museums and galleries. *Publications:* Under The Influence: catalogue to accompany retrospective, 1997. *Clubs:* Chelsea Arts, Double Crown. *Signs work:* "Eileen Hogan." *Address:* 102 Coleherne Ct., Old Brompton Rd., London SW5 0ED.

**HOGARTH, Arthur Paul,** O.B.E., R.A., Dr. R.C.A., R.D.I., R.E.; illustrator, printmaker and draughtsman; senior tutor, Royal College of Art (1964-71), visiting lecturer (1971-85); *b* Kendal, Cumbria, 4 Oct., 1917. *Studied:* Manchester School of Art and St Martin's School of Art, London. *Exhib:* regularly at Francis Kyle Gallery, London. *Work in collections:* city art galleries of Bradford, Bury, Blackburn, Carlisle, Kendal, Manchester, Newcastle-on-Tyne; Library of Congress, Washington D.C., Boston Public Library (U.S.),

Fitzwilliam Museum, Cambridge, Imperial War Museum, V. & A., B.M. *Publications:* Creative Pencil Drawing (1964), Drawing Architecture (1973), Arthur Boyd Houghton (1981), Artist as Reporter (revised enlarged edn., 1986); illustrator of Brendan Behan's Island and Brendan Behan's New York (with Brendan Behan); Majorca Observed (with Robert Graves); Russian Journey (with Alaric Jacob); America Observed (with Stephen Spender); Graham Greene Country (with Graham Greene); The Mediterranean Shore (with Lawrence Durrell); The Illustrated Year in Provence (with Peter Mayle). *Signs work:* "Paul Hogarth" or "P.H." *Address:* c/o Tessa Sayle, 11 Jubilee Pl., London SW3 3TE.

**HOLCH, Eric Sanford,** artist in oil, printmaker of limited edition serigraphs; *b* Andover, Mass., 17 Sept., 1948. *m* Elspeth R. Holch. one *s.* one *d. Educ:* Trinity-Pawling School. *Studied:* Hobart College (1969-70), mostly self taught in serigraphy. *Exhib:* one-man shows: Geary Gallery, Connecticut (1996), Gallery 39, Osaka, Japan (1990, 1994), Martha Lincoln Gallery, Florida (1987), The Little Gallery, Nantucket (1986), D. Christian James Gallery, N.J. (1985), Portfolio Gallery, C.T. (1982-87). *Work in collections:* Champion International, Chesebrough-Ponds, E. F. Hutton, First National Bank of Boston, Merrill Lynch, Societé General, Bermuda National Gallery. *Signs work:* "Eric Holch." *Address:* 11 Wauwinet Rd., Nantucket, M.A. 02554, U.S.A.

**HOLISTER, Frederick Darnton,** M.A. (Cantab.) (1957), M.Arch. Harvard (1953), A.R.I.B.A., Wheelwright Fellowship, Harvard (1952); Fellow, Clare College, Cambridge; Director of Studies in Architecture, Clare College, Cambridge; University Lecturer, Department of Land Economy, Cambridge University (retd. 1994); architect in private practice; Consultant Architect to Clare College, Cambridge, Consultant Architect to University of Buckingham (retd. 1997); *b* Coventry, 14 Aug., 1927. *m* Patricia Ogilvy Reid (marriage dissolved). two *s.* two *d. Educ:* Bablake School. *Studied:* Birmingham School of Architecture under A. Douglas Jones (1944-46, 1948-51), Harvard University under Prof. Walter Gropius (1951-53). *Address:* Clare College, Cambridge CB2 1TL.

**HOLLAND, Claerwen Belinda,** N.D.D. (1964); David Murray landscape studentship (1963); artist in ink, water-colour, pastel and oils; *b* Cwmdauddwr, 4 Mar., 1942. *Educ:* Miss Lambert's School, Queens Gdns., London. *Studied:* Byam Shaw School of Art (1960-64, Maurice de Sausmarez). *Exhib:* R.A., N.E.A.C., Bath Contemporary Art Fair (1991); one-man shows: Sue Rankin Gallery, Countryworks Gallery, Montgomeryshire, Thackeray Rankin, Thackeray Gallery (1996). *Work in collections:* The Library, University College, Cardiff. *Commissions:* various. *Publications:* illustrations to A Year and a Day by J.L.G. Holland (Hodder and Stoughton). *Signs work:* "C.B. Holland." *Address:* Dderw, Cwmdauddwr, Rhayader, Powys LD6 5EY.

**HOLLAND, Harry,** artist in oil on canvas, printmaking; *b* Glasgow, 11 Apr., 1941. *m* Maureen. two *d. Educ:* Rutlish School, Merton. *Studied:* St.

Martin's School of Art (1964-69). *Exhib:* extensively in Britain, France, Belgium, U.S.A.; one-man shows: Jill George Gallery (1988, 1990, 1992, 1994, 1996); retrospective travelling Britain Nov. 1991-Jan. 1993. *Work in collections:* Newport Museum and A.G., National Museum of Wales, Tate Gallery Print Coll. *Commissions:* portrait of Lord Callaghan (1990). *Publications:* Painter in Reality (1991). *Clubs:* Chelsea Arts. *Signs work:* "Harry Holland." *Address:* c/o Jill George Gallery, 38 Lexington St., London W1R 3HR.

**HOLLAWAY, Antony Lynn,** A.T.D. (1953), A.R.C.A. (1956), F.R.S.A., F.C.S.D.; stained glass designer; *b* Kinson, Dorset, 1928. *Educ:* Poole Grammar School. *Studied:* Bournemouth College of Art, and R.C.A., London. *Exhib:* Whitechapel Gallery, John Moores Liverpool and in U.S.A. *Work in collections:* include collection of Baroness Alix de Rothschild Paris, and others. *Commissions:* major new work designing and making new stained glass for Manchester Cathedral. *Publications:* work repro.: Architectural Press and elsewhere. *Signs work:* "Hollaway." *Address:* Home Farm House, Bottesford Rd., Allington, nr. Grantham, Lincs. NG32 2DH.

**HOLLEDGE, Bryan Raymond,** A.R.C.A., F.R.S.A., M.I.P.R., A.F.B.A.; part-time lecturer, Hammersmith School of Art (1949); part-time teacher, St. Hubert's Special School, Brook Green; lecturer, London School of Printing and Graphic Arts; part-time teacher, Chelsea School of Art; graphic designer, Metal Box (1955); Head of Graphics, Swiss Co. Sulzer Bros. (1958); freelance corporate design/mural, Chelsea Arts Club (1950); *b* Ealing, Middx., 1919. *m* Maria Haid. two *d. Educ:* Ealing College. *Studied:* Ealing College of Art (1937-40); H.M.F. 1940-46; Royal College of Art (1946-49). *Exhib:* painting in National Gallery Exhbn. for Young Artists, Whitechapel Gallery (1953), Arts Council U.K. tour, Mural painting, Shipping Co. and Theatres joint exhbn., London (1984); one-man show, London (1955) in assoc. with Atomic Energy Soc. Exhib. regularly at London galleries for painting/etching/wood engraving; recent exhbn. of wood engraving at Syon House, Isleworth. A Companion of Western Europe Dip. *Signs work:* "Bryan R. Holledge." *Address:* 5 The Green, Feltham, Middx. TW13 4AF.

**HOLLICK, Kenneth Russell,** F.C.S.D.; designer; *b* Essex, 5 Jan., 1923. *Studied:* Central School of Arts and Crafts, London. *Publications:* work repro.: trade marks, symbols, logotypes, corporate identity programmes, vehicle livery, booklets. Designs shown in books on graphic design published in Japan, Italy, Switzerland and Britain. *Address:* 4 Knighton House, 102 Manor Way, Blackheath, London SE3 9AN.

**HOLLOWAY, Douglas Raymond,** A.R.I.B.A., R.W.A.; architect retd.; artist in water-colour, pen and wash; *b* W. Hampstead, London, 25 Aug., 1923. *m* Marjorie Cynthia. three *s. Educ:* Haberdashers Aske's Hampstead, and Reading School. *Studied:* Royal West of England Academy School of Architecture. *Exhib:* R.Cam.A., various mixed and one-man exhbns. in England and Wales. *Work in collections:* R.W.A. *Signs work:* "D.R.

Holloway." *Address:* Longton Forge, 61 Liverpool Rd., Longton Preston, Lancs. PR4 5HA.

**HOLLOWAY, Edgar,** R.E., R.B.A.; painter, etcher; *b* 6 May, 1914. *m* (1) Daisy Hawkins; three *s.* one *d.*; (2) Jennifer Boxall. *Educ:* Doncaster Grammar School (1926-28). *Studied:* Slade School (1934). *Exhib:* one-man shows, London (1931, 1934, 1979, 1993), Brighton and Oxford (1980), Doncaster (1982), Edinburgh (1986), Abergavenny (1989), U.S.A. (1972, 1973, 1974, 1975); retrospective Ashmolean (1991-92). Touring exhbn. at 80 (1994) National Library of Wales, Hove A.G., Abbot Hall A.G., Kendal, Graves A.G., Sheffield and London (Cork St.). Wolsely Fine Art W11 (1996). *Work in collections:* B.M., V. & A., Ashmolean, Fitzwilliam, New York Public Library, Birmingham City A.G., Scottish Gallery of Modern Art, Scottish National Portrait Gallery, National Museum of Wales, National Library of Wales, University College of Wales, Oxford and Cambridge colleges. *Publications:* book launch, "The Etchings & Engravings of Edgar Holloway" (Scolar Press,1996); work repro.: Dictionary of 20th Century British Art (1991), British Printmakers, 1855-1955. *Address:* Woodbarton, Ditchling Common, Sussex BN6 8TP.

**HOLLOWAY, Laura Ellen,** S.W.A. (1994), Post.Dip.F.A. (R.A.); painter in water-colour and tempera; *b* Worcester, 1960. *Educ:* Worcester Girls' Grammar School. *Studied:* Glos. College of Art (1978-82), R.A. Schools (1985-88, Norman Blamey, R.A., Jane Dowling). *Exhib:* solo shows at Mason-Watts Fine Art, Warwick (1992); mixed shows in London and Birmingham. *Signs work:* "L.H." *Address:* 404 Wyld's Lane, Worcester WR5 1EF.

**HOLTAM, Brenda,** R.W.S., B.F.A.Hons. (1983), R.A. Schools Postgraduate Dip. (1986); painter in oil, gouache, water-colour; figurative painter of landscape, still life, interiors and portraits; Tutor in water-colour; *b* Whiteway, Glos., 2 Oct., 1960. *m* Howard Vie. one *s. Educ:* Stroud Girls' High School. *Studied:* Glos. College of Art and Design (1979, T. Murphy), Falmouth School of Art (1980-83, F. Hewlett), R.A. Schools (1983-86, Peter Greenham, C.B.E., R.A.). *Exhib:* R.A. Summer Exhbn., N.E.A.C. Annual Exhbn., R.P., R.W.S. Members Exhbn. Bankside Gallery; two-person exhbn. Cadogan Contemporary (1994). Elected A.R.W.S. (1987), elected to full membership (1992). *Signs work:* "Brenda Holtam" or "Holtam." *Address:* 39 Ashburnham Rd., Richmond, Surrey TW10 7NJ.

**HOMES, Ronald Thomas John,** D.F.C., F.C.S.D.; artist/industrial designer; winner of R.S.A. industrial design bursaries (1948-49); Central School of Arts and Crafts Dip for Industrial Design; Associate, Guild of Aviation Artists; *b* London, 3 Oct., 1922. *m* Ione Winifred Amelia. two *d. Educ:* Willesden Technical College. *Studied:* Central School of Arts and Crafts. *Signs work:* see appendix. *Address:* 69 Linden Pk., Shaftesbury, Dorset SP7 8RN.

**HOMESHAW, Arthur Howard,** R.W.A., A.T.D.; artist in water-colour, pastel, colour prints; *b* 27 Nov., 1933. *m* Wendy Bennetto. two *s. Educ:*

# WHO'S WHO IN ART

Chipping Sodbury Grammar School. *Studied:* West of England College of Art (1951-54, 1956-57). *Exhib:* R.A., R.W.A., R.E.; one-man show, Patricia Wells Gallery (1981), Exeter Arts Centre (1992). *Work in collections:* R.W.A., Bristol Educ. Com., Devon County Hall, Stoke-on-Trent Educ. Com., B.P. International, South Glamorgan Educ. Authority, Walsall Educ. Authority, Avon Schools Service, Exeter University. *Signs work:* "HOMESHAW." *Address:* Arwen, Alexandra Rd., Crediton, Devon EX17 2DH.

**HONE, David,** P.P.R.H.A., Hon. R.A., H.R.S.A.; portrait and landscape painter in oil; *b* Dublin, 1928. *m* Rosemary D'Arcy. two *s.* one *d. Educ:* St. Columba's College; Univ. College, Dublin. *Studied:* National College of Art, Dublin (1947-50), under J. Keating and M. MacGonical. *Work in collections:* Portrait Collection, National Gallery, Dublin, Cork Municipal Gallery. *Signs work:* "D. Hone." *Address:* 25 Lr. Baggot St., Dublin, 2.

**HOOKE, Robert Lowe, Jr.,** sculptor of figures, wild animals and birds in bronze; art dealer; investment adviser; Managing Director: Research Vision Ltd.; Director: Blaines Fine Art Ltd.; *b* Canton, Ohio, 12 Sept., 1942. *Educ:* Bowdoin College, Brunswick, Maine (B.A.); Columbia University, N.Y. (M.B.A.). *Studied:* N.Y. School of Visual Arts (1973-75, Herbert Kallem). *Exhib:* one-man shows: London, Geneva, Basel, Baden-Baden, Sydney, Johannesburg, Cape Town; group shows: Paris, Zurich, Amsterdam, San Francisco. *Work in collections:* Compton Acres, Poole; Oppenheimer Collection, S. Africa. *Commissions:* various private, Bowdoin College (U.S.A). *Clubs:* Hurlingham, Royal Ocean Racing, Ascot Park Polo, Annabels. *Signs work:* see appendix. *Address:* 61 Holland Pk., London W11.

**HOPE HENDERSON, Eleanora,** D.A., S.S.A., Post Grad. Scholarship, Guthrie Award (1940); artist in oil; *b* Edinburgh, 1917. *m* David Hope Henderson. two *s. Educ:* St. George's, Edinburgh. *Studied:* Edinburgh College of Art under Sir William Gillies, Sir W. MacTaggart, Westwater, Maxwell. *Exhib:* S.S.A., R.S.A., R.A., R.P., Dumfries Art Soc., McGill Duncan Gallery and Harbour Gallery, Kircudbrightshire; one-man shows: Chelsea A.G., Kirkcudbright Harbour Gallery, Woodstock Gallery, Pittenweem A.G. Fife, Coach House, Norwich, Ropner Gallery, London. Work in private collections. *Signs work:* "E. Hope Henderson", before marriage "BORRIE." *Address:* Achie, New Galloway, Kircudbrightshire DG7 3SB.

**HOPE-KING, Christopher Stewart,** A.R.M.S. (1993), S.M. (1991), H.S. (1994), Gold Bowl Hon. mention R.M.S. (1993), Fairman Members subject miniature award (1995); miniaturist in water-colour and acrylics (paints unique duck miniatures); *b* Leeds, Yorks., 16 Sept., 1951. *Educ:* Homefield School, Bournemouth. *Studied:* with grandfather, Hector King. *Exhib:* R.A. Summer Show, Mall Galleries, British Painters, Westminster Gallery (R.M.S.); many one-man shows. *Publications:* included in: Techniques of Miniature Painting (Sue Barton, Batsford), R.M.S. One Hundred Years (Suzanne Lucas, Lucas Art). *Signs work:* "H.K."joined. *Address:* Staddle Cottage, 1 Mill St., Corfe

# WHO'S WHO IN ART

Mullen, Wimborne Minster, Dorset BH21 3RQ.

**HOPKINS, Clyde David F.,** B.F.A.(Hons.) (1969); painter; Professor; Head of Painting, Chelsea College of Art; *b* Sussex, 24 Sept., 1946. *m* Marilyn Hallam. *Educ:* Barrow-in-Furness, Cumbria. *Studied:* University of Reading (Claude Rogers, Terry Frost). *Exhib:* Serpentine Gallery, Hayward Gallery, Ikon Gallery, Francis Graham-Dixon Gallery, Joan Prats Gallery, N.Y.C., U.S.A. etc. *Work in collections:* A.C.G.B., etc. Studio: London and Hastings. *Clubs:* Chelsea Arts. *Signs work:* "Clyde Hopkins." *Address:* 55 Marischal Rd., London SE13 5LE.

**HOPKINS, Peter,** painter, teacher, writer; Dean of Men, Emeritus, New York-Phoenix School of Design; Lecturer, Art Students League of New York; grantee, American Academy and National Institute of Arts and Letters (1950); Correspondent, Christian Science Monitor; *b* New York, 1911. *m* Gertrude L. Beach. *Educ:* Art Students League of New York. *Work in collections:* Museum of City of New York. *Publications:* work repro.: The American Heritage History of the 1920s and 1930s; The USA, a History in Art; The Complete Book of Painting Techniques; National Museum of American Art, Smithsonian Institution. *Address:* 36 Horatio St., New York, N.Y. 10014, U.S.A.

**HORE, Richard Peter Paul,** A.R.C.A. (Painting 1959, Mural Painting, Silver Medal 1960), N.D.D. (Illustration 1955), F.R.S.A. (1964), R.C.A. (Cambrian 1978); painter in gouache and mixed media; *b* Clacton-on-Sea, 1935. *m* Janice Hart. one *s.* one *d. Educ:* Colebaynes High School, Clacton. *Studied:* Colchester School of Art (1951-55, John O'Conner), R.C.A. (1956-60, Carel Weight, Ruskin Spear, Leonard Rosoman). *Exhib:* R.A.; Minories, Colchester; Welsh Arts Council; W.A.G., Liverpool; Mostyn, Llandudno; Artist in an Industrial Landscape, N. Wales Arts. *Work in collections:* R.C.A., Cheshire and Clwyd C.C., National Maritime Museum, Dept. of the Environment, various private collections. *Signs work:* "RICHARD HORE." *Address:* 65 Parkgate Rd., Chester, Ches. CH1 4AQ.

**HORNE, Cleeve,** O.C., O.Ont., R.C.A., O.S.A., S.S.C.; pres. Ontario Soc. of Artists (1949-51); painter, sculptor and artist consultant; *b* Jamaica, B.W.I., 9 Jan., 1912. *m* Jean Horne (sculptor). three *s. Educ:* England and Canada. *Studied:* sculpture under D. Dick of England (1928); painting at Ontario College of Art, Toronto (1930); R.A.I.C. Allied Arts Medal for 1963; Europe in 1936. *Exhib:* Canada, U.S.A. and England. *Work in collections:* portraits of leading Canadians; memorials and architectural sculpture. *Clubs:* Art and Letters (Pres. 1956-57), York Club, Toronto. *Signs work:* "Cleeve Horne." *Address:* 181 Balmoral Ave., Toronto, Canada M4V 1J8.

**HOROVITZ, Isabel,** B.A.(Hons.) (1978), Dip.Cons. (1982); paintings conservator; freelance conservator and consultant to Royal Academy of Arts; *b* London, 1957. *m* Jonathan Blake. three *s.* one *d. Educ:* St. Paul's Girls' School. *Studied:* University of London (History of Art), Courtauld Inst. of Art (Conservation of Easel Paintings). *Exhib:* Conservator for R.A. Loans Exhbns.

*Publications:* contributions to various catalogues and conservation literature. Special interest in history, techniques and conservation of paintings on copper supports. *Address:* The Painting Conservation Studio, Belgravia Workshops, 157-163 Marlborough Rd., London N19 4NP.

**HORSBRUGH, Patrick B.,** A.A. (Hons.) Dipl., F.A.I.A., A.C.I.P., A.P.A., F.R.G.S., F.R.S.A., F.B.I.S.; Hon. Mem. A.S.L.A.; Hon. Mem. A.S.I.D.; architect; town planner and artist in ink, water-colour, gouache, etc.; Visiting Prof. of Architecture, Universities of Nebraska and Texas; organized Texas Conference on Our Environmental Crisis (1966) and International Conference, Cities in Context; Cultural, Ethical and Natural (1968); Founder and Chairman of the Board, Environic Foundation International Inc; V.P., Channel Tunnel Assoc. (1975-91); Co-chairman, Earthday (International); Prof. Emeritus of Architecture, Former Director of Graduate Programme in Environic Design, University of Notre Dame; *b* Belfast, 21 June, 1920. *Educ:* Canford and A.A., School of Architecture, Dept. of Civic Design, University of London. *Signs work:* "Patrick Horsbrugh." *Address:* 916 St. Vincent St., South Bend, Indiana 46617, U.S.A.

**HORTON, Antony Brian,** landscape painter in oil and gouache; *b* Birmingham, 21 Aug., 1933. *m* Sheila Horton. three *d. Educ:* Shrewsbury School and Exeter College, Oxford. *Studied:* Cheltenham College of Art (R.S. Dent). *Exhib:* R.A., David Messum Gallery, and local exhbns. *Clubs:* M.C.C. *Signs work:* "A. B. Horton" or "Brian Horton." *Address:* The Old Rectory, Taplow, Bucks. SL6 0ET.

**HORTON, Ernest Charles,** R.B.S.A. (1988); artist in oil, pastel, water-colour; Curator, Royal Birmingham Soc. of Artists; *b* 8 Jan., 1935. *m* Maureen. one *s.* one *d. Studied:* Moseley Rd. School of Art (C.H. Adams, E. Mason), Margaret St. College of Art, B'ham (R. Ball). *Exhib:* R.B.S.A., P.S., R.W.A., also Germany, France, Italy, New York, Hong Kong. *Work in collections:* R.B.S.A. *Clubs:* B'ham Art Circle (Past Pres.), Sutton Coldfield Soc. of Art (Past Pres.), B'ham Water-colour Soc., B'ham Easel, R.B.S.A. *Signs work:* "E.C. Horton." *Address:* 29 Redacre Rd., Sutton Coldfield, W. Midlands B73 5EE.

**HORTON, James Victor,** M.A. (R.C.A.) (1974), R.B.A. (1979); artist in oil and water-colour; *b* London, 24 July, 1948. *m* Rosalind. two *s. Studied:* Sir John Cass School of Art (1964-66), City & Guilds Art School (1966-70), Royal College of Art (1971-74) . *Exhib:* widely in Britain and abroad, ten - oneman shows. *Publications:* seven books on painting and drawing; numerous articles for art magazines. Taught in art schools and summer schools in Britain and abroad. *Address:* 11 Victoria Rd., Cambridge CB4 3BW.

**HORWITZ, Angela Joan,** N.S. (1982), R.A.S. (1983); sculptress in stone, bronze, painter in oil and pastel; steward, A.G.B.I. (1985-86); *b* London, 14 Oct., 1934. two *s.* one *d. Educ:* Colet Court Girls' School, Rosemead Wales, Lycée Français de Londres. *Studied:* Marylebone Inst. (1978), Sir John Cass

College (1983), Hampstead Inst. (1990-92). *Exhib:* Grand Palais, Paris (1985, 1986), R.B.A., N.S., S.W.A. (Mall Galleries), Civic Centre, Southend, S.E.F.A.S., Guildhall, Ridley Soc., City of Westminster Arts Council, Alpine Gallery, Smiths Gallery Covent Gdn., Wintershall Gallery, nr. Guildford, The Orangery, Holland Pk. W8, Hyde Park Gallery (Winchester Cathedral, 1993), Beaux Arts, South of France (1997), Salon International du Livre et de la Presse à Genèva (1997). *Work in collections:* Sculpture in stone for Winchester Cathedral; Well Woman Centre, The United Elizabeth Garrett Anderson Hospital for Women, London; Zurich Switzerland private collection. Listed Who's Who in International Art. *Signs work:* "A.H." or "Angela Horwitz." *Address:* 6 Wellington House, Aylmer Drive, Stanmore, Middx. HA7 3ES.

**HOSKINS, Stephen,** M.A. (1981), A.R.E. (1989), R.E. (1995), B.A. (Hons.) (1977); printmaker in silkscreen, lithography and drawing; *b* Eastleigh, Hants., 31 Aug., 1955. *m* Barbara Munns. one *s. Educ:* Barton Peveril Grammar School. *Studied:* W. Surrey College of Art and Design (1974-77), R.C.A. (1978-81). *Exhib:* R.A., R.E., mixed exhbns. worldwide. *Work in collections:* V.&.A., Tate Gallery. *Publications:* A pop-up book ($5^3$). *Signs work:* "S. Hoskins." *Address:* 62 Monk Rd., Bishopston, Bristol BS7 8NE.

**HOUSE, Ceri Charles,** artist in oil; gilding restorer; *b* London, 20 Mar., 1963; partner: Amanda Wainwright. one *d. Educ:* St. Christopher School, Herts. *Studied:* with father, Gordon House. *Exhib:* N.P.G., B.P. Portrait awards (1994), R.A. Summer Shows (1992, 1993, 1995). *Commissions:* Numerous private commissions. *Publications:* R.A. Illustrated catalogue (1993). *Signs work:* see appendix. *Address:* 109 Highbury New Park, London N5 2HG.

**HOUSTON, Ian,** A.R.C.M., President, East Anglian Group of Marine Artists, Associate, French Soc. of Artists, F.R.S.A.; Silver medal, Paris Salon, Gold medal, F.N.C.F.; artist in oil and water-colour; *b* Gravesend, Kent, 24 Sept., 1934. *m* Angela Adams. one *s.* one *d. Educ:* St. Lawrence College, R.C.M., London. *Exhib:* over 30 one-man shows U.K., U.S.A., Australia. *Work in collections:* U.K. and abroad. Official artist to "Young Endeavour"; limited edition prints, 15 signed by Premiers Thatcher and Hawke, sold to raise funds for project. *Signs work:* "Ian Houston." *Address:* c/o Portland Gallery, 9 Bury St., St. James's, London SW1Y 6AB.

**HOWARD, Ian,** M.A. (Hons.), A.R.S.A.; artist in acrylic, oil, mixed media, printmaking; Prof. of Fine Art, Duncan of Jordanstone College of Art, University of Dundee; *b* Aberdeen, 1952. *m* Ruth D'Arcy. two *d. Educ:* Aberdeen Grammar School. *Studied:* Edinburgh University, Edinburgh College of Art (1970-76). *Exhib:* numerous one-man and group exhbns. *Work in collections:* S.A.C., A.C.G.B., Aberdeen A.G., Dundee A.G., Hunterian A.G., City Art Centre Edinburgh, Contemporary Art Soc., Warwick University Art Centre. *Publications:* Ian Howard, Painting, Prints and Related Works (Third Eye Centre Glasgow/Peacock Printmakers, Aberdeen), Heretical Diagrams (Peacock Printmakers, Aberdeen 1997). *Signs work:* "I.H." or "Ian

Howard." *Address:* 66 Camphill Rd., Broughty Ferry, Dundee DD5 2LX.

**HOWARD, Ken,** R.A. (1992), Hon. R.B.S.A. (1991), R.W.S. (1983), R.W.A. (1981), R.O.I. (1965), N.E.A.C. (1961); Appointed Official Artist Northern Ireland Imperial War Museum (1973-78); *b* London, 26 Dec., 1932. *Educ:* Kilburn Grammar School. *Studied:* Hornsey College of Art (1949-53), Royal College of Art (1955-58). *Exhib:* New Grafton Gallery (1971, 74, 76, 78, 81, 83, 86, 88, 90, 93, 95), Manya Igel Fine Art (1987-97). *Signs work:* "Ken Howard." *Address:* 8 South Bolton Gdns., London SW5 0DH.

**HOWARD-JONES, Ray,** Fine Art Dip. University of London, Slade Scholar; 1st class Hons. History of Art; painter, poet, mosaics; *b* Lambourne, Berks., 30 May, 1903. *Educ:* London Garden School. *Studied:* Slade School, University of London (1921) under Henry Tonks, Wilson Steer, Elliot-Smith (anatomy), Tancred Borenius (History of Art); Postgraduate School of Painting, Arbroath. *Work in collections:* National Museum of Wales, National Museum of S. Australia, Glynn Vivian Gallery Swansea, Contemporary Art Society, Museum and Gallery Glasgow, Imperial War Museum, Arts Council for Wales, M. of W., City Art Galleries of Aberdeen, Glasgow, Burton-on-Trent, large mosaic exterior Thomson House Cardiff and Grange Church Edinburgh. *Publications:* various contributions to The Anglo-Welsh Review. Heart of The Rock Poems 1973-92 (Rocket Press, 1993). *Signs work:* "Ray." *Address:* Studio House, 29 Ashchurch Park Villas, London W12; and St. Martin's Haven, Marloes, W. Wales. Agents: Rocket Gallery, 13 Old Burlington St., London W1X 1LA.

**HOWARTH, Constance M.,** B. of E. intermed. (1946), N.D.D. (1947); winner, Vogue Cotton Design Competition 1960 designer hand painted dresses; *b* Rochdale, Lancs., 14 May, 1927. *Educ:* Merchant Taylors' School for Girls, Crosby; Bolton School. *Studied:* Manchester Regional College of Art. *Exhib:* Rayon Design Centre, London. *Work in collections:* V. & A. New works: mixed media abstract mirror windows, wall scenics and ornamental flower trees, decoupage furniture. *Signs work:* "Constance Howarth" and "Constanza." *Address:* 17 Upper Wimpole St., London W1M 7TB.

**HOWELL, David,** self taught painter in water-colour, oil and pastel; *b* Markyate, 14 July, 1939. *m* Jenny. one *d*. *Educ:* St. Albans Grammar. *Exhib:* R.S.M.A., S.Eq.A., many mixed and one-man shows in London, England, Wales, Saudi Arabia and Bahrain. *Work in collections:* United Biscuits, Provident Financial, Charterhouse Bank, Albank Alsaudi Alhollandi. *Publications:* City of the Red Sea (Scorpion, 1985). *Signs work:* "David Howell." *Address:* North Barwick, Iddesleigh, Winkleigh, Devon EX19 8BP.

**HOWELLS, Patricia Frances,** A.T.D. (1954), N.D.D. (1953); artist in oil and water-colour, teacher; Head of Art, St. John's-on-the-Hill; *b* London, 27 July, 1929. *Educ:* P.N.E.U. Hazlemere, Brecon Grammar School. *Studied:* Cardiff College of Art, London Central St. Martin's College of Art. *Exhib:* annually for S.B.A., S.W.A. Mall Galleries, Guernsey Coach House Gallery,

University of Leicester, W.A.C., Museum of Wales, Gallery 20 Brighton, etc. *Clubs:* S.B.A. *Signs work:* "PAT" with date of year. *Address:* 5 Mount Pleasant, Chepstow, Gwent NP6 5PS.

**HOWSON, Peter,** D.Litt., Honoris Causa, Strathclyde University, B.A. (Hons.), G.S.A.; painter in oil; *b* London, 27 Mar., 1958. *m* Terry. one *d. Educ:* Prestwick Academy. *Studied:* Glasgow School of Art (1975-77 and 1979-81, Alexander Moffat). *Exhib:* widely in Europe and the U.S.A. *Work in collections:* Tate Gallery, V. & A., Metropolitan Museum of Modern Art, N.Y., M.O.M.A., N.Y., Oslo Museum of Modern Art, Glasgow Art Galleries. *Commissions:* Official war artist, Bosnia (1993). *Clubs:* The Caledonian, London. *Signs work:* "Howson." *Address:* c/o Flowers East, 199-205 Richmond Rd., London E8 3NY.

**HOYLAND, John,** artist; *b* Sheffield, 12 Oct., 1934; divorced. one *s. Studied:* Sheffield College of Art (1951-56, Eric Jones), R.A. Schools (1956-60). *Exhib:* numerous exhbns. including one-man: Marlborough New London Gallery, Whitechapel A.G., Waddington Galleries, Robert Elkon Gallery N.Y., Nicholas Wilder Gallery, Los Angeles, Andre Emmerich Gallery, N.Y., Austin Desmond Fine Art, London, also in Canada, Germany, Italy, Portugal, Australia, Sweden; two-man shows: Brazil, London, U.S.A.; group shows: R.A. Summer Exhbns., R.B.A. Gallery, John Moores, Liverpool, Ulster Museum, Belfast, Edinburgh Open, Chichester Natural Art, Barbican A.G., Francis Graham-Dixon Gallery, R.C.A., McLellan Galleries, Glasgow, etc. *Publications:* John Hoyland (1990). Television and radio broadcasts. *Signs work:* see appendix. *Address:* 41 Charterhouse Sq., London EC1M 6EA.

**HUBBARD , Deirdre,** B.A. (Summa cum Laude) (1957), A.R.B.S. (1981); Sohier prize (1957), Wapping Arts Trust 'Art and Work' (1987); sculptor in bronze; *b* N.Y.C., 1935. *m* Dr. John L. Wilson. three *s.* one *d. Educ:* Radcliffe College, Harvard University (1953-57). *Studied:* painting with Andreas Feininger (1954-55), Chelsea Art School (1957-61, sculpture with Willi Soukop and Bernard Meadows). *Exhib:* R.A., R.B.S., R.W.A., Essex University, Bristol Cathedral, Camden Arts Centre, National Museum of Wales, Bloomsbury Gallery, Barbican Centre, etc. *Work in collections:* Royal Free Hospital, Inst. of Educ. London University, Towner A.G., Usher Gallery, Lincoln, Bryn Mawr College, Bryn Mawr, P.A., U.S.A. *Signs work:* "D.H." *Address:* 101 Woodsford Sq., London W14 8DT.

**HUCKVALE, Iris,** R.M.S., S.B.A., S.M.; miniaturist in oil on ivorine, wood, card; *b* Northampton, 27 Sept., 1930. *m* John Huckvale, O.B.E. one *s.* one *d. Educ:* Northampton Grammar School for Girls. *Studied:* Nottinghamshire Evening Inst., but mainly self taught. *Exhib:* R.A., R.M.S., S.W.A., S.B.A., S.WL.A., Medici, S.M., M.A.S.-F., M.A.S.-N.J.; one-man show, Coach House Gallery, Guernsey. *Publications:* work repro.: Medici greetings cards. *Signs work:* see appendix. *Address:* 4 Heath Green, Heath and Reach, Leighton Buzzard, Beds. LU7 0AB.

**HUDSON, Eleanor Erlund,** R.W.S. (1949), R.E. (1946), A.R.C.A. (1937); graphic artist, portraitist, figure subjects, water-colourist; costume designer, artistic adviser to Brooking Ballet School, Marylebone; *b* S. Devon. *Educ:* Wentworth Hall, Surrey. *Studied:* R.C.A. (School of Engraving) under Professors Malcolm Osborne, R.A., R. S. Austin, R.A., Drawing Prize, 1936, Continuation Schol. (4th year) 1938, Travelling Schol. 1939. *Exhib:* R.A. and international. *Work in collections:* Boston Pub. Library, Fogg Museum, U.S.A., Imperial War Museum, London, War Artist's Advisory Comm. *Signs work:* "ERLUND HUDSON." *Address:* 6 Hammersmith Terr., London W6.

**HUDSON, Thomas Roger Jackson,** Teachers' Cert. (1951), Teachers' Dip. (1961), M.Coll.H. (1962), Mem. A.W.G.; self employed furniture maker and designer; *b* Bicester, Oxon., 24 July, 1929. *m* Ragnhild Ann Schanche. one *s.* two *d. Educ:* Bicester Grammar School. *Studied:* Oxford School of Art (1947), Shoreditch College (1949-51), Camberwell School of Art (1961), Goldsmiths' College (1962). *Publications:* Wheelstocks and Ploughshares (Tabb House, 1988). *Signs work:* carved into all major works (cow), see appendix. *Address:* The Barn, 117 High St., Odell, Bedford MK43 7AS.

**HUGHES, Christine,** Dip.Ed. (1968), Dip.F.A. (1994); painter in oil, printmaker, teacher; *b* London, 20 Feb., 1946. *m* D.C.C. Hughes. two *d. Educ:* Homerton College, Cambridge. *Studied:* Southampton College of Art (1989-94). *Exhib:* many mixed and solo shows in S.W. England and Cumbria. *Signs work:* "C. Hughes" or H within a C. *Address:* Linmoor Cottage, Highwood, Ringwood, Hants. BH24 3LE.

**HUGHES, Jim,** D.A. (1954), S.G.A. (1972), A.T.C. (1955), T.G.C. (1956); artist/designer/calligrapher; former teacher of art and design, Adult Educ. Dept., University of Glasgow; *b* Glasgow, 1934. *Educ:* Ayr Academy. *Studied:* Glasgow School of Art (1950-54); Jordanhill College (1954-56) under Sam Black, D.A., R.S.W. *Work in collections:* Glasgow Art Gallery, other work in private collections throughout the world. *Publications:* Graphic Design for S.S.A.E. and Ayr Adult Educ. Booklets. Work featured in B.B.C. TV series "The Quest"(1989). *Signs work:* initials on work, name on back, see appendix. *Address:* 32 Macadam Pl., Ayr KA8 0BZ.

**HUGHES, Kevin Michael,** B.Sc. (1969), A.L.A. (1971); artist in water-colour, oil and pastel; *b* Colwyn Bay, 4 Sept., 1947. *m* Teresa Vonesch. one *s.* one *d. Educ:* Reading University, Polytechnic of N. London. *Studied:* Balham and Clapham A.E.I. (1977-78, Caroline Clough). *Exhib:* R.W.S., R.W.A.; one-man shows: many since 1980 including four at Rooksmoor Gallery Bath. *Signs work:* "Kevin Hughes." *Address:* Edge Hill, Helscott Rd., Marhamchurch, Bude, Cornwall EX23 0JE.

**HUGHES, Malcolm,** A.R.C.A., D.A. (Manc.); artist (painter) and lecturer; Hon. Fellow, University College, London, Emeritus Reader in Fine Art, University of London, Hon. Research Fellow, Slade School of Fine Art; *b* Manchester, 1920. *Studied:* Regional College of Art, Manchester, Royal

College of Art, London. *Work in collections:* Tate Gallery, Arts Council of Great Britain, Contemporary Arts Society, Walker Art Gallery, Liverpool, Ashmolean Museum, Oxford, etc. Works and lives in London. *Signs work:* name written on the back of each work. *Address:* c/o The Slade School of Fine Art, Gower St., WC1E 6BT.

**HUGHES, Robert,** H.S. (1986), R.M.S. (1989), S.M. (1991), S.Lm. (1993); artist in oil and gouache; *b* London, 5 Nov., 1934. *Exhib:* R.M.S., H.S., S.M. *Publications:* co-author of How to Paint Miniatures; Magic of Miniatures compiled by Jo Clay. *Signs work:* "Robert Hughes" or "R. HUGHES." *Address:* Easton Barns, Easton Royal, Pewsey, Wilts. SN9 5LY.

**HULME, Ursula,** M.B.E., N.R.D., F.P.S., B.A.A.T.; artist in oil, watercolour, pastel, felt pen and collage; textile designer; art therapist; Founder of 'Conquest' The Society for Art for the Physically Handicapped (1979); *b* Cottbus, 5 Mar., 1917. *m* Ernest Hulme. *Educ:* Berlin. *Studied:* Reimann School, Berlin under Maria May. *Exhib:* one-man shows: Woodstock Gallery, London (3), Talent Store, London (1990); group shows: F.P.S., Mall Galleries, Loggia Gallery, Nimes, France, Leatherhead Theatre, Richmond Art Group, etc. *Publications:* entries in London Diary in book form from 1970-72. ABC book, and three videos on Conquest Teaching Methods produced 1988-96; book, Guide for Group Leaders. *Signs work:* "Ursula Hulme." *Address:* 3 Beverley Cl., E. Ewell, Epsom, Surrey KT17 3HB.

**HUMPHREYS, David,** B.A. (Dunelm); Thomas Penman Scholar and State Scholar at Durham University (1958-62); painter and constructor; *b* London, 27 Oct., 1937. *Educ:* Battersea Grammar School and King's College, Durham University (Dept. of Fine Art). Elected mem. Royal Cam. Academy (1994). *Work in collections:* Arts Council, Leicester, Newcastle, London Universities, Ministry of Works, Bishop Otter College, Ashridge College, Nuffield Foundation, I.C.I., J. Sainsbury, Shell, American Express Bank (London and N.Y.), P. & O., Financial Times, H.M. the Queen Mother, their Royal Highnesses, the Prince and Princess of Wales. *Address:* Maudlin Hill House, Sopers La., Steyning, W. Sussex BN443PU.

**HUMPHREYS, John Howard,** R.O.I.(1977, resigned 1992; elected Hon. Senior Mem. 1994); artist in oil; Press Officer, R.O.I. (1978-81); Winner of Stanley Grimm Prize (1981); *b* Bethlehem, S. Africa, 20 Oct., 1929. *m* Mary Mack. one *s.* one *d. Educ:* King Edward VII School, Johannesburg. *Studied:* Heatherley's Art School (Iain Macnab), and privately under Stanley Grimm (1953-57). *Exhib:* R.A., R.O.I., R.B.A., R.I., R.S.M.A., S.WL.A., Paris Salon, etc.; also in the U.S.A. and Japan. *Signs work:* "J. Humphreys." *Address:* 94 Kings Ave., Greenford, Middx. UB6 9DD.

**HUNDERTWASSER, (Friedrich Stowasser),** *b* Vienna, 15 Dec., 1928. *Exhib:* (1952-81): Vienna, Paris, Tokyo, Hanover, Bern, Amsterdam, Stockholm, London, Geneva, Berlin, U.S.A., N.Z., Australia, Luxembourg, Marseille, Cairo, Tel Aviv, Warsaw, Reykjavik, Copenhagen, Dakar,

# WHO'S WHO IN ART

Yokohama, Hong Kong, Cape Town, Pretoria, Rio de Janeiro, Brasilia, Sao Paulo, Caracas, Mexico City, Montreal, Toronto, Brussels, Budapest, Madrid, Rome, Milan, Oslo, Cologne, Graz, Helsinki, Bucharest. *Publications:* Verlag Galerie Welz, Salzburg (1965), Buchheim Verlag, Feldafing (1965), Bruckmann Verlag, Munich (1972). Cassette of graphic works: Look at it on a rainy day (1972); first Japanese colour woodcut portfolio Nana Hiaku Mizu (1973); Midori No Namida portfolio (1975). Matura (1948). *Signs work:* see appendix. *Address:* P.O. Box 28, A-1182 Vienna, Austria.

**HUNDLEBY, A. R.,** designer-packaging and graphics, artist in water-colour; *b* 1923. *m* Marion Smallshaw, A.T.D. *Studied:* Lincoln and Leicester. *Signs work:* "HUNDLEBY." *Address:* 35 Kelross Rd., London N5 2QS; and Hill House, Binham, Norfolk NR21 0DW.

**HUNKIN, Sally Elizabeth,** painter, printmaker in etching and water-colour, gardener; Organizer and teacher at Kew Studio; *b* Herts., 1924. *m* Oliver Hunkin, ex-TV producer. one *s.* one *d. Educ:* St. Mary's Calne; Dartford College; Richmond Adult College. *Exhib:* solo shows locally and in Suffolk and Manchester; group shows include Royal Soc. of Artist Printmakers, and R.A. *Work in collections:* St. Thomas's Hospital. *Commissions:* two friezes for St. Thomas's Hospital. *Publications:* work repro.: posters and cards for Kew Gdns. *Signs work:* "Sally Hunkin." *Address:* 31 Leyborne Pk., Kew, Richmond, Surrey TW9 3HB.

**HUNT, Emma,** B.A. (Hons.), M.A.; Sen. lecturer, Art and Design History; Course Director, Cultural Studies, Bournemouth and Poole College of Art; adviser to Southern Arts; *b* Bideford, 27 July, 1962. *m* Martin. two *s. Educ:* Leicester and Birmingham. *Exhib:* curated small college exhbns. and at Russell-Cotes Museum. *Publications:* contributor to design history articles. *Signs work:* "E.F. Hunt." *Address:* Shepherds Cottage, Henfords Marsh, Warminster, Wilts. BA12 9PA.

**HUNT, Geoffrey William,** R.S.M.A. (1989); marine artist and illustrator in oil, acrylic, water-colour; *b* Twickenham, 11 Mar., 1948. *m* Vivienne Anne Hobbs. two *s. Educ:* Hampton Grammar School. *Studied:* Kingston School of Art (1966-67), Epsom School of Art (1967-70). *Exhib:* R.S.M.A. since 1977; Solent Gallery, Lymington; Mystic Maritime Gallery, U.S.A.; also Oliver Swann Gallery SW3. *Work in collections:* Royal Naval Museum, Portsmouth; R.N. Submarine Museum, Gosport; H.M.S. Neptune, Faslane; Ferens A.G., Hull. *Publications:* illustrated many book covers including complete series of Patrick O'Brian's Aubrey/Maturin novels. *Signs work:* "Geoff Hunt." *Address:* 66 South Park Rd., Wimbledon, London SW19 8SZ.

**HUNT, Susie,** B.A. (Hons.) Fine Art (1980); artist in water-colour and mixed media, and framer; *b* Fareham, Hants., 18 Dec., 1957. *m* Anthony Paul Duley. one *s.* one *d. Studied:* Canterbury College of Art (1976-77), West Surrey College of Art (1977-80). *Exhib:* many mixed and solo shows in London and Home Counties. *Signs work:* "Susie Hunt." *Address:* 33 Knoll Rd., Dorking,

Surrey RH4 3ES.

**HUNTER, Alexis,** Dip.F.A. Hons. (Painting) (1970), Teaching Dip. (1971); painter in oil on canvas (used photography and xerox 1976-81); lecturer; *b* Auckland, N.Z., 4 Nov., 1948. *m* Baxter Mitchell, I.B.M.S. *Educ:* Auckland Girls Grammar. *Studied:* Elam School of Fine Arts, Auckland (1965-69, Colin McCahon). *Exhib:* over 150 exhbns. including Hayward, Serpentine, Musee d'Art Moderne, Paris, Auckland City A.G., etc. *Work in collections:* Imperial War Museum, Scottish National Gallery of Modern Art, Zurich Museum, Auckland City A.G., Museum of N.Z., etc. *Publications:* From the Interior, editor Fran Lloyd (Kingston University Press 1997). *Signs work:* "Alexis Hunter." *Address:* 13 Hiller Ho.46, Camden Sq., London NW1 9XA.

**HUNTER, Christa,** S.W.A.; sculptor in terracotta, porcelain, bronze resin, bronze; *b* Stuttgart, Germany, 18 Aug., 1943. *m* Robin Hunter. one *s.* one *d. Educ:* Ostheim Stuttgart. *Studied:* Sculpture course by Major Tugwell/Judy Cousins (1983). *Exhib:* regularly with art socs. in Berks. and Surrey, annually S.W.A. at Westminster Hall, Medici Gallery (1994), Surrey Sculpture Soc. Sculpture Trail Wisley (1997). *Work in collections:* Holme Grange A.G., Wokingham. *Commissions:* several private Foundry Bronze. *Signs work:* "C.H." or "Christa." *Address:* 26 Cavendish Meads, Sunninghill, Berks. SL5 9TD.

**HUNTER, Janet Claire (Jan),** S.W.A. (1997), F.E.T.C. (1987), Dip. in Advertising and Design (1965); artist in water-colour, dry and acrylic media; lecturer in drawing and water-colour, Surrey Adult and Continuing Educ. Service; *b* Reading, Berks., 2 July, 1946. *m* Ian Hunter. one *s.* one *d. Educ:* Westwood Grammar School, Reading. *Studied:* Berks. College of Art, Reading (1962-65). *Exhib:* S.W.A,, Guildford Art Soc., Woking Soc. of Arts and other local venues *Signs work:* "Jan Hunter" and date. *Address:* 9 Willow Green, West End, Woking, Surrey GU24 9HR.

**HUNTINGTON-WHITELEY, James,** B.A. (Hons.) Manchester (1985); Modern British and Contemporary Art Exhbn. Organizer; *b* 14 Aug., 1963. *m* Magdelen Evans. *Address:* 106 Tennyson Rd., London NW6 7SB.

**HUNTLEY, Dennis,** N.D.D. (1951), A.T.C. (1952), F.R.B.S. (1970); sculptor in bronze, plastics, stone, wood; educationalist; Head of Sir John Cass School of Art; Governor, City of London Polytechnic; *b* Weybridge, Surrey, 6 Dec., 1929. *m* Gillian Huntley. one *s.* two *d. Educ:* Wallington Grammar School for Boys. *Studied:* Wimbledon School of Art (1947-51), Gerald Cooper (principal), London University Senior House (1951-52). *Exhib:* several galleries. *Work in collections:* 6 major works (4 stone, 2 wood) Guildford Cathedral, 7ft. metal fig. for L.C.C. Patronage of the Arts Scheme at Henry Thornton School, Clapham, life-sized wood fig. of Anne Boleyn, London Borough of Sutton, awarded Sir Otto Beit medal in open competition for best work, 1967, in United Kingdom and Commonwealth. *Publications:* book reviews for L.C.C. and Studio Vista and various articles for Education. *Clubs:*

Arts, Chelsea Arts. *Signs work:* "D. W. Huntley" on prints and drawings, "D. HUNTLEY" on sculptured work. *Address:* The Studio, 30 Hawthorn Rd., Sutton, Surrey.

**HUNTLY, Moira,** A.T.C. (Lond.), P.S. (1978), R.I. (1981), R.S.M.A. (1985), R.W.A. (1995); artist in acrylic, oil, pastel, water-colour; Vice-Pres., Pastel Soc.; *b* Motherwell, Scotland, 7 Nov., 1932. *m* Ian E. Buchanan Huntly. one *s.* two *d. Educ:* Wirral County School for Girls, Harrow Weald County School. *Studied:* Harrow School of Art (1948-53, Christopher Sanders, R.A.), Hornsey College of Art (1953-54). *Exhib:* Young Contemporaries, R.O.I., N.E.A.C., R.I., P.S., R.W.A., R.S.M.A., F.C.A., Pastellistes de France; numerous solo shows, Mystic Maritime Museum, U.S.A. *Work in collections:* Ferens A.G., Hull (R.S.M.A. Coll.). *Publications:* 'Imaginative Still Life', 'Painting and Drawing Boats', 'Painting in Mixed Media', 'Learn to Paint Gouache', 'Learn to Paint Mixed Media', 'The Artist's Drawing Book'. *Signs work:* "Moira Huntly." *Address:* "Alpha", Collin Cl., Willersey, Broadway, Worcs. WR12 7PP.

**HURDLE, Robert Henry,** painter; senior lecturer until 1981, Faculty of Fine Art, Bristol Polytechnic; *b* London, 1918. two *s.* one *d. Studied:* Richmond School of Art (1935-37), Camberwell School of Arts and Crafts (1946-48) under Coldstream. *Exhib:* one-man shows, University College of Swansea (1973); Albany Gallery, Cardiff (1974); New Ashgate Gallery, Farnham (1977); City A.G., Bristol (1977); Pao Sui Loong Galleries, Hong Kong Arts Centre (1978); King St. Gallery, Bristol (1982); Farnham Maltings (1983); Pelter/Sands Gallery (1988); Cleveland Bridge Gallery, Bath (1989); Retrospective exhbn. R.W.A. (1995). *Work in collections:* University College, Swansea; R.W.A.; City Art Gallery, Bristol; Bath University; Hong Kong Arts Centre; Wessex Collection, Longleat and various private collections. *Signs work:* signature or seal. *Address:* 14 Oxford St., Kingsdown, Bristol BS2 8HH.

**HURN, J. Bruce,** A.T.D. (1946), F.R.S.A. (1966), P.P.R.B.S.A. (President 1973); painter/designer in oils, acrylic, gouache; former teacher, examiner and H.M.I. (Art), mem. advisory com. N.E.C.A.; *b* Spalding, 18 May, 1926. *m* June Barbara. one *s.* three *d. Educ:* King Edward's, Camp Hill, B'ham. *Studied:* Birmingham College of Art (1942-46). *Exhib:* Universities: B'ham, Aston, Keele, Oxford, Leicester, Kent; group shows: municipal art galleries, R.B.S.A., R.A. *Work in collections:* private, colleges, universities, schools, industrial collections in U.K., private collections in U.S.A., Europe, Australia. *Publications:* Practical Biology (Dodds and Hurn). *Signs work:* see appendix. *Address:* Sandy Ridge, 64 Lubbock Rd., Chislehurst, Kent. BR7 5JX.

**HURST, Stephanie,** Dip. in illustration (1974), R.A. Dip. of advanced studies - B.A. equivalent (1984); painter in oil on board with gesso ground; *b* Wimborne, Dorset, 3 July, 1952. *Educ:* Convent of the Sacred Heart, Weymouth. *Studied:* Bournemouth and Poole College of Art (1970-71), Hornsey College of Art (1971-74), Byam Shaw School of Painting and

Drawing (1976-77), R.A. Schools (1981-84). *Exhib:* R.A., Royal Festival Hall, Spirit of London Competition (awarded prize), South Bank Show, Camden Arts Centre - Druce Competition (awarded prize), Bath Contemporary Arts Fair, Elgin Fine Art, Bath, Jonathan Poole Gallery, London. *Signs work:* "S. Hurst" on back of painting. *Address:* 3 King's Ave., Muswell Hill, London N10 1PA.

**HUSON, Cedric Nigel,** Dip.A.D. (1973), R.A. Schools Post. Grad. Cert. (1978); painter; *b* Salop, 1 June, 1951. *m* Kitta Potgieter. *Educ:* Marlborough Grammar School, Wilts. *Studied:* Salisbury School of Art (1967-68), Swindon School of Art (1968-69), Winchester School of Art (1970-73), Royal Academy Schools (1975-78). *Exhib:* group shows: Piccadilly Gallery (1987-97), Lamont Gallery (1994-95), R.A. Summer Exhbn. (1988-94, 1997), Hunting Group Open (1989, 1990, 1994), Cleveland Bridge Gallery, Bath (1990), The London Group Open (1990, 1992, 1993), The Discerning Eye (1992, 1995), National Trust Centenary Exhbn. (1995), Everard Read Gallery, Cape Town (1997). *Signs work:* "Cedric Huson." *Address:* 11b Camberwell Green, London SE5 7AF.

**HUSSEY, John Denis,** F.R.B.S., R.W.A.; sculptor of assemblages; principal lecturer, Director of Studies, Fine Art Dept., Bristol Polytechnic (retd. 1983); *b* Slough, 26 Apr., 1928. *m* Katherine Hiller. two *s. Educ:* Slough Grammar School. *Studied:* Goldsmiths' College (1946-49); research Diploma in Fine Art/Sculpture at Bristol Polytechnic (1969-70). *Exhib:* R.A., R.W.A. *Work in collections:* Tallboys, R.W.A. *Signs work:* "J. Hussey." *Address:* Sanderling, 21 Colne View, Point Clear, St. Osyth, Essex CO16 8LA.

**HUSTON, John I.,** History's Most Significant Artist; in oil, egg tempera, pastels, sculptures, landscapes, figures, abstracts, upon canvas, wood, masonite; writer; scientist; artist; planner; Finance Innovate; *b* Saltillo, Penna., U.S.A., 22 Jan., 1915. *Educ:* Juniata College and University Special Studies; completely self-trained in art via Commercial Art, Industrial Art, Cinema Art, Fine Art. Work in private collection. *Publications:* The Art of Life as permanent.*Clubs:* International Directory of Arts, Who`s Who World Wide. *Signs work:* see appendix. *Address:* 1215 Jackson Tower, Harrisburg, Pa. 17102.

**HUTCHESON, Tom,** D.A. (1949) R.G.I.; artist in mixed media; principal art lecturer; *b* Uddingston, Lanarkshire, 13 Nov., 1924. *m* Mary McKay. *Educ:* Motherwell. *Studied:* Glasgow School of Art (1941-49) under Hugh Adam Crawford, R.S.A., David Donaldson, R.S.A. *Exhib:* R.S.A., G.I., R.S.W., Moores; three one-man shows. *Work in collections:* H.M. the Queen, H.R.H. Prince Philip, Arts Council, Liverpool and Glasgow Universities, Scottish Educ. Authorities. *Clubs:* Art, Glasgow. *Signs work:* "Tom Hutcheson." *Address:* 73 Woodend Dr., Glasgow G13.

**HUTCHISON, Sidney Charles,** C.V.O., F.S.A., F.M.A., F.A.A.H., F.R.S.A., London Univ. Dip. in Hist. of Art, Lt.-Cdr. (S), R.N.V.R.; Antiquary and Hon. Archivist, R.A. of Arts; on administrative staff of R.A. from 1929 (Librarian 1949-68, Secretary 1968-82); Chantrey Bequest Trustee; President,

Southgate Soc. of Arts. Lecturer for Univ. of London Extension Courses (1957-67); *b* London, 26 Mar., 1912. *Educ:* Holloway School, London. *Publications:* The Homes of the Royal Academy (1956), The History of the Royal Academy, 1768-1968 (1968) and updated edition 1768-1986 (1986). *Clubs:* Athenaeum, Arts. *Address:* 60 Belmont Cl., Cockfosters, Barnet, Herts. EN4 9LT.

**HUXLEY, Paul,** R.A., Cert.R.A.S. (1960), Harkness Fellow (1965-67); painter in acrylic, oil, printmaking; Professor of Painting, Royal College of Art; *b* London, 12 May, 1938. *m* Susie Allen. two *s. Studied:* Harrow School of Art (1951-56, Edward Middleditch), R.A. Schools (1956-60, Peter Greenham). *Exhib:* over sixteen one-man shows and numerous group shows worldwide. *Work in collections:* Tate Gallery, V. & A., plus various museums in the U.K., Europe, U.S.A. and Australia. *Publications:* Exhibition Road - Painters at the Royal College of Art. *Clubs:* Chelsea Arts. *Signs work:* "Paul Huxley" in bottom margin of prints and small works on paper, verso on larger works on canvas. *Address:* 2 Dalling Rd., London W6 0JB.

**HYATT, Derek James,** A.R.C.A.; painter/writer; *b* Ilkley, Wharfedale, Yorkshire, 1931. *Educ:* Ilkley Grammar School. *Studied:* Leeds College of Art (1948-52), Royal College of Art (1954-58). *Exhib:* London one-man shows include Austin Desmond/Gillian Jason Gallery (1987, 1989). Waddington Galleries (1974, 1977), New Art Centre (1960, 1961, 1963, 1966); group shows include John Moores, Cincinnati Bienniale, Arts Council Travelling Exhbns., and two Critics Choice exhbns. *Work in collections:* Museum of Modern Art, New York, Contemporary Art Soc., Carlisle, Hull, Bradford, Sheffield and Bootle Art Galleries and Nuffield Foundation. *Publications:* Edited ARK (1958); articles Modern Painters (1987-97); Alphabet Stone (1997). Video "Circles on the Dark Rock" Mappin Gallery, Sheffield (1995). *Address:* Rectory Farm House, Collingham, Wetherby LS22 5AS.

**HYMAN, Timothy,** painter in oil, pastel and drawing, writer, lecturer; *b* Hove, 17 Apr., 1946. *m* Judith Ravenscroft. *Educ:* Charterhouse. *Studied:* Slade (1963-67). *Exhib:* Narrative Paintings (I.C.A., Arnolfini, 1979), Blond Fine Art (1981, 1983, 1985), Austin Desmond (1990), Manchester Castlefield (1993), Gallery Chemould Bombay (1994), Gallery M [Flowers East] (1994). *Work in collections:* Arts Council, British Museum, Museum of London, Contemporary Art Soc., Bristol, Sheffield, Lincoln A.G.'s, Government Art Collection, etc. *Commissions:* Lincoln Cathedral, Sandown Racecourse. *Publications:* Bonnard (Thames & Hudson, 1998); numerous articles in T.L.S., etc. *Signs work:* "Timothy Hyman," "T.H." or "HYMAN." *Address:* 62 Myddelton Sq., London EC1R 1XX.

# I

**I'ANSON, Charles,** F.R.B.S. (1967), F.R.S.A. (1956), R.B.S.A. (1966), M.Sc. (1980), O.L.J. (1981); sculptor in steel; *b* Birmingham, 1924. *Studied:*

Birmingham College of Art. *Exhib:* F.P.S., London Group, Commonwealth Inst., New Vision and Alwyn Galleries, London; "Sculpture 1971", York, etc. *Work in collections:* Cardiff Civic Centre, Midlands Art Centre, Bristol and Leeds Universities, Trinity and All Saint's College, Leeds; Birmingham, Bradford and Wakefield A.G.'s, R.D.C., Walmley, Bristol, Minard Castle, Inveraray, Argyll; R.A. Gamecock Barracks, Nuneaton; Dore School, Sheffield; Windmill Hill School, Stourport; St. Paul's Church, Doncaster; St. Winefrid's Church, Wibsey, Bradford, etc. *Signs work:* "I'ANSON." *Address:* April Cottage, Mount Pleasant Rd., Morcott, Oakham, Rutland LE15 9DP.

**IBBETT, Vera,** R.M.S. (1990), Grenfell Silver medal - botanical illus. (1970), F.S.S.I. (1970); painter and illustrator in oil, water-colour, pastel; *b* Kingswood, Surrey, 30 May, 1929. *m* Raymon Strank. *Educ:* Banstead Central School. *Studied:* City and Guilds of London Art School (1955-63, Innes Fripp, John Nash, R.A.), Reigate School of Art (1968-70). *Exhib:* R.A., R.M.S., S.W.A., R.H.S. *Work in collections:* R.A.F. Chapel of Remembrance, Biggin Hill. *Publications:* Flowers in Heraldry (Alcuin Soc. Vancouver B.C., 1977), La Revue Moderne (1960), European Illustrators (1974-75). *Signs work:* "Vera Ibbett" and see appendix. *Address:* 89 Chipstead La., Lower Kingswood, Surrey KT20 6RD.

**INCHBALD, Michael,** F.C.S.D.; Architectural and Interior Designer; twice married; two children; *Studied:* A.A. *Commissions:* work includes 1st Class Lounge "Queen's Room" and Library on Q.E.2, and other Liners, Ballroom, all banquet areas and suites at Berkeley Hotel, Post House, Heathrow, Claridges' Penthouse, Savoy's River Room and Lincoln Room, Crown Commissioner's H.Q., Carlton House Terr., Banks of America and Trust Hanover, Player's and Plessey's H.Q. Offices, Justerini and Brooks, Boardroom etc. for Imperial Group, Law Society's Lady's Annexe, Dunhill's, Jermyn Street and Worldwide; Residential: Duc de la Rochefoucauld, Duke of St. Albans, Marquess of Ailesbury, Earls of Dartmouth and St. Aldwyn, Countess of Lonsdale, etc. *Address:* 10 Milner St., London SW3 2PU.

**IND, John William Charles,** F.R.S.A.; painter in oil, water-colour, sculptor in wood, designer, illustrator; *b* London, 1927. *m* Greta Bambridge-Butler. two *s. Educ:* London and Cambridge. *Studied:* in London and Oslo. *Exhib:* Royal Exchange, Madden Gallery, Barle Gallery, Harrods Gallery; one-man shows: Halford House, Newton Gallery, Kensington Ct. Gdns. *Work in collections:* Harris Bank, Barclays Bank, Hays Allan, Ind Coope, Texaco London, Taylor Hall; private collections in France, Germany, U.S.A., Britain, N.Z., Scandinavia. 1994, painting commissioned for 105th Regiment, Royal Artillery. *Signs work:* "Ind." *Address:* Atelier; Aller, Som., TA10 0QN.

**INGHAM, Alan Everard,** Lt. Cdr. R.N. retd. (1965), A.R.I.C.S. (1971); painter of landscapes in water-colour; *b* Skipton, 25 Oct., 1932. *m* Rose. one *d. Educ:* Ermysteds Grammar School, Skipton; Royal Naval College, Dartmouth. *Exhib:* R.I., R.B.A., Harrods, Selfridges, etc.; one-man shows: Granby Gallery, akewell (1980-90), Halcyon Gallery Birmingham, etc. *Work in collections:* olls Royce Motor Co., Rank Hovis McDougall, Ind Coope, etc. *Publications:* Under a Water-colour Sky (Washington Green, 1996); work repro.: work published extensively as fine art editions, calendars, etc. *Signs work:* "ALAN ING-HAM" mid horizontal strokes of letters extended. *Address:* Farthings, The Cherry Orchard, Staverton Village, Cheltenham GL51 0TR.

**INGHAM, George Bryan,** A.R.C.A.; artist; *b* Preston, Lancs., 11 June, 1936. *Studied:* St. Martin's School of Art; R.C.A.; British Academy, Rome. *Exhib:* Francis Graham-Dixon Gallery, London. *Work in collections:* V. & A., Ashmolean, Kunsthalle, Bremen, etc. *Publications:* illustrated catalogue Anthony Gross. *Clubs:* Blue Anchor, Helston. *Signs work:* "B. Ingham" on back. *Address:* c/o Francis Graham-Dixon Gallery, 17-18 Gt. Sutton St., London EC1V 0DN.

**INGLIS, John,** R.S.W. (1984), F.S.A. (Scot.) (1983), D.A. (1974), Post. Grad. (1975), Travelling scholar (1976); painter in water-colour, acrylic, lecturer; *b* Glasgow, 27 July, 1953. *m* Heather Binnie. two *s.* two *d. Educ:* Hillhead High School, Glasgow. *Studied:* Gray's School of Art, Aberdeen (1970-75, William Littlejohn, Frances Walker, Alexander Fraser). *Exhib:* R.S.A., R.S.W., R.G.I.F.A., S.S.A., Compass Gallery, Glasgow, Open Eye Gallery, Edinburgh, Park Sq. Gallery, Leeds, Venice, Rome, Canada, Regensberg, Illinois, U.S.A. *Work in collections:* Aberdeen A.G., Scottish Arts Council, University of Aberdeen, Argyll and Bute Educ. Authority, Scottish Television, Inst. for Cancer Research, Aberdeen Hospitals Collection, Clackmannan District Council Collection, Royal Scottish Academy, Clackmannan College, Scottish Arts Club. *Signs work:* "John Inglis" usually on back. *Address:* 21 Hillview Rd., Larbert, Stirlingshire FK5 4RL.

**INNES, William Henry,** P.S., U.A.; artist in pastel and oil; President, S.E. London Art Group; Life mem. Pastel Soc. Council; *b* London, 23 Feb., 1905. *m* Violet Gertrude. *Educ:* L.C.C. School. *Exhib:* R.A., P.S., U.A., R.S.M.A., N.E.A.C., R.O.I., several one-man shows. *Work in collections:* Southwark and Lambeth Councils, Courbeviou, and many countries worldwide and private collections. *Clubs:* London Sketch. *Signs work:* "INNES." *Address:* 38 Ruskin Walk, London SE24 9LZ.

**INSALL, Donald W.,** C.B.E., F.S.A., R.W.A., F.R.I.B.A., F.R.T.P.I., A.P.Dip. (Hons); architect; Chairman, Donald Insall Assocs. (Architects and Planning Consultants), London SW1; Ex-Commissioner, The Historic Buildings and Monuments Commission for England, Visiting Prof. University of Leuven, Service as Consultant to City of Chester in National Pilot City Conservation Programme, Architects for post-fire restoration of Windsor Castle; *b* Clifton, Bristol, 1926. *Exhib:* R.A., R.W.A., R.I.B.A. *Publications:* The Care of Old Buildings Today (Architectural Press); 'Architectural Conservation' Encyclopaedia Britannica; Conservation in Action. Consultancy has received over 60 Conservation and Craftmanship Awards/Commendations.

*Clubs:* Athenaeum. *Address:* 73 Kew Green, Richmond, Surrey TW9 3AH.

**IRENE:** see FRÖHLICH-WIENER, Irene.

**IRVIN, Albert,** painter; *b* London, 21 Aug., 1922. *m* Beatrice Nicolson. tw.
*d. Educ:* Holloway County. *Studied:* Northampton and Goldsmiths' School o.
Art; taught at Goldsmiths' College School of Art (1962-82). *Exhib:* one-ma.
shows: Gimpel Fils, London; New Art Centre, London; Acme, London; 5
Gallery, Edinburgh; Aberdeen A.G.; Third Eye Centre, Glasow; Ikor
Birmingham; Bede, Jarrow; Goldsmiths' College Gallery; Newcastl
Polytechnic; Manchester Polytechnic; De Marco, Edinburgh; Skulima, Berlin
Lüpke, Frankfurt; Galerie 2, Stuttgart; Städtische Kunstsämmlunger
Ludwigshafen; Berlin Opera House; Galerie im Griechenbeisl, Vienna
Coventry Gallery, Sydney; Kilkenny Castle; Hendriks, Dublin; Carine Campc
Antwerp; Monochrome, Brussels; Gimpel and Weitzenhoffer, N.Y.
Serpentine, London; Talbot Rice, Edinburgh; Oriel and Chapter, Cardiff
Spacex, Exeter; Royal Hibernian Academy, Dublin; Wasserman, Munich
Stühler, Berlin, etc. *Work in collections:* include: Tate Gallery; Arts Council
British Council; other British and international public collections. Mem
London Group. *Signs work:* see appendix. *Address:* c/o Gimpel Fils, 30 Davie
St., London W1Y 1LG.

**IRVIN, Magnus,** Dip.F.A. (1973), R.E. (1993); artist in woodcuts, etching
mixed media and shoes made from bananas; *b* London, 6 Dec., 1952; partner
Chris Stubbs. *m* one *s. Educ:* Creighton School, Muswell Hill. *Studied*
Hornsey Art College (1970), N.E.L.P. Walthamstow (1971-74). *Exhib*
Redfern Gallery, Whitechapel Open, Cleveland Drawing Biennale, Bradfor.
Print Biennale, Ljubljana Print Biennale, Xylon Museum Germany, A.
Cologne. *Work in collections:* A.C.G.B., B.M., V. & A., International Centre o.
Graphic Art, Slovenia. *Commissions:* Tunstall Western Bypass, Stoke on Tren
- concrete aeroplanes to bypass environment. *Signs work:* "M. Irvin." *Address*
11 Lancaster Rd., London N4 4PJ.

**IRWIN, Flavia,** artist in acrylic on canvas, mixed media on paper, tutor
Head of Decorative Arts Dept., City & Guilds of London Art School; *b* London
*m* Roger de Grey. two *s.* one *d. Educ:* Hawnes School, Ampthill. *Studied*
Chelsea School of Art (Graham Sutherland, Henry Moore, Robert Medley
*Exhib:* Zwemmers, London Group, R.A., Ansdell Gallery, Gallery 1.
Grosvenor St., Phoenix Gallery, Curwen Gallery, Peoples Theatre, Newcastle
Arts Council Gallery, Bury St. Edmunds, Taranman Gallery. *Work in collec
tions:* Carlyle A.G., D.O.E., Chelsea & Westminster Hospital. *Commissions*
Daniel Galvin, George St., London. Dealers: Studio 3, 75 Leonard St., Londo
EC2A 4QS. *Signs work:* "Flavia Irwin" back of canvas, pencil on drawings
*Address:* Camer Street, Meopham, Kent DA13 0XR.

**IRWIN, Gwyther,** painter: oil paint, water-colour and acrylics; *b* Cornwal
7 May, 1931. *m* Elizabeth. two *s.* one *d. Educ:* Bryanston. *Studied:* Centr.
School of Art (1952-55). *Exhib:* Redfern Gallery, London. *Work in collections*

Tate Gallery, British Council, Arts Council, Contemporary Art Soc., Arts Council of N. Ireland, Calouste Gulbenkian, City Art Gallery, Bradford, Albright-Knox, Yale University, Peggy Guggenheim, Peter Stuyvesant. *Signs work:* "Gwyther Irwin." Studios in London and Cornwall. *Address:* 21 Hillbury Rd., London SW17.

**ISOM, Graham Michael,** N.D.D. (1965), A.A.E.A., S.E.A.; artist in oil; *b* Kent, 5 Mar., 1945; married. one *s.* two *d. Educ:* Dartford. *Studied:* Ravensbourne College of Art (1961-65). *Work in collections:* Kentucky Derby Museum of Racing, Churchill Downs, Louisville. *Commissions:* Household Cavalry (Officer's Mess). *Publications:* Racing in Art/John Fairley. *Signs work:* see appendix. *Address:* 5 Neville Pk., Baltonsborough, Som. BA6 8PY.

**ITHIER, Jean R.F.,** artist in oil, water-colour, pen and pencil; retd. architect; *b* Montpellier, France, 16 Apr., 1921. *m* Jacqueline. one *s.* one *d. Educ:* Royal College, Mauritius (1934-38). *Studied:* Hammersmith School of Building and Arts and Crafts (1949-53). *Exhib:* Ripley Arts Centre, Bromley, Bromley Library. *Clubs:* West Wickham Arts Assoc., S.G.F.A., Bromley Arts Soc. *Signs work:* "Jean R.F. Ithier." *Address:* 2 Downsway, Orpington, Kent BR6 9NU.

**IZZARD, Pam,** artist in oil, acrylic and mixed media, etching; *b* London, 1926. *m* (1) K.Lucas; two *s.* one *d.* (decd.). (2) Jack Millar; *Educ:* Old Palace School, Croydon, Torquay Grammar School. *Studied:* Beckenham, Bromley Schools of Art, and Croydon. *Exhib:* R.A., London Group, N.E.A.C., R.B.A., Curwen Gallery, Linton Ct. Gallery, Ashgate Galleries and various provincial galleries. One-man shows, Ashgate Galleries, Abbot Hall, Kendal. Has taught in art schools in London and the provinces. *Work in collections:* local authorities. *Signs work:* "P. Izzard" on back. *Address:* 10 Overhill Rd., Dulwich, London SE22 0PH.

# J

**JACK, Kenneth William David,** A.M. (1987), M.B.E. (1982), R.W.S. (1977), A.W.I. (1955), A.T.D. (1951), A.T.C. (1949); landscape and architectural painter and printmaker in water-colour, acrylic, pastel and most drawing media, lithography, silk-screen; Patron, O.W.S.C. (Australian branch); *b* Melbourne, 5 Oct., 1924. *m* Betty Dyer. one *s.* two *d. Educ:* Melbourne High School. *Studied:* R.M.I.T. (John Rowell, Harold Freedman). *Exhib:* R.W.S. annually at Bankside Gallery, Leicester Galleries (1975), Fine Art Soc. London, A.W.I.; many one-man shows in Australia. *Work in collections:* National Galleries of all Australian capital cities; 500 works Australian War Memorial, Canberra. *Publications:* many folios and large reproductions of paintings; Kenneth Jack by L. Klepac; Kenneth Jack - World War II Paintings and Drawings (text, K.J.); Kenneth Jack by D. Dundas; The Flinders Ranges paintings, text by K.J.); The Melbourne Book by C. Turnbull; Charm of

Hobart by C. Turnbull. *Clubs:* O.W.S.C. *Signs work:* "Kenneth Jack." *Address.* P.O.Box 1, Doreen 3754, Victoria, Australia.

**JACKLIN, Bill,** M.A., R.C.A. (1967), A.R.A. (1989); artist in oil paintings, etching; *b* London, 1 Jan., 1943. *m* (1) Lesley (divorced); (2) Janet Russo. *Educ:* Walthamstow Technical College. *Studied:* Walthamstow School of Art (1962-64), R.C.A. (1964-67, Carel Weight). *Exhib:* one-man shows, London Nigel Greenwood (1970, 1971, 1975), Hester Van Royen Gallery (1973, 1977) Marlborough Fine Art (1980, 1983, 1988, 1992, 1995, 1997), Marlborough Gallery, N.Y. (1985, 1987, 1990, 1997), M.O.M.A. Oxford (1992), Museo de Pobo Galego, Santiago de Compostela, Spain (1993), University of Northumbria, Newcastle upon Tyne, England (1994), Hong Kong Arts Centre, Hong Kong (1995); numerous group shows. *Work in collections:* A.C.G.B. British Council, B.M., Government Arts Coll., Metropolitan Museum, N.Y. M.O.M.A. (N.Y.), Museum Boymans-Van Beuningen, Rotterdam, Tampa Museum, Museum of N.S.W., V. & A., Tate Gallery, Yale Centre for British Art. *Commissions:* by Bank of England for painting (Futures Market, London) (1988); Ivy Restaurant in London for painting (The Ivy) (1988); De Beers for Tapestry - "The Park" - 6ft. x 17ft. (1993); Metropolitan Washington Airport Authority for new terminal at Washington National Airport (1994-97) Design Architect, Cesar Pelli & Ass.; mural - "The Rink" - 6ft. x 25ft. (1997). Artist in Residence, British Council Hong Kong (1993-94). *Publications:* Monograph Bill Jacklin by John Russell-Taylor (Phaidon Press, London, 1997); gallery catalogues and numerous articles and broadcasts. *Clubs:* Chelsea Arts. *Signs work:* "Jacklin." *Address:* Apt. 7a, 155 Perry St., N.Y.C., N.Y. 10014, U.S.A.

**JACKSON, Ashley,** F.R.S.A., U.A.; artist in water-colour; lecturer and demonstrator in w/c throughout Britain, U.S.A., Valencia, Milan and Madrid; *b* Penang, Malaysia, 22 Oct., 1940. *m* Anne. two *d. Educ:* St. Joseph's, Singapore Holyrood, Barnsley. *Studied:* Barnsley School of Art (1955-60) under F Adams, A. Critchley, T. Long. *Exhib:* R.I., R.B.A., R.W.S., Britain in Water colour, U.A.; one-man shows: Upper Grosvenor Gallery, Mall Galleries Christina Foyle Gallery, Huddersfield 1987-opened by H.R.H. Prince of Wales Huddersfield A.G. (1990), Patchings A.G. Nottingham (1993), Rotherham A.G. (1994), Barnsley A.G. (1995), Brighouse A.G. (1995), Doncaster A.G. (1995), Benninborough Hall (1996), Wakefield A.G. (1996), Sewerby Hall (1996), Salford A.G. (1997). *Work in collections:* Royal Navy, Sir Harold Wilson, Sir Yehudi Menuhin, Lord Mason of Barnsley, Rt. Hon. Edward Heath, Yorkshire Bank, Yorkshire Television, N.C.B., Rt. Hon. John Major, Sir Bernard Ingham. *Publications:* autobiography "My Brush with Fortune" (Secker and Warburg, 1982); "An Artists Notebook" (Luddites, 1982), "Painting in the Open Air" (Harper Collins, 1992), "A Brush with Ashley" (Boxtree, 1993), "Painting the British Isles: a water-colourist's journey" (Boxtree, 1994). Featured in Y.T.V. documentary "My Own Flesh and Blood" (1981); own series on B.B.C. "Pebble Mill at One"; series of "How to Paint" on Channel 4, titled "Making the Most of" (1982); own series on Y.T.V. "A Brush

Vith Ashley" (1990, 1992, 1993, 1995). Founder Member of Yorkshire Watercolour Soc. "Ashley Jackson Art Gallery" - Barnsley College - Permanent collection of 30 of Ashley's works open to the public. *Signs work:* ee appendix. *Address:* Ashley Jackson Galleries, 13-15 Huddersfield Rd., Holmfirth, Huddersfield HD7 1JR.

**JACKSON, H. J.,** R.E., S.W.E., N.D.D.; full time printmaker using lino etc.; b Kings Lynn, Norfolk, 7 Dec., 1938; married. one d. *Educ:* Melton Constable. *Studied:* Norwich School of Art (1954-58) under G. Wales, R.E. *Exhib:* Touring Print Exhbns. America and United Kingdom; one-man and group shows throughout East Anglia, print and mixed shows in London. Work included in a number of public collections, and private collections worldwide; and various educational authorities. *Address:* 12 Whitehall Rd., Norwich NR2 3EW.

**JACKSON, Maz,** B.A.(Hons.) (1976); artist in oil, water-colour, drypoint, charcoal, pen and ink; b Norwich, 6 Aug., 1953. m Paul Hill. two s. one d. *Educ:* Notre Dame High School, Norwich. *Studied:* Norwich School of Art 1972-76, Edward Middleditch). *Exhib:* R.A. (Stowells Trophy), Mall Galleries, Birmingham Arts Centre, Fermoy Centre King's Lynn, Ellingham Mill Suffolk, Assembly Rooms Norwich, Chimney Mill Gallery, West Stow, "All That Jazz" Wymondham, Blickling Hall, Norfolk, Grapevine Gallery, Norwich, Knapp Gallery, London, Art Cunnoisseur, London. *Clubs:* S.G.F.A., Norwich Artists. *Signs work:* "MAZ." *Address:* Friends House, Church Rd., East Harling, Norwich NR16 2NB.

**JACKSON, William Alexander,** A.T.D., P.P.R.B.S.A. (President R.B.S.A. 1983-87); Chairman B'ham Pastel Soc. (1984-95); artist in pastel, oil, acrylic; retd. Principal, Bournville College of Art (1964-81), teacher of drawing and painting since 1947; b B'ham, 11 Sept., 1919. m Mary Elizabeth. one s. one d. *Educ:* W. Bromwich Grammar School. *Studied:* Ryland Memorial School of Art (1936-40), B'ham College of Art (1946-47). *Exhib:* R.B.S.A, Mall Galleries, Perugia, Alexandria; private galleries: Worcester, Malvern, Broadway. *Work in collections:* Dudley A.G. Prizewinner Mid-Art Dudley. *Clubs:* President, Redditch Art Soc. *Signs work:* "Alex Jackson." *Address:* 18 Moss Lane Cl., Beoley, Redditch B98 9AU.

**JACOBSON, Ruth Taylor,** D.F.A.Lond. (1963); 1st prize, figure drawing at the Slade (1961); painter/printmaker/stained glass artist; b London, 1941. m U. Jacobson, F.R.C.S., M.R.C.O.G. two s. one d. *Studied:* Slade School of Fine Art (1959-63, Peter Brooker, Andrew Forge). *Exhib:* Agnews, Wildenstein, Royal Festival Hall, Barbican Centre; one-man shows: Camden Arts Centre, Poole Arts Centre, Zionist Confederation House, Jerusalem. *Work in collections:* Panstwowe Muzeum Oswiecim Brzezinka, Poland, Yad Vashem Museum, Israel, Ben Uri Gallery, London. *Commissions:* portrait of H.M. Queen Elizabeth the Queen Mother for the Museums Association. *Clubs:* British Soc. of Master Glass Painters. *Signs work:* "Ruth B. Jacobson."

*Address:* 25 Holne Chase, London N2 0QL.

**JAFFE, Harold,** A.S.A. (1973), F.S.V.A. (1978); artist in acrylic and mixed media; interior designer and muralist, teacher and antiquarian; certified fine arts appraiser; President, Louis Comfort Tiffany Soc.; Past President, L.I. Chapter American Society of Appraisers; Faculty, New York University, George Washington University; *b* New York City, 26 Mar., 1922. *m* Gisèle Jaffe. one *s. Educ:* Pratt Institute, Parsons School. *Studied:* Cape Ann, Gloucester under Maxwell Starr. *Work in collections:* Denton Greens Housing Development Dr C. MacCormick, Mr. and Mrs. S. Berman, Dr. D. Bernstein, Mr. and Mrs. A Adler. *Publications:* work repro.: Interiors Magazine, Years Work. *Signs work* "Harold." *Address:* 5 Devon Rd., Great Neck, New York 11023, U.S.A.

**JAFFE, Ilona Lola Langdorfl,** artist in monotype (oil), tapestries; *b* Krakow, Poland. *Studied:* P.F. Art College, S. Africa under Joan Wright *Exhib:* solo shows: Orchid Fine Arts, Lymington, Swanage, Berlin Johannesburg, Munich, Boston, Freising, Cape Town Eching, Sasolburg Rustenburg, Antwerp, Van Eck Gallery; group shows: Johannesburg, Paris London. *Work in collections:* King George VI A.G. and Museum, Port Elizabeth, Pretoria A.G. and Museum, Pretoria, R.A.U. Johannesburg, Dom Gymnasium, Freising, Franz Mark Gymnasium, Markt Schwaben, Germany also private collections and institutions. *Address:* Flat 3, 5 St. Winifred's Rd. Meyrick Pk., Bournemouth BH2 6NY.

**JAFFÉ, Lois,** R.D.S. medal (1934); artist in pastel, water-colour, oil; *b* Axminster, 16 Sept., 1918. *m* Eric Jaffé. one *s. Educ:* Essex County High School. *Studied:* St. Martin's School of Art (1939). *Exhib:* Pastel Soc. (1976 82), Trends, Mall Gallery (1976), Westward TV Plymouth (1975), Civil Service; one-man, Kings Arm Gallery Dorchester, Harbour Gallery, W. Bay Dorset V. & A. (1937-39), City of London Guildhall. *Work in collections* Philpot Museum, Lyme Regis. *Signs work:* "LOIS JAFFÉ." *Address:* The Old Coach House, Bellair, Charmouth, Dorset DT6 6RD.

**JAGGAR, Margaret Leah,** Hon.Retd. R.C.A.; wood engraver, mural painter, commercial artist; *b* 9 July, 1907. *m* Robert Jaggar (decd.). one *s.* one *d. Educ:* Cheltenham Ladies' College; Liverpool Art School. *Exhib:* Soc. of Wood Engravers, etc. *Commissions:* murals for Cunard White Star Liner s.s. Caronia, National Trust, etc. *Publications:* work repro.: Murals in Architect Building News, Architects Journal, Design; W. H. Smith and Sons, Ltd., etc *Address:* Croes Efa, Rhydwyn, nr. Holyhead LL65 4EL.

**JAGO, Joan E.,** F.R.S.A. (1989), F.F.P.S. (1992), Wilfred Sirrell Award (City of Westminister Arts Council) 1989, Dip. in Creative Textiles (1985) fibre artist/paper maker; *b* Leeds, 22 Mar., 1930. *Educ:* Aireborough Grammar School, W.Yorks. *Exhib:* solo show: Marks & Spencer plc H.Q. Bldg., London (1993); group shows in London, Hong Kong and the U.S.A. *Signs work:* "Joan Jago." *Address:* 606 Nelson House, Dolphin Sq., London SW1V 3NZ.

**JAKOBER, Ben,** sculptor in stone, iron, bronze; winner of The Pilar

Juncosa and Sotheby's Special Prize for 1993 awarded by the Fundació Pilar i Joan Miró a Mallorca; *b* Vienna, 31 July, 1930. *m* Yannick Vu, with whom he now works and signs jointly. one *s*. *Educ:* Mill Hill School; La Sorbonne, Paris. *Exhib:* 1982: Fundación March, Palma; 1984: Palais des Beaux Arts, Brussels; Louisiana Museum, Humlebaek; Städtische Kunsthalle, Mannheim; Museum Moderner Kunst, Vienna; 1985: Salon de Montrouge; Recklinghausen Museum; Biennale de Sculpture Belfort; Galería Maeght, Barcelona; 1986: Capella de la Misericordia, Palma; Salon de Montrouge; Biennale di Venezia; 1987: Künstlerhaus, Vienna; 1988: Minos Art Symposium, Greece; Olympiad of Art, Seoul; 1990: Galerie Montenay, Paris; Jeune Sculpture, Paris; 1991: MVSEV, Palma; Palacio de Fortea, Zaragoza; Padiglione d'Arte Contemporanea, Ferrara; Musée d'Art Moderne, Pully (VD); Musée de la Poste, Paris; Musée des Jacobins, Morlaix; XV Biennale Internazionale del Bronzetto, Padova; 1992: IMF Center, Washington; Spanish section EXPO 92, Seville; "La Salerniana", Erice; Museo Civico de Gibellina; 1993: Arnolfini, Bristol; Musuem Moderner Kunst Stiftung Ludwig Palais Liechtenstein, Vienna; Sala Bramante, Rome; "MEDIALE", Hamburg; 6 Biennale d'Arte Contemporanea, Marostica; XLV Biennale di Venezia; 1994: Instituto Italiano de Cultura, Madrid; Centre Cultural Contemporani Pelaires, Palma de Mallorca; Fundació Pilar i Joan Miró a Mallorca, Palma de Mallorca; Ses Voltes, Palma de Mallorca; La Salerniana, Erice, Sicily; 1995: Galerie Montenay, Paris; Salle delle Reali Poste, Gli Uffizi, Firenze; Fundación Cultural COAM, Madrid; 1996: Istituto Italiano di Cultura, Paris; Galerie Pièce Unique, Paris; "Universalis", XXIII Bienal International de São Paulo, Brazil. *Work in collections:* Museo Nacional Centro de Arte Reina Sofía, Madrid; Musée d'Art Moderne, Brussels; Museum of Modern Art, Palais Liechtenstein, Vienna; Museum of Austrian Art of the XIX and XX Centuries, Vienna; Kunsthalle Bremen; Kunsthalle, Hamburg; Musée d'Art Moderne F.A.E., Pully (VD); Colombe d'Or, St Paul de Vence; Fattoria di Celle, Pistoia; E.P.A.D., Paris; Seoul Olympic Park; Fondation Vincent Van Gogh, Arles; Fundació Pilar i Joan Miró a Mallorca, Palma de Mallorca; Gabinetto Disegni e Stampe degli Uffizi, Firenze; Museum Beelden aan Zee, Scheveningen. *Signs work:* "B.J." *Address:* 205 St Ursula St., Valletta 06, Malta.

**JAMES, Donald,** painter, designer; exhibits internationally; P.E., Commonwealth of Massachusetts; M.I.E., Australia; *b* New York, 1932. *Educ:* M.A. (1960) University of California, B.Sc. (1953) University of New York, San Francisco Art Institute, California School of Fine Arts, San Francisco State College, American University, Corcoran School of Art, Union University, Union College. *Signs work:* "James." *Address:* 6 Eccleston St. Belgravia, c/o Eccleston B.O., London SW1W 9LS.

**JAMES, Kim,** M.A.(R.C.A.), M.Sc., Ph.D., N.D.D., A.T.C.; Consultant to the French National Inst. for training psychiatric personnel, Dijon, France; Director P.S.I. International Ltd.; *b* Wollaston, Northants, 31 July, 1928; married. two *d*. *Educ:* Wellingborough Grammar School. *Studied:* Borough

Polytechnic under David Bomberg and Tom Eckersley; Royal College of Art; Brunel University, School of Applied Biology; and Division of Cybernetics. Special research field psychology of perception. *Exhib:* R.A., Scottish Arts Council; Middleheim Biennale, Antwerp. *Publications:* Writings include critical essays and reviews on current theories of Perception and Philosophy (Leonardo, vols. 8, 9, 10, 11, 13, 14). Gallery: Grosvenor Gallery, London. *Signs work:* "Kim James." *Address:* Hickmire, Wollaston, Northants NN29 7SL.

**JAMES, Simon,** M.A.(R.C.A.) (1989); artist in oil, charcoal and printmaking; *b* 22 Jan., 1965. *Educ:* Northampton School for Boys. *Studied:* R.A. Schools (1984-87), R.C.A. (1987-89). *Exhib:* R.A., N.E.A.C., Marks and Spencer Young Artist award (1992), prizewinner in the 10th Cleveland International Drawing Biennale (1991), numerous exhbns. in England, U.S.A., and Berlin. *Work in collections:* Lloyd's of London, Cleveland C.C., The Foreign Office. *Signs work:* "SIMON JAMES" or "S.J." *Address:* Houseboat Clifton, Blomfield Rd., London W9 2PB.

**JAMESON, Norma Marion,** R.B.A., R.O.I., N.D.D., A.T.D., Goldsmiths' Advanced Dip., textiles; painter, lecturer; *b* Burslem, 18 Jan., 1933. *m* Kenneth Ambrose Jameson (decd.). *Educ:* Thistley Hough Grammar School, Stoke-on-Trent. *Studied:* Bath Academy of Art (1951-55); Liverpool University (1955-56); Goldsmiths' College (1978). *Exhib:* R.A.; various one-man shows in London and the South East. Mem. Royal Society of British Artists and The Royal Inst. of Oil Painters. *Signs work:* "Norma Jameson." *Address:* 111 Hayes Way, Beckenham, Kent BR3 6RR.

**JAMILLY, Victor,** painter, oil and water-colour; art gallery director; *b* 31 May, 1927. *m* Audrey. two *s.* one *d. Educ:* Highgate and Cranleigh Schools. *Studied:* St. Martin's School of Art. *Exhib:* New English Art Club, R.S.B.A., various group and gallery shows. *Work in collections:* Euston Gallery, London. *Signs work:* "V. Jamilly." *Address:* Wendover, 13 Hampstead Way, London NW11.

**JAMISON, Paul,** B.A.Hons. (1979), P.G.C.E./A.T.D. (1982); artist in oil and water-colour; *b* Middlesbrough, 16 Sept., 1954. *Educ:* St. Mary's College, Middlesbrough. *Studied:* University of Newcastle upon Tyne (1975-79), University of Bristol (1981-82). *Exhib:* Hatton Gallery, Newcastle (1979), Alpine Gallery, London (1980, 1983), Bayswater Gallery (1987, 1989, 1991). Work in private hands throughout the world. *Work in collections: Signs work:* "Jamison" with year, i.e. '98. *Address:* 16 Cosway St., London NW1 5NR.

**JAMMET, Lin,** painter in gouache on paper, oil on canvas; *b* 22 May, 1958. *m* Valerie Jammet. two *s. Educ:* French Lycée, London; C.E.G. d'Anduze, France; Millfield, Somerset. *Studied:* Chelsea School of Art (sculpture course 1976). *Exhib:* one-man shows: Beaux Arts Gallery, Bath, St. Jude's Gallery, London, Contemporary Fine Art Gallery, Eton, Bohun Gallerie Henley, Beaux Arts Gallery, London. *Clubs:* Chelsea Arts. *Signs work:* "Lin Jammet."

# WHO'S WHO IN ART

*Address:* Woolland House, Woolland, Blandford Forum, Dorset DT11 0EP.

**JANACEK, Mirice:** see MATTAROZZI DI THARASH, Mirella.

**JANES, Violeta,** portrait painter, still-life, artist in oil, pastel and water-colour; Directed art studies at Alma College, Ontario, Canada; *b* Buenos Aires, Argentina. *Educ:* Giffen School, Viña del Mar, Chile. *Studied:* Regent St. Polytechnic School of Art under S. Tresilian, Middleton Todd, E. Osmond. *Exhib:* R.A., R.O.I., S.W.A., R.S.A., N.E.A.C., R.P., Paris Salon and the provinces; two-man show in the West End, one-man, Broomfield Museum. Member United Society of Artists. *Signs work:* "Violeta Janes." *Address:* 2 Salisbury Ave., Harpenden, Herts, 5AL 2QQ.

**JAQUES, Norman Clifford,** D.A. (Manc., 1941), M.S.I.A. (retd.); Sen. Lecturer, Manchester Polytechnic (1950-82); President, Manchester Academy of Fine Art (1984-90); Visiting Lecturer, Cleveland, U.S.A. (1979); freelance artist; *b* 23 Apr., 1922. *m* Marjorie Hovell. two *s. Educ:* Manchester College of Art (J. M. Holmes, P. W. Keen, 1937-42); R. M. I. Heywood Prize; Proctor Travelling Scholarship (1948) Italy, France. *Exhib:* London, Manchester, Glasgow, Edinburgh, U.S.A. and Canada, etc. *Work in collections:* V. & A. Museum, M/Cr City A.G., Westminster Bank, Rochdale, Stoke, Manchester, Newcastle Education Committees, etc. *Commissions:* United Steel Co., Post Office, B.B.C., British Transport, Odhams, Macmillan, etc. Agents: R.P. Gossop, London (1946-89). *Address:* 6 Wardle Rd., Sale, Ches. M33 3BX.

**JARAY, Tess,** D.F.A. (Lond., 1960), F.R.I.B.A.; painter and etcher, environmental artist; Reader in Fine Art; *b* Vienna, 31 Dec., 1937. two *d. Educ:* Alice Ottley School, Worcester. *Studied:* St. Martin's School of Art (1954-57), Slade School of Fine Art (1957-60). *Exhib:* solo exhbns.: Whitworth A.G., Manchester, Ashmolean Museum, Oxford, Serpentine Gallery, London. *Work in collections:* Stadtisches Museum, Leverkusen, Walker Art Gallery, Liverpool, Arts Council of Gt. Britain, Tate Gallery, Graves Art Gallery, Sheffield, Warwick University. *Commissions:* Floor for Victoria Station, London, Centenary Square, Birmingham, Cathedral Precinct pedestrianisation, Wakefield. *Signs work:* "Tess Jaray." *Address:* 29 Camden Sq., London NW1.

**JARMAN, Anne Nesta,** H.R.M.S. (1981), Hon. R.M.S (retd.); prizewinner for miniature portrait, National Eisteddfod of Wales; artist of miniature portraits in water-colour and pastel; *b* Sutton, Surrey. *Educ:* Penarth County School, Bedales School, Petersfield. *Studied:* Cardiff School of Art; Heatherley's, London; privately with the late Alfred Praga in miniature painting. *Exhib:* R.A., Paris Salon, R.M.S., R.W.A., R.C.A., S. Wales Art Soc., etc. *Work in collections:* Apothecaries Hall, London. *Signs work:* "Nesta Jarman." *Address:* 4 Ellenborough Ct., 17 Ellenborough Park N., Weston-super-Mare, Somerset BS23 1XQ.

**JARVIS, Gloria,** N.D.D.; Médaille d'Argent Paris (1976); Académicien d'Italie, Médaille d'or (1980); artist in oil, water-colour, pastel, ink, gouache; lecturer on historic costume and instructor in costume drawing, Polytechnic,

Regent St. (1950-63); *m* A. Raymond Smith, B.A. (1964). *Educ:* Heathfield-Norris School, Harrow; Aylesbury Grammar School. *Studied:* St. Martin's School of Art, London, under James Bateman, R.A., A.R.W.S., for drawing, painting and composition; the history of art at Florence University. *Exhib:* R.A., N.E.A.C., N.S., Leicester Galleries; one-man show, Brussels (1970. . .). *Work in collections:* Abbot Hall A.G., Kendal; Museum of the Dynasty, Brussels; International Museum of Carnival and Mask, Binche, Belgium; and private collections. *Commissions:* numerous portraits and genre paintings, Brussels. *Publications:* work repro.: Macmillan, Brussels Times. Short stories published; broadcast by B.B.C. *Clubs:* Soc. of Women Writers and Journalists. *Signs work:* "Gloria Jarvis." *Address:* The Bungalow, Tyler Cl., Canterbury, Kent CT2 7BD.

**JASINSKI, Alfons B.,** R.S.W. (1978), Latimer award R.S.A. (1975), D.A. Travelling scholar (1969); artist in oil, acrylic, water-colour, pastel (seashore/figure/landscape); *b* Falkirk, 1945. *m* Ann Conlan. one *s.* two *d. Studied:* Edinburgh College of Art (1964-68, Philipson, Houston, Blackadder, Cumming). *Exhib:* Loomshop Gallery, Lower Largo, Scottish Gallery, Kirkcaldy A.G., Artis: Flying Colours. *Work in collections:* S.A.C., Edinburgh Schools Collection, Aberdeen City A.G., Duke of Devonshire, P.I.H. Scotland. *Signs work:* "A. B. Jasinski." *Address:* 15 Normand Rd., Dysart, Fife KY1 2XN.

**JASON, Gillian,** Art Gallery Director, Jason & Rhodes, London; *b* U.K., 30 June, 1941. *m* Neville. one *s.* one *d. Educ:* Royal Ballet School/London Opera Centre. *Address:* 40-42 Inverness St., London NW1 7HB.

**JEFFERSON, Alan,** A.R.C.A.; painter; retired from teaching at Dept. of Fine Art, University of Portsmouth (1983); *b* S. Kensington, 7 Apr., 1918. one *s.* one *d. Educ:* Mitcham County School. *Studied:* Wimbledon School of Art and R.C.A. *Exhib:* R.A., Redfern, Piccadilly and provincial galleries; one-man exhibitions Bear Lane Gallery, Oxford, Hiscock Gallery, Portsmouth, City A.G., Portsmouth. *Work in collections:* U.K., South Africa, U.S.A., Portsmouth Corp. *Signs work:* "ALAN JEFFERSON." *Address:* 22 Bell Rd., Cosham, Hants. PO6 3NX.

**JEFFERSON, Annelise,** M.A. (1990), A.R.O.I. (1993); fine art painter in oil on canvas; *b* Pembury, 1965. *Educ:* Chichester High School. *Studied:* West Surrey College of Art and Design (Stephen Farthing), Royal Academy (Norman Adams). *Exhib:* R.A. Summer Exhbn. (1988, 1989, 1990, 1991), Bonhams: The New Generation (1990), Royal Overseas League (1990), Rubicorn Gallery, Dublin (1991), The Hunting Art Prizes finalist (U.K. and Paris, 1991), N.E.A.C., Mall Galleries (1991-92). *Work in collections:* South East Arts, Lloyds of London, Leics. C.C.; also private collections in U.K., Eire, Canada. *Signs work:* see appendix. *Address:* Maycotts Lodge, The Green, Matfield, Tonbridge, Kent TN12 7JU.

**JEFFERY, Juliet,** N.D.D., President's medal S.Eq.A. (1993); artist and calligrapher in water-colour, gouache; *b* Bognor Regis, 5 Mar., 1943. *Educ:* Warren, Worthing. *Studied:* Brighton College of Art and Crafts (Dennis Flanders, R.W.S.). *Exhib:* S.Eq.A. Annual, R.W.S. Open, locally and Cumbria, S.S.I. (1996). *Publications:* Gypsy Poems and Ballads by Lavengro; Appley Fair; Bender Tents; and Sarah's Tales (Dragon Press). *Clubs:* S.Eq.A., S.S.I., C.L.A.S. *Signs work:* "Juliet Jeffery." *Address:* The Providence, Compton, Chichester, Sussex PO18 9HD.

**JELLICOE, Colin,** painter in oils and acrylics; art gallery director; *b* 1 Nov., 1942. *Educ:* Heald Place School. *Studied:* Manchester Regional College of Art. *Exhib:* one-man shows: Monks Hall Museum, Eccles (1970), Stockport A.G. (1981), Salford A.G. (1981), Jellicoe Gallery (1983, 84, 85, 90, 95), Buxton Museum and A.G. (1997); group shows: Northern Images Manchester (1974), North West One Chenil Galleries, London (1976), North West Two National Theatre, London (1979), Contemporary Art Fair, Bath (1981, 82, 83), with Micheal Goddard Royal Exchange Theatre Manchester (1985), Edinburgh Festival Fringe (1983, 84, 85), Contemporary Art Fair, London (1984, 85, 86); Open shows: Manchester Academy City A.G. (1970, 73, 75, 76, 81, 84, 85, 88, 92, 95), R.A. Summer Exhbn. (1981); many others in Preston, Accrington, Bolton, Southsea, Wimbledon and Manchester. *Signs work:* see appendix. *Address:* 82 Portland St., Manchester M1 4QX.

**JENKINS, Christopher,** Slade Dip. (Painting) (1957), A.T.C. (1958); potter in thrown and glazed oxidised stoneware, artist in water-colour; Mem. C.P.A., N.P.A.; *b* B'ham, 1933; divorced. one *s.* one *d. Educ:* Harrogate Grammar School. *Studied:* Harrogate School of Art (1949-52), Slade School of Fine Art (1952-54 and 1956-57), Central School (ceramics, 1957-59). *Exhib:* V. & A., Crafts Centre, C.P.A., York, Scarborough, Kendal, Nottingham, Manchester, Liverpool, Tokyo, Copenhagen, Paris. *Work in collections:* North West Arts, L.E.A's: London, Leicester, Bucks., N. Yorks, Kirklees. *Signs work:* see appendix. *Address:* 19 Towngate, Marsden, Huddersfield HD7 6DD.

**JENKINS, Heinke,** R.B.S.A. (1967), R.B.A. (1977); printmaker in linocut, art teacher; *b* Heilbronn, W.Germany, 2 Jul., 1937. one *s. Educ:* Heilbronn Grammar School. *Studied:* Stuttgart Academy of Arts (Prof. Henninger), Stuttgart College of Graphic and Illustration (Prof. Leo Schobinger). *Exhib:* Germany, U.S.A., England. *Work in collections:* Heilbronn A.G., Stuttgart A.G. *Commissions:* 1993: drawings and linocuts by B'ham University Maternity Hospital in Memory of the old Sorrento Maternity Hospital, B'ham. *Publications:* illustrated, Arts Review, 'Ambit' poetry magazine, 'Circle' poems, M. Armstrong. *Clubs:* R.B.S.A., R.B.A., Heilbronn Kunstler Bund. *Signs work:* "HEINKE." *Address:* 26 Allesley Cl., Sutton Coldfield, Birmingham B74 2NF.

**JENNINGS, Walter Robin,** artist in oil; portraits, landscape, and equestrian pictures; *b* Old Hill, Staffs., 11 Mar., 1927. *m* Barbara Wilkinson. *Educ:* Macefields Secondary School. *Studied:* Dudley and Staffordshire Art School,

Brierley Hill School of Art, Birmingham School of Art. *Exhib:* R.B.S.A., R.W.A., R.Cam.A., Royal Institute Galleries, Utd. Soc. of Artists, N.E.A.C., etc. *Work in collections:* Allison House, Mr. H. Woodhouse; Enville Hall, Mr. and Mrs. J. Bissel; Brierley Hill A.G. *Publications:* work repro.: Royle, Medici, Solomon and Whitehead, etc. *Signs work:* see appendix. *Address:* Kestrels, Caunsall, Cookley, nr. Kidderminster, Worcs. DY11 5YJ.

**JENNISON, Robert William,** R.W.A., N.D.D. (1954), A.T.D. (1958); painter in oil, occasional printmaker, lecturer; *b* Grantham, 8 June, 1933. *m* Angela Cook. one *s.* two *d. Educ:* Grammar School, Weston super Mare. *Studied:* West of England College of Art, Bristol (1950-54, 1957-58, Paul Feiler). *Exhib:* frequent solo and group shows since 1962: London, South-West, N. Ireland, including R.W.A., R.U.A. *Work in collections:* public and private collections in Britain, Europe, U.S.A. etc. *Signs work:* "Robert Jennison," "R. Jennison" or "R.J." *Address:* The Old Church School, Talaton, E. Devon EX5 2RQ.

**JERVIS, Sharon,** Dist. Wildlife Illustration (1978), M.A. Graphic Design (1982), M.S.I.A.D. (1980), A.R.S.M. (1996); artist in water-colour and gouache; M.D. Sharon Jervis Ltd.; *b* Leicester, 5 May, 1956. one *s.* one *d. Studied:* Dyfed College of Art (wildlife illustration), Leicester Polytechnic (now De Montfort University). *Address:* Farndon Grange, East Farndon, Market Harborough, Leics. LE16 9SL.

**JESTY, Ronald,** artist in water-colour and acrylic, part-time lecturer; Pres. Somerset Soc. of Artists; *b* Weymouth, Dorset, 7 May, 1926. *m* Margaret Johnson. *Educ:* Weymouth Grammar School; no formal art training. *Exhib:* R.I., R.W.A., R.W.S., R.B.A., R.A., Singer & Friedlander/Sunday Times water-colour competition; nine one-man shows. *Work in collections:* Somerset C.C. *Publications:* "Learn to Paint Seascapes" ( Harper Collins, June 1996). *Clubs:* Artists 303, Somerset Soc. of Artists. *Signs work:* "R. Jesty" and year. *Address:* 24b Brunswick St., Yeovil, Som. BA20 1QY.

**JOBSON, Patrick,** landscape and marine painter and draughtsman in oil, water-colour and pastel; illustrator in black and white; heraldic artist and designer; demonstrator - oils, water-colour, pastel, charcoal. Signs for many of princ. London brewers; *b* 5 Sept., 1919. *m* Lillias Bettina. one *s. Educ:* Sir George Monoux Grammar School, Walthamstow. *Studied:* Under my father, Frank Mears Jobson, and Sir Frank Brangwyn. *Exhib:* generally. *Commissions:* mural panels "The Arts" in Harrison Art Centre. *Publications:* "A Celebration of Marine Art" (Blandford), "20th Century British Marine Painting", "Dictionary of British Book Illustrators", illustrations (O.U.P., Blackie, Macmillan), etc., "The Wapping Group of Artists" (Heron Press). *Clubs:* Langham Sketch (Past President), Wapping Group (Past President). *Signs work:* see appendix. *Address:* 117 Eton Ave., N. Wembley, Middx. HA0 3BA.

**JOEL, Judy,** self taught artist in gouache and acrylic; Curator, St. Ives Soc. of Artists, Hon. Sec., Molesey Art Soc.; *b* London, 30 Aug., 1946. *m* Paul Joel.

one *s.* one *d. Exhib:* solo shows: London, Surrey, Sussex and Cornwall. *Commissions:* Simon Weston, Nerys Hughes, etc. *Signs work:* "J.S Joel." and a little mouse. *Address:* Noah's Ark Studio, Abbey Pl., Mousehole, Cornwall TR19 6PQ.

**JOHANNESON, Steven Thor,** artist in most painting mediums, but especially water-colour and gouache, painting land and sea-scapes, weather and wildlife, i.e. "Nature"; has work published both as cards and Limited Edition Prints; *b* Minneapolis, Minn., 16 June, 1948. *Educ:* Menominee High School, Michigan; Bethel College, St. Paul, Minn. *Studied:* Heatherly-Wilson School of Art (1970-73, Clive Duncan, Helen Wilson, David Ufland). *Exhib:* R.S.M.A., S.WL.A., several mixed and one-man shows in the West Country and London; galleries include St. Ives Gallery; Mid-Cornwall Galleries; Gallerie Marin Appledore; Arty Crafts, Wadebridge; St Breock Gallery; Chagford Gallery; Higher Street Gallery, Dartmouth and White Oak Gallery, Edina, Minneapolis. *Signs work:* "S.T. Johanneson" in vermilion. *Address:* Flat 4, Brentwood Ct., Treyarnon Bay, nr. Padstow, Cornwall PL28 8PL.

**JOHN, Samuel,** B.A. (Lond. 1958), M.B.I.M. (1968), I.P.M. (1960), M.Inst.M. (1970), M.Inst.Ex., former Overseas Marketing Manager, Glaxo Group (1972), R.L.S.S.Inst. (1953); artist in oil, pastel, water-colour, writer, former medical student, business entrepreneur; *b* Newport, Mon., 9 Feb., 1935. *m* Anne Drummond-Leigh, actress. three *s.* one *d. Educ:* Newport High School; London University; Ashridge and Sundridge Management Colleges (Marketing). *Studied:* Chelsea (St. Mark and St. John College) (1955-58, P. G. Roberts, R.A.); qualified as teacher (1957). *Exhib:* Thames Gallery (1978), Chenil Galleries (1956), The Clement, Oxford (1977-79), Oxford Art Soc. (1977-78), Barclay Gallery, Chester (1980), St. Martin's, London (1983), Royal Overseas League, London (1983). *Work in collections:* St. Helen's Convent, Oxford; Blackfriars, Oxford; Mr. R. Bradon, Australia. *Commissions:* Films: (Equity Mem.) Coronation Street, Pardon the Expression, The Jewel in the Crown, The Man in Room 17, etc. *Publications:* The Sacred and The Profane (1980), The Proitiation (1980), The Act of Love (1983); awarded Koestler Prize for Verse (1980). Literary Agent: Curtis Brown, London. Theatrical: Joan Reddin, London. *Clubs:* Royal Overseas, Oxford and Cambridge. *Signs work:* "John." *Address:* c/o Browse Darby, 19 Cork St., London W1X 2LP.

**JOHNS, Phil,** artist in water-colour and oil; Director of Art Publishing Co.; *b* Brentwood, Essex, 15 Feb., 1950. one *s.* one *d. Studied:* Southend Art School, Royal Wanstead School. *Exhib:* over six one-man shows since 1989 worldwide. *Work in collections:* British Petroleum; Forest Healthcare Trust; Intercontinental Hotel, Park Lane. *Commissions:* numerous. *Publications:* work repro.: Limited Editions. *Address:* c/o Nevill Gallery, 43 St. Peter's St., Canterbury, Kent CT1 2BG.

**JOHNSON, Annette,** S.W.A. (1987), N.S.; painter-etcher in water-colour, oil and etching; mem. National Soc. of Painters, Sculptors and Printmakers, and

Soc. of Women Artists; *b* London, 24 March., 1943. *m* Alan. one *s*. one *d*. *Studied:* etching at Morley College; painting at Sir John Cass College of Art. *Exhib:* N.S.P.S. (1985), R.S.M.A. (1985), R.I. (1981), R.A. (1985), S.W.A. annually, N.S. annually. *Signs work:* "Annette Johnson." *Address:* 3 Ballast Quay, Greenwich, London SE10 9PD.

**JOHNSON, Ben,** artist in acrylic; *b* Llandudno, 24 Aug., 1946. *m* Sheila Johnson. two *s*. *Studied:* R.C.A. (1965-69). *Exhib:* one-man shows: New York, London, Bradford; group shows: England, Scotland, Ireland, Belgium, U.S.A., Poland, Yugoslavia, Spain, Australia, France, Germany, Switzerland, Portugal, Italy. *Work in collections:* Boymans-van Beuningen Museum Rotterdam, British Council, Tate Gallery, Contemporary Art Soc., De Beers/CSO Coll., R.I.B.A., Glasgow City A.G., Whitworth Gallery Manchester, Centre Georges Pompidou Paris, V. & A., B.P., Deutsche Bank. Numerous publications. *Commissions:* For last 10 years has worked exclusively to commission for both public and private collections. *Signs work:* "Ben Johnson." *Address:* 4 St. Peter's Wharf, Hammersmith Terr., London W6 9UD.

**JOHNSON, Brian Robert,** R.I. (1988) Bronze Medal Award (1987), Hon. Citizen, Victoria B.C.; Graduated with distinction from The Art Center College of Design, Los Angeles, Calif. with a Bachelor of Professional Arts (1962); artist in water-colour; *b* Victoria, B.C., Canada, 4 Apr., 1932; married. two *s*. one *d*. *Educ:* Victoria High School, Victoria College; Art Center College of Design, Los Angeles. *Exhib:* R.I., R.B.A., A.W.S., F.C.A, C.S.P.W.C., N.W.W.S., C.S.M.A., numerous one-man and group exhbns. in Canada and U.S. *Work in collections:* Canada, U.S., Australia, U.K. and Europe. *Signs work:* "Brian R. Johnson." *Address:* 1766 Haultain St., Victoria, B.C., V8R 2L2, Canada.

**JOHNSON, Joy Alexandra,** B.F.A. (Hons.) (1980), Higher Dip. (Lond.); artist in oils, water-colour; *b* Hull, 26 Aug., 1958. *Educ:* Hatfield High School, Yorks. *Studied:* Newcastle upon Tyne Polytechnic (1977-80), Slade School of Fine Art (1982-84, Lawrence Gowing). *Exhib:* Northern Young Contemporaries (1979), Sainsbury Centre (1980), Mappin Gallery Open Art (1984, 1985), R.A. Summer Exhbn. (1985), several solo exhbns. in London. Received award from Swiss based Vordemberge Gildewart Foundation (1986). *Signs work:* "J.A. Johnson." *Address:* 17 Bempton La., Bridlington, E. Yorks. YO16 5EJ.

**JOHNSTON, Brenda,** painter in oil and scraperboard; *b* London, 8 Dec., 1930. *m* David Johnston. two *s*. one *d*. *Educ:* Rosebery Grammar School, Epsom. *Studied:* Epsom School of Art (1948-49, 1955-60) under Michael Cadman, Leslie Worth; Reigate School of Art (1961-65) under Eric Waugh. *Exhib:* R.A., R.B.A., Nimes and Avignon, Arts Council Exhbn. Midlands and East Anglia; nine one-man shows. *Work in collections:* Ryder Memorial Bequest. *Clubs:* F.P.S., Thames Valley Art, Leatherhead Art. *Signs work:* "Brenda Johnston" or "BJ." *Address:* Russells, 36 Oakfield Rd., Ashtead,

Surrey KT21 2RD.

**JOHNSTON, Duncan,** sculptor in lignum vitae, bronze, ceramics; *b* Liverpool, 9 Mar., 1924. *Studied:* commercial art Liverpool School of Art, self-taught sculptor since demobilisation in 1946, teacher trained 1948, Royal Academy Scholarship 1966, left teaching 1967. Organiser of M-S.S.E. with special reference to blind and partially-sighted visitors. *Exhib:* London, Edinburgh, Paris, Belfast. *Work in collections:* Arts Council of Northern Ireland, R.N.I.B., Kingston-upon-Hull Education Committee, Exhall Grange School, The Argory (National Trust), St. George's Church, Museo Michelangelo, Tel Aviv Museum of Modern Art. *Signs work:* see appendix. *Address:* 151 Craddocks Ave., Ashtead, Surrey KT21 1NR.

**JOHNSTON, George Bonar,** D.A. (Edin.), R.S.W.; artist in oil, gouache and water-colour; formerly adviser in art, Tayside Region Educ. Authority; *b* Edinburgh, 14 June, 1933. *Educ:* Bathgate Academy. *Studied:* Edinburgh College of Art (1951-56) under William Gillies, P.P.R.S.A., R.S.W., and Robin Philipson, P.P.R.S.A., A.R.A., R.S.W. *Exhib:* regular exhibitor R.S.A., R.S.W., R.G.I.; one-man shows: Perth, Kirkcaldy, Glasgow, Dundee; mixed shows: Edinburgh, Aberdeen, London, Paris, Toronto, New York. *Work in collections:* Glasgow, Strathclyde, Edinburgh, Dundee, London, Toronto, U.S.A., France, Australia. *Signs work:* "Johnston." *Address:* 10 Collingwood Cres., Barnhill, Dundee DD5 2SX.

**JOHNSTONE, John,** D.A. (Edin.), A.R.S.A.; painter in oil, lecturer; *b* Falkirk, Stirlingshire, 11 Sept., 1937. *m* Gwen Rodger. one *s.* two *d. Educ:* Graeme High School, Falkirk. *Studied:* Edinburgh College of Art (1957-61, Sir William Gillies). *Work in collections:* Scottish Arts Council; Arts Council of G.B.; Hamilton A.G., Canada; Olinda Museum, Sao Paulo, Brazil; Aberdeen A.G.; Liverpool University; Watson Trust, Edinburgh; Campden Burgh Council, London; Dunbartonshire Educ. Trust, Dunbarton. *Signs work:* "John Johnstone." *Address:* The Luggie, Lauder, Berwickshire TD2 6QT, Scotland.

**JOLL, Evelyn,** B.A. (Oxon.) (1949); art dealer, Agnew's (retd. 1994); *b* London, 6 Feb., 1925. *m* Pamela. one *s.* three *d. Educ:* Dragon School, Oxford; Eton College; Magdalen College, Oxford. *Publications:* The Paintings of J.M.W. Turner (with Martin Butlin) Yale U.P. 2 vols. 1977; awarded Mitchell Prize for History of Art (1978), Revised Edn. (1984). *Clubs:* Boodle's, Hurlingham. *Address:* Flat 3, 42 Tregunter Rd., London SW10 9LQ.

**JONCZYK, Prof. Dr. Leon,** painter, graphic artist, art historian, author of publications about theory of art, experimental printing; Memb., National and International Academies for Arts, Sciences and Humanities, Paris, Bordeaux, Naples, Rome; JSAST, San Francisco; University Prof., Academia Polona Artium; Head of Graphic Art Dept., Munich; President, Assoc. of Graphic Artists, W. Germany; *b* Katowice, Poland, 25 July, 1934. *Educ:* High School, Poland. *Studied:* in Poland, Netherlands, Gt. Britain. *Exhib:* Czechoslovakia, France, Italy, E. and W. Germany, Gt. Britain, Netherlands, Poland, Sweden,

311

Switzerland, Tasmania, Turkey, Yugoslavia, U.S.A. *Work in collections:* more than 30 galleries and museums in Europe, public and private collections in Europe, Australia, U.S.A. *Publications:* illustrated monographs in different languages. *Signs work:* "L. Jonczyk." *Address:* Franz-Joseph-Str. 30/IV, 80801 München, Germany.

**JONES, Aldwyn Douglas,** O.B.E., M.A., F.R.I.B.A., R.W.A., Dip. with Distinction Liverpool University (1933), R.I.B.A. Athens Bursary (1938); architect; Professor Emeritus, University of Bristol; formerly Head, Birmingham School of Architecture (1947-62); *b* Caernarfonshire, 2 Apr., 1910. *m* Phyllis Catharine Jones-Parry. two *s. Educ:* Dragon School, Oxford; Malvern College. *Studied:* architecture: Liverpool School of Architecture (1928-33, Sir Charles Reilly). *Publications:* editor: Colston Papers (1 Edn.), A History of Architecture. *Address:* Senate House, The University, Bristol BS8 1TH.

**JONES, Allen,** N.D.D. (1959), A.T.D. (1960), R.A. (1984); painter, sculptor, printmaker; Trustee, British Museum (1990); *b* Southampton, 1 Sept., 1937; divorced. two *d. Studied:* Hornsey College of Art (1955-59), R.C.A. (1960-61). *Exhib:* since 1961 numerous museum and group shows. *Work in collections:* public museums and private collection worldwide. *Commissions:* public sculpture commissions in the U.K. Represented by Waddington Galleries, London; James Corcoran, Santa Monica, U.S.A.; Thomas Levy, Hamburg; Patrice Trigano, Paris; Charles Cowles, N.Y.C. *Signs work:* "Allen Jones." *Address:* 41 Charterhouse Sq., London EC1M 6EA.

**JONES, Aneurin M.,** N.D.D. (1950), A.T.D. (1955); artist in oil, acrylic, mixed media; retd. Head of Art Dept., Preseli Comprehensive School, N. Pembrokeshire; *m* Julie Jones. one *s.* one *d. Studied:* Swansea College of Art (Principal: Kenneth Hancock, A.R.C.A., Head of Fine Art: William Price, A.R.C.A.), Prix de Rome Scholar. *Exhib:* numerous one-man and mixed shows England and Wales. Welsh representative at the Celtic Festival, Lorient, Brittany. *Work in collections:* National Library of Wales, Aberystwyth; Welsh Arts Council; West Wales Assoc. for the Arts; Dyfed County Council; Ceredigion County Council; The Welsh Office, Cardiff. *Commissions:* three full-length studies of Welsh Archdruids for Gorsedd of Bards permanent collections; mural to commemorate 'Owain Glyndwr' the last native Prince of Wales's struggle for independence in the 13th Century. *Publications:* numerous Welsh/English periodicals, magazines and books. *Clubs:* lecturer for various clubs, societies and educational establishments. *Signs work:* "ANEURIN M. JONES"; 1993 onwards "ANEURIN." *Address:* Heulwen, Aberystwyth Rd., Cardigan, Ceredigion SA43 1LU.

**JONES, Barry Owen,** R.W.S., R.E., N.D.D.; artist in water-colour, etching/aquatint; Gallery Director; *b* London, 11 Sept., 1934. *m* Alexandria Virginia, née Parsons. one *s.* one *d. Educ:* Friern Barnet Grammar School. *Studied:* Hornsey College of Art (1950-55). *Exhib:* R.W.S., R.E., Coach House

Gallery, Guernsey, Bankside Gallery. *Work in collections:* Guernsey Museum and A.G., South London A.G. *Signs work:* see appendix. *Address:* Les Douvres Vineries, La Fosse, St. Martin, Guernsey C.I. GY4 6EF.

**JONES, Edward Scott,** R.C.A. (1964); artist in oil, water-colour, gouache, acrylic; *b* Liverpool, 6 June, 1922. *m* Althea. one *s.* one *d. Educ:* Anfield Road Elementary School. *Studied:* Liverpool College of Art. *Exhib:* R.C.A., Williamson A.G., Bluecoat A.G., R.I., R.S.M.A. *Work in collections:* Merseyside Council Libraries, Blackpool Corp. A.G., Salford A.G., Bolton A.G., Williamson A.G., Birkenhead, also works in private collections. *Signs work:* "E. Scott Jones." *Address:* 18 The Fairway, Knotty Ash, Liverpool L12 3HS.

**JONES, Geraldine M.L.,** Dip.A.D.(Hons.) (1972), Post Grad. Cert. R.A. Schools (1975); freelance artist and illustrator in water-colour, oil, pencil, charcoal; *b* Ampleforth College, Yorks., 23 Nov., 1949. *m* Nigel Jones. *Educ:* The Bar Convent, York. *Studied:* Hull Regional College of Art (1969-72, John Clarke, Michael Chiltern), R.A. Schools (1972-75, Peter Greenham, Anthony Eyton). *Exhib:* York, Hull, Peterborough, Oxford, London, Norwich. *Work in collections:* Bradford Cathedral Chapter House. *Commissions:* Bradford Cathedral. *Publications:* 'Stories from Yorkshire Monasteries' (J. & B. Spence). 'The Yorkshire Journal', 'Against the Tide', Marjorie Bourne. *Clubs:* S.G.F.A. *Signs work:* "G. Jones." *Address:* Fleet House, Hoffleet Stow, Bicker, Boston, Lincs. PE20 3AF.

**JONES, Ian,** B.F.A.(Hons.) (1979), M.F.A. (1982); artist; lecturer in Fine Art; *b* B'ham, 3 July, 1947. *m* Carole A. Jones. two *s. Educ:* Queensbridge Secondary Modern, Moseley. *Studied:* B'ham Polytechnic School of Fine Art (1975-78, Roy Abel, Trevor Halliday), R.C.A. (1979-82, Peter de Francia). *Exhib:* regular exhbns. since 1981, group and individual shows. *Work in collections:* Britain, Europe, America. *Signs work:* "Ian Jones." *Address:* Anderson O'Day Gallery, 255 Portobello Rd., London W11 1LR.

**JONES, Joan,** A.R.B.S.A. (1970); painter in oil and water-colour, also paper collage; painting instructor in still life, portraits, flowers and landscape; *b* Solihull, 16 Apr., 1924; married. one *s. Educ:* Malvern Hall, Solihull. *Studied:* Sutton Coldfield, Bourneville, Birmingham (1950-60, Dennis Greenwood, A.T.D., Alex Jackson, A.T.D., R.B.S.A.). *Exhib:* B'ham, Sutton Coldfield, Worcester, etc. *Signs work:* "Joan Jones" sloping upwards towards right hand side. *Address:* Elms Cottage, Grafton Flyford, Worcester WR7 4PG.

**JONES, John Edward,** N.D.D. (1951), A.T.D. (1952), Dip.F.A. (Slade 1954), R.W.A.; painter in oil, pen, etc.; University senior lecturer; Regional Director of Open College of the Arts; London University Moderator G.C.E. 'O', 'A' level and G.C.S.E. Art; President, Leeds Fine Art Club; *b* Bristol, 19 Aug., 1926. *m* Gabriela Jones. two *d. Educ:* Winterbourne Elementary; Colston's School, Stapleton. *Studied:* West of England College of Art (1942-44 (army intervened) 1948-52, George Sweet), Slade School (1952-54, Rogers,

Coldstream, Wittkower). *Exhib:* R.W.A., Leeds Fine Art, and private galleries. *Work in collections:* University of Leeds, R.W.A. *Publications:* author, Wonders of the Stereoscope. *Clubs:* Chelsea Arts. *Signs work:* "J.E. Jones" or "Jones" (and date). *Address:* 20 Hollin La., Leeds LS16 5LZ.

**JONES, Joyce Margaret (née Mellor),** illustrator, miniature painter of portraits, animals, floral; *b* Bangalore, India. *Studied:* Regional College of Art, Manchester (1954-57), St. Martin's School of Art (1957-59), Italy (1959-60). *Publications:* illustrated books for Longmans, University of Wales Press, Cambridge School Classics, N.W. Arts Assoc., Thames and Hudson, Encyclopedia Britannica, Nature Conservancy. Work purchased: by Indian Army (portraits), miniature collectors, commercial dealers in U.K., U.S.A., S. Africa, Australia. *Address:* 3 Queens Park, Colwyn Bay LL29 7BG.

**JONES, Karen,** S.Eq.A.; equine water-colourist; *b* 11 Aug., 1942. *m* Mike Eaton. two *d*. *Educ:* Godolphin and Latymer. *Exhib:* R.A., England, Wales and U.S.A. *Work in collections:* England, Wales, Scotland, Ireland, U.S.A., Canada, France, Italy, Germany, Portugal, Holland, W.I., New Zealand, Spain, Australia. Gallery at home: open Summer. *Signs work:* "K.J.'98." *Address:* Blaenllyn, Llangolman, Clunderwen, Pembs. SA66 7XR.

**JONES, Leslie,** A.R.E., A.R.C.A., D.A.(Manc.), H.R.Cam.A., Rome Scholar; painter, printmaker, illustrator; taught at Hornsey, Kingston, St. Martin's Schools of Art (1961-67); H.M.I. (1967-83); Bangor (1987-89); *b* Tremadoc, 26 June, 1934. *Studied:* Regional College of Art, Manchester (1951-55), Royal College of Art (1955-58), British School at Rome (1958-60); visitor at Belgrade Academy (1959). *Exhib:* London, Rome, U.S.A., Austria. *Work in collections:* V. & A., Arts Council, University of Oregon, University of Wales, National Library Wales, L.E.As. *Publications:* illustrated books for Lion & Unicorn, Longmans, University of Wales Press, Cambridge School Classics Project. *Address:* 3 Queens Park, Colwyn Bay LL29 7BG.

**JONES, Lucilla Teresa,** Cert.F.A. (Oxon.); painter in oil, water-colour, mixed media; *b* Exmouth, 30 June, 1949; divorced. one *s*. *Educ:* St David's Ursuline Convent, Brecon. *Studied:* Ruskin School of Fine Art and Drawing (1968-71). *Exhib:* many solo and mixed shows including Ashmolean Museum, Monaco Fine Arts Monte Carlo, Chapter Gallery Cardiff, Upton Lodge Galleries, Tetbury, Weatherall, Green & Smith, London, Osborne Studio Gallery, London, Julian Davies Gallery, San Diego, Louis C. Morten Gallery, Mexico City, Capriole Gallery, Virginia, Mall Galleries, Inst. of Contemporary Arts, Warwick Arts Trust Galleries, London, Roy Miles Gallery, London. *Work in collections:* Royal Artillery and Royal Marines, Brecknock Museum and A.G.; private collections in U.K., U.S.A., Singapore, S. Africa, Holland and Ireland including those of Prince Kais al Said and Ravi Tikoo. *Publications:* Horse Breeding in Ireland, Horses, Hounds and Hunting Horns by Dr. Colin Lewis (Allen, 1980). *Signs work:* "L.T.J." or "Lucilla Jones." *Address:* Dan-y-Parc, Llandefalle, Brecon, Powys. LD3 0UN.

# WHO'S WHO IN ART

**JONES, Malcolm,** H.Dip.A.D. (1973), B.A. (Hons.) (1971); artist in painting and installation; administrator, Cafe Gallery, London SE16; *b* Merseyside, 12 May, 1949. *Studied:* Chelsea School of Art (1972-73), University of Reading (1967-71). *Exhib:* six solo shows in London public galleries since 1980, internationally in group exhbns. since 1972. Work reviewed in The Architects Journal, The Times, Neue Bildende Kunst, Neues Deutschland, The Guardian, Artscribe, BBC Critics Forum, Arts Review, NRC Handelsblad, Der Tagesspiegel, Frankfurter Rundschau, Het Parool and Tu Times. *Address:* 64 Chisenhale Rd., London E3 5QZ.

**JONES, Mary Lloyd,** N.D.D. (1955), A.T.D. (1956); artist in water-colour and oil; Chairman, Wales Artists Development Centre Assoc.; *b* Devil's Bridge, Ceredigion, Wales, 21 Aug., 1934. *m* John Jones. two *d*. *Educ:* Ardwyn Grammar School, Aberystwyth. *Studied:* Cardiff College of Art (1951-56, Eric Malthouse). *Exhib:* Montserrat Gallery, N.Y., Martin Tinney Gallery, Cardiff, Gallery of Modern Art, London. *Work in collections:* Tabernacle Museum of Modern Art, Wales, W.A.C., Crawford Museum and Gallery, Cork, Tyrone Guthrie Centre, Ireland, B.B.C. Wales, Ceredigion C.C., S4C Centre. *Publications:* The Mountains of Wales (Univ. of Wales Press), Our Sisters Land (Univ. of Wales Press). *Clubs:* Gweled (Welsh Artists Assoc.), Water-colour Soc. Wales, R.Cam.A. *Signs work:* "Mary Lloyd Jones." *Address:* Yr Hen Ysgol, Aberbanc, Llandysul, Dyfed, Wales SA44 5NP.

**JONES, Olwen,** R.A.S. (1968), R.E. (1978), R.W.S. (1989); painter in oil and water-colour, printmaker in relief and etching; *b* London, 1 Mar., 1945. *m* Charles Bartlett. *Educ:* Harrow School of Art (1960-65). *Studied:* Royal Academy Schools (1965-68), engraving under Gertrude Hermes. *Exhib:* first one-man: Zaydler Gallery, London (1971). *Work in collections:* National Museum of Wales, Norwich Castle Museum, Reading Museum, Nuffield Foundation. *Signs work:* "Olwen Jones." *Address:* St. Andrews House, Fingringhoe, nr. Colchester, Essex CO5 7GB.

**JONES, Rosamund,** N.D.D. (Painting), R.E.; artist in etching, water-colour; shepherd; *b* Harrogate, 1944; married. one *s*. three *d*. *Educ:* Harrogate. *Studied:* Harrogate College of Art (Mr. Pemsil), Leeds College of Art (1960-64, Mr. Taylor). *Exhib:* Cartwright Hall Bradford, Oxford Gallery, Zella 9 Gallery, R.A., R.S.A., Bankside Gallery. *Signs work:* "Rosamund Jones." *Address:* New Bridge Farm, Birstwith, Harrogate HG3 2PN.

**JONES, Royston,** Dip. A.D. (1968), M.F.A. (Illinois, 1971); photographer; human interface design; computer art and design; Assistant Development Director, St. Helens College; *b* Wolverhampton, 15 Jan., 1947. *m* Sheila Donoghue. one *d*. *Studied:* Birmingham College of Art and Design (1965-68, John Walker, Trevor Halliday), University of Illinois (1969-71, Jerome Savage, Art Sinsebaugh, Bart Parker). *Exhib:* regularly in Britain and U.S.A. *Address:* St. Helens College, Brook St., St. Helens, Merseyside WA10 1PZ.

**JONES, Selwyn,** R.C.A., A.T.C., A.T.D., N.D.D., D.A. (Manc.); painter in oil, mixed media, water-colour, former lecturer; *b* Llanberis, 3 May, 1928. *m* Sarah Jones. *Educ:* Caernarfon Grammar School. *Studied:* Regional College of Art, Manchester (1948-53). *Exhib:* U.C.N.W., Howard Roberts Gallery, Cardiff, Oriel, Bangor, Albany Gallery, Cardiff, Rhyl Art Centre, Glyn-y-Weddw, National Museum of Wales (North), Art Spectrum Wales, Anglesey Observed, Face of Wales, Rochdale A.G. *Work in collections:* G.L.C. Rochdale, Gwynedd, Glamorgan, Denbighshire, U.C.N.W., W.A.C., C.A.S.W.I., National Library of Wales. *Signs work:* "Selwyn Jones" or "S.J." or not at all. *Address:* Anglesey LL61 6NJ.

**JONES, Stanley Robert,** A.T.D. (1950), F.S.A.; printmaker and archaeologist; *b* Birmingham, 9 June, 1927. *Educ:* Elementary School; Yardley Grammar School, Birmingham. *Studied:* Birmingham College of Art under Harold Smith, B. Fleetwood-Walker, A.R.A. (1942-45, 1948-50), R.A. Schools under B. Fleetwood-Walker, A.R.A., Henry Rushbury, R.A. (1950-55). *Exhib:* R.A., R.B.S.A., Printmakers' Council Venues, South Yorkshire Open. *Work in collections:* Graves Art Gallery, Sheffield. *Signs work:* see appendix. *Address:* 118 Totley Brook Rd., Sheffield S17.

**JONES, Steven,** Dip. in Illustration (1981); artist/illustrator in oil and water-colour; *b* Chester, 5 Apr., 1959. *m* Sian. one *s.* one *d. Educ:* Colwyn High School, Colwyn Bay. *Studied:* Wrexham College of Art (1976-81, Keith Bowen). *Exhib:* one-man show: Oriel Môn, Anglesey (1996). *Publications:* book covers, magazine illustrations, company reports, film posters and B.P. Calendar. Specialises in figures in landscape scenes particularly beach scenes and golf scenes. Many paintings sold through auctions in Britain including Christies, Bonhams and Chrystals. Works from his own gallery in Felinheli. *Signs work:* "Steven Jones." *Address:* 16 Stad Eryri, Bethel, Gwynedd, N. Wales LL55 1BX.

**JONES, Trevor,** N.D.D. (1953), A.T.C.(Lond.) (1954), Fellow, Designer Bookbinders, Founder Mem. and President (1983-85); artist craftsman in bookbinding; on Crafts Council Index of Selected Makers; *b* Wembley, 15 July, 1931. *m* Pauline Jones. two *d. Studied:* Harrow School of Art (1947-49, 1952-53), Hornsey College of Art (1953-54). *Exhib:* Britain and internationally with Designer Bookbinders since 1956. *Work in collections:* British Library, V. & A., Royal Library Copenhagen, University of Texas, Pierpoint Morgan Library N.Y., Lilly Library Indiana, Keatley Trust Collection of 20c. British Art, Shipley A.G. Gateshead. *Publications:* articles in The New Bookbinder, Bookbinder, Crafts, Fine Print, Magnus. *Signs work:* "T.R.J." or "Trevor Jones." *Address:* 48 Burton Stone Lane, York YO3 6BU.

**JONES, Yvonne,** B.A.Hons.F.A.; painter; *b* Holywell, N. Wales, 9 Oct., 1946. *m* Peter M. Jones. two *s. Educ:* Holywell Grammar School. *Studied:* Liverpool College of Art. *Exhib:* mixed: Mall Gallery, Liverpool Festival of Arts, Wrexham Arts Centre, R.A. Summer Exhbns. (1989, 1990), Portsmouth City Gallery, Doncaster City Gallery; European tour: one-man shows:

Bridewell Studios Liverpool (supp Eastern Arts), Quay Arts Centre (supp Southern Arts). *Work in collections:* Welsh Arts Council, Merseyside Arts Trust, New Hall, Cambridge, Contemporary Women Artists; private collections: U.K. and Germany. *Address:* Hazelwood, Waters Green, Brockenhurst, Hants. SO42 7RG.

**JONES, Zebedee,** B.A. (Hons.) Fine Art (1992), M.A. (Hons.) - Fine Art (1993); painter in oil on canvas and board; *b* London, 12 Mar., 1970. *Studied:* Norwich School of Art and Design, Chelsea College of Art and Design. *Exhib:* Arts Council, Southampton City A.G., Leeds City A.G., Unbound at the Hayward Gallery (1994), Real Art (Southampton 1995, Leeds City A.G. 1996); two solo exhbns. (1995, 1997). *Publications:* 'Affective Light' Rear Window (1994), Unbound Possibilities in Painting, Hayward Gallery (1994), From Here Exhbn. Cat., Essay by Andrew Wilson, Waddington Galleries (1995), Foundations for Fame, The London Inst. (1997). *Address:* 1 Albert Bridge Rd., London SW11 4PX. *2nd Address*c/o Waddington Galleries, 11 Cork St., London W1X 2LT.

**JONES-ROWE, Avril,** N.D.D., D.F.A.(Slade), M.F.P.S.; painter in oil and acrylic, sculptor in bronze, landscape gardener, teacher, art historian; *b* New Forest, Hants., 1934. *Studied:* Southampton Art College (1951-55), Sander Theatre School, Southampton (1952-54), Slade School (1955-57), Perugia University (1959). *Exhib:* group shows: Young Contemporaries, London Group, Loggia Gallery, Trends, Bloomsbury Gallery, Bougton Aluph Church, Stroud Festival; one-man shows: Bailey House, Canterbury (Artist in Residence, 1965), B'ham University (1967), St. Pancras Hospital (1975), Loggia Gallery (1987). *Signs work:* "Jones-Rowe." *Address:* 25 Station Rd, Alderholt, Fordingbridge, Hants. SP6 3AF.

**JONZEN, Karin,** F.R.B.S.; annual award trophy for 'Action Research' and R.A.D.A. (1979); gold medal, Academie Italia delle Arte (1980); gold medal, International Parliament for Safety and Peace, U.S.A. (1983); silver medal, R.B.S. (1983); sculptor (terracotta, bronze, and stone); *b* 1914. *m* Basil Jonzen. one *s. Educ:* Wimbledon High School. *Studied:* Slade School, Stockholm Royal Academy. Slade Scholarship and Diploma (1934); Prix de Rome (1939). *Exhib:* Cambridge, Cork St., R.A. since 1934, Geneva. *Work in collections:* Tate Gallery (1985), Brighton, Bradford, Glasgow, Liverpool, Southend and Melbourne A.G. Official purchases: Arts Council; Selwyn College, Cambridge; L.C.C. housing estate at Lewisham (1960); St. Michael's Church, Golder's Green (1961); Guildford Cathedral (1962); World Health Organization Headquarters, New Delhi (1963), World Health Organization Headquarters, Geneva (1965). Exhibited three works for City of London Festival (1968), one work retained, Madonna and Child, purchased for St. Mary-le-Bow (1969). Exhibited New York, one torso acquired by Andrew White Museum, Cornell University (1969). *Commissions:* Life-size bronze figure commissioned by London Co-operation for site at the Barbican (1970); over

# WHO'S WHO IN ART

life-size group for Guildhall Square. Gift of Lord Blackford to London Co-operation (1972); ¾ life-size Pièta for Swedish Church, Marylebone (1975); ¾ life-size figure Young Girl purchased for Cadogan Estate erected in Sloane Gdns.; over life-size bronze portrait bust of Samuel Pepys purchased for Seething Lane Garden (1983); Madonna and Child purchased for St. Mary and St. Gabriel Church, S. Harting, Hants (1985); Madonna and Child purchased for St. Saviours Church, Maida Vale (1985). Portrait busts include: Malcolm Muggeridge, Sir Alan Herbert, Sir Hugh Casson, Dame Ninette de Valois, Donald Trelford, Sir Monty Finiston, Paul Scofield. *Publications:* Karin Jonzen, Sculptor (Bachman & Turner, 1976). Who's Who in International Art (Geneva, 1997). *Signs work:* "K. Jonzen." *Address:* 6a Gunter Gr., London SW1 0UJ.

**JOPE, Anne,** B.A.Hons. (1970), A.R.E. (1979), R.E. (1984), Central Postgrad. Printmaking Dip. (1981), S.W.E. (1984); painter in oil paint and water-colour, printmaker in wood engraving, woodcut and linocut, illustrator; *b* Corfe Mullen, Dorset, 31 Jan., 1945. *m* John Anthony Jope. *Studied:* Ealing Art College (1966-67), Central School of Art and Design (1967-70, 1980-81). *Exhib:* eleven one-man shows, R.A., N.E.A.C., R.B.A., Camden Arts Centre, Ferens A.G., Graffiti, Morley Gallery, Royal Western Academy, St. David's Hall, Cardiff. *Work in collections:* Liverpool public libraries, B.M., Malcolmson Collection at Hereford City A.G., Ashmolean Museum, Leics. Educ. Com., N.P.G. *Publications:* The Song of the Reeds and Rushavenn Time, The Honey Gatherers, Animals at the Table, Nightlife Poems. *Signs work:* "Anne Jope." *Address:* 14 Millwood End, Long Hanborough, Witney, Oxon. OX8 8BX.

**JORDAN, Maureen Ann,** S.B.A., U.A.; designer/artist in pastel, water-colour, acrylic; *b* 14 Apr., 1941. *Educ:* Escourt High School, Kingston upon Hull. *Studied:* Kingston upon Hull College of Art and Crafts. *Exhib:* P.S., S.B.A., U.A., New Trends Hong Kong, Art Mart, also in many galleries mainly in the London area. *Publications:* art magazines, art books, greetings cards, prints and limited editions. *Address:* 26 Manor Gdns., London SW20 9AB.

**JOSEPH, Jane,** painter, draughtsman, printmaker; *b* Surrey, 7 June, 1942. *Studied:* painting: Camberwell School of Art and Crafts (1961-65, Robert Medley, E. Uglow, F. Auerbach, R. Kitaj, R.D. Lee, F. Bowling). *Exhib:* solo shows: Morley Gallery (1973), Minories, Colechester (1982), Angela Flowers (1987), Flowers East (1989, 1992), Edinburgh Printmakers (1994). *Work in collections:* Arts Council of Wales, Government Picture Collection, Castle Museum, Norwich, Unilever House, Imperial College, London, University of Northumbria, Chelsea and Westminster Hospital, British Musuem, Paintings in Hospitals. *Commissions:* Chelsea and Westminster Hospital. *Clubs:* Chelsea Arts. *Signs work:* "Jane Joseph" or "JEJ." *Address:* 105 Cambridge Gdns., London W10 6JE.

**JUKES, Edith Elizabeth,** F.R.B.S., A.R.C.A. (1932), S.R.N. (Bart's, 1945);

sculptor in clay, wood, stone; teacher of sculpture, Sir John Cass School of Art, City of London Polytechnic (1946-75); *b* Shillong, Assam, 19 Dec., 1910. *Educ:* Norland Pl. School, Kensington. *Studied:* R.C.A. (1928-32) under Profs. Richard Garbe, R.A., Henry Moore, and Herbert Palliser. *Exhib:* R.A., etc. *Signs work:* see appendix. *Address:* The Studio, 347 Upper Richmond Rd., London SW15 6XP.

# K

**KALASHNIKOV, Anatoly Ivanovich,** Hon. R.E. (1988), Hon. S.W.E. (1993); Russian wood engraver; *b* Moscow, Russia, 5 Apr., 1930. *m* (1) Iulia Borisovna 1957 (died 1980); (2) Ludmila Nikolaevna 1980 (died 1994); (3) Ludmila Ivanovna 1994. *Educ:* Moscow Art Inst. (formerly Stroganoff Art School), disciple of Academician Ivan Pavlov Freelance designer for many Soviet publishing houses and Ministry of Communications (postal designs) 1960-80; created over 100 postage stamps and 500 commemorative envelope designs, more than 900 bookplates. *Exhib:* more than 160 solo exhbns. worldwide. Academician, International Academy of the Book and Art of the Book, Moscow (1992); Merited Artist of Russian Federation; first prizes in international bookplate design competitions: Barcelona, Budapest, Kronach (Germany), Como, Genoa, Pescara, San Vito al Tagliamento (Italy), Helsingor (Denmark), Carlisle (USA). *Work in collections:* B.M., London; Cabinet of Engraving, Biblioteque Nationale, Paris; National Museum, Prague. *Publications:* Anglo-Russian Relations (1983); War and Peace: A suite of Wood Engravings, based on the novel by Leo Tolstoy (1991); 500 Exlibrisis (1993); The Dostoyevsky Suite (1994); Omar Khayam in xylographies by A. Kalashnikov (1994); Golden Ring of Russia (1995); many other albums and suites. Leisure interest: travelling, bookplate design. *Clubs:* Lions Club, Moscow. *Signs work:* see appendix. *Address:* Leninsky prospect 44, Apt.124, 117334 Moscow, Russian Federation.

**KALEDKIEWICZ, Zdzisław Lucjan,** M.F.A. (1955); painter and teacher; Lecturer, Technical University, Gdansk, State Schools in Gdansk and Gdynia; *b* Czestochowa, Poland, 31 Aug., 1913. *m* Irena. two *s*. one *d*. *Studied:* Cracow Academy of Fine Art (1936-39). M.A. in Fine Art, Gdansk (1955). *Exhib:* representative exhbns. of Polish art abroad (1945-90). *Work in collections:* Gdansk, Oliwa, Cracow. *Publications:* "Muse on Bidet" aphorisms (Gdynia, 1958). *Clubs:* Freedom and Democracy Union. *Signs work:* "Z. Kaledkiewicz." *Address:* 80-322 Gdansk-Oliwa, Ul.Lesna 9/2, Poland.

**KALKHOF, Peter Heinz,** painter, lecturer in fine art; *b* Stassfurt, Germany 20 Dec., 1933. *m* Jeanne The. one *s*. *Educ:* Germany. *Studied:* School of Arts and Crafts, Braunschweig; Academy of Fine Art, Stuttgart; Slade School of Fine Art, London; Ecole des Beaux Art, Paris (1954-62). *Exhib:* Annely Juda Fine Art (1970-79, 1990, 1997), Scottish Arts Council, Edinburgh, Glasgow,

Juda-Rowan Gallery (1983), Landesmuseum Oldenburg (1988), Camden Arts Centre (1989), Galerie Rösch, Neubrunn (1993)/Karlshruhe (1994), Germany. *Work in collections:* Northern Ireland Trust, Arts Council of Gt. Britain, Leics. Educ. Authority, European Parliament, Landesmuseum Oldenburg, Ostpreussen Museum, Lüneburg. *Commissions:* 1987 Treaty-Centre: Mural (Taylor Woodrow), Hounslow, London. *Signs work:* "Peter Kalkhof." *Address:* c/o Annely Juda Fine Art, 23 Dering St., London W1R 9AA.

**KANE, Martin,** B.A.(Hons.) (Edin. 1987); artist in oil on canvas, pastel; *b* Cardiff, 3 June, 1958. *Educ:* St. Andrew's High School, Clydebank, Glasgow. *Studied:* Glasgow School of Art (1981-82), Edinburgh College of Art (1982-87, David Michie). *Exhib:* Angela Flowers Gallery (1988), Jill George Gallery (1990), Thumb Gallery, Atlanta, U.S.A. (1990), Kasen Summer Coll., N.Y.; one-man shows: Jill George Gallery (1992, 1993), Beaux Arts, London (1996). *Work in collections:* Cleveland, Middlesbrough; Cleveland, Ohio; Glasgow Museums and A.Gs.; Unilever PLC; Gartmore Investments. *Signs work:* "Martin Kane." *Address:* Dovehill Studios, 15 East Campbell St., Glasgow G1 5DT.

**KANIDINC, Salahattin,** awarded High Moral Prize (1954); artist in pencil, pen, brush, ink, oil, polymer; letterer, calligrapher, designer, expert on historical writing systems (hieroglyphs to Roman alphabet) and modern letter forms; owner-creative director, Kanidinc International; and consultant designer for major corporations; *b* Istanbul, Turkey, 12 Aug., 1927. *m* Seniha Kanidinc. two *s. Educ:* 22nd Elementary School of Uskudar, Uskudar 1st High School, Istanbul, Turkey. *Studied:* Defenbaugh School of Lettering, Minn. (1954), Zanerian College of Penmanship, Ohio (1963), State University of Iowa (1963), University of Minnesota (1964), University of California (1963-64). *Work in collections:* Peabody Inst. Library, Baltimore; W.C.C., N.Y.C.; and in private collections. *Publications:* participant designer, Alphabet Thesaurus, Vols. 2-3. Listed in 'Who's Who' publications throughout the world. *Clubs:* S.S.I., W.C.C., International Assoc. of Master Penmen and Teachers of Handwriting, American Inst. of Graphic Arts, International Center for the Typographic Arts, National Advisory Board of the American Security Council. *Signs work:* see appendix. *Address:* 33-44 93rd St., Jackson Heights, New York 11372, U.S.A.

**KAUFFMANN, C. Michael,** PhD. (1957), F.B.A. (1987), F.M.A., F.S.A.; Art historian and museum curator (formerly V. & A.); Emeritus Prof. of the History of Art, and former Director; Courtauld Inst., University of London; *b* Frankfurt a/M, 5 Feb., 1931. *m* Dorothea. two *s. Educ:* St. Paul's School; Merton College, Oxford (1950-53); Warburg Inst., London (1953-57). *Publications:* The Baths of Pozzuoli: medieval illuminations of Peter of Eboli's poem (1959); An Altarpiece of the Apocalypse (1968); V. & A. Catalogue of Foreign Paintings; British Romanesque Manuscripts 1066-1190 (1975); Catalogue of Paintings in the Wellington Museum (1982); John Varley (1984);

Studies in Medieval Art (1992). *Address:* 53 Twyford Ave., London W3 9PZ.

**KAY, Nora,** A.R.C.A., M.C.S.D.; decorative studio pottery, lino-cuts, book jackets; designer for Yardley's, Jenners Ltd.; teacher at St. Martin's School of Art, Newland Park College, Maltman's Green School; *Educ:* Wycombe High School, St. Martin's School of Art, R.C.A. *Exhib:* R.B.A., N.E.A.C. *Publications:* children's books; work repro.: general advertising work, London Transport posters, Christmas cards, book jackets. *Signs work:* "N.K." *Address:* Flat 5, Ethorpe Cres., Gerrards Cross, Bucks SL9 8PW.

**KEANE, John,** B.F.A. (1976); painter in oil and mixed media on canvas, P.V.A. and mixed media on paper; Official War artist, Gulf (1991); *b* Herts., 12 Sept., 1954. *m* Rosemary McGowan. one *d*. *Studied:* Camberwell School of Art (1972-76). *Exhib:* twenty five one-man shows in U.K., Europe and U.S.A. since 1980. *Work in collections:* Imperial War Museum, Contemporary Art Soc., Rugby Museum, Cleveland Gallery, The Guardian, Harris Museum, Preston, Glasgow Museum and A.G., Aberdeem A.G., Wolverhampton Museum and A.G., Christies Corporate Collection, British Coal, Financial Times, Unilever PLC, Detroit Art Inst. *Publications:* Conflicts of Interest by Mark Lawson (Mainstream Pub. 1995). *Clubs:* Groucho. *Signs work:* "John Keane." *Address:* c/o Flowers East, 199-205 Richmond Rd., London E8 3NJ.

**KEANY, Brian James,** R.S.W. (1977), D.A. (Edin. 1967); artist in oil, acrylic, water-colour; art teacher; *b* Forfar, Scotland, 16 Jan., 1945. *m* Christina Nicol Herd, D.A.(Edin.). one *s*. two *d*. *Educ:* Brechin High School. *Studied:* Edinburgh College of Art (1963-67, Sir William Gillies, Sir Robin Philipson, William J. L. Baillie). *Exhib:* R.S.A., R.S.W., R.G.I., and several one-man shows and group exhbns. *Signs work:* "BRIAN KEANY." *Address:* 27 Solway Pl., Glenrothes, Fife KY6 2NS.

**KEARNEY, Joseph,** D.A.Glas. (1961); painter in various media; *b* Glasgow, 14 Sept., 1939. *Educ:* St. Aloysius' College, Glasgow. *Studied:* Glasgow School of Art. *Exhib:* several one-man shows in Glasgow. *Work in collections:* Glasgow A.G. and Museum and in many private collections. *Commissions:* Portrait of Most Rev. J.D.Scanlan, Archbishop of Glasgow, and many other private commissions. *Clubs:* Glasgow Art. *Signs work:* "Kearney." *Address:* 97 Elmore Ave., Glasgow G44 5BH.

**KEIR, Sally,** B.A.(Hons.) (1984), M.S.B.A. (1989); designer jeweller/botanical artist in gouache; *b* Guildford, 29 Sept., 1938. *m* Peter Benson. two *d*. *Educ:* Sydenham School, Devon. *Studied:* Hereford College of Art (1979-81), Duncan of Jordanstone College of Art (1981-84). *Exhib:* R.H.S. gold, silver gilt and silver medals, S.B.A. (1989-97), Linnean Soc. (1990-91), Discerning Eye (1991), Del Bello Gallery, Toronto (1988-90), R.S.M. (1990), Tregaquelle (1994), S.W.A. (1991). *Work in collections:* Hunt Inst. of Botanical Art, Chicago, Shirley Sherwood Coll. *Publications:* Collin's Artists Manual, Contemporary Botanical Artists, Drawing and Painting Course. *Signs work:* "S.A.K." *Address:* 36 Woodcock Gdns., Featherstone, Wolverhampton WV10 7TQ.

**KELLY, Deirdre,** B.Ed.(Hons.) (1984), M.A. (1987), R.E.; printmaker; *b* London, 1 May, 1962. *Studied:* Wimbledon School of Art. *Exhib:* B.P. International, Contemporary Art Soc., Galerie Luc Queryel, Harriet Green Gallery. *Work in collections:* Sedgewick Gp. International, Atlantis Paper Co., King's College School, Museuda Gravura, Brazil. *Publications:* work repro.: Big Issue (1995). *Signs work:* "Deirdre Kelly" or "D.K." *Address:* c/o Hardware Gallery, 162 Archway Rd., London N6 5BB.

**KELLY, Felix,** artist in oil; *b* Auckland, N.Z., 1916. *Exhib:* Lefévre Gallery (1943, 1944, 1946), Leicester Gallery (1950, 1952), Portraits Inc., N.Y. (1947), Charleston, S.C. (1948), Washington, D.C. (1949), Arthur Jeffress Gallery (1959-62), Arthur Tooth & Sons (1965, 1968, 1971), Kennedy Galleries Inc., N.Y. (1970), Delgado Museum of Art, New Orleans (1970), Partridge Fine Arts, London (1978, 1981). *Work in collections:* Lord Rothermere, Sir Herbert Read, Lord Faringdon, Charles Engelhard, Esq., The Earl of Mountbatten, David Bruce, Esq., Chester Beattie, Esq., The Duke of Buccleuch, Walter Annenberg, Esq., John Hay Whitney, Esq., Lord Aberdare, four murals for Lord Howard at Castle Howard, York. *Publications:* Paintings by Felix Kelly, by Sir Herbert Read; illustrations for Longmans, Macmillans, Hutchinsons, Chatto & Windus. Theatre sets for Haymarket, Phoenix, Sadlers Wells, Old Vic. *Signs work:* "Felix Kelly." *Address:* 49 Princes Gate, London SW7.

**KELLY, Phil,** painter in oil and charcoal; *b* Dublin, 7 Sept., 1950. *m* Ruth. *Educ:* Rugby School. *Studied:* Bristol University (1970-73). *Exhib:* U.K., U.S.A., Portugal, Mexico. *Work in collections:* Museum of Contemporary Art, Centro Cultural Arte Contemporaneo Mexico. *Signs work:* "Kelly" or "P.K." *Address:* Emscote Lawn, Warwick CV34 5GD.

**KELLY, Victor Charles,** R.B.S.A. (1983), R.C.A. (1991); painter in water-colour, acrylic, pastel, lecturer, teacher; Past Hon. Sec. Royal Birmingham Soc. of Artists, Past Vice President R.B.S.A.; *b* B'ham, 6 Sept., 1923. *m* Sylvia. two *s. Educ:* B'ham Teachers Training College. *Studied:* Liverpool College of Art (1949-50). *Exhib:* R.B.S.A., R.I., Manchester Academy of Art, Chelsea Art Soc., R.Cam.A., Dudley Mid Art, Laing, London, New York. *Work in collections:* R.B.S.A. *Clubs:* Past Pres. B'ham Water-colour Soc., Easel Club, B'ham Art Circle. *Signs work:* "Victor C. Kelly." *Address:* 90 Sandringham Rd., Perry Barr, B'ham B42 1PH.

**KEMPSHALL, Kim,** R.B.S.A. (1985), A.R.C.A. (1960); painter/printmak-er oil, acrylic, water-colour, etching, lithography; *b* 1934. *m* Sylvia. one *s.* one *d. Studied:* Manchester College of Art (1951-55); Royal College of Art (1957-60). *Exhib:* R.A., Scottish Royal Academy, Arts Council, one-man shows. *Work in collections:* Edinburgh City Coll., Scottish Modern A.G., Aberdeen A.G., Dundee A.G., Arts Council, V. & A., Herbert A.G., Whitworth A.G., Birmingham A.G., Wolverhampton A.G., Bradford A.G., City of Lyon, City of Frankfurt, Ecole de Beaux Art, Toulouse; many private collections worldwide. *Signs work:* "K.K." *Address:* Mere House, 49 Henley Ave., Iffley, Oxford OX4 4DJ.

**KENDALL, Alice R.,** D.A. (Edin.), F.R.Z.S. (Scot.), S.W.A., F.R.S.A., P.P.S.W.A. (1977-82); artist in oil, water-colour, pen and ink, writer; *b* N.Y.C. *Educ:* New York and Edinburgh. *Studied:* Edinburgh under Sir Wm. Gillies, Sir Wm. MacTaggart. *Exhib:* R.A., Paris Salon, R.B.A., N.E.A.C., R.I., S.W.A., etc. and with the late Alice Kendall (Mother) at Cooling Galleries (1948, 1956) and Chelsea Gallery (1949). *Work in collections:* The Royal Society of Edinburgh: Official portrait of Father (1956). *Publications:* children's book 'Funny Fishes'; articles and poems, many illustrated, in Punch, Poetry Review, The Artist, The Voice of Youth, etc. *Signs work:* "A.R. Kendall." *Address:* 35 Beaufort Gdns., London SW3 1PW.

**KENDALL, Kay Thetford,** R.M.S., S.W.A.; sculptor and portrait sculptor in bronze, bronze resin, gold and silver, specialising in cats, miniature sculpture and sculptural jewellery; *b* Manchester. *m* D. Wilmer Kendall. *Educ:* Cheadle Hulme Schools. *Studied:* Malvern College of Art; Hertfordshire College of Art and Design. *Exhib:* Mall Galleries, London; S.W.A., R.M.S.; one man shows, Welwyn Garden City, Hatfield, Knebworth, Wembley, Bishop's Stortford. Awards: 1st Prize for sculpture, Grolla d'oro, Venice (1981); Bidder & Borne award for sculpture R.M.S. (1986). *Clubs:* R.M.S., S.W.A. *Signs work:* see appendix. *Address:* The Studio, 45 Orchard Rd., Tewin, Welwyn, Herts AL6 0HL.

**KENNEDY, Cecil,** flower and portrait painter in oils; *b* Leyton, Essex, 4 Feb., 1905. *m* Winifred Aves. one *s. Studied:* in London, Paris, Antwerp, Zürich. *Exhib:* R.A., R.S.A., R.H.A., Doncaster, Oldham, Bradford, Southport, etc., and many London galleries; also U.S.A. and S. African galleries. Awarded Silver Medal, Paris Salon (1956) and Gold Medal, Paris Salon (1970). *Work in collections:* H.M. Queen Mary, Merthyr Tydfil Art Gallery, Rochdale Art Gallery. *Publications:* Numerous. *Signs work:* see appendix. *Address:* Manor Garden House, 135 Fishpool St., St. Albans, Herts. AL3 4R7.

**KENNISH, Jenny,** R.M.S. (1985), S.W.A., F.S.B.A.; self taught sculptress in porcelain of wild flowers and animals; school teacher; *b* England, 11 Mar., 1944. one *s.* one *d. Educ:* Nonsuch County Grammar School for Girls; Whitelands Teacher Training College. *Studied:* Zoology, botany and art. *Exhib:* Westminster Galleries with the R.M.S., S.B.A., S.W.A. and local societies. *Signs work:* "J.K." *Address:* Kinghern, Silchester Rd., Little London, nr. Basingstoke, Hants. RG26 5EX.

**KENNY, Michael,** R.A., F.R.B.S. (1992), D.F.A.(Lond.); sculptor in plaster, metal, wood, and stone, also painted reliefs; Principal, City & Guilds School of Art (1995-); Director of Fine Art Studies, University of London Goldsmiths' College (1983-88); *b* Liverpool, 10 June, 1941. *m* Angela Smith (marriage dissolved); re-married Susan Rowland, 1993; one *s.* two *d.* (by previous marriage to Rosemary Flood). *Educ:* St. Francis Xavier's College, Liverpool. *Studied:* Liverpool College of Art (1959-61, Phillip Hartas, Arther Ballard), Slade School of Fine Art (1961-64, Reg Butler, Michael Kellaway, F.E. McWilliam).

*Exhib:* retrospective exhbn. (work between 1963-84) Wilhelm Lehmbruck Museum, Duisburg, W. Germany (1984-85); numerous one-man shows and mixed exhbns. in England, Europe, S. America, Australia and Japan. *Work in collections:* V. & A., B.M., Tate Gallery, A.C.G.B., British Council, Staatsgalerie Stuttgart, Lehmbruck Museum, Duisburg, W. Germany, London Borough of Camden, Leics. Educ. Com., Contemporary Art Soc., Hara Museum of Contemporary Art, Tokyo, Leeds City A.G., Walker A.G. Liverpool, etc. *Commissions:* work at Lumsden, Aberdeenshire; Addenbrookes Hospital, Cambridge; Le Parc de la Courneuve, Paris; Yokohama Business Park, Japan; Muraoka-Cho, Japan (1992); Limehouse Link Tunnel (Eastern Entrance) Docklands, London (1993); Prittlewell School, Essex (1993-94). *Publications:* illustrated, I Know the Place by Harold Pinter, Contemporary Artists (1977), Contemporary British Artists (1979, 1989), Monograph by Peter Davies (Scolar Press, London 1997), etc. *Signs work:* "Michael Kenny," bronze casts sometimes initialled "M.K." and date. *Address:* Studio: 71 Stepney Green, London E1 3LE.

**KENT, Colin,** R.I. (1971); self taught painter in water-colour, acrylic, mixed media; *b* 10 Feb., 1934. *m* Joan. *Educ:* Romford County Technical School; S.W. Essex Technical College and School of Art. *Exhib:* R.A., R.I., Mall Galleries, Shell House Gallery, Ledbury, Adam Gallery, Bath, Blackstone Gallery, Pinner, Manor House Gallery, Chipping Norton. *Work in collections:* in Britain, U.S.A., France, Germany, Finland. *Signs work:* "Colin Kent." *Address:* 64 Forest Rd., Romford, Essex RM7 8DT.

**KERN, Doreen,** sculptor in bronze; consultant to B.M. Replica Dept.; *b* 9 Aug., 1941; divorced. two *s. Educ:* Hampstead Garden Suburb Institute; studio assistant at the Morris Singer Art Bronze foundry. *Studied:* under Howard Bates, R.A. *Exhib:* Waterloo Fine Arts, Talma Gallery, Tel-Aviv, Ryder Gallery, L.A., Galerie Nichido, Tokyo, London University, Bath Festival, National Museum of Archaeology, Valletta, Malta, Design Centre, St. Paul's Cathedral, Edinburgh Festival (1995). *Work in collections:* Dr Kwame Nkrumah, Guyana, Emperor Haile Selassie (Palace of Addis Ababa), Anne Frank for Anne Frank house, Amsterdam, Clint Eastwood. *Signs work:* see appendix. *Address:* 38 Canons Drive, Edgware, Middx. HA8 7QT.

**KERR, Bernadette,** B.F.A. Hons. (1981), P.G.C.E. (1982), Slade School Higher Dip. Postgraduate (1984); painter in oil on canvas, lecturer; Winchester School of Art Fellow (in painting) (1987-88), Lecturer in Art, Goldsmiths' College, University of London; *b* Fontainebleau, France, 21 June, 1958. *Educ:* Loreto Grammar School, Nottingham. *Studied:* Mansfield School of Art (1977-78), Trent Polytechnic (1978-81, D. Curruthers), Institute of Education (1981-82), Slade School of Art (1982-84, Lawrence Gowing). *Exhib:* New Contemporaries I.C.A. (1981, 1983), British Drawing, Hayward Annual (1982), Spirit of London, Royal Festival Hall (1983, 1985), Camden Annual (1983-85), Stowells Trophy, R.A. (1984), London Group, R.C.A. (1984),

Contemporary Art Soc. Market (1984-87), Whitechapel Open (1985), two-man Vortex Gallery (1985), Leics. Schools Collection (1986), Monuments in Light, Swiss Cottage Exhbn. Hall (1987), R.A. Summer Show (1987), Pacesetters 7, Peterborough Museum and A.G. (1987). *Work in collections:* London Borough of Camden Arts and Entertainment Dept. *Signs work:* "Bernadette Kerr." *Address:* 31 Belsize Ave., London NW3.

**KERSHAW, Walter,** B.A. Hons. Fine Art (Dunelm); mural painter and freelance artist in oil, water-colour, mosaic; occasional visiting lecturer in Environmental Art at Universities in the U.K., Brazil and W. Germany; *b* Rochdale, 7 Dec., 1940. *Educ:* De la Salle College, Salford. *Studied:* Durham University (1958-62). *Exhib:* Large scale, public, external murals in Manchester, Trafford Park and N.W. Museum of Science and Industry; Norwich; Brazil, Sao Paulo and Recife. Internal murals for British Aerospace, Manchester United F.C., P. & O., Sarajevo, Salford University, the C.E.G.B., Hollingworth Lake Visitors Centre and Italian Consulate Manchester. Photos of murals at the Serpentine, Whitechapel and Tate galleries. *Work in collections:* V. & A., British Council, Arts Council, Gulbenkian Foundation, 'Cultura Inglesa', Museum of Art, São Paulo, and other public galleries in the U.K. Films: 'Terra Firma' BBC 2 (1976), 'First Graffiti Artist' (1977), 'Nationwide' (1982), '5 x 5' W. Germany (1984), 'Folio' Anglia TV (1987), Bosnia TV (1996), International Arts Festival. Recorded: 'Conversation Piece' with Sue MacGregor, Radio 4 (1983), 'Kaleidoscope' Radio 4 (1986). *Signs work:* "Walter Kershaw." *Address:* 193 Todmorden Rd., Littleborough, Rochdale OL15 9EG.

**KETCHER, Jean,** B.A.Hons. Fine Art Painting (1976); painter in oil, water-colour, etc.; art teacher, Copleston High School, Ipswich; *b* 6 July, 1955. *Studied:* Ipswich School of Art (1971-73), Maidstone College of Art (1973-76). *Exhib:* Halesworth Gallery, Ellingham Mill, Bungay, Corn Exchange, Ipswich. *Signs work:* "Jean Ketcher." *Address:* 46 Sandown Rd., Ipswich IP1 6RE.

**KEY, Geoffrey,** D.A. (1960); painter in oil, sculptor; *b* Manchester, 13 May, 1941. *Educ:* High School of Art, Manchester. *Studied:* Regional College of Art, Manchester (1958-61), under Harry Rutherford, William Bailey. *Exhib:* Salford A.G., Clermont Ferrand France, London, Nancy France, Germany, Madison Ave., N.Y., Lausanne Switzerland, Dublin, Saint Ouen France, Hong Kong, Moret-sur-Loing France, Barbizon France. *Work in collections:* Salford A.G., Manchester City Gallery, Bolton A.G., Granada Television, Wigan Corp., Manchester University, North West Arts, Jockey Club of Hong Kong, Perrier, Society Roquefort, Mandarin Hotel, Hong Kong, Chateau de St. Ouen, Chateaux Relais. *Publications:* G.Key: Drawings (Margin Press), Dictionary of British Art (Collectors Club Press), European Painters (Clio Press). *Clubs:* Manchester Academy, Portico Manchester. *Signs work:* see appendix. *Address:* 59 Acresfield Rd., Pendleton, Salford M6 7GE.

**KHALIL: see NORLAND (NEUSCHUL), Khalil.**

# WHO'S WHO IN ART

**KHAN, Keith Ali,** B.A.(Hons.); sculptor in large scale exterior/interior constructions, using fabric and many people; Director, Carnival Designer; *b* Trinidad, 4 Dec., 1963. *Educ:* King's College, Wimbledon. *Studied:* Wimbledon School of Art, Middlesex Polytechnic (Dante Leonelli), The Street, Port of Spain, Trinidad. *Exhib:* Houston International Festival, Harris Museum, Preston, Arnolfini, Bristol; one-man shows: Bluecoat Gallery, Liverpool, Greenwich Citizen Gallery; on the streets of Notting Hill, as well as numerous designs on TV and stage. *Signs work:* "Khan." *Address:* 79 Grand Drive, Raynes Pk., London SW20 9DW.

**KHANNA, Balraj,** M.A. (1962); awarded Winnifred Holtby prize by R.S.L. (1984); painter in acrylic and oil, novelist; *b* 4 Oct., 1940. *m* Francine Martine. two *d. Educ:* Punjab University, Chandigarh. *Exhib:* forty-five one-man shows including Ashmolean Museum, Oxford (1968), City A.G., Bristol (1969), Galerie Transposition, Paris (1966, 1968, 1974, 1975), Herbert Benevy Gallery, N.Y. (1971, 1972), Serpentine Gallery (1979), Richard Demarco (1986), Royal Festival Hall (1990), Arnolfini (1991). M.O.M.A. Wales (1993), Berlin and Frankfurt (1994), De La Warr Pavilion (1996). *Work in collections:* Arts Council; Musee d'Art Moderne, Paris; Ville de Paris; Ashmolean Museum; National Gallery of Modern Art, New Delhi; City A.G., Bristol; City A.G., Bradford; V. & A.; Calouste Gulbenkian Foundation, Lisbon. *Publications:* Nation of Fools (Michael Joseph and Penguin), Sweet Chillies (Constable), Kalighat, Popular Indian Painting, 1800-1930 (Redstone Press), Krishna - The Divine Lover (South Bank Centre Publication).*Signs work:* "Khanna." *Address:* 3a Pindock Mews, London W9 2PY.

**KIDNER, Michael,** B.A. (Cantab); paintings and constructions; *b* Kettering, 1917. *m* Marion Frederick. *Educ:* Bedales School. *Studied:* self-taught. *Exhib:* widely. *Work in collections:* Tate Gallery, Arts Council of G.B., British Council, W.A.G., Huddersfield A.G., Manchester City A.G., Contemporary Art Soc., London, Sussex University, University of Wales, Gulbenkian Foundation, V. &. A., Museum Sztuki, Lodz, and Poznan Museum, Poland, Museum of Modern Art, N.Y., Southampton City A.G., Anios Anderson Museum, Helsinki, Norrkopings Konstmuseum, Malmo Konsthall. *Publications:* Elastic Membrane. *Signs work:* "Michael Kidner." *Address:* 18 Hampstead Hill Gdns., London NW3 2PL.

**KIFF, Ken,** artist in painting and printmaking; *b* 29 May, 1935; married .one *s.* one *d. Studied:* Hornsey School of Art (1955-61). *Exhib:* many one-man and mixed exhbns. *Work in collections:* Tate Gallery and other museums. *Clubs:* Chelsea Arts. *Signs work:* unobtrusively. *Address:* c/o Marlborough Fine Art, Albemarle St., London W1X 4BY

**KINAHAN, Lady Coralie,** U.S.W.A., U.W.A., R.U.A. (resigned); artist in oil and water-colour; Lady Mayoress of Belfast (1959-62); President, Co. Antrim Red Cross (1955-67); *b* Surrey, 1924. *m* Sir Robin Kinahan. two *s.* three *d. Educ:* by 14 governesses and 4 schools. *Studied:* John Hassall, and Chelsea

326

Schools of Art (1943-46); private portrait classes under Sonia Mervyn, A.R.A. (1946-49). *Exhib:* R.A., R.P., R.O.I., S.WL.A., R.S.A., R.U.A.; solo exhbns. annually, Belfast, Dublin, Wexford, Galway, Bristol and London (1964-85). Opened own gallery (1985) Templepatrick, exhibiting landscapes, wildlife, horses and portraits. *Commissions:* include Lord Bishop of Durham, Rt. Hon. Humphrey and Mrs. Atkins, Rt. Hon. James Prior, General Sir Ian Freeland, Capt. Torrens-Spence, D.S.O., R.N. (H.M. Lord Lt. for Armagh), Lord Cooke of Islandreagh, Gen. Sir John and Lady Waters and many children's portraits; Army commissions for The Black Watch Regt., The Grenadier Guards, Imperial War Museum, The Royal Highland Regt., The 2nd Parachute Regt., The 9/12th Royal Lancers and the Ulster Defence Regt.; Sporting pictures for Mr. Victor McCalmont and The Master Beagler, Terence Grainger. *Publications:* historical novels: You can't shoot the English (1982), After the war, came Peace? (1987), Memoirs: Behind every great man - ? (1998); work repro.: limited edns. 200 prints of Belfast Harbour; and Patrol looking over Belfast. Husband made H.M.'s Lord Lieut. for Belfast (1985). *Signs work:* "C. de B.K." oils; "Coralie Kinahan" water-colours. *Address:* Castle Upton, Templepatrick, Co. Antrim, N. Ireland BT39 0BE.

**KINDER, Joan,** S.G.F.A. (1965), F.F.P.S. (1960); painter and printmaker in ink and water-colour of mono prints in abstract expressionism; *b* Yorkshire, 19 June, 1916. *m* K.J. Kinder. two *d. Educ:* Bridlington High. *Studied:* Scarborough School of Art (1932-36, Edward and Ethel Walker) specialising in textile. *Exhib:* S.G.F.A., Mall Galleries, C.W.A.C., and solo shows. *Work in collections:* U.K. and U.S.A. *Signs work:* "(Joan) Kinder." *Address:* 8 Upper Woodcote Village, Purley, Surrey CR8 3HE.

**KING, Andrew Norman,** B.F.A. (Hons.) (1978), N.S. (1984), R.O.I. (1992); David Murray Scholarship, R.A. Schools (1978); landscape and marine artist in oil and water-colour, interested in light and atmosphere in landscape; *b* Bedford, 1956. *Educ:* Barnfield College, Luton. *Studied:* Hornsey College of Art. *Exhib:* Britain in Water-colour, R.I., N.E.A.C., N.S., R.S.M.A., R.O.I., R.W.S., R.P., Laing; one-man shows, Luton, Hitchin, Linslade, Stowe, London and Aldeburgh. *Work in collections:* Luton Art Council, Beds. C.C., Eagle Star Offices, and in private and royal collections in Britain and abroad. Finalist, Winsor and Newton Young Artists award (1985). *Signs work:* "Andrew King." *Address:* Pond Cottage, Long Rd., Colby, Norwich NR11 7EF.

**KING, Christabel Frances,** B.Sc.Hons.(Lond.) (1971), F.S.B.A.; R.H.S. Grenfell Silver Gilt medal (1974), Linnean Soc. Jill Smythies award for Botanical Illustration (1989); botanical artist in water-colour; part-time lecturer, Capel Manor Horticultural and Environmental Centre, Enfield; *b* London, 1950. *Educ:* Sherborne School for Girls. *Studied:* scientific illustration: Middlesex Polytechnic (1973-74). *Exhib:* Messrs. Agnew (1980), Kew Gdns. Gallery (1993). *Work in collections:* R.B.G. Kew. *Publications:* contributed illustrations to Curtis's Botanical Magazine since 1975; illustrations in:

Flowering Plants of the World, ed. V.H. Heywood (Elsevier 1978), All Good Things Around Us by Pamela Michael (Ernest Benn 1980), World Book Encyclopaedia (Childcraft International, U.S.A.), Kew Magazine Monographs: The Genus Pleione, The Genus Echinocereus, The Genus Lewisia; Africa's Mountains of the Moon by Guy Yeoman (Savitri Books 1989). *Clubs:* S.B.A. (Founder mem. 1985). *Signs work:* "C.F.K." or "C.F. King." *Address:* 149 Fulwell Park Ave., Twickenham, Middx. TW2 5HG.

**KING, John Gregory,** S.E.A.; artist in oil, water-colour, bronze; *b* West Tytherley, 16 Apr., 1929. *m* Mary Rose. one *s.* one *d. Educ:* Canford School. *Studied:* briefly at Salisbury Art College. *Exhib:* nine one-man shows in London. *Work in collections:* Gordon Highlanders Museum, Perth, Royal Fusilier Museum, Tower of London. *Publications:* illustrated: They Meet at 11, They Still Meet at 11, The Golden Thread, The Fox and the Orchid, Gallant Horses and Horsemen. *Clubs:* The Arts, The Farmers. *Signs work:* "John King." *Address:* Church Farm House, West Tytherley, Salisbury, Wilts. SP5 1LB.

**KING, Mary,** A.T.C. (1947), S.W.A. (1979), N.S. (1984), F.R.S.A. (1988); artist in mixed media, water-colour and collage; lecturer, North East Surrey College of Technology (1968-80) and Surbiton Adult Education Centre; *b* London, 17 Oct., 1926. *m* Ralph King. one *s.* three *d. Educ:* Wallington Grammar School. *Studied:* Chelsea College of Art (1946, painting, Ceri Richards; 1948-49, stained glass, Francis Spear), Central School of Arts and Crafts, London, Whitelands College, Putney. *Exhib:* Fairfield Halls, Croydon, Bourne Hall, Ewell, F.B.A., S.W.A., R.B.A., Mall Galleries, Westminster Gallery (1988-97 annually), R.A. Summer Exhbn. (1981, 1982), Bankside Gallery, London (1985, 1986, 1996), National Soc., Whiteleys Atrium (1995-97), Munich (1997); solo shows, Farnham Maltings (1983, 1985, 1987, 1990), Epsom Playhouse, Ashley Gallery, Epsom, Conway Hall, London (1984), Loggia Gallery (1983, 1984, 1986), many London exhbns. including Heifer Gallery, Islington (1990-96), Hyde Park Gallery, Fine Arts, Bond St. (1991), Bonhams Knightsbridge, Smiths Galleries, Covent Gdn. (1990-93), Windsor (1997). *Signs work:* "Mary King" or "M. King." *Address:* 42 Reigate Rd., Ewell, Epsom, Surrey KT17 1PX.

**KING, Phillip,** C.B.E. (1974), R.A.; sculptor in steel, bronze, fibreglass; Prof. of Sculpture, Royal Academy of Art, Prof. Emeritus, Royal College of Art; *b* Tunis, 1934; married; one *s..* one *s.* (decd) *Educ:* Mill Hill School; Christ College, Cambridge. *Studied:* St. Martin's School of Art. *Exhib:* Rowan Gallery London, Richard Fergen Gallery N.Y., Venice Biennale, Whitechapel Gallery London, Kunsthalle Mannheim. *Work in collections:* Tate Gallery, M.O.M.A. (N.Y.), National Gallery of Australia, Kroller Muller Museum, New Museum of Contemporary Art Hiroshima, Yorkshire Sculpture Pk., Kunsthalle Mannheim, etc. *Publications:* The Sculpture of Phillip King by Tim Hilton. *Signs work:* see appendix. *Address:* c/o New Rowan Gallery, 25 Dover St.,

London W1X 3PA.

**KING, Robert,** R.I. (1970); Mem. Leicester Soc. of Artists (1960); painter in oil, water-colour; etcher and lithographer; *b* Leicester, 28 June, 1936. *m* Christine James. *Educ:* Fosse Boys' School, Leicester. *Studied:* Leicester College of Art (1956-58). *Exhib:* one-man shows, six at Gadsby Gallery, Leicester (1970-80) and Medici Gallery (1980-89); three with Burlington Paintings (1989-97); annually with R.I., R.A., R.S.M.A., Leicester Soc. of Artists. *Work in collections:* Nottingham Educ. Com., Leicester Royal Infirmary, Leicester University, Fishmongers Hall London, Royal Yacht Squadron, Cowes, I.O.W. *Publications:* illustrated Denys Brook-Hart's 20th Century British Marine Painting. *Signs work:* "ROBERT KING." *Address:* 2 Coastguard Cottages, Lepe, nr. Exbury, Hants. SO45 1AD.

**KINGS, Tarka Huxley,** M.A.; painter/printer in oil, silkscreen; *b* London, 24 May, 1961. *Educ:* St. Paul's Girls School. *Studied:* City and Guilds, R.A. Schools (1982-87, Peter Greenham, Norman Adams). *Exhib:* Creative Salvage (1985), R.A., Gallery 24, Phoenix Gallery, Langton Gallery, St. Paul's, Cadogan Contemporary (1988), Bill Thomson Gallery, Rebecca Hossack Gallery (1991, 1993, 1994, 1995). Asst. to Leonard Rosoman, Lambeth Palace Chapel ceiling. *Work in collections:* private collections in U.S.A. and England. Artwork for films: 'Secrets' (Dir. Phillip Savile), 'The Dream' (Dir. Con Mulgrave). *Clubs:* Congress. *Signs work:* "THK." *Address:* 35 Beethoven St., London W10.

**KINGSTON, Angela Hoppe,** painter; Chairman, Water-colour Soc. of Wales; Lectures and Workshops; *b* Mumbles, nr. Swansea, 1936. *m* Dr. Gordon (Ph.D.). three *s.* two *d. Educ:* Llwyn y Bryn High School, Swansea. *Studied:* Bath Academy of Art, Corsham, Wilts. (1955-58, Adrian Heath, Martin Froy, William Scott). *Exhib:* solo shows: Mistral Gallery, London (1992), St. David's Hall, Cardiff (1991), etc.; group shows: W.A.C. Touring (1993-95), St. Donats Arts Centre, Wales (1992), A.A.D.W. Cardiff Arts Festival (1988-89), S.B.A., W.S.W., Welsh Group. *Work in collections:* Glynn Vivian A.G., Swansea. *Clubs:* W.S.W. (Chair), S.B.A. (founder mem.), The Welsh Group. *Signs work:* "A. Hoppe Kingston" or "A.H.K." *Address:* Monks, Dimlands Rd., Llantwit Major, Vale of Glam. CF61 1SJ, Wales.

**KINMONT, David Bruce,** b Kent, 1932. *Educ;* St. John's College, Cambridge. Was Senior member of the University of Bristol where, in 1971, he delivered the George Hare Leonard Memorial Lecture. Visiting professorships: George Washington University, Washington D.C. (1974); universities in Beijing, Shanghai (1986), and Hebei (1989), in China; and at the University of Leningrad in 1990. Recent lectures include New Jersey, and Gulbenkian Museum, Lisbon (1996); *Exhib:* one-man shows include, Ferens City A.G., Hull (1963); City A.G., Bangor (1960); St. John's College, Cambridge (1969); Churchill College, Cambridge (1976); University of Durham (1981); University of Exeter (1986); Georges, Bristol (1987). *Address:* The Lent

House, Clevedon Rd., Flax Bourton, Bristol BS19 1NQ.

**KIRBY, Michael,** M.F.P.S.; fine art restorer, artist in oil; *b* Farnham Common, Bucks., 30 Dec., 1949; married. two *s.* two *d. Studied:* High Wycombe School of Art (1967-71) under G. G. Palmer, Romeo Di Gerolamo R.B.A., Eric Smith, R.B.A., R.W.S., Henry Trivick, R.B.A. *Exhib:* R.B.A. Open Salon, F.P.S., H.U.A.S. *Signs work:* "M. Kirby." *Address:* 30 Sycamore Rise, Bracknell, Berks. RG12 3BU.

**KIRK, Barry,** N.D.D. (1954), A.R.C.A. (1959), F.R.S.A. (1989); Travelling scholarship R.C.A. (1959); painter, draughtsman; Canterbury College of Art 1959-1988 (Vice-Principal 1974-87, Principal 1987-88); thereafter full-time art practice; *b* Deal, Kent, 17 Feb., 1933. *m* Pleasance Kirk, A.R.C.A., M.S.D.C. two *s. Educ:* Westminster School. *Studied:* Canterbury College of Art (1950-54), R.C.A. (1956-59). *Exhib:* R.A., Francis Kyle Gallery; one-man shows Alwin Gallery, etc. *Work in collections:* V. & A., Kent C.C., Canterbury C.C., Glasgow C.C. *Signs work:* "Barry Kirk." *Address:* 13 High St., Bridge Canterbury, Kent CT4 5JY.

**KIRK, Douglas William,** painter in oil and water-colour; lecturer, City of London Polytechnic (1976-89); *b* Edinburgh, 22 Feb., 1949. *m* Jacqueline Adams. one *s. Educ:* George Heriot's School, Edinburgh. *Studied:* Duncan of Jordanstone College of Art, Dundee (1967-71), Royal College of Art, London (1971-74). *Exhib:* S.S.A., Compass Gallery, Glasgow, Fine Art Soc., 57 Gallery, Edinburgh, Fruit Market Gallery, Edinburgh. *Work in collections.* Carlisle Museum and Gallery. *Signs work:* "douglas kirk." *Address:* 146 Darnley Rd., Gravesend, Kent DA11 0SN.

**KIRK, Robert Joseph,** B.A. (1973), M.Sc. (1978), N.A.P.A. (1988); painter in acrylic and pastel; Executive Council mem., N.A.P.A.; *b* Walsall, 7 Jan. 1932. *m* Sheila M. two *d. Studied:* Walsall and Stafford Schools of Art (1955 Angus Macauley, David Bethel). *Exhib:* N.A.P.A. Annual since 1989. *Clubs.* N.A.P.A., Ludlow Art Soc. *Signs work:* "Robert Kirk." *Address:* West Fortune Ashford Carbonell, Ludlow, Salop. SY8 4DB.

**KIRKWOOD, John Sutherland,** artist, mixed media, photography and etching; *b* Edinburgh, 6 Apr., 1947. *Educ:* George Watson College, Edinburgh *Studied:* Dundee College of Art. *Exhib:* one-man shows: 57 Art Gallery Edinburgh Printmakers Workshop, A.I.R. Gallery, Talbot Rice Art Centre Demarco Gallery, "Scottish Art Now". *Work in collections:* S.A.C. Loan Hunterian Museum, University of Glasgow, Scottish Museum of Modern Art Imperial War Museum. *Signs work:* "J. S. Kirkwood." *Address:* 15 Leopold Pl. Edinburgh.

**KITSON, Linda Frances,** B.A. (1967), M.A., R.C.A. (1970); official war artist, Falkland Islands Task Force (1982); artist/tutor; Pres. Army Arts and Crafts Soc. (1983); *b* London, 17 Feb., 1945. *m* Hon. Barnaby Howard (1996) *Educ:* Tortington Pk., nr. Arundel, Sussex. *Studied:* St. Martin's School of Art (1965-67), R.C.A. (1967-70). *Exhib:* Workshop Gallery, Illustrators A.G.

Imperial War Museum (Falkland's War Exhbn. U.K. tour), National Theatre, R.A. *Work in collections:* Imperial War Museum. *Publications:* Picnic (Jill Norman); The Falklands War, a Visual Diary (Mitchell Beazley); The Plague; Sun, Wind, Sand and Stars (Folio Soc.). *Clubs:* Chelsea Arts. *Signs work:* "Linda Kitson." *Address:* Flat 3, 25 Onslow Sq., London SW7 3NJ.

**KITSON, Prof. Michael,** M.A.; art historian; on staff of Courtauld Inst. (1955-85), becoming Dep. Director (1980-85); Director of Studies, Paul Mellon Centre for Studies in British Art (1986-92); *b* 30 Jan., 1926. *Educ:* Gresham's School; King's College, Cambridge. *Studied:* history of art: Courtauld Inst. of Art (1950-52, Anthony Blunt, Johannes Wilde). *Exhib:* organized: 'The Art of Claude Lorrain' (Newcastle and London, Hayward Gallery, 1969); 'La Peinture Romantique Anglaise' (Paris, Petit Palais, 1972); 'Salvator Rosa' (London, Hayward Gallery, 1973); 'Zwei Hunderte Englische Malerie' (Munich, Haus der Kunst, 1979). *Publications:* Turner (1964), The Age of Baroque (1965), Caravaggio (1969), Rembrandt (1969, revised 1992), Claude Lorrain, Liber Veritatis (1978). *Address:* 72 Halton Rd., London N1 2AD.

**KITTS, Barry Edward Lyndon,** N.D.D. (1964), F.R.S.A. (1972); landscape painter and writer on art; visiting lecturer at Central St. Martin's College of Art and Design; *b* Bath, 18 Oct., 1943. *Educ:* Sutton East County Secondary School (Surrey Special Art Course under George Mackley, M.B.E., R.E.). *Studied:* Kingston School of Art (1959-61) under J. D. Binns, A.R.C.A., D.A. Pavey, A.R.C.A., Wimbledon School of Art (1961-64) under Gerald Cooper, A.R.C.A. *Exhib:* N.E.A.C., R.B.A., Wessex Artists' Exhbn. *Publications:* Coauthor of a Graphic Design Sourcebook (1987). *Signs work:* "Barry Kitts." *Address:* 500 Kingston Rd., London SW20 8DT.

**KLEIN, Anita,** B.A.Hons. (1983), M.A. (1985), R.E. (1991); painter/printmaker in drypoint, woodcut, oil on board; *b* Sydney, Australia, 14 Feb., 1960. *m* Nigel Swift. two *d*. *Educ:* Hampstead School. *Studied:* Chelsea School of Art (1978-79), Slade School of Fine Art (1979-83, Mick Moon, Paula Rego; 1983-85, Barto dos Santos). *Exhib:* I.C.A., Hayward, R.I., Blond Fine Art; one-man shows: London: Creaser Gallery, Leigh Gallery, Tall House Gallery, Wilson Hale; Print Works, Colchester, Cambridge Contemporary Art, Beaux Arts, Bath, C.C.A. Oxford. *Work in collections:* A.C.G.B., R.E., Ashmolean Museum. *Clubs:* Greenwich Printmakers, Royal Soc. of Painter Printmakers. *Signs work:* see appendix. *Address:* 82 Tressillian Rd., London SE4 1YD.

**KNAPP-FISHER, John,** R.C.A. (1992); painter; *b* London, 2 Aug., 1931. *m* Sheila Basset (divorced). one *s*. one *d*. *Educ:* Eastbourne College. *Studied:* Maidstone College of Art (1951-53), Designer in Theatre. *Exhib:* R.A., Business Art Galleries, Oriel, Welsh Arts Council, Upper Grosvenor, Agnews, Fry, Marjorie Parr, Johannesburg, Toronto, N.Y., Pembrokeshire Museums Touring (1984), Beaux Arts, Bath (1986), Henry Thomas Gallery, Faculty of Art and Design, Carmarthan (1989), National Museum of Wales, Lichfield Festival (1995), Attic, Swansea, Martin Tinney, Albany, Cardiff. *Work in col-*

*lections:* B.B.C. Cardiff, National Library of Wales, Beecroft A.G., W. Wales Assoc. for the Arts, Swansea University, Haverfordwest Museum, prize winning panel, Withybush Hospital Haverfordwest. *Publications:* illustrated Pembrokeshire Churches (1989); included in: Cymru'r Cynfas by Hywel Harries (Lolfa Press, 1983); wrote and illustrated John Knapp-Fisher's Pembrokeshire (Senecio Press, 1995), 'Welsh Painters Talking' by Tony Curtis (Seren Books, 1997). Films: Anglia T.V. The Artist and his Work (1963), H.T.V. (Merlin T.V.) 'A Word In Your Eye' (1997). *Signs work:* "John Knapp-Fisher." *Address:* Trevigan Cottage, Croesgoch, Haverfordwest, Pembrokeshire SA62 5JP.

**KNEALE, Bryan,** R.A. Rome Scholar; sculptor in steel and all metals, wood, etc.; Mem. C.N.A.A. Fine Arts Panel, Royal College of Art, Professor of Sculpture, Royal Academy (1980-83), Head of Sculpture R.C.A. (1985-90), Professor of Drawing (1990), Chairman A.S.G.; *b* Douglas, I.O.M., 19 June, 1930. *m* Doreen Kneale. one *s.* one *d. Educ:* Douglas High School. *Studied:* Douglas School of Art (1947) under W. H. Whitehead; R.A. Schools (1948-52) under Philip Connard, Henry Rushbury. *Exhib:* John Moores, Art d'aujourd'hui, Paris, Battersea Park, Whitechapel Retrospective, Cardiff, Leics. Educ. Com., Whitechapel, City of London, Peter Stuyvesant, Southampton, British Sculptors, R.A. Holland Park, Royal Exchange Sculpt., Hayward Gallery, R.A., London Group, Redfern Gallery, New Art Centre. *Work in collections:* Tate, Arts Council, C.A.S., W.A.G., Fitzwilliam Museum, B.M., City Art Galleries of Manchester, Birmingham, Sheffield, Bradford, Wakefield, Leicester, York and Middlesbrough, Sao Paulo, Brazil, Museum of Modern Art, N.Y., National Galleries of N.Z., Queensland and S. Australia, Manx Museum and A.G., Abbot Hall Gallery, Cumberland, Beaverbrook Foundation, Frederickton, Bochum Museum, W. Germany, Bahia Museum, Brazil. *Clubs:* Chelsea Arts. *Signs work:* "BRYAN KNEALE" (die stamp), "Bryan Kneale" (drawings, etc.). *Address:* 10a Muswell Rd., London N10 2BG.

**KNIGHT, Clifford (Edgar Levi),** U.A. (1955); painter in oil, water-colour and mixed media, lecturer; *b* Kempston, Beds., 8 Mar., 1930. *m* Sherri. one *s.* one *d. Educ:* Kempston Secondary Modern School. *Studied:* under William Twybel, A.R.C.A. (1948-54), L.C.C. Central School (1955-57, William Roberts, Merlyn Evans, Paul Hogarth, S.R. Badmin). *Exhib:* U.A., N.E.A.C. one-man shows, Upper St. Gallery (1973), Carlton House Terr. (1983), Bedford, Luton, Letchworth, Northampton, Retford, Wellingborough, Welwyn Garden City, Abbotsholme School, Bedford School. *Work in collections:* Northampton, Luton and Letchworth A.Gs, Crown Commissioners, Texas Instruments, Beds. C.C.; private collections: U.S.A. *Commissions:* N.G.A., Bedford Rowing Club, Bedford, U.S.A., Paris, London. *Publications:* work repro.: Leisure Painter. *Signs work:* "Clifford Knight." *Address:* Brushwood, 29 Milton St., Higham Ferrers, Northants. NN10 8BG.

**KNIGHT, Geoffrey Snowden,** F.R.I.B.A.; ret. architect; landscape and marine artist in water-colour of landscape and traditional sailing craft; has worked in Africa and Caribbean; *b* Parkstone, Dorset, 1920. *Educ:* Canford School. *Studied:* painting: Poole Art School. *Exhib:* London, Sydney Australia, Chichester. *Address:* 3 The Orchard, Aldwick Bay, Bognor Regis, W. Sussex PO21 4HX.

**KNIGHT, Sophie,** R.W.S. (1992), A.R.W.S. (1990), B.A.(Hons.) Fine Art (1986), Post Grad. Dip. (1989); Ian Tragarthen Jenkins award (1986), Fred Ellwin award (1987), David Murray Scholarship (1988), Erik Kennington award (1989), Hunting Group Student prize (1989), R.W.S. award (1989); painter in water-colour and oil; *b* London, 20 Mar., 1965. *Educ:* The New School, Kings Langley. *Studied:* Herts. School of Art, St.Albans (1982), Camberwell School of Art and Design (1983-86), R.A. Schools (1986-89). *Exhib:* numerous exhbns. including R.A. Summer Exhbn. (1988), Royal Festival Hall (1988), Mall Galleries (1989), Boundary Gallery (1989), Whitechapel Open (1994); one-man shows include Cadogan Contemporary (1991), Waterman Fine Arts (1993), Reutlingnen Gallery, Germany (1996). *Work in collections:* B.M. *Signs work:* "Sophie Knight." *Address:* Flat 5, 28 West Nicolson St., Edinburgh EH8 9DD.

**KNOWLER, Ann Patricia,** S.W.A. (1993); artist in oil and soft pastels; *b* Pinner, 3 June, 1940. *m* Jonathan Knowler. one *s.* one *d. Educ:* Northwood Secondary Modern School. *Studied:* F.E. classes and privately under Claude Murrills. *Exhib:* S.W.A. Westminster Gallery, David Curzon Gallery. *Clubs:* Weald of Sussex Art, The Adventurers Art, Assoc. of Sussex Artists, Guild of Sussex Artists. *Signs work:* "Ann Knowler." *Address:* Sundown, 7 Western Rd., Newick, E. Sussex BN8 4LE.

**KNOWLER, Brian,** R.I.; artist in acrylic and water-colour; Director, Alresford Gallery; *b* London, 10 Aug., 1937. *Exhib:* R.A., R.I., R.W.A., N.E.A.C., R.B.A., R.P. Various public and private collections. *Clubs:* Winchester Art. *Signs work:* "Knowler." *Address:* Alresford Gallery, Alresford, Hants.

**KNOWLES, Arthur Morris,** Dip.P.W. (1952), R.C.A., A.R.S.A.; landscape painter/poster artist in pencil, pastel, oil, design crafts; *b* Wolverhampton, 1923; married. two *s. Educ:* Graiseley (Sen. Boys) School. *Studied:* Wolverhampton School of Art and Crafts (1937-39, A. Willetts), Holborn 1948-52, E. Oldham), E.M.I. Inst., Chiswick (1952-54, J.M. Higginson). *Exhib:* Wolverhampton, Dudley, Bridgnorth, Norwich, Tettenhall and Wolverhampton stores, Moxley-Darlaston. *Commissions:* Local posters and sign boards - church posters, small paintings. *Clubs:* (Professional Associate), Society of Amateur Artists (Nottingham). *Signs work:* "Knowles" or "M.K." joined. *Address:* 48 Bromford Rise, Oaklands Rd., Penn, Wolverhampton WV3 9ES.

**KNOX, Jack,** R.S.A. (1979), R.G.I. (1981), R.S.W. (1987), Hon. R.I.A.S. 1997); painter in oil, acrylic, pastel; Head of Painting, Glasgow School of Art

(1981-92); *b* Kirkintilloch, 1936. *m* Margaret. one *s*. one *d*. *Educ:* Lenzie Academy. *Studied:* Glasgow School of Art (1952-58, William and Mary Armour). *Exhib:* one-man shows: Scottish Gallery (1966, 1989), Demarco Gallery, Edinburgh (1969), Serpentine, London (1971), Glasgow School of Art (1982), Retrospective (1983), Glasgow A.Gs. (1990), Open Eye Gallery Edinburgh (1991), Festival Exhbn., Open Eye Gallery, Edinburgh (1993). *Work in collections:* Scottish National Gallery of Modern Art, Manchester City A.G. Scottish National Portrait Gallery, Glasgow A.Gs., Arts Council. *Publications* The Scottish Bestiary by George Mackay Brown (Charles Booth Olibborn/Paragon Press, 1986), Lapotiniere and Friends by David and Hilary Brown (Century Editions/Random Century Group Ltd., 1990). *Signs work* "Jack Knox." *Address:* 31 North Erskine Pk., Bearsden, Glasgow G61 4LY.

**KOLAKOWSKI, Matthew Edmund Czeslaw,** B.A. (1978), M.A. (1979) artist/painter in oil; Foundation tutor, Woolwich College, and Central St Martin's; visiting lecturer, Wolverhampton University; *b* Ruislip, Middx., 12 Mar., 1956. *m* Philomena Marmion. one *s*. *Educ:* Douay Martyrs School Ickenham. *Studied:* Watford School of Art (Michael Werner, Peter Schmidt Charles Harrison), Ravensbourne College of Art (Brian Fielding, Victor Kwell Kit Twyford), Chelsea School of Art (Anthony Wishaw, Ian Stevenson). *Exhib* London Group since 1989; one-man show: Duncan Campbell Gallery (1993 1995), Mid Pennine Art Centre (1997). *Clubs:* London Group (Vice-Pres. since 1996). *Signs work:* "M" in circle or triangle, and see appendix. *Address* Brightside Studios, 9 Dartford St., London SE17 3UQ.

**KONDRACKI, Henry Andrew,** artist in oil on canvas; *b* Edinburgh, 12 Feb., 1953. *m* Sara. three *s*. *Educ:* Bellevue School, Edinburgh. *Studied:* Slade School of Fine Art (Ron Bowen, Jeffrey Camp, Jock McFadyen, Patrick George). *Exhib:* Vanessa Deveureux Gallery (1987, 1989), William Jackson Gallery (1991). Flowers East (1995). *Work in collections:* British Council A.C.G.B., University College London, Manchester A.G., City Art Centre Edinburgh, Glasgow Museums. *Publications:* Contemporary Scottish Painting by Bill Hare. *Signs work:* "H. Kondracki." *Address:* 20 Marchmont Cres. Edinburgh EH9 1HL.

**KOPEL, Harold,** R.O.I. (Hon. Treasurer, 1984-94); painter in oil, acrylic and pastel; art master, lecturer, Further Education I.L.E.A.; *b* Newcastle upon Tyne. *Educ:* Rutherford Grammar School, Newcastle; University College London. *Studied:* Central School of Arts, London. *Exhib:* several one-man shows, numerous mixed shows including R.A., R.B.A., N.E.A.C., R.W.A. Paris Salon (Silver medal), Barcelona biennial, R.G.I., Contemporary Art International, Olympia (1989), many private galleries; Cornelissen prize. *Work in collections:* University College, London, Nuffield Foundation, I.L.E.A *Signs work:* "Kopel." *Address:* 13 Hampstead Gdns., London NW11 7EU.

**KORALEK, Paul George,** C.B.E., R.A.; architect; Director, Ahrends Burton and Koralek; *b* 7 Apr., 1933. *m* Jennifer Chadwick. one *s*. two *d*. *Educ.*

Aldenham. *Studied:* architecture: Architectural Assoc. *Exhib:* Heinz Gallery, R.I.B.A. (1982), R.A. Summer Show (annually since 1987). *Publications:* Monograph "Ahrends Burton and Koralek". *Address:* Unit 1, 7 Chalcot Rd., London NW1 8LH.

**KORDA, Vincent Henry,** artist in oil and pastel; *b* London, 4 May, 1957. *Studied:* City and Guilds, London; R.A. Schools. *Exhib:* one-man shows: Cylinder Gallery (1984-85), Quinton Green Fine Art (1986). *Signs work:* "KORDA." *Address:* 9 Pembroke Studios, Pembroke Gdns., London W8 6HX.

**KOSTER, David,** D.F.A. (Lond.), N.D.D., A.T.D., S.WL.A.; printmaker and painter; *b* London, 5 Nov., 1926. *m* Katherine Macrae. one *d. Educ:* Clayesmore. *Studied:* Slade School. *Work in collections:* Aberdeen City A.G., Royal Ulster Museum, Belfast, Berliner Graphothek, U.C.L., Dept. of Environment, All Soul's College, Oxford, Hokin Gallery, U.S.A., Hamilton Public Library, Canada, University New South Wales, S. London Gallery, Towner A.G., Eastbourne, numerous County Council and Educ. Com. Collections, Ministry of Agriculture, S.W.A.N. *Publications:* Wood engraved illustrations 'Down to Earth', drawings 'Fellow Mortals'. *Signs work:* "David Koster." *Address:* 5 East Cliff Gdns., Folkestone, Kent CT19 6AR.

**KOWALSKY, Elaine Gloria,** Dip. of Art, M.A.; artist in relief, litho, ceramics; Henry Moore Fellow in Printmaking, Leeds Polytechnic; *b* Winnipeg, Manitoba, 24 Sept., 1948. *m* Elton Bash, painter. *Educ:* Charleswood Collegiate, Winnipeg. *Studied:* University of Manitoba, St. Martin's School of Art, Brighton Polytechnic. *Exhib:* R.A., and numerous one-man shows. *Work in collections:* V. & A., Birmingham A.G., Worcester A.G., Leeds A.G., Manchester A.G., Canada Council Art Bank, University of Manitoba, National Gallery of Australia, Smithsonian Inst. *Commissions:* banners, Dover Castle. *Publications:* Wood engraving and the Woodcut in Britain c.1890-1990, J. Hamilton (Barrie & Jenkins Ltd. 1994). *Signs work:* "Elaine Kowalsky." *Address:* 27 Aberavon Rd., London E3 5AR.

**KOZARZEWSKA, Magda,** L.C.A.D. (1977), S.I.A.D. (1977), B.A.Hons. (1981); artist in oil, charcoal, pencil; *b* Warsaw, 7 Oct., 1952. *m* Jonathan Goldberg. one *s. Educ:* Grammar School, Warsaw. *Studied:* Chelsea School of Art (1974-77), Slade School of Fine Art (1977-81, Prof. Sir L. Gowing, Patrick George, Euan Uglow). *Exhib:* solo shows: Polish Cultural Inst. (1975), Sue Rankin Gallery (1988), Thackeray Gallery (1991); major retrospective, Polish Cultural Inst. (1991), Thackery Gallery (1993), Duncan Campbell Fine Art (1995, 1997), Konrad Bayer Gallery, Munich (1996); group shows: Hayward Gallery (1982), N.P.G. (1986), Zacheta Gallery, Warsaw (1991), R.A. (1995), Konrad Bayer Gallery, Munich (1995), Polish Cultural Inst., London (1996). *Work in collections:* U.K., Europe, U.S.A., Canada, S. Africa. *Signs work:* "M.K." or "Kozarzewska." *Address:* 15 Woodlands Ave., New Malden, Surrey KT3 3UL.

**KRUT, Ansel Jonathan,** M.A. (1986), B.F.A. (1982); painter in oil; awarded Rome prize (1987); *b* Cape Town, 1959. *m* Felicity Powell. two *d. Studied:* University of the Witwatersrand (1979-82), R.C.A. (1983-86). *Exhib:* R.A., John Moores, London Group, Cité des Arts, Paris; one-man shows Fischer Fine Art (1989, 1990), Gillian Jason Gallery (1994), Jason and Rhodes Gallery (1995, 1996) *Work in collections:* Arts Council London, British Council, Government Art Collection, Harris Museum of Art Preston, Mercer A.G. Harrogate, Ben Uri Collection, Johannesburg A.G. *Signs work:* "A. Krut." *Address:* Jason and Rhodes Gallery, 4 New Burlington Pl., London W1X 1FB.

**KUHFELD, Peter,** N.E.A.C., R.P., B.A.; artist in oil and pencil; *b* Glos., 4 Mar., 1952. *m* Cathryn Showan, artist. two *d. Educ:* Gateway School, Leicester. *Studied:* Leicester (1972-76), R.A. Schools (1977-80, Peter Greenham, Jane Dowling, Norman Blamey). *Exhib:* R.A., N.E.A.C., R.P., R.B.A., R.W.A., N.P.G., Accademia Italiana, New Grafton Gallery, Agnews, W.H. Patterson, Christie's, Fine Art Soc. *Work in collections:* H.M. The Queen, Baring Bros., Lazards, Cable and Wireless, Hammerson Group, National Trust, Elizabeth Greenshield Foundation, Hambros, Mercury Asset Management, Sabanci Bank. *Signs work:* "Kuhfeld." *Address:* The Corner House, Upper Bridge St., Wye, nr. Ashford, Kent TN25 5AW.

**KUO, Nancy,** author, art critic and painter; gold medallist; Member of International Assoc. of Art Critics, P.E.N., British Actors' Equity; Adviser, British Assoc. of Writers in Chinese; Founder/Director, Chinese Arts Inst. since 1964; *b* Shanghai, China. *Studied:* Xinhua Art Academy, Shanghai. *Exhib:* in many countries in Asia, Africa and Europe. *Work in collections:* private collections all over the world, National Museums of Burma and Leyden. *Publications:* author of "Chinese Paper-cut Pictures", "The Sky is Singing" and many other books, essays etc. in Chinese and English. *Signs work:* "Nancy" in Chinese; see appendix. *Address:* Sea-Breeze Studio, 35 Artillery Rd., Ramsgate, Kent CT11 8PT.

# L

**LABAN, Keith Maurice,** Surrey Dip. (1970); artist in water-colour; Sir Alec Issigonis Prize for Art (1969); *b* London, 22 May 1949. *m* Vivienne Jane Laban (née Ferne). *Studied:* Reigate College of Art (1996-70). *Exhib:* mixed exhbns. London, U.K., Holland. *Signs work:* "Laban." *Address:* 2 Bolsover Grove, Merstham, Surrey RH1 3NU.

**LACEY, Mary Elliot,** A.T.D., S.WL.A.; wildlife painter and illustrator in oils, water-colour and conté chalk; *b* Birmingham, 26 Sept., 1923. one *s.* two *d. Educ:* Birmingham. *Studied:* Birmingham College of Art (1939-44). *Exhib:* Tryon Gallery, Birdland Wildlife Gallery, S.WL.A., Mall Galleries. *Work in collections:* Sultan of Oman, Eric Hosking, Miss Eleanor MacDonald, Rolf Harris. *Publications:* book illustrations for Hamlyn Publishing, South Leigh Press, Balberry Publishing, Royle and Medici. *Signs work:* "Mary Elliot

,acey." *Address:* Meadowbank, Snape Rd., Sudbourne, Woodbridge, Suffolk P12 2BA.

**LACK, Barbara Dacia,** A.R.C.A. Lond.; artist in oil, engraving, textile esign, draughtswoman. *Educ:* Perse School, Camb. *Studied:* Camb. School of rt, R.C.A. *Exhib:* paintings and engravings, R.C.A. Assoc. Exhbn. at the R.A. 1948) and provinces; painting at Colchester Castle (1950); paintings in eicester (1963); Norwich (1966); Peterborough (1969-1973); Sudbury (1969-975); Cambridge, Ely, etc.; textiles, etc., in London, Edinburgh and 'openhagen. *Work in collections:* two purchased by Messrs J. and P. Coats 1945). *Publications:* Modern Embroidery, Embroideress, etc. *Signs work:* "B. ). LACK." *Address:* Acorn Bank, Temple Sowerby, Penrith, Cumbria.

**LACKNER, Suzanne O.,** F.I.L., M.F.P.S.; sculptor in marble, onyx, labaster, soapstone, portland stone, etc. and recently bronze and wood; *b* erlin, 10 Feb., 1908; widow. one *d. Educ:* Berlin Technical University (archi-cture), in France since 1933. *Studied:* Camden Main Institute. *Exhib:* Camden nstitute (1975), Camden Arts Centre (1976), City of Westminster Arts Council 1976), Burgh House (1992), etc. *Work in collections:* England, France, iermany, U.S.A., Japan. *Signs work:* see appendix. *Address:* 49 Eton Hall, ton College Rd., London NW3 2DR.

**LA FONTAINE, Thomas Sherwood,** painter in oil, water-colour and black nd white of portraits and animal subjects; *b* 21 Dec., 1915. *Educ:* Rottingdean nd Tonbridge School. *Studied:* Regent St., Polytechnic (Harry Watson, S. resilian, since 1934); City and Guilds, Kennington (Innes Fripp, James Grant, liddleton Todd, since 1936); Spenlove School (Reginald Eves, since 1939). *igns work:* in printed capitals. *Address:* East Cottage, Burton Hill, lalmesbury, Wilts. SN16 0EL.

**LAGO, Darren,** B.A. (Fine Art), M.A. (Fine Art); sculptor in installation nd object based artworks; Tutor, Kingsway College, London; *b* 22 Sept., 1965. *'duc:* King Edward VI School, Lichfield. *Studied:* Portsmouth University (Don lopes), Chelsea School of Art and Design (Shelagh Cluett). *Exhib:* New 'ontemporary I.C.A. London, Annely Juda Gallery. *Work in collections:* nnely Juda Fine Art Gallery, Unilever House, Unilever plc. *Signs work:* see ppendix. *Address:* 23b Lonsdale Rd., London NW6 6RA.

**LAIN, Graham E.W.,** S.G.F.A.; architectural technician and self taught rtist in water-colour, pen and ink; *b* Wymondham, Norfolk, 18 Sept., 1938. *m* 'arol Mary Phipps. one *d. Exhib:* one-man shows biennially. *Signs work:* G.L." *Address:* Nesbit Cottage, 2 Granary Loke, Spooner Row, Wymondham, lorfolk NR18 9JW.

**LAING, Gerald Ogilvie-,** N.D.D. (1964), F.R.B.S. (1994); artist: figurative Pop) painting (1962-65), highly finished abstract painting/sculpture (1966-69), bstract 3-dimensional sculpture in the landscape (1970-72), formal figurative culpture (1973-82), figurative sculpture (1983-to date); Commissioner, Royal ine Art Commission for Scotland; *b* Newcastle-upon-Tyne, 11 Feb., 1936. *m*

Adaline Havemeyer Frelinghuysen. four *s*. one *d*. *Educ:* Berkhamsted School R.M.A. Sandhurst. *Studied:* St. Martin's School of Art. *Exhib:* more than 30 one-man shows worldwide. Major retrospective, Fruitmarket Gallery Edinburgh (1993). *Work in collections:* National Gallery,Tate Gallery, V. & A. N.P.G., M.O.M.A., N.Y., Whitney Museum, N.Y., and many others *Commissions:* 'Callanish' Glasgow, 'Fountain of Sabrina' Bristol, 'Wise and Foolish Virgins', 'Axis Mundi', 'Conan Doyle Memorial' Edinburgh and 'eight dragons', Bank Underground Station, London, 'Four Rugby Players' Twickenham, 'John Paul Getty III', National Gallery, London. *Publications:* Kinkell :The Reconstruction of a Scottish Castle. *Clubs:* Chelsea Arts. *Sign work:* "Gerald Laing." *Address:* Kinkell Castle, Ross-shire IV7 8AT, Scotland and 901 Lexington Ave., N.Y. 10021, U.S.A.

**LAING, Gordon James,** I.S.O., Ph.D., M.Sc.; painter in acrylic and oils (or crayon, chalk, pastels for small sketches); *b* Oldham, Lancs., 12 Jan., 1923 divorced. one *s*. *Educ:* Eltham College and Oldham Hulme Grammar School Manchester University, Sussex University and London University. *Exhib:* R.A., Paris Salon, International Centre in Washington and Hong Kong. *Sign work:* signs canvas on rear of painting, and sometimes on front also. *Address:* Senlac House, 42 York Way, Fort George, St. Peter Port, Guernsey, C.I. GY1.

**LAIRD, Michael Donald,** O.B.E., F.R.S.A., F.C.S.D., F.R.I.A.S., (McLaren Fellow 1956-58), R.I.B.A.; R.S.A. Architecture Medal (1968); Awards from Civic Trust, British Steel Corp., Saltire Society, etc.; architect and design consultant; Governor, Edinburgh College of Art; *b* 1928. *m* Hon. Kirsty Noel Paton. two *s*. one *d*. *Educ:* Loretto School. *Studied:* Edinburgh College of Art and University under Prof. R. Gordon Brown. *Commissions:* Buildings: include Standard Life Assurance Head Office, Royal Bank Computer Headquarters Edinburgh University Kings Buildings Centre, Restoration, Maxwelton House and Blairquhan Castle. *Clubs:* New (Edinburgh). *Address:* 22 Moray Pl. Edinburgh; and Brock, Isle of Tiree, Argyllshire.

**LAKE, C. Elisabeth Matheson,** R.M.S. (1989), F.H.S. (1982-95); miniature painter in water-colour (interiors); *b* Norwich, 12 Apr., 1939. *m* Geoffrey N Lake. one *s*. three *d*. *Studied:* West of England College of Art (1957-60). *Exhib:* H.S. (1982-95), R.A. Summer Exhbn. (1986), R.M.S. (1984-), many N American and Canadian exhbns. (1985-89). *Work in collections:* England, N America and Europe. *Publications:* books, magazines. *Signs work:* see appen dix. *Address:* Hollow End, Hollow Marsh, Farrington Gurney, Somerset BS18 5TX.

**LALLY, Richard,** painter in oil, pastel and water-colour; *b* London, 2 Oct. 1928. *Educ:* Brixton College of Building and Architecture (1942-45). *Studied* Hammersmith School of Art (1955-59, Leon Underwood, Dennis Gilbert) *Exhib:* one-man shows, Real Club Nautico, Tenerife (1961), Manolette Gallery, Richmond (1977); R.O.I., N.S., U.A., S.WL.A. *Signs work:* "LALLY." *Address:* Strathcroy, Drumbeg, Lairg, Sutherland, Scotland IV27

4NG.

**LAMB, Elspeth,** D.A. (Glas.) (1973), H.Dip.A.D. (Manc.) (1974), A.R.S.A. (1990); lecturer/printmaker in printmaking, papermaking, drawing; Lecturer in drawing and painting, Edinburgh College of Art; *b* Glasgow, 28 Mar., 1951. *Educ:* Kings Pk. Senior Secondary School, Glasgow. *Studied:* Glasgow School of Art (Philip Reeves), Manchester Polytechnic, The Tamarind Inst. of Lithography, University of New Mexico, U.S.A. (Lynn Allen). *Exhib:* Mercury Gallery (1988, 1990), Conservative Management (1990), Marlborough Graphics (1991), Glasgow Print Studio (1990). *Work in collections:* S.A.C., British Council, Japanese Consular Coll., Perth A.G., Glasgow A.G., City Arts. *Address:* Bon a Tirer Editions, 15 E. Campbell St., Glasgow G1 1DG.

**LAMBERT, Colin Joseph,** sculptor in bronze and stone; *b* Guantanamo Bay, Cuba, 17 Jan., 1948. *m* Catherine Finn. *Studied:* Chouinard Art Inst., Los Angeles (1966-68); apprenticed with Karl Gomez in Amsterdam (1980-83). *Work in collections:* Stamford Forum, Stamford, Conn.; London United Bldg., London; Renaissance Vineyard and Winery, Calif.; Warminster Market Centre, Warminster, Wilts. *Signs work:* see appendix. *Address:* Flint Barn Studio, West End, nr. Essendon, Hatfield, Herts. AL9 5RQ.

**LAMBIRTH, Alan,** R.B.A. (1986), R.A. Gold medal (1982), R.A. Schools Advanced Dip. (1983), Higher Surrey Dip. A.D. (1980), De Laszlo medal awarded by R.B.A. (1991); artist in oil, pastel, gouache and water-colour; *b* Cuckfield, 19 Feb., 1959. *Educ:* Hazelwick School, Crawley. *Studied:* W. Sussex College of Design (1975-77), Epsom School of Art (1977-80, Peter Peterson), R.A. Schools (1980-83, Peter Greenham, R.A.). *Exhib:* R.A., R.B.A., N.E.A.C., Soc. of Landscape Painters; one-man shows: Odette Gilbert Gallery (1984, 1986), Solomon Gallery (1988), Sheila Harrison Fine Art (1989, 1991), Enid Lawson Gallery (1997); four-man show: Hallam Gallery (1990). *Address:* 22 Brushwood Rd., Roffey, Horsham, W. Sussex RH12 4PE.

**LAMONT, Ian James,** painter in oil; *b* Carshalton, 16 May, 1964. *Educ:* Nork Pk. School; N.E. Surrey College of Technology; Sutton College of Liberal Arts. *Studied:* Kingston Polytechnic School of Art and Design; also portrait painting under Ronald Benham, N.E.A.C., R.B.A. (1982-86). *Exhib:* R.A., N.E.A.C., R.B.A., R.O.I. (Winsor and Newton Young Artist award finalist 1983-88), Royal Portrait Soc. *Work in collections:* United Racecourses. *Signs work:* "Ian Lamont." *Address:* 25 Woodgavil, Banstead, Surrey SM7 1AA.

**LANCASTER, Brian Christy,** R.S.M.A. (1997), F.R.S.A. (1995), G.R.A. (1990); artist in water-colour, occasional acrylic, illustrator (mainly architectural); *b* Atherton, nr. Manchester, 3 Aug., 1931. *m* Pauline Carol Wheler Lancaster. *Educ:* Lee St. School, Atherton. *Studied:* Bolton College of Art (1946-49), Southport College of Art (1949-52). *Exhib:* Atkinson A.G., Southport, Bristol Savages, R.W.A., R.I., R.B.A., R.W.S., G.R.A., R.S.M.A. *Work in collections:* Duke and Duchess of Beaufort, Badminton, Glos., Bristol

Savages. *Commissions:* Second Severn Crossing Bridge Under Construction painting, Sir Charles Halcrow Co. Ltd., Nuclear Electric (Calendar), Grant Thornton (Chartered Accountants), calendars, R.N.L.I., Napier Brown. *Publications:* work repro.: two art books (David & Charles), Countryside Commission annual report '94 & '95 illustrations, Post Office commemorative cover: Forth Bridge Centenary, two page spread in book '100 years of Railways'. Reproductions of paintings in several magazines, book jacket for Scottish Steam in the 1950's and 60's (OPC). *Clubs:* Bristol Savages. *Signs work:* "Brian C. Lancaster." *Address:* Galloway, Waterley Bottom, N. Nibley, Glos. GL11 6EF.

**LANCASTER, John Maurice,** N.D.D., M.Phil., Ph.D.; painter, calligrapher, heraldic artist; *b* Wigan. *Studied:* Leeds College of Art (1946-51), advanced painting with Victor Pasmore. *Exhib:* one-man shows: Leicester, Nottingham, London, Keele, Bristol, Decatur, U.S.A., Columbus, U.S.A., Thatcher, Az., U.S.A., Guild Gallery, Bristol, Stowe, Wadhurst; three two-man shows; R.W.A., R.B.A., Hesketh Hubbard, Mod. Art in Yorkshire, W. Riding Artists, John Noott 20th C. Gallery, Kenulf Galleries, Guild Gallery, Bristol, Upton Lodge Gallery and other galleries. *Work in collections:* Europe, Scandinavia and U.S.A. *Publications:* 16 books. Visiting Prof. U.S.A.; Gila Valley Arts Council Visiting artist, Az., U.S.A. *Clubs:* S.S.I., S.H.A. *Signs work:* "John Lancaster." *Address:* 10 Walnut Cl., Cheltenham, Glos. GL52 3AG.

**LANDAU, David,** M.D. (1978), M.A. (1980); Chairman, Loot Group of Cos.; Editor, Print Quarterly; Trustee: National Gallery and N.A.C.F.; Treasurer, Venice in Peril Fund; *b* 22 Apr., 1950. *Publications:* Georg Pencz (1978); Federica Galli (1982); The Renaissance Print (with P.Parshall) (1994). *Address:* 80 Carlton Hill, London NW8 0ER.

**LANDERS, Linda Anne,** B.A.(Hons.) (1986), A.R.E. (1995); painter/printmaker/writer, oil, etching, wood engraving, hand-made books; *b* Herts., 27 Dec., 1959. two *s.* *Studied:* Central School of Art (1979-86, Cecil Collins). *Exhib:* national and international group shows; solo shows nationally; artist and 'Fine Press' book fairs. *Work in collections:* British Art Library, V. & A., Ashmolean Museum, R.C.A., Musuem Van Het Boek, Netherlands, University of California L.A., University of Plymouth. *Commissions:* wood engraving for Circle Press, and for Delos and Redlake Press. *Publications:* published seven Limited Edn. artists books under imprint: Spoon Print Press. Writes and performs own poetry. *Signs work:* "L.A. Landers" and see appendix. Signature varies according to size of work. *Address:* 337 Westbourne Park Rd., London W11 1EG.

**LANE-DAVIES, Hugh John,** Dip. Arch. (Dist. in Thesis) R.I.B.A. (1951); architect/artist in water-colour; *b* Ramsgate, 20 Dec., 1927. *m* Wendy Isabel (née Pierce). one *s.* *Educ:* King's College, Taunton, and (now) University of Westminster. *Exhib:* numerous exhbns. in London and Home Counties, including R.I.B.A., Cider House Gallery Bletchingley, Llewellyn Alexander Fine Art,

Bourne Gallery Reigate, World of Drawings and Water-colours, London, Fine Art and Antiques Fair, London. *Work in collections:* private and corporate collections worldwide, including Tokai Bank of Japan, I.B.M., Price Waterhouse, Furness Withy, Trafalgar House, W.S. Atkins. *Publications:* work repro.: Christmas cards, calendars and limited edition prints. *Signs work:* "H. Lane-Davies." *Address:* White Rose Cottage, White Hill, Bletchingley, Surrey RH1 4QT.

**LANG, Wharton,** R.S.M.A. (1948), now Hon. Mem., F.R.S.A. (1983); sculptor in wood; ex Mem. S.WL.A.; *b* Oberammergau, Bavaria, 13 June, 1925. *m* Ingrid. *Educ:* Newquay Grammar School. *Studied:* Leonard Fuller School of Painting (1946) and privately under Faust Lang (1946-49). *Work in collections:* Ulster Museum, Belfast, R.S.M.A. Diploma Collection, National Maritime Museum, Greenwich, Carving in Relief 'Castle of Mey' presented to H.M. Queen Mother (1967). *Signs work:* "W. LANG," "Wharton Lang" and see appendix. *Address:* Fauna Studio, Mount Zion, St. Ives, Cornwall.

**LANGFORD, Martin James,** A.R.E. (1996); artist in mezzotint; *b* Kingston upon Thames, 2 June, 1970. *m* Therese Langford. *Studied:* University of Plymouth (B.A. (Hons.) Fine Art 1993); Post Grad. Advanced Printmaking, Central St. Martin's College of Art (David Gluck, R.E.). *Exhib:* National Print (1995, 1996, 1997); one-man shows, 'A Trifle Greedy' through Alternative Arts (1995), The Mansion House, Hackney (1996-97). *Work in collections:* For Art's Sake, Ealing, W. London; Will's Art Warehouse, Parson's Green, London; Cupola Gallery, Sheffield; Barleycorn Antiques, Berkhampsted; Bankside Gallery, London. Awards: Gwen May R.E. Student Award - National Print (1995), Gwen May R.E. Commemorative Award for outstanding print-making - National Print (1996). *Address:* 2 Norfolk House, The Farmlands, Northolt, Middx. UB5 5EU.

**LARGE, George Charles,** R.I. (1986), A.T.C.; artist in oil and water-colour; *b* London, 20 Jan., 1936. *m* Pamela Parkinson; three *s.* two *d.* (one *s-s.* one *s-d.*). *Educ:* Downhills Central School, Tottenham. *Studied:* Hornsey College of Art (1958-63, Maurice de Sausmarez, John Titchell, Alfred Daniels). *Exhib:* R.I., R.B.A., S.W.E.; one-man shows, Mall Galleries, National Gallery Malta, Duncan Campbel Fine Arts, Melitensia A.G., Malta, Llewellyn Alexander. *Work in collections:* British Rail, National Gallery Malta, British Consulate Malta, Cranfield Inst., I.C.I. *Publications:* illustrated, Laughter in the Kitchen, and various magazines, Taste of History, Food of the Knights of Malta, Pamela Parkinson-Large; The Cartographer, David Mackenzie. Awards: Windsor Newton Award, R.I. Singer Friedlander/Sunday Times. *Signs work:* "LARGE 98." *Address:* 13/14 Market Pl., Woburn, Beds. MK17 9PZ.

**LARMONT, Eric,** N.D.D., A.T.C.; painter in oil, etcher; part-time art lecturer; *b* South Shields, 27 Sept., 1943. *Studied:* Sunderland College of Art (1963-65); Goldsmiths' School of Art (1965-66), Post-grad. Belgian Scholarship (1968-69). *Exhib:* one-man shows, London: 273 Gallery (1969), Scribes Cellar (1978), Holsworthy Gallery (1981), Galerie Blankenese,

Hamburg (1983), Pump House Gallery, London (1997); two-man show, Jonathan Poole Gallery (1986). *Work in collections:* Carlisle Corporation; private collections: various. Prizes and awards: Reeves Bi-centenary Premier Award (1966); Second Non-purchase Prize, Northern Painters Exhibition (1966). *Signs work:* see appendix. *Address:* 20 Rainville Rd., London W6 9HA.

**LARUSDOTTIR, Karolina,** R.E., R.W.S., N.E.A.C.; painter in oil and water-colour, etcher and printmaker; *b* Reykjavik, Iceland, 1944. *Studied:* Ruskin School of Art, Oxford University and Barking College of Art. *Exhib:* Bankside Gallery, R.E., R.A., R.B.A.; one-man shows: Kjarvalsstadir Reykjavik (1982, 1986), Gallerie Gammelstrand, Kobenhagen, Gallery 10 (1984, 1987, 1991), Cambridge Contemporary Art (from 1994), John Brandler Galleries, Brentwood. *Work in collections:* Cartwright Hall Museum, Bradford; The Vatican Collection, Rome; Nelson Atkin Museum, Kansas City, U.S.A.; British Museum, London; Ashmolean Museum, Oxford; Fitzwilliam Museum, Cambridge; Pompidou Museum, Paris. Prizes and awards: The Dicks and Greenbury Award, Bankside Gallery (1989). Special award: Premio Internazionale Biella per l'incisione, Italy. *Signs work:* "LARUSDOTTIR." *Address:* 27 Portugal St., Cambridge, CB5 8AW.

**LASDUN, Sir Denys (Louis),** C.H. (1995), Kt. (1976), C.B.E. (1965); architect. Principal works: include: housing and schools for Bethnal Green and Paddington; London H.Q., N.S.W. Govt.; Flats 26 St James's Place; Royal College of Physicians; University of East Anglia; London University (SOAS, I. of E., Law Inst.); work for Universities Leicester and Liverpool; Fitzwilliam College, and Christ's College extension, Cambridge; National Theatre and IBM South Bank; European Investment Bank, Luxembourg; Hurva Synagogue project, Jerusalem; Cannock Community Hospital; Genoa Opera House project; offices Fenchurch Street, EC4 and Milton Court, EC2. Member Academician: Paris (1984); San Luca, Rome (1984); Bulgaria (1986). Hon. F. American Institute of Architects (1966), Royal Gold Medal for Architecture, R.I.B.A. (1977); R.A. (1991); Wolf Prize in Arts (Architecture) Wolf Foundation (1992); R.I.B.A. Trustees' Medal (1992): Hon. F.R.I.A.S. (1994); Hon. Dip. Architecture Assoc. (1994); The Architects' Journal Centenary Medal (1995); *b* 8 Sept., 1914. *m* Susan Bendit. two *s.* one *d. Educ:* Rugby School. *Studied:* Architectural Association. *Exhib:* Royal Academy. *Publications:* include: A Language and a Theme (1976); Architecture in an Age of Scepticism (1984); publication on Sir Denys Lasdun: Denys Lasdun: Architecture, City, Landscape by William Curtis (Phaidon Press, 1994). *Address:* 146 Grosvenor Rd., London SW1V 3JY.

**LAUDER, Kenneth Scott,** A.R.C.A. (1939); painter in oil and water-colour; *b* Edinburgh, 1916. *m* (1) Sylvia Morgan (1946);one *s* (m dissolved); (2) Marian Mills (1966); two *s. Educ:* King Alfred's Grammar School (Albert Rutherston). *Studied:* Chelsea School of Art (1933-36, H.S. Williamson, G. Sutherland, R. Medley), R.C.A. (1936-39, P.H. Jowett, Gilbert Spencer, Percy

Horton). *Exhib:* R.A., Agnews, Scottish Gallery London and Edinburgh, Liverpool Academy, Newcastle Laing Gallery, Bristol R.W.A., Stratford-on-Avon Ruskin Gallery, Bear Lane Gallery Oxford, William Jackson Gallery London, Galeries Cloots Brussels. *Work in collections:* The School of Design in Providence, Rhode Island, U.S.A. *Signs work:* see appendix. *Address:* Moreton Lodge, Eye, Leominster, Herefordshire HR6 0DP.

**LAW Enid:** see CHAUVIN, Enid.

**LAWRENCE, Gordon Robert,** Dip.A.D. (1951), Teacher's Cert. (1952), 1st Class Hons. Rome Accademia de Belle Arte (1962), M.Ed. Liverpool (1975), Ph.D. (1979); painter/sculptor in acrylic, water-colour, stone; *b* Glasgow, 1930; divorced. three *s. Educ:* Hillhead High School, Glasgow. *Studied:* Glasgow School of Art, Accademia de Belle Arte, Rome. *Exhib:* Britain, France, Germany, Spain, Ireland and U.S.A. *Signs work:* see appendix. *Address:* Camboulit, 46100 Figeac, France.

**LAWRENCE, John,** winner, Francis Williams Book Illustration award (twice); freelance illustrator in wood engraving and water-colour; part time lecturer, Camberwell School of Art; external assessor, Exeter College of Art; Duncan of Jordanstone College of Art; Edinburgh College of Art; Kingston School of Art; Visiting Professor in illustration at the London Inst.; *b* Hastings, 15 Sept., 1933. *m* Myra. two *d. Educ:* Salesian College, Oxford. *Studied:* Hastings School of Art and Central School of Art and Design. *Exhib:* R.E., S.W.E. *Work in collections:* V. & A., Ashmolean Museum, National Museum of Wales and several provincial galleries. *Publications:* over 100 books. *Clubs:* A.W.G., S.W.E., Double Crown. *Signs work:* "John Lawrence." *Address:* 22a Castlewood Rd., London N16 6DW.

**LAWRENCE, Mary R.,** painter in oil and water-colour; *b* Wimbledon, 17 June, 1922. *m* F.R.M. Lawrence. one *s.* two *d. Educ:* Downe House, Cold Ash, Newbury. *Studied:* Epsom School of Art and Design (1970-80, John Morley, Alan Dodd, Leslie Worth). *Exhib:* R.A. Summer Shows (1974-87), N.E.A.C. (1972-76). *Address:* 15 Jackson Cl., Epsom, Surrey KT18 7RA.

**LAWSON, Gillian,** painter in water-colour and oil, printmaker in etching; *b* 6 May, 1936. married. one *s.* two *d. Educ:* Parliament Hill Grammar School. *Studied:* Camden Institute (silk screen printing, Ingrid Greenfield), Camden Art Centre (1971-75, etching, Dorothea Wight). *Exhib:* Cape Town, S.A., Georgetown, Washington, U.S.A., R.A., Halesworth Gallery, Burgh House, Hampstead, The Ice House, Holland Park, Hinton Gallery, nr. Horley, Ninth British International Print Biennale. *Signs work:* "Gillian Lawson." *Address:* 7 Oak Hill Way, Hampstead, London NW3 7LR.

**LAWSON, Simon Nicholas,** B.A. Hons. (1985); artist in oil, etching, photography; *b* Waltham, Lincs., 2 Aug., 1964. *Educ:* Waltham Toll Bar Comprehensive. *Studied:* Grimsby School of Art (1980-82, Peter Todd), Wimbledon School of Art (1982-85, Bernard Cohen), R.A. Schools (1985-88, Norman Adams). *Exhib:* Symondsbury Gallery, Bridport (1986), Royal

Festival Hall (1986), R.A. (1986-87). *Signs work:* "S.N. Lawson." *Address:* 22 Bursar St., Cleethorpes, S. Humberside.

**LAWSON, Sonia,** R.A., R.W.S., R.C.A., M.A.(1st) (1959); artist in oil, water-colour, etching; Tutor R.A. Schools; *b* Wensleydale, Yorks., 2 June, 1934. *m* Charles Congo. one *d. Studied:* Royal College of Art (1956-59, Prof. Carel Weight), Post-graduate year (1959-60), Travelling Scholarship, France. *Exhib:* retrospective tour, Leicester Polytechnic, Mappin Gallery Sheffield, Ferens Hull, Cartwright Bradford, Central Gallery Milton Keynes (1982-83); selected solo exhbns. Kirklees (1985), Manchester (1987), Wakefield (1988), Bradford (1989), London, Boundary Gallery (1989, 1995); mixed shows, New York, Fragments against Ruin tour, China, British Council tour, Arts Council, Tolly Cobbald, John Moores, Edinburgh, R.A. London, Haywards Annual London, Subjective Eye, Midland Group Nottingham. *Work in collections:* Arts Council, Sheffield, Carlisle, Belfast, Bradford, Middlesbrough, Bolton, Harrogate, Rochdale, Wakefield and Huddersfield A.G.'s, Open University, M. of W., Leeds University, R.C.A., Nuffield, Cranfield, Imperial War Museum, R.A., Vatican. *Signs work:* "S. Lawson," "Sonia Lawson" or "Lawson." *Address:* c/o Royal Academy, Piccadilly, London W1.

**LAWSON-BAKER, Auriol,** muralist, sculptor in bronze; Director, L.B.P. Sculpture and Design; owner "Scene Inside" Mural Co.; *b* 7 Sept., 1963. *m* Neil Lawson-Baker. one *s. Educ:* Ditcham Park, Petersfield, Hants. *Exhib:* R.A., sculpture project managed throughout U.K. and Europe including Houses of Parliament Arts Com., London International Financial Futures Exchange; British Gas plc., etc. *Signs work:* "A. Lawson-Baker." *Address:* Graingers, West Ashling, W. Sussex PO18 8DN.

**LAWSON-BAKER, Dr. Neil,** M.B., B.S. (Lond.), B.D.S., L.D.S. (Lond.), L.D.S., R.C.S. (Eng.); dental surgeon and sculptor in bronze; Director, L.B.P. Sculpture and Design; *b* Watford, 8 Nov., 1938. *m* Auriol Lawson-Baker. one *s. Educ:* Merchant Taylors and London University. *Exhib:* one-man show: Watermans Gallery, London (1991). *Commissions:* Sterling House, Albert Bridge, London SW11; Entrance and trading floor at London International Financial Futures Exchange; British Gas plc, 7 metre bronze flame, Reading and Loughborough; Entrance Hall, 1 Parliament Street, London SW1; Entrance Gibran Library, Beirut University, Lebanon; Inauguration Sculpture for Channel Tunnel, Eurotunnel plc; Magna Carta Fountain, Runnymead Borough Council, Egham; 14 metre Keris, National Stadium, Kuala Lumpur, Malaysia. *Publications:* Visual Times, a private Journal of sculpture. *Clubs:* Arts, R.A.C. *Signs work:* "Neil Lawson-Baker." *Address:* Graingers, West Ashling, W. Sussex PO18 8DN.

**LAYCOCK, Allan Bracewell,** A.T.D. (1951), F.S.A.I. (1975), R.W.A. (1986); landscape painter in acrylic, in situ; lecturer in graphics and illustration; *b* Sutton-in-Craven, 4 June, 1928. *Educ:* Keighley Grammar School. *Studied:* Keighley School of Art (1945-46, 1948-50), Sheffield College of Art (1950-

51), Norwich School of Art (1951). *Exhib:* one-man and group shows in eastern and S.W. England. Work in private collections in U.K. and overseas. *Signs work:* "Allan Laycock." *Address:* Tararua, Broad St., Hartpury, Glos. GL19 3BN.

**LAYZELL, Peter,** B.A.(Hons.) Fine Art; artist in oil; part-time lecturer in art at Blackpool College and Lancaster University; *b* Hitchin, Herts., 1962. *m* Jean Palmer. one *s*. *Studied:* Mander College, Bedford and Coventry Polytechnic (1981-84). *Exhib:* R.A. Summer Exhbn. from 1986-97 (prizewinner, 1990); various group exhbns. in London etc. *Work in collections:* Morgan Grenfell, St. Martin's College, Lancaster, Warrington Arts Council. Dealers: James Huntington-Whiteley, London. *Signs work:* "P. Layzell" on reverse. *Address:* 72 Vale Rd., Lancaster LA1 2JL.

**LEACH, D.,** potter in stoneware and porcelain; *b* Tokyo, 7 May, 1911. *m* Elizabeth Mary; three *s*. (all potters). *Educ:* Dauntsey's School. *Studied:* with Bernard Leach. *Exhib:* numerous in U.K., Germany, Japan, Australia, Turkey, Belgium, U.S.A., Craftsmans Art at V. & A. (1973), British Crafts Centre (1979); one-man, Craftsmen Potters Assoc. (1966, 1981, 1990, 1994). *Work in collections:* V. & A., Exeter Museum and A.G., Wakefield Museum, Liverpool Museum and A.G. Extensive lecture tours in U.S.A., Canada, Germany, Spain, Italy and Greece. *Signs work:* seal in foot of pots, see appendix. *Address:* Lowerdown Pottery, Bovey Tracey, Devon TQ13 9LE.

**LEACH, Mark Alan,** P.S. (1994); self taught artist in pastel, charcoal, acrylic; *b* Bromley, Kent, 10 Apr., 1952. *m* Gabrielle Janice. three *s*. *Educ:* Dulwich College; Bromley Grammar School. *Exhib:* P.S., Mall Galleries, various one-man and mixed shows London and South East. *Signs work:* see appendix. *Address:* The White House, Pannel Lane, Pett, Hastings, E. Sussex TN35 4JB.

**LEACH, Ursula Mary,** A.R.E. (1996), B.A. (Hons.) (1992); printmaker/painter in etching and oil paint; *b* Woking, 14 May, 1947. *m* John Leach (separated). one *s*. one *d*. *Studied:* Winchester, Wimbledon and Farnham Schools of Art. *Exhib:* Attendi, London W4, Mall Galleries, London, Redfern, London, Southampton City A.G. *Work in collections:* Diploma Collection, Ashmolean, Oxford. *Commissions:* Worthing Hospital Postgraduate Medical Centre, Dorset County Hospital. *Publications:* work repro.: review: Contemporary Art Vol. 2. No.3., several exhbn. catalogues. *Signs work:* "U. Leach." *Address:* 14 The Square, Cranborne, Dorset BH21 5PR.

**LEAPER, Landreth Francis,** R.W.A.; self taught artist in water-colour and mixed media; *b* Horsham, 22 Dec., 1947. *Exhib:* numerous in South and S. West England. *Signs work:* "LEAPER" or "L. LEAPER" or double LL within a circle, sometimes above the year. *Address:* 28 Gerald Rd, Ashton, Bristol BS3 2DN.

**LE BAS, Rachel Ann,** R.E., N.E.A.C.; Mem. A.W,G., Somerset Guild of Craftsmen; painter, line-engraver, etc.; *b* 9 Apr., 1923. *Educ:* W. Heath School, Sevenoaks. *Studied:* City and Guilds of London Art School (A.R. Middleton

Todd, R.A., R.W.S., R.E., N.E.A.C.). *Exhib:* R.A., N.E.A.C., R.E., etc. *Work in collections:* Ashmolean Museum, Exeter Museum, Southampton Civic Centre, R.A. Graphics. *Clubs:* Arts, Dover St. *Signs work:* "R. A. LE BAS." *Address:* Winsford, nr. Minehead, Som. TA24 7JE.

**LE BROCQUY, Louis,** H.R.H.A. (1983), F.C.S.D. (1960), Hon. Litt.D., Dublin (1962), Hon. Ll.D. National University of Ireland (1988), Chevalier de la Légion d'Honneur (1975); *b* Nov., 1916. *Studied:* self-taught. *Exhib:* Gimpel Fils (London, N.Y.), Galerie Jeanne Bucher (Paris), Taylor (Dublin). Retrospective exhbns.: Municipal Gallery of Modern Art, Dublin (1966, 1978), Ulster Museum, Belfast (1967, 1987), Fondation Maeght, St. Paul (1973), Arts Council, Belfast (1975, 1978), Musée d'Art Moderne, Paris (1976), New York State Museum (1981), Palais des Beaux Arts, Charleroi (1982), Festival Centre, Adelaide (1988), Westpac, National Gallery of Victoria, Melbourne (1988), Museum of Contemporary Art, Brisbane (1988), Musée Picasso, Antibes (1989), Museum of Modern Art, Kamakura (1991), Itami Museum of Art, Osaki (1991), City Museum of Contemporary Art, Hiroshima (1991); Irish Museum of Modern Art, Dublin (1996). *Address:* c/o Gimpel Fils, 30 Davies St., London W1Y 1LG.

**LE BRUN, Christopher Mark,** Dip. F.A. Slade (1974), M.A. Chelsea (1975), R.A. (1996); painter, printmaker, sculptor; Trustee National Gallery (since 1996), Trustee Tate Gallery (1990-95); *b* Portsmouth, 20 Dec., 1951. *m* Charlotte Verity. two *s.* one *d. Studied:* Slade School of Fine Art, Chelsea School of Fine Art. *Exhib:* numerous mixed exhbns., one-man shows world-wide since 1978. *Work in collections:* Tate, V. & A., B.M., M.O.M.A. New York, Arts Council, Fitzwilliam Museum, Courtaulds, Oslo, Sydney, Yale, S.N.G.M.A., Edinburgh, Whitworth, Southampton, etc. *Commissions:* The Parables, Liverpool Cathedral (1996). *Clubs:* Groucho, Chelsea Arts. *Address:* c/o Marlborough Fine Art, 6 Albemarle St; London W1X 4BY.

**LEDER, Carolyn,** M.A. (1968); Curator, Old Speech Room Gallery, Harrow School (1989-); Trustee, Stanley Spencer Gallery, Cookham (1978-90); formerly Lecturer in History of Art, University of London, Dept. of Extra-Mural Studies (1972-88); *b* Melbourne, 5 Mar., 1945. *m* Professor Malcolm Leder. two *s. Studied:* Courtauld Inst. of Art, University of London. *Publications:* book, Stanley Spencer: The Astor Collection (1976); articles; numerous catalogues including 'Victor Pasmore', 'John Piper', 'English Watercolourists'. Historical Adviser, BBC 2 Television, 'Stanley', drama-documentary on Stanley Spencer (1988). Specialist commentator in Stanley Spencer Gallery's video 'Stanley Spencer: A Painter in Heaven' (1996). *Address:* The Steps, Hill Close, Harrow on the Hill, Middx. HA1 3PQ.

**LEE, Rern,** painter in oil colour; *b* Jakarta, Indonesia, 19 Sept., 1938. *m* Siew Pui-Sam. two *d. Educ:* Singapore and Jakarta. *Studied:* Nanyang Academy of Fine Arts, Singapore. Trainee for several years in father's studio, then travelled and worked in England, France, Italy, Holland, Germany and

Singapore (1969-72); Australia and New Zealand (1976); U.S.A. and Canada (1981). *Exhib:* one-man shows: Singapore (1970) and Jakarta (1980), etc. *Work in collections:* Nanyang University Museum, Singapore; Indonesia Palace Museum, Jakarta; The Asia and Pacific Museum, Warsaw, etc. Awards: Academic of Italy with Gold Medal; International Parliament U.S.A. Gold Medal of Merit; conferred Honorary Prize with Memorial Medal of Golden Centaur 1982; Diploma of Honoris Causa "Master of Painting" from the International Seminar of Modern and Contemporary Art and Diploma of Merit from Italian University of Arts. *Signs work:* "R. Lee." *Address:* Jalan Gedong 11-A, Jakarta Barat, Indonesia.

**LEE, Rosie,** D.F.A. (1957); painter in oil; *b* Rotterdam, 23 Dec., 1935; married. four *s. Educ:* Abbeydale Girls' Grammar School, Sheffield. *Studied:* Sheffield College of Art (1953-55), Slade School (1955-58). *Exhib:* Piccadilly Gallery, London. *Work in collections:* Walker A.G. (Schools Collection), Hull Educ. Authority, W. Riding of Yorks. Educ. Authority, Surrey Educ. Authority, Dept. of Environment, Coventry City A.G., Sheffield City A.G. *Signs work:* see appendix. *Address:* High Tor View, Brunswood Rd., Matlock Bath, Matlock, Derbyshire DE4 3PA.

**LEE, Sidney Edward,** graphic artist and painter in oil and charcoal/chalks; *b* London, 22 Nov., 1925. *m* Amy Gwendoline Aston (decd.). *Studied:* Harrow School of Art, Willesden School of Art. *Exhib:* R.W.A., R.O.I., R.S.M.A., Guildhall and Mall Galleries London; exhib. marine paintings regularly with the R.S.M.A. (1979-85) - see 20th Century British Marine Painting by Denys Brook-Hart. Recent work includes charcoal and conté drawings of the Cornish landscape. *Clubs:* St. Ives Soc. of Artists. *Signs work:* see appendix. *Address:* Rose Lea, Rose Hill, Marazion, Cornwall TR17 0HB.

**LEE, Terry Glyn,** D.F.A. (Lond.), 1957; artist in oil; *b* Sheffield, 28 Oct., 1932. four *s. Educ:* King Edward VII School, Sheffield. *Studied:* Sheffield College of Art; Slade School of Fine Art (1955-58); Sir William Coldstream. *Exhib:* New Art Centre, Agnews, Piccadilly Gallery, Wildenstein, R.A., Van Rijn Maastricht, Bühler Gallery Stuttgard. *Work in collections:* Liverpool Art Gallery, Ferens Art Gallery, Hull, Coventry Art Gallery, Oldham Art Gallery, The Arts Council, Financial Times, Contemporary Art Soc., Sheffield Art Galleries, Duke of Devonshire, Government Art Collection. *Signs work:* "Terry Lee." *Address:* Calton Houses, Calton Lees, Beeley, nr. Matlock, Derbyshire DE4 2NX.

**LEECH, Raymond Ian,** R.S.M.A. (1986), L.S.I.A.D. (1969); mem. E.Anglian Group of Marine Artists; landscape and seascape painter in oil and water-colour; partner in a design group, Pencil Point Studio; *b* Gt.Yarmouth, 1949. *Educ:* Edward Worledge School, Alderman Leach High School. *Studied:* Gt.Yarmouth College of Art and Design (1965-69). *Exhib:* R.S.M.A., Hunting Group, Mystic U.S.A., Assembly Rooms Norwich, Ladygate Gallery, and other provincial galleries. *Work in collections:* National Maritime Museum, The

Sheik of Oman, Mystic Maritime Gallery U.S.A., etc. *Publications:* represented in Tonal Painting (Quarto). *Signs work:* see appendix. *Address:* 1 The Staithe, Oulton Broad, Lowestoft, Suffolk.

**LEES, Stewart Marshall,** D.A. (Edin.) (1952), R.O.I. (1987), R.S.W. (1992), R.W.S. (1991); *b* Auchtertool, Fife, 15 Jan., 1926. *Educ:* Edinburgh College of Art (1947-52). *Exhib:* R.A. Summer Exhbn., Royal Scottish Academy, R.S.W., R.W.S., and privately. *Work in collections:* Glenrothes New Town, Liverpool Educ. Com., Fife Educ. Com., University of Glasgow, University of Nottingham, Nuffield Foundation, Imperial Tobacco Co., Sheffield City A.G., Leverhulme Foundation, Scottish Arts Council, Esso Ltd., Leeds Educ. Com. *Clubs:* Arts, London. *Signs work:* "Stewart Lees." *Address:* Southlands, Arlington Drive, Mapperley Pk., Nottingham NG3 5EN.

**LEES, Susan Jane,** artist in gouache, water-colour, oil; Wildlife illustrator at Bristol Zoo; *b* Bristol, 23 June, 1961. *Educ:* Hengrove Comp. Bristol. *Studied:* Glos. College of Art and Design (1980-82). *Exhib:* Soc. of Amateur Artists, Soc. of Women Artists, British Soc. of Painters, The Wild Arts Soc., and local exhbns. *Clubs:* Soc. of Amateur Artists '93, Wildlife Art Soc.'94, Soc. of Women Artists '95, '96, British Soc. of Painters '95, '96, Whitchurch Art Club '92. *Signs work:* "Susan Jane." *Address:* 163 Avonvale Rd., Redfield, Bristol BS5 9RY.

**LEGG, Owen,** M.F.P.S.; printmaker and artist in oil on board, lino-cut prints, abstract constructions; *b* London, 1 Aug., 1935. *Educ:* Alleyns School, Dulwich. *Studied:* Tunbridge Wells Adult Education Centre. *Exhib:* York University, Tunbridge Wells Library, Loggia Gallery. *Work in collections:* Greenwich Library, Graphotek, Berlin. *Publications:* York Mystery Play The Armourers Play, Cut in the Chalk, Rubaiyyat of Omar Khayaam; The Garden by V. Sackville West (1989), On First Seeing Iceland (1992), Christmas letters from a Friend (1997). *Signs work:* "Owen Legg." *Address:* Woodcraft Press, 152 Hadlow Rd., Tonbridge, Kent TN9 1PB.

**LEHMANN, Olga,** S.G.F.A., N.S., F.R.S.A.; painter; designer; *b* Catemu, Chile, 1912. *m* Carl E.R. Huson (decd.). one *s. Educ:* Santiago College, Chile. *Studied:* Slade School of Fine Art (Prof. Schwabe, Alan Gwynne Jones, V. Polunin). In 1941 joined the film industry as scenic artist, later became a designer of sets and costumes. Credits include "Tom Thumb", "Guns of Navarone", "Man in the Iron Mask", "Kidnapped." *Exhib:* London Group, N.E.A.C., S.G.F.A., N.S., Suffolk Art Soc., Gainsborough House, Thaxted Guildhall, and many others; one-man shows: John Whibley Gallery, A.I.A. Gallery, Rushmore Rooms, and Heffer's Gallery, Cambridge, Guildhall, Finchingfield, County Library, Saffron Walden, Augustine Gallery, Holt, Guildhall Thaxted, etc. *Work in collections:* Imperial War Museum, R.A.F. Museum. *Commissions:* Portraits include: Prince Harry, Faucigny Lucinge, Vice Admiral Sir Gilbert Stephenson, Sir Vivian Fuchs, Mrs Parker Bowles, Dame Betty Paterson, C.B.E., etc. *Signs work:* "Olga Lehmann." *Address:* 1

Artisans Dwellings, Saffron Walden, Essex CB10 1LW; and 7 Windsor Mans., Luxborough St., London W1M 3LS.

**LEHRFREUND, Denise,** artist, mainly landscape, in acrylic and charcoal; *b* London, 3 May, 1944. one *s*. two *d*. *Educ:* N.W. London Grammar School. *Studied:* calligraphy: Hornsey College of Art (1960). *Exhib:* London: Loggia Gallery, Barbican Centre (1984), Bloomsbury Gallery (1989), R.A. Summer Exhbn. (1989), Bowmoore Gallery (1989), Waterman Fine Art Ltd. (1989, 1990), Llewellyn Alexander Gallery (1994), Mall Galleries; Usher Gallery, Lincoln, Lauderdale House, Highgate (1992), Boxfield Gallery, Stevenage (1994). *Clubs:* F.P.S. *Signs work:* "Denise Lehrfreund" or "DENISE." *Address:* Tregony, 71 Lower St., Norwich, Norfolk NR12 8AA.

**LEIGH, David Roy,** M.A.(Oxon.) (1972), F.S.B.A. (1986); botanical artist in water-colour; former official artist to the Orchid Com. of the R.H.S.; *b* Leeds, 2 June, 1945. *m* Vaila Mary Eastabrook. one *s*. one *d*. *Educ:* City of Leicester Boys' School, and Oxford University (Worcester College). *Exhib:* S.B.A. at Mall Galleries, R.H.S. *Publications:* illustrated Aroids (Century, 1988), author: Orchids (Cassell, 1990). *Signs work:* "David R. Leigh" or more often "D.R.L." with year. *Address:* West Hill House, Plush, Dorset DT2 7RQ.

**LEK, Karel,** R.C.A., A.T.D.; artist in oil, water-colour and graphic media; *b* Antwerp, 7 June, 1929; married; two children. *Studied:* Liverpool College of Art. *Exhib:* National Museum for Wales, R.A., R.C.A., Cardiff, Woodstock Gallery, W.1, Arts Council, Bangor Gallery, Mostyn Gallery, Llandudno, Retrospective (1994) Oriel Ynys Môn, Anglesey, Breknock Museum Brecon (1997). *Work in collections:* University Coll. of N. Wales, Contemporary Art Soc. for Wales, National Library of Wales, Anglesey C.C. Welsh Collection, Michael Forte Collection. Half hour documentary "Prime Time" H.T.V. (9 May & 9 Oct. 1994). *Address:* Studio House, Beaumaris, Anglesey LL58 8EE.

**LEMAN, Martin,** artist in oil; former graphic design teacher, Hornsey College of Art (1961-77); *b* London, 25 Apr., 1934. *m* Jill. *Educ:* Royal Masonic School. *Studied:* Worthing School of Art, and Central School of Arts and Crafts. *Exhib:* twenty exhbns. *Commissions:* many cat portraits. *Publications:* twenty-four books, mainly cat paintings. *Signs work:* "Leman." *Address:* 1 Malvern Terr., London N1 1HR.

**LENEY, Sheila,** S.B.A. (1987); floral artist in water-colour and embroidery; *b* London, 23 Nov., 1930. *m* Edward W. Leney. two *s*. one *d*. *Educ:* St. Helen's School, Streatham. *Studied:* Croydon School of Art (1947-49), Epsom A.E.C. (1982). *Exhib:* Mall Galleries; Outwood Gallery, Surrey; Linnean Soc.; Lannards Gallery, Sussex; Westminster Gallery, Knapp Gallery, London; McEwan Gallery, Scotland. Work in private collections. *Publications:* greetings cards for Medici Soc. *Signs work:* "Sheila Leney." *Address:* Invermene, 107 Newton Wood Rd., Ashtead, Surrey KT21 1NW.

**LENG-SMITH, Barbara,** Hon. Mention, Paris Salon, Silver Medal; portrait painter in oil, water-colour and pastel specialising in children; *b* Isle of Man, 7

Mar., 1922. *m* Ralph Leng-Smith. one *s.* four *d. Educ:* Sheffield. *Studied:* Manchester under Harry Rutherford. *Exhib:* one-man show: Tib Lane Gallery, Manchester; Royal Society of Portrait Painters, London; Paris Salon; R.S.A., Edinburgh. *Signs work:* "Leng-Smith." *Address:* Miramar, Arthog Rd., Hale, Altrincham, Cheshire WA15 0LS.

**LENNON, Stephen,** F.I.G.A. (1995), B.W.S. (1994), Y.M.S. (1997); artist in water-colour and mixed media; *b* Burnley, Lancs., 10 Mar., 1953. *m* Laila (née Wesenlund). one *s.* one *d. Studied:* mostly self taught, life classes in Burnley in the 1970's. *Exhib:* Laing Finalist (1989); one-man show: Bradford University (1990); mixed shows: Mercer Harrogate, Ginnel Manchester, Salford City A.G. Many private commissions. *Publications:* work repro.: B.W.S. catalogue (1997), articles in the Yorkshire Journal. *Clubs:* Yorkshire Water-colour Soc. *Signs work:* "Stephen Lennon." *Address:* 24 Ickornshaw, Cowling, nr. Keighley, W. Yorks. BD22 0DE.

**LEONARD, (Douglas) Michael,** painter and illustrator; *b* Bangalore, India, 25 June 1933. *Educ:* Stonyhurst College. *Studied:* St. Martin's School of Art (1954-57). Worked as an illustrator from 1957-72 and subsequently as a painter. *Exhib:* one-man shows: Fischer Fine Art London (1974, 1977, 1980, 1983, 1988), Harriet Griffin, New York (1977), Gemeentemuseum, Arnhem (1977-78) (retrospective), Artsite, Bath (1989) (retrospective), Stiebel Modern New York (1992), Thomas Gibson Fine Art, London (1993, 1997); mixed shows: "Realismus und Realitat" Darmstadt (1975), John Moores, Liverpool (1976, 1978), "The Craft of Art" Walker A.G. (1979), "Nudes" Angela Flowers, London (1979/80), "The Real British", Fischer Fine Art (1981), "Contemporary British Painters", Museo Municipal, Madrid (1983), "Self Portrait: A Contemporary View", Artsite, Bath (1987), "In Human Terms", Stiebel Modern, New York (1991). *Work in collections:* The Boymans Van Beuningen Museum Rotterdam, De Beer/C.S.O., N.P.G., V. & A., Fitzwilliam Museum Cambridge, Ferens A.G., Hull. *Commissions:* Painted H.M. Queen Elizabeth II for Readers Digest (1986). *Signs work:* "Leonard" or "ML." *Address:* 3 Kensington Hall Gdns., Beaumont Ave., London W14 9LS.

**LETTS, John Barry,** sculptor in clay; *b* Birmingham, 20 Aug., 1930. *m* Patricia Letts. two *s.* one *d. Educ:* Sharman Cross Senior School, Birmingham. *Studied:* Birmingham College of Art (1945-49) under William Bloye. *Exhib:* London, Birmingham, Nuneaton, Solihull, Stratford-upon-Avon, Stoke-on-Trent. *Work in collections:* Nuneaton and Stratford-upon-Avon galleries. *Commissions:* one and a half times life-size statue of George Eliot (authoress) for Nuneaton Town Centre (1985); 1994: portrait bust of H.M. The Queen, unveiled by Her Majesty 8 Dec. 1995, commissioned by Warwickshire Health Authority. *Signs work:* "John Letts." *Address:* Tilehouse, Green Lane, Knowle, Solihull, W. Midlands B93 9EJ.

**LEVEE, John,** B.A., Grand Prix, Academie Julian (1951), Biennal de Paris (1959); Ford Fellowship (1969); Grand Prix, Wodmark Foundation (1975);

painter in oil, gouache, crayon; visiting Professor of Art, University of Illinois (1965), N.Y. University (1967-68), University Southern Calif. (1970-72); *b* Los Angeles, 10 Apr., 1924. *Educ:* University Calif., New School for Social Research, N.Y. *Studied:* New School; Academie Julian, Paris (Grand Prix 1952). *Work in collections:* Kunst Museum, Basle; Smith College Museum; Museum of Modern Art, N.Y.; Stedelijk Museum, Amsterdam; Musée du Havre; Towner A.G.; Baltimore Museum; Columbus Gallery of Fine Art, etc. *Publications:* 16 Painters of Young, School of Paris, Abstract Art, Dictionary of Abstract Art, Concise History of Modern Art, L'école de Paris 1945-1965 Harumbourg. *Signs work:* "Levee." *Address:* 119 rue Notre Dame des Champs, Paris 75006.

**LEVEN, Marian,** D.A. (1966), R.S.W. (1993); artist in water-colour, gouache, acrylic; *b* Edinburgh, 25 Mar., 1944. *m* Will MacLean. two *s.* one *d.* *Educ:* Bell-Baxter, Cupar, Fife. *Studied:* Gray's School of Art, Aberdeen (1962-66). *Exhib:* R.S.A., R.S.W., R.G.I., Aberdeen Artists. *Work in collections:* Arts in Fife. *Signs work:* "Marian Leven." *Address:* Bellevue, 18 Dougall St., Tayport, Fife DD6 9JD.

**LEVENE, Ben,** A.R.A. (1975), R.A. (1986); painter (genre) in oils, water-colours; Curator, Royal Academy Schools since 1995; *b* London, 23 Dec., 1938. *m* Susan. one *s.* two *d.* *Studied:* Slade School of Fine Art (1956-61), Boise Scholarship (1961-62). *Exhib:* regularly at R.A., and Browse and Darby Gallery, London.; work in many private and public collections. *Publications:* Oils Masterclass by Sally Bulgin. *Signs work:* Usually signed on back; since 1975 with monogram "B.L." *Address:* c/o The Royal Academy, Burlington House, Piccadilly, London W1V 0DS.

**LEVI, Edgar:** see KNIGHT, Clifford.

**LEWENSTEIN, Eileen,** A.T.D., F.S.D.C., F.C.P.A.; potter (stoneware and porcelain); Chair U.K. Com., World Crafts Council; co-editor, Ceramic Review; council mem., Craft Potters Assoc.; *b* London, 1925. *m* Oscar Lewenstein (decd.). two *s. Educ:* Red Maids School, Bristol. *Studied:* West of England College of Art; University of London Institute of Education. *Exhib:* I.A.C., Istanbul (1992), Studio Ceramics (1994), V. & A. (1994-95), British Ceramics, Athens (1996), etc. *Work in collections:* V. & A., Glasgow A.G. and Museum, Museum of Decorative Arts, Prague, etc. *Publications:* New Ceramics (Studio Vista 1974). *Signs work:* "Eileen Lewenstein" and see appendix. *Address:* 11 Western Esplanade, Portslade, Brighton, E. Sussex, BN41 1WE.

**LEWIS, Ann,** Royal Cambrian Academician, B.A.; artist/illustrator in gouache, water-colour, mixed media, pencil, ink; *b* St. Asaph, N. Wales, 29 Aug., 1962. *Studied:* Exeter College of Art and Design (1985-88). *Exhib:* Royal Cambrian Academy - Conwy, W.A.C., National Library of Wales, Mostyn Gallery, Wales Open, Clwyd Open, Mercier Gallery, Albany Gallery - Cardiff, Tegfryn Gallery - Anglesey, Hanover Galleries - Liverpool, Royal Exchange Theatre - Manchester. *Publications:* books illustrated: eight children's books, one collection of poetry, numerous illustrations for published articles. *Clubs:* R.Cam.A. *Signs work:* "Ann Lewis." *Address:* 6 Well St. 2, Gerlan, Bethesda, Gwynedd, LL57 3TW. http://www.oriel-cambria.co.uk

**LEWIS, Charles Walter Edward,** A.R.C.A., F.R.B.S., A.W.G., Royal Exhibition and Continuation Scholarship (1946); sculptor in stone and wood; Head of Sculpture, Kingston College of Art (1947-78); *b* Southsea, 18 July, 1916. *m* Margaret Parkinson. two *s.* one *d. Educ:* Portsmouth Southern Secondary School. *Studied:* Portsmouth College of Art (1932-36), Royal College of Art, under Prof. Richard Garbe (1936-39). *Exhib:* retrospective, Weston Press Gallery, New York (1983). *Commissions:* sculpture commissioned by the Ministry of Public Building and Works, The G.L.C. and several private architects. *Address:* Chemin de Font Fresque, 11120 Bize Minervois, France.

**LEWIS, Dennis Reginald,** R.W.A. (1979), F.C.S.D. (1986); artist in oil, acrylic, water-colour; Design Group Chairman (retd.); *b* Bristol, 2 Apr., 1928. *m* Irene Margaret. one *s.* two *d. Educ:* F.A.S. Bristol. *Studied:* No. 3 Army College (1948, Mervyn Levy), West of England College of Art (1948-52). President, Bristol Savages (1972, 1979, 1989). *Signs work:* "Dennis Lewis." *Address:* 4 Redcliffe Parade E., Redcliffe, Bristol BS1 6SW.

**LEWIS, John,** A.K.C., B.Sc. (1950), ex F.L.S., M.F.P.S. (1974), Dip.V.A. (Lond.) (1980); phanerogamic taxonomist, poet and amateur artist in oil; International Conifer Registrar (R.H.S.); *b* Chingford, 25 Nov., 1921. *Educ:* City of London School, Kings College, London. *Studied:* Richmond Adult College and Field Studies Council. *Exhib:* F.P.S. and privately. *Publications:* numerous scientific papers and one poem. *Signs work:* uses ideogram, a rhomboid with two verticals included. *Address:* Shoothayes, Sheepway, Shepton Beauchamp, Somerset TA19 0JZ.

**LEWIS, Kit,** painter in oil; *b* Lichfield, Staffs., 27 Sept., 1911. *m* 1st, Morland Lewis, decd.; 2nd, Sir James Richards, decd., formerly editor of The Architectural Review. *Educ:* at home. *Studied:* Chelsea School of Art. *Exhib:* London and provincial galleries and in America, one-man exhbn., Leicester Galleries (1953 and 1971), Holsworthy Gallery (1982), Sally Hunter, Motcomb St. (1988). *Work in collections:* Arts Council, National Museum of Wales, Cambridge and Sussex Schools, Carlisle City A.G., Sir Roland Penrose Collection, Sir Geoffrey Jellicoe Collection. *Signs work:* "KIT LEWIS." *Address:* c/o 29 Larpent Ave., London SW15 6UU.

**LEWIS, Stephen,** B.F.A.(Hons.); sculptor in steel; *b* 11 Jan., 1959. *Educ:* Deyes High School, Maghull, Merseyside. *Studied:* Southport College of Art (1976-77), Manchester Polytechnic (1977-80), Jan van Eyck Academie, Maastricht, The Netherlands. *Exhib:* New Contemporaries, I.C.I. London (1979), Kunst Europa, Germany (1991); one-man shows: Francis Graham-Dixon Gallery (1988, 1990, 1993), Holden Gallery, Manchester (1990). *Signs work:* "Stephen Lewis." *Address:* 76 Royal Hill, Greenwich, London SE10 8RT.

**LEYDEN, John Michael,** hon. mem., S.A. Assoc. of Draughtsmen; cartoonist in black and white; artist in water-colour and etching; staff cartoonist, Daily News, since 1939; S.A. Cartoonist of the Year (1981); awarded Papal Cross, "Pro Pontifice et Ecclesia" (1986); *b* Grangemouth, Scotland, 21 Nov., 1908. *m* Annabel Eugenie Wishart. one *s*. three *d*. *Educ:* St. Aloysius College, Glasgow. *Studied:* Durban School of Art, Heatherley's, Central Schools of Arts and Crafts. *Exhib:* Natal Soc. of Artists, Durban Art Gallery (one-man shows). *Work in collections:* Africana Museum, Johannesburg, Durban A.G. and University of Natal (cartoons and caricatures). *Publications:* thirteen books of cartoons. *Clubs:* Patron, Natal Motorcyle and Car Club. *Signs work:* see appendix. *Address:* 233 Nicholson Rd., Durban, Natal, S.A.

**LEYGUE, Louis,** Président de l'Académie des Beaux-Arts (1976 and 1982); Membre de l'Institut; sculptor; Prof., head of studio, L'École Nationale Supérieure des Beaux-Arts since 1945; *b* Bourg-en-Bresse, Ain, 25 Aug., 1905. *m* Marianne Cochet, painter. two *s*. *Educ:* Lycée Charlemagne, Paris. *Studied:* L'École Nationale des Arts décoratifs, Paris, L'Ecole Nationale des Beaux-Arts, Paris, Villa Medicis, Rome. *Work in collections:* Museum of Modern Art, Paris, Phenix Université de Caen, Auditorium Maison de la Radio, Paris, French Embassy, Ottawa, Fontaine des Corolles, Paris la Défense, Palais de Justice, d'Abidjan, Piave, Nantua, "Le Soleil" Autoroute Nancy-Dijon (1983). *Signs work:* "LOUIS LEYGUE." *Address:* 6 rue de Docteur Blanche, Paris XVIe.

**LIDDELL, John,** A.T.D. (1946), D.A.E. (1974); art lecturer, printmaker in relief print, woodcut, lino, wood engraving; part-time lecturer, Bournemouth and Poole College of Art; *b* London, 6 July, 1924. *m* Jo Witchalls. two *s*. one *d*. *Educ:* Minchenden School, London N14. *Studied:* Hornsey College of Art (1941-46, Russell Reeve, Norman Janes, D.P. Bliss). *Exhib:* R.A., R.W.A., Scribes, London EC4, Dorset Galleries. *Work in collections:* Print Club, Philadelphia, U.S.A., Poole Art Centre, Dorset (mural). *Publications:* work repro.: for own press, Onzello Press. *Clubs:* N.S.E.A.D., S.W.E., Printmakers' Council, Founder, Poole Printmakers (1990). *Signs work:* "John Liddell" with date. *Address:* 90 Richmond Pk. Ave., Bournemouth BH8 9DR.

**LILLEY, Geoffrey Ivan,** U.A.; painter in oil, author and illustrator in line; seascapes, still life, animal portraits, experimental work; *b* Cambridge, 1 May, 1930. *m* Marguerite E. one *d*. *Educ:* Cambridge. *Studied:* Cambridge Technical College. *Exhib:* regularly at major London exhbns., including R.O.I., R.S.M.A., N.S., and U.A., etc., St. Ives, Cornwall, and major galleries in Sussex; one-man shows at London, Oxford, Bourton-on-the-Water. *Publications:* Artist, Art Review, Leisure Painter, etc.; author of several books and over 250 articles on art and craft subjects; over 1,000 drawings published. *Signs work:* see appendix. *Address:* Roosters at Golden Cross, Chiddingly, Lewes, Sussex BN8 6JE.

**LIM, Kim,** D.F.A.(Slade) (1960); sculptor, printmaker; *b* Singapore, 16 Feb., 1936. *m* William Turnbull. two *s*. *Studied:* St. Martin's School of Art

(1954-56), Slade School of Fine Art (1956-60). *Exhib:* Waddington Galleries (1973, 1990), M.O.M.A. (Oxford, 1975), Tate Gallery (1977), National Museum A.G., Singapore (1984) and group exhbns. worldwide. *Work in collections:* Arts Council, Nagaoka Museum of Modern Art, Japan, Tate Gallery, etc. *Signs work:* "Kim Lim" and see appendix. *Address:* c/o Waddington Galleries, 11 Cork St., London W1X 1PD.

**LIMBREY, John Nigel Stephens,** N.D.D. (1953), M.C.S.D. (1969); Freeman of the Worshipful Company of Goldsmiths, City of London; silversmith and product designer; artist in water-colour and oil; landscape, architectural and marine subjects; *b* Hatfield, 2 Feb., 1933. *Educ:* King Edward's School, B'ham. *Studied:* B'ham College of Art (1949-53). *Exhib:* R.I., R.W.S., R.S.M.A. *Signs work:* "Limbrey." *Address:* Silk Mill Cottage, Chipping Campden, Glos. GL55 6DS.

**LINDGREN, Carl Edwin,** M.Ed., Ed.S., F.C.P., Hon.D.Litt., F.R.S.A., F.R.A.S., F.Coll.P. (Essex), A.S.I.I.P.C. (New Delhi); Faulknerian landscape photographer, art historian, antiquarian; *b* 20 Nov., 1949. *m* Penni Bolton, M.I.Sc.T. (Lond.), Senior Research Technician. *Educ:* University of Mississippi, College of Preceptors (Essex). *Exhib:* Center for Faulkner Studies, Center for the Study of Southern Culture, The Cossett Gallery, Northwest College Art Gallery, The University of Mississippi, India Intl. Photographic Council (New Delhi), Manipur University Museum, etc. *Signs work:* "C.E. Lindgren." *Address:* London (occasionally) or P.O.B. 8161, University, MS 38677 U.S.A.

**LINDLEY, Brian,** artist in pastel; *b* Sheffield, 21 Jan., 1932. *m* Gabrielle. two *s.* four *d. Educ:* Salford College of Art. *Exhib:* four one-man shows; N.E.A.C., Pastel Soc. *Address:* c/o John Noott Galleries, 14 Cotswold Court, Broadway, Worcs. WR12 7AA.

**LINFIELD, John Leslie,** R.W.S. (1988), N.E.A.C. (1982), A.R.C.A. (1953); painter in oil and water-colour; *b* Carshalton Beeches, Surrey, 5 Jan., 1930. *Educ:* Sutton County School. *Studied:* Wimbledon School of Art, R.C.A. *Exhib:* R.A., R.B.A., R.P., N.E.A.C.; one-man shows, Trafford Gallery (1961, 1963), Ditchling Gallery (1964, 1965), Halifax House, Oxford (1972), Waterman Fine Art (1991), "Venice in Peril" W.H. Patterson since 1992. *Commissions:* Spink & Sons Ltd., Milton Abbey School, Dorset, Hove Museum and A.G., John Dickinson Ltd., Winsor and Newton Ltd. *Signs work:* "JOHN LINFIELD." *Address:* The Old Armoury, Court Barton, Crewkerne, Somerset TA18 7HP.

**LINTON, Robert George,** D.A., A.T.D., A.R.U.A., C.E.M.A. Travel Scholarship to Italy (1955); N.I. Arts Council Travel Grant to Holland (1968); artist in oil and sculpture; retd. Head of Art Dept., Limavady Grammar School; *b* Co. Donegal, 4 Feb., 1930. *m* Doreen Mary Shaw, B.A. *Studied:* Belfast College of Art and L.C.C. Central School of Art and Crafts. *Exhib:* four one-man exhbns. in Belfast and Londonderry; I.L.A. Dublin. Illuminated scrolls from Ballymena Borough Council to Royal Irish Rangers. *Clubs:* Royal Ulster Academy. *Signs work:* "Linton" followed by date. *Address:* 100 Glenhead Rd., Limavady, Co. Londonderry BT49 9LZ.

**LISTER, Caroline Nicola Josephine,** B.A.Hons. (1980), A.R.B.A.; painter and printmaker; printmaking tutor, Guildford College of Art (1980); Director and tutor, Tyger, Tyger Printmaking, Cambridge (Intaglio Printmaking Workshop); Steering Group mem. Cambridgeshire Regional College (1989); *b* Cambridge, 30 Mar., 1958. *Educ:* Perse School, Cambridge. *Studied:* Cambs. College of Arts and Technology (1976-77), W. Surrey College of Art and Design (1977-80). *Exhib:* R.B.A., R.E., R.I., P.S., R.W.S., S.W.A., C.D.S. *Signs work:* "Nicola Lister." *Address:* 79 St. Philips Rd., Cambridge CB1 3DA; studio: Tyger, Tyger Printmaking, Studio One, 37 City Rd., Cambridge CB1 1DP.

**LISTER, Raymond George,** P.R.M.S. (1970-80), M.A., Litt.D. (Cantab.); Governor, Federation of British Artists (1972-80); Fellow, Wolfson College, Cambridge; a syndic, Fitzwilliam Museum Cambridge (1981); painter; author; *b* Cambridge, 28 Mar., 1919. *m* Pamela Brutnell. one *s.* one *d. Educ:* Cambs. High School; St. John's College School, Cambridge. *Studied:* privately. *Publications:* Raymond Lister, by C. R. Cammell and others (1963). Edward Calvert (1962); William Blake (1968); Samuel Palmer and His Etchings (1969); The Letters of Samuel Palmer (1975); George Richmond (1981); The Paintings of Samuel Palmer (1985); Catalogue Raisonné of Samuel Palmer (1988); With my Own Wings: Memoirs (1994). *Address:* 9 Sylvester Rd., Cambridge CB3 9AF.

**LITTLEJOHN, William Hunter,** D.A., R.S.A., R.S.W., R.G.I.; painter in oil and water-colour; former Head of Fine Art Dept., Gray's School of Art, Aberdeen; retd. from teaching 1986; *b* Arbroath, Angus, Scotland, 16 Apr., 1929. *Educ:* Arbroath High School. *Studied:* Dundee College of Art. *Work in collections:* National Gallery of Modern Art, Edinburgh, Arbroath Art Gallery, Aberdeen Art Gallery, Arts Council Collection, Abbot Hall Art Gallery, Kendal, Edinburgh Civic Collection, Edinburgh Education Authority, Paisley Art Gallery, Perth Art Gallery, Towner Art Gallery, Eastbourne. *Signs work:* see appendix. *Address:* 16 Colvill Pl., Arbroath, Angus DD11 1RB, Scotland.

**LLOYD, Reginald,** R.I.; self taught artist in water-colour, oil, acrylic; *b* Hereford, 21 Dec., 1926. *m* Diana van Klaveren (decd.). four *s.* three *d. Educ:* Dawlish Boys and County Senior School. *Exhib:* 'Portrait of the Artist' Tate Gallery, etc. *Work in collections:* Tate Gallery, V. & A., National Maritime Museum, Hatton Gallery Newcastle, Burton Gallery Bideford. *Publications:* illustrated: What is the Truth by Ted Hughes, The Cat and the Cuckoo by Ted Hughes, The Mermaid's Purse by Ted Hughes. *Signs work:* "R.J. LLOYD," "R.J.L." or "R.J. Lloyd." *Address:* Iffield, North Rd., Bideford, Devon EX39 2NW.

**LOBANOV-ROSTOVSKY, Princess Roxane,** S.W.A.; water-colourist sculptor in alabaster, marble; *b* Athens, 3 Oct., 1932. two *s.* one *d. Educ:* St. George's Ascot, Pretoria Girls High School. *Studied:* Carlton University, Ottawa; Brighton Polytechnic (Norma Weller, Norman Clarke, R.W.S.). *Exhib:* numerous exhbns., one-man show: The Grange, Rottingdean (1987), etc. *Signs work:* "R. Lobanov-Rostovsky." *Address:* Swallowdale, 67 Woodruff Ave., Hove, E. Sussex BN3 6PJ.

**LOCHHEAD, Thomas,** D.A.; potter; *b* Milngavie, Glasgow, 28 Nov., 1917. *m* Anne T. Wilson. three *s.* two *d. Educ:* Dumfries Academy. *Studied:* Edinburgh College of Art under Princ. Wellington, A.R.C.A., and Alick Wolfenden, A.R.C.A. *Exhib:* S.S.A. *Work in collections:* Glasgow Art Gallery, Paisley Art Gallery. *Signs work:* "Lochhead." *Address:* Ashbank, Kirkcudbright.

**LOCKHART, David,** R.S.W. (1969), D.A. (Edin.) (1944); artist in acrylics, oil and water-colour; *b* Leven, Fife, 4 Nov., 1922. *m* Jean Lockhart. one *s.* two *d. Educ:* Beath High School, Cowdenbeath (1934-40). *Studied:* Edinburgh College of Art (1940-46). *Exhib:* Shed '50 (1974), Carnegie Dunfermline Trust Festival of Arts (1972), Douglas and Fowlis Gallery, Edinburgh (1963) with James Barclay, Byre Theatre (St. Andrews) (1996), Richmond Hill Gallery (1997), Billcliffe Gallery Glasgow (1997), 'Loomshop' Gallery. Lower Largo Fife (1988), 'Frames' Gallery Perth (1994). *Work in collections:* Scottish Committee of the Arts Council, W. Riding of Yorkshire Educ. Authority, Carnegie Dunfermline Trust, Fife County Council, Dunbartonshire Educ. Authority, Harry Cruden Coll. (Pitlochry Festival Theatre), E.I.S. award, R.S.W. (1984). *Commissions:* 19 x 12ft. mural "Many Mansions" Benarty Primary School, Fife (1963). *Signs work:* "David Lockhart" (paintings), and see appendix. *Address:* 2 Burnside North, Cupar, Fife KY15 4DG.

**LODGE, Jean,** R.E., B.A. (Miami), M.A. (Oxon.); painter/printmaker; *b* U.S.A., 1941. *Educ:* Miami University, Ohio, Oxford University. *Studied:* Beaux Arts de Paris, Atelier 17 with S.W. Hayter. *Exhib:* solo shows: Europe, Japan, India, Argentina, Venezuela, U.S.A., etc.; numerous international print shows. *Work in collections:* Museums in Europe and N. and S. America. *Address:* 52 Granville Ct., Cheney Lane, Headington, Oxford OX3 0HS.

**LOFTHOUSE, Hermione Thornton,** U.A. (1975), N.S.; painter in water-colour, oil and pastel; tutor, Moor Park College (1968-82); Master Classes for Richmond-upon-Thames Arts Council (1982, 1983), Adult Educ., Univ. of Surrey; V.P., Ridley Art Soc.; *m* F.H. Lockyer. three *s. Educ:* St. Paul's Girls' School. *Studied:* Heatherleys' (1946-50) under Iain Macnab, Académie Julian and La Grande Chaumière (1950); cert. History of Art, Courtauld Inst. *Exhib:* Paris, Germany, N.Z. Academy, Wellington Architectural Centre, Bombay Museum, W.A.G., Artists of Chelsea, R.B.A., R.O.I., etc.; eleven solo shows, Upper St. Gallery, Mall Galleries, Ice House - Holland Park, Surrey Univ. *Work in collections:* Richmond Parish Charity Lands, R.A.M., Surrey Univ., Guildford House Museum etc. *Publications:* The Art of Drawing and Painting.

*Signs work:* "H. Thornton Lofthouse." *Address:* 48 Compton Way, Farnham, Surrey GU10 1QU.

**LOGAN, Andrew,** Dip.Arch.(Oxon.); sculptor in glass; *b* Witney, 11 Oct., 1945. *Educ:* Lord Williams' Grammar School; Burford Grammar School. *Studied:* architecture: Oxford School of Architecture (1964-70). *Exhib:* numerous exhbns. including I.C.A. (1970), Whitechapel A.G., Beverly Hills, L.A., Ebury Gallery, Space Gallery, Faerie Fair, Norfolk, Crafts Council, Sandbeck Hall, Yorks., Sculpture Pk., Portland Bill, Commonwealth Inst., German Film Museum, Frankfurt, Hotel Meridian, Singapore, Botanical Gdns., Rome, Angela Flowers (Ireland) Inc., Flowers East (1991), Old Library, Cardiff (1991); first one-man show: New Art Centre, London (1973); retrospective: Museum of Modern Art, Oxford (1991), 'The Happy Heart show', Manchester City Art Galleries (1995), Moscow Art Fair (1996). *Work in collections:* Andrew Logan's Museum of Sculpture, Berriew, Powys. *Signs work:* see appendix. *Address:* The Glasshouse, Melior Pl., London SE1 3QP.

**LOIZOU, Renos,** painter in oil on canvas, oil on paper and board; *b* Cyprus, 24 Jan., 1948. *m* Susan. one *s.* two *d. Educ:* Shrubbery School, Cambridge. *Studied:* Cambridge School of Art (1963-66, Alec Heath). *Exhib:* Kettles Yard, Cambridge (1974, 1981), I.C.A. (1975), Orangerie, Cologne (1976), Peterborough Museum of Art (1982), Christopher Hull Gallery, London (1982, 1985, 1987, 1989, 1991), Fine Art Soc. (1990), Fitzwilliam Museum, Cambridge (1990); many mixed shows and overseas exhbns. *Work in collections:* Kettles Yard, Fitzwilliam College, Gonville and Caius College, Magdalene College, Cambridge, M. of E. Cyprus, Arts Council Denmark, University of Surrey, B.P. Coll., Baring Bros., W.H. Smith plc. *Publications:* book cover, Voices of Czechoslovak Socialists. *Clubs:* Chelsea Arts, National Arts N.Y. *Signs work:* "Renos Loizou." *Address:* Girton Gate, Cambridge CB3 0LH.

**LOKER, John Keith,** D.A. Graphic Design (1958), A.R.C.A. Fine Art (1963); painter in oil; *b* Leeds, 15 Sept., 1938; divorced. two *s. Studied:* Bradford Regional College of Art (1954-58), Royal College of Art (1960-63). *Exhib:* over 30 one-man exhbns. in U.K. and abroad. *Work in collections:* Tate, Arts Council, Power Inst., etc. *Commissions:* Watmough Holding, Bradford, Essex General Hospital, I.T.N. Building (Norman Foster). *Clubs:* Chelsea Arts. *Signs work:* "John Loker," occasionally "J.L." *Address:* Union Workhouse, Guilt Cross, Kenninghall, Norfolk NR16 2LJ.

**LONGBOTHAM, Charles Norman,** R.W.S.; painter in water-colour and other media, model maker (specialist in landscape models); Mem. A.W.G; *b* Carlton, Notts., 6 July, 1917. *m* Eleanor née Nairn-Allison (died 1972); one *d.* re-married Jeanie Campbell-Taylor née Goodacre, 1979. *Educ:* Portsmouth Grammar School and H.M.S. Conway, Birkenhead. *Exhib:* R.A., R.W.S. Galleries, and other London exhbns.; one-man exhbns. London and provinces. *Work in collections:* water-colours: V. & A., Fitzwilliam, Laing A.G., Norwich

Castle Museum, Merseyside Maritime Museum, Southampton City Museum, Nottingham Castle Museum, Abbot Hall A.G., Kendal; models in Imperial War Museum, Commonwealth Inst., etc. *Signs work:* see appendix. *Address:* 35 Owlstone Rd., Cambridge CB3 9JH.

**LONGUEVILLE, James,** P.S. (1983), R.B.S.A. (1989); landscape painter in oil, pastel and water-colour; lecturer and demonstrator; *b* Waverton, Chester, 22 Sept., 1942. *m* Elizabeth Mary Smith. two *s.* one *d. Educ:* Sedbergh School, Cumbria. *Exhib:* R.O.I., P.S., R.I., R.C.A., R.B.S.A., galleries in U.K., Eire, Australia, Canada. *Clubs:* R.B.S.A. *Signs work:* "James Longueville." *Address:* The Studio, Shocklach, Malpas, Cheshire SY14 7BW.

**LOPEZ-REY, Jose,** Ph.D. (Madrid, 1935); Doctor of Humane Letters (honorary, Southern Methodist University, 1979); art historian; Prof. Emeritus, New York University; Prize, Elie Faure, Paris, 1981; *b* Madrid, 14 May, 1905. *m* Justa Arroyo López-Rey. *Educ:* Universities of Madrid, Florence, and Vienna. *Publications:* Antonio del Pollaiuolo y el fin del Quattrocento; Realismo é impresionismo en las artes figurativas españolas del siglo XIX; Goya y el mundo a su alrededor; Goya's Caprichos; Beauty, Reason and Caricature; A Cycle of Cycle of Goya's Drawings: The Expression of Truth and Liberty; Velázquez: A Catalogue Raisonné of his oeuvre; Velázquez' Work and World; Velázquez: The artist as a maker. With a catalogue raisonné of his extant works (1979); Vélasquez, artiste et créateur. Avec un catalogue raisonné de son oeuvre intégral (1981); Views and Reflections on Murillo (1987). *Address:* Callejón Sierra, 3, 28120 Ciudad Sto. Domingo (Madrid), Spain.

**LOUDON, Irvine,** A.R.E. (1995), B.M.B.Ch. (1951), D.M.(Oxon.) (1973), D.R.C.O.G. (1961), F.R.C.G.P. (1976); medical practitioner, medical historian, artist in etching and drawing; *b* Cardiff, 1 Aug., 1924. *m* Jean Loudon. two *s.* three *d. Educ:* Dauntseys School, Oxford University. *Studied:* Oxford Printmakers Co-operative (1983). *Exhib:* mixed shows with Oxford Art Soc., Oxford Printmakers Co-operative; one-man shows in Oxford and London. *Publications:* Medical Care and the General Practitioner 1750-1850 (O.U.P. 1986), Death in Childbirth (O.U.P. 1992), Western Medicine: An Illustrated History (O.U.P. 1997). *Clubs:* Oxford Art Soc. *Signs work:* see appendix. *Address:* The Mill House, Locks Lane, Wantage, Oxon. OX12 9EH.

**LOVELL, Margaret,** Dip. F.A. (Slade, 1962), F.R.B.S. (1973), R.W.A. (1972); sculptor in bronze, marble, slate; *b* Bristol, 1939; married. two *s.* two *d. Studied:* West of England College of Art, Bristol, Slade School of Fine Art, Academy of Fine Art, Florence (Italian Scholarship 1962-63), Greek Government Scholarship (1965-66). *Exhib:* City Art Gall., Bristol, Arts Council of G.B., Marjorie Parr Gall., London (4 one-man shows), also one-man shows inc. Park Square Gall., Leeds, Fermoy A.G., King's Lynn, Univ. of Bath, Bruton Gall., Somerset, 1st retrospective Plymouth City A.G. (1972), Hot Bath Gallery, Bath (1995), McHardy Sculpture Co. London, Bruton St. Gallery, London (1996-97). *Signs work:* "M. Lovell." *Address:* Greenlane Farm,

Compton Dando, Bristol BS18 4JU.

**LOVETT, Eleanor Selwyn,** R.A. Dip.; painter and sculptor in terracotta; mem. Hesketh Hubbard Art Soc. *Educ:* Goldsmiths' College and R.A. Schools. *Exhib:* R.A. Summer Exhbn., Arnhem Gallery, Croydon, Carlton House Terrace. *Work in collections:* landscapes and murals, Robert Fleming (Merchant Bankers). Started horse painting in 70's. Sold some terracottas, also large horse picture. Now has agent. *Signs work:* unsigned. *Address:* 12 Elgin Rd., East Croydon.

**LOW, Bet,** A.R.S.A., R.S.W., R.G.I.; artist in oil and water-colour; *b* Gourock, Renfrewshire, 27 Dec., 1924. *Educ:* Greenock Academy. *Studied:* Glasgow School of Art. *Exhib:* regularly at Royal Scottish Academy, Water-colour Soc., Royal Glasgow Inst., Fine Art Soc., and widely in U.K. and Europe. Retrospective exhbn. 'Paintings and Drawings 1945-85', Third Eye Centre, Glasgow (1985). *Work in collections:* Scottish Arts Council, Glasgow, Aberdeen, Abbot Hall, Hunterian, Lillie, Perth, Waterford A.G.'s, Fife and Dunbarton Educ. Authorities, Glasgow and Strathclyde Universities, Cruden Collection, Britoil, Clyde Shipping Co., Clydesdale Bank, Flemings, London. *Clubs:* Glasgow Art. *Signs work:* "LOW." *Address:* 53 Kelvinside Gdns., Glasgow G20 6BQ.

**LOW, Jack,** artist in oil and water-colours, stone- and wood-carver, carpet designer; L.C.C. art instructor (1945-48); *b* Brondesbury, 17 Oct., 1903. *Studied:* City & Guilds School of Art (1941-42), and Goldsmiths' School of Art (1946-50) under Adrian Ryan. *Exhib:* R.A., R.B.A., A.I.A., Northbank Artists, Leicester Gallery, Redfern Gallery, London, Neville Gallery, Canterbury; one-man show, Theatre Club, Shaftesbury Avenue, London (1953), Civil Defence Exhbn. (1941), Hammersmith Town Hall (1959). *Work in collections:* private: England, France, Rome, Germany, America. *Commissions:* various. *Address:* Little Stour Cottage, West Stourmouth, nr. Canterbury, Kent CT3 1HS.

**LOWE, Adam,** M.F.A. (Oxon.), M.A. (R.C.A.); artist in oil, printmaking; *b* Oxford, 18 Feb., 1959. *m* Yuka. *Studied:* Ruskin School of Drawing, Oxford; R.C.A. (Peter de Francia). *Exhib:* regularly at Pomeroy Purdy Gallery, also exhbns. in England and America. Commissioned work in Japan. *Work in collections:* Contemporary Art Soc., Atkinson A.G. *Publications:* A Resurgence in Contemporary Painting (Alistair Hicks, Phaidon 1989). *Signs work:* "ADAM LOWE." *Address:* Reeds Wharf, Mill St., London SE1.

**LOWE, Ian,** M.A., Hon.R.E, (1975); Museum Curator, Ashmolean Museum (1962-87); *b* London, 18 Apr., 1935. *m* Mary Howard. one *s. Educ:* Oriel College, Oxford. Laurence Binyon prize (1958). *Publications:* author: The Etchings of Wilfred Fairclough (1990). *Address:* Spring Ford, Newton Reigny, Penrith, Cumbria CA11 0AY.

**LOXTON PEACOCK, Clarisse,** painter in oil; *b* 7 May, 1926. *m* (1st) G. Loxton Peacock; one *s.* one *d.* (2nd) Sir Anthony Grover. *Educ:* Budapest University. *Studied:* Chelsea School of Art (Dip. course); Central School of

Arts and Crafts (Post. Grad. course); St. Martin's School of Art. *Exhib:* one-man shows, Walker Gallery, London, Grosvenor Gallery, O'Hana Fine Art (two), Bodley Gallery, N.Y., Frost and Reed, Gallerie des Arts, Düsseldorf (three), Salisbury Arts Festival, Fox Gallery, London, Wylma Wane Fine Arts, Old Bond St., London (1982), Petöti Museum, Budapest (1988 - sponsored by Hungarian Government), Cadogan Contemporaries, London (1989), Makepiece Art Centre, Dorset (1989), King's Lynn Art Festival (1994), Osborne Studio Gallery (1994), University of East Anglia, John Innes Exhbn. Centre (1996). *Work in collections:* V. & A. (Directors' Room), U.S.A., Spain, Germany, England, S. Africa (Queen's Gallery), France, Japan. *Publications:* Handbook of Modern British Painting 1900-1980. *Clubs:* Arts, London. *Signs work:* "C. Loxton Peacock." *Address:* 85 Bedford Gdns., London W8 5EQ.

**LUCAS, Suzanne,** F.L.S., Médaille de la France Libre, R.H.S. Gold Medal (1975, 1976, 1977, 1978, 1979, 1980, 1982, 1983, 1984, 1985, 1986, 1987, 1988); painter and miniaturist in water-colour; President, Royal Society of Miniature Painters, Sculptors and Gravers; Founder-President, Society of Botanical Artists; Vice President, Dorset Arts and Crafts Soc; *b* Calcutta, 10 Sept., 1915. *m* Admiral Louis Lucas, C.B.E., Commandeur Legion of Honour. *Educ:* Roedean School, Edinburgh University; Munich and Grenoble Universities; Berlin School of Art with Professor Schmidt. *Exhib:* R.A., Paris Salon, R.I.; one-man shows in London: Cooling Galleries (1954), Sladmore Gallery (1973), Mall Galleries (1975, 1979), Liberty's (1977). *Publications:* author and illustrator of large art volume "In Praise of Toadstools" Vol. 1 (1992) and Vol. 2 (1997), a botanical work; author and editor of highest quality art book "The Royal Society of Miniature Painters, Sculptors and Gravers -One Hundred Years" the official celebratory volume. *Clubs:* Royal Automobile, Overseas League. *Signs work:* see appendix. *Address:* Ladymead, Manor Rd., Mere, Wilts. BA12 6HQ.

**LUCKAS, Joy Heather,** S.B.A. (1991); botanical artist in water-colour; *b* Cambridge, 1926. *m* John Richard Ainley Luckas. one *s.* two *d. Educ:* Perse Girls' School, Cambridge. *Studied:* Cambridge College of Art (1943-46, G. Stevenson, Mr. Huffer). *Work in collections:* Hunt Inst. for Botanical Documentation, Pittsburg, R.H.S. Library, London. *Publications:* illustrated: Introduction to Drawing Flowers by Margaret Stevens. *Signs work:* see appendix. *Address:* Ty'n Rhos, Llydan Rd., Rhosneigr, Anglesey, N. Wales LL64 5JE.

**LUNCH, John,** C.B.E. (1975), V.R.D. (1965), F.C.A. (1946), F.R.S.A. (1976); artist in water-colour and oil; retd. Director General, Port of London Authority; Hon. Art Adviser to R.N.L.I.; Life V.P. R.N.L.I. (1994); *b* Eastbourne, 11 Nov., 1919. *m* (1st) Joyce Barbara Clerke (decd.); two *s.* (2nd) Fiona Charis Elizabeth Fleck. *Educ:* Roborough School, Eastbourne. *Exhib:* Mall Galleries. *Work in collections:* R.N.L.I. Collection (170 Years of Lifeboat History). *Clubs:* Army and Navy. *Signs work:* "John Lunch." *Address:* Martins,

East Ashling, Chichester, W. Sussex PO18 9AX.

**LUPTON, Lewis F.,** preacher, writer, historian, painter in oil and water-colour; b London, 18 July, 1909. *Studied:* Sheffield College of Arts (1923-30). Practised commercial art in Strand advertising agency before the war. Freelance since 1940. Exhibition designer during and just after the war. Many paintings in the R.A. at this period. Then turned to the illustration of Christian literature. Numerous exhibitions of own, and wife's work held in recent years. Publisher under the Olive Tree imprint of own History of the Geneva Bible (25 vols.) and other related literature. *Address:* 2 Milnthorpe Rd., London W4 3DX.

**LYELL:** see ROBINSON, Peter Lyell.

**LYNCH, James,** Greenshield Foundation Award (1983), Pimms Prize, R.A. 1986), Spectator prizewinner (1993); b Hitchin, 12 July, 1956. m Kate Armstrong. two s. one d. *Educ:* Devizes School. *Exhib:* R.A., R.W.S., Portal, Bath Festival Art Fairs; one-man shows: Linfields, Bradford-on-Avon (1982-3), Nevill, Bath (1984), Odette Gilbert, London (1988), Maas Gallery, London 1991, 1993, 1995, 1997). *Work in collections:* Longleat House, Chatsworth House, National Trust. *Publications:* illustrated "Wind in the Willows" (Folio Soc., 1995). *Signs work:* "J. Lynch." *Address:* The Dairy House, North Cadbury, Som. BA22 7DE.

# M

**MACARA, Andrew,** R.B.A. (1983), N.E.A.C. (1984); self taught figurative painter in oil; b Ashbourne, Derbyshire, 4 Apr., 1944. m Ann. two s. *Educ:* Derby College of Technology. *Exhib:* New Academy Gallery, London, Contemporary Fine Art Gallery, Eton, Fosse Gallery, Stow-on-the-Wold. *Work in collections:* Derby Museum and A.G. *Commissions:* Palace of Westminster Paintings for Members Dining Room). *Signs work:* "Andrew Macara." *Address:* Aberfoyle, 32 Farley Rd., Derby DE23 6BX.

**MACARRÓN, Ricardo,** R.P. (1962); 1st prize National Fine Art Exhbn. 1962), Prize Direction of Fine Art (1954); artist in oil of figures, dead nature, landscapes, portraits; b Madrid, 9 Apr., 1926. m Alicia. two d. *Studied:* Fine Art School of San Fernando, Madrid (1942); scholarship to study in France by French Institute (1950). *Work in collections:* Contemporary Art Museum, Madrid, University of Oslo, National Gallery (Cape Town), Güell Foundation Barcelona), and several private collections. *Signs work:* see appendix. *Address:* Augustin de Bethencourt 5, Madrid 3, Spain.

**MacARTHUR, Ronald Malcolm,** R.S.W. (1982), D.A. Painting (1937); painter in water-colour and oil; Principal teacher of Art, Portobello High School, Edinburgh (1952-79); b Edinburgh, 1914. m Dorothy Stephenson. *Educ:* Royal High School of Edinburgh. *Studied:* Edinburgh College of Art 1933-37, William Allison, R.S.A., David Foggie, R.S.A., William MacTaggart, R.S.A.). *Exhib:* R.S.W. (1948-60 and 1976 onwards). *Work in*

WHO'S WHO IN ART

*collections:* Lothian Schools Collection, Strathclyde Schools Collection, and private collections. *Signs work:* "Ronald MacArthur, R.S.W." *Address:* Morden, 1 Duddingston Rd., Edinburgh EH15 1ND.

**MACCABE, Gladys,** H.R.O.I., M.A.(Honoris Causa), F.R.S.A., H.R.U.A., Founder and Past-Pres. Ulster Society of Women Artists; Academician with gold medal Italian Academy; Diploma of Merit, University of Arts, Parma; Hon. Academician, Royal Ulster Academy; Hon. Mem. Ulster Water-colour Soc.; Hon. Mem. Ulster Soc. of Miniaturists, Mem. Water-colour Soc. of Ireland; painter in oil and water-colour and various other media; art lecturer, writer and broadcaster; pianoforte soloist; *b* Randalstown, N. Ireland. *m* Max Maccabe. two *s. Educ:* Brookvale Collegiate School, Ulster College of Art France and Italy. *Exhib:* London, Dublin, U.S.A., Canada, Belfast, Scotland, France, etc. *Work in collections:* Irish National Self-portrait Collection, Limerick University (3 works), Imperial War Museum, Ulster Museum, Arts Council of Northern Ireland, The Queen's University, Belfast, Ulster Office, London, Longford County Library, Thomas Haverty Trust, County Dublin Educ. Authority, B.B.C., Cyril Cusack, Esq., Miss Beatrice Lillie, Lady Wakehurst, the late Adlai Stevenson, Esq., Dr. James White, Director, National Gallery of Ireland, B.B.C. (N.I.), Royal Ulster Academy, etc. *Commissions* numerous. *Publications:* Many important publications; T.V. programmes at home and abroad. *Signs work:* "GLADYS MACCABE." *Address:* 1a Church Rd., Newtownbreda, Belfast BT8 4AL.

**MACCABE, Max,** F.R.S.A., W.C.S.I., Hon. Mem. R.U.A.; Diploma of Merit, University of Arts, Parma; painter in oil and water-colour; art critic and lecturer; orchestral violinist; lecturer, Carnegie U.K. Trust, and Irish School of Landscape Painting; *b* Belfast, 16 Aug., 1917. *m* Gladys Chalmers. two *s. Educ:* Royal Belfast Academical Inst. *Exhib:* London, U.S.A., Canada, Scotland, Belfast, Dublin. *Work in collections:* The Hon. Mrs. McClintock, The Countess of Antrim, Lady Clark, The Ana M. Berry Memorial Fund, Ernest Milton, Lady Wakehurst, Ulster Museum, Swan Hunter Tyne Shipbuilders, Allied Irish Banks, Dr. James White, Director, National Gallery of Ireland, Limerick University, etc. *Commissions:* UNICEF acquired reproduction rights for 1997 Christmas card (oil painting). *Publications:* work repro.: Art News and Review, The Listener, Irish Tatler and Sketch, Sunday Independent, The Studio, International Who's Who in Art and Antiques, etc.; Radio and T.V. programmes on Art matters. *Signs work:* "MAX MACCABE." *Address:* 1a Church Rd., Newtonbreda, Belfast BT8 4AL.

**McCANN, Brian,** B.A. Sculpture (1980), M.A. (R.C.A.) (1983), Picker Fellow (1983), Rome Scholar (1984-86); sculptor in bronze, mixed media, installations; part-time lecturer in sculpture, Royal College, Chelsea College, Kingston University, Royal Academy Schools; External examiner, sculpture University of Hull; British School at Rome Assoc. Mem.; *b* Glasgow, 2 July 1955. *Studied:* Duncan of Jordanstone, Dundee (1977-80), R.C.A. (1980-83)

# WHO'S WHO IN ART

*Exhib:* Serpentine Gallery Summer Show (1983), Hilderbrandtstrasse, Dusseldorf (1982), Salo Uno, Rome (1988), Tate Gallery, Liverpool (1989), William Jackson Gallery, London (1992), Coexistence Gallery, London (1992), Museum of St. John, London (1995). *Work in collections:* Arts Council, Government Collection. *Publications:* 'Sojourn' poetry (1980), 'Plumage of Recognition' catalogue (1991). *Signs work:* "Brian McCann." *Address:* 11 Chandlers House, 38 London Rd., Kingston, Surrey KT2 6QF.

**McCARTER, Keith,** D.A.(Edin.) (1960), F.S.I.A. (1968), F.R.S.A. (1969), A.R.B.S. (1991); sculptor in bronze, stainless steel, concrete; *b* Edinburgh, 15 Mar., 1936. *m* Brenda Schofield. one *s.* one *d. Educ:* Royal High School, Edinburgh. *Studied:* Edinburgh College of Art (1956-60, Eric Schilsky, Helen Turner). *Exhib:* R.A., Monaco, Burleighfield Gallery, Alwin Gallery, Berkeley Sq. Gallery. *Work in collections:* Numerous countries worldwide. *Commissions:* many public sited sculptures in U.K., U.S.A., Europe, Africa; Moody Gardens, Galveston, U.S.A., with Sir Geoffrey Jellicoe. *Clubs:* Farmers, London. *Signs work:* "McCarter"; small works, see appendix. *Address:* Ottermead, Church Rd., Gt. Plumstead, Norfolk NR13 5AB.

**McCLOY, William Ashby,** Henry B. Plant Emeritus Prof., Connecticut College; painter, sculptor, printmaker; *b* Baltimore, Md., 2 Jan., 1913. *m* Patrica C. *Educ:* Phillips Academy, Andover, Mass., University of Iowa. *Studied:* University of Iowa. *Exhib:* N.A., Whitney Museum of American Art, Pennsylvania Academy of Fine Arts, Chicago Art Inst., Carnegie Inst., Walker Art Centre, Kansas City Art Inst., Cincinnati Art Museum, Joslyn Mem. Art Museum, Library of Congress, Milwaukee Art Inst. *Signs work:* "WILLIAM A. McCLOY." *Address:* 376 Kitemaug Rd., Uncasville, Connecticut.

**McCLURE, David,** D.A. (Edin.), R.S.A. (1971), A.R.S.A. (1963), R.S.W. (1965); painter in oils and water-colours; teacher of painting, College of Art, Dundee (1957-85); *b* Lochwinnoch, Scotland, 20 Feb., 1926. *m* Joyce Dixon Flanigan. two *s.* one *d. Educ:* Queen's Park School, Glasgow, Edinburgh Univ. *Studied:* Edinburgh College of Art (1947-52), Travelling Scholarship (1952-53), Fellow of Edinburgh College of Art (1955-57). *Work in collections:* Arts Council (Scotland), Dundee Art Gallery, Glasgow Art Gallery, Aberdeen Art Gallery, Scottish National Gallery of Modern Art, Towner Art Gallery, Eastbourne, Edinburgh and St. Andrew's University Staff Clubs, Queen's College, Dundee. *Signs work:* "D. McClure" or "McClure." *Address:* 16 Strawberry Bank, Dundee.

**McCOMB, Leonard William,** R.A., R.E. (1993), Slade Dip. (1960); artist-painter, sculptor, printmaker; visiting teacher: R.A. Schools; *b* Glasgow, 3 Aug., 1930. *m* Barbara Elenora. *Studied:* Manchester School of Art (Harry Sutcliffe), Slade School (Sir William Coldstream, Prof. A.H. Gerrard). Removed Golden Man sculpture _ Lincoln Cathedral Travelling Exhbn. *Work in collections:* Tate Gallery, Arts Council Collection, V. & A., B.M., Towner A.G., Belfast A.G., B'ham, Manchester, Sheffield, Swindon and Worcester city galleries. *Commissions:* commemorative plaque bronze gold leaf Brookes University, Oxford (1993); tapestry 'Fishes and Invertebrates in the Sea' Boots plc (1994). *Publications:* Arts Council Catalogue (1983), Painting from the South Catalogue (1989), Catalogue Drawings and Paintings, Browse and Darby Gallery (1993), Gillian Jason Gallery; Video Film Arts Council 'Flow of Life (1983). *Signs work:* "McCOMB" and "L.M" within circle and date. *Address:* 6 St. Saviours Rd., Brixton Hill, London SW2 5HD.

**McCOMBS, John,** N.D.D., R.O.I., A.R.B.A., F.R.S.A.; landscape artist ir oil; *b* Manchester, 28 Dec., 1943. *Educ:* Manchester High School of Art *Studied:* St. Martin's School of Art (1962-67) under F. Gore, Reynolds Kossoff. *Exhib:* R.A., Mall Galleries, Manchester City A.G., Saddleworth Museum, John McCombs Gallery. R.A. Scholarship and 'College prize' St Martin's (1966); Stanley Grimm prize R.O.I. (1990); 'People's prize' Manchester Academy (1991). *Work in collections:* Manchester, Salford, Oldham A.G.'s, Saddleworth Museum. *Clubs:* R.O.I., R.B.A., M.A.F.A. *Signs work:* "J. McCombs," sometimes "J.Mc." *Address:* 12 King St., Delph, Oldham OL3 5DQ.

**McCRUM, Bridget,** sculptor in stone, bronze-abstracted figurative; *b* Yorks., 27 Apr., 1934. *m* Robert McCrum. three *d. Studied:* painting at Farnham (1951-55, Musjynski; 1980-82 stone carving Joekes). *Exhib:* solo shows: Vanessa Deneveux, Phoenix, Plymouth School of Architecture, Dartington Hall Gdns., Wattis Fine Art, Hong Kong; mixed shows: R.A., R.S.A., R.W.A., Roche Court, Deans Court. *Work in collections:* Frink, Golden Door Foundation, National Trust. *Signs work:* "Bridget McCrum" or "McC." *Address:* Hamblyns Coombe, Dittisham, Dartmouth, Devon TQ6 0HE.

**McCULLOCH, Ian,** D.A. (1957), S.S.A. (1964), A.R.S.A. (1989); painter in acrylic on canvas, and printmaker; Fine Art Fellow, University of Strathclyde (1994-); *b* Glasgow, 4 Mar., 1935. *m* Margery Palmer. two *s. Educ:* Glasgow School of Art (1953-57). 1st prize Stirling Smith Biennial (1985), painted murals for Italian Centre, Glasgow (1989), winner Glasgow Concert Hall murals competition (1990). *Exhib:* recent one-man exhbns.: Peacock Printmakers, Aberdeen (1995), Aberdeen A.G. (1992), Aberystwyth Arts Centre, Wales (1991), Glasgow Print Studio (1989), Odette Gilbert Gallery, London (1987), Camden Arts Centre London and Richard Demarco Gallery Edinburgh (1986); many group exhbns. including New North, Tate Gallery Liverpool (1990), John Moores, Liverpool (1989). *Work in collections:* Saatchi Collection, Contemporary Arts Soc., S.A.C., Glasgow A.G., Dundee A.G. Edinburgh City A.G., Universities of Glasgow and Liverpool. *Signs work:* "Ian McCulloch." *Address:* 51 Victoria Rd., Lenzie, Glasgow G66 5AP.

**McCULLOUGH, George,** M.S.Exc., hons. M. of E. dipl.; artist in oil water-colour, gouache, pastel; Founder and Tutor, Donegal School of Landscape Painting, Dunfanaghy, Co. Donegal, Rep. of Ireland; *b* Belfast, 2 Oct., 1922; married. two *d. Educ:* Belfast College of Technology and Belfast

College of Art (1940-47). *Studied:* as above. *Exhib:* R.U.A., United Nations, N.Y., Oriel Gallery, Dublin, Cambridge Gallery, Dublin, Eaton Gallery, Toronto, Flowerfield Art Centre, Portstewart, Yonge Gallery, Chicago, Bell Gallery, Belfast. *Signs work:* see appendix. *Address:* 20 Joanmount Drive, Carrs Glen, Belfast BT14 6PB.

**MacDONALD, Alastair James Henderson,** R.M.S., A.S.M.A. (Vic.), F.R.S.A., H.U.A.; Gold Bowl Hon. Men. (1991, 1992, 1993); Llewellyn Alexander Masters Award (1995); miniature painter; elected Hon. Treas. R.M.S. (1981); *b* Tighnabruaich, Argyll, 5 July, 1934. *m* Juliet Anne Mead. two . three *d. Educ:* Pope Street School, New Eltham. *Studied:* Woolwich Polytechnic School of Art and Crafts. *Exhib:* R.M.S., U.A., A.S.M.A. (Vic.), NSW., QLD., TAS. *Signs work:* see appendix. *Address:* 63 Somers Rd., North Mymms, Herts.

**MACDONALD, Frances,** A.R.C.A., (1938); artist in oil, water-colour, pencil and ink, lithography; *b* Wallasey, Ches., 12 Apr., 1914. *m* Leonard Appelbee, A.R.C.A. one *d. Educ:* Wallasey High School. *Studied:* Wallasey School of Art (Gordon Macpherson), R.C.A. (Barnett Freedman). *Exhib:* Wildenstein, Brod Gallery. *Work in collections:* Tate Gallery, National Gallery of: Wales, Melbourne and Adelaide, Australia; Newport, Arts Council, Imperial War Museum, War Artist work and Pilgrim Trust drawings in V. & A. and provincial galleries, and work in many private collections. At present, painting landscape, portrait, etc. *Commissions:* Courtalds, Curwen Press, Baynard Press, and other private people. *Signs work:* "Frances Macdonald." *Address:* Rosemount, Toll Rd., Kincardine-on-Forth, Fife FK10 4QZ.

**McDOWELL, Leo,** B.A.Hons., C.Ed., R.I.; Winsor and Newton R.I. award Mall Galleries (1990); self-taught artist in water and acrylic colour; Council Mem. R.I.; *b* 19 Jan., 1937. *Educ:* Keighley Grammar School; Manchester University; Innsbruck University; Cambridge University. *Studied:* Modern Languages, History of Art. *Exhib:* Shell House Gallery, Ledbury, Blackstone Gallery, Pinner, Albemarle Gallery, London, The British Gallery, Los Gatos, Calif., La Difference Gallery, Dinslaken, Germany, Lisette Alibert Gallery, Paris. *Work in collections:* H.R.H. The Prince of Wales, Hertfordshire C.C., Reuters. *Signs work:* "Leo McDowell." *Address:* Craigleith, Hanbury La., Essendon, Hatfield, Herts. AL9 6AY.

**McENTAGART, Brett,** B.A. (1961), M.F.A. (1963), R.H.A. (1980), W.C.S.I. (1974); artist in oil, water-colour, etching, pastel; Head of Printmaking, National College of Art and Design, Dublin; Board Mem. National Gallery of Ireland; Council Mem. Royal Hibernian Academy; *b* Dublin, 27 May, 1939. *m* Miriam O'Hara. two *s.* one *d. Educ:* St. Columba's College, Rathfarnham, Dublin. *Studied:* Dartmouth College, N.H., U.S.A., University of Colorado, U.S.A., Salzburg Academy, Austria. *Exhib:* R.H.A., W.C.S.I., R.W.A., R.U.A.; one-man shows Dublin. *Work in collections:* Board of Works Dublin, H.E.A. Dublin, W.C.S.I. Collection, Limerick, National Self

Portrait Collection, Limerick. *Publications:* covers for: 'Blooms' - Joyce anthology, 'At Europe's La Terrasse' by Gerard Duffy. St. Columba's College, Rathfarnham, Dublin; *Signs work:* "B.McE." *Address:* 5 Sandycove Ave. West, Sandycove, Co. Dublin, Ireland.

**McEWAN REID, Marjorie,** M.A. (1942), B.A. (Oxon.) Hons. Zoology (1939), Dip.Ed. (1940), S.W.A. (1994); winner, Seifas Cup (1991); artist in oil; immunologist in medical research (retd.); *b* Uckfield, Sussex, 1917. *m* Robert. one *s*. one *d*. *Educ:* Talbot Heath, Bournemouth; Somerville College, Oxford *Studied:* Bletchingley A.E.I. (1977-80, Arthur Easton, R.O.I., N.S.), Elmers End Art Centre (1992-97) and at Edinburgh College of Art (1994, George Donald); also privately (1980-86) with the late Edmond Perini and (1987-97) with Richard Walker, S.G.F.A., U.A. *Exhib:* S.W.A.; many mixed shows; three two-man shows with husband. *Clubs:* The Croydon, Tandridge and Old Coulsdon Art Socs. *Signs work:* see appendix. *Address:* 21 Byron Ave. Coulsdon, Surrey CR5 2JS.

**McEWEN, Elizabeth Alexandra,** N.D.D. (1960), A.T.D. (1961), U.S.W.A (1980), U.W.S., R.U.A. (1990), S.B.A. (1987); R.U.A. Gold medallist (1991); painter in water-colour, gouache and acrylic; *b* Belfast, 13 Dec., 1937. *Educ:* Belfast Royal Academy. *Studied:* Belfast College of Art (1956-60), Reading University (1960-61). *Exhib:* many mixed and solo shows throughout N. Ireland, S.B.A. London, Laing London. *Work in collections:* Royal Ulster Academy, National Self Portrait Collection, Limerick University. *Signs work:* "E.A. McEwen." *Address:* 43 King's Drive, Belfast, N.Ireland BT5 6PS.

**MACEY, Julian Bernard,** R.M.S. (1995); retired Divisional Youth and Commuinty Officer; self taught artist in oils, water-colour, pastel, pencil; *b* Minehead, Som; 13 Apr., 1920; widower. one *s*. *Educ:* Duke of York's Royal Military School, Dover. *Work in collections:* Gt. Yarmouth and District Soc. of Artists. *Address:* 119 Beccles Rd., Bradwell, Gt. Yarmouth, Norfolk NR31 8AB.

**MACEY, Leo,** C.B.E. (1979), H.S. (1988); picture restorer, painter of miniatures in oil on ivorine and board; Director, Penn Prints Ltd.; *b* Minehead, 23 Feb., 1922. *m* Isabella. two *s*. one *d*. *Educ:* English Military School, Cairo. *Studied:* Frobisher School of Painting (1964-66, Lucy Frobisher). *Exhib:* R.W.A., H.S., Armed Forces Art Soc. *Work in collections:* Sultan of Negri Sembilan, Malaysia; Officers Mess R.M.P.; and others. *Clubs:* Professional/Businessmen, Warminster. *Signs work:* see appendix. *Address:* 56 Upper Marsh Rd., Warminster, Wilts. BA12 9PN.

**McFADYEN, Jock,** B.A., M.A.; artist in oil on canvas, plaster, wax and bronze; *b* Paisley, 1950. *m* (1) Carol (divorced); one s. ; (2) Susie. one *s*. one *d*. *Educ:* Renfrew High School. *Studied:* Chelsea School of Art (1973-77, Anne Rees Mogg, Ron Bowen, Ian Stephenson). *Exhib:* 27 one-man shows including Blond Fine Art, Scottish Gallery, Imperial War Museum, William Jackson Gallery, Camden Arts Centre. *Work in collections:* 28 public collections including British Council, Imperial War Museum, Kunsthalle, Hamburg, National Gallery, V. & A. *Commissions:* Designed sets and costumes for Sir Kenneth McMillan's last ballet 'The Judas Tree', Royal Ballet, Royal Opera House, Covent Gdn. (1992). *Clubs:* Vintage Japanese Motorcycle. *Address:* 284 Globe Rd., Bethnal Green, London E2 0NS.

**McFALL, David,** R.A.; sculptor in stone and bronze; *b* Glasgow, 1919. *m* Alexandra Dane, actress. one *s.* one *d. Educ:* English Martyrs, Spark Hill. *Studied:* Birmingham, R.C.A. and Lambeth. *Work in collections:* Bullcalf (Tate), Churchill (Burlington House), Balfour (House of Commons), Vaughan Williams (Royal Festival Hall), Lord Attlee (Imperial War Museum), bronze study of Prince Charles (Buckingham Palace), Oedipus and Jocasta (W. Norwood Library), Pocahontas, Sir Godfrey Allen (bust) in crypt of St. Paul's Cathedral, 'Son of Man', Canterbury Cathedral. *Signs work:* see appendix. *Address:* 10 Fulham Park Gdns., London SW6 4JX.

**MacFARLANE, Sheila Margaret,** D.A. (Edin.) 1964; artist, printmaker and engraver; lecturer in printmaking, Duncan of Jordanstone College of Art, Dundee (1970-76); founder and director, Printmakers Workshop at Kirkton of Craig (1976-90); *b* Aberdeen, 2 May, 1943; divorced. one *d. Work in collections:* national and private collections in U.K. and private collections Overseas. Presently working with children with special needs and as a freelance artist. *Signs work:* "Sheila M. MacFarlane." *Address:* 1 Tangleha', St. Cyrus, Kincardineshire.

**McGOWAN, Hilary,** M.A., F.M.A., M.B.I.M.; Museums and Heritage Director, Museums and Art Gallery, Bristol; *Address:* City of Bristol Museum and Art Gallery, Queen's Rd., Bristol BS8 1RL.

**MacGREGOR, David Roy,** M.A. (Cantab). 1948, F.S.A., F.R.Hist.S.; architect, ship draughtsman, author, artist in oil, water-colour and pen; *b* Fulham, 1925. *m* Patricia M.A.P. Gilpin. *Educ:* Eton and Trinity College, Cambridge. *Studied:* under Julius Olsson, R.A., R.O.I. and Cdr. G. F. Bradshaw, R.S.M.A. *Exhib:* R.O.I., N.E.A.C., R.B.A., R.S.M.A.; one-man shows: Woodstock Gallery, London (1974), Digby Gallery, Mercury Theatre, Colchester (1976), Old Butchers Bookshop, Cley (1994). *Publications:* illustrations to his own books. *Signs work:* "D. R. MacGregor." *Address:* 12 Upper Oldfield Park, Bath BA2 3JZ.

**MacGREGOR, Robert Neil,** M.A., Ll.B.; Director, The National Gallery; *b* 16 June, 1946. *Educ:* New College, Oxford, University of Edinburgh, Courtauld Institute of Art. *Signs work:* "Neil MacGregor." *Address:* National Gallery, Trafalgar Sq., London WC2N 5DN.

**McGUINNESS, Michael,** R.W.S. (1993); painter in water-colour and oil; Senior typographic and book designer with Readers Digest and, subsequently, Art Editor of The Independent and The Independent on Sunday (1986-91); *b* Essex, 20 Mar., 1935. *Studied:* S.E. Essex Technical College (illustration and typography, Harry Eccleston, O.B.E.), Royal Academy Schools (painting,

Fleetwood Walker, R.A.), Walthamstow School of Art (Stuart Ray). *Publications:* The Encyclopaedia of Water-colour Techniques (two paintings), Einstein for Beginners (illustration), Jung for Beginners (illustration). *Clubs:* Wynken de Worde Soc. *Signs work:* "McG." *Address:* 4 Denmark Rd., London W13 8RG.

**McINTOSH, Iain,** A.R.S.A.; sculptor; *b* Peterhead, 4 Jan., 1945. *m* Freida. two *d. Educ:* Peterhead Academy. *Studied:* Gray's School of Art (1962-67). *Signs work:* "I.M." plus year. *Address:* 53 Kilry-mont Rd., St. Andrews, Fife, Scotland KY16 8DQ.

**McINTYRE, Donald,** R.I., R.C.A.; landscape painter in acrylic, oil and water-colour; *b* Yorkshire, 1923. *m* Lauren Lindee. . *Educ:* Scarborough College, Skipton Grammar School. *Studied:* studio of James Wright, R.S.W. *Work in collections:* H.R.H. Duke of Edinburgh, National Library of Wales, Welsh Arts Council, Robert Fleming Holdings plc, Birkenhead A.G., Newport (Gwent) A.G., Merthyr Tydfil Gallery, Welsh Contemporary Art Soc. *Signs work:* see appendix. *Address:* 3 Waen-y-Pandy, Tregarth, Bangor, Gwynedd LL57 4RB.

**MACKAY, Arthur Stewart,** R.O.I. (1949); artist in oil; former lecturer, Hammersmith College of Art and Building; *b* Dulwich, London, 25 Feb., 1909. *Educ:* Wilson's Grammar School, Camberwell, Regent St. Polytechnic School of Art. *Studied:* Regent St. Polytechnic School of Art. *Exhib:* R.A., R.S.A., Paris Salon and London galleries. *Work in collections:* Imperial War Museum (2 paintings), and many private collections in Britain and Australia. *Publications:* articles on figure painting and outdoor sketching written for the publication, Artist. *Signs work:* "A STEWART MACKAY" or "STEWART MACKAY." *Address:* 4 Dog Kennel Hill, East Dulwich, London SE22 8AA.

**MACKAY CLARK, Deirdre,** N.D.D.; painter in gouache, oil, mixed media; tutor; *b* Ilford, 18 Sept., 1937. *m* John Clark. three *s.* one *d. Educ:* Copthall Grammar. *Studied:* Hornsey College of Art (1954-59, Alfred Daniels, Colin Sorensen). *Exhib:* Minories, Colchester, R.A. Summer Exhbns., R.W.S., Chris Beetles, R.I., M.O.M.A. (Wales). Work in private and business collections. Designed/painted ceramics. (1977-82). *Publications:* Artists Cards (1984), R.A. Pubs. (1985), card and print; Pimms Prize for Drawing R.A. (1985), book jackets (1988), range of Fine Art cards and prints (1989-90). Family ran BOURLETS -1965 *Signs work:* "D.M." or "Deirdre Mackay." *Address:* Brierley Cottage, Brierley, Leominster, Herefordshire HR6 0NT.

**McKEAN, Lorne (Miss),** F.R.B.S.; sculptor; silver medal for sculpture combined with architecture; Feodora Gleichen and Leverhulme Scholarships; *m* Edwin Russell, F.R.B.S. *Exhib:* four one-man shows, London W1. Portrait sculptures include: the late Marquess of Salisbury, Hatfield House; H.R.H. Prince Philip on polo pony 'Portano', H.M. The Queen's personal Silver Wedding gift to her husband; the late Prince William of Gloucester, Kensington Palace; Earl of Lichfield for BBC programme 'Portrait'; Prince Charles on

'Pans Folly'. Public works: A.A. Milne public memorial of bear cub at London Zoo; Shearwaters, Shearwater House, Richmond Green; Girl and Swan 17 ft. bronze in Reading; 'Galoubet' French show jumping stallion; H.M. The Queen, Drapers Hall. *Signs work:* "Lorne McKean." *Address:* Lethendry, Polecat Valley, Hindhead, Surrey GU26 6BE.

**McKELLAR, Robert,** painter in oil and acrylic specialising in abstract and still life; *b* Gravesend, 2 July, 1945. *Educ:* Gravesend Technical School. *Studied:* Medway College of Art, Camberwell School of Art. *Exhib:* R.A., Hong Kong, London, Singapore, Los Angeles. Works with Northcote Gallery, 110 Northcote Rd., London SW11. *Commissions:* British Consulate. *Signs work:* "R. McKellar." *Address:* The Stable, Staplehurst, Kent TN12 0RW.

**McKENNA, Laurence,** artist in oil, water-colour, pastel and pencil; *b* 20 Nov., 1927. *m* Carmel Beattie. two *s.* one *d. Educ:* St. Kevin's, Belfast. *Studied:* self-taught. *Exhib:* Belfast, Dublin, Cork, London, U.S.A. *Publications:* work repro.: Revue Moderne, Paris (drawing, 1947), Sunday Independent, Dublin (drawing, 1956), Irish News (drawing, 1958), Ulster Illustrated (drawing, 1958), Sunday Independent (drawing, 1965). *Signs work:* "LAURENCE McKENNA." *Address:* 23 Grangeville Gdns., Belfast BT10 0HJ.

**MACKENZIE, Phyllis Edith,** Slade Dip.; artist in oil, pastel, water-colour, pen and wash, sanguine, pencil, gouache; *b* 3 Aug., 1911. *m* K. E. Mackenzie, C.M.G. one *s. Educ:* Cheltenham Ladies' College, Slade School of Art, London, and in Brussels. *Exhib:* R.A., R.P., N.E.A.C., S.W.A., P.S., etc.; one-man shows: Beaux Arts, Brussels; Iran; Egypt; Singapore; Stockholm; Margery Parr, Chelsea; Bury St. Edmunds; Cheltenham; Berthe Hess Museum, London; Century Gallery, Henley-on-Thames; Century Gallery, Datchet. *Clubs:* East India *Signs work:* "Phyllis Mackenzie." *Address:* 11 St. James Cl., Pangbourne, Berks. RG8 7AP.

**McKENZIE, Winifred,** D.A. (Glas.); for fourteen years lecturer in Duncan of Jordanstone College of Art, Dundee; artist in oil; wood-engraver; *b* Bombay, 23 Aug., 1905. *Educ:* Prior's Field. *Studied:* Glasgow School of Art and Grosvenor School of Modern Art under Iain MacNab. *Exhib:* R.S.A., S.S.W.A., etc.; retrospective exhbn. (50 years) English Speaking Union Gallery, Edinburgh (1984). *Work in collections:* Liverpool, Perth, Cork, Modern Arts Assoc. *Publications:* in Studio, Image and A History of British Wood-engraving; The McKenzie Sisters (a biography by A. Clark) *Signs work:* "Winifred McKenzie." *Address:* 3b Playfair Terr., St. Andrews, Fife KY16 9HX.

**McKENZIE SMITH, Ian ,** O.B.E., D.A., R.S.A., P.R.S.W., LL.D. (Aberdeen University, 1991), F.R.S.A., F.S.S., F.M.A., F.S.A. Scot; artist in oil and water-colour; *b* Montrose, 3 Aug., 1935. *m* Mary Rodger Fotheringham. two *s.* one *d. Educ:* Robert Gordon's College, Aberdeen. *Studied:* Gray's School of Art (1953-59) under Ian Fleming and R. Henderson Blyth; Hospitalfield College of Art, Arbroath (1958 and 1959). *Exhib:* Royal Scottish Academy, Fine Art Soc., Royal Glasgow Inst. *Work in collections:* Scottish National

Gallery of Modern Art, Scottish Arts Council, Abbot Hall Gallery, Kendal, Aberdeen A.G., Glasgow A.G., City Arts Centre, Edinburgh, Perth A.G., Royal Scottish Academy, Arts Council of Northern Ireland, Contemporary Art Soc., IBM, Robert Fleming Holdings. *Clubs:* Royal Northern *Signs work:* normally unsigned, labelled on reverse. *Address:* 70 Hamilton Pl., Aberdeen AB15 5BA.

**MACKEOWN, James Martin,** B.A. (Open Univ.); painter in oil, acrylic, water-colour and pastel; *b* London, 3 Nov., 1961. *m* Marie Lestang. two *s.* two *d. Educ:* Gresham's School, Norfolk. *Studied:* self taught, first one-man show (1997). *Exhib:* numerous, in London, Paris, Rouen, and Belfast. Works permanently on show at: Galerie Rollin, Rouen; Galerie Alfa, Le Havre; Galerie Colette Dubois, Paris; West Wales Art Centre,; Fishguard, Bank Street Gallery, Sevenoaks; Bell Gallery, Belfast. *Signs work:* "James Mackeown." *Address:* Clos Saint-Pierre. Vattetot s/Mer, 76111 Yport, France.

**MacKEOWN, Martin,** D.A. (Edin.) (1952); painter in oil; *b* Belfast, 14 May, 1931. *m* Ann Carr. four *s.* two *d. Educ:* Campbell College, Belfast. *Studied:* Belfast College of Art (1948-49), Edinburgh College of Art (1949-52, W.G. Gillies, W.MacTaggart, Leonard Rosoman, R. Philipson). *Exhib:* numerous. *Work in collections:* National Self-Portrait Collection of Ireland, Clare College Cambridge, Arts Council (N. Ireland), Ulster Television. *Publications:* illustrated several, including ten of his wife's cookery books, e.g. 'Ann Carr's Recipe Collection' (1987). *Signs work:* "M. MacKeown." *Address:* Manor House, Itteringham, Norfolk NR11 7AF.

**McLAREN, Sally,** French Government Scholarship; painter and printmaker; taught at Goldsmiths' School of Art; *b* London, 1936. *Studied:* Central School, London, Atelier 17, Paris. *Exhib:* R.A., R.E., one-man show, Bear Lane, Oxford, Studio Prints, London; widely in group shows internationally; Llubjana Print Biennale, Seoul Biennale; North-west Printmakers U.S.A.; Cabo Frio Biennial, Brazil; R.E.; Edinburgh Festival; Atelier 17 Group Show, Paris, La Jeune Gravure Contemporaire, Paris, etc. Work in many important international collections. *Clubs:* Printmakers' Council, Royal Soc. of Painter Printmakers. *Signs work:* "Sally McLaren" or "McLaren." *Address:* Clouds Cottage, E. Knoyle, Wilts. SP3 6BE.

**McLEAN, John,** self-taught painter in acrylic; *b* Liverpool, 10 Jan., 1939. *m* Janet. *Educ:* Reform Street School, Kirriemuir, and Arbroath High School. *Exhib:* over twenty one-man shows worldwide. *Work in collections:* Tate Gallery, Scottish National Museum of Modern Art, Hunterian Collection, Glasgow University, Swindon, Southampton, Glasgow, and Basildon A.G's. *Signs work:* "John McLean" or "J.M." *Address:* c/o Francis Graham Dixon Gallery, 17-18 Gt. Sutton St., London EC1V 0DN.

**McLEAN, Mary,** R.M.S. (1994), H.S. (1990); miniature painter in water-colour; *b* Farnborough, Kent, 1944. *m* John S. McLean. two *s.* one *d. Educ:* Marion Vian School, Beckenham. *Studied:* privately with Ronald Jesty, A.R.B.A. *Exhib:* R.A., R.M.S., Llewellyn Alexander (Fine Arts), The Market

Cross Gallery, Sturminster Newton, Dorset, Japan and U.S.A., Lannards Gallery, Billingshurst, Sussex, Hilliard Soc.; Work in private collections. *Publications:* front cover illustration for specialist poultry magazine, Artist and Leisure Painter magazines, Royal Miniature Society, 100 years book. *Signs work:* "Mary McLean." *Address:* 24 Plover Rd., Milborne Port, Sherborne, Dorset DT9 5DA.

**MACLEAN, W.J.,** D.A., R.S.A.; Professor, fine art, Dundee College, Univ. of Dundee; *b* Inverness, 12 Oct., 1941. *m* Marian Leven. two *s*. one *d*. *Educ:* Inverness Royal Academy, H.M.S. Conway, N. Wales. *Studied:* Grays School of Art, Aberdeen (1961-66); British School at Rome (1966). *Exhib:* one-man shows: Edinburgh, New 57 Gallery, Richard Demarco Gallery, R.H.W. London; group shows: Scottish Arts Council, Art First, London, 3rd Eye Gallery. *Work in collections:* Aberdeen A.G., Scottish Arts Council, Contemporary Art Society, Scottish National Gallery of Modern Art, Hull A.G., Fitzwilliam Museum, Cambridge, B.M. *Signs work:* "W. J. Maclean." *Address:* 18 Dougall St., Tayport, Fife DD6 9JD, Scotland.

**MacLENNAN, Alastair MacKay,** M.F.A. (1968), D.A. (1965); intermedia artist in mixed media installations, actuations, time-based work, conceptual orientation; Prof. of Fine Art, University of Ulster (1992-); *b* Blairatholl, Scotland, 3 Feb., 1943. *Educ:* Perth Academy, Scotland. *Studied:* School of the Art Institute of Chicago, U.S.A. (1966-68), Duncan of Jordanstone College of Art, Dundee, Scotland (1960-65). *Exhib:* national and international festivals of performative and time-based work throughout America, Canada, Britain, E. and W. Europe. *Work in collections:* British Arts Council; private collections in Britain, America, Canada, Germany, Switzerland and Poland. *Commissions:* Representing Ireland at the Venice Biennale (1997), with 'Body of (D) Earth'. *Publications:* reviews and interviews in art publications and periodicals. *Address:* c/o University of Ulster, Faculty of Art and Design, York St., Belfast BT15 1ED, N. Ireland.

**MACLEOD, Duncan,** D.A. (1974), R.S.W. (1980); artist in mixed media, water-colour, school teacher; S.A.C. Lecturers Panel; *b* Glasgow, 5 Apr., 1952. *m* Maretta Macleod, artist (divorced). one *s*. one *d*. *Educ:* Clydebank High School. *Studied:* Glasgow School of Art (1970-74, David Donaldson). *Exhib:* R.S.A., R.S.W., R.G.I., and many mixed and one-man shows in Britain. *Work in collections:* U.K., U.S.A., France, Sweden, and the Far East. *Signs work:* "Duncan Macleod." *Address:* 25 Taylor St., Clydebank, Glasgow.

**MACLEOD, Flora,** B.W.S. (1951-56), S.S.W.A. (1955-67), S.W.A. (1960-78); *b* Forres, 24 Mar., 1907. *Educ:* privately. *Exhib:* R.B.A. (Open Assembly), R.I., R.S.W., S.S.W.A., S.W.A., R.G.I., R.W.S. Art Club, Ridley Art Club, R.B.S.A., Paisley Art Inst., Aberdeen Artists, Britain in Water-colours. *Signs work:* "FLORA MACLEOD." *Address:* Meadowlark Nursing Home, Manachie Rd., Dalvey, Forres, Morayshire IV36 0JT.

**MACLUSKY, Hector John,** Slade Dip. (London); painter; illustrator; lecturer, Stevenage College; art master, Highgate School (1948-50); *b* Glasgow, 20 Jan., 1923. *Educ:* Roundhay and Warwick Schools. *Studied:* Leeds College of Art (1939-40) and Slade School (1945-48). *Exhib:* R.A., R.B.A., London and provinces, Barbican Foyer Exhbn., The Face of Bond (1996). *Work in collections:* America and Australia. *Publications:* freelance cartoonist and illustrator for Press and television. *Signs work:* "John McLusky." *Address:* Hollybush Studio, Baines Lane, Datchworth, Herts. SG3 6RA.

**MACMARTIN, John Rayment,** D.A., F.R.S.A.; Diploma of Merit, Italy; D.M.D.A.; F.S.A.(Scot.); Industrial Design Consultant and Architectural Designer; Director (Tackle & Guns); artist in oils; inventor; *b* Glasgow, 3 Oct., 1925; Creamola Kid (1936-37). *m* Evelyn Margaret Lindsay Macmartin, embroideress. two *s.* one *d. Educ:* Allan Glen's School, Glasgow. . *Studied:* Glasgow School of Art (A past president of the Graduate Association). *Exhib:* oil paintings - Product design, Scottish Inventions of the year - (finalist). *Work in collections:* throughout the world. Structural Building MODULE, designed after a visit to Pompeii; invited to Leningrad, Moscow (1985), U.S.A. (1987), China (1988), Florida (1988), France (1989, 1994) and Norway (1991). National Trust for Scotland: V.P., Lanarkshire (1992-95), Probus Mem. (1992-95). Scottish Core of Retired Executives. *Address:* Rosebank, 2 Markethill Rd., East Mains, East Kilbride G74 4AA.

**MACMIADHACHÁIN, Pádraig,** R.W.A.(resigned 1996); artist, Travelling Prize to Moscow (1957), winner, Laing National Painting Competition (1991), winner Daler Rowney award in Royal West of England Academy (1992), Polish Govt. to Poland (1961); *b* Downpatrick, Ireland, 2 Mar., 1929. *m* Hazel McCool; two children; divorced; m. Ann Slacke; one child; divorced; Charlotte Kockelberg (T.A. Charlotte Kienitz); divorced ; m. Bonnie Brown, painter; divorced; m. Jane Hobday, painter. *Educ:* Bangor Grammar School; Portora Royal School, Enniskillen. *Studied:* Belfast College of Art (1944-48), National College of Art, Dublin (1948-49), Academy of Art, Krakow, Poland (1960-61). *Exhib:* one-man: Belfast, Dublin, London, Madrid, Krakow, Seattle, Los Angeles, Vancouver, Las Palmas; group shows: R.A., R.W.A., R.U.A., Gorky Park, Moscow, Irish Exhbn. Living Art. *Work in collections:* Arts Council, Ireland, Ronald Alley, Bob Monkhouse, Sam Wanamaker, Peter Sellers collection, Lord Briggs, King Carlos of Spain, the late President Chernenko of the U.S.S.R., Hertford College, Oxford, Sussex University, The Bank of China, Irish Allied Bank, S.G. Warburg and Kobe Steel. *Publications:* three collections of poems. *Signs work:* see appendix. Work always in New Academy Gallery, 34 Windmill St., London, New Craftsman, St. Ives and Wills Lane Gallery, St. Ives. *Address:* MacIntyre Saul Studio, 4 Commercial Lane, Swanage, Dorset BH19 1DE.

**McPAKE, John A.,** N.D.D., A.T.D., R.E.; painter/printmaker working in a variety of drawing and painting media in addition to etching, relief and mixed media printmaking; *b* Burnley, Lancs., 28 June, 1943. *m* Anne Genner

Crawford. *Educ:* St. Anselm's College, Birkenhead. *Studied:* Wallasey School of Art and Crafts (1961-65), Liverpool Polytechnic (1965-66), Birmingham Polytechnic (1966-67), Leeds Polytechnic (1977-78). *Exhib:* various group shows including R.E's, R.A. Summer shows, Seoul Print Biennale (1986, 1988), etc. *Work in collections:* Bankside Gallery (R.E's.); Rufford Craft Centre, Notts.; Leeds Craft and Design Gallery; various collections in England and abroad. *Signs work:* "John A. McPake." *Address:* 21 Ingbirchworth Rd., Thurlstone, nr. Sheffield S36 9QN.

**MACPHAIL, Ian S.,** F.I.P.R.; artist in typography and print design; European Co-Ordinator, International Fund for Animal Welfare and editor; asst. music controller, E.N.S.A., specializing in publicity; asst. music director, Arts Council of Gt. Britain, responsible for all printing and publicity design; *b* Aberdeen, 11 Mar., 1922. *m* Michal Hambourg. one *s.* one *d. Educ:* Aberdeen Grammar School. *Studied:* with Charles W. Hemmingway. *Exhib:* Exhbns. of posters, Council of Industrial Design. *Publications:* You and the Orchestra (McDonald & Evans), editor and designer of Dexion News, Good Company and The Griffith Graph, designed literature for the first world conference on gifted children (1975); work repro.: British Printer. *Clubs:* Savile. *Signs work:* "Ian Mac. Phail." *Address:* 35 Boundary Rd., St. John's Wood, London NW8 OJE.

**MACPHERSON, Hamish,** A.R.B.S.; sculptor; teacher, Central School of Arts and Crafts, London (1948-52), Sir John Cass School of Art, London (1948-53); *b* Hartlepool, 20 Feb., 1915. *Educ:* New Zealand. *Studied:* Elam School of Art, Auckland, N.Z. (1930-32), Central School of Arts and Crafts, London (1934-39). *Exhib:* one-man exhbns., Picture Hire, Ltd., London (1938), Chelsea Gallery, London (1947), Apollinaire Gallery, London (1950, 1952), Alwin Gallery, London (1968), London Group, N.S., New York, Paris, the Colonies and provinces; work for Festival of Britain (1951). *Signs work:* "Hamish Macpherson." *Address:* Casa Mia, Mitchel Troy Common, Monmouth, Gwent NP5 4JB.

**MacSWEENEY, Dale Pring,** Dip.A.D.; painter in oil on canvas; *b* London, 1949. *m* David MacSweeney, writer, psychiatrist. *Educ:* Burlington Grammar, W. London; Greycourt Secondary School, Ham, Surrey. *Studied:* Wimbledon School of Art (1966), Waltham Forest College (1967-70). *Exhib:* R.A., N.E.A.C., Piccadilly Gallery, Cork St., London; Henry Wyndham Fine Art, Jermyn St., London. *Clubs:* Chelsea Arts. *Signs work:* "Dale Pring MacSweeney" or "Dale MacSweeney." *Address:* 30 King Edward's Mans., 629 Fulham Rd., London SW6.

**MADDISON, John Michael,** B.A. (1974), Ph.D. (1978), F.S.A. (1991); painter in oil, distemper, gouache; former architectural adviser to Victorian Soc. (1979-81), and historic buildings representative, National Trust East Anglia (1981-92); *b* St. Andrews, Fife, 17 Nov., 1952. *m* Jane Kennedy, architect. two *s. Studied:* University of Manchester. *Exhib:* R.A., R.I., many mixed exhbns. and one-man shows in London, Norfolk, Cambridge, Salisbury and Bury St. Edmunds. *Commissions:* distemper panels for National Trust restaurant Felbrigg Hall. *Publications:* articles on medieval architecture and books on country houses. *Signs work:* "J.M." *Address:* 88 St. Mary's St., Ely, Cambs CB7 4MM.

**MADDISON, Robert,** S.G.F.A. (1985), M.E.N.S.A. (1987); painter in water-colour, pastel, graphite; *b* Newcastle upon Tyne, 6 May, 1946. *m* Elizabeth Finch. one *s*. one *d*. *Educ:* Heaton Grammar School. *Studied:* Newcastle College of Art (1962-64, John Crisp), Manchester College of Art (1964-65). *Exhib:* S.G.F.A., N.S.; numerous one-man shows. *Work in collections:* Durham University; numerous private collections including H.R.H. The Prince of Wales. *Publications:* The Northern Pennines - An Artist's Impressions; articles; television broadcasts. *Signs work:* "R. Maddison." *Address:* Spring Cottage Studio, Dovespool, Allenheads, Northumberland NE47 9HQ.

**MADDOX, Ronald,** P.R.I., Hon. R.W.S., F.C.S.D., F.S.A.I., F.R.S.A.; illustrator, consultant designer, artist in water-colour, line, gouache, specialising in architecture and landscape; *b* Purley, Surrey, 5 Oct., 1930. *m* (1st) Camilla Farrin, 1958 (decd. 1995); two *s*. (2nd) Diana Goodwin (1997). *Studied:* St Albans School of Art, Hertfordshire College of Art and Design, London College of Printing and Graphic Arts. Design/art direction 1951-61; freelance from 1962. *Exhib:* R.A., R.I., F.B.A. galleries, national and provincial exhbns., one-man shows. *Work in collections:* Britain, U.S.A., Canada, Germany. Elected President R.I. (1989), Governor F.B.A. (1989). Designer, British Commemorative stamps (1972/78/84/89); Design Council award (1973); Isle of Man Europa stamps, Prix de l'Art Philatelique (1987); Winsor & Newton R.I. Award (1981, 1991); finalist Hunting Group Art Prizes (1980-81-83); R.I. Rowland Hilder Award (1996). *Publications:* work repro.: national and international publications. *Signs work:* "RONALD MADDOX." *Address:* Herons, 21 New Rd., Digswell, Welwyn, Herts. AL6 0AQ.

**MADERSON, Arthur Karl,** N.D.D. (1964); painter in oil, pastel, acrylic and water-colour; *b* London, 27 Dec., 1942. *Educ:* Battersea County Comprehensive. *Studied:* Camberwell School of Art (1960-64, Robert Medley). *Exhib:* regularly at R.W.A. (Cornelissen prizewinner 1986), R.A., R.H.A. (Abbey Studio prizewinner 1992), represented in Co. Dublin by the James Gallery, Dalkey. *Work in collections:* Europe and abroad. *Publications:* work repro.: contributor to many journals and art publications including The Artist. Mem. Cork Arts Soc. *Signs work:* "A.K. Maderson," or "A.K.M" on picture and reverse. *Address:* Derriheen House, Cappoquin, Waterford, Rep. of Ireland.

**MADGWICK, Clive,** S.E.A. (1991), R.B.A. (1983), U.A. (1976); self-taught artist in oil, acrylic and water-colour; *b* London, 31 Oct., 1934. *m* Joan Patricia. one *s*. one *d*. *Educ:* Epsom College and London University. *Exhib:* 32

one-man shows; R.A., R.B.A., R.O.I., U.A., Royal Soc. of Miniature Artists and Sculptors. Winner Royle Landscape Prize (1978), Higgs & Hill Bursary F.B.A. (1986), Daler Rowney Award Equestrian Soc. (1987), specializing country sports, Britain Painters Royle Landscape prize (1991), Liquitex Award U.A. Exhbn. (1996). Works in public and private collections throughout the world. *Signs work:* "C. MADGWICK" and see appendix. *Address:* Newton House, Newton Rd., Sudbury, Suffolk CO10 6RN.

**MAER, Stephen,** F.S.D.C.; Council Mem. Soc. of Designer Craftsman, Designer Jewellers Group: Founder-Member and Chairman (1980-83, 1992-95), Crafts Council, Index of Executive Mem. Crafts Occupational Standards Board (1991-96), Assoc. for Contemporary Jewellery; designer jeweller; *b* London, 1933. *m* Janet Eddington. two *d. Educ:* Clayesmore School. *Studied:* jewellery design at R.C.A. under Prof. R. Goodden. *Exhib:* group shows: British Crafts Centre, R.S.A., Design Centre, Goldsmiths Hall, Barbican Centre. *Signs work:* "SM" (hallmark). *Address:* 18 Yerbury Rd., London N19 4RJ.

**MAGOR, William Laurence,** A.R.C.A. (1939), A.T.D. (1940); Principal, Berkshire College of Art (1960-74); artist in water-colour; *b* Mountain Ash, S. Wales, 30 Apr., 1913. *m* Marie Alexander. one *s.* two *d. Educ:* Crypt Grammar School, Gloucester. *Studied:* Gloucester Art School (1932-36) and R.C.A. (1936-39) under E. Bawden, Paul Nash. *Exhib:* R.A. *Signs work:* "W. L. Magor." *Address:* Gwenville, Sellars Rd., Hardwicke, Glos.

**MAI, Jinyao:** see MAK, Kum Siew.

**MAK, Kum Siew, (Mai, Jinyao),** A.R.C.A. (1967); full-time artist in Chinese and Western media; *b* Singapore, 21 Apr., 1940. two *s. Educ:* Singapore. *Studied:* St. Martin's School of Art (1961-64) under Frederick Gore, R.C.A. (1964-67) under Carel Weight. *Exhib:* R.A., I.C.A., R.C.A., Serpentine Gallery, Tate Gallery, Whitechapel Gallery. *Work in collections:* Tate Gallery, London; National Gallery, Singapore; Museum of Modern Art, Hyogo, Japan; Arts Council of G.B. *Publications:* Talking Pictures. *Address:* Alvernia, The Street, Mortimer, Berks. RG7 3PE.

**MAKEPEACE, John,** O.B.E. (1988), F.C.S.D., F.I.Mgt., F.R.S.A.; designer and furniture maker since 1961; Founder and Director: The Parnham Trust (1977-); *b* 6 July, 1939. *m* 1983 Jennie Moores. *Work in collections:* Cardiff; Fitzwilliam; Leeds; Frankfurt; Sidney and Frances Lewis. *Commissions:* Furniture commissions for Nuffield Foundation; Portals plc; Post Office; Royal Society of Arts; Directors' Forum; Boots plc; Banque Generale du Luxembourg. *Publications:* "A Spirit of Adventure in Craft and Design" by Jeremy Myerson. Study/Consultancy Tours: Scandinavia; N.America; W.Africa; Australia and Japan. V. & A.; Royal Museum of Scotland; The Art Inst. of Chicago; Lewis College, Richmond, Va. Featured in numerous books, articles and films internationally. *Address:* Parnham House, Beaminster, Dorset DT8 3NA.

**MAKLOUF, Raphael,** sculptor in bronze; painter; *b* Jerusalem, 10 Dec., 1937. *Studied:* Camberwell School of Art (1953-58) under Dr. Karel Vogel. *Work in collections:* Life-size bronze bust of H.M. Queen Elizabeth II for Royal Society of Arts, John Adam St., London (1986); life-size bronze bust of General Sir John Mogg for Army Benevolent Fund (1987); Tower of London; Carnegie Hall, N.Y., etc. New portrait effigy of H.M. The Queen on all U.K. coinage from 1985. *Signs work:* see appendix. *Address:* 3 St. Helena Terr., Richmond, Surrey.

**MALCLES, Jean-Denis,** Mem. Salon d'Automne, Salon des Artistes Décorateurs, Salon de l'Imagerie, Officier ordre des Arts et Lettres; Chevalier de la Légion d'honneur; painter in oil, gouache and pastel; lithographer; stage and costume designer; *b* Paris, 15 May, 1912. *m* Janine Malcles. *Educ:* École Boulle and Académies Peinture. *Studied:* under Louis Sognot and Rulhmann. *Work in collections:* Musée d'Art Moderne, City of Paris, French Government. Theatre decor: Opéra de Paris, Comedie-Francaise, Scala de Milan, Opéra de Hambourg, Cie Renaud-Barrault, Festival musique d'Aix en Provence, Le Théâtre de Jean Anouilh, Covent Garden. *Publications:* Bel Ami, Lettres de Mon Moulin, La Muse au Cabaret, Affiches, Expositions Galerie des Orfèvres, Paris; work repro.: Vogue, Femina, Plaisir de France, Graphis, Ballets des Champs-Elysées, Art et Style, Style en France. *Signs work:* see appendix. *Address:* 152 rue L. M. Nordmann, Paris 13.

**MALCOLM, Ellen,** R.S.A. (1976), Guthrie Award (1952); artist in oil; teacher; *b* Grangemouth, 28 Sept., 1923. *m* Gordon S. Cameron, R.S.A. *Educ:* Aberdeen Academy. *Studied:* Gray's School of Art, Aberdeen (1940-44) under Robert Sivell, R.S.A., and Dr. D. M. Sutherland, R.S.A. *Work in collections:* Perth City Gallery, Art Gallery, Southend, Lillie Gallery, Milngavie, Edinburgh City Collection, Palace of Holyrood House, Thorburn-Ross and Dr. Arnott Hamilton Collections, Edinburgh. *Signs work:* "E. Malcolm." *Address:* c/o 4 Deemount Gdns., Aberdeen AB11 7UE.

**MALCOLMSON, Joe,** artist in oil and gold leaf, water-colour; *b* Lanarkshire, 28 June, 1932. *m* Joyce Franklin. *Studied:* Medway College of Art (1959-61). *Exhib:* R.A., R.W.S., R.I., R.O.I., N.E.A.C., N.S. *Signs work:* "J.L. MALCOLMSOn" capitals except for last letter. *Address:* The Cottage, Woodland Way, Kingswood, Surrey KT20 6NU.

**MALENOIR, Mary,** R.E. (1984); R.A. Schools Dip. (1964), Rome Scholar in Engraving (1965-67); artist in mixed media; *b* Surrey, 29 July, 1940. *m* Michael Fairclough, artist. two *d. Studied:* Kingston School of Art (1957-61), R.A. Schools (1961-64), S.W. Hayter's Atelier 17, Paris (1967). *Exhib:* Prizewinner in:- P.M.C. National Print Competition (1987), Hunting Group Competition (1987), Humberside Printmaking Competition (1987), Bankside Gallery Open Print Competition (1989), R.A.Summer Exhbns., R.E. and P.M.C. Exhbns. *Work in collections:* Ashmolean Museum, Ipswich Museum, Graves A.G. Sheffield. *Signs work:* "MALENOIR." *Address:* Tilford Green

Cottages, Tilford, Farnham, Surrey GU10 2BU.

**MALIN, Suzi,** Slade Post. Grad. (1975); painter in tempera; *m* David Hames. one *s.* one *d. Educ:* Badminton, Bristol. *Studied:* Slade School of Art (1969-75, John Aldridge, R.A.). *Exhib:* one-man shows, J.P.L. Fine Arts, London (1977), Achim Moeller, London (1978), Coe Kerr, N.Y. (1978), Galerie d'Eendt, Amsterdam (1983), Gimpel Fils, London (1982). *Work in collections:* N.P.G.; Raby Castle; Gt. Hall, Christchurch, Oxford; Hull University; East Anglia University; Midland Bank. *Commissions:* Lord Home, Alistair Morton, Queen of Greece, Elton John. *Clubs:* Chelsea Arts. *Signs work:* "S. Malin." *Address:* The Meeting Hall, 158a Mill La., London NW6.

**MALINS, Margery Helen,** A.T.D., D.A. (Reading), R.C.A., M.F.P.S.; artist in oil, water-colour; *b* Reading. *m* F. M. Malins, A.T.D., D.A. (Reading), R.C.A., M.F.P.S. four *s. Educ:* Abbey School, Reading. *Studied:* Reading University under Prof. A. Betts and Walter Bayes, Liverpool College of Art. *Signs work:* "M. Malins." *Address:* The Mill House, Sandy Cross, Heathfield, E. Sussex TN21 8BS.

**MANCHOT, Melanie,** M.A. Fine Art (Photography) (1992); artist/part-time lecturer/photographer; part-time Lecturer, Bournemouth and Poole College of Art and Design; Visiting Lecturer, London colleges; *b* Germany, 7 July, 1966; partner: Stuart Haygarth. one child *Studied:* Royal College of Art (1990-92). *Exhib:* England and abroad regularly, solo and group shows. *Work in collections:* Saatchi. *Address:* 144a Union St., London SE1 0LH.

**MANDL, Anita,** R.W.A. (1978), F.R.B.S. (1980), Ph.D. (1951), D.Sc. (1960); sculptress, formerly University Reader, Medical School, Birmingham; carvings in wood and stone (alabaster, soapstone); also bronzes made from original carvings; *b* Prague, 1926. *m* Dr. Denys Jennings (decd.). *Studied:* part-time at Birmingham College of Art. *Exhib:* R.A., R.B.A., R.W.A., R.G.I.F.A., R.S.M.A., New Academy Gallery, Llewellyn-Alexander Gallery, Alresford Gallery, Adam Gallery, etc. and U.S.A. *Work in collections:* Ulster Museum; Royal West of England Academy; National Maritime Museum. *Signs work:* Mostly unsigned. (Highly polished carvings are marred by signature). Bronzes marked A.M. *Address:* 21 Northview Rd., Budleigh Salterton, Devon EX9 6BZ.

**MANIFOLD, Debra,** P.S.; artist in pastel, oil, water-colour, acrylic; urban landscapes and interiors; Council Mem. Pastel Soc.; *b* London, 28 Aug., 1961. *Studied:* Harrow School of Art (1978-83), Central School of Art and Design (1983-84), Advanced Printmaking Postgrad. Dip. *Exhib:* P.S., R.I., Mall Galleries, R.W.A., Barbican Centre, Société des Pastellistes de France; widely exhib. in and around London including Linda Blackstone Gallery, Bank Street Gallery, Orleans House, Edward Day Gallery, Ontario, Canada. *Publications:* Pastels Masterclass; Encyclopedia of Pastel Techniques; articles in 'The Artist'. Lectures throughout U.K. and in Canada. *Signs work:* "Manifold." *Address:* 8 Spring Gdns., E. Molesey, Surrey KT8 0JA.

**MANLEY, Jim,** A.R.U.A.; Patron's prize, E.V.A. Limerick (1984); painter in water-colour, pastel, collage; *b* St. Helen's, 1934. *m* Margaret. three *s. Educ:* West Park Grammar School, St. Helen's; De La Salle College, Middleton. *Exhib:* over twenty exhbns. in Ireland and England, including London Gallery, Duncan Campbell Fine Arts, Dublin, Solomon Gallery. *Work in collections:* Abbot Hall Kendal, U.T.V. Belfast, Walker Liverpool, Bank of Ireland Dublin. *Clubs:* United Arts, Dublin. *Signs work:* "J. Manley." *Address:* Coastguard Cottages, Killough, Downpatrick, Co. Down BT30 7QS, N. Ireland.

**MANN, Alex,** painter of 'visual-sound' (music) - portraits, landscapes, castles, homes; *b* Ayr, Scotland, 26 Feb., 1923. *m* Joyce. four *d. Studied:* Sidcup School of Art, Fine Art (paintings and sculpture). *Exhib:* London, Birmingham, Edinburgh, Germany, U.S.A etc. *Work in collections:* worldwide. *Commissions:* worldwide. *Signs work:* "Alex Mann." *Address:* Braemar Studio, 3 Chapel Brae, Braemar AB35 5YT.

**MANN, Caryl J.,** S.W.A. (1994), N.D.D. (1960); artist in water-colour, pastel, acrylic; *b* London, 31 Mar., 1938. *m* Christopher Mann. one *s. Educ:* Eastbourne High School. *Studied:* Eastbourne School of Art (1956-60). *Exhib:* S.W.A. annually since 1991, David Curzon Gallery since 1988; various mixed and solo shows in Sussex. *Signs work:* "C. Mann." *Address:* Six Birches, Upper Hartfield, Hartfield, E. Sussex TN7 4DT.

**MANN, Sargy,** H.N.D. Mech. (1958), N.D.D. (1964); landscape painter; *b* Hythe, Kent, 29 May, 1937. *m* Frances Carey. two *s.* two *d. Educ:* Dartington. *Studied:* Camberwell School of Arts and Crafts (1960-64, Frank Auerbach, Euan Uglow, Francis Hoyland) (1967, Dick Lee). *Exhib:* R.A., Hayward Annual (1983), London Group, International Drawing Biennale; one-man shows, Salisbury Festival of Arts, Cadogan Contemporary. *Work in collections:* Arts Council of G.B., Contemporary Art Soc., Cleveland C.C. *Publications:* Drawings by Bonnard (Arts Council, 1984), Pierre Bonnard Drawings (J.P.L. Fine Art, 1981), Pierre Bonnard Drawings Vols. 1-2 (J.P.L. Fine Art, 1987), Raoul Dufy (J.P.L. Fine Art, 1987), Pierre Bonnard (Nottingham Castle Museum, 1984), Introduction Past and Present (Arts Council, 1987), Bonnard Drawings (John Murray J.P.L. Fine Arts, 1991). *Signs work:* "Sargy Mann" or "Sargy." *Address:* Lawn Meadow, Bridge St., Bungay, Suffolk.

**MANOUK:** see BAGHJIAN, Manouk.

**MANSER, Michael John,** C.B.E., R.A., P.P.R.I.B.A., R.W.A. Dip.Arch., Hon. F.R.A.I.C.; architect; Principal, Manser Assoc.; *b* 23 Mar., 1929. *m* José Manser, journalist. one *s.* one *d. Educ:* Polytechnic Regent St. School of Architecture (now Westminster University). *Exhib:* R.A., R.W.A., Japan, Hong Kong, U.S.A., Singapore, Canada, Italy. *Publications:* Planning Your Kitchen, co-author with wife José Manser (C.I.D.); part author: Psychiatry in the Elderly (O.U.P.), House Builder Reference Book (Newnes), The Nature of Architecture (Routledge), Innovative Trends in Psychogeriatrics (Karger, Switzerland). *Clubs:* Brooks. *Signs work:* "Michael Manser." *Address:* Bridge Studios,

Hammersmith Bridge, London W6 9DA.

**MANTLE, Ruth,** S.G.F.A. (1984), C.F.A. (Oxon.) (1949); artist in pencil, ink, water-colour of buildings and botanical subjects; illustrator and teacher of drawing; *b* Newbury, Berks., 27 Aug., 1925. *m* Ian Mantle, M.A. two *s.* one *d. Educ:* St. Catherine's School, Bramley, Surrey. *Studied:* Ruskin School of Drawing, Oxford (1946-50, Albert Rutherston, Percy Horton; History of Art, Sir Kenneth Clark). *Exhib:* S.G.F.A. Annual, provincial exhbns. Work mainly in private collections, in Britain and abroad. *Publications:* illustrated, The Necklace Villages, Cambridge Itself, My Cambridge (Robson Books). *Clubs:* S.G.F.A., Shropshire Art Soc., Ludlow Art Soc., The Marches Artists. *Signs work:* "Ruth Mantle." *Address:* 35 Central Ave., Church Stratton, Shropshire SY6 6EF.

**MAPP, John Ernest,** A.R.C.A. (1948); artist in oil, acrylic, illustrator, etc.; *b* Northampton, 26 Mar., 1926. *m* Margaret Trayler. one *s.* one *d. Educ:* Eaglehurst College, Northampton. *Studied:* Northampton School of Art (1941-45), R.C.A. (1945-48) under Barnett Freedman and Gilbert Spencer. *Exhib:* Various galleries. *Signs work:* see appendix. *Address:* 64a Vineyard Hill Rd., Wimbledon Pk., London SW19 7JJ.

**MARA, Pam,** M.C.S.D. (1970), N.D.D. (1958), F.F.P.S. (1997); illustrator, designer, painter, printmaker in oil, pastel, acrylic, water-colour, lithography; *b* London, 12 May, 1928. *Educ:* Henrietta Barnett School, London. *Studied:* Willesden School of Art, Central School of Art. *Exhib:* mixed shows: Mall Galleries, Barbican, National Theatre, Bloomsbury Gallery, Loggia Gallery, St. Martin in the Fields Crypt Gallery, Royal Festival Hall, Holland Park Orangery. *Publications:* illustrated over 100 books, work published in England, America, several European countries, W. Africa, Near and Far East, South Africa and Australasia. *Signs work:* "Pam Mara." *Address:* 5 Gloucester St., London SW1V 2DB.

**MARAIS, (Mary Rachel Brown),** Mem. Visual Artist and Gallery Assoc.; self-taught artist in oil; *b* New York City, 24 Sept., 1921. *Educ:* New York University. Lived in Paris several years and painted warm, charming nostalgic scenes of Paris completely capturing the ambiance in a very personal style. *Exhib:* Paris, New York, Switzerland; Centre d'Art Contemporain, Paris (1984), Galerie Chantepierre Auboune, Switzerland; seen on NYC Channel 13 TV (1979, 1980). *Work in collections:* Jean Aberbach, Theodora Settele, Hugo Perls, Dr. M. Reder, Jacques Bellini. *Signs work:* "Marais." *Address:* 33 W. 67th St., New York 10023, N.Y.

**MARCHANT, Leonard,** R.E.; artist in oil painting, etching, mezzotint; *b* Cape Town, S. Africa, 23 Oct., 1929. *m* Teressa. *Educ:* St. Joseph's College, Cape Town. *Studied:* St. Martin's School of Art (1956), Central School of Art and Design (1960-63). *Exhib:* numerous including, one-man shows: Argus Gallery, Cape Town (1950, 1957), Lidchi Gallery, Johannesburg (1957), Angela Flowers (1975), The Pigeonhole, London (1977, 1980), Hogarth

Galleries, Sydney (1983), Pretoria Museum, S.A. (1988), Hurlingham Gallery, London (1989), Ludlow Assembly Rooms (1994), etc.; group shows: S.W.E., R.E., Bradford City A.G., International Print Biennale, Florence, Wolpe Gallery, Cape Town, R.A. Summer Shows, R.C.A. Gallery, Thumb Gallery, London, Mall Galleries, etc. *Work in collections:* V. & A., National Gallery of S.A., Cape Town, Museum of Fine Art, Boston, British Council, Churchill College, Cambridge, Albertina, Vienna, Pretoria Art Museum, Technikon, Johannesburg, etc.; private collections in U.K., U.S.A., France, Italy, Switzerland, Holland, S. Africa, Australia, etc. *Clubs:* Chelsea Arts. *Signs work:* "L. Marchant." *Address:* Radnor House, Pountney Gdns., Bell Vue, Shrewsbury SY3 7LU.

**MARDEL-FERREIRA, Elizabeth Gilchrist,** painter in acrylic, ink and wash, silk-screen printer; *b* Nottingham, 5 May, 1931. *m* Joseph Charles Mardel-Ferreira. one *s.* two *d. Educ:* Headington School, Oxford. *Studied:* Nottingham College of Art (1949-53). *Exhib:* Emsworth Group (7), R.A. (1978). Work in private collections. *Clubs:* Emsworth Group. *Signs work:* "E. Mardel" or "Elizabeth G. Mardel.' *Address:* 15 Warblington Ave., Havant, Hants.

**MARDI:** see BARRIE, Mardi.

**MAREK, Jerzy,** self-taught primitive painter in oil; *b* Poland, 1925. *m* Margaret Baird. one *s. Exhib:* Portal and Grosvenor Galleries, London, also in a number of International and Arts Council Exhbns. for primitive painters. *Work in collections:* Salford A.G., Bolton A.G., Abbotts Hall Museum, Kendal, Lancaster Museum, Glasgow Gallery of Modern Art, Sydney Janis Coll., N.Y. *Publications:* Naive Kunst by Ida Niggli, The Rona Guide to the World of Naive Art, Twentieth Century British Naive and Primitive Artists by E. Lister and S. Williams; many postcards. *Signs work:* "J. Marek." *Address:* 7 Pittville St., Portobello, Edinburgh EH15 2BZ.

**MARGRIE, Victor,** C.B.E., F.C.S.D.; potter; Visiting Prof. University of Westminster; Director, Crafts Council (1977-84); External Advisor, School of Fine Art, Cardiff Institute (1993-); Mem. of Board of Studies in Fine Art, University of London (1989-); Mem. UK National Commission for UNESCO (1984-85); Fine Arts Advisory Committee British Council (1983-86); *b* London, 29 Dec., 1929. *Work in collections:* V. & A., and private collections. *Publications:* contributed to: Oxford Dictionary of Decorative Arts (1975); Europaischt Keramik Seit (1950, 1979); Lucie Rie (1981); contrib. specialist publications and museum catalogues. *Signs work:* see appendix. *Address:* Bowlders, Doccombe, Moretonhampstead, Devon TQ13 8SS.

**MARINKOV, Sasa (Alexandra),** R.E.; artist in printmaking, lecturer, teacher; *b* Belgrade, Yugoslavia, 12 Jan., 1949. *m* Michael Jones. one *d. Studied:* Fine Art: Leeds University (1967-71), Advanced Dip. printmaking: Central St. Martin's. *Exhib:* Biennales at Cleveland, Bradford, Brazil, Korea, Spain, Xylon 13, Whitechapel and Riverside Open, London Group, Kunsthaus

Zug, Prints from Wood (Arts Council). *Work in collections:* Leeds University; London University; Brazil; Skopje; Clare College, Cambridge; London Hospital; British Rail Freight; Bank of China; Winchester Hospital; Dept. of Transport; Arts Council/South Bank Centre. Awards: G.L.C., South Bank picture show, R.A. Summer Show (twice), Ministry of Transport, London Arts Board. *Signs work:* "S. Marinkov." *Address:* Woodcut, Riverside, Twickenham TW1 3DJ.

**MARJ:** see BOND, Marj.

**MARKS, Laura Anne Celia,** Greenshields Foundation award (1982, 1983); artist in oil, water-colour and pencil; *b* Toronto, Canada, 1954. *Educ:* Forest Hill Collegiate, Toronto. *Studied:* Central Technical School, The Three Schools of Art, Art's Sake, and Ontario College of Art (1971-80, Paul Young). *Exhib:* one-man shows: Evans Gallery, Toronto (1973), Prince Arthur Gallery, Toronto (1980), October Gallery, London (1982), Alberta House, London (1982), Gallery Gabor, Toronto (1984), International Exhbn., Monte-Carlo (1985), John Denham Gallery, London (1991). *Work in collections:* Ontario House, London. *Signs work:* "MARKS." *Address:* 26 West End La., London NW6.

**MARR, Leslie,** M.A. (1947); painter and draftsman in oil, water-colour, etc.; Secretary, Borough Group (1947-49); *b* Durham, 14 Aug., 1922. *Studied:* Borough Polytechnic under David Bomberg. *Exhib:* one-man shows: Everyman Gallery, Drian Galleries, Laing A.G., Newcastle upon Tyne, Woodstock Gallery, Maddermarket Norwich, Fermoy Gallery, Kings Lynn, "Bomberg and the Family" exhbn. Ben Uri Gallery, London, Catto Gallery, London. *Work in collections:* Laing A.G., Newcastle upon Tyne, University of Haifa, Graves A.G., Sheffield. *Publications:* From My Point of View (Acorn Editions 1979). *Signs work:* see appendix. *Address:* 20 Gordon Rd., Melton Constable, Norfolk NR24 5BW.

**MARRIOTT, Michael,** F.R.B.S. (1974), N.D.D. (1960); sculptor in stainless steel, glass, G.R.P., stone, clay, plaster, bronze; *b* London, 3 May, 1940. *Educ:* Latymer Foundation and Christopher Wren Secondary. *Studied:* St. Martin's School of Art (1956-60, Elizabeth Frink, Anthony Caro, Edward Paolozzi). *Exhib:* one-man shows: Cockpit Theatre, London (1971), Alwin Gallery, London (1976); two-man show: Europa Gallery, Surrey (1978); group exhbns.: annually all over U.K. since 1960, Margam Park, S. Wales, Barbican Centre, Hannah Peschar Gallery, Surrey; also in U.S.A. and Europe. *Work in collections:* I.B.M. Cosham, Hunting Engineering Bedford, Heron House London, Crown House London. *Signs work:* see appendix. *Address:* 16 Seymour Rd., London SW18 5JA.

**MARSHALL, Dunbar:** see MARSHALL MALAGOLA, Dunbar.

**MARSHALL, Joan,** S.W.A. (1994); equestrian and portrait artist in oils; *b* Yorks., 8 Jan., 1931. *Studied:* Hull Art School. *Exhib:* S.W.A., S.Eq.A. *Signs work:* "Joan Marshall." *Address:* The Studio, Oldhay Farm, Altarnun,

Launceston, Cornwall PL15 7RN.

**MARSHALL, John,** landscape painter in water-colour; *b* Colchester. *Educ:* Rugby School. *Studied:* pupil of Cedric John Kennedy (1898-1968). *Exhib:* British Art Centre, New York, Leicester Galleries, London; one-man exhbns.: Leicester Galleries WC2 (1956-59-62), Anthony Reed's Gallery W1 (1981). *Work in collections:* Wadsworth Atheneum, U.S.A., Columbia Museum of Art, U.S.A., Norwich Castle Museum, Hull Education Committee. *Publications:* Cedric Kennedy memorial Catalogue and Monograph (1969 and 1972); work repro.: The Studio (July, 1956, Feb., 1960); monographs: Arts Review (June, 1956), The Studio (Feb., 1960). *Signs work:* "John (J) Marshall." *Address:* 41 Campden Hill Rd., London W8.

**MARSHALL, Maria Heléne,** B.A.Hons. (1986); sculptor in steel, stone, wood and canvas; *b* India, 14 Feb., 1964; married. *Educ:* Millfield School, Somerset, Ardingly College, Sussex. *Studied:* Chelsea Foundation (1982), Wimbledon School of Art (1986, Glyn Williams), Ecole des Beaux Arts, Geneva. *Exhib:* Gallerie Eric Frank (Geneva, Chicago, Basel); one-man shows: Odette Gilbert Gallery (London and Madrid), Crucral Gallery. Public sculpture 'Goddess' Princes Ct., Brompton Rd. *Signs work:* "Maria Marshall." *Address:* The Workshops, 23 Theatre St., London SW11.

**MARSHALL, Richard,** P.S. (1983); painter in oil, pastel, gouache, part-time lecturer; *b* Goring, Sussex, 29 Jan., 1943. two *d*. *Educ:* West Sussex College of Art. *Studied:* under William Cartledge, R.I., R.S.M.A. (1969-72), Gyula Sajo (1973-89). *Exhib:* internationally; mixed shows, France, London and Sussex; one-man show, Croydon; two-man show, Arundel and Worthing. *Clubs:* Worthing Atelier Art Group. *Signs work:* "R. Marshall." *Address:* 17 Harsfold Cl., Rustington, W. Sussex BN16 2QQ.

**MARSHALL MALAGOLA, Dunbar,** R.B.A.; painter; mem. Salon d'Automne, Paris (1972); former Sec.-General International Assoc. of Art, UNESCO; *b* Florence, 1918. *m* Daphne Chart. *Studied:* Westminster and Chelsea Schools of Art under Gertler, Meninsky, Robt. Medley, Ceri Richards. *Exhib:* one-man shows, Grabowski, London (1961, 1964), UNESCO House (1985), Prévôt Gallery, Paris IV (1986, 1989). *Work in collections:* Museums of Contemporary Art: Skoplje and Bihac Yugoslavia; Lodz, Poland; Baghdad, Iraq; Pori, Finland; Academy Savignano, Italy; University of Liverpool; Japan Artists' Centre, Tokyo; Imperial War Museum, Lambeth. *Signs work:* "DMM" or "Marshall Malagola." *Address:* 14 Cross Hayes, Malmesbury, Wilts. SN16 9BG.

**MARTIN, David McLeod,** R.S.W., R.G.I., D.A. (Glasgow) (1948), Hon. Professional Mem. S.S.A. (1949), Past Vice-Pres. R.S.W.; *b* Glasgow, 30 Dec., 1922. *m* Isobel A.F. Smith. four *s*. *Educ:* Glasgow. *Studied:* Glasgow School of Art, 1940-42 (R.A.F. 1943-46), 1946-48. *Exhib:* R.A. (1984), Bath Contemporary Art Fair (1987), numerous group shows; one-man shows in Glasgow, Edinburgh, Perth, Greenock, Stone Gallery, Newcastle and London.

Work in numerous public and private collections. Special Award of merit, Robert Coloquhoun memorial art prize exhbn., Kilmarnock (1974); prizewinner, Friends of the Smith Art Gallery, Stirling (1981); May Marshall Brown award, R.S.W. Exhbn. (1984); Mabel McKinlay award, R.G.I. (1990); prizewinner, Laing Exhbn., Mall Gallery, London (1990, 1993). *Signs work:* "DAVID M. MARTIN." *Address:* The Old Schoolhouse, 53 Gilmour St., Eaglesham, Glasgow G76 0LG.

**MARTIN, John,** R.B.A., B.A.(Hons.), R.A. Post Dip. (1983); painter in oil, gouache and water-colour; *b* London, 25 Jan., 1957. *Educ:* Houndsfield School, London. *Studied:* Exeter College of Art (Micheal Garton, Alexander MacNeigh), R.A. Schools (Peter Greenham). *Exhib:* numerous one-man shows in England; mixed shows in France and Canada. *Work in collections:* Norfolk County Collection, Art in Hospital Fund. *Signs work:* "J.M." *Address:* 4 Ship St. Gardens, Brighton, Sussex BN1 1AJ.

**MARTIN, Marie-Louise,** D.F.A. (1982), B.F.A. (1983); artist printmaker in etching; Director, Black Church Print Studio, Dublin; *b* Dublin, 29 Mar., 1960. *Studied:* National College of Art, Dublin (1978-83). *Exhib:* R.A. (1987, 1988), R.H.A. (1985-97), R.U.A. (1987, 1996), An T-Oireachtas (1984-96), E.V.A. (1984, 1986, 1988); print exhbns. in Ireland, England, Japan, America, Germany, Spain, Taiwan; exchange print exhbns. to China, Finland, Cuba. Print prizewinner R.H.A. (1989). *Work in collections:* B.P. Oil (Brussels); Kilkenny Castle; Guinness Peat Aviation; National Self portrait Coll.; Contemporary Arts Soc.; Office of Public Works. *Clubs:* United Arts, Dublin. *Signs work:* see appendix. *Address:* 9 Estate Cottages, Shelbourne Rd., Dublin 4.

**MARTIN, Nicholas Gerard,** B.A. (Hons.) (1980); artist in oil-stained acrylics, paper collage and paper mosaics, mural mosaics; educational project artist, Glyndbourne Touring Opera (1987); *b* Edinburgh, 5 July, 1957. *m* Marion Brandis. two *s. Educ:* Edinburgh Academy. *Studied:* Edinburgh College of Art (1975-80, Ian Davidson). *Exhib:* R.S.A., Traverse Theatre, Gardner Art Centre, Brighton Polytechnic A.G., Royal Pavilion A.G., Brighton, Dryden St. Gallery, Horsham Arts Centre, Royal Festival Hall A.G., Ramsgate Library Gallery, Booth Natural History Museum, Brighton. *Work in collections:* S.E. Arts, Royal Pavilion A.G., Forestry Commission, Edinburgh, Royal Festival Hall, Towner A.G., mosaic mural for Channel Tunnel, Ashford Library (1990), Herne Bay Sea Front Mosaic Fountain (1993), Govan Shipyard Mural, Glasgow (1993), Queen Elizabeth Queen Mother Hospital Mural (1996), Maps for Rochester City Council. Educational residencies with: Glyndebourne Touring Opera, Destafford School, Hextable School, Spinney School. *Signs work:* "Nicholas Martin." *Address:* The Shieling, Kingstonridge, Kingston, nr. Lewes, E. Sussex BN7 3JX.

**MARTINA, Toni,** B.A. (Hons.) (1978), Prix de Rome scholar (1987), R.E. (elected 1992); many prizes and awards including 1st prize Dept. of Transport

National Art Competition (1992), Christie's Contemporary Art award at R.A. (1987), N.Y. National Academy of Design Summer Exhbn. (1986), Lloyds Bank Printmakers award at R.A. (1986); painter/printmaker; *b* London, 7 Mar., 1956. *m* Tessa. one *d. Studied:* Harrow College of Art (1974-75), Kingston Polytechnic (1975-78), Central School of Art (1986). *Exhib:* Europe and the U.K. including R.A. Summer Show, R.E., Barbican Centre, British School at Rome, Royal Festival Hall, National Academy of Design N.Y. *Work in collections:* Cambridge libraries, Plymouth Museum, Rochdale Museum, Oldham Museum, Dept. of Transport., Museum of London, The London Hospital, Ashmolean Museum. *Signs work:* "Toni Martina." *Address:* 302 Plumstead Common Rd., London SE18 2RT.

**MARX, Enid C. D.,** R.D.I. (1942), F.C.S.D., Hon. F.R.C.A.; designer to the Board of Trade Utility Furniture Design Com.; *b* 20 Oct., 1902. *Educ:* Roedean School. *Studied:* Central School, Royal College of Art. *Exhib:* Burlington House, Paris, Leipzig, Boston Museum. *Work in collections:* Arts Council, V. & A., Leipzig, U.S.A., Ontario, Canada. *Publications:* Popular and Traditional Art in England (with Margaret Lambert); Victorian Scrapbook (with Margaret Lambert); twelve children's books; work repro.: Graphis, International Textiles, etc. Designed the definitive stamps on the accession of H.M. Queen Elizabeth II, Christmas stamps (1976). *Address:* 39 Thornhill Rd., Barnsbury Square, London N1 1JS.

**MASCO, Pam,** artist in oil and water-colour; *b* Springfield, Mass., 19 Mar., 1953. *m* John Heseltine. *Studied:* School of the Boston Museum of Fine Art, U.S.A. (Grad. Dip.) 1976. *Exhib:* Bourne Gallery, Reigate (1983-current), Clarendon Gallery, London (1986), David Messum, London (1990), R.B.A. (1992), R.W.S. (1992), Sunday Times Singer Friedlander Water-colour (1992), Priory Gallery, Cheltenham (1993, 1995), W.H. Patterson, London. *Work in collections:* private and corporate collections; other collections Wentworth Club. *Publications:* illustrations for many major London publishers (1981-88). *Signs work:* "P. MASCO." *Address:* East House, East St., Petworth W. Sussex GU28 0AB.

**MASON, Cyril Harry,** M.C.S.D. (1966), F.C.S.D. (1979), M.S.T.D. (1966), A.R.B.S.A. (1983), R.B.S.A. (1986); landscape and marine painter in water-colour and oil; chartered designer; *b* Halesowen, Worcs., 30 May, 1928. *m* Barbara Hill. one *s.* one *d. Educ:* Halesowen Grammar School. *Exhib:* R.I., R.W.S., R.S.M.A., R.B.S.A., R.C.A., R.W.A., Clarges Gallery and Llewellyn Alexander, London and midland galleries. *Work in collections:* Wyre Forest (Kidderminster), Wychavon, Marks & Spencer. *Clubs:* B'ham Water-colour Soc. *Signs work:* until 1986 "Mason"; after 1986 "Cyril H. Mason." *Address:* Bank Cottage, Shenstone, nr. Kidderminster, Worcs. DY10 4DS.

**MASON, Michael,** A.T.D., D.A. (Manc.) (1956), Fellow in Sculpture B.S. Rome (1976), F.R.B.S. (1992); sculptor in ceramics/bronze; former PR/lecturer sculpture, Manchester University; *b* Lancs., 1 June, 1935. *m* Barbara. one *s.*

one *d*. *Studied:* Manchester College of Art, British School, Rome. *Exhib:* Whitworth A.G., Serpentine Gallery, etc. *Work in collections:* V. & A., A.C.G.B., Zagreb A.G., A.V.A.F. Caracas. *Commissions:* Manchester Business School, Hackney Empire. *Publications:* Art International, Ceramic Review. *Signs work:* "Michael Mason" or "M.M." in rectangle. *Address:* 89 Park Rd., Hale, Altrincham, Ches. WA15 9LE.

**MASON, Richard,** M.F.P.S. (1969); sculptor of constructions in metals, wood and perspex, painter in oil and acrylic; *b* Ipswich, 20 June, 1931. *Educ:* Ipswich Grammar School. *Exhib:* one-man show: Woodbridge A.G. (1967); regular exhib. with F.P.S. Trends and Ipswich Art Club. *Clubs:* Ipswich Art, F.P.S., Felixstowe Art Group. *Signs work:* "Richard Mason." *Address:* Upland Gate, 39 Bishops Hill, Ipswich 1P3 8EW.

**MASTER, Jean,** R.O.I. (1987); painter in oil and acrylic; *b* London; married. two *s*. one *d*. *Educ:* St. Joan of Arc Convent, Rickmansworth, Herts. *Studied:* St. Martin's School of Art (Kenneth Martin), also in Hamburg under Prof. Karl Kluth. *Exhib:* Royal Academy, London, Royal West of England, Bristol, Mall Galleries London and other mixed exhbns. *Signs work:* see appendix. *Address:* Eaton House, Clifton Down, Bristol BS8 3HT.

**MATANIA, Franco,** U.A., S.G.F.A., S.E.A.; First prize 'Talens' award Mall Galleries (1984), Soc. Equestrian Art prize for drawing (1986, 1988), United Soc. of Artists award (1993); artist in all media; *b* Naples, 1922 (British subject 1935). *Educ:* Salesian College. *Studied:* at studio of artist relative, the late Fortunino Matania, R.I. (Chevalier): distinguished artist (Imperial War Museum: Benizet, etc.); student apprentice 1947-55 after military service. *Exhib:* mixed shows, R.I., R.O.I., N.S., P.S., U.A., S.G.A., S.E.A.; one-man shows, Campbell and Franks Fine Art, Bajazzo Gallery, Marlborough, Alpine Gallery, Guild Fine Arts; (abroad 1980's), Galleria Maitani, Orvieto, Italy, Galleria Treves, Milan, Italy, Galleria Alandaluz, Granada, Spain, Tanisia Gallery, N.Y. Galleria Toison, Madrid. *Work in collections:* Centro Hogar, Granada, Knight Inc. Conference Centre, Boston, Industria Marmo Design of Italy. *Signs work:* see appendix. *Address:* Little Venice Studio, 20 Clarendon Gdns., Maida Vale, London W9 1AZ.

**MATCHWICK, Beryl A.,** Hon. R.M.S.; artist in oil and water-colour; *b* London, 1907. *m* Anthony M. Tew (decd.). *Educ:* privately. *Studied:* Redhill School of Art under W. Todd-Brown, R.O.I. *Exhib:* R.A., R.I., R.M.S., R.S.A, Paris Salon, Hull, etc. *Signs work:* "Matchwick." *Address:* 8 Castle Ct., River Pk., Marlborough, Wilts. SN8 1NH.

**MATHESON, Andrew Kenneth Mackenzie,** D.A., R.B.S.A., Cert. Ed.; artist/potter and teacher works mainly in stoneware/porcelain - from studio in Lichfield, Staffs; *Educ:* Riland Bedford High School, Sutton Coldfield. *Studied:* Madeley College of Education (1968-71), Grays School of Art, Aberdeen (1974-79), Dip. in Art (1978), postgrad. Dip. in Art (1979). *Exhib:* in Scotland and England. *Clubs:* R.B.S.A., B'ham Art Circle, Midland Potters

Assoc. *Signs work:* "Andrew K.M. Matheson" and see appendix. *Address:* 7 Driffold, Sutton Coldfield, W. Midlands.

**MATHEWS, Alister,** B.Sc,; botanical painter in water-colour; *b* Prestbury, 25 Feb., 1939. *m* Carl Mathews, Ph.D. one *s.* one *d. Educ:* James Allen's Girls' School, Dulwich; University of Wales. *Exhib:* S.B.A., S.W.A., Malcolm Innes; solo show: Hitchin Museum, Westminster Gallery annually. *Work in collections:* Hunt Inst. for Botanical Illustration, Carnegie Mellon University, Pittsburg, Shirley Sherwood Collection. *Signs work:* "Alister Mathews." *Address:* 4 Bramshott Close, London Rd., Hitchin, Herts. SG4 9EP.

**MATHEWS, Binny,** Greenshield Foundation Award (1989); painter in oil, specialising in portraiture, tutor; *b* Dorset, 25 June, 1960. *m* Stuart Martin, architect. two *s. Studied:* Bournemouth and Poole College of Art (1977-78), West Surrey College of Art (1978-81), Brighton Polytechnic (1981-82). *Exhib:* N.E.A.C., Hunting Award, R.P., Mall Galleries, N.P.G. (1981, 1982 1985, 1988, 1990, 1993), R.A., etc., numerous one-woman shows in the provinces and London. *Work in collections:* La Sainte Union College, Southampton; National Trust, Castle Drogo; Seagrams; British Gas; Carpenters Hall; American Embassy. *Clubs:* Chelsea Arts. *Signs work:* "Binny Mathews." *Address:* 13 Crescent Pl., Brompton Rd., London SW3 2EA.

**MATTAROZZI DI THARASH, Mirella (Mirice Janàcêk),** artist-painter, fine arts professor, writer; Diploma, Istituto Belle Arti di Bologna, Accademia di Belle Arti di Bologna; *b* Bologna. *Exhib:* Italy, Europe, South America. *Work in collections:* museums, Palazzo Vecchio, Firenze, Castello Sforzesco, Milano, Museo S. Matteo, Pisa, etc. Associate of Incisori d'Italia (I.D.IT.), Ex Libristi d'Italia (E.L.D.IT.). *Publications:* Il Comanducci, Annuario Internazionale di Belle Arti (Berlin), Guida all'arte Italiana, Who's Who in Europe, ed. Feniks, etc., Knight of the Tommaso da Vico Order; Academician of the Accademia dei 500, Rome. Lady-in-waiting of the Corporazione Internazionale della Stella Croce d'Argento (C.I.S.C.A.) dei Cavalieri del Bene. *Address:* via Sigismondo n$^0$33, Cattolica Forlì, Italy.

**MATTHEWS, Anton,** R.C.A. (1960), N.D.D., A.T.D., painter in oil; formaly lecturer Flintshire School of Art, Head of Rugby School of Art (1965-85); *b* 5 Dec 1925. *m* Janet. three *s. Studied:* Cheltenham College of Art, and University of Reading. *Exhib:* R.A., R.B.A., R.W.A., R.C.A., and many mixed exhbns. and one-man shows. *Work in collections:* Pictures for Scools and Welsh Arts Council. *Signs work:* "Anton Mathews" or "AM" *Address:* 8 Elizabeth Way, Chard, Som. TA20 1BY.

**MATTHEWS, Peter Jeffrey,** N.D.D. (1962), R.E. (1983); artist/printmaker in water-colour, etching and lithography; Senior Lecturer in Printmaking, Wimbledon School of Art; *b* London, 29 July, 1942. *m* Caroline Moore. one *s.* one *d. Studied:* Ealing School of Art (1958-62). *Exhib:* numerous mixed shows in G.B. and abroad. *Work in collections:* V. & A., Bibliotheque Royal, Brussels, Albertini Museum, Vienna, Morandi Museum, Bologna, Italy. *Signs* *work:* "Peter Matthews." *Address:* 1 Manor Rd., London SW20 9AE.

**MATTHEWS, Sharyn Susan,** S.W.A.; self taught artist in water-colour, acrylic, gouache, oil; *b* Bristol, 13 Jan., 1951. one *s.* one *d. Exhib:* numerous one-man shows at home and abroad, including Mall Galleries. Work permanently on show Park Lane Fine Arts, Ashtead, Surrey. *Signs work:* "Sharyn Matthews." *Address:* 19 Longdown La. North, Ewell, Surrey KT17 3HY.

**MAYER, Charlotte,** A.R.C.A. (1952), F.R.B.S. (1980); sculptor in bronze, steel and wood; *b* Prague, 4 Jan., 1929. *m* Geoffrey Salmon. one *s.* two *d. Studied:* Goldsmiths' College School of Art (1945-49, Wilson Parker and Roberts Jones), R.C.A. (1949-52, Frank Dobson). *Exhib:* R.A., R.W.A., V. & A.;Selected Galleries: Belgrave, Bruton, Hagen, Pangolin, Sladmore. *Work in collections:* Wadham College Oxford; Merseyside C.C.; Basingstoke and N. Hants. Health Authority; Cement and Concrete Assoc.; British Petroleum. *Commissions:* Tree of Life,North London Hospice; Ascent, Barbican, City of London; Journey 2, Nene College, Northants.; Wind and Fire, Marylebone Gate, London. *Publications:* illustrated, The Mystery of Creation by Lealman and Robinson; Patronage and Practice, Tate Gallery Liverpool. *Signs work:* "C.M." or "Mayer." *Address:* 6 Bloomfield Rd., Highgate, London N6 4ET.

**MAZ:** see JACKSON, Maz.

**MAZZOLI, Dino (Leopoldo),** artist in oil and water-colour; *b* Terni, Italy, 10 May, 1935. one *s.* one *d. Educ:* Oriani College, Rome. *Studied:* Villa Massimo, Rome (1953-54, Renato Guttuso), Villa Medici, Rome (1954-56), Eastbourne College of Art, and with Dorothy Swain, R.C.A. *Exhib:* Don Orione, Farnesina, Rome, Heathfield A.G., E. Grinstead Autumn Show, Towner Museum and A.G., Eastbourne, Brighton Museum and A.G., Star Gallery, Lewes, Blackheath Gallery, London; also in Dusseldorf, Germany, St. Laurent en Grandvaux, France, Birmingham, Alabama U.S.A., etc. *Work in collections:* La Charbonniere, St. Laurent en Grandvaux 39150 France; Premier Gallery, Eastbourne. Mem. of the Eastbourne Group. *Signs work:* "D. Mazzoli." *Address:* 11 Summerdown Rd., Eastbourne, E. Sussex BN20 8DS.

**MEACHER, Neil,** N.D.D. (1955), A.R.C.A. (1960), R.I. (1981); artist/illustrator in ink and water-colour, coloured pencils, teacher; senior lecturer, Ealing C.H.E.; *b* Sandwich, Kent, 20 Dec., 1934. *m* Margaret Joyce. one *s.* one *d. Educ:* Sir Roger Manwood's Grammar School. *Studied:* Canterbury College of Art (1951-55), R.C.A. (1957-60, Humphrey Spender, John Drummond, Julian Trevelyan, Edward Ardizzone, Alistair Grant, Geoffrey Ireland). *Exhib:* Rye Gallery, John Neville Gallery, New Ashgate Gallery, Edwin Pollard Gallery, Mall Galleries. *Clubs:* R.I., Assoc. of Illustrators. *Signs work:* "NEIL MEACHER." *Address:* 7 Mervyn Rd., Shepperton, Middx. TW17 9HG.

**MEADOWS, Anthony William,** A.R.M.S. (1984); self-taught painter and illustrator in oil, wood engraving; *b* Aldershot, 28 Aug., 1957. *m* Dawn Hardy (jeweller). *Educ:* Fanshawe School, Ware. *Exhib:* R.A., R.I., R.M.S. and several one-man shows. *Work in collections:* Hertford Museum. *Signs work:* "A. W.

Meadows". *Address:* 27 Victoria Rd., Oswestry, Salop. SY11 2HT.

**MEDHURST, Doreen,** R.M.S. (1993), S.B.A. (1989), S.W.A. (1989); self taught painter in acrylic and oil; *b* London, 5 Aug., 1929. *m* Cyril Medhurst. two *s. Educ:* Sydenham High School. *Exhib:* R.M.S., S.B.A., S.W.A., Llewellyn Alexander Gallery, Alfriston Gallery, Elan Art Centre, and several one-man shows. *Signs work:* "D Medhurst." *Address:* 45 Blenheim Rd., Orpington, Kent BR6 9BQ.

**MEEK, Elizabeth R.,** R.M.S., H.S., S.W.A.; portrait artist in oil; *b* London, 7 May, 1953. two *d. Educ:* Beaconsfield High School. *Exhib:* R.M.S., Hunting/Observer, Mall Galleries, Smith Gallery, Yorks., L'Espace Pierre Cardin, Paris, British Painters, Barbican Centre, S.W.A., H.S., Llewellyn Alexander Gallery, London, R.A. Summer Exhbn.; one-woman show in Valletta, Malta, Africa '97 London. *Publications:* 'The Techniques of Painting Miniatures' by Sue Burton; '100 Years of Miniatures' by Suzanne Lucas. Awards: winner, R.M.S. Gold Memorial Bowl (1995); The Bell Award (1992, 1997) (best portrait in exhbn.); H.S. (1993, 1994) (best in exhbn. twice); R.M.S. (1992, 1994) (runner-up for Gold Memorial Bowl, twice); R.M.S. (1993) Gold Bowl hon. mention, The Mundy Sovereign Award (1995). *Signs work:* "E.R. Meek." *Address:* 482 Merton Rd., Southfields, London SW18 5AC.

**MELAMED-ADAMS, Alicia,** U.A. (1965), Gold medallist, Academie Italia belle arti el Lavore (1981), Art in Edinburgh (1984), Gallery Internationale, Paris (1984); artist in oil; *b* Borystaw, Poland, 26 Sept., 1927; married. one *s. Studied:* St. Martin's School of Art (1960-63); Academie Chaumiere, Paris; Sir John Cass College of Art. *Exhib:* Foyles A.G., R.B.A., Augustine Gallery, Flower Paintings of Today, Flower Paintings of the World, 100 Years of British Drawing, Galerie Solombo, Paris (1987-89), Crypt Gallery, London, R.A. (1988), Hunting Group, Mermaid Theatre (1991), Real Art Gallery (1992), Intaglio Gallery, Manchester (1993), Crocodile Gallery (1993), Leicester City Gallery (1993), Laudersdale House (1994); two artists, two views, Bird and Davis Ltd. (1996); Sackville Gallery mixed (1996, 1997). *Work in collections:* Brazil, Paris, London; permanent collection, Ben Uri. *Signs work:* "Alicia Melamed." *Address:* 17 Edmunds Walk, London N2 0HU.

**MELLAND, Sylvia,** R.E.; painter-etcher; *b* Altrincham. *m* Brian Mertian Melland. one *s. Educ:* Altrincham Grammar School. *Studied:* Manchester College of Art, Byam Shaw, London, Euston Road, Central School (Graphics). *Exhib:* one-man shows, Wertheim and Jackson's Galleries, Manchester, Zwemmer Gallery, London, Galleria S. Stefano, Venice, Galerie Maurice Bridel, Lausanne, Galerie Bürdeke, Zürich, Agi Katz Fine Art, London. *Work in collections:* Rutherston Collection, S. London A.G., N.Y. Library, Leeds A.G., Brighton Museum, Coventry Educ. Council, Twickenham Educ. Council, Greenwich Library, Ferens A.G., Hull, V. & A., R.A. (Stott Foundation), Talmuseum des Münstertals, Switzerland, New Hall College, Cambridge and in private collections here and abroad. *Signs work:* prints, "Sylvia Melland," oils,

"S.M." *Address:* 68 Bedford Gdns., London W8.

**MELLOR, Mary,** LL.B., A.K.C. (1961), Called to Bar (1962), B.A. Graphics (1984), M.F.P.S.; artist in oil, teacher; *b* Swansea, 1939. *m* His Hon. Judge David Mellor. two *d. Educ:* Bolton School, Newcastle-on-Tyne Church High School, Sutton High School, G.P.D.S.T., King's College, London, Inner Temple. *Studied:* Norwich School of Art (1979-84). *Exhib:* Norwich Artists' Group, Norwich Gallery (Norfolk Inst. of Art and Design), Dixon Gallery, London, Loggia Gallery, London, Castle Museum, Norwich (Norfolk Art Now), Advice Arcade Gallery, Norwich. *Signs work:* "Mary Mellor." *Address:* The Old Hall, Mulbarton, Norwich.

**MELLOR, Pamela,** F.R.S.A.; painter in oil, writer; Hon. Sec., Chelsea Art Society (1971-1978); Com., Armed Forces Art Society; *b* Sydney, Australia. *m* Lt.Col. Gerard Mellor, Royal Signals, retd. *Educ:* at home and abroad. *Exhib:* U.A., R.W.S., R.M.S., Artists of Chelsea, Chelsea Art Soc., Leighton House, Ridley Art Soc., Armed Forces Art Soc., Dowmunt Gallery, Qantas Gallery. *Work in collections:* H.R.H. The Prince of Wales, The Agent General of N.S.W., The Agent General of Queensland and other private collections. *Publications:* author, The Mystery of X5 (pub. William Kimber). *Signs work:* "Pam Mellor." *Address:* 44 Stanford Rd., Kensington, London W8 5PZ.

**MENDEL, Renée,** sculptor and potter; *b* Elmshorn, 22 Sept., 1908. *Educ:* Lichtwark School, Hamburg; universities of Berlin, Frankfurt, Paris. *Studied:* Berlin under Ernest de Fiori, Paris under Pablo Gargallo. *Exhib:* Salon d'automne, Paris, R.A., Hertford House; one-man show at Royal Copenhagen Porcelain Co., 6 Bond St., Heal & Son Exhbn. Sculpture for the Home, Camden Arts Centre, Royal Exchange (1977). *Work in collections:* sculpture (wood carving) of James Joyce, National Portrait Gallery. *Commissions:* Dm. H. Winsley-Stolz, S.P. (bronze portrait 1989). *Publications:* work repro.: The Studio, Evening Standard, Semaine à Paris, Artistes d'aujourd'hui, Hampstead and Highgate Express and News, Hornsey Journal. Sculpture of 'Beatles' sold by Sotheby's (21 May 81), Sculpture of James Joyce, N.P.G. (Feb. 1987). *Signs work:* "Renée Mendel." *Address:* 27 Onslow Gdns., London N10 3JT.

**MENDOZA, Edwin,** portrait and muralist painter in oil and water-colour, interior designer; *b* Alexandria, Egypt, 11 Jan., 1936. *m* Katherina. two *d. Educ:* Victoria College, Alexandria. *Studied:* St. Martin's School of Art. *Signs work:* see appendix. *Address:* 59 The Ridgeway, London NW11 8QL.

**MENDOZA, June,** R.P., R.O.I.; portrait painter; *b* Melbourne, Australia; musician parents. *m* Keith Mackrell. one *s.* three *d. Educ:* Lauriston Girls' School, Australia. *Studied:* St. Martin's School of Art. *Work in collections:* government; H.M. Forces; industry; commerce; medicine; academic and legal professions; theatre; sport, and private collections internationally. Portraits include: H.M. The Queen; H.R.H. Prince Charles; H.R.H. Princess of Wales; H.M. Queen Mother; Mrs. Margaret Thatcher; Mr John Major; Prime Ministers of Australia and Fiji; Presidents of Philippines and Iceland; series of musicians inc. Sutherland, Solti, Menuhin. Group portraits include: House of Commons in Session; Council of Royal College of Surgeons; House of Representatives, Canberra. Hon. D.Litt. Bath University; Hon.D.Litt. Loughborough University; A.O.(Australia); lectures; T.V. *Signs work:* "MENDOZA" and see appendix. *Address:* 34 Inner Pk. Rd., London SW19 6DD.

**MENZIES, Gordon William,** D.A.; Josef Sekalski Award for Printmaking; Head of Pottery Dept., Community Centre, Edinburgh; established Iona Pottery, 1982 (Workshop/Gallery) with own ceramics, engravings, landscapes; *b* Motherwell, Scotland, 9 Jan., 1950. *Educ:* Dalziel High School, Motherwell. *Studied:* Duncan of Jordanstone College of Art, Dundee (1969-73) under Sheila Green, Ron Stenberg; Atelier 17, Paris (1974) under S. W. Hayter. *Exhib:* Edinburgh, Printmakers Workshop, Compass Gallery, Glasgow, Montpelier Art Institute, France, R.S.A., S.S.A., Edinburgh, many others within Edinburgh and surrounding area. *Publications:* books illustrated mainly within Children's Educational area. *Address:* Lorne Cottage, Isle of Iona, Argyll PA76 6SJ.

**MEREDITH, Julian Nelson,** artist in woodcut print; *b* Bath, 4 Mar., 1952. *m* Jane. three *d. Educ:* Clifton College. *Studied:* Exeter College of Art (1972, 1974). *Exhib:* Mall Galleries (1988, 1989), R.A. Summer Exhbn. (1989), Henry Brett Galleries (1989). *Signs work:* "J.Meredith." *Address:* c/o Jonathan Meredith, 1 Clifton Villas, Balmoral Rd., St. Andrews, Bristol 6.

**MEREDITH, Norman,** A.R.C.A.; illustrator; tutor University of Aberystwyth (1935) and St. Martin's School of Art; war service M. of A.P. (Farnborough); *m* Violet Mary Brant. *Studied:* Liverpool College of Art and R.C.A.; travelling scholar. *Exhib:* frequently at Chris Beetles Gallery, London SW1, since 1984. *Work in collections:* H.R.H. The Duke of Gloucester, etc. Textiles for Moygashel, Crowson Fabrics; designs for Metal Box Co., greetings cards, gift wraps, nursery pictures for Brunott of Holland; nursery china. *Publications:* work repro.: Punch, Tatler, Bystander; books illus. most British publishers, strip cartoonist. Hobbies: Recording piano music, photography, travel, (two world tours). *Signs work:* "NORMAN MEREDITH." *Address:* The Elders Epsom Road Ewell Surrey KT17 1JT.

**MERTON, John Ralph,** M.B.E. (1942); painter; *b* 7 May, 1913. *m* 1939 Viola Penelope von Bernd; two *d.* (and one *d.* decd.). *Educ:* Eton; Balliol Coll. Oxford. Served War of 1939-45 (MBE); Air Photo reconnaissance research, Lieut-Col. 1944. Works include Mrs Daphne Wall (1948); The Artist's daughter Sarah (1949); altar piece (1952); The Countess of Dalkeith (1958); A Myth of Delos (1959); Clarissa (1960); Mrs Julian Sheffield (1970); Sir Charles Evans (1973); Iona Duchess of Argyll (1982); Sir David Piper (1985, N.P.G.); H.R.H. The Princess of Wales in Cardiff City hall (1987); Professor James Meade, Nobel Prize Winner (1987); H.M. The Queen (1989) as head of the Order of Merit. Head Master of Eton (1990), Triple portrait of The Duke of Grafton for the National Portrait Gallery (1992), Paul Nitze (1992); Legion of

Merit (USA) 1945. Recreations: music, making things, underwater photography. *Address:* Pound House, Oare, nr. Marlborough, Wilts. SN8 4JA.

**MESSELET, Jean,** Conservateur honoraire du Musée Nissim de Camondo; *b* Paris, 22 Feb., 1898. *Educ:* Lycée Louis le Grand. *Studied:* Ecole du Louvre. *Publications:* monographs on French painters; articles in Archives de l'Art Francais, Beaux-Arts, Bulletin Monumental, Bulletin des Musées, etc. *Address:* 2 rue Léonce-Reynaud, Paris XVIe.

**MICAH, Lisa,** M.F.P.S. (1989), N.A.P.A. prize (1988); artist in acrylic; Council mem. Cambridge Drawing Soc. (1988-91), Consultant, Galeries d'Attente, London (1989-91); *m* M.J. Chapman, F.C.I.Arb. four *d. Educ:* in Europe and Africa. *Exhib:* solo-shows: Cambridge (1987, 1988), London (1991), Lyon (1992, 1993, 1994), Château du Cingle (1994). Artiste invitée d'honneur, St.Galmier (1996). *Work in collections:* private: Austria, Belgium, England, Finland, France, Germany and Switzerland; public: England, France, United States. *Clubs:* Farmers' London. *Signs work:* "L. Micah" and see appendix. *Address:* BP19, 69881 Jonage Cédex, France.

**MICHAELS, Jane,** P.G.Dip. (1994), B.A.(Hons.) (1993); artist in oil, acrylic, print; founder, Art in Life; *b* Yorks., 5 Jan., 1964. *Educ:* South Axholme School; Bristol University. *Studied:* University of the West of England. *Exhib:* many mixed and solo shows in London, Bristol, Bologna, Stockholm, Glos. and Somerset. *Publications:* Maps in Contemporary Art. *Signs work:* "Jane Michaels" or "Michaels." *Address:* c/o Park View, Ladymead Lane, Langford, Bristol BS18 7ED.

**MICHIE, David Alan Redpath,** O.B.E. (1997); painter; Prof. Emeritus, Heriot Watt University (1991); Head, School of Drawing and Painting, Edinburgh College of Art (1982-90); *b* St. Raphael, Var, France, 1928. *m* Eileen Michie. two *d. Educ:* Hawick High School. *Studied:* painting: Edinburgh College of Art (1946-1953), Italy (1953-1954). *Exhib:* one-man shows, Mercury Gallery, London (1967, 1969, 1971, 1974, 1980, 1983, 1992, 1996), Mercury Gallery, Edinburgh (1986), Lothian Region Chambers (1977), The Scottish Gallery, Edinburgh (1980, 1994), Kasteel de Hooge Vuursche, Netherlands (1991). *Work in collections:* Scottish National Gallery of Modern Art. *Signs work:* "David Michie." *Address:* 17 Gilmour Rd., Edinburgh EH16 5NS.

**MICKLEWRIGHT, Robert Flavell,** D.F.A. (London), R.W.S.; graphic designer, illustrator, painter in oil, water-colour; *b* Staffordshire, 1923. *Studied:* Croydon School of Art (1939), Wimbledon School of Art (1947-49), Slade School (1949-52). *Exhib:* regular exhibitor in London, provinces and U.S.A. *Work in collections:* pictures in public and private collections. *Publications:* illustrated numerous books. Work reproduced in the following reference books: Artists of a Certain Line (Bodley Head), Designing a Book Jacket (Studio), Designers in Britain, 5, 6, 7 (Andre Deutsch), Drawing for Radio Times (Bodley Head), Illustrators at Work (Studio), Royal Academy

Illustrated, Underground Art (Studio Vista). *Address:* Mount Hill, Mogador, Tadworth, Surrey KT20 7HZ.

**MIDDLETON, Michael,** A.R.E. (1981), R.E. (1986), Dip.A.D. (1971), H.D.A. (1974); lecturer/painter/printmaker in oil, water-colour, etching, wood-cut; teaches print-making, art history, Colchester Inst. School of Art and Design; *b* Louth, Lincs., 25 June, 1950. *Educ:* Heron Wood, Aldershot. *Studied:* West Surrey College of Art and Design (1966-68), Sheffield Polytechnic (1968-71), Chelsea School of Art (1973-74). *Exhib:* R.A., R.E., and several one-man shows. *Work in collections:* Harlow Town Corp., R.E., Ashmolean Museum Oxford, Fitzwilliam Museum Cambridge. *Commissions:* Print Collectors Club. *Signs work:* "M. Middleton." *Address:* 104 Maldon Rd., Colchester, Essex CO3 3AP.

**MIDDLETON, Michael Humfrey,** C.B.E., F.C.S.D., Hon. F.R.I.B.A., Hon. F.L.I.; Assistant Editor/Editor of Picture Post (1949-53); Lilliput (1953-54); House and Garden (1955-57); Deputy Director, the Civic Trust (1957-69), Director (1969-86); art critic, Spectator (1946-56); *b* London, 1 Dec., 1917. *m* Julie Harrison. one *s.* two *d. Educ:* King's School, Canterbury; Heatherley's. *Publications:* Group Practice in Design; Man Made the Town; Cities in Transition; contributor to many periodicals, etc., on art, design and environ-ment. *Address:* 84 Sirdar Rd., London W11 4EG.

**MIDDLETON, Renée,** S.G.F.A., S.B.A., S.W.A.; Rexel prizewinner (1984), Rotring prizewinner (1994); artist in pen and ink specialising in natural forms of stipple and/or line; *b* 19 Mar., 1920; married. one *s.* one *d. Educ:* Old Palace School for Girls, Croydon. *Exhib:* R.B.A., S.W.A., S.G.F.A., S.B.A., 'Flowers and Gardens' Mall Galleries and Central Hall, Westminster; three-man show, Fairfield Halls, Croydon. *Clubs:* S.G.F.A., S.B.A., S.W.A., local Sussex Socs. *Signs work:* see appendix. *Address:* Merryhill Corner, Thakeham, W. Sussex RH20 3HB.

**MIDGLEY, Julia,** Dip.A.D. (1969); mem.: P.M.C., Manchester Academy of Fine Arts (Vice President, 1994-96); painter, printmaker; senior lecturer, Liverpool John Moores University; *b* 1948; married. two *s. Studied:* Northwick School of Art and Design (1965-66), Manchester College of Art and Design (1966-69). *Exhib:* Manchester Academy annually since 1979, R.A. (1983, 1986, 1987, 1997), R.E. (1987, 1990), Business A.G's. (1981, 1982, 1983, 1985), New Academy (1987-94), National Print Exhbns. Blackpool (1979, 1981, 1985), Chelsea Arts Club, P.M.C. Exhbns. (1984-93). *Work in collec-tions:* national, international, public and private collections. *Commissions:* cor-porate and public. *Clubs:* Chelsea Arts. *Signs work:* "Julia Midgley." *Address:* 140 Chester Rd., Northwich, Ches. CW8 4AW.

**MIERS, Christopher John Penrose,** R.B.A. (1986); artist in oil and water-colour; Secretary, The Arts Club (1986-90); Trustee, The Water-colour Foundation (1988-91); *b* 26 Sept., 1941. *m* (1) 1967 Judith Hoare; one *s.* one *d.*; (2) 1993 Liza Thynne.*Educ:* Wellington College and R.M.A. Sandhurst. *Exhib:*

R.A., R.B.A., N.E.A.C., The Minories, Colchester (1964), Ansdell Gallery, Kensington (1967, 1968), Fortescue Swann, Brompton Rd. (1976), C.D. Soar & Son, Launceston Pl. (1986, 1988), Sally Hunter Fine Art (1990, 1993, 1995), Mall Galleries (1991), Jerram Gallery (1994, 1996), Grosvenor House (1996). *Work in collections:* Imperial War Museum, House of Commons, Sultanate of Oman. *Clubs:* Arts, Chelsea Arts, Fadeaways. *Signs work:* "C. MIERS." *Address:* 114 Bishop's Mans., Bishop's Park Rd., Fulham, London SW6 6DY.

**MILES, June,** R.W.A.; painter; Mem. Penwith Society of Artists and Newlyn Society of Artists; *b* London, 4 July, 1924. *m* Paul Mount, sculptor; one s. two d. by previous marriage. *Educ:* Portsmouth High School. *Studied:* Slade School (1941-43) under Randolph Schwabe. *Work in collections:* Bristol City, A.G., Plymouth City A.G., R.W.A., Nuffield Foundation, Durham University, Sussex Educ. Com. *Signs work:* "June Miles" (on back of painting). *Address:* Nancherrow Studio, St. Just, Penzance TR19 7LA.

**MILLAIS, Raoul,** painter in oil, pastel, ink and pencil of equestrian, Spanish, figure and landscape subjects; *b* Horsham, Sussex, 4 Oct., 1901; wife deceased. three *s. Educ:* Winchester College. *Studied:* Byam Shaw School of Art (1919-20), R.A. Schools (1921-25). *Exhib:* Fine Arts (1930), Tryon Gallery (4), Spain, U.S.A. *Work in collections:* Racing Museum, Sandringham, many in America. *Publications:* Life to be published Feb., 1998. *Signs work:* "Raoul Millais." *Address:* Westcote Manor, Church Westcote, Chipping Norton, Oxon. OX7 6SF.

**MILLAR, Jack Ernest,** A.R.C.A. (1950), R.B.A. (1954); artist in oil; former Head of Fine Art, Kingston Polytechnic (retd. 1986); *b* London, 28 Nov., 1921. *m* (1) Pauline Sawyer one *s.* one *d.* (2) Pamela Izzard. *Studied:* Clapham School of Art (1939), St. Martin's School of Art (1941), Royal College of Art (1947-50, 1st Class Dip., awarded Andrew Lloyd Scholarship for landscape painting). *Exhib:* Odette Gilbert Gallery; one-man shows, Linton Court Gallery, Duncan Campbell Fine Art, Mason-Watts Fine Art. *Work in collections:* Royal Academy (work purchased by President and Council. Shown at London Group), Leicester Galleries, Piccadilly Gallery, Trafford Gallery, Brighton Art Gallery, Roland, Browse and Delbanco, Alton Gallery. *Clubs:* Arts. *Signs work:* "J. Millar." *Address:* 10 Overhill Rd., East Dulwich, London SE22 0PH.

**MILLAR, Sir Oliver Nicholas,** G.C.V.O., F.B.A., F.S.A.; Director of the Royal Collection and Surveyor of H.M. The Queen's pictures (retd. 1988); Surveyor Emeritus of The Queen's Pictures; *b* Standon, Herts., 26 Apr., 1923. *m* (1954) Delia Dawnay. one *s.* three *d. Educ:* Rugby, Courtauld Inst. *Publications:* English Art (1625-1714), with Dr. M. D. Whinney; Abraham van der Doort's Catalogue; Tudor, Stuart and early Georgian Pictures in the Collection of H.M. the Queen; Zoffany and His Tribuna; Later Georgian Pictures in the Collection of H.M. the Queen; Inventories and Valuations of the King's Goods; The Queen's Pictures; Victorian Pictures in the Collection of

# WHO'S WHO IN ART

H.M. the Queen; catalogues; articles in various journals. *Clubs:* Brooks'; M.C.C. *Address:* The Cottage, Rays Lane, Penn, Bucks. HP10 8LH.

**MILLER, David,** R.B.A. (1994), N.D.D. (1958); artist in oil; I.L.E.A. Head of Dept. for Art in A.E.I. (1971-87); *b* Belfast, 25 Feb., 1931. *m* Monica Miller. one *s*. one *d*. *Educ:* Trinity College, Glenalmond, Perthshire. Studied Polytechnic School of Art, Regent St. London (1954-60, Norman Blamey R.A.). *Exhib:* R.A., R.B.A., R.P., New Soc. of Portrait Painters, and other mixed exhbns. *Signs work:* "DAVID MILLER." *Address:* Whiteswood Cottage, Back Lane, Nazeing, Essex EN9 2RS; and Flat 2, 76 Auckland Hill London SE27.

**MILLER, David T.,** D.A. (Edin.), F.R.B.S., Latimer Award, R.S.A. (1961 Prof. Member S.S.A.; sculptor on wood, stone, bronze, steel, fibreglass resin lecturer, Moray House College; *b* Bo'ness, 1931. *m* Morag Macmurray. one one *d*. *Educ:* Mortlach School, Dufftown. *Studied:* Gray's School of Art Aberdeen, Edinburgh College of Art (Eric Schilsky), Paris, Vallauris. *Work i collections:* public sculpture in Edinburgh, Selkirk, Dalkeith, Alyth, Linwood Moray House, Scottish Arts Council. *Signs work:* see appendix. *Address* Northend House, Pathhead, Ford, Midlothian.

**MILLER, Ingrid,** printmaker, painter in etching, drypoint, oil, acrylic water-colour; *b* Copenhagen, 1940. *m* R.G. Miller, printmaker. *Educ* Copenhagen University. *Studied:* Malmö Printmaking School. *Exhib:* R.A R.S.A., Mall Galleries, Leighton House Gallery, Guildhall Gallery, R.A Copenhagen, National Museum Gdansk, Wainö Aaltonen Museum Finland Liljevalchs Stockholm, Print Triennales Malmö and Gothenburg, Internationa Print Biennales: Cracow, Ljubljana, Rockford, Horgen, Cadaques, Varna Maastrich, Biella, Berlin, Fredrikstad; Museums: Kalmar, Eksjö, Kristianstad Vetlanda, Växjö. *Work in collections:* Cabo Frio, Brazil; Swedish States Art Council; Kalmar Museum. *Clubs:* Swedish and Danish Federations o Printmakers, G.S., D.G. and K.R.O., S.K., K.K.S., F.S.K., Grant Swedish State *Signs work:* "Ingrid Miller." *Address:* Bolmen, 34194 Ljungby, Sweden.

**MILLER, Ronald George,** printmaker, painter in etching, mezzotint engraving, acrylic; sculptor in wood; *b* London, 1938. *m* Ingrid, printmaker *Educ:* Haverstock Hill Secondary School. *Studied:* Ingrid Miller's Prin Workshop, Ljungby, Sweden. *Exhib:* R.A., R.S.A. Edinburgh, Internationa Print Biennales in Ljubljana, Krakow, Grenoble, Cadaques, Varna, Biella Maastrich, Majdanek, Frechen, Berlin, Fredrikstad; museums in Kristiansta Vetlanda, Kalmar, Växjö, Liljevalchs, 4th National Exhbn. of British Prints Grundy Gallery, Blackpool. *Work in collections:* Majdanek Museum Poland Museums in Växjö, Vetlanda, Swedish Arts Council. *Clubs:* Federation o Swedish Printmakers, G.S., K.R.O., S.K., Grant Swedish State. *Signs work* "Ronald Miller." *Address:* Bolmen, 34194 Ljungby, Sweden.

**MILLINGTON, Terence,** painter/printmaker in oil, water-colour, etching *b* B'ham, 20 Oct., 1942. *m* Patricia. one *s*. *Educ:* Moseley Secondary School o rt. *Studied:* painting: B'ham College of Art (1958-63), and printmaking at Manchester College of Art (1965-66). *Exhib:* many group and one-man exhbns. throughout Europe and the U.S.A. *Work in collections:* various private and public including Tate Gallery, and V. & A. *Commissions:* Royal Mail stamp commission 1997 (100th Anniversary of sub post offices). *Publications:* Editions of etchings regularly published by C.C.A. London and Behr-Thyssen Ltd. New York. *Signs work:* "Terence Millington." *Address:* 146 Church St., Kingsbridge, Devon TQ7 1DB.

**MILLIS, Susan M.,** S.W.A. (1987), S.E.A. (1995); pyrographic artist specializing in wildlife, equestrian and pictorial subjects on hand turned wooden paper-weights, pomanders, plaques, jewellery, paper and now blowtorch fire painting; Vice-Pres. Soc. of Women Artists; *b* Tidworth, Hants., 14 Nov., 1953. m Gareth Hughes Millis. one *s.* one *d. Educ:* Upbury Manor, Gillingham. *Exhib:* R.M.S., S.W.A., S.E.A. annually, Francis Iles Galleries, Rochester throughout the year. Work in private collections worldwide. *Publications:* A Burning Art (Popular Crafts, May 1989). *Signs work:* "S.M. Millis." *Address:* 10 Buxton Cl., Lordswood, Chatham, Kent ME5 8UP.

**MILLMORE, Mark Alexander,** R.E., B.A. (Hons.) Fine Art; artist in etching, painter in oil and water-colour; *b* Shanklin, I.O.W., 13 Jan., 1956. *Studied:* Falmouth School of Art (1977-80, Prof. Lionel Miskin). *Exhib:* C.C.A. Galleries, and around the U.K. (1990-95); mixed shows: Japan, U.S.A., Sweden, Taiwan, Australia, Spain, Canada, Kenya and the U.K. *Work in collections:* Ashmolean Museum, Habikino City Hall Japan, Crown Court, Bristol, Victoria A.G. Bath, Kanagawa Prefectural Gallery Japan, Auburn University Contemporary Art Collection U.S.A., International Centre for Wildlife Art Gloucester. Theatre designer: Stinkfoot, a comic opera by Vivian Stanshall Bristol 1985, London 1988); Rawlinson Dogends, starring Vivian Stanshall London 1991). *Signs work:* "Millmore." *Address:* Upper Jury Farm, Wormbridge, Herefordshire HR2 9EE.

**MILLNER, Etienne Henry, de la Fargue,** figurative sculptor in plaster and clay for bronze; *b* Penang, Malaysia, 15 Jan., 1954. *m* Mary Castle. one *s.* one *d. Educ:* Stowe School. *Studied:* Goldsmiths' College (Michael Kenny, R.A., Ivor Roberts-Jones, C.B.E., R.A.), R.A. Schools. *Exhib:* R.A. Summer Shows 1979, 1982, 1984, 1985, 1986, 1988), N.P.G. 'New Faces' (1987), 'Art for Sale' Whiteleys (1992), Chelsea Harbour (1993), Cadogan Gallery Summer Show (1993); one-man show Cadogan Contemporary (1994). S.P.S. Annual Exhbn. (1995, 1996, 1997). *Work in collections:* N.P.G., Wellington College, Harris Manchester College, Oxford. *Commissions:* Field Marshal Sir Claude Auchinleck for Wellington College (1992), Capt. Charles Harris, M.C., Statue for Harris Manchester College, Oxford (1997), Rumer Godden (1996). *Clubs:* Chelsea Arts. *Signs work:* see appendix. *Address:* Montana Cottage, 7 Priory Gr., London SW8 2PD.

**MILLS, Clive,** B.A.Hons. (1987); painter in oil on canvas; *b* Shoreham,

Sussex, 7 Mar., 1964. *Educ:* Portslade College. *Studied:* Brighton Polytechnic (1984-87), R.A. Schools (1987-90). *Exhib:* Mall Galleries (group show 1988, Post Grad. show 1989), R.A. Summer Exhbn. (1989). *Work in collections:* South East Arts and private collections including Switzerland. *Signs work* "Clive Mills." *Address:* 22 Easthill Drive, Portslade, Brighton, E. Sussex BN4 2FO.

**MILLS, John W.,** A.R.C.A., F.R.B.S.; sculptor in bronze; *b* London, 1933; *m* Josephine Demarne. one *s.* one *d. Educ:* Bec School, Tooting. *Studied* Hammersmith School of Art (1947-54), R.C.A. (1956-60, John Skeaping). *Exhib:* Arts Council, R.A., Alwin Gallery London, Simsar Gallery Michigan, Beaux Arts Gallery Bath. *Work in collections:* Wellcome Foundation, Chicago Inst. of Fine Art, University of Cambridge, University of Michigan, Orient Express, City of London. *Publications:* 8 books on sculpture techniques recent - Encyclopedia of Sculpture Technique. *Signs work:* "John W. Mills." *Address:* Hinxworth Pl., Hinxworth, Baldock, Herts. SG7 5HB.

**MILLWARD, Michael,** M.A., A.M.A.; museum curator; Curator and Museum Manager, Blackburn Museum and Art Gallery; *b* Oldham, 9 Nov. 1944. *m* Dorothy. one *s.* one *d. Educ:* King George V Grammar School, Southport; St. John's College, Cambridge. *Publications:* Victorian Townscape (with Brian Coe) 1974. *Address:* Blackburn Museum and Art Gallery, Museum St., Blackburn, Lancs. BB1 7AJ.

**MILNE, Judith Erica,** N.D.D. (1965), A.T.D. (1966); painter of botanical landscape and garden scenes in water-colour; publisher; tutor; *b* Malvern, 30 Oct., 1943. *m* J.A.S. Milne. one *s.* one *d. Educ:* St. Mary's Convent, Worcester. *Studied:* B'ham College of Art and Crafts. *Exhib:* London and various galleries in British Isles. *Work in collections:* V. & A., Traynor Fine Arts, Berks. *Commissions:* nationally and internationally. *Publications:* Flowers in Water-colour (B.T. Batsford); Wildflowers in Water-colour (B. T. Batsford, 1995); greetings cards and prints, regular articles for Leisure Painter magazine. *Clubs:* S.G.F.A. *Signs work:* "Judith Milne." *Address:* 20 Colemans Moor Rd. Woodley, Reading RG5 4DL.

**MILNE, Robert Wilson,** artist in water-colour (landscape, historic bldgs., still life), oil (landscape), pen and ink (bldgs. and figure); *b* Hitchin, 4 Mar., 1950; married. one *s.* one *d. Educ:* Hitchin Boys' Grammar School. *Studied:* St. Albans College of Art. *Exhib:* one-man shows: Cheltenham, Hereford, Worcester, R.I.B.A. (1983), Ludlow Festival, Olivia Rumens Gallery (1990). *Work in collections:* Hereford City A.G. *Signs work:* "Robert Milne." *Address:* 2 Pedwardine Cottages, Brampton Bryan, Bucknell, Shropshire SY7 0DW.

**MINERS, Neil,** artist in oil, water-colour; *b* Redruth, Cornwall, 19 June, 1931. *m* Wendy Noak. two *d. Studied:* Falmouth School of Art under Jack Chalker (1948) drawing only. *Exhib:* R.I., R.O.I., and Britain in Water-colours; one-man shows and various in Cornwall. *Work in collections:* R.N.L.I., Trinity House and H.R.H. Prince Charles. Official designs and medals, illustrated book nd Flags for Tall Ships start from Falmouth (1966). *Signs work:* see appendix. *address:* 23 Arwenack St., Falmouth, Cornwall TR11 3JA.

**MIRECKI, Wladyslaw,** painter in water-colour; co-Proprietor of Chappel Galleries; *b* Chelmsford, 1956. *m* Edna Church, née Battye. *Exhib:* N.E.A.C. 1988), Epping Forest District Museum 'Artists in Essex' (1989), Southend-on-Sea 31st Open (1989), Foyles A.G. (1991), Dept. of Transport Art Competition 1992), Deuxième Salon Biennale de L'Aquarell, Hirson, France (1992), Singer & Friedlander/Sunday Times Water-colour Competition (1997); solo shows: Chappel Galleries (1990, 1996). *Work in collections:* Essex C.C. *Signs work:* "Mirecki." *Address:* 15 Colchester Rd., Chappel, Essex CO6 2DE.

**MISTRY, Dhruva,** R.A., M.A. (1981), M.S. University, M.A. (R.C.A. 1983), F.R.B.S. (1993); artist in Residence, Kettle's Yard, Cambridge (1984-85); sculptor in plaster, bronze, stone; *b* Kanjari (Gujarat) India, 1 Jan., 1957. *Exhib:* over 15 one-man shows worldwide, U.K., India, Japan. *Work in collections:* Tate Gallery, National Museum of Wales, Fukuoka Art Museum, British Council, etc. *Publications:* exhbn. catalogues: Kettle's Yard (1985), Nigel Greenwood Gallery (1990), Fukuoka Art Museum (1994). *Signs work:* "Dhruva Mistry" or "D.M." *Address:* c/o Royal Academy, Burlington House, Piccadilly, London W1V 0DS.

**MITCHELL, Brian,** R.S.M.A.; painter in oil, water-colour, acrylic; *b* St. Ives, Cornwall, 12 Oct., 1937. *m* Marion. one *s*. *Educ:* Penzance Grammar School. *Studied:* Penzance (1958-60, Bouverie Hoyton), Falmouth (1960-62), nst. of Educ. London University (1962-63). *Exhib:* R.W.A., R.W.S., R.I., R.B.A., R.S.M.A. *Signs work:* "MITCHELL." *Address:* Gwaynten, Porthrepta Rd., St. Ives, Cornwall TR26 2NZ.

**MITCHELL, Enid G. D.,** F.R.B.S.; Dip.A.D. (Ceramics), Visual Arts Diploma, London University; Ghilchrist Prize; sculptor of portraits and figures cast in bronze, cement and resin, art ceramics in porcelain and stoneware; one s. two *d*. *Educ:* Lady Eleanor Holles School, Hampton, Middx. *Studied:* Ealing School of Art (sculpture tutors, Tom Bailey and Robert Thomas, A.R.C.A.). *Work in collections:* Leamington Spa, Islip Manor and Drayton Green Primary Schools and private collections: England, Holland, Israel, Denmark, U.S.A., etc. *Clubs:* Royal Society of British Sculptors. *Signs work:* "MITCHELL" or "Enid G. D. Mitchell." *Address:* 32 Stanier St., Swindon, Wilts. SN1 5QX.

**MITCHELL, Gordon Kinlay,** Dip.Art (Edin.), awarded Post.Dip. Scholarship and Travelling Scholarship; surrealist artist in water-colour, acrylic, oil; full-time professional artist; *b* Edinburgh, 16 Nov., 1952. *m* Catriona A.C. Mitchell. one *s*. one *d*. *Studied:* Edinburgh College of Art (Sir Robin Philipson, David Michie). *Exhib:* many major exhbns. in the British Isles; one-man shows, Henderson Gallery, Edinburgh (1978, 1981), Open Eye Gallery, Edinburgh (1992), Roger Billcliffe Fine Art, Glasgow (1993). *Work in collections:* Scottish Arts Council, Kansas City Art Inst., Educational Inst. for Scotland, Old City A.G., Jerusalem, Paisley Art Inst., Teachers Whiskey,

Scottish Brewers, Alliance & Leicester Bldg. Soc. *Signs work:* "Gordon K Mitchell." *Address:* 10 Argyll Terr., Haymarket, Edinburgh EH11 2BR.

**MITCHELL, John,** R.S.W. (1967); lecturer and teacher; artist in water colour, silkscreen; Mem. S.S.A.; *b* Glasgow, 21 Dec., 1937. *Educ:* Glasgow Academy, Royal High School of Edinburgh. *Studied:* Edinburgh College of Ar (1956-61). *Work in collections:* Scottish Arts Council, Fife Education Com. British Transport Hotels. *Signs work:* "JOHN MITCHELL." *Address:* Wes Gowanbrae, 4 The Temple, Lower Largo, Fife.

**MITCHELL, S. M.,** P.P.S.P.S., F.R.B.S., A.R.C.A., N.D.D.; sculptor in clay, wood, stone, fibreglass, resins, concrete, bronze; *b* Farnham. *m* Charles Bone, artist. two *s. Educ:* Seager House School, Farnham G.G.S. *Studied.* Farnham School of Art (1946), under Charles Vyes, Guildford School of Art (1947), under Willi Soukop, R.A., Royal College of Art (1948-51), under Frank Dobson, R.A., John Skeaping, R.A., Edward Folkard, F.R.B.S. *Exhib:* R.A. S.P.S., N.E.A.C., W.I.A., Ashgate Gallery, Furneaux Gallery, Canalette Gallery, Chenil Gallery; 20 one-man exhbns., Medici Gallery, Ashgate Gallery Gainsborough's House, University of Surrey, Guildford House, Malta, G.C. Tarrystone Gallery. Majorca, Spain, Pasadena, U.S.A. *Commissions:* portrai commissions in bronze, terracotta. Recent portraits: H.R.H The Duchess o Kent, Sebastian Coe, Robert Bolt, Sarah Miles, Sir Edward Tuckwell, Si George Edwards, and over 200 bronze portrait sculptures. Two 9ft. sculpture for Majorca Legend of Chertsey, forecourt of Thorn PLC, bronze 11ft. high etc. Designer: ceramic sculpture, including Royal Worcester Porcelain. Electe first woman president Society of Portrait Sculptors (1977). *Signs work:* "S Mitchell." sometimes (B) after signature. *Address:* Winters Farm, Puttenham nr. Guildford, Surrey GU3 1AR.

**MOCKFORD, Harold,** self taught artist in oil; *b* 25 Jan., 1932. *Exhib:* one-man shows: Towner A.G. (1970, 1987), Hove Museum (1980, 1985) Thackeray Gallery, London (1978); R.A. Summer Exhbns., London Group Newport (Gwent) A.G. (1995). *Work in collections:* Tate Gallery, Chantry Bequest, Towner Gallery, Hove Museum of Art, Government Art Collection *Signs work:* "H. Mockford" on back of board. *Address:* 45 Hillcrest Rd. Newhaven BN9 9EE.

**MOGER, Jill,** A.S.W.L.A. (1996); ceramic sculptor (wildlife) in stoneware porcelain clay; *b* London, 1946. *m* Dr. Philip Moger. two *s.* two *d. Educ.* Ursuline High School, Ilford, and Saffron Walden County High. *Exhib:* S.WL.A., Bonham's "Art of Living World", Singapore, Yorkshire Sculpture Park; many mixed and two solo exhbns. *Work in collections:* Stoke on Tren City Museum and A.G. *Commissions:* Leeds Playhouse, Yorkshire Museum o Farming. *Signs work:* "Jill Moger" (and date) etched into clay. *Address:* The Studio, 75 Millfield Lane, Nether Poppleton, York YO2 6NA.

**MOLLOY, Sylvia,** M.A.; painter in oil and other media; *b* 27 Mar., 1914. *m* Patrick Molloy. two *s. Educ:* Durham, M.A. (English and Art). *Studied.*

Johannesburg College of Art (1949-52). *Exhib:* R.A., R.B.A., R.O.I., S.W.A., W.S.; solo shows, six in London, Letchworth, Hitchin, Lavenham and others. *Work in collections:* stained glass in Johannesburg and Pretoria, paintings in East London, Bloemfontein, Pretoria; U.K.: Letchworth A.G., Sax House, Heritage Foundation. *Commissions:* Archbishop Edinburgh, other portraits. *Publications:* autobiography 'Burma Bride' (1995) illustrated with own pictures. Entry in Dictionary of S. African Painters and Sculptors. *Clubs:* N.S., F.P.S. (Fellow). *Signs work:* "Sylvia Molloy." *Address:* 41 Field Lane, Letchworth, Herts. SG6 3LD.

**MONCHER-DUNKLEY, Anthea,** Mem. S.B.A.; scientific illustrator (botanical and geological) in oil; University illustrator/cartographer and muralist and botanical painter; *b* Isle of Wight, 10 Oct., 1945. *Educ:* private school. *Studied:* Southampton College of Art (part-time). *Exhib:* S.B.A., Soc. of Floral Painters, Wessex Artists. *Work in collections:* commissioned paintings: Dept. of Geology, Southampton University, and educational establishments; commissioned work in private collections: Egypt, Japan, India, Syria, U.S.A., France and Australia. *Publications:* scientific journals. *Address:* 'The Studio', 7 Lawn Rd., Portswood, Southampton, Hants. SO17 2EX.

**MONTAGUE, Lucile Christine,** L.C.A.D. (1974); painter; *b* London, 1950. *m* (1) Michael Montague (divorced); (2) David Greene. one *s. Educ:* Fyling Hall School, Yorks. *Studied:* Plymouth College of Art (1967-69), Byam Shaw School of Art (1971-74). *Exhib:* R.A., Whitechapel Open, London Group, Spirit of London, Leicester Exhbn., South Bank Show, Thumb Gallery; group shows: Ikon Gallery touring, 'Ways of Telling' Mostyn Gallery, Llandudno, 'Subjective City' touring, 'Witnesses and Dreamers' touring; one-man shows, Mario Fletcher Gallery, London; Clayton Gallery, Newcastle; The Studio Gallery, London. *Work in collections:* Bankers Trust, Coopers and Lybrand, Camden Council, Herbert Museum and A.G., Coventry. *Publications:* Women Artist's Diary (1989). *Signs work:* "L.C. Montague." *Address:* 47 Hargrave Pk., London N19 5JW.

**MONTAGUE-GRAINGER, Bernard,** A.R.C.A., F.R.S.A., Membre Associé de la Société des Artistes Français; design consultant and engineer; Instrument maker Geophysics Survey; silversmith, mine surveying, etc.; sapper, R.E. Field Survey; retd. Hon. Lecturer in Freehand Drawing, Faculty of Architecture, Sheffield University; at opening of School of Tropical Medicine appointed Extra Mural Member by Prof. Sigmund Freud; *b* Paddock Wood, Kent, 16 July, 1907. *m* Pattie Revell. two *s.* one *d. Educ:* Ardingly College, Minor Holy Order: Door-keeper. *Studied:* Maidstone School of Art, scholarship to R.C.A. (Post dip. 4th year); Ordained Reader and Exorcist by Archbishop Leadbeater (Minor Holy Order and Theosophy). *Exhib:* Paris Salon, R.A., Biarritz, Sheffield, Manchester, Derby, N.Y., Gallery Mouffe Paris. *Work in collections:* Canada, France, U.S.A., New Zealand, Spain, Sweden, Australia, Iran, British Isles, Goldsmiths' Hall. *Publications:* written work, letters and essays in private circulation: adolescent development, theology, sexual and sociological studies, military studies, etc. *Clubs:* Past President: Sheffield Soc. of Art, Derbyshire Pennine Club, Craven Pothole Club; Founder mem.: British Spaeological Assoc., Cave Research Group, Peveril Underground Survey Assoc. *Signs work:* "B.M. Grainger." *Address:* Belmont, Terrace Rd., Tideswell, Derbyshire SK17 8NA.

**MONTANÉ, Roger,** painter in oil; Prix Bethouard (1948); President, Groupe 109 (1982); *b* Bordeaux, 21 Feb., 1916; married. two *s. Educ:* Toulouse. *Studied:* self-taught. *Exhib:* Chicago (1964), New York (1965), Musée de Toulon (1965). *Work in collections:* Musée d'Art Moderne (Paris), Musées de la Ville (Paris), de St. Denis (Paris), de Toulouse, d'Albi, Ishibashi (Tokyo), Groupe International d'Art Figuratif (Japan, 1960), Exposition Particulière la Maison de La Pensée Française, Paris (1961), Aberdeen Museum and Art Gall., Musées de Valence, de Rodez, de Sete, de Bagnols s/Cèze, Wellington Museum (N.Z.), de Grenoble. President, Salon d'Automne (1966-68), Musées de Narbonne, Prague, du Sport (Paris). *Signs work:* see appendix. *Address:* 33 rue Charcot, Paris 13.

**MONTGOMERY, Iona Allison Eleanor,** B.F.A.(Hons.) (1987), Post.Grad. D.F.A. (1988), R.S.W. (1991); Alexander Graham Munro travel award (1990), Lauder award (1991); artist in painting and printmaking; *b* Glasgow, 14 Apr., 1965. *Educ:* Boclair Academy, Bearsden, Glasgow. *Studied:* Glasgow School of Art (Philip Reeves), Tamarind Inst., Albuquerque, U.S.A. *Exhib:* one-man shows including Galerie Seghaier, Vienna, Ancrum Gallery, Edinburgh Gallery, Lillie A.G., various group shows including R.S.A., R.S.W., R.G.I., G.P.S., Consument Art, also U.S.A., Europe and U.S.S.R. *Work in collections:* Lillie A.G., Milngavie, B.B.C., Hilton Hotels, etc. Various teaching including part-time lecturer Grays School of Art. *Clubs:* R.S.W., G.P.S., G.S.W.A., S.A.C. *Signs work:* "Iona A.E. Montgomery." *Address:* 171a Maryhill Rd., Flat 2/3, Glasgow G20 7XL.

**MONTGOMERY, James Alexander,** artist in water-colour, pen and ink, oil; Leader of Complex of Rehabilitation Units, including Art Therapy; *b* Glasgow, 3 Oct., 1928. *m* Isabelle, artist. two *s.* one *d. Educ:* Woodside School, Glasgow. *Studied:* Glasgow School of Art (David Donaldson, Edward Powell), apprenticed to industrial artist. *Exhib:* Columbus City Museum, U.S.A., Carrollton Nova Lomason A.G., Atlanta. *Clubs:* Glasgow Art. *Signs work:* "Hamish Montgomery." *Address:* 13 Avon Ave., Bearsden, Glasgow G61 2PS.

**MOOD, Kenneth,** B.A. (Hons,); artist/writer; *b* Gateshead, 24 Nov., 1950. *m* Margaret. one *s.* one *d. Educ:* Gateshead. *Studied:* Sunderland Art College. *Exhib:* Mail Art shows worldwide. *Work in collections:* Arts Council, Whitney Museum (N.Y.), twenty-five U.K. art galleries and museums. *Address:* 1 Burns Cres., Swalwell, Tyne and Wear NE16 3JE.

**MOODIE, Stuart,** Artist-designer in pen and ink, water-colour, acrylic and mixed media; *b* Aberdeen, 7 Apr., 1922. *m* Christine Bou. two *d. Educ:* Robert

Gordon's College, Aberdeen; autodidactic in painting but greatly influenced by Robin Philipson. *Exhib:* Douglas and Foulis Gallery, Edinburgh, Pitlochry Festival Theatre, Craon, La Mayenne, France. *Work in collections:* Britain, America, Canada, Denmark, Spain, France. With his wife, co-owned and ran two private art galleries in Scotland. Taught art to adults in the artists' town of Altea on Spain's Costa Blanca. *Signs work:* "Stuart Moodie" and see appendix. *Address:* 4 rue de la Grotte, Bourg de Coesmes, 35134 France.

**MOODY, Catherine Olive,** A.T.D. (1944), P.S. (1960), R.B.S.A. (1965), Exhbn. Scholarship R.C.A. (1941); painter in oil and pastel, writer, designer; Head of School of Art, Malvern Hills College (1962-80); President, Malvern Art Club, Editorial Consultant, Leisure Painter periodical; *b* London, 27 Nov., 1920. *Educ:* Stroud High and Thornbank Schools. *Studied:* Malvern School of Art (1935-41, Victor Moody), Royal College Art (1941), Birmingham School of Art (1944, Fleetwood-Walker). *Exhib:* R.A., P.S., R.P., R.B.S.A., R.I.B.A. *Work in collections:* Worcester City A.G., British Rail Archives. *Publications:* Silhouette of Malvern; Painter's Workshop, and articles. *Clubs:* Malvern Art. *Signs work:* "C.O. MOODY" or "C.M." *Address:* 1 Sling La., Malvern, Worcs. WR14 2TU.

**MOON, Liz,** B.A./M.A. Oxon. (Engineering) 1964, S.W.A. (1987); painter in acrylic, water-colour; Adult Tutor in Art; *b* India, 4 Oct., 1941. *Educ:* Sherborne Girls' School; St. Hugh's College, Oxford; Redlands College, Bristol. *Studied:* San Francisco Art Inst. *Exhib:* R.S.M.A., R.W.A., R.B.A., R.I.; solo shows: Barbican Level 5 West, Royal Opera House, Covent Gdn., John Russell Gallery, Ipswich, and Heffer Gallery, Cambridge. "Liz Moon paints the world she knows with amused intensity. Her everyday scenes of people in action are infused with energy and humour." *Publications:* article in The Artist (1987). *Address:* 21 Bermuda Terr., Cambridge CB4 3LD.

**MOON, Michael,** First prize, John Moores Liverpool Exhbn. (1980), print award, Gulbenkian (1984); painter in mixed media; *b* Edinburgh, 9 Nov., 1937. *m* Anjum Moon. two *s. Educ:* Shoreham Grammar School, Sussex. *Studied:* Chelsea School of Art (1958-62), R.C.A. (1963). *Exhib:* one-man shows in U.K., Australia and U.S.A. including Tate Gallery (1976); numerous group exhbns. worldwide. *Work in collections:* Tate Gallery, Arts Council, Saatchi Collection, provincial and overseas. *Signs work:* "Mick Moon." *Address:* 10 Bowood Rd., London SW11 6PE.

**MOON, Tennant,** A.R.C.A., F.S.A.E., F.R.S.A., Principal, Cumbria College of Art and Design (1957-78); Principal, Gravesend School of Art and Crafts (1949-57); Lecturer, Leicester College of Art (1946-49); President, National Society for Art Education (1972-73); Chairman, Association of Art Institutions (1976-77); Chairman, Standing Advisory Committee for Art & Design, Associated Examining Board (1970-86); *b* Penarth, S. Glamorgan, 12 Nov., 1914. *m* (1) Barbara Ovenden (decd.); one s. one d.; (2) Joan Whiting. *Studied:* Cardiff School of Art, Royal College of Art under Sir William

Rothenstein. *Exhib:* R.A., Leicester Galleries, National Museum of Wales, South Wales Group, Newport (Gwent) A.G., Leicester A.G., etc. *Work in collections:* Cumbria Educ. Com. and private collections. *Clubs:* The New (Cheltenham). *Address:* 15 Lansdown Parade, Cheltenham, Glos. GL50 2LH.

**MOORE, Bridget,** R.A.S.Dip., R.B.A., Greenshield Foundation (1985), painter in oil and gouache; *b* Whitstable, 2 Aug., 1960. *m* Alistair Milne. one *s* one *d. Educ:* The Sir William Nottidge School, Whitstable. *Studied:* Medway College of Design, Epsom School of Art, R.A. Schools. *Exhib:* R.A., R.B.A. *Clubs:* Reynolds. *Signs work:* "BRIDGET MOORE" on back. *Address:* 29 Sylvan Rd., Upper Norwood, London SE19 2RU.

**MOORE, Gerald John,** N.D.D. (1958), A.T.C., A.T.D. (Manc.) (1959), B.A.(Hons.Theol.) (1969), F.R.S.A. (1985); traditional painter in water-colour and oil: landscapes, animals, birds, buildings, historical genre and portraits; *b* Ratby, Leics., 1938. *Educ:* Broom Leys School, Leics. *Studied:* Loughborough (1955-58), Manchester Regional College of Art (1958-59), University of Exeter (Theology 1966-69; History of Art 1974-75). *Exhib:* Teignmouth, Tiverton, Taunton, Widecombe-in-the-Moor, Braunton, Bournemouth, Salisbury and Bristol. *Signs work:* "G.J.M." or "G.J. MOORE." *Address:* Lower Huntham Farm, Stoke St. Gregory, Taunton, Som. TA3 6EY.

**MOORE, Heather Ruth,** S.B.A.; botanical painter in water-colour and oil; *b* Scarborough, 9 May, 1925. *m* James K.L. (decd.). three *s. Studied:* Scarborough School of Art (1939-41), A.E.C. Tunbridge Wells (Maurice Weidman). *Exhib:* Mall Galleries, Westminster Gallery, Camden Arts Centre, Linnean Soc., Burlington House, etc. *Signs work:* "H.R. MOORE" (initials H.R. linked). *Address:* 2 Newlands, Langton Green, Tunbridge Wells, Kent TN3 0BU.

**MOORE, Jean Marigold,** R.M.S. (1993); Hon. Mention R.M.S. (1995); painter in oil and water-colour, writer; *b* Valletta, Malta, 24 Nov., 1928. divorced. three *s. Educ:* privately. *Studied:* Lowestoft School of Art. *Exhib:* Mall, Westminster and Llewellyn Alexander Galleries; also in Brussels at the American Embassy; solo shows in Sussex. *Signs work:* "J.M. MOORE" (oils) "J.M.M." (water-colours and miniatures). Also painted under Dunbar (maiden name) and Seabrook (1st married name). *Address:* 17 Garrod House, Charles Rd., St. Leonards, Sussex TN38 0QD.

**MOORE, Ken,** painter in oil; director, Commonwealth Biennale of Abstract Art London (1963); *b* Melbourne, Australia, 1923. *Studied:* St. Martin's School of Art under Derrick Greaves, Kenneth Martin, Russell Hall. *Work in collections:* New Britten Museum, Connecticut, Phoenix Art Museum Arizona, Cedar Rapids Art Museum, Iowa, Keppe Gallery, Denmark, Lynam Allen Museum, Connecticut, Finch College Museum, N.Y., Tweed Gallery Minneapolis, Witchita University, Kansas, Bertrand Russell Foundation, The Australian Ballet, University of Sydney, University of Melbourne, University of New England Armidale, H.R.H. Princess Margaret, King George VI and

Queen Elizabeth Foundation, Windsor, The American Legation Museum, Tangier. *Signs work:* "Ken Moore." *Address:* 33 Vicarage Ct., Vicarage Gate, London W8 4HE.

**MOORE, Leslie Lancelot Hardy,** R.I.; artist in water-colour; *b* Norwich, 1907. *m* daughter of Col. J. Plunkett. two *s*. *Educ:* City of Norwich School, University of Reading. *Studied:* mainly self-taught, otherwise University of Reading and Norwich School of Art. *Exhib:* R.A., N.E.A.C., Mall Galleries, Edwin Pollard Gallery, Wimbledon, Mandells Gallery, Norwich. *Publications:* illustrated Old Guns and Pistols, Norwich Inns, Call Me at Dawn; work repro.: in colour commercially. *Signs work:* "Leslie L. H. Moore." *Address:* 26 Suffield Cl., N. Walsham, Norfolk NR28 0HN.

**MORESCHI, Maria,** A.B.A., F.P.S.; art teacher, portrait artist in oil, pastel and water-colour; art teacher The American School, Cobham; *b* Florence, 18 July, 1949; married. one *s*. two *d*. *Educ:* SS. Ma. Annunziata. *Studied:* Academia delle Belle Arti; taught portraiture by Annigoni in Florence. *Exhib:* America, Italy, Holland, England. *Work in collections:* La Loggia, Oxshott, Walton, Epsom, Studio 54 Cobham, The Investment Gallery. *Publications:* in the process of illustrating an animal and wildlife drawing book. *Clubs:* Epsom, Oxshott, Walton, Mosley, Cobham, London. *Signs work:* "M. Moreschi." *Address:* A.C.S. Middle School, Heywood, Portsmouth Rd., Cobham, Surrey.

**MORETON, Nicolas,** B.A.(Hons.) (1985), A.R.B.S. (1995); fine art sculptor in English stones, plaster, clay, bronze, pencil drawing; Resident Sculptor, Manorbier Castle; *b* Watford, Herts., 22 Oct., 1961. *m* Julie Rose Bills. *Educ:* Weston Favell Upper School, Northampton. *Studied:* Nene College, Northampton (1981-82, Frank Cryer), Wolverhampton Polytechnic (1982-85, John Paddison, R.C.A.). *Exhib:* Leics. Schools and Colleges, Albermarle Gallery, Hobart and Maclean Gallery London, Hannah Peschar Gallery Ockley, British Stone Carving, Angel Row; one-man shows: Mall Galleries (1989, 1991), Lamont Gallery (1992), Hunt Jennings (1993), Goldmark Gallery (1995, 1997). Anglia Television 'Moving Art'. *Commissions:* Double public commission, Milton Keynes (1995). *Signs work:* drawing "Nicolas Moreton"; sculpture see appendix. *Address:* 4 West Lodge Cottages, London Rd., Courteenhall, Northampton NN7 2QA.

**MORGAN, Glyn,** Mem. S.B.A.; painter in oil, water-colour, collage; *b* Pontypridd, 16 July, 1926. *m* Jean Bullworthy. *Educ:* Pontypridd Grammar School. *Studied:* Cardiff School of Art (1942-44, Ceri Richards), Camberwell School of Art (1947), East Anglian School (1944-82, Cedric Morris). *Exhib:* one-man shows: Gilbert Parr, London (1978, 1980), Alwin, London (1982, 1983), Richard Demarco Gallery, Edinburgh (1973), Minories, Colchester (1971, 1981), Archway Gallery, Houston, Texas, Chappel Gallery, Essex (1991, 1996), Rhondda Heritage Park, Y Tabernacl, Wales (1997); organised 'The Benton End Circle' exhbn. of work by pupils of Cedric Morris and Lett Haines, Bury St. Edmunds Gallery (1985). *Work in collections:* Auckland and

Brisbane A.G's, Derbyshire, Monmouthshire, Oxford and West Riding Educ. Coms., Welsh Arts Council, Contemporary Art Soc. for Wales, Ipswich Borough Museum and A.G., Newport Museum and A.G. *Signs work:* "MOR-GAN." *Address:* Hunters, 120 High St., Hadleigh, Suffolk IP7 5EL.

**MORGAN, Helena Frances,** Dip. in Textiles (1985), F.F.P.S. (1997), L.C.G.I. (1992); fibre artist in felt; *b* Mountain Ash, Mid Glam., 11 Feb., 1938. *m* Hugh. one *s*. two *d*. *Educ:* Mountain Ash Grammar School. *Studied:* Gloucs. College of Art (1957-61), Regent St. Polytechnic (1963-64), London College of Furniture (1983-85). *Exhib:* group shows in London, France, Hong Kong and Hungary. Work in private collections. *Signs work:* "Helena Morgan." *Address:* Lansbury, 51a High St., Langford, Beds. SG18 9RU.

**MORGAN, Howard James,** M.F.A., R.P.; painter in oil, water-colour, casein; *b* 21 Apr., 1949. *m* Susan Ann. two *s*. one *d*. *Educ:* Fairfax High School. *Studied:* Newcastle-upon-Tyne University (Ralph Holland, Charles Leonard Evetts). *Exhib:* Anthony Mould, Claridges, Agnews, Richmond Gallery. *Work in collections:* N.P.G. *Clubs:* Chelsea Arts, Beefsteak. *Signs work:* roman numerals of month, followed by arabic year and surname, i.e. "MORGAN II 98." *Address:* (studio) 401 Wandsworth Rd., London SW8; (home) 12 Rectory Grove, Clapham, London SW4.

**MORGAN, Jennifer Frances,** N.D.D. (1962), A.R.S.M.A.; freelance artist-painter, mostly in oil/gouache, specializing in marine painting, ships, sailing craft, etc.; *b* Woolwich, London, 22 June, 1942. *Studied:* Camberwell School of Art (1960-64, Robert Medley). *Exhib:* various exhbns. in U.K. including Mall Galleries, London, Ferens Gallery, Hull. *Commissions:* several private commissions over years. *Publications:* work repro: catalogues, book illustrations, calendar publications, Limited. Edn. prints. Finely detailed work sold work Sotheby's, London. *Address:* The Nest, Highgate Lane, Sutton-on-Sea, nr. Mablethorpe, Lincs. LN12 2LH.

**MORGAN, Ronald,** R.B.A. (1984), R.O.I. (1984); draughtsman, painter in water-colour, black and white, oil and pastel, illustrator, linguist, teacher; Mem. Chelsea Art Soc.; *b* Landywood, Staffs., 28 Feb., 1936. *Educ:* Landywood Junior School, Great Wyrley Secondary School, Staffs. *Studied:* Walsall School of Art (1951-53, George Willott, A.R.C.A.). *Exhib:* R.A., R.I., R.B.A., N.E.A.C., S.G.F.A., R.W.A., R.B.S.A., R.S.M.A., R.O.I., Paris Salon, Britain in Water-colours and touring exhbns., etc. *Work in collections:* London Boroughs of Islington, and Tower Hamlets, Graves A.G., Sheffield, Sultan of Oman. *Publications:* work repro.: Leisure Painter, La Revue Moderne (Paris, 1963, 1965), Royal Academy Illustrated. *Signs work:* "R. MORGAN. 1990." *Address:* 8 Marina Ct., Alfred St., Bow, London E3 2BH.

**MORPETH, Vivienne Helen Bland (née Totty),** B.A. Hons. Fine Art (1984), A.M.A. (Art) (1990); curator/fine art; Fine Arts Officer, Middlesbrough Art Gallery (1985-88), Exhbns. Officer, Scunthorpe Museum (1989-92), County Arts and Museums Officer, Cleveland C.C. (1992-95), freelance curator (1995-); *b* Edinburgh, 16 Feb., 1962. *Educ:* The Rudolph Steiner School, Edinburgh. *Studied:* history of art and architecture: University of E. Anglia, Norwich (1981-84). *Exhib:* curated numerous exhbns. at Middlesbrough A.G. and Scunthorpe Museums, local, national, international art and artists tours. *Publications:* exhbn. catalogues. *Address:* 28 Westfield Rd., Barton-upon-Humber, South Humberside DN18 5AB.

**MORREAU, Jacqueline,** artist in oil; Prof. of Art, Regent's College, London; lecturer, Royal College of Art; *b* Wisconsin, U.S.A. *m* Patrick Morreau. two *s.* two *d. Educ:* Chouinard Art Inst., L.A.; Jepson Art Inst., L.A., (Rico Lebrun); University of California Medical School, San Francisco. *Exhib:* one-person shows: Odette Gilbert (1989, 1990), Art Space, London (1986, 1988), Ferens A.G. (1997), retrospective, Ferens A.G., Hull (1988); group shows: Museum of Modern Art, Oxford, `Women's Images of Men' I.C.A. London and tour, Rochdale A.G., Lamont Gallery, London (1997). *Work in collections:* A.C.G.B., B.M., V. & A., Open University, Nuffield College Oxford, City Art Galleries, Hull, etc. *Publications:* Women's Images of Men with Sarah Kent (1985, 1989), Bibliography Jacqueline Morreau, drawings and graphics (1985), From the Interior (Kingston U. Press, 1997), Themes and Variations, (Artemis Press, 1996). *Signs work:* "J. Morreau." *Address:* 40 Church Cres., London N10 3NE.

**MORRELL, Peter John,** N.D.D. (Painting, 1956), A.R.C.A. (Painting, 1959), Rome Scholar in Painting (1959), R.W.S. (1983), Mem. London Group (1990); painter in oil and water-colour, lecturer; *b* Newton Abbot, 28 Feb., 1931. *m* Helene Halstuch. one *s.* one *d. Educ:* Worthing High School for Boys. *Studied:* Kingston-upon-Thames College of Art (1952-56), R.C.A. (1956-59, Ruskin Spear, Carel Weight, John Minton, Colin Hayes). *Exhib:* R.A., John Moores, Grabowski Gallery, New Art Centre, London Group, Beaux Arts Gallery, Arnolfini Gallery, Six Young Painters, Gimpel Fils, R.W.S., Arts Council Touring Exhbns., Gallery Appunto Rome. *Work in collections:* Arts Council, L.C.C., Charterhouse Boys' School, Science Museum. *Commissions:* P. & O. Shipping. *Signs work:* "MORRELL." *Address:* The Mill House, Little Sampford, nr. Saffron Walden, Essex CB10 2QT.

**MORRIS, Anthony,** R.P., N.D.D. (1958), R.A.S. (1961), N.E.A.C. (1995); painter/illustrator in oil and water-colour; *b* Oxford, 2 Aug., 1938. *m* Aileen. *Studied:* Oxford School of Art, R.A. Schools (Peter Greenham). *Exhib:* R.A., R.P., Medici Gallery. *Work in collections:* Bodleian Library, Open University, King's College Hospital. *Publications:* B.B.C. and major publishers. *Signs work:* "MORRIS." *Address:* Church House, Cloduck, Longtown, Herefordshire HR2 0NY.

**MORRIS, James Shepherd,** R.S.A., M.L.A., F.R.I.A.S., A.R.I.B.A.; Mem. Arts Council of Gt. Britain (1973-80), Vice-Chairman, Scottish Arts Council (1976-80), Arts Council Enquiry into Community Arts (1974), Trustee, Nat. Mus. of Antiquities (1980-86), Past Chairman, Scottish Arts Council Art Com.;

Convenor Fellowship Com. R.I.A.S. (1982-87); Mem. Council R.S.A., Hon. Treasurer R.S.A. (1990); Partner, Morris and Steedman, Architects and Landscape Architects, Edinburgh; *b* St. Andrews, Fife, 22 Aug., 1931. *m* Eleanor Kenner Smith. two *s.* one *d. Studied:* Edinburgh College of Art, University of Pennsylvania. R.I.B.A. Award (1974), European Heritage Award (1975), Nine Civic Trust Awards (1962-90), two highly commended Geraldine Scott Design Awards (1995), two R.I.B.A. awards for Scotland (1989, 1974), three A.P.R.S. Awards (1977-89). *Exhib:* R.S.A. *Work in collections:* R.S.A. *Clubs:* New (Edinburgh), Philadelphia Cricket (Philadelphia), Valderrama (Spain). *Address:* Woodcote Pk., Fala, Midlothian, Scotland EH37 5TG.

**MORRIS, John,** Mem., Water-colour Soc. of Wales; painter in water-colour; *b* Deiniolen, N. Wales, 27 Sept., 1922. *m* Eluned Mary. one *s.* one *d. Educ:* Brynrefail County School, Bangor Normal College. *Studied:* Bangor Normal (1955-57, H. Douglas Williams), Press Art School, London (1958-60, Percy V. Bradshaw). *Exhib:* Williamson A.G. Birkenhead, Oriel Theatre Clwyd Mold, Wrexham Arts Centre, Albany Gallery Cardiff, R.I., N.S., Royal National Eisteddfod of Wales, Water-colour Soc. of Wales. *Work in collections:* Royal Welsh Agricultural Soc., National Library of Wales, Midland Bank Ltd., Burnley Building Soc., Clwyd C.C., Shotton Paper Co. *Publications:* Newid Aelwyd, Newid Bro. *Signs work:* "John Morris." *Address:* Elidir, 46 Bryn Awelon, Yr Wyddgrug (Mold), Clwyd CH7 1LU, N. Wales.

**MORRIS, Mali,** B.A. (1968), M.F.A. (1970); artist in acrylic on canvas, water-colour etc. on paper; Senior lecturer, Chelsea School of Art. *Studied:* University of Newcastle upon Tyne (1963-68), University of Reading (1968-70). *Exhib:* 16 solo shows since 1979, including Francis Graham-Dixon Gallery (1997), many group shows worldwide. *Work in collections:* A.C.G.B., British Council, Contemporary Arts Soc., Eastern Arts Assoc., Lloyds of London, National A.G., Botswana, Northern Arts, W.A.C., etc. and private collections. *Signs work:* "Mali Morris." *Address:* c/o Francis Graham-Dixon Gallery, 17-18 Gt. Sutton St., London EC1V 0DN.

**MORRIS, Stanley William,** M.Ed. (1976), A.T.D. (1951), A.R.B.S.A., M.F.P.S.; *b* 1922. *Studied:* Birmingham College of Art. *Exhib:* Paris Salon, R.O.I., N.E.A.C., U.A.S., R.B.S.A., Birmingham University, Keele University. *Work in collections:* Midlands Arts Centre, wood carving for Prince of Wales Regt., Leeds Permanent Building Soc., Alexander Ross. *Address:* Bromley Cottage, Ashbrook La., Abbots Bromley, Staffs. WS15 3DW.

**MORRISON, James,** R.S.A., R.S.W., D.Univ., D.A.; painter in oil and water-colour; *b* Glasgow, 1932; married. one *s.* one *d. Educ:* Hillhead High School, Glasgow School of Art. *Work in collections:* Glasgow, Dundee and Aberdeen Art galleries, Arts Council, Argyll, Dundee and Edinburgh Educ. Committees, Glasgow, Edinburgh, Strathclyde and Stirling Universities, H.R.H. the Duke of Edinburgh, Dept. of the Environment, various embassies, Kingsway Technical College, Vaughan College, Leicester, Municipality of the

Hague, Earls of Dalhousie, Moray, Airlie, Robert Fleming, Merchant Bankers, BBC, Grampian Television, General Accident, Scottish Amicable, Life Assoc. of Scotland; Banks: Royal, Scotland, Clydesdale, T.S.B. *Publications:* author, Affthe Squerr. *Signs work:* "Morrison" and date. *Address:* Craigview House, Usan, Montrose, Angus DD10 9SD.

**MORROCCO, Leon,** D.A., (Edin.), A.R.S.A., R.G.I.; painter in oil and mixed media; *b* Edinburgh, 4 Apr., 1942. *m* Jean Elizabeth Selby. two *s*. *Educ:* Harris Academy, Dundee. *Studied:* Duncan of Jordanstone College of Art, Dundee (1960, Alberto Morrocco, R.S.A.), Slade School of Fine Art (1960-61, Sir William Coldstream), Edinburgh College of Art (1961-65, Sir Robin Philipson, R.S.A.). *Exhib:* 20 one-man shows since 1966, Scotland, London, Melbourne, Sydney. *Work in collections:* U.S.A., Britain, Australia, etc. *Clubs:* Chelsea Arts. *Signs work:* "Leon Morrocco." *Address:* c/o Royal Scottish Academy, The Mound, Edinburgh EH2 2EL.

**MORROW, Elizabeth Eleanor,** D.A. (Belfast, 1954), U.S.W.A. (1961), U.W.S. (1967); housewife, painter in water-colour; Hon. Sec. Ulster Soc. of Women Artists; *b* Enniskillen, Co. Fermanagh, 14 Apr., 1926. *m* T.A. Morrow (decd.). one *s*. two *d*. *Educ:* Enniskillen Collegiate Grammar School. *Studied:* Belfast College of Art. *Exhib:* R.I., R.U.A., U.S.W.A., U.W.S. *Clubs:* U.S.W.A., U.W.S. *Address:* 33 Kensington Gardens South, Belfast BT5 6NN, Northern Ireland.

**MORSE, Colin Benjamin Scale,** Dip.A.D. (1982), M.C.S.D.; illustrator in water-colour and mixed media; *b* Pembrokeshire, 6 Aug., 1942. *m* Roberta Wilson; one *s-d*. *Educ:* Haverfordwest Grammar School. *Studied:* Dyfed College of Art, Carmarthen (1978-82). Work on display in various commercial galleries throughout U.K. *Publications:* Limited Edition prints. *Signs work:* "Colin Morse." *Address:* Priskilly Fawr Farm, Hayscastle, Haverfordwest, Pembrokeshire SA62 5QF.

**MORTIMER, Martin Christopher Fortescue,** Consultant, Delomosne & Son Ltd. Specialist in English Porcelain, English and Irish Glass, particularly English glass lighting fittings, and articles on these subjects in various art journals; *b* London, 4 July, 1928. *m* Sara Ann Proctor. *Educ:* Shrewsbury School. *Address:* Court Close, North Wraxall, Chippenham, Wiltshire SN14 7AD.

**MORTON, Cavendish,** R.I., R.O.I., Hon. S.G.A., Hon. N.S.; painter of landscape, marine, in oil, water-colour, black and white; Vice Pres., Gainsborough's House Society, Vice-Pres., Norfolk Contemporary Arts Society; Past Chairman, Isle of Wight Council for the Arts, Vice-Pres., Isle of Wight Art Society; *b* Edinburgh, 17 Feb., 1911. *m* Rosemary Britten. one *s*. two *d*. *Exhib:* R.A., R.B.A., U.S.A., Canada, Australia, Bermuda; one-man shows: London, York University, Norwich, King's Lynn, Sudbury, Ipswich, Aldeburgh, Henley, Portsmouth. *Work in collections:* B.M., Norwich Castle Museum, Wolverhampton A.G., Contemporary Arts Society, Eastern Arts Assoc., I.O.W. Cultural Services, Glasgow City A.G., Royal Naval Museum,

Gustav Holst Museum. *Commissions:* Review of The Cumberland Fleet, Royal Thames Yacht Club. *Publications:* illustrations for Dorothy Hammond Innes' Occasions (Michael Joseph, 1972), What Lands are These (Collins, 1981), and The Bembridge Redwings, David Swinstead (1997). *Signs work:* "CAVENDISH MORTON." *Address:* 6 Fairhaven Cl., Bembridge, I.O.W. PO35 5SX.

**MOSELEY, Austin Frank,** R.B.S.A. (1988), C.A.S. (1987), C.Eng.M.I.Mech.E. (1958); painter in oil, ink, pastel, charcoal; *b* Tividale, Staffs., 25 Apr., 1930. *m* Sylvia. two *s. Educ:* Dudley Technical College. *Studied:* Dudley School of Art. *Exhib:* R.B.S.A., Chelsea Arts Soc., Dudley Mid. Art, Llewellyn Alexander (London), John Noott (Broadway), R.O.I. *Work in collections:* Dudley Metropolitan County Borough, R.B.S.A, and many private and commercial collections. *Signs work:* "Austin Moseley." *Address:* 24 Raglan Cl., Sedgley, Dudley, W. Midlands DY3 3NH.

**MOSELEY, Malcolm,** B.A. (1969), M.A. (1973); painter; *b* Birmingham, 1947. *Studied:* Birmingham College of Art (1965), Winchester School of Art (1966-69), Central School of Art (1969-70), R.C.A. (1970-73). *Exhib:* R.A., R.S.W., London Group, Mall Galleries, Barbican, Eastern Open, New English, Laing Landscape. *Work in collections:* Ipswich Museums, P. & O., McDonalds, Hammersmith and Fulham Council. *Clubs:* Ipswich Art Soc. *Signs work:* "M.M." *Address:* 133 Norwich Rd., Ipswich, Suffolk IP1 2PP.

**MOUNT, Paul,** A.R.C.A. (1948), R.W.A. (Hon.); sculptor in stainless steel, bronze, G.R.P. concrete; *b* 8 June, 1922. *m* (1st) Jeanne Martin (div.), (2nd) June Miles. one *s.* one *d. Educ:* Newton Abbot Grammar School. *Studied:* Paignton School of Art (1937-40), R.C.A. (1940-41, 1946-48). *Exhib:* one-man shows, Drian Gallery, John Whibley, Marlborough, New Art Centre, Galerie Ruf, Munich, Galerie Contemporaine, Geneva; mixed shows, R.A., R.B.S., London Group. *Work in collections:* Harlow Art Trust, D.O.E., Cornwall Educ. Coll. *Commissions:* Fibreglass Ltd., B.S.C., Government House, Nigeria, Cabinet Offices, Accra, Swiss Embassy, Lagos, C.R.S., York House, Bristol. *Clubs:* Penwith, R.W.A. *Signs work:* "Paul Mount." *Address:* Nancherrow Studio, St. Just, Cornwall TR19 7LA.

**MOUNTFORD, Derylie Anne,** S.W.A. (1988); artist in pencil, etching, oil and water-colour; *b* London, 17 June, 1943. *m* Malcolm Mountford, B.A.(Oxon.). two *s. Educ:* Montessori, Wimbledon. *Studied:* Byam Shaw School of Art (1960-62, Peter Greenham, Bernard Dunstan), St. Martin's School of Art (1963). *Exhib:* R.A., R.B.A., R.M.S., S.W.A., N.S.P.S., C.D.S.; one-man shows: Japan (1986, 1988), Lyric Theatre, Hammersmith (1990), Cambridge (1988); group shows: Cambridge, Ely, Saffron Walden, Salisbury, etc. *Work in collections:* Addenbrookes Hospital Trust. *Signs work:* "Derylie Mountford" (etchings), "D. Mountford" (paintings). *Address:* 3 Belle Vue Gdns., Brighton, Sussex BN2 2AA.

**MOWAT, Jane Catherine,** B.A. (Hons.) History of Art, P.G.C.E. (Art);

artist/printmaker in woodcuts; co-ordinator for Art Curriculum, Danesfield Community, Som.; *b* Stamford, Lincs., 5 Apr., 1956. one *s.* one *d. Studied:* Courtauld Inst. of Art - Art History (1975-78, Anita Brookner, George Zarnecki). *Exhib:* many Open Exhbns. in South East, including R.W.A. *Publications:* illustrated: You and Your Child's Behaviour (Birmingham and Redditch Health Authority, 1984). *Clubs:* Printmakers Council. *Signs work:* "Jane Mowat." *Address:* 5 Palmerston Rd., Taunton, Som. TA1 1ES.

**MOXLEY, Ray,** F.R.I.B.A., R.W.A., Hon. F.(W.Eng.), of Moxley Jenner and Partners; architect of Chelsea Harbour and Exhibition Centres; Vice-president R.I.B.A. (1971-74), Chairman A.C.A. (1974-76); *b* 28 June, 1923. *m* Jacqueline. one *s.* two *d. Educ:* Caterham. *Studied:* architecture: Oxford (1940-42 and 1946-49). *Exhib:* R.W.A. annual 1960 onwards, A.C.A. Salons at the Royal Academy (1982, 1984, 1986). *Publications:* Building Construction (Batsford), Fee Negotiations (A.P.), Architects Eye (G.P.C.), Building Management by Professionals (Butterworth). *Signs work:* "Ray Moxley." *Address:* 1 Hobhouse Ct., Suffolk St., London SW1Y 4HH.

**MOYSE, Arthur,** artist in collage, water-colour, pen and ink; art critic for Freedom Press, London Correspondent for Chicago Industrial Worker; *b* London, 21 June, 1914. *Educ:* Addison Gardens L.C.C. Primary School. *Exhib:* Angela Flowers Gallery, Woodstock and others. *Work in collections:* Transport Museum. *Publications:* More in Sorrow, Zero One, Revolutionary Manifesto, Peterloo. *Clubs:* Hon. Mem. Chelsea Arts. *Signs work:* "Arthur Moyse." *Address:* 39 Minford Gdns., W. Kensington, London W14 0AP.

**MUIR, Jane,** artist, in mosaic and stone, etching and water-colour; *b* 1929. *m* A. W. E. Muir. two *s. Educ:* Rye St. Antony School. *Studied:* Oxford University, Teesside College of Art. M.A. Oxon (1950), Dip. Architectural Decoration (1969), F.C.S.D. (1974). *Exhib:* numerous. Founder Mem. International Assoc. of Contemporary Mosaic Artists, U.K. exhibitor Ravenna (1980), Trier (1984), Louvain (1986), Tokyo (1994), Alexandria (1996). *Work in collections:* Public: Oxon County Museum, Buckinghamshire County Museum, Glynn Vivian A.G., Open University, St. Anne's College, Oxford; Ruskin Gallery, Sheffield. *Commissions:* major: St. Anne's College Oxford; Open University; Princes Sq., Glasgow; Longmarket, Canterbury; Becket's Well, Northampton; Doha, Arabian Gulf. *Clubs:* Art Workers' Guild, Soc. of Designer Craftsmen. *Signs work:* "Muir." *Address:* Butcher's Orchard, Weston Turville, Aylesbury, Bucks. HP22 5RL.

**MULLEN, Kay,** S.W.A. (1993), S.B.A. (1995); self-taught painter in gouache and pastel ; *b* Mottingham, Kent, 3 Sept., 1959. one *d. Educ:* Nonsuch High School for Girls, Cheam, Surrey. *Exhib:* S.W.A. and S.B.A. at Westminster Central Halls, many mixed exhbns. *Publications:* work repro.: Medici and The Paper house Group. *Address:* 1b Parkhurst, Epsom, Surrey KT19 8QZ.

**MULLETT, Vivien,** A.R.M.S. (1992), H.S. (1990), B.A. Fine Art (1974);

artist in water-colour, graphic designer; *b* Oxford, 1952. *Educ:* Milham Ford School, Oxford. *Studied:* Reading University (1970-74). *Exhib:* R.A. Summer Show, R.M.S., H.S., M.A.S.-F. *Publications:* illustrated The Night Watchma-collection of stories. *Signs work:* "VM." *Address:* 111 Penwith Rd., Earlsfield, London SW18 4PY.

**MULLINS, Edwin Brandt,** B.A., M.A. (Hons.) Oxford University (1957); writer and film-maker, mainly on art subjects; *b* London, 1933. *m* Gillian Brydone (d. 1982); one s. two d.; Anne Kelleher (1984). one *s.* two *d. Educ:* Midhurst Grammar School and Oxford University. *Publications:* numerous books and over 200 television films. *Address:* c/o Curtis Brown Ltd., 28-29 Haymarket, London SW1Y 4SP.

**MUMBERSON, Stephen Leonard,** R.E. (1995), M.A. (1981), B.A. (Hons.) (1977); Programme leader/Head printmaking in print/paint/mixed media; *b* Beaconsfield, 16 Feb., 1955. *Educ:* Secondary Modern School, Bucks. *Studied:* Brighton Polytechnic (1977-78), R.C.A. (1978-81, Prof. Grant, Chris. Orr), Cité des Arts, Paris (1980). *Exhib:* R.E., Bankside London, Art Now London. *Work in collections:* V. & A., U.S.A., Japan, S.America, Europe, Canada, Zambia, Zimbabwe. *Signs work:* "Stephen Mumberson" or "S. Mumberson." *Address:* c/o Fine Art Dept., Faculty of Performance, Art and Design, Middlesex University, Quicksilver Pl., Western Rd., London N22 6XH.

**MUNDY, William Percy,** R.M.S., M.A.A., M.A.S.-F.; self-taught artist in water-colour and oil, miniaturist, portrait and Trompe l'oeil painter; *b* Wokingham, 30 Oct., 1936. *Educ:* Forest School, Berks. *Exhib:* R.A., R.M.S., R.P. Awarded "Exhibit of the Year" at 1980 and 1982 R.A. Summer Exhbns; Silver medal, Paris Salon (1982); Gold Memorial Bowl, R.M.S. (1986); Bell Award (1987); Best of Show M.A.S.-F. (U.S.A.) 1997; Bell Award (1996). *Work in collections:* H.R.H. The Duke of Edinburgh; H.M. King Bhumipol Aduladej of Thailand; The Yang di Pertuan Agong of Malaysia; H.R.H. The Sultan of Johor; Quaboos Bin Said, The Sultan of Oman; V. & A., London; Cincinatti Museum of Art, U.S.A. *Clubs:* Tanglin, Singapore; Phyllis Court, Henley. *Signs work:* "W. P. Mundy." *Address:* 2 Marsh Mills, Wargrave Rd., Henley-on-Thames, Oxon. RG9 3JD.

**MUNSLOW, Angela E.,** H.N.C., Grad.R.I.C., B.Ed.Hons.; sculptor in bronze, resin, terracotta, ceramic, cement and plaster, glass; figurative painter in oil, water-colour and pastel; *b* Sandbach, Ches. *m* Peter. two *s. Educ:* Ravenscroft Hall School, Cheshire; N.Staffs. Polytechnic (now Staffs. University); Crewe and Alsager College of C.H.E. (now Manchester University). *Studied:* sculpture: Sir Henry Doulton School of Sculpture. *Exhib:* Expo '92 Seville; group shows: St. Martin in the Fields, Mall Galleries, Westminster Gallery, and galleries in the North-West and Midland regions. *Work in collections:* Royal Doulton Museum, Stoke-on-Trent, Stapeley Water Gdns., Nantwich Ches. *Commissions:* for 'Heredities'; Garden Sculpture - a series of figures. *Clubs:* S.W.A., Soc. of Staffordshire Artists. *Signs work:*

"A.E. Munslow" and see appendix. *Address:* 65 Station Rd., Alsager, Stoke-on-Trent ST7 2PD.

**MURISON, Neil,** A.T.D. (1951), R.W.A. (1979); painter in oil and acrylic; Co-ordinator, Dept. of Foundation Studies, Bristol Polytechnic (1961-87); previously art master, Queen Elizabeth's Hospital, Bristol (1952-61); *b* Bath, 10 Oct., 1930. *m* (1) Valerie Elizabeth John; one *s.* one *d.*; (2) Sheila May Tilling (1985). *Educ:* Bristol Grammar School. *Studied:* West of England College of Art (1946-51). *Work in collections:* Nuffield, Wills Tobacco Co., Bank of America, Skopje Modern Art Museum, Yugoslavia, Trumans Breweries, Bridgwater Public Library, Bristol, Devon, Leeds, Herts., Hull, Leics., Liverpool, Surrey and West Riding of Yorks, Educ. Authorities. *Signs work:* "Murison." *Address:* 110 Redland Rd., Redland, Bristol BS6 6QU.

**MURRAY, Dawson Robertson,** D.A. (1965); Post-grad (1966); B.A. Hons. (1982); R.S.W. (1988); R.G.I. (1995); Head of Art and Design, Bolcair Academy (1976-94); President, Glasgow Group of Artists (1990-94); Vice President, R.S.W. (1993-96); painter in water-colour, acrylic, etching; atmospheric abstractions of garden themes; *b* Glasgow, 25 June, 1944. *m* Liz Murray. two *d. Educ:* Albert Senior Secondary, Glasgow. *Studied:* Glasgow School of Art (1961-66), L'Accademia delle Belle Arti, Venice (1966). *Exhib:* solo: Nancy Smillie Gallery, Glasgow (1997), Richard Demarco Gallery (1995, 1990); group shows: Encuentro Acuarela Santa Cruz (1994), Scottish Etching, G.P.S., (1994), 5th Drawing Triennale, Wroclaw (1992), Mini-print Cadaques (1988), Winter Festival Sarajevo (1988), Galleria del Cavallino, Venice (1983). *Work in collections:* S.A.C., B.B.C. Scotland. *Signs work:* "Dawson Murray." *Address:* The Old Post Office, Kilmany, Cupar, Fife KY15 4PT.

**MURRAY, Donald,** B.A., D.A.; artist and designer in calligraphy, water-colour and pastel; Head of Art, Robert Gordon's College, Aberdeen; *b* Edinburgh, 1940. *m* Mary F. Low. two *s. Educ:* George Heriot's School, Edinburgh. *Studied:* Edinburgh College of Art (1958-63). *Exhib:* R.S.W., S.S.A., Pitlochry Festival Theatre, Aberdeen Artists' Society. *Work in collections:* Edinburgh District Council, Heriot-Watt University, Moray House College of Education, Edinburgh Merchant Company. *Commissions:* Illuminated scrolls and miscellaneous formal calligraphy: Aberdeen City Council; Orkney Islands Council. *Publications:* illustrated Growing up in the Church, Christian Symbols, Ancient and Modern. *Signs work:* "Donald Murray." *Address:* Manorlea, Commerce St., Insch, Aberdeenshire AB52 6JB.

**MURRAY, Liz,** D.A. (1965), S.S.A. (1991), R.S.W. (1992); painter in mixed media - collage including stitched and moulded paper; *b* Aberdeen, 1943. *m* Dawson Murray. two *d. Educ:* Dundee High. *Studied:* Duncan of Jordanstone College of Art, Dundee (1961-65). *Exhib:* regularly at R.S.A., R.S.W., S.S.A., R.G.I., S.A.A.C.; work featured in many touring exhbns. in Scotland, and selected for group exhbns. in Italy, Poland, Germany, Bosnia and Canaries. *Work in collections:* Scottish Arts Council, Renfrewshire Educ.

Authority, Lanarkshire Educ. Authority, Hamilton District Libraries,Motherwell District Libaries, City Art Space, plc. *Signs work:* "Liz Murray" or "L.M." *Address:* The Old Post Office, Kilmany, Cupar, Fife KY15 4PT.

**MUSGRAVE, Barbara,** N.D.D.; sculptress specialising in portraiture and animals; painter in oil; *b* London 1937. *m* Peter Musgrave. one *s.* two *d. Educ:* Maltman's Green, Gerrards Cross. *Studied:* Regent St. Polytechnic (1955-59) under Mr. Deeley. *Exhib:* Harrow Art Soc., Mall Galleries, Compass Theatre, Ickenham, Smiths Covent Garden, Cow Byre Ruislip. *Signs work:* "B. Musgrave" or "B.M." *Address:* 25 Bury St., Ruislip, Middx. HA4 7SX.

**MUSZYNSKI, Leszek Tadeusz,** D.A. (Edin.); artist in oil, pastel, water-colour, drawing, lithograph; Retd. Head of Painting School, West Surrey College of Art and Design; *b* Poland, 19 Apr., 1923. *m* Patricia. one *s. Educ:* in Poland. *Studied:* Edinburgh College of Art (W. Gillies, J. Maxwell, W. MacTaggart); Travelling Scholarship to Paris, Florence, Arezzo, Assisi. *Exhib:* R.S.A. Edinburgh; one-man shows: London, Edinburgh, Copenhagen, Basle, Dallas, Texas, Warsaw, Cracow, Poznan. *Work in collections:* V. & A., N.P.G., L.C.C., National Museum, Poland, Museum of Art, Dallas, Texas, Museum, Durban, S. Africa. *Signs work:* see appendix. *Address:* West Wing, Bramshott Ct., Liphook GU30 7RG.

**MYERS, Bernard,** N.D.D. (1951), A.R.C.A. (1954), Hon. F.R.C.A., Hon. Prof. R.C.A.; painter in oil, water-colour, oil pastel, printmaker; taught at various London art schools and R.C.A.; Visiting Prof., Indian Inst. of Technology, New Delhi (1968-72), Prof., Brunel University (1980-85); *b* London, 22 Apr., 1925. *m* Pamela Blanche Fildes. *Studied:* St. Martin's (1947-49), Camberwell School of Art (1949-51), R.C.A. (1951-54). *Signs work:* "B. Myers" or "B.M." *Address:* 5 St. Peter's Wharf, Hammersmith Terr., London W6 9UD.

**MYERS, Mark Richard,** B.A.(Hons.), R.S.M.A. (1975), President R.S.M.A. (1993), A.S.M.A. (1978), C.S.M.A. (1985); marine artist in oils and acrylic on canvas and water-colour; *b* San Mateo, Calif., U.S.A., 19 Nov., 1945. *m* Peternella Bouquet. one *s.* two *d. Educ:* Pomona College, Calif. *Exhib:* R.S.M.A., A.S.M.A., New York, London, Seattle. *Work in collections:* National Maritime Museum, Greenwich, San Francisco Maritime Museum, N. Devon Maritime Museum. *Publications:* various maritime books illustrated. *Signs work:* "Mark Myers," "Mark Richard Myers" or "Myers." *Address:* The Old Forge, Woolley, Bude, Cornwall EX23 9PP.

**MYNOTT, Gerald P.,** S.S.I.; topographical artist, printmaker and calligra-pher; *b* London, 1957. *Studied:* Reigate College of Art; College of Arms, London; Vienna Kunstlerhaus, Austria. *Exhib:* Francis Kyle Gallery, London, continuously from 1980, New York (1984), Bath Festival (1983), Arts Club, London (1987). *Work in collections:* V. & A., Tate Gallery (Curwen Archive), The Savoy Group, Chevening Estate, U.S.A., Tokyo. Lloyds Printmakers Award (1981). *Publications:* work repro.: The Times, The Observer, Tatler, Radio Times, Weidenfeld and Nicolson, Penguin Books, V. & A. Publications,

The Field, B.B.C. *Clubs:* Arts. *Address:* 3 Belgrave House, 157 Marine Parade, Brighton, Sussex.

**MYNOTT, Katherine S.,** B.A.; illustrator/printmaker in gouache, line and lino; *b* London, 1962. one *s. Studied:* Heatherley School of Art, Central School of Art and St. Martin's School of Art. *Publications:* work repro.: Vogue, Radio Times, Daily Telegraph, Tatler, Harpers and Queen, B.B.C., Palace Pictures, Cosmopolitan, Time Out, Over 21, 19, The Observer, The Listener, I.P.C., New Society, Economist, etc. *Signs work:* "K. Mynott." *Address:* 23 Mount Park Rd., London W5.

**MYNOTT, Lawrence,** M.A. (R.C.A.), A.O.I.; portrait painter, illustrator in water-colour, oil, line and gouache; lecturer and art writer; *b* London, 1954. *Studied:* Chelsea School of Art (1972-76), Royal College of Art (1976-79). *Exhib:* R.A., European Illustrators, Folio Soc., Thames Television; two one-man shows of portraits at Cale Art, Chelsea. *Work in collections:* N.P.G., National Gallery of Wales, Hull A.G., Arts Council. Awarded D. & A.D. silver award (1985). Lecturer at V. & A., 'The Sitwells as Patrons', Neo-Romanticism, The Rococo Revival. *Publications:* work repro.: Radio Times, Vogue, Tatler, Harpers and Queen, The Observer, Penguin Books, Macmillans, Hamish Hamilton, etc. *Clubs:* Chelsea Arts. *Signs work:* "Lawrence Mynott," "Mynott" or monogram "L.M." *Address:* c/o "The Organisation", 69 Caledonian Rd., London N1. (Agent).

**MYNOTT, Patricia,** film designer, illustrator and natural history artist working in water-colour, line and gouache; *b* London, 1927. *m* Derek Mynott, N.E.A.C. (d. 1994). two *s.* one *d. Educ:* Dominican Convent, Chingford. *Studied:* S.W. Essex School of Art. Films: National Screen Service, National Savings, Film Producers Guild. *Publications:* illustrated, Marine Life of the Caribbean, Guide to the Seashore, Beaches and Beachcombing, Folklore of Fossils, The Curious Lore of Malta's Fossil Sharks Teeth, Edible Seaweeds; children's books: Encyclopedias, Educational Teaching Alphabet. Publishers: Blackies, Readers Digest, Paul Hamlyn, Michael Joseph, Macdonalds, Pitmans, Sacketts. *Signs work:* "Patricia Mynott" or "Barton." *Address:* The Arts Club, 40 Dover St., London W1X 3RB.

# N

**NALECZ, Halima,** F.F.P.S.; Dip. U.S.B. (Wilno), Dame Chevalier d'Honneur (18 May, 1957); Bronze Medal, Europe prize for painting, Kursaal, Ostend,Belgium (1969, 1971); painter in oils and mixed media; Founder and Director of Drian Galleries, London; *b* Wilno, Poland, 2 Feb., 1917. *m* Zygmunt Nalecz, writer. *Educ:* Lycée, Wilno. *Studied:* under Professor Roube, Professor Szyszko-Bohusz, Professor Zahorska, and in Paris under H. J. Closon. *Exhib:* most municipal and public galleries in England, and W.I.A.C., A.I.A., Free Painters and Sculptors, London Group, Salon de Réalités

# WHO'S WHO IN ART

Nouvelle, Galerie Collette Allendy, Salon des Divergences, Galerie Creuze (Paris); one-man exhbns. at Walker Galleries, London (1956), New Vision Centre, London (1957, 1959), Ewan Phillips, London (1967), County Town Gallery, Lewes (1967), Drian Galleries, London (1968-69), R.A. Summer Exhbn. (1967, 1968, 1969), S.S.W.A., Edinburgh. *Work in collections:* Britain, France, Spain, Italy, Germany, Australia, U.S.A., Sweden, Nuffield Foundation, London, National Gallery of Israel, Bezalel, Jerusalem, National Museum in Warsaw, Gdansk, Poznan. *Publications:* work repro.: Quadrum, Apollo, Arts Review, Art and Artists, Wiadomosci, Art International, etc.; prefaces to catalogues by Denis Bowen and Pierre Rouve. Paintings featured in film, The Millionairess. *Clubs:* A.I.A., W.I.A.C., Hampstead Artists Association, Free Painters and Sculptors, Polish Hearth. *Signs work:* see appendix. *Address:* 7 Porchester Pl., Marble Arch, London W2 2BT.

**NAPP, David,** Dip. C.S.D., Elizabeth Greenshields Foundation award (1986, 1990); artist in chalk, pastel, oil and water-colour; sessional lecturer, Kent Inst. of Art and Design; *b* London, 5 Mar., 1964. *Educ:* Queen Elizabeth's School, Faversham. *Studied:* Canterbury College of Art (1981-85). *Exhib:* Bourne Gallery, Reigate (1987-), Art London (1989, 1990, 1991), Walker Galleries, R.W.S., R.B.A., P.S., Napier Gallery Jersey. *Publications:* illustrations: Encyclopaedia of Pastel Techniques (Headline); Colour: How to see it, how to paint it; How to Paint Trees, Flowers and Foliage; Pastels Workshop. *Signs work:* "David Napp" and date. *Address:* Windmill Cottage, Mill La., Barham, Canterbury, Kent CT4 6HH.

**NAPPER, Helen,** B.A. (1980), M.F.A. (1983), P.G.C.E. (1985); painter in oil on board; *b* Wivenhoe, 29 Mar., 1958. *Educ:* Friends School, Saffron Walden; Colchester County High School for Girls. *Studied:* Colchester Art School, Wimbledon Art School (Maggi Hambling, Colin Cina), Reading University (Adrian Heath, Terry Frost), London University Central School of Art (Norman Ackroyd, Bernard Cheese). *Exhib:* Sue Rankin Gallery (1989-91), L.A. Contemporary Art Fair (1989, 1990), Olympia Art, London (1990, 1991) with Sue Rankin Gallery, Tatistcheff and Co., N.Y. and L.A. (1992, 1993). *Work in collections:* Citicorp Bank, London. *Signs work:* "Helen Napper." *Address:* 5 Castle Hill, Orford, Suffolk.

**NASH, David,** B.A. (Hons.) Fine Art (1967); artist/sculptor in wood; *b* Esher, Surrey, 14 Nov., 1945. *m* Claire Langdown. two *s. Studied:* Kingston College of Art Foundation Course (1963-64), Brighton College of Art (1964-65, painting), Kingston College of Art (1965-67, sculpture), Chelsea College of Art (1969-70, post-grad.). *Exhib:* Forest of Dean, Sculpture Trail, Walker Art Center, Minneapolis, U.S.A., Nagoya City Museum, Japan. *Commissions:* 'Eighteen Thousand Tides' Eastbourne, public sculpture (1996), 'Divided Oaks' and 'Turning Pines' (planted sculptures) Ottorlo, Netherlands (1985). *Publications:* The Sculpture of David Nash by Julian Andrews; Forms into Time (with essay by Marina Warner). *Address:* Capel Rhiw, Blaenau

Ffestiniog, Gwynedd LL41 3NT.

**NASH, Tom,** A.T.D., R.C.A.; artist in oil, P.V.A., gouache, collage, murals in retroreflective plastics, etc.; awarded the Geoffrey Crawshay Memorial Travelling Scholarship; West Wales Association for the Arts, Research Award; *b* Ammanford, 1931. *m* Enid Williams. two *d. Educ:* Llandeilo. *Studied:* Swansea, Paris, Provence; associated with Paul Jenkins in Paris. *Exhib:* one-man and mixed exhibitions in London, provinces, Washington, D.C., Argentine, Toronto, Japan. *Work in collections:* National Museum of Wales, Nuffield Foundation, Arts Council, Clare, Churchill, Pembroke Colleges, Cambridge, various county collections, Caerleon College of Education, Glynn Vivian Art Gallery, Swansea, Steel Company of Wales, C.A.S., Caiman Museum, Argentina, Wadham College, Oxford, University of Wales, India Rubber Co., Macco Corp., California, Brasenose College, Oxford, Trinity College of Education, 3M United Kingdom Limited, University of Bradford, Church of Wales Collection, I.T.V., British Petrolium Co., B.B.C.; private collections in Britain, France, Germany, U.S.A., Canada, New Zealand. *Commissions:* 3M U.K. Ltd., B.B.C., University of Bradford, Brecon Jazz Festival, P.T.P. Ltd., S.W. Police Authority, Prestige Hotels, Cardiff Festival, Brasenose College Oxford. *Publications:* I.T.V. biographical films, B.B.C. biographical films, national and international publications, 3M/UK/France publications. *Clubs:* Brecon *Signs work:* "Tom Nash." *Address:* Clydfan, Llandeilo, Dyfed, Wales SA19 6HY. Internet web site http:/www digitrol.coma/abulafia

**NEAGU, Paul,** sculptor, painter, Anglo-romanian; lecturer (1972-91); *b* Bucharest, 1938; divorced. *Educ:* Inst. 'N. Grigorescu' Bucharest (1959-65). *Exhib:* over forty one person shows. Major works: 'Palpable and tactile objects' (1965-90), 'Anthropocosmos (1968-81), 'Performance' (1969-77), 'Hyphen' (1974-93), 'Nine Catalytic Stations' (1975-87), 'Unnamed' (1983-92), 'Newhyphen' (1991-93), 'Ten right angles' (1994), 'Unnamed (Eschaton) (1997). *Work in collections:* U.K., U.S.A., Japan, Germany, Romania, France, Ireland. Outdoor sculpture: Middlesbrough, London, Bucharest, Scotland. *Publications:* 'Palpable Art' (1969), 'Generative Arts' (1977), 'Hyphen' (1985), 'Deep Space and Solid Time' (1988), 'Epagoge' (1993), 'Reorganisation of nothing' (1996). *Signs work:* "Paul Neagu" or "P. Neagu." *Address:* 31c Jackson Rd., London N7 6ES.

**NEAL, Arthur Richard,** Dip.A.D.; painter/printmaker in oil, water-colour and etching; *b* Chatham, 15 Mar., 1951. *m* Jane. one *s.* one *d. Educ:* Reeds School. *Studied:* Camberwell School of Art. *Exhib:* R.A. Summer Shows, Cadogan Contemporary. *Publications:* Illustrated Poems of Edward Thomas. *Clubs:* N.E.A.C. *Signs work:* "ARN" or "ARNEAL" or not at all. *Address:* 32 Duke St., Deal, Kent CT14 6DT.

**NEAL, Charles William,** B.Sc. Hons. (1980); landscape painter in oil; *b* Carshalton, 27 Nov., 1951. *m* Susan Ann. one *s. Educ:* Highview High School/City of London University. *Studied:* initially private tuition with

Malcolm Domingo and Francis Lane-Mason; later self taught to perfect style and technique. *Exhib:* Omell Gallery (1982); R.B.A.: Omell Gallery (1983), Godalming Gallery (1984), Harrods Picture Gallery (1985); annual, national, international exhbns.: Campbell's of Walton Street and Astley House Fine Art, Glos. *Work in collections:* one royal and many private and commercial collections both national and international. Gallery affiliation: Campbell's of Walton Street, 164 Walton St., London SW3 2JL; Astley House Fine Art, Moreton-in-Marsh, Glos. GL56 0LL. *Signs work:* C. Neal." *Address:* Woodside Cottage, 4 Cotswold Park, Woodmancote, Cirencester, Glos. GL7 7EL.

NEAL, James, A.R.C.A. (1939); artist; *b* Islington, 18 Jan., 1918. *m* Doreen Barnes. two *s.* one *d. Educ:* St. John Evangelist. *Studied:* St. Martin's School of Art; R.C.A. *Exhib:* R.A., R.S.A., N.E.A.C., London Group, Redfern Galleries; one-man shows Trafford Gallery, Wildensteins, etc. *Work in collections:* Nottingham A.G., Wakefield A.G., Ferens A.G., Hull, Beverley A.G., Graves A.G., Sheffield, London County Council, Hull Educ. Com., W. Riding Educ. Com., East Riding Educ. Com., Derbyshire Educ. Com., Durham Educ. Com., etc. *Signs work:* "James Neal." *Address:* 205 Victoria Ave., Hull, N. Humberside HU5 3EF.

NEAL, Trevor, self-taught artist in oil; *b* York, 1947. *m* Sharon. one *d. Exhib:* Graves A.G. (1972-75, 1977), White Rose Gallery Bradford (1974), R.A. (1975, 1980, 1981, 1992), Art Centre St. Petersburg, U.S.A. (1980, 1982), Anderson Marsh Galleries St. Petersburg (1983), Ginnel Gallery Manchester (1988), Evander Preston Gallery St. Petersburg (1988, 1989, 1991), S. Yorks. Open Cooper A.G. Barnsley (1989), Ferens A.G., Hull (1995, 1996, 1997), Roy Miles, London (1994, 1995). *Work in collections:* U.K., U.S.A., France, Germany, Israel. *Commissions:* U.K., U.S.A., Germany. *Publications:* "Dreams" (The Bridgewater Book Co., 1996). *Signs work:* see appendix. *Address:* Fossdale Towers, 23 Fossdale Rd., Sheffield S7 2DA.

NEALE, John, self-taught landscape and seascape painter in oil and water-colour; *b* 13 Sept., 1944; divorced. two *s.* one *d. Studied:* self-taught, but privately helped by Edward Seago. *Exhib:* Omell Galleries, Quantas Galleries, Frost and Reed, Bristol, John Noott, Broadway, Chime Gallery, N.Y., etc. *Work in collections:* in Europe and U.S.A. *Signs work:* "John Neale." *Address:* Maple Leaf House, 59 Maidenhead Rd., Stratford-on-Avon CV37 6XU.

NEASOM, Norman, R.W.S. (1978), R.B.S.A. (1947), Hon.S.A.S. (1976); artist in water-colour and gouache; retd. art master; *b* Tardebigge, 7 Nov., 1915. *m* Jessie Mary. two *d. Educ:* Redditch County High. *Studied:* Birmingham College of Art (1931-35, Harold H. Holden, Michael Fletcher, Fleetwood Walker, R.A., W.F. Colley, H. Sands). *Exhib:* R.A. (1970, 1974, 1976), R.W.S., R.B.S.A., Stratford Art Soc., Mall Galleries. *Work in collections:* West Midland Arts Council and various private collections. *Publications:* work repro.: articles for Leisure Painter, covers for Readers' Digest. *Clubs:* Redditch Sailing (founder). *Signs work:* "N. NEASOM" and date. *Address:* 95 Bromfield

# WHO'S WHO IN ART

Rd., Redditch, Worcs. B97 4PN.

**NEILAND, Brendan,** R.A. (1992), Dip.A.D. (1966), M.A. (1969), Silver Medal R.C.A. (1969); painter in acrylic on canvas, printmaker in silkscreen, lithography; Prof. of Painting, University of Brighton (1996); *b* Lichfield, 23 Oct., 1941. *m* Hilary. two *d*. *Educ:* St. Philip's G.S., B'ham; St. Augustine's Seminary, Ireland. *Studied:* B'ham College of Art (1962-66, William Gear, John Walker, Ivor Abrahams), R.C.A. (1966-69, Carel Weight, Roger de Grey). *Exhib:* Angela Flowers Gallery, Fischer Fine Art, Redfern Gallery. *Work in collections:* Tate Gallery, V. & A., British Council, Arts Council. *Commissions:* National Bank of Dubai (1997). *Publications:* "Brendan Neiland on Reflection" (Motivate Publishing, Oct. 1997). *Clubs:* Chelsea Arts. *Signs work:* "Brendan Neiland" on all prints and paper work; "NEILAND" stencilled onto back of canvas on stretcher. *Address:* 24 The Chase, London SW4 0NH; and Crepe, La Greve sur Mignon, Courcon 17170, France.

**NEILL, Errol James,** LL.B. (Lond.), Paris Salon: Silver Medallist (1980), Gold Medallist (1981); solicitor; artist in oil and pastel; *b* Doune, Perthshire, 15 Aug., 1941. *m* Audrey Bradbury. one *s*. two *d*. *Educ:* Christ Church, Preston. *Exhib:* R.B.A., R.O.I., R.S.M.A., N.E.A.C., U.A., S.E.A., Lancashire Art, Société des Artistes Francais, Paris, Deauville, N.Y., Melbourne, Australia. *Work in collections:* Britain, France, Eire, U.S.A., S. America. *Publications:* Travelling the Turf 1987 to 1992. *Clubs:* Law Soc. Art Group, New Longton Artists. *Signs work:* "ERROL NEILL." *Address:* Bridge House, 217 Chapel La., New Longton, Preston, Lancs. PR4 4AD.

**NEILL, William Andrew Knight,** Dip.A.D. (Fine Art) Leeds (1966), A.T.C. Goldsmiths' (1967), S.WL.A. (1990); wildlife and landscape artist in water-colour; Director, Taigh Chearsabhagh, Museum and Art Centre, Lochmaddy; *b* Middlewich, Ches., 22 Aug., 1943. *Educ:* Sandbach School. *Studied:* Leeds College of Art, Goldsmiths' College. *Exhib:* annually with S.WL.A. *Work in collections:* Nature in Art, Wallsworth Hall. *Commissions:* Scottish Natural Heritage, and The Western Isles Health Board. *Publications:* illustrations in: British Birds, Scottish Birds, etc.; illustrated, Scottish Wildlife Trust, Discovery Book of Western Isles. *Address:* Rannachan, Askernish, South Uist., Western Isles HS8 5SY.

**NELLENS, Roger,** painter in oil on canvas; *b* Liege, Belgium, 11 May, 1937. one *s*. two *d*. *Educ:* College St. Michel et St. Louis, Brussels, and London Academy; autodidact. *Work in collections:* Collection de l'Etat Belge; Musée d'Ostende; Collection de la Flandre Occidentale, Bruges; Museum Boymans-van Beuningen, Rotterdam; Musée d'Art et d'Industrie, St. Etienne France; CNAC, Paris; McCrory Corp., N.Y.; Tate Gallery, London; Musée d'Art Moderne, Brussels; The Menil Foundation, Houston; Centre Pompidou, Paris. *Signs work:* on the back; see appendix. *Address:* Fort St. Pol, Zoutelaan, 280, 8300 Knokke-Heist, Belgium.

**NELSON, Kathleen,** R.M.S. (1984), H.S.F. (1982); Hon. Men. Gold

Memorial Bowl award R.M.S. (1985, 1994), Drummond award R.M.S. (1984), Llewellyn Alexander subject miniature award R.M.S. (1996); wildlife, equestrian and natural history artist in water-colour and oil; *b* Durham City, 12 Mar., 1956. *Educ:* Whinney Hill Secondary School, Durham, and Durham Wearside. *Exhib:* R.M.S., H.S., Medici Gallery, Llewellyn Alexander Gallery; solo shows: Darlington A.G., Durham A.G. *Work in collections:* Darlington A.G. *Publications:* chapter with illustrations, The Techniques of Painting Miniatures by S. Burton (B.T. Batsford Ltd., 1995). *Signs work:* "Kathleen Nelson." *Address:* 18 Beverley Gdns., Chester-le-Street, Co. Durham DH3 3NB.

**NESSLER, Walter H.,** Gold and Silver Medal, Academy Campanella, Rome; landscape painter in oil, polyester resin, reliefs; teacher; *b* Leipzig, 19 Jan., 1912; married. one *s. Studied:* Castelli, Italian Art School at Dresden (1933-35), and self-taught. *Exhib:* R.A., R.B.A., Leger Galleries, Redfern Gallery, Arcade Gallery, Twenty Brook St. Gallery, Galerie des Beaux-Arts (Paris), Bradford City Art Gallery, New Vision Gallery, Gallery One, Obelisk Gallery, John Whibley Gallery, O'Hana Gallery, Molton Gallery, Hendon Group, New End Gallery, Madden Galleries, Harlow Festival, Alwin Gallery, Gallery Petit, Rotunda Gallery, Erica Bourne Gallery, German Embassy, M. Fisher Gallery, London, Galerie Grigerson, Hamburg, Centaur Gallery, Pentonville Gallery, John Denham Gallery, Art in Exile Berlin-London. *Work in collections:* C.A.S., Municipal Museum, Leicester, R.A.F. Museum, Hendon, Ein Harod Museum (Israel); and private collections in America, S. Africa, England, Norway. *Clubs:* C.A.S. *Signs work:* "Nessler." *Address:* 16 Somali Rd., London NW2 3RJ.

**NEUENSCHWANDER, James Brody,** Ph.D., M.Phil., A.B.; calligrapher, lettering artist, graphic designer; *b* Houston, Texas, 8 Sept., 1958. *Educ:* Princeton University, Courtauld Inst. *Studied:* Roehampton Inst. under Ann Camp. *Exhib:* Princeton University Library, Museum of Fine Arts, Houston, Gallerie Comptoir des Ecritures Paris, Torre di Malta, Padua. *Work in collections:* Princeton University, Westminster Cathedral. *Publications:* Modern German Calligraphy - Special issue of Letter Exchange Magazine; Letterwork-Creative Letterforms for Graphic Design (Phaidon, London 1993). Collaborated with Director Peter Greenaway on several films, including Prospero's Books, The Baby of Mâcon and The Pillow Book. *Signs work:* "Brody Neuenschwander." *Address:* Spinolarei 2, 8000 Bruges, Belgium.

**NEVE, Margaret,** R.W.A. (1995); painter in oil on wood panels; *b* Wolverhampton, 29 Mar., 1929. *m* James Sutton. two *s. Educ:* privately. *Studied:* Birmingham College of Art (1946-49), R.A. Schools (1949-55, B. Fleetwood Walker). *Exhib:* Hamilton Gallery (1967), Marjorie Parr Gallery (1976), Gilbert Parr Gallery (1977, 1979), New Grafton Gallery (1981), Montpelier Studio (1987, 1990, 1994). *Work in collections:* Birmingham A.G. *Signs work:* "M. Neve." *Address:* 18 Greville Pl., London NW6 5JH.

**NEVETZ:** see COX, Stephen B.

**NEVIA:** see ROGERS, Joseph Shepperd.

**NEWBERRY, John Coverdale,** R.W.S. (1995), B.A. Dunelm (1960), M.A.Oxon. (1989); Water-colour Foundation prize R.W.S. Open (1990); painter of landscapes in water-colour and figure compositions in oil; tutor, Ruskin School of Drawing, Oxford (1963-89); *b* Horsham, 8 May, 1934. *Educ:* Kingswood School, Bath; School of Architecture, Cambridge. *Studied:* King's College, Newcastle upon Tyne (1957-60, Lawrence Gowing, Victor Pasmore). *Exhib:* R.W.S., O.A.S., R.A., R.I., N.E.A.C., numerous one-man shows mostly in Oxford: Ashmolean (1978), Chris Beetles (1990, 1991), Duncan Campbell (1993, 1994, 1996). *Signs work:* "Newberry." *Address:* Moulin de Sourreau, 24230 Vélines, France.

**NEWBURY, Brian James,** F.R.S.A., Mem. B.A.D.A.; specialist in marine, military, sporting and topographical prints, paintings and water-colours, ship models, etc.; Chairman and Managing Director of the Parker Gallery; *b* London, 24 Dec., 1941; widower. one *s. Educ:* Bembridge School, I.O.W. *Clubs:* Naval. *Address:* 49 Peplins Way, Brookmans Park, Herts. AL9 7UR.

**NEWCOMB, Mary,** painter; B.Sc. Natural Sciences; *b* Harrow-on-the-Hill, 25 Jan., 1922. *m* Godfrey Newcomb. two *d. Signs work:* "Mary Newcomb." *Address:* Rushmeadow, Newton Flotman, Norwich, Norfolk NR15 1QX.

**NEWICK, John,** lecturer in education, University of London Institute of Education (1968-86); lecturer in art education, Birmingham College of Art and Design (1952-62, 1964-65); lecturer then reader in art education, University of Science and Technology, Ghana (1962-64); lecturer, Faculty of Education, Makerere University College, Uganda (1965-66); staff exchange, School of Education, University of California, Berkeley (1969); visiting lecturer, University of British Columbia (summer 1970, 1975-76) and Stanford University (summer 1973); *b* Bristol, 30 Nov., 1919. *Educ:* The Grammar School, Bristol. *Studied:* West of England College of Art. *Address:* Beechwood Lodge, Bannerdown Rd., Bath BA1 7NE.

**NEWLAND, Anne,** Edwin Abbey Major Scholarship (1938); *b* Wilts., 11 Jan., 1913. *Educ:* Byam Shaw Art School (1934-38). *Address:* 4 Vaughan Rd., London SE5 9NZ.

**NEWMAN, Colin Ralph,** artist in water-colour and pen and ink; 30 years litho-artist Mardon Son & Hall, (retd.); *b* Chipping Sodbury, 1923. *m* Hylda. one *d. Educ:* St. John's Chipping Sodbury. *Studied:* Academy of Art, Florence and West of England Academy; printing at Merchant Venturers, Bristol. *Exhib:* R.W.A., R.W.S., S.B.A., and many west country galleries. *Work in collections:* Barclays Bank Head Office, D.R.G. Head Office; private collections in Europe, America, S. Africa and U.K. *Publications:* work repro.: greetings cards and calendars. *Signs work:* "Colin Newman" or "C.N." *Address:* 28 Field View Drive, Downend, Bristol BS16 2TT.

**NEWTON, Joanna Dawson,** Dip. in Art (1982); artist in oil on canvas, charcoal drawing; *b* Oxford, 24 Apr., 1958. *Educ:* Headington School, Oxford. *Studied:* Byam Shaw School of Art (1979-82, P. Gopal-Chowdhuny, N. Volley). *Exhib:* Whitechapel Open, N.P.G., John Player award, R.A. Summer Exhbn., Picture Brokers Exhbn. *Clubs:* Chelsea Arts. *Signs work:* "Joanna D. Newton." *Address:* 60 St. Dionis Rd., Fulham, London SW6.

**NEWTON-DAVIES, Diana Elizabeth:** see WHITESIDE, Diana Elizabeth Hamilton.

**NG, Kiow Ngor,** Dip.F.A. (1989); artist in painting and printmaking; *b* Singapore, 6 Apr., 1963. *Studied:* Nan Yang Academy of Fine Arts (1986-89), Slade School of Fine Art (1991-93). *Exhib:* London Group (1992), R.A. Summer Show (1992, 1993). *Signs work:* see appendix. *Address:* 9a Kang Choo Bin Rd., Singapore 1954.

**NGUYEN, Tân-Phuoc,** Mem. Confédération Internationale des Associations des Experts et du Conseils auprès du Conseil Economique et Social de l'Onu; Président Asia-Africa Museum (fondé en 1961); Président de la Chambre Internationale de Commerce Vietnam-Suisse; art expert on Asiatic archaeology and Africa Art, specialised in the founding of Fine Art Collections and Muséums, historian, writer; *b* 11 Oct., 1932. *m* Hélène Gerber. two *s. Educ:* Saigon, S. Vietnam, and Paris. *Studied:* l'Institut Hautes, Etudes Indochinoises, and Ecole du Louvre. *Publications:* Archéologie asiatique, Netzuke, La Culture de Ban-Chiang (Siam) 7.000-5.000 ans, Fouilles archéologiques à Ban-Chiang. Conférencier invité à Davos Symposium (from 1985) by W.E.F. *Clubs:* Musée d'Ethnographie, Musée des Collections Baur-Duret, Union Internationale des Experts, Croix Rouge Suisse, Intérêt de Genève, Kiwanis International, Président, Asia-Africa Museum (GVA) (1993), Chevalier du Tastevin. *Address:* 30 Grand Rue, Genève 1204. Switzerland

**NICHOLAS, Peter,** N.D.D. (1956), A.R.C.A. (1962), F.R.B.S. (1993); sculptor in stone, bronze, G.R.P.; *b* Ebbw Vale, S. Wales, 1934. *m* Marjorie (decd.); one *s.* two *d.* ; *m.* Annie. one *s. Educ:* Ebbw Vale County Grammar School. *Studied:* Cardiff College of Art (1951-56, Frank Roper, Geof Milsom), R.C.A. (1958-61, John Skeaping). *Exhib:* Jonathan Poole Fine Art. *Work in collections:* U.K., Europe, U.S.A. *Publications:* Art in Architecture an Architects Choice (Eugene Rosenberg), The Encyclopedia of Sculpture Techniques (John Mills), Teaching Art in Wales (Alan Torjussen). *Signs work:* "P.W. NICHOLAS." *Address:* Craig-y-Don, Horton, Gower, W. Glam. SA3 1LB.

**NICHOLLS, Howard John,** B.A. (Hons.) (1975), R.B.A. (1983); painter in oils, drawings mixed media, lecturer; Lecturer in Fine Art, Epsom School of Art and Design (1979-84); *b* 14 Jan., 1950. *Educ:* Selhurst Grammar School. *Studied:* Camberwell School of Art (1972-75), R.A. Schools (1975-78). *Exhib:* R.A., R.B.A. *Work in collections:* S.I.U. Cooke Fund (1979). *Publications:* work repro.: Home Artist. *Signs work:* "H. Nicholls." *Address:* 19 Drakefield Rd., London SW17.

**NICHOLS, Patricia Mary,** R.M.S., S.W.A.; portrait painter in miniature and full-size portrait drawings in sanguine, chalk; *Mem.* Royal Society of Miniature Painters; and Soc. of Women Artists; teaches miniature painting at the West Norfolk Art Centre; *m* the late John Trevor Nichols, M.C.I.T. one *s.* one *d. Educ:* innumerable private schools. *Studied:* Central School of Arts and Crafts London. *Exhib:* R.I., Mall Galleries, Westminster Gallery and many others. *Commissions:* has undertaken many important, including royal, commissions. *Publications:* work repro.: The Artist, Illustrated county magazines and newspapers. *Signs work:* "Patricia Nichols." *Address:* Sealand, Wodehouse Rd., Old Hunstanton, Norfolk PE36 6JD.

**NOAKES, Michael,** P.P.R.O.I., R.P., C.P.S., Hon. N.S., Hon. U.A., Cert. R.A.S., N.D.D.; landscape and portrait painter (subjects include H.M. the Queen, other members royal family, etc.); Chairman (1971) Contemporary Portrait Society; Pres. Royal Institute of Oil Painters (1972-78); art critic (1964-68), B.B.C. Television; *b* Brighton, 28 Oct., 1933; married. two *s.* one *d. Educ:* Downside. *Studied:* R.A. Schools. *Exhib:* R.A., R.O.I., R.P., R.B.A., N.S., etc. *Work in collections:* H.M. the Queen, H.R.H. the Prince of Wales, B.M., National Portrait Gallery, etc. *Publications:* A Professional Approach to Oil Painting (Pitmans, 1968); work repro.: widely. *Signs work:* "Michael Noakes," with date underneath. *Address:* 146 Hamilton Terr., London NW8 9UX.

**NOELLE:** see SIMPSON, Noelle.

**NOOTT, Edward John,** B.A.; painter in oil; *b* W. Midlands, 4 Oct., 1965. *m* Denise Cardone. one *s.* one *d. Educ:* Cheltenham College. *Studied:* Gloucestershire College of Art, Cheltenham, Trent Polytechnic College, Nottingham, State University of N.Y. *Exhib:* John Noott Galleries, R.B.S.A. *Publications:* work reproduced by The Art Group, Robertson Collection. *Signs work:* "Edward Noott." *Address:* c/o 14 Cotswold Ct., Broadway, Worcs. WR12 7AA.

**NORBURY, Ian,** B.A. (1979); sculptor in wood, metal, semi precious stones; *b* Sheffield, 21 Aug., 1948. *m* Betty Ann. two *s.* one *d. Educ:* Andover Grammar; St. Paul's College, Cheltenham. *Studied:* St. Paul's College, Cheltenham (Harold Sayer, R.E., R.W.A., A.R.C.A.). *Exhib:* annual one-man. *Work in collections:* Tower of London, Fine Art Museum of the South of Mobile, U.S.A., many private collections. *Publications:* Techniques of Creative Woodcarving, Projects for Creative Woodcarving, Relief Woodcarving and Lettering, Fundamentals of Figure Carving, Carving Facial Expressions. *Signs work:* "IAN NORBURY," "I. NORBURY" or "I.N." *Address:* Ballycommare, Tournafulla, Co. Limerick, Eire.

**NORDEN, Gerald,** A.R.C.A. (1937); still-life painter in oil; *b* Hampstead, London, 28 June, 1912. *m* Lilian Moorhead. one *s.* two *d. Educ:* Arnold House, NW8. *Studied:* Thanet School of Art (J. Moody, B. Willis), R.C.A. (Gilbert Spencer, Percy Horton). *Exhib:* Trafford Gallery (1969-75), King St. Gallery (1976-86), Catto Gallery (1991-93). *Publications:* A Practical Guide to Perspective (Longman). *Signs work:* "NORDEN." *Address:* 11 Julian Rd.,

Folkestone, Kent CT19 5HP.

**NORLAND (NEUSCHUL), Khalil,** M.A. Physics (Oxon.); artist-painter in mixed media; *b* Aussig (Usti), Czechoslovakia, 25 Mar., 1934. *m* Layla Shamash. three *s*. *Educ:* Merton College, Oxford. *Studied:* Ruskin College of Art, Oxford (1953-57), Slade School of Art London University (1959-60). *Exhib:* Artist House, Jerusalem (1959), Woodstock Gallery, London (1961), Gallerie Lambert, Paris (1964), Camden Arts Centre, London (1987), Queen Elizabeth House, Oxford (1987), Loggia Gallery, London (1988), Haus am Lützowplatz, Berlin (1991). *Signs work:* see appendix. *Address:* 25 Southmoor Rd., Oxford OX2 6RF.

**NORMAN, Barbara,** Paris Salon bronze medal (1975), silver medal (1976); glass engraver in diamond point, flexible drive drill; *b* London. *Studied:* Stanhope Institute and glass engraving at Morley College under Mary Stevens. *Exhib:* Bourne Hall, Ewell, New Ashgate Gallery, Farnham, Florida Gulf Coast Art Center, Clearwater, Florida, Tampa Bay Art Center, Florida. *Publications:* Engraving and Decorating Glass (David and Charles 1972, McGraw Hill, U.S.A. 1972); Glass Engraving (David and Charles 1981, ARCO, U.S.A. 1981, A. H. & A. W. Reed, Australia 1981). *Signs work:* "Barbara Norman." *Address:* 9 Downs Lodge Court, Church St., Epsom, Surrey. KT17 4QG.

**NORMAN, Michael Radford,** R.S.M.A. (1975); artist/model maker, in pen and water-colour, often of river and coastal scenes; *b* Ipswich, 20 Aug., 1933. two *d*. *Educ:* Woodbridge School. *Studied:* Bournemouth School of Art. *Exhib:* R.I., R.S.M.A.; one-man shows, Colchester, Ipswich, Norwich, etc. *Work in collections:* water-colour at D.O.E. *Publications:* illustrated, The Suffolk Essex Border by John Salmon. *Signs work:* "Michael Norman" usually in black ink. *Address:* The Studio, Woolverstone, Ipswich, Suffolk IP9 1AX.

**NORMAN, Richard,** D.A. (1978), R.S.W. (1994); Cargill award R.G.I. (1991), Travelling Scholarship, Venice (1995); artist in water-colour and oil; teacher; *b* Glasgow, 15 June, 1956. *Studied:* Glasgow School of Art (1974-78, Dr. David Donaldson, James Robertson, Leon Morrocco). *Exhib:* regularly at R.G.I. and R.S.W.; one-man shows 1990-92: Kelly Gallery, Glasgow, Blythswood Gallery, Glasgow. *Clubs:* Glasgow Art. *Signs work:* "Richard Norman." *Address:* 185 Bath St., Glasgow G2 4HU.

**NORRIS, David,** Cert. R.A.S., F.R.B.S.: sculptor in bronze; Vice-Pres. Royal Soc. of British Sculptors; *b* São Paulo, Brazil, 26 Sept., 1940. *m* Carol. three *d*. *Educ:* Millfield. *Studied:* Guildford School of Art and R.A. Schools. *Exhib:* R.A., Mall Galleries, Royal Mint. *Work in collections:* 'Women and Doves' Stevenage Town Park; 'Britannia' for the Falklands Monument; 'Mother and Child' Portland Hospital; Sir Barnes Wallis, R.A.F. Museum Hendon; 'Spindrift' 3.5m. high stainless steel spiral with bronze gulls for P. & O. liner Royal Princess; two life-size bronzes for Royal Caribbean Cruise Line; group of 'Flying Flamingos', Arndale Centre, Luton; bronze portrait of Maria Callas for the Royal Opera House, London; bronze relief portrait of General Sir

David Fraser, Grenadier Guards; bronze 'Birds of Prey' for the Middle East. Awarded the Sir Otto Beit medal. *Signs work:* "David Norris." *Address:* The Orchard House, Cranleigh, Surrey GU6 8LR.

**NORRIS, Katharine,** B.A.(Hons.) graphic design and illustration; decorative mural artist and stenciller and fine artist of figurative work, landscape, life, decorative still life in acrylic, oil, pastel, coloured pencil, charcoal; *b* Worthing. *Educ:* Trinity School, Carlisle. *Studied:* Cumbria College of Art and Design (1977-78), Norwich School of Art (1978-81). *Clubs:* Life Drawing, Penrith. *Signs work:* "Kate Norris." *Address:* 30 Esk Bank, Longtown, Carlisle, Cumbria CA6 5PT.

**NORTON, Maureen Joan,** R.S.M. (1982), S.M. (1981); marine and landscape artist in oil on canvas and oil on ivorine; *b* Norwich, 1928. *m* Denis Norton. one *d. Exhib:* three one-man shows at Ancient House, Holkham, also soc. exhbns. at Mall Galleries, The Westminster Gallery; R.S.M. Golden Bowl Hon. mention (1996). *Work in collections:* America, Germany, Australia and Mexico. *Signs work:* "M.J. Norton." *Address:* 179 Wroxham Rd., Sprowston, Norwich NR7 8AG.

**NOSWORTHY, Ann Louise,** N.D.D. (1952), A.T.D. (1953); painter in oil, gouache, pastel and charcoal; *b* Stonehaven, Scotland, 24 Aug., 1929. *m* T. C. Nosworthy. one *s. Educ:* Beacon School, Bridge-of-Allan, Scotland. *Exhib:* one-man shows: Redcar, Yorks. (1968), Castle de Vide, Portugal (1966). *Work in collections:* Municipal Art Gallery, Port Allegre, Portugal. *Signs work:* "A. L. Nosworthy." *Address:* Brackengarth, Lealholm, Whitby, Yorks. YO21 2AE.

**NOT, Philip James,** self-taught artist in oil; Proprietor of Galerie Not; *b* 28 Feb., 1938. *m* Violet Vidot 'Une Belle Seychelleoise'. one *s.* two *d. Educ:* Holloway Grammar School. *Work in collections:* Etablisement de Rue (Arras, France), Lloyds Bank Plc. (Hampstead Village Branch). Noted for legal still life, and local West Hampstead and Hampstead landscapes. *Signs work:* "P.J. Not" or "PJN" *Address:* 54 Mill Lane, West Hampstead, London NW6 INJ.

**NOYES, Margot,** N.D.D. (1960); painter in oil; *b* London, 17 Aug., 1939; divorced. one *s.* one *d. Educ:* Fulham County Grammar School. *Studied:* Camberwell School of Arts and Crafts (1956-60, Robert Medley, Anthony Eyton, Richard Lee, Michael Salaman, Richard Eurich, Henry Inlander). *Exhib:* Many one-man shows and mixed shows nationwide. A founder member of the Suffolk Group. *Signs work:* "M. Noyes," very small works initials only. *Address:* Marsh Cottage, Wenhaston, Halesworth, Suffolk IP19 9EL.

# O

**OATES, Bennett,** painter in oils, specialising in flowers and landscape; President, Guild of Norwich Painters; *b* London, 1 Jan., 1928. *m* Phyllis Mary, Art Historian and Designer A.R.C.A. two *d. Educ:* Raynes Park Grammar School. *Studied:* Wimbledon School of Art (1943-46, Gerald Cooper), R.C.A.

(1948-51, Robin Darwin and Ruskin Spear). *Exhib:* three Continents. *Work in collections:* Stacy-Marks Gallery. *Clubs:* City Club, Norwich. *Signs work:* "Bennett Oates." *Address:* The Grange, Little Plumstead, Norwich NR13 5DJ.

**O'BRIEN, Brigid:** see GANLY, Rosaleen Brigid.

**OCEAN, Humphrey,** winner Imperial Tobacco Award (1982); artist; *b* Pulborough, 22 June, 1951. *m* Miranda Argyle. two *d*. *Educ:* Ampleforth. *Studied:* Tunbridge Wells Art School (1967-69), Brighton College of Art (1969-70), Canterbury College of Art (1970-73). *Exhib:* R.A., Whitechapel Open, Haus der Kunst Munich, British Council; one-man shows: N.P.G. (1984), Ferens A.G. Hull (1987), Dulwich P.G., Whitworth A.G. and Tate Gallery, Liverpool (1991), Whitworth A.G., Manchester, Ormeau Baths Gallery, Belfast and Kapil Jariwala Gallery, London (1997-98). *Work in collections:* N.P.G., Imperial War Museum, Ferens A.G., Scottish N.P.G., R.A.F. Museum, Royal Collection, Hertford College, Oxford, Southwark Collection, Wolverhampton A.G., U.E.A. *Commissions:* Neptune Court Project, National Maritime Museum (1997-98). *Publications:* The Ocean View (Plexus 1982), Big Mouth (Fourth Estate 1990, and Brown Trout, San Francisco 1994). *Address:* 22 Marmora Rd., London SE22 0RX.

**OCKENDEN, John Richard,** B.Ed. (Hons.) (1978); artist in water-colour and acrylic; Vice Chairman, Deeside Art Group; *b* Cheltenham, 6 Aug., 1946. one *d*. *Educ:* Alsager C.H.E., Chester C.H.E. *Exhib:* one-man shows: Theatr Clwyd Gallery since 1988; many mixed shows in England and Wales, including International Spring Fair, N.E.C. B'ham. *Publications:* limited editions. *Signs work:* "John R. Ockenden." *Address:* 29 Marksway, Pensby, Wirral L61 9PB.

**O'CONNELL, Richard Marcus,** Dip. A.D. (Hons.) Norwich (1969), Cert. F.A. (Oxon. 1972); figurative painter of maritime subjects, and townscapes in oil, acrylic, water-colour, poet; *b* Mumbles, Swansea, 19 July, 1947. *m* Heather Green. two *d*. *Studied:* Swansea College of Art (1965-66), Norwich School of Art (1966-69), Ruskin School of Drawing, University of Oxford (1971-72). *Exhib:* one-man shows: Marlborough Fine Art, London (1974), St. David's Hall, Cardiff (1989, 1996), National Museum of Wales, Turner House, Penarth (1994). *Work in collections:* Bailiol College, The Welsh Industrial and Maritime Museum, Cardiff, Vale of Glamorgan Council, Barry. *Publications:* poetry book: 'Cardiff my Cardiff' (Inika Press, Penarth, 1997). *Signs work:* "R.M. O'Connell." *Address:* 53 Windsor Rd., Penarth, Vale of Glamorgan, Wales CF64 IJE.

**O'CONNOR, John,** R.W.S., A.R.C.A.; painter, illustrator, wood engraver and author; *b* Leicester, 11 Aug., 1913. *m* Jenny Tennant. one *s*. *Educ:* Wyggeston School. *Studied:* Leicester College of Art; Royal College of Art. *Exhib:* one-man shows, Zwemmer Gallery (1955-68), Clare College (1965), New Grafton Gallery (1970-80), Broughton Gallery, Borders (1978 onwards); mixed shows, R.A., Bankside Gallery, London SE1 (R.W.S.), Rocket Gallery

W1. *Work in collections:* N.Y. Public Library, Columbia University; public galleries, Oxford, Cambridge, and other Universities and Colleges. *Publications:* written and illustrated: Canals, Barges and People (Shenval Press), A Pattern of People (Hutchinson); books illustrated for Golden Cockerel Press, Dropmore Press, Boston Imprint, Limited Editions Club, N.Y., Florin Press, Whittington Press, Foulis Archives Pree, Glasgow. Technical, several books on Graphic Arts. *Clubs:* Double Crown. *Signs work:* "John O'Connor." *Address:* Craigmore, Parton, Castle Douglas DG7 3NL, Scotland.

**O'CONNOR, Marcel,** B.A. (Hons.) Fine Art; artist/teacher in oil and wax encaustic painting; *b* Lurgan, Co. Armagh, 19 Nov., 1958. *Educ:* St. Michael's High School, Lurgan. *Studied:* Liverpool Polytechnic (1977-78), Brighton Polytechnic (1978-81), Cyprus College of Art (1983-84). *Exhib:* Scotland, Ireland, England, Cyprus, Hungary, Germany. *Work in collections:* City Arts Centre, Edinburgh. *Publications:* catalogues: 'Boundaries' in Edinburgh and Belfast; 4 Artists in Hungary; 'Europe 24' in Hungary; 'Europe 24 no.2' in Germany, bookcover artwork 'Scotland and Ulster'. *Signs work:* "Marcel O'Connor." *Address:* W.A.S.P.S. Studios (115), Patriothall, Stockbridge, Edinburgh.

**ODDY, Mercy,** seascape painter in water-colour, miniaturist; Council Mem. Soc. of Women Artists, Mem. Hilliard Soc. of Miniaturists, Sec. Christchurch Arts Guild; *b* Southsea. *m* David Oddy. two *d. Exhib:* solo show: Red House Museum and A.G., Christchurch, Dorset (Mar./Apr. 1994). *Commissions:* National Gallery Dublin, Guildhall London, Bristol University. *Signs work:* "Mercy Oddy" larger works; "M.O." miniatures. *Address:* 1 Lyme Cres., Highcliffe, Dorset BH23 5BJ.

**O'DONOGHUE, Declan,** M.C.S.D. (1986), F.S.C-D. (1991), M.Inst.P.I. (1991), M.S.D.I. (1991); designer and furniture maker in wood, metal, stone, glass; Director, Wilcogold Ltd. (1985), Adviser, Connemara West plc. (1992), Partner, S.F. Furniture (1980), Principal visiting tutor, Furn. Coll. Letterfrock (1988); *b* Cork, 18 Oct., 1960. *m* Fiona Mary Curry. two *d. Educ:* St. Vincent's College, Castleknock, Dublin. *Studied:* Parnham College (1978-80, R. Ingham). *Exhib:* National Theatre, Barbican, Camden Arts Centre, Mall Galleries, Bath Festival, Kilkenny Design Dublin, British Crafts Centre, British Crafts, Cheltenham. *Commissions:* National Gallery Dublin, Guildhall London, Bristol University. *Publications:* numerous exhbn. catalogues, articles, book features, B.B.C. (1981), H.T.V. (1992-93). Freeman City of London (1994), Liveryman Worshipful Co. of Furn. Makers (1994). *Clubs:* Royal Cork Yacht. *Address:* Street Farm, Acton Turville, Badminton, Glos. GL9 1HH.

**O'FARRELL, Bartholomew Patrick,** B.Ed.Hons. (Wales), Dip.A.D.; landscape painter and Demonstrator in acrylic, pastel, water-colour; Lecturer in illustration, Faculty of Art, W.G.I.H.E., Swansea (1981-85); *b* Ogilvie, mid-Glamorgan, 11 Aug., 1941. *Educ:* Caerphilly Grammar School. *Studied:* Cardiff College of Art (1959-62), Polytechnic of Wales, Barry (1974-78).

*Exhib:* Cornwall and S. Wales; annual one-man shows in Cornwall from 198
onwards at Trelowarren, Helston Folk Museum, Camborne School of Mine
Museum and Gallery, St. Austell Arts Centre, Falmouth A.G.; selected
National Museum of Wales, Albany Gallery, Cardiff, Celtic Art, Falmouth
Manor House Fine Arts, 3 Spires, Truro, Royal Cornwall Museum, Truro
*Work in collections:* National Library of Wales. *Publications:* The
Encyclopedia of Acrylic Techniques; The Best of Acrylic Painting
Inspirational Portraits; Encyclopedia of Water-colour Landscape Painting
Water, How to paint it. *Signs work:* "Bart O'Farrell." *Address:* Treleague Farm
St. Keverne, Helston, Cornwall TR12 6PQ.

**OFFEN, John,** B.A.(Hons.); designer and author; partner Ken Moor
Design Associates; *b* 15 Mar., 1951. *Educ:* University of Exeter. Positions held
British Council, UNESCO, Attache, British Embassy, Tunis. *Publications:* 
History of Irish Lace, Thoroughbred Style. *Address:* 33 Vicarage Ct
Kensington Church St., London W8 4HE.

**OGDEN, Catherine,** A.R.B.S.A. (1992), R.M.S. (1993), S.W.A. (1988)
miniature seascape painter and flower pastelist; *b* London, 10 Apr., 1951. *Educ*
Plashet Secondary Modern, Kingsway College. *Exhib:* R.M.S., S.W.A., R.I
R.B.S.A., R.W.S., Mid 'Art' 86 Dudley, Laing Art collection competition, Joh
Noott Gallery, Llewellyn Alexander Gallery. *Signs work:* "C. Ogden.
*Address:* Forge House, Brimfield, Ludlow, Shropshire SY8 4NG.

**O'HARA, D. Patrick,** botanical sculptor (original works in porcelain
engraving and enamelling on crystal); *b* Windsor, 17 June, 1936. *m* Ann
Greenwood, landscape painter. one *s.* one *d. Educ:* Haileybury and Reading
University. *Studied:* Malvern Art School (1969-71). *Exhib:* Cartier, N.Y
(1972), Tryon and Moorland Gallery (1973), Chicago Flower Show (1975
Wexford Festival (1976), Victor Zelli (1978), R.H.S. (1979), Bank of Ireland
(1980), Meister Gallery, Zurich (1980, 1981), Chester Beatty Library, Dublin
(1984), United Nations (1984), EXPO, Osaka (1990), Royal Bot. Gdns. (1994)
*Work in collections:* Lewis Ginter Botanical Gdn., Richmond, Va.; Flagle
Museum, Florida; Jones Museum, Maine; International Museum of Wildlif
Art, Gloucester; Chicago Horticultural Soc.; Gloucester City Museum; Adach
Inst., Tokyo; Smithkline Beecham Corp., Sumitomo Group; Jefferson Smurfi
Foundation. *Signs work:* "Patrick O'Hara." *Address:* Manor House
Currabinny, Carrigaline, Co. Cork, Ireland.

**OHL, Gabrielle,** painter in oil, inks, stained glass; *b* Diego-Suarez, Malagsy
*Studied:* Paris Academie Julian (1949-50), Madrid Beaux Arts (1950-51)
Melbourne Technical College of Arts (1951-53), Paris. *Exhib:* Paris salons
Independents, Marine, Automne, Femmes Peintres; Maison de l'Alsac
Germany, U.S.A. One-man shows, Paris, Belgium, London, Italy, Malaya
Korea, Kuwait, Luxemburg, Sardinia, La Coupole, Paris, Stasburg, Rosheim
Barr, Alsace, MDIAC, Paris. Awards: Medaglia "Nuova Critica Europea" Ital
(1969); Gold Medal, Paternoster Academy, London (1971), Palmes d'or, Paris

Critique (1977), Gold Medal, Baden Baden (1981), Bronze Medal, New York (1983), Gold Medal, Milan (1989), Prix Special, Nouvelle Figurtion, MDIAC. Paris (1995). *Signs work:* see appendix. *Address:* 10 Rue des Halles, Paris 75001.

**OLDFIELD, Joy M.,** A.T.D. (1943); painter, sculptor and potter in oil, pastel, charcoal, clay and stone; *b* Hampstead, 1920. *m* John Oldfield. one *s.* two *d.* *Educ:* Camden School for Girls. *Studied:* Westminster and Central Schools of Art (1938-40, K. Jamieson, R. Millard), Regent St. Polytechnic Art School (1940-42, S. Tresillian), Hornsey School of Art (1943). *Exhib:* R.P., S.W.A.; one-man show, Watatu Gallery, Nairobi (1980), Castle Park Frodsham (1994), Northwich Soc. of the Arts annual exhbns. *Work in collections:* England, Scotland, Ireland and Kenya. *Signs work:* "Joy M. Oldfield." *Address:* White Lodge, West Rd., Weaverham, Ches. CW8 3HL.

**OLIN, Leon,** N.D.D. (1962), A.T.D. (1963); artist and illustrator in oil, water-colour, line drawing; Resident Artist and co-Proprietor, Gallery One, Fishguard, Dyfed; *b* Leicester, 28 May, 1939. *m* Sylvia Gainsford. *Educ:* Gateway School, Leicester. *Studied:* Leicester and Brighton Colleges of Art (D.P. Carrington). *Exhib:* Numerous exhbns. *Work in collections:* Portsmouth Civic Gallery, Kallis Foundation, Beverly Hills. *Publications:* Pembrokeshire Architecture (Rosedale Pub.), Wildlife of St. James' Park (Brick by Brick L.H.A.G.), Food from the Countryside, Where have all the Cowslips gone, Out of This World (all Bishopsgate Press), The Country Kitchen (Bell and Hyman), From our Garden (Hawthorn Pub.). *Signs work:* "LEON OLIN." *Address:* Fron Haul, Rhos-y-Caerau, Goodwick, Pembrokeshire SA64 0LB.

**OLIVER, Charles William,** A.R.C.A. (1933), Liverpool Academy (1938); artist in oil; Vice-Principal, Laird School of Art, Birkenhead (retd.); *b* Youngstown, Ohio, U.S.A., 21 Apr., 1911. *m* Ena Landon Davies. two *s. Educ:* Wade Deacon Grammar School, Widnes, Cheshire. *Studied:* City School of Art, Liverpool, and R.C.A. under Sir W. Rothenstein (1930-34). *Exhib:* R.P.S., R.B.A., R.Scot.A., Liverpool Academy of Arts, Southport, R.Cam.A., Wirral Soc. of Arts. *Work in collections:* Liverpool, Birkenhead A.G.; Portraits: Liverpool University & John Moores Univ., Birkenhead School, Society of Anaesthetists, Chester Cathedral Library, etc. *Publications:* Anatomy and Perspective (Studio Vista, 1972). *Signs work:* "C. W. OLIVER" and date. *Address:* 1 South Bank, Oxton, Birkenhead L43 5UP.

**OLIVER, Kenneth Herbert,** R.W.S., R.E., A.R.C.A., R.W.A.; etcher, lithographer, artist in water-colour; taught at Gloucestershire College of Arts and Technology, Cheltenham; *b* Norwich, 7 Feb., 1923. *m* Joyce Margaret Beaumont, A.R.C.A., R.W.A. three *d. Educ:* King Edward VI Grammar School, Norwich. *Studied:* Norwich School of Art and R.C.A. *Exhib:* R.W.S., R.W.A., R.A., R.E., provincial galleries and abroad. *Work in collections:* Royal West of England Academy, Bristol, Cheltenham A.G. *Signs work:* "KENNETH H. OLIVER." *Address:* Vyners, Halfway Pitch, Pitchcombe, Stroud,

Glos. GL6 6LJ.

**OMAN, Julia Trevelyan,** C.B.E. (1986), Hon. D.Litt. (1987), R.D.I. F.C.S.D., Des.R.C.A. Royal Scholar, R.C.A.; 1st Class; Silver Medal R.C.A. Designer of the Year Award (1967); designer for films, theatre, television books; Director, Oman Productions Ltd.; *b* 11 July, 1930. *m* Sir Roy Strong former Director, V. & A. *Educ:* R.C.A., London. *Exhib:* design of productions for: National Theatre, Royal Opera Covent Garden, Royal Ballet, Royal Shakespeare Co., Hamburg Opera, West End Theatres, Burg Theater Vienna Boston Ballet, Stockholm Opera, Kassel Opera, Glyndebourne, B.B.C Television, films. *Work in collections:* V. & A. *Publications:* Street Children (photographs); Elizabeth R. (design); Mary Queen of Scots (design); Merchant of Venice (Folio Society), etc. *Signs work:* "Julia Trevelyan Oman." *Address* The Laskett, Much Birch, Hereford HR2 8HZ.

**ONIANS, Richard (Dick) Lathbury,** M.A.(Cantab.), A.R.B.S. (1989); City and Guilds Art School Cert. of Merit (1968); sculptor in wood and stone, lecturer; Senior Carving Tutor, City and Guilds of London Art School; *b* Chalfont St. Giles, 19 May, 1940. *m* Frances Clare Critchley. *Educ:* Merchant Taylors School, Northwood; Trinity College, Cambridge. *Studied:* City and Guilds of London Art School (1966-68). *Exhib:* Mall Galleries, Marjorie Parr Gallery Century Galleries, Henley-on-Thames, Galleria Renata, Chicago, Clement House Gallery, Edith Grove Gallery, Bow House Gallery, London *Publications:* Essential Woodcarving Techniques: (G.M.C. Publications Ltd. 1997). *Signs work:* "R.L.O." *Address:* Woodside, Commonwood, King's Langley, Herts. WD4 9BA.

**ORAM, Ann Alexandra,** B.A.(Hons.) 1980, Post Grad. Dip. in Fine Art (1981), R.S.W. (1986); painter in water-colour, mixed media and oil; *b* London 3 May, 1956. *m* David Cemery. one *s. Educ:* Grantown Grammar School Inverness Royal Academy. *Studied:* Edinburgh College of Art/Heriot Watt University (1976-82). *Exhib:* one-man shows include: Thackeray Gallery, Scottish Gallery, Portland Gallery, Loomshop and Macauley Gallery; group shows: R.S.A., R.S.W., R.G.I., R.A., Stowell's Trophy, Royal Oversea League, Compass Gallery - New Generation, Corrymelia Scott, Duncan Miller Fine Art, Roger Billcliffe, S.T.V. Student Show. Air Fairs Bath, London Manchester, New York. *Work in collections:* Britain and abroad. *Signs work:* "Ann Oram." *Address:* Gardener's Cottage, Nigg Mains, by Tain, Easter Ross IV19 1QR.

**O'REILLY, Faith,** N.D.D., Dip. R.A., A.T.C.; oil and water-colourist; *b* Boston, Mass., U.S.A., 6 Aug., 1938. *Educ:* in U.S.A. and England. *Studied:* Berkshire College of Art, Royal Academy Schools, Hornsey and University of London. *Exhib:* group and solo shows: Midland Group Gallery; 273 Gallery, London; shows in Universities, Surrey, Sussex, Montpellier, Paris and Dieppe *Work in collections:* U.S.A., France, Australia, Singapore, Britain *Commissions:* 'Roman' Mosaic, Moorgate, London, Helped to found Stanley

Spencer Gallery, Cookham, Berkshire. *Clubs:* N.A.A. *Signs work:* "F.O.R." and "Faith O'Reilly." Returned to "O'Reilly" from adoptive name "Gibbon" in 1975. Studio in S. France; Le Vernet, 34240 Combes, and in Kemptown, Brighton, U.K. *Address:* 13 Walpole Terr., Kemptown, Brighton, Sussex BN2 2EB.

**O'REILLY, Richard,** F.P.S.; artist in oil, water-colour, ink, wood; *b* London, 11 May, 1932. *m* P. Turner. two *s.* one *d. Educ:* Avondale School, Cheadle Heath, Ches. *Studied:* under William Redgrave, sculptor-draughtsman 'One to One'. *Exhib:* Guildhall London, Ragley Hall, Foyles's King's College, Vienna 9th International, P.S., Tattershall Castle, Cambridge Union, University of Essex, House of Commons, B.A.C., St. Martin-in-the-Fields, London. *Work in collections:* Loggia Gallery, The Investment Gallery, Paris, Berlin, Vienna. *Publications:* work repro.: Arts Review. *Signs work:* "O'Reilly." *Address:* 12 Acanthus Rd., Battersea, London SW11 5TY.

**ORGAN, Robert,** D.F.A. (Lond.), R.W.A.; painter in oil, water-colour, sometimes tempera; *b* Hutton, Som., 27 Jan., 1933. *m* Valerie Barden. one *s.* three *d. Studied:* West of England College of Art, Slade School. *Exhib:* Beaux Arts, Bath (1983-95), Browse & Darby (1981-96), R.W.A. (1995), Belloc Lowndes, Chicago (1995-97). *Work in collections:* Plymouth City A.G., Brighton and Hove A.G., Exeter Royal Albert Museum, Devon Educ. Com., Cornwall Educ. Com., R.W.A. Collection, S.W.A. Collection, Universities: Edinburgh, Exeter, Reading, Illinois. *Publications:* various articles, art and architectural journals. *Signs work:* "Robert Organ" usually on back. *Address:* Lower Ridge, Wambrook, Chard, Som. TA20 3ES.

**ORR, Chris,** M.A. (1967), R.A. (1995); artist in painting, etching, lithography; visiting lecturer, Royal College of Art; *b* London, 1943. *m* Catherine Terris. one *s.* one *d. Educ:* Penge Academy. *Studied:* R.C.A. (1964-67). *Exhib:* R.A. Summer Exhbn.; one-man shows: London, America, Australia, France, Japan, Canada. *Work in collections:* V. & A., British Council, Arts Council, Science Museum. *Publications:* John Ruskin (1976), Arthur (1977), Many Mansions (1990), The Small Titanic (1994). *Signs work:* "Chris Orr." *Address:* 7 Bristle Hill, Buckingham MK18 1EZ.

**OSBORNE, Stuart John,** A.R.C.A., A.T.D., M.F.P.S.; sculptor, models portraits, figures and animals; stone and wood carver; *b* Weston-s-Mare, Som. *m* Margaret Cole, A.T.D., portrait and animal painter. one *d. Educ:* Kingsholme School, Weston-s-Mare. *Studied:* Bristol College of Art, and Royal College of Art, London. *Exhib:* societies: F.P.S., Galerie Salammbo, Paris, Vallombreuse, Biarritz, International, New York, Geneva, Mall, London, Loggia Gallery. *Signs work:* "Osborne." *Address:* 64 Burton Manor Rd., Stafford ST17 9PR.

**OSMOND, Edward,** A.T.D., M.S.I.A., Carnegie Award; artist in oils, wash, line, illustrations, commercial drawing and book design; *m* C. M. ("Laurie") Osmond, sc. and painter. *Signs work:* in full, block caps. *Address:* Downland Cottage, Lullington Cl., Seaford, E. Sussex BN25 4JH.

**OTTEY, Piers Ronald Edward Campbell,** B.A.(Hons.); painter in oil on canvas and panel, teacher/lecturer; *b* London, 27 Sept., 1955. *m* Annelise. two *s.* one *d. Educ:* King's College School, Wimbledon. *Studied:* Chelsea School of Art (1974-78, the late Patrick Symons, Myles Murphy). *Exhib:* R.A., Bath Contemporary Arts Fair, London, Sussex, Paris; one-man shows: Brighton (1988), Midhurst (1991), Stansted House (1994), Seaford College (1994), The Mill Studio, Sussex (1996). *Work in collections:* England, France, Denmark, Canada. *Commissions:* Grant Thornton, Chichester Hospital. *Signs work:* "Ottey." *Address:* Bishop's Hill Cottage, Graffham, nr. Petworth, W. Sussex GU28 0QA.

**OWEN, Glynis,** B.A. (Fine Art) (1966), A.T.C. (1967), F.R.B.S. (1990); sculptor in stone and bronze; *b* Gravesend, Kent , 22 May, 1945; married. two *s.* one *d. Educ:* Portsmouth High School, G.P.D.S.T. *Studied:* Portsmouth College of Art (1962-66), Goldsmiths' College (1966-67). *Exhib:* R.I.B.A (1991), McHardy Sculpture Company (1996), Glyndebourne Festival Opera (1996). *Work in collections:* Alton College, Hants. purchased by Hants Architects Dept.; Stevenage Town Centre, life-size family group, commissioned by Stevenage Development Corp.; Portrait of Jacqueline du Pre for Music Bldg. St. Hilda's College, Oxford. *Commissions:* private: Lake Como, Switzerland (1992), Nick Mason (Pink Floyd) (1997). *Publications:* Carving Techniques by Glynis Beecroft (Batsford 1976), Casting Techniques by Glynis Beecroft (Batsford 1979). *Signs work:* "Glynis Owen." *Address:* The Studio, 52 Pilgrim's Lanc, Hampstead, London NW3 1SN.

**OWEN, Muriel Sylvia,** N.D.D., A.T.D., S.W.A., U.A., F.R.S.A.; painter in water-colour, lecturer; Head of Art and Deputy Principal, Dixon and Wolfe Tutors, London SW1 (1969-82); Vice-Pres., Soc. of Women Artists; *b* Welwyn Garden City. *m* Edward Eardley Owen, M.A.; three *s.* by previous marriage. *Educ:* Welwyn Garden City Grammar School. *Studied:* St. Albans School of Art (1946-50 under Gwen White and Christopher Sanders, R.P., R.A.), London University (1951). *Exhib:* R.I., S.W.A., U.A., Llewellyn Alexander Gallery, London; ten one-man shows, London, Fairfield Halls, Croydon, Yarmouth Castle, I.O.W. official galleries. *Work in collections:* 38 paintings English Heritage, I.O.W. Arts Council, Bank of England, Queen Elizabeth Military Hospital, Woolwich, Atomic Energy Commission, London. *Publications:* work repro.: St.Paul's, Westminster, floral, (Henry Ling), calendars 1988, 1989 and 1991 (I.O.W. County Press), series of 4 art teaching videos (1992). *Signs work:* "Muriel Owen." *Address:* Briarwood House, Church Hill, Totland, I.O.W. PO39 0EU.

**OXENBURY, Helen Gillian,** illustrator/writer in water-colour; Kate Greenaway medal (1969), Smarties award (1989), Boston Globe award, Kurt Maschler award (1985); *b* 2 June, 1938. *m* John M. Burningham. one *s.* two *d. Studied:* Ipswich School of Art and Central School of Arts and Crafts, London. *Publications:* illustrated: The Three Little Wolves and the Big Bad Pig (1993).

Farmer Duck (1991), We're Going on a Bear Hunt (1989). *Signs work:* "Helen Oxenbury." *Address:* c/o Walker Books, 87 Vauxhall Walk, London SE11 5HJ.

**OXLADE, Roy,** N.D.D., M.A., R.C.A.; painter in oil; *b* 13 Jan., 1929. *m* Rose Wylie. one *s.* two *d. Studied:* Bromley College of Art and with David Bomberg. *Exhib:* Young Contemporaries (1952-54), Borough Bottega Group (1954, 1955), Winnipeg Biennial (1st prize drawing, 1960), John Moores (1963, 1991), Hayward Annual (1982), Norwich Gallery 'Rocks and Flesh' (1985), Waddington Schiel, Toronto (1987), Jan Turner, Los Angeles (1988), Cleveland International (1989), Norwich Gallery, 'EAST' (1991, 1994); Art Fairs: Olympia (1986), Chicago (1987), Los Angeles (1987), Seattle (1996); one person shows: Vancouver A.G. (1963), New Metropole, Folkestone (1983), AIR Gallery (1983), Odette Gilbert Gallery (1985, 1987, 1988), Gardner Centre, University of Sussex (1990), Reed's Wharf Gallery, London (1993). *Work in collections:* South East Arts. *Publications:* David Bomberg (R.C.A. Papers 3 1981). *Clubs:* Chelsea Arts. *Signs work:* "R. Oxlade" on reverse. *Address:* Forge Cottage, Newnham, Sittingbourne, Kent ME9 0LQ.

**OXLEY, Ursula Frances,** Board of Educ. drawing exam. (1937); artist in black and white, crayon, conte, pastel and water-colour; specialist in child portraiture; *b* Ealing, 4 May, 1918. *m* Laurence Oxley. one *s.* one *d. Educ:* privately. *Studied:* Winchester School of Art under E. E. Anderson, A.R.C.A. (1935-39). *Exhib:* P.S., S.W.A., S.G.A., R.I., Guildford Art Soc., Woking Art Soc., N.S., Alresford Art Soc. *Publications:* illustrated 1971 and subsequent editions of History of Alresford, and Sketches of My Cat. *Clubs:* Alresford Art Soc. *Signs work:* "Ursula Oxley." *Address:* The Studio Bookshop, Alresford, Hants. SO24 9AW.

**OXLEY, Valerie Mary,** Cert.Ed. (1969), A.N.E.A. (1983), S.B.A. (1987); self taught botanical illustrator in pencil, water-colour, pen and ink; Tutor, botanical illustration, University of Sheffield A.E.C.; *b* Manchester, 26 Sept., 1947. *m* Michael Oxley, M.Sc., C.Eng. one *d. Educ:* Abbeydale Girls' Grammar School, Sheffield; Hereford College of Educ. *Exhib:* S.B.A., R.H.S., Linnean Soc., Portico Gallery, Manchester, Durham A.G., Museum of Garden History, London. *Clubs:* President, Northern Soc. of Botanical Art. *Signs work:* "Valerie Oxley." *Address:* Brookside, Firbeck, Worksop, Notts. S81 8JZ.

# P

**PACE, Shirley,** sculptor and artist in bronze, charcoal, pen and ink, conté, monochrome, the Ashling Collection representational, equestrian sculptor to Susse Fondeur, Paris; *b* Worthing, Sussex, 16 Feb., 1933. *m* Roy Pace. two *d. Educ:* Worthing Convent. *Studied:* Worthing School of Art (1948-51). *Exhib:* Mall Galleries, Alwin Gallery, many provincial and overseas galleries. *Work in collections:* Life and a quarter dray-horse, London; private collections: England, U.S.A., Bermuda, New Zealand, Australia, Hong Kong. *Clubs:*

S.E.A., Chichester Art Soc. *Signs work:* "Shirley Pace." *Address:* Field House, Newells La., West Ashling, Chichester, W. Sussex PO18 8DD.

**PACKARD, Gilian E.,** Des.R.C.A. (1962), F.S.D.C. (1963), F.R.S.A. (1975), F.C.S.D. (1977); first woman freeman of Goldsmiths' Company by special grant (1971); designer of jewellery in gold, platinum, silver and stones; Senior Lecturer, Sir John Cass Dept. of Arts, Design and Manufacture, London Guildhall University; *b* Newcastle upon Tyne, 16 Mar., 1938. *Educ:* Claremont School, Esher. *Studied:* Kingston-upon-Thames School of Art (1955-58), Central School of Arts and Crafts (1959), Royal College of Art (1959-62). *Work in collections:* Goldsmiths Hall, De Beers, V. & A. *Signs work:* "G.E.P." within oval, (Hallmark). *Address:* 8.2 Stirling Ct., 3 Marshall St., London W1V 1LQ.

**PACKER, William John,** N.D.D. (Painting), A.T.C., Hon. F.R.C.A., Hon. R.B.A.; painter in oil and water-colour; Art Critic, The Financial Times (since 1974); *b* Birmingham, 19 Aug., 1940. *m* Clare Winn. three *d. Educ:* Windsor Grammar School; Wimbledon School of Art (1959-63), Brighton College of Art (1963-64). *Exhib:* R.A.; group exhbns.: Angela Flowers, Cadogan, Contemporary and many other galleries. *Publications:* The Art of Vogue Covers (Octopus, 1980), Fashion Drawing in Vogue (Thames & Hudson, 1983), Henry Moore (with Gemma Levine) (Weidenfeld & Nicolson, 1985). *Clubs:* Chelsea Arts. *Signs work:* "W.P." or "W. PACKER." *Address:* 39 Elms Rd., Clapham, London SW4 9EP.

**PADDEN, Daphne,** artist and graphic designer in water-colour and gouache; *b* London, 21 May, 1927. *Educ:* Rosebery County School. *Studied:* Epsom and Ewell School of Art (1944-49, David Birch, R.O.I., R.O. Dunlop, R.A., Leslie Worth, A.R.C.A., Ronald Benham). *Exhib:* R.M.S., Medici Gallery, Bourne Gallery, Reigate, Edwin Pollard Gallery, Wimbledon, Llewellyn Alexander (Fine Paintings) Ltd., London, Kingsmead Gallery, Great Bookham. *Work in collections:* U.K. and overseas. *Signs work:* see appendix. *Address:* 30 Marshalls Cl., Epsom, Surrey KT19 8HZ.

**PAES, Rui,** M.A., R.C.A. (1988), Dip. E.S.B.A.P. (1976-81); painter in oil and water based media; *b* Pemba, Mozambique, 13 July, 1957. *m* Anabela Riberio da Cunha. one *s. Educ:* Escola de Belas Artes do Porto, Portugal (1976-81), Royal College of Art, London (1986-88). Calousie Gulbenkian Scholarship (1986-1988) and the Beal Foundation Grant. *Exhib:* England, Germany, Portugal and Spain. *Work in collections:* Museu de Arte Moderna, Oporto, Portugal, The Beal Collection, U.S.A., and the Royal College of Art Permanent Collection. *Commissions:* Mural painting in Egypt, England, France, Germany, Norway and Portugal. *Publications:* illustrations for "..do tempo inutil" by Gloria de Sant'anna (1975). *Signs work:* see appendix. *Address:* 2 Chelsea Farmhouse Studios, Milmans St., London SW10 0BY.

**PAGE, Charles,** R.I. (1988), M.S.I.A. (1955); painter, illustrator and graphic designer in water-colour, acrylic, mixed media, collage; *b* Leighton Buzzard, 17 Apr., 1910. *m* (1) Jessie Stevens (decd.); (2) Beryl Sheaves (decd.). one *s.*

*Educ:* Luton Grammar School. *Studied:* Central School of Art and Crafts (1928-29). *Exhib:* R.I., R.W.S., R.S.A., R.B.S.A. and several provincial galleries. First recipient of Rowland Hilder Award at R.I. (1994). *Work in collections:* Luton A.G., Letchworth A.G. *Signs work:* "Charles Page." *Address:* 13 Carisbrooke Rd., Harpenden, Herts. AL5 5QS.

**PAGE-ROBERTS, James,** painter in oil, sculptor, artist in black and white, and writer; *b* Silchester, 5 Feb., 1925. *m* Margaretha Klees. *Educ:* Wellington College, and Taft, U.S.A. *Studied:* Central School of Arts and Crafts and Old Vic School of Theatre Design. *Exhib:* one-man shows at Galerie de Seine, Reid Gallery, Kintetsu Gallery, Osaka, Qantas Gallery, Cambridge, Loft Gallery. *Publications:* author, Vines in your Garden (Argus); writer/illustrator first four editions of The Best Wine Buys in the High Street (Foulsham); The Oldie Cookbook (Carbery Press); Vines and Wines in a Small Garden (Herbert Press); Guide to a Dockland of Change (Mudlark Press). *Signs work:* "P R" and "PAGE-ROBERTS." *Address:* 37 St. Peter's Grove, London W6 9AY.

**PAINE, Ken,** P.S., S.P.F.; portrait artist in pastel, oil, water-colour; Master Pastellist of France; *b* 2 Nov., 1926. one *s.* two *d.* Worked with R.Q. Dunlop, R.A.; studied at Twickenham College of Art. *Exhib:* annually P.S., R.P., R.O.I., R.I. at Mall Galleries London, R.W.A., widely exhib. in and around London, U.S.A., France, Canada, Germany; solo exhbns. include Llewellyn Alexander Gallery, London; Edward Day Gallery, Ontario, Canada. *Commissions:* many which include Sir David Atkinson Air Marshal, Trevor McDonald broadcaster. *Publications:* (Biography) "Ken Paine - His Life and Work" by Michael Simonow. *Signs work:* "PAINE." *Address:* 8 Spring Gdns., E. Molesey, Surrey KT8 0JA.

**PAINE, Ula,** R.D.S. teacher-artist cert. (1931); painter in oil and water-colour; *b* Surbiton, 26 Sept., 1909. *Educ:* St. Winifred's, Eastbourne; Oak Dene, Beaconsfield. *Studied:* Queen Anne's Studio, Chelsea (1929-31, Lettuce MacMunn), Chelsea Polytechnic (H.S. Williamson, O.B.E.), and later under Vivian Pitchforth, R.A. *Exhib:* R.A., R.B.A., R.O.I., W.I.A.C., Britain in Water-colours, Mall Galleries, U.A., Phoenix Gallery, Lavenham, Paris Salon, South Bank Picture Show; one-man show: Gallery 10, London W1. *Publications:* work repro.: The Artist, The Tatler, Arts Review, The Illustrated London News, The Artist's and Illustrator's Magazine, Portrait, Chelsea News. *Signs work:* "Ula Paine." *Address:* 32 Astell St., Chelsea, London SW3 3RU.

**PAINTER, Tom,** F.R.B.S., R.B.A., A.R.C.A. (Sculpture, 1949) Travelling Scholar; sculptor in bronze, concrete, resin/fibre glass, wood, stone; *b* 29 Nov., 1918. *m* Muriel Jeffery, A.R.C.A. one *d.* *Educ:* Wolverhampton. *Studied:* Wolverhampton School of Art (R.J. Emerson). *Exhib:* R.B.S., R.B.A., R.A. *Work in collections:* U.K., U.S.A., Canada, Italy. *Signs work:* "Tom Painter." *Address:* 5 Garlies Rd., Forest Hill, London SE23 2RU.

**PALMER, Prof. Herbert Ralph,** awarded Scholarship of Art, Johannesburg, S. Africa (1932-36); F.R.B.S.; sculptor in all known media and painter in oil and water-colour; worked in the Art Dept., V. & A.; art teacher Tower Bridge Institute, London (1950-51), Senior Professional Officer and Curator of Art, McGregor Museum, Kimberley, Cape Province (1974-76) Curator, Zululand Historical Museum, Eshowe, Natal (1980-); *b* Richmond Surrey, 13 Dec., 1915. *Studied:* Johannesburg Art School, and one-time pupil of Anton Van Wouw and P. H. Jowett. *Exhib:* in twenty leading galleries in London, New York, South Africa, Portugal. *Work in collections:* (1947 worked with Sir William Reid Dick, K.C.V.O., R.A., on the Roosevel Monument. *Commissions:* numerous, including two ecclesiastical figures, St James Church, Fulham, London; bronze Mother and child, South Africa House London; Dr. Basil Merriman Bronze, Carter Foundation, London, etc *Publications:* There must be Sculpture (1989). Hobby: Violin-making. *Clubs* Chelsea Arts. *Signs work:* "R. Palmer." *Address:* 91 Vausedale Rd. Queensburgh 4093, Natal, S. Africa.

**PALMER, Jean C.,** B.A. (Hons.) Fine Art; painter in oil; part-time Tutor Adult College, Lancaster; *b* Southport, 1961. *m* Peter Layzell. *Studied* Southport College of Art (1977-79), University of Central Lancs. (1979-82) *Exhib:* R.A. Summer Shows (1992, 1993, 1994, 1995, 1996, 1997), variou London exhbns. with Houldsworth Fine Art, Gillian Jason Gallery, etc. *Work in collections:* Manchester City A.G., NatWest Coll., Warrington Arts Council Jerwood Foundation. *Signs work:* "J.Palmer" on reverse *Address:* 72 Vale Rd. Lancaster LA1 2JL.

**PALMER, John Frederick,** R.W.A. (1991); Cornelissen prize R.W.A annual exhbn. (1985); graphic designer; artist in oil, water-colour, gouache P.P., Bristol Savages; *b* Bristol, 11 Aug., 1939. *Educ:* Carlton Park, Bristol *Studied:* West of England College of Art (1955-56, J. Arnold). *Exhib:* Bristo Artists, Arnolfini. *Work in collections:* Bristol Savages, Leeds Bldg. Soc. NatWest Assurance, British Aerospace, Atomic Energy Authority *Publications:* Drawing & Sketching (1993). *Clubs:* Bristol Savages. *Sign work:* "J.F. Palmer." *Address:* 18 Haverstock Rd., Knowle, Bristol BS4 2BZ.

**PALMER, Juliette,** N.D.D. (1950), A.T.D. (1951); painter in water-colour illustrator, author; *b* Romford, 18 May, 1930. *m* Dennis Palmer. one *d. Educ* Brentwood County High School. *Studied:* S.E. Essex School of Art (1946-50 Alan Wellings, William Stobbs, Bernard Carolan). *Exhib:* R.A., R.I., N.E.A.C. R.O.I., R.W.A.; group gallery shows, Philadelphia, U.S.A., Sheffield, Windsor Henley, Barnes, Bloomsbury; one-man shows, S. Australia, Tokyo Cambridge, Chipping Norton, Cookham. Finalist in Hunting, Laing, Singer & Friedlander/Sunday Times National Art Competitions. *Work in collections* Barking Library, Leicestershire Educ. Com. *Publications:* 60 children's book: illustrated; author/illustrator, 6 children's picture/information book: (Macmillan). *Signs work:* "Juliette Palmer." *Address:* Melmott Lodge, The Pound, Cookham, Maidenhead, Berks. SL6 9QD.

**PALMER, Margaret,** A.T.D., P.S., N.S.; portrait painter in oil and pastel animal and genre painter, book illustrator; *b* London, 10 Sept., 1922. *m* R. G. W. Garrett. two *d. Studied:* Hornsey School of Art (1938-39), Salisbury School of Art (1939-41), Bournemouth College of Art (1941-42). *Exhib:* R.P., R.O.I., etc.; one-man shows in London, Guildford, Farnham, Leatherhead, works in worldwide collections. *Publications:* written and illustrated, Honeypot and Buzz; also illustrated books published by Harrap, Heinemann, etc. *Signs work:* "Margaret Palmer." *Address:* Robins Oak, Wonersh, nr. Guildford, Surrey.

**PALMER, Robert Derrick,** R.O.I. (1978), R.B.A. (1983); painter in oil; *b* Cambridge, 13 June, 1927. *m* Jean Parker. one *s.* one *d. Educ:* Central School, Cambridge. *Studied:* Cambridge School of Art (part-time 1951-58). *Exhib:* one-man shows, Richard Bradley Atelier, Norwich (1968), Fermoy Gallery, Kings Lynn (1980). Awarded De Laszlo Medal at R.B.A. exhbn. (1990). *Signs work:* "R. PALMER" or "R.P." *Address:* Flat E, 151 Longfleet Rd., Poole, Dorset BH15 2HS.

**PALTENGHI, Julian Celeste,** B.F.A.; Winner 1993 Hunting/Observer art prizes: Travel award - Australia; painter in oil, sculptor in plaster and bronze; *b* London, 28 Aug., 1955. *m* Katy. one *d. Educ:* Stowe, Bucks. *Studied:* Cambridge (1976-77), Loughborough College of Art (1978-81). *Exhib:* 'Critic's Choice' Clare Henry: Cooling Gallery, Beaux Arts Galleries, London and Bath, Swiss Artists in Britain: October Galleries, Stephen Bartley, Chelsea, Camden Annual, G.L.C. Spirit of London Festival Hall, Centre Georges Pompidou, Paris, Royal West of England Academy, (purchased by) Christie's Cooperate Collection. *Clubs:* Chelsea Arts. *Signs work:* "PALTENGHI." *Address:* 143 Old Church St., London SW3.

**PANCHERI, Robert,** A.R.B.S., Dip. (1977); sculptor in wood and stone; *b* Bromsgrove, 22 June, 1916. *m* Bridget Milligan. two *s.* two *d. Educ:* Bromsgrove School. *Studied:* Birmingham School of Art (1934-39, William Bloye). *Work in collections:* statues: Winwick Lancs; Great Malvern Priory; Franciscan Friary, Chester; St. Peter's Church, Swinton, Manchester; sculpture panel, Sheldon Fire Station. *Signs work:* "R. Pancheri" lower case letters. *Address:* 12 Finstall Rd., Bromsgrove B60 2DZ.

**PANNETT, Juliet,** M.B.E. (1992), F.R.S.A.; portrait painter; Special artist to the Illustrated London News from 1958-64; *b* Hove, Sussex. *m* Major M. R. D. Pannett (died 1980). one *s.* one *d. Studied:* Brighton School of Art. *Exhib:* R.A., R.P., R.I. *Work in collections:* 22 portraits in National Portrait Gallery, Hove Art Gallery. Portraits include: H.M. The Queen; H.R.H. Prince Andrew and H.R.H. Prince Edward for H.M. The Queen; Lord Goodman; Lord Tonypandy; Lavinia Duchess of Norfolk for Arundel Castle; Oxford and Cambridge colleges. *Publications:* work repro.: illustrated London News, The Times, Daily Telegraph, Radio Times, Birmingham Mail. Awarded freedom of Worshipful Company of Painter Stainers; Freeman of City of London (1960). *Signs work:* "Juliet Pannett." *Address:* Pound House, Poundstone Lane, Angmering Village, Sussex BN16 4AL.

**PAOLOZZI, Sir Eduardo Luigi,** Kt. (1989), C.B.E. (1968), R.A. (1979), Hon. Dr. (R.C.A.), D.Litt. (Glas.); sculptor; Visiting Professor, Royal College of Art; *b* Leith, Scotland, 7 Mar., 1924. *Studied:* Edinburgh College of Art, Slade School. *Exhib:* one-man shows, Mayor Gallery (1947), 30th Venice Biennale (1960), M.O.M.A. New York (1964), Rijksmuseum, Otterlo (1967), Stadtische Kunsthalle Dusseldorf, Tate Gallery (1971), V. & A. (1973, 1977), Nationalgalerie Berlin (1975), Kolnischer Kunstverein (1979), Royal Scottish Academy (1984), Museum Ludwig (1985). *Publications:* Eduardo Paolozzi by Winfried Konnertz (Dumont Verlag, 1984). *Signs work:* "Eduardo Paolozzi." *Address:* 107 Dovehouse St., London SW3 6JZ.

**PARFITT, Margaret,** C.B.E. (1980), S.R.N., S.W.A., C.A.S., S.E.L.A.S.; sculptor in wood and metal; *b* Romford, 23 Oct., 1920. *m* Ronald Parfitt. two *d.* *Educ:* Brentwood County High School. *Studied:* Evening Classes (Don Smith). *Exhib:* Sun Lounge, Fairfield (1991), Outwood Gallery (1988-90), Soc. of Women Artists. *Signs work:* "Margaret Parfitt' or "M.P." joined. *Address:* The White House, 165 Shirley Church Rd., Shirley, Croydon CR0 5AJ.

**PARKER, Constance-Anne,** A.T.D., F.R.B.S.; Lecturer, Archivist and Travelling Exhbns. Organiser, Royal Academy (1986-), Librarian, Royal Academy of Arts (1974-86), Assistant Librarian (1958-74); Landseer Scholar, Sir David Murray Scholarship, Leverhulme Scholarship; painter in oil, sculptor in wood and clay; *b* London, 19 Oct., 1921. *Educ:* privately. *Studied:* Polytechnic School of Art and Royal Academy Schools (four silver and three bronze medals). *Exhib:* R.A., London galleries and provinces. *Publications:* Mr. Stubbs the Horse Painter (1971), Royal Academy Cookbook (1981), Stubbs Art Animals, Anatomy (1984). *Clubs:* Reynolds (Chairman). *Address:* 1 Melrose Rd., Barnes, London SW13 9LG.

**PARKER, Gill,** S.Eq.A. (1987); winner President's Medal S.Eq.A. (1992); sculptress in bronze, silver; *b* Amesbury. *Educ:* South Wilts. Grammar School. *Exhib:* solo shows: Sladmore Gallery, London (1984, 1987, 1989), S.Eq.A. (1984-96), National Horse Racing Museum, Newmarket (1991), Chute Standen (1992). *Work in collections:* National Horse Racing Museum, Newmarket. *Commissions:* Habibti, Mrs.Moss, Precocious, Rainbow Quest, Sir Wattie, Dancing Brave, Middleroad. *Signs work:* "G. Parker" or "Gill Parker." *Address:* 18 Tibbs Meadow, Upper Chute, Andover, Hants. SP11 9HG.

**PARKER, Walter F.,** A.R.C.A., M.S.I.A.D., A.T.D., F.R.S.A.; Principal, Hartlepool College of Art (1953-78); War Service in Middle East as F/Lieut. in R.A.F.; senior posts held at Preston and Hastings Schools of Art; since retirement in 1978 takes a number of regular painting schools in Britain specialising in water-colours and printmaking; *b* Carlisle, 11 May, 1914. *m* Joy E. Turk, contralto, Guildhall School of Music. *Educ:* Carlisle Grammar School (1922-30). *Studied:* Carlisle Art School (1930-35), R.C.A. (1935-38), Courtauld Inst. (1938-39). *Clubs:* Pres., Lake Artists' Soc. and Life mem. (1996). *Signs work:* "Walter F. Parker." *Address:* 19 The Cliff, Seaton Carew, Hartlepool TS25

# WHO'S WHO IN ART

1AP.

**PARKIN, Ann,** artist in oil and pastel of impressionist paintings; *b* Bristol, 11 Aug., 1939. two *s. Exhib:* Clifton Gallery, Bristol and Rooksmoor Gallery Bath; R.I. Mall Galleries (1988). *Work in collections:* Lord Bath. Limited edition prints of selected paintings from: Rubicon Studios Ltd. at Lailey's Gallery, 24 Bridge St., Bradford on Avon BA15 1BY. *Signs work:* "Ann Parkin" or "A.P." *Address:* 10 Priston Village, Bath, Avon BA2 9EB.

**PARKIN, Jane Maureen,** S.Eq.A., S.W.A.; artist in oil and pastel; *b* Sheffield, 29 Aug., 1936. *m* Frank. one *d. Educ:* Wath Grammar School, S. Yorks. *Studied:* mainly self taught with five years tuition by P.K.C. Jackson, A.R.C.A. *Exhib:* S.Eq.A., Westminster Gallery, Christie's, Carisbrooke Gallery. *Publications:* Limited edn. prints and Open prints by Rosensteils London. *Signs work:* "Jane M. Parkin." *Address:* 103/109 Main St., Haworth, Keighley, W. Yorks. BD22 8DP.

**PARKIN, Michael Robert,** art dealer; chairman/managing director, Michael Parkin Fine Art Ltd.; *b* London, 1 Dec., 1931. three *d. Educ:* Mill Hill and St. George's Schools; Magdalen College, Oxford. *Exhib:* at Michael Parkin Gallery, 11 Motcomb St., SW1. Cover British Art 1850-1950, have included The Cafe Royalists, Four for Whistler, The Fitzrovians, Claude Flight, A Salute to Marcel Boulestin and J. E. Láboureur, Jean Cocteau, Cecil Beaton Memorial Exhbn., Artists of the Yellow Book, Nina Hamnett, Walter Sickert, Walter Greaves, Rex Whistler and Stephen Tennant, Walter Bayes, Jaques Emile Blanche, Artists of Corsham - a Celebration, Sylvia Gosse, Therese Lessore, the 7 & 5 Society, Paul Stevenson and John Pawle, Hermione Hammond, Gwyneth Johnstone, Roland Collins, Philip Jones, Damian O'Brien. *Publications:* Old Chelsea (Newson, London 1975), Louis Wain's Cats (Thames & Hudson, London 1983), Louis Wain's Edwardian Cats (Thames & Hudson, New York 1983); in preparation: Modern British Art 1860-1960; Walter Greaves. *Clubs:* Beefsteak, Bucks, B.A.F.T.A., Chelsea Arts. *Address:* Gunton Hall, Hanworth, Norfolk.

**PARKINSON, Gerald,** painter in oil, gouache and water-colour; *b* Shipley, Yorks., 5 Nov., 1926. *m* Sylvia Mary. one *s. Educ:* Woodhouse Grove School, nr. Leeds. *Studied:* Bradford College of Art (1951-54). *Exhib:* R.A., West of England Academy, John Moores, Sussex Artists, Yorks. Artists, S.E.A.; one-man shows: London, Bologna, Stockholm, Brighton, York, Bristol, Monte Carlo, Lewes, Bradford, Hove, Tunbridge Wells. *Work in collections:* Glasgow, Brighton, Leicestershire C.C., L.C.C., Surrey C.C., West Riding C.C. *Commissions:* Mural for NatWest Bank. *Signs work:* "Gerald Parkinson." *Address:* The Gate House, Wootton Manor, Polegate, Sussex BN26 5RY.

**PARKINSON, Richard Henry,** Dip. A/D (1967); painter in oil on canvas/board, restorer, critic, designer, frame maker; Prop./M.D. The Studio, tutor for Pitman's Correspondence Courses since 1967, judge at Royal College for Parkinson/Henderson Prize since 1988, and Cheltenham Correspondence

College; *b* Epsom, 23 Mar., 1947. *m* Susan Sanders. one *s*. one *d*. *Educ:* Ewell Castle, Epsom. *Studied:* Folkestone School of Art (1963-67), Heatherleys School of Art (1968-71). *Exhib:* R.A. since 1967, Wye, Henley, Wimbledon, R.W.A., Mall Galleries, R.B.A., Stockbridge, etc. *Work in collections:* Woolworth Holdings, various Boardrooms. *Publications:* Introductory Art (Pitman), Mounting Water-colours (The Artist). *Clubs:* Chelsea Arts. *Signs work:* "R.H.P." or "Richard Parkinson." *Address:* The Studio House, 113 Bridge St., Wye, Kent TN25 5ED.

**PARROTT, Denis William,** N.D.D.(Painting) (1953), A.T.C. (1958), Ph.D. (1993), Fulbright Scholar, U.S.A. (1970-71), F.R.S.A. (1977), F.S.A.E. (1980); painter, printmaker; lecturer, Nene College, Northampton; *b* Dewsbury, Yorks., 22 Mar., 1931. *m* Kathleen Hendry. one *s*. *Educ:* Dewsbury Technical College. *Studied:* Dewsbury and Batley School of Art (1948-51), Camberwell School of Art (1951-53), Leeds College of Art (1957-58). *Exhib:* R.A., Mall Gallery, U.S.A., Centre International d'Art Contemporain de Paris and Galerie Salammbo, Paris. *Work in collections:* England, Europe and U.S.A. *Publications:* author for Schools Council. *Signs work:* "Denis W. Parrott." *Address:* 37 Bowling Green Rd., Kettering, Northants. NN15 7QN.

**PARRY, David,** S.WL.A.; wildlife artist in water-colour; *b* Liverpool, 23 June, 1942. *Educ:* in Tunbridge Wells. *Studied:* Tunbridge Wells School of Art, Central School of Art, London. *Exhib:* one-man shows, Brasted, Kent, Lanhydrock House, Cornwall PL22 0JN. *Signs work:* "David Parry." *Address:* Castle Cottage, Lostwithiel, Cornwall.

**PARRY, Leigh,** M.A. (1946), P.S. (1966), P.P.S. (1983-88), R.B.A. (1988), P.S. (Canada) (1987), S.E.A. (1983); painter in pastel, oil and water-colour of equestrian subjects, landscapes, buildings, etc.; *b* London, 12 Apr., 1919. *Educ:* Uppingham; Pembroke College, Cambridge. *Studied:* St. Martin's School of Art (1945). *Exhib:* R.A., Paris Salon, New Grafton, Linda Blackstone, Pinner, R.B.A., N.E.A.C., P.S.; one-man shows, Canada and London. *Work in collections:* Kesteven C.C., Essex C.C., Lincolnshire museums, Midland Bank. *Publications:* illustrated Climbing and equestrian publications. *Signs work:* "Leigh Parry." *Address:* 6 Wharf Rd., Stamford, Lincs. PE9 2DU.

**PARRY, Sheila Harwood,** R.M.S. (1971), F.R.S.A. (1971), Dip. M.H. Societé des Artistes Français, Paris Salon (1971), Mem. H.S., Mem. American Soc. of Miniaturists, Washington; artist in gouache on vellum, oils on canvas; artist member of Fine Arts Trade Guild; *b* Salford, 5 Mar., 1924. *m* Alan Parry, Eng. Director. one *s*. three *d*. *Educ:* Salford Technical College (1937-39). *Studied:* Salford College of Art (1940-42), under Leslie F. N. Reid, D.A. Edin. *Exhib:* group exhbns.: Moreton Gallery, Australia, Suffolk St. Galleries, S.M.; flower exhbns.: R.W.S., Royal Society of Miniaturists, Royal Academy, Washington and Florida, U.S.A., Societé des Artistes Français (Paris Salon). *Work in collections:* Southport Municipal (Atkinson) Gallery, mainly held in private collections of art dealers and art publishers including W. H. Patterson

(Albemarle); also in private collections in Canada, Holland, Belgium, U.S.A., Spain and Australia. Works published by Royles. *Signs work:* "S. Harwood Parry" and see appendix. *Address:* Lezayre Mount, Bay View, Ramsey, I.O.M.

**PARSONS, Denis Alva,** M.B.E. (1993), A.R.B.S. (1992); sculptor in wood, stone and bronze; *b* Polesworth, Warwickshire, 14 Nov., 1934. one *s.* one *d. Educ:* Tamworth Secondary Modern; apprenticeship to R. Bridgemen Ltd. (1950-55); Birmingham College of Art (1953-55, part-time). Work in various churches and public buildings. *Signs work:* see appendix. *Address:* Alderways, Fosseway La., Pipe Hill, Lichfield, Staffs. WS13 8JX.

**PARTINGTON, Peter Norman,** N.D.D., A.T.C., S.WL.A.; painter in water-colour, oil, drypoint etching, art lecturer; Com. mem. S.WL.A.; *b* Cambridge, 29 Sept., 1941. *m* Josephine. two *s.* one *d. Educ:* Poole Grammar School. *Studied:* Bournemouth College of Art and Design (1960-66), Middlesex Polytechnic (1967-68). *Exhib:* various galleries in London including Tryon Gallery, Glos., Wilts. *Work in collections:* Nature in Art Museum. *Publications:* illustrations, 'Down the River' H.E. Bates (Gollancz 1987), 'Painting Birds in Watercolour' (Collins 1989), 'A Floating World' own poetry and illustration. *Signs work:* "Peter Partington." *Address:* 15 Primrose Terr., Gravesend, Kent DA12 1JN.

**PARTRIDGE, John Arthur,** antique dealer; Chairman, Partridge Fine Arts PLC; Chairman, Fine Art and Antiques Export Com.; Hon. Treasurer, Society of London Art Dealers; *b* London, 6 July, 1929; married. two *s.* one *d. Educ:* Elstree and Harrow. *Address:* 144-146 New Bond St., London W1.

**PASCOE, Ernest,** D.F.A. (London Univ.), F.R.B.S., R.W.A.; sculptor and painter; Former Head of Fine Art, Bristol Polytechnic and Executive Vice-Pres., Royal West of England Academy (retd. 1987); *m* Jean Denwood. four *d. Studied:* Carlisle (1938-41), R.A.F. 1941-45, Slade School (1945-48) awarded Wilson Steer Medal, Tonks drawing Prize, Robert Ross Scholarship. *Exhib:* Arts Council, R.A., London Group, R.B.A, R.W.A., provincial galleries. etc. *Work in collections:* Chantrey Bequest, Oxford University, Royal College of Surgeons, City Art Gallery Bristol, R.W.A. and many private collections. *Signs work:* "E. Pascoe" or "Ernest Pascoe." *Address:* The Old Rectory, Weston-in-Gordano, Bristol BS20 8PZ.

**PASCOE, Jane,** B.A.(Hons.) Fine Art (1977), A.T.C. (1978), R.W.A. (1988); painter/sculptor/printmaker, teacher (Head of Art Dept.); *b* Bristol, 9 May, 1955. one *s. Educ:* The Redmaids School, Bristol (Bristol Foundation Scholarship 1966-73). *Studied:* Bristol Polytechnic Faculty of Art and Design, Dept. of Fine Art (1974-77). *Exhib:* R.W.A., Eye Gallery, Bristol, Parkin Fine Art, Mall Galleries, London, Salisbury Arts Centre, Swindon Museum and A.G., Victoria Gallery, Beaux Arts Gallery Bath. *Work in collections:* R.W.A., Avon County Art Collection, Cheltenham and Gloucester Bldg. Soc. Art Collection. *Signs work:* "Jane Pascoe." *Address:* 42 Shaftesbury Rd., Wilton, Salisbury, Wilts. SP2 0DR.

**PASMORE, Wendy,** painter; teacher of painting at Sunderland College of Art, (1955-58), and at Leeds College of Art (1958-67); *b* Dublin, 1915. *m* Victor Pasmore (decd.). one *s.* one *d. Educ:* privately. *Studied:* art: privately. Mem. London Group. *Work in collections:* Tate Gallery, Arts Council, Leeds Education Committee. *Clubs:* Arts. *Address:* Dar Gamri, Gudja 2TN, Malta, and 12 St. Germans Pl., Blackheath, London SE3 0NN.

**PASS, Derek Percy,** artist in ceramic enamels, water-colour; ceramic artist, Royal Doulton (retd.); *b* Newcastle, Staffs., 19 Apr., 1929. *m* Doreen Odell. two *d. Educ:* Knutton Elementary School; Burslem School of Art. *Studied:* Stoke-on-Trent College of Art (1942) under Gordon Forsyth, R.I. and Reginald Haggar, R.I. *Exhib:* Trends, Britain in Water-colours, N.S. *Signs work:* "Derek Pass," "D. Pass" (ceramic). *Address:* 12 Thirlmere Pl., Clayton, Newcastle, Staffs. ST5 3QJ.

**PASS, Donald James,** N.D.D.; portrait and landscape painter in oil, pastel and water-colour; noted for large works of a visionary nature; *b* Congleton, Ches., 9 Sept., 1930. *m* Anne Jacqueline Whitelegge. two *s.* three *d. Educ:* Macclesfield Kings School. *Studied:* Macclesfield School of Art, Stoke-on-Trent Regional College of Art, R.A. Schools (silver medal). *Exhib:* Drian Gallery - New Art Centre, Premio Lissone, Milan, etc. *Work in collections:* Gdansk National Museum, Poland, Stoke-on-Trent A.G., Yorkshire Educ. Com., Gallery of Contemporary Art Skopje, Yugoslavia, Gallery of Art Lissone, Milan, University of Keele, Church of St. Mary the Virgin, Elmley Castle, Worcs., Graves A.G., Sheffield, Sir John Rothenstein. *Commissions:* Sir Compton Mackenzie, Brigadier Sir Alex Stanier, Bt., D.S.O., M.C. (portraits), Lt. Col. Sir John Miller, G.C.V.O., D.S.O., M.C. *Publications:* Apollo Magazine article by Sir John Rothenstein, Quarto Press, work included in Encyclopedia of Water-colour Techniques and others. *Clubs:* Reynolds. *Signs work:* "D. Pass" or "DONALD PASS." *Address:* 2 Green Lane Lodge, Old Rd., Wheatley, Oxford OX33 1NY.

**PATERSON, Donald M.,** D.A.; artist in water-colour, teacher; elected Mem. Royal Scottish Soc. of Painters in Water-colour; *b* Kyleakin, Isle of Skye, 28 Nov., 1950. *m* Alexandra. two *s. Educ:* Portree High School. *Studied:* Glasgow School of Art (1969-73). *Exhib:* one-man show: Fair Maids Gallery, Perth; mixed shows: 'Artists under 30' Third Eye Centre, Glasgow, Glasgow Herald Exhbn. Collins Gallery, Strathclyde University, R.S.A. Annual, G.I. Annual. *Signs work:* "D.M. Paterson." *Address:* Blaven, Torr Rd., Bridge of Weir, Renfrewshire PA11 3BE.

**PATERSON, Michael Hugh Orr,** B.A., F.R.S.A.; art restorer; freelance lecturer and archivist; trainee, City A.G., Birmingham (1953-54); asst., City A.G., Hereford (1954-55); asst.-in-charge, Municipal A.G., Oldham (1956); asst. keeper, City A.G., Leicester (1957-58); Curator, Russell-Cotes A.G. and Museums, Bournemouth (1958-66); Curator of Art, London Borough of Enfield (1966-81); Hon. Curator, Thomas Coram Foundation for Children to

1995; *b* London, 7 Dec., 1927. *m* Maureen Robinson. *Educ:* Kirkcudbright Academy; Cranleigh School; Manchester and Edinburgh Universities. *Address:* 24 Adamsrill Cl., Enfield, Middx. EN1 2BP.

**PATRICK, (James) McIntosh,** R.O.I., A.R.E., R.S.A., O.B.E.; painter and etcher; *b* 1907. *m* Janet Watterston (d. 1983). one *s.* one *d. Educ:* Morgan Academy, Dundee; Glasgow School of Art. Awarded Guthrie Award R.S.A. (1935). *Work in collections:* Chantrey Bequest; Scottish National Gallery of Modern Art; Tate Gallery; National Gallery of S. Africa, Cape Town; Art Gallery of S. Australia; Scottish Contemporary Art Assoc.; and Municipal collections Manchester, Aberdeen, Hull, Dundee, Liverpool, Glasgow, Greenock, Perth, Southport, Newport (Mon.), Arbroath, Lady Leverhulme A.G., etc.; etchings in B.M. and other print collections. Served War of 1939-46, N. Africa and Italy; Captain (General List). Fellow: Duncan of Jordanstone College of Art, Dundee (1987), Glasgow School of Art (1994); Hon.LL.D. Dundee (1973), O.B.E (1997). *Signs work:* "McINTOSH PATRICK." *Address:* c/o Fine Art Soc., 148 New Bond St., London W1Y 0JT.

**PATTON, Eric Samuel,** R.H.A. (1982); self-taught painter in oil and watercolour; *b* Dundalk, Ireland, 29 Jan., 1925. *Educ:* Wellington National School, Dundalk Grammar School. *Exhib:* one-man shows: Dublin, Belfast, Galway, Longford, Wales, New York, Jeddah. *Work in collections:* Jeddah, Saudi Arabia. *Clubs:* United Arts, Dublin. *Signs work:* "Eric Patton." *Address:* 35 Kildare St., Dublin 2.

**PAVEY, Don,** F.R.S.A., A.R.C.A.; director, Micro Academy producing art education videos and computer art software; author; lecturer in design and colour; a founder of the National Art Education Archive (Leeds Univ.). Freedom of the City of London, (July, 1987). *Publications:* The Artist Colourmen's Story (Winsor & Newton's Museum of Colour Guide, 1985), Color (Architectural Digest of America, 1980), Art-based Games (Methuen, 1979), Methuen Handbook of Colour and Colour Dictionary (Methuen, 1961, 1967, 1978). Mem., Colour Group (Great Britain) - awarded the Isaac Newton Medal for research into the history and theroy of colour (1997). *Address:* Studio House, 30 Wayside, Sheen, London SW14.

**PAYNE, David,** N.D.D., A.T.C. (1954); painter in oil and water-colour (triptychs); formerly senior lecturer in painting, Bedford College of Educ.; *b* Dover, 29 July, 1928. *m* Iris. one *s.* one *d. Studied:* Canterbury, Farnham and Brighton Colleges of Art until 1954, R.A. Schools (1980-81) (Guest student/Peter Greenham). *Exhib:* R.A. (1976, 1978-89, 1991-92, 1995-97), Singer Friedlander/Sunday Times (1991-94), N.E.A.C. (1992-96), R.W.S. (1992-96), Portal Gallery (1984), Laing Gallery (1984), Ellingham Mill (1979, 1982), Ash Barn Gallery, Sotheby's (1981); one-man show, The Gallery, Wellingborough (1983-85), New Ashgate Gallery, Farnham (1987), Discerning Eye (1996). *Work in collections:* Beds. Educ. Loan Service and private collections. *Publications:* reviews, I.T.V. (1982), B.B.C.2 (1983), Academy Illustrated

(1983, 1984, 1991). *Clubs:* Reynolds. *Signs work:* "David Payne." *Address:* 25 Willmers Cl., Bedford MK41 8DX.

**PAYNE, Margaret A.,** N.D.D. (1959), A.T.C. (1960), B.A.(Hons.) History of Art (1981), M.A. (Art Educ.) (1983), R.E. (1975); graphic artist including computer graphics, painter in oil, etcher; Art teacher at Sarum Hall School, London NW3; Currently researching children's learning in N.C. Art at KS1 & 2; *b* Southampton, 14 Apr., 1937. *Educ:* St. Helen's School, Northwood, Middx. *Studied:* Harrow School of Art (1955-59), Goldsmiths' College (1959-60). *Exhib:* R.A., R.E., Paris Salon, Society of Women Artists, Young Contemporaries, R.I. *Work in collections:* Sheffield and Nottinghamshire C.C., Pictures for Schools circulation. *Publications:* in Journal of Art and Design Education (1993), Froebelian Principles and the Art National Curriculum. *Address:* 11a Wallorton Gdns., London SW14 8DX.

**PAYNTER, Hilary,** N.D.D. (1964), A.T.C. (1965), M.A. (Psych.Ed., 1982), A.R.E. (1984), F.R.S.A. (1986); wood engraver; educational psychologist; Hon. Sec. S.W.E., Council Mem. R.E.; *b* Dunfermline, 16 June, 1943. *m* Gerry Bradley. one *s.* one *d. Studied:* Portsmouth College of Art (Gerry Tucker). *Exhib:* S.W.E., R.E., Xylon, Switzerland; major engraving exhbns.: Durham (1982), Medici (1980), Hereford (1982), Sydney, Australia (1986-87), Ex Libris Internationals; one-man: Buckden (1976) and Kew (1985), R.A., etc. *Work in collections:* Hereford City A.G., Ashmolean Museum. *Publications:* contributions to: The Imprisoned Heart (Gryphon, 1979), Hilary Paynter's Picture Book (Carr, 1985). *Signs work:* "Hilary Paynter." *Address:* P.O. Box 355, Richmond, Surrey TW10 6LE.

**PAYNTON, Colin Frank:** see SEE-PAYNTON, Colin Frank.

**PEACE, Dr. David,** M.B.E., D.Sc.Tech., F.S.A., A.R.I.B.A., F.R.T.P.I.; glass engraver, lettering and heraldic designer; Master, A.W.G. (1973); first Chairman, Guild of Glass Engravers (1975), President (1980-86); Liveryman, Glaziers Co. (1977); *b* Sheffield, 13 Mar., 1915. *m* Jean Margaret Lawson, A.R.C.A. two *d. Educ:* Mill Hill; University of Sheffield, Hon.D.Sc.Tech. (1991). *Studied:* under Clarence Whaite. *Exhib:* 12 one-man shows; Retrospective (1990). *Work in collections:* V. & A., Fitzwilliam, Kettle's Yard, Brierley Hill Glass Museum, Corning Museum, N.Y., etc.; much presentation glass; windows in many churches; also engraved screens and doors - e.g. St. Nicholas, Liverpool, St. Albans Abbey, Westminster Abbey; memorial to G.M. Hopkins and John Betjeman, Poets Corner. Since 1986, much architectural glass in partnership with Sally Scott, e.g. St. John's College, Cambridge, Norwich Cathedral, Lancaster and Sheffield Universities. *Clubs:* Arts. *Signs work:* see appendix. *Address:* Abbots End, Hemingford Abbots, Huntingdon, Cambs. PE18 9AA.

**PEACOCK, Brian,** A.R.C.A. Silver medal (1960), Prix de Rome, painting (1960); painter in oil on board; Head of Painting and Printmaking, Sheffield Polytechnic until 1988; *b* London, 1934. *Educ:* Sir Joseph Williamsons

Mathematical School, Rochester. *Studied:* R.C.A. (1957-60, Carel Weight, Roger de Grey). *Exhib:* R.A., John Moores, Bristol Art Show; one-man shows include Piccadilly Gallery, John Davies Fine Art, Stow, Mistral Galleries, Dover St. *Work in collections:* Contemporary Arts Soc., Government Collection, D.O.E., M. of W., Nuffield Foundation, Free University Amsterdam, Pembroke College Oxford, many provincial and overseas galleries. *Signs work:* "B. Peacock." *Address:* 107 Meersbrook Pk. Rd., Sheffield S8 9FP.

**PEACOCK, Carlos (Charles Hanbury),** B.A.(Cantab.); writer and art critic; *b* 6 Oct., 1909. *m* Cynthia Howell. *Educ:* Uppingham and Cambridge. *Exhib:* Arranged: Constable Exhbn. at Aldeburgh Festival (1948), Pre-Raphaelite Exhbn. at Bournemouth (1951). *Publications:* Painters and Writers (Tate Gallery), co-author (with John Rothenstein) of essay on Tate Gallery in The Nations Pictures (Chatto and Windus, 1951), John Constable (John Baker Ltd.), Samuel Palmer (John Baker Ltd.), Richard Parkes Bonington (Barrie & Jenkins). *Address:* 26 Brompton Sq., London SW3 2AD.

**PEARCE, Antony,** B.A. (Exeter) (1963), F.R.S.A. (1990), A.N.S. (1991); teacher/full time artist in water-colour and acrylic since 1980; *b* Leigh, Essex, 21 July, 1933. *Educ:* Mayfield College, Sussex. *Studied:* self taught, but inspired principally by Rowland Hilder and Edward Seago. *Exhib:* Edwin Pollard Gallery, Wimbledon (annually), numerous one-man shows. *Publications:* by Sharpe's, Castlebar Graphics, Kingsmead Publications. *Clubs:* R.S.A. *Signs work:* "Antony Pearce." *Address:* 16 Sandra House, Hansler Gr., E. Molesey, Surrey KT8 9JL.

**PEARCE, John Allan,** Vice-Pres., Turner Society; painter in oils; retd. solicitor; *b* Sidcup, Kent, 1912. *m* Raffaella Baione. two *s. Educ:* Charterhouse and B.N.C. Oxon. *Studied:* with Giorgio de Chirico and privately. *Exhib:* R.A., N.E.A.C., R.B.A., R.O.I., Chelsea Art Soc., etc. *Clubs:* Travellers. *Signs work:* "A.P." *Address:* 32 Brompton Sq., London SW3 2AE.

**PEARCEY, Eilean,** B.A. Melb. (1922), M. Univ. Surrey (1987); figure and landscape painter in oil, water-colour, etching, Indian ink, conté, writer; specialized in drawing dancers in action (classical - Pavlova, Dolin, Ulanova, Kirov and Bolshoi; African, Indian and Far East); *b* Melbourne, Australia, 28 May, 1901; *m* A. Ramsay Moon, B.A., B.Sc. (Melb.), M.I. Struct.E. one *s.* (decd.).*Educ:* P.L.C. Melbourne; Melbourne University (1919-21). *Studied:* National Gallery School, Melbourne (1922-25, L. Bernard Hall); Académie LHote, Paris (1932); Iain Macnab London School of Modern Art. *Exhib:* Melbourne and Sydney, Australia (1938, 1955), Paris Salon, London, Galerie Apollinaire (1952, 1953), R.A., U.A., India House (1974, 1980), 'The Place' L.C.D.T. (2), University of Surrey, Guildford (3); various mixed shows. *Work in collections:* University of Surrey Dance Centre, Marcel Marceau Museum; Robin Howard, C.B.E. (Martha Graham drawings), Ram Gopal (ten drawings of himself). *Publications:* drawings published in U.S.A. 'The Christian Science

Monitor' and 'Dance Observer', N.Y.; 'Marg' Bombay; 'Sangeet Natak Academi Journal' Delhi; David Bolland's 'Guide to Kathakali'; Massey's 'Dances of India' (1989); The Times, Sunday Telegraph, Ballet Annual, Soviet Weekly, and wrote for seven years on Indian dance for Dance and Dancers. *Clubs:* F.P.S., V. & A. *Signs work:* "Eilean Pearcey," before 1952 "EILEAN PEARCEY." *Address:* 6a Shaftesbury Villas, Allen St., London W8 6UZ.

**PEARSON, Bruce Edward,** B.A. Fine Art (1973), S.WL.A. (1978); painter in water-colour and oil; President, Soc. of Wildlife Artists (1994); *b* Newmarket, Suffolk, 20 Sept., 1950. *m* Sara Oldfield. two *d. Studied:* pre-Dip. Gt. Yarmouth College of Art and Design (1969-70), Leicester Polytechnic (1970-73). *Exhib:* many solo exhbns. in U.K., and group shows in Wales, Holland, U.S.A. and France. *Commissions:* Artists for Nature Foundation, Holland; Ministre de L'Environment, France; Natural History Museum, London. *Publications:* chapter with illustrations in 20th Century Wildlife Artists, Nick Hammond (Croom Helm, 1981); author and illustrator: An Artist on Migration (Harper Collins, 1991). *Signs work:* "B.P." (on some illustrative work), "BRUCE PEARSON" (on all other work). *Address:* The Old Plough, Caxton Rd., Great Gransden, Sandy, Beds. SG19 3BE.

**PEARSON, James E.,** artist in oil, clay, bronze; William Boyd Andrews, Best of Show, 1961; Gold Keys, 1951, 1954, 1956; Scholastic Art Awards, Carnegie Institute; art instructor, Woodstock, Comm. High School, Woodstock, Illinois, U.S.A.; Bachelor of Science in Education (1961), Master of Science in Education (1962), Master of Fine Art (1964); *b* Woodstock, Illinois, U.S.A., 12 Dec., 1939. *Educ:* McHenry Community High School, McHenry, Illinois; Northern Illinois University, Dekalb, Illinois. *Studied:* Northern Illinois University, Dekalb, Illinois. *Work in collections:* Northern Illinois University; over 100 private collections (company and individual). *Publications:* McHenry County, 1832-1968. *Signs work:* see appendix. *Address:* 5117 Barnard Mill Rd., Ringwood, Illinois, 60072, U.S.A.

**PEARSON, Yvette L.,** B.A.Hons.; freelance graphic designer in oil and water-colour, fashion designer; visiting lecturer, South Devon College of Art and Design; *b* 16 May, 1962. *Studied:* South Devon College and Ravensbourne College of Art and Communication (1985). *Exhib:* South Devon. Work manufactured: Kirtle, Jester Dress. *Address:* 22 Central Ave., Paignton, S. Devon.

**PEART, Tony,** B.A. (Hons.) (1983), M.A. (1986); painter in oil; associate lecturer, Cumbria College of Art and Design; *b* Darlington, 23 June, 1961. *m* Sharyn Brown. one *d. Educ:* Eastbourne School. *Studied:* Cheltenham College of Art, Leeds Polytechnic, Newcastle Polytechnic. *Exhib:* Piccadilly Gallery (1988-). *Work in collections:* Carlisle A.G., Darlington A.G., Government Painting Coll., Rank Xerox, Newcastle University, Northern Arts. *Signs work:* "Tony Peart" always on reverse. *Address:* 4 Beanley Ave., Lemington, Newcastle upon Tyne NE15 8SP.

**PECKHAM, Barry Arthur,** S.E.A. (1984); landscape, marine and equestrian artist in oil, water-colour, pastel, etching; *b* New Forest, Hants., 30 Dec., 1945; divorced. three *d. Educ:* Bartley School. *Studied:* Southampton College of Art. *Exhib:* R.A., R.I., R.O.I., P.S., R.S.M.A., S.E.A., N.E.A.C., R.W.A. *Work in collections:* Royal Marines, Poole. Awards: Royle prize (1984), Cuneo medal (1989), Crossgate Gallery award (1989), Pastel award (1990), Champagne Mumm Marine Artist (1990). *Signs work:* "B.A. PECKHAM." *Address:* Fletchwood Cottage, Busketts Way, Ashurst, Southampton, Hants. SO40 7AE.

**PEDLEY, Nada Marija,** R.M.S. (1994); sculptor in clay and terracotta; freelance sculptor, Royal Doulton; *b* 1 Aug., 1944. *m* John Pedley. two *s.* one *d. Studied:* Slovenija Ljubljana Commercial Art (1964-67), Horsham Art School (1974-78, ceramics: John Green). *Exhib:* R.M.S. (1987-), Doulton Gallery, Stoke-on-Trent. *Work in collections:* Doulton Gallery, Stoke-on-Trent. *Publications:* Royal Doulton Figures (Richard Dennis, 1994). *Signs work:* "Nada Pedley." *Address:* 9 Garrick Rd., Worthing, Sussex BN14 8BB.

**PELL, Robert Leslie,** N.D.D. (Painting) (1948), F.R.S.A. (1968); painter in oil and gouache and lecturer; *b* Northampton, 24 Nov., 1928. *m* Pamela Crake. one *s.* one *d. Educ:* Technical High School, Northampton. *Studied:* Northampton School of Art and Camberwell School of Art and Crafts. *Exhib:* R.C.A. Galleries, R.B.A., Foyle's Gallery, Canaletto Gallery, Leicester Gallery (Artists of Fame and Promise), Piccadilly Gallery, Bear Lane Gallery, Oxford. *Work in collections:* University College and Balliol College, Oxford, Leicestershire, Reading, Surrey and Northumberland Education Committees, The John Lewis Organisation, Northampton Art Gallery, Coventry City Art Gallery, private collections in England, America and Finland. *Publications:* work repro.: La Revue Moderne, Art Review, The Artist, The Oxford Magazine, The Studio. *Clubs:* Royal Society of Arts. *Signs work:* "Pell" (written in italic script). *Address:* The Studio House, 141 High St., Brackley, Northants. NN13 7BN.

**PELLING, John Arthur,** A.R.C.A.; painter in oil on canvas; clergyman, Church of England; *b* Hove, 9 Aug., 1930; divorced. four *s. Educ:* Brighton, Hove and Sussex Grammar School. *Studied:* Brighton College of Art (1946-49) and Royal College of Art (1951-55). *Exhib:* eight one-man shows, London, Sussex University, Manchester. *Work in collections:* National Gallery Poland, Nuffield Foundation, Vittorio 'de Sica private collection, Italy. At present full time painter in France and London. *Clubs:* Chelsea Arts. *Signs work:* "PELLING" (on paintings), "John Pelling" (on drawings). *Address:* 44 Redcliffe Rd., London SW10 9NJ.

**PELLY, Frances,** R.S.A., D.A.; sculptor in wood, stone, clay, paper; *b* Edinburgh, 1947. *Educ:* Morrisons Academy, Crieff. *Studied:* Duncan of Jordanstone, Dundee (1965-71, Scott Sutherland, Alistair Smart). *Exhib:* R.S.A., S.S.A., R.G.I.; solo shows, Collective Gallery, Edinburgh (1986), Crawford Art Centre, St.Andrews (1987), 'Nousts', travelling exhbn. in

Highland Region and Norway (1992-93). *Work in collections:* Fine Art Soc., Scottish Arts Council, Dundee, BBC Glasgow, Perth, Dumfries, Orkney, Aberdeen, Royal Concerthall Glasgow, Banff, City Halls Glasgow and Fort William. *Commissions:* North Inch Perth, Orkney Art Soc., Parcelforce Glasgow, Mobil North Sea Banff, Strathclyde Regional Council Glasgow, Highland Regional Council Fort William. *Signs work:* Uses symbol of gibbous moon or red throated diver. Never signs work. *Address:* Costa Schoolhouse, Evie, Orkney KW17 2NJ.

**PELZ, Peter,** M.A. (Cantab.) (1968); artist in oil, tempera, water-colour, drawing and etching; *b* Oxford, 18 Sept., 1945. *Educ:* King's College, Cambridge. *Studied:* Wigan, Lancs. (1957-63, Theodore Major). *Exhib:* Rebecca Hossack Gallery, London and permanently at The Coffee house/Gallery, 11 Sheep Street, Charlbury, Oxon. *Work in collections:* on commission (chief works): triptych at St. James's, Piccadilly; mural at St. Peter's, Morden. *Publications:* Prayer for the Day (Cairns). *Signs work:* "Peter Pelz" and date. *Address:* Chimney Cottage, Dancers Hill, Charlbury, Oxon. OX7 3RZ

**PEMBERTON, Christopher Henry,** M.A. (1948); landscape, portrait and still life painter and draughtsman in oil, pencil, pen, water-colour and gouache; Head of Foundation Studies, Camberwell School of Art (1982-85; taught at Camberwell 1958-85); *b* London, 14 Mar., 1923. *m* Hester Riddell. four *s.* one *d. Educ:* Eton College, Christ Church Oxford. *Studied:* Camberwell School of Art (1948-50, Claude Rogers). *Exhib:* one-man shows: Woodlands, Blackheath (1977), Bury St. Edmunds A.G. (1977), Wells Centre, Norfolk (1987), Quay Theatre, Sudbury (1988), Gainborough's House (1989), Cadogan Contemporary (1989, 1992). *Work in collections:* Newnham College, Cambridge; Christ Church, Oxford. *Publications:* Gasquet's Cézanne (Thames & Hudson, 1991). *Signs work:* "C. Pemberton." *Address:* Place Farmhouse, Bardwell, Bury St. Edmunds, Suffolk IP31 1AQ.

**PENDERED, Susan Marjorie Anne,** M.C.S.P., R.I. (1983); painter in water based medium; Winner of the Winsor & Newton R.I. Award (1988); *b* London, 15 June, 1925. *m* John H. Pendered, G.P., M.B.E., M.B., B.S. one *s.* two *d. Educ:* Lillesden School for Girls, Hawkhurst, Kent. *Studied:* part-time at Brighton Polytechnic (1975-82, Norma Weller). *Exhib:* Mall Galleries, R.I., R.A. Summer Exhbn., R.W.A., Bristol, participated in travelling exhbn. to Vancouver, Canada and Seattle, U.S.A. (1986). *Clubs:* Sussex Water-colour Soc., Attic Club Ditchling. *Signs work:* "S. Pendered." *Address:* Littleway, West Furlong La., Hurstpierpoint, W. Sussex BN6 9RH.

**PENDERY, Carroll,** S.W.A. (1997); artist in pastel, water-colour, oil, and gardener; *b* Leicester, 30 Dec., 1935. *m* Terence Pendery, B.Sc. two *s. Educ:* Gateway Girls School, Leicester. *Exhib:* by selection in Yorkshire, Birmingham, Peterborough and London. *Signs work:* "C. Pendery" or "Carroll Pendery." *Address:* 134 Station Rd., Cropston, Leicester LE7 7HE.

**PENKETH-SIMPSON, Barbara,** R.M.S. (1996), R.G.N.; Mundy

Sovereign Portrait award (1989), R.M.S. President's Special Commendation (1996); self-taught artist and miniaturist, larger oils and portraiture; *b* Crewe, Ches., 17 Apr., 1948. *m* F.W. Simpson. one *s*. one *d*. *Exhib:* S.W.A., R.M.S. *Publications:* featured on Flier For, and included in Royal Society of Miniature Painters, Sculptors and Gravers 100 years of Miniatures. *Signs work:* see appendix. *Address:* 31 Meadowview Rd., Bexley, Kent DA5 1HP.

**PEPYS, Rhoda Gertrude,** N.A.T.C. (South Africa); artist, portrait painter, tutor; *b* Port Elizabeth, 12 Mar., 1914 (née Kussel). *m* Prof. Jack Pepys (1938); two children. *Educ:* Collegiate, School of Arts and Crafts, Port Elizabeth; Silver Medal (1934). *Exhib:* one-man shows: S.A.; Italy; Paris (1962); London: Hampstead Art Cellar (1963), Barbican (1982), Studio 36 (1967-89); U.S.A.: Washington (1985); group shows in London: R.A. Summer Exhbn. (1966, 1989), Images of Italy (1987-89), Israel Paintings (1988). *Commissions:* Univ. of London, Portrait of (1) Prof. G. Scadding (1974); (2) Prof. Jack Pepys (1979). Awards: Academie International de Lutèce, Paris, Silver Medal, (1978); Accademia Italia, Gold Medal (1980); Centauro D'Oro (1982). *Clubs:* Accademia Italia. *Signs work:* "Pepys" and "Rhoda Pepys." *Address:* 34 Ferncroft Ave., London NW3 7PE.

**PEPYS, Sandra Lynn,** B.A. (Hons.), London; artist, art historian, journalist, illustrator, art teacher and lecturer; *b* Cape Town, 27 Jan., 1942. *m* A. Heidecker (1969). *Educ:* South Hampstead and S.O.A.A.S., Univ. of London; awarded 1st Prize, Univ. of London Exhbn. (1966). *Exhib:* one-man shows: London: Hampstead Art Cellar (1962); Everyman (1963); Mermaid Theatre (1966); Studio 36 (annually from 1966-1976); Oxford: Halifax House (1963); Paris: Galerie Tedesco (1962); Italy: Sperlonga (1962, 1965); Rome: Galleria Coppella (1965); Artists House, Jerusalem (1979-1982); group shows: H.A.C., W.A.C. Univ. of London, Guildhall, R.A. Summer Exhbn. (1973, 1977, 1978). *Commissions:* mural paintings, London University (1966) and Brit. Railways (1967). *Clubs:* Florentine Assoc., Italy, Jerusalem Artists Assoc. *Signs work:* "Sandra Pepys." *Address:* 34 Ferncroft Ave., London NW3.

**PERKINS, Stuart M.G.,** R.M.S. (1991), M.A.A. (1990), A.T.D., N.D.D. (1956), M.P.S.G., M.A.S.-F., M.A.S.-N.J.; miniaturist in water-colour and gouache; *b* Leicester, 4 July, 1935. *m* Joan Chatterley, A.T.D. three *d*. *Educ:* Alderman Newton Boys G.S., Leicester. *Studied:* Leicester College of Art (1952-56, Albert Pountney). *Exhib:* R.M.S., R.W.A., R.W.S. Summer Show, W.A.C.; many mixed exhbns. in England and Wales, miniature exhbns. in U.K., Canada, U.S.A. *Work in collections:* M.A.S.-F., G.M.A.S. *Signs work:* "S. PERKINS, R.M.S, M.A.A.," (dated), "Stuart Perkins." *Address:* The Old School, Scowles, Coleford, Glos. GL16 8QT.

**PERRIN, Brian,** A.R.C.A., Rome Scholar (1954); painter/etcher; Head of Printmaking Dept., Wimbledon School of Art; Mem. C.N.A.A. Fine Art Board; *b* 19 Aug., 1932. *m* Jane Lisle. two *s*. *Educ:* Whitgift Middle School. *Studied:* Croydon School of Art (1948-51), R.C.A. (1951-54). *Exhib:* extensively in

# WHO'S WHO IN ART

Europe and U.S.A., including international print Biennales. *Work in collections:* Library of Congress, Washington, V. & A., Arts Council, British Council; Museums of Art: Metropolitan N.Y., Perth, Jerusalem, Boston, Cincinatti, Glasgow. *Signs work:* "Brian Perrin." *Address:* 293 Kings Rd., Kingston-upon-Thames, Surrey KT2 5JJ.

**PERRY, Roy,** R.I. (1978); painter in oil, water-colour and acrylic; awarded R.I. Medal (1978), R.I. Council (1979); *b* Liverpool, 1935. *m* Sallie Charlton. one *s*. one *d*. *Educ:* John Lyon School, Harrow and Southampton University. *Exhib:* R.A., R.I., R.B.A., R.S.M.A., etc.; one-man shows, Oxford, Guildford, London, Henley and Cambridge. *Work in collections:* many large business corporations; The Fleet Air Arm Museum; H.R.H. The Duke of Edinburgh and other private collections throughout the world. *Publications:* work repro.: Lithographs, New York, Industrial Reviews and Laings Calendar. *Signs work:* "Roy Perry." *Address:* The Mill House, Donhead St. Mary, Shaftesbury, Dorset SP7 9DS.

**PESKETT, Eric Harry,** A.T.D. (1934), A.R.C.A. (1938), R.C.A. travelling scholar (1939), F.R.B.S. (retd); sculptor; *b* Guildford, 31 Jan., 1914. *m* Marjorie Ayling. one *s*. *Educ:* Brighton, Hove and Sussex Grammar School. *Studied:* Brighton College of Art (1929-35), R.C.A. (1935-39). *Work in collections:* (drawings) V. & A.; (brick reliefs) Congress Theatre, Eastbourne; Church of Holy Cross, Patricroft, Lancs.; Veterinary Bldg., Liverpool University; (altar Crucifixes) St. Mary's Church Denton, Lancs.; Church of the Holy Cross, Patricroft; (fountain pool) Tower Block, Borough Polytechnic, London. *Clubs:* Architectural Association. *Signs work:* "Peskett." *Address:* 12 Court Bushes Rd., Whyteleafe, Surrey CR3 0BG.

**PESKETT, Tessa,** B.A. (Hons.) Fine Art (1979), P.G.C.E. (1982), H.Postgrad.Dip.Painting (1992), R.O.I. (1994); Chadwick Healey prize for painting (1992), Anne LeClerc Fowle medal (1993); artist in oil, water-colour, charcoal; *b* Three Bridges, Sussex, 25 Apr., 1957. *Educ:* Beaumont School, St. Albans. *Studied:* Reading University (1975-79), City & Guilds of London Art School (1992). *Exhib:* R.A. Summer Shows, R.B.A., R.O.I., Linda Blackstone Gallery, Mall Galleries, Trinity A.G. Arundel, Parkview, Bristol, Laing Art Competition, London (1994-97), Atrium Gallery, Bournemouth University, solo show (1996), Albemarle Gallery, London (1996-97).*Work in collections:* Espace Darvil, Paris. *Signs work:* "Tessa D. Peskett" and "T.P." *Address:* 63 Swanmore Rd., Boscombe, Bournemouth, Dorset BH7 6PD. Internet: art.com/gallery

**PETERSON, Peter Charles,** N.D.D., V.P.R.B.A. (1988), R.B.A. (1978); mem. Landscape Soc. (1989), Vice Chairman, Soc. of Landscape Painters; Daler Rowney Prize (1983), First Prize (1988), De Laszlo medal (1994); artist in oil, water-colour and gouache; lecturer, Visual Research Dept. Chesterfield College of Art; senior lecturer, Fine Art Dept. Epsom College of Art; visiting lecturer, Falmouth College of Art (1986); *b* 4 Apr., 1934. *Studied:* Hornsey

College of Art. *Exhib:* R.A. Summer Exhbn. since 1968, R.B.A. since 1978, Falmouth A.G., Hallam Gallery, N.E.A.C., Crossgate Gallery, U.S.A.; one-man shows, Portal Gallery, Highgate, Southwell-Brown Gallery, Richmond, Gt.Yarmouth Museum; group shows, Odette Gilbert Gallery (1983-84), Southwell-Brown Gallery, Richmond, Alexander Gallery London. *Signs work:* "Peter Peterson." *Address:* 101 Selhurst Rd., S. Norwood, London SE25 6LH.

**PETHERS, Ian Peter Andrew,** S.B.A. (1989); artist in ink and wash, water-colour and acrylic of botanical, marine and architectural subjects; *b* London, 23 Jan., 1956. *Educ:* Langley County School, Slough. *Studied:* at school under Thomas McCabe (1967-73). *Exhib:* 12 one-man shows since 1985, Westminster Gallery, S.B.A., R.S.M.A., Mall Galleries. *Publications:* work repro.: greetings cards; illustrated 'Healthy options' and 'Four Seasons' Food and Travel Guides by Joy David (1997). *Clubs:* S.B.A. *Signs work:* "Ian Pethers." *Address:* Glenrock, Drakewalls, Gunnislake, Cornwall PL18 9EE.

**PETO, Michael James,** B.A. (Arch.) (Lond.), M.I.A.Z., Donaldson Medal (1950), Dip. T.P. (1952); architect; artist in water-colour, ink; *b* Jaffna, Ceylon, 9 Feb., 1928. *Educ:* St. John's, Leatherhead. *Studied:* Canterbury School of Art under Robert W. Paine and Gerald Norden (1944-45); Bartlett School of Architecture, London University, under Prof. H. O. Corfiato (1945-51). *Exhib:* Canterbury, St. John's Wood, Zimbabwe. *Publications:* work repro.: Christmas cards, etc. *Signs work:* "James Peto." *Address:* P.O. Box 270, Harare, Zimbabwe.

**PETTERSON, Melvyn Lawrence,** R.E. (1991), B.A. (1986); painter/print-maker in oil, etching, water-colour; partner, Artichoke Print Workshop; *b* Cleethorpes, 7 July, 1947. *m* Glynis. one *d. Educ:* Cleethorpes-Beacon Hill Sec. Modern. *Studied:* Grimsby Art School (Peter Todd, Alf Ludlam, Nev Tipper), Camberwell School of Art (Graham Giles, Francis Hoyland, Anthony Eyton, R.A., Ben Levene, R.A.). *Exhib:* R.A., N.E.A.C., R.O.I., Bankside Gallery, museums and galleries in U.S.A., France, Russia, China, Spain, Sweden, Finland, Mont Carlo. *Work in collections:* Oxford, Leicester, galleries in U.S.A. *Publications:* British Painters/Sculptors, Painting and Drawing, Art Review, Drawing and Painting the Landscape (Collins-Brown). *Clubs:* R.E. *Signs work:* "M.L. Petterson" or "M.L.P." *Address:* 92 Grove Park, Camberwell, London SE5 8LE.

**PETTY, Anthony,** A.A. (Hons.) Dip. (1948), S.P. Dip. (1949); architect and painter in water-colour, gouache and mixed media; *b* Southampton, 1918. *m* Christine Durell. two *d. Studied:* Southern College of Art (1934-38, William Dring), Architectural Assoc. School (1946-48, Gordon Brown). *Exhib:* R.A., and many provincial galleries. *Signs work:* "Anthony Petty." *Address:* Curtle, Blackhill, Lindfield, Sussex.

**PETZSCH, Helmut Franz Günther,** D.A. (Edin.) 1951; F.S.A. Scot.; painter in oil and water-colour; *b* Berlin, 13 Dec., 1920. *m* Catherine Oag Craigie. one *s.* two *d. Educ:* Hamburg and London. *Studied:* Edinburgh College of Art (1947-51). *Exhib:* R.S.A., S.S.A., '57 Gallery, Edinburgh. *Publications:* author of Architecture in Scotland (Longman). *Signs work:* "Helmut Petzsch." *Address:* 32 Canaan Lane, Edinburgh EH10 4SU.

**PHILLIPS, Aubrey,** R.W.A., P.S.; Gold Medal, Paris Salon (1966); artist in pastel, water-colour and oil, teacher; *b* Astley, Worcs., 18 June, 1920. *m* Doris Kirk. three *s. Studied:* Stourbridge School of Art (E. M. Dinkel), Kidderminster School of Art (W. E. Daly, C. J. Lavenstein). *Exhib:* F.B.A. Galleries, National Library of Wales, City A.G.'s of Worcester, Hereford and Gloucester. *Work in collections:* Worcester A.G., Worcester County Museum. *Publications:* Two works on pastel and one on water-colour publ. by Search Press; work repro.: Leisure Painter and Artist. *Signs work:* "Aubrey R. Phillips." *Address:* 16 Carlton Rd., Malvern, Worcs. WR14 1HH.

**PHILLIPS, Francis Douglas,** painter and illustrator in water-colour, oil, acrylic, pastel, ink; *b* Dundee, 19 Dec., 1926. *m* Margaret Parkinson. one *d. Educ:* Dundee. *Studied:* Dundee College of Art (J. Milne Purvis). *Exhib:* R.S.A., R.S.W., R.G.I.; two 'Grampian' T.V. appearances (Feb. and July 1987) 'Tayside Artist'. *Work in collections:* National Trust for Scotland, English Speaking Union, Northern College of Educ., Aberdeenshire Health Board; Watson and Philip Plc., Glasgow Port Authority; private collections worldwide. *Publications:* work repro.: Limited Edn. Prints; illustrated over 100 books; covers on British and French Reader's Digest; The Artist. *Signs work:* "Phillips." *Address:* 278 Strathmore Ave., Dundee DD3 6SJ.

**PHILLIPS, Frederick David,** B.A. (Hons.) Fine Art (1974); painter in oil, colour pencil, limited edition serigraphs, lithographs; *b* Stoke-on-Trent, Staffs., 4 July, 1953. *m* Patricia Phillips. two *s-s. Studied:* Burslem College of Art, Staffs. (1970-74). *Exhib:* one-man shows: England, Hong Kong and the United States. Born in England, but working and living in Chicago since 1990. *Signs work:* "F.D. Phillips" or "Frederick Phillips." *Address:* 718 Green Bay Rd., Winnetka, Ill. 60093, U.S.A.

**PHILLIPS, John Edward,** N.D.D. (Sculpture) 1958, A.T.C. (Lond.) 1961; full-time sculptor and Artist in Residence; *b* Ealing, London, 28 June, 1937. *m* Valerie Maughan. one *s.* one *d. Educ:* Ealing College. *Studied:* Ealing School of Art (1953-58), Hornsey College of Art (1960-61). *Exhib:* various galleries, art centres, libraries, schools in London, Southern England and France. *Work in collections:* Hillingdon Civic Centre, Uxbridge Library and various schools in the London area, Bucks., Herts. and Oxford. *Signs work:* "John Phillips." *Address:* Lanhael, Hedgerley Hill, Hedgerley, nr. Slough SL2 3RW.

**PHILLIPS, John Henry,** A.T.D., M.C.C.Ed. (1947), F.R.S.A.; finalist, City and Guilds (handicrafts), Lond. (1948); artist in oil, water-colour; lately, Administrator, School Examinations Dept., University of London, responsible for art, technical subjects (retd. 1980); Head of Art, Handicraft, Harold Hill Gram. Sch., Romford (1957-65), Chatham House Gram. Sch., Ramsgate (1952-57), Luton Gram. School (1947-52); *b* Horsham, Sussex, 26 May, 1920. *m*

Gladys Phillips, S.R.N. one *s.* one *d. Educ:* Gram. Sch., Cowbridge, Glam. *Studied:* College of Art, Cardiff, from 1936, under Evan Charlton, William Pickles. *Exhib:* New Herts. Art Soc., Ramsgate Art Soc. *Signs work:* "J. Phillips." *Address:* 3 Priory Rd., Noak Hill, Romford, Essex RM3 9AT.

**PHILLIPS, Karen Erica,** D.A.T.E.C. (1982), B.A.Hons. (1985), M.F.A. (1987); painter in oil, ink, charcoal, acrylic; *b* Kidderminster, 1 Nov., 1962. *Educ:* Franche Middle School, Kidderminster; Ilfracombe Comprehensive. *Studied:* North Devon College (1979-82, Robin Wiggins), Bristol Polytechnic (1982-85, Ernest Pascoe), Newcastle University (1985-87, Norman Adams). *Exhib:* New Theatre Gallery, Barnstaple (shared exhbn. with father), Zetland Studios, Bristol, Burton A.G., Bideford, Jigsaw, Barnstaple, Long Gallery, Newcastle, R.W.A., R.A., Vicarage Cottage Gallery, North Shields. *Signs work:* "K. Phillips." *Address:* 6 Laburnum Ct., Guidepost, Northumberland.

**PHILLIPS, Rex,** Cdr.R.N. (retd.); marine and landscape artist in oil and water-colour; *b* March, Cambs., 19 July, 1931. *m* Shirley Chadwick. one *s.* two *d. Educ:* Nautical College, Pangbourne. *Exhib:* R.S.M.A., A.F.A.S., and various one-man shows. *Work in collections:* Royal Naval, Royal Marines and Fleet Air Arm Museums, London and provincial galleries; private collections in U.K. and abroad, naval ships and establishments, R.N.L.I. and other institutions. *Signs work:* "Rex Phillips." *Address:* 15 Westbourne Ave., Emsworth, Hants. PO10 7QT.

**PHILLIPS, Tom,** R.A. (1988), R.E., M.A. (Oxon.), N.D.D.; artist in oil, water-colour, book productions, television director (A TV Dante, etc.); *b* London, 25 May, 1937. *m* (1st) Jill (divorced). one *s.* one *d.*; (2nd) Fiona Maddocks, 1995. *Educ:* St. Catherine's, Oxford. *Studied:* Camberwell School of Art (Frank Auerbach). *Work in collections:* Tate Gallery, B.M., V. & A., Moma, N.Y., etc. Gallery (Graphics) Alan Cristea Gallery. *Clubs:* S.C.C.C., Groucho. *Signs work:* "Tom Phillips." *Address:* 57 Talfourd Rd., London SE15 5NN; and Alan Cristea Gallery, 31 Cork St., London W1X 2NU.

**PHIPPS, Howard,** B.A.(Hons.), R.W.A., S.W.E.; wood engraver, painter and illustrator; *b* Colwyn Bay, 1954. *Studied:* Fine Art, Cheltenham Art College (1971-75). *Exhib:* R.W.A., S.W.E., also at R.A. Summer Exhbns. where in 1985 awarded Christies Contemporary Print prize; one-man exhbns. include Dorset County Museum, Salisbury Museum (1993), Victoria Gallery, Bath (1994), Cassian de Vere Cole Fine Art, London (1996), Cheltenham Art Gallery (1997). *Work in collections:* Cheltenham A.G., V. & A. London, Dorchester Museum, R.W.A. *Publications:* illustrated books for: Bloomsbury, Century, Perdix, Folio Soc. (Shakespeare, Bronte, Tennyson) and Whittington Press who published the artist's own books Interiors (1985) and Further Interiors (1991). Contributor to Country Life. *Address:* Hilfield, Homington Rd., Coombe Bissett, Salisbury SP5 4ND.

**PICHÉ, Roland,** 1st Class N.D.D., A.R.C.A., Medal for Work of Distinction, R.C.A.; sculptor in resin, fibreglass, stainless steel, stone and bronze; lecturer in sculpture; Principal Lecturer, Canterbury College of Art; *b* London, 21 Nov., 1938. one *s.* two *d. Educ:* Romsey College, Embley Park, Hants. *Studied:* Hornsey College of Art (Mr. C. Anderson, A.R.C.A., 1956-60), Royal College of Art (Mr. B. Meadows, A.R.C.A., 1960-64). *Work in collections:* The Arts Council of Great Britain and Wales, São Paulo Museum, Gothenburg Museum, Sweden, National Gallery of Western Australia, M.O.M.A. New York, Aberdeen Scotland, Nene College, Northampton. *Publications:* Private View (B. Robertson and T. Armstrong-Jones), Dada, Surrealism (W. S. Rubin). *Signs work:* see appendix. *Address:* Victoria Studios, Tollesbury, Essex CM9 8RG.

**PICKEN, Mollie,** N.D.D. (1963), A.T.C. (1964); freelance artist in illustration, embroidery and fabric collage; *b* 13 Oct., 1940. *Studied:* Goldsmiths' College School of Art (1959-64) under Constance Howard and Betty Swanwick. *Work in collections:* Education Authorities. *Publications:* Illustrated books by Constance Howard; collaborated with Christine Bloxham to produce Love and Marriage (Pub. date: Feb. 1990). Art work for Oxfordshire Museum Services, Embroiderers Guild. *Clubs:* S.D.C.; Embroiderers' Guild, Assoc. of Illustrators. *Address:* The Old Post Office, Sibford Gower, Banbury, Oxon. OX15 5RT.

**PICKING, John,** N.D.D. (1960), D.A. Edin. (1962), A.T.D. (1966); painter and lecturer; Mem. Manchester Academy; ex Senior Lecturer in Fine Art, Manchester Polytechnic. *Studied:* Wigan School of Art, 1956-60 (Governors Medal); Edinburgh College of Art, 1960-63 (Postgrad. Scholarship); Scholarship to Spain 1963-64; Goldsmiths' College, London, 1965-66. *Exhib:* Scottish Gallery, Edinburgh, Colin Jellicoe Gallery, Manchester, Mercury Gallery, London, La Barcaccia galleries in Rome, Naples, Palermo etc.; since 1989 exclusive with Telemarket (Brescia) with galleries in Milan, Rome, Bologna etc.; many group exhibitions including Royal Academy, London and Galleria Borghese, Rome. *Work in collections:* Salford and Manchester Universities, Edinburgh Corp., Palermo Museo Regionale, private collections over the world. Work reflects interest in mixing painting languages, mythology, geology. Since 1979 painting full-time. Studios in Brescia and Sicily. *Address:* c/o Colin Jellicoe Gallery, 82 Portland St., Manchester M1 4QX.

**PIDOUX, Janet Anne,** S.W.A. (1992); painter in pastel; *b* High Wycombe, Bucks., 2 Sept., 1950. *m* Derek. one *s.* one *d. Educ:* Wellesbourne. *Exhib:* S.W.A., S.WL.A., P.S. *Publications:* work repro.: greetings cards. *Signs work:* "JANET PIDOUX." *Address:* c/o Penn Barn Gallery, By the Pond, Elm Rd., Penn, Bucks. HP10 8LB.

**PIERSON, Rosalind,** R.M.S., H.S.F., M.A.S.-F.; Paris Salon silver medal (1978), gold medal (1981); artist in water-colour; *b* Tavistock, Devon, 14 Sept., 1954. *Educ:* St. Audries School, West Quantoxhead, Som. *Studied:* Ruskin School of Drawing and Fine Art (John Newberry). *Exhib:* R.A., Paris Salon, Bilan de l'Art Contemporain, Paris, Quebec, New York, Florida, W. Virginia,

Montana, Bath, Wells, Tavistock, Monaco, Ulster. *Work in collections:* Miniature Art Soc., Florida. *Clubs:* Royal Soc. Miniature Painters, Sculptors and Gravers, Hilliard Soc. (Co-founder), Miniature Art Soc. of Florida, W.W.F., R.S.P.B., I.F.A.W. *Signs work:* "R. Pierson." *Address:* Brangwyn House, Kilworthy Hill, Tavistock, Devon PL19 0EP.

**PIKE, Jonathan,** B.A. (1971), A.R.B.A. (1995); painter in water-colour and oil; *b* Leatherhead, 17 Jan., 1949. *m* Roselind McClinton. two *d. Studied:* Central School of Art and Design, Falmouth School of Art. *Exhib:* one-man shows: London; mixed shows: throughout England and U.S.A. *Commissions:* Oxford University Press, The Clockworkers' Co. *Signs work:* "JONATHAN PIKE." *Address:* 26 Manor Lane Terr., London SE13 5QL.

**PIKE, Septimus:** see WATTS, Michael Gorse.

**PIKESLEY, Richard Leslie,** N.E.A.C., Dip. A.D. (1973), A.T.C. (1974); finalist, Hunting Group Prize (1981 and 1989), winner, E.F. Hutton Prize (1987), W.H. Patterson Prize (1988); painter in oil and water-colour; *b* London, 8 Jan., 1951. *m* Susan Margaret Stone. *Studied:* Harrow School of Art (1969-70), Canterbury College of Art (1970-73). *Exhib:* R.A., R.O.I., R.W.A., R.I.; one-man shows include New Grafton Gallery London (1990), Linfield Gallery, Bradford-on-Avon (1986), St. James's Gallery, Bath Festival (1986). *Clubs:* N.E.A.C. *Signs work:* "Richard Pikesley." *Address:* Middlehill Farm, Marrowbone Lane, Bothenhampton, Bridport, Dorset.

**PILCHER, Terence John,** A.R.C.A. (1953); landscape and portrait painter in oil and water-colour; *b* Barnehurst, Kent, 1926. *m* Mary. four *s.* two *d. Studied:* Sidcup School of Art (1940-44, 1947-49), R.C.A. (1951-53, Ruskin Spear, John Minton). *Exhib:* R.A., R.W.A. *Work in collections:* Mermaid Inn, Rye, Sussex; private collections in Australia, Britain and U.S.A. *Signs work:* "Terry Pilcher." *Address:* 2 White Horse Cottages, Washford, Watchet, Som. TA23 0JZ.

**PILKINGTON, Richard Godfrey,** M.A. (Cantab.); art dealer and publisher; Partner (Co-founder) Piccadilly Gallery, 16a Cork St., W1, since 1953; Chairman of Society of London Art Dealers (1974-77); editor The Art Bulletin (1951-60); Governor, Wimbledon School of Art (1991-); *b* Stafford, 8 Nov., 1918. *m* Evelyn (Eve) Vincent. two *s.* two *d. Educ:* Clifton and Trinity College, Cambridge. *Address:* 45 Barons Court Rd., London W14 9DZ.

**PILKINGTON, Ruth Jane,** R.O.I. (1976), S.W.A. (1985); painter in oil; *b* Manchester, 2 May, 1924. *m* Eric W. L. Pilkington (decd.). one *s.* (decd.). one *d. Educ:* Ladybarn House School, Manchester and Maltman's Green, Gerrard's Cross. *Studied:* Johannesburg Technical College (1947-48), Macclesfield C.F.E. (1962-65). *Exhib:* R.B.A., R.O.I., Paris Salon, Manchester Academy, etc., other group exhbns., one-man show in Channel Islands (1976). *Work in collections:* Barreau A.G., Société Jersiaise, Jersey. *Signs work:* "Ruth J. Pilkington." *Address:* Sondela, La Rue à Don, Grouville, Jersey, JE3 9DX, C.I.

**PILLOW, Lorna Mary Carol,** A.R.C.A.; Sir Frank Warner Memorial Medal; freelance textile, exhibition and graphic designer; taught, Croydon and Berkshire Colleges of Art; senior lecturer, West Surrey College of Art and Design (retd.); *b* Cork, Eire. *m* widow of Peter John Palmer. one *s. Educ:* Wolverhampton and Leeds. *Studied:* Leeds, Hull and the Royal Colleges of Art. *Exhib:* Beverley Art Gallery, Ferens Art Gallery, Guildhall, R.W.S. Galleries, Mall Galleries, London, W.S.C.A.D. Gallery, Farnham, R.S.A. Travelling Exhibition, Design Centre, London. *Publications:* International Textiles; illustrated Geography of Flowering Plants. *Signs work:* "Lorna Pillow." *Address:* 33 Havelock Rd., Maidenhead, Berks. SL6 5BJ.

**PINCUS, Helen Frances,** B.A. Hons. (1982), M.F.P.S. (1984), M.S.D.C. (1993), Adult Educ. Dip. (1979); fibre and textile artist, designer, embroiderer in fibres, yarns, aluminium mesh, wood, piano wire and pure silk; freelance lecturer, writer and musician; *b* Acton, London, 22 Oct., 1938. *Educ:* Haberdashers' Aske's Acton Girls' School; The Arts Educational Schools. *Studied:* Nottingham University; Loughborough College of Art and Design. *Exhib:* numerous one-man shows and mixed exhbns. both in the U.K. and abroad including Commonwealth Inst. A.G., Cork St. Fine Arts, Leighton House, Savaria Muzeum (Hungary), Westminster Abbey, Galeria Bellas Artes (Spain), Smith's Gallery, University of Surrey, Loggia Gallery, Contemporary Arts (Hong Kong), Hampton Court Palace, Guild Gallery, Heifer Gallery, Bloomsbury Gallery, Vincent A.G. (Australia), Southwark Cathedral, Cecilia Colman Gallery, Metro Toronto Convention Centre (Canada), Del Bello A.G. (Canada), The Fourth Annual International Exhbn. of Miniature Arts in Toronto, Canada, awarded a special distinction (1989), Strathclyde University, Barbican Centre, The Rotunda Gallery Hong Kong. *Work in collections:* Savaria Muzeum, Hungary. *Clubs:* F.P.S., Embroiderers' Guild, New Embroidery Group, London Symphony Chorus, St. Endellion Festival Chorus, The Colour Group (G.B.), Soc. of Designer Craftsmen, Registered with the Crafts Council. *Signs work:* see appendix; or occasionally embroiders initials and year. *Address:* Rock Cottage, Treknow, Tintagel, N. Cornwall PL34 0EN.

**PINE, Diana,** Assoc. Sussex Artists (1974, Hon. Sec. 1978-83); artist in water-colour, pastel and oil; documentary film director, Crown Film Unit, Wessex, etc. B.B.C.; part-time teacher, Mole Valley A.E.C. and Day Centre; *b* London. *Educ:* Jersey, France, London, P.N.E.U. *Studied:* Regent St. Polytechnic (1936-37) under Clifford Ellis, Chelsea Art School under H. S. Williamson, Central School; apprentice Edward Carrick for Art Direction, Films (-1940), Ernest Savage, Aubrey Sykes (1968-75). *Exhib:* R.I., P.S., S.W.A. (1976-86), Assoc. Sussex Artists, Horsham, Barns Green, Dorking Group. *Signs work:* "D. Pine." *Address:* 2 Lodge Close, North Holmwood, Dorking, Surrey RH5 4JU.

**PINKNEY, Richard,** N.D.D., A.T.D.; painter, sculptor and printmaker in oil, acrylic, gouache, intaglio, etc.; teacher, Ipswich, Colchester and St.

Martin's Schools of Art, and Kingsway College; Director, Lady Lodge Arts Centre, Peterborough; *b* 22 July, 1938. *m* Judith Foster, A.R.C.A. two *s. Educ:* Ipswich School. *Studied:* Ipswich Civic College, School of Art; West of England College of Art, Bristol. *Exhib:* solo shows: A.I.A. Gallery, London; Traverse Theatre, Edinburgh; Paperback Bookshop, Edinburgh; St. Martin's School of Art, London; Lady Lodge Arts Centre, Peterborough; Manor School of Ballet, Edinburgh; University College Suffolk; Christchurch Mansion, Ipswich; Sans Walk Gallery, London; group shows: graphics and mailart widely, U.K., Europe, U.S.A., Japan, S. America. *Work in collections:* Tate Gallery, V. & A., B.M.; public and private collections U.K. and worldwide. *Publications:* Circle, Tetrad, Trivia & Bad Presses. *Clubs:* Suffolk Group, Ipswich Arts Soc. *Signs work:* "R.P.," "R. Pinkney," "Richard Pinkney." *Address:* 10 The Street, Bramford, Ipswich, Suffolk IP8 4EA.

**PINSKY, Michael,** M.A.(R.C.A.), B.A. (Hons.) Fine Art (1991); artist in photography, sculpture, site-specific installation; *b* Scotland, 24 Nov., 1967. *Educ:* James Gillespies High School. *Studied:* Manchester Polytechnic (1987-88), Brighton Polytechnic (1988-91, Bill Beach), R.C.A. (1993-95). *Exhib:* one-man shows: Collective Gallery Edinburgh, Traverse Theatre Edinburgh, The Warehouse Amsterdam, The Gantry Southampton, Open Eye Gallery Liverpool, Viewpoint Gallery Manchester, Stockport A.G., Crawford Arts Centre St. Andrews, Quay Arts Centre, I.O.W., Gatwick Airport, Metropole A.G. Folkestone, Gracefield Art Centre, Dumfries, McLellan A.G. Ayr, Dean Clough A.G. Halifax, Towner A.G. Eastbourne, Photofusion, London, Duncan of Jordanstone A.G. Dundee, Delfina London, Bonnington Gallery Nottingham, Laing Gallery Newcastle, Chapter Cardiff, Tramway Glasgow, etc.;group shows:U.K., U.S.A., and Europe. *Address:* 47 Earlsferry Way, London N1 0D2.

**PIOTTI, Vittorio,** Dip. of Artistic Maturity, Art-Liceum, Carrara (1967), Knighthood of Italian Republic (Cav.) (1978), R.W.A. (1983); Major Alpini Parachutists; sculptor in iron; *b* Brescia, Italy, 5 Mar., 1935. *m* Andreina. one *s.* one *d. Studied:* Art Liceum of Venezia; Art-Liceum of Carrara. *Exhib:* (1967-93): Brescia, Trento, Padova, Vicenza, Mantova, Cremona, Bari, Pavia, Biarritz and Parigi (France), Venezia, Pompeii, Cassino, Bolzano, Verona, Bergamo, Torino, Bristol (England), Genova, Monaco and Mainz (Germany). *Work in collections:* in Italy, Libya, France, England, Germany. Public monuments: in Italy and Germany, etc. *Signs work:* "V. PIOTTI" or "Vittopiotti." *Address:* via Columbaia 17, 25050 Rodengo, Saiano, Brescia, Italy.

**PITFIELD, Thomas Baron,** N.R.D., Hon. F.R.M.C.M.; artist in water-colour, reed-pen, lino-cut, lettering; composer; art master; *b* Bolton, Lancs., 5 Apr., 1903. *m* Alice Maud Astbury. *Educ:* Bolton and Manchester. *Studied:* Municipal School of Art, Bolton (apprenticed in Engineer's drawing-office). *Exhib:* R.A., Northern Academy of Fine Arts, and various one-man exhbns. *Publications:* Junior Course in Art Teaching, Senior Course in Art Teaching,

The Poetry of Trees, Bowdon and "Limusicks" (40 limericks), (texts, script, illustrations), Recording a Region (drawings and hand-lettered script), and a large number of musical compositions; autobiographies: A Cotton Town Boyhood, No Song, No Supper, A Song after Supper; work repro.: Artist, Countryman, and other periodicals, calendars, etc. C.D. issued by R.N.C.M., of chamber music and songs. *Signs work:* see appendix. *Address:* Lesser Thorns, 21 East Downs Rd., Bowdon, Ches.WA14 2LG.

**PITMAN, Primrose Vera,** S.G.A. (1953), L.R.A.M., Gold Medal for Design; painter in water-colour, commercial artist in pencil; etcher. *Educ:* St. Hilda's School. *Studied:* Royal Albert Memorial School of Art under Burman Morrall and James Sparks. *Exhib:* R.W.A. and provincial galleries. *Work in collections:* Royal Albert Memorial Museum, City of Exeter. *Publications:* work repro.: of pencil drawing of Exeter Cathedral for Preservation Fund organized by Mayor of Exeter. Etchings and pencil drawings in This Jewel Remains (1942). *Clubs:* Exeter Art Soc., Kenn Group. *Signs work:* "Primrose V. Pitman." *Address:* Marlands, 4 Victoria Park Rd., Exeter.

**PLATT, Eric Warhurst,** A.R.C.A., Silver Medallist (1940); artist in line and wash, water-colour, etching, graphic design, and creative cut card relief; Vice Principal Doncaster College of Art; Head of Design, Doncaster M.Inst. of H.E. (retd. July 1980); *b* Cudworth, Yorks., 2 May, 1915. *m* Mary Elizabeth. one *s.* one *d. Educ:* Wakefield and Doncaster School of Art. *Studied:* R.C.A. under Malcolm Osborne, R.A., and Robert Austin, R.A. (1937-40). *Exhib:* R.A., Brighton, West Riding Artists exhbn., Yorkshire Artists exhbn., Doncaster A.G., Feren's Gallery, Hull, Graves Gallery, Sheffield, etc. *Signs work:* "Eric Platt." *Address:* 18 Warren Hey, Spital, Bebington, Wirral L63 9LF.

**PLINCKE, J. Richard,** R.I. (1984), R.I.B.A., A.A.Dip. (1951); painter in water-colour and mixed media; work includes designs for tapestries, and stained glass windows at St. Mark's Church, Kempshot; *b* Woldingham, Surrey, 29 Oct., 1928. *m* Rosemary D. Ball. two *d. Educ:* Stowe, Bucks. *Studied:* art: Southampton Inst. of Higher Educ., gaining Higher Cert. (Distinction); architecture: Architectural Assoc. School of Architecture, London *Exhib:* R.A., R.W.A., R.I., R.S.M.A., Manor House Gallery, Chipping Norton, Linda Blackstone Gallery, Pinner, Shell House Gallery, Ledbury. Work included in a number of private collections. *Signs work:* "R.P." followed by the date. *Address:* The Studio, 2 St. Thomas Mews, Winchester, Hants. SO23 9HG.

**PLUMLEY, Richard Harry,** interior designer, painter in oil, water-colour and gouache, early sculpture, stage and theatre design, consultant; co-Director, Personal Choice Interiors; *b* Harrow, Middx., 5 Mar., 1944. *m* Snezana Nikolic. one *s.* one *d. Educ:* Orange Hill, Edgware. *Studied:* Harrow College of Art (1962). *Exhib:* one-man shows: George St. London (1969, 1972), Isle of Man (1994); mixed shows: Windsor (1976), Douglas (1984). Currently preparing retrospective exhbn. for 1998. *Work in collections:* London, Chicago, Spain,

Isle of Man, private collections *Commissions:* interiors Avon Castle, Ringwood. *Publications:* Manx Life, Isle of Man Examiner and Courier. *Clubs:* Legion Players. *Signs work:* "R.H. Plumley" or "R.P." *Address:* 4 Seaforth House, Crown St., Peel, I.O.M. IM5 1AJ.

**PLUMMER, Brian,** R.A.S.; painter in acrylic and water-colour relief; *b* London, 1934. *Studied:* Hornsey College of Art, R.A. Schools. *Exhib:* R.A., Expo Montreal, Barcelona Bienal (prize winner), Toronto, Abbot Hall, Kendal, Lucy Milton, Galerie van Hulsen, Amsterdam, Rex Irwin Sydney, Sloane St. Gallery, Audun Gallery, The Macquarie Galleries, Sydney, Gallerie St. Pierre, Bordeaux. *Work in collections:* D.O.E., St. Thomas' Hospital, Power Collection Sydney, Ministero Cultura Madrid, Mobil Oil Co., Lancaster University, Abbot Hall, Kendal, Armidale N.S.W. *Signs work:* "BRIAN PLUMMER" on acrylics, hand written on water-colours. *Address:* 89 Palmerston Rd., London N22 4QS.

**POLLARD, Malcolm,** sculptor, draughtsman, teacher; *b* Raunds, Northants, 14 Mar., 1941. *m* Elke Kairies Addis. two *s*. *Signs work:* "MALCOLM POL-LARD" - christian name above surname. *Address:* 42 East Park Parade, Northampton NN1 4LA.

**POLLOCK, (Sir) George F.,** Bt., M.A. (Cantab.), Hon. F.R.P.S., F.R.S.A., F.B.I.P.P., E.F.I.A.P.; artist-photographer, a-v producer; past President, Royal Photographic Society; *b* 13 Aug., 1928. *Educ:* Eton College and Trinity College, Cambridge. *Exhib:* numerous. *Work in collections:* British Council, R.P.S., National Gallery of Victoria, Musée de Photographie, Bièvres, Towner A.G., Eastbourne, Texas University, University of Surrey. *Commissions:* murals for Lloyds Bank, British Petroleum. *Publications:* numerous articles on photography; "The Limits of Photography" - Prizewining essay. *Signs work:* "George F. Pollock." *Address:* 83 Minster Way, Bath BA2 6RL.

**POLLOCK, Helen,** D.A. (Edin.); painter in acrylic and mixed media; theme of work includes abstract and semi abstractions based on natural and man made objects; *b* Limavady, Co. Derry, 23 Mar., 1945. *m* Laurence Roche, D.A. (Edin.). *Studied:* Edinburgh College of Art (1963-67). *Exhib:* R.S.A., R.W.A., S.S.A., R.S.W., S.S.W.A., and numerous other exhbns. *Work in collections:* private collections in Britain and abroad. *Signs work:* "Helen Pollock." *Address:* 16 Belmont Rd., Stroud, Glos. GL5 1HH.

**POMERANCE, Fay,** painter; *b* 1912. *m* Ben Pomerance. *Educ:* King Edward's High School; Art School, Birmingham. *Exhib:* one-man: "Lucifer Theme - The Sphere of Redemption" and other works 1949-1983, Archer and Ben Uri Galleries, St. James's and St. Botolph's Churches, London; Liverpool, Wakefield, Batley, Derby, Middlesbrough, Newcastle, Gateshead municipal galleries, R.B.S.A., Birmingham, Theatre and University Centres, Oxford, Sheffield, Leicester, Nottingham, Cambridge, Durham, Solihull. Represented London exhbns.: Leicester, Redfern, Molton. *Work in collections:* Trevelyan and Grey College, Durham, Hull, Staffordshire Educ. Committees, Batley, Gateshead Picture Lending, Ben Uri, Israel; reproduced work in books by Fred

Gettings, Douglas Baker, Francis X. King. Designed stained glass window Birmingham Synagogue. *Address:* 92a Ranmoor Rd., Sheffield SI0 3HJ.

**POND, Edward Charles,** N.D.D. (1955), Des.R.C.A. (1958), R.C.A. Royal Scholar (1956) Silver medal (1958), F.R.S.A.; C.O.I.D. Design of the Year (1959), National Paper Box U.S.A. two 'firsts', three 'excellence' (1988), International Advertising N.Y. two golds' (1990); P.P.C.S.D. (1981-83); chartered designer in paper collage, oil, acrylic, water-colour, ceramic glaze; Chairman, Met. Police C.C.G.; artist to B.R. Network South-East; *b* 12 Mar., 1929. *m* Jane Pond, M.A. one *s.* two *d. Educ:* Royal Liberty School, Gidea Park. *Studied:* S.E. Essex (1951-55, Charles Handley Read), R.C.A. (1955-58). *Exhib:* Young Contemporaries, Bangor University, Portmeirion, Whitworth A.G., Scott Howard, Bournemouth/Medway Colleges of Art, Concert Hall Blackheath, Avalon/Crows Nest Cornwall. *Work in collections:* British Rail - murals, Armada mural - Plymouth; numerous private collections. *Publications:* A.H. Mackmurdo (Anti-Rationalists), articles in Design (Crafts Press). *Clubs:* Blackheath F.C., Design and Industries Assoc. *Signs work:* "Edward Pond." *Address:* Long Loft, Cadgwith, Cornwall TR12 7JY.

**POOLE, David James,** R.P. (1969), A.R.C.A.; artist; President, Royal Soc. of Portrait Painters (1983-91); Senior lecturer in Painting and Drawing, Wimbledon School of Art (1962-77); *b* 5 June, 1931. *m* Iris Mary Toomer. three *s. Educ:* Stoneleigh Secondary School. *Studied:* Wimbledon School of Art, R.C.A. *Exhib:* one-man shows: Zurich and London. Portraits include: H.M. The Queen, H.R.H. The Duke of Edinburgh, H.M. The Queen Mother, H.R.H. Prince Charles, H.R.H. Princess Anne, H.R.H. Princess Margaret, Earl Mountbatten of Burma and The Duke of Kent; also distinguished members of govt., industry, commerce, medicine, the academic and legal professions. *Work in collections:* H.M. The Queen and H.R.H. The Duke of Edinburgh; and in Australia, S. Africa, Bermuda, France, W. Germany, Switzerland, Saudi Arabia, U.S.A. *Address:* Trinity Flint Barn, Weston Lane, Weston, Petersfield, Hants. GU32 3NN; *2nd Address* Studio 6, Burlington Lodge, Rigault Rd., Fulham, London SW6 4JJ.

**POOLE, Greg,** B.Sc. Zoology (1983, Mem. S.WL.A.; artist/illustrator in printmaking and collage; *b* Bristol, 26 Oct, 1960. *Studied:* Foundation Course, Manchester Polytechnic (1989-90). *Exhib:* many mixed exhbns., annually withS.WL.A. *Work in collections:* Nature in Art Museum, Glos. *Publications:* work repro: book covers for Blackwells, C.U.P. and Reed International, many magazine illustrations. Participant in Artists for Nature Foundation Projects on the Loire Estuary, France, and Bhamragarh, India. Recent residences in France, Ireland and Barbados. *Address:* 31 Burlington Rd., Redland, Bristol BS6 6TJ.

**POOLE, Monica,** A.R.E. (1967), R.E. (1975); Central School Diploma (1949); Member of the Art Workers' Guild; wood engraver; *b* Canterbury, 20 May, 1921. *m* Cmdr. A. G. M. Small, R.N., F.I.H.V.E. *Educ:* Abbotsford, Broadstairs. *Studied:* Central School of Arts and Crafts (1945-49). *Exhib:* R.A.

R.E., etc. *Work in collections:* Fitzwilliam Museum, B.M., S.N.G.M.A., V. & A., Ashmolean Museum, Museum Boymans van Beunegen, Rotterdam, Hunt Botanical Museum, Pittsburgh, U.S.A., Pistoia A.G., National Museum of Wales. *Publications:* The Wood Engravings of John Farleigh (1985). *Signs work:* "MONICA POOLE." *Address:* 67 Hadlow Rd., Tonbridge, Kent TN9 1QB.

**POPE, Perpetua,** D.A. (Edin.) 1947; painter in oil; lecturer in visual arts, Moray House College of Education (1968-73); *b* Solihull, Warwicks., 29 May, 1916. *Educ:* Albyn School, Aberdeen. *Studied:* Edinburgh College of Art under W. G. Gillies, John Maxwell, Leonard Rosoman. *Exhib:* one-man shows: Scottish Gallery, Edinburgh; mixed shows: R.A., R.S.A., S.S.A., S.S.W.A., Aberdeen Artists, Stirling Gallery. *Work in collections:* H.R.H. The Duke of Edinburgh, Scottish Arts Council, Nuffield Trust, Argyll County Council, Robert Fleming Plc. *Signs work:* "Perpetua Pope." *Address:* 27 Dean St., Edinburgh EH4 1LN.

**PORTEOUS WOOD, James,** R.S.W. (1945); landscape, mural and portrait artist in oils, water-colour, black and white; specialist in architectural subjects; art director and chief designer Asprey, Bond St. (1956-1980); designer of important gold and silver and objets d'art - works in many of the premier world contemporary collections; murals and paintings in royal and presidential palaces in Near, Middle and Far East; *b* Edinburgh, 1919. married. one *s. Educ:* George Heriot's School. *Studied:* Edinburgh College of Art (1935-40) (Travelling Scholarship). *Exhib:* R.A., R.S.A., R.S.W., G.I., and several one-man shows. *Publications:* private editions with miniatures and calligraphy mainly on vellum, Midland Riches (Hancock), Yorkshire Sketchbook; work repro.: many editorial drawings mainly architectural, industrial, and portrait in national Press, top magazines and prestige books. *Signs work:* "PORTEOUS WOOD." *Address:* Caimbe Bridge, Arisaig, Inverness-shire PH39 4NT.

**PORTMAN, Joanne Merle,** landscape painter in water-colour and water soluble pens; *b* Worcester, 21 Feb., 1965. *Studied:* ceramic art: Boehm of Malvern. *Exhib:* Malvern Arts (1989, 1991, 1993). *Work in collections:* Malvern Galleries, Worcester Antiques Centre; private collections in Europe and U.S.A. *Clubs:* Malvern Art. *Signs work:* "J.M. Portman." *Address:* Flat 1, Scarsdale, 22 Priory Rd., Malvern, Worcs. WR14 3DR.

**PORTSMOUTH, Delia,** painter of landscapes, portraits, flowers, birds, wildlife in oils; *b* Mottram, Ches., 6 Aug., 1939. *m* A. C. Portsmouth. four *d. Educ:* Hyde and Bala Grammar Schools. *Studied:* self taught. *Exhib:* R.O.I., Hesketh Hubbard, Flower Painters' Summer Salon; one-man shows: Chester, Lampeter, Bala, Brantwood, St. Davids, Usher Gallery, Lincoln, Public Gallery, Oldham. *Work in collections:* National Library of Wales, National Museum of Wales, Liverpool Corp. and numerous private collections world-wide. *Clubs:* founder member, Modern Millais Association. *Signs work:* "Delia Portsmouth." *Address:* 14 Saffron Park, Kingsbridge, Devon TQ7 1RL.

**POTTER, Donald,** F.R.B.S.; sculptor in stone, wood and ivory; *b* Newington, Kent, 21 Apr., 1902. *m* Mary Potter. one *s*. one *d*. *Studied:* pupil of Eric Gill. *Work in collections:* Sculptures in St. George's Chapel, Windsor, St. Paul's Cathedral, Zomba Cathedral (Nyasaland), The Baden-Powell Statue (Queens Gate), St. Sebastian, Winchester College. *Signs work:* see appendix. *Address:* Bryanston, Blandford, Dorset.

**POTTINGER, Frank,** D.A. Sculpture (1963), R.S.A. (1991); sculptor in bronze, stone, wood, clay; *b* Edinburgh, 1 Oct., 1932. *m* Dr. Norah Smith, 1991. one *s-s*. one *d-d*. *Educ:* Boroughmuir School. *Studied:* Edinburgh College of Art (1958-63). *Exhib:* Richard Demarco Gallery, Yorkshire Sculpture Park, Landmark Scottish Sculpture Trust, Camden Arts Centre, Pier Arts Centre Orkney, Kildrummy Castle, S.S.W. Open, Royal Scottish Academy. *Work in collections:* Heriot Watt University, Hunterian Museum, I.B.M., Scottish Development Agency, Leeds Educ. Authority, Scottish Arts Council. *Commissions:* L.A.S.M.O., The Woodland Trust, Motherwell District Council, Ellon Development, Aberdeenshire, Dundee University. *Address:* 30/5 Elbe St., Leith EH6 7HW.

**POTTS, Kenneth Arthur,** A.R.B.S. (1988), Dip.A.D., B.A. (1972), C.I.C. (1969); sculptor in bronze, stoneware, terracotta and fine porcelain; *b* Macclesfield, 16 Mar., 1949. *m* Anne. one *s*. one *d*. *Educ:* Stockport C.F.E. (1966). *Studied:* Stafford College of Art (1969), Stoke-on-Trent College of Art (1972). *Exhib:* R.A. Summer Show, Festival Hall, Sladmore Gallery, Art Expo N.Y., R.B.S. West of England Academy, Tokyo, etc. *Work in collections:* Dyson Perrins Museum, Raphael Djanogly Trust. *Commissions:* Bronze statue, Sir Edward Elgar, Worcester; bronze statue, A.E. Housman, Bromsgrove; mosaic panels, Holy Trinity, Sutton Coldfield; "Spitfire" mural, Longton, Stoke on Trent; Cassidy Memorial, Tamside Metropolitan Borough; Hogg Memorial, Edinburgh. *Signs work:* "Kenneth Potts." *Address:* Clater Pk., Bringsty, Worcester WR6 5TP.

**POUNTNEY, Monica (née Brailey),** cup for oils S.E.I.F.A.S. (1976); free-lance artist in oil, water-colour, acrylic, pastel, etc.; *b* London. *m* D. H. Pountney. one *s*. *Studied:* Hammersmith School of Arts and Crafts (Carel Weight and Ruskin Spear), Central School (John Farleigh). *Exhib:* Federation of British Artists, U.A., S.W.A., R.I., N.S., and various mixed exhbns. *Work in collections:* landscapes in London, Moscow and U.S.A. *Commissions:* various. *Publications:* work repro.: books illustrated for Heinemann, Blackie and others. *Clubs:* U.A., L.A.G., Essex A.C. *Signs work:* "M.P." or full name. *Address:* 3 Thickwood House, Bedford Rd., S. Woodford, London E18 2AH.

**POVER, Emma,** R.B.A.; sculptor (largely figurative and portraiture) in bronze, plaster, cement; *b* Plymouth, 1 Apr., 1950. two *s*. *Educ:* Devonport High, St. John's, Singapore. *Exhib:* numerous provincial galleries, Woodlands, R.A., Mall Galleries, Islington Art Fair. *Work in collections:* life-sized bronze Lambeth Palace; various private collections. *Signs work:* "E. Pover" or

"Pover." *Address:* 78 Inverine Rd., Charlton, London SE7 7NL.

**POVEY, Edward,** B.Ed. (1978), R.C.A.; artist in oil, pencil and conté; *b* London, 1 May, 1951. *m* Alison Bone. two *s. Educ:* Crown Woods Comprehensive School, Eltham. *Studied:* Eastbourne College of Art and Design (1972-73), University of Wales (1974-78, Selwyn Jones). *Exhib:* Martin Tinney Gallery, Cardiff; Meridian Contemporary Arts, Hay-on-Wye; Mostyn Gallery, Llandudno; Jan de Maere Galleries, Brussels; Gallery Gerard, The Hague; Midtown Payson Galleries, N.Y.; Horwitch Newman Gallery, Scottsdale, U.S.A. *Work in collections:* University of Wales at Bangor, Laguna Gloria Museum in Austin, Texas. *Publications:* chapters and photographs in: Painting The Town by Cooper and Sargent (Phaidon Press 1979), Wales on Canvas by Hywel Harries (Lolfa Press 1983), Gwynedd by Ian Skidmore Robert Hale 1987). *Signs work:* "Edward Povey" or "Povey." *Address:* Vale Barn, Lower Chapel, Brecon, Powys LD3 9RE.

**POWELL, Christopher Alan,** LL.B. (1957); former journalist; painter mainly in oil with occasional water-colour and tempera of landscapes, seascapes, city scenes, still life and flower studies; former sub-editor on The Times (1968-92); *b* Newcastle upon Tyne, 11 July, 1935. *Educ:* Queen Elizabeth Grammar, Hexham. *Studied:* part time at City Literary Inst., London (Cecil Collins). Studied law at King's College, Newcastle upon Tyne. *Exhib:* Mall Galleries, Leighton House, various art societies in London. *Work in collections:* U.K., U.S.A., Japan. *Signs work:* "C.A. POWELL." *Address:* Flat A7, Sloane Ave. Mans., Chelsea, London SW3 3JF.

**POWELL, John,** A.R.C.A.; painter; *b* Nottingham, 27 Aug., 1911. *m* Freda Heathcote. one *d. Studied:* R.C.A. under Gilbert Spencer (1935-39) and Nottingham Art College (1932-35). *Exhib:* R.A., R.B.A., R.O.I., N.E.A.C., London Group, S.M.A., N.S., United Artists, Pastel Society, also mixed and travelling exhbns. in London and provincial galleries. Main exhbns.: New Ashgate Gallery, Farnham (1981), Bosham Walk Gallery, W. Sussex (1990), Eastgate Gallery, Chichester (1994). *Work in collections:* Bristol Educ. Com. (Harbour, Tenby), Manchester Educ. Com., (Child at Breakfast, Fair at Twilight); and private collections. *Signs work:* "John Powell" on back or under mat. *Address:* Fishbourne Farmhouse, Fishbourne, Chichester, W. Sussex PO18 8AW.

**POWELL, Sir Philip,** C.H., O.B.E., R.A., F.R.I.B.A., A.A. Dip. (Hons.), R.I.B.A. Gold Medallist (1974); Treasurer R.A. (1985-95), Member, Royal Fine Art Commission (1969-94); architect (Powell, Moya, 1946-91); *b* Bedford, 15 Mar., 1921. *m* Philippa (née Eccles). *Educ:* Epsom College. Works include Churchill Gdns., Pimlico; South Bank Skylon; British Pavilion, Expo. 70, Osaka; Hospitals at Swindon, Slough, High Wycombe, Maidstone, Great Ormond Street; Wolfson College, Oxford; new buildings at Brasenose, Christ Church and Corpus Christi, Oxford, and St. John's and Queens' Colleges, Cambridge; Chichester Festival Theatre; Museum of London; Queen Elizabeth

II Conference Centre, Westminster. *Address:* 16 The Little Boltons, London SW10 9LP.

**POWELL, Roy Owen,** N.D.D. (1956), A.T.D. (1959); landscape figure and still life artist in oil on canvas, charcoal and pencil drawings; retd. art teacher; *b* Chepstow, 3 Dec., 1934. *Educ:* Monmouth School and West Mon School, Pontypool. *Studied:* Cardiff College of Art (1952-56, Eric Malthouse, J.C. Tarr). *Exhib:* one-man show Brecknock Museum (1994); various group shows in England, Wales and Scotland including 'Celtic Vision'. *Publications:* articles for 'Planet' magazine. *Clubs:* The Welsh Group. *Signs work:* "R.O. Powell." *Address:* 10 Mill St., Brecon, Powys LD3 9BD.

**POWER, Philip Ian,** B.A.(Hons.) (1980), M.F.A. (1983); works in light, digital imaging, sound; lecturer, University of Edinburgh Architecture Dept.; *b* Swansea, 26 Apr., 1955. *m* Maggie Bolt. one *s. Educ:* King Edward's School, Witley. *Studied:* Maidstone College of Art (1977-80, Kerry Trengove, Mike Upton), University of Reading (1981-83, Marc Chaimowicz, Bill Culbert, Ron Haselden). *Exhib:* New Contemporaries (1982, 1983), "Shape and Form" British touring show, Fruitmarket Edinburgh, C.C.A. Glasgow, etc. *Commissions:* collaboration with Phoenix Dance Co. (1987) and Architects City as a Work of Art, Edinburgh (Consultant) Scottish Sculpture Trust (1995) and Edinburgh Festival Theatre (gable end installation). *Signs work:* "Power" or "P.P." *Address:* 20a Rankeillor St., Edinburgh EH8 9HY.

**PRENDERGAST, Peter,** D.F.A. (1967), M.A. (1970); painter draughtsman/landscape painter in water-colour, oil, charcoal, pencil and ink on paper, canvas, board; prizewinner, Singer Friedlander/Sunday Times Water-colour competition (1996); *b* 27 Oct., 1946. *m* Lesley. two *s.* two *d. Educ:* Cardiff *Studied:* Slade School of Fine Art (William Coldstream, Frank Auerbach, Jeffery Camp), Reading University. *Exhib:* Mostyn Gallery touring to Swansea, Durham, London, Tate Gallery, Norwich A.G., A.C.G.B. touring show, National Parks Exhbn., V. & A., also toured U.S.A., Land and Sea exhbn. with Len Tabner, Scarborough (1992), National Museum of Wales (1993-94), Agnews, London, Boundary Gallery, London, Royal Academy and Barcelona tour. *Work in collections:* Tate Gallery, B.M., A.C.G.B., W.A.C. Contemporary Art Soc., National Museum of Wales, etc. *Publications:* Paintings from Wales - Agnews London (1994). Agents: Boundary Gallery London NW8 0RH. *Signs work:* "Peter Prendergast." *Address:* Tan-y-Craig Deiniolen, Caernarfon LL55 3EE.

**PRENTICE, David,** painter in oil, pastel, water-colour; co-founder/director Ikon Gallery, B'ham. (1964-71); taught at School of Fine Art, B'ham (1968-86), Ruskin, Oxford (1986-87), U.C.E., Birmingham and Fine Art B.A., Trent Polytechnic (1986-93); *b* Solihull, 4 July, 1936. *m* Dinah Prentice, artist. four *d. Educ:* Moseley School of Art, B'ham. *Studied:* B'ham College of Art and Crafts. *Exhib:* Serpentine, M.O.M.A., N.Y., Betty Parsons, N.Y., Albright Knox, Buffalo. Winner of the Singer & Friedlander/Sunday Times water-colour prize (1990 and 1996). *Signs work:* "David Prentice." Represented by Cowleigh Gallery, Malvern, Art First, 9 Cork St., London W1X 1PD; and John Davies Gallery, Stow-on-the-Wold. *Address:* Ashdown Villa, 9 Hanley Terr., Malvern, Worcs. WR14 4PF.

**PRESTON-GODDARD, John,** Professional painter in oil, water-colour, gouache; *b* Liverpool, 5 May, 1928. *m* Kathleen Preston-Goddard, art gallery owner (Who's Who World of Women). *Educ:* privately. *Studied:* Croydon School of Art (1948-50). *Exhib:* foremost London galleries; one-man shows Beaux Arts, Leicester, Redfern, Royal Academy. *Work in collections:* Britain, U.S.A., Europe, Australia, Japan and S.Africa. *Commissions:* 1997:"Skaters Winter Fantasy" large oil, The Children's Society, London. Painting for children's charities. *Clubs:* Chelsea Arts Trust, London. *Signs work:* "PRESTON-GODDARD." *Address:* Studio Hse., 46 Selborne Rd., Croydon CR0 5JQ.

**PRETSELL, Peter,** D.A. (Edin.); artist in printmaking, painting; lecturer in printmaking, Nene College, Northampton; lecturer, Edinburgh College of Art (1985); *b* Edinburgh, 1942. *m* Philomena Pretsell. three *s*. *Educ:* George Heriots School, Edinburgh. *Studied:* Edinburgh College of Art (1960-65). *Exhib:* New 57 Gallery, Printmakers Workshop, S.S.A. and Fruitmarket Gallery (Edinburgh), Northampton, Birmingham, Newcastle, Kettering, Bedford, Thumb Gallery, London, Bradford Print Biennale Prizewinner. *Work in collections:* V. & A., Scottish Arts Council, Edinburgh Corp., Hull, Northampton A.G. *Signs work:* "Pretsell." *Address:* c/o Edinburgh College of Art, Edinburgh.

**PRICE, E. Jessop,** H.R.S.W.A. (1987), S.W.A. (1951), Mem. of Council (1956); painter in oils; *b* Ashby-de-la-Zouch. *m* Rev. A. Jessop Price. four *s*. *Educ:* Ashby and Versailles. *Studied:* St. Ives School of Art (Leonard Fuller), St. Martin's School of Art (Archibald Zeigler), Heatherley's (Iain Macnab). *Exhib:* one-man show at R.W.S. Gallery (1949), S.W.A., R.O.I., Bradford Art Gallery, City of London Guildhall, etc.; awarded Freedom of the Worshipful Company of Painter Stainers in 1957. *Work in collections:* St. Paul's Cathedral, Chase National Bank, N.Y., Newton Chambers, etc. *Publications:* work repro.: The Soho Gallery, Daily Telegraph, etc. *Signs work:* "E. Jessop Price." *Address:* Sefton, Stade St., Hythe, Kent CT21 6DY.

**PRICE, Trevor,** A.R.E., B.A.Hons.; artist/printmaker; *b* Cornwall, 18 July, 1966. *Educ:* Truro School, Cornwall. *Studied:* Falmouth School of Art (1984-85), Winchester School of Art (1985-88). *Exhib:* widely throughout Europe including R.A. Summer Show, Christie's Contemporary Arts. *Publications:* art work used for Encyclopedia of Printmaking Techniques (Headline Publication 1993). *Signs work:* "Trevor Price." *Address:* 53 Back Road East, St. Ives, Cornwall TR26 1NW.

**PRIESTNER, Stephen Miles,** artist in acrylic paint, collages; sign-writer, life-guard, shop assistant; *b* Altrincham, Ches., 1 May, 1954. *m* Annabel, née Warburton. *Educ:* Dodoma School, Tanzania (1959-61), Ellesmere College,

Salop. (1967-70), Blackpool College of Art (1971-72), Manchester Polytechnic (1972-74). *Studied:* École des Beaux Arts, Paris (1978, B. Neiland). *Exhib:* Olympian Arts, London (1993), Salford Museum (1988), Studio 54, New York City, Art Competition Winner (1994). *Work in collections:* Whitworth A.G.; drawings: Ghent Museum, Belgium; M.O.M.A., New York (prints); Musée d'Art Moderne, Paris; paintings in private collections Europe. *Publications:* work repro.: The Artist, Apollo Magazine, New York Post (review) etc. *Clubs:* Chelsea Arts. *Signs work:* "Stephen M. Priestner" or "Stephen Miles." *Address:* c/o 44 Towerhill, Dover, Kent.

**PRITCHARD, Marion Ruth,** S.W.A. (1987), S.O.F.A. (1994); painter and illustrator in oil and water-colour; *b* London, 10 Nov., 1934. *m* Ronald Pritchard. two *s.* one *d. Educ:* Minchenden Grammar School. *Studied:* Hornsey College of Art and Crafts (1951-56, graphic design). *Exhib:* R.A., R.B.A., R.I., R.O.I., S.W.A., S.WL.A., S.G.A., S.B.A., R.S.M., S.O.F.A.; mixed exhbns. at several London galleries. *Publications:* work repro.: greetings cards for Medici, Royle, Bucentaur, Camden Graphics. *Signs work:* "Marion Pritchard." *Address:* 50 Arnos Grove, Southgate, Londn N14 7AR.

**PROCKTOR, Patrick,** R.A., R.W.S., R.E.; painter and etcher; *b* Dublin, 12 Mar., 1936. *m* Kirsten Benson, née Bo-Andersen (decd.). one *s. Studied:* Slade School (1958-62). *Exhib:* since 1963 seventeen one-man shows at Redfern Gallery, London, and other one-man shows abroad. Works represented in numerous public collections. *Publications:* author of One Window in Venice, publ. 1974 (16 water-colour views, published by Galleria Cavallino, Venice); new edition of The Rime of the Ancient Mariner by S. T. Coleridge with twelve etching illustrations, publ. 1976 by Editions Alecto, London; A Chinese Journey, suite of acquatint landscapes of China, publ. 1980 by Editions Alecto; Patrick Procktor, monographs by Patrick Kinmonth publ. by Cavallino 1986; Self portrait, memoir publ. 1993 by Weidenfeld & Nicholson; P.Proctor, monograph by John McEwen, publ. 1997 by Scolar Press. *Clubs:* Garrick. *Address:* 26 Manchester St., London W1.

**PROCTER, (née PALMER), Marjorie,** A.T.D. (1940); artist in water-colour, pencil and wash; art teacher, Ealing School of Art (1943-74); art teacher, Liverpool Inst. for Boys (1941-43); *b* Birmingham, 17 Feb., 1918. *m* Kenneth Procter, painter (1964). *Educ:* Wade Deacon Grammar School, Widnes. *Studied:* Liverpool City School of Art (1935-40). *Exhib:* R.A., R.I., R.B.A., Nat. Soc., United Soc. of Artists, S.M.A., S.W.A., R.I. Summer Salon, Britain in Water-colour. *Signs work:* "Marjorie Procter," either written or in block capitals. *Address:* Spring Cottage, Woonton, Almeley, Herefordshire HR3 6QL.

**PROUD,, Alastair Colm,** artist in oil and water-colour, specialising in wildlife and landscape; *b* Dublin, Rep. of Ireland, 2 Oct., 1954. *m* Jill Paula. one *s.* one *d. Work in collections:* Sultan of Oman. *Publications:* illustrator: Birds of Prey of British Isles; Wildfowl of British Isles and North West Europe.

*Clubs:* S.WL.A. *Address:* Plas Bach, Newchurch, Carmarthen, Carms. SA33 6EJ, S. Wales.

**PROWSE, Alexander Reginald,** P.S., R.M.S.; painter and printmaker in pastel, water-colour and oil; *b* London, 23 June, 1949. *m* Janet Prowse. *Studied:* Harrow School of Art (Christopher Saunders, R.A., Ken Howard, R.A.). *Exhib:* one-man shows: London, Mexico, Venezuela; N.E.A.C., P.S., R.S.M.A., R.P., R.I., R.M.S. *Work in collections:* Royal Academy of Dancing, Hotel de Ville, Paris, General Motors S.A. *Address:* Barge 'Bloom', Little Venice Studio, Blomfield Rd., London W9 2PA.

**PRYSE: see SPENCER PRYSE, Tessa.**

**PULLAN, Margaret Ida Elizabeth,** Paris Salon: Gold Medal (1972), Silver Medal (1967); artist in oil; *b* Saharanpur, U.P., India, 6 Nov., 1907. *Educ:* Highfield, Oxhey Lane, Watford, Herts. *Studied:* privately. *Exhib:* Paris Salon (1957-58, 1963 (hon. mention), 1965-71), R.P., R.B.A., Leicester Galleries, Bournemouth, Bradford, Cartwright Memorial Hall, United Soc. of Artists. *Work in collections:* Rugby A.G. *Signs work:* see appendix. *Address:* Cedars Rest Home, 90 Warwick Park, Tunbridge Wells, Kent TN2 5EN.

**PULLAN, Tessa,** S.Eq.A. (1988), A.R.B.S. (1994); sculptor in wood, clay, stone, bronze; *b* London, 20 Dec., 1953. married. one *s.* one *d. Educ:* Tudor Hall. *Studied:* apprenticeship with John Skeaping, R.A. (1971-74), City & Guilds of London Art School (1974-77, James Butler), R.A. Schools (1977-80, Willi Soukop, R.A.). *Exhib:* Guildhall London, R.A. Summer Shows, Cork St. Fine Arts, Ackermann (London and N.Y.), Bath Contemporary Arts Festival, S.Eq.A., Cleveland Bridge Gallery Bath, Tryon and Moorland Gallery, Gallery Les Hirondelles Geneva, London Contemporary Art Fair, Bruton St. Gallery, etc.; solo shows: Quinton Green Fine Arts, London, John Hunt Gallery, Sussex. *Work in collections:* N.P.G., National Horse Racing Museum, Newmarket, Yale Center for British Art, Clare College, Cambridge, Virginia Museum of Fine Art, Paul Mellon Center for Studies in British Art, Virginia Historical Soc. *Signs work:* "Tessa Pullan" and see appendix. *Address:* Granby House, Kings Lane, Barrowden, Rutland LE15 8EF.

**PULLEE, Edward,** C.B.E. (1967), A.R.C.A. (1929), F.S.A.E. (1945), N.E.A.C. (life mem.); artist in oil and water-colour; retd. Chief Officer, N.C.D.A.D. (1967-74); *b* London, 19 Feb., 1907. *m* Margaret, A.R.C.A., N.E.A.C. one *s. Educ:* St. Martin's School, Dover. *Studied:* Dover School of Art (1922-26), R.C.A. (1926-30, Profs. William Rothenstein, Randolph Schwabe, Malcolm Osbourne). *Exhib:* R.A., N.E.A.C., London and provincial galleries. *Work in collections:* Leeds City A.G., Leicester City A.G. *Signs work:* "Pullee." *Address:* 3 March Sq., The Drive, Summersdale, Chichester, W. Sussex PO19 4AN.

**PULLÉE, Michael Edward,** Des.R.C.A., F.C.S.D., N.E.A.C., F.R.S.A.; artist in oil, designer and educational consultant; former H.M. Inspector of

Schools; *b* London, 8 Sept., 1936. *m* Sheila Mary Threadgill. two *d. Educ:* Bootham School, York. *Studied:* Leeds College of Art, R.C.A. *Exhib:* New English Annual, Pattersons, R.A. Summer Exhbn., Bankside. *Clubs:* N.E.A.C. *Signs work:* "Michael E. Pullée." *Address:* White Gables, 48 Wray Common Rd., Reigate, Surrey RH2 0NB.

**PURNELL, John,** B.A.Hons., M.A., F.B.P.A., A.R.P.S., M.Ph.E.; painter, printmaker, photographer; photography tutor, University researcher; *b* Birmingham, 8 Jan., 1954. *Studied:* Bournville College of Art; Cardiff Inst. of Higher Education University of Wales Institute, Cardiff. *Clubs:* Mensa. *Signs work:* "John Purnell" and see appendix. *Address:* Flat 3, 4 West Luton Place, Adamsdown, Cardiff CF2 1EW.

**PUTMAN, Salliann,** B.A. (Hons.) Fine Art, A.R.W.S.; painter/teacher in oil and water-colour; *b* London, 20 Apr., 1937. *m* Michael. one *s.* one *d. Studied:* West Surrey College of Art and Design, Farnham (1988-93). *Exhib:* one and two-man shows: London, Windsor, Stockbridge; R.A., Mall Galleries, N.E.A.C., R.B.A., R.O.I., R.I., P.S., Bankside Gallery, and at galleries in Bristol, Barnes and U.S.A. *Signs work:* water-colours: "Salliann Putman," oils: "S.P." *Address:* 3 Pinecote Drive, Sunningdale, Berks. SL5 9PS.

**PYE, Patrick,** Mem. of Aosdana and R.H.A.; painter in tempera and oil, stained glass artist, etcher - An artist of the sacred theme; *b* Winchester, 1929. *m* Noirin Kennedy. two *d. Studied:* National College of Art, Dublin (1951-54), Jan van Eyck Akad., Maastricht (1957-58). *Exhib:* many one-man shows, (Jorgensen Fine Art), Dublin, R.H.A. Annual, etc. *Work in collections:* Municipal Gallery Dublin, Crawford Gallery, Cork. *Commissions:* Stations of the Cross, Killerney; Life of Mary, Cork North Cathedral and many others. *Publications:* author: Apples and Angels; The Time Gatherer (on El Greco). *Signs work:* "Patrick Pye." *Address:* Pyerstown, Tallaght, Dublin 24, Ireland.

**PYE, William,** A.R.C.A., F.R.B.S., Hon.F.R.I.B.A.; sculptor, film; *b* 16 July, 1938. *m* Susan. one *s.* two *d. Educ:* Charterhouse. *Studied:* Wimbledon School of Art (1958-61) under Freda Skinner, R.C.A. Sculpture School (1961) under Prof. B. Meadows. *Work in collections:* Arts Council, Museum of Modern Art, N.Y., Contemporary Art Soc., G.L.C., Royal Albert Memorial Museum, Exeter, Graves City A.G., Sheffield, Middlesbrough City A.G., Birmingham City A.G., Szépmúvészeti Muzeum, Budapest, National Museum of Wales, Wakefield A.G. *Commissions:* Slipstream and Jetstream Gatwick Airport; Chalice, Fountain Square, London WC1; Cristos, St. Christopher's Place, London; Derby Cascade. *Signs work:* see appendix. *Address:* 43 Hambalt Rd., Clapham, London SW4 9EQ.

**PYNE, Doris Grace,** A.T.D. (1934), oil painting cert., Slade School; free-lance artist in water-colour, art teacher; *b* Wealdstone, 8 Oct., 1910. *Studied:* Hornsey School of Art (1930-34, Norman Janes, A.R.C.A., R.E., Douglas Percy Bliss, M.A.), Slade School (Randolph Schwabe). *Exhib:* one-man show, Salon des Nations, Paris (1984), Mall Galleries, London (1982); Norwich

(1967, 1969, 1972, 1978), Park Gallery, Chislehurst (1973), Aldeburgh (1974), International Art Centre, London (1975), frequent exhib. R.I., Graphic Artists, Mall Galleries. *Clubs:* F.B.A., Bromley Art Soc. *Signs work:* "PYNE." *Address:* 32 Clarendon Way, Marlings Pk., Chislehurst, Kent BR7 6RF.

**PYTEL, Walenty,** N.D.D. (1961), A.R.B.S.; sculptor in bronze and mild steel; *b* Poland, 10 Feb., 1941. *m* Janet Mary. one *s.* one *d.* *Studied:* Hereford College of Art (1956-61). *Exhib:* Tokyo (1988), Marbella (1985), U.S.A., Germany, France, Jersey, S.WL.A. Mall Galleries (award winner 1988). *Work in collections:* Hereford, Worcester and Stockport; permanent: New Palace Yard Westminster, B'ham International Airport, Beaulieu, Berkeley Hotel London, J.C.B. Uttoxeter, County Hall, Llandrindod Wells. *Commissions:* South Herefordshire District Council 1997 'Landing Ducks'; 'Swans'; 'Leaping Salmon'. Gracemount Developments Ltd. Royal Caribbean Cruiseline; Lloyds Bank Trophy; Lloyds of London; Yamazaki Machinery Ltd. *Publications:* London Art and Antiques Guide (1991), Debrett's Distinguished People of Today (1988-95), Into the New Iron Age (Amina Chatwin 1995). *Signs work:* "WALENTY PYTEL," "W. Pytel" or "W.P." *Address:* Hartleton, Bromsash, Ross-on-Wye HR9 7SB.

# Q

**QUANTRILL, David James,** artist in oil, pastel, water-colour; *b* Lowestoft, 11 July, 1938. *m* Angela. one *s.* one *d.* *Studied:* Lowestoft College (part-time). *Exhib:* C.C.A. Gallery Cambridge, Barnes Gallery London, John Russell Gallery Ipswich, Frederick Gallery Norfolk, P.S. since 1985, First Britains Painters (1988), Eastern Open (1985, 1988, 1990, 1993), Work on tour (1988). *Work in collections:* Norwich Castle. *Signs work:* "Quantrill." *Address:* 18 Carlton Sq., Lowestoft, Suffolk NR33 8JL.

**QUINN, Mary P. (née McLAUGHGLIN),** Hons. sculpture (1986); sculptor in bronze portrait busts and statues; *b* Co. Down, N.I., 26 May, 1943. three *d.* *Educ:* St. Dominic's High School, Belfast. *Studied:* Richmond Adult College (1982-89). *Exhib:* many group shows since 1985. *Work in collections:* Archbishop Cranmer (bronze bust) at St. James Garlickhythe, London EC4; John Wesley (bronze bust) editions at Wesley's Chapel, City Rd., London, Leeds, Peterborough, Methodist museums in N. Carolina, New Jersey, Nashville, Georgia, Texas, California and Germany; George Whitefield in Billy Graham's Seminary in Boston and Savannah, Georgia; Cardinal John Henry Newman (bust) in St. Mary's College, Twickenham and Oratory School, Reading; Mother Teresa (bust) in Westminster Cathedral, London; Sir Edward Appleton (bust) in Bradford University; Our Lady of Walsingham (statue) in St. Mary's Church, Teddington; Lord Learie Constantine (bust) at Willesden Green, London; private collections in Ireland and England. *Commissions:* life. size statue of John Wesley for Virginia Wesleyan College, Virginia, U.S.A.

*Clubs:* F.P.S., S.C.A. *Signs work:* "Mary Quinn." *Address:* 1 Exeter Rd., Hanworth, Feltham, Middx. TW13 5PE.

# R

**RACZKO, Julian Henryk,** Dip. Eng. (Warsaw, 1963); artist; *b* Warsaw, 2 Jan., 1936. *m* Malena Raczko, architect. two *d*. *Educ:* Warsaw Technical University. *Studied:* voluntary basis at Warsaw Academy of Fine Art (1963-65, Prof. Alexander Kobzdej). *Exhib:* one-man shows: Poland, Denmark, Norway, Sweden, France, Germany, C.K. Norwid art critics award 1980. *Work in collections:* National Museums of Warsaw, Wroclaw, Poznan, Arts Museum Lodz, galleries of Chelm, Bydogoszcz, National Gallery of Arts, Washington, Arts Museum Norrköping, Museum of Modern Art, Hünfeld, Van Reekum Museum of Apeldoorn, Fyns Kunstmuseum, Odense. *Signs work:* "Julian H. Raczko." *Address:* J. Bruna 34 m 35, 02-594 Warsaw, Poland.

**RAE, Fiona,** B.A. Fine Art Goldsmiths' (1987); artist in oil and acrylic on canvas; *b* Hong Kong, 10 Oct., 1963. *Studied:* Croydon College of Art (1983-84), Goldsmiths' College, London (1984-87). *Exhib:* solo shows: 1997: Saatchi Gallery, London (with Gary Hume), The British School at Rome; 1996: Contemporary Fine Arts, Berlin; 1995; Waddington Galleries, London; 1994: John Good Gallery, N.Y., Galerie Nathalie Obadia, Paris; 1993-94: Inst. of Contemporary Arts, London; 1992: Kunsthalle Basel, Basel; 1991: Waddington Galleries, London; 1990: Third Eye Centre, Glasgow, Pierre Bernard Gallery, Nice. *Work in collections:* includes Tate Gallery, London; Arts Council; Walker A.G., Liverpool; Musée Départemental de Rochechouart, Haute-Vienne; Hamburger Bahnhof, Berlin; Sintra Museum of Modrn Art, Portugal. *Publications:* work repro: numerous exhbn. catalogues, articles and reviews. *Address:* c/o Waddington Galleries, 11 Cork St., London W1X 2LT.

**RAE, John,** works in mixed media, often in combination with PVA, and also makes screen and mono prints and etchings, and draws in conté and pencil. Subjects include landscape, plants and trees, buildings, people, and life paintings. Formerly a lecturer in Architecture at University College London, the Architectural Association, and at Hornsey College of Art. He has travelled and painted in Australasia, Africa, and the New World; *b* Exeter, 1931. *Exhib:* Australian and British galleries. *Publications:* Sketch Book of the World. *Signs work:* "John Rae." *Address:* 14 Orchard St., St. Albans, Herts. AL3 4HL.

**RAEBURN, Kenneth Alexander,** D.A.(Edin.) (1966); Post Grad. Scholarship (1966-67); sculptor in bronze, resins and wood, of free-standing figures, portraits and relief murals; principal teacher of art, Comprehensive School; *b* Haddington, E. Lothian, 9 June, 1942. *m* Helen Raeburn. one *s*. one *d*. *Educ:* Trinity Academy, Edinburgh. *Studied:* School of Sculpture, Edinburgh College of Art under Eric Schilsky. *Exhib:* R.S.A., S.S.A., various group exhbns. in Scotland, Salon des Nations Exhbn., Paris (1983); one-man show, Metropolis Galerie d'Art, Geneva (1985). *Work in collections:* commissioned panel depicting Baptism of Christ by St. John, in St. John the Baptist Primary School, W. Lothian (awarded Saltire Society Commendation, 1972); commissioned woodcarving of St. Columba in St. Columba's Church, Boghall, West Lothian; commissioned life-sized seal, with her pup, (concrete), South Queensferry; work in numerous private collections in U.K. *Signs work:* "Raeburn." *Address:* 46 Belsyde Ct., Linlithgow, W. Lothian EH49 7RW.

**RAINE, Sarah Lamar (Woodie),** portrait artist, illustrator, graphic designer in chalk, conté, charcoal, pastel, pencil; Publicity Designer, Methuen General Books; *b* Atlanta, Georgia, U.S.A., 30 June, 1940. *Studied:* The Lovett School, Atlanta (Jan Savage), University of Georgia (Lamar Dodd), Stratford College, Va. (David Clarke), Atlantic College of Art (Mr. Grecco). *Exhib:* Sesame Club (1982), Saville Club (1983). *Clubs:* Friend of Federation of British Artist. *Signs work:* see appendix. *Address:* 61 Stanlake Rd., London W12.

**RAMSDEN, Eric,** N.D.D. (1950), A.R.E. (1960), Hon. R.E. (1985), Fellow, Society of Wood Engravers; artist in gouache, oil, wood engraving; *b* Cheshire, 22 June, 1927. *m* Anna Maria. one *s. Studied:* Liverpool College of Art (1943-45, 1948-50). Studio Manager and Chief Designer, Portals Ltd., papermakers to The Bank of England (retd. 1992). *Exhib:* R.A., R.W.S. Galleries, South London Gallery, provincial galleries, Liverpool Walker Art Gallery. *Work in collections:* in the U.K. and abroad. *Signs work:* "Eric Ramsden." *Address:* The Priory, Freefolk, Whitchurch, Hants. RG28 7NL.

**RANDALL, Edward Mark,** graphic designer, painter in oil, pastel, watercolour; *b* Coventry, 24 Feb., 1921. *m* Marjory. two *s.* one *d. Educ:* Coventry Technical College. *Studied:* Coventry Art School, Hornsey and Central Schools. *Work in collections:* Marks and Spencer, Plessey Co. private collection, R.C.M. Printing Group. *Signs work:* "Mark Randall." *Address:* B7 Argyll House, Seaforth Rd., Westcliff-on-Sea, Essex SS0 7SH.

**RANDLE, Susan Ann,** Dip.H.E.; painter, muralist and graphic artist in oil, water-colour, gouache, pen and ink; *b* Portsmouth, 16 June, 1936. *m* Dave Randle, writer. one *s.* one *d. Educ:* Dominican Convent, Harare, Zimbabwe. *Studied:* Dartington College of Art, Totnes (1978-80, Chris Crickmay, John Gridley). *Exhib:* Carlos Gallery, London, Arnolfini, Bristol; one-man show: Bruyas Gallery, Torquay. *Signs work:* "Sue Randle." *Address:* 2a Granville Rd., Sidcup, Kent DA14 4BN.

**RANK-BROADLEY, Ian,** H.D.F.A. (Lond.) (1976), Boise scholar (1976), F.S.N.A.D. (1990), F.R.B.S. (1994), F.R.S.A. (1995); sculptor and medallist in bronze; *b* Walton-on-Thames, 4 Sept., 1952. *m* Hazel Rank. one *s.* one *d. Studied:* Epsom School of Art (1970-74, Bruce McLean), Slade School of Fine Art (1974-76, Reg Butler). *Exhib:* Coombs Contemporary, Adonis Art. *Work in collections:* B.M., University of Surrey, Fitzwilliam Museum, Cambridge, States Museum, Berlin, Rijksmuseum, Leiden, N.P.G. London, Royal Swedish Coin Cabinet, Royal Mint, Goldsmiths' Hall, London, H.M. The Queen Mother.

Freeman of the Goldsmiths' Company; Granted Freedom of City of London (1996). *Signs work:* see appendix. *Address:* Stanfields, Kingscourt La., Rodborough, Stroud, Glos. GL5 3QR.

**RANKIN, Stella,** painter in oil; *b* London, 1915. *m* A. C. Rankin. one *d.* *Educ:* St. John's Priory, Banbury. *Studied:* St. Martin's, London (1956-58), Goldsmiths' College of Art (1958-61, Kenneth Martin). *Exhib:* Royal Festival Hall, Barbican, (F.P.S.) Guardian, (Art for Sale), Whiteley's, Christie's (Imperial Cancer Research) London, The London Group, Artists International, Studio Club, W1, Market Cross Gallery, Bury St. Edmunds, Galerie Internationale, New York, Library, U.S.A.A.F., Lakenheath, Inst. of Education; one-man shows: Oriel Gallery, Aberystwyth, Halesworth Gallery, Suffolk, Mercury Gallery, Colchester, Loggia Gallery Buckingham Gate, SW!, Chappel Gallery, Essex Cinema Gallery, Aldburgh. *Work in collections:* Chelmsford Museum; and private collections. *Signs work:* "Stella Rankin." *Address:* 106 High St., Kelvedon, Colchester CO5 9AA.

**RASMUSSEN, Roy,** F.F.P.S. (1961); sculptor in hand beaten and welded aluminium; Director, Loggia Gallery, London (1984 to present); Co-Director, Woodstock Gallery, London (1958-67);*b* London, 29 Apr., 1919 . *Exhib:* British Council, Berlin (1961); Réalités Nouvelles, Paris (1966); John Whibley Gallery, Cork St., London (1968-77); F.P.S. exhbns. (1957-95); and many London galleries, including one-man shows. *Work in collections:* Towner Gallery and Museum, Eastbourne, Paris, Berlin and U.S.A. *Publications:* The Free Painters and Sculptors 1952-1992 (author). *Signs work:* "RASMUSSEN." *Address:* 123 Canterbury Rd., N. Harrow, Middx. HA1 4PA.

**RAVERA, John,** P.P.R.B.S., F.R.S.A.; President, R.B.S. (1988-90); sculptor in clay; *b* Surrey, 27 Feb., 1941. *m* Daphne. one *s.* *Studied:* Camberwell School of Art (1954-62). *Exhib:* R.A. (1975, 1976), Alwin Gallery (1977), Woodlands (1977), Bexleyheath (1985), Haywards Heath (1985), Johannesburg S.A. (1995), Chris Beatles Gallery (1996). *Commissions:* Major commissions: Academy of Arts Hong Kong (1982), Morgan's Walk London (1983), London Dockland Development, bronze bust (1986), Bayswater London, bronze group of children (1987), Barbican London, bronze group dolphins (1989), Elstree London, stainless steel abstract (1989), Tokyo (1994), Maidenhead (1996), Reading (1996). *Signs work:* "John E. Ravera." *Address:* Studio, 82 Latham Rd., Bexleyheath, Kent DAG 7NQ.

**RAWLINS, Janet,** N.D.D. (Illustration), A.T.D.; book illustration, fabric collage, gouache, water-colour; *b* Horsforth, Leeds, 3 May, 1931. *m* John G. Leyland, F.C.A. one *s.* *Educ:* Gt. Moreton Hall, Ches. *Studied:* Leeds College of Art. *Exhib:* R.A., northern galleries. *Work in collections:* Bradford, Harrogate and Batley Art Galleries, Leeds, Huddersfield, West Riding, Leicester and Essex Education Committees, Leeds Permanent Building Society, I.W.S., N.C.B., I.C.I. *Publications:* children's books by William Mayne and Jane Gardam; compiled and illustrated A Dales Countryside

Cookbook (1993). *Signs work:* "Janet Rawlins." *Address:* West End House, Askrigg, Wensleydale, N. Yorks. DL8 3HN.

**RAY:** see HOWARD-JONES, Ray.

**RAY, Karen,** painter in oil, water-colour, pencil, coloured pencil, lecturer; *b* Queensland, Australia, 8 Dec., 1931. *m* Stuart Ray (decd.). three *s. Studied:* Walthamstow School of Art (Stuart Ray, John Tichell, Fred Cuming); R.A. Schools (Peter Greenham). *Exhib:* many times in the R.A. Summer Exhbn. *Signs work:* "K. Ray." *Address:* 91 Mountview Rd., London N4 4JA.

**RAYMENT, Brenda,** A.R.M.S. (1991); artist in oil on ivorine; *b* Paddock Wood, Kent, 5 May, 1951. *m* Laurence Rayment. one *s.* one *d. Educ:* Kidbrooke School. *Studied:* Bexley A.E.C. (1980-90, Barry Shiraishi, R.M.S.). *Exhib:* S.W.A., R.M.S. *Address:* Heather Cottage, 5 Gwel-an-Garrek, Mullion. Cornwall TR12 7RW.

**RAYNER, Desmond,** L.G.S.M., F.R.S.A.; self-taught artist in gouache, charcoal, pencil, oil; literary agent, writer, actor; *b* London, 31 Oct., 1928. *m* Claire Rayner. two *s.* one *d. Educ:* theatre: Guildhall School of Music and Drama. *Exhib:* Heals, London; Embankment Gallery, Tattershall Castle, London; Grays, Mayfair; Talent Store, Belgravia; October Gallery, U.S.A.; Mall Galleries, London; Seven Dials Gallery, London; Barbican Centre, London; Wylma Wayne Fine Art, London; Building Centre, London, etc. *Work in collections:* U.S.A., Canada, Australia, U.K. *Publications:* The Dawlish Season, The Husband. *Signs work:* "RAYNER." *Address:* Holly Wood House, Roxborough Ave., Harrow-on-the-Hill, Middx. HA1 3BU.

**RAYNOR, Trevor Samuel,** Mem. Associé, Société des Artistes Français (1977); textile designer, artist in oil and water-colour and floral subjects in gouache; *b* Oldham, 13 May, 1929. *m* Margaret Joyce Marwood. one *s. Educ:* Werneth Council School. *Studied:* Oldham School of Art (1942-45), Manchester School of Art (1945-49). *Exhib:* Paris Salon (1975, 1976, 1977); one-man shows, Salford City A.G., Swinton Memorial A.G. Work in private collections. *Publications:* work repro.: prints of floral work. *Signs work:* "RAYNOR" or "T.S. RAYNOR." *Address:* 1 Hollin Cres., Greenfield, Oldham OL3 7LW.

**READ, Sue,** R.I. (1985), N.D.D. (1963), A.T.D. (1964); artist in water-colour; *b* Slough, 1941. *m* Robert Read (divorced). three *s. Educ:* Aylesbury Grammar School. *Studied:* High Wycombe School of Art (1959-63), Royal West of England College of Art (1963-64). *Exhib:* Mall Galleries, R.A. Summer Exhbn., Shell House Gallery, Ledbury. *Signs work:* "S.R." *Address:* The Old Surgery, West St., Buckingham MK18 1HP.

**REAL, Jacqueline,** F.F.P.S. (1992); contemporary painter in acrylic, collage and mixed media; *b* Zürich, 5 Oct., 1931. *m* Christopher Butler. one *s.* one *d. Studied:* in Zürich (1975-78), Academy of Modern Art, Masterclass, Salzburg (1979), Painting Course in Meran (1980). *Exhib:* solo and group shows:

Switzerland, London, U.S.A. and Germany. *Work in collections:* Switzerland, England, U.S.A., Germany, including Mark Rich Switzerland, Union Bank of Switzerland Zürich and London, Zürich Insurance, Credit Swiss Bank Zürich, British Government, Johnson & Johnson, Tokai Bank. *Publications:* New Visions, St. Ives Painters. Represented by: International Art Consultants, London, Wills Lane Gallery, St. Ives, and Contemporary Art Gallery, Bonstetten (Zurich), New Millenium Gallery, St. Ives, Artescona, Ascona. *Clubs:* F.P.S., Soc. of Swiss Painters, Sculptors and Architects, Eastbourne Group of Artists. *Signs work:* "J. Real." *Address:* 7 Bath Court, Kings Esplanade, Hove BN3 2WP.

**REDDICK, Peter,** D.F.A. (Slade, 1951), R.E. Hon. Retd., R.W.A.; printmaker and wood-engraver, freelance illustrator; *b* Essex, 1924. *Studied:* Slade School of Fine Art (1948-51); Gregynog Arts Fellow (1970-80). Chairman, Bristol Printmakers Workshop. *Signs work:* "Peter Reddick." *Address:* 18 Hartington Park, Bristol BS6 7ES.

**REDFERN, June,** D.A. (1972); prizewinner, Scottish Young Contemporaries; Artist in Residence, National Gallery (1985); painter in oil and water-colour; *b* St. Andrews, Fife, 16 June, 1951. *Educ:* Dunfermline High School, Fife. *Studied:* Edinburgh College of Art (1968-73, Robin Philipson, David Michie, Elizabeth Blackadder, John Houston). *Exhib:* many throughout Britain and U.S.A. including National Gallery, London (1985). *Work in collections:* S.N.G.M.A., National Gallery London, B.B.C. Television, Robert Fleming plc, Arthur Andersen, Texaco, Hiscox Holdings. *Signs work:* "June Redfern" on reverse of oils only. *Address:* 12 Lawley St., London E5 0RJ.

**REDGRAVE-RUST, Graham,** artist (muralist, illustrator and botanical painter) in water-colour and water-based paints;; *b* Hatfield, 17 Feb., 1942. *m* Inez Andrade Paes, artist. *Educ:* St. Dominics School. *Studied:* Regent St. Polytechnic (1958-60, Sir Lawrence Gowing, and Norman Blamey, R.A.), Central School of Arts and Crafts (1960-61), National Academy of Art, N.Y. (1962). *Exhib:* First exhib. R.A. (1965), over 20 one-man exhbns. worldwide since 1964. *Commissions:* Private mural commissions in various country houses in England. Largest work, the South staircase, Ragley Hall, Warwickshire for the Marquess of Hertford (1969-83). Public mural commission, The Theatre, Chipping Norton, Oxon. (1996). *Publications:* The Painted House (1988), Decorative Designs (1996); illustrated: The Story of the Maison Moet & Chandon by Patrick Forbes (1969), Recipes from a Chateau in Champagne by Robin McDouall and Sheila Bush (1982), The Secret Garden by Frances Hodgson Burnett (1986), A Little Princess by J.H.B. (1989), Little Lord Fauntleroy by J.H.B. (1993), Some Flowers by Vita Sackville West (1993), The Fine Art of Dining (1995). Artist in Residence, Woodberry Forest School, Virginia (1967-68). *Clubs:* Brooks. *Signs work:* "GRAHAM RUST" or "G.R. Rust." *Address:* Studio 7, 49 Roland Gdns., South Kensington, London SW7 3PG.

**REDINGTON, Simon,** B.A. (Fine Art), Postgrad.Dip. in Art Therapy, Cert. of Advanced Printmaking; artist/printmaker in etching, woodcuts, letterpress, painting, mixed media; *b* London, 28 Sept., 1958. *Educ:* Pimlico School. *Studied:* Goldsmiths' College, Hertfordshire College of Art, Central St. Martin's College of Art. *Exhib:* N.P.G., R.A. Summer Show, Slaughterhouse Gallery, Southbank Picture Show, Royal Festival Hall, Bankside Gallery. *Work in collections:* V. & A., Theatre Museum, Ashmolean Museum, N.Y. Public Library, Harvard University, Yale Center for British Art, Museum of London, Newberry Library, Chicago. *Commissions:* Peter O'Toole as Jeffery Bernard, Shaftesbury Theatre, London. *Publications:* "Hangman" Edn. 20-boxed set of 20 prints (woodcut/letterpress) Kamikaze Press. *Clubs:* R.E. *Signs work:* "S. Redington." *Address:* 149 Archway Rd., London N6 5BL.

**REDPATH, Barbara,** D.A. (Edin.); works in oils and water-colour; *b* London 1924. *Educ:* Streatham. *Studied:* Edinburgh College of Art under W. G. Gillies, P.R.S.W. *Exhib:* R.S.A., S.S.A., S.S.W.A., R.G.I., Edinburgh, Glasgow, London, Cannes, Paris. *Work in collections:* Dept. of Fine Art, University of Glasgow, University of Strathclyde. *Signs work:* "Babs Redpath." *Address:* 32 Glasgow St., Glasgow, G12.

**REDVERS, John Stephen,** (formerly PIGGINS, John Redvers Stephen, changed 1979), Slade Dip. (1948), P.S. (1984); portrait painter in pastel, oil; *b* Birmingham, 18 July, 1928. *m* Mary Pennel. one *s.* two *d. Educ:* Solihull School, Warwickshire. *Studied:* Slade School of Art (1945-48, Prof. Randolph Schwabe), Ruskin School of Art, Oxford (1950, Prof. Albert Rutherston). *Exhib:* R.P., P.S., Hopetoun House, W. Lothian (1977); one-man show, Chakrabongse Palace, Bangkok (1962). *Signs work:* "JOHN REDVERS" or "REDVERS" ("J.R.S. Piggins" or "John Piggins" pre 1979). *Address:* Tweenhills, Hartpury, Gloucester GL19 3BG.

**REES, Darren,** B.Sc. (Hons.) (1983), S.WL.A. (1985); self-taught artist in water-colour of natural history particularly birds; *b* Andover, Hants., 15 Mar., 1961. *m* Gwynneth Jane Rees (Kenny). one *s. Educ:* Southampton University. *Exhib:* S.WL.A., Artists for Nature Foundation, Holland, Sweden, Poland, U.S.A. *Work in collections:* Lloyds, Les Ecrins National Park, Leigh Yawkey Museum Wisconsin, Stirling Council. *Commissions:* Awards: B.B.C., R.S.P.B., Lloyds. *Publications:* Bird Impressions, Portrait of Wildlife on a Hill Farm, Birds by Character. Awards: R.S.P.B. Fine Art Award, Natural World Award, Young European Bird Artist Award. *Signs work:* "Darren Rees" or "DR" *Address:* New East Frew, Thornhill, Stirling FK8 3QX.

**REES-DAVIES, Kay,** A.L.C.M. (1976), S.B.A. (1994), R.H.S. Silver Grenfell Medal (1992); R.H.S. Silver-Gilt Grenfell Medal (1993); R.H.S. Gold Medal (1996); Cert. of Botanical Merit, S.B.A. (1994); freelance botanical artist in water-colour; *b* Brighton, 17 June, 1936. *m* John Rees-Davies. one *s.* one *d. Educ:* Bretton Hall College (1954-56), attended courses of Botanical Art, Adult Study Centre, Gwynedd (1988-89, Margaret Stevens). *Exhib:* several

# WHO'S WHO IN ART

solo and joint exhbns. in N. Wales; S.B.A., London; R.H.S. *Work in collections:* R.H.S. Lindley Library; Hunt Inst. for Botanical Documentation, Carnegie Mellon University, Pittsburgh U.S.A.; Library, R.B.G., Kew. *Publications:* illustrated 'Plantas Endémicas e Avores Indigenas de Cabo Verde (1995). *Address:* 6 Balmoral, The Promenade, Llanfairfechan, Conwy LL33 0BU.

**REEVE, Marion José,** N.D.D. (1953), M.F.P.S. (1968); landscape painter in acrylic and gouache; retd. civil servant, Building Research Establishment; life mem. International Assoc. of Art; *b* Watford, 26 Sept., 1926. *m* Albert Edward Butcher (decd.). *Educ:* St. Joan of Arc Convent, Rickmansworth. *Studied:* Watford College of Technology, School of Art (1947-53) under Alexander Sutherland, M.A. *Exhib:* one-man show: Loggia Gallery (1974), Young Contemporaries (1954), F.P.S. Annual and Travelling exhbns. at Kings Lynn Festival, South of France, etc. *Work in collections:* St. Michael and All Angels Church, Watford (Stations of the Cross), also design for Christ in Majesty. *Clubs:* Watford and Bushey Art Soc. *Signs work:* "M. Reeve" and date. *Address:* 10 Kelmscott Cres., Watford, Herts. WD1 8NG.

**REEVES, Philip Thomas Langford,** A.R.C.A. (1954), R.E. (1963), R.S.W. (1959), A.R.S.A. (1971), R.S.A. (1976), R.G.I. (1981); painter-etcher; *b* Cheltenham, 7 July, 1931. *m* Christine MacLaren (decd.). one *d. Educ:* Naunton Park Senior Secondary School, Cheltenham. *Studied:* Cheltenham School of Art (1945-49), Royal College of Art (1951-54). *Work in collections:* Arts Council of Gt. Britain, V. & A., Contemporary Art Soc., Gallery of Modern Art, Edinburgh, Glasgow A.G., Glasgow University Print Collection, Aberdeen A.G., Paisley A.G., Milngavie A.G., Dundee A.G., Edinburgh University, Stirling University, Dept. of the Environment. *Signs work:* "Philip Reeves." *Address:* 13 Hamilton Drive, Glasgow G12 8DN.

**REGO, Paula,** F.R.C.A.; painter in various mediums; *b* Lisbon, Portugal, 26 Jan., 1935. *m* Victor Willing (decd.). one *s.* two *d. Educ:* St. Julian's, Portugal. *Studied:* Slade School of Fine Art. *Work in collections:* Gulbenkian Foundation, Lisbon; National Gallery, London; Tate Gallery, London; Saatchi Collection, London. *Publications:* Paula Rego by John McEwen (Phaidon Press), Peter Pan (Folio Soc.), Nursery Rhymes (Thames & Hudson). *Address:* c/o Marlborough Fine Art, 6 Albemarle St., London W1X 4BY.

**REID, Sir Norman Robert,** Kt. (1970), D.A. (Edin., 1937), D.Litt., F.M.A., F.I.I.C., joined Tate Gallery, 1946; appointed Director, 1964; Chairman, British Council Fine Arts Committee; Fellow and Vice-Chairman, International Institute for Conservation of Historic and Artistic Works; Member, British National Cttee. of I.C.O.M.; Mem. Culture Adv. Cttee.; President, Council of the Rome Centre; *b* London, 27 Dec., 1915. *m* Jean Bertram. one *s.* one *d. Educ:* Wilson's Grammar School. *Studied:* Goldsmiths' College, Edinburgh College of Art (1933-38) and Edinburgh University. *Work in collections:* paintings in Tate Gallery, S.N.G.M.A. and the Government Art Collection. *Clubs:* Arts.

*Signs work:* "Reid." *Address:* 50 Brabourne Rise, Beckenham BR3 6SH.

**REILLY-DEAS,Anne,** self-taught artist in oil, water-colour, pastel, mixed media; writer, accounting executive;business studies, qualified for "Mensa" genius score; *b* Mullingar, 28 Nov., 1950. *m* Arthur Deas, scientist (divorced). *Exhib:* Tullynally Castle, R.H.A., Westmeath County Library, Alliance Francaise, etc. Work in private collections at home and abroad. *Publications:* work repro.: catalogues, articles, exhbns. *Signs work:* "Anne Deas", "Reilly-Deas." *Address:* "Greenville", Dublin Rd., Castlepollard, Co. Westmeath, Ireland.

**REITER, Laura,** B.A. (Hons.) (1986), M.A. (1989), R.E. (1989); painter in oil, acrylic and water-colour, printmaker mainly in silkscreen/linocut; teacher/lecturer; *b* London, 25 Aug., 1950. three *d. Educ:* Brondesbury and Kilburn High School. *Studied:* Kingston School of Art (1983-86), Wimbledon School of Art (1986-89). *Exhib:* Bankside Gallery, Barbican, London, Manchester Royal Exchange Theatre Gallery, Brunel University Gallery. *Signs work:* "Laura Reiter." *Address:* 52 Gatehill Rd., Northwood, Middx. HA6 3QP.

**RELFE, Elizabeth Anne Harvey (Liz),** S.W.A. (1993), F.E.T.C. (1980); painter in water-colour and pastel, teacher; lecturer in drawing, water-colour and mixed media: Surrey Adult and Continuing Educ. Service; *b* Harrow, Middx., 21 Dec., 1943. *m* John Relfe (divorced). two *d. Educ:* Paddington and Maida Vale High School for Girls. *Studied:* with John Kingsley Sutton (1972-75), Edward Wesson (1977-82). *Exhib:* S.W.A., Britain's Painters, numerous mixed and solo shows in London and South East. *Work in collections:* Surrey Heath Museum. *Publications:* four teaching videos. *Signs work:* "Liz Relfe" or "L.R." *Address:* 12 Riverside Ave., Lightwater, Surrey GU18 5RU.

**REMFRY, David,** R.W.S.; painter, Mercury Gallery, London; oil, water-colour; *b* Sussex, 30 July, 1942. *Studied:* Hull College of Art (1959-64). *Exhib:* solo shows: Mercury, London (1978/80/82/84/86/88/90/92/94/97), Edinburgh (1983), New Grafton Gallery (1973), Editions Graphiques (1974), Old Fire Engine House, Ely (1975/77/79/81/83/86/90/92/94), Ferens A.G., Hull (1975), New Art Centre, Folkestone (1976), Ankrum Gallery, Los Angeles (1980/81/83/85/87), Bohun Gallery, Henley (1978/81/83/85/87/89/91/93/96), Galerie de Beerenburght, Holland (1979/80/83/86), Middlesbrough A.G. (1981), Zack Shuster Gallery, Florida (1986/88/90), Margaret Lipworth Fine Art, Florida (1992/93/97), N.P.G. (1992), Portal Gallery, Bremen, Germany (1993/95), Tatistcheff Gallery, N.Y. (1996). *Work in collections:* N.P.G., V. & A., Middlesbrough A.G., Minneapolis Museum of Art, U.S.A., Swarthmore College, Pennsylvania, U.S.A., Museo Rayo, Colombia, South America, Boca Raton Museum of Art, Florida, U.S.A., Royal Collection, England. *Clubs:* Chelsea Arts, Groucho, Colony. *Signs work:* "David Remfry." *Address:* 19 Palace Gate, London W8 5LS.

**REMINGTON, Mary,** A.R.C.A. (Lond., 1933), N.E.A.C. (1954), R.O.I. (1962); painter in oil; *b* Reigate, Surrey, 1910. *Educ:* privately. *Studied:* Redhill

School of Art; awarded scholarship to Royal College of Art (1930) under Sir William Rothenstein; later at Académie de la Grande Chaumière, Paris. *Exhib:* R.A., N.E.A.C., R.O.I., R.B.A., Arts Council and principal provincial galleries. *Work in collections:* Grundy Gallery, Blackpool; Brighton Municipal Gallery; Kensington Public Library; Tower Hamlets Public Library; private collections: Italy, Germany, Belgium, Persia, Switzerland, Canada and Gt. Britain. *Signs work:* "Mary Remington." *Address:* White Post Studio, 13 Stanley Rd., Sutton, Surrey SM2 6TB.

**RENNIE, Neil,** M.C. (1945), B.Sc.(Econ.), F.F.P.S. (1988); expressionist artist in pastel, water-colour, acrylic and collage; Treasurer, F.P.S.; *b* Wandsworth, London of Scottish lineage, 25 Apr., 1921. *Educ:* Rutlish, Merton Park and London School of Economics. *Studied:* privately since 1980 with Elyn Carleton, founder of Creators. *Exhib:* regularly at the Loggia Gallery, 15 Buckingham Gate, London SW1E 6LB. *Work in collections:* Australia, England and France. *Signs work:* "Neil Rennie," "N.R.R." or "N.R." *Address:* Flat E, 10 King's Rd., London SW19 8QN.

**RENTON, Joan,** D.A., R.S.W.; painter and teacher in oil, water-colour and mixed media; *b* 1935. *m* R. S. Renton, D.A. two *s.* one *d. Educ:* Dumfries Academy and Hawick High School. *Studied:* Edinburgh College of Art, Post.Dip. Travelling Scholarship. *Work in collections:* H.R.H. the Duke of Edinburgh, Yorkshire Educ. Dept., Scottish Hospitals, Lothian Region Collection, Royal College of Physicians, Paintings in Hospitals and Jean Watson Trust; private collections in Europe, U.K., U.S.A. and N.Z. *Signs work:* "Joan Renton." *Address:* Holmcroft, 4 Tweeddale Ave., Gifford, E. Lothian EH41 4QN.

**REYNOLDS, Daphne,** Chairman, Women's International Art Club (1964-67); Fellow, Printmaker's Council (1973); Founder, Gainsborough's House Printworkshop (Chairman 1978-79); painter in oil, gouache, and engraver in mezzotint; *b* Huddersfield, 12 Jan., 1918. *m* Graham Reynolds (q.v.). *Educ:* Wentworth School, Huddersfield. *Studied:* Huddersfield School of Art (1934-36). *Exhib:* Galerie Creuze, Paris (1959), Drian Galleries (1961, 1964), City of Oldham A.G. (1969, 1975), Angela Flowers (1975), Gainsborough's House, Sudbury, Suffolk (1976, 1989), Ipswich City A.G. (1977), Bill Thomson, Albany Gallery, London (1991, 1993,), Haylett Gallery, Colchester (1995), Chappel Gallery, Essex, (1996), etc. *Work in collections:* Arts Council, V. & A., B.M., D.O.E., Bibliotheque Nationale, Paris, I.C.I., National Galleries in Australia and N.Z., Minneapolis Inst. of Fine Art, New Orleans Museum, Library of Congress, Washington D.C., etc. *Signs work:* "Daphne Reynolds." *Address:* The Old Manse, Bradfield St. George, Bury St. Edmunds, Suffolk IP30 0AZ.

**REYNOLDS, Graham,** O.B.E. (1984), B.A. (1935), F.B.A. (1993); keeper, Dept. of Prints and Drawings, and Paintings, V. & A. (1959-74); *b* 10 Jan, 1914. *m* Daphne Reynolds (q.v.) née Dent. *Educ:* Highgate School and Queens'

College, Cambridge. *Publications:* Twentieth-century Drawings (1946), Nicholas Hilliard and Isaac Oliver (1947) 2nd edition (1971), English Portrait Miniatures (1952) 2nd edition (1988), Painters of the Victorian Scene (1953), The Constable Collection, Victoria and Albert Museum (1960) 2nd edition (1973), Constable, the Natural Painter (1965), Victorian Painting (1966) 2nd edition (1987), Turner (1969), A Concise History of Water-colours (1971), Portrait Miniatures, Wallace Collection (1980), Constable's England (1983), The Later Paintings and Drawings of John Constable (1984), awarded Mitchell Prize (1984), English Watercolours (1988), The Early Paintings and Drawings of John Constable (1996). *Address:* The Old Manse, Bradfield St. George, Bury St. Edmunds. Suffolk IP30 0AZ.

**REYNOLDS, Ruth Evelyn Millicent,** F.R.S.A.; sculptor and artist in oil and water-colour; *b* India, 4 Oct., 1915. *m* Lt.-Col. D. L. C. Reynolds, O.B.E. one *s.* two *d. Educ:* abroad and Conamur, Sandgate, Kent. *Studied:* Guildford School of Art under Victor Burnand, A.R.C.A.; Prof. Arthur Pan of Academie Authentique, Budapest; Wycombe School of Art. *Exhib:* one-man shows: Halifax House, Oxford University Graduate Centre (1965), English-Speaking Union (1967), County Museum, Aylesbury, sponsored by Bucks C.C. (1976), Loggia Gallery (1982), Century Galleries, Henley-on-Thames (1987); group show: Amnesty International Sculpture Exhbn. *Work in collections:* Anne, Duchess of Westminster's Arkle Coll.; Rev. J. Studd, M.A.; Guinness (Park Royal) Ltd.; Mrs Jenny Hopkinson, Palo Alto, California; Mr Fuad Mulla Hussein, Kuwait Planning Board; R.A.F. Halton, Bucks; St. Dunstan's Church, Monks Risborough, Aylesbury; Welch Regiment Museum, Cardiff Castle; BBONT, Oxford; Stoke Mandeville Hospital, Aylesbury; Lambeth Palace Garden, SE1.; Mrs. Charlotte Steel. *Signs work:* "RUTH REYNOLDS" or "R.R." *Address:* 30 The Retreat, Princes Risborough, Bucks. HP17 9NG.

**REYNOLDS, Vicki,** B.A.(Hons.) (1976), Dip.R.A.S. (1979); British Inst. award (1978), Richard Ford scholarship (1980), S.J. Solomon silver medal for painting (1979); prizewinner, The Spirit of London; painter in oil, water-colour, charcoal, sculptress in clay; part-time assistant, Royal Academy; *b* Portsmouth, 8 June, 1946. divorced. *Educ:* Paulsgrove and Southsea Schools, Portsmouth. *Studied:* Goldsmiths' College (1972-76, John Thompson), R.A. Schools (1976-79, Peter Greenham). *Exhib:* Stowells Trophy, New Contemporaries, Three College Show, R.A. Summer Exhbn., Vortex Gallery; group shows, R.A., The London Group, Gallery 10. *Signs work:* "V.R." *Address:* 4 Whidborne Cl., St. John's Vale, London SE8.

**RHOADES, Peter G.,** C.F.A.Oxon. (1958), N.D.D. Painting (1959), M.A. Cardiff (1992), R.E. (1989); artist/lecturer in printmaking, drawing, photography; Tutor in Art, Christ Church College, Oxford, Visiting Tutor in Drawing, Ruskin School of Drawing, University of Oxford; *b* Watford, 6 May, 1938. partner: Jane Harrison;. one *s.* three *d. Educ:* Bryanston School. *Studied:* Ruskin School of Drawing (1955-59, Percy Horton), Central School of Art and

Crafts (1960-61, William Turnbull, Alan Davie), Cardiff Inst. of Higher Educ. (1990-92, John Gingell). *Exhib:* periodic one-man shows, numerous selected exhbns. in Britain, Europe and U.S.A. *Work in collections:* Ashmolean Museum Oxford, John Radcliffe Hospital Oxford, Art in Hospitals. *Signs work:* "PETER RHOADES" or "P.G.R." *Address:* Seven Stars, Spurt St., Cuddington, Aylesbury, Bucks. HP18 0BB.

**RHODES, Marion,** R.E., F.R.S.A., S.G.A., Paris Salon, Hon. Mention, bronze, silver and gold medals, Silver Medal and Diploma, Rome (1970), Associate Artistes Français (1971-81); artist in black and white, water-colour, oil; *b* Huddersfield, 1907. *Educ:* Greenhead High School, Huddersfield Art School, Leeds College of Art, Central School of Arts, London. *Exhib:* R.A., Paris Salon, R.S.A., W.A.G. and provincial galleries, S. Africa and U.S.A. *Work in collections:* British Museum and V. & A. print room, Bradford, South London, Brighouse, Huddersfield. *Signs work:* "Marion Rhodes." *Address:* 2 Goodwyn Ave., Mill Hill, London NW7 3RG.

**RHYS-JAMES, Shani,** B.A.Hons.; Hunting/Observer first prize (1993), Gold medal, Eisteddfod (1992), B.P. Portrait prize (1994), B.B.C. Wales Visual Artist of the Year (1994); artist in oil on canvas, gesso and linen; *b* Melbourne, Australia, 2 May, 1953. *m* Stephen West, artist. two *s. Educ:* Parliament Hill Girls' School. *Studied:* Loughborough (1972-73), St. Martin's (1973-76, Freddie Gore, Jennifer Durrant, Gillian Ayres, Albert Herbert). *Exhib:* mixed shows: Disclosures, Touring to Barcelona, Reclaiming the Madonna, Intimate Portraits Glyn Vivian, In the Looking Glass, solo shows: Blood Ties Touring, Beaux Arts Bath, Martin Tinney, Cardiff.Usher; Facing the Self, Mostyn Llandudno, touring. *Work in collections:* National Museum of Wales, Newport Museum, Contemporary Art Soc., Glyn Vivian, Swansea, B.B.C., Lincoln Museum. *Publications:* Art Today: (Phaidon,) Edward Lucie-Smith: Facing the Self. *Clubs:* 56 Group, R.Cam.A. *Signs work:* "Shani Rhys-James." *Address:* Dolpebyll, Llangadfan, Powys SY21 0PU, Wales.

**RICE, Elizabeth Helen,** S.B.A., R.H.S. Gold Medal; botanical painter in water-colour; illustrator; *b* Canterbury, 4 Apr., 1947. *Educ:* Ashford School, Kent. *Studied:* Exeter College of Art (1963-65), bursary to study wallpaper design with Arthur Sanderson & Sons (1965-70). *Exhib:* Mall Galleries, Medici Gallery, Pawsey & Payne, St. James's, Jersey Wildlife Preservation Trust, C.I., McEwan Gallery, Scotland, etc. *Work in collections:* H.R.H. The Princess of Wales, Sultan of Oman, Sissinghurst Castle, Kent. *Publications:* contributor to Collins Fieldguide to Crops of Britain and Europe, Reader's Digest Fieldguide to Butterflies, Collins Gem Guide to Herbs, etc. *Signs work:* "Elizabeth H. Rice." *Address:* 33 Peel St., London W8 7PA.

**RICE, Seán,** Prix de Rome (1953-55); sculptor/painter in bronze, mixed media, oil and water-colour; *b* London, 5 Nov., 1931. *m* Janet Teniers. two *s.* one *d. Educ:* Brighton and Hove County Grammar School. *Studied:* Brighton College of Art (1947-51, James Woodford, R.A.), R.A. Schools (1951-53,

Maurice Lambert, R.A.), British School at Rome (1953-55). Winner of Constance Fund Sculpture competition (1970). *Exhib:* R.A.; one-man shows: 15 in G.B. and Italy, eight at Alwin Gallery London; Art Scene London. *Commissions:* Noah Fountain, Chester Zoo; Poseidon Fountain, Gravesend; Atlantic Tower Sculptures, Liverpool; Stations of the Cross, Metropolitan Cathedral, Liverpool. *Signs work:* "Rice" or not at all. *Address:* 72 Mandeville St., Liverpool L4 5TL.

**RICHARDS, E. Margaret (née Turner),** exhbn. scholarship R.C.A. (1940), Drawing prize (1943), A.R.C.A. (Painting) (1943), M.F.P.S. (1976); artist in oil and water-colour; *b* Kingston, Surrey, 29 Dec., 1918. *m* E. M. Richards, LL.B. three *s.* one *d. Educ:* St. Paul's Convent, Teddington. *Studied:* Kingston School of Art (1935) under Reginald Brill, R.C.A. (1939-40) under Gilbert Spencer. *Exhib:* R.A., R.O.I., London Group, R.B.A., N.E.A.C., Trends. *Clubs:* F.P.S. *Signs work:* "E. Margaret Richards" on back, sometimes "Peggy E. M. Turner." *Address:* 3 Cheapside, Horsell, Woking GU21 4JG.

**RICHARDS, Patricia,** N.D.D.; freelance display artist, art tutor with Adult Educ. including art for the handicapped, pre-school toddlers and paper sculpture for primary school children; diversional therapist for the elderly, Clare House Nursing Home, Walton, Surrey; artist in oil, water-colour, pencil and pen work; demonstrator of varied crafts; *b* New Malden, Surrey, 9 Nov., 1935. divorced. one *s.* one *d. Educ:* Wimbledon County Grammar School. *Studied:* Kingston Art School (1950-55, Reginald Brill). *Exhib:* Graphic Artists (1984), Heritage '84 (National Trust), R.A. (1984), Mall Galleries, Festival Hall, London, Guildford House, Blaydon Gallery, Parkshot Gallery, Richmond, Garden Gallery, Kew, Boathouse Gallery, Walton; one-man show, Trends (F.P.S.) and Esher. Work in private collections. *Signs work:* "P. Richards" or "P.RICHARDS." *Address:* 39 Woodlands, Meadowlands Pk., Weybridge Rd., Addlestone, Surrey KT15 2RQ.

**RICHARDSON, Barbara E.,** B.A. (Hons.), A.R.B.A. (1996); painter in oil and water-colour; *b* 29 June, 1944. two *s. Studied:* Chelsea School of Art (1975-79, Patrick Symons). *Exhib:* N.P.G. Portrait Award, R.A., N.E.A.C., London Group Open, Discerning Eye, R.O.I., R.P., R.B.A., R.W.S., Singer & Friedlander/Sunday Times. *Signs work:* "B.R." (oils), "Barbara Richardson" (water-colours). *Address:* 27 Potterne Cl., London SW19 6RX.

**RICHARDSON, Geoffrey Philip,** landscape artist in oil, water-colour, etching, drypoint; *b* Woodbridge, 15 Apr., 1928. *Educ:* Woodbridge Elementary School. *Studied:* Ipswich School of Art (1940-44) under A. Ward, A.R.C.A., A. W. Bellis, A.R.C.A., Miss E. Wood, A.R.C.A. *Exhib:* R.I., N.S. Summer Salon; one-man shows, Haste Gallery, Ipswich, Deben Gallery, Woodbridge; and various group shows. *Work in collections:* England, America, Germany, Turkey, New Zealand. *Clubs:* Ipswich Art. *Signs work:* "G. Richardson", followed by date and monogram, paintings, and "G" engraved in etchings and drypoint. *Address:* 21 Old Barrack Rd., Woodbridge, Suffolk IP12 4ET.

**RICHARDSON, Ilana,** Dip. A.D. (1968); painter in water-colour and screen printer; *b* Haifa, Israel, 1946. *Studied:* Betzalel Academy of Art, Jerusalem (1963-67), Hornsey College of Art (1967-68). *Exhib:* C.C.A. Galleries London, Oxford, Bath, Amalgam Gallery London, Window Gallery Brighton, R.A., and many exhbns. abroad. *Publications:* participated as artist in The New Guide to Screen Printing by Brad Faine. Prints published by C.C.A. since 1982 printed at the artist's studio and Coriander Studio London. Posters published by the art group. *Signs work:* "Ilana Richardson." *Address:* 12 Dalebury Rd., London SW17 7HH.

**RICHARDSON, John Frederick,** A.T.D., Dip. Art History (London), F.S.A.I.I., S.B.A., F.R.S.A.; artist in water-colour, pastels, oils; Head of Art Dept., Emanuel School, London (1951-74), Hove Grammar School (1938-50), University College School (1934-37); *b* London, 23 Apr., 1912. *Educ:* Wilson's Grammar School. *Studied:* Camberwell School of Art (1928-31); London Day Training College (1931-32). *Exhib:* R.P., R.S.M.A., R.S.A., R.H.A., P.S., N.E.A.C. Galleries; one-man show: Ickworth (1971, 1973). *Clubs:* Langham. *Signs work:* "John F. Richardson." *Address:* 32 Oakland Rd., Mumbles, Swansea SA3 4AH.

**RICHMOND, Donald Edward,** N.D.D., painting (1952), A.T.C., London (1953); painter and theatrical designer; hon. treas. (1952), hon. adviser (1953), Young Contemporaries; senior lecturer in stage design, West Midlands College (since 1966); *b* Ilford, Essex, 13 Aug., 1929. *Educ:* Ilford County High School. *Studied:* S.W. Essex Technical College and School of Art (1946-48 and 1950-52), Brighton College of Art (1952-53). *Exhib:* Young Contemporaries, R.B.A. galleries (1952-53). Designer: Tower Theatre, N.1 (1956-61); English première Goyescas (Granados), Morley College (1965-66). *Signs work:* "DON RICHMOND." *Address:* Portsea House, 3 Sea Lane Cl., E. Preston, W. Sussex BN16 1NQ.

**RICHMOND, Robin,** B.A., M.A.; artist in water-colour, pastel, mixed media, oil; writer and broadcaster; *b* Philadelphia, U.S.A., 7 Nov., 1951. *m* Dr. James Hampton. one *s.* one *d. Educ:* St. George's English School, Rome. *Studied:* Chelsea School of Art (1969-74). *Exhib:* (selected) Mercury Gallery (1989, 1990, 1992), Barbican Centre (1992); group shows: (selected) Cleveland Biennale (1990), Southwestern Arts, Dallas (1993), etc. *Work in collections:* San Francisco Fine Art Museum, Middlesbrough A.G., M.O.M.A. (N.Y.). *Publications:* (selected) illustrated: The Magic Flute (Faber); author: Michelangelo and the Creation of the Sistine Chapel (Barrie and Jenkins, 1992), Introducing Michelangelo (Little Brown, 1992), Story in a Picture, Vols. I, II (Ideals, 1992, 1993), Frida Kahlo in Mexico (Pomegranate, 1993). *Signs work:* "Robin Richmond." *Address:* c/o Rebecca Hossack Gallery, 35 Windmill St., London W1.

**RIDLEY, Martin Friedrich,** H.N.D.; artist and wildlife illustrator; *b* Liverpool, 9 Aug., 1967. *Educ:* Calday Grange Grammar School, Wirral.

*Studied:* Carmarthenshire College of Technology and Art (1985-88). *Exhib:* S.WL.A., 'Wild in de Natur' Enschede, Holland, Theatre in the Forest, The Grizedale Soc. Cumbria, St. Helier Gallery, Jersey, John Noott Galleries, Patricia Wells Gallery, Carousel Gallery, 'Nature in Art' Wallsworth Hall, Glos. *Signs work:* "Martin Ridley." *Address:* c/o John Noott Galleries, 14 Cotswold Ct., Broadway, Worcs. WR12 7AA.

**RIDLEY, Philip,** B.A.(Hons.); artist in oil and charcoal; *b* London, 29 Dec., 1962. *Educ:* St. Martin's School of Art. *Exhib:* The Vinegar Blossoms. *Signs work:* "Philip Ridley." *Address:* c/o Lamont Gallery, 65 Roman Rd., Bethnal Green, London E2 0GN.

**RIGDEN, Geoffrey,** N.D.D. (1963), A.R.C.A. (1966); painter/sculptor in acrylic, oil, canvas, wood; visiting artist, Cyprus College of Art; *b* Cheltenham, 22 July, 1943. *Educ:* King's School, Gloucester, Grammar School, Weston-super-Mare. *Studied:* Somerset College of Art, Taunton (1960-63, Terence Murphy), R.C.A. (1963-66). *Exhib:* John Moores Liverpool (prize, 1965), Tolly Cobbold (prize, 1977), Hayward Annual (1980-82); one-man shows: Francis Graham-Dixon Gallery (1988, 1990, 1993, 1995). *Work in collections:* Arts Council, Contemporary Art Soc., Eastern Arts Assoc. *Signs work:* "Rigden." *Address:* c/o Francis Graham-Dixon Gallery, 17 Gt. Sutton St., London EC1V 0DN.

**RILEY, Bridget,** C.B.E. (1972), A.R.C.A.; 1st English painter to win the major Painting Prize at Venice Biennale (1968); painter; *b* London, 1931. *Studied:* Goldsmiths' College of Art; Royal College of Art. *Work in collections:* Arts Council, Tate Gallery, V. & A., British Council, Museum of Modern Art, New York, Albright Knox Gallery, Buffalo, Gulbenkian Foundation, Art Gallery of Victoria, Melbourne, Stuyvesant Foundation, Chicago Institute, Whitworth A.G., Manchester, Power Gallery of Contemporary Art, Sydney, Walker A.G., Liverpool, Dept. of the Environment, Fitzwilliam Museum, Cambridge, Scottish National Gallery of Modern Art, Edinburgh, Ulster Museum, Belfast, Museum Boymans van Beuningen, Rotterdam, Stedilijk Museum, Amsterdam, Ohara Museum, Okayama-Ken, National Gallery of Australia, Canberra. *Address:* Karsten Schubert Ltd., 41-42 Foley St., London W1P 7LD.

**RIMMINGTON, Eric,** artist in oil and charcoal; *b* Portsmouth, 14 June, 1926. *m* Sonia Michaels. one *d*. *Studied:* Slade School of Fine Art. *Exhib:* many mixed exhbns. in public and private galleries since 1963, R.A., Mercury Gallery (1983-96). *Work in collections:* Bradford City A.G., Gulbenkian Foundation, University of Wisconsin. *Signs work:* "E.R." "Eric Rimmington" or not at all. *Address:* c/o Mercury Gallery, 26 Cork St., London W1X 1HB.

**RISOE, Paul Schjelderup,** Dip. A.D. (Painting) (1968), A.T.C. (1972); painter in acrylic on board, work based on landscape; Head of Art History Dept., Downe House; *b* Calcutta, 19 Mar., 1945. *m* Clare Perry. two *s*. one *d*. *Educ:* Christ College, Brecon. *Studied:* Epsom (1963-65, Leslie Worth),

Chelsea (1965-68, Brian Young, Jeremy Moon). *Exhib:* Young Contemporaries, R.A.; one-man shows, London, Middlesbrough, Newbury; various mixed exhbns. *Work in collections:* B.P. International, Leicester Educ. Authority etc. *Signs work:* "Paul Risoe." *Address:* Fencewood House, Slanting Hill, Hermitage, Berks. RG18 9QQ.

**RITCHIE, Paul Stephen,** Dip.A.D. (1972); etcher and intaglio printmaker; established and runs, Manchester Etching Workshop; formerly ran, Two Rivers Paper Co. (1984-88); *b* Chatham, 29 Oct., 1948. *Educ:* Taunton School. *Studied:* Somerset College of Art, Manchester College of Art and Design (Norman Adams, Brendan Neiland), Croydon College of Art. *Exhib:* R.A., R.S.A., S.A.C., M.A.F.A., Whitworth A.G. *Work in collections:* Arts Council, S.A.C., Johnsonian, S.N.G.M.A., Hunterian, Aberdeen A.G., Salford A.G., Bradford A.G; Oldham A.G., Rochdale A.G. *Publications:* in conjunction with V. & A. and B.M.: facsimile edition of William Blake's Songs of Innocence and of Experience (1983). *Signs work:* "Paul Ritchie." *Address:* 91 Northern Gr., West Didsbury, Manchester M20 2JL.

**RIZVI, Jacqueline Lesley,** R.B.A. (1992), R.W.S. (1986), A.R.W.S. (1983), N.E.A.C. (1982), Dip.A.D. (1966); painter; *b* Dewsbury, Yorks., 25 June, 1944. *m* Syed Muzaffar Rizvi. one *d. Educ:* Whitley Bay Grammar School. *Studied:* The Polytechnic, Regent St. (1962-63), Chelsea School of Art (1963-66, Patrick Symons, R.A., Norman Blamey, R.A.). *Exhib:* R.A., R.I., R.S.M.A., N.E.A.C., R.W.S., City of London Exhbn., Barbican Centre, Exhbn. of Contemporary Art, B.P., Britannic House, I.C.A.F., Bath Festival, London Chamber of Commerce, Sothebys, World of Watercolours, Park Lane, Lineart, Ghent, 20th Century British Art Fair, Minton Fine Art Toronto, Ruthven Gallery, Ohio, Glyndebourne, The Upstairs Gallery, R.A., New Grafton Gallery, The New Academy Gallery, Agnews, National Trust Foundation for Art, Fosse Gallery, Patterson Gallery, Milne and Moller, Tokyo, St. James' Art Group, The Arts Club, The Hague, Castle Museum, Norwich, Catto Gallery, Waterman Fine Art, Exchange Quay, Manchester, Visions of Venice; S.A.V.E., The Heart of the City, Enchanted Gardens; Duncan Miller; King St. Galleries; Albany Gallery, Cardiff; Driffold Gallery, Sutton Coldfield; Wherry Key Gallery, Ipswich; Malcolm Innes, Edinburgh; Bilbao; Seville; Barcelona; Gorstella Gallery, Chester; City Gallery; Duncan Cambell; Thompsons Gallery; six one-man shows: The Sallyport Tower, Newcastle-upon-Tyne, Cale Art, Chelsea, New Grafton Gallery, The Upstairs Gallery, R.A., The New Academy Gallery. *Work in collections:* murals for The Medical School, St. Mary's Hospital, Paddington; London Underground Ltd., London Clubs Ltd., Shell, Amoco, Davy Corporation. *Commissions:* three murals for The Medical School, St. Mary's Hospital, Paddington; London Underground Ltd.; London Clubs Ltd. *Clubs:* The Arts, Dover Street. *Signs work:* "J.L.R." and year. *Address:* 24 Sunny Gardens Rd., Hendon, London NW4 1RX.

**RIZZELLO, Michael Gaspard,** O.B.E. (1977), Prix de Rome (1951),

P.P.S.P.S. (1968-73), P.P.R.B.S. (1976-86), F.C.S.D. (1977); sculptor and chartered designer; *b* London, 2 Apr., 1926. *m* Sheila Semple Maguire. one *d*. *Educ:* Oratory Boys School. *Studied:* R.C.A. (1947-50), British School in Rome (1951-53). *Work in collections:* London, Cardiff, Dublin and Saudi Arabia, etc.; Welsh National Memorial: David Lloyd George; busts: Sir Thomas Beecham: Royal Opera House, Royal Festival Hall and St. Helens, Lancs.; Nelson Mandela: Dublin, Tanzania and London. *Clubs:* Reform. *Signs work:* "Rizzello." *Address:* Melrose Studio, 7 Melrose Rd., London SW18 1ND.

**ROBARDS, Audrey,** R.D.S.Hons.; freelance artist in water-colour, oil, collage; *b* B'ham, 1924. *m* Jack Robards. two *s*. one *d*. *Educ:* Park House School, Malvern. *Studied:* B'ham College of Art (Alex Jackson), Sutton Coldfield College of Art (Dennis Greenwood), Bournville College of Art (Alex Jackson). *Exhib:* numerous one-man shows in the Midlands. *Work in collections:* hotels, boardrooms, theatres in G.B. and various European venues. *Clubs:* Stratford on Avon Art Soc., Sutton Coldfield Soc. of Arts, Worcs. Soc. of Arts. *Signs work:* "Audrey Robards." *Address:* Ivy Cottage, Main St., Wick Pershore, Worcs. WR10 3NU.

**ROBERT, Mary,** M.A. R.C.A. (1985), B.A. (1973); photographer and graphic artist in photographic and mixed media; Senior lecturer and Lens Media Programme Co-ordinator at Richmond International University, London; Tutor in Photography, Royal College of Art; *b* Atlanta, Georgia, 11 Dec., 1951. *Educ:* Miami University, Oxford, Ohio; University of Akron, Akron, Ohio; R.C.A., London. *Work in collections:* Bibliothéque Nationale, Paris, N.P.G. London, and private collections in U.S.A., Britain, Europe, Asia. *Signs work:* "Mary Robert." *Address:* 47 Creffield Rd., London W5 3RR.

**ROBERTS, Gladys Gregory,** R.C.A.; artist in oil and acrylic; *b* Rhyl. *m* Prof. E. J. Roberts, M.A., M.Sc. (decd.). one *d*. *Educ:* Pendre Private School, Prestatyn. *Studied:* Bangor Technical College (1959-63). *Exhib:* Royal Cambrian Academy of Art, Tegfryn Gall., Menai Bridge, Anglesey. *Signs work:* "G. Roberts." *Address:* "Bryn Llinos", Victoria Drive, Bangor LL57 2EY.

**ROBERTS, John Vivian,** R.W.S., R.E., A.R.C.A., R.C.A.; artist in acrylic, mixed intaglio media, water-colour; *b* Tredegar, Mon., 26 Jan., 1923. *m* Gwendoline Thomas. one *s*. one *d*. *Educ:* Cathays High School, Cardiff. *Studied:* Cardiff School of Art (1939-42), Royal College of Art (1947-51), Engraving School under Prof. Robert Austin. *Work in collections:* Arts Council, Nat. Mus. of Wales. *Publications:* books illustrated for a variety of publishers. *Signs work:* "John Roberts." *Address:* Ty Meini 16 Cross Sq., St. Davids, Dyfed.

**ROBERTS, Marguerite Hazel:** see HARRISON, Marguerite Hazel.

**ROBERTS, Phyllis Kathleen,** R.O.I. (1961); Paris Salon Silver Medal (1959) and Gold Medal (1964); portrait and landscape painter in oil, and sculptor; *b* London, 11 June, 1916. *m* A. Gwynne Roberts, F.C.I.I. *Educ:* Clifton College, London. *Studied:* Hornsey College of Art. *Exhib:* R.A., Paris Salon, R.O.I., N.E.A.C., R.B.A., R.P., Contemporary Portrait Society, and principal provincial municipal art galleries, etc. *Work in collections:* British Isles, France, Portugal, Spain, etc. *Publications:* articles in Leisure Painter. *Signs work:* see appendix. *Address:* 17 Providence Place, Chapel St., Chichester, W. Sussex PO19 1BS.

**ROBERTS, Walter James,** F.R.S.A.; artist in water-colour, oil, polymer and black and white; retired civil servant; Agricola Art Club (1956-), Soc. of Staffordshire Artists (1961-), chairman, Crewe Music and Arts Soc. (1964-75) (President 1987); *b* Doncaster, 10 Dec., 1907. *m* Edith Wareing. two *s. Educ:* Doncaster Grammar School. *Studied:* Doncaster School of Art under F. J. Glass. *Exhib:* London and provincial galleries, SS. Queen Mary, Laguna Beach, London Gallery, L.A., Art Collectibles, Ventura, California. *Work in collections:* Stoke-on-Trent, Santa Paula, California; National Trust, Cheshire C.C., Crewe and Nantwich Borough Council. *Signs work:* see appendix. *Address:* 591 Crewe Rd., Wistaston, Crewe CW2 6PU.

**ROBERTS, Will,** R.C.A.; Bynge-Stamper Prize (awarded by Lord Clark, 1962); Welsh expressionist painter; draws and paints figures in landscape, religious themes, flowers; born and lives in Wales; *b* Ruabon, Denbighshire, 1910. married. one *d. Studied:* Swansea School of Art (1930's); began painting after war service in R.A.F. *Exhib:* first one-man shows, London (1954); Arts Council tour (1962-63); London Group, John Moores; retrospective exhbn. Llandaff Festival (1973), N.E.A.C., R.A.; retrospective tour, Wales (1993-94). *Work in collections:* National Museum of Wales, City of Coventry, City of Hereford, Contemporary Art Soc., Arts Council and private collections; film features B.B.C. and H.T.V. Wales. *Publications:* Artists in Wales (Meic Stephens, 1977), Planet International (1994). *Signs work:* "Will R." *Address:* 10 Bilton Rd., Neath SA11 1YU.

**ROBERTSON, Anderson Bain,** D.A. (1955), A.T.C. (1956), B.A.Hons. (1982); painter in oil and water-colour; formerly Principal Art Master, Prestwick Academy; *b* Bristol, 22 Oct., 1929. *m* Mary M.M. Christie. two *s. Educ:* Ardrossan Academy, Ayrshire. *Studied:* Gray's School of Art, Aberdeen (1951-52, Robert Sivell), Glasgow School of Art (1952-55, 1981-82, David A. Donaldson, William Armour, Jack Knox). *Exhib:* R.S.A., R.S.W., R.G.I., S.S.A., R.P. Work in Many private collections. Elected professional member of S.A.A.C. (1996). *Clubs:* Glasgow Art. *Signs work:* "Anderson B. Robertson." *Address:* "Window Rock", Sandy Beach, Innellan, Argyll PA23 7TR.

**ROBERTSON, Barbara Janette,** D.A. (1970), S.S.A. (1974), Lily MacDougall, S.S.W.A. (1975); printmaker in linoprint, part-time lecturer; *b* Broughty Ferry, Dundee, 16 Aug., 1945. *Educ:* Blairgowrie High School. *Studied:* Duncan of Jordanstone College of Art, Dundee (1965-71) under Ron Stenberg, Josef Sekalski. *Exhib:* Aberdeen Art Centre, Print Exchange, Galerie

Tendenz; Contributor R.S.A. (1973-75), Prints in Folios of Compass Gallery, Glasgow, Glasgow Print Workshop, Molesey Gallery, Kingston on Thames. *Work in collections:* Leeds, Aberdeen, Glasgow, Stirling, Angus. *Publications:* illustrated The Cuckoo's Nest by Carl McDougall; The Oath Takers, Sea Green Ribbons, by Naomi Mitchison. *Signs work:* "Barbara Robertson." *Address:* 10 The Row, Douglastown, Forfar DD8 1TL, Scotland.

**ROBERTSON, Richard Ross,** F.R.B.S. (1963), R.S.A. (1977); sculptor in clay, wood, stone; retd. lecturer, Aberdeen Art College; *b* Aberdeen, 1914. *m* Kathleen Matts. two *d. Studied:* Glasgow and Aberdeen Schools of Art (1934-38, Benno Schotz, T.B. Huxley Jones). *Exhib:* R.S.A. Edinburgh, Glasgow Inst., Open Eye Gallery, Kingfisher Gallery Edinburgh. *Work in collections:* Aberdeen A.G., Peterhead A.G., Metropolitan Gallery, N.Y., Boston University. *Signs work:* "R.R. Robertson." *Address:* Creaguir, Rosemount, Woodlands Rd., Blairgowrie.

**ROBERTSON, Seonaid Mairi,** Dip. in Design and Crafts, Edinburgh (1935), A.T.D., Postgrad. Dip. in Psychology, London University (1947); educator, lecturer, craftswoman; fellow of Edinburgh College of Art (1944-47), and senior lecturer, Bretton Hall (1948-54), Senior Research Fellow in Educ., Leeds University (1954-57), Deputy Head A.T.C. Goldsmiths' College, London (retd.); *b* Perth, Scotland. *Educ:* Edinburgh University and College of Art. Visiting Prof. or Lecturer in six U.S.A. Universities, and in Brazil. Founder/Mem. W.C.C., I.N.S.E.A., British Soc. of Aesthetics. *Exhib:* London, Manchester, Edinburgh and the U.S.A. *Publications:* Creative Crafts in Education, Rosegarden and Labyrinth, Dyes from Plants, Using Natural Materials, articles in Craftsman Potter, Studio Potter, Parabola, etc. *Signs work:* "S.M.R." *Address:* 3 Seaview Ct., Selsey PO20 0JS.

**ROBERTSON, Sheila Macleod,** R.S.M.A., Mem. St. Ives Society of Artists; artist in oil, water-colour and animal studies in wire sculpture; *b* London, 1927. *Educ:* St. Michael's School, Leigh-on-Sea. *Studied:* Watford Art School, Central School of Arts and Crafts. *Exhib:* R.O.I., R.S.M.A., S.W.A. and St. Ives. *Work in collections:* R.S.M.A. Diploma Collection. *Signs work:* "S. M. ROBERTSON" and see appendix. *Address:* Flat 7, 1 Pentland Drive, Edinburgh EH10 6PU.

**ROBINSON, Barbara,** Prize for Portrait, Marlborough Fine Art, Prize and Medal, City of Monaco/Medal, City of Rodez; painter in oil, gouache, pencil; *b* London, 7 Mar., 1928. *m* Walter Robinson (decd.). two *s. Educ:* Lycée Français du Royaume Uni, Kensington High School. *Studied:* Slade and Ruskin Schools (1943-45), Ruskin School of Drawing (1945-47, Prof. Randolph Schwabe). *Exhib:* New Art Centre, London (1959-74), French, Swiss and American Galleries (1975-94), John Campbell Gallery, London (1995), Nîmes (1987), Sommieres (1994), Galerie Reno Montpellier, Galerie d'Hippocampe, St. J. Cap Ferrat. *Work in collections:* Contemporary Art Soc. London; City Halls Monaco, Sommieres, Rodez and Pamiers; Museums of La Rochelle,

Frontignan, Nimes. *Publications:* Lumières du Barbara Robinson by Geneviève Conte (1985), D'Autres Lumières du Barbara Robinson by Marc Moulin (1997). *Signs work:* see appendix. *Address:* Vic-le-Fesq (Gard), France.

**ROBINSON, Basil William,** F.B.A., F.S.A., M.A., B.Litt. (1938); museum curator (retd. 1976); deputy keeper, Victoria and Albert Museum (1954), keeper (1966), Keeper Emeritus (1972); President, Royal Asiatic Society (1970-73); *b* London, 20 June, 1912. *m* 1st., Ailsa Mary Stewart (decd. 1954); 2nd, 1958, Oriel Hermione Steel. one *s.* one *d. Educ:* Winchester, Corpus Christi (Oxford). *Publications:* A Primer of Japanese Sword Blades (1955), Descriptive Catalogue of the Persian Paintings in the Bodleian Library (1958) and other books, booklets, articles and reviews on Persian and Japanese Art. *Address:* 41 Redcliffe Gdns., London SW10 9JH.

**ROBINSON, Hilary,** B.A.(Hons.) (1979), M.A. (1987); lecturer, writer, artist; lecturer, University of Ulster; *b* U.K., 25 June, 1956. *m* Alastair MacLennan. *Educ:* John Mason School, Abingdon. *Studied:* University of Newcastle upon Tyne (1975-79, Prof. Kenneth Rowntree), R.C.A. (1985-87, Prof. Christopher Frayling). *Exhib:* U.K., Italy, Hungary. *Publications:* author: Visibly Female: Feminism and Art Today (Camden Press 1987, Universe (N.Y.) 1988), The Rough Guide to Venice (1989, 1993); many catalogue essays including: Mothers, Ikon Gallery, Birmingham (1990), Sounding the Depths, I.M.M.A., Dublin (1992), Louise Bourgiois, M.O.M.O. Oxford (1996); Editor, Alba (1990-92). *Address:* School of Fine Art, University of Ulster, Belfast BT15 1ED.

**ROBINSON, Ivor,** M.B.E., artist-bookbinder; Hon. Fellow of Oxford Brookes University, Fellow of Designer Bookbinders (President 1968-73); *b* 28 Oct., 1924. *m* Olive Trask. one *s.* one *d. Studied:* Bournemouth School of Art (1939-42). Royal Navy (1942-45). Lecturer: Salisbury School of Art (1946-52), London School of Printing and Graphic Arts (1953-58), Oxford Polytechnic (1959-89). *Exhib:* major one-man shows: Hantverket, Stockholm (1963), Galleria del bel Libro, Ascona (1969), Prescote Gallery, Cropredy (1981). *Work in collections:* B.M., V. & A., Bodleian Library, Crafts Council, Keatley Trust, Danish Royal Library; Royal Library, The Hague; Swedish Royal Library, Röhsska Museum, Gothenburg. Awards: Triple Medallist, Prix Paul Bonet, Switzerland (1971). *Signs work:* "IR" and date. *Address:* Trindles, Holton, Oxford OX33 1PZ.

**ROBINSON, Jim,** F.B.S.P. (1988); line artist (printing industry) in acrylic, pencil, scraperboard; *b* Leeds, 12 Apr., 1928. *m* Anne. one *s.* one *d. Studied:* Leeds College of Art (1941-43). *Exhib:* Yorkshire Artists Ilkley, Yorkshire Itinerants, numerous venues throughout Yorkshire. *Commissions:* various. *Clubs:* Horsforth Arts Soc. *Address:* 33 Grove Farm Cl., Cookridge, Leeds LS16 6DA.

**ROBINSON, Peter Lyell,** B.A.(Hons.) (Geog. Geol.); sculptor in clay, plaster, bronze, stone; *b* Melbourne, Australia, 12 Apr., 1962. *m* Kate MacNab. one *s.* one *d. Educ:* King's School, Bruton. *Studied:* Durham University. Apprenticed to sculptor John Robinson (1987-90). *Exhib:* London: Alwin Gallery, Harrods F.A. Gallery, McHardy Sculpture Co., Art Scene; Arlesford Gallery Hants., Beaver Galleries, Australia, Mc Hardy Sculpture Company at Butler's Wharf, The Garden Door at Ladbroke Sq., Alwin Gallery at Tunbridge Wells. *Signs work:* "LYELL." *Address:* Bralorne, Charlton Horethorne, Sherborne, Dorset DT9 4PQ.

**ROBINSON, Sonia,** N.S.A. (1977), R.S.M.A. (1979), S.W.A. (1990), Past Chairman of St. Ives Soc. of Artists; paints in oil, water-colour and gouache; *b* Stockport, 24 May, 1927. *Educ:* Glasgow High School; Manchester High School; Copthall School, Mill Hill, London. *Studied:* Manchester School of Art (1943-45), Hornsey Art School (1945-47). *Exhib:* London: R.S.M.A., R.I., Singer and Friedlander (Mall Galleries), S.W.A. (Westminster Galleries), Orangery, Holland Park, St. Katharine's Dock, Thackeray Gallery, R.A. Summer Exhbn. and Heals, shared R.S.M.A. exhbns. at Century Gallery, Datchet, Bruton St. Gallery London, Guildford House Gallery, Guildford. Solo show at Coach House Gallery, Guernsey and the Mariners' Gallery, St. Ives (1990-94 and 1996). Exhibits regularly at the St. Ives Soc. of Artists Norway Gallery, Lyonesse Gallery, Lands End, and the Passmore Edwards Gallery, Newlyn Cornwall. Exhbns. abroad: Mystic Maritime Gallery, Connecticut, U.S.A., Prouds, Sydney, Australia, Vancouver, Canada and Pont Aven, France. *Publications:* A Celebration of Marine Art (Fifty Years of the Royal Society of Marine Artists), and Marine Painting by James Taylor. *Signs work:* "SR" on oils; "Sonia Robinson" on gouaches and water-colours. *Address:* 3 Paul La., Mousehole, Penzance, Cornwall TR19 6TR.

**ROBINSON, Virginia Susanne Douglas,** artist in pastel, oil, acrylic; *b* London, 27 July, 1933. *m* Lowther. *Educ:* privately. *Studied:* Brighton College of Art, R.A.S. *Exhib:* R.A., Bradford, York, Cheltenham, Gottingen, Annecy. *Clubs:* Cheltenham Group of Artists. *Signs work:* "Virginia S.D. Robinson." *Address:* 49 The Green, Southwick, Brighton BN42 4FY.

**ROBOZ, Zsuzsi,** painter in oils, acrylics, pencil and charcoal, sculptor in clay; *b* Budapest. married. *Studied:* Regent St. Polytechnic, R.A. under Peter Greenham, and in Florence under Annigoni. *Work in collections:* Museum of Fine Arts, Budapest, National Portrait Gallery, Tate Gallery, V. & A., Royal Festival Hall, London, Bradford Museum, Graves A.G., Sheffield. *Publications:* Eux et Elles, Dix ans d'Arts Graphiques, La Femme dans l'art contemporain, Les Arts en Europe, Women and Men's Daughters, Chichester 10 - Portrait of a Decade, British Ballet To-day, British Art Now with E. Lucie-Smith (1993). *Clubs:* Chelsea Arts, Arts Club, Dover St. *Signs work:* "Roboz." *Address:* The Studio, 76 Eccleston Sq. Mews, London SW1.

**ROBSON, Hugh Mather,** artist in oil, gouache, pen and ink; *b* Hinckley, Leics., 28 June, 1929. *m* Barbara Ann Mills. four *d. Educ:* Hinckley Grammar

School. *Studied:* Fine art: St. Martin's School of Art (1945-49, William Craig, Russell Hall); Slade School of Art (1949-53, Lucien Freud, Sam Carter, tutor). *Exhib:* Arthur Jeffress, Trafford Gallery, Windsor Fine Arts, King St. Gallery, Mallets at Bourdon House, Colefax and Fowler, Nina Campbell's and Stephanie Hoppens Gallery. Murals include Crockfords, Park Lane Hotel, Belfry Club, Capital Hotel, 45 Park Lane, Croix des Gardes and many private houses. Visuals of gardens for Peter Coats; visuals of interiors for Interior decorators including John Siddley, Nina Campbell and Colefax and Fowler. Fabric designs for Nina Campbell. Bookplates, letterheads and tile designs. A series of Genre Singerie water-colours (96 to date), also a series of 20 military pansy figures (signed EWL).*Publications:* articles in House and Garden, Country Life, Connaissance des Arts, World of Interiors, Harpers, Southern Accents, etc. *Signs work:* "Hugh Robson." or "H. M. Robson." *Address:* 47 Loraine Rd., London N7 6HB.

**ROCHE, Laurence,** N.D.D., D.A.(Edin.), G.R.A.; marine, landscape and industrial painter in oil and acrylic; *b* Goodwick, Pembs., 1 May, 1944. *m* Helen Pollock, D.A.(Edin.). *Educ:* Fishguard County Secondary School; Swansea College of Art (1961-65); *Studied:* Edinburgh College of Art (1965-68); Postgrad. scholarship; Moray House College of Educ., Edinburgh (1969-79). *Exhib:* many group and one-man exhbns. *Work in collections:* in U.K. and abroad. *Signs work:* "Laurence Roche." *Address:* 16 Belmont Rd., Stroud, Glos. GL5 1HH.

**RÖDER, Endre Zoltán Eugene,** painter in oil on canvas and board; formerly art teacher in secondary schools, art gallery educ. officer, senior lecturer (Art History); *b* Budapest, 17 Aug., 1933. *m* Carole. two *s. Educ:* St. John's College, Southsea. *Studied:* Sheffield College of Art (1956-60, W.S. Taylor, Eric Jones). *Exhib:* R.O.I., various Open Shows (provinces), but generally in private galleries in England, Scotland and U.S.A. *Work in collections:* Sheffield City A.Gs., Sheffield University, etc. *Signs work:* "RÖDER." *Address:* 50 Clifford Rd., Sheffield S11 9AQ.

**RODGER, Willie,** A.R.S.A. (1989), R.G.I. (1994); artist in lino and woodcuts; *b* Kirkintilloch, 3 Mar., 1930. *m* Anne Henry, illustrator. two *s.* two *d. Educ:* Lenzie Academy. *Studied:* Glasgow School of Art (1948-53, Lennox Paterson). *Exhib:* many one-man since 1964, also group in U.K. and abroad, including R.S.A., R.A., S.S.A., R.G.I.F.A., Glasgow Group, 'In Between the Lines' retrospective, Collins Gallery, Glasgow (1986). *Work in collections:* V. & A., S.A.C., numerous public collections in U.K. *Commissions:* Enamel mural, Exhibition Station, Glasgow (Scot Rail, 1987); illustrations and mural, Dallas D.H.U. Distillery, Forres (Historic Scotland, 1987-88); designs, stained glass windows, St. Mary's Parish Church, Kirkintilloch (1987-93); street banners, 200th Anniversary, Union St., Aberdeen (1994). *Publications:* Scottish Historical Playing Cards (1975); illustrated, The Field of Thistles (1983); Willie Rodger, Open Eye Gallery, Edinburgh (1996); Willie Winkie,

Strathpride Universality Ltd., Glasgow (1997). Artist in Residence, University of Sussex (1971); Saltire Awards for Art in Architecture (1984-87). *Signs work:* "Willie Rodger." *Address:* Stenton, Bellevue Rd., Kirkintilloch G66 1AP.

**RODGERS, Harry Stewart,** painter in acrylic, pastel; *b* Stamford, 18 July, 1920. *m* Pamela Codd (decd.). *Educ:* Stamford School. *Studied:* with Ian Macnab (1951-52). *Exhib:* Boston, Stamford, London, Dublin. *Work in collections:* Lincolnshire Arts. *Clubs:* R.A.F.A. *Signs work:* "H.S. Rodgers" or "Roger." *Address:* 1 Tinwell Rd., Stamford, Lincs. PE9 2QQ.

**ROGERS, John Boydell,** M.A.; Welsh National Eisteddfod First prize (1980), Hunting Art prizes (1995), Arts Council of Wales Travel grant (1995); painter in acrylic and oil, teacher; retd. teaching Goldsmiths' College (1987); *b* Leigh, Lancs., 13 Sept., 1934. *m* Johanna Willson. three *s*. one *d*. *Educ:* Hyde County Grammar School. *Studied:* Bretton Hall, University of Birmingham, University of London, Goldsmiths' College. *Exhib:* one-man and mixed shows throughout U.K. including Arnolfini (1962-63), Camden Arts Centre (1980), Sheffield City Gallery Mappin (1977), Glyn Vivian Gallery, Swansea (1997), Barbican Arts Centre (1996), Islington International Arts Fair '95. *Work in collections:* Museum of Modern Art, Wales, private collection in U.S.A. and Europe. Glider pilot with International licence flies in France and Spain. *Signs work:* "J.B. Rogers" on back of painting, or "J.B.R." and date on front of drawings. *Address:* 28a Spilman St., Carmarthen SA31 1LQ.

**ROGERS, John Rowland,** painter, mainly landscapes, in water-colour and oil; Art Com., W.A.C., Mem. W.C.S.W.; *b* Cardiff, 28 May, 1939. married. three *s*. *Studied:* Cardiff (John Roberts, Phil Jennings, David Tinker). *Exhib:* R.S.M.A., I.C.A., W.A.C. (touring), Mostyn Gallery, Wales, Edwin Pollard Gallery, London, John Rogers' retrospective touring (1991). *Work in collections:* Haverfordwest County Museum, West Wales Arts, W.A.C., Museum and A.G., Newport, Gwent, National Library of Wales, Aberystwyth. *Signs work:* "John Rogers." *Address:* Peter's La., St. Davids SA62 6SD, Wales.

**ROGERS, Joseph Shepperd (Nevia),** B.A. (1967), M.F.A. (1969), Instructor, Corcoran School of Art, Columbia Inst. of Art (1970-72), M.P.S.G.S (Jamieson Award, 1982); artist in oil and collage; V.P., American Art League Admission Com., Arts Club of Washington; *b* Washington, D.C., 10 Mar., 1943. *Educ:* Longfellow School for Boys, Bethesda, Md. *Studied:* Corcoran School of Art, D.C., Greensboro College, N.C., (Irene Cullis, U.N.C.G., M.F.A., Gilbert Carpenter, Peter Agostini, Stephen Antonakos), American University (Dr. Turak). *Exhib:* "Five American Artists" Galerie Geilsdorfer, Köln, W. Germany (1982), "Art on Paper" Weatherspoon Gallery, U.N.C.G. (1970-80), "New Members" Spectrum Gallery, Georgetown, D.C.: seven one-man shows, etc. *Work in collections:* University of Maryland, "Maryland Collection", main altar collage, Chapel, Bishop Dennis J. O'Connell School, Arlington, Va. *Clubs:* Soc. of Architectural Historians, Arts Club of Washington, N. Va. Fine Arts Assoc., American Assoc. of Museums. *Signs* *work:* see appendix. *Address:* Bealls Pleasure, P.O. Box 1268, Landover, Md. U.S.A.

**ROGERS, Richard George, (Rogers of Riverside)** Baron 1996 (Life Peer) Kt 1991; M.Arch., R.I.B.A.; Richard Rogers Partnership, Rogers P.A. Technical and Science Centre; Piano and Rogers, France; *b* 23 July, 1933. married three *s m* Ruth Elias (1973). two *s Educ:* Architectural Assoc. (graduate Dip.); Yale Univ. (Fulbright, Edward D. Stone, and Yale Scholar, M.Arch) R.I.B.A. Chairman, Tate Gallery (1984); Royal Gold Medal for Architecture (1985); Royal Academician; Hon. Fellow Royal Academy of the Hague; Hon Fellow American Institute of Architects; Saarinen Professor Yale University (1985); Mem. United Nations Architects Committee; IBM Fellow; Mem R.I.B.A. Council; Visiting Lecturer/Professor: U.C.L.A., Princeton, Harvard Berkeley, Cornell U.S.A., McGill Canada, Hong Kong University, Aachen Germany, Cambridge University England. Winner of internat. competition from 680 entries for Centre Pompidou (1 million sq. ft. in Paris for Min. of Culture) (1977); winner of Lloyd's internat. competition for 600,000 sq. ft Headquarters in City of London (1978). Projects include: Music res. centre for Pierre Boulez and Min. of Cultural Affairs, Paris (1977); B. & B. Factory Como, Italy (1972); P.A. Science Lab. Princeton, U.S.A. (1984); Urban Conservation, Florence Italy (1984); HQ Wellcome Pharmaceuticals Eshe U.K. (1984); Cummins/Fleetguard factory, Quimper, France (1980) Electronics Factory for Reliance Controls Ltd., Swindon U.K. (1967); P.A. Technology Centre, Phases 1, 2 and 3, near Cambridge U.K. (1975); Inmo: semi-conductor manufg. facilit, Newport, S. Wales (1982). Prizes: include: Fin Times Indust. Arch. Award for Most Outstanding Indust. Bldg. 1967, (Reliance Controls, Swindon), and 1976 (Patscentre) and 1983 (Inmos); Auguste Perre Prize, Internat. Union of Architects (1978), Premier Europeo Umberto Biancamano (1979), Royal Institute of British Architects Research Award (1970), Royal Institute of British Architects Commendations (1976), British Steel Structural Design Award (1975, 1982), Eurostructpress Award (1983) Architectural Design Awards (1964, 1965, 1968). Subject of BBC documen tary, Building for Change (1980). *Publications:* incl. contribs. to Architectura Design, Global Arch. and Arch. and Urbanism. Monograph. G.A. Beaubourg *Address:* (offices and studios) Thames Wharf, Rainville Rd., London W6 9HA

**ROGERSON, Joyce,** R.M.S. (1996), S.W.A. (1996), H.S. (1996); wildlife artist and miniaturist in water-colour, for miniatures vellum; Vice Pres. S.W.A (1997-); *b* Yorkshire. *m* Ronald Rogerson, A.M.R.Ae.S., I.Eng.Cei., retd. aero nautical engineer; one *s.* one *d. Educ:* Mayfield Girls School, Walton-on Thames. *Studied:* art: Chertsey Inst *Exhib:* R.M.S., S.W.A., H.S., M.A.S.-F (U.S.A.), G.M.A.S. (U.S.A.), U.S.M. (Ulster), Mall Galleries, Westminste Gallery, Medici Gallery, Llewellyn Alexander Gallery, Soc. of Wildlife Art o the Nations. *Commissions:* worldwide, and designs for greetings cards *Publications:* Included in: Technique of Painting Miniatures, Royal Miniature Society 100 Years, Magic of Miniatures. *Signs work:* "Joyce Rogerson."

*Address:* 84 Cobham Rd., Fetcham, Surrey KT22 9JS.

**ROMER, Caroline Eve,** Byam Shaw Dip. (Painting); painter in oil, water-colour, etching; *b* Braughing, Herts., 25 Sept., 1955. *m* David Marzo. three *d.* *Educ:* Ware Grammar School for Girls. *Studied:* Cambridge Polytechnic (1972-73), Byam Shaw School of Art (1974-76). *Exhib:* R.A., R.B.A., N.E.A.C.; one-man shows, Brotherton Gallery (2), Prades Festival, Thackeray Gallery (1989, 1991, 1993), Lineart, Belgium, 20th Century British Art Fair, France, Spain. *Signs work:* "C.E. Romer." *Address:* Casa Moline, Escalarre, Esterri de Aneu, Prov. de Lerida, Spain.

**ROMER, Philippa Maynard,** portrait painter in oil; *b* Hitchin, Herts. *Studied:* Cambridge School of Art and R.A. Schools. *Exhib:* R.A., R.P., R.B.A., N.E.A.C., S.W.A. *Signs work:* "Philippa Romer." *Address:* North End Farm, Littlebury, Saffron Walden, Essex CB11 4TW.

**RONN:** see HILL, Ronald James.

**ROONEY, Michael John,** N.D.D. (1964), A.R.C.A., M.A. (1967), A.R.A. (1990); painter in gouache, water-colour, tempera, oil; Lecturer in painting, Royal Academy Schools; *b* Epsom, 1944. *m* (1) Patricia Anne (divorced); one s. one *d.*(2) Alexandra. one *s. Studied:* Sutton School of Art (1959-62, E. Bulley, C. Clairmonte), Wimbledon School of Art (G. Cooper, N. Stokoe), R.C.A. (Prof. C. Weight, C.B.E., Ruskin Spear, Roger de Grey, Peter Blake). *Exhib:* R.A. Summer Shows (1978-90), Mercury Gallery, Arts Council touring, Hunting Group annual, Tolly Cobbold, also Amsterdam, The Hague, etc. *Work in collections:* Hove Museum, Towner Museum, S.E. Arts, Rye A.G., University of Aston, Museo Ralli, Uraguay. *Clubs:* Chelsea Arts, Dover St. Arts. *Signs work:* "Rooney." *Address:* The Old Sorting House, 19 Alder Rd., Mortlake, London SW14 8ER.

**ROPER, Geoffrey John,** painter in oil and water-colour; *b* Nottingham, 30 July, 1942. *Educ:* Nottingham Sec. Art School. *Studied:* Nottingham College of Art (1958-60); Edinburgh College of Art (1960-65) under Sir Robin Philipson, P.R.S.A. *Exhib:* Figurehead Gallery, Edinburgh (1992), Murray Motor Co., Edinburgh (1994), Open Eye Gallery, Edinburgh (1995), Fine Art Society (1972, 1974, 1975, 1977, 1980, 1988), Teesside A.G. (1972), Great King St. Gallery, Edinburgh (1970, 1971, 1972), Middlesbrough Civic A.G. (1968), King St. Gallery, Dublin (1968), David Letham, Edinburgh (1968, 1969), Douglas Foulis Gallery, Edinburgh (1967), William St. Gallery, Edinburgh (1964, 1965, 1966), Silver Coin Gallery, Harrogate (1965, 1966). *Work in collections:* Middlesbrough Civic Art Galleries, Edinburgh New Town Conservation Com., New University of N. Ireland. *Signs work:* see appendix. *Address:* Whinstane Cottage, Midcalder, W. Lothian EH53 0HR.

**ROSCINI, Count M.,** F.R.S.A. (1967), M.F.P.S. (1985), B.A. (1960); sculptor in bronze; *b* Rome, 22 Dec., 1933 divorced. one *d. Educ:* Rome and Cambridge University. *Studied:* Accademia dell'Art Rome. *Exhib:* Hamilton Gallery, Drian Gallery, Loggia Gallery, Salon de Provence, Grenoble, Tevere

Expo Rome. *Work in collections:* Morristown N.J., Manilla, Lambeth Palace. *Publications:* Sounds of the Cross by David Owen. *Signs work:* "Roscini." *Address:* 19a Annandale Rd., Greenwich, London SE10 0DD.

**ROSE, Christopher Andrew,** Biology B.Sc. Hons. (1981); artist in acrylic and oils; *b* Uganda, 27 Aug., 1959. *m* Elaine Smith. *Educ:* Rydens County Secondary School, Hersham, Surrey; Nottingham University. *Exhib:* S.WL.A.; Wildlife A.G., Lavenham; many mixed exhbns. in U.K., France, Holland, Spain, U.S.A., Japan, Singapore. *Publications:* Swallows and Martins of the World (Christopher Helm, 1989), Complete Book of British Birds (R.S.P.B. and A.A., 1988), and many other publications. *Signs work:* "Chris Rose." *Address:* Maple Cottage, Holydean, Bowden, Melrose, Scotland TD6 9HT.

**ROSE, Diana Cecilia,** M.F.P.S. (1976); artist in oil; *b* Chiswick, 12 June, 1921. *m* Donald Rose. *Educ:* Lourdes Mount Convent, Ealing and Westcliff High School for Girls, Westcliff-on-Sea. *Studied:* Southend-on-Sea Art School (1948-60 part-time) under Leo Hardy; St. Martin's Art School (1946-47) under A. Ziegler. *Exhib:* Whitechapel A.G., Mall Galleries, Trends, Barbican A.G., Beecroft A.G., Southend-on-Sea. *Work in collections:* Britain, U.S.A. and Sweden. *Address:* 19b Cliff Parade, Leigh-on-Sea, Essex SS9 1AS.

**ROSE, Jean Melville,** artist/painter in water-colour and powdered colour; retired art teacher; *b* 29 Apr., 1929. married. two *s. Studied:* Bath Academy of Art, Corsham (Kenneth Garlick, William Scott, Peter Potworowski, Clifford Ellis, Kenneth Armitage) *Exhib:* Portal Gallery, London, Woodstock Gallery, London, Ancrum Gallery, Los Angeles,(three shows) and many others. *Work in collections:* H.S. Ede Kettles Yard permanent collection, Cambridge. *Commissions:* Fresco through Country Works Gallery, Montgomery, Wales. *Clubs:* Cambridge Soc. of Painters and Sculptors. *Signs work:* "JEAN ROSE." *Address:* 1 Wingfield House, Wingfield, Trowbridge, Wilts. BA14 9LF.

**ROSE, Muriel (Miss),** R.O.I. (1966), R.B.A. (1968), W.I.A.C. (1967), F.F.P.S., N.S.; painter in oils, designer, printmaker, ceramic sculptor, potter; Lecturer in ceramics and painting in Adult Education; *b* London, 1923. *Educ:* Richmond Grammar School. *Studied:* Richmond School of Art, pottery at Hammersmith College of Art. *Exhib:* R.A., R.B.A., R.O.I., Royal Scottish Academy, R.W.A., Paris Salon, Gallery Creuze, Paris, U.S.A., South Africa, National Museum of Wales, Glasgow Institute of the Fine Arts. *Work in collections:* Oxford, Nottingham E.C., Herts E.C., Welsh E.C., Univ. of Texas A.G., Danish Court of Justice, Lady Docker, Mrs. Michael Foot, etc. *Signs work:* "Muriel Rose." *Address:* 9 Temple Sheen, London SW14 7RP.

**ROSEMAN, Stanley,** B.F.A. (1967), M.F.A. (1972); painter, engraver, draughtsman and sculptor in oil, drypoint, engraving, chalk, pen and ink, bronze; *b* Boston, Mass., 4 Sept., 1945. *Studied:* The Cooper Union for the Advancement of Science and Art, N.Y.C. (1965-67), Pratt Inst., N.Y.C. (1970-72). *Exhib:* (among others) N.Y.C., Zurich, Vienna, Oxford, Dublin, London, Bordeaux, Haarlem, Brussels, Washington, Paris. *Work in collections:* (among

# WHO'S WHO IN ART

others) V. & A.; Ashmolean; National Gallery of Art, Washington D.C.; Los Angeles County Museum of Art; California Palace of the Legion of Honor, San Francisco; Bibliothèque Nationale, Paris; Musée des Beaux-Arts, Rouen; Cabinet des Dessins, Strasbourg; Musée des Beaux-Arts, Bordeaux; Musée Ingres, Montauban; Museum of Modern Art, Brussels; Bibliothèque Royale, Brussels; Teylers Museum, Haarlem; Prentenkabinet der Rijksuniversiteit, Leyden; Museum of Modern Art, Rio de Janeiro; National Museum of Wales, Cardiff; National Gallery of Ireland, Dublin; Vatican Museum, Rome; Staatliche Graphische Sammlung, Munich; Museum of Fine Art, Budapest; Israel Museum, Jerusalem; Albertina, Vienna; China Museum of Fine Arts, Beijing; H.M. The Queen. *Publications:* Stanley Roseman and the Dance-Drawings from the Paris Opera (Ronald Davis, Paris, 1996). *Signs work:* see appendix. *Address:* 1 rue Davioud, 75016 Paris, France.

**ROSEN, Hilary,** B.A. (1976), M.A. (1980); painter in water-colour; part-time art lecturer; *b* London, 3 Sept., 1953. married. one *s.* one *d. Educ:* J.F.S. Comprehensive School, London. *Studied:* Trent Polytechnic (1973-76, Derek Carruthers), R.C.A. (1978-80, Peter de Francia). *Exhib:* solo shows: Royal National Theatre, Galerie Rose Hamburg, Strausberg Galerie Berlin, Galerie Fischinger Stuttgart; mixed shows: R.A., Singer and Friedlander, Arthur Andersen, Boundary Gallery, London. *Work in collections:* Neville Burston Coll., Zeiss, Hamburg, Imperial College; private and public collections in Munich, Hamburg, New York, Paris, Arthur Andersen, B.T., British Gas, Liberty. *Publications:* Dorling Kindersely: Water-colour Still Lives. *Clubs:* Chelsea Arts. *Signs work:* "H. Rosen." *Address:* Chisenhale Studios, 64-84 Chisenhale Rd., London E3.

**ROSEN, Ismond,** M.B., B.Ch. (1946), D.P.M. (1951), Witwatersrand M.D. (1954), Associate Mem. British Institute of Psycho-analysis (1959), (Member, 1971), F.R.C.Psych. (1971); psychiatrist, sculptor, painter, photographer; *b* Johannesburg, S. Africa, 2 Aug., 1924. *Educ:* Witwatersrand University. *Studied:* mainly self-taught and at Academie Julien and Ecole des Beaux Arts, Paris (1952), Regent St. Polytechnic. *Exhib:* S. African Academy; private shows, Johannesburg (1949); Pretoria (1951); one-man shows: John Whibley Gallery, Cork St., London (1972), "Genesis" Borough of Camden, Camden Arts Centre, (1974), "Sinai as Inspiration" Camden Arts Centre, Royal Free Hospital, Nikon Gallery, London (1982), St. Mary's Church, Nottingham, R.A. *Work in collections:* in many London medical insts. especially Royal Society of Medicine, Royal College of Psychiatrists; full-size bronze figure - "The Revelation" presented by CCJ to Pope John-Paul II and is in The Vatican; "Holocaust Sculptures" exhbn., St. Paul's Cathedral, London (Oct. 1992-May 1993). *Clubs:* Fellow Soc. of Portrait Sculptors. *Signs work:* "Ismond Rosen." *Address:* Charlecote, 3 Hampstead Hill Gdns., London NW3 2PH.

**ROSMAR:** see BOOTH, Rosa-Maria.

**ROSOMAN, Leonard,** O.B.E. (1981), A.R.A. (1960), R.A. (1970); artist and teacher; teacher of illustration, Camberwell School of Art; teacher of mural decoration, Edinburgh College of Art; tutor at the Royal College of Art, London; *b* Hampstead, London, 27 Oct., 1913. *Educ:* Deacons School, Peterborough. *Studied:* King Edward VII School of Art, Durham University; Central School of Arts and Crafts; R.A. Schools. *Exhib:* Fine Art Society, Roland, Browse & Delbanco, Leicester Galleries, Leger Gallery, St. George's Gallery, Sheffield, Bradford, Edinburgh, Dublin, and provincial galleries, and Lincoln Center, N.Y., State University of New York at Albany. *Work in collections:* Tate Gallery, London, Nat. Portrait Gallery, London, Royal Academy, London, Aberdeen A.G., Royal College of Art, London, Bradford City A.G. *Commissions:* murals: vaulted ceiling, Lambeth Palace Chapel, Royal Academy Restaurant, London. *Publications:* Mad Meg, Pieter Breughel; illustrated: Old Testament, Exodus (O.U.P.); Aldous Huxley's Brave New World, and Point Counterpoint; Thomas Mann's Buddenbrooks; Evelyn Waugh's Brideshead Revisited (all Folio Soc.). *Clubs:* Arts Dover St.,Chelsea Arts. *Signs work:* "Leonard Rosoman." *Address:* 7 Pembroke Studios, Pembroke Gdns., London W8 6HX.

**ROSS, Alastair Robertson,** O.St.J., F.R.B.S., A.R.S.A.; sculptor; Lecturer in Fine Art, Duncan of Jordanstone College of Art, Dundee; D.A. (1965), Postgrad. (1966), F.R.S.A. (1966), F.S.A.Scot. (1971), A.R.B.S. (1968), F.R.B.S. (1975), A.R.S.A. (1980), Mem. of Council, S.S.A. (1972-75), Scottish Mem. of Council, R.B.S. (1972-), Vice Pres., R.B.S. (1988-90); *b* Perth, Scotland, 1941. *m* Kathryn Wilson. one *d. Educ:* St. Mary's Episcopal School, Dunblane, McLaren High School, Callander. *Studied:* Duncan of Jordanstone College of Art, Dundee Work in numerous collections in this country and abroad. Awards: Dickson Prize (1962), Holokrome Award (1962), S.E.D. Travelling Scholarship (1963), R.S.A. Chalmers Bursary (1964), R.S.A. Carnegie Travelling Scholarship (1965), Duncan of Drumfork Scholarship (1965), S.E.D. Post-grad. Scholarship (1965-66), bronze and silver medallist Paris Salon, Sir William Gillies award of R.S.A. (1989), Sir Otto Beit Medal of R.B.S. (1989), Freeman of the City of London (1989). *Signs work:* see appendix. *Address:* Ravenscourt, 28 Albany Terr., Dundee DD3 6HS.

**ROSS, Michélle,** S.B.A. (1987), H.Dip. (1985); freelance illustrator/artist in water-colour; *b* Morpeth, Northumberland, 9 Mar., 1964. *Educ:* Hustler Comprehensive, Middlesbrough. *Studied:* Cleveland College of Art (1980-82), Harrow School of Art (1982-85). *Exhib:* solo shows: Talent Show Gallery, London (1988), S.B.A. *Publications:* work repro.: illustrated numerous books for adults and children. *Clubs:* S.B.A. *Signs work:* "Michelle Ross." *Address:* c/o The Conifers, Moorsholm, Saltburn-by-the-Sea, Cleveland TS12 3JH.

**ROSS-CRAIG, Stella,** F.L.S.; artist in water-colour, pencil, and pen and ink; *b* Aldershot, Hants, 19 Mar., 1906. *m* J. Robert Sealy, B.Sc., F.L.S. *Educ:* privately. *Studied:* Thanet Schools of Art, and botany at Chelsea Polytechnic. *Work in collections:* Reference Collection, Herbarium of Royal Botanic Gdns.,

Kew (approx. 500 water-colours, several hundred pen-and-ink and pencil drawings); Hunt Botanical Library, Pittsburgh, Penn., U.S.A. *Publications:* work repro.:Drawings of British Plants in Hooker's Icones Plantarum, Botanical Magazine, and many other scientific publications. *Signs work:* "SR-C" or "Stella Ross-Craig." *Address:* 15 Grosvenor Rd., Richmond, Surrey TW10 6PE.

**ROSSER, John,** N.D.D. (1952); painter; *b* London, 8 June, 1931. *m* Margaret Rosser. *Studied:* Regent St. Polytechnic and Watford School of Art (1947-52) under A. J. B. Sutherland. *Exhib:* R.A., R.B.A., N.E.A.C., R.I., Young Contemporaries, Medici Gallery, Compton Gallery, Windsor, Neville Gallery, Sandford Gallery, Paris Salon; one-man shows: Brian Sinfield Gallery, Burford (1987), Hallam Gallery, SW14 (1989); finalist in the Hunting Group art prizes (1981); Chelsea Library (1992). *Work in collections:* Watford Museum, Goodwood House. *Publications:* work repro.: Elgin Court, Simon and Schuster, Australia, Foyles Books, Rosenstiels, Medici, Reader's Digest Publications. *Signs work:* capital R. *Address:* 4 Beachview, 91 Banks Rd., Sandbanks, Poole, Dorset BH13 7QQ.

**ROSSIE, Kay,** Dip.F.A., A.Dip., F.F.P.S.; abstract painter/sculptor in acrylic, water-colour, oil, wood, metal constructions; *b* Porthcawl, 1940. *Studied:* Croydon College (1983-86), one year advanced sculpture (1986-87). *Exhib:* one-man show, Loggia Gallery, London; many mixed exhbns. of painting and sculpture, including Trends, Phillips, G.E.C. Management College, Business Design Centre, Royal Academy of Birmingham Artists. *Work in collections:* Croydon College, Price Waterhouse. *Commissions:* Kenetic Sculpture for First Light Ltd. *Clubs:* F.P.S., London, Reigate Soc. of Artists. *Signs work:* "Kay Rossie." *Address:* 12 Brokes Cres., Reigate, Surrey RH2 9PS.

**ROSSITER, Anthony,** M.C.S.D. (1963), R.W.A. (1964), Arts Council awards, Literature (1967, 1970), T.V. James Mossman's Review (1970); painter in oil and water-colour, writer, lecturer; Lecturer, Bristol Polytechnic (early retirement 1983); started Dalesford Studio, teaching small groups painting within own studio (1983); *b* London, 29 Mar., 1926. *m* Anneke. one *s.* one *d.* *Educ:* Eton. *Studied:* Chelsea Polytechnic (1947-51). *Exhib:* Artists in National Parks (1988-90). *Work in collections:* V. & A., Bristol City Art Gallery, Reading City Art Gallery, London Transport, John F. Kennedy Centre, Smithsonian Institute, U.S.A., Ministry of Works, etc. *Publications:* The Pendulum (Gollancz, 1966), The Golden Chain (Hutchinson, 1970), The Pendulum, A Round Trip to Revelation (Garrett Publications, U.S.A.; Foreword W. H. Auden); illustrated Elizabeth Jennings's Poems A Dream of Spring (Celandine Press, 1980). B.B.C. TV documentary, Work as Painter, Lecturer, Writer (1981). Represented British Landscape and Figure Painting 1930-1985 Irma Stern Museum, Cape Town, S. Africa (1987). *Signs work:* "A.R." *Address:* Dalesford House, Litton, nr. Bath, Somerset.

**ROWAN, David Paul,** R.B.A. (1979), R.A. Schools Post. Grad. Cert. (1972-

75), Dip.A.D. (Painting, 1969-72); artist in acrylic; *b* Colne, Lancs., 28 Apr., 1950. *Studied:* Maidstone College of Art (1969-72, D. Winfield, R.B.A., W. Bowyer, R.A.), R.A. Schools (1972-75, P. Greenham, C.B.E., R.A., Margaret Green, John Holden). *Exhib:* R.B.A., Mid-Pennine Arts, Colne. *Work in collections:* F. Kobler, London; A. Whalley, Windsor. *Signs work:* "DAVID ROWAN" or "D.P. Rowan." *Address:* 1 Sandown Rd., London SE25 4XD.

**ROWAN, Evadné Harris,** M.C.S.D. (1952), A.I.A. (1949); freelance artist in pen and ink, water-colour, oil, lithography; *b* Warsash, Hants. *m* F. H. Paul. *Studied:* Gloucester School of Arts and Crafts and Central School of Arts and Crafts, Southampton Row. *Exhib:* Senefelder Club and Artists International Assoc. *Publications:* work repro.: Radio Times, Sunday Times, Heinemann, Macmillan, Penguin Books, Methuen, Harvill Press, Rupert Hart-Davis, Odhams, Collins, Putnams, G.P.O., Dents, O.U.P., Michael Joseph, Ward Lock, Longmans, B.B.C. *Signs work:* "Evadné Rowan." *Address:* Flat 7, 35 Elm Pk. Gdns., London SW10 9QF.

**ROWBOTHAM, Mark A.,** Dip.A.D., P.S. (1992); painter in oil and pastels; Mem. Pastel Soc., winner Patterson Award; *b* Sarawak, Borneo, 1959. *m* Sherree E. Valentine-Daines. one *s.* two *d. Studied:* Epsom School of Art (1977-81). *Exhib:* R.B.A., R.O.I., R.W.S., R.P., N.E.A.C., P.S. *Signs work:* "M.A.R." *Address:* Misty Ridge, 126 The Street, Ashtead, Surrey KT21 1AB.

**ROWE-EVANS, Prue,** B.A. (Lond.), Dips. in Painting and Printmaking (mid-Warwickshire C.F.E.), F.F.P.S.; painter; *b* London, 30 July, 1921. *m* Adrian. one *s. Educ:* Frognal School, Hampstead; University College, London. *Studied:* Slade, and mid-Warwickshire C.F.E. *Exhib:* numerous mixed and one-man exhbns. in the Midlands, and in London at the Loggia Gallery and Llewellyn Alexander. *Clubs:* Fellow, Free Painters and Sculptors, Coventry and Warwickshire Soc. of Artists, Assoc. of Midland Artists. *Signs work:* "P. ROWE-EVANS" or "Prue Rowe-Evans." *Address:* 48 New St., Kenilworth CV8 2EZ.

**ROWLAND, Dawn,** F.R.B.S.; sculptor in stone and bronze; Council mem. R.B.S. and M.A.F.A.; *b* London, 24 Sept., 1944. *m* Prof. Malcolm Rowland. two *d. Educ:* Orange Hill Girls' Grammar School. *Exhib:* Chelsea Harbour Sculpture (1993), Chichester Festival (1994), Konishi Gallery Kyoto, R.A. Summer Show, Salford A.G., Hannah Peschar Sculpture Garden. *Signs work:* "DAWN" in semicircle with date under. *Address:* The Pines, 39 Bramhall Park Rd., Bramhall, Stockport, Ches. SK7 3NN.

**ROWLETT, George Goldie,** painter of land and seascapes, portrait and figure in oil; *b* Troon, Ayrshire, 29 June, 1941. *m* Marion Sneller. two *s. Educ:* De Aston Grammar, Market Rasen. *Studied:* Grimsby School of Art (1960-62), Camberwell School of Art (1962-65), R.A. Schools (1965-68). *Exhib:* one-man shows: Grimsby Museum (1962), Greenwich Theatre Gallery (1975), Woodlands Gallery (1982), Zur Torkel Zehn, Konstanz (1985, 1986, 1987, 1991), D.M. Gallery (1987), Everard Read Gallery, Johannesburg (1987, 1988,

1990), Smith-Jariwala Gallery (1989), Cleveland Bridge Gallery, Bath (1989), Albemarle Gallery (1990, 1992, 1995), Art Space Gallery (1993, 1995, 1997), Belloc Lowndes, Chicago (1995), Grant Fine Art, Newcastle, N. Ireland (1996); mixed shows: R.A., Whitechapel Open, Cleveland Drawing Biennale, N.P.G., Hayward Annual 'A Singular Vision', Hunting Group, Spirit of London, South Bank Picture Show, London Group, Druce-Constable, Zur Torkel Zehn, Read Stremmel San Antonio, Everard Read, Architectural Arts Co. Dallas, Elizabeth Gordon Durban, Cleveland Bridge, Albemarle, Henry Wyndam, National Trust Centenary - Christies, Grant Fine Art, Belloc Lowndes, Art Space Gallery, Chicago Art Fair, Glasgow Art Fair. *Work in collections:* Grimsby Museum, Northern Arts, Cleveland Museum Service, Nuffield Foundation, Baring Bros., Manny Davidson Discretionary Trust, Equitable Real Estate Investment, Atlanta, Ga., Kelmac Group, Price Forbes Ltd., Auto & General Ltd., Innovative Marketing Ltd., Ken Solomon Ltd., African Salt Works Ltd., Weedon Minerals, Anglo American Ltd., A.G. Diamond Cutters, Mesquite Investments, Philip Loot's Assoc., Sumrie of London, Stephen Fauke Interiors, Altron Ltd., Charles Glass Soc., Rose Gardens Ltd., Nedfin Bank Ltd., Head Interiors, Momentum Components, Grinrod Unicorn Group Ltd., Voicevale Ltd. Gallery: Art Space Gallery, 84 St. Peter's St., London N1 8JS. *Signs work:* "George Rowlett." *Address:* 23 Farrins Rents, London SE16 1NF.

**ROWSELL, Joyce (née Gwyther),** B.A., H.S.F., M.A.S.-F.; painter, miniaturist, illustrator, mostly in oil; *b* S. Wales, 20 Nov., 1928. *m* Geoffrey N. Rowsell. two *s. Educ:* Coborn School, Bow, and Bishop Fox's School, Taunton. *Studied:* privately, History of Art degree from Courtauld Inst. *Exhib:* Hilliard Society of Wells (1982-97), Miniature Art Soc. of Florida (1994-97), Royal Soc. of Miniature Painters, Sculptors and Gravers (!993-94), Llewellyn Alexander Gallery, London (1993-97), Royal Birmingham Soc. Artists Prize Exhbn. (1997). *Commissions:* Includes portraits of people, houses, racehorses. *Publications:* pen and ink illustrations, full colour book jackets. *Clubs:* Hilliard Soc. (Founder Mem.), M.A.S.-F. *Signs work:* "Joyce Rowsell." *Address:* Spring Grove Farm, Milverton, Som. TA4 1NW.

**ROWSON, Hugh Thomas,** B.A., D.A., R.S.W.; artist in water-colour, acrylic, printmaking, educationalist; former Educ. Officer, Aberdeen A.G.; former V.P., Aberdeen Artists Soc., mem. Peacock Printmakers, Aberdeen; *b* Aberdeen, 4 Aug., 1946. *m* Lesley (divorced). two *s. Studied:* Grays School of Art, The Robert Gordon University (1965-70, Alexander Fraser, Ian Fleming), Aberdeen College of Education (1970-71), Open University (1972-76). *Exhib:* Aberdeen University, Aberdeen Arts Centre, Peacock Printmakers (1997). *Work in collections:* Aberdeen Royal Infirmary. *Publications:* Childrens' Guide to Aberdeen Art Gallery. *Clubs:* R.S.W. *Signs work:* "Hugh T. Rowson" or "H.T.R." *Address:* Peacock Printmakers, 21 Castle St., Aberdeen AB11 5BQ; and 276 Union Grove, (Ground Floor Flat), Aberdeen AB10 6TQ, Scotland.

**ROXBY, Brian,** R.O.I. (1993); painter in oil, acrylic and water-colour; *b* 25 Oct., 1934. *m* Christina Mary. one *s.* two *d. Educ:* St. Cuthbert's Grammar School, Newcastle upon Tyne. *Studied:* Sunderland College of Art (1951-55, Harry Thubron), R.C.A. (1955-58, Leonard Rosoman, Robert Buhler). *Exhib:* R.B.A., N.E.A.C., R.I., R.O.I., Contemporary British Painters, Wildenstein (1958); one-man shows: Queen's Hall Gallery, Hexham (1988), Trevelyan College, Durham (1989). *Work in collections:* National Gallery of Wales and Government Art Collection. *Signs work:* "B. Roxby." *Address:* The Chestnuts, 21 High St., Walcott, Lincoln LN4 3SN.

**ROY, Michael (Michael Roy Presley-Roy),** A.T.C. (1970, Reading University, D.A.E., (1976) London University; artist (mixed media) land-scapes, religious studies, figurations, flower-pieces and fantasy themes; *b* London, 20 Apr., 1928. *Educ:* Upton Grammar, Berks. *Studied:* Newland Park College (1967-70, David Bowers), and later at Hornsey College of Art (Eric Sonntag). *Exhib:* London, Windsor and Southhampton Civic A.G. *Work in collections:* various private and public, U.K. and abroad. *Publications:* author: "The rôle of the Art Teacher" (1976); "The Art Lark" (1992). Profile/feature p.61 British Contemporary Art (Gagliardi, London 1993). *Signs work:* "Michael Roy" with symbol of small spider and date, see appendix. *Address:* 53 Lyon St., Southampton SO14 0LW.

**RUDD, Bob,** B.A. (1973), R.I. (1995); painter in water-colour; *b* Ipswich, Suffolk, 18 Jan. 1944. *m* Jennifer Cuff. two *s. Studied:* Ipswich Art School (1960-63), Bath Academy of Art (1969-73, Adrian Heath). *Exhib:* R.A., R.I., R.W.A. and many mixed exhbns. and one-man shows in London and Edinburgh. *Work in collections:* several (14) works in the permanent collection of the House of Commons. *Address:* 38 The Causeway, Chippenham, Wilts. SN15 3DB.

**RUFFING, A. E.,** professional artist in water-colour; *b* Brooklyn, N.Y. *m* George Ruffing. one *d. Educ:* Cornell University, Drexel Institute of Technology. *Studied:* under John Pike (1964). *Work in collections:* Metropolitan Museum of Art, Smithsonian Institute, Library of Congress, Brooklyn Museum, Harvard University, Institute of Early American History and Culture, Albany Institute of History and Art, Atwater Kent Museum, Johnston Historical Museum, N.Y. Historical Society. *Signs work:* "A. E. Ruffing." *Address:* P.O. Box 125, Bloomington, N.Y. 12411.

**RUNAYKER, Irene,** N.D.D. (1958); painter in acrylic, Chinese ink; *b* London, 11 May, 1937. two *s. Educ:* Sarah Bonnell Grammar School, London. *Studied:* Camberwell School of Art (1954-58, Dick Lee, Tony Fry, Michael Salaman). *Exhib:* Swiss Cottage, Camden Borough Gallery (1985), Woodlands A.G., London (1990), Stadtiches Museum, Gelsenkirchen, Germany (1992), Cumberland Lodge, Windsor (1993), Jeu de Paume, Albert, France (1995), Cable and Wireless, London (1996-97). *Work in collections:* London Borough of Camden, Insearch Unit, University of Technology, Sydney, Australia, Our

Lady of Dolours, London. *Publications:* ref. in: Camberwell Students and Teachers 1943-1960 (Antique Collectors, Woodbridge, 1995), Edgell Rickword by Charles Hobday (Carcarnet Press). *Clubs:* Ridley Art Soc., I.N.I.V.A.,Women Artist Slide Library. *Signs work:* "Runayker"; before 1982 "Runacre." *Address:* 1 Matlock Rd, Eastbourne BN20 7RA.

**RUNSWICK, Eddie,** Director of Community and Leisure Services, Borough of Blackburn. *Address:* Town Hall, Blackburn BB1 7DY.

**RUSH, Maureen Elizabeth,** S.B.A. (1989); freelance artist in water-colour and pastel; Adult Educ. teacher; *b* Surrey, 1938. *m* Christopher John Rush. three *s. Educ:* Rosebery County Grammar School, Epsom. *Studied:* primarily self taught, influenced by Edward Wesson and the English Water-colour Impressionist School. *Exhib:* many mixed shows, five solo shows. *Work in collections:* Royal Tunbridge Wells A.G. *Publications:* work repro.: greetings cards for Henry Ling (London) Ltd. *Signs work:* "Maureen Rush." *Address:* Weaver's Cottage, 3 New Row, Birstwith, Harrogate, N.Yorks. HG3 2NH.

**RUSHMER, Gordon,** landscape painter in oils and water-colour; *b* Petersfield, 12 July, 1946. *m* Shirley Ann Holland. one *s.* one *d. Educ:* Petersfield School. *Studied:* Farnham School of Art (1962-67). *Exhib:* Furneaux Gallery, Edwin Pollard Gallery, Ceri Richards Gallery, R.I., Ashbarn Gallery, New Ashgate Gallery, Farnham, Peter Hedley Gallery, Wareham, Kingsmead Gallery, Gt. Bookham, Ucheldre Centre, Holyhead, Dragon St. Gallery, Petersfield, Gallery East, N.Y., David Curzon Gallery, Wimbledon. *Work in collections:* National Library of Wales, I.C.I., Leach Group, Nelson Mandela. *Publications:* Art Business News U.S.A., Artists and Illustrators Magazine. *Signs work:* "Gordon Rushmer." *Address:* 2 Sherwood Cl., Liss, Hants. GU33 7BT.

**RUSHTON, James,** A.R.C.A., R.W.S., N.E.A.C.; artist in oil and water-colour; principal lecturer (retd.); *b* Newcastle-u-Lyme, 15 Jan., 1928. widower. one *s.* one *d. Studied:* Burlem School of Art; Royal College of Art. *Exhib:* R.A., R.W.S. and N.E.A.C. annual exhbns. Work in private collections. *Commissions:* portrait, Dr. Derek Ferrington. *Publications:* illustrations for, Maxwells Ghost, On a Shoe String to Coorg, Archaeology Publications (Quality Book Club, London). *Signs work:* "J Rushton." *Address:* 17 Gower St., Newcastle-u-Lyme, Staffs. ST5 1JQ.

**RUSSELL, Christine Gillian,** S.W.A., U.A.; self taught artist specialising in figurative still life, in pastel, water-colour; *b* London, 4 Apr., 1952. *m* Sidney Stephen Russell. one *s.* one *d. Educ:* Tollington Park School, London (1963-68). *Exhib:* S.W.A., U.A., P.S., R.B.S.A.; Century Gallery, Datchet, Alexander Gallery, Bristol, Gallery 21, Nailsworth; many mixed exhbns. Many works in private collections. *Publications:* entry in S.W.A. Exhibitors 1855-1996, editor Charles Baile de la Perrière (Hilmarton Manor Press, 1996). *Signs work:* "C.G. Russell." *Address:* 58 St. Davids Rd., Thornbury, South Glos. BS12 1AJ.

**RUSSELL, Edwin John Cumming,** F.R.B.S., Cert. R.A.S., R.A. Gold

Medal for sculpture; Sir Otto Beit Medal for sculpture (1991); sculptor in bronze, stone, wood; *b* Heathfield, 4 May, 1939. *m* Lorne McKean, sculptor. two *d*. *Studied:* Brighton College of Art and Crafts (1955-59), Royal Academy Schools (1959-63). *Work in collections:* Crucifix, and St. Michael, St. Paul's Cathedral; Bishop, Wells Cathedral; Dolphin Sundial, Greenwich; Sundials for Oman University and Dubai Parliament Sq.; Mad Hatters Tea Party, Warrington; Lion and Lamb, best shopping centre (1987); Alice and White Rabbit, Guildford; Panda, W.W.F., H.Q.; Forecourt Sculpture, Rank Xerox U.K., H.Q. *Signs work:* "E.R." *Address:* Lethendry, Hindhead, Surrey GU26 6BE.

**RUSSELL,  Jim,** R.B.A.; painter and illustrator in oil and water-colour; *b* Walsall, Staffs., 30 June, 1933. *m* Becky. one *s*. one *d*. *Educ:* Royal School, Wolverhampton. *Studied:* Birmingham College of Art. *Exhib:* R.A., John Moores, R.B.A., F.B.A., Bankside, Laing, Singer & Friedlander, Hunting, etc.; one-man shows: Amalgam, Drian London, Alpha House Sherborne, Boxfield Stevenage. *Work in collections:* Liverpool University, various L.E.A.'s. *Commissions:* various theatre rehearsal drawings, Wine Soc. *Publications:* work repro.: Radio Times, Punch, newspapers, theatres, etc. *Address:* 10 Milton Rd., London SE24 0NP.

**RUSSELL, Kathleen Barbara,** D.A.Edin. (1962); Membre Associé Société des Artistes Français; artist in oil, pastel, gouache and water-colour; *b* Edinburgh, 1940. *m* John Caskey. *Educ:* The Mary Erskine School for Girls. *Studied:* Edinburgh College of Art (1958-63) under Sir Wm. Gillies, R.A., R.S.A. and Sir Robin Philipson, P.R.S.A. *Exhib:* one-man shows since 1965. *Work in collections:* Watson Coll., Edinburgh Corp. Schools Coll., Nuffield Collection, Durham University, Kings College, London, Royal Botanic Gardens, Kew. *Publications:* illustrated Magnus the Orkney Cat. *Signs work:* "Kathleen Russell" or "K. Russell" or "K." *Address:* 113 Laleham Rd., Catford, London SE6 2JD.

**RUSSELL, Pat,** F.S.S.I., F.C.L.A.S.; textile artist in fabric collage, lettering artist, calligrapher; *b* Wembley, 17 Aug., 1919. *m* Birrell Russell. one *s*. one *d*. *Educ:* Farnborough Hill. *Studied:* Chelsea College of Art under M. C. Oliver. *Exhib:* Oxford Gallery and various group exhbns. *Work in collections:* V. & A., Oxford City and County Museum, Reading Museum. *Publications:* Lettering for Embroidery (Batsford); Decorative Alphabets Throughout the Ages (Bestseller Publications). *Signs work:* "Pat Russell." *Address:* 48 East Saint Helen's St., Abingdon OX14 5EB.

**RUSSON, Mary Georgina,** N.D.D. (1963), A.T.D. (1971); artist in ink, gouache, acrylic; art teacher, B'ham (1971-79); *b* Hockley, B'ham, 1937. one *d*. *Educ:* Holly Lodge Grammar School, Smethwick. *Studied:* B'ham College of Art and Crafts (1960-63, Glyn Griffiths). *Exhib:* Central Hall, Westminster (1960's). *Publications:* illustrated many children's books, some magazine and other work. *Address:* 4 The Hawthorns, Woodbridge Rd., Moseley,

Birmingham B13 9DY.

**RYAN, Adrian,** painter in oil, water-colour; teacher, Goldsmiths' School of Art (1948-83); Cambridge School of Art (1969-85); *b* Hampstead, 3 Oct., 1920. *m* 1st. Peggy Rose, one *d*; 2nd. Barbara Pitt, two *d*; 3rd. Susan Curnow. *Educ:* Eton. *Studied:* Slade School. *Exhib:* R.A., London Group, Tate, etc. *Work in collections:* Tate Gallery, V. & A., Belfast Art Gallery, Manchester Art Gallery, National Gallery of New Zealand, Plymouth Art Gallery, Gulbenkian Foundation, Chantrey Bequest, Arts Council of G.B., Contemp. Art Soc., etc. *Publications:* author, Still Life Painting Techniques. *Signs work:* "Ryan." *Address:* 8 Camden Studios, Camden St., London NW1 0LG.

**RYAN, John Gerald Christopher,** freelance artist, illustrator, writer and cartoon film-maker; *b* Edinburgh, 4 Mar., 1921. married. one *s*. two *d. Educ:* Ampleforth College. *Studied:* Regent St. Polytechnic. *Exhib:* R.A. Creator "Captain Pugwash" "Sir Prancelot" and various other children's cartoon characters. *Publications:* work repro.: internationally in various magazines and picture-books. Cartoonist 'Catholic Herald' since 1967. *Signs work:* "JOHN RYAN." *Address:* Gungarden Lodge, The Gungardens, Rye, E. Sussex TN31 7HH.

**RYAN, Thomas,** P.P.R.H.A., D.Litt., A.N.C.A.D., Hon.R.A., Hon.R.S.A.; painter in oil, water-colour, pastel, red chalk, medal designer; President, United Arts Club, Dublin, and Limerick Art Soc.; Council mem. Stamp Design Com.; *b* Limerick, Ireland, 16 Sept., 1929. *m* Mary Joyce. four *s*. two *d. Educ:* Christian Brothers School, Limerick. *Studied:* Limerick School of Art (Richard Butcher, A.R.C.A.), National College of Art, Dublin (Seán Keating, Maurice McGonigle). *Exhib:* many one-man and mixed shows in Ireland, G.B., Ukraine, U.S.A., Latvia. *Work in collections:* National Gallery of Ireland, President of Ireland, Cardinal's residence Armagh, European Court, E.E.C. Brussels, St. Patrick's College, Maynooth, Kings Inns, Dublin, Royal College of Surgeons, Trinity College Dublin, University College, Dublin, University College, Galway, Limerick University, Dublin Castle, Leinster House (Dáil Eireann), National University of Ireland, Royal Hibernian Academy, Archbishop of Cashel, McKee Barracks (Chief of Staff), Government Buildings (Taoiseachs Office), Pro-Cathedral, Christ Church Cathedral, N.C.E.A.; Office Public Works. *Clubs:* Arts Dublin, Friendly Brothers of St. Patrick, Dublin. *Signs work:* "Thomas Ryan." *Address:* Robertstown Lodge, Robertstown, Ashbourne, Co. Meath, Ireland.

**RYDER, Betty Pamela Dorothy,** landscape painter in oil on canvas and board; *b* London, 5 Jan., 1924. *m* P.B.H. Furlong, D.F.C., F.R.I.C.S. two *s*. one *d. Educ:* L.M.S., Parsons Green. *Studied:* Epsom School of Art - mature student (1969-75, John Morley). *Exhib:* N.E.A.C., R.B.A., R.A., Kingsmead Gallery, Bookham, David Curzon Gallery, Church Rd., Wimbledon. *Signs work:* "B. Ryder." *Address:* 22 Lansdowne Rd., Wimbledon, London SW20 8AW.

**RYDER, Margaret Elaine,** H.V.P.R.M.S., S.W.A., S.M., F.S.B.A., H.S.,

Member of the Royal Society of Miniature Painters, Sculptors and Gravers (1963); portrait, flower and landscape painter in oil, pastel, and water-colour, and miniaturist on ivory; for 20 years a freelance commercial artist; *b* Sheffield, 1908. *m* Norman Vint. *Educ:* Sheffield High School. *Studied:* Sheffield College of Art; numerous scholarships. *Exhib:* R.A., Paris Salon, Pastel Society, Royal Institute, Exhbn. of Flowers and Gardens, Manchester Academy, Aberdeen Society of Arts, Sheffield Society of Artists, Australia, U.S.A.; five one-man shows in Sheffield. *Signs work:* see appendix. *Address:* 26 Bents Dr., Sheffield S11 9RP.

**RYDER, Susan,** R.P. (1992), N.E.A.C. (1980), N.D.D. (1964), David Murray Travel scholarship (1964); N.E.A.C. Critics prize (1990, 1993), Barney Wilkinson prize (1990), Alexon Portrait Competition (1991); painter in oil and water-colour; *b* Windsor, 1944. *m* Martin Bates. one *s.* one *d. Studied:* Byam Shaw School of Painting (1960-64, Maurice de Sausmarez, A.R.A., Bernard Dunstan, R.A.). *Exhib:* R.A., Portrait Painters, N.E.A.C.; one-man shows, Haste Gallery, Ipswich (2), W.H. Patterson, Albemarle St., W1. (1989, 1995). *Work in collections:* "Miss Pears 1984" Pears Collection, several at Allen and Overy, and James Capel Co. Ltd. *Commissions:* H.R.H. The Princess of Wales (1982); H.M. The Queen (1997). *Signs work:* "Ryder." *Address:* 17 Queen's Gate Place, London SW7 5NY.

**RYLAND, Christopher,** B.A. Fine Art (1972), A.T.C. (1975), S.B.A. (1995); artist specializes in flower paintings in water-colour, printmaking; and teacher *b* Eastbourne, Sussex, 2 Feb., 1951. *m* Pamela Ryland. *Studied:* Goldsmiths' College School of Art, University of London. *Exhib:* The Barbican, London, Antony Dawson Fine Art, London, Medici Galleries, London, R.B.A., Mall Galleries, London, John Russell Gallery, Ipswich. *Commissions:* Wedgewood, Royal Doulton. *Signs work:* "Ryland" or "RYLAND." *Address:* 35 Gainsborough St., Sudbury, Suffolk CO10 6EU.

# S

**SADDINGTON, Donald William,** painter in oil, pastel, water-colour, acrylic, specialising in landscape and marine; Tutor in Art Workshops; *b* Dartford, 31 Aug., 1935. *m* Vivienne Crouch (decd.). one *s.* one *d. Educ:* Wordsworth Secondary. *Studied:* London College of Printing and Graphic Arts (1950-55), Cricklade College, Andover. *Exhib:* R.I., P.S., R.W.S., R.W.A., City A.G., Southampton; Guildhall Gallery, Winchester; Wykeham Galleries, Stockbridge; Linda Blackstone Gallery, many one-man shows in England and France. *Work in collections:* G.P.M.U., Salisbury. *Clubs:* S.G.A. *Signs work:* "D. Saddington." *Address:* 85 Highlands Rd., Andover, Hants. SP10 2PZ.

**SAHAI, Virendra,** O.B.E., Dip.T.P., A.R.I.B.A.; painter in oil and water-colour; *b* Shahjehanpur, India, 25 June, 1933. *m* Ingrid Clara Marie. one *s. Educ:* trained as an architect and townplanner, Polytechnic, Regent St.,

London. *Studied:* painting: Central School of Art. *Exhib:* one-man shows: New Vision Centre and Biggins Gallery, London (1961), Commonwealth Institute, London (1966), Galerie Suzanne de Coninck, Paris (1967), Bear Lane Gallery, Oxford (1967), Horizon Gallery, London (1991); group and mixed exhbns.: Redfern Gallery, London, Commonwealth Biennale of Abstract Art (1961-67), Kettle's Yard, Cambridge (1996), Reading Museum, Bradford Museum, Brighton Museum, Beaune Gallery, Paris, and several others. *Work in collections:* Bradford Museum, Councils for Art Education, Leicester and Oxford; private collections in England, Nigeria, U.S.A., Canada, Germany, Hong Kong and Spain. *Publications:* Guardian, Art International, Discovering an Historic City - Cambridge. *Signs work:* see appendix. *Address:* 39 New Rd., Barton, Cambs. CB3 7AY.

**SAILO, Nina,** sculptor and designer; *b* St. Petersburg, 26 July, 1906. *m* Alpo Sailo, sculptor (died 6 Oct., 1955). three *s.* one *d. Studied:* Drawing School, Viipuri (1921-24), Technical school in Harrow-on-the-Hill (1930-31), pupil of Alpo Sailo from 1932. *Exhib:* Kalevalatalo, Helsinki. *Work in collections:* Kalevala Ladies' Soc., Helsinki, in museums (Finland) and in Sweden; memorial medals in Finland, Sweden and Norway; public monuments at Helsinki, Lappeenranta, Seinäjoki, Tornio, Rauma, Ammansaari, Vierumäki and Imatra and Porvoo, Svulrya, Norway, Boras, Sweden. *Clubs:* Charter mem. of Kalevalatalo Foundation, mem. of Kalevala Ladies' Soc. *Signs work:* "Nina Sailo." *Address:* Kotikuja 02420 Jorvas, Finland.

**ST. JOHN ROSSE,, Nicholas David,** figurative artist in oil, pencil, pastel, gouache, tempera; twice Elizabeth Greenshields Foundation; *b* London, 18 Sept., 1945. *m* Chantale. two *s. Educ:* University College School. *Studied:* under Pietro Annigoni, Florence, and at the Scuolo del Nudo of the Florence Academy, early 60's. *Exhib:* regular one-man shows and group shows London, nationwide and the Continent. *Work in collections:* E. Greenshields Foundation, Montreal. *Commissions:* portrait/figure, religious, houses. *Publications:* series of illustrated articles on egg tempera painting 'Artist' magazine (1980). *Clubs:* St. Ives Soc. of Artists. *Address:* St. Adwen, Trethevy, Tintagel, Cornwall PL34 0BE.

**SALAMAN, Christopher,** artist in oil, bronze and resin bronze; *b* Dorking, 4 Nov., 1939. married. one *s. Educ:* Bedales School. *Studied:* Camberwell School of Art and Crafts under Karel Vogel. *Exhib:* Woodstock Gallery, Upper Street Gallery, Mall Galleries, Margaret Fisher Gallery. *Signs work:* "Christopher Salaman." *Address:* West Park Lodge, High Ongar, Essex.

**SALMON, Martin,** artist in water-colour and gouache; designer (Advertising); *b* Barnehurst, Kent, 19 Apr., 1950. *m* Janice. *Educ:* Dartford Technical School. *Exhib:* Edwin Pollard Gallery, Limpsfield Water-colours. *Work in collections:* Hong Kong, N.Z., Italy, N. America, etc. *Signs work:* "Martin Salmon." *Address:* 17 Dome Hill, Caterham, Surrey CR3 6EE.

**SALMOND, Ronald,** A.T.D. (1938), S.G.A. (1967); wood engraver, etcher, painter, etc.; Head of Art Dept., Preston Manor High School, Wembley (retd.); *b* Hornsey, 30 Dec., 1912. *m* Mary. one *s*. *Educ:* Tollington Grammar School. *Studied:* Hornsey College of Art (print-making under Norman Janes). *Exhib:* R.A., R.E., R.B.A. *Work in collections:* South London A.G., Ashmolean Museum. *Signs work:* "Ronald Salmond." *Address:* 13 Treve Ave., Harrow, Middx. HA1 4AL.

**SALTER, Anthony,** graphic designer and printmaker in etching; graphic designer, University of Greenwich; *b* London, 2 Mar., 1949. *Studied:* Goldsmiths' College of Art (1966-69). *Exhib:* R.A., R.S.P.E.E., P.M.C. *Work in collections:* Rank Zerox, London Borough of Greenwich. *Signs work:* "ANTHONY SALTER." *Address:* 34 Lizban St., London SE3 8SS.

**SALTER, Rebecca,** B.A. Art and Design; artist in acrylic on canvas, works on paper, woodcut prints; *b* Sussex, 24 Feb., 1955. *m* Geoffery Winston. *Educ:* Bristol Polytechnic (1974-77). *Exhib:* extensively in Britain and Japan; solo shows: Jill George Gallery (1994, 1996), New York (1997), Russell Cotes Museum (1998). *Work in collections:* Tate Gallery, British Museum, Portland Museum and San Francisco Museums of Modern Art, Library of Congress, Washington, British Council. *Publications:* Exhibition catalogue (1996). *Signs work:* "REBECCA SALTER." *Address:* c/o Jill George Gallery, 38 Lexington St., London W1R 3HR.

**SALTZMAN, William,** B.S. Education, University of Minnesota (1940); easel and mural painter, designer, teacher; Prof. Emeritus, Macalester College (since 1984); Director-resident artist, Rochester Art Centre, Rochester, Minn. (1948-63), Freelance Studio, Minneapolis, Minn. (since 1963); Prof. of Art, Macalester College, St. Paul, Minn. (since 1966); currently painting and designing stained glass and sheet copper sculpture reliefs for many architectural commissions; exhibiting paintings widely coast to coast; (3) I.F.R.A.A. National awards; Regional/National awards; *b* Mpls., Minn., 9 July, 1916. *m* Muriel. one *s*. two *d*. *Educ:* University of Minnesota; Art Students League, N.Y.C. *Studied:* as above. *Signs work:* see appendix. *Address:* Studio: 5916 Walnut Drive, Edina, Minn. 55436-1750.

**SAMPE, Prof. Astrid,** Hon. Doctor (1989), Hon. R.D.I., London (1949), S.I.D., Dame of the Order of Vasa (1961); Member of A.I.D., New York (1963); designer; director, A.B. Nordiska Kompaniet's design studio since 1937; designer for contract interiors, textile designer for industries making carpets, curtains, upholstery; *b* Stockholm. divorced. one *s*. one *d*. *Educ:* Konstfackskolan, Stockholm; R.C.A., London. *Studied:* Atelier Vignal, Paris (1933), and on scholarship to Germany (1934), Italy (1936). *Exhib:* one-man show, Nationalmuseum, Stockholm (1984); other exhbns. Sweden, Tokyo, New York, etc. *Publications:* Textile Bilderbok, with Vera Djurson (1948). *Clubs:* Faculty of Royal Designers in Royal Society of Arts, London. *Signs work:* "Astrid Sampe, Professor." *Address:* Consult Interior and Industrial Design, Karlaplan 4, 114 60 Stockholm, Sweden.

**SANCHA, Carlos,** R.P.; portrait painter in oil; *b* London, 27 Apr., 1920. *m* Sheila Neal Green. two *s.* one *d. Educ:* Lindisfarne College. *Studied:* Central School of Arts & Crafts under Rodrigo Moyniham, A.R.A., J. Grant; Byam Shaw School under Patrick Philips, R.P. *Exhib:* R.A., R.P. *Signs work:* "C. SANCHA." *Address:* 8 Melbury Rd., London W14 8LR.

**SANDERS, Rosanne Diana,** S.B.A.; R.H.S. gold medal (1981, 1984, 1985, 1988), R.H.S. silver gilt medal (1977, 1980), R.A. miniature award (1985); botanical artist; *b* Stoke Poges, Bucks., 21 June, 1944. one *s. Educ:* Roedean. *Studied:* High Wycombe College of Art for one year, otherwise self taught. *Exhib:* 'Flowers and Gardens' exhbn. Westminster Gallery annually. *Publications:* Portrait of a Country Garden (Aurum Press, 1980), The Art of Making Wine (Aurum Press, 1982), Painting the Secret World of Nature (Search Press, 1987), The English Apple (Phaidon Press, 1988). *Signs work:* "R.D.S." *Address:* Mattiscombe Cottage, Stokenham, Kingsbridge, Devon TQ7 2SR.

**SANDERS, Susan Mary,** D.F.A. (1968), R.A. Schools Post Grad. Cert. (1971); painter in oil, water-colour, pencil, chalk and gouache; Partner, The Studio, Wye Art Gallery; *b* Haslemere, 11 Aug., 1946. *m* Richard Henry Parkinson. one *s.* one *d. Educ:* St. Mary's School, Baldslow Hastings. *Studied:* Byam Shaw School (1964-68), R.A. Schools (1968-71). *Exhib:* R.A. Summer Exhbn. (1971-89), R.W.A., (1983-88), Mall Galleries (1986-89), Bath, Bristol, Stockbridge, etc. *Work in collections:* Merchant Navy Pensions London, B.& Q. Southampton, and various boardrooms and offices. *Publications:* work repro.: Whatmans Ltd. Calendar (1989), advertising of B.& Q. Southampton. *Clubs:* Reynolds, R.A. Schools. *Signs work:* "S. Sanders," "Susan Sanders," or "S.S." *Address:* The Studio House, 113 Bridge St., Wye, Kent TN25 5ED.

**SANDERSON, C. J.,** 1st prize Corfu Landscapes (1967); Dip. d'Honneur Salon International Biarritz (1974); artist in oil, acrylic, water-colour, pastel, gouache, pencil, etching, Indian ink, stone, clay and wood; *b* London, 18 Aug., 1949. *Educ:* Millfield. *Studied:* Byam Shaw School of Art (1967-71) under Maurice de Sausmarez and Ruskin Spear, R.A. *Exhib:* one-man shows: Woodstock Gallery (1974), Gallery Vallombreuse (1974), Gallery Mouffe (1974), Drian Gallery (1979); mixed shows: John Neville (1974), Ashgate Gallery (1973, 1974), Paris Salon (1974), R.A. (1970, 1972, 1973, 1983, 1984, 1985), Wylma Wayne Gallery (1983), Roy Miles Gallery (1995), Grosvenor Gallery (1995), Bruton St. Gallery (1995) and other mixed shows London and abroad. *Work in collections:* D. J. Redwood White, London, and Paris. *Publications:* Noo 1995 Critics Choice Sunday Telegraph. *Clubs:* The Organ. *Signs work:* "C.J. Sanderson." *Address:* 7 Gordon Pl., London W8 4JD.

**SANDERSON, Roger,** N.D.D. (1951), S.G.F.A. (1985), A.O.I. (1980), S.C.A. (1986); painter in water-colour, illustrator, designer (landscapes, figurative, humorous); Senior tutor, Linguaphone Institute's Paris School of Art (1982-94); *b* London, 23 Nov., 1923. *m* Hilde Kokorz. one *s.* three *d. Educ:*

Dulwich College. *Studied:* Croydon and Epsom Art Schools (Barbara Jones, Michael Cadman, Leslie Worth, Ray Evans). *Exhib:* R.I., R.W.S. Open, R.B.A., P.S., U.A., etc. H.W. Peel prizewinner - drawing S.G.F.A. (1992). private and corporate collections. *Publications:* illustrations for leading publishers. *Signs work:* "ROGER SANDERSON," see appendix. *Address:* Bucklers Lodge, St. Ives, Ringwood, Hants. BH24 2NY.

**SANDLE, Michael Leonard,** R.A., F.R.B.S., D.F.A. (Lond.); artist in water-colour and ink, sculptor in bronze; Prof. at The Academy for Visual Arts, Karlsruhe, W. Germany; *b* Weymouth, 18 May, 1936. divorced; one *s*; *m* Demelza Spargo, 1988. *Educ:* Douglas High School. *Studied:* Douglas School of Art, I.O.M. (1951-54), Slade School of Fine Art (1956-59). *Exhib:* group: Young Contemporaries (1957-59), Grabowski Gallery, London (1964, 1966), British Sculptors '72, R.A. (1972), Hayward Annual (1978), Träume vom Frieden, Recklinghausen (1982), etc.; one-man: Drian Gallery (1963), Haus am Lützowplatz, Berlin (1975), Allen Gallery, Vancouver (1975), Fischer Fine Art (1981, 1985), Wilhelm Lehmbruck Museum (1984), Whitechapel (1988), Württembergischer Kunstverein, Stuttgart (1989), Ernst Museum, Budapest (1990), etc. *Work in collections:* Arts Council, British Council, B.M., Imperial War Museum, Leics. A.G., Leics. Educ. Authority, Metropolitan Museum, N.Y., Museum des 20. Jahrhunderts, Vienna, Neuberger Museum of Modern Art, U.S.A., Neue Sammlung, Munich, National-Galerie, Warsaw, Preston Art Museum, Tate Gallery, V. & A., W. German Government, etc. *Signs work:* "Michael Sandle." *Address:* Schloss Scheibenhardt, D 71635 Karlsruhe, W. Germany.

**SANDWITH, Noelle,** artist in egg tempera, water-colour, line, etching, oil, acrylic. *Studied:* Kingston-on-Thames, Croydon and Heatherley's. *Exhib:* R.A., R.B.A., S.W.A., Brighton A.G., Waldorf Astoria, New York; one-man show: Foyle's Art Gallery. *Work in collections:* Royal Naval College, Greenwich, Starr Commonwealth, Albion, Michigan, U.S.A., Royal Free Hospital, London, Auckland Inst. and Museum, N.Z., National Museum of Australia, Museum of Mankind, London (B.M.). *Publications:* work repro.: The Times, Sydney Morning Herald, R.A. Illustrated, Revue Moderne, Frost & Reed, etc. *Signs work:* "Noelle Sandwith." *Address:* 15 Sobell Court, Church St., Henfield, W. Sussex BN5 9NP.

**SANFORD, Sheila,** R.I., R.M.S., M.A.A., H.S.; water-colour artist, miniaturist; *b* Singapore, 1922. *m* Roy Sanford. three *s*. *Educ:* Brentwood School, Southport. *Studied:* St. Martin's School of Art. *Exhib:* Kingsmead Gallery; Llewellyn Alexander (Fine Paintings) Ltd.; M.A.S.-F.; R.I.; R.M.S.; H.S.; R.A. Summer Exhbn. *Work in collections:* M.A.S.-F., Llewellyn Alexander (Fine Paintings) Ltd., M.A.A., R.M.S. *Signs work:* "Sheila Sanford." *Address:* Sheepwash Cottage, Uploders, Bridport, Dorset DT6 4PH.

**SANZ-PASTOR Fz. de PIÉROLA, Consuelo,** Doctor of History; Chairman of I.C.O.M. National Committee (1981-84); Mem. Hispanic Society of America (since1959); Directora Museo Cerralbo (1942-86); Inspectora Museos Bellas Artes (1963-69); Chairman of Sup. Council of Museums (1980-82); Mem., Trustees the Prado Museum (1980-85); Directora Honoraria Museo Cerralbo (since 1986); *b* Madrid. *Publications:* Guia Museo Cerralbo (4th ed. 1981), Catálogos Exposiciones A. Berruguete (1960), San Pablo en el Arte (1963), Francisco de Zurbarán (1964), Museos y Colecciones de España (5th ed. 1990). Guia Museo Casas Reales (Rep. Dominicana 1976), Museo Cerralbo: Catálogo de Dibujos (1976). *Address:* Juan Hurtado de Mendoza 9-28036 Madrid.

**SAPIEHA, Christine,** S.W.A., A.P.A.; painter in acrylic, portraits, sculpture; therapist; *b* Vienna, 5 May, 1934. *m* Adam Fremantle. two *s. Educ:* The Brearley, N.Y.C., Georgetown University, Washington D.C. *Studied:* Abbott School of Art, Washington D.C. (1951-52), Parsons School of Design, N.Y.C. (1952-56). *Exhib:* Mall Galleries, Spirit of London, R.A. Summer Show, Francis Kyle, Stable Gallery, Ice House, Bush House, Beach Thomas Gallery, Burford, Gallery East, N.Y., Westminster Gallery. *Work in collections:* Sheldon Weisfeld, Brownsville, Tex., W.A.S.L. *Publications:* illustrated science and fiction for children. *Signs work:* see appendix. *Address:* 20 Macduff Rd., Battersea, London SW11 4DA.

**SAPP, Prudence Eugenie (née Williams),** School Cert. with Hons. in Art and English (1945); painter in oil; *b* London, 11 Mar., 1928. *m* Reginald Walter. *Educ:* Wycombe Abbey; Benenden School, Kent; English School of Languages, Chateau d'Oex, Switzerland. *Studied:* C.F.E. Bognor Regis (1964), portraiture at Epsom A.E.C. (1974, Reg Sapp). *Exhib:* one-man shows: Hyde Park Gallery (1992, 1993); two-man shows: Barnes Gallery, SW13 (1994, 1995), Mall Galleries since 1974; R.A. Summer Exhbn. (1987, 1992-95). *Work in collections:* America, Sweden, Japan. *Clubs:* Chelsea Art Soc. *Signs work:* "Prue Sapp." *Address:* 19 Waterer Gdns., Tadworth, Surrey KT20 5PB.

**SAUMAREZ SMITH, Romilly,** Fellow of Designer Bookbinders; bookbinder; *b* London, 10 Feb., 1954. *m* Charles Saumarez Smith. two *s. Studied:* Camberwell School of Art and Crafts (1975-78). *Exhib:* many bookbinding exhbns. since 1982. *Work in collections:* Crafts Council, V. & A., N.Y. Public Library, H.R.C., Austin Texas, British Museum. *Publications:* reviews and articles for Crafts Magazine. *Address:* 13 Newell St., Limehouse, London E14 7HP.

**SAUNDERS, Jutta Gabrielle,** Slade Dip. (1951); painter in oil and watercolour, sculptor in clay; tutor; *b* 10 July, 1929. *m* Vernon Saunders. one *s.* one *d. Educ:* The Hall School, Somerset, St. Maurs, Weybridge. *Studied:* Kingston School of Art (1945-48), Slade School of Fine Art (1948-51) under William Coldstream, John Piper; sculpture under F.E. McWilliam. *Exhib:* R.A., R.W.A., Leicester, London and provincial galleries; sculpture in London. *Work in collections:* England, U.S.A., Brazil, Germany and France. *Signs work:* "J. SAUNDERS." or "J.G.S." *Address:* Flint House, Oatlands Mere, Weybridge,

Surrey KT13 9PD.

**SAVAGE, Judith,** L.D.A.D.; artist in oil on canvas; *b* Sydney, Australia. one *s. Educ:* Australia. *Studied:* Interior Design and Decoration and Mural Design, Chelsea College of Art (1977-80). *Exhib:* London: Loggia Gallery, Leighton House, C.W.A.C., etc. Specialises in colour: therapeutic, psychological, symbolic aspects. Studies in art therapy, psychology, sociology (1991-92). Guest Lecturer Chelsea College of Art. Currently working St. Bernards Psychiatric Hospital, Ealing. *Signs work:* "J. Savage." *Address:* 32 Mansell Rd., The Vale, London W3 7QH.

**SAVEGE, Roma,** painter in oil, gouache, tempera, sculptor in welded steel and glass: sand, blasting, gilding, colouring and engraving; Hon. mem. N.S.; *b* Christchurch, N.Z., 17 July, 1907. *m* R.M. Savege, O.B.E., M.C., F.R.C.S. six *s. Educ:* Queenwood, Eastbourne. *Studied:* Canterbury College of Art, N.Z., and Richmond and Hounslow Colleges, England. *Exhib:* one-man shows, Richmond Hill Gallery, R.A.G., Contemporary Portrait Soc., Circuit Painters, N.E.A.C., Guildhall, etc. Now working in computer graphics with Don Pavey. *Clubs:* N.S., F.P.S., I.P.I., R.A.S. *Signs work:* "Roma Savege." *Address:* Pembroke House, The Green, Richmond, Surrey TW9 1QF.

**SAWYERS, David Robert,** A.T.C. (1964), A.R.E. (1964), M.A. (1983); topographical draughtsman in pen and ink with water-colour washes; *b* Brighton, 29 Apr., 1941. married *Educ:* Varndean Grammar School, Brighton. *Studied:* Brighton College of Arts and Crafts (1959-64), University of Sussex (1982-83). *Exhib:* Gardner Centre, Bankside Gallery, Corn Exchange and Gallery, Brighton Museum and Library. Work held by A.R. Whibley and Son, Fine Art Dealers, Worthing. *Signs work:* "D.R. Sawyers." *Address:* 19 Foundry St., Brighton BN1 4AT.

**SAYCE, Harry H.,** F.I.A.L., N.D.D.; painter; Head of the Art Department, Paddington School; *m* Oonagh McCarthy. one *s.* three *d. Educ:* Trent Park College. *Studied:* Hammersmith School of Art; lithographic artist with the R.E. Field Survey (Reproduction Unit) in North Africa and Italy, Colchester School of Art (1942), Harrow School of Art (1938), Instituta Delle Arte, Florence (1945). *Exhib:* R.A., R.B.A., New Burlington Galleries, Square and Mirror, A.I.A., Football and the Fine Arts, Arts Council Tours, Portsmouth, Worthing, Graves Gallery, Sheffield, Brighton, Piccadilly Gallery. *Clubs:* Chelsea Arts. *Signs work:* "Sayce." *Address:* 9 Brackley Rd., Chiswick, London W4.

**SAYERS, Brian,** B.A. (1978); painter in oil on canvas; *b* Bromley, Kent, 3 Oct., 1954. one *d. Educ:* St Olave's Grammar School, Kent. *Studied:* Slade School of Fine Art (1974-78, Jeffery Camp, Patrick George). *Exhib:* R.A., N.P.G., Long & Ryle, Hohental & Littler, Munich, Discerning Eye, Mall Galleries (1st Prize). *Signs work:* "Brian Sayers" on reverse. *Address:* 27a Walterton Rd., London W9 3PE.

**SCARFE, Laurence,** A.R.C.A.; painter, graphic artist, writer. Murals for the Festival of Britain; s.s. Orcades and Oriana; Jamestown Museum, Virginia;

Royal Garden Hotel, London; penthouse mural, New York, etc. *Exhib:* West End and provincial galleries, U.S.A., Italy; prints for Curwen Gallery. Work in V & A., Tate Gallery, R.I.B.A. Library, Imperial War Museum, Science Museum, Brighton A.G. Lecturer, London Central School of Art & Design (1945-70) and Faculty of Art, Brighton Polytechnic. *Publications:* Rome (1950), Venice (1952), Alphabets (1954), Italian Baroque (Motif, 1961). Sometime art editor and contributor for The Saturday Book. Ceramic design for Carters, Wedgwood, K. Clark. *Address:* (studio) 4 Jeffreys St., London NW1.

**SCHAVERIEN, Pat,** B.A. Hons. in Fine Art (1974), Slade Higher Dip. in F.A. (1976); printmaker in etchings-collographs and linocuts; *b* London, 12 Oct., 1951. *m* Charles Frydman. *Educ:* Middlesex Polytechnic (1970-74). *Studied:* Slade School of Fine Art (1974-76). *Exhib:* V.&A., Museum of London, British Council, Guildhall Library, City of London (R.A.) and mixed exhbns. *Commissions:* The site of Bracken House, London, by the Museum of London, Henderson Assoc. Bldg., Broadgate, London. *Address:* 12 Frognal Lane, London NW3 7DU.

**SCHILSKY, Mrs. Eric:** see FOOT, Victorine Anne.

**SCHLEE, Anne H.,** P.P.N.S.; artist in water-colour, acrylic, ink; Cert. Fine Art (1972); Hon. Officer, National Soc. Painters, Sculptors and Printmakers (1989); *b* Shanghai, China, 1931. *m* Charles A. Schlee. three *d. Educ:* Katharine Branson School, California. *Studied:* International School (1962-65, Chinese art: Chow Chian-Chui), Famous Artists' School (1970-72, Charles Reid, John Pellew, Joseph Laskar, Ray Peese). *Exhib:* Hong Kong, N.S., Chelsea Art Soc., Ridley Art Soc., Women Painters of Washington. *Work in collections:* Guildford House Museum and Gallery; private collections in U.S.A., Canada, Australia, U.K., etc. *Publications:* work repro.: House and Garden. *Signs work:* "Anschlee." *Address:* 6554 Monte Vista Drive N.E., Bainbridge Island, W.A. 98110, U.S.A.

**SCHLEE, Nick,** M.A. (Oxon.); painter in oils; *b* 17 July, 1931. *m* Ann Acheson Schlee;. one *s.* three *d. Educ:* Rugby School (1942-47), Oxford (1952-55). *Studied:* Evening Classes, Art Students League, New York, Central School London, Morley College, Putney Art School, Slade. *Exhib:* one-man, Flying Colours Gallery, Edinburgh (1992), Barbican Centre, University of Liverpool (1994), Christchurch Picture Gallery, Oxford (1996). *Address:* Galvey, Upper Basildon, nr. Reading RG8 8LU.

**SCHWARZ, Hans,** R.B.A. (1981), R.W.S. (1982), N.E.A.C (1982), R.P. (1990), Hunting Group Prize (1981); painter in water-colour and oil; *b* Vienna, 29 Dec., 1922. *m* Lena. two *s. Educ:* Vienna. *Studied:* Vienna Kunstgewerbeschule (1937-38), Birmingham College of Art (1941-43). *Exhib:* R.W.S., R.A., R.B.A., N.E.A.C., R.P.; eighteen one-man shows since 1960: A.I.A., Camden Arts Centre, Cambridge, Thackeray Gallery. *Work in collections:* Glasgow A.G., National Maritime Museum, Newport A.G., Halifax N.Z. A.G., Oxford University, N.P.G. *Publications:* Studio Vista: Figure Painting;

Colour for the Artist; Painting in towns; four for Pitmans, etc. *Signs work:* see appendix. *Address:* c/o R.W.S., Bankside Gallery, 48 Hopton St., London SE1 9JH.

**SCOTT,, Dafila Kathleen,,** S.WL.A. (1991), M.A. (1975), Ph.D. (1978); painter in oil, water-colour; *b* London, 9 June, 1952. *m* Tim Clutton-Brock. one *s*. one *d*. *Educ:* Badminton School, Millfield School, Oxford University. *Studied:* in the studios of Peter Scott (since childhood), Thomas Newbolt and Robin Child (1993). *Publications:* illustrated Antarctica: A Guide to the Wildlife by Tony Soper (Bradt Publications, 1994). *Signs work:* "Dafila Scott" or "DKS." *Address:* White Roses, The Hythe, Reach, Cambs. CB5 0JQ.

**SCOTT, David Henry George Montagu Douglas,** landscape painter and illustrator in oil and water-colour; *b* Edinburgh, 29 Jan., 1945. *m* Laura Harmsworth. two *d*. *Educ:* Eton. *Studied:* Byam Shaw School of Art (1963-66, Maurice de Sausmarez), R.A. Schools (1966-67, Peter Greenham). *Exhib:* R.A., R.B.A., R.P., Rutland Gallery, Thomas Gibson Fine Art, Maclean Gallery, The Scottish Gallery, French Embassy, Wildenstein 'Venice Observed', etc. *Work in collections:* Dublin Art Museum, Thameside Council. *Publications:* illustrated five children's books for Walker Books and Methuen; contributed to 'The Children's Book' (Walker Books), 'Open Door' Series (Thomas Nelson). *Signs work:* "D.S." and date on back of picture. *Address:* 19 Petworth St., London SW11.

**SCOTT, I. Borg,** Associate, Société des Artistes Français, F.R.S.A.; artist in oil and sanguine chalk; *b* 4 Feb., 1940. *Studied:* under Leonard Boden, R.P., and F. Wyatt, V.P.S.W.A., R.M.S. *Exhib:* Salon des Artistes, France; Salon Sony, Osaka, Japan; European Art, Auckland, N.Z.; Roy Miles, London; group shows: Westminster Gallery; Gagliardi Gallery, etc. *Signs work:* "I. Borg Scott." *Address:* 8 Colinwood, Colinwood Rd., Farnham Common, Berks. SL2 3LN.

**SCOTT, Irene Mary,** D.A. (Edin.) (1965), B.A.(Hons.) (1990), M.A. (1994), R.S.W. (1989); artist in water-colour, oil, etching; elected professional mem. S.S.A. (1987); *b* Penicuik, Midlothian, 31 Dec., 1942. *m* Brian S. Duffield. four *s*. one *d*. *Educ:* Lasswade High School. *Studied:* Edinburgh College of Art (1961-65). *Exhib:* R.S.A., R.S.W., S.S.A., various group exhbns., etc. *Work in collections:* Britain, Canada, N. Ireland, Norway, Poland and U.S.A. *Commissions:* Iona Abbey Ltd. (1997). Member of Board of Directors AXIS (Visual Arts Information Service, 1997). *Signs work:* "Irene M. Scott." *Address:* The Old Farmhouse, Tomnacross, Kiltarlity by Beauly IV4 7HW.

**SCOTT, John Edward,** A.T.D., R.C.A.; Senior lecturer, College of Art, N. Wales; artist in acrylic and mixed media; *b* Beckenham, Kent, 21 Apr., 1934. *Educ:* Windsor Grammar School. *Studied:* Reading University School of Fine Art (1954-57) under Prof. J. Antony Betts. *Work in collections:* owned privately in Europe, esp. London. *Signs work:* "John Scott." *Address:* 8 Halkyn Rd., Chester CH2 3QE.

**SCOTT, Judy,** N.D.D. (1961), C.S.D. (1962); figurative painter in gouache; *b* Herts., 7 Nov., 1939. *Studied:* Maidstone College of Art (1956-58, Dick Lee), Central School of Arts and Crafts (1958-62), mid 80's, Dick Lee. *Exhib:* mixed shows: New Grafton, Abbott & Holder London, N.E.A.C., R.P., R.W.S., R.I., Alresford Gallery, nr. Winchester; R.W.S. Abbott & Holder Travel award (1993), Cadogan Gallery, London, Wells Centre and Bircham Gallery, Norfolk, Barn Gallery, Suffolk. *Signs work:* "J. Scott." *Address:* 4 Church Cottage, Bale, Fakenham, Norfolk NR21 0QZ.

**SCOTT, Sally,** painter in oil, pastel, drawing, glass engraver in sandblasting and engraving on flat glass; Partnership with David Peace, Peace and Scott (1986); *b* London, 28 Jan., 1939. *m* Tony Guy, graphic designer (decd.). one *s.* one *d. Educ:* Benenden School, Kent. *Studied:* Croydon College of Art (1957-59), R.A. Schools (1959-62). *Work in collections:* glass work in Norwich, Leicester, Llandaff, St. Albans Cathedrals, Westminster Abbey, Lancaster, Sheffield, Oxford and Cambridge Universities; private collections in France and England. *Publications:* contributed to Drawing, Seeing and Observing by Ian Simpson (1992), co-author, Engraved Glass in Architecture (Peace and Scott, 1995). *Clubs:* A.W.G., Associate Fellow, Guild of Glass Engravers, Art and Architecture. *Signs work:* "Sally Scott." *Address:* The Cottage, Cambalt Rd., London SW15 6EW.

**SCOTT-KESTIN, Colin,** R.M.S. (1995), H.S. (1989), A.S.Eq.A. (1994); painter in oil, water-colour and gouache of landscapes, equestrian and other animal subjects, especially miniatures; *b* 14 Jan., 1921. *m* Mary Widdows. *Educ:* St. Giles School, St. Leonards-on-Sea. *Studied:* Beckenham School of Art (1938-39, Henry Carr, R.P.). *Exhib:* R.M.S., H.S., S.Eq.A., Llewellyn Alexander (Fine Art), where awarded a Commendation of Excellence (1995). *Work in collections:* war sketches, Royal Signals Museum, Blandford. *Signs work:* "C. SCOTT-KESTIN." *Address:* Strapp Cottage, Skillgate La., Chiselborough, Som. TA14 6TP.

**SCOTT-TAGGART, Elizabeth Mary Josephine,** N.D.D.; sculptor working mainly as wood-carver; *b* nr. Croydon, 10 Oct., 1927. *Educ:* Old Palace School, Croydon. *Studied:* Central School of Arts and Crafts, and St. Martin's, London (1945-49). *Exhib:* R.A.; group shows: R.B.A., Trends at Mall Galleries, Loggia Gallery, Wooburn and Cookham Festivals; one-man shows at Century Galleries, Henley-on-Thames. Full mem. F.P.S. Has recently started studying and practising Chinese Brush Painting. *Signs work:* "est." *Address:* 96 Gregories Rd., Beaconsfield, Bucks. HP9 1HL.

**SCROPE-HOWE, Pat,** Sociétaire of Société des Artistes Indépendants Paris (1973); Sociétaire of Artistes Français Le Salon Paris (1975); painter in oil, pastel, acrylic, water-colour; sculptor in cire perdue and GRP/bronze; *b* London, 27 Jan., 1926. married two *s. Studied:* Torbay Art School (1958-59), Saskatchewan Art Council (1959-60), Bourneville Art School (1961-62), Manchester Fine Arts (1963-69), Florence, Rome and Venice. Also travelled and painted in France, U.S.A., Spain, Egypt, Far East, South America and the Caribbean. Studied under Harry Rutherford (pupil of Sickert) for portraiture and studies in pastel and oils, Terry McGlynn for abstract and experimental art, Ian McDonald Grant for History of Art, life and composition. *Exhib:* Paris: Salon des Nations (1984), Grand Palais (Indépendants and Artistes Français) since 1973; provinces: Salford Open (1964), Withington, Liverpool Open (bi-annual), Colin Jellicoe Gallery, Manchester College; London: R.S.M.A. Boat Show and National Tour (1969-73). Painting rented via R.S.M.A. for a Polaris Submarine which went under North and South Poles (1973); London International Open, S.W.A. and their National Tour (1972), Laing Competition (1975), Hesketh Hubbard Soc., U.A., Long Gallery, Isleworth (solo show), Royal Horticultural Art Exhbn., Festival of Paintings and Graphic Art (1972); Ireland: Kilkenny (solo show), Dunmore East, Waterford (Studio, permanent solo show). *Work in collections:* Canada, Australia, Gt. Britain, Ireland and the continent. Has appeared on CKBI TV (Canada) to talk on art. *Signs work:* "Pat Scrope-Howe." *Address:* Chandos, 185 Spring Grove Rd., Isleworth, Middx. TW7 4AL.

**SCRYMGEOUR WEDDERBURN, Janet,** F.R.B.S. (1980), R.S.A. Ottillie Helen Wallace Scholarship (1972), R.S.A. Benno Schotz Prize (1973), Paris Salon bronze medal, silver medal; sculptor in clay and bronze, stained glass window designer; *b* Winchester, 14 Aug., 1941. *m* Mervyn Fox-Pitt. one *s.* two *d. Educ:* Kilgraston, Convent of the Sacred Heart, Bridge of Earn, Perthshire. *Studied:* with Alastair Ross, F.R.B.S. (1970-71). *Exhib:* R.S.A. (1971-76, sculpture); Paris Salon (1972, 1973, sculpture). *Work in collections:* East Window of the Episcopal Church of St. James the Great, Cupar, Fife; West Window the Chapel Royal, Falkland Palace; Meditation Window Bedale Church, Yorks.; Victory and Freedom Windows, R.A.F. Leuchars, St. Paul's Church (1993), Sir Nicholas Fairbairn, M.P. (Scottish National Portrait Gallery), (posthumous) The Marquis of Bute, National Museum of Scotland. *Commissions:* St. Columba 1997 (Diocese of Dunkeld), Admiral Lord Duncan, 1997 (Camperdown Trust), Dundee Sea Gate (seven foot high). *Signs work:* "J.S.W." *Address:* Grange Scrymgeour, Cupar, Fife. KY15 4QH.

**SCULL, Paul Harvey,** B.F.A.Hons. (1975), H.D.F.A.Lond. (1978), R.E. (1986), M.Ed. (1988); artist; Head of Fine Art, Herefordshire College of Art and Design; *b* London, 1953. *Educ:* Kimbolton School, Cambs. *Studied:* Northampton School of Art (1971-72), Maidstone College of Art (1972-75, Stuart Brisley, William Bowyer, Joan Williams), Slade School of Fine Art (1976-78, David Leverett). *Exhib:* R.A. Summer Exhbns., R.E., National Exhbn. of Prints, Blackpool, Humberside Printmaking Competition. *Work in collections:* Rank Xerox, Sheffield Metropolitan Borough, Bedfordshire, Kent, Hereford and Worcester C.C's. *Signs work:* "Paul Scull." *Address:* Fair View, Brockhampton, Hereford HR1 4SQ.

**SEAGER, Harry Abram,** A.T.D. (Birm., 1955); sculptor in glass and mixed media, cast and constructed metals; Senior Lecturer, College of Art, Stourbridge, W.Midlands; *b* Birmingham, 9 May, 1931. married. two children. *Educ:* Holly Lodge Grammar School, Smethwick, Warley, W.Midlands. *Studied:* College of Art, Birmingham. *Work in collections:* City Art Gallery, Leeds, C.A.S., London, Joseph H. Hirshorne Coll., U.S.A., D.O.E. London, V. & A., W.Midlands Arts; private collections in Canada, U.K., U.S.A., Holland, Italy. two children. *Address:* 1 Baylie St., Stourbridge, W.Midlands DY8 1AZ.

**SEAL, Norman,** painter in oil, ink, water-colour, calligrapher; *b* Warsop, Notts., 26 Feb., 1921. one *s.* one *d. Educ:* Mansfield Technical College. *Studied:* Mansfield College of Art (1963). *Exhib:* Nottingham Castle (1965), Fermoy, Kings Lynn (1978), Hudson Gallery, Wisbech (1978), Assembly House, Norwich (1978, 1990), Municipal Gallery, Mansfield (1981), Angles Theatre, Wisbech (1988), Central Library, Cambridge (1988). *Clubs:* Cambridge Arts Forum. *Signs work:* "N. Seal" and see appendix. *Address:* 15 Westfield Rd., Wisbech, Cambs. PE13 3EU.

**SEARLE, Ronald,** *b* Cambridge, 3 Mar., 1920. *Studied:* Cambridge School of Art (1936-39). *Exhib:* Leicester Galleries (1948, 1950, 1954 and 1957); Kraushaar Galleries, New York (1959); Bianchini Gallery, New York (1963); Kunsthalle, Bremen (1965); Wilhelm-Busch Museum, Hanover (1965, 1976); Wolfgang Gurlitt Museum, Linz, Austria (1966); Galerie La Pochade, Paris (1966, 1967, 1968, 1969, 1971, 1976); Galerie Carmen Cassé, Paris (1975, 1977), Galerie Gurlitt, Munich (1967, 1969, 1970, 1971 and 1973); retrospectives: Bibliothèque Nationale, Paris (1973), Prussian National Gallery (1976), etc. *Clubs:* Garrick. *Signs work:* see appendix. *Address:* c/o Tessa Sayle, 11 Jubilee Pl., London SW3 3TE.

**SEDDON, Richard Harding,** P.R.W.S., A.R.C.A., Ph.D.; painter in oil and water-colour, and writer on art. *Educ:* King Edward VII School and Reading University. *Studied:* Sheffield College of Art (1932-36); Royal College of Art (1936-39). *Exhib:* R.A., R.W.S. *Work in collections:* H.M. The Queen, V. & A., Imperial War Museum, Sheffield, Leeds, Derby, Southport, Reading, Philadelphia (U.S.A), Neufchatel (France). *Publications:* The Academic Technique of Oil Painting (1960), A Hand Uplifted (War Artist Memoirs) (1963), Art Collecting for Amateurs (1965), A Dictionary of Art Terms (1982) (with K. Reynolds), The Artist's Studio Book (1983); art criticism in The Guardian and most art journals; London art critic of Birmingham Post (1961-70); of Yorkshire Post since 1974. *Address:* 6 Arlesey Cl., London SW15 2EX.

**SEE-PAYNTON, Colin Frank,** R.C.A. (1993), R.E. (1986), S.WL.A. (1986), S.W.E. (1984), A.R.E. (1983); painter, etcher and engraver in water-colour, etching and wood engraving; *b* 1946. *m* Susie See. *Educ:* Bedford. *Studied:* Northampton School of Art (1963-65, Henry Bird). *Exhib:* R.A., R.E., R.W.S., S.W.E., S.WL.A. *Work in collections:* Ashmolean Museum Oxford, Beecroft A.G., Southend, Bedford C.C., Fremantle Museum, Australia, National Museum of Wales, National Library of Wales, S.W.A.N., and many others. *Publications:* illustrations in many private press and commercial publications. *Signs work:* see appendix. *Address:* Oerle Hall, Berriew, Powys, Wales, SY21 8QX.

**SEGAL, Hyman,** R.B.A.; artist in charcoal and all mediums; founder mem. Penwith Soc.; *b* London, 26 May, 1914. *m* Diane Christie. *Educ:* Elementary and J.F.S., London. *Studied:* St. Martin's (Leon Underwood, Vivian Pitchforth). *Exhib:* one-man shows: Bankfield Museum, Halifax, Batley, Nairobi, E. Africa, International Club, Manchester, Downings Bookshop, Heffer Gallery, Castle Gallery, St. Ives, The Crypt, St. Ives, Penwith Soc., St. Ives Soc. of Artists. *Work in collections:* 'Bernard Leach' National Museum of Wales, 'Study of a Footballer' Manchester City A.G., The Sloop Inn, St. Ives permanent exhbn. since 1948. *Publications:* "Familiar Faces of St. Ives"; Art Colony"; "As I was Going to St. Ives." *Clubs:* Chelsea Arts. *Signs work:* "H. Segal." *Address:* 10 Porthmeor Studios, St. Ives, Cornwall TR26 IHE.

**SELBIE, Rosy,** artist in oil, water-colour, pastel; *b* Wales, 1 Oct., 1930. *m* Robert, civil engineer. one *s.* one *d. Educ:* Birtwhistles, London SW1. *Studied:* Sir John Cass Foundation (Roy Marsden). *Exhib:* solo shows: Knapp Gallery, Burghclere Manor; numerous mixed shows including Mall Galleries. *Work in collections:* Regents College, London, Test Valley Hampshire. *Clubs:* Sloane. *Signs work:* "Selbie." *Address:* Fellowes Cottage, Hurstbourne Priors, Whitchurch, Hants. RG28 7SE.

**SELBY, William,** A.R.B.A. (1988), A.R.W.S. (1987), R.O.I. (1982); painter; *b* Fitzwilliam, nr. Pontefract, Yorks., 25 Dec., 1933. *m* Mary. *Educ:* Fitzwilliam Secondary Modern. *Work in collections:* Mapin Gallery, Sheffield. Prizes: Christina Leger award R.O.I. (1985, 1987), Chris Beetle award (1986), L. Cornelissen & Son award R.O.I. (1988). *Clubs:* Leeds Fine Art. *Signs work:* "SELBY" or "WILLIAM SELBY." *Address:* 22 Sandringham Rd., Byrom, Knottingley, Yorks. WF11 9NS.

**SELL, Richard,** A.T.D. (1949); artist in lithography, water-colour, drawing; Vice Pres. Cambridge Drawing Soc.; *b* Berkhamsted, 26 Jan., 1922. *m* Jean Bryant. one *s.* one *d. Educ:* Berkhamsted School. *Studied:* Chelsea School of Art (Brian Robb, Morland Lewis, Harold Jones, Ceri Richards, Ella Griffin). *Exhib:* one-man shows: Old Fire Engine House Ely, Heffer Gallery Cambridge, Trumpington Gallery Cambridge; R.A. Summer Shows, National Exhbn. Prints and Drawings R.I. Gallery (1964), E. Anglian Art Today R.I. Gallery (1969), Mall Prints (1971, 1972, 1973), Art in Business, Arthur Young, Cambridge (1987, 1988). *Commissions:* portrait drawings for several Cambridge colleges; lithographs for Lloyd's Register of Shipping, Emmanuel College Cambridge, Pembroke College Cambridge. *Signs work:* "Richard Sell 1998." *Address:* 22 Station Rd., Fulbourn, Cambridge CB1 5ES.

**SEMMENS, Jennifer,** B.A.(Hons.) (1986); painter in mixed media on paper and etcher; *b* Penzance, 12 Jan., 1964. *m* Roger Asbury. one *d. Educ:* in Penzance, Cornwall. *Studied:* Falmouth School of Art (1982-83),

# WHO'S WHO IN ART

Gloucestershire College of Arts and Technology, Cheltenham (1983-86). *Exhib:* New Ashgate Gallery, Farnham; Coram Gallery, London; Marsden Contemporary Art, London; Gibbs Gallery, Canterbury; On Line Gallery, Southampton. *Publications:* 'Twenty-Two Painters (who happen to be women) St. Ives' by Marion Whybrow; 'Drawing Towards the End of the Century' by Newlyn Society of Artists. *Clubs:* Penwith Soc. of Artists, Newlyn Soc. of Artists. *Signs work:* "J. Semmens." *Address:* Higher Barn, Bone Farm, Bone Valley, Heamoor, Penzance, Cornwall TR20 8UJ

**SEMPLE, Patricia Frances,** S.S.A. (1980), R.S.W. (1987); painter of expressionist landscape in water-colour, ink, oil, charcoal; tutor, Open College of the Arts; *b* Kintyre, Argyll, 3 July, 1939. *Educ:* Lasswade Grammar. *Studied:* Edinburgh College of Art (1958-63), post. grad. (1963-64). *Exhib:* Stirling Gallery, Art Space Aberdeen, Edinburgh University, Aberdeen University, Dundee College of Art, Open Eye Gallery Edinburgh, regularly with R.S.A., S.S.A., R.S.W.; group shows: Glasgow Group, Scottish Gallery, Compass Gallery, Arts Council Travelling Exhbn. Scotland and Yugoslavia. *Work in collections:* S.A.C., Aberdeen A.G., B.B.C., Globus, Gateway Inc. N.Y., Educ. Inst. of Scotland, Grampian TV, Aberdeen Hospitals, Shell U.K. *Signs work:* "Pat Semple." *Address:* Tigh-Nan-Uiseagan, By Drumnadrochit, Inverness-shire.

**SENFT, Nadin,** A.R.B.S. (1980), City and Guilds D.F.A. (1968); sculptor in bronze, stone, wood, perspex; *b* London, 8 Mar., 1932. *m* Dr. Paul Senft (decd.). *Educ:* St. Mary's Abbey, London; Eversley, Lymington, Hants. *Studied:* Leicester College of Art; City and Guilds of London College of Art, Kennington. *Exhib:* R.A., Alwin Gallery, Royal Exchange, Jordan Gallery, Annely Juda Fine A.G., Hertford Museum, Sutton College of Art, Natalie Stern Gallery, Richard Demarco Gallery, Edinburgh, Scone Palace, Perth, Herbert Museum and A.G. Coventry, Aim Gallery, Milton Keynes. *Commissions:* 'St. George and the Dragon', St. George's Centre, Preston; 'Seated Bronze Figures' Guildhall Sq., Portsmouth; Royal Inst. of Chartered Surveyors Trophy (sculpture of Logo in perspex for annual presentation); The Fasson Trophy (6 aluminium sculptures). *Publications:* Sixteen Stories as they Happend by Michael Bullock. *Signs work:* "Nadin Senft" and see appendix. *Address:* Willowbrook, Cotswold Cl., Tredington, Warwicks. CV36 4NR.

**SENIOR, Bryan,** painter of figures, landscape, still-life; *b* Bolton, 1935. *Exhib:* one-man shows include: Crane Kalman Gallery, London (1965, 1968, 1971), Demarco, Edinburgh (1970, 1973), Vaccarino, Florence (1968, 1970, 1975), Pucker-Safrai, Boston, U.S.A. (1968), Bolton A.G. (1961), Fieldborne Galleries, London (1972), Ashgate Gallery, Farnham (1973), Exeter Museum (1974), Exeter University (1975), Galleria Acropoli, Milan (1976), Lad Lane Gallery, Dublin (1977), Architectural Assoc., London (1982), Hampstead Museum (1983), Manor House, Finchley (1989), Tricycle Gallery (1990), Hooper Gallery, London (1991). Prizes: G.L.C. 'Spirit of London'; Druce

Competition. *Address:* 134 Upper Grosvenor Rd., Tunbridge Wells, Kent TN1 2EX.

**SEROTA, Nicholas Andrew,** Director, Tate Gallery (since 1988); *b* 27 Apr., 1946. *m* Angela Mary Beveridge (marr. diss. 1995); two *d*; *m* Teresa Gleadowe (1997). *Educ:* Haberdashers' Askes School, Hampstead and Elstree; Christ's College, Cambridge (B.A.). *Studied:* Courtauld Inst. of Art, London (M.A.). *Publications:* Experience or Interpretation: The Dilemma of Museums of Modern Art 1996 (Neurath Lecture, National Gallery, !996). Hon. Fellow, Queen Mary and Westfield College; Univ. of London (1988), Hon. D. Arts, City of London Polytechnic (1990), Hon. F.R.I.B.A. (1992), Hon. D.Litt. Plymouth University (1993), Hon. D.Litt. Keele University (1994), Hon. F.G.C.L. (1994), Hon. D.Litt. South Bank University (1996), Hon. D.Univ., University of Surrey (Wimbledon School of Art, 1997). Regional Art Officer and Exhbn. Organiser, Arts Council of G.B. (1970-73); Director, Museum of Modern Art, Oxford (1973-76); Director, Whitechapel A.G. (1976-88). Mem., Fine Art Advisory Com., British Council (1976-), Chairman 1992; Trustee, Public Art Development Trust (1983-87); Trustee, Architecture Foundation (1992-). Selector 'A New Spirit in Painting', R.A. (1981), Carnegie International, Carnegie Museum of Art, Pittsburgh (1985, 1988). *Address:* Tate Gallery, Millbank, London SW1P 4RG.

**SETCH, Terry,** D.F.A. (Lond., 1959); painter; Senior Lecturer in Fine Art, University of Wales Inst. Cardiff (1964); *b* London, 11 Mar., 1936. *m* Dianne Shaw. one *d. Educ:* Sutton and Cheam School. *Studied:* Sutton School of Art (1950-54), Slade School of Fine Art (1956-60). *Work in collections:* Tate Gallery, Arts Council of G.B., Welsh Arts Council, Aberystwyth University, Contemporary Arts Soc. of Wales, V. & A., University College, London, Gallery of Modern Art, Lodz, Poland, Swansea University, British Council, National Museum of Wales, Contemporary Arts Soc., Coleg Harlech, Wakefield City A.G., Glynn Vivian Museum and A.G., Northampton A.G., Rugby Borough Council, Leicestershire Educ. Authority, Cardiff C.C., Glamorgan Educ. Authority, Normal College Bangor. *Commissions:* National Museum and Galleries of Wales, painting for the restaurant, Cardiff. *Publications:* New Work by Terry Setch, pub. Welsh Arts Council, National Museum of Wales, Camden Arts Centre (1992). *Clubs:* Chelsea Arts, London. *Signs work:* "Terry Setch." *Address:* 111 Plymouth Rd., Penarth, Vale of Glamorgan CF64 5DF, S. Wales.

**SEUPHOR, Michel,** writer, painter (in Chinese ink, and coloured paper collage), art historian, poet; *b* Antwerp, 10 Mar., 1901. *m* Suzanne Plasse. one *s. Educ:* Antwerp and University of Louvain. *Exhib:* Galerie Berggruen, Paris; Galerie Denise Renée, Paris; Rose Fried Gallery, New York; Galleria Lorenzelli, Milan; Moderne Galerie, Basel; Galerie der Spiegel, Cologne; Documenta II, Kassel; Galerie St. Stephen, Wien; Galerie Saint Laurent, Brussels; Galerie Ziegler, Zürich; Robles Galleries, Los Angeles; Galerie

# WHO'S WHO IN ART

Martano, Turin; Musée National d'Art Moderne, Paris; Musée de le Boverie, Liége. *Publications:* Seuphor: Un siècle de libertés, Entretiens, Hazum, Paris (1996). Centre Pompidou, Paris. Tapestries, mosaics and ceramics (Sèvres). *Signs work:* see appendix. *Address:* 83 avenue Emile Zola, F. 75015 Paris, XV.

**SEWARD, P.,** A.R.C.A., Hon. Retd. A.R.E., R.W.S., Rome Scholar, Dip. in Paper Conservation; artist in pen and ink, water-colour, etching and lithography; *b* London, 1926. *Studied:* Royal College of Art, Camberwell School of Art and Crafts (Conservation of Prints and Drawings). *Exhib:* R.A., Bankside Gallery, Curwen Gallery, Barbican, London, Flitcroft Gallery, London. *Publications:* children's books, cookery books. *Signs work:* "P. Seward." *Address:* 30 Sekforde St., London EC1R 0HH.

**SEWELL, Peggy Joan Kearton,** M.F.P.S. (1986); painter of landscapes and flowers in oil on canvas; Freeman of the Worshipful Company of Painter-Stainers, London; *b* London, 18 Dec., 1920. *m* Robert H. Sewell, Ch.M., F.R.C.S. two *d*. *Educ:* Manchester High School, and Merchant Venturers College, Bristol. *Studied:* Croydon Art College and privately with Richard Walker, N.D.D., A.T.D. *Exhib:* Guildhall London, Royal Exchange, Fairfield Halls Croydon, Loggia Gallery, London and Painters Hall, London. *Clubs:* Croydon Art Soc., Purley Art Group, F.P.S., Tandridge Art Soc. *Signs work:* "Joan Sewell." *Address:* 4 Bayards, Warlingham, Surrey CR6 9BP.

**SEYMOUR, Jack,** N.D.D. (1954), Ad.Cert.Ed. (1962); painter of landscapes, interiors and portraits in oil, pencil and water-colour; *b* London, 23 Apr., 1928. one *s*. two *d*. *Educ:* Southall Technical School. *Studied:* Harrow School of Art (1948-52, C. Sanders, T. Ward), Gloucester College of Art (1952-54, R.S.G. Dent), St. Paul's College, Cheltenham (1960-62, H.W. Sayer). *Exhib:* R.B.A., R.P., R.A., R.W.A.; one-man show, Stroud, Gloucs.; provincial galleries, travelling exhbns. and abroad. *Work in collections:* Britain and abroad. *Signs work:* "SEYMOUR" and year. *Address:* 3 Holeground, School Hill, Wookey Hole, Som. BA5 1BU.

**SHACKLETON, Keith Hope,** R.S.M.A., S.WL.A., Hon.Doctor of Laws; oil painter, writer, naturalist, T.V.; *b* Weybridge, 16 Jan., 1923. *m* Jacqueline. two *s*. one *d*. *Educ:* Melbourne, Australia, Oundle. *Work in collections:* R.S.M.A. Maritime Museum, Greenwich, Birkenhead, Belfast A.G., LYW Art Museum Wisconsin, U.S.A. *Publications:* Wake, Tidelines, Wild Animals in Britain, Ship in the Wilderness, Wildlife and Wilderness. *Signs work:* see appendix. *Address:* Woodley Wood Farm, Woodleigh, Kingsbridge, Devon TQ7 4DR.

**SHANKS, Duncan Faichney,** D.A., A.R.S.A. (1972), R.G.I. (1983), R.S.W. (1987), R.S.A. (1990); artist in oil; *b* Airdrie, 30 Aug., 1937. *m* Una Brown Gordon. *Studied:* Glasgow School of Art. *Exhib:* Art Spectrum, Contemporary Art from Scotland (1981-82), Five Glasgow Painters, Scottish Painting - Toulouse, About Landscape - Edinburgh Festival, Scottish Painting - Rio de Janeiro, Ten Scottish Painters - London, Scottish Painting - Wales, Bath, Basle,

London Art Fairs; one-man shows: Stirling University, Scottish Gallery, Fine Art Soc. - Glasgow and Edinburgh, Talbot Rice Gallery, Edinburgh (cat.), Crawford Centre, St. Andrews, Maclaurin Gallery, Ayr, Glasgow A.G. (1990), Touring Exhbn. Wales (1991-92) (Cat.), Billcliffe Fine Art (1992). *Work in collections:* A.C.G.B., Scottish Art Council, Glasgow, Dundee and Swansea A.Gs., Hunterian Museum, Edinburgh University, City Art Centre, Edinburgh, Lillie A.G., Government Art Collection, Scottish TV., 'Talking Pictures', STV film. *Signs work:* "SHANKS." *Address:* Davingill House, Crossford By Carluke, Clyde Valley ML8 5RA.

**SHANKS, Una Brown,** D.A. (Textiles) (1962), R.S.W. (1988); artist in water-colour, pen and ink; *b* Hartwood, 9 June, 1940. *m* D.F. Shanks. *Educ:* Wishaw High School. *Studied:* Glasgow School of Art (1958-62). *Exhib:* Scottish Artists Shop (1987), Fine Art Soc. (1988, 1989, 1993). Awards: Alexander Stone R.G.I. (1990, 1991), Betty Davies R.S.W. (1993). *Signs work:* "Una B. Shanks." *Address:* Davingill House, Crossford By Carluke, Clyde Valley ML8 5RA.

**SHARP, Elizabeth,** S.Eq.A. (1988), A.S.E.A. (1984), S.W.A. (1986), B.H.S.A.I. (1969); artist in oil and acrylic, China and silk painting, also sculptor specializing in golfing, animal and equestrian subjects; *b* 7 Jan., 1947. *Educ:* Kesteven and Grantham Girls' High School. *Studied:* Leicester College of Art and Design (1965-66), Stoke Rochford College (1966-70). *Exhib:* regularly with S.E.A. and S.W.A. in London; occasionally one-man shows, Napier Gallery, St. Helier, Jersey. *Work in collections:* sculpture in Victoria Centre, Sydney, Australia; Flying Horse Centre, Nottingham; Reindeer Court, Worcester. *Commissions:* Lord's Cricket Club. *Publications:* work repro.: numerous prints and cards. Breeds American Morgan horses, avid golfer. *Clubs:* B.C.P.A.A., British Horse Soc. *Signs work:* "Elizabeth Sharp." *Address:* Stanton Court, Denton, Grantham, Lincs. NG32 1JT.

**SHAVE, Terry,** B.A.(Hons.), H.D.F.A. (Slade); artist in oil, acrylic on canvas, etching; lecturer; Head of Painting, Staffordshire Polytechnic; *b* 8 June, 1952. *Studied:* Loughborough College of Art (1972-75), Slade School of Fine Art (1975-77). *Exhib:* Anderson O'Day Gallery. *Work in collections:* A.C.G.B., Unilever, B'ham City Museum and A.G., Stoke Museum and A.G. "Terry Shave." *Address:* c/o Anderson O'Day, 255 Portobello Rd., London W11 1LR.

**SHAW, Barbara Nancy,** R.H.S. Gold medallist (1980), Grenfell medals (1976, 1977); botanical artist in water-colour; *b* Dartmouth, Devon, 28 Sept., 1922. *m* Denis Latimer, surgeon. three *s.* one *d. Educ:* Fairview College and Hampton Court School. *Exhib:* Chagford Galleries (1977), Thompson Gallery, Aldborough and London, etc. *Work in collections:* U.K., U.S.A., Germany, Japan. *Publications:* author and illustrator: The Book of Primroses (David & Charles 1991), illustrations in The Plantsman, illustrator: Foliage and Form by Phillipa Rakusen, and others. *Clubs:* S.B.A., S.M. *Signs work:* see appendix. *Address:* Tan Cottage, West Lane, Cononley, nr. Keighley, N. Yorks. BD20

8NL.

**SHAW, Sax Roland,** D.A. (Edin.), F.M.G.P.; former Head of Stained Glass Dept., Edinburgh College of Art (retd. 1984); works in tapestry, stained glass, mural decoration, water-colour paintings; *b* Huddersfield, 5 Dec., 1916. *m* Mary. two *s. Educ:* Almondbury Grammar School. *Studied:* Huddersfield, Edinburgh, Paris. *Work in collections:* private and public buildings in Edinburgh, London, New York, San Francisco, Iceland. At present working on windows and tapestries for the Marquis of Bute. *Signs work:* "Shaw." *Address:* 25 Howe St., Edinburgh EH3 6TF.

**SHEARS, Marcelle Dorothy,** R.M.S., P.V.P.S.W.A., H.S.F.; silhouette artist and miniature painter in water-colour on vellum, ivory, plaster, glass and card; *b* Croydon, 16 May, 1926. *m* Arthur D. Shears. two *d. Educ:* Chipstead Valley School, Surrey. *Studied:* with George H. Tozer. Hunting Group finalist (1981), U.S.A., M.A.S.F. (1981, 1983), G.M.A.S. (1992, 1993), H.S., Lucas award (1985), Cert. of Excellence (1994), R.M.S. Hon. Mention gold memorial bowl (1986, 1994, 1996), Llewellyn Alexander Masters award (1995) Outstanding Excellence (1993, 1997). *Exhib:* R.A., Mall Galleries, Westminster Gallery, Southampton A.G., Medici A.G., Portsmouth A.G., Llewellyn Alexander A.G., U.S.A.: M.A.S. Florida, Georgia, Tampa Museum of Art, New York Art Expo (1993). *Work in collections:* Royal Soc. of Miniature Painters, Sculptors and Gravers, Fareham Museum, Hants. *Publications:* R.M.S., One Hundred Years, Painting Miniatures by Burton. *Signs work:* see appendix. *Address:* Trout Cottage, Two Bridges, nr. Princetown, Yelverton, Devon PL20 6SW.

**SHEATH, Janet,** A.R.M.S. (1994), S.W.A. (1995), H.S. (1992); self taught artist in miniatures, water-colour and dry mediums; *b* Portsmouth, 1952. *m* Robert J.C. Sheath. two *d. Educ:* Cowplain Secondary Modern School for Girls. *Exhib:* R.A., R.M.S., S.W.A., S.B.A., H.S., Llewellyn Alexander. *Signs work:* "Janet Sheath" or "J. SHEATH." *Address:* 4 Cupressus Ave., Winford, Sandown, I.O.W. PO36 0LA.

**SHELLEY, Alan William,** Dip.Arch.(Hons.) (1975), R.I.B.A. (1976); artist in water-colour, pen and wash, screen printing; *b* Sidcup, Kent, 13 Feb., 1935. *m* Angela Williams. one *s.* two *d. Educ:* Chislehurst and Sidcup Grammar School. *Studied:* architecture: Medway College of Art (1951-55), Polytechnic of N. London (1971-75). *Exhib:* S.WL.A., R.S.M.A. Mall Galleries, numerous one-man shows since 1984. *Work in collections:* Bexley Museum and Library, Lewisham Library Loan Scheme. *Publications:* book jackets for private publications, and for library edn. of 'Voices in Summer' by Rosemary Pilcher (Severn House Publishing). *Signs work:* "Alan Shelley." *Address:* Ashleigh, 36 Oaklands Rd., Bexleyheath, Kent DA6 7AJ.

**SHEPHARD, Rupert,** Hon. A. L'Accademia Fiorentina; R.P., N.E.A.C.; painter, graphic artist; Slade Dipl.; lecturer, Central School, St. Martin's School of Art (1945-48); Professor of Art, University of Cape Town (1948-63); *b* 12

Feb., 1909. *m* 1st, Lorna Wilmott (decd., 1962); one *s*. two *d*. 2nd, Nicolette Devas (1965). *Exhib:* one-man: Calmann Gall. (1939), Agnews (1962, 1980), Upper Grosvenor Gall. (1966, 1970), Kunsthalle, Bielefeld, Germany (1973), Collectors Gall., Johannesburg (1975), Patrick Seale Gall. (1975, 1979), Sally Hunter Gall. (1985, 1987, 1989, 1991), National Museum of Wales, Parkin Gallery (1977), Cape Town (seven) and Johannesburg (three) (1949-63); general: London: R.A., R.P., etc.; Venice Biennale (1958), São Paulo Bienal (1957), Ljubljana Biennale (1955, 1957, 1959, 1961). *Work in collections:* C.E.M.A. British Museum, War Artists, National Portrait Gall., National Museum of Wales, South African National Gall., Johannesburg Municipal Gall. *Publications:* illustrated: Capescapes (1954), Passing Scene (1966). *Address:* 68 Limerston St., London SW10 0HJ.

**SHEPHEARD, Sir Peter (Faulkner),** Kt. (1980), C.B.E. (1972), B.Arch., Liverpool (1936), P.P.R.I.B.A., M.R.T.P.I., P.P.I.L.A.; architect, town planner, landscape architect, draughtsman and illustrator. In private practice (Shepheard, Epstein & Hunter) (1948-1989); Prof. of Environmental Design (and Dean 1971-76) of the Graduate School of Fine Arts, University of Pennsylvania, Philadelphia (1959); mem. National Parks Commission (1966-68), Countryside Commission (1968-71), Royal Fine Art Commission (1968-71), Artistic adviser, Commonwealth War Graves Commission (1977-); *b* Birkenhead, 1913. *m* Mary Bailey. one *s*. one *d*. *Educ:* Birkenhead School. *Studied:* Liverpool School of Architecture and Dept. of Civic Design. *Exhib:* R.A., etc. *Publications:* Modern Gardens (Arch. Press, 1953), Gardens (C.O.I.D., 1969); illustr.: A Book of Ducks and Woodland Birds. *Signs work:* "Peter Shepheard." *Address:* 21 Well Rd., London NW3 1LH.

**SHEPHERD, David,** O.B.E. (1979), F.R.S.A. (1986), F.R.G.S. (1988); artist; ; *b* 25 Apr., 1931. *m* Avril Gaywood. four *d*. *Educ:* Stowe. *Studied:* under Robin Goodwin (1950-1953); started career as aviation artist, founder member of Guild of Aviation Artists; many worldwide trips for aviation and military paintings for Services; began specializing in African wildlife subjects (1960). *Exhib:* R.A., R.P.; one man exhbns. London (1962, 1965, 1971, 1978), Johannesburg (1966, 1969), New York (1967). *Work in collections:* 15ft reredos of Christ for Army Garrison Church, Bordon, Hants (1964). Portraits: H.E. Dr Kenneth Kaunda, President of Zambia (1967), H.M. The Queen Mother (1969), H.E. Sheikh Zaid of Abu Dhabi (1970). In 1984 David founded The David Shepherd Conservation Foundation, a registered charity, to raise funds and awareness for endangered animals. Awards: Order of Golden Ark by H.R.H. Prince Bernhard of The Netherlands (1973), Hon.D.F.A.Pratt Inst. N.Y. (1971), Hon. Doctor of Science, Hatfield Polytechnic (1990), Member of Honour, World Wildlife Fund (1979), Order of British Empire (1979), Officer (Brother) of the Order of St. John (1996).Life story subject of BBC TV documentary "The Man Who Loves Giants" (1971), Harlech TV documentary, "Elephants and Engines", etc. Auctioned five wildlife paintings in U.S.A. in 1971 and raised funds for Bell Jet Ranger Helicopter for anti-poaching work in

Zambia, in return President Kaunda presented an 1896 steam locomotive, it's return to Britain subject of BBC TV documentary "Last Train to Mulobezi" (1974); painted "Tiger Fire" 1973, raised £127,500 for Operation Tiger (1973). Purchased two mainline steam locomotives 92203 Black Prince, and 75029 The Green Knight (1967) and founded The East Somerset Steam Railway, Cranmore, Somerset, a registered charity and fully operational steam railway. *Publications:* Artist in Africa (1967), The Man who Loves Giants (1975), Paintings of Africa and India (1978), A Brush with Steam (1983), David Shepherd: The Man and his Paintings (1985), An Artist in Conservation (1992), David Shepherd, My Painting Life (1995). Videos: The Man who Loves Giants: The Most Dangerous Animal; Behind the Scenes, In Search of Wildlife I and II. Ambition: to drive Black Prince into Waterloo Station. Recreations: driving steam locomotives and raising money for wildlife. *Address:* Winkworth Farm, Hascombe, Godalming, Surrey GU8 4JW.

**SHEPHERD, Gerald,** F.F.P.S. (1990); painter and graphic artist in oil, acrylic, ink and pencils; currently co-ordinating the 'Artists for Animals' project; Director, Ionist Art Group; *b* 1955. *Exhib:* solo and group exhbns. in London and south of England, including Loggia Gallery, London. *Work in collections:* Surrey University, Stevenage Art and Leisure Centre; private collections. *Publications:* edited, Ion Exchange Magazine. *Clubs:* Founded: Ionist Art Group, Process Art, Artists for Animals; F.P.S., Marlborough Artists. *Signs work:* usually "G.S." occasionally "GERALD SHEPHERD"; signature often incorporated into composition. *Address:* 18 Ham Cl., Aughton, Collingbourne Kingston, nr. Marlborough, Wilts. SN8 3SB.

**SHEPHERD, Philip,** R.W.S. (1977); Gold medal Paris Salon (1976); artist in water-colour, oil, wood engraving; *b* London, 4 May, 1927. two *d. Studied:* Harrow College of Arts and Crafts (1941-45), Birmingham College of Arts and Crafts (1948-50). *Exhib:* R.W.S. *Work in collections:* Fitzwilliam Musem Cambridge, Whitworth A.G. Manchester (wood engravings). *Signs work:* "Philip Shepherd, R.W.S." *Address:* 52 Aston Cantlow Rd., Wilmcote, Stratford-upon-Avon, Warwickshire CV37 9XZ.

**SHEPHERD, Valerie Mary,** S.W.A. (1987), Cert.A.D.; graphic artist and printmaker in monotype with gouache, water-colour, oil, linocuts, etching; *b* Orpington, Kent, 5 Feb., 1941. *m* Norman Shepherd, dental surgeon. one *s.* two *d. Educ:* St. Philomena's Convent. *Studied:* Gyula Sajo Atelier; Brighton Polytechnic. *Clubs:* S.W.A., Soc. of Sussex Painters, W. Sussex Art, Arun Art Soc., Atelier Art, Assoc. of Sussex Artist. *Signs work:* "Valerie Shepherd." *Address:* Bacon Hall, Poling, nr. Arundel, Sussex BN18 9PO.

**SHEPPARD, Faith Tresidder,** landscape and marine painter; Médailles d'Or (1978) and d'Argent Paris Salon (1975), Men.Hon. (1970), Diplôme d'Honneur, Cannes (1974), First Prize Herts. Countryside (1975); Welwyn Trophy (1982, 1989), Prize water-colour Bury A.G. (Granada TV); *b* London. *Studied:* under Mother, Nancy Huntly (R.A. Schools 1910-1914 frequent exhibitor R.A. two Silver Medals Nat.Comp.); R.A. Schools; Byam Shaw Chelsea. *Exhib:* R.A., Harrods, B.B.C., Mall Galleries, home and abroad. *Work in collections:* Buckingham Palace, Prime Minister Thatcher, Barbara Cartland Sir Derrick Holden-Brown, Home Counties Newspapers. *Publications.* "Bruges"; "Caernarfon", "20th Century British Marine Painting" (Brook-Hart) Laing's Calendar "Chartres." *Clubs:* Reynolds, Chelsea Art, W.G.C., Hertford St. Alban's (Vice-President). *Signs work:* "Faith Sheppard." *Address:* Studio. 29 Digswell Rd., Welwyn Garden City, Herts.

**SHEPPARD, Liz,** Intermediate in Arts Crafts (1953), N.D.D. Painting (1955), A.T.D. (Lond. 1956), Scholarship Pratt bequest (1956, to Italy); painter printmaker in etching; *b* Tonbridge, 20 Dec., 1933. *m* Clive Sheppard, sculptor (decd.). two *s.* one *d. Educ:* St. Albans Girls Grammar School. *Studied:* St. Albans School of Art (1950-52); St. Martin's College of Art (1952-55) under Frederick Gore, Derrick Greaves; London University Institute (1955-56) *Exhib:* Digswell House, Bear Lane Gallery, Oxford, City Gallery, Milton Keynes, R.A. Summer Exhbn. (1977, 1978), Cartoon (1978), Wavendor Festival (1979), Margaret Fischer (1980), Bedford School (1990), Leighton Buzzard Arts Centre (1990), Milton Keynes Exhbn. Gallery (1991), Bromham Mill Gallery, Bedford (1992), S.W.A. (1993), Art in Milton Keynes (1993). *Work in collections:* H.R.H. The Princess Margaret; John Dankworth and Cleo Laine; The Open University; Milton Keynes Development Corp.; M.K Hospital; Anglian Water, Huntingdon; Bedford Art Loan Collection: Bedfordshire Library; Leicester Royal Infirmary; Ernst and Young, etc. *Clubs:* Friends of Royal Academy. *Signs work:* "Liz Sheppard." *Address:* 6 Leighton St., Woburn, Milton Keynes, MK17 9PJ.

**SHEPPARD, Maurice,** P.P.R.W.S., M.A. (R.C.A.), Dip.A.D.; professional painter in oil and water-colour; *b* Llangwm, Pembrokeshire, 25 Feb., 1947. *Educ:* Haverfordwest Grammar School. *Studied:* Loughborough College of Art; Kingston College of Art under Alfred Heyworth; R.C.A. under Hamilton-Fraser, Buhler, Spear, Weight. *Exhib:* London and abroad. *Work in collections:* V. & A., National Museum of Wales, Cardiff, B'ham Museum and A.G., B.M. *Publications:* Old Water-colour Soc. Club Annual Vol. 59. *Signs work:* "Maurice Sheppard." *Address:* 33 St. Martin's Pk., Crow Hill, Haverfordwest, Pembrokeshire SA61 2HP, Wales; and 14 Apsley St., Rusthall Common, Tunbridge Wells, Kent TN4 8NU.

**SHEPPERSON, Patricia Ann,** artist in pastel, wildlife, still life and landscape; *b* London, 1929. *m* Desmond Vereker. one *s.* one *d. Educ:* Holy Trinity Convent, Bromley. *Studied:* Heatherly School of Art (1959-62, Patrick Larking, R.O.I.), Sir John Cass School of Art (1963-67), studied drama at Guildhall School of Music and Drama (1946-49) *Exhib:* one-man shows, London and The Hague, mixed exhbns., R.A., Mall Galleries. *Work in collections:* U.K. and abroad. *Signs work:* "Patricia Shepperson." *Address:* 2 Grange Rd., Norwich, Norfolk NR2 3NH.

**SHERLOCK, Siriol Ann,** B.A.Hons. (1977), S.B.A. (1988); R.H.S. Gold Medal (1993, 1994, 1995); textile designer, water-colour painter, botanical artist; *b* Nantwich, 28 Aug., 1954. *m* Stephen Paul Sherlock. two *d*. *Educ:* Fernhill Manor School; Brockenhurst College. *Studied:* Winchester School of Art (1973-77). *Exhib:* many galleries in south of England, The Hillier Gdns. and Arboretum (1990, 1993, 1996), Kew Gdns. Gallery (1992). *Work in collections:* The Hunt Inst., Pittsburgh, U.S.A., The Hillier Gdns. and Arboretum, Romsey, The Royal Horticultural Soc, The Shirley Sherwood Collection. *Publications:* work repro.: in The Kew Magazine, The New Plantsman, Contemporary Botanical Artists. *Signs work:* "Siriol Sherlock." *Address:* Elizabethan Cottage, Michelmersh, nr. Romsey, Hants. SO51 0NW.

**SHETLAND, Ilric (alias),** Hornsey Dip., S.I.A.D. (1969); artist in pencil, ink, sprayed pictorial sculpture, mixed media; *b* London, 24 Oct., 1946. *m* Naurika Lenner. *Educ:* Forest Hill Comprehensive School. *Studied:* Hornsey College of Art (1966-69). *Exhib:* International Cultural Centre, Antwerp, Gamstyl, Brussels, Basle '75, Serpentine Gallery, London, Treadwell Gallery, London, Patrick Seale Gallery, London. *Clubs:* A.I.R., A.M.P. *Signs work:* "Ilric Shetland." *Address:* 38 Chalcot Rd., London NW1.

**SHIELD, George William,** B.Sc., Lond.; sculptor, particularly in wood and concrete, terracotta, metal, plaster, little stone; head, Mexborough G.S.; *b* Leicester, 7 July, 1919. *m* Jean. one *s*. two *d*. *Educ:* Gateway School; University College, Leicester. *Studied:* College of Art, Leicester, under A. Pountney and A. T. White (1948-52). *Exhib:* R.A., R.S.A., R.B.A., R.I., Glasgow, S.S.A., Contemp. Artists, Bradford. *Work in collections:* Joan Farrier bust in Paisley A.G., portrait head, Warden Harrison, Merton College, Oxford. *Clubs:* Midland Group, Leicester Soc. of Artists. *Signs work:* "SHIELD" inscribed with modelling tool. *Address:* 30 Lewes Rd., Conisborough, S. Yorks.

**SHIELDS, Christopher Ronald,** Dip.A.D. (1973), B.W.S. (1985); artist in water-colour, gouache and acrylic; *b* Sale, Ches., 7 June, 1954. divorced. one *d*. *Educ:* Sale Moor Secondary School. *Studied:* Northwich College of Art and Design (1970-73). *Exhib:* Warrington Museum and A.G. (1983, 1986, 1989, 1992), Wildfowl Trust Martin Mere (1985), Towneley Hall A.G. and Museum, Burnley (1988), Stockport A.G. (1991), plus several other one-man shows in private art galleries throughout Gt. Britian. *Work in collections:* Trafford Borough Council's Art Archives, City of Wakefield Educ. Resource Service Collection. *Publications:* published in Gt. Britain, Europe, N. America and Japan. Illustrated over 80 books including Collins Guide - Seashore of Britain and Europe, Collins New Generation Guide - Wild Flowers, Collins Gem Guide - Pond Life, Tracks and Signs of the Birds of Britain and Europe (Helm Publishing); plus commissions for B.B.C. publications, the R.S.P.B. and the Worldwide Fund for Nature. *Signs work:* "Chris Shields" - always includes moth or butterfly in every work. *Address:* 2 Bramble Walk, Sale, Ches. M33 5LL.

**SHIPSIDES, Frank,** M.A.; painter in oil and water-colour, specialising in marine painting; President, Bristol Savages (1974-75); *b* Mansfield, Notts., 1908. *m* Phyllis. one *s.* one *d. Educ:* King Edward School, Mansfield. *Studied:* Mansfield College of Art (1923) under Buxton; Nottingham College of Art (1925) under Else. *Exhib:* Alexander Gallery, Bristol 8. *Work in collections:* Bristol Maritime Heritage Centre "Visit of H.M. The Queen", Bristol Council House, H.M.S. Bristol paintings 1653-1983. *Publications:* Frank Shipsides Bristol; Somerset Harbours; Bristol Impressions; Original Graphic - Days of Steam & Sail; Bristol: Portrait of a City; Bristol: Maritime City. *Clubs:* Bristol Savages (Pres. 1983-84). *Signs work:* see appendix. *Address:* 5 Florence Pk., Bristol BS6 7LS.

**SHIRAISHI, Barry Toshio,** teacher (painting and sculpture);Vice Pres. Royal Soc. of Miniature Painters, Sculptors and Gravers; *b* Woolwich, London, 5 May, 1938. *m* Colleen Powell. two *s.* three *d. Studied:* Woolwich Polytechnic School of Arts (1950-54, Heber Matthews). *Exhib:* Geneva, Frankfurt, Paris and London. *Work in collections:* Franklin Mint Museum, Philadelphia. *Commissions:* Channel Tunnel Products and Franklin Mint. *Address:* 34 Paget Rise, Plumstead, London SE18 3QQ.

**SHIRLEY, Rachel,** B.A.Hons. (1986); animal and landscape artist in oil; Daler Rowney art prize winner (Spring 1995); *b* Nuneaton, 26 May, 1965. *Studied:* N. Warwickshire College of Art, Nuneaton (1981-83), Kingston Polytechnic School of Fine Art (1983-86). *Exhib:* one-man shows: Museum and A.G., Nuneaton (1987), Hinckley Municipal A.G., Leics. (1988), Whitmoors Fine A.G., Leics. (1989); group shows: Hurlingham Gallery, London, Warwick University, Twycross Zoo Gallery, Leics. *Work in collections:* Midland private collections. *Publications:* work repro.: Rosenstiels Fine Art Ltd. *Signs work:* "Rachel Shirley." *Address:* 65 Gipsy Lane, Whitestone, Nuneaton, Warwickshire CV11 4SH.

**SHIRLEY, Sidney Raymond,** Médaille d'Argent (Paris Salon, 1981); still-life artist in oil; *b* Coventry, 27 Nov., 1930. *m* Sylvia Denise Elizabeth. six *d. Studied:* privately. *Exhib:* one-man shows, Museum and A.G., Nuneaton (1968, 1974, 1982, 1993); group shows, R.A., N.E.A.C., R.B.A., R.O.I., R.B.S.A., New King's Rd., and 20th Century Galleries, London. *Work in collections:* Australia, N.Z., France, Austria, U.K. *Publications:* work repro.: R.A. Illustrated, La Revue Moderne, Le Monde, etc. Work reviewed BBC-CWR (1993). *Clubs:* Membre Associé, Société des Artistes Français, Founder mem, Bedworth Civic and Arts Soc. (1969). *Signs work:* "R. SHIRLEY" or "R.S." *Address:* 65 Gipsy Lane, Whitestone, Nuneaton, Warwickshire, CV11 4SH.

**SHIRREFF, Jack Robert,** N.D.D., A.T.D., A.R.E.; artist in intaglio; Director of 107 Workshop; *b* Sri Lanka, 11 July, 1943. *m* Patricia. *Educ:* Sutton Valence. *Studied:* Brighton Polytechnic. Lecturer, Bath Academy of Art (1965-85). Currently engaged in producing and publishing work by Howard Hodgkin, Joe Tilson, Jim Dine, Oleg Kudryashov, David Inshaw, Gillian Ayres.

*Publications:* S.W. Hayter: Eluard; S.W. Hayter: Death of Hektor; produced The Way We Live Now: Hodgkin/Sonntag. *Signs work:* "J. Shirreff." *Address:* 107 Workshop, The Courtyard, Bath Rd., Shaw, nr. Melksham, Wilts. SN12 8EF.

**SHOA, Nahem,** B.A.(Hons); artist in oil; *b* 4 Oct., 1968. *Educ:* Holland Park Comprehensive. *Studied:* London College of Printing (1987-88), Manchester School of Art (1988-91). *Exhib:* R.A. Summer Show (1992, 1993), Discerning Eye Mall Galleries (1992), winner Carol Foundation award R.P., Mall Galleries (1992), B.P. National Portrait award N.P.G. (1993), Elizabeth Greenshield award (1994), The Sacred Body, James Colman Fine Art (1996), Modern British Art Show, R.C.A. (1996, 1997). *Commissions:* Peter Mandelson, M.P., Dr. Mary Cowling. *Signs work:* "N. Shoa." *Address:* 69 Princes Sq., London W2 4NY.

**SHORE, Jack,** A.T.D. (1943); artist in collage, drawing in various media; President, Royal Cambrian Academy of Art (1976-82); *b* Ramsbottom, Lancs., 17 July, 1922. *m* Olive Brenda Shore. one *s.* one *d. Educ:* Haslingden Grammar School. *Studied:* Accrington and Manchester Schools of Art (1938-43, S. V. Lindoe, John M. Holmes). *Exhib:* R.Cam.A.; one-man shows, Theatre Clwyd, N. Wales (1979), R.Cam.A., Conwy (1980), Oriel Gallery, Bangor (1984). *Work in collections:* Bury A.G., and University College, N. Wales. *Signs work:* "J. Shore." or "J.S." *Address:* 11 St. George's Cres., Queen's Pk., Chester.

**SHORES, Margot,** painter in oil and acrylic; lecturer in painting, University of Newcastle upon Tyne (1985-90); visiting lecturer, R.A. Schools (1987-88); *b* 1961. *Exhib:* 'Young Masters' Solomon Gallery (1985), R.A. Summer Show (1986-87), Cleveland Drawing Biennale (1989). *Signs work:* "Margot Shores." *Address:* 70 On the Hill, Old Whittington, Chesterfield, Derbyshire S41 9HA.

**SHORTHOUSE, G. Sydney,** R.M.S., M.A.A., M.A.S.-F., H.S., F.I.D. (1969-83); retd. Company Director; artist in water-colour, mainly miniature portraiture; Display and Advertising Manager, Leicester Corp., Area Design Manager, E. Midlands Gas Board, Design Director, City Design and City Leather Companies; *b* Whitwick, Leics., 1925. married one *s.* one *d. Educ:* Hugglescote School. *Exhib:* R.M.S., Hilliard Soc., Florida and Washington D.C. *Commissions:* The Garter Principal King of Arms, Lady Hilda Swan, The Governor of Anguilla, The Lord Provost of Perth, Scotland, The Pro-Chancellor of Edith Cowan University, W. Australia, Anastasia, Baroness Peter Hatvany. *Publications:* R.M.S. - One Hundred Years; The Techniques of Painting Miniatures; The Magic of Miniatures. Awards: Hon. men. (1988, 1989, 1991, 1994, 1995, 1996) R.M.S. Gold Bowl award; 1st International Portrait award Washington D.C. (1989); 2nd International Portrait award Florida (1990); Best In Exhbn. (1987), Bell award (1989) Hilliard Soc.; Suzanne Lucas award (1985); Mundy Sovereign Awards R.M.S. (1991); Excellence in all Entries award and 1st International Portrait award Florida (1995). *Signs work:* see appendix. *Address:* The Barn, Main St., Wilson,

Derbyshire DE73 1AD.

**SHRAGER, Ann Jessica,** N.E.A.C. (1975); artist in oil and water-colour;; *b* London, 9 Jan., 1948. *m* Martin Anderson. two *s. Studied:* Byam Shaw (1967-70, Maurice de Sausmarez), R.A. (1970-73, Peter Greenham). *Exhib:* Mixed: R.A., N.E.A.C., New Grafton, Erica Bourne, British Art at Auction, Bilan de L'Art Contemporian, Paris; one-man, Michael Parkin (1976, 1978, 1979, 1996). *Publications:* work repro.:book cover design for Remember Your Gramer! (Winged Lion Publishers). *Signs work:* "A.J.S." *Address:* 3 Maids of Honour Row, The Green, Richmond, Surrey TW9 1NY.

**SHUKMAN, Barbara Benita,** Jacox Students Painting Prize, Edmonton, Canada (1968), John Radcliffe Purchase Prize, Oxford (1983); painter in acrylic on paper and canvas, and inks on silk, and printmaker, etchings, etc.; *b* London, 25 Nov., 1934. *m* (1) Harold Jacobs; one *s.* two *d.* (2) Harold Shukman. *Educ:* U.S.A. primary schools; Queen's College, London. *Studied:* University Saskatchewan, Regina, Canada (1963-65), University Alberta, Edmonton, Canada (1966-70). *Exhib:* group shows: Canada, U.K., Spain; solo shows: U.K., U.S.A. *Work in collections:* U.S.A.: Solomon Guggenheim Museum, N.Y.; Georgia Museum of Art; New Orleans Museum. Turkey: Sheraton Voyager, Antalya. U.K.: Sedgwick Group; British and Commonwealth; Sarm Film Studios; Bain and Co.; Jardine and Co.; Strutt and Parker; Chartwell Land: Christiana Bank, (all London). John Radcliffe Hospital Oxford. *Signs work:* "Barbara Shukman." *Address:* 11 Cunliffe Cl., Oxford OX2 7BJ.

**SHURROCK, Christopher,** A.T.D.; painting, sculpture, print; *b* Bristol, 1939. *Studied:* painting: West of England College of Art, Postgraduate Cardiff, A.T.D.(Dist.). Art Adviser, University Settlement, Bristol (1961), Cardiff College of Art, Foundation Dept. 1962-91 (Senior Lecturer/Director). Consultant Art and Design. *Work in collections:* National Gallery of Slovakia, Bratislava. National Museum and Gallery of Wales, University of Wales, A.C.W., C.A.S.W., John Caroll University, Ohio, etc. *Publications:* Studio International (June, 1966) D'Ars Agency N36-37 (1967), Art and Artists (Jan. 1969), Art in Britain, 1969-70 (Dent), Studio International 991/2 (1981), Art in Wales 1850-1980 (U.W.P.). *Address:* 9 Min-y-Nant, Rhiwbina, Cardiff CF4 6JR.

**SIDERY, Vera Ethel,** painter in pastel and oil; *b* 3 Aug., 1916. *m* Albert Sidery (decd.). two *s.* two *d. Educ:* Tottenham High School. *Studied:* with Leonard and Margaret Boden. *Exhib:* P.S., Mall Galleries, Enfield; one-man show, Broomfield Museum, Southgate. *Clubs:* P.S., Enfield Art Soc. *Signs work:* "V.E. Sidery." *Address:* 8 Roedean Cl., Enfield EN3 5QR.

**SIDOLI, Dawn Frances,** R.W.A. (1987), N.E.A.C. (1990), Teacher's Cert. (1956); painter, printer; *b* Gosport, Hants., 24 Nov., 1933. *m* Frank Sidoli. two *s.* one *d. Educ:* Wigton High School, Cumbria; Notre Dame Convent, Northampton. *Studied:* Northampton Art School (1949-52). *Exhib:* R.A. from

1977, R.W.A., N.E.A.C., Cardiff, etc. Finalist, Laing '85, '86, Hunting Group '86, '87, '89, Inveresk, Singer and Friedlander w/col. Comp., Laing National First Prize '88. *Work in collections:* R.W.A., Mid-Glamorgan C.C., Cardiff School of Economics (Schools Art, Avon, Cardiff, Salisbury). *Clubs:* Bath Soc. of Artists, Clifton Arts. *Signs work:* "Dawn Sidoli" or "SIDOLI." *Address:* 10 Elgin Pk., Redland, Bristol BS6 6RU.

**SILBER, Evelyn Ann,** Ph.D.(Cantab.), M.A.(Cantab.), M.A. (University of Pennsylvania), F.M.A.; art historian and museum curator; Director, Leeds Museums and Galleries; *b* Welwyn Garden City, 22 May, 1949. *Educ:* Hatfield Girls' Grammar School. *Studied:* history of art: New Hall, Cambridge (1968-72), University of Pennsylvania (Thouron Fellowship, 1972-73), Clare Hall, Cambridge (Leverhulme Fellowship, 1975-78). *Exhib:* organised: Jacob Epstein, Sculpture and Drawings, Leeds City A.G., and Whitechapel A.G. (1987). *Publications:* The Sculpture of Jacob Epstein (Phaidon, 1986), Gaudier-Brzeska: Life and Art (Thames and Hudson, 1996); catalogues, articles, lectures. *Clubs:* Royal Overseas League. *Address:* c/o Leeds Museums and Galleries, Town Hall, Headrow, Leeds LS1 3AD.

**SILLMAN, Norman H.,** A.R.C.A., F.R.B.S.; sculptor, coin and medal designer, Royal Mint; Fine Art Dept. (retd.), Nottingham Polytechnic; *b* May, 1921. *m* Gillian M. one *d. Educ:* Pyramid Hill, Australia. *Studied:* Blackheath Art School, Royal College of Art. *Exhib:* R.A., R.B.A., London Group, Midland Group, Arts Council "Sculpture in the Home" Exhbn., R.C.A. Open Air Exhbn.; medals exhib. in Europe and U.S.A. *Work in collections:* B.M., Derby Educ. Coll., Kelham Hall, Notts. Designed R.I.B.A. Awards (1990), British coins: £2 (1986), four £1 (1994), various overseas. *Commissions:* sculpture 16ft. Staythorpe Power Station, Notts. and various. *Publications:* articles, Saeculum (1981), Tubingen; Jour. Indian Anthrop. Soc. (1983). *Signs work:* "N. Sillman." *Address:* 33 Church St., Eye, Suffolk IP23 7BD.

**SILVERTON, Norma,** M.A., N.S., H.N.D., F.E.T.C.; artist/printmaker in etching, lithograph, silkscreen, 2D and 3D; *b* Birmingham, 1941. married one *s.* two *d. Educ:* in Birmingham. *Studied:* Byam Shaw School of Art, Camberwell College of Art. *Exhib:* solo shows: Tel Aviv, Israel and London; and continually in group shows in U.K. and abroad. Curated print exhbns. between U.K., Israel and Germany. *Work in collections:* Scarborough Municipal A.G., Ben Uri Museum Collection. *Publications:* Eye Music - a collection of nine lithographs, Unspoken Poems - a collection of ten etchings. *Clubs:* Printmakers Council, N.S.P.S. *Signs work:* "Norma Silverton." *Address:* 13 Linden Lea, London N2 0RF.

**SIMCOCK, Jack,** painter; *b* Biddulph, Staffs., 6 June, 1929. *m* Beryl Shallcross (decd.). one *s.* one *d. Educ:* Stoke-on-Trent. *Exhib:* over 50 one-man shows, England and abroad. Sole agent from 1997: John Hunt, 15 King Street, St. James's, London. Work in many public art galleries and private collections at home and abroad. *Publications:* Simcock, Mow Cop, autobiography (1975),

Midnight Till Three, volume of poems (1975). *Signs work:* "SIMCOCK." *Address:* 13 Primitive St., Mow Cop, Stoke-on-Trent ST7 3NH.

**SIMEON, Margaret,** A.R.C.A. (1933), R.C.A. Travelling Scholar (1934), M.S.I.A. (1945); textile and wallpaper designer; teacher of Textile Design and Printing, R.C.A. (1936-40); teacher of textile design and history of art at Wimbledon School of Art (1934-84); *b* 1910. *Educ:* Chelsea School of Art, R.C.A. *Exhib:* International Exhbn. at Paris, Stockholm, New York, Arts and Crafts Exhbn. Soc. (1935-54), Britain Can Make It Exhbn. (1946), Festival of Britain (1951). *Publications:* The History of Lace; How to Draw Garden Flowers; work repro.: in International Textiles, Architectural Review, Studio, Designers in Britain, Decorative Art. *Address:* Springfield House, 6 Stoke Rd., Cobham, Surrey KT11 3AS.

**SIMMONDS, Jackie,** H.N.D.; artist in pastel and water-colour; *b* Oxford, 27 Dec., 1944. *m* Geoffrey Simmonds. two *d. Educ:* Preston Manor Grammar. *Studied:* Harrow School of Art (1978-82). *Exhib:* Linda Blackstone Gallery, Pinner, P.S., R.I., R.W.A., R.S.B.A., Britain's Painters (1992). *Publications:* Pastels Workshop (Harper Collins, 1994). *Signs work:* "Jackie Simmonds." *Address:* 23 Linksway, Northwood, Middx. HA6 2XA.

**SIMMONS, Fay,** N.D.D. (1959), Cert.R.A. (1963), Leverhulme Scholarship (1963), A.R.B.S. (1976); sculptor in bronze or gesso composition with mixed media; V.S.O. Business/Social Development, Uganda; *b* New Zealand, 1938. *m* Sean Mullaney. *Educ:* Stella Maris Convent, Bideford. *Studied:* Bideford School of Art; Hammersmith College of Art; R.A. Schools. *Exhib:* R.A., Nicholas Treadwell Gallery, A.I.A., Alec Mann Birmingham, XVIII Gallery Knightsbridge, Jersey, Guernsey, Gallery Oste Hamburg, New York, Washington. *Clubs:* R.B.S. *Signs work:* "F.S." *Address:* 54 Coburg Cl., Greencoat Pl., London SW1P 1DP.

**SIMMONS, Rosemary,** N.D.D. (1953), Hon. R.E. (1990); artist in relief printmaking, water-colour; writer; Editor, Printmaking Today; *b* Brighton, 19 Oct., 1932. *m* Anthony Christie, M.A., F.S.A. *Studied:* Chelsea School of Art (1949-53). *Exhib:* International Gdn. Festival (1984), Museum of Gdn. History (1985), St. John's, Smith Sq. (1987). *Work in collections:* Tate Gallery print collection. *Publications:* Collecting Original Prints (1980), Complete Manual of Relief Printmaking with Katie Clemson (1988). *Signs work:* "Simmons." *Address:* 14b Elsworthy Terr., London NW3 3DR.

**SIMPSON, Alan John,** R.S.M.A., I.S.M.P.; marine and landscape artist in oil, water-colour, pastel; *b* Basingstoke, 22 July, 1941. *m* Denise. two *s. Studied:* informal training at College of Art, Bournemouth. *Exhib:* R.S.M.A., R.O.I., R.I., Britain in Water-colour, Mystic, Seaport, U.S.A., Richard Beard Gallery, Vancouver, Harrison Galleries, Vancouver. *Signs work:* "Alan Simpson." *Address:* 24 Waltham Rd., Bournemouth BH7 6PE.

**SIMPSON, Cathy,** B.A.(Hons.), A.R.B.S.A., R.M.S., H.S.; freelance illustrator in water-colour and gouache; Head of Art, Bromsgrove School; *b*

# WHO'S WHO IN ART

Kingston on Hull, 15 Nov., 1959. *Educ:* Christ's Hospital Girls' School, Hertford; Leicester University. *Studied:* Central St. Martin's School of Art. *Exhib:* R.I., S.WL.A., S.W.A., S.B.A., R.M.S., H.S., R.B.S.A., M.A.S.-F. *Signs work:* see appendix. *Address:* 23 The Dock, Catshill, Bromsgrove, Worcs. B61 0NJ.

**SIMPSON, Ian,** A.R.C.A. (1958); Abbey Travelling Scholar (1958); free-lance artist-writer in oil, acrylic and drawing media; Principal, St. Martin's School of Art (1972); Assistant Rector, The London Institute, Head of School, St. Martin's School of Art (1986-88); Course Director, Open College of the Arts (1997-); b Loughborough, Leics., 12 Nov., 1933. *Educ:* Bede Grammar School, Sunderland. *Studied:* Sunderland College of Art (1950-53); Royal College of Art (1955-58). *Work in collections:* Glasgow City A.G., Nuffield Foundation, Hull Education Authority, Northumberland Education Authority. *Publications:* Eyeline (B.B.C.), Picture Making (B.B.C.) Drawing: Seeing and Observation (Van Nostrand Reinhold) 3rd Revised Edn. (A. & C. Black 1992), Ian Simpson's Guide to Painting and Composition (Warnes), Painters Progress (Allen Lane), The Encyclopedia of Drawing Techniques (Headline), The Challenge of Landscape Painting (Collins 1990), The New Guide to Illustration (Chartwell Books 1990), Anatomy of Humans (Studio Editions 1991), Collins Complete Painting Course (Harper Collins 1993), Collins Complete Drawing Course (Harper Collins 1994). T.V. Programmes written and presented: Eyeline (B.B.C. 1968), Picture Making (B.B.C. 1972), Reading the Signs (B.B.C. 1976). *Clubs:* Suffolk Group. *Signs work:* "Simpson." *Address:* Motts Farm House, Chilton St., Clare, Sudbury, Suffolk CO10 8QS.

**SIMPSON, Leslie,** F.R.S.A. (1985); portrait artist in oil and water-colour working to commission on all subjects; Director, Soc. of Miniaturists, British Water-colour Soc., British Soc. of Painters; Founder, Yorkshire Artists Exhbn. (1981); Principal, International Guild of Artists; b Horsforth, 28 May, 1930. *m* Margaret. one *s. Educ:* Bridlington School. *Studied:* Hull College of Art. *Work in collections:* portrait of the full Wakefield City Council (1974); portraits of the Lady Lord Mayors of Leeds, Bradford, Sheffield and London; 'The Winning Throw' portrait of Tessa Sanderson, Los Angeles Olympics (1984). Descendant of James Simpson (1791-1864) leading non-conformist architect in the North, and John Simpson official portrait artist to Queen Donna Marie II of Portugal (1837). *Signs work:* "Leslie Simpson." *Address:* Briargate, 2 The Brambles, Victoria Drive, Ilkley, W.Yorks. LS29 9DH.

**SIMPSON, Noelle,** painter, colourist of joyous landscapes, nudes, interiors and portraits in oil on canvas, original limited edition prints; b Auckland, N.Z., 10 Aug., 1950. one *d. Educ:* Chatelard, Switzerland; Moreton Hall, Shropshire. *Studied:* under Philip Sutton, R.A., and Frederick Deane, R.P. (1985), Van Wieringen, Bali (1986-90). *Exhib:* J. Weston Gallery, London (1985), Symon Gallery, Bali (1987), Bowmoore Gallery, London (1991), Hilton International, Bali (1992), Gagliardi Gallery, London (1992, 1994), Pacific Rim Gallery, San Diego (1993), Los Angeles (1995), Turning Point Gallery, Singapore (1997).

*Work in collections:* Agung Rai Museum, Bali. *Publications:* Then Till Now - Noelle Simpson. *Signs work:* see appendix. *Address:* 18 Cottesmore Gdns., London W8 5PR.

**SIMS-WILLIAMS, Dorothy Audrey Constance,** F.R.S.A., Hon. Mention, Paris Salon, R.A.S. Cert., Leverhulme Leaving Scholar Silver and Bronze medal; artist in oil and pastel, teacher, lecturer; *b* Disley, Ches., 26 May, 1909. *m* Rev. L. T. Sims-Williams. three *s.* one *d. Educ:* privately. *Studied:* Stockport Art School (1926-28), R.A. Schools (1928-33) under W. W. Russell, R.A. and F. E. Jackson, A.R.A. *Exhib:* R.P and various London exhbns., R.W.A. Bristol, Dorset Art Weeks. *Work in collections:* St. Matthew's Church, Stockport; St. John's Church, Hopwood, Lancs.; St. Andrew's Church, Dearnley, Lancs. Bridport Museum. *Commissions:* portraits. *Clubs:* Reynolds. *Signs work:* "D. Sims-Williams." *Address:* Stonehays, Westcliff Rd., Charmouth, Dorset DT6 6BG.

**SINCLAIR, Elizabeth,** N.D.D. (1950), A.T.D. (1958), M.F.P.S. (1986), Visual Arts Dip. (1969), Dip. in History of Art (1972); painter in oil, pastel, acrylic and water-colour; *b* Glasgow, 18 Jan., 1933. *Educ:* 'Wings', Charlton Pk., Wilts. *Studied:* Plymouth School of Art, Bath Academy of Art, London University. *Exhib:* one-man shows: Hong Kong, Italy; group shows: Hong Kong, Germany, Plymouth, London, Reigate, etc. *Work in collections:* Plymouth A.G. *Clubs:* Reigate Soc. of Artists, North Weald Group, F.P.S. *Signs work:* "E. Sinclair." *Address:* 10 Cockshot Hill, Reigate, Surrey RH2 8AE.

**SINCLAIR, Frances,** painter in oil; *b* 18 Jan., 1913. *m* Rear Admiral Sinclair, C.B., D.S.C. (decd.). two *s. Educ:* privately. *Studied:* under John Tichell, A.R.A. *Exhib:* R.A. for many years, also at Easton Rooms, Rye, Wykeham Galleries at Stockbridge and Barnes and others in the South West. *Publications:* work repro.: paintings by Medici Soc. *Signs work:* "F. Sinclair." *Address:* Castle Cottage, Castle St., Winchelsea, E. Sussex TN36 4EL.

**SINCLAIR, Helen,** B.F.A.(Hons.) (1976); sculptor in cast stone and metal; *b* S.Wales, 27 Feb., 1954. *m* Terry Ryall, sculptor. *Educ:* Llanelli Girls' Grammar School. *Studied:* Dyfed School of Art, Wimbledon School of Art (1973-76, Peter Startup, Jim Turner). *Exhib:* Heifer Gallery, Highbury, Montpellier Gallery, Cheltenham and Stratford-upon-Avon, Online Gallery, Southampton, Gordon Hepworth Gallery, Exeter. Edith Grove Gallery, Fulham, Flying Colours Gallery, Chelsea, Fairfax Gallery, Tunbridge Wells. *Work in collections:* Bultarbo Estate, Sweden, Grand Theatre, Swansea. *Commissions:* Trophy for W. Wales Tec Management Awards; Wall Reliefs, Castle Square, Swansea. *Signs work:* "Helen Sinclair" or "H.S." *Address:* Rhossili Farmhouse, Rhossili, Gower, Swansea SA3 1PL.

**SINCLAIR, N. T.,** M.A., F.M.A.; Senior Curator *Address:* Museum and Art Gallery, Borough Rd., Sunderland, SR1 1PP.

**SINNOTT, Kevin,** artist in oil on canvas; *b* Wales, 1947. *m* Susan. three *s.* one *d. Studied:* Cardiff College of Art (1967-68), Gloucester College of Art

(1968-71), R.C.A. (1971-74). *Exhib:* one-man shows: Ikon Gallery (1980), Blond Fine Art (1982, 1984), Chapter Arts Centre, Cardiff (1984), Bernard Jacobson Gallery (1986, 1987, 1988, 1990), Flowers East (1992, 1994, 1996). *Work in collections:* British Council, B.M., A.C.G.B., R.C.A., Whitworth Manchester, Wolverhampton City Gallery, Unilever, Deutsche Bank A.G. London, Metropolitan Museum of Art, N.Y., National Museum of Wales. *Clubs:* Chelsea Arts. *Signs work:* initials right hand corner. *Address:* c/o Flowers East, 199 Richmond Rd., London E8 3NJ.

**SITWELL, Pauline,** S.W.E., R.A. Dip. (1937), L.I.S.T.D., F.R.G.S.; painter, printer, poet and lecturer; oil, water-colour, wood engraving, lithography, etc.; *b* Malta, 5 Oct., 1916. *Educ:* full stage training and young career. *Studied:* St. John's Wood School of Art (1930), Royal Academy Schools of Art (1933-37). *Exhib:* S.W.E., R.S.M.A., and Mall Prints tour of G.B., etc.; Laureat Paris Salon de Printemps, Auribeau s/Siagne, France (1988); one-man show sponsored by Westminster City Council, many others. *Work in collections:* works in seven countries. *Commissions:* many and various. *Publications:* Green Song; Train Journey to Deal and other Poems (Outposts, 1981). *Clubs:* Royal Academy, Reynolds (Hon. Treasurer, retd. after 20 years), S.I.A.C., B.S.C.G., S.W.E., etc. *Signs work:* "Pauline Sitwell" and see appendix. *Address:* 46 Porchester Rd., London W2 6ET.

**SKEA, Janet,** B.F.A. (1968); painter in water-colour, tempera and oils; *b* Johannesburg, S.Africa, 15 Sept., 1947. *Educ:* Parktown Girls' High, Johannesburg. *Studied:* Stellenbosch University (1965-68, Prof. Otto Schröder). *Exhib:* widely in the U.K., including St. Ives Soc. and Mariners; Look, Helmsley; Bourne, Reigate; R.W.A., Bristol; London: Bankside, Chursee Studio, Llewellyn Alexander, Mall, Medici; solos: Museum of Garden History (1985), Heifer (1994), Financial Times (1995). *Signs work:* "Janet Skea" dated on reverse. *Address:* 30 Queen St., Penzance, Cornwall TR18 4BH.

**SKELTON, John,** M.B.E.; sculptor, letter cutter, stone, wood, all metals; *b* 1923. married. one *s.* two *d. Educ:* Norwich Cathedral Choir School; Bablake, Coventry; School of Art and Architecture, Coventry; apprenticed Eric Gill; army, Far East; own Workshop-Studio (1950). *Exhib:* R.A. regularly; Herbert (Coventry), Battersea Park, Sussex University, Hamburg, Washington, Paris Salon, Brighton Festival, U.N. Pavilion and International Sculpture Symposium, Yugoslavia, representing Gt. Britain (1964). Served Arts Council, Scotland; Royal Soc. of British Sculptors; R.S.A. *Work in collections:* Norwich, Lincoln, Hereford, Chichester, Portsmouth and St. Paul's Cathedrals; museums: Toledo, U.S.A., Chichester and Coventry; Glyndebourne Opera. *Commissions:* many Royal lettering commissions. *Signs work:* "John Skelton" *Address:* Blabers Mead, Streat, Hassocks, Sussex BN6 8RR.

**SKILLINGTON, Nancy:** see TALBOT, Nancy Wilfreda Hewitt.

**SKINNER, John,** B.A. (Hons.) Fine Art (Painting); artist in oil painting; *b*

531

Kent, 19 Aug., 1953. *m* Mary Skinner. one *s. Educ:* Brighton Polytechnic (1973-76). *Address:* The Abbotsbury Studio, 11a Rodden Row, Abbotsbury, Dorset DT3 4JL.

**SLADE, Roy,** N.D.D., A.T.D., G.S.M. (British Army); Kt. First Class of the Order of the White Rose of Finland (1985); artist in acrylics; Chairman, Commission on Art in Public Places for the State of Michigan (1984-85); President, Cranbrook Academy of Art (1977-94); Director, Corcoran Gallery of Art (1972-77); Dean, Corcoran School of Art (1970-77); *b* Cardiff, Wales, 1933; American citizen (Oct. 1975). *Educ:* University of Wales (1953-54), Cardiff College of Art (1949-54), Royal Army School of Education (1954). *Work in collections:* A.C.G.B., Contemporary Art Soc., Westinghouse Corp., Cadbury Bros. Ltd., Nuffield Foundation. *Publications:* work repro.: articles published: Studio International, "American Art Education" (Nov., 1972); Art Journal, "Atlantic Storm" (Spring, 1972); Studio International, "Up the American Vanishing Point" (Nov., 1968); Detroid News, "Speaking of Art - In the Future Tense" (Mar., 1985); N.A.S.A.D. and A.A.M.D., "Toward Understanding and Collaboration" (1982); N.C.A.A., "The Temple Flourishes" (1980); Lewis and Clark College, "The Gallery Symposium" (1978); "Art Gallery" (Jan. 1975). *Address:* P.O. Box 48, Harsens Island, Michigan 48028.

**SLANEY, Noël,** R.S.W.; artist in Batik oils and water-colour; *b* Glasgow, 26 Dec., 1915. *m* George Frederick Moules, painter. four *d. Educ:* Girls' High School, Glasgow. *Studied:* Glasgow School of Art under the late Hugh Adam Crawford, R.S.A., D.A. (1937), Post Dip. with distinction (1939). *Work in collections:* water-colours in Aberdeen and Dundee; oils in Arts Council, Glasgow A.G., Lillie A.G. Milngavie, Hunterian Museum Glasgow. *Signs work:* "Slaney." *Address:* c/o MacKinnon, 12 Woodvale Ave., Giffnock, Glasgow G46 6RQ.

**SLICER, Sheila Mary,** A.R.M.S. (1978); first prize M.A.S.-F. (1983, 1986, 1992); President, A.S.M.A. (Vic.); freelance miniature portraitist in water-colour; miniature restorer, lecturer; *b* Yorks., 26 Sept., 1930. *m* Robert Slicer. two *d. Educ:* Bradford Girls Grammar School. *Studied:* Bradford Regional College of Art (1946-49). *Exhib:* R.M.S., M.A.S.-F., Andorra, Yorks. Water-colour Soc., Brighouse and Bradford Art Clubs, Victoria, New South Wales, Queensland and Tasmania, Australia, Hilliard Soc., Royal Pastel Soc., and Sweden. *Work in collections:* England, Bermuda, Florida, Australia, Hong Kong, Andorra, America. *Clubs:* R.M.S., M.A.S.-F., H.S., M.A.A., Victoria, N.S.W. and Queensland Miniature Socs., Australia, Tasmania. *Signs work:* "Sheila M. Slicer." *Address:* Faraway, 1655 Don Rd., Launching Pl., Victoria 3139, Australia.

**SLOWE, Vikki,** R.E., P.M.C.; printmaker in etching; *b* London, 24 May, 1947. *m* Martin Slowe. two *d. Educ:* Camden School for Girls. *Studied:* London College of Fashion; Camden Arts Centre. *Exhib:* R.A., R.E., Bradford Biennale. *Work in collections:* Smithsonian Inst., Washington, Tel Aviv

Museum, Israel, Ashmoleum Museum, Oxford. *Signs work:* "Vikki Slowe."
*Address:* 35 Ornan Rd., London NW3 4QD.

**SMAIL, Elizabeth Ann,** F.L.S. (1991), F.S.B.A. (1985); Cert. of Botanical
Merit (S.B.A. Exhbn. 1993); botanical artist in water-colour, gouache;
Personnel Officer, Council Mem. (Ex-officio), Soc. of Botanical Artists (1988-
95); *b* Ross-on-Wye, 5 Mar., 1942. *m* Norman Smail. *Educ:* Ross-on-Wye.
*Studied:* Hereford College of Art (1958-62). *Exhib:* Mall Galleries (1986,
1987), Westminster Gallery (1988), Hereford Museum and A.G. (1991),
Sevenoaks Wildfowl Trust annually since 1994; 19 other centres worldwide
since 1984. *Work in collections:* Hunt Inst. of Botanical Documentation,
Pittsburg; Marine Soc., London; private collections throughout the world.
*Publications:* work repro.: illustrations for articles in various publications;
designs for reproduction on greetings cards and ceramics. *Signs work:*
"Elizabeth Smail." *Address:* 25 Walton Rd., Tonbridge, Kent TN10 4EF.

**SMART, Jeffrey,** painter in oil, pen and ink; *b* Adelaide, S. Aus., 26 July,
1921. *Educ:* Pulteney Grammar School, Adelaide. *Studied:* S.A. School of
Arts, Adelaide (1940), Grand Chaumiere (1948) under McEvoy, Academie
Montmartre (1949) under Fernand Leger. *Exhib:* Whitechapel (1962), Tate
Gallery (1963); one-man shows: Redfern Gallery (1967, 1979, 1982), Galleria
88 Rome (1968), Leicester Galleries (1970). *Work in collections:* National
Galleries of Sydney, Melbourne, Adelaide and Perth, Mertz Coll., Corcoran
Gallery, Washington, Yale University, Von Thyssen Coll., Lugano, De Beers
Coll., 20th Century Art, London. *Publications:* work repro.: Art International
(May, 1968), Present Day Australian Art (Ure Smith), Masterpieces of
Australian Art (1970), 200 Years of Australian Art (1971), The Moderns
(Phaidon Press, 1976), Jeffrey Smart (S. McGrath, Art International Vol.
XXI/I, 1977), Jeffrey Smart (David Malouf, Art International, Nov. 1982);
Jeffrey Smart by Peter Quartermaine (Gryphon Press, 1983). Documentary film
BBC "Omnibus" (1984). *Signs work:* "Jeffrey Smart." *Address:* c/o Redfern
Gallery, Cork St., London.

**SMITH, Barry Edward Jervis,** B.A.; artist/illustrator in water-colour; *b*
Sydney, Australia, 27 Apr., 1943. *Educ:* Coburg High School; University of
Melbourne (1961-66). *Exhib:* group shows in London; one-man shows: Nantes,
Edinburgh, Sweden and Australia. *Publications:* written and illustrated several
children's books. http://www.rom.net/barry *Signs work:* "B. Smith" or "Barry
Smith." *Address:* P.O. Box 846, London E8 1ER

**SMITH, Basil,** M.C.S.D. (1958), M.S.T.D. (1965), F.S.B.A. (1985),
M.G.M.A. (1992); freelance artist in water-colour and acrylic; *b* Hove, 1925. *m*
Mavis Grant. three *s.* one *d. Educ:* Xaverian College, Brighton. *Studied:*
Brighton College of Art and Crafts (1940-42, 1946-48, Charles Knight). *Exhib:*
R.I., Mall Galleries, Sussex Artists, Wildlife Artists, Westminster Gallery,
Donnington, Limerock U.S.A. *Publications:* illustrated: The Principles of
Gardening, The Good Cook, Vegetables, Graham Hill's Motoring Racing

Book, Food from your Garden. *Signs work:* "BASIL" and see appendix. *Address:* 53 Davigdor Rd., Hove, E. Sussex BN3 1RA.

**SMITH, C. Philip,** A.R.C.A. (1st Class) (1954), M.D.E. (1970), Fellow of Designer Bookbinders; Presidium of Honour (Czech) (1989); several international Gold and Silver Medals; book artist, bookbinder, painter, author, inventor (Patents for maril, and lap-back book-structure); Past President of Designer Bookbinders (1977-79); an Editor of The New Bookbinder (1980-95); British Museum team Florence flood 1966-67; *b* Southport, Merseyside, 10 June, 1928. *m* Dorothy M. Weighill, artist. three *s. Educ:* Ackworth School, Yorks. *Studied:* Southport School of Art (1949-51), R.C.A. (1951-54, Roger Powell); Sydney Cockerell bindery (1957-61). *Exhib:* several solo U.K. and abroad, over 150 book-art and binding exhbns. U.K., U.S.A., France, Germany, Holland, Belgium, Luxembourg, Spain, Norway, Czechoslovakia, S. America, Canada, Japan, S. Africa, etc.; painting exhbns. include John Moores, R.B.A., etc. *Work in collections:* V. & A., B.M. (B.L.), Royal Collection, Royal Library Holland, and other major public collections U.K., U.S.A., France, Spain and around the world. *Publications:* The Lord of the Rings and Other Bookbindings, (1970); New Directions in Bookbinding (London and N.Y. 1975); The Book: Art & Object (1982); Book Art: Concept and Making, in prep.; numerous exhbn. catalogues, articles and reviews internationally. *Clubs:* Designer Bookbinders, Meister der Einbandkunst, Canadian G. of B.B.A., Soc. of Bookbinders, Center for Book Arts, N.Y. *Signs work:* "Philip Smith." *Address:* The Book House, Yatton Keynell, Wilts. SN14 7BH.

**SMITH, Caryl,** S.B.A. (1997); mainly self-taught artist in pastel and watercolour, mostly flowers and gardens.; *b* Wiltshire, 21 Oct., 1943. *m* V. J. Smith. two *s. Exhib:* galleries in the Cotswolds, Wiltshire and Sussex. *Clubs:* S.B.A., Fosseway Artists. *Signs work:* paintings: "CARYL." *Address:* 20 Beech Lea, Blunsdon, Swindon, Wilts. SN2 4DE.

**SMITH, Colin Hilton,** B.A.(Hons.), M.A.(R.C.A.); Harkness Fellow (Yale University), Royal Overseas League joint first prize winner; painter in oil on canvas, acrylic etc. on paper; part-time lecturer, Canterbury School of Art; *b* Harpenden, Herts., 21 Feb., 1953. *m* Rosemary Victoria. one *s. Educ:* Hitchin Boys Grammar School. *Studied:* St. Albans School of Art (1971-72, Arnold Van Praag), Falmouth School of Art (1972-75, Karl Weschke), R.C.A. (1975-79, John Walker), Yale (1983-85, Andrew Forge). *Exhib:* Nicola Jacobs Gallery (1982, 1984, 1987, 1989), Ruth Siegal, N.Y. (1986), Anderson O'Day (1991), Kunst Europa (1991), Gallery 30, N.Y. (1993), Barbican Concourse Gallery, London (1993), Art Itinera 83 Italy, 14th International Festival of Painting, France (1982), etc. *Work in collections:* R.C.A., Unilever, A.C.G.B., Contemporary Art Soc., Prudential, Pepsi Cola, Arthur Anderson, B.A., etc. Obituary for Richard Diebenkorn, Artscribe (1991). *Clubs:* Chelsea Arts. *Signs work:* "Colin Smith." *Address:* c/o Anderson O'Day Fine Art, 255 Portobello Rd., London W11 1LR.

# WHO'S WHO IN ART

**SMITH, David Henry,** M.Art, R.C.A. (1971), Hugh Dunn Plaque (1971); artist in oil and water-colour; *b* Cleethorpes, 29 Oct., 1947. *m* Irena Ewa Flynn. *Educ:* Elliston Secondary Modern School, Cleethorpes. *Studied:* Grimsby School of Art (1965-68); R.C.A. (1968-71). *Exhib:* one-man shows, New Art Centre, London (1970-72), Fischer Fine Art, London (1974, 1976, 1978, 1981), Vienna (1976), W. Germany (1976), Sweden (1979). *Work in collections:* Arts Council, Contemporary Art Soc. *Signs work:* "D. H. Smith." *Address:* Hall Lodge, Holton-cum-Beckering, Wragby, Lincoln.

**SMITH, Edward John Milton,** A.T.D. (1952), N.D.D. 2nd Cl. Hons. (1951), F.S.A.E.; artist in lettering, writing and illumination; Principal Lecturer, Subject Leader (Art) P.G.C.E. Course, Leeds Polytechnic 1963-85 (now retd.); art teacher, West Monmouth School, Pontypool (1952-62); visiting lecturer, Newport College of Art (1954-62); President N.S.A.E. (1972); *b* Stonehouse, Glos., 3 May, 1922. *m* Doreen. one *s.* two *d. Educ:* Central School, Stroud, Glos. *Studied:* Stroud School of Art (1936-38), Gloucester College of Art (1939-40), Leeds College of Art (1946-52). *Signs work:* see appendix. *Address:* Glevum, 30 Burnham Rd., Garforth, Leeds, Yorks. LS25 1LA.

**SMITH, Gregor,** R.S.W., D.A. (1966), Post-grad. scholarship (1967); artist in oil and water-colour, teacher; *b* Renton, Dunbartonshire, 15 July, 1944. *m* Elizabeth. *Educ:* Wishaw High School. *Studied:* Edinburgh College of Art (1962-67). *Exhib:* R.S.A., R.S.W., Compass Gallery, Glasgow, numerous group and one-man shows. *Work in collections:* H.R.H. The Duke of Edinburgh, S.A.C., numerous educ. authorities and district councils. *Signs work:* "Gregor Smith." *Address:* Auchendarroch House, Shore Rd., Kilcreggan, Helensburgh, Dunbartonshire G84 0HQ.

**SMITH, Ivor Stanley,** M.A., LL.D., R.I.B.A., A.A. Dip.; consultant architect; educational consultant, The Caribbean School of Architecture, Kingston, Jamaica; *b* Leigh-on-Sea, Essex. *m* Audrey. one *s.* three *d. Educ:* Southend School of Art; Bartlett, Cambridge; A.A. Schools of Architecture. *Signs work:* "Ivor Smith." *Address:* The Station Officer's House, Prawle Point, Kingsbridge, Devon TQ7 2BX.

**SMITH, Jack,** artist in oil; *b* Sheffield, 18 June, 1928. *m* Susan. *Educ:* Nether Edge Grammar School. *Studied:* R.C.A. (1949-52). *Exhib:* twenty one-man shows in England. *Work in collections:* Tate Gallery, Arts Council, Berlin Internatioal Gallery, Guggenheim Museum, Gottenburg Museum. *Signs work:* "Jack Smith" or "Jacksmith." *Address:* 29 Seafield Rd., Hove, Sussex BN3 2TP.

**SMITH, Joan,** M.A. (Hons.) (1987), Postgrad. Dip. in Painting (1988), M.F.A. (1989); artist in acrylic, oil and mixed media on canvas and paper, lithography; Lecturer in Drawing and Painting, Edinburgh College of Art; *b* Dundee, 28 June, 1964. *Educ:* Monifieth High School, Dundee. *Studied:* Edinburgh University (1982-87, Prof. Fernie), Edinburgh College of Art (1982-89, Prof. David Michie). *Exhib:* solo shows: Collective Gallery, Edinburgh

535

(1992), Crawford Art Centre, St. Andrews (1993); many group shows, Pier Art Centre, Orkney (1994), Christopher Boyd Gallery, Galasheils (1995). *Work in collections:* R.S.A., Edinburgh College of Art, Edinburgh City Art Centre, Heriot Watt University, Glasgow Museums and Art Galleries. *Publications:* Drawing Comparisons (1997). *Signs work:* "Joan Smith." *Address:* 14 Coillesdene Gdns., Edinburgh EH15 2JS.

**SMITH, Peter William,** D.F.C.; artist in oils and water-colour; *b* New Malden, Surrey, 3 July, 1920. *Educ:* Whitgift, Croydon. *Studied:* Reigate Art School. *Exhib:* East Sussex Art Club, Hastings (1947 and 1948), International Amateur Art (1969). *Signs work:* "Peter Smith." *Address:* Dean Cottage, Blanks Lane, Newdigate, Surrey RH5 5ED.

**SMITH, Richard Michael,** B.A. (Hons.) (1993); winner, Carroll Foundation award (R.P.); painter in oil on canvas, pastel, pencil; *b* Warlingham, Surrey, 15 June, 1957. two *s.* one *d. Educ:* Caterham School. *Studied:* Coventry Art School (1977-80, Colin Saxton, Harry Weinberger), and in studio of John Ward, R.A. *Exhib:* R.A. Summer Exhbns., R.P., Brian Sinfield Gallery, Burford, Portland Gallery, London. *Work in collections:* G.L.C. *Signs work:* "Richard Smith," "R.S." or "R.M.S." *Address:* Flat 5, Stangrave Hall, Godstone, Surrey RH9 8NB.

**SMITH, Rita,** B.A. (Hons.) (1978), H.D.F.A. (Lond.) (1980), Boise Travelling Scholarship (1980); artist in water-colour; *b* London, 9 Mar., 1946. two *s. Educ:* Collingwood School for Girls. *Studied:* Camberwell School of Art (1974-78), Slade School of Fine Art (1978-80). *Exhib:* solo: University of Surrey, Plymouth Arts Centre; selected mixed shows include, The Whitechapel, R.A., South London A.G., Grundy Gallery, Blackpool, Plymouth and Truro Museums, Singer and Friedlander/Sunday Times Water-colour Competition, Gallery 27, Cork Street, Gillian Jason Gallery. Winner, The Guinness award at R.A. (1993). *Signs work:* "RITA SMITH." *Address:* 1 Gnaton Terr., Albaston, nr. Gunnislake, Cornwall PL18 9AG.

**SMITH, Stan,** R.W.S.; painter/draughtsman; Hon. Life President, London Group; former Head of Fine Art, Ruskin School, University of Oxford; Fellow, Linacre College, Oxford (1981); Chairman, Chelsea Arts Club (1994); *b* Hull, 1929. *Exhib:* widely in U.K. and abroad. Work in national, corporate and private collections worldwide. Prizewinner: R.A. and Hunting Group. *Publications:* include books, articles and videos on art and art theory. Consultant on magazines, TV and radio programmes. *Clubs:* The Arts Club, Chelsea Arts, Grouchos. *Address:* 1 Brunswick Cl., Twickenham, Middx. TW2 5ND.

**SNELLING, John,** F.R.S.A. (1966); landscape and marine artist in water-colour and oils; *b* Greenwich, 15 Nov., 1914. *m* Margaret Snelling. three *s.* one *d. Educ:* Camberwell School of Art. *Studied:* under Horace Brodzky. *Exhib:* Mall Galleries, Guildhall Gallery and numerous one-man shows. *Work in collections:* Great Britain, U.S.A., S.A., Finland, Norway, Germany, Italy, etc.

*Publications:* written and illustrated: Painting Defects (Spon), Painters Book of Facts (Technical Press). *Signs work:* see appendix. *Address:* 306 Wennington Rd., Rainham, Essex.

**SNOW, Graham,** Dip.A.D. (1968), H.Dip. (1972); Mombusho scholar, Japan (1974-77), Artist in Residence, Cambridge University (1977-81); artist in oil and water-colour; *b* Exeter, 28 Oct., 1948. *Educ:* Colfox School, Dorset. *Studied:* Bournemouth College of Art (1966-68), Hornsey College of Art (1968-70), Slade School of Fine Art (1970-72). *Exhib:* one-man shows in London, New York and Tokyo. *Work in collections:* Arts Council, Chase Manhattan Bank, Texaco, etc. *Signs work:* "G. SNOW." *Address:* c/o Grob Gallery, 20 Dering St., London W1R 9AA.

**SNOWDEN, Hilda Mary,** B.A. (Hons.) Open University, F.I.A.L.; artist in pastels, oils, water-colour, embroidery, sculpture; *b* Bradford, 13 Apr., 1910. *Educ:* Grange Upper School, Hillcroft College, Surbiton. *Studied:* Regional College of Art, Bradford, Positano Art Workshop, Italy. *Exhib:* London, Bradford, Harrogate, Ilkley. *Publications:* author and illustrator, Dalesman (Nov. 1985); Under Stag's Fell - A History of Simonstone-Wensleydale (1989); author, Bradford Antiquary (1987). *Signs work:* see appendix. *Address:* Flat I, Victoria Mans., Dawson St., Thackley, Bradford BD10 8LH.

**SNOWDON, Brian Robert,** private Fine Art Dealer and adviser specialising in modernist, post-war and contemporary paintings and sculpture; Quality stock holdings: enquiries and commissions by institutions and private clients for major works welcomed and undertaken; *b* Darlington, 27 June, 1942. *Educ:* Darlington C.F.E. *Address:* Nepenthe Cottage, 7 Park St., Stow-on-the-Wold, Glos. GL54 1AQ.

**SOAR, John Richardson,** M.A. (1966), B.Sc. (1952), A.R.M.S. (1996), U.A. (1989), H.S. (1989); landscape painter in pastel (from miniature to large size pastel paintings); Principal, Swindon Technical College and School of Art (retd. 1984); Inspector of Further Education for Essex C.C. (1965-70); *b* London, 30 May, 1927. *m* Miriam Theresa. one *s.* one *d. Educ:* West Ham Municipal College; King's College, London. *Exhib:* U.A. (annually), Westminster Gallery; Hilliard Soc. of Miniaturists (annually), Wells; R.M.S. Westminster Gallery (annually); Wantage Museum Gallery (1987, 1988, 1989, 1995); regular contributor to Medici Gallery and Llewellyn Alexander Gallery, London. *Work in collections:* mostly in West of England, U.S.A., Canada and various European countries. *Clubs:* Guild of Wiltshire Artists, Fossenay Artists. *Signs work:* "JOHN SOAR." *Address:* 81 Chestnut Springs, Lydiard Millicent, Swindon, Wilts. SN5 9NB.

**SOBIEN, Inka,** Grand Prix Humanitaire de France avec Medaille d'Argent (1977), La Palme D'or, Belgo-Hispanique (1977); artist; lecturer, Hornsey College of Art and Central Academy of Film, Art and Drama, London (1963-66), St. Martin's School of Art (1963-67); *b* 25 Feb., 1939. *m* Stewart Steven. one *s. Studied:* St. Martin's School of Art (1959-63). *Exhib:* one-man shows:

Upper St. Gallery, London (1974), Gallerie Raymond Duncan, Paris (1975), New Jersey (1975), Ligoa Duncan, N.Y. (1975), Philadelphia (1975), Florida (1976), Festival International de Peinture et d'Art Graphico-Plastique de St. Germain-des-Pres, Paris (1976), Scribes Writers' Club, London (1978), Little Palace, Warsaw (1979), B.W.A. Gallery, Cracow (1979), Avant Garde Gallery, Wroclaw (1979), Barbican Centre (1985), Budapest (1985), Camden Arts Centre (1989); mixed shows: Grande Palais Paris; London: Marjorie Parr Gallery, Gallery XVIII, Annely Juda Fine Art, Leinster Fine Art, Salomon Gallery. *Work in collections:* National Museum, Warsaw and Cracow, Museum of Modern Art, Budapest. *Signs work:* "Inka Sobien." *Address:* 29 Priory Ave., London W4.

**SOKOLOV, Kirill Konstantinovich,** painter, printmaker, illustrator, sculptor, engraver; co-editor, "Leonardo"; *b* Moscow, 27 Sept., 1930. *m* Avril Pyman. one *d. Educ:* Special Art School, Moscow (1942-49). *Studied:* Surikov Institute, Moscow (1949-56). *Exhib:* Gulbenkian Gallery, Newcastle, Durham University, St. Helier, C.I., London University, Bishopsgate Foundation, Academy of Art, Riga, House of Artists, Krymskaia Naberezhnaia, Moscow, Art Gallery, Perm, Hatton Gallery and Laing Gallery, Newcastle, and various venues in U.S.S.R., China, U.S.A., Norway, Germany. *Work in collections:* Pushkin Museum, Trediakov Gallery, Latvian State Museum of Arts, Graphic Archive, Munich, Perm Gallery, Optyno-Pustyn, Taras Shevchenko, Dostoevsky and Aleksandr Blok Memorial Museums, Shakespeare Memorial Museum, Stratford-on-Avon, V. & A., Faust Soc., Knittlingen, Lyric Theatre, Hammersmith, Theatre Royal, Newcastle, Hatton Gallery, Newcastle. *Publications:* over 60 titles in Russian and English. *Signs work:* "Kirill Sokolov," also "K.S." and "K.C." (until 1974 in cyrillic). *Address:* 213 Gilesgate, Durham DH1 1QN.

**SONNIS, Alexander,** A.R.C.A., lithographer R.C.A.; painter in various mediums; part-time instructor, St. Martin's School of Art (1946-73); also periods at other art schools; *b* 1904. *Educ:* L.C.C., part-time student of Bernard Meninsky, Central School of Arts and Crafts (1924-27); textile designer B.C.P.A. (1927-29); Royal College of Art award (1929-32). *Exhib:* N.E.A.C. (London Group), R.A., miscellaneous galleries. *Work in collections:* War Advisory Committee (1942). *Signs work:* "Alex Sonnis" or "A. SONNIS." *Address:* 51 Cresswell Rd., Twickenham, Middx. TW1 2EA.

**SOREL, Agathe,** R.E., Churchill Fellow (1967), Fellow, Printmakers Council; printmaker, sculptor, lecturer; *b* Budapest, 1935. *m* G. Sitkey. one *s. Studied:* Academy of Fine Art, and Academy of Applied Art, Budapest; Camberwell School of Art and Crafts (Michael Rothenstein, S.W. Hayter); Atelier 17, Paris. *Exhib:* one-man shows: Curwen Gallery, London, Arleigh Gallery, San Francisco, Philadelphia Print Club, Camden Arts Centre, O.U.P., Robertson Gallery, Ottawa, Mälargalleriet, Stockholm, Sculpture at Paul Kõvesdy Gallery, N.Y., Galerie Geiger Kornwestheim, Germany, Städtische

# WHO'S WHO IN ART

Galerie Filderstadt, Germany; retrospective exhbn. Herbert Read Gallery, Canterbury. *Work in collections:* in 33 major museums including B.M., Tate Gallery, Los Angeles Museum of Art, Philadelphia Museum of Art, Chicago Art Inst., National Gallery, Washington. *Publications:* illustrated: Jean Genet, Le Balcon. *Clubs:* R.E., Printmakers Council. *Signs work:* "Agathe Sorel." *Address:* Dorrell Hall, 43 London Rd., London SE23 3TY.

**SORRELL, Adrian,** sculptor in wax and clay cast in bronze, painter; lecturer, Bolton College of Art (1961-75); *b* Salford, 1932. *Studied:* Salford School of Art (1949-54). *Exhib:* Sladmore Gallery, London (1972-78), Les Animaliers, 150 Years of Animal Sculpture, Sladmore Gallery (1976), Morris Singer Exhbn., Dubai (1977), Sportsmans Edge Gallery, N.Y. (1978), Moorland Gallery, London (1979), Dominion Gallery, Montreal (1980), R.A. Summer Exhbn. (1980-89), Tryon Moorland Gallery, London (1983, 1987), Liverpool Museum (1985), Church St. Gallery, Stow (1987), Reid Stremmel Gallery, Texas (1986-87). *Signs work:* "SORRELL." *Address:* 74 Ringley Rd., Whitefield, Lancs. M25 7LN.

**SORRELL, Richard,** Dip.A.D. (1969), R.A. Schools Post. Grad. Cert. (1972), R.W.S. (1978), R.B.A. (1989); artist in oil, water-colour and acrylic; *b* Thundersley, Essex, 24 Sept., 1948. *m* Doreen Burke. two *s. Educ:* Eton House School, Thorpe Bay, Essex. *Studied:* Walthamstow Art School (1965-66), Kingston College of Art (1966-69), R.A. Schools (1969-72). *Exhib:* R.A., R.W.S., R.B.A., The Lane Studio, New Grafton Gallery, Agnews, Cadogan Gallery. *Work in collections:* V. & A., Museum of London, Beecroft A.G., Southend-on-Sea. *Publications:* The Artist, Country Life. *Signs work:* "Richard Sorrell." *Address:* East Side, Syers Rd., Beeston, King's Lynn, Norfolk PE32 2NJ.

**SOULAGES, Pierre,** painter; *b* Rodez, France, 24 Dec., 1919. *m* Colette Llaurens. *Exhib:* one-man shows in Museums of Hannover, Zurich, Essen, De Hagen (1960-61), Copenhagen (1963), Houston (1966), Paris (1967, 1979), Buffalo, Pittsburgh, Montréal (1968), Mexico, Caracas, Rio de Janeiro, Sao Paulo (1975-76), Liège et Salzburg (1980), Tokyo (1984), Kassel, Valencia, Nantes (1989), Séoul, Pekin, Taipei (1994), Paris, Montréal, Sao Paulo (1996), Hamburg, Zaragoza (1997). *Work in collections:* Centre G. Pompidou, Paris, Museum of Modern Art, Guggenheim Museum, N.Y., National Gallery, Washington, National Gallery of Australia, Canberra, Museo de Arte Moderna, Sao-Paulo, Tate Gallery, London, etc. *Signs work:* see appendix. *Address:* 18 rue des Trois-Portes, 75005 Paris, 5.

**SOUZA, F. N.,** painter; founder of Progressive Artists Group, Bombay (1948); *b* Goa, 12 Apr., 1924. *m* 1st. Maria Figuereido (divorced); one d; 2nd. Liselotte Kristian (in common law); three *d*; 3rd. Barbara Zinkant (divorced). one *s s. Educ:* St. Xavier's College. *Studied:* Sir J. J. School of Art; Central School of Art; Ecole des Beaux Arts *Exhib:* one-man shows, London, Paris, Stockholm, Copenhagen, Johannesburg, Germany, U.A.E., U.S.A., etc.; retrospective exhbns., London, New Delhi, Leicester, Detroit; Minneapolis Int. Art (1972); Expo '67, Montreal; Commonwealth Inst., London (1977); Contemporary Indian Artists (N.Y., 1978); Festival of India, R.A. and Oxford (1982), etc. *Work in collections:* New Delhi, Tate, Haifa, Melbourne, etc. *Publications:* Words and Lines (autobiography); The White Flag Revolution (1982); New Poems (1985). *Signs work:* see appendix. *Address:* 148 West 67 St., New York, N.Y. 10023.

**SPACKMAN, Sarah,** B.A. (1981); painter in oil, water-colour, gouache, charcoal; *b* Reading, Berks., 19 Feb., 1958. *Educ:* Abbey School, Reading. *Studied:* Byam Shaw School of Art (1977-78), Camberwell School of Art (1979-81). *Exhib:* Austin Desmond Fine Art, Cadogan Contemporary, New Ashgate Gallery, Farnham, Solomon Gallery, Dublin, Mitchell Gallery, Toronto, Canada. *Work in collections:* Contemporary Art Collection, Allied Irish Bank. *Publications:* four paintings as posters by The Art Group. *Signs work:* "S.S." *Address:* 12 Henley St., Oxford OX4 1ER.

**SPAFFORD, George,** M.A., B.C.L., R.C.A. (1990); artist in acrylic; *b* Manchester, 1 Sept., 1921. *m* Iola. one *s.* one *d. Educ:* Rugby, Oxford. *Signs work:* "G.S." *Address:* 57 Hawthorn La., Wilmslow, Ches. SK9 5DQ.

**SPAFFORD, Iola Margaret,** D.F.A. (1953), R.C.A. (1984), mem. M.A.F.A.; artist in oil, pen and ink, water-colour, etching; *b* Cambridge, 24 Aug., 1930. *m* George Spafford. one *s.* one *d. Educ:* Queen Anne's, Caversham. *Studied:* Bristol Art School (1947), Nottingham Art School (1948-50), Slade School of Fine Art (1950-54). *Exhib:* one-man shows, Tib Lane Gallery, Manchester (4). *Work in collections:* Manchester A.G. (Rutherston Collection), Salford A.G., and many private collections. *Signs work:* "Iola Spafford." *Address:* 57 Hawthorn La., Wilmslow, Ches. SK9 5DQ.

**SPALDING, Julian,** F.M.A. (1983); Director, Glasgow Museum and Art Galleries; *b* London, 15 June, 1947. *m* (1) Frances Crabtree (divorced); one *s;* (2) Gillian Tait. *Educ:* Chislehurst and Sidcup Grammar School for Boys. *Studied:* University of Nottingham (B.A.Hons. Fine Art). *Address:* Glasgow Art Gallery and Museum, Kelvingrove, Glasgow G3 8AG.

**SPENCER, Charles Samuel,** lecturer and art critic; *b* London, 26 Aug., 1920. Former editor, Art and Artists: Former editor, Editions Alecto Collectors Club; Lecturer, Theatre and Art. *Publications:* author: Erté (1970); A Decade of Print Making (1973); Leon Bakst (1973), enlarged and revised (1995); Cecil Beaton (1975), enlarged and revised (1995); The World of Serge Diaghilev (1974); editor: The Aesthetic Movement (1973); The World of Flo Ziegfeld (1974); Alecto Monographs on Kenneth Armitage, Colin Lanceley, Tom Phillips, Achilles Droungas, Ed Meneely, Harald Becker, Igino Legnaghi. *Address:* 24a Ashworth Rd., London W9 1JY.

**SPENCER, Claire,** N.D.D. (1958), A.R.C.A. (1963), A.T.D. (1973), R.B.S.A. (1980), P.S. (1985); Council mem. and Publicity Sec. Pastel Soc.; painter in oil, water-colour and pastel; *b* Kingsbury, Middx., 17 May, 1937. *m*

Christopher Postins. one *s. Educ:* Harrow County School for Girls. *Studied:* Hornsey College of Art (1954-58), R.C.A. (1960-63), Accademia di Belle Arti, Perugia (1966). Numerous individual and group exhbns. *Work in collections:* Nuffield Collection, West Midlands Arts Collection. *Publications:* contributor to The Artist Magazine. *Signs work:* "Claire Spencer" and see appendix. *Address:* Rotherwood, 17 Summerfield Rd., Clent, Stourbridge, Worcs. DY9 9RG.

**SPENCER, Gwen,** N.S.; painter in oil, pastel and gouache; Hon. sec., National Soc. of Painters, Sculptors and Printmakers; *b* Argentine, 2 Oct., 1927. *m* Christopher Spencer, F.C.A. two *s.* one *d. Educ:* St. Hilda's College, Buenos Aires. *Studied:* Atelier Josse, Buenos Aires, and Putney School of Art. *Exhib:* N.S., R.O.I., P.S., Ridley Soc. *Work in collections:* U.K., N. and S. America, Italy, Holland, Denmark, India and Australia. *Publications:* work repro.: Medici Soc. *Signs work:* "Gwen Spencer" or "G. Spencer." *Address:* 122 Copse Hill, Wimbledon, London SW20 0NL.

**SPENCER, Liam David,** B.A.; artist in oil paint; *b* Burnley, 1964. *m* Heather Walker. two *s. Educ:* Manchester Polytechnic (1983-86). *Exhib:* 'Windows on the City' touring exhbn. (1996-97). The Mancunian Way touring exbn (199-98).*Work in collections:* Towneley Hall A.G. and Museum, Burnley, Manchester City A.G., Readers Digest, N.Y. *Commissions:* Price Waterhouse, Manchester, U.S.S. Liverpool. *Publications:* 'Articles of Faith' Richard Kendal Art Review (Oct. 1996), 'The Landscape Next Door' Laura Gascoigne Artists and Illustrators (Sept. 1997). *Signs work:* "L.S." (reverse) or not at all. *Address:* 52 Audley Rd., Manchester M19 3FQ.

**SPENCER, Pamela Mary,** artist in oil, water-colour, pencil; *b* Manchester, 11 Jan., 1924. *Educ:* P.N.E.U. Schools, Queen's College, Radbrook College of Domestic Science (Shrewsbury). *Studied:* St. Martin's School of Art under J. Bateman, Barry Craig, J. L. Wheatley, H. A. Freeth, K. Martin (1945-51). *Exhib:* R.A., N.E.A.C., S.W.A., N.S., R.B.A., R.O.I., P.S., Russell-Cotes Museum, and other provincial galleries. *Signs work:* "Pamela M. Spencer" or "P. M. Spencer." *Address:* 33 Damer Gdns., Henley-on-Thames, Oxon. RG9 1HX.

**SPENCER, Sarah,** B.A. (Hons.) (1988), Post. Dip. R.A. Schools (1991); painter in oil, charcoal, pastel; part-time lecturer, Canterbury College; *b* Sevenoaks, 26 Sept., 1965. *Educ:* Tonbridge Grammar School, West Kent College of F.E. *Studied:* Camberwell School of Art and Crafts (1985-88), R.A. Schools (1988-91). *Exhib:* solo shows: New Grafton Gallery, Waterman's Fine Art; many mixed shows. *Work in collections:* West Wales Arts Council. *Signs work:* full signature on reverse of works, sometimes "S.S." on front. *Address:* 7 Marine Terr., Whitstable, Kent CT5 1EJ.

**SPENCER PRYSE, Tessa,** R.B.A. (1986); painter of portraits, landscapes and interiors in oil, water-colour, lithography; *b* Highcliff on Sea, 28 Sept., 1939. *m* E.D.A. Cameron. one *s.* one *d. Educ:* France and Switzerland. *Studied:*

Byam Shaw School of Art (1960-64, Peter Greenham, Bernard Dunstan). *Exhib:* R.A., R.P., R.B.A., N.E.A.C., R.S.A., R.W.S.; one-man shows: Phoenix Gallery, Lavenham, Hayletts Gallery, Colchester, Alpine Gallery, London, Digby Gallery, Colchester, John Russell, Ipswich, Arthur Andersen, London, Llewellyn Alexander, London. *Work in collections:* Essex Museum. *Signs work:* "PRYSE." *Address:* 9 Anchor Hill, Wivenhoe, Colchester, Essex CO7 9BL.

**SPENDER, Humphrey,** Hon. Des. R.C.A.; painter, photographer; designer; textiles, wallpapers, carpets; four C.O.I.D. Awards; *b* London, 19 Apr., 1910. *m* Pauline Wynn. two *s. Studied:* Architectural Assoc. *Exhib:* one-man: Redfern, Leicester Galleries, New Art Centre, Windsor, Farnham, Colchester, Bristol; group: C.A.S., Arts Council, John Moores, Bradford, Aldeburgh, R.A. *Work in collections:* V. & A., N.P.G., M. of W., Southampton, Wolverhampton, Brighton, Manchester, Johannesburg. Murals: Festival of Britain, P. & O. Liners Orcades, Orsova, Oriana, Canberra, Shell Centre, Pilkingtons. *Publications:* Worktown People (Falling Wall Press, 1982), Lensman (Chatto & Windus, 1987). *Address:* The Studio, Ulting, Maldon, Essex CM9 6QX.

**SPENDLOVE, Gerald Hugh,** A.T.D. (Dist.) (1954), F.S.D.C. (1972); designer- craftsman in calligraphy, lettering, illumination and ceramics; formerly Head of Ceramics, Herts. College of Art, St. Albans; *b* Derby, 1929. *m* Valerie Spendlove. one *s.* three *d. Educ:* Salisbury School of Art (1949-51), L.C.C. Central School of Art (1951-53), N.D.D. Pottery and Calligraphy. *Exhib:* Nottingham, Southampton, Bath, York, St. Albans, London, Winchester. *Work in collections:* H.M. the Queen, Herts. C.C., Nevers (France); private collections in U.S.A., France, Norway, Germany, Nigeria, U.K. *Commissions:* numerous commissions, hand produced, all forms of lettering; stoneware and porcelain. *Signs work:* "G. H. Spendlove", stamp GHS in square. *Address:* The Sycamores, New Rd., Swanmore, Hants. SO32 2PE.

**SPRAKES, John,** R.O.I., R.B.A., F.R.S.A.; Andrew Grant scholarship, D.A. (Edin.) post grad.; prizewinner Singer Friedlander/Sunday Times water-colour (1992); artist in tempera, oil, acrylic; *b* 17 Oct., 1936. *m* Barbara Ann. three *s. Studied:* Doncaster College of Art, Edinburgh College of Art (1954-57). *Exhib:* R.A., Mem. of The Manchester Academy; Manchester Academy (prize 85), Barclays Bank award (1986, 1991), P/P award (1989), group and one-man shows. Work in public and private collections. Agent in London, J. Corless, Blackheath Gallery. *Signs work:* "John Sprakes" or "J. Sprakes." *Address:* 39 Douglas Rd., Long Eaton, Nottingham NG10 4BH.

**SPURRIER, Raymond,** R.I., R.W.A.; writer, illustrator, painter, printmaker; Hon. Secretary R.I.; *b* Wellingborough, 1920. *Educ:* Wellingborough Grammar School. *Studied:* part-time at St. Martin's and Central School. Practising town planner until 1980 and part-time freelance illustrator and writer. *Exhib:* R.A., R.W.A., R.I., etc.; finalist Hunting Group prize competition (1980, 1982); Winsor & Newton R.I. Award (1984). *Work in collections:* Dept. of the

Environment and private. *Publications:* work repro.: R.A. Illustrated and calendar; contributor: The Artist Magazine and instructional art books; author: Sketching with Raymond Spurrier; part author: Mastering Water-colour. *Signs work:* "Raymond Spurrier." *Address:* Halstead Cottage, Halstead, Sevenoaks, Kent.

**SQUIRE, Geoffrey,** D.F.A. (Lond.) 1948, A.R.S.A. (1977), R.G.I. (1980), R.S.W. (1983); painter in oil, acrylic, water-colour, pastel; retd. senior lecturer, Glasgow School of Art (1988); *b* Yorks., 21 Feb., 1923. *m* Jeanmarie. one *s*. one *d*. *Studied:* Leeds College of Art (1939-41); Slade School of Art, Oxford (1941-42), London (1946-48, Randolph Schwabe). *Exhib:* Yorks., Glasgow, Fife, Edinburgh. *Work in collections:* Glasgow A.G., Greenock A.G., Paisley A.G., Dunkeld A.G., Jordanhill College of Educ., Royal Scottish Academy. *Clubs:* Lagonda. *Signs work:* "SQUIRE." *Address:* The Studio, Links Pl., Elie, Fife.

**STABELL, Waldemar Christian,** painter in oil, wax drawings; *b* Hillsboro, N.B., Canada, 1913. *m* Margit Baugstö. one *s*. one *d*. *Educ:* Canada, Norway. *Studied:* Scandinavia, Anglo-French Art Centre, London, Brighton College of Art (etching). *Exhib:* first one-man show in London (1947), St. George's Gallery; several one-man shows and mixed exhibitions. *Publications:* Edvard Munch and Eva Mudocci; Bernt Tunold 1877-1977; Phillip King - En Engelsk Billedhugger (1969); British Artists at the Voss Summer School of Fine Arts; work repro.: Studio, Canada's Weekly, Contact Book, Arts Review, London. Founder of the Voss School of Fine Arts (1964) Voss, Norway. *Signs work:* "Stabell." *Address:* Sydneskleven 31, 5010 Bergen, Norway.

**STAFFORD, C. Carolyn,** C.P.S., S.G.F.A., P.M.C., N.S. (1996), N.D.D., D.A. (Manc.) (1955), Dip. Fine Art (1957); painter in oil and water-colour, printmaker in etching, woodcut, lino; tutor; *b* Bolton, 1935. *m* Gordon Clough, broadcaster. one *s*. three *d*. *Educ:* Bolton School. *Studied:* Bolton School of Art, Manchester College of Art (Ralph Downing, Ian Grant), Slade School of Fine Art (William Coldstream, Claude Rogers, Anthony Gross), Esmond Scholar British Inst. in Paris, etching with S.W. Hayter (1957-58). *Exhib:* John Moores, Liverpool. R.A., Bankside Open Prints, London Group, Arts Council tours, R.I., R.B.A., Printmakers Council, Malta, U.S./U.K., Art Olympia (1990-93), Pump House (1993), Contemporary Portrait Soc., Northern School (Pelter-Sands and touring exhbn.), Lvov (1991), New Academy Gallery (1991), Paris (1994, 1996), Universities of Bristol, Cambridge, London, Oxford and Surrey (1980-90), Tel Aviv, Ben Uri, Curwen, F.P.S., Munich (1997). *Work in collections:* Slade School, D.O.E., Bolton School (Girls Div.), Bolton A.G., Lvov A.G., Landau A.G. *Signs work:* "Carolyn Stafford," "Carolyn Stafford Clough" or "C. STAFFORD." *Address:* 52 Ellerton Rd., London SW18 3NN.

**STAHL, Andrew,** Slade D.F.A., Slade H.D.F.A.; painter in oil, water-colour, acrylic; part-time lecturer, Chelsea College of Art, Slade School of Fine Art; *b* London, 4 July, 1954. *m* Jean Oh. one *s*. two *d*. *Studied:* Slade School of Fine Art. *Exhib:* many one-man and group shows in U.K. and abroad. *Work in* *collection:* Arts Council, British Council, British Museum, Contemporary Arts Soc., City Museum Peterborough, Leics. Educ. Authority, Metropolitan Museum of Art, New York. Ex Rome Scholar and Wingate Scholar. Represented by Angela Flowers Gallery. *Signs work:* back of work usually "ANDREW" or "A. STAHL". *Address:* 38 Powis Sq., London W11 2AY.

**STAINTON, Frances:** see EASTON, Frances.

**STANDEN, Peter,** D.A. (Edin.); works in oil, acrylic, etching, lithography: subjects allegorical, imaginary future ruins, and cats; Mem. Edinburgh Printmakers Workshop (Council 1974-87; Chairman 1979-82); Mem. Soc. of Scottish Artists (Council 1990-93); Scottish Art Council Awards incl. 'Artist in Industry' Ferranti plc (1987); *b* Carshalton, 3 Apr., 1936. *m* Helen. one *s*. one *d*. *Educ:* Epping Secondary. *Studied:* Nottingham College of Art (1954-56), Edinburgh College of Art (1956-59). *Exhib:* one-man shows: 'Up the Nile' Commonwealth Inst., Edinburgh (1965), 'Paintings' New 57 Gallery, Edinburgh (1977), 'Mr. Cat' Traverse Theatre Club, Edinburgh (1985), 'Looking Back to the Future' P.M.W. Edinburgh (1988); group shows: 'Art into Landscape' I and III Serpentine Gallery, London (1974, 1979), '5 Scottish Printmakers' selected by Peter Fuller, P.M.W. Edinburgh Festival (1983), 'Ljubljana Biennial' Yugoslavia (1987), 'Festive City' Fine Art Soc., Edinburgh Festival (1988). *Work in collections:* H.M. The Queen, Windsor Castle, Hamilton A.G., Ontario, Scottish Arts Council, City of Edinburgh, International Club London, Moray House College Edinburgh, Eastern General Hospital Edinburgh, The University of Edinburgh, Royal Bank of Scotland. *Publications:* etchings included in "Edinburgh Suite" (1992) and "The Sea, the Sea" portfolios (Pub. by E.P.M.W., Edinburgh). *Signs work:* prints: "P. Standen" (pencil signature); paintings: "P. STANDEN." *Address:* 5 Lee Cres., Portobello, Edinburgh EH15 1LW.

**STARR, Marion,** artist in oil; *b* Hitchin, Herts., 19 Apr., 1937. *m* Christopher Fielder. two *d*. *Educ:* various Grammar Schools in U.K. and abroad. *Studied:* Chinese brush painting and the Sogetsu School discipline of flower arrangement while in the Far East. *Exhib:* R.A. Summer Exhbn. (since 1979), R.W.A., R.O.I., R.B.A., N.E.A.C., Laing, Spirit of London, Rye Soc. of Artists, Chichester City of Culture Open Art Exhbn., 'A Celebration of the Romney Marsh' at Sassoon Gallery, Folkestone and Marsh Gallery, New Romney; New Grafton Gallery, Easton Rooms and Stormont Studio, Rye, Neville Gallery, Canterbury, Attendi Gallery, Chiswick, Anna-Mei Chadwick Gallery, Fulham, andTalents Fine Arts, Malton. Major winner, Laing Landscape Painting competition (1994). *Signs work:* "M.S." or "Marion Starr." *Address:* 23 Military Rd., Rye, E. Sussex TN31 7NX.

**STAUVERS, Feliks,** R.V.D.S. Arts Academy School (Riga, Latvia); Diploma of Merit, University of Art, Italy; artist in oil, water-colour, dry pigments, restorer, art historian, lecturer in Art and Old Master Paintings; *b* Riga, Latvia, 22 Apr., 1926. *m* M. E. Stauvers. two *s*. *Educ:* Latvia. *Studied:* Riga

Government Arts Academy School (1939-44) under, Prof. Brumel, Dr. V. Luans, Daluns Paks, R.V.D.S. *Exhib:* Nuneaton, Coventry, London. *Work in collections:* Nuneaton Museum A.G., Riga Government A.G., Latvia. *Clubs:* Former Associate of I.I.C. London. *Signs work:* "Feliks Stauvers." *Address:* 83 Windmill Rd., Exhall, Coventry CV7 9GP.

**STEPHENS, Ian,** N.D.D. (1961), R.E. (1984), S.W.E. (1984) (Chairman 1992-95); artist in wood engraving, water-colours; *b* Gt. Linford, Bucks., 19 May, 1940. *m* Valerie. two *s. Educ:* Wolverton Technical School. *Studied:* Northampton School of Art (1956-61). *Exhib:* R.E. (1975 onwards), Fremantle, Jeune Gravure Contemporaine, Paris, Humberside (1985); one-man show Daventry (1989, 1993), British Miniature Print International, Bristol (1989, 1997), Cadaqués (1991, onwards). *Work in collections:* Northants C.C., Notts. C.C., Surrey C.C., Warwicks. Museums, Kettering B.C., Daventry D.C., Fremantle Arts Centre. *Signs work:* "I. Stephens" or "Ian Stephens." *Address:* 46 Yardley Drive, Northampton NN2 8PE.

**STEPHENS, Nicholas Anthony,** N.D.D. (1960), A.R.C.A. (1963), Harkness Fellowship, U.S.A. (1963-65), Arts Council Major award (1977), A.R.B.S. (1981); sculptor in bronze; Principal Lecturer in Fine Art, Glos. College of Art and Technology; visiting teaching: U.C. Davis, California (1971), Victoria College, Prahran, Australia (1983); *b* Nottingham, 6 June, 1939. *m* Jenifer Beesley (divorced 1984). two *s. Educ:* Nottingham High School. *Studied:* Central School (Wm. Turnbull), R.C.A. (1960-63, Lord Queensbury), Pratt Inst., N.Y. (1964), San Francisco Art Inst. (1965, James Melchert). *Exhib:* Davis Cal. (1971), S.W. Arts (1978), The State of Clay (1978-80), R.A. (1980, 1981, 1983, 1984), R.B.S. Scone Palace (1983), Park Gallery Cheltenham (1982, 1985), St. Donat's Castle, Wales (1983), Nicholas Tredwell Gallery (1985), Air Gallery, Harkness Arts (1985), St. David's Hall, Cardiff (1988). *Signs work:* "N.A. STEPHENS." *Address:* The Red House, Bredon, Tewkesbury, Glos. GL20 7LM.

**STEPHENSON, Christine,** N.D.D. (1957), A.T.D. (1958), S.B.A. (1997), R.H.S. Silver Medal (1996), Gold Medal (1997); botanical artist in water-colour; *b* Winchester, 3 Apr., 1937. *m* Jack Stephenson, artist. two *s. Educ:* St. Swithun's School, Winchester. *Studied:* Bournemouth College of Art (1953-58). *Exhib:* R.H.S., S.B.A., Lucy B. Campbell Gallery, London. *Signs work:* "C.F.S." *Address:* 3 Causeway Cottages, Middleton, nr. Saxmundham, Suffolk IP17 3NH.

**STEPHENSON, Prof. Ian,** B.A.Hons.(Dunelm), R.A.; painter; former Studio Demonstrator (pioneered 1st foundn. course in U.K. dedicated to new creativity in art) and Dir. of Foundn. Studies (introd. 1st alternating approach between perceptual and conceptual studies to an academic syllabus), Fine Art, Ncle. Univ.; former Dir. of Postgrad. Painting (created 1st M.A. fine art course in London), Chelsea School of Art; taught many distinguished British artists; *b* nr. Meadowfield, Co. Durham, 11 Jan., 1934. *m* Kate Brown. one *s.* one *d.*

# WHO'S WHO IN ART

*Educ:* Blyth Grammar School, Northld. *Studied:* King Edw. VII School of Art, King's College, Durham Univ., Ncle. *Exhib:* (Retrospectives) Laing A.G., Ncle. (1970); Hayward Gallery (1977); City A.G., Birmingham (1978); often repr. U.K. abroad. *Work in collections:* worldwide. *Publications:* work repro.: in numerous publications; Cubism & After, B.B.C. Michael Gill film; Blow-up, M.G.M. Antonioni film. *Address:* c/o Royal Academy of Arts, Piccadilly, London W1V 0DS.

**STETTLER, Michael,** D.Sc.; art historian; architect; Director of Bernese Historical Museum from 1948 to 1961; Director Abegg Foundation (1961-77); P. Helvetia Foundation (1965-71); *b* Berne, 1 Jan., 1913. *m* Barbara von Albertini. four *d. Educ:* Berne. *Studied:* Zürich Inst. of Technology and University under J. Zemp and H. Wölfflin, and at Rome. *Publications:* Das Rathaus zu Bern (1942), Inventory of Historical Monuments of Canton Aargau (Vol. I, 1948, Vol. II, 1953); Swiss Stained Glass of the 14th Century (English Edition, 1949); Of Old Berne (1957); Rat der Alten (1962); Bernerlob (1964), Neues Bernerlob (1967); Aare, Bär und Sterne (1972); Machs na (1981); Ortbühler Skizzenbuch (1982); A la Rencontre de Berne (1984); Sulgenbach (1992), Lehrer und Freunde (1997). *Address:* Ortbühl, CH-3612 Steffisburg, Switzerland.

**STEVENS, Chris,** B.F.A. (Hons.); artist in oil; *b* Basingstoke, 1956. *Studied:* University of Reading (1974-78). *Exhib:* one-man shows: U.K., London and Holland; group shows: London, Germany and U.S.A; shows with Sue Williams, London. *Work in collections:* National Gallery of Wales. *Address:* Space Studios, Deborah House, Retreat Pl., London E9.

**STEVENS, Helen M.,** S.W.A. (1989); artist in pure silk hand embroidery, writer; *b* Belmont, Surrey, 2 Oct., 1959. *m* Brian Rayner. *Educ:* Bury St. Edmunds County Grammar School. *Exhib:* S.W.A., Soc. of Wildlife Art in Nature; numerous solo shows every two years. *Work in collections:* Palace of Westminster. *Publications:* author and illustrator: 'The Embroiderers Countryside', 'The Embroiderers Country Album' and 'The Timeless Art of Embroidery' (David & Charles). *Signs work:* "Helen Stevens." *Address:* The Mill House, Market Weston, Diss, Norfolk IP22 2PE.

**STEVENSON, David John,** painter in egg tempera and oil; *b* Leicester, 26 Nov., 1956. *m* Alison Wilkins. two *s. Educ:* Guthlaxton College, Leicester. *Exhib:* Leicester Museum, Loseby Gallery, Leicester, Tettenhall Gallery, R.A. *Clubs:* Leicester Soc. of Artists. *Signs work:* "D. Stevenson." *Address:* 15 Wartnaby St., Market Harborough, Leics.

**STEVENSON, Richard Lee,** etcher, printmaker, painter in intaglio, relief printing, oils; *b* Penzance, 9 Apr., 1955. *Studied:* Falmouth School of Art, North Staffs. Polytechnic, Penzance School of Art (Sue Lewington). *Exhib:* R.W.A. Mall Galleries, London, Victoria Galleries, Bath, Small Print Works, Penzance. *Commissions:* Linocut cover design for the 18th International Celtic Film and Television Festival catalogue. *Publications:* Ten Penwith Printmakers

(1998). *Clubs:* St. Ives Soc. of Artists, Cornwall Crafts Assoc., Penwith Printmakers. *Signs work:* "Richard Lee Stevenson." *Address:* Little Trevarrack, Brandy Lane, Rosudgeon, Penzance, Cornwall TR20 9QB.

**STEWART, Charles William,** taught at Byam Shaw School (1950-58); artist and illustrator in water-colour, pen and ink; *b* Ilo-Ilo, Panay, Philippine Islands, 18 Nov., 1915. *Educ:* Radley College:. *Studied:* The Byam Shaw School of Drawing and Painting (1932-38) under Ernest Jackson. *Publications:* illustrated: Pendennis (Thackeray), Limited Editions Club, N.Y.; Vathek (Beckford), Bodley Head; The Lady of the Linden Tree (Barbara Leonie Picard), O.U.P.; Grimbold's Other World (Nicholas Stuart Gray), Faber; The Visiting Moon (Celia Furse), Faber; Uncle Silas (Sheridan LeFanu) Folio Soc.; Mistress Masham's Repose (T.H. White) Folio Soc., etc. *Signs work:* "Charles W. Stewart." *Address:* Flat 1, Ritchie Court, 380 Banbury Rd., Oxford OX2 7PW.

**STEWART, John Dunlop,** M.S.I.A. (1947-70), N.R.D. (1945), probationer, R.I.B.A. (1944); industrial designer and product design consultant; founder and hon. sec., Paisley Rocketeers' Society (1936-39 and from 1968); designer and producer of multiple originals - numbered and initialled rocket mail flown in experimental models; draughtsman-designer, Universal Pulp Containers Ltd. (1941-48); designer-photographer, H. Morris & Co. Ltd., Glasgow (1948); designer, Design Industries, Beckenham (1949-52); Burndept-Vidor Ltd., Erith (1952-56); Scottish Aviation Ltd (1956-59); *b* Paisley, 3 Sept., 1921. *Educ:* John Neilson Inst., Paisley. *Studied:* Glasgow School of Art, Glasgow School of Architecture and Royal Technical College, Glasgow, and Govt. Training Centre, Thornliebank. *Address:* Greystone, 15 Bushes Ave., Paisley PA2 6JR.

**STEWART-JONES, Elizabeth,** painter, mainly of portraits, in oil and gouache; *b* Lewes, 10 Nov., 1910. *m* Major F.H.D. Pulford. two *d. Studied:* Chelsea School of Art. *Exhib:* pre-war open: S.W.A. (1932, 1934, 1936, 1938), R.A. (1935), R.O.I. (1937, 1938), N.E.A.C., London Group, Artists International (1938), Paris (1939); post-war open: R.B.A., R.A., R.W.A., N.S., F.P.S., etc. Current paintings mostly abstract portraits based on the colour of sound. *Commissions:* various. *Signs work:* "E.S-J." or "E. Stewart-Jones." *Address:* Penlanole, nr. Llandrindod-Wells, Powys LD1 6NN.

**STEYN, Carole,** sculptor/painter/engraver uses organic, and inorganic material in bas reliefs also oils and pastels; *b* Manchester. divorced. two *s. Educ:* Wycombe Abbey. *Studied:* Académie Julian, Paris (1954), St. Martin's School of Art (1955-57). *Exhib:* seven solo shows: Drian Galleries (1971, 1975, 1981 (First Retrospective Exhbn.), 1985), Jablonsky Galleries, London (1987), Galerie Harounoff, London (1991); twenty group shows: all in London (1968-97). *Work in collections:* National Museum, Warsaw, Poland (Nalecz Collection), Sheffield City Museum, National Museum, Gdansk, Poland, Ben Uri Collection. *Commissions:* British Telecom (1985). *Publications:* work repro.: in Apollo "The Select Few"(1975), Arts Review (1981), etc. Radio broadcast B.B.C. (1971), twice (1975), Open House and "WHAM" B.B.C. Manchester (1985). Television B.B.C. 1 (1971) and B.B.C. 2 (1989). *Signs work:* "C. Steyn." *Address:* 12 Rosecroft Ave., London NW3 7QB.

**STIEGER, Jacqueline,** sculptor/jewellery/medals - lost wax technique, casting, bronze and precious metals; *b* London, 26 Jan., 1936. two *s-s.. Educ:* Bedales, Hants; The Mount School, York. *Studied:* Edinburgh College of Art (1952-58) under W. Gillies. *Exhib:* Goldsmiths' Hall, Galerie Riehentos, Basel. *Work in collections:* Eidgenosische Kunstkommission, Bern Ch; Museum of Medallic Art, Cracow, Poland; Goldsmiths' Hall Collection; B.M. *Commissions:* Plaque to commemorate Second World War, The Reform Club, London (1995), Bronze Sculpture, St. Clare's Oxford (1997). *Signs work:* "J. Stieger." *Address:* Welton Garth, Welton, N. Humberside.

**STOBART, Jane,** R.E. (1986); artist printmaker specialising in etching; part-time lecturer at Goldsmiths' College and Harlow College; Fellow, Royal Society of Printmakers; *b* S. Shields, Tyne and Wear, 10 Nov., 1949. *m* Mustafa Sidki. *Educ:* S.E. Essex Technical School, Dagenham. *Studied:* Hornsey College and Central School. Exhibits internationally. *Work in collections:* Ashmolean Museum, Suffolk County, Enfield & Newham Boroughs, Smithsonian Inst., U.S.A. *Commissions:* National Grid (1995), Smithsonian Inst., U.S.A. (1996), Florence Nightingale Health Centre, Harlow (1997). *Address:* 47 Potter St., Harlow, Essex CM17 9AE.

**STOCK, Andrew Nicholas,** S.WL.A.; Richard Richardson award for bird illustration (1980); P.J.C. award for individual merit (1990), prizewinner in Natural World fine art awards (1989, 1990), runner-up in BBC World Magazine's Wildlife Artist of the Year (1991); Bird Illustrator of the Year (1995); Council mem. S.WL.A. (1992-94), secretary (1995-); self taught painter in water-colour, etching, oil, pen and ink; *b* Rinteln, W. Germany, 25 Mar., 1960. *m* Melanie Vass (divorced 1995). one *d. Educ:* Sherborne School, Dorset. *Exhib:* S.WL.A., etc.; one-man shows, Malcolm Innes Gallery, London (4), Alpine Club Gallery, London (2), Gallery in Cork St., London (1) The Mall Galleries (1), Edinburgh and Cerne Abbas, Dorset (2). *Commissions:* M.A.F.F., 29 Commando R.A., The Sultan of Oman. *Publications:* illustrated Driven Game Shooting by D. Bingham (Unwin Hyman, 1989). *Signs work:* "Andrew Stock." *Address:* The Old School House, Ryme Intrinseca, Sherborne, Dorset DT9 6JX.

**STOCKHAM, Alfred Francis,** A.R.C.A. (1966), Rome Scholar (1967), Granada Arts Fellow (1968), R.W.A. (1992); painter in oil; *b* London, 1 Jan., 1933. *m* Catherine Bellow. *Studied:* Camberwell School of Art (1960-63, Robert Medley), R.C.A. (1963-66, C. Weight), Rome Scholar (1966-67). *Exhib:* Il Capittello, Rome, Munster, Germany, Arts Fair, New York, R.A., R.W.A. *Work in collections:* Bradford City Museum, Bristol City Museum, G.L.C., M. of W., Arts Council (N.I.), York City A.G. *Signs work:* "A.S." front; "A.F. Stockham" back. *Address:* 75 Woodhill Rd., Portishead, Bristol BS20

9HA.

**STOCKHAUS, Eva H. M., R.E.;** artist in wood-engraving; Mem. Swedish Printmakers' Assoc.; Mem. British Soc. of Wood Engravers; *b* Gothenburg, Sweden, 4 Apr., 1919. *m* Bengt Stockhaus. one *s.* one *d. Educ:* Stockholm University; art studies Stockholm and London. *Work in collections:* V. & A., London; National Museum, Stockholm; Nasjonalgalleriet, Oslo; New York Public Library; Graphische Sammlung Albertina, Vienna; various museums Scandinavia etc. Recipient artist's grant of the Swedish State (1975, 1976). *Signs work:* "Eva Stockhaus." *Address:* Appelbovagen 10, 16771 Bromma, Sweden.

**STOKER, Richard,** J.P. (1995), F.R.A.M. (1973); self employed artist in oils, poster paint, pen, pencil; composer, auther; Com. mem. and treasurer, R.A.M. Guild; *b* Castleford, Yorks., 8 Nov., 1938. *m* Dr. Gillian Stoker, Ph.D., M.A., B.A. (Hons.). *Studied:* Huddersfield School of Art (now University) under Sugden and Reginald Napier (1954-58) and privately under H.R.M. Irving, Huddersfield (1958-59); in Paris with Madame Nadia Boulanger (1962-63). *Exhib:* Lawrence House (two one-man shows), Lewisham Soc. of Arts Summer Exhbn. (1992), Tudor Barn, Eltham (1990), Blackheath Art Soc. Exhbn.(1989, 1990, 1991), Lewisham Arts Festival (1990, 1992). Work in: private collections. *Commissions:* Arts Council, London. *Publications:* Open Window - Open Door (Regency); Words Without Music (Outposts, 1971); Tanglewood (novel) (Merlin); Diva (novel) (Minerva); Collected Short Stories (Minerva, 1997). Portrait painted by John Bratby, R.A. (1983). Steering Group mem. and treasurer, Lewisham Visual Arts Festival (1990, 1992). Nominated: 'Man of the Year 1997' by the American Biographical Soc. (1997), two Editors Awards: National Library U.S.A. *Clubs:* Blackheath Art Soc. (1988), Lewisham Arts Soc. (1990), elected to P.E.N. International and London P.E.N. (1996), R.A.M. Guild (1986), Founder mem. Atlantic Council (1993), Euro - Atlantic Group (1993). *Signs work:* "Stoker" or "R.S." or not at all. *Address:* 38 Lee Rd., Blackheath, London SE3 9RU.

**STOKES, Vincent,** B.A. (Hons.) Photography and Semiotics; designer/photographer; art director; *b* 9 Jan., 1964. *Studied:* London College of Printing (1986-89, Ann Williams, Peter Osborn). *Exhib:* Camera Work U.K., Camera Work San Francisco, Photographers Gallery, Arnolfini Bristol, New Orleans, Buffalo, Vancouver, N.Y. *Signs work:* see appendix. *Address:* 14 Beckley House, Hamlets Way, London E3 4SZ.

**STOKOE, Michael Arthur,** N.D.D. (1957); painter; mem. Printmakers Council; senior lecturer, Ravensbourne College of Design; *b* London, 1933. *m* Gillian Stacey. *Educ:* King's School, Bruton. *Studied:* St. Martin's School of Art (1953-57). *Exhib:* R.A., R.B.A., R.O.I., R.S.O.P.P., Young Contemporaries, Arts Council, Belfast, Piccadilly Gallery, Arnolfini Gallery, Hamilton Gallery, John Moores, New Gallery, Belfast etc.; one-man shows: Temple Gallery, Drian Galleries, Bear Lane Gallery, Nottingham City A.G.,

Oxford Gallery, Anna Mei Chadwick Gallery, London SW6. *Work in collections:* Arts Council of N. Ireland, V. & A., W.A.G., Ferens A.G., Hull, Leeds City A.G., etc., and 20 educational authorities. *Signs work:* "STOKOE." *Address:* 44 Stockwell Park Cres., London SW9 0DG.

**STONES, Anthony,** F.R.B.S. (1992), V.P.S.P.S.; sculptor in clay for bronze; *b* Glossop, Derby., 8 Feb., 1934. *Educ:* St. Bede's College, Manchester. *Studied:* Manchester Regional College of Art (1950-51). *Work in collections:* bronze portrait heads: John Piper in Reading Civic Centre; Prof. Dorothy Hodgkin, O.M., Somerville College, Oxford; Sir Ronald Syme, O.M. and Sir Isaiah Berlin, O.M., Wolfson College, Oxford; Liam Ó Flaherty, National Gallery of Ireland; Sean Ó Faolin, Irish Writers Museum, Dublin. *Commissions:* commemorative bronze figures: The Hon. Peter Fraser, Wellington, N.Z.; Lord Freyberg, V.C., Auckland, N.Z.; Jean Batten, Auckland International Airport; Victorian Navvy (1992), Gerrards Cross Railway Station; Seven Pacific Explorers for New Zealand Pavilion Expo 92 Seville; Captain James Cook, Gisborne, New Zealand (1994); The Pioneer Wine Maker, Waitakere City, New Zealand (1995); equestrian statue of "Bonnie Prince Charlie", Derby (1995); Captain James Cook, National Maritime Museum, Greenwich (1997); Blair 'Paddy' Mayne, Newtownards, Northern Ireland (1997); 'King' and 'Queen', 'Orpheus and Eurydice', four bronze statuettes for Royal Caribbean Cruise Line A/S (1997). *Publications:* edited: Celebration (Penguin Books, 1984); wrote and illustrated: Bill and the Ghost of Grimley Grange (Wolfhound Press, 1988; Puffin Books, 1994), Bill and the Maze at Grimley Grange (Wolfhound Press, 1990); 'Venus and Cupid': a relief carving by Michelangelo? papers of The British School at Rome Vol. LXI (1993). *Signs work:* "Anthony Stones." *Address:* 42 Beauchamp Pl., Oxford OX4 3NE.

**STONES, Thomas Fiendley,** O.B.E. (1981), B.A. (Admin.), F.M.A.; *b* Astley, Lancs., 25 July 1920. *m* Elizabeth Mackie (decd.). one *d*. *Educ:* Leigh Grammar School and Manchester University. Served R.A.F. (1941-46); Keeper of the Rutherston Collection, Manchester City Art Galleries (1946-52); Keeper of Modern European Dept. and Print Dept., Royal Ontario Museum of Archæology, Toronto; special lecturer in art and archæology, University of Toronto (1953-54); British Council, Fine Arts Dept., Fine Arts Officer, Paris; Cultural Attaché, British Embassy, Budapest; etc. *Address:* c/o National Westminster Bank, P.O. Box 2162, 20 Dean St., London W1A 1SX.

**STOPS, John,** N.D.D., A.T.D., R.W.A.; retd. lecturer, landscape painter in oil, water-colour, lino, gallery organiser; Gallery Organiser, Guild Gallery, Bristol; *b* Radlett, 24 Mar., 1925. *m* Susan. one *s*. one *d*. *Educ:* Repton School. *Studied:* Northampton, Leeds (1947-52, Alicia Boyle, Henry Bird). *Exhib:* numerous, mainly Bristol, own gallery St. Davids (1969-89). *Work in collections:* Northampton A.G., Royal West of England Academy. *Clubs:* R.W.A., Bath Soc. of Artists. *Signs work:* "John Stops" and year. *Address:* 9 Freeland

Pl., Hotwells, Bristol BS8 4NP.

**STOREY, Terence,** P.P.R.S.M.A., F.R.S.A.; marine and landscape artist in oils and water-colour; *b* Sunderland, 17 Apr., 1923. *Educ:* Sunderland Art School and Derby College of Art. *Exhib:* N.S., R.B.A., R.S.M.A., R.O.I., N.E.A.C. and S.WL.A. *Work in collections:* H.R.H. the Prince of Wales, R.S.M.A. Diploma Collection, The Picture collection of the Port of London Authority, and private collections in U.S.A., Canada, Australia, New Zealand, Germany and the U.K. *Commissions:* Sultan of Oman, The Royal Eagles Club, The Royal Burnham Yacht Club. Works published by Winsor and Newtons, Rolls-Royce Limited, 20th Century British Marine Painting, and numerous Shipping lines. *Signs work:* see appendix. *Address:* Merlewood, 6 Queensway, Derby DE22 3BE.

**STOREY, Warren,** R.W.A. (1976), V.P.R.W.A. (1988-Mar.93), A.T.D. (1950), Brit. Inst. Scholarship (1948); painter, general and ecclesiastical designer, mural artist; Head of Weston-super-Mare School of Art (1958-84); extra mural art history lecturer, Bristol University; *b* S. Shields, 19 Aug., 1924. *m* Lilian Evans. five *d. Educ:* S. Shields High School. *Studied:* S. Shields School of Art under Ernest Gill, A.R.C.A. (1941-44), and Regent St. Polytechnic School under Wm. Matthews and Norman Blamey (1947-50). *Exhib:* R.A., R.B.A., R.W.A., etc. *Work in collections:* R.W.A., St. Monica Home, Bristol, Somerset C.C., Walsall, Casa Piccolo Valletta, Weston-super-Mare Museum. *Commissions:* Harvey's Sherry Bristol, various churches, Windwhistle Junior School mural, private portraits. *Publications:* contributor to Leisure Painter since 1987. *Signs work:* "Storey" and date. *Address:* 14 Leighton Cres., Weston-super-Mare, BS24 9JL.

**STOWASSER, Friedrich:** see HUNDERTWASSER.

**STRAIN, Robert William Magill,** Commander, Order of St. John, B.Sc., M.D., Ph.D., F.R.C.P.I.; physician; artist in oil and water-colour; *b* Belfast, 1907. *m* Eileen Mary Clapham. *Educ:* Royal Belfast Academical Inst.; The Queen's University of Belfast. *Exhib:* R.U.A., Walker's Gallery, London (Medical Art Soc.). *Work in collections:* decorated maps, Ulster Museum. *Publications:* The Heraldry of Medicine (Ulster Medical Journal), Belfast and Its Charitable Society (O.U.P.); work repro.: End Papers, Book of Belfast by Robert Marshall (1937). *Signs work:* "R.W.M. Strain." *Address:* Flat 3, 5 Royal Parade, Bayshill Rd., Cheltenham GL50 3AY.

**STREVENS, Bridget Julia,** M.A. (Cantab., 1979); artist and illustrator in oil, water-colour, line, and multimedia designer; *b* Ongar, Essex, 24 Sept., 1956. *m* (1) Stephen Romer; one s. (2) Michael Finch; one d. *Educ:* King's College, Cambridge University. *Studied:* Ecole Nationale Superieure des Beaux Arts, Paris. *Work in collections:* Epping Forest District Museum. *Publications:* CD-Rom 'Star Act' (Herisson Fox/Hachette), 'Toto's Travels' (Little, Brown & Co.), 'En Route' (Albin Michel, Fr.). *Signs work:* "B. Strevens" or "Biddy Strevens." *Address:* 59 Rue de Meaux, 60300 Senlis, France.

**STRONG, Sir Roy,** Ph.D. Fellow Ferens (1976), Prof. of Fine Art (1972), Hon.D.Litt. (Leeds) (1983), Hon.D.Litt. (Leele) (1984); writer and historian; Director, Victoria and Albert Museum (till Dec. 1987); *b* London, 23 Aug., 1935. *m* Dr. Julia Trevelyan Oman. *Educ:* Edmonton County Grammar School; Queen Mary College, London; Warburg Inst., London. *Publications:* author: Portraits of Queen Elizabeth I (1963), Holbein - Henry VIII (1967), Tudor - Jacobean Portraits (1969), The English Icon: English - Jacobean Portraiture (1969), Van Dyck: Charles on Horseback (1972), Splendour at Court: Renaissance Spectacle - the Theatre of Power (1973), Nicholas Hilliard (1975), The Cult of Elizabeth: Elizabethan Portraiture - Pageantry (1977), And When Did You Last See Your Father? (1978), The Renaissance Garden in England (1979), Britannia Triumphans: Inigo Jones, Rubens and Whitehall Palace (1980), The English Renaissance Miniature (1983), Art - Power (1984), Strong Points (1985), Henry, Prince of Wales - England's Lost Renaissance (1986), Creating Small Gardens (1986), Gloriana, Portraits of Queen Elizabeth I (1987), A Small Garden Designer's Handbook (1987), Cecil Beaton, The Royal Portraits (1988), Creating Small Formal Gardens (1989), Small Period Gardens (1992), A Celebration of Gardens (1992), Successful Small Gardens (1994), A Country Life (1994), William Larkin (1994), The Tudor and Stuart Monarchy, I, Tudor, II, Elizabethan (1995), The Story of Britain (1996), The Roy Strong Diaries 1967-1987 (1997); other books jointly with Julia Trevelyan Oman, J.A. van Dorsten, Stephen Orgel, Colin Ford and J. Murrell; contributor to numerous books and learned journals. *Clubs:* Garrick. *Address:* The Laskett, Much Birch, Herefordshire HR2 8HZ.

**STUART, Kiel,** A.P.S.; artist in papier mache, mixed media and fibre, writer; Editor, Keystrokes; *b* N.Y.C., 1951. *m* Howard Austerlitz. *Studied:* Suny New Paltz, Suny Stony Brook. *Exhib:* Lynn Kottler Galleries, N.Y.C.; Gallery II RSVP, Virginia; Artforum, Mills Pond House, N.Y.; Myths, Music and Magic, East End Arts Council, N.Y.; Gallery North, Setauket, N.Y. *Work in collections:* National Museum of Women's Art, Washington DC. *Publications:* cover, Island Women Anthology (N.S.W.W.A. Press). *Signs work:* see appendix. *Address:* 12 Skylark Ln., Stony Brook, N.Y. 11790, U.S.A.

**STUART-SMITH, Susanna J.,** B.Mus., Dip.Ecol., Gold medal (R.H.S.); botanical artist in water-colour, pencil, ink; freelance botanical illustrator working at R.B.G. Kew; especially interested in fieldwork abroad (Oman, India), orchid illustration; botanical illustration tutor; *b* B'ham, 26 May, 1943. *m* (1) L.M. Stuart-Smith. one *s*. two *d*. (2) Richard Clymo, ecologist. *Educ:* Universities of London, Cambridge, Kent. *Studied:* trained: R.B.G. Edinburgh (1984), R.B.G. Kew (1993). *Exhib:* R.H.S. London; R.B.G. Edinburgh; R.B.G. Kew; Linnean Soc. London; Hunt Inst., U.S.A.; World Orchid Conference, Glasgow. *Work in collections:* R.B.G. Edinburgh, R.B.G. Kew. *Publications:* illustrated: 'Plants of Dhofar, Southern Region of Oman', Miller and Morris (Sultanate of Oman 1988); 'The New R.H.S. Dictionary of Gardening'

Macmillan Press Ref. Books 1992); 'The Orchids of Belize' (1996); reference books and scientific publications. *Signs work:* "Susanna Stuart-Smith" or "S.S.S." *Address:* 49 High St., Robertsbridge, E. Sussex TN32 5AL.

**STUBBS, Constance,** A.R.C.A.; painter and etcher in collage and acrylic; *b* Cheltenham, 6 Aug., 1927. *m* Harold Yates. two *s.* one *d. Studied:* Cheltenham School of Art, Royal College of Art (1949-51, Carel Weight, Ruskin Spear, John Minton, Barnett Freedman). *Exhib:* mixed shows: R.A., Hayward, Mall Galleries, C.P.S., S.C.A., Print Biennale-Berlin, Cracow and Rijeka; solo shows: Anglo Hellenic League Athens, John Russell Ipswich, Chappel Essex, Market Cross and St. Johns St., Bury St. Edmunds, Oxford Gallery. *Work in collections:* the late Princess Marina, Christchurch Mansions Ipswich, Unilever, Prudential, etc. *Signs work:* "C. STUBBS." *Address:* The Old School, Church Hill, Pakenham, Bury St. Edmunds, Suffolk IP31 2LN.

**STUBLEY, Trevor Hugh,** D.A. (Edin.) (1951), R.P. (1974) Vice-President (1994), R.S.W. (1990), R.B.A. (1991), R.W.S. (1995); painter; *b* Leeds, 27 Mar., 1932. *m* Valerie Churm. four *s. Studied:* Leeds College of Art (1947-49); Edinburgh College of Art (1949-53). *Exhib:* Edinburgh, London. *Work in collections:* N.P.G., M.of.D., I.E.E., Palace of Westminster, British Library, B.M., Windsor Castle, five Oxford Colleges, Art Galleries: Doncaster, Harrogate, Huddersfield, Hull, Leeds, Lincoln, Manchester, Sheffield, Wakefield, nine University collections. *Publications:* work repro.: illustrated over 400 children's books. Prizes: Hunting Group (1986), Singer & Friedlander (1990). *Clubs:* Arts. *Signs work:* "Stubley." *Address:* Trevor Stubley Gallery, Greenfield Rd., Holmfirth, nr. Huddersfield HD7 2XQ.

**STULTIENS, Jeff,** Dip.A.D. (1966), R.P. (1990); First Prize - The Portrait Award, National Portrait Gallery (1985); Hon. Sec. R.S.P.P.; Senior Lecturer at Hertfordshire College of Art and Design (1974-1987); painter in oil; *b* Blackpool, 12 Sept., 1944. *m* Catherine Knowelden. *Educ:* Hutton and Tiffin Schools. *Studied:* Kingston School of Art under Alfred Heyworth and Camberwell School of Art under Robert Medley R.A. (1961-1966). *Exhib:* John Player Portrait Award - N.P.G., British Portraiture 1980-85, Drawings for All, R.S.P.P., Hunting/Observer, Nikkei Exhbn. - Tokyo, The Portrait Award 1980-89. *Work in collections:* N.P.G., Merton and Oriel Colleges - Oxford, National Heart and Lung Inst., R.N.L.I., Royal Medical Foundation, R.A.M. Many other public and private commissions. *Signs work:* "Stultiens." *Address:* 26 St. George's Cl., Toddington, Beds. LU5 6AT.

**SULLIVAN, Jason,** B.A. (1979); painter in oil; *b* Poole, Dorset, 31 Mar., 1958. *m* Una. one *s. Educ:* Queen Elizabeth Grammar School, Horncastle, Lincolnshire. *Studied:* Grimsby College of Art (1974-76, Mr. Todd), Sheffield College of Art (1976-79, Mr. Peacock). Numerous exhbns. *Signs work:* see appendix. *Address:* 19 Meersbrook Pk. Rd., Sheffield, S. Yorks.

**SULLIVAN, Wendy,** poet, painter; *b* London, 18 May, 1938. *Educ:* Notre Dame High School, Battersea; largely self-taught in art but attended Sir John

Cass and Goldsmiths' Colleges; life drawing with Leonard McComb, R.A. anatomy with Prof. Pegington, F.R.S. (U.C.H.). *Exhib:* R.A. Summer Shows, Galerie Dagmar, Portobello Opens, South Bank Show, Tamsins, Satay Cooltans, Paperworks IV, Brixton Gallery, Le Creole, The Carrot Cafe, W Norwood Library, The Ritzy, Banner Project - London Printworks Trust. *Work in collections:* on loan/and collections: Galerie Dagmar, Breast Screening Clinic Camberwell, St, John's Church, Angell Town, Lambeth Archives, Brixton Academy. *Signs work:* "Wendy Sullivan" and see appendix. *Address:* 127 Crescent La., London SW4 8EA.

**SUMMERS, Leslie John,** F.F.P.S. (1968); sculptor in bronze, perspex (acrylic); *b* London, 2 Nov., 1919. *m* Prof. Janet Margaret Bately. *Educ:* Dulwich College and London University. *Studied:* Chelsea School of Art. *Exhib:* R.A., R.B.A., Walker A.G., Cork St. Gallery, Alwin Gallery, Richmond Gallery London, Brussels Exhbn., Vth International Bienal Barcelona (Prizewinner). *Work in collections:* National Museum of Wales (purchased by Contemporary Art Soc. of Wales); Hull University, U.S. Atomic Energy Commission, Nat. Exhbn. Centre, Birmingham, Brighton Centre, Rochester Museum of Western Art, N.Y., G.L.C., British Tourist Authority, etc. *Publications:* work repro.: Studio International, Exploring Sculpture, Creative Plastics. *Signs work:* see appendix. *Address:* 86 Cawdor Cres., London W7.

**SUMSION, Peter Whitton,** A.R.C.A. (1955); painter in oil and printmaker in relief and mono prints, drawing, lecturer; Lecturer, Glasgow School of Art (retd. 1995); *b* Gloucester, 23 Aug., 1930. *m* Sarah Noble. two *s.* two *d. Educ:* St. George's Choir School, Windsor, St. Thomas' Choir School, New York City, Rendcomb College, Glos. *Studied:* Cheltenham School of Art (1949) Chelsea School of Art (1950-52), R.C.A. (1952-55, Carel Weight, John Minton, Robert Buhler). *Exhib:* one-man, Drawing Schools Gallery, Eton College (1960, 1978), Bury St. Edmunds Gallery; group shows, R.P., R.G.I. *Work in collections:* Brewhouse Gallery, Eton College. *Signs work:* "Peter Sumsion." *Address:* Bachie Bhan House, Cairndow, Argyll PA26 8BE.

**SUNAR, Mina,** A.R.B.S; sculptor in bronze and stone; *b* Tokat. *Studied:* Paris, and Sir John Cass and Ealing Schools of Art. *Exhib:* R.I.B.A. exhbn Cardiff and London, also various parts of Britain, the U.S.A., Austria and Germany. *Work in collections:* United Nations Bldg., Vienna; Queen Elizabeth Hall, London; 1.½ x life bronze of The Pope at Castel Gandolfo, Rome; 2 ½ x life size of President Inonu in Ankara. *Clubs:* The Hurlingham, Les Ambassadeurs, Institute of Directors. *Address:* The Studio, Queen Anne's Gdns., London W3 0TG.

**SUNLIGHT, Benjamin Clement,** professional artist; painter in oils and printmaker; *b* Brighton, 7 Apr., 1935. *m* Vivien Baskin. *Educ:* Clifton and Magdalene College, Cambridge. *Studied:* London Central School of Art and Design (Mural Diploma, 1962) under Alan Davie, Hans Tisdall, Harold Cohen and Tony Harrison. Part-time teacher, Hornsey College of Art (1964-65)

Cranfield Institute of Technology (1973-74); Fellow and Vice-Chairman, Free Painters and Sculptors (1965-68); Mem., International Arts Guild; Gold Medallist, International Academy, Rome, and Italian Academy, Palma. *Signs work:* "Ben Sunlight." *Address:* 227 Kingston Rd., Teddington, Middx. TW11 9JJ.

**SURREY, Kit,** Dip.A.D. Theatre design (1968); theatre designer and artist in several media, mainly pastel and charcoal drawing; *b* B'ham, 23 June, 1946. *m* Meg Surrey (née Grealey). one *s.* one *d. Educ:* Tauntons Grammar School, Southampton. *Studied:* Southampton College of Art (1963-65), Wimbledon School of Art (1965-68). *Exhib:* R.A., International Drawing Biennale Cleveland (1991), Cheltenham International Open (1994), Soc. of British Theatre Designers (1976, 1978, 1983), International Organisation of Scenographers, Berlin (1981), Moscow (1982). *Work in collections:* R.S.C. Coll., Stratford. *Publications:* included in British Theatre Design - The Modern Age. *Signs work:* "KIT SURREY" or not at all. *Address:* 77 Queens Rd., St. Thomas, Exeter, Devon EX2 9EW.

**SUTHERLAND, Carol Ann,** B.A.Hons. (1973); artist in water based mixed media, oil; *b* Greenock, Scotland, 16 Mar., 1952. three *s. Educ:* St. Columba School for Girls, Kilmacolm, Renfrewshire. *Studied:* Glasgow School of Art (1969-73, Donaldson, Goudie, Grant, Robertson). *Exhib:* Mercury Gallery. *Work in collections:* McNay Museum, San Antonio, Tex., Middlesbrough A.G., Paintings in Hospitals. *Publications:* Leafy and Adam at the Seaside (handmade artist's book). *Signs work:* "Carol Ann Sutherland" or "C.A.S." *Address:* c/o Mercury Gallery, 26 Cork St., London W1X 1HB.

**SUTTON, Linda Olive,** M.A. (R.C.A.) (1974); painter in oil on canvas, etching, water-colour; *b* Southend-on-Sea, 14 Dec., 1947. *Educ:* Southend College of Technology. *Studied:* Winchester School of Art (1967-70), R.C.A. (1971-74). *Exhib:* one-man shows, Galerij de Zwarte Panter, Antwerp; Bedford House Gallery, London; L'Agrifoglio, Milan; World's End Gallery, London; Ikon Gallery, Birmingham; Chenil Gallery, London; Royal Festival Hall, London; Stephen Bartley Gallery, London (1986); Beecroft Gallery, Westcliff-on-Sea (1987); Christopher Hull Gallery (1988); Jersey Arts Centre (1988); Beaux Arts, Bath (1988); Austin/Desmond, Bloomsbury (1989); Isis Gallery, Essex (1993); Lamont Gallery, London (1993); Pump House Gallery, Battersea Park (1994); Sutton House (National Trust) (1994); Chappel Galleries, Essex (1995); Bromham Mill, Beds. (1995); Piers Feetham Gallery, London (1995); Lamont Gallery, London (1996); John Bloxham, Fine Art (1996); Emscote Lawn, Warwick (1996); Six Chapel Row, Bath (1997). *Signs work:* "Linda Sutton." *Address:* 192 Battersea Bridge Rd., London SW11 3AE.

**SUTTON, Philip,** R.A. (1989); artist in oil and water-colour; *b* Poole, Dorset, 20 Oct., 1928. *m* Heather. one *s.* three *d. Studied:* The Slade School of Fine Art. *Exhib:* Roland, Browse & Delbanco (1954-79), Australia, S. Africa and U.S.A., Berkeley Square Gallery, London. *Work in collections:* Tate

Gallery, etc. *Signs work:* "Philip Sutton." *Address:* 3 Morfa Terr., Manorbier, Tenby, Pembrokeshire SA70 7TH, Wales.

**SWAIN, Dorothy Louisa,** artist in oil; private art teacher; *b* Wimbledon, 2 July, 1922. *m* A.C. Swain. two *s.* two *d. Educ:* Wimbledon College of Art *Studied:* Royal College of Art (Charles Mahony, Gilbert and Stanley Spencer Paul and John Nash). *Exhib:* R.A., R.C.A., Russell Cotes Gallery. *Work in collections:* Premier Gallery, Eastbourne. *Signs work:* "D.L. Swain." *Address* Hawthorn, West St., Mayfield, E. Sussex TN20 6DR.

**SWAN, Ann,** S.B.A., S.G.F.A.; R.H.S. Silver-gilt medal (1990), Gold medal (1991, 1993, 1997); botanical artist in pencil, coloured pencil, oil pastel, water colour; *b* England, 7 Apr., 1949. *Educ:* Gravesend Grammar School for Girls *Studied:* Manchester College of Art and Design. *Exhib:* Hampton Ct International Flower Show (1990, 1991, 1994-97), S.B.A. (1991, 1992, 1994 97), R.H.S. (1990, 1991, 1993, 1997), Century Gallery Henley (1991), Lyric Theatre Hammersmith (1992), R.B.G., Kew (1994), Hunt Inst. of Botanical Documentation, Pittsburgh, U.S.A. (1996). *Work in collections:* The Shirley Sherwood Collection. *Publications:* work repro.: limited edns. prints, and greetings cards. *Signs work:* "Ann Swan." *Address:* 55 Railway Rd. Teddington, Middx. TW11 8SD.

**SWANN, Marilyn,** F.F.P.S.; painter; Women's Art Library, Fulham; *b* Kent 1932. *Studied:* Woolwich Poly. (1945-50), Central, Chelsea and Sidcup (evenings). *Exhib:* Trends (Mall, Wieghouse, Barbican, Bloomsbury Galleries etc.), F.P.S. shows since 1973, St. Martin's Crypt, Trafalgar Sq.; solo shows Brangwyn Studio (1976/7), Univ. of Surrey, Old Bull, Barnet (1978), Loggia Gallery (1984), Holland Park Orangery (1987), Hall Place and various venues in Bexley. *Work in collections:* Univ. of Surrey, Wilfred Sirrel Collection Westminster Arts Council, Queen Mary's Hospital, Sidcup. *Clubs:* A.C.S.A.C *Signs work:* "SWANN." *Address:* Cheltenham GL52 2JJ.

**SWANN, Peter C.,** M.A. (Oxon.), LL.D. (Brock, Queens, Waterloo and Wilfred Laurier); keeper, Department of Eastern Art, Ashmolean Museum Oxford; Director Royal Ontario Museum, Toronto, Canada (1966-72); Director East Asian Studies, Waterloo, Ontario, Canada; *b* London, 1921. *m* Elizabeth Hayden (divorced); three *s.* two *d. m* Susan MacPhee. *Educ:* Tottenham Grammar School, Oxford University, London University, Leiden University *Publications:* Introduction to the Arts of Japan (1958), Chinese Painting (1958), Hokusai (1959), Two Thousand Years of Japanese Art (with Y Yashiro, 1959), The Monumental Art of China (1963), The Arts of China Korea and Japan (1963); editor of Oriental Art (1955-68). *Signs work:* "Peter C. Swann." *Address:* 133 Claremont Ave., Kitchener, Ont. N2M 2P9, Canada.

**SWEET, George,** painter; *b* London, 20 Nov., 1909. *m* Audrey Hannam (decd.). one *d. Studied:* Slade School of Fine Art (1929-33, Orpen Bursary 1932), Paris, Barcelona and Madrid. *Exhib:* London Group, R.A., etc., retrospective: Browse and Darby (1987). *Signs work:* "G.S." *Address:* 30

Cornwallis Cres., Clifton, Bristol BS8 4PH.

**SWETCHARNIK, Sara Morris,** Fulbright Fellow, Spain (1987-88, 1988-89); painter, sculptor; *b* Shelby, N. Carolina, 1955. *m* William Swetcharnik. *Studied:* Art Students League, N.Y.; Schuler School of Fine Art, Baltimore, Maryland. *Exhib:* Arts in Embassies, Honduras (1997-98). Residency Fellowship, Virginia Center for Creative Arts, Sweet Briar, Virginia (1990); Workshop instructor, Landon School, Washington D.C. (1991-96); Artist's Residency Fellowship, American Numismatic Assoc. Conference, The American Numismatic Museum, Colorado Springs, Colorado (1994). *Clubs:* Fulbright Assoc., Delaplaine Visual Art. *Signs work:* "Sara Morris Swetcharnik." *Address:* 7044 Woodville Rd., Mt. Airy, Maryland 21771, U.S.A.

**SWETCHARNIK, William Norton,** P.S.A., Fulbright Fellow: Spain (1987-89), Honduras (1994-95), Yaddo Foundation (1987), Cintas Foundation (1985), Millay Colony for the Arts Fellowship (1983), Stacey Foundation (1983); painter in oil, pastel, tempera, encaustic; *b* Philadelphia, Pennsylvania, 1951. *m* Sara Morris. *Educ:* Sandy Spring Friends School, Maryland. *Studied:* Rhode Island School of Design, University of California, New York Art Students League. *Exhib:* Springville (Utah) Museum of Art, Butler Inst. of American Art, Youngstown, Ohio, Washington County (Maryland) Museum of Art, National Arts Club, N.Y.C., Hermitage Museum, Norfolk, Virginia. *Signs work:* "Wm. Swetcharnik." *Address:* 7044 Woodville Rd., Mt. Airy, Maryland 21771, U.S.A.

**SWINGLER, Brian Victor,** N.D.D., A.T.D., R.B.S.A. (1986); artist in water-colour and acrylics; part time teacher at Birmingham, Hereford and Worcester; *b* Birmingham, 8 July, 1939. divorced. two *s. Educ:* Yardley Grammar School. *Studied:* Birmingham Art School (1962-65, Gilbert Mason, Roy Abell). *Exhib:* mainly at Potter Clarke Gallery, St. Ives, also at Compendium Gallery, Ombersley Gallery, R.B.S.A., Timaeus Gallery, Helios Gallery, Cedric Chivers Gallery, Pictures, Henry-Brett Gallery, Richard Hagen Gallery, New Gallery, Moseley Gallery, Bankside, Frames, Noott Gallery. *Work in collections:* R.B.S.A. Gallery. *Commissions:* many public and private portrait commissions. *Publications:* work repro.: Artist Magazine and Leisure Painter. *Clubs:* R.B.S.A., Art Circle. *Signs work:* "B.V. Swingler." *Address:* 17 Beverley Rd., Rubery, Birmingham B45 9JG.

**SYKES, Sandy (Ms.),** B.A.Hons. (1966), R.E. (1987), M.A. (1987); print-maker in wood, lino, etching and silkscreen, painter and lecturer in art; *b* Wakefield, 13 Mar., 1944. *m* Martin Cropper. *Studied:* Leeds College of Art (1962-66), Middlesex Polytechnic (1966-67), Wimbledon College of Art (1984-87). *Exhib:* recent solo shows: Crossley Gallery Dean Clough (1995), Brahm Gallery, Leeds (1995), Pentonville Gallery (1988), Creaser Gallery (1988), Hardware Gallery (1988, 1991, 1995, 1997), Wakefield A.G. (1988-89); many mixed shows in Britain, America, Russia and Europe. *Work in col-*

*lections:* A.C.G.B., V. & A., Wakefield A.G., Rank Xerox, Petro-Diamond, U.K., National Art Collections Fund, Mappin A.G. *Commissions:* Oxfam (1992), B.B.C. (1990), London Ecology Centre (1990), Artists Book Yearbook (1996). *Publications:* Lament for Ignacio Sanchez Mejias by Federico Garcia Lorca; 'Blank White Page', Netscape Printworks Mag. on Internet (Apr. 1997). Represented in video 'Etching' Brighton University; 'The Wood Engraving and Woodcut in Britain 1890 to 1990,' by James Hamilton; Digital Data Bases 'Art View', New York and 'Axis'. *Clubs:* Chelsea Arts. *Signs work:* "Sandy Sykes." *Address:* 12 Kirkley Rd., London SW19 3AY.

**SYKES, Steven,** R.C.A.; designer and sculptor; *b* Formby, Lancs., 30 Aug., 1914. *m* Jean Judd. two *s.* one *d. Educ:* Oratory, Caversham. *Studied:* R.C.A. *Exhib:* Galerie Apollinaire, Hanover Gallery; one-man shows Guillaume Gallozzi, N.Y., Redfern Gallery. *Work in collections:* V. & A.; Walker Gallery, Liverpool; Ashmolean, Oxford; Ceramic Museum, Faenza. Sculpture: Coventry Cathedral; U.S. National War Memorial, Washington Cathedral; water sculpture, British Pavilion, Expo 67; tapestry, Hammersmith and W. London Coll. Library (1980); decorative relief panels J. Sainsbury, Braintree (1982); Pallant House Gallery, Chichester (1996). *Commissions:* Hanging Crucifix, 16 ft. 6 ins. All Saints, Queensbury. *Publications:* work repro.: Drawings of Normandy Invasion (pub. Sunday Times Magazine, June 1984); garden sculpture featured Crafts Magazine (Nov./Dec. 1990); "Deceivers Ever" (Spellmount) 1990 written and illustrated war memoirs. *Signs work:* "Steven Sykes." *Address:* Studio, Hopkiln Bepton, Midhurst, Sussex GU29 0HX.

**SYLVESTER, Diana,** R.W.A. (1986), R.O.I.; artist in oil; Ex. Wilts. County Council part-time lecturer; Sec. Bath Soc. of Artists; *b* Bath, Som., 16 Mar., 1924. *m* Robin Sylvester. three *s.* one *d. Educ:* Bath High School. *Studied:* Chippenham Technical College, Corsham and Bristol Polytechnic. *Exhib:* R.A., R.W.A., R.O.I., etc. *Work in collections:* R.W.A., Bristol Schools Art Service. *Clubs:* Bath Soc. of Artists. *Signs work:* "DIANA SYLVESTER." *Address:* Upper Farm, South Wraxall, nr. Bradford-on-Avon, Wilts. BA15 2RJ.

**SYMONDS, Ken,** N.D.D., P.S.; artist in pastel, oil, water-colour; *b* 18 Jan., 1927. *m* Jane. one *s.* one *d. Educ:* Euclid St. Grammar School, Swindon. *Studied:* Regent St. Polytechnic, London (1948-52, Norman Blamey, R.A.). *Exhib:* regularly in Cornwall, Mall Galleries, Europe, U.S.A. *Work in collections:* Government Collection, Plymouth C.C., Guernsey, etc. *Publications:* Around the Penwith. *Signs work:* "Symonds." *Address:* St. Andrew's Studio, Fore St., Newlyn, Cornwall TR18 5LD.

**SYNGE, Pamela:** see de MEO, P.T.

# T

**TABER, A. Lincoln,** artist; *b* Colchester, 1970. *Studied:* City and Guilds School of Art (1989-92). *Exhib:* R.A. Summer Show, New Grafton Gallery.

*Commissions:* murals, portraits. *Clubs:* Chelsea Arts. *Address:* 6 Hermes House, Arodene Rd., London SW2.

**TABER, Jacqueline,** artist and picture restorer; *b* London, 1946. *m* the late A. Lincoln Taber, painter. one *s. Educ:* Paris (one year). *Studied:* Florence (Signorina Simi), Gabinetto del Restauro, Offizi Museum. *Exhib:* R.A. Summer Exhbn., New Grafton Gallery, Hayletts Gallery, Colchester. *Clubs:* Chelsea Arts. *Address:* 33 Cleveland Gdns., London SW13 0AE.

**TACHON, Miriam M.,** M.B.E.; silver and gold medallist Paris Salon (1977, 1980); painter in water-colour and oil; retd. nurse; tutor, Dover Soc. of Miniature Painters; *b* Guernsey, C.I., 1909. *Educ:* in Guernsey. *Studied:* Dover Art School (H. Busby, T. Greville). *Exhib:* R.M.S., Mall Galleries, Société des Artistes Français, Paris Salon. *Work in collections:* S.M., R.W.S. Galleries. *Clubs:* Dover Art. *Signs work:* "M.M. Tachon." *Address:* 56 Rokesley Rd., Dover, Kent CT16 2EH.

**TAIT, Renny,** painter; *b* Perth, Scotland, 27 June, 1965. *m* Valerie Anderson. one *d. Studied:* Edinburgh College of Art, Royal College of Art. *Exhib:* regularly with Flowers East, London. *Signs work:* "Renny J. Tait" on back of painting. *Address:* 26a Lygon Rd., Edinburgh EH16 5QA.

**TAIT, Wendy Ann,** water-colour artist and demonstrator; *b* Derby, 19 Apr., 1939. *m* H.D.L. Tait. two *s.* two *d. Studied:* Joseph Wright School of Art, Derby (1952-55), Adult Educ. (1974-78, Roy Berry). *Exhib:* numerous Derbyshire galleries; demonstrations regularly given to local clubs and societies and for 'Maimeri' artists materials at N.E.C. and Business Design Centre, London. *Publications:* work repro.: greetings cards by Robertson Collection. *Clubs:* B.W.S. *Signs work:* "W.A. Tait." *Address:* Harwen, 1 Chevin Rd., Duffield, Derbys. DE6 4DS.

**TAJIRI, Shinkichi,** William and Noma Copley Award for sculpture (1959); John Hay Whithey Found. Opp. Fellowship (1960); Mainichi Shibum Prize, Tokyo Biennale (1963); sculptor in bronze and brass; Prof. of Sculpture, Hochschule für Bildende Kunste, W. Berlin (retd. 1989); *b* Los Angeles, 7 Dec., 1923. *m* Ferdi (decd.). two *d.m* Suzanne Van Der Kapellen (1976). *Educ:* Los Angeles. *Studied:* under Donald Hord, San Diego (1948-51); O. Zadkine and F. Leger, Paris. *Work in collections:* Stedelijk Museum, Amsterdam, Gemeente Museum, Den Haag, Modern Museum, Stockholm, Town of Arnhem, Holland, Museum of Modern Art, N.Y., etc. *Signs work:* see appendix. *Address:* Kasteel Scheres, 5991 NC Baarlo, Limburg, Holland.

**TAKEDA, Fumiko,** B.A. (1989), M.A. Hons. (1991); artist in etching; lecturer since 1970, Tokyo Y.M.C.A. Inst. of Design; *b* 26 July, 1996. *Studied:* Tokyo University of Fine Art and Music (1985-89), The Graduate School of Tokyo University of Fine Art and Music (1989-91). *Exhib:* over seventeen solo exhbns. since 1990, R.A. (1997), The 2nd and 3rd Sappro International Print Biennial Exhbn. (1993, 1995). *Work in collections:* Tokyo University of Fine Art and Music. *Signs work:* "TAKEDA, F." *Address:* 2-10-21, Takagi-cho,

Kokubunji-shi, Tokyo 185, Japan.

**TALBOT, Nancy Wilfreda Hewitt,** D.A. (Lond.) (1948); painter in oil and stage designer; consultant, Talbot Film Productions; teacher of painting for Hampshire (1950-66); *b* Coventry, 31 Aug., 1925. *m* Major Leon Talbot. *Educ:* Leamington High School, Leamington Spa. *Studied:* Ruskin Drawing School, Oxford (1945) (Albert Rutherston), Slade School, London (1945-48) (Randolph Schwabe, Vladimir Polunin). *Exhib:* first one-man show, Alfred Herbert Gallery, Coventry (1965). *Work in collections:* mural and portrait commissions, privately owned. *Signs work:* "Nancy Talbot" or "Nancy Skillington." *Address:* Greensleeves, Avon Castle, Ringwood, Hants. BH24 2BE.

**TALBOT KELLY, Chloë Elizabeth,** M.C.S.D. (1968), S.WL.A. (1964), M.B.O.U. (1960); freelance bird artist/illustrator in water-colour, gouache and black and white; *b* Hampstead, 15 July, 1927. *m* Jeffrey Smith. one *s. Educ:* St. George's School for Girls, Convent of the Sacred Heart; adviser, father and Bird Room, B.M.N.H. *Exhib:* S.WL.A. and provincial galleries in U.K. and Australia. *Commissions:* various. *Publications:* work repro.: Field Guides to Birds N.Z., Seychelles, Fiji, Tonga and Samoa; contributor to New Dictionary of Birds, African Handbook of Birds etc. *Clubs:* British Ornithologists. *Signs work:* "C.E. Talbot Kelly" semi printed in paint or written, or initials only. *Address:* 22 St. Philip's Rd., Leicester LE5 5TQ.

**TAMBLYN-WATTS, Harold,** artist and illustrator in water-colour and line; *b* Settle, Yorks, 1900. married. two *s. Educ:* Stanstead School. *Studied:* Southend School of Art; Emmett Group Studio Manager (1935-48). *Exhib:* Fleet St. Artists, Croydon Art Soc., Private Art Exhbn., Bouverie St. (1948), Fairfield Halls Croydon (1974). *Publications:* work repro.: in Modern Publicity in War, Aeroplane, Flight; books illustrated, The Young Naturalist, Wonderful Plants, and children's books; book jackets, etc. *Signs work:* see appendix. *Address:* 25 Bennett's Way, Shirley, Surrey CR0 8AE.

**TAMBURRINI, Mosé,** sculptor, direct carver in marble, stone and wood - bronze casts from these; International Affiliate Royal Soc. of British Sculptors; *b* Buenos Aires, 29 Nov., 1905. *Educ:* St. Martin's School of Art. *Exhib:* recent one-man shows: Bexhill Museum, Redchurch Gallery, London. *Work in collections:* John Hunt Galleries; Nicholas Bowlby Gallery; private collections in U.K., Europe and U.S.A. *Signs work:* "M. TAMBURRINI" carved on marble, stone pieces; engraved on bronzes. *Address:* 21 Glenleigh Pk. Rd., Bexhill, E. Sussex TN39 4EE.

**TAMPLIN, Heather,** M.F.P.S. (1984); artist in oil and water-colour; *b* Caterham, 4 Aug., 1950. one *s.* one *d. Studied:* Wimbledon College of Art (1967). *Exhib:* Loggia Gallery and Barbican with F.P.S., Mall Galleries, Fermoy Centre, King's Lynn; one-man shows locally. *Signs work:* "H. TAMPLIN." *Address:* Orchard House, The Green, Aldborough, Norfolk NR11 7AA.

**TARRANT, Olwen,** R.O.I., N.S.; oil painter, sculptor, lecturer, art teacher;

Council R.O.I.; *b* Newport, Gwent, 1927. *m* John Tarrant, BBC and Fleet St. journalist and author. *Educ:* Newport High School, Gwent. *Studied:* Sir John Cass School of Art. *Exhib:* R.O.I. (winner, Cornelissen Prize, 1987), R.B.A., N.S., Albermarle, Medici, City, Fosse, Century and others. *Work in collections:* London Polytechnic, Warburg, the late Sir Charles Wheeler, P.P.R.A. *Publications:* work repro.: Art text books, cards, calendars, Artists and Illustrators, Leisure Painter. *Signs work:* "Olwen Tarrant." *Address:* High Ridge, 4 Yew Tree Lane, Upper Welland, Malvern, Worcs. WR14 4LJ; and Las Encinas de Siller, 3, Calle Urxella, 33, Puerto Pollensa, Mallorca.

**TARRANT, Peter Rex,** F.N.D.D.; artist in oil; *b* Shropshire, 1943. *Educ:* Morville School. *Studied:* Shrewsbury Art School. *Work in collections:* Birmingham City Museum and A.G. *Address:* 10 Lower Bromdon, Wheathill, Burwarton, nr. Bridgnorth, Salop. WV16 6QT.

**TARRANT, Terence Richard,** F.M.A.A.; medical artist; ophthalmic artist at Theodore Hamblin Ltd. (1945-48); ophthalmic artist at Queen Alexandra's Military Hospital, Millbank (1948-50); medical artist at Inst. of Ophthalmology, London (1950-84); *b* London, 7 Jan., 1930. married. one *s*. two *d*. *Educ:* London. *Studied:* Camberwell School of Arts and Crafts. *Work in collections:* Moorfields Eye Hospital. *Publications:* Stallard's Eye Surgery, Roper-Hall; Clinical Ophthalmology, J.J. Kanski; System of Ophthalmology, Duke-Elder; Management of Vitreoretinal Disease, Chignell and Wong; Contact Lens Complications, N. Efron. *Signs work:* "TARRANT" with tops of the Ts joined. *Address:* 11 Portman Drive, Child Okeford, Blandford Forum, Dorset DT11 8HU.

**TATE, Barbara,** P.S.W.A., R.M.S., F.S.A.B.A., F.R.S.A., I.A.A., Ass. Société des Artistes Français; Silver Medal, Paris Salon (1968); Gold Medal, Paris Salon (1969); Prix Marie Puisoye (1971); Special Mention Palme d'or des Beaux-Arts, Monte Carlo (1972); Laureat Grand Prix de la Côte d'Azur (1972); painter in oil; President, Society of Women Artists; Hon. Prof. Thames Valley University; *b* Uxbridge, Middlesex. *m* James Tate, also a painter. one *d*. *Educ:* Dormers Wells School, Southall. *Studied:* Ealing School of Art (1940-45, under T. E. Lightfoot, A.R.C.A., T. Bayley, A.R.C.A., J. E. Nicholls, A.R.C.A.) and Wigan Art School (1945-46). 1957-58, under Peter Coker, R.A., A.R.C.A. *Exhib:* BBC2 Television, Royal Academy, Royal Society of Portrait Painters, Royal Institute of Oil Painters, Royal Society of British Artists, New English Art Club, National Society, Royal Society of Miniature Painters, Sculptors and Gravers, United Society of Artists, Society of Women Artists, Hesketh Hubbard Art Society, Royal Institute, Free Painters and Sculptors, R.W.S. Galleries' Flower Painting Exhbn., Chenil Galleries, Chelsea, Paris Salon, Salon Terres Latines, Salon du Comparaisons, Ville Eternal, Rome, Nice, Monte Carlo, Royal Festival Hall. *Publications:* work repro.: The Green Shawl, Clematis, Nasturtiums, Golden Girl, Marigolds, King's Pawn, Moon Goddess, Josephine, Marigold, Daisy, Scabious, Poppy, as prints for hanging, published by Solomon & Whitehead, London, and Marigold published by Felix Rosenstiel's Widow and Son. *Signs work:* see appendix. Some work done in collaboration with husband (see appendix). *Address:* Willow House, Ealing Green, London W5 5EN.

**TAULBUT, John Maurice,** R.W.A.; Jack Goldhill award for sculpture R.A. (1987); sculptor in stone, wood and bronze, teacher; *b* Gosport, 19 Jan., 1934. *m* Janet Marian Rickards. three *s. Educ:* Portsmouth College of Art, Highbury Technical College. *Studied:* Eaton Hall College of Educ., Retford. *Exhib:* R.A., R.B.A., R.W.A., S.WL.A., R.S.M.A., Sotheby's, Southampton A.G., Swindon A.G., Oxford Soc., Cheltenham Soc., 3D Gallery, Bristol, Rooksmoor Gallery, Bath, Ceri Richards Gallery, Swansea, Ash Barn, Petersfield, Swansea Arts Workshop, Barry Keene Gallery, Henley on Thames, The McHardy Sculpture Co. *Work in collections:* Royal West of England Academy, Grand Pavilion, Porthcawl, and private collections. *Commissions:* Madonna and Child, Parish Church, Llansteffan. *Signs work:* "John Taulbut." *Address:* Cambria House, Llanstephan, Carmarthen, Carmarthenshire SA33 5JQ.

**TAVENER, Robert,** R.E., A.T.D., N.D.D.; illustrator and printmaker; formerly Deputy Principal, Eastbourne College of Art and Design; *b* London, 1920. married. one *d. Studied:* Hornsey College of Art (1946-50). *Exhib:* 30 one-man exhibitions; work selected for eight Arts Council exhibitions. *Work in collections:* over 2000 prints purchased for national collections in U.K. and abroad by galleries, museums, local educational authorities. *Publications:* illustrated series of children's books for Longmans Green and Oxford University Press; and commissioned work for B.B.C., London Transport, G.P.O., Shell, I.C.I., Nuffield Foundation, etc. *Clubs:* Senior Fellow, Royal Soc. of Painter Printmakers (retd.). *Signs work:* see appendix. *Address:* Tussocks, Link Rd., Meads, Eastbourne BN20 7TA.

**TAYLOR, Alan,** N.D.D. (1954), A.R.C.A. (1957); artist in water-colour, gouache, ink, chalks; T.V. Designer/Art Director; retd. from T.V., painting full time, now producing computer art; *b* India, 5 June, 1930. *m* Rachel Taylor. *Studied:* R.C.A. (Prof. John Skeaping, Leon Underwood). *Exhib:* one-man shows: three in Wales, one in Holland; mixed shows: Wales, England, France, Holland and U.S.A.; one-man show in computer art: Newport (Nov., 1997). *Work in collections:* University of Wales, Bangor, University of Wales, Cardiff, B.B.C. *Commissions:* Computer landscape and portrait commissions (private), computer images for T.V. Channel S4C. *Publications:* illustrated Song of the Harp (Christopher Davies); illustrations for B.B.C. T.V. and H.T.V. Listed in Welsh Arts Council and Axis slide libraries. *Signs work:* see appendix. *Address:* 75 Preston Ave., Newport, Gwent NP9 4JD.

**TAYLOR, Alan,** B.A.(Hons.) (1973), A.T.C. (1974); painter in acrylic; *b* Wembley, Middx., 1942. *m* Josephine. one *d. Educ:* Hornchurch Grammar School. *Studied:* Colchester School of Art (1963-65, drawing: John Nash), Stourbridge College of Art (1965-68 and 1972-73), University of Sussex Art

Teachers' Certificate (1973-74). *Exhib:* Midland Young Contemporaries (1966-67), London, Trends in Modern Art (1966), Corning Museum, N.Y. (1968), numerous mixed and one-man shows Birmingham, London, Colchester, Wivenhoe, Exeter, Chudleigh, Sidmouth, Normandy. *Work in collections:* U.K., Europe, Middle East, Australia, U.S.A. Works mainly to commission. *Signs work:* "ALAN TAYLOR." *Address:* La Chapelle, Foulognes, 14240 Caumont L'Evente, Calvados, Normandie, France.

**TAYLOR, Eric,** R.E., A.R.C.A. (1934); painter, sculptor and printmaker; teacher of art at Camberwell School of Art (1936-39), Willesden School of Art (1936-39 and 1945-49), Central School of Arts (1946-48); Head of Design School, Leeds (1949-56); Principal, Leeds College of Art (1956-69); Assistant Director, Leeds Polytechnic (1969-71); *b* 6 Aug., 1909. widower. one *s.* one *d. Educ:* William Ellis School, Hampstead; R.C.A. (1932-35). *Exhib:* R.A., London Group, N.E.A.C. *Work in collections:* Washington A.G., Art Institute Chicago, Imperial War Museum, B.M. and V. & A. Print Rooms, Leeds A.G., Ashmolean Museum. *Signs work:* "Eric Taylor." *Address:* Linton Springs Farm, Sicklinghall, Wetherby LS22 4AQ.

**TAYLOR, James Spencer,** A.R.C.A., B.Sc.(Econ.) (Hons.), F.R.S.A., M.M.A.F.A.; painter; lecturer, Bolton College of Art (1948-79); *b* Burnley, 7 May, 1921. *m* Joyce B. Haffner. one *s.* one *d. Studied:* Burnley School of Art, Slade School of Fine Art, Royal College of Art (1945-48). *Exhib:* Red Rose Guild of Craftsmen, Crafts Centre of Gt. Britain, Society of Designer Craftsmen, Arts Council Touring, R.A., R.W.S., R.B.A., R.I., V. & A., C. of I.D., and many provincial galleries. *Work in collections:* Towneley Hall A.G., Burnley; Bolton A.G. Executed many commissions in Great Britain and abroad. *Signs work:* "JT" (books, 1948-70), "J. S. Taylor" or "JST" (paintings). *Address:* 7 Leaverholme Cl., Cliviger, Burnley, Lancs. BB10 4TT.

**TAYLOR, Jane Winifred,** A.R.C.A. (1946), R.W.S. (1988), R.B.A. (1988); artist in gouache, private tutor; *b* Sheffield, 20 June, 1925. *m* Leslie Worth. one *s.* three *d. Educ:* Sheffield High School G.P.D.S.T. *Studied:* Sheffield College of Art (1941-43, Eric Jones), R.C.A. (1943-46, Gilbert Spencer). *Exhib:* R.B.A., R.W.S., R.A., Linfield Gallery, Jon Leigh Gallery, and others. *Work in collections:* Graves A.G. Sheffield, and various Educ. authorities. *Publications:* magazine articles on drawing and painting. *Signs work:* "Jane Taylor." *Address:* 11 Burgh Heath Rd., Epsom, Surrey KT17 4LW.

**TAYLOR, Jo,** B.A. Hons. (illustration); artist in mixed media, oils, etching; *b* Blackburn, Lancs., 25 Aug. 1969. *Educ:* Moorland School, Clitheroe. *Studied:* Leeds Metropolitan University (1988-91). *Exhib:* R.A., various exhbns. in U.K., Ireland and U.S.A.; several one-man shows. Represented by Courcoux and Courcoux, Stockbridge, Hants. *Publications:* The R.A. Exhibition Catalogue, various articles and reviews; cover for 'The Classical Rider' by Sylvia Loch (J.A. Allen 1997). *Signs work:* "Jo Taylor." *Address:* Brook Bottom Barn, Stonyhurst, Clitheroe, Lancs. BB7 9QY.

**TAYLOR, Joan D.,** A.T.D. (1946); textile designer and printer and painter; instructor in printed textiles, Laird School of Art, Birkenhead (1946-67). *Educ:* St. Edmund's College, Liverpool. *Studied:* Liverpool College of Art. *Exhib:* R.A., N.E.A.C., Liverpool Academy of Arts, Bluecoat Display Centre, Liverpool. *Signs work:* paintings: "J. D. Taylor." *Address:* 79 Grosvenor Rd., Birkenhead L43 1UD.

**TAYLOR, John Russell,** B.A.(Cantab.1956), M.A.(Cantab.1959); writer; Art Critic, The Times since 1978; *b* Dover, 19 June, 1935. *Educ:* Jesus College, Cambridge; Courtauld Inst., London. *Publications:* The Art Nouveau Book in Britain; The Art Dealers; Impressionism; Edward Wolfe; Bernard Meninsky; Impressionist Dreams; Ricardo Cinalli; Claude Monet: Impressions of France; Bill Jacklin; etc. *Address:* The Times, 1 Virginia St., London E1 9BD.

**TAYLOR, Joyce Barbara,** Oxford Delegacy, A.T.D., C.G.L.I. (Embroidery); lecturer, Bolton College of Adult Education; artist in embroidery and water-colour; *b* Burnley, 6 Aug., 1921. *m* James S. Taylor. one *s.* one *d.* *Educ:* Burnley High School. *Studied:* Burnley School of Art, Manchester College of Art. *Exhib:* Red Rose Guild of Craftsmen, Embroiderers Guild, Whitworth A.G., R.W.S. Galleries, London, Manchester and Hereford Cathedrals. *Work in collections:* Altar Frontals etc. for Bolton and Walmsley Parish Churches, and other churches; Banners and other work in private collections in England and U.S.A. *Signs work:* "J.B.T." and "Joyce B. Taylor." *Address:* 7 Leaverholme Cl., Cliviger, Burnley BB10 4TT.

**TAYLOR, Kate Dornberger,** B.A. (1948), R.M.S., M.P.S.G.S., H.S.F., M.A.S.-F., G.M.A.S., C.P.A.; painter in water-colour, acrylic and oils, housewife; *b* Pittsburgh, Pa., U.S.A., 26 July, 1926. *m* Kenneth T. Taylor, retd. Antique Dealer. *Studied:* Chatham College (1944-48, Charles Le Clair): later under Murray Hantman in Maine and N.Y.C. (1955-60) and Walter Houmère. *Exhib:* R.M.S., M.P.S.G.S., M.A.S.-F., G.M.A.S., C.P.A. and several galleries and art shows. *Work* in many private collections. *Signs work:* "DORNBERGER" or monogram "KTD." *Address:* Jokers, High St., Curry Rivel, Som. TA10 0ET.

**TAYLOR, Mrs. M.:** see BRIDGE, Muriel Elisabeth.

**TAYLOR, Martin,** B.A.(Hons.) (1975), A.T.D. (1976); artist in water-colour and acrylic, etcher; *b* Hayes, Middx., 10 May, 1954. *m* Marianne Read. one *s.* one *d.* *Studied:* Ealing School of Art, Wimbledon School of Art, Goldsmiths' College. *Exhib:* Bankside Gallery (1986-94), Contemporary British Water-colours (1983-93), Mercury Gallery, Cork St., Catto Gallery, Hampstead, London, Edwin Pollard Gallery, Wimbledon, Linda Blackstone Gallery Pinner, Savage Fine Art, Northampton, R.A. Exhbns. (1982, 1985), Singer & Friedlander/Sunday Times water-colour exhbns. (1987-97). *Work in collections:* The Prudential. *Publications:* contributor to: Encyclopaedia of Water-colour Techniques (Quarto), Buildings (Quarto), Acrylics Masterclass (Quarto), Encyclopaedia of Drawing Techniques (Quarto); articles in The

Artist magazine. *Signs work:* "Martin Taylor." *Address:* 13 St. Georges Ave., Northampton NN2 6JA.

**TAYLOR, Michael John,** Dip.Arch. (1953), A.R.I.B.A. (1955), V.P.S.G.F.A., F.S.A.I.; architectural illustrator in water-colour, gouache, linocuts; *b* Scarborough, 22 Sept., 1930. *m* Molly Crowther. one *s.* one *d. Educ:* Scarborough Boys High School. *Studied:* Leeds College of Art, School of Architecture (1948-53). *Exhib:* R.A., R.I., R.S.M.A., S.G.F.A., "Not the RA" Llewellyn Alexander Gallery, Laing, Singer and Friedlander and Hunting competitions; one-man shows: Bath, Canterbury, Harrogate. *Work in collections:* R.A.C. Pall Mall, Hertfordshire C.C. Museums Service. *Publications:* book jackets for Foyle, Hodder and Stoughton. *Signs work:* "Michael J. Taylor" and see appendix. *Address:* 4 Sewell Ave., Wokingham, Berks. RG41 1NS.

**TAYLOR, Michael Ryan,** B.A.Hons.(Lond.); artist in oil; *b* Worthing, 17 Feb., 1952. *m* Caroline. one *s.* one *d. Educ:* Worthing High School for Boys. *Studied:* Goldsmiths' School of Art (1970-73). *Exhib:* Morley Gallery, N.P.G. John Player Award (winner 1983), Millfield Open (winner 1989), Hunting Group Art Prize (1989), R.A., Worthing A.G., Quay Arts Centre, I.O.W., Beaux Arts, Bath and London. *Work in collections:* N.P.G., Christchurch Hall, Oxford. *Address:* 1 Upper St., Child Okeford, Blandford Forum, Dorset DT11 8EF.

**TAYLOR, Newton:** see TAYLOR, William Henry.

**TAYLOR, Pam,** A.R.B.S. (1980), S.P.S. (1975); sculptor in bronze, resin bronze; *b* Pontypridd, 13 May, 1929. *m* Peter William Taylor. two *s. Educ:* South Shields and Wick High Schools. *Studied:* Sir John Cass College School of Art (1947-50, Bainbridge Copnall, M.B.E., P.R.B.S., and Beth Jukes, F.R.B.S.). *Exhib:* Mall Galleries, Guildhall, Royal Exchange. *Work in collections:* Principal works: R.A.F. and Allied Air Forces WW2 Monument, Plymouth Hoe; R.A.F. and Battle of Britain Museums, Hendon; Shakespeareplatz, Berlin; Chalmers Bequest Coll.; Colgate-Palmolive Head Office; Bancrofts School; Tobacco Dock London; Georgetown Guyana; bronze bust of Shakespeare in Shakespeare's Globe Theatre, London. *Commissions:* All the above were commissions as well as numerous portrait commissions. *Clubs:* Royal Soc. of British Sculptors. *Signs work:* see appendix. *Address:* Merrydown, 88 Haltwhistle Rd., S. Woodham Ferrers, Chelmsford, Essex CM3 5ZF.

**TAYLOR, Sean,** Hons.D.F.A. (1982), M.A.F.A. (1983), F.F.A. (1989); sculptor in mixed media; Senior Lecturer in Sculpture, Limerick School of Art and Design, Ireland; Vice Chairman, Artists Assoc. of Ireland; Director, Real Art Project, Limerick, Ireland; *b* Cork, 16 Aug., 1959. *Educ:* Presentation Brothers College, Cork. *Studied:* Crawford College of Art and Design, Cork (1979-82), University of Ulster, Belfast, N.I. (1982-83), Kunstenacademie, Rotterdam (1988-89). *Exhib:* 13 one-man shows since 1983 worldwide. *Work in collections:* museums in Poland, Mexico; commissions in Glasgow. *Signs* *work:* "Sean Taylor." *Address:* Lismullane, Ballysimon, Co. Limerick, Rep. of Ireland.

**TAYLOR, W. S.,** A.R.C.A., M.Phil.; painter; editor of Manuals Series for Thames and Hudson Ltd.; Dean of Faculty, Sheffield Polytechnic (1972-75)(now Sheffield Hallam University); *b* 26 Sept., 1920. *m* Audrey Wallis. one *d. Educ:* City Grammar School, Sheffield. *Studied:* Sheffield College of Art and R.C.A. (1939-43). *Exhib:* R.A., etc. *Work in collections:* various. *Publications:* Catalogue of Burne-Jones Exhbn., Sheffield City Art Galleries (1971). *Address:* Lower Manaton, South Hill, Callington, Cornwall PL17 7LW.

**TAYLOR, Wendy Ann,** C.B.E. (1988); sculptor; Mem. Royal Fine Art Commission since 1981; Specialist Adviser, Com. for Arts Design since 1988; Mem. Advisory Group P.C.F.C. (1989-90); F.Z.S. (1989-); Mem. Design Advisory Panel, London Docklands Development Corp. (1989-); Trustee, L.A.M.A. (1993-), F.Q.M.W. (1993-), F.R.B.S. (1994-); *b* 29 July, 1945. *m* 1982, Bruce Robertson. one *s. Educ:* St. Martin's School of Art, L.D.A.D. (1st Dist.). *Exhib:* ten one-man shows: (1970-92); over 100 group exhbns. (1964-82). *Work in collections:* G.B., U.S.A., Eire, N.Z., Germany, Sweden, Qatar, Switzerland, Seychelles. *Commissions:* Major commissions: over forty throughout the U.K. *Publications:* 'Wendy Taylor' monograph by Edward Lucie-Smith (1992). *Signs work:* see appendix. *Address:* 73 Bow Rd., London E3 2AN.

**TAYLOR, William Henry (Newton Taylor),** A.R.C.A. (1934), A.R.E. (1957), Free Studentship (1932), Prix-de-Rome Finalist in Engraving (1935); artist in oil (portrait and landscape), water-colours, etching and engraving on metal and wood; Head (retd.) School of Art, Amersham; lecturer, demonstrator, critic; *b* Normanton, Yorks., 31 Aug., 1911. *m* Elsie May Newton. three *s. Educ:* Normanton Boys' Grammar School, Yorks. *Studied:* Wakefield School of Art; Leeds School of Art; R.C.A. *Exhib:* Yorks. Artists Soc., Bucks. Art Soc., R.P.E., R.B.A., R.A. *Signs work:* "NEWTON TAYLOR" in two lines. *Address:* Newstone Bungalow, Bovingdon Green, Marlow, Bucks. SL7 2JR.

**TAYLOR WILSON, Joanne,** M.A. Fine Art (Edin. 1977), A.T.C. Goldsmiths' College (1978), R.A. Schools Post. Grad. Cert. (1981), Elizabeth Greenshields Scholarship (1981-82); still life, landscape and portrait painter in oil and water-colour; Mem. of Manchester Academy of Arts (1985); *b* Bolton, Lancs., 12 Sept., 1953. *m* Ivan Wilson, R.I.B.A. one *s.* one *d. Educ:* Canon Slade Grammar School, Bolton. *Studied:* Edinburgh College of Art (1972-77), R.A. Schools (1978-81, Peter Greenham, R.A.). *Exhib:* Royal Scottish Academy (1975, 1987), R.A. (1979, 1980, 1982, 1983, 1986, 1987), R.B.A. (1980), Manchester Academy (1979-83, 1985-97), Manchester; one-man show, Bolton A.G. (1979). *Work in collections:* Bolton A.G., West Midlands College of Education. *Signs work:* "J. TAYLOR WILSON" or "J.T.W." *Address:* 4 Beechwood Ave., Clitheroe, Lancs. BB7 1EZ.

**TEASDILL, Miss Caroline Nova,** Dip. in Fashion; fashion designer; *b*

Dewsbury, 31 Oct., 1965. one *s. Educ:* Stourfield and Beaufort Schools, Bournemouth, and the School of Fashion, Bournemouth and Poole College of Art and Design. Practices as Caroline Nova Fashions. *Address:* 99 Carbery Ave., Southbourne, Bournemouth BH6 3LP.

**TEASDILL, Graham,** F.R.S.A., F.R.N.S., F.Z.S., F.M.A.; Museum and Art Gallery Curator (retd.); *b* Horsforth, 5 Oct., 1935. *m* Nova Ann Pickersgill of Horsforth, 22 July, 1960. one *s.* two *d* (see Teasdill, Caroline Nova; Andrews, Pauline Ann). *Educ:* Ilkley Grammar School. Assistant at Ilkley (1950-55), Leeds (1955-56) and Huddersfield (1956-60); assistant curator, Cheltenham (1960-62); Curator, Batley (1962-66), Russell-Cotes A.G. and Museum, Bournemouth (1966-88). President, Yorkshire Federation of Museums (1966-67); South-Eastern Federation (1969-70). *Address:* 99 Carbery Ave., Southbourne, Bournemouth BH6 3LP.

**TEBBS, Margaret,** R.H.S. Silver gilt medal (1995); freelance botanical illustrator in ink and water-colour; freelance artist: R.B.G. Kew, Natural History Museum, New Plantsman, etc.; *b* 5 Sept., 1948. *Educ:* Manor School, Ruislip. *Studied:* Ealing College of Art. *Exhib:* Westminster Gallery, London, Everard Read Gallery, South Africa. *Publications:* numerous scientific papers illustrated for Kew Bulletin, Flora of Arabia, B.S.B.I. Publications, Wild Flowers of Europe (New Holland), Flora Zambesiaca. *Signs work:* "M. Tebbs." *Address:* 29 Casewick Rd., West Norwood, London SE27 0TB.

**TEED, John,** actor, antique dealer, landscape painter in water-colour, portrait artist in pastel; *b* London, 18 Jan., 1911. *Educ:* Westminster School. *Studied:* L.C.C. School of Art, Westminster. *Exhib:* R.A., P.S., R.I., Blackpool. *Work in collections:* National Gallery, N.S.W. *Publications:* illustrated, Owens Second Story Book. *Signs work:* "John Teed." *Address:* The Old Manor House, Bradford-on-Avon, Wilts. BA15 1JU.

**TEMPEST, Victor,** A.R.C.A. (1935); artist in oil and tempera; *b* Swaffham, Norfolk, 23 Mar., 1913. *Studied:* Woolwich Polytechnic School of Art (1927-32), R.C.A. (1932-36, Sir William Rothenstein). *Exhib:* R.A., R.B.A., N.E.A.C., and provincial galleries. *Work in collections:* City of Leicester A.G., Wolverhampton Municipal A.G., R.A., New York, Tokyo. *Signs work:* "Tempest." *Address:* 12 Forest Ridge, Keston Pk., Keston, Kent BR2 6EQ.

**TEMPLE, Nigel Hal Longdale,** Ph.D., M.Litt. in Architecture, N.D.D., A.T.D., F.S.A.E., R.W.A.; painter; architectural and garden historian; Registrar of Research, Garden History Soc., Companion of the Guild of St. George; Visiting lecturer, A.A. School of Architecture; *b* Lowestoft, 1926. *m* Judith Tattersill. one *s.* one *d. Studied:* Farnham, Sheffield, Bristol, Keele. *Exhib:* R.W.A.; Städtisches Museum, Göttingen; Musée du Château d'Annecy; Cheltenham Festivals; University of Reading; University of Bristol; New Ashgate; Cheltenham A.G. *Publications:* author: Farnham Inheritance (1956, 1965), Farnham Buildings and People (1963, 1973), Looking at Things (1968), Seen and Not Heard (1970), John Nash and the Village Picturesque

(1979),(chronologically). George Repton's Pavilion Notebook: a catalogue raisonné (1993) contributor: Porzellan aus China und Japan (1990). *Signs work:* "Nigel Temple" and date. *Address:* 4 Wendover Gdns., Christchurch Rd., Cheltenham GL50 2PA.

**TENGBERG, Violet,** City of Gothenburg award for cultural achievement (1966), Bronze Medal, Europe Prize for painting (1971), Ostende, Belgium; Accademico Tiberino, Rome, Il Premio Adelaide Ristori, Rome (1984); City of Gothenburg Hon. Award (1987); Swedish Artists Foundation (1995); artist in oil and graphic work, and enamels on iron; poet, has published poetry books, 'Vision of the World Egg' (1996, 1997); *b* Munktorp, Sweden, 21 Feb., 1920. *m* J. G. A. Tengberg, D.H.S. one *s.* one *d. Educ:* Dipl. Academy of Fine Arts, Gothenburg (1958-63) "Valand". B.A. in Art History, Dept. of Art History, Gothenburg. *Exhib:* 19 one-man shows, Stockholm, Helsinki, London, Brussels, Paris, Rome, Viterbo, etc.; nearly 200 group shows all over Europe; Riksutställningar travelling exhbn.; 2nd Enamel Triennial, Trondheim, Norway (1993); group exhbn.: Enamel Artists from the Northern Countries, Kecskemet (1993); Szegred, Budapest, Hungary; Vienna, Austria; Germany (1994); 3rd International and mailausstellung, Coburg, Germany (1995). Official invite to exhbit in India, New Delhi and The Government Museum of Chandigarh. *Work in collections:* Museums and official collections in Sweden including: Museet i Halmstad, Kalmar Art Museum; Institut Tessin, Paris; Musée de Pau and Musée de Caen, France; Bibliothèque Nationale, Paris; Musée Vatican, Italy; Tate Gallery, London; Museo Nationale, Gdansk, Poland; Galleria Nationale, Varsavia, Poland; Museo di Viterbo, Italy; National Gallery of Modern Art, New Delhi, India. *Publications:* Swedish Art Lexicon, part V, Allhem; Enciclopedia Universale "SEDA" della Pittura Moderna, Milano, etc. (colour ill.); "Violet Tengberg - Paintings, drawings, graphics and poems" (1982) in three languages and with 45 colour reproductions; Creative Mysticism - a Psychological Study of Violet Tengberg's religious visions and artistic creations by Prof. Antoon Geels (University of Lund, 1989). Essays by (Prof.) J.P. Hodin, Teddy Brunius (Prof. art History, University of Copenhagen) and Benkt-Erik Benktson (Prof. University of Gothenburg); Violet Tengberg: paper on William Blake's poem "The Tygor" of "Songs of Innocence and of Experience" (Gothenburg University of Art Dept. 1994). *Clubs:* A.I.A., W.I.A.C., F.P.S., K.R.O. *Signs work:* "VT," "Violet Tengberg." *Address:* Götabergsgatan 22, 41134 Gothenburg, Sweden.

**TERRY, John Quinlan,** F.R.I.B.A. (1962); architect, artist in pen and ink, water-colour, linocut; *b* London, 24 July, 1937. *m* Christine. one *s.* four *d. Educ:* Bryanston School. *Studied:* architecture: Architectural Assoc., London. *Exhib:* R.A. Summer Show since 1962, Biennale in Venice (1980), San Francisco (1982), Paris (1981), Real Architecture Building Centre (1987); one-man shows: Rye A.G. (1980), Architectural Design (1981), Anthony Mould Gallery (1986), Judd St. Gallery (1987), Vision of Europe, Bologna (1992). *Address:* Old Exchange, Dedham, Colchester, Essex. CO7 6HA.

**THELWELL, Norman,** A.T.D. (1950); cartoonist and freelance illustrator in pen, line and wash, water-colour and gouache; teacher of design and illustration, College of Art, Wolverhampton (1950-56); now freelance; *b* Birkenhead, Ches., 3 May, 1923. *m* Rhona E. Ladbury. one *s*. one *d*. *Educ:* Rock Ferry High School, Birkenhead. *Studied:* Liverpool College of Art under H. P. Huggill, A.R.C.A., M.A., A.R.E., principal, and G. H. Wedgwood, A.R.C.A., teacher of graphic design (1947-50). *Signs work:* see appendix. *Address:* Herons Mead, Timsbury, Romsey, Hants. SO51 0NE.

**THEXTON, Ronald,** painter in oil; retd. oral surgeon; *b* Burton, Westmoreland, 21 Feb., 1916. *m* Barbara J. Stevens. one *s*. one *d*. *Educ:* Solihull School, Birmingham and Edinburgh Universities. *Studied:* Edinburgh (evenings); private assistance from James Cowie, R.S.A., Hayward Veal, Allen Gwynne-Jones, R.A. *Exhib:* R.A., R.B.A., R.W.A., S.S.A. *Work in collections:* Newport (Gwent) Corp., Thamesdown Corp., Frank Slide Interpretive Centre, Alberta, Canada. *Signs work:* "Thexton." *Address:* Tallett Steps, Barnsley, Cirencester, Glos. GL7 5EF.

**THICKE, Thelma Gwendoline,** N.D.D., A.T.D., Dip. H.E., M.F.P.S.; dealer in fine art, restorer and painter in oil and water-colour; principal: Thicke Gallery, and Swansea Antique Club; retd. lecturer, Faculty of Art and Design, W. Glamorgan Inst. of Higher Educ., Swansea, also Swansea University, Faculty of Educ.; *b* 20 Aug., 1921. *Educ:* St. Leonards-on-Sea. *Studied:* Hastings School of Art (Vincent Lines), West of England College of Art, Bristol University, B'ham University (1966-67). *Exhib:* R.A., R.B.A., N.E.A.C., F.P.S., R.W.S. *Clubs:* Royal Overseas League, L.A.P.A.D.A. *Signs work:* "T.G. Thicke." *Address:* 14 Valley View, Sketty, Swansea SA2 8BG, S. Wales.

**THISTLETHWAITE, Ann,** N.D.D. painting; artist, landscape painter in oil, pastel and charcoal; *b* Birmingham, 22 Oct., 1944. *Educ:* Edgbaston Church of England College. *Studied:* Birmingham College of Art and Design (1961-66) under Gilbert Mason and Mr. Francis. *Exhib:* one-man shows: London, Birmingham, Worcester, Tunbridge Wells, Malvern, R.B.A., R.O.I., R.S.M.A., P.S., Contemporary Art. (Royal Overseas Commonwealth Art 1st Prize (1969) presented to H.M. the Queen). *Signs work:* "Ann Thistlethwaite." *Address:* 4 King George Ave., Droitwich, Worcs. WR9 7BP.

**THOMAS, David Arthur,** B.A. (1972), P.G.C.E. (1982); artist in oil and acrylic; retd. teacher; *b* Croydon, 30 Apr., 1928. *Educ:* Wallington County Grammar School. *Studied:* Croydon Polytechnic (1949-53), Farnborough Technical College (1962), Roehampton Adult Inst. (1982). *Exhib:* Compass Theatre Co., Sheffield; several one-man shows. *Clubs:* F.P.S. *Signs work:* "D. THOMAS." *Address:* 21 Baileys Rd., Southsea, Hants. PO5 1EA.

**THOMAS,, Glynn David Laurie,** L.S.I.A. (1967), R.E. (1975); freelance artist in etching; taught printmaking, Ipswich Art School (1967-79); *b* Cambridge, 7 Apr., 1946. *m* Pearl. one *s*. one *d*. *Studied:* Cambridge College of

Art (1962-67). *Exhib:* mixed and one-man shows incl. R.A., National Print Exhbn. Pall Mall Gal., Barbican, Cambridge Contemporary Art, John Russell, Ipswich, Printworks, Colchester, Royal Exchange, Manchester, Lyric, Hammersmith, Aldephi, New York, Toronto, Hong Kong. *Work in collections:* Museum of London, Ashmolean and Ipswich Museum. *Commissions:* Christies Contemporary Art. *Publications:* Victorian Cambridge, Illustrated Journal of Nepal. *Address:* Lodge Cottage, Bluegate Lane, Capel St. Mary, Ipswich IP9 2JX.

**THOMAS, Jean,** Dip.A.D. Fine Art (Bristol, 1974); painter/printmaker in oil on canvas; *b* Haverfordwest, 1950. *m* Paul Preston, goldsmith. one *s.* one *d. Educ:* Taskers, Haverfordwest. *Studied:* Newport College of Art (1969-71), Bristol Polytechnic (1971-74). *Exhib:* Welsh National Eisteddfod, R.S.P.P., R.S.B.A., R.S.P.M., Galerie d'Or Hamburg, Fountain Fine Art Llandeilo, Manor House Cardiff; and numerous exhbns. G.B.H, Germany, Austria. *Commissions:* portraits for: Earl of Halifax, Lady Brooksbank, Judge Haworth, plus commissions for Christie's, and Northallerton Council for Duke and Duchess of York. Recently worked on large mural and now flag/banner sculpture. *Address:* The Old Smithy, Llandeilo, Haverfordwest, Pembrokeshire SA62 6LD.

**THOMAS, Margaret,** R.W.A., R.B.A., N.E.A.C.; painter; *b* 26 Sept., 1916. *Studied:* Slade School (1936-38), R.A. Schools (1938-39). *Exhib:* R.A., R.W.A., and R.S.A.; one-man exhbns. include Leicester Galleries (1949 and 1950); Aitkin Dott's Edinburgh (1952, 1955 and 1966); Canaletto Gallery (1961); Howard Roberts, Cardiff (1963); Minories, Colchester (1964); Queen's University, Belfast (1967); Mall Galleries (1972); Octagon, Belfast (1973); Scottish Gallery, Edinburgh (1982), Sally Hunter Gallery, London (1988, 1991, 1995), Royal West of England Academy (1992). *Work in collections:* H.R.H. Duke of Edinburgh; Chantrey Bequest; Arts Council; Exeter College, Oxford; Min. of Educ.; Min. of Works; Paisley, Hull and Carlisle Art Galleries; G.L.C.; Edinburgh City Corporation; Steel Company of Wales; Financial Times; Nuffield Foundation Trust; Scottish National Orchestra; Robert Fleming; Lloyds of London, and the Warburg Group. *Signs work:* see appendix. *Address:* Ellingham Mill, Bungay, Suffolk NR35 2EP; and 8 North Bank St., Edinburgh EH1 2LP.

**THOMAS, Norma Marion,** B.A. (1980), N.S.A.M., Cert. in Art; artist in oil; *b* Hawarden, Ches., 9 Jan., 1922. *m* Leslie Gurwin Thomas, A.T.D. (decd.). three *s. Educ:* Hawarden Grammar School; Normal College, Bangor. *Studied:* Liverpool School of Art, Goldsmiths' and Hornsey College of Art. Art mistress in Liverpool, Wisbech and Wirral Grammar School. Own studio and exhbn. gallery. Paintings in Gt. Britain and abroad. *Signs work:* "Norma M. Thomas." *Address:* Old School Studio, Blaenporth, Cardigan SA43 2AP.

**THOMAS, Robert John Roydon,** A.R.C.A. (1952), Otto Beit Medal R.B.S. (1963), R.B.S. Silver Medal (1966); sculptor in bronze, stone; Past-President,

Society Portrait Sculptors; Past V.P.R.B.S.; *b* Cwmparc, Treorchy, Rhondda, Glam., 1 Aug., 1926. *m* Mary Gardiner, Des. R.C.A. two *s.* one *d. Educ:* Pentre Grammar School, Rhondda. *Studied:* Cardiff College of Art (1947-49), R.C.A. (1949-52). *Exhib:* R.A. and various London galleries. *Work in collections:* Sculptures at Coalville, Leics., Birmingham City Centre, Blackburn Town Centre, Ealing Broadway Centre, London, Cardiff, Swansea, Rhondda; portraits include, H.R.H. Princess Diana, Viscount Tonypandy, Lord Parry, Lord Chalfont, Aneurin Bevan, Cliff Morgan, Sir Geraint Evans, Sir Julian Hodge, Dame Gwyneth Jones, Gwyn Thomas, Ryan, Carwyn James. *Signs work:* "Robert Thomas sculptor." *Address:* Villa Seren, 23 Park Rd., Barry, Vale of Glam. CF62 6NW.

**THOMAS, Shanti,** artist in oil, pastel and charcoal, teacher; Artist in Residence, Gatwick Airport (1993); *b* London, 3 Dec., 1949. *Studied:* School of Signa Simi (1965), Academy of Fine Arts, Florence (1965-67), Camberwell School of Art and Crafts (1971-73, Sargy Mann). *Exhib:* Commonwealth Inst. (1987), Ikon touring (1984, 1989), Whitechapel Open (1987, 1989), Athena Arts Award Open, Barbican (1987), 'Critical Realism' Nottingham, Camden Arts Centre (1988), 'Black Art, Plotting the Course' Oldham (1988), 'The Artist Abroad' Usher Gallery, Lincoln (1989). *Work in collections:* A.C.G.B., Leicester Schools, and private collections. *Publications:* Birthday Book, Women's Artist Diary (1988), catalogues, Critical Realism, Black Art, The Artist Abroad, etc. *Signs work:* "Shanti Thomas." *Address:* 18 Cornwall Rd., London N4 4PH.

**THOMPSON, Hilli,** B.A.Hons. (1967), M.Phil. (1971), P.G.C.E. (1977); artist/botanical illustrator in linocut, etching, pen, pastel; *b* London, 3 Apr., 1946. *Educ:* Brondesbury and Kilburn Grammar School; Universities of Newcastle (1964-67), Ulster (1968-71), Leeds (1971-77). *Exhib:* frequently at botanical socs. of British Isles, S.B.A.; solo shows: Ipswich/E. Anglia. *Work in collections:* Norwich City Museum. *Publications:* The New Flora of British Isles by C.A. Stale (C.U.P.). *Signs work:* "Hilli." *Address:* 42 Dover Rd., Ipswich, Suffolk IP3 8JQ.

**THOMPSON, Kevin Barry,** self-taught artist in oil, acrylic, water-colour; *b* Dorking, Surrey, 11 Mar., 1950. *m* Vanessa Jane. one *s.* one *d. Educ:* Roman Hill School, Lowestoft; studied general design at Lowestoft College (1985-87). *Exhib:* R.O.I., R.S.M.A.; one-man shows: Norwich (1982), Aldeburgh (1986), Southwold (1989), Gt. Yarmouth (1991). *Work in collections:* Many works are held in private collections, both in Gt. Britian and abroad. *Clubs:* Norfolk and Norwich Art Circle, Oulton Broad Art Circle. *Signs work:* "KEVIN.B. THOMPSON." *Address:* 24 Pound Farm Drive, Lowestoft, Suffolk NR32 4RQ.

**THOMPSON, Liam,** B.A. Hons. (1978); self employed artist in water-colour and oil; Adult Educ. tutor, creative studies curriculum leader; *b* Larne, Co. Antrim, 20 Nov., 1956. *Educ:* Campbell College, Belfast. *Studied:*

Newcastle College of Art and Design (1974-75), Chelsea School of Art (1975-78), City and Guilds of London Art School (1978-79, Peter Coker, R.A.). *Exhib:* R.A. Summer Shows (1983-97). *Work in collections:* National Trust, U.T.V. Collection. *Commissions:* National Trust, Storm Damage at Nymans, Sussex, Mount Stewart House, Co. Down. *Publications:* work repro.: Leisure Painter Magazine (1990-97). *Signs work:* water-colours and oils: signed on back. *Address:* Stone Cottage, Hogbens Hill, Selling, Faversham, Kent ME13 9QU.

**THOMSON, Diana,** B.A., F.R.B.S.; sculptor in bronze, terracotta, wood, resin; *b* Manchester, 1939. *Studied:* Kingston Polytechnic Sculpture Dept. *Exhib:* R.A., R.W.A., New College, Oxford, Margam Park, S. Wales, and various group shows. *Commissions:* 'Woking Market' bronze plaque 7'3" x 4'6" at Network House, Bradfield Cl., Woking; 'Father and Child' bronze over life-size at Central House, off New St., Basingstoke; 'The Swanmaster' 7' bronze at Fairfield Ave., Staines; 'The Hurdler' bronze life-size, at APC International, The Lodge, Harmondsworth, Middx.; 'The Inheritors' bronze life-size group; 'Portrait of Yvonne de Galais and her daughter' life-size group; 'The Bargemaster' bronze 7' at Data-General Tower, Brentford, Middx.; 'Portrait of D.H. Lawrence' bronze life-size, at Nottingham University. *Signs work:* "D.C. Thomson" or "D.C.T." *Address:* The Summerhouse, 64 Mincing La., Chobham, Surrey GU24 8RT.

**THOMSON, George L.,** D.A. (Edin.), S.S.A., F.S.S.I.; calligrapher; principal art teacher (retd.); *b* Edinburgh, 15 Dec., 1916. *Studied:* Edinburgh College of Art (1932-37). *Publications:* Better Handwriting (Puffin, 1954), Traditional Scottish Recipes (1976), New Better Handwriting (1977), Scribe (1978), Christmas Recipes (1980), Rubber Stamps (1982), Traditional Irish Recipes (1983), (Canongate), Dear Sir, (1984), The Calligraphy Work Book (1985), The Calligrapher's Book of Letters (1990) (Thorsons), The Art of Calligraphy (1987, Treasure Press), My Life as a Scribe (Canongate, 1988), others in preparation. *Signs work:* "George L. Thomson." *Address:* The White Cottage, Balgrie Bank, Bonnybank, by Leven KY8 5SL.

**THORN, Mary Elizabeth,** N.S. (1980), mem. Bucks. Art Soc. (1975); painter in oil, water-colour, sculptor in stone, bronze; *b* Egypt, 25 Jan., 1928. *m* Royston Thorn. two *s.* one *d. Educ:* Sacre Coeur (Egypt), Notre Dame, Grey Coat Hospital, Barrett St. Technical College. *Studied:* Amersham C.F.E. and art oils with D. Berryman; sculpture, A. Southwell. *Exhib:* in mixed exhbns., also one-man shows. *Signs work:* "Mary Thorn" or "M.E.T." *Address:* Morten House, First Avenue, Amersham, Bucks.

**THORNBERY, Mary,** painter in oil; *b* Bredhurst, Kent, 23 May, 1921. *m* Michael Dobson, F.R.A.M. one *s. Studied:* painting: London, Florence, Rome. *Exhib:* R.A., London Group, W.I.A.C., New English Art Club, Royal West of England Academy, Bristol (permanent collection). *Signs work:* "MARY THORNBERY." *Address:* Rose Hill, Brechfa, Carmarthen, W. Wales SA32

7RA.

**THORNE, Angela Rosemary,** (pre-1945 Angela Deane), mem. Academia Italia (gold medal, 1979); Hon. N.S., Hon. Mention Soc. des Artistes Français, Paris Salon (1969); painter, sculptress, illustrator; *b* London, 1911. *m* Major C. B. Thorne, M.C. (died 1981). *Studied:* Winchester School of Art (1921-23), Academie Julien, Paris (1928-29) under Stanley Grimm. *Exhib:* Paris Salon, R.S.A., R.P., P.S., R.S.M.A., R.O.I., N.S. Major works incl: 34 portrait illustrations presentation book H.R.H. Prince of Wales, Duchy of Cornwall (1933); oil portraits incl: H.M. The Queen and H.R.H. Prince Philip, commd: 1976; H.M. The Queen Mother, commd: 1980; altarpiece, Prestbury Church, Cheshire (1977). *Work in collections:* U.K., Europe, U.S.A., Canada, S. Africa. *Signs work:* "Angela Thorne" (paintings and illustrations), "A. Thorne" (sculpture). *Address:* 4 Fullerton Manor, Andover SP11 7LA.

**THORNTON, Leslie,** A.R.C.A. (1951); *b* Skipton, 1925. *Studied:* Leeds College of Art (1945-48), R.C.A. (1948-51). *Exhib:* One-man shows, Gimpels Fils (1957, 1960, 1969); Retrospective, Manchester (1981); I.C.A. (1955); Berne (1955); British Council Young Sculptors Exhbn. (Germany, 1955-56), Sweden (1956-57); São Paolo Biennal (1957); Holland Park (1957); C.A.S. Religious Theme Exhbn., Tate Gallery; British Embassy, Brussels (1958); Middelheim Biennial, Antwerp (1959). *Work in collections:* Museum of Modern Art, New York; Arts Council of Gt. Britain; Leeds Art Gallery; Felton Bequest, Australia; Albright Museum; Fogg Art Gallery; National Gallery of Scotland; private: U.K., Europe, U.S.A. and S. America. *Address:* Stable Cottage, Chatsworth Pl., Harrogate HG1 5HR.

**THURGOOD, Gwyneth,** N.D.D. (1958), A.T.D. (1959), F.N.S.E.A.D. (1970); artist/teacher in painting, etching, stained glass; *b* Swansea, 2 Apr., 1938. *m* Anthony Thurgood. one *s. Educ:* Neath Girls' Grammar School. *Studied:* Swansea College of Art, B'ham College of Art. *Exhib:* eight solo shows: art/science (1987-97) including B.A. Meeting (1993), Science Museum, London (1995). *Work in collections:* Universities of Surrey, Manchester, Kent and Warwick. *Publications:* illustrated: papers - three international journals, catalogues; Meridian Television The Gallery (1994, 1995), Meridian Tonight, interview (1997). *Signs work:* "Gwyneth Thurgood" or "Thurgood." *Address:* Serengeti, Pilgrims Way, Harrietsham, Maidstone, Kent ME17 1BT.

**THURSBY, Peter,** P.R.W.A., F.R.B.S., Hon. D.Art; sculptor in bronze; *b* Salisbury, 1930. *m* Maureen Suzanne Aspden. *Educ:* Bishop Wordsworth's School, Salisbury. *Studied:* West of England College of Art, Bristol and Exeter College of Art. *Exhib:* solo shows: Arnolfini Gallery; A.I.A. Gallery; Plymouth City A.G. (2); Marjorie Parr Gallery (3); Westward TV Studios, Plymouth; Northampton Museum and A.G.; Sheviock Gallery; Royal Albert Museum and A.G., Exeter; University of Sheffield; Haymarket Theatre, Leicester; Nottingham Playhouse; University of Exeter; Alwin Gallery; R.W.A. Bristol, Bruton St. Gallery London. 1987 awarded R.B.S. Silver Medal. *Work in col-*

*lections:* Arnolfini Gallery; A.T.E.I. London; Gloucester Regt.; Plymouth City A.G.; R.W.A. Bristol; University of Exeter; Westminster College Oxford; National Guard of Saudi Arabia; Newcastle College of Arts and Technology; Wates Built Homes Ltd. 1995 elected President, Royal West of England Academy, Bristol. *Commissions:* Croydon, Exeter, Dallas and New York State, U.S.A., Harrow, London (2), Plymstock, Tunbridge Wells, Uxbridge. *Clubs:* Chelsea Arts. *Address:* Oakley House, Pinhoe, Exeter EX1 3SB.

**THYNN, Alexander (7th Marquess of Bath),** B.A., M.A.(Oxon.); painter in oil, novelist; *b* London, 6 May, 1932. *m* Anna Gael. one *s.* one *d. Educ:* Eton and Christchurch, Oxford. *Studied:* Paris: Grande Chaumiere (Henri Goetz), Academie Julian (Andre Planson), Academie Ranson (Roger Chastel). *Work in collections:* murals at Longleat House. *Publications:* Lord Weymouth's Murals by Alexander Thynn; novels, The Carry-Cot (W. H. Allen 1972), The King is Dead (Longleat Press 1976), Pillars of the Establishment (Hutchinson 1981). *Address:* Longleat House, Warminster, Wilts. BA12 7NN.

**TIDMARSH, Roy John Eric,** painter in oil (mainly interiors); *b* Birmingham, 15 Feb., 1944. *m* Joan Patricia Lakin. one *s.* one *d. Educ:* Moseley School of Art (1956-59). *Studied:* College of Art, Birmingham (1960-63). *Exhib:* N.E.A.C., R.B.A., R.A., R.O.I. *Work in collections:* throughout the U.K. and U.S.A. *Signs work:* "Roy Tidmarsh" (always bottom left). *Address:* 27 Sunnyside Lane, Balsall Common, Warwickshire CV7 7FY.

**TIDNAM, Nicholas Rye,** N.D.D. (1961); painter in oil and water-colour, illustrator, lecturer; visiting lecturer, Medway College of Design; *b* Oadby, Leics., 13 May, 1941. *m* Ruth Murray. one *s.* one *d. Educ:* Kings Park, Eltham. *Studied:* Camberwell School of Art (1957-61, Michael Rothenstein, Frank Martin, Henry Inlander, Richard Lee, Bernard Dunstan). *Exhib:* Mercury Gallery, London, R.A., N.E.A.C., R.B.A., Drew Gallery, Canterbury, The Peter Hedley Gallery, Wareham. *Work in collections:* Unilever, Leics., Notts. and W. Riding Educ. authorities and numerous private collections. *Publications:* work repro.: magazine illustrations. *Clubs:* Savage. *Signs work:* "Nicholas Tidnam" or "N.T." *Address:* 16 Roebuck Rd., Rochester, Kent ME1 1UD.

**TIERNEY, James Richard Patrick,** Dip.A.D.(1966), Postgrad. Dip. in Printmaking (1967); artist in all painting and printmaking media; principal lecturer; *b* Newcastle upon Tyne, 23 May, 1945. *m* Janet Rosemary. one *d. Educ:* The Royal Grammar School, Newcastle. *Studied:* Sunderland Polytechnic (1961-66, David Gormley), Brighton Polytechnic (1966-67, Jennifer Dickson). *Address:* Laburnum Cottage, 29 Mill La., Lindford, Hants. GU35 0PE.

**TIERNEY, Robert,** D.A.Dip. (1956); International artist, Cos.; textile designer/graphics, etc.; artist in water-colour, oil, design colours; début U.K. and Paris (1958); since 1958 annually engaged by numerous companies throughout three continents; *b* Plymouth, 9 Aug., 1936. *Studied:* Plymouth College of Art (Joan Lee, A.T.D.), Central School, London (1956-58, Alan Reynolds). *Exhib:* from 1959, London Design Centre, Paris, Vienna, Italy,

Australia, Sweden, Denmark, U.S.A., Canada, Munchen, Switzerland; five tours of Japan (1977-81), U.S.A. tour (1981), exhbns. in European, U.S.A., Far East cities (1982, 1983, 1984, 1985). *Work in collections:* Boston Museum of Fine Arts (1981), honoured by five works accepted by V. & A. Museum (1986), etc., and private collections. *Signs work:* "Tierney" or "Robert Tierney." *Address:* Chub Cottage, 31 Church St., Modbury PL21 0QR.

**TILL, Michael John,** S.G.F.A.; artist in graphic, engraving, etching, pastel; Insurance Broker; *b* Sri Lanka, 23 Mar., 1939. *m* Kathleen Margaret. one (decd.). *s.* (decd.). two *d. Educ:* St. George's College, Weybridge. *Studied:* City and Guilds (1970-72 part-time). *Exhib:* S.G.F.A. *Clubs:* Bosham S.C., R.C.Y.C., Royal London Y.C. *Signs work:* see appendix. *Address:* 57 Southway, Carshalton Beeches, Surrey SM5 4HP.

**TILLING, Robert,** R.I. (1985); painter in water-colours and acrylic; lectures include Tate Gallery and Exeter University; awarded R.I. Medal (1985); prizewinner, International Drawing Biennale (1989); *b* Bristol, 1944. *m* Thelma, N.D.D. two *d. Educ:* Bristol; studied art, architecture and education Bristol and Exeter. *Exhib:* one-man exhbns. include London, Bristol, Exeter, Southampton, Guernsey, and Jersey; various mixed exhbns. include the R.A., R.W.S., Barbican Centre (1988). *Work in collections:* include Lodz Museum, Poland and the States of Jersey. *Publications:* illustrations to 'Twenty One Poems', by Charles Causley C.B.E., (Cellandine Press); various reviews/criticism on jazz and blues in many magazines. *Signs work:* "Robert Tilling." *Address:* Paul Mill, La Rosiere, St. Saviour, Jersey, C.I.

**TILLYER, William,** artist in acrylic on canvas and panel, water-colour, print; French Government Scholarship (1962); Artist in Residence, Melbourne University (1981-82); *b* Middlesbrough, 1938. *m* Judith. one *s.* one *d. Studied:* Slade School of Fine Art (1960-62, William Coldstream, Anthony Gross), Atelier 17, Paris (1962, gravure under William Hayter). *Exhib:* one-man shows: Bernard Jacobson Gallery (1978-80, 1983, 1984, 1987, 1989, 1991), Wildenstein & Co. (1991, 1994), Andre Emmerich, N.Y. (1994). *Work in collections:* V. & A., A.C.G.B., Tate Gallery, M.O.M.A. (N.Y.). *Publications:* illustrations for A Rebours by J.K. Huysmans. *Signs work:* surname on back. *Address:* c/o Bernard Jacobson Gallery, 14a Clifford St., London W1.

**TILMOUTH, Sheila,** Dip.A.D. (Hons.), A.T.C.; artist in oil on gesso panel; *b* London, 25 Sept., 1949. two *s.* one *d. Educ:* Latymer Grammar School, London. *Studied:* Hornsey College of Art (1969-72, Jack Smith, Nigel Hall, Norman Stevens), Byam Shaw School (1974-75, Bill Jacklin). *Exhib:* R.A. Summer Exhbn. (1978 to present day), Anna-Mei Chadwick Gallery, London, Hart Gallery Nottingham, Alresford Gallery, Leeds, etc. *Work in collections:* Calder Museums. *Publications:* Limited Edn. prints (Buckingham Fine Arts, and Contemporary Arts Group). *Signs work:* "ST '98" *Address:* 9 Ridge Bank, Todmorden, Lancs. OL14 7BA.

**TILSON, Joe,** painter, sculptor; *b* London, 24 Aug., 1928. *m* Joslyn. one *s.*

two *d*. *Studied:* St. Martin's School of Art (1949-52), R.C.A. (1952-55). *Exhib:* Venice Biennale (1964), Marlborough Gallery (1960-77), since 1977 Waddington Galleries, internationally since 1961. *Work in collections:* major museums in Gt. Britain, U.S.A., Italy, S. America, Australia, Germany, Holland, Denmark, Belgium, N.Z., etc. *Signs work:* "Joe Tilson." *Address:* The Old Rectory, Christian Malford, Wilts. SN15 4BW.

**TINDLE, David,** R.A. (1979), Hon. F.R.C.A. (1984), M.A. (Oxon.) (1985); painter in egg tempera; Ruskin Master of Drawing, University of Oxford (1985-87), Hon. Fellow at St. Edmund Hall, Oxford; Hon. mem. R.B.S.A.; *b* Huddersfield, 29 Apr., 1932. *Studied:* Coventry School of Art (1945-47). *Exhib:* Fischer Fine Art since 1985, Piccadilly Gallery (1954-83), Galerie XX, Hamburg (1974, 1977, 1980), Redfern Gallery (1994). *Work in collections:* Tate Gallery, Manchester City A.G., Wakefield, Coventry, Whitworth, A.G.'s., Bradford, Huddersfield, R.A., N.P.G. Agents: Redfern Gallery, Cork St., London. *Signs work:* "David Tindle" or "D.T." *Address:* 16 Place de la Mairie, 56580 Rohan, Morbihan, France.

**TINSLEY, Francis,** M.A. (1971); lecturer, painter in oil, etching, woodcut; Sen. lecturer, Camberwell College of Arts;; *b* Liverpool, 30 Mar., 1947. *m* Jennifer. *Studied:* Camberwell College of Arts (1967-70), Chelsea College of Art (1970-71). *Exhib:* one-man and mixed shows in London. *Work in collections:* Fylde Museum, Blackpool, Hereford Museum, and Liverpool. *Publications:* Practical Printmaking. *Clubs:* Chelsea Arts. *Signs work:* "FRANCIS TINSLEY." *Address:* 28 Ewell Court Ave., Epsom, Surrey. KT19 0DZ

**TIPPETT, Jane,** freelance artist in water-colour, tempera, also lithography, and teacher; *b* London, 25 Feb., 1949. *Studied:* Gloucestershire College of Art and Design, R.A. Schools (1977-80). Artist in Residence, Oundle School (1980-82). *Exhib:* R.A. Summer Exhbn. (1978-90), Agnew's Albermarle St. Gallery (1982), Church St. Gallery, Saffron Walden (1983, 1984, 1986); 14 lithographs made at the Curwen Studio. *Signs work:* "Jt." *Address:* 56 Searle St., Cambridge CB4 3DB.

**TISDALL, Hans,** painter and designer; *b* 1910. *Exhib:* London, Paris, Rome, Brussels, Germany, Spain, Switzerland. *Commissions:* murals, tapestries. *Signs work:* see appendix. *Address:* 7 Brunel House, 105 Cheyne Walk, London SW10 0DF.

**TITCHELL, John,** R.A. (1993), A.R.C.A. (1951), A.R.A. (1986); artist in oil and water-colour; *b* Crayford, Kent, 6 Aug., 1926. *m* Audrey Ward. one *s*. one *d*. *Educ:* Crayford Elementary School. *Studied:* Sidcup School of Art (1940-44), R.C.A. (1947-51). *Address:* Frith Farm, Pluckley, Kent TN27 0SY.

**TITCOMBE, Cedric Anthony,** N.D.D. (1962); painter and screen-printer in charcoal, oil, screenprints; *b* Gloucester, 11 Dec., 1940. divorced. two *s*. two *d*. *Educ:* Crypt Grammar School, Gloucester. *Studied:* Gloucester College of Art (1959-63, James Tucker, John Whiskerd, Gordon Ward). *Exhib:* R.A., R.W.A., and numerous mixed shows. *Work in collections:* Trevor Barnes, etc. *Signs* *work:* "TITCOMBE." *Address:* 72 Priory Rd., Gloucester GL1 2RF.

**TITHERLEY, Hazel M.,** R.C.A. (1985), A.T.C., A.T.D.(Manc.); painter in oil, acrylic and water-colour; *b* Little Singleton, Lancs., 4 Mar., 1935. *m* Philip Titherley, F.R.I.B.A., M.R.T.P.I. one *s. Educ:* Queen Mary School, Lytham. *Studied:* Blackpool School of Art (1953-58), Manchester Regional College of Art (1958-59). *Exhib:* over 30 solo, many open and groups shows, incl. International Art Symposium, W. Germany. *Work in collections:* Salford A.G. and private collections in Europe, U.S.A., and Far East. Teaches painting; studio-gallery open by appointment. *Clubs:* Founded New Longton Artists (1969). *Signs work:* "Hazel Titherley." *Address:* Woodside, Woodside Ave., New Longton, Preston, Lancs. PR4 4YD.

**TODD, Daphne Jane,** R.P. (1985), N.E.A.C. (1984), F.R.S.A. (1997), Hon. S.W.A. (1996), H.D.F.A.(Lond.) (1971); awards: 2nd prize John Player award (1983), G.L.C. prize (1984), 1st prize Hunting Group (1984); painter in oil on panel; Hon. Sec. R.P. (1990-91); Director of Studies, Heatherley School of Art, Chelsea (1980-86); President R.P. (1994-); Governor, Heatherley School of Art (1986-); Governor, Federation of British Art (1995-); *b* York, 27 Mar., 1947. *m* Lt.Col. P.R.T. Driscoll. one *d. Educ:* Simon Langton Grammar School, Canterbury. *Studied:* Slade School (1965-71). *Exhib:* R.A., R.P., N.E.A.C., Patterson Gallery, retrospective Morley Gallery (1989). *Work in collections:* Chantrey Bequest; University College, London; Royal Hollaway A.G. and Museum; H.Q. Irish Guards; Pembroke College, Cambridge; Lady Margaret Hall, Oxford; St. David's University; N.P.G; St. Catharine's College, Cambridge; Science Museum; De Montfort University; N.U.M.A.S.T.; Institution of Civil Engineers; Bishop's Palace, Hereford. *Commissions:* incl.: H.R.H. The Grand Duke of Luxembourg, K.G.; Dame Janet Baker, D.B.E.; Spike Milligan, Hon. C.B.E. *Publications:* occasional articles in The Artist. *Clubs:* Chelsea Arts, The Arts. *Signs work:* "D. Todd." *Address:* Salters Green Farm, Mayfield, E. Sussex TN20 6NP.

**TODD, James Gilbert,** M.A. (1965), M.F.A. (1970), A.R.E. (1995); artist in painting and wood relief printmaking; Prof. of Art and Humanities, University of Montana; *b* Minneapolis, Minn., 12 Oct., 1937. *m* Julia. three *s. Educ:* Chicago Art Inst., College of Great Falls, University of Montana (1965-70, Rudy Antio, Donald Bunse, James Dew). *Exhib:* North and South America, England, Europe, Russia, Asia. *Work in collections:* U.S.A., England, Europe, Asia, Canada. *Publications:* numerous articles on artists and art theory, and four books illustrated. *Clubs:* Northwest Print Council, S.W.E., R.E., American Assoc. of University Professors. *Signs work:* "James G. Todd" or "TODD." *Address:* 6917 Siesta Drive, Missoula, Montana 59802, U.S.A.

**TODD, Peter William,** A.R.C.A. (1949); artist in oil; Head of Grimsby School of Art (1956-86); *b* Sheffield, 13 May, 1921. *Studied:* Sheffield College of Art, Royal College of Art (1946-49). *Exhib:* R.A., London Group, R.B.A., N.E.A.C., New Grafton Gallery. *Clubs:* Caterpillar. *Signs work:* "Peter Todd."

# WHO'S WHO IN ART

*Address:* School House, Walesby, nr. Market Rasen, Lincs. LN8 3UW.

**TODD WARMOTH, Pip,** B.A.(Hons.), M.A.; artist in oil. *Educ:* Caistor Grammar School. *Studied:* Grimsby, Camberwell, R.A. Schools. *Exhib:* Catto Gallery, New Grafton, John Martin, Bellock- Lowndes, Chicago, Albemarle, L.K.F. Gallery, Hong Kong, China Club, Hong Kong, C.A.C.; group shows: R.A., Bonhams, Thompson Gallery. *Work in collections:* Franklin Trust, Kingston Lacey, Montecute - National Trust, London Transport. *Commissions:* poster for London Underground. *Publications:* work repro.: Country Life, House and Garden, Evening Standard, South China Morning Post, Hong Kong Standard, Artist Illustrators, Art Review. B.B.C. Breakfast Show, H.K. Radio 4 and 5, C.B.S., News International *Clubs:* Dover St. Arts, Chelsea Arts. *Signs work:* "Pip T.W." *Address:* 396 Brixton Rd., London SW9 7AW.

**TOLLEY, Sheila,** R.W.A.; artist in all media; *b* Birmingham, 28 June, 1939. *Educ:* Richard C. Thomas School for Girls, Staffs. *Studied:* Bournemouth and Poole College of Art (1972-74, Edward Darcy Lister, R.C.A.). *Exhib:* R.A. Summer Exhbns. (1978-95), R.W.A. (1976-77, 1980-87). Twice winner of the Cornelissen Prize for Painting. *Work in collections:* U.K. and abroad. *Signs work:* "sheila tolley" and see appendix. *Address:* Flat 16 Hollybush House, 3 Wollstonecraft Rd., Boscombe Manor, Bournemouth, Dorset BH5 1JQ.

**TOLSON, Roger Nicholas,** B.A.; painter in oil; Collections Manager, Dept. of Art, Imperial War Museum; *b* Sheffield, 2 Dec., 1958. *Educ:* King Edward VII School, Sheffield; Oriel College, Oxford. *Studied:* Sir John Cass College of Art (1986-90). *Exhib:* R.A. Summer Show (1986-87), Hunting Group (1987), Whitechapel Open (1988, 1989, 1992), N.E.A.C. (1988); one-man show: Cadogan Contemporary (1990). *Address:* 4 Kelross Rd., London N5 2QS.

**TOMALIN, Peter John,** R.I.B.A. Dip.Arch. (Leics. 1964), F.S.A.I. (1978), U.A. (1978); first prize in B.B.C. Christmas painting competition (1977); self employed architectural illustrator and water-colour artist; *b* Kettering, 18 Oct., 1937. *m* Marjorie Elizabeth. two *s. Educ:* Kettering Technical College, Leicester School of Architecture. *Studied:* Northampton School of Art (1976-79, Peter Atkin, Frank Cryer). *Exhib:* Mall Galleries, U.A., R.I., Grosvenor Gallery, Hitchin, Northampton A.G. *Clubs:* Northampton Town and County Art Soc., S.A.I. *Signs work:* "Peter Tomalin." *Address:* 170 Sywell Rd., Overstone, Northampton.

**TOMS, Peter Edward,** R.M.S. (1995), A.R.M.S. (1991), H.S. (1991); marine and landscape painter, principal designer, British Aerospace, to 1982; full time painter since then; *b* Hayes, Middx., 28 May, 1940. *m* Patricia Mary Toms. four *s.* three *d. Educ:* Mellow Lane School, Hayes. *Studied:* engineering and design: Southall Technical College (1956-63). *Exhib:* R.S.M.A., R.I., R.M.S., R.B.A., N.S., U.A., numerous London and provincial one-man and other exhbns. including Alpine Club, Century, Edwin Pollard, Oliver Swann, Omell, Skipwith, Solent and Wykeham Galleries. *Work in collections:* P. & O. "SS Canberra", Royal Hampshire Regt., Royal Navy (H.M.S. "Osprey"), NV

Amev Group (Utrecht), H.M. Land Registry, Astrid Trust and many other corporate and private collections. *Publications:* biographical note, R.M.S. Centenary Book '100 Years'. *Clubs:* Dorchester (President). *Signs work:* "Peter Toms." *Address:* Stoneways, Springfield Rd., Broadwey, Weymouth, Dorset DT3 5DX.

**TONG, Belinda Josephine,** S.W.A., U.A.; painter in oil, pastel, watercolour; *b* Woodford, Essex, 8 Sept., 1937. *m* Bernard Tong. two *s.* one *d. Educ:* Loughton County High School for Girls, Havering College. *Studied:* Open College of the Arts. *Exhib:* R.O.I., S.B.A., S.W.A., U.A. *Signs work:* "B. Tong" (oil and pastel), "Belinda Tong" (water-colour). *Address:* Grazebrook, Theydon Mount, nr. Epping, Essex CM16 7PW.

**TONKS, John,** A.T.D., F.R.B.S., V.P.R.B.S.; freelance sculptor in stone, wood, terracotta, bronze; part-time lecturer, Birmingham University; V.P., Royal Soc. of British Sculptors (1990-91); *b* Dudley, Worcs., 14 Aug., 1927. *m* Sylvia Irene. one *s.* one *d. Educ:* Dudley Grammar School. *Studied:* Wolverhampton and B'ham Colleges of Art specialising in sculpture (William Bloy, Albert Willetts, Tom Wright). *Exhib:* one-man shows: University of B'ham (1974, 1984), Ombersley Gallery, Worcs. (1983), Helios Gallery, B'ham (1984); V.B. Gallery, St. Louis, U.S.A. (1981), Poole Willis Gallery, N.Y. (1983), Liverpool International Gdn. Festival (1984), Gardens of New College, Oxford (1988), Garden Festival, Wales (1992). *Commissions:* Alexandre Hospital, Redditch; Pendrell Hall, Stafford; Gretna Green; B'ham Botanical Gdns. *Signs work:* "J.T." joined. *Address:* Downshill Cottage, Comhampton, Stourport-on-Severn, Worcs. DY13 9ST.

**TOOKEY, John Michael,** P.S. (1982); commercial artist in oil, watercolour and pastel; *b* Ilford. *Educ:* Gearies Secondary Modern School. *Studied:* Sir John Cass School of Art. *Exhib:* R.I., R.B.A., R.O.I., R.W.S. Art Club. *Work in collections:* Bowes Museum Educ. Service, Gateshead County Library, Hackney Borough Council. *Publications:* illustrations for 'The Countryman', 'East Anglia', 'The Yorkshire Ridings', 'Kent, Surrey & Sussex', 'The Cotswolds'. *Signs work:* "John Tookey." *Address:* 1a Calne Ave., Clayhall, Ilford, Essex.

**TOOP, Bill,** R.I. (1979), M.C.S.D. (1971); artist and illustrator in watercolour, line and wash, line, with own gallery in Salisbury; *b* Bere Regis, Dorset, 27 May, 1943. *m* Elizabeth Thurstans. one *s.* one *d. Educ:* Weymouth Grammar School, Blandford Grammar School. *Studied:* Bath Academy of Art (1961-63, Robyn Denny, Howard Hodgkin), Southampton College of Art (1964-66, Peter Folkes), Bristol Polytechnic Art Faculty (1967-68, Derek Crowe). *Exhib:* R.I., R.W.A., numerous one-man shows. *Work in collections:* The Sultan of Oman, Northern Telecom, British Gas, Whitbread Inns, Coutts & Co., The Sedgwick Group, N.F.U. Mutual and Avon Insurance, Royal School of Signals, Atomic Energy Authority, Inst. of Directors, etc. *Publications:* illustrated Portrait of Wiltshire (Pamela Street), National Gardens Scheme Handbook, etc. *Signs* *work:* "Bill Toop." *Address:* Bill Toop Gallery, 5 St. John's St., Salisbury, Wilts. SP1 2SB.

**TOPHAM, John,** F.P.S., I.A.A., Assoc. Internationale des Arts Plastiques; painter; *b* Hampstead, London. *m* Hazel Grimsey, painter. two *s. Studied:* Melbourne, Australia; Harrow and Ealing Schools of Art. *Exhib:* R.W.A., R.B.A., F.P.S., R.S.B.A., U.A., H.A.C., Camden Art Centre, Allsop Gallery, Anglo-French Exhbn., Poole Art Centre, Seldown Gallery, Hambledon Gallery, Archer Gallery, Minstrel Gallery, Colne Group, Parkway Gallery, Questers Gallery, Swiss Cottage Library, Olympus Gallery, Upton House Gallery, Poole Art Centre Open Exhbn. *Work in collections:* Nuffield Foundation, Camden Council; private collections in U.K. and U.S.A. *Clubs:* F.P.S., life mem. I.A.A., Assoc. Internationale des Arts Plastiques. *Signs work:* "Topham." *Address:* Holmstoke, West Milton, Bridport, Dorset DT6 3SJ.

**TOPLIS, Valma Maud,** M.F.P.S.; artist in etching and aquatint, teacher; *b* Maidenhead, 18 June, 1946. *Educ:* Clark's College, Ilford; Beal Grammar School for Girls. *Studied:* St. Osyth's Training College (1964-67, Graham Eccles, Michael Kaye), Barking Technical College (1967-80, Harry Eccleston, O.B.E.). *Exhib:* Loggia Gallery, Bankside Gallery, R.E., The Barbican. *Work in collections:* Britain and America. *Clubs:* Ilford Art Soc., Essex Art. *Signs work:* "VALMA TOPLIS." *Address:* 62 Chadville Gdns., Chadwell Heath, Romford, Essex RM6 5UA.

**TOVEY, Robert Lawton,** A.T.D. (1947); painter in oil; *b* Birmingham, 3 Apr., 1924. *m* Annette Suzanne Hubler. *Educ:* The George Dixon Grammar School, Birmingham. *Studied:* Birmingham College of Art under B. Fleetwood-Walker (1939-43, 1946-47). *Exhib:* R.B.S.A., R.B.A., A.I.A., N.E.A.C., R.O.I., R.W.A., one-man shows, Geneva (1957, 1962, 1964, 1980, 1981, 1982, 1983, 1984, 1985, 1995), Baden (1973, 1976), Nyon (1978, 1985). *Work in collections:* Musée d'Art et d'Histoire, Geneva; Dudley A.G.; oil painting, The Red Scarf, for above (1953). *Signs work:* "R. L. TOVEY." *Address:* 2 Place de L'Octroi, 1227 Carouge, Geneva, Switzerland.

**TOWER, Meriel Theresa,** F.S.D.C.; freelance textile designer, painter, teacher; on technical staff, Campbell Fabrics (1936-39); teacher, Upton House School, Windsor (1948-72), St. George's School, Windsor Castle (1953-70), from 1974 part-time teacher, Bucks. County Council Adult Educ.; *b* Windsor, 1911. *Educ:* St. Paul's Girls' School. *Studied:* Westminster School of Art (1929-31) and Chelsea School of Art under Boris Heroys (1931-34). *Exhib:* one-man show, Museum of Oxford (1978), R.A. (1984). *Publications:* British Textile Designers Today (Lewis), British Designers: Their Work, Series I (Lewis), Designers in Britain, 1947 (published for S.I.A.), Decorative Art, 1950-51 (The Studio Publications), Design for Applied Decoration in the Crafts, by John Farleigh (Bell). *Address:* The Thatch, Aston Rowant, Watlington, Oxon. OX9 5SS.

**TOWNSEND, Storm Diana,** N.D.D. (Sculpture) (1960), A.T.C. (1962),

Siswa Lokantara Foundation Resident Fellowship Award, Indonesia (1960-61), Huntington Hartford Foundation Resident Fellowship Award, Calif. (1963); sculptor in bronze, cements; sculpture instructor, Albuquerque University, New Mexico, University of New Mexico in Albuquerque and The College of Santa Fe, New Mexico; *b* London, 31 Aug., 1937. *Studied:* London University, Goldsmiths' College (1955-60) under Harold S. Parker, Ivor Roberts-Jones. *Exhib:* throughout U.S.A. *Work in collections:* Museum of New Mexico and the City of Albuquerque, public works, many private collections. *Commissions:* over life-size bronze "To Serve and Protect" commissioned by the City of Albuquerque and others, New Mexico (1984). *Publications:* many and various articles and interviews in local and national publications. 1964 Resident Fellowship Award, Helene Wurlitzer Foundation, Taos, New Mexico. *Signs work:* "STORM." *Address:* P.O. Box 1165, Corrales, New Mexico, 87048, U.S.A.

**TOWSEY, Mary,** T.D.; artist in oil and mixed media; *b* Epsom, 24 July, 1936. *m* Robin Towsey. three *d*. *Educ:* Clare Park, Farnham. *Studied:* Goldsmiths' College (1955-57), part-time, Epsom College of Art (1960-67, Leslie Worth, Peter Oliver). *Exhib:* Fairfield Halls Croydon, Lizard Gallery Farnham, Wintershall Gallery Bramley, Hallam Gallery London, Edwin Pollard Gallery, Ebury Gallery London, Wykeham Gallery London, Jonleigh Gallery Wonersh, Galerie de Vétheuil, France, R.B.A., R.O.I., N.E.A.C., R.W.S., S.W.A., S.B.A. B.B.C.2 television series 'Painters'. *Signs work:* "Mary Towsey." *Address:* Ambelor, Lands End La., Lindford, Bordon, Hants. GU35 0SS.

**TRANT, Carolyn,** D.F.A.(Lond.) (1973); artist in egg tempera, drawings, etchings and lithographs, artists books under imprint 'Parvenu Press'; *b* Middx., 29 Oct., 1950. two *s*. one *d*. *Educ:* North London Collegiate School. *Studied:* Slade School of Fine Art (1969-73). *Exhib:* New Grafton Gallery, Business Arts Gallery, Brighton Festival, Artists Bookfair, Barbican, and throughout S. East. *Work in collections:* R.A., E.S.C.C./S.E. Arts commission: 'Rituals and Relics' - Earthworks on the Downs. *Signs work:* "Carolyn Trant" on back of work. *Address:* 17 St. Anne's Cres., Lewes, E. Sussex BN7 1SB.

**TRAPPE, Paul,** sculptor in stone; *b* Göttingen, Germany. *m* G. Schaeffter. one *s*. *Educ:* Göttingen, Northeim Düsseldorf. *Exhib:* Canberra, Adelaide, Bonn, London, Milwaukee. *Work in collections:* Düsseldorf, Canberra, Adelaide, Tanunda, Milwaukee, Sydney, Dubuque, Baden-Baden, Northeim, West Bend, Saskatoon. *Commissions:* Germany, U.S.A., Australia. *Publications:* Vantage, Adelaide; Kunstreport, Berlin; Art Works of Canberra, Düsseldorf Creativ; Wondabyne, Paul Trappe-Sculpture 1969-1989; Living Stone; Paul Trappe-Sculpture 1990-1995. *Signs work:* "tr." *Address:* 11 Mac Donnell St., Tanunda, S. Australia 5352; and Wildenbruchstr. 15, 40545 Dusseldorf.

**TRATT, Richard,** S.WL.A. (1981), S.B.A. (1987); painter in oil; *b* Enfield,

19 Oct., 1953. *m* Hilary Wastnage. *Educ:* Crewe Grammar School. *Studied:* Northwich College of Art (1970-72), Dartington College of Arts (1972-74). *Exhib:* R.A., Mall Galleries, Robert Perera Fine Arts, Alresford Gallery, Peter Hedley Gallery, British Artists Show, Spirit of London, etc.; nineteen one-man shows. *Work in collections:* S.W.A.N., Royal Palace of Oman. *Publications:* work repro.: Reynard Fine Art, Royles, McDonald, Rosenstiel's. *Signs work:* "Tratt." *Address:* 10 Sharpley Cl., Fordingbridge, Hants. SP6 1LG.

**TRAYHORNE, Rex,** R.M.S. (1988); artist in water-colour and gouache; art teacher, demonstrator and writer; exhbns. organiser, Wessex Artists Exhbns.; *b* 13 Oct., 1931. *m* Geraldine. two *s* (one *s-s*), two *d* (one *s-d*). *Educ:* Newbury Grammar School. *Studied:* Reading College (1958). *Exhib:* R.I., R.M.S., R.W.S., local art societies, Wessex Artists Exhbns., etc. *Publications:* Adventure into Water-colour. *Clubs:* Romsey Art, Ringwood Art Soc. *Signs work:* "Rex Trayhorne." *Address:* Stable House Studio, Newton Lane, Romsey, Hants. SO51 8GY.

**TRAYNOR, Mary,** J.P.; artist in pen and ink, water-colour and mixed media; *b* 23 Mar., 1934. *m* Brian Traynor (decd.). one *s*. two *d*. *Educ:* Walthamstow Hall, Sevenoaks. *Studied:* Birmingham College of Art and Crafts, Theatre Design: Findlay James, Roy Mason. *Exhib:* National Museum of Wales, Welsh National Eisteddfod; one-man: Welsh Industrial and Maritime Museum (1988), St. David's Hall, Cardiff (1990), Manor House Fine Arts, Cardiff (1997). *Work in collections:* Welsh Industrial and Maritime Museum, Cardiff, Cardiff Magistrates, Professional Offices, County of Cardiff, Gwent Health Authority. *Commissions:* public and private commissions inc. C.A.D.W. and various companies. *Publications:* illustrated: Wales Tourist Board, Western Mail, National Museum of Wales, Cardiff City Council, C.A.D.W. *Clubs:* The Victorian Soc., Cardiff Architectural Heritage Soc., Cardiff Civic Soc. *Signs work:* "Mary Traynor." *Address:* 72a Kimberly Rd., Penylan, Cardiff CF2 5DN.

**TREANOR, Frances,** P.S. (1978), A.T.C. (1967), N.D.D. (1966); L'Artiste Assoifee awards winner (1975), Diplome d'Honneur, Salon d'Antony, France (1975), George Rowney award (1982), Frank Herring award (merit) (1984), Conté (U.K.) award (1986), Government Print Purchase (1987); *b* Penzance, Cornwall, 1944. *m* (1) Frank Elliott, (2) Anthony Taylor (divorced). one *d*. *Educ:* Assumption Convent, Kensington; Sacred Heart Convent, Hammersmith. *Studied:* Goldsmiths' College (1962-66) Hornsey College of Art (1966-67). *Exhib:* London, Paris, Yugoslavia, Berlin. Stage set design commission 'As You Like It' O.U.D.S. Summer Tour (Japan, U.S.A., U.K.) 1988. *Publications:* Vibrant Flower Painting (David & Charles). *Signs work:* "Treanor" or "F.T." *Address:* 121 Royal Hill, London SE10 8SS.

**TREE, Michael Lambert,** portrait painter, etcher, draughtsman and illustrator; *b* New York, 5 Dec., 1921. *m* Lady Anne Tree. two *d*. *Educ:* Eton. *Studied:* Slade School of Fine Art. *Exhib:* Hochmann Gallery, N.Y. (1982), Fine Arts,

London (1984), St. Jame's Gallery (1989), Lumley Cazalet (1995). *Publications:* illustrations to Summoned by Bells by John Betjeman (1960). *Clubs:* White's. *Signs work:* "M. Tree." *Address:* 29 Radnor Walk, London SW3.

**TRELEAVEN, Richard Barrie,** S.WL.A. (founder member), M.B.O.U.; artist in oil on canvas, alkyd, gouache, specialises in painting birds of prey; company director of family business; *b* London, 16 July, 1920. *m* Margery (decd.). *Educ:* Dulwich College (1932-36). *Studied:* under G. E. Lodge. *Exhib:* S.WL.A. Art Exhbns. Bureau, Moorland Gallery, etc.; one-man show, Bude (1953), Launceston (1973, 1980). *Work in collections:* Batley and many private collections. *Publications:* Peregrine (1977); and ornithological journals. *Clubs:* British Falconers. *Signs work:* "R. B. Treleaven." *Address:* Blue Wings, South Petherwin, Launceston, Cornwall.

**TRESS, David,** painter in water-colour based mixed media, including gouache, ink and oil crayon, charcoal, oil; *b* London, 11 Apr., 1955. *Educ:* Latymer Upper School, Hammersmith. *Studied:* Harrow College of Art (1972-73), Trent Polytechnic, Nottingham (1973-76). *Exhib:* regularly in Wales, England, Holland and France, recently 'Five Leading Welsh Artists' San Francisco; Boundary Gallery, London; W. Wales Arts Centre. *Work in collections:* National Library of Wales, C.A.S.W. *Signs work:* "David Tress." *Address:* 17 Castle St., Haverfordwest, Pembrokeshire SA61 2ED.

**TREVENA, Shirley,** R.I. (1994); self taught artist in water-colour; *b* London, 11 Sept., 1934. *m* Michael Pickerill. *Educ:* Drayton Manor Grammar School, Middx. *Exhib:* R.I. Mall Galleries, R.W.S. Bank St. Gallery, Nicholas Bowlby Gallery, Tunbridge Wells. *Publications:* numerous articles and reviews; examples of work in several books on water-colour painting and drawing. *Signs work:* "S. Trevena." *Address:* 27 Montpelier Cres., Brighton, E. Sussex BN1 3JJ.

**TRIBE, Barbara,** F.R.B.S., R.W.A. Disciplines: sculpture, painting, drawing and ceramic sculpture; *b* Sydney, Australia. *m* John Singleman, architect, artist, potter (decd.). *Studied:* Trained in sculpture, student of G. Rayner Hoff, East Sydney Technical College; graduated with honours, awarded Diploma and Bronze Medal for sculpture. Won the New South Wales travelling art scholarship for sculpture to the Royal Academy Schools, London. Elected: Fellow of the Royal Society of British Sculptors, Member of the Society of Portrait Sculptors, Academician of the Royal West of England Academy. *Work in collections:* works represented: Anzac War Memorial, Sydney, Australia; National Gallery of Australia, Canberra; Australian War Memorial Museum, Canberra; Art Gallery of New South Wales, Sydney, Australia; Art Gallery of South Australia, Adelaide; Bathurst Regional Art Gallery, New South Wales; Spode Potteries Museum and Art Gallery, Stoke-on-Trent; Stoke-on-Trent City Museum and Art Gallery; Doncaster Museum and Art Gallery, Yorkshire; R.A.F. Museum, Hendon, London; in many private collections in U.K., U.S.A.,

Canada, Australia, Far East - Japan and Thailand. Exhibited widely and worked abroad. *Exhib:* Royal Academy, London; Royal West of England Academy; Royal Scottish Academy; Cambrian Academy of Art; Paris Salon; Galarie Artica, Cruxhaven, W. Germany; Royal Society of British Sculptors; Society of Portrait Sculptors; Sladmore Gallery, London; Corbally Stourton Contemporary Art - Australian Art in London; London Group; Fieldborne Galleries, London; Newlyn and St. Ives Society of Artists; Penwith Society of Artists, St. Ives; Prouds Gallery, Sydney; Barry Stern Gallery, Sydney; Holland Fine Art Gallery, Double Bay, Sydney; David Angeloro Gallery, Sydney; MacQuarie Galleries, Sydney; Blaxland Galleries, Sydney. Major retrospective exhibitions: Stoke-on-Trent City Museum and Art Gallery; Guildford House Galleries, Guildford; Mall Galleries, London. *Publications:* represented in: 'British Sculpture' by Eric Newton; 'On View' ' acquisitions in Britain; 'Art and Australia' - Sam Ure Smith; 'A Matter of Taste' - investing in Australian art by Terry Ingram; 'Australian Sculptors' by Ken Scarlett; Encyclopaedia 'British Pottery and Porcelain Marks' by Geoffrey A. Godden; 'Heritage' - the National Women's art book - 500 works by 500 Australian women artists, edited by Joan Kerr. Instructor of modelling and sculpture, Penzance School of Art (1948-88). *Signs work:* "Barbara Tribe" see appendix. *Address:* The Studio, Sheffield, Paul, Penzance, Cornwall TR19 6UW, England.

**TROITZKY, Nina,** B.A. Hons., A.R.O.I. (1987); painter in oil, installations, mixed media. *Studied:* Icon painting, Chelsea School of Art (part time), London Guildhall University and Chichester Inst. - Degree course. *Exhib:* R.O.I., Mall Galleries, London Contemporary Art Fair, British Painters, Discerning Eye, Mall Galleries, Anna Mei, Clifford St. Fine Arts, Halkin Arcade Galleries 'Women and Art', Abbot & Holder, Llewellyn Alexander, Wykham, Chelsea Arts Club, Century Windsor, Hann Bath, Example Art London, River Gallery Arundel, S.W.A.N. Sydney, Australia, and many provincial and European galleries. *Work in collections:* V. & A., St. Richard's Hospital Chichester, California State University of Long Beach U.S.A., Bishop Otter College, Chichester. *Publications:* work repro.: Medici card. *Clubs:* Chelsea Arts. *Signs work:* "N.T." *Address:* Trinity House, 91 Tarrant St., Arundel, W. Sussex BN18 9DN.

**TROTH, Miriam Deborah,** B.A. Hons. (1983); multi-media environmental artist and sculptor; Mem. Eco-design Assoc., and N.A.A.; *b* Edgbaston, 1 Oct., 1951. *Studied:* W. Surrey College of Art and Design (1980-83). *Exhib:* Barbican, British Commonwealth Inst., Swansea A.G., Bradford House Glass Museum, Coleridge Gallery, Bristol A.G., R.A., Bankside Gallery, Smiths Gallery, Royal Soc. of Artists Gallery, Salisbury Museum, Windsor Arts Centre, Christchurch Museum, Bournemouth University. *Work in collections:* London, Sydney, Detroit, Frankfurt, Wiltshire C.C. *Signs work:* "Miriam Troth." *Address:* 125 Seafield Rd., Bournemouth, Dorset BH6 3JL.

**TROWELL, Jonathan Ernest Laverick,** N.D.D. (1959), R.A.S.Dip.

(1962), F.R.S.A. (1983), N.E.A.C. (1986); painter in oil, pastel and water-colour; *b* Easington Village, Co. Durham, 1938. *m* Dorothea May Howard. *Educ:* Robert Richardson School. *Studied:* Sunderland College of Art, R.A. Schools. *Exhib:* New Bauhaus Cologne, Young Contemporaries, John Moores, R.A., Lee Nordnes N.Y., Bilan de Contemporain Paris, R.B.A., N.E.A.C.; one-man shows, Brod Gallery London, Century Gallery, Culham College Oxford, Richard Stone-Reeves New York, Osborne Gallery London, Stern Galleries Australia. *Work in collections:* Bank of Japan; Culham College, Oxford; de Beers (Diamond Co.); Oriental Diamond Co.; Ciba-Geigy; Imperial College of Science; R.C.A.; B.P. *Clubs:* Chelsea Arts. *Signs work:* "TROWELL." *Address:* Blenheim House, Litcham, Norfolk PE32 2NS.

**TRUZZI-FRANCONI, Jane,** B.A. (1977); Angeloni prize (1979), Discerning Eye prize (1990); sculptor in bronze; Supervisor, Fiorini Fine Art Foundry; *b* London, 26 July, 1955. one *d. Educ:* Sydenham School. *Studied:* Goldsmiths' College of Art (1973-74), Ravensbourne College of Art (1974-77), R.C.A. (1978-79). *Exhib:* R.A., Mall Galleries, many mixed shows in London, E. Anglia, Kent and Surrey. *Signs work:* "J.E.T.F." *Address:* 4 Wolsey Cottages, Strickland Manor Hill, Yoxford, Suffolk IP17 3JE.

**TUCKER, Patricia Rosa, (née Madden),** N.D.D. (1950), A.T.D. (1951); oil and water-colour painter, art teacher; Past Chairman, Bromley Art Soc.; Visual Arts Officer, Bromley Arts Council (1970-87); Sec. Chelsea Open Air Art Exhbn. (1967-87); *b* London, 2 Jan., 1927. *m* L. Tucker. two *s.* one *d. Educ:* Mayfield, Putney, St. Catherines, Swindon. *Studied:* Swindon School of Art, West of England College of Art. *Exhib:* R.A., Bankside, Mall, etc.; one-man shows, London, Blackheath, Greenwich, Bromley, Chelsea, Gloucester and Denmark. *Work in collections:* Bromley, Gloucestershire, Kensington and Chelsea, Swindon. *Commissions:* portraiture, architectural landscapes. *Publications:* illustrations, Parenting Plus. *Clubs:* Croydon, Blackheath, Bromley, S.E.F.A.S. *Signs work:* "Patricia Tucker." *Address:* 5 Bromley Ave., Bromley, Kent BR1 4BG.

**TUCKWELL, George Arthur,** D.F.M. (1942), A.T.D. (1952), N.D.D. (1951); painter in oil and water-colour, sculptor in wood, metals and ivory, illustrator, teacher; *b* Burwell, Cambs., 4 Mar., 1919. *m* Joyce. three *d. Educ:* Sir George Monoux Grammar School. *Studied:* Sir John Cass (1947-51), Goldsmiths' College (1951-52). *Exhib:* R.B.A., R.I., R.O.I., London Group, R.W.S., N.S., Arts Council, U.S., Piccadilly Gallery, Gimpel Fils, Stone Gallery, Newcastle, John Hunt Gallery, Lewes Gallery, Weald Gallery Cranbrook. *Work in collections:* Ashmolean Museum - War Artists Collection, Oxford, Cambridge, Surrey and London Universities; public and private collections in U.K., U.S.A., Australia, N.Z., S. Africa, S. America. *Signs work:* see appendix. *Address:* 38 Geers Wood, Heathfield, E. Sussex TN21 0AR.

**TULLY, Joyce Mary,** U.A. (1978), A.M.N.S. (1974); artist in oil and water-colour, teacher; speaker at local societies; teaches calligraphy and exhibits examples of work; *b* Wooler, Northumberland. *Educ:* Duchess Grammar School, Alnwick. *Studied:* Hammersmith Art College (part-time) and private tuition with Mr. Harold Workman, R.O.I., R.B.A., R.S.M.A. *Exhib:* Paris Salon, R.O.I., R.B.A., Chelsea Artists, N.S., U.A., Ridley Soc. and in Australia, British Painting in 1979, Paxton House, Berwickshire. *Work in collections:* Copeland Castle, and private collections in England, Europe and America. *Signs work:* "J. M. Tully." *Address:* Kia-or, 26 Tenter Hill, Wooler, Northumberland NE71 6DG.

**TURNBULL, William,** sculptor and painter; *b* Dundee, 11 Jan., 1922. *m* Kim Lim. two *s. Studied:* Slade School of Fine Art (1946-48). *Exhib:* I.C.A. (1957), Waddington Galleries (1967, 1969, 1970, 1976, 1978, 1981, 1985, 1987, 1991), Tate Gallery (1973); one-man and major group shows worldwide. *Work in collections:* Arts Council, Tate Gallery, Scottish National Gallery of Modern Art; numerous provincial and overseas collections. *Signs work:* see appendix. *Address:* c/o Waddington Galleries, 11 Cork St., London W1X 1PD.

**TURNER, Cyril B.,** M.P.S.G. (1985), M.A.A. (1988), I.G.M.A. (Fellow Fine Art 1994); Fine Art master miniaturist in most categories including illuminated miniatures; inventor of Lumitex, an acid free, ultra-violet proof substitute for ivory as a miniature base; introduced cold enamel as a medium for miniature paintings; miniaturist in oils, cold enamel, soft pastel, gouache, acrylic, egg tempera, water-colour, pigmented inks, silverpoint; *b* Aldeby, Norfolk, 10 Sept., 1929. *Educ:* Beccles Area School. *Exhib:* since 1983 annual one-man exhib. 100-150 original fine art miniature paintings Museum Galleries Gt. Yarmouth. Many other U.K. one-man miniature shows, R.A., Salon des Nations Paris, annually International Miniature Shows, Arts Club Washington D.C., New York, Colorado, New Jersey, Nevada, Montana, Wyoming, Georgia, Florida, New Mexico, Ulster, Washington, Tasmania, N.S.W., Queensland, Victoria; others W. Virginia, S/N Carolinas, Ohio, Pennsylvania, Arizona, Kentucky, Jersey, Canada, France. *Work in collections:* Private, corporate and representative miniature permanent collections throughout the world. Awards: 79 miniatures have won awards, including Best of Show, Highest Merit, 1st Place. *Publications:* author: Painting Miniatures in Acrylics (1990), miniature section of Painting in Acrylics (English and French edns. 1991). Currently engaged in writing and publishing a 21 pocket book Informative Series 'Painting Original Fine Art Miniatures' 1 Bases (Lumitex), 2 Bases Various (1993): 3 Landscapes in Water-colours, 4 Landscapes in Oils, 7 Selecting Subjects and Categories (1994): 5 Landscapes in Cold Enamel on Lumitex, 6 One Twelfth Scale Miniatures in Water-colour on Lumitex Fino, 8 Miniatures in Water-colour on Lumitex Fino (1995), 9 Miniatures in Oils on Lumitex Fino, 10 One Twelfth Scale Miniatures in Oils on Lumitex Fino (1997): 11 Miniatures in Soft Pastel, 12 Miniatures in Gouache, 13 Miniatures in Silverpoint, 14 Miniatures in Oils, 15 Miniatures in Water-colour (1997-98), 2 Miniature books (Limited Edns.) of Miniatures Paintings (1997). *Signs work:* "C.B. Turner." *Address:* 6 Gablehurst Ct., Long Lane, Bradwell, Gt. Yarmouth,

Norfolk NR31 7DS.

**TURNER, Jacquie,** B.A.; painting in mixed media and collage on paper; *b* 27 Mar., 1959. *m* Nigel Wheeler. three *s. Educ:* Rickmansworth School, Herts. *Studied:* Winchester School of Art (1979-81, Gillian Ayres). *Exhib:* Linda Blackstone Gallery, Pinner, Middlesex. *Work in collections:* Leics. Coll. for schools and colleges, Norsk Hydro Oslo, Adam Bank London, Shangri La Hong Kong. *Publications:* The Encyclopaedia of Acrylic Techniques by Hazel Harrison (Headline), How to Capture Movement in Your Paintings by Julia Cassels (Northlight Books), Artists Manual (Collins), Mixed Media Pocket Palette by Ian Sidaway (Northlight Books). *Signs work:* "Jacquie Turner." *Address:* Fairview House, Chinnor Rd., Bledlow Ridge, Bucks. HP14 4AJ.

**TURNER, Lynette,** Hons.B.Sc. (Zoology, 1968), H.N.D.D. (Graphic design, 1970); printmaker in coloured etchings using zinc; *b* London, 28 May, 1945. *Educ:* Hall School, Wincanton, Som., Manchester University. *Studied:* Brighton Art School (1963), City and Guilds Art School (1969, etching Henry Wilkinson, Tim Edmunds), Manchester Art School. *Exhib:* Century Gallery, Henley (1976), Margaret Fisher Gallery (1976), R.A. (1977), S.E. London Art Group, Y.M.C.A., Gt. Russell St., WC1, (1983), R.A. Summer Show (1987), December 1989 exhbn. in Crypt of St. Martin-in-the-Fields. (etchings and water-colours) Herge's "Tintin" influence. *Clubs:* Falmouth's Royal Cornwall Polytechnic Society's Members' Annual Exhbn. (1996, 1997). *Signs work:* "Lynette Turner." *Address:* Pendynas, Minnie Pl., Falmouth, Cornwall TR11 3NN.

**TURNER, Martin William,** N.D.D. (1961), R.O.I. (1974), N.S. (1975); painter in oil, acrylic and water-colour, printmaker; *b* Reading, 3 Oct., 1940. *Educ:* Gravesend Technical School. *Studied:* Medway College of Art under David Graham, C. Stanley Hayes. *Exhib:* R.A., R.O.I., R.B.A., N.S., R.S.M.A., R.E. *Work in collections:* Abbot Hall Gallery, Swansea University, Cardiff Museum, Glamorgan Educ. Com., Liverpool A.G. *Publications:* work repro.: articles for Leisure Painter. *Clubs:* R.I., N.S.P.S., Hampstead Artists' Council. *Signs work:* "Martin Turner." *Address:* 24 Marshall Rd., Rainham, Kent ME8 0AP.

**TURNER, Peggy E. M.:** see RICHARDS, E. Margaret.

**TURNER, Prudence,** freelance artist in oil on canvas; Scottish landscape painter specifically since 1966; plus portraiture, seascapes and dream-fantasies; *b* 15 Mar., 1930. *Studied:* in India, Egypt, France and England, learning from artists already famous. Nationally recognized in England in 1934. Fine Art Publication copyrights purchased from 1967 onwards and given international circulation, including limited editions of signed prints. *Work in collections:* U.K., and Overseas. *Commissions:* Professional: Constant, including royalty. *Signs work:* "Prudence Turner." *Address:* 49 Romulus Ct., Justin Cl., Brentford Dock Marina, Brentford, Middx. TW8 8QW.

**TURNER, Silvie,** publisher, writer, artist, original print paper and book arts;

*b* 19 Oct., 1946. two *d. Studied:* Corsham (1965-68), University of Brighton (Post grad., 1968-70). Work in permanent collections worldwide. *Publications:* about 20 on various print, paper, book subjects. *Clubs:* Chelsea Arts. *Signs work:* "Silvie Turner." *Address:* 204 St. Albans Ave., London W4 5JU.

**TURNER, William Ralph,** R.C.A., F.R.S.A.; artist in oil and water-colour; *b* Chorlton-on-Medlock, 30 Apr., 1920. *m* Anne Grant (decd.). one *d. Studied:* Derby College of Art (1945). *Exhib:* R.B.A., R.I., R.C.A., O'Mell Galleries London, Christopher Cole Galleries, Henley-on-Thames, Pitcairn Galleries, Knutsford, Boundary Gallery, London. *Work in collections:* Manchester Educ. Com., Stockport A.G., Saab (Manchester) Ltd.; private collections in New York, Los Angeles, Kenya, Portugal, Switzerland, Zaire. *Publications:* Cheshire Life Magazine. *Signs work:* "William Turner" and see appendix. *Address:* (studio) Renrut, 23 Gill Bent Rd., Cheadle Hulme, Cheadle, Ches.

**TURPIN, Louis,** Dip.Ad.(Hons.) Fine Art (1971); painter in oil on canvas; *b* 25 Apr., 1947. *m* Davida Smith. two *s. Educ:* Alleyns, Dulwich; Sunbury Grammar School, Sunbury-on-Thames. *Studied:* Guildford School of Art (1967-68), Falmouth Art School (1968-71). *Exhib:* Beaux Arts, Bath, N.P.G., Bohun Gallery, Henley-on-Thames, Rye A.G., R.A., Oddfellows Gallery Kendal, R.S.P.P. *Work in collections:* Rye A.G., South East Arts, Towner A.G., Bath University, John Radcliffe Hospital, Oxford. *Commissions:* Miss Pears, Bedruthan Steps Hotel. *Publications:* The Painted Garden by Huxley. *Clubs:* Rye Soc. of Artists. *Signs work:* "Louis Turpin." *Address:* 19 Udimore Rd., Rye, E. Sussex TN31 7DS.

**TUTE, George William,** N.D.D. Illustration, N.D.D. Painting, R.A.Cert., M.A. (R.C.A.), R.E., R.W.A., S.W.E.; artist in oil, water-colour, printmaking; freelance graphic designer; *b* Hull, 23 Mar., 1933. *m* Iris Tute. two *s. Educ:* Bainse Grammar School, Lancs. *Studied:* Blackpool School of Art (1951-54); Royal Academy Schools (1954-59); Royal College of Art (1981-82). *Exhib:* R.A., R.W.A., R.E.; private and public galleries. Exhibits prints and paintings, book illustration and general illustration for commissions. *Signs work:* "G. W. Tute." *Address:* 46 Eastfield, Westbury-on-Trym, Bristol BS9 4BE.

**TWEED, Jill,** F.R.B.S., F.R.S.A., Slade B.A.; sculptor in bronze; *b* U.K., 7 Dec., 1931. *m* Philip Hicks. one *s.* one *d. Studied:* Slade School of Art (F. E. McWilliam). *Exhib:* Marjorie Parr Gallery, London, Ladlane Gallery, Dublin, Bruton St. Gallery, London, Flowers East Gallery, London, Poole-Wills Gallery, N.Y. *Work in collections:* H.M. The Queen; Corps of the Royal Military Police, Chichester; Royal Engineers, Mill Hill, London; Austin Reed Ltd., London; Picker Collection, Kingston-upon-Thames; Hampshire C.C.; Amec U.K. Ltd., London; Conseil Regionale de Normandie, Caen, France; K.C.C.; Oxon. C.C.; Gosport D.C. *Signs work:* "Jill Tweed." *Address:* Royal Society of British Sculptors, 108 Old Brompton Rd., London SW7 3RA.

**TYSON, Rowell,** A.R.C.A., R.B.A.; painter in oil and water-colour; *b* London, 5 Jan., 1926. *m* Monica Lyon. *Studied:* Tunbridge Wells School of

Art, Beckenham School of Art, Royal College of Art (1946-1950), fourth year scholarship (1949-1950). Senior Mem of Royal Soc. of British Artists. *Exhib:* R.A., R.S.A., R.B.A., R.O.I., R.S.M.A., provincial galleries and touring exhbns. *Work in collections:* include Leo-Burnett, Miles Laboratories, Shell, Lopex, Leicester Educ. Com., Carlisle City A.G., K.C.C., Paxus, Sumicorp Finance Ltd., Merrill Lynch, Arthur Andersen & Co., Qatar National Bank, Inst. of Directors. *Signs work:* "ROWELL TYSON." *Address:* 29 Fisher St., Sandwich, Kent CT13 9EJ.

**TYSON EDWARDS, Marian,** D.F.A.; sculptor in bronze, cement fondu, terracotta; *b* Manchester, 2 Oct., 1937. *m* John T. Sharples. one *s.* one *d.* *Studied:* Liverpool College of Art and High Wycombe College of Art. *Exhib:* Mall Galleries, galleries in Henley, Birmingham, Chalfont, etc. *Work in collections:* Windsor and Eton Fine Art. *Signs work:* "M. Tyson Edwards." *Address:* Wispington House, Worster Rd., Cookham, Berks. SL6 9JC.

# U

**UGLOW, Euan,** painter in oil; First Prize John Moores (1972); awarded Austin Abbey Premiere Scholarship; artist Trustee, National Gallery, London; teacher at Slade School of Art; *b* London, 10 Mar., 1932. *Educ:* Strand Grammar School for Boys. *Studied:* Camberwell School of Art and Slade School. *Work in collections:* Tate Gallery, Arts Council, Glasgow Art Gallery, Southampton Art Gallery, South Australia National Gallery, Liverpool University, Ferens A.G., Hull. Gallery & Agent: Browse & Darby, Cork St., W1. *Signs work:* "Euan Uglow." *Address:* 11 Turnchapel Mews, Cedars Rd., London SW4 0PX.

**UHT, John,** R.I. (1976); painter in oil and water-colour, sculptor in bronze, marble, wood, lead sheet; *b* Dayton, Ohio, 30 Aug., 1924. *m* Jill Gould. two *s.* one *d. Educ:* Danville High School, Illinois. *Studied:* University of Illinois Fine and Applied Arts College (1943-47, Marvin Martin, John Kennedy) and Ishmu Naguchi (1948). *Exhib:* Art, U.S.A. (1958), Reading Museum (1970), Edwin Pollard Gallery, Barry M. Keene Gallery, R.A., R.I. *Work in collections:* R.A. (bronze), Nelson Rockefeller (bronze). *Clubs:* R.I., Sherborne Arts. *Signs work:* painting, "JOHN UHT," sculpture, "UHT." *Address:* 44 Dorchester Rd., Weymouth, Dorset.

**UNDERWOOD, Keith Alfred,** Leverhulme Research Award in Fine Art (France, 1957-58); realist painter in oil and water-colour; sculptor, restorer, designer; *b* Portsmouth, 21 June, 1934. *Educ:* Monmouth School (1946-53). *Studied:* Newport College of Art (1953-57) under the late Tom Rathmell, A.R.C.A, and the late Hubert Dalwood; West of England College of Art (1960-61). *Exhib:* Welsh Arts Council, Pictures for Schools, British Art for Moscow, Young Contemporaries, Mall Galleries, Chepstow locale. *Work in collections:* Margaret Cleyton Memorial restoration (St. Mary's, Chepstow 1984), Onitsha

Cathedral, Nigeria (portrait bronze 1985), Earl of Worcester armorial sculpture (Chepstow Town Gate 1988); large historical mural, Drill Hall, Chepstow, and town map (1991); Caldicot town map (1994); twelve stained glass cartoons for windows in SS. Richard and Alexander, Bootle (1994); paintings in private collections: U.K., U.S.A., Australia, S. Africa and Netherlands. *Clubs:* The Heraldry Soc. *Signs work:* "KAU" until c1974, "K. Underwood" and "Keith Underwood" thereafter, see appendix. *Address:* 1 Madocke Rd., Sedbury, nr. Chepstow, Monmouthshire NP6 7AY.

**UPTON, Michael,** Cert. R.A.S. (1962), Abbey Scholar (Rome Scholarships); artist in mixed media, lecturer; lecturer, Royal Academy Schools (1980-); visiting lecturer various art colleges; *b* 5 Feb., 1938. *m* Susan E. Young. one *s.* one *d. Educ:* King Edward VI School, Birmingham. *Studied:* Birmingham College of Art (1954-58) under Gilbert Mason; R.A. Schools (1958-62) under Peter Greenham. *Exhib:* Various London and touring exhbns. *Work in collections:* include Arts Council, British Council and private collections. *Publications:* work repro.: Studio International, Artscribe, Flash Art, etc. *Clubs:* Chelsea Arts. *Signs work:* "Michael Upton." *Address:* c/o Anne Berthoud Gallery, 10 Clifford St., Bond St., London W1.

**UTERMOHLEN, William C.,** painter; *b* Philadelphia, Pa., 1933. *Studied:* Pennsylvania Academy of Fine Art, Philadelphia; Ruskin School of Drawing, Oxford. *Exhib:* one-man shows: Traverse Theatre Gallery, Edinburgh Festival (1963), Bonfiglioli Gallery, Oxford (1965, 1967), Nordness Gallery, N.Y. (1967), Marlborough New London Gallery (1969), Galerie d'Eendt, Amsterdam (1970, 1971), Mead Art Museum, Amherst College, Amherst, Massachusetts (1974). Visiting artist, Amherst College (1972-74). Mural, Liberal Jewish Synagogue, St. Johns Wood, London (1981); mural, Royal Free Hospital, Hampstead (1985). *Publications:* illustrated, Ten war poems by Wilfred Owen (1995). *Signs work:* "Utermohlen." *Address:* 35 Blomfield Rd., London W9 2PF.

# V

**VAIZEY, Marina (Lady Vaizey),** B.A. Radcliffe, M.A. (Cantab.); Art Critic, Sunday Times (1974-91); Editor, N.A.C.F. (1991-94), Editorial Consultant, N.A.C.F. (1994 -); Art Critic, Financial Times (1970-74); Trustee, National Galleries and Museums on Merseyside, Imperial War Museum, South Bank Centre, Geffrye Museum; *b* New York City, 16 Jan., 1938. *m* Lord Vaizey (decd. 1984). two *s.* one *d. Exhib:* Painter as Photographer, Arts Council (1982-85). *Publications:* 100 Masterpieces of Art (1979); Andrew Wyeth (1980); Artist as Photographer (1982); Peter Blake (1985); Christo (1990); Christiane Kubrick (1990); organised Critic's Choice, Tooth's (1974), Shining Through (Crafts Council, 1995). *Address:* 24 Heathfield Terr., London W4 4JE.

**VALENTINE-DAINES, Sherree E.,** Dip. A.D., U.A. (1983), S.W.A.;

painter in oil; *b* Effingham, 1956. *m* Mark Alun Rowbotham. one *s*. two *d*. *Studied:* Epsom School of Art and Design (1976-80, Leslie Worth, Peter Petersen). *Exhib:* R.B.A., R.A., Tate Gallery, R.O.I., R.W.S., R.P., Royal Overseas League, N.E.A.C., U.A., P.S., Olympic Games Exhbn., Royal Festival Hall, Barbican, Laing Landscape, N.S.P.S. *Commissions:* include Test Cricket, 5 Nations Rugby, Royal Ascot, Henley Royal Regatta. *Signs work:* "S.E.V.D." *Address:* Misty Ridge, 126 The Street, Ashtead, Surrey KT21 1AB.

**VANGO, David,** self taught artist in oil and mixed media; *b* London, 18 Feb., 1950. *Studied:* private studies at the Courtauld Inst. and Witt Library, and galleries and museums in the U.K. and abroad. Mem. Lincoln Art Soc. *Exhib:* one-man shows: Vidal Gallery, Barcelona (1977), Picture Workshop (1979), Gallery Three (1983), Loggia Gallery (1989); group shows: F.P.S. (1988, 1989), Black, White and Grey (1989, 1990), Trends, Bloomsbury Gallery (1989), Brighton Polytechnic A.G. (1989), Nina Hosali Award Exhbn. (1989, 1991), Selected work for the Arts Centre, Hemel Hempstead (1989) and St. Martin's Gallery, Trafalgar Sq. (1990), Stevenage F.P.S. (1991), Heads (1990), Loggia Gallery, F.P.S. (1992), Fairfield Halls, Croydon (1992), Loggia Gallery (1992), Lauderdale House (1992), Usher Gallery, Lincoln (1993, 1994), Scunthorpe Museum and A.G. (1993), Gagliardi'Dynamic Structure and Form (1993), Paxhaven Studio (1993). *Work in collections:* Japan, France, Spain, Germany, Italy, Australia, America, etc. *Publications:* contributor to British Contemporary art (1993). *Signs work:* see appendix. *Address:* 68 Alexander Terr., Lincoln LN1 1JE.

**VAN NIEKERK, Sarah Compton,** R.E. (1976), S.W.E. (1974), R.W.A. (1992); wood engraver; Tutor, City and Guilds of London Art School since 1978, R.A. Schools (1976-86); *b* London, 16 Jan., 1934. *m* Chris Van Niekerk. one *s*. two *d*. *Educ:* Bedales. *Studied:* Central School of Art, Slade School of Fine Art. *Exhib:* R.A., Bankside Gallery, Duncan Campbell, U.S.A., 28 one and two-man exhbns. *Work in collections:* V. & A., Fitzwilliam, Ashmolean, National Museum of Wales, National Library of Wales, U.C.L.A., Wood Engravers Soc. U.S.S.R., Fremantle Arts Centre, Graves, Hereford Museum. *Publications:* illustrations for Folio Soc., Gregynog, O.U.P., Readers Digest, Pavilion, Virago, Silent Books, Rider. *Signs work:* "Sarah van Niekerk" in pencil. *Address:* Priding House, Saul, Glos. GL2 7LG.

**VAN ROSSEM, Ru,** Hon. Mem., Academy of Fine Arts, Florence; Premio Milano (1988); Euro-medal in gold, Bonn; Gold Medal Biennale, Perugia; M.A.I. International Graphic Prize, Biennales Gorizia, Italy, Malbork, Poland; Head of Graphic Department, Tilburg Academy of Fine Art, Holland; *b* Amsterdam, 19 Mar., 1924. *m* 1st Miriam Pollock (decd.); two *s*. one *d*. 2nd Marianne van Dieren; one *s*. *Educ:* Rijksmuseumschool of Fine Art; Grammar School, Zaandam. *Exhib:* most European countries and U.S.A. *Work in collections:* Rijksmuseum and Municipal Museum, Amsterdam, Boymans Museum, Rotterdam, Bibliothèque Nationale, Paris, Museum of Modern Art, New York,

National Museum, Cracow, Cincinnati Museum, etc. *Commissions:* sculpture for St. John's Cathedral, 's Hertogenbosch. *Publications:* biography written by Frans Duister (1977, 1994). *Signs work:* "Ru Van Rossem." *Address:* Burg, Vonk de Bothstr. 54, 5037NL Tilburg, Holland.

**VEALE, Anthony McKenzie,** self taught painter in oil and acrylic, sculptor (surrealist and figurative work) in bronze, wood, marble and stone; also abstract painting and minimalist work; *b* Tonbridge, 20 Oct., 1941. *m* Susan. one *s.* two *d. Educ:* Sevenoaks School. *Exhib:* Tryon Gallery (1979), 20th Century Gallery (1985), Mall Galleries (1992). Permanent exhbn. of bronzes in sculpture garden at Buckstone House. *Publications:* cartoon illustrations: 'Hippo, Potta and Muss' (Chatto, Boyd & Oliver U.K., 1969), 'A Lemon Yellow Elephant called Trunk' (Harvey House Inc. U.S.A., 1970). *Signs work:* "Tony Veale," "Anthony Veale" or "A.V." *Address:* Buckstone House, Upton Hellions, nr. Crediton, Devon EX17 4AE.

**VENNING, Virginia,** Mem. S.W.A.; sculptor in stone, wood, clay for bronze, terracotta, including portraits; painter in water-colour; *b* London, 1913. *m* Capt. E. D. T. Churcher, C.B.E., R.N. (decd.). *Educ:* privately. *Studied:* Paris and Florence; Regent St. Polytechnic (1931), R.A. Schools (1934-39). *Exhib:* R.A. Summer Exhbn. (from 1933), S.W.A. Annual. *Work in collections:* wood and stone carvings for churches, (mostly in Somerset) and other buildings, portraits. *Signs work:* "V.M. Venning." *Address:* 26 Bimport, Shaftesbury, Dorset SP7 8AZ.

**VERDIJK, Gerald,** Silver Medal, Prix Europe (1966), Maris Prize (1964, 1967); painter; *b* Boxmeer, Holland, 1934. *Exhib:* one-man shows: Galerie Gunar, Düsseldorf, Galerie Orez, The Hague (1961, 1962, 1964, 1965, 1967, 1971, 1979), Galerie Potsdammer, Berlin, Casino Ostende, Museum Municipal, The Hague (1967), Von der Heidt Museum, Wuppertal (1968), Galerie Palette, Zürich Galerie Lock St. Gallen (1984), Groninger Museum (1970), Gemeente Museum, The Hague (1972), Galerie Peccolo Livorno (1978), Galerie La Citta, Verona, Galerie La Polena, Geneva, Galerie Jeanneret, Geneva (1979), Galerie E. München (1981), Brenda Taylor Gallery, New York (1996); Abbemuseum Eindhoven (1985), Stedelijk Museum, Amsterdam 1993 (retrospective), Noord Brabants Museum, Den Bosch (retrospective of works on paper) 1998; group shows: Amsterdam, Delft, The Hague, Berlin, Wuppertal, Brussels, Belfast, Dublin, Cork; Bienale de Paris (1961), World Fair, Montreal (1967), London, Liverpool, Paris, Stockholm, Los Angeles, Frankfurt, Tokyo, Copenhagen. *Work in collections:* Museums of The Hague, Schiedam, Brussels, Wuppertal, London, Ostend, Rotterdam, Amsterdam, Osaka. *Signs work:* see appendix. *Address:* "Les Places" Marcillac-St. Quentin, par 24200 Sarlat, Dordogne, France.

**VERITY, Colin,** A.R.I.B.A. (1965), R.S.M.A. (1975); architect, artist in oil, water-colour and gouache; retd. principal architect, Humberside C.C., Pres., Hornsea Art Soc., Mem. Fylingdales Group of Artists (N. Yorks.), Guild of

Aviation Artists; *b* Darwen, Lancs., 7 Mar., 1924. *m* Stella Elizabeth Smale. one *s*. three *d*. *Educ:* Malet Lambert High School, Hull and privately. *Studied:* Hull School of Architecture. *Exhib:* R.S.M.A., Mystic Maritime Gallery, Connecticut, U.S.A., Francis Iles Gallery, Rochester, Ferens Gallery, Hull. *Work in collections:* National Maritime Museum, Greenwich, Sultanate of Oman, Ben Line, Harrison Line, P. & O. Line, Town Docks Museum, Hull, - 16 countries. *Signs work:* "Colin Verity." *Address:* Melsa, Meaux, Beverley, E. Yorks. HU17 9SS.

**VERNON-CRYER, Joan,** A.R.C.A., R.W.S. (1970); painter in watercolour; *b* Blackburn, 21 Mar., 1911. *m* W. Fairclough. one *s*. one *d*. *Educ:* Blackburn High School and Blackburn Technical College. *Studied:* Royal College of Art (Painting School). *Exhib:* Hunting Group Competition, Mall Galleries (1990), Sunday Times Water-colour Exhbn., Mall Galleries, Glasgow Cultural Year (1990). *Publications:* work repro.: in Old Water-colour Society's volumes, Visions of Venice (Michael Spender, 1990); Water-colour Drawings and Artists Magazine (1991); La Exposicion Internacional de Acuarela (1992, 1995). *Signs work:* "Joan Vernon-Cryer." *Address:* 12 Manorgate Rd., Kingston-upon-Thames, Surrey KT2 7AL.

**VERRALL, Nicholas Andrew,** N.D.D. (1965); artist in oil, pastel, watercolour, etching and litho; *b* Northampton, 4 Jan., 1945. *m* Alayne Page. one *s*. one *d*. *Studied:* Northampton College of Art (1960-65). Full-time artist since 1970. Prizes: R.W.S. Barcham Green Prize for Water-colour, Royal Horticultural Grenfell Medal, R.A. Committee Prize from B.A.T. *Exhib:* R.A., R.W.S., R.E., R.B.A. and N.E.A.C.; mixed shows: Tryon Gallery, R.A. Upstairs Gallery, Abbott & Holder, Gallery 10; one-man shows: Upper Grosvenor, Langton Gallery Chelsea, Railings Gallery, Scene Gallery and Catto Gallery. *Work in collections:* City of London, B.A.T. Coll., Crown Life, Painshill Park Trust, Coys of Kensington. Private collections in Britain, France, America and Japan. *Signs work:* "N Verrall." *Address:* The Orchard, Ivy La., Woking, Surrey GU22 7BY.

**VICARY, Richard Henry,** R.E., R.W.A.; printmaker, (woodcuts etc.), painting, typography; late Head Printmaking Dept., Shrewsbury School of Art; *b* Sutton, Surrey, 1918. *m* Deirdre Vicary. one *s*. one *d*. *Educ:* Judd School, Tonbridge. *Studied:* Medway School of Art (1936-39); Brighton College of Art (1946); Camberwell School of Art and Crafts;, Central School of Art *Exhib:* A.I.A., Whitechapel, R.W.S., R.W.A. (Bristol) and many private galleries. *Work in collections:* various Universities and Education Authorities. *Publications:* Manual of Lithography and Manual of Advanced Lithography, (Thames & Hudson, 1976, 1977). *Signs work:* "Richard Vicary." *Address:* The Holding, Dunns Heath, Berwick, Shrewsbury SY4 3HY.

**VIGG, Bob,** B.Ed. Fine Art (Exeter,1973); landscape/seascape artist in oil; Com. mem.St. Ives Soc. of Artists; *b* Plymouth, 20 Oct., 1932. *m* Sandy Vigg. three *s*. *Studied:* Rolle College, Exeter (Alan Cotton). *Exhib:* Tregeseal Gallery,

St. Just, Penwith, R.O.I. (1983), St. Ives Soc. of Artists, Rooksmoor Bath, Penlee House Penzance, Dartington Devon, etc. *Publications:* Thomas Luny, marine artist (National Maritime Museum, Greenwich, 1981). *Signs work:* "Vigg" *Address:* The Old Chapel, Botallack, St. Just, Penzance, Cornwall TR19 7QG.

**VINE, Edward,** landscape artist in acrylic, water-colour, oil, pastel; *b* Weymouth, Dorset, 10 May, 1943. *Exhib:* regular one-man shows at Peter Hedley Gallery, Wareham and Market Cross Gallery, Sturminster Newton, Dorset; mixed exhbns. at Daler Gallery, Bournemouth, Wykeham Gallery, Stockbridge and Robert Perera Fine Art, Lymington, Hants. Artist-in-Residence at "Max Gate", Thomas Hardy's Dorchester home now owned by the National Trust. *Address:* 90 Easton St., Portland, Dorset DT5 IBT.

**VOGEL, Suzi,** S.B.A., S.W.A.; self taught botanical and landscape artist in oil on panel; b Kent, 1950; one *s.*. regularly with S.B.A. and S.W.A.; Suzi Vogel paints to celebrate the beauty of the natural world. She belongs to a long established Kentish family of passionate writers, gardeners and horticultural-ists. Now living and working in Dorset and working only in oils, she uses the finest traditional methods and materials, following in the footsteps of the Dutch and French masters of the sixteenth and seventeenth centuries. Her paintings combine the classically decorative with the botanically accurate and are appre-ciated and collected by connoisseurs of fine representational oil painting. *Publications:* example of work, picture and caption on page nine of "Drawing Flowers" by Margaret Stevens. *Signs work:* see appendix. *Address:* Flat 1, 22 Victoria Grove, Bridport, Dorset DT6 3AA.

**VOLLER, Peter Robert,** painter in oils, acrylic polymer, painted wood and paper collage; *b* Fleet, Hants., 26 Sept., 1943. *m* Tessa Philpot. two *s.* one *d.* *Studied:* Farnham School of Art. *Exhib:* R.A., London and provinces. *Signs work:* "Voller" or "Peter Voller." *Address:* 53 The Street, Wrecclesham, Farnham, Surrey GU10 4QS.

**von HARTMANN, Sylvia,** D.A. (Edin.) (1965), Post. Dip. (1966), R.S.W. (1983); artist in wax; *b* Hamburg, Germany, 8 Dec., 1942. *m* Hamish Dewar. one *s.* one *d. Educ:* Walddoerfer Schule, Hamburg-Volksdorf. *Studied:* Werkkunstschule, Hamburg (1961-63), Edinburgh College of Art (1963-66), Royal College of Art, London. *Exhib:* R.A., R.S.A. Edinburgh, R.S.W., R.G.I.F.A., The Scottish Gallery, Edinburgh, National Trust of Scotland, Grosvenor Gallery, London, Open Eye Gallery, Edinburgh, etc. *Work in col-lections:* Scottish Arts Council, Scottish National Gallery of Modern Art, City of Edinburgh Art Collection, Dundee Museum and Art Galleries, National Westminster Bank, Edinburgh, The Royal Infirmary, Edinburgh, H.M. The Queen, St. John's Hospital, Livingstone. *Publications:* Living Light, Books II and III (Holmes McDougall), The Scots Magazine (June, 1984), The Green Book Press Ltd., Bath. *Signs work:* "Sylvia von Hartmann." *Address:* Rhododendron House, 5 Whitehorse Cl., Canongate, Edinburgh EH8 8BU.

# W

**WADDELL, Heather,** M.A. St. Andrews (1972), D.F.A. (1976), Cert. Ed. London (1977); author, photographer, art critic; *b* Scotland, 1950. *Exhib:* N.S.W. House A.G., (1980), ACME Studio (1977-80), Battersea Arts Centre (1979). *Publications:* Articles on art: Artnews, Art and Australia, The Artist, Art Monthly, Glasgow Herald (1978-94), London correspondent, Vie des Arts (1979-89), The Independent, The European, The Times; author/photographer: London Art and Artists Guide (7th ed. 1997); co-author, The Artists Directory (3rd edn. 1988); photographer: Glasgow Arts Guide, N.P.G. 20th c. Archives; contributor: Encyclopaedia of London (Macmillan), Henri Goetz (1986), Time Out Publications (1987-92), L'Ecosse (1988), Londres (1997), Edns. Autrement, Paris. *Address:* 27 Holland Park Ave., London W11 3RW.

**WADSWORTH, Freda Muriel,** M.B.E. (1979), F.M.A.A. (1968), F.F.P.S. (1984); painter of geometrical abstracts, using unique technique in gouache; lecturer in medical art, University of London (1956-79); Hon. Newsletter Editor, F.P.S.; *b* London, 31 Jan., 1918. *Educ:* Vardean School, Brighton. *Studied:* Brighton School of Art (1935-39, Charles Knight, R.W.S.). *Exhib:* one-man shows: Loggia Gallery (1979, 1982, 1985, 1988); numerous London group shows including Mall Galleries and the Barbican. *Signs work:* "Freda Wadsworth." *Address:* 11 Burnham Ct., Moscow Rd., London W2 4SW.

**WADSWORTH, Hilda Marjorie,** F.F.P.S. (1988); painter in gouache of 17th and 18th c. architectural and sculptural features in historic parks and gardens; design and display executive, British Cellophane Ltd. (1949-71), freelance design (1972-80), Hon. sec. Free Painters and Sculptors (1981-87); *b* London, 5 July, 1911. *Educ:* Brighton Polytechnic (1927-29). *Studied:* Brighton School of Art (1929-34, Charles Knight, R.W.S.). *Exhib:* solo shows: Loggia Gallery (1988, 1992); group shows in London at Mall Galleries, Barbican, Loggia Gallery. *Commissions:* six paintings purchased by P. & O. Cruises for the Oriana (1994). *Signs work:* "M. Wadsworth." *Address:* 11 Burnham Ct., Moscow Rd., London W2 4SW.

**WALBOURN, Peter,** U.A. (1982); portrait painter in oil and water-colour; *b* Chingford, 22 Aug., 1910. *m* Gweneth. one *d. Educ:* Bishop's Stortford. *Studied:* Heatherleys, R.A. Schools (1928-32, Gerald Kelly, Walter Russel, Gerald Brockhurst, Fredrick Whiting). *Exhib:* R.P. R.O.I., U.A., P.S. *Work in collections:* Old Bailey, Middle Temple, University of Coleraine, American, Arab and Iranian banks. *Commissions:* portraits: H.M. Queen Elizabeth the Queen Mother for Middle Temple; Lord Denning, Master of the Rolls; Sir Hugh Wontner, Lord Mayor of London; The Duke of Abercorn and Sir Wilfred Cockcroft, Chancellors of universities; Sir James Steel and Col. Ingleton-Webber, High Sheriffs of counties; etc. *Signs work:* "`Peter Walbourn." *Address:* 1 Fair Green, Sawbridgeworth, Herts. CM21 9AG.

# WHO'S WHO IN ART

**WALCH, Kenneth Charles Crosby,** N.D.D. (1955); artist in oil, water-colour, woodwork; former A.E. art tutor with I.L.E.A. Hounslow, Bognor; *b* Wimbledon, 16 Sept., 1927. *m* Olive Winifred (decd.). *Educ:* Bradfield College. *Studied:* National Gallery Art School, Melbourne (1952-53, Murray Griffin), St. Martin's School of Art (1953-55, Bateson Mason, F. Gore). *Exhib:* Belgium (Hof de Bist), London, Germany (Unna), Hong Kong (Nishiki), Dublin. *Work in collections:* Hof de Bist, Antwerp, Chichester Centre of Arts; private collections in U.K., Europe, America, Australia. *Clubs:* Chichester Centre of Arts, Friends of Pallant Ho, Chichester Art Soc., Quaker Fellowship of Arts. *Signs work:* block letters with pencil into wet paint. *Address:* 193 Oving Rd., Chichester, W. Sussex PO19 4ER.

**WALDRON, Dylan Thomas,** B.A.Hons.; artist in egg tempera, acrylic, pencil and water-colour; *b* Newcastle-under-Lyme, 21 Aug., 1953. *Educ:* King Edward VI Grammar School, Stourbridge. *Studied:* Stourbridge College of Art (1971-72), Wolverhampton Polytechnic, Faculty of Art and Design (1972-76). *Exhib:* R.A. Summer Exhbn. (1983 to 1996), Piccadilly Gallery, Cork St., London (1981-96). *Work in collections:* West Midlands Arts. *Clubs:* Leicester Soc. of Artists *Signs work:* "Dylan Waldron" paintings initialled "D.W." *Address:* 2 Hallaton Rd., Slawston, nr. Market Harborough, Leics. LE16 7UA.

**WALES, Patricia Ann,** S.W.A. (1995), S.F.P. (1997); artist in water-colour - flower paintings; *b* Hamilton, Ontario, 27 Feb., 1933. *m* Graham Wales. two *s. Exhib:* London, Paris and Wessex Region. *Work in collections:* paintings in private collections in Australia, Americas and Western Europe. *Publications:* work repro.: greetings cards. *Clubs:* Lymington Art Group, Lyndhurst Art Group, Lymington Palette. *Address:* Willowbank, Widdow Close, Sway, Hants. SO41 6AX.

**WALKER, Edward Donald,** marine artist in oil, publisher; owner, Sumar Publications; *b* 2 Aug., 1937. *m* Susan. one *s.* one *d. Educ:* Warbreck School, Liverpool. *Studied:* Liverpool College of Art (1950-56). *Exhib:* R.S.M.A., Paris Salon, Talbot Gallery, Ethos Gallery, Lancs., Harrods London, Fulmar Gallery, N. Wales, and galleries throughout U.S.A. *Work in collections:* Liverpool Museum and private collections worldwide. *Clubs:* Liverpool Nautical Research Soc., Fine Art Trade Guild. *Signs work:* "E.D. Walker." *Address:* 1 Richmond Grove, Lydiate, Merseyside L31 0BL.

**WALKER, Jeffery,** Dip. (1982), B.A.Hons. (1985), S.D.C. (1985), F.P.S. (1989), I.S.A.S.T. (1991); painter in oil, charcoal and computer; P/T lecturer, Farnham, Worthing, Bournemouth and Winchester; *b* Scunthorpe, 11 May, 1962. *Educ:* Brumby Comprehensive, N. Lindsey Technical College, Lincoln College. *Studied:* Grimsby College (1982), Brighton Polytechnic (1985). *Exhib:* De Richter Gelder, Arnhem (1989), Diamond Valley, Australia (1989), Barbican (1991), Erte, Czechoslovakia, Wroclaw, Poland, Leningrad, U.S.S.R. *Signs work:* "J.W." and usually signed and dated on back. *Address:* 41 Waldegrave Rd., Brighton, E. Sussex BN1 6GR.

**WALKER, Richard Ian Bentham,** N.D.D. (1947), A.T.D. (1949); Mem. United Soc. of Artists, Armed Forces Art Soc., Soc. of Graphic Fine Arts; portrait and landscape painter; teacher of oil painting, Croydon Art School (1948-53); *b* Croydon, 18 Mar., 1925. *Educ:* Canford School, Dorset; Queen's College, Oxford; Founder's Prize, Royal Drawing Soc. (1938). *Studied:* Croydon School of Art (1945-48), London University (1949), Slade School. *Exhib:* R.A., R.P., R.B.A., R.O.I., Paris Salon, Imperial Institute, etc.; one-man shows, Oxford, Croydon, Mall Galleries (1978), Alpine Galleries (1981). *Work in collections:* Portraits of: Dr. Herbert Howells for Royal College of Music (1972); A. K. Chesterton (1973); Sir Reginald Wilson for the Brompton Hospital; Sir Thomas Holmes Sellors for the Middlesex Hospital; C.B. Canning (1989), John Hardie (1990), Ian Wallace (1991), all for Canford School; Sir William Penney, Reading A.G. (1953); London panorama, Museum of London (1978); Croydon Landscape (1939), for the Croydon Collection. *Publications:* drawings of Stokowski, Havergal Brian, etc., published Triad Press, London (1971-73); illustrations to C. Palmer's biography of Herbert Howells (1993). *Signs work:* "RICHARD WALKER" and see appendix. *Address:* 72 Coombe Rd., Croydon CR0 5SH.

**WALKER, Roy,** A.R.E. (1975); painter/etcher; Director, Print Workshop, Penwith Society of Arts, St. Ives, Cornwall; *b* Welling, Kent, 25 Aug., 1936. *m* Margaret Anne Walker. two *s.* one *d. Studied:* Gravesend School of Art (1951-52), Regent St. Polytechnic (1952-54); Central School of Art (1957-60). *Exhib:* one-man shows: Camel Gallery, Wadebridge, Orion Gallery, Penzance, Plymouth Art Centre; three-man show: Marlborough Graphics; joint shows: Penwith Society of Arts, Wills Lane Gallery, St. Ives, Newlyn Gallery. *Work in collections:* Print Room, V. & A. *Signs work:* "Roy Walker." *Address:* Warwick House, Sea View Terr., St. Ives; Studio: 6 Porthmeor Studios, Back Rd. West, St. Ives.

**WALKER, Sandra,** artist in water-colour; *b* Washington D.C., U.S.A. *Exhib:* many mixed and one-man shows: Singer & Friendlander (1st Prize); R.I., R.W.S., R.B.A., Galerie Mensch, Hamburg; Bourne Gallery; Alresford Gallery; Mall Galleries; Watermans, London; Gallery Henoch, N.Y., U.S.A., Franz Bader Gallery, Washington .D.C., Corcoran Gallery, Washington .D.C., Smithsonian Inst., National Geographic, *Publications:* work illustrated: Watercoulor Step by Step (Harper Collins, 1993), How to Draw and Paint Texture (Harper Collins, 1993), Collins Complete Painting Course (Harper Collins, 1993), Shapes and Edges (Sandstone Books, 1996), Houses and Buildings (Cassells Press 1991), Encyclopedia of Water-colour Techniques (Healine Press, 1990)*Address:* 39 Stewkley Rd., Wing, Leighton Buzzar, Beds.

**WALKLIN, Carol,** A.R.C.A. (1953), F.R.E. (1986); graphic artist and printmaker; *m* Colin Walklin, A.R.C.A., co-Director 'Mullet Press' tutor-lecturer in printmaking. *Studied:* Beckenham School of Art and Royal College of Art. *Exhib:* widely in U.K. including Bankside Gallery and Beatrice Royal Gallery.

*Work in collections:* U.K., U.S.A., Europe and the Far East. *Commissions:* British Council, BBC T.V. 'Jackanory', Post Office U.K. (stamp designs and air letters). *Clubs:* Senior Fellow, Royal Soc. of Painter-Printmakers. *Signs work:* "Walklin." *Address:* 2 Thornton Dene, Beckenham, Kent BR3 3ND.

**WALLACE, Donald Ian Mackenzie,** B.A. (Economics, Law), Cantab.; company director; artist in pencil, ink, gouache; *b* Gt. Yarmouth, Norfolk, 14 Dec., 1933. *m* Wendy. three *d. Educ:* Loretto School. *Commissions:* several annually. *Publications:* Birds of the Western Palearctic (Field Characters, plates); five other books; many papers. *Clubs:* Soc. of Wildlife Artists. *Signs work:* "dim wallace" *Address:* Mount Pleasant Farm, Main Rd., Anslow, Burton-on-Trent, E. Staffs. DE13 9QE.

**WALLER, Jonathan Neil,** B.F.A. (Hons.), M.A. (Painting); artist in oil and charcoal; *b* Stratford upon Avon, 16 Apr., 1956. *Educ:* Cherry Orchard High, Northampton, Northampton Grammar School. *Studied:* Nene College, Northampton (1979-80), Coventry (Lanchester) Polytechnic (1980-83), Chelsea School of Art (1984-85). *Exhib:* one-man shows: Paton Gallery, London (1986, 1988), Flowers East, London (1990); group shows: 1984: New Contemporaries, I.C.A. London, Midland View 3 (major prizewinner), 1988: London, Glasgow, N.Y., Metropolitan Museum, N.Y., New British Painting, Cincinnati (touring), 1989: The Thatcher Years, Flowers East, 1991: Kunst Europa, Karlsruhe, Germany. *Publications:* Jonathan Waller (Flowers East, 1990). *Signs work:* "J.W.98." *Address:* Basement Flat, 166 Amhurst Rd., London E8 2AZ.

**WALLER, Margaret Mary,** F.I.A.L. (1958, mem. of Council), A.T.D., Mem. Liverpool Academy (1953); painter in oils, portrait, landscape, and decorative church work in gold leaf, also water-colour and egg tempera; *b* Yorks., 13 Nov., 1916. *m* Stephen Bryant, 1989. *Educ:* Friary Convent School (Venice), Belvedere School (Liverpool). *Studied:* Liverpool College of Art (1934-37) and R.A. Schools (1937-39). *Exhib:* R.A., S.W.A., R.P., Paris Salon, Funchal, Madeira (1992); executed Altar-piece for the Chapel of St. John, Guernsey (1960); also large decorative panels for St. Stephen's Church (1964). Invited to U.S.A. (1986) to give exhbn. of water-colours. Commissioned to paint in St. Malo, France (1993). *Clubs:* Sandon Studios Soc. (Liverpool), Reynolds (London). *Signs work:* "MARGARET WALLER." *Address:* Les Sauterelles, St. Jacques, Guernsey GY1 1SW; and Mayfield Studio, Sark.

**WALPOLE, Josephine Ailsa,** artist specialising in flower painting and botanical illustration; *b* Cockfield, Suffolk, 27 Apr., 1927. *m* Derek Walpole. one *s. Educ:* East Anglian School for Girls, Bury St. Edmunds; Notre Dame High School, Norwich. *Studied:* privately under Stuart Somerville. *Exhib:* London and East Anglia. *Publications:* 'Anna' Memorial, Biography of Anna Zinkeisen; Biography of Leonard Squirrell, R.W.S., R.E.; Leonard Squirrell, Etchings and Engravings; Life and Work of Martin Kidner; Vernon Ward (Biography); 'Roses in a Suffolk Garden'. *Signs work:* "J. Walpole." *Address:*

The Green House, 15 Cooper's Rd., Martlesham Heath, Ipswich, Suffolk IP5 3SJ.

**WALTON, Barbara Louise,** M.F.A. (Hons.) (1981), Post.Grad. Dip. Painting and Drawing (1982); painter in oil and acrylic paint on canvas and paper; *b* Bishop Auckland, 30 Dec., 1955. *m* Dursun Cilingir, doctor. *Educ:* Queen Anne Grammar School. *Studied:* Edinburgh University/College of Art (Elizabeth Blackadder, David Michie). *Exhib:* York University (1982), Gloucester College of Art (1983), Paisley Art Inst. drawing competition (1987), N.P.G. portrait competition (1987, 1989), Mall Galleries Open (1989); solo shows: Mercury Gallery (1988, 1993), Grape Lane Gallery, York (1989); regular exhib. with Mercury Gallery since 1986. *Signs work:* "B.L. Walton" *Address:* 31 St. John's Rd., Exeter EX1 2HR.

**WALTON, John,** D.F.A. (Lond. 1949), R.P. (1976); portrait painter in oil and tempera; Principal, Heatherley School of Fine Art, London; Governor, Federation of British Artists, Mem., Royal Soc of Portrait Painters; *b* Birkenhead, 5 Dec., 1925. *m* (1) Annette d'Exéa; two *s*. one *d*. (2) Alice Low. *Educ:* Birkenhead School, Edge Grove School, Aldenham School. *Studied:* Ruskin School of Fine Art (1944-45, Albert Rutherston), Slade School of Fine Art (1945-49, Randolph Schwabe). *Exhib:* R.A., R.P., Paris Salon (Hon. mention), Academie des Beaux Arts, Institut de France. *Clubs:* Chelsea Arts. *Signs work:* "John Walton." *Address:* 30 Park Rd., Radlett, Herts. WD7 8EQ.

**WANG, Elizabeth,** F.S.B.A. (1987); Founder mem. Soc. of Botanical Artists, Medalife Art award (1990); artist in water-colour, oil, pencil, writer; *b* Slough, 1942. *m* M.K. Wang. two *s*. one *d*. *Educ:* Dr. Challoner's Grammar School, Amersham. *Studied:* part-time at St. Albans College of Art. *Exhib:* F.B.A. Mall Galleries; mixed shows: still-life and botanical works: S.B.A., R.A., R.I., Fine Art (Solihull); solo shows: recent religious works: Harpenden, Westminster Cathedral, Bar Convent Museum, York. *Publications:* illustrated: The Way of the Cross (Collins Liturgical 1988). *Signs work:* "Wang" or "E.W." *Address:* 25 Rothamsted Ave., Harpenden, Herts. AL5 2DN.

**WARD, Frank C.,** A.R.C.A.; painter; *b* Stradbroke, Suffolk, 1914. *m* Kathleen Walne, painter; three children. *Educ:* Stowmarket Grammar School. *Studied:* Ipswich Art School, R.C.A. *Exhib:* R.A., Essex County Art (1936), N.E.A.C. (1946), Chelsea Arts Club, Cooling Gallery (1953), Compendium 2 (1972), Brighton (1975), Stradbroke (1980). *Work in collections:* Garman Ryan Art Collection, Walsall, donated by Lady Epstein (1973). Produced war drawings, The Guns of 6 A.G.R.A. Included in Artillery Commemoration Book 1939-45. Recreated Black Oil, used by Dutch and Venetian Schools. *Publications:* Mixed Palette (Frank Ward and Kathleen Walne) by David Buckman (Sansom & Company, 1997). *Signs work:* "F.C. Ward." *Address:* 39 Kensington Pl., Brighton, E. Sussex BN1 4EJ.

**WARD, Gordon,** D.F.A. Lond., R.W.A.; artist in all mediums; formerly Head of Painting, Gloucestershire College of Arts and Technology; *b* N.

Walsham, Norfolk, 1932. *m* Maureen Liddell. one *s*. two *d*. *Educ:* Paston Grammar School, N. Walsham, Norfolk. *Studied:* Norwich School of Art (1949-53), Slade School of U.C.L. (1955-57). *Work in collections:* Royal West of England Academy, Robert Fleming Holdings, The Royal Bank of Scotland, Prudential Assurance and various private collections in Europe, America and Australia. *Signs work:* "GORDON WARD" and date. *Address:* Prospect House, Oakridge Lynch, Stroud, Glos. GL6 7NZ.

**WARD, J. S.,** A.R.C.A., V.P.R.P., R.A.; painter in oil and water-colour; *b* Hereford, 1917. *m* Alison Ward. four *s*. two *d*. *Educ:* St. Owens School, Hereford. *Studied:* R.C.A. under Gilbert Spencer. *Work in collections:* H.M. the Queen, N.P.G., R.A., Preston A.G., Maas Gallery, Hereford. *Publications:* Alphonse by George Ward; Cider with Rosie by Laurie Lee; Little Kingdom by Richard Church; Autobiography of H. E. Bates. *Clubs:* Athenæum. *Signs work:* "John Ward." *Address:* Bilting Ct., Bilting, nr. Ashford, Kent.

**WARD, Joan,** A.R.C.A. (1949), N.S. (1979); sculptor in resins, wood, stone, etc.; *b* London, 10 Jan., 1925. *m* T. W. Ward. one *s*. one *d*. *Educ:* Croydon High School for Girls. *Studied:* Bromley Art School, Royal College of Art (1945-48, Willi Soukop, Frank Dobson). *Exhib:* R.B.A, N.E.A.C., N.S., Coach House Gallery, C.I. (1987); group exhbns. in London Parks and Questers, Ealing, Wherry Quay and Grove House, Ipswich, Digby Gallery, Colchester, Chappel Galleries, Essex. *Clubs:* N.S., Suffolk Group and Ipswich Art Soc. *Signs work:* "Joan Ward." *Address:* Hollydene, Ipswich Rd., Holbrook, nr. Ipswich, Suffolk IP9 2QT.

**WARD, Nicholas,** Dip.A.D. (1971), R.A. Schools (1974), R.E. (1992); artist and printmaker in etching and pencil; *b* Gt. Yarmouth, 10 Jan., 1950. *m* Elizabeth Somerville. one *s*. *Educ:* Lowestoft County Grammar School. *Studied:* Lowestoft School of Art (1967-68), St. Martin's School of Art (1968-71, Alan Cooper, James Stroudley), R.A. Schools (1971-74, Denis Lucas, Peter Greenham). *Exhib:* R.A. Summer Shows (1982, 1984-87, 1990, 1994), R.E. Annual (1988-97), British Miniature Print (1989, 1994, 1997), Bradford Print Biennale (1990), National Print Exhbn. (1995, 1996, 1997); one-man shows 1974-97. *Work in collections:* Norfolk Museums, Ipswich Museum. *Signs work:* "N. Ward." *Address:* 38 Bulmer La., Winterton-on-Sea, Gt. Yarmouth, Norfolk NR29 4AF.

**WARD, Thomas William,** A.R.C.A. (1949), R.E. (1953), R.W.S. (1957); water-colour painter, draughtsman, etcher, illustrator of maritime subjects; one time Director of Studies (Illustration) Harrow C.H.E.; *b* Sheffield, 8 Nov., 1918. *m* Joan. one *s*. one *d*. *Educ:* Nether Edge Grammar School, Sheffield; Sea Service 1936-37. *Studied:* part time, Sheffield (1937-39, Eric Jones, A.R.C.A.); Military Service (1939-46); R.C.A. (1946-50, (Silver Medal 1949), R.S. Austin, R.A., Malcolm Osborne, R.A.). *Exhib:* Walker Gallery (1957-60), Wakefield City A.G. (1962), Shipley A.G. (1962), Middlesbrough A.G. (1963), St. John's College, York (1965), Bohun Gallery (1974, 1982), Digby Gallery

(1981), Coach House Gallery, C.I. (1987), Bankside Gallery (1987), Chappel Gallery. *Work in collections:* National Gallery of New Zealand, V. & A., Oxford University Junior Common Room, S. London A.G. *Publications:* illustrated, Fast Sailing Ships, Merchant Sailing Ships 1775-1815, Merchant Sailing Ships 1815-1850, Merchant Sailing Ships 1850-1875, Schooners in Four Centuries (all by D.R. MacGregor), Country Life Book of Nautical Terms under Sail. *Signs work:* see appendix. *Address:* Hollydene, Ipswich Rd., Holbrook, Ipswich IP9 2QT.

**WARDEN, Peter Campbell,** A.R.B.A. (1982), R.B.A. (1994), D.A. (1976), Post. Dip. (1977); award, Robert Colquhoun (1976); 1st prize Devon and Cornwall Figurative Art competition (1992); painter in oil, water-colour, pen, pencil; *b* Vancouver, Canada, 19 Mar., 1950. *m* Lorna Hawes. one *d. Educ:* Lancing College. *Studied:* Glasgow School of Art (1972-77). *Exhib:* R.A., R.B.A., R.S.A., R.G.I., R.S.W.; one-man shows: Malaga, Marbella, Dumfries, Sterts. *Work in collections:* Kilmarnock and Loudon D.C.; Sociedad Economica, Malaga. *Publications:* work repro.: various art magazines. *Signs work:* "Peter C. Warden" and date. *Address:* 57 Sunrising, East Looe, Cornwall PL13 1ND.

**WARMAN, Oliver Byrne,** R.B.A., R.O.I.; painter in oil of landscapes, houses, gardens, boats, cattle; Chief Executive, Federation of British Artists; Director, Arts News Agency (1983-92); *b* London, 10 June, 1932. Former regular officer Welsh Guards. *Educ:* Stowe, Exeter University, Royal Military College of Science, Staff College Camberley, Balliol College, Oxford. *Studied:* Exeter University. *Exhib:* R.A., R.B.A., R.W.A., N.E.A.C., R.S.M.A., R.O.I. *Work in collections:* Lancaster House, all major Banks, Sultan of Oman, Emir of Kuwait, American Embassy. *Publications:* Royal Society of Portrait Painters (joint, 1984), Arnhem, 1944 (1971). *Clubs:* Cavalry and Guards, Chelsea Arts, Royal Cornwall Yacht. *Signs work:* "O.B.W." or "Oliver Warman." *Address:* 1 and 2 The Row, Mollington, nr. Banbury, Oxon. OX17 1BH.

**WARMAN, Sylvia (Mrs.),** Ass. des A. Francais; portrait sculptor and painter; Wells Prize in Fine Art Reading University (1952); Owen Ridley Prize in Fine Art Reading University (1954); Bronze Medal (Sculpture) Paris Salon (1969); Silver Medal (Sculpture) Paris Salon (1973); Gold Medal Accademia Italia (1981); Hon. Sec. National Society Painters, Sculptors Printmakers (1978-83) Vice-President (1984/5); *b* St. Leonards on Sea, Sussex. *m* J. Royce Warman. three *d. Studied:* Reading University (1947-54). *Exhib:* various including R.A., London, and West of England R.A., five times Paris Salon. *Address:* 1 Chester St., Caversham, Reading RG4 8JH.

**WARNER, Robert,** artist in oil and water-colour; *b* Colchester, 14 Sept., 1947. *Studied:* Colchester School of Art (1964-71, John Nash, Peter Coker). *Exhib:* R.O.I., N.E.A.C., R.I., R.A. (1974-84, 1986, 1988, 1991, 1992, 1993), Athena Art Awards (1987), Hunting Group (1988), Sunday Times Exhbns. (1988, 1990, 1992, 1996, 1997), Laing Art Competition (1990, 1991, 1992,

1994, 1996), Mall Galleries, prizewinner 32nd Essex Open and 35th best water-colour; one-man shows: The Minories, Colchester (1973), Mercury Theatre (1972, 1980, 1985), Chappel Gallery, Essex. *Work in collections:* Epping Museum, private collections in Britain and America. *Publications:* work repro.: R.A. Illustrated (1980, 1988). *Clubs:* Colchester Art. Soc. *Signs work:* "R. Warner." *Address:* St. Elmer, Queens Rd., W. Bergholt, Colchester, Essex CO6 3HE.

**WARNES, Robin,** B.A.(Hons), R.A. Schools Cert. (Postgrad.); painter in oil, charcoal, pastel, acrylic, pencil; David Murray Studentship, Turner Gold medal for Landscape Painting (1980), regional prize winner, Laing Landscape Exhbn. (1990); Artist in Residence, Ipswich Museums and Galleries (1989-90); *b* Ipswich, 13 Mar., 1952. *m* Vanessa. two *s*. one *d*. *Studied:* Ipswich School of Art (1972-74, Colin Moss), Canterbury College of Art (1974-77, Tom Watt), R.A. Schools (Peter Greenham, C.B.E., R.A.). *Exhib:* R.A., Federation of British Artists, Laing Landscape, John Russell Gallery Ipswich, Cadogan Gallery London, Chappel Gallery Colchester. *Work in collections:* Ipswich Borough Council, Suffolk C.C. *Signs work:* "R. Warnes" or "R.W." *Address:* 77 Rosehill Rd., Ipswich, Suffolk IP3 8ET.

**WARREN, Michael John,** N.D.D. (1958), S.WL.A. (1971); *b* Wolverhampton, 26 Oct., 1938. *m* Kathryne. one *s*. one *d*. *Educ:* Wolverhampton Grammar School. *Studied:* Wolverhampton College of Art (1954-58). *Exhib:* one-man shows, Moorland Gallery (1972, 1974, 1977, 1979), Carl Battaglia Galleries, N.Y. (1978), Barbican Art Centre (1984), Jane Neville Gallery (1988), Wildlife A.G. Lavenham (1994). Designed 1980 issue British Post Office stamps 'Birds'; designed Audubon U.S.A. stamps 1985-97. Designed 1990/1 issue Republic of Marshall Islands postage stamps; U.K. Habitat stamp (1996-97); 1997 Republic of Marshall Islands, W.W.F. postage stamps. *Work in collections:* S.W.A.N. *Commissions:* 1985-87 Unicover Corporation U.S.A., paintings from 50 States; 1990-92 Unicover / Ducks Unlimited U.S.A., 50 paintings North American Wildfowl; Tarmac Calendar since 1995; work for R.S.P.B. *Publications:* Shorelines. Bibliography: 20th Century Wildlife Artists. Works with artists for Nature Foundation. *Clubs:* Nottinghamshire Birdwatchers (President). *Signs work:* "warren" (paintings), "Michael Warren" (prints). *Address:* The Laurels, The Green, Winthorpe, Notts. NG24 2NR.

**WASIM, L.,** painter in oil and water-colours; nominated as an "Academic of Italy with Gold Medal" and Gold Plaque "Premio d'Italia 1986"; awarded Golden Centaur 1982 Prize with Gold Medal; and International Parliament U.S.A. Gold Medal of Merit; conferred Honoris Causa diploma "Master of Painting" from Salsomaggiore International Seminar of Modern and Contemporary Art, and Diploma of Merit from Italian University of Arts; Institute of Art Contemporer at Milano conferred the Great Gold Medal with the Institute's emblem in 24 carat gold on brass with box and relative certificate of merit for "Premio Milano 1988"; 20th Century Award Medal Achievement '96 from International Biographical Centre Cambridge, England; *b* Bandung, Java, 9 May, 1929. *Studied:* Graduated from The Central Academy of Arts, Beijing (1956). Instructor of Shanxi Provincial College of Fine Arts, Xian (1956-59). Court painter in Indonesian Presidential Palaces, Jakarta and Bogor (1961-67). Study tour in Asia and Europe (1975-80); participated several art exhbns. in Indonesia and Europe. *Work in collections:* Indonesian Palaces Museums, Jakarta and Bogor; The Asia and Pacific Museum, Warsaw, etc. *Signs work:* "L. Wasim" and see appendix. *Address:* J1 Tanah Sereal V no. 6, Jakarta Barat 11210, Indonesia.

**WATANABE, Naohiko,** M.A. (1996), A.R.E. (1996); Julian Trevelyan Hon. R.E. Memorial Award, National Print Exhbn. (1996); student in print-making and photo media (screen printing); Research Degree student at Central St. Martin's College. *Studied:* Central St. Martin's College of Art and Design. *Address:* 1-81 Kasatori-Cho, Nishi-Ku, Nagoya City, Aichi, Japan 451; and 40 Parade Mansions, Watford Way, London NW4 3JJ.

**WATERFIELD, Ken,** S.WL.A. (1972); landscape and wildlife artist in oil and acrylics; *b* Watford, 7 Nov., 1927. *m* Enid. two *s.* two *d. Studied:* Watford School of Art (1940-43). *Exhib:* Mall Galleries, Medici, Guildhall London, Southern Regional Galleries; major one-man show, Winchester City Gallery (1979). *Work in collections:* Oxford C.C., King Alfred's College, Winchester. *Publications:* work repro.: illus. profiles, R.S.P.B. Magazine 'Birds' (Autumn, 1978); Oxford Mail (28 Oct., 1976). Winner, Natural World Art Award (1988, 1995). *Signs work:* "Waterfield." Later work displays strong abstract characteristics. *Address:* Plaintiles, Uploders, Bridport, Dorset DT6 4NR.

**WATERS, Linda Mercedes,** B.A.Hons. (1977); painter, illustrator and designer in water-colour, pen and ink, wood engraving; *b* Monmouthshire, 10 Nov., 1955. *Educ:* Chepstow School. *Studied:* Gwent C.H.E. Faculty of Art and Design, Newport (1974-77). *Exhib:* Royal West of England Academy, Medici Gallery, Oriel Cardiff, etc. *Work in collections:* historic reconstructions of Chepstow in Chepstow Museum; many private collections. *Publications:* several books and magazines illustrated. *Signs work:* "Linda Waters" or "L. Waters." *Address:* 41 Hardwick Ave., Chepstow, Monmouthshire NP6 5DS.

**WATKINS, Frances Jane Grierson (Peggy),** oil, water-colour, pencil artist; speciality, pencil portraiture; jewellery; instructor silverwork and jewellery Hereford College of Art (1957-72); *b* 24 July, 1919. *m* Rev. Alfred Felix Maceroni Watkins; one *s* (decd). one *d. Educ:* Elms Private School, Herefordshire School of Art, Birmingham School of Jewellery. *Exhib:* R.A., R.S.A., R.B.A., R.W.A., R.B.S.A., National Eisteddfod, Herefordshire Arts and Crafts. *Work in collections:* Hereford A.G.; Lady Hawkins Grammar School; Agric. Exec. Com.; Hereford City Art Gallery; Hereford RDC (badge of office). *Signs work:* "PEGGY WATKINS." *Address:* Leylines, 26 Southbank Rd., Hereford HR1 2TJ.

# WHO'S WHO IN ART

**WATSON, Arthur James,** D.A., A.R.S.A.; sculptor/printmaker; Course Director, Master of Fine Art, Duncan of Jordanstone College of Art and Design, Dundee; *b* Aberdeen, 6 June, 1951. *Educ:* Aberdeen Grammar School. *Studied:* Grays School of Art, Aberdeen (1969-74). *Exhib:* Venice Biennale (1990), New Directions, Sarajevo (1988), Common Ground, Utrecht (1995). *Work in collections:* Aberdeen A.G. and Museum, Scottish Arts Council. *Commissions:* North of Scotland Hydro Electric Board, University of Aberdeen, P. & O. Cruises, Monklands District Council, Forest Enterprise. *Signs work:* see appendix. *Address:* 16 Pilot Sq., Footdee, Aberdeen AB11 5DS.

**WATSON, Heather,** A.R.M.S. (1992), H.S. (1989); miniaturist painter in water-colour; *b* Coventry, 10 Mar., 1939. *m* William James Egerton Smith. *Educ:* Stoke Park School, Coventry. *Exhib:* R.A., R.M.S., Llewellyn Alexander (Fine Arts) Ltd., Medici Gallery, London, Linda Blackstone Gallery, Pinner, Hilliard Exhbns. Wells; solo shows: Dorset and N. Yorks, Nunnington Hall, National Trust Property, N. Yorks. *Signs work:* see appendix. *Address:* Dale Cottage, Dale End, Kirkbymoorside, N. Yorks. YO6 6EQ.

**WATSON-GANDY, Basia,** B.A.Hons., S.W.A., I.P.A., Grollo d'Ora Silver Medal (1980), Gold Medal (1981); painter on china, porcelain and ceramics using glazes, lustres, goldwork; lecturer and researcher in the Industry; lecturer. Founder Com. mem. and past president, B.C.P.A.A. Commissioned work in private collections throughout the world.; *Publications:* many magazine articles; appearances on TV and radio. *Clubs:* S.W.A., Confraternity of Polish Artists, Virginia Water Art Soc., Visual Images Group. *Signs work:* see appendix. *Address:* Squirrel Court Studio, Hare La., Little Kingshill, Gt. Missenden, Bucks. HP16 0EF.

**WATSON STEWART (née GIBB), (Lady) Avril Veronica,** D.St.J. (1997), F.R.S.A. (1969), Hon.F.B.I.D. (1979), Hon.M.Aust.S.C. (1983); artist/calligrapher/lettering designer on vellum, glass, metals, stone; worldwide lecturer; *b* Glasgow. *m* Sir James Watson Stewart, Bt. (decd. 1988). *Educ:* Glasgow High School for Girls, Glasgow and West of Scotland College of Commerce (now University of Strathclyde). *Studied:* Glasgow School of Art (1950, Prof. Colin Horsmann). *Exhib:* California, Norfolk, Va., St. Andrews, Dunfermline, Greenock A.G., National Library of Scotland, Australia. *Work in collections:* V. & A., and private collections. *Clubs:* Royal Scottish Automobile. *Signs work:* owl followed by maiden name - see appendix. *Address:* Undercliff Court, Wemyss Bay. PA18 6AL Scotland.

**WATT, Gilbert,** D.A. (1946), A.R.B.S. (1982), Landseer bronze medal; Cert. of Merit (R.A. 1952), Prix de Rome (1952); sculptor in clay, stone, steel, wood; *b* Aberdeen, 19 Sept., 1918. *m* Irene Mae. *Studied:* Gray's School of Art, Aberdeen, under T.B. Huxley-Jones; R.A. Schools under Maurice Lambert; British School at Rome. *Exhib:* R.A.; R.S.A.; Rome; Leicester Galleries; Royal Festival Hall; Arts Council Travelling Exhbn.; G.I.; Aberdeen A.G.; Scone Palace; Shakespeare Birthplace Trust Exhbn.; Taliesin Art Centre, Swansea

University; one-man show, Inverurie, Aberdeenshire. *Work in collections:* Britain, America, W. Germany. *Signs work:* "Gilbert Watt." *Address:* Riverside, 4 Ellon Rd., Bridge of Don, Aberdeen AB2 8EA.

**WATTS, Mrs. Dorothy,** S.W.A. (1952), Mem. Federation of British Artists; artist in water-colour; early years, fashion designer for London and Northern papers; *b* London, 3 Apr., 1905. *m* A. Gordon Watts, LL.B., solicitor. *Studied:* Brighton College of Arts under J. Morgan Rendle, R.I., R.B.A. *Exhib:* R.A., R.I., R.B.A., S.W.A., Britain in Water-colours and provincial galleries. *Work in collections:* Hove Art Collection. *Publications:* work repro.: in Londoner's England, various Christmas cards and in newspapers, London and provincial. *Clubs:* S.W.A. *Signs work:* see appendix. *Address:* Southwoods, 65 Surrenden Rd., Brighton, Sussex BN1 6PQ.

**WATTS, Joan Alwyn,** A.R.M.S.; portrait miniatures and water-colour landscapes; *b* Birmingham, 19 Dec., 1921. *m* Ronald O. Watts. one *s.* one *d. Educ:* Birmingham College of Art. *Exhib:* Birmingham Soc. of Artists, Royal Miniature Soc., Paris Salon, various exhbns. in America and Australia; permanent exhbn. Art Bureau, London. *Publications:* The Royal Miniature Society 100 Years (a portrait min. requested for this publication). *Address:* Dial Cottage, Bannut Tree La., Bridstow, nr. Ross-on-Wye, Herefords. HR9 6AJ.

**WATTS, Michael Gorse,** (otherwise PIKE, Septimus - cartoonist), A.R.I.B.A. (1965), M.F.P.S. (1989); artist, cartoonist, illustrator, in ink, acrylic, water-colour; *b* Stepney, London, 3 Dec., 1934. *m* Meg Wattson Dean; three s. one *d* by first marriage. *Educ:* St. Edward's School. *Studied:* Oxford School of Technology and Art (1951-54), S.W. Essex School of Art (1960-62). *Exhib:* Group, solo, etc., in London, the home counties and the provinces. Work in private collections at home and abroad. *Publications:* work repro.: numerous articles, cartoons and illustrations. *Clubs:* Free Painters and Sculptors, Chichester, Lewisham, Selsey. *Signs work:* see appendix. *Address:* 27 Sutherland St., London SW1V 4JU.

**WATTS, Peter,** F.R.B.S. (1970); sculptor in wood and stone; *b* Chilcompton, Bath, 12 Oct., 1916. *m* Anne Mary Coulson. two *s.* one *d. Educ:* Downside School. *Studied:* Bath School of Art (1937) under Clifford Ellis, apprenticed (1938) to Lindsey Clark, F.R.B.S., in London; also at City and Guilds School of Art, Kennington (1938-39). *Commissions:* Principal commissioned works in U.K.: Oban Cathedral (1951), St. Mary and St. Joseph's Church, Poplar, (1952), St. Mary's Church, Highfield St., Liverpool (1953), Bath Abbey, (West Front) (1959-60), Prinknash Abbey (1971), Downside Abbey (1974); in U.S.A.: Gethsemani Abbey, Kentucky (1955-64), St. John's Abbey, Collegeville, Minn. (1962), Sun of Justice Church, Benson, Vermont (1962-65), private collection of Mr. Chauncey Stillman, Amenia, N.Y. (1965-1970). *Signs work:* carved monogram, see appendix. *Address:* The Maltings, Wellow, Bath, Avon. BA2 8QJ.

**WATTSON DEAN, Meg,** H.S.; specialist in miniatures and glass engraving;

artist/sculptor; *b* Luton, 11 Nov., 1929. *m* Michael Watts. one *s*. one *d*. *Educ:* Bedford High School. *Studied:* Rolle College, Exmouth (1968-70). *Exhib:* with R.M.S. (1989-96), Hilliard Soc., 'A Million Brushstrokes' at Llewellyn Alexander Galleries, Florida, Washington and Georgia Miniature Art Socs. (1991-94), Guild of Glass Engravers, Westminster Arts Council; two-person exhbns. with Michael Watts. *Work in collections:* Chelsea and Westminster Hospital, private collections U.K. and U.S.A. *Clubs:* Hilliard Soc., Guild of Glass Engravers, Miniature Art Soc. of Florida. *Signs work:* "Meg Wattson Dean" and see appendix. *Address:* 27 Sutherland St., London SW1V 4JU.

**WAUGH, Eric,** A.R.C.A. (1953), R.I. (1990); artist in water-colour; *b* London, 15 Dec., 1929. *Studied:* Croydon School of Art (1946-50), R.C.A. (1950-53). *Exhib:* Ashgate Gallery, Farnham (1965-67), Geffrye Museum (1968), Roland, Browse & Delbanco (1971), Arte Benimarco, Spain (1980), Galeria de Arte Denia, Spain (1981), Galeria de Arte Javea, Spain (1982), R.A., R.I., R.B.A., London Group, Sport in the Fine Arts, Madrid. *Work in collections:* Mexico, U.S.A., Australia, Spain, U.K. *Publications:* articles written for various magazines; Painting in Acrylics - A Correspondence Course (Pitmans). *Signs work:* "Eric Waugh." *Address:* 9 Mead Rd., Edenbridge, Kent TN8 5DD.

**WAUTERS, Jef,** artist (painter); *b* B9910 Mariakerke, 26 Feb., 1927. *m* Denise D'hooge. one *s*. one *d*. *Studied:* Sup. Inst. St. Lucas and Academy of Fine Arts, Ghent. *Exhib:* numerous one-man and group exhbns. *Work in collections:* New York, Chicago, San Francisco, Los Angeles, Paris, München, Brussels, Rome, Bern, The Haegue e.o. Diff. museums. *Publications:* Palet (300 numb. ex.), "Paris-Roma" sketch-book, (500 numbered ex.), Jef Wauters by J. Murez, Jef Wauters (Ed. Aro, Roma) by G. Selvaggi, Jef Wauters (ed. Arben Press Switzerland). *Signs work:* see appendix. *Address:* 7 Rode Beukendreef, 9831 St. Martens Latem, Belgium; and 3 rue Chérubini, Paris 2.

**WEBB, Elizabeth,** A.R.C.M., (1953), G.R.S.M. (London) (1955); artist in oil on canvas or board; music teacher; *b* Fakenham, 7 Sept., 1931. *m* (1) Frank Rayer (decd.), (2) Graham Webb (decd.). two *s*. *Educ:* The Park School, Yeovil; Royal College of Music, London. *Studied:* Evening Classes with Mary Bairds (1989-93). *Exhib:* R.A., Paris Salon, Meridian International Center, Washington, Sui Loung Gallery, Hong Kong. *Signs work:* "Elizabeth Webb" and see appendix. *Address:* La Guelle, Guelles Rd., St. Peter Port, Guernsey, C.I. GY1 2DE.

**WEBB, Kenneth,** N.D.D., A.T.D.Hons., N.S., F.R.S.A., R.W.A.; artist in oil and acrylic; Head of Painting School, Ulster College of Art (1953-60); *b* London, 1927. *m* Joan Burch. two *s*. two *d*. *Educ:* Bristol Grammar School; Lydney Grammar School and School of Art. *Studied:* Gloucester College of Art and University College, Swansea. *Exhib:* one-man shows 1954 to 1994: Verhoff Washington D.C., Arts Council Belfast, Walker Galleries London, Toronto, San Francisco, Ritchie Hendricks Dublin, Kenny Galleries, Alexander Gallery Bristol, Geneva, Solomon, etc. *Publications:* Kenneth Webb (Shenval

Press, London), Profile of an Artist by Thomas Kenny (Pub. 1990). *Signs work:* figurative work: "Kenneth Webb," non figurative work: "Webb." *Address:* Portland House, Chagford, Devon TQ13 8AR.

**WEBB, Sarah Ann,** B.A.(Hons.) (1978), S.W.A. (1994); Best of Show (1987) and Athena award (1992) Central South Art competition (U.S.A.); artist in oil; *b* Nashville, TN, 19 Feb., 1948. *m* Gary A. Webb, attorney. *Educ:* University of Tennessee. *Studied:* University of Tennessee and Vanderbilt University. *Exhib:* regular exhib. S.W.A. and Central South Art competition (U.S.A.), winner American Artists National Art competition, Grand Central Gallery (N.Y. 1985), Tennessee All State competition, numerous national and international group and solo shows; P.B.S. Television (U.S.A. 1994, 1995), Radio (U.S.A. 1985). Work in corporate and private collections worldwide. *Signs work:* "Sarah Webb." *Address:* P.O. Box 50134, Nashville, TN 37205, U.S.A.

**WEBBER, Angela Mary,** S.C.A.; painter and maker of religious images, writer on and tutor of animal painting; founder and secretary, S.S.S.A.; *b* London, 4 Jan., 1931. *m* Russell Arlen Bedingfield, art and antiques collector. *Studied:* Hull College of Art (1949-52). *Exhib:* O'Mell Gallery (1976), Solange de la Bruyere Gallery, Saratoga Springs, U.S.A. (1976-77), S.E.A. (1981), N.S. (1980), N.E.A.C. (1983). *Work in collections:* Martin S. Vickers, Stella A. Walker, Miss Wiesenthall, U.S.A. *Commissions:* various. *Publications:* work repro.: The Webber Prints, Quartilles International, etc. *Signs work:* "A. M. WEBBER." *Address:* 2 Marina Cottage, Willingdon Lane, Jevington, Polegate, Sussex BN26 5QH.

**WEBBER, Michael H.,** A.T.D.; Music Adviser, English Heritage; mem. Ben Uri Gallery; Concert promoter (Louis Armstrong and Duke Ellington Anniversary Concerts, etc); Chairman, London Lyric Orchestra; freelance writer, critic, journalist; Catalogues: East Anglian Art Today (1969), Artists in Camera (1972), Ipswich Arts Club Centenary Ex. (1975), "Critics Choice" (1983), Anna Airy Exhbn. (1985); *b* London, 30 June, 1926. *m* Miriam Broughton. two *d. Educ:* Kilburn Grammar School (1937-43). *Studied:* Northampton School of Art; Chelsea School of Art; Central School of Arts. *Address:* 19 Netherhall Gardens, London NW3 5RL.

**WEBSTER, John Robert,** A.T.C., D.A.E.; W.A.C. travel grant to Ireland (1991); artist in etching, printmaking, gouache; senior lecturer, St. Mary's College, Bangor, N. Wales (1968-75); Dip. in Art Educ., Leeds University Inst. (1975-76); Lecturer in Art Educ., U.C.N.W. Bangor (1977-89); part-time Curator, U.C.N.W. Art Gallery (1982-); *b* Bridlington, E. Yorks., 22 May, 1934. *m* Dorothy Lloyd Webster. one *s.* four *d. Educ:* Leeds G.S. *Studied:* Leeds College of Art (1951-55-57). *Exhib:* Mold, Conway (1969-), National Eisteddfod Llangefni (1983), Cardiff, Aberystwyth Open (from 1986), Birkenhead (1986), Anglesey Eisteddfod (1986), etc. *Work in collections:* Schools Museum, Cardiff, D.O.E., National Library, Aberystwyth. *Address:*

Tyn' Cae, Paradwys, Bodorgan, Anglesey, Gwynedd LL62 5PF.

**WEBSTER, Norman,** R.W.S., R.E., A.R.C.A.; painter etcher; *b* Southend-on-Sea, 6 May, 1924. *m* Joan W. Simpson, A.R.C.A. three *s. Educ:* Dover Grammar School; Tunbridge Wells School of Art (1940-43, E. Owen Jennings, R.W.S.); Royal Navy (1943-46); R.C.A. School of Engraving (1946-49, Malcolm Osborne, C.B.E., R.A., Robert Austin, R.A.). *Exhib:* Painter Etchers, R.W.S., R.A., Yorkshire Artists at Leeds, Bradford, Wakefield and Hull City A.G.'s., with Yorkshire Printmakers in Britain, U.S.A., Israel and Canada. *Work in collections:* Ashmolean Museum; Salford University; Leeds City A.G. and Arts Council of G.B. *Signs work:* "Norman Webster." *Address:* 48 The Drive, Cross Gates, Leeds, LS15 8EP.

**WEEKS, John Lawrence Macdonald,** L.R.M.S. (1984), A.R.M.S. (1987), F.N.C.M. (1984); artist in oil and water-colour; private music teacher and organist; *b* Chelmsford, 28 Apr., 1954. *Educ:* Moulsham High School, Chelmsford. *Studied:* Colchester Inst. of H.E. (1973-74, John Buhler). *Exhib:* R.M.S. annual, Medici Gallery and one-man shows. *Signs work:* name followed by date and device (see appendix). *Address:* 47 Prescott, Hanworth, Bracknell, Berks. RG12 7RE.

**WEGNER, Fritz,** M.C.S.D., Mem. Art Workers' Guild; freelance artist, retired lecturer, St. Martin's School of Art; *b* Vienna, 15 Sept., 1924. *m* Janet Wegner. two *s.* one *d. Studied:* St. Martin's School of Art. *Publications:* work repro.: bookjackets and illustrations for British, American and Continental publishers; cover designs and illustrations for magazines; educational publications; G.P.O. Christmas and Anniversaries sets of stamps. Examples of work reproduced in several manuals on illustration. *Clubs:* Chelsea Arts. *Signs work:* "Wegner." *Address:* 14 Swains Lane, London N6 6QS.

**WEIL, Hanna,** N.T.D. (1943); painter in oil, water-colour, gouache; tutor, Hammersmith School of Arts and Crafts (1945-48); St. Martin's School of Art (1945-87); *b* Munich, 19 May, 1921. *m* R. S. Strauss, Dr.Ing. one *d. Educ:* North London Collegiate School. *Studied:* St. Martin's School of Art (1940-43). *Exhib:* R.A., Leicester Galleries, Liverpool, Brighton, London Transport (posters), Pro Arte Kasper Gallery, Switzerland, Arthur Jeffress (Pictures) Ltd., 4 galleries Munich, Portal Gallery, Elaine Benson Gallery, U.S.A. *Publications:* work repro.: Amalgamated Press, The Queen, Art News and Review, The Studio, The Artist; postcards, calendars, prints of paintings. *Signs work:* "H. Weil." *Address:* 34 Christchurch Hill, London NW3 1JL.

**WEINBERGER, Harry,** artist in oil and all kinds of drawing; *b* Berlin, 7 Apr., 1924. one *d. Educ:* Continent and England. *Studied:* Chelsea School of Art under Ceri Richards, and privately with Martin Bloch. *Exhib:* 33 one-man shows, including fifteen in London, one in Berlin and three in Stuttgart. Present gallery: Duncan Campbell Fine Art, 15 Thackeray St., Kensington Sq., London. *Signs work:* "HW." *Address:* 28 Church Hill, Leamington Spa, Warks. CV32 5AY.

**WELCH, Robert Joseph,** B.A. (1979), M.A. (1981); painter in oil and acrylic on canvas; *b* 22 Feb., 1956. *Educ:* Regis Comprehensive, Wolverhampton. *Studied:* Hull C.H.E. (1976-79, John Clarke), Manchester Polytechnic (1980-81, David Sweet). *Exhib:* Castlefield Gallery, Manchester, Showroom Gallery, London, Winchester School of Art, Mall Galleries; one-man shows: Patricia Brown, Dulwich, Smith-Jariwala, London. *Signs work:* "Welch, R.J.W." *Address:* 4a Husbourne House, Chilton Grove, London SE8 5DZ.

**WELCH, Rosemary Sarah,** S.Eq.A., S.W.A.; artist in oil and pastel; *b* 24 May, 1943. *m* Anthony Crockford. *Educ:* private school Bournemouth, American High School, N.Y. *Studied:* St. Ives School of Painting (Leonard Fuller, R.A., R.O.I.). *Exhib:* Belfast, Mall Galleries, Omells, John Davies, St. Ives Soc. of Artists, American Academy Equine Art. *Work in collections:* Russell-Cotes Museum, Bournemouth. *Signs work:* "Rosemary Sarah Welch." *Address:* Forest Way, Valley Lane, Bransgore, Dorset BH23 8DX.

**WELLINGS, Tricia,** self taught artist in gouache, charcoal and ink and gouache; *b* Guildford, 20 Mar., 1959. *Educ:* Horsham High School. *Exhib:* Painters Hall, London EC2, Mall Galleries, London SW1, Edith Grove Gallery, London SW10, Wattis Fine Art, Hong Kong, Ramsay Galleries, Honolulu, Hawaii, Ropner Gallery, London SW6, Bartley Drey Gallery, London SW3. *Work in collections:* U.S.A., Australia, Mexico, U.K., Hong Kong, Ireland (Eire). *Clubs:* The Nine Elms Group of Artists. *Signs work:* "T. Wellings." *Address:* 5a Pentland Gdns., Wandsworth, London SW18 2AN.

**WELLS, Peter,** Dip.Soc. (Lond.) (1970), M.F.P.S. (1987); painter in oil, poet; *b* London, 12 Jan., 1919. *m* (1) Elisabeth Van der Meulen (decd.); (2) Gillian Anne Hayes-Newington. one *d. Educ:* privately, and Universities of London and Manchester. *Studied:* Hornsey School of Art - part-time (1952-54, J.D. Cast). *Exhib:* Hornsey Artists (1953), Ellingham Mill Art Soc. (1981), The Crest Gallery, London (1982), Minsky's Gallery, London (1982), Wells Arts Centre, Norfolk (1982), Loggia Gallery (1988), Fermoy Gallery, King's Lynn (Eastern Open Competition 1992), School House Gallery, Wighton, Norfolk (1991-). *Publications:* The One Time Press - illustrated edns. of the artist's own work. *Clubs:* P.E.N. *Signs work:* see appendix. *Address:* Model Farm, Linstead Magna, Halesworth, Suffolk IP19 0DT.

**WELTMAN, Boris,** Nature micro miniaturist, draughtsman, stylus; painter, water-colour; *b* London, 29 Nov., 1921. *m* Phyllis Joyce. *Educ:* Chatham House, Ramsgate; Folkestone College; art and light craft. Work in collections worldwide. *Signs work:* on back of micro miniature drawings and paintings, see appendix. *Address:* Temptye Farmhouse, Worth, Deal, Kent, CT14 0DJ.

**WELTON, Peter,** B.A.; artist in water-colour; Emertis Prof. of Fine Art, De Montfort University, Leicester; *b* Barnetby, Lincs., 15 Mar., 1933;. *m* Liza. two *s. Studied:* King's College, Newcastle (Gowing, Pasmore and Hamilton). *Exhib:* Keele University (1997), Laing Gallery, Newcastle, Bar Convent

Museum, York, Buxton Art Gallery. *Work in collections:* Wimbledon 1997 "The New No. 1 Court", H.M. The Queen "Moored Boat" (1992), Peter Ogden: "The Jethou Suite" (1997), *Publications:* "See What I Mean" with John Morgan (Edward Arnold, London, 1986), "Paint in Water-colour" (Patchings Farm, Nottingham); work repro.: illustrated London News , The Artists Magazine. Video "Peter Welton's Way with Water-colour", (1997). *Signs work:* "Peter Welton". *Address:* Orchard Cottage, Arnesby, Leics. LE8 5WG.

**WERGE-HARTLEY, Alan,** N.D.D. (Leeds) 1952, A.T.D.; painter in oil, pen and wash of marine landscapes, lecturer; senior lecturer Dept. of Education, Portsmouth Polytechnic (1962-90); *b* Leeds, 1931. *m* Jeanne Werge-Hartley. two *d. Studied:* Leeds College of Art (1947-53) under Maurice de Sausmarez and E. E. Pullée; Hornsey College of Art (1972-73) (sabbatical). *Exhib:* in group exhbns. and one-man shows in Hampshire from 1962. *Work in collections:* Portsmouth City Gallery and numerous private collections in England and abroad. *Signs work:* see appendix. *Address:* 5 Maisemore Gdns., Emsworth, Hants. PO10 7JU.

**WERGE-HARTLEY, Jeanne,** N.D.D., F.S.D.C., F.R.S.A.; designer/jeweller/goldsmith; Founder Mem., Designer Jewellers Group; Vice-President and past Chairman, Soc. of Designer Craftsmen; *b* Leeds, 1931. *m* Alan Werge-Hartley. two *d. Educ:* Leeds Girls' High School. *Studied:* Leeds College of Art (1948-52) under Eric Taylor, A.R.C.A. *Exhib:* nationally and internationally. *Commissions:* U.K., U.S.A., Europe, New Zealand, Japan. Freeman of the Worshipful Company of Goldsmiths and the City of London (1986). Included on Craft Council Index and represented on the BBC Domesday Project. *Signs work:* see appendix. *Address:* 5 Maisemore Gdns., Emsworth, Hants. PO10 7JU.

**WERNER, Max,** B.A., M.A.; printmaker in etching, acrylic, pencil on paper; *b* Ghent, Belgium, 17 Oct., 1955. *m* Shireen. two *d. Educ:* College de la Berlière (Belgium). *Studied:* Byam Shaw School of Art (1979-82, Winn Jones, Chris Crabtree, John Lewis), Slade School of Fine Art (1983-85, B. dos Santos). *Exhib:* mixed and one-man shows in U.K., Belgium, France, Portugal, Switzerland, Germany, Ireland, Pakistan, Taiwan, Argentina. *Commissions:* collaborated with B. dos Santos to the decoration of the "Enter Campos" underground station, Lisbon, and to an etched limestone panel for the Nyombashi station, Tokyo. *Signs work:* "M. Werner." *Address:* Grenada 774, Acassuso 1641, Prov. de Buenos Aires, Argentina.

**WESSELMAN, Frans,** R.E. (1986); painter and etcher; *b* The Hague, Holland, 1953. *Studied:* printmaking and photography at Groningen College of Art (1976-78). Work concerned with the human figure, emotions and interactions. Sometimes literary sources (Shakespeare) are a starting point, from where my paintings develop into valid graphic, pictorial statements with strong colours and compositions. *Exhib:* R.E., R.A., R.W.S., R.W.A., Catto Gallery, London, Ombersley Gallery, Ombersley, Manor House Gallery, Chipping

Norton. *Work in collections:* Fitzwilliam, Ashmolean Museum. *Address:* 119 Watling St. South, Church Stretton SY6 7BJ.

**WESSELOW, Eric,** M.A., M.F.A., Prix de Rome, R.C.A., S.C.A., F.R.S.A.; past Pres. Independent Art Assoc. and Quebec Soc. for Educ. through Art; painter, artist in water-colour, acrylic, chalk and glass (patented system of coloured glass lamination), of portraits, landscapes, abstracts; teacher, linguist; *b* Marienburg, Germany, 12 Sept., 1911. *Educ:* Academy of Fine Arts, Koenigsberg. *Studied:* Philology, University Koenigsberg. *Exhib:* one-man shows: Montreal Museum of Fine Arts; Waddington Gallery, Montreal; N.Y. State University, Plattsburgh; Inaugural Exhbn. Eaton A.G., Montreal; Robertson Galleries, Ottawa; Toronto Dominion Centre; Ontario Assoc. of Architects, Toronto, etc. Represented in numerous national and international art exhbns. *Work in collections:* architectural laminated coloured glass relief windows and screens: Montreal Airport Dorval; Hospital Dortmund, W. Germany; Sanctuaries Congregation Beth-El, Montreal; Temple Emanu-El-Beth Sholom, Montreal; Temple Sinai, Toronto; Humbervalley United Church, Toronto; St. Dunstan of Canterbury Anglican Church, West Hill, Ontario; Baptistery Church of the Resurrection, Valois, Quebec. *Publications:* Sparks, illustrated own aphorisms (1980); New Sparks (1985 and 1992). *Signs work:* "Wesselow" or "W" followed by date or year. *Address:* 5032 Victoria Ave., Montreal, Quebec, Canada H3W 2N3.

**WEST, Steve,** Dip.A.D. (1969), R.A.S. Higher Cert. (1972), Prix de Rome (1972), A.R.B.S. (1992); sculptor in bronze, glass fibre, wood; *b* Warrington, 6 Apr., 1948. *m* Jenny. one *s.* one *d.* *Studied:* Liverpool College of Art and Design (1965-69), R.A. Schools (1969-72, Willi Soukop). *Exhib:* Crescent Gallery Scarborough, Oldknows Gallery Nottingham, Lanchester Gallery Coventry, Tabor Gallery Canterbury, Woodlands Gallery Blackheath, Prediger Schwabisch Gmund, Hart Gallery London. *Commissions:* undertakes ecclesiastical commissions. *Signs work:* "Steve West." *Address:* 17 Swift St., Barnsley, S. Yorks. S75 2SN.

**WESTLEY, Ann,** artist, sculptor and printmaker in etching, relief printing, mixed media; part-time lecturer in printmaking, Colchester School of Art and Design; *b* Kettering, 5 Mar., 1948. *Educ:* Bedford High School. *Studied:* Northampton School of Art (1965-67), Bristol Polytechnic (1967-70, Ernest Pascoe, Ralph Brown, Bob Clatworthy), Gulbenkian Rome Scholarship in Sculpture (1970-71). *Exhib:* Serpentine Gallery (1976), Out of Print, South Hill Arts Centre, Bracknell (1983), British Miniature Print Biennale (1990), A New Generation of British Printmakers, Xylon Museum, Germany (1992). *Work in collections:* Gulbenkian Foundation, Ashmolean Museum, Fredrikstaad Museum Norway. *Clubs:* R.E. *Signs work:* "Ann Westley." *Address:* Gore Cottage, 4 Gore La., Rayne, Braintree, Essex CM7 8TU.

**WESTON, David J.,** B.A. (Hons.) Fine Art, R.M.S., B.W.S., H.S., S.M., U.A., F.R.S.A.; seascape and landscape painter in water-colour and other media; miniaturist; *b* 21 Sept., 1936. *Studied:* St. Albans School of Art and Design (University of Hertfordshire). *Exhib:* one-man shows: Clare Hall Cambridge, Grosvenor Gallery, Old Fire Engine House Ely. Has exhibited at New Academy, Llewellyn Alexander and Medici galleries; frequently with U.A., R.M.S., R.S.M.A., R.B.A., R.I., N.E.A.C. and H.S. at Mall and Westminster Galleries, also with B.W.S. and S.M. at Ilkley. *Signs work:* "DAVID J. WESTON" or "D.J.W." (miniatures and small works). *Address:* Little Glebe, 11 Longcroft Ave., Harpenden, Herts. AL5 2RD.

**WESTWOOD, John,** A.R.C.A. (1948); designer and consultant on corporate identity, logos, heraldry; Head of Typographic Design, later Director of Graphic Design, at Her Majesty's Stationery Office, London (1960-1978); *b* Bromley, 26 Sept., 1919. *m* Margaret Wadsworth. two *s*. *Educ:* Bromley County Grammar School. *Studied:* Bromley College of Art (1936-39) and R.C.A. (1940 and 1947-48). *Exhib:* South Bank (1951). *Commissions:* Binding designs for The Folio Society. *Publications:* articles on graphic design; International Meccanoman; printing trade press, etc. *Address:* The Malt House, Church La., Streatley, Reading RG8 9HT.

**WHALLEY, Ann Penelope,** N.D.D., A.T.D., A.T.C., S.W.A.; artist in water-colour and pastel; tutor and organiser for painting holidays abroad; *b* Yorks., 1 Apr., 1935. *m* Theo Whalley, N.D.D., A.T.D., A.T.C. four *s*. *Educ:* Pontefract Girls' High School. *Studied:* Leeds College of Art (1950-55, Mr. Pullé). *Exhib:* one-man shows: Albany Gallery, Cardiff, Fountain Gallery Llandeilo, Library Hall, Haverfordwest annually since 1981, Workshop, Wales (1983), Bloomfield Hall (1986), Coachhouse (1987), Henry Thomas Gallery, Carmarthen, Patricia Wells Gallery (1987); group shows: St. Ives Gallery (1984), Beacon Gallery, Painswick (1985), B.W.S. (1986), Laing Comp. (1987), S.W.A. (1987), R.I. (1986), Albany Gallery, Cardiff, Century Gallery, Henley-on-Thames, Bromley Gallery, Kent, Fountain Gallery, Llandeilo, Wold Gallery, Bourton on the Water. *Publications:* illustrated, About Pembrokeshire; author, Painting under a Blue Sky; author, Painting Water in Water-colour (Batsfords); articles for Artist and Illustrator, and Leisure Painter. *Signs work:* "Ann Whalley." *Address:* Haroldston House, Haverfordwest, Pembs. SA61 1UH.

**WHEELER, Colin,** S.G.F.A. (1986); graphic artist, illustrator and cartographer in ink, pencil and pastel; *b* Amersham, Bucks., 4 July, 1946. *Educ:* Alleyne's Grammar School, Stevenage. *Studied:* privately. *Exhib:* S.G.F.A., various one-man shows including Fermoy Gallery, King's Lynn, Lion Yard, Cambridge, Theatre Royal, Norwich, Denington Gallery, Stevenage. *Work in collections:* B.Ae., Stevenage and N. Herts. Museum. *Publications:* travel and tourist brochures. *Signs work:* "Colin Wheeler." *Address:* 39 Plash Drive, Stevenage SG1 1LN.

**WHEELER, Sir H. Anthony,** Kt. (1988), O.B.E. (1973), P.P.R.S.A., P.P.R.I.A.S., F.R.I.B.A., M.R.T.P.I., B.Arch. (Strath.), Hon. R.A., Hon. R.G.I.,

Hon. R.B.S., Hon. Doc.Des., Robert Gordon's Inst. of Technology, P.R.I.A.S. (1973-75), P.R.S.A. (1983-90), Hon. Pres. Saltire Soc. (1995); architect and planner, Consultant, Wheeler & Sproson, Edinburgh and Kirkcaldy since 1986 when ceased to be senior partner; mem. of the Royal Fine Art Commission for Scotland, (1967-85); trustee of the Scottish Civic Trust (1970-83); *b* Stranraer, Scotland, 7 Nov., 1919. *m* Dorothy Jean Wheeler. one *d. Studied:* architecture: Glasgow School of Architecture under Prof. W. J. Smith, and Glasgow School of Art; graduated 1948; John Keppie Scholar, Rowand Anderson Studentship R.I.A.S. (1948); R.I.B.A. Grissell Gold Medallist (1948); R.I.B.A. Neale Bursar (1949); 22 Saltire Awards and Commendations for Housing and Reconstruction; 12 Civic Trust Awards and Commendations. *Exhib:* R.S.A., R.A., R.G.I. *Clubs:* Scottish Arts, New Club. *Signs work:* "H. A. Wheeler." *Address:* South Inverleith Manor, 31/6 Kinnear Rd., Edinburgh EH3 5PG.

**WHEELER, Zona Lorraine,** B.F.A., F.I.A.L., N.S.M.P.; advertising designer, painter, sculptor, white sheet-vinyl; proprietor, 3-D Studio; senior Art Director, McCormick-Armstrong Co. (1970-79); *b* Lindsborg, Kansas, 15 Feb., 1913. *Studied:* under Dr. Birger Sandzen, Bethany Coll., Lindsborg, American Academy of Art, Chicago, Wichita Art Assoc. School. *Exhib:* Rugby, Boston, England, San Francisco Art Assoc.; solo shows in white sheet-vinyl, Sandzen Memorial Gallery, Lindsborg, Kansas, Fort Hays Kansas State University, Wichita Art Assoc. (retrospective 1987). *Clubs:* Nat. League American Pen Women, Nat. Soc. Mural Painters. *Address:* 230 South Belmont, Wichita, Kansas 67218.

**WHEELER-HOPKINSON, John Samuel,** S.G.A. (1983); graphic artist in pen and ink, pencil and colour wash; *b* Prestatyn, N. Wales, 1 Mar., 1941. *m* Claire Follett. two *d. Educ:* Grammar School, Colne, and King's College, London. *Exhib:* Mall Galleries, London. *Signs work:* "J.W-H." and date as ideogram. *Address:* Le Champ Peron, Bayet 03500, St. Pourçain sur Sioule, France.

**WHIDBORNE, Timothy Charles Plunket,** artist in oil, tempera, sanguine, lithography, sculptor; Director, Pheasantry Studios Ltd.; *b* Hughenden, Bucks., 25 July, 1927. *m* Wendy. *Educ:* Stowe School. *Studied:* St. Martin's Art School (1944), La Grandè Chaumiere, Paris (1948), with Mervyn Peake, Chelsea (1945) and Pietro Annigoni, Florence (1949). *Exhib:* R.A., R.P. (1986), S.P.S., etc.; one-man show: Upper Grosvenor Galleries (1969). *Work in collections:* portrait of H.M. The Queen, H.Q. Irish Guards, London; St. Katherine of Alexandria, Worshipful Company of Haberdashers, London; H.M. The Queen Mother, the Inspection of the In-Pensioners Founder's Day at the Royal Hospital, Chelsea, 1991; The Duke of Devonshire, Proprietor of Pratt's Club, 1994; collection of J. Paul Getty K.B.E. and Mrs. Getty. *Clubs:* Chelsea Arts. *Signs work:* "T. Whidborne" or "T.W." *Address:* The Studio, 30 Albert Rd., Deal, Kent CT14 9RE.

**WHISHAW, Anthony,** R.A., R.W.A., A.R.C.A. (1955), Travelling

Scholarship, R.C.A., Abbey Premier Scholarship (1982), Lorne Scholarship (1982-83), John Moores minor prize; *b* 22 May, 1930. *Exhib:* one-man shows: Madrid (1956), Roland, Browse and Delbanco (1960, 1961, 1963, 1965, 1968), I.C.A. (1971), New Art Centre (1972), Hoya (1974), Hayward Annual (1980), Nicola Jacobs (1981, 1983, 1984), Mappin A.G. (1985). *Work in collections:* National Gallery, Melbourne, Australia, Seattle Museum, Arts Council, Coventry Museum, Leicester Museum, Chantrey Bequest, Bolton A.G., Bayer Pharm., Western Australia A.G., Museo de Bahia, Brazil, Power A.G., European Parliament, Ferens A.G., Tate Gallery, Graves A.G. Sheffield. *Address:* 7a Albert Pl., Victoria Rd., London W8 5PD.

**WHISKERD, Jennifer,** B.A. Hons. Fine Art (Chelt.); painter; *b* Gloucester, 23 Mar., 1962. *Exhib:* international and national. Work in public and private collections. Fine Art tutor. *Signs work:* "J.H. Whiskerd." *Address:* Springfield Cottage, Kilcot, Newent, Gloucs. GL18 1NS.

**WHISTLER, Laurence,** C.B.E., D.Litt.Oxon. (1992); *b* 1912. *Educ:* Stowe and Balliol. *Work in collections:* V. & A.; Ashmolean, Oxford; Fitzwilliam, Cambridge; Brighton A.G.; Cecil Higgins, Bedford; Corning Museum, N.Y., etc. *Commissions:* Engraved panels and church windows: Moreton, Dorset; Hannington and Wootton St. Lawrence, Hants.; Salisbury Cathedral; Eastbury and Radley College, Berks.; Thornham Parva, Suffolk; Balliol, St. Hilda's and St. Hugh's Colleges, Oxford, etc. *Publications:* The Engraved Glass of Laurence Whistler (1952), Engraved Glass 1952-58 (1959), The Initials in the Heart (1964), Pictures on Glass (1972), The Image on the Glass (1975), Scenes and Signs on Glass (1985), The Laughter and the Urn: The Life of Rex Whistler (1985), Enter (Poetry, 1986). *Signs work:* "LW" with year date. *Address:* Watlington, Oxford OX9.

**WHITAKER, Rita Elizabeth,** R.M.S., M.A.S.F.; professional artist specialising in stoving enamel on copper, and with her husband owns a gallery in Newport, Dyfed; *b* 3 Sept., 1936. two *s. Educ:* Sion Convent, Worthing. *Studied:* Regent St. Polytechnic under Stuart Tresilian. *Exhib:* Royal Miniature Soc., R.A., Medici's, Assoc. of Sussex Artists, Georgia and Florida Miniature Socs. and various galleries throughout England and Wales. *Work in collections:* Royal Exchange and Baltic Exchange, London, and Carningli Centre, Newport, Dyfed; private collections throughout the world. *Signs work:* "R. E. Whitaker." *Address:* Scholars' Brook, College Sq., Newport, Pembrokeshire SA42 0QB Wales.

**WHITCOMBE, Susan Anne Clare,** painter in oil and water-colour of equestrian portraits; *b* London, 17 June, 1957. *m* Robin Marriott. two *s. Educ:* N. Foreland Lodge, Hants. *Studied:* Heatherley School of Fine Art (John Walton, Bernard Hailstone). *Exhib:* S.E.A.; one-man shows: London (1981, 1988, 1993), Tokyo (1985, 1987), Melbourne (1982). *Signs work:* "Susie Whitcombe." *Address:* Redwood Cottage, West Meon, Hants. GU32 1JU.

**WHITE, Charles,** D.F.A. (Lond.), F.R.S.A.; Pres. European Group; former

Head of Art Department, United World College; *b* London, 11 Feb., 1928. *m* Mary White, calligrapher, potter. *Educ:* Stoneleigh. *Studied:* 1941-50: Sutton School of Art and Crafts, Newport, Kingston-upon-Thames, Slade, London University. *Exhib:* one-man shows in England, Wales, France and Germany; Landes Vertretung Rheinland-Pfalz & Europa. *Work in collections:* Her Majesty Queen Elizabeth II, H.R.H. Prince Charles, Secretary of State for Wales, Mayor of Zürich, Contemporary Art Society, National Museum of Wales, England, America, Canada, Germany, Belgium, France, Sweden, Holland and Luxembourg. First Prize, Salon International, France (1990). *Signs work:* "Charles White." *Address:* Zimmerplatzweg 6, 55599 Wonsheim, Germany.

**WHITE, David,** Des.R.C.A. (1959); potter, producing individual porcelain pots for sale in most of the leading galleries throughout the country; Joint Winner of the Duke of Edinburgh's Prize for Elegant Design (1960); *b* Margate, Kent, 27 June, 1934. *m* (1962) Diana Groves. one *s.* one *d. Studied:* Thanet School of Art (1950-54) and Royal College of Art (1956-59). Accepted as Full mem. Craftsmen Potters' Assoc. (Apr. 1991). *Address:* 4 Callis Court Rd., Broadstairs, Kent CT10 3AE.

**WHITE, James,** LL.D. (N.U.I.); Chairman, Irish Arts Council (1978-84); Director, National Gallery of Ireland (1964-80), Curator, Municipal Gallery of Modern Art, Dublin (1960-64); lecturer, Dublin and National Universities; *b* Dublin, 16 June, 1913. *m* Agnes Bowe. three *s.* two *d. Educ:* Belvedere College, Dublin. *Publications:* The National Gallery of Ireland (Thames & Hudson); Irish Stained Glass (Gill & Co.); Jack B. Yeats (Martin Secker & Warburg); John Butler Yeats and the Irish Renaissance (Dolmen Press); Masterpieces of the National Gallery of Ireland (Jarrolds, Norwich); Pauline Bewick, Painting a Life (Wolfhound Press); Gerard Dillon, A Biography (Wolfhound Press). *Address:* 15 Herbert Pk., Dublin 4.

**WHITE, John Norman,** N.D.D. (1951); painter, illustrator, oil, gouache, and water-colour; *b* Chipperfield, Herts., 27 Mar., 1932. *Educ:* Belmont Senior Modern School. *Studied:* Harrow School of Art (1945-51). *Exhib:* R.A., Young Contemporaries. *Signs work:* "JOHN - WHITE." *Address:* Northwood Lodge, Bullockstone Rd., Herne, Herne Bay, Kent.

**WHITE, Laura,** B.A.(Hons.); sculptor in stone, wood and bronze; *b* Worcester, 10 Mar., 1968. *Educ:* Alice Ottley School, Worcester. *Studied:* Worcester Art College, Loughborough College of Art and Design. *Exhib:* various mixed and solo shows in U.K. *Work in collections:* Art Scene London, Gallery Shurini London. *Signs work:* "LAURA WHITE" or not at all. *Address:* Flat B, 4 Corporation Oaks, Woodborough Rd., Nottingham NG3 4JY.

**WHITE, Mary,** A.T.D.; ceramic artist and calligrapher; awarded Rheinland-Pfalz Staatspreis (1982); *b* Croesyceiliog, Wales, 1926; née Rollinson. *m* Charles White, artist. *Studied:* St. Julian's High School; Newport College of Art; Hammersmith College of Art; London University Goldsmiths' College of

Art. *Exhib:* Europe, U.S.A. *Work in collections:* British Museums: V.&.A., Fitzwilliam Cambridge, Newport, Cardiff, Winchester, Bristol, Norwich Castle, Swindon; Collections: Bath Study Centre, Leicester Educ. Authority, Aberystwyth Univ., Welsh Arts Council; U.S.A.: Pennsylvania State Museum; Museums in Germany: Kunstgewerbemuseum Köln, Veste Coburg, Westerwald, Berlin, Keramion, Deidesheim, Stuttgart, Mainz, Darmstadt. Many private collections. *Commissions:* many, including British Government and German Bundestag. *Publications:* work repro.: Ceramic Review, Letter Arts Review, German Keramik Magazines; work included in many books in G.B., Germany, France, Belgium and U.S.A. *Clubs:* Fellow C.P.A., Fellow S.S.I, Deutscher Handwerkskammer, Fellow C.L.A.S. *Signs work:* see appendix. *Address:* Zimmerplatzweg 6, 55599 Wonsheim, Germany.

**WHITEFORD, Joan,** N.D.D. (1963), A.T.D. (1964); artist in etching and wood engraving; *b* St. John, Cornwall, 5 May, 1942. *m* David Whiteford. *Educ:* Grammar School, Tavistock, Devon. *Studied:* Plymouth College of Art (1958-63, William Mann, Jeff. Clements), Bournemouth College of Art (1963-64). *Exhib:* R.A., R.E., N.S., S.W.A., N.E.A.C., R.I., Mall Print. *Signs work:* "J. Whiteford." *Address:* Meadowside, Cockwells, Penzance, Cornwall TR20 8DB.

**WHITEFORD, Kate,** Dip.A.D. (1973), Dip.F.A. (1976) History of Art; Sargant Fellow, British School at Rome (1993-94); artist in oil on gesso, also land drawings; *b* Glasgow, 9 Mar., 1952. *m* Alex Graham. *Educ:* Glasgow High School. *Studied:* Glasgow School of Art (1969-73), Glasgow University (1974-76, History of Art, Prof. Martin Kemp). *Exhib:* Institute of Contemporary Art (1983), Riverside Studios (1986), Whitechapel A.G. (1988), Glasgow Museum and A.G. (1990). *Work in collections:* Tate Gallery, British Council, C.A.S., A.C.G.B., National Gallery of Modern Art Edinburgh, S.A.C., Glasgow Museum and A.G. *Publications:* artists books published by Whitechapel A.G. (1988), Tetra Press and Advanced Graphics (1992), Cairn Gallery (1992), Sitelines (1992), Graeme Murray Gallery (1992). *Signs work:* "Whiteford" or "Kate Whiteford." *Address:* c/o Frith St. Gallery, 60 Frith St., London W1V 5TA.

**WHITELEY, Alfred,** A.R.C.A. (1952); Arts Council major award (1977); painter in oil; *b* Chesterfield, 18 Nov., 1928. *m* Ottoline Reynolds. one *s.* one *d.* *Educ:* Tapton House, Chesterfield. *Studied:* Chesterfield School of Art (1945-47), R.C.A. (1949-52). *Exhib:* R.A., Odette Gilbert Gallery; one-man shows Odette Gilbert, Vorpal Gallery, N.Y. and Pride Gallery. *Work in collections:* U.K., U.S.A., Germany. *Publications:* work repro.: The Times, Sunday Times, Art Line, etc. *Signs work:* "Alfred Whiteley." *Address:* Fairfield, Mogador Rd., Tadworth, Surrey KT20 7EW.

**WHITE-OAKES, Sue,** M.C.S.D.; metal sculptor in copper and bronze; *b* 26 May, 1939. *m* Roger Oakes. two *s.* *Educ:* St. Martin's High School, London. *Studied:* Central School of Art. *Exhib:* Edinburgh, Glasgow, St. Andrews,

London. *Publications:* articles: Craftsman Magazine and The Scotsman colour supplement. *Clubs:* C.S.D. *Signs work:* "Sue White-Oakes." *Address:* Tarfhaugh Farmhouse, West Linton, Peeblesshire EH46 7BS.

**WHITESIDE, (formerly Newton-Davies), Diana Elizabeth Hamilton,** miniature painter in water-colour; *b* London, 13 Jan., 1942. *m* John Newton Davies (1964-87). two *d*. *Educ:* Lycée Français de Londres, Glendower School, Sydenham House, Devon. *Studied:* Simi's and L'Accademia delle Belle Arti, Florence (1959-60), Camberwell School of Art (1961-62). *Exhib:* R.A., R.M.S., R.H.S., Tate Gallery, Mall Galleries, Anna-Mei Chadwick's, Westminster Gallery, Medici Gallery. *Commissions:* animal portraits. *Signs work:* "19 D.E.N.D. 85" (or relevant year pre 1987); "D.E. 1993 H.W." (or relevant year from 1987). *Address:* Chapel Lands, Chailey, nr. Lewes, Sussex BN8 4DD.

**WHITFORD, Christopher,** artist in water-colour and acrylic; *b* Malvern, Worcs., 18 Feb., 1952. *m* Filippa. two *d*. *Studied:* Malvern. *Exhib:* R.M.S., John Noott, Broadway. *Signs work:* "C. Whitford" or "C.W." *Address:* c/o John Noott Twentieth Century, 14 Cotswold Ct., Broadway, Worcs. WR12 7DP.

**WHITFORD, Filippa,** artist in water-colour; *b* Italy, 22 Jan., 1951. *m* Christopher Whitford. two *d*. *Exhib:* R.M.S, R.W.S., John Noott, Broadway. *Signs work:* "Filippa Whitford." *Address:* c/o John Noott Twentieth Century, 14 Cotswold Ct., Broadway, Worcs. WR12 7DP.

**WHITTEN, B. Janice E.,** Dip.Bact. (1960), F.R.S.H. (1990); bacteriologist and freelance artist in oil; *b* Middx., 15 July, 1937. *m* Don Whitten, designer (decd.). two *d*. *Educ:* Torquay Girls' Grammar School, Greenford Grammar School. *Studied:* Regent St., Chelsea, Harrow School of Art. *Exhib:* R.I. Gallery, mixed exhbns., Devon County Show, Royal Bath and West. *Publications:* illustrated: Modern Cereal Chemistry; Countryside Commission: The East Devon Way; Science of Bread; catalogues, articles. *Signs work:* capital W supporting initials - see appendix. *Address:* Hardy's Hill, Colyton, E. Devon EX13 6RU.

**WHITTEN, Jonathan Philip,** B.A. Hons. (1977), P.G.C.E. (1978); teacher and potter in ceramic; Head of Art, Sir James Smith's School, Camelford; *b* Eastbourne, 23 Sept., 1954. *m* Sally Bowler. two *s*. *Educ:* Eastbourne Grammar School. *Studied:* Eastbourne College of Art and Design (1972-73, Geoffrey Flint, A.R.C.A.), University of E. Anglia (1974-77, Prof. Andrew Martindale), University of London (1977-78, William Newland); apprentice potter to Michael Leach (1978-79) and Roger Cockram (1980-81). *Exhib:* Brewhouse Gallery, Taunton (1979), Devon Guild of Craftsmen (1981), Leics. Guild of Craftsmen (1983-87), etc. *Address:* Hale Farmhouse, St. Kew, Bodmin, Cornwall PL30 3HE.

**WHITTEN, Miranda M.A.,** B.Sc.(Hons.) (1994), M.R.S.H. (1994); biologist, artist/illustrator in acrylic, pencil, ink; nature artist commissioned by E. Devon District Council; Ph.D. student (immunology); *b* London, 25 Sept.,

1972. *Educ:* Colyton Grammar School; Aston University; Swansea University *Exhib:* mixed shows: Christie's, Devon County Show, Bath and West *Publications:* illustrated: Countryside Commission: The East Devon Way Nature in East Devon; Elefriends Recipe Book; catalogues, posterwork. *Sign. work:* "M. Whitten." *Address:* Hardy's Hill, Colyton, E. Devon EX13 6RU.

**WHITTEN, Philip John,** A.R.C.A. (1949), F.R.S.A. (1952); painter in oil pastel; teacher, London University Inst. of Educ. (1968); senior lecturer; exam iner, Cambridge and London University Insts. of Educ. (retd.); *b* Leyton, Essex 19 June, 1922. four *s.* one *d. Educ:* Bishopshalt, Hillingdon. *Studied:* Hornsey College of Art (1937-40), R.C.A. (1946-49). *Exhib:* R.B.A., Dowmunt Gallery Bond St., Towner Gallery, Cecil Higgins; Bedford, Shoreditch Colleges, pri vate galleries in Weybridge, Walton and Eastbourne areas. *Work in collections* Towner Gallery, Brunel University. Work sold by Christie's and Sotheby's *Signs work:* "Philip Whitten." *Address:* 10 Beechwood Cres., Eastbourne BN20 8AE.

**WHITTEN-LOCKE, Helena M.J.,** freelance artist in pen and ink, water colour; scientific proof reader; *b* London, 9 Oct., 1970. *m* Tony Locke. *Educ* Colyton Grammar School. *Exhib:* mixed shows: Devon County Show, Roya Bath and West; exhbn. designer: The Business Shop Agency. *Commissions.* sign writing, various house and pub exteriors in pen and ink. *Publications* illustrated: Countryside Commission: The East Devon Way; catalogues, arti cles, posterwork. *Signs work:* "H.W.," "H.L." or "H. LOCKE." *Address:* 'The Rosary', Godford Cross, Awliscombe, E. Devon EX14 0PP.

**WHITTINGHAM, Dr. Selby,** B.A. (1964), M.A., Ph.D. (1975); art historian founded Turner Soc. 1975 (Hon. Sec. 1975-76, 1980-84; Vice Chairman 1984- 85); and Watteau Soc. 1984 (Sec. General and Editor); and J.M.W. Turner R.A. (Co-Editor), 1988; *b* Batu Gajah, Malaya, 8 Aug., 1941. *m* Joanna Dodds *Educ:* Shrewsbury School; Universities of Oxford and Manchester *Publications:* An Historical Account of the Will of J.M.W. Turner, R.A. (1989 1996); The Fallacy of Mediocrity: The Need for a Proper Turner Gallery (1992); World Directory of Artists' Museums (1995). *Address:* Turner House 153 Cromwell Rd., London SW5 0TQ.

**WHITTLESEA, Michael,** R.W.S. (1985), N.E.A.C.; painter; *b* London, 6 June, 1938. *m* Jill. *Studied:* Harrow School of Art. *Exhib:* prizewinner, Singer Friedlander/Sunday Times Water-colour Competition. *Publications:* The Complete Watercolour Course (1987). *Clubs:* Chelsea Arts. *Signs work:* "Michael Whittlesea." *Address:* Richmond Cottage, High St., Hurley, Berks. SL6 5LT.

**WIELICZKO, Jan Staniskaw,** painter, sculptor and designer; Director. Centaur Gallery, London; lecturer and demonstrator, Slade School (1949); *b* Wilno, Poland, 1921. *m* Dinah Wieliczko. two *s. Educ:* Wilno, Poland. *Studied:* Slade School, London (1945-48) (1st prize Decorative Painting). *Exhib:* Irving Gallery (1953), Redfern Gallery (1954), Centaur Gallery, John Denham

Gallery (1992), Centaur Retrospective (1994); all the principal mixed exhbns. in London. Film, "Artistic biography of Jan Wieliczko" for Polish Television (1995). *Clubs:* Chelsea Arts. *Signs work:* "J. Wieliczko." *Address:* 82 Highgate High St., London N6.

**WILD, David Paul,** D.F.A. Slade (1955), Abbey Major Scholarship to Rome (1955); artist in oil and water-colour; Founder, Friends of the Weavers Triangle; *b* Burnley, 14 Apr., 1931. *Educ:* Burnley Grammar School. *Studied:* Burnley School of Art, Slade School of Fine Art. *Exhib:* extensively in the north of England since 1957; Woodstock Gallery (1965), John Moores (1965, 1970), R.A. (1972-74), Arts Council 'Drawings of People' Serpentine Gallery. *Work in collections:* W.A.G., Manchester City A.G., Rutherston Coll., Granada TV, Arts Council of G.B., Salford A.G., Bolton, Blackburn and Burnley Municipal galleries. *Signs work:* "D. Wild." *Address:* 66 Rosehill Rd., Burnley.

**WILDE, Louis,** N.D.D. (1955), A.T.C. (1956), D.A.E. (1970), M.A. (1980); painter in oil and acrylic; ex-Principal, Halifax School of Art; *b* London, 14 Mar., 1921. *m* Janet Wilde. one *s.* one *d. Educ:* The Millbank School, Westminster. *Studied:* Leeds College of Art (1951-55, Tom Watt, Gavin Stuart), Leeds University (1955-56 and 1969-70), B'ham Polytechnic (1977-78), privately under George Dafters. *Exhib:* Chiltern Gallery, London; New Art Centre, Chelsea; Seven Dials Gallery, London; Edinburgh Festival; Manchester Academy; Piece Hall Gallery, Halifax; Contemporary British Art touring U.S.A./Canada; Lane Gallery, Bradford; City A.G. Bradford. *Work in collections:* Bradford City Art Galleries, International Shakespeare Globe Centre. *Publications:* contributor to: Systems Art Enquiry Two (B'ham Polytechnic), Index of British Studies in Art Education (Allison). *Clubs:* S.G.F.A. *Signs work:* "Louis Wilde," "L.W.W.," "L. Wilde" or "Louis." *Address:* 60 Park Lane, Baildon, Shipley, W. Yorks. BD17 7LQ.

**WILES, Gillian,** A.R.B.S., I.B.H.S.; sculptor/painter/illustrator; *b* Johannesburg, 1942. *m* Dr. Robin Catchpole. *Educ:* Royal Veterinary College, London. *Studied:* Cape Town University, and Heatherley, London. *Exhib:* one-man shows: Sladmore, London, John Pence, San Francisco, The Collector, Johannesburg; exhib. at Tryon, London, R.B.S., Denis Hotz, London, Sportsmen's Edge, N.Y., Collector's Covey, Dallas. *Work in collections:* bronze sculptures: Genesee Museum, N.Y.S., Toyota S.A., Nikon S.A. *Commissions:* many, international. *Publications:* work repro.: illustrations for advertising. *Signs work:* "Gill Wiles." *Address:* c/o R.B.S., 108 Old Brompton Rd., London SW7 3RA.

**WILKINS, William Powell,** A.R.C.A.; artist in oil, lecturer and consultant; *b* Kersey, Suffolk, 4 Apr., 1938. *m* Lynne Brantly. two *d. Educ:* Malvern College. *Studied:* Swansea and Royal College of Art. *Exhib:* London, New York, San Francisco, Swansea. *Work in collections:* National Museum of Wales, Glynn Vivian Museum Swansea, Hirshorn Museum Washington D.C. *Address:* c/o Piccadilly Gallery, 16a Cork St., London W1X 1PF.

**WILKINSON, John Charles,** R.B.A.; artist in oil, water-colour, pen and ink, pencil; *b* Barnes, London, 20 July, 1929. *m* Sarah Goodwin, artist. one *s* one *d*. *Educ:* Bradford College; University College, London. *Studied:* R.A. Schools (1954-59). *Exhib:* two one-man shows, numerous mixed exhbns. *Signs work:* "J.C.W." and on back of work signs full name. *Address:* Garretts, Martin, Fordingbridge, Hants. SP6 3LN.

**WILKINSON, Ronald Scotthorn,** M.A., B.M., B.Ch. (Oxon.); physician, playwright, novelist, artist in oil, water-colour; *b* Melton Mowbray. two *d*. *Educ:* Shrewsbury School, Merton College, Oxford. *Studied:* under H. B. Hewlett. *Exhib:* Public Schools Exhbn., Leicester Soc. of Artists' Exhbn., R.A. Summer Exhbn. (1977); one-man show, Fine Art Trade Guild (1986). *Address:* 50 Hanover Steps, St. George's Fields, Albion St., London W2 2YG.

**WILKINSON-CLEMENTSON, William Henry,** R.E., A.R.C.A., F.I.A.L. (1946), Ph.D. (1980); line engraver and painter; Head of Dept. Engraving, City and Guilds of London Art School; *b* Bath, 1921. *m* Lady Margaret Ewer. one *d*. *Educ:* Winchester. *Studied:* Royal College of Art under Malcolm Osborne and Robert Austin, Heidelberg and Lindau, Germany, Fiorenza, Italy. *Work in collections:* Holland, Switzerland, Italy and America. *Clubs:* Chelsea Arts, Aviemore, Scotland, Swiss Alpine. *Signs work:* "HENRY WILKINSON." *Address:* Crane Cottage, Tatsfield, Westerham, Kent TN16 2JT.

**WILLIAMS, Alex,** N.D.D., A.T.D.; artist in oil on canvas; *b* Reading, 1942. *m* Celia. one *s*. two *d*. *Educ:* St. Peter's School, Cambs. *Studied:* St. Martin's School of Art (1962-66, Frdk. Gore, Peter Blake, Peter de Francia, David Tindle). *Exhib:* Helen Greenberg Gallery, Los Angeles (1977, 1982), Retrospective Hereford City Museum (1987), Fosse Gallery Stow on the Wold, The Kilvert Gallery, Clyro. *Work in collections:* National Library of Wales, National Trust, Hurst Newspapers, Hereford and Worcester City Museums, public and private collections in U.S.A. *Commissions:* has designed (restaurants) and painted many portraits of country houses. *Publications:* illustrated The Bird who Couldn't Fly (Hodder & Stoughton, 1988). Extensive collection of prints, greetings cards published and over 100 fine bone china designs distributed worldwide. *Signs work:* "Alex Williams '98." *Address:* Pemberton Cottage, St. John's Pl., Hay-on-Wye, Hereford HR3 5BN.

**WILLIAMS, Charles,** B.A. (Hons.) (1989), M.A. (R.A.S.) (1992); oil painter; *b* Evanston, Ill., U.S.A. *m* Alice Smith, artist. *Studied:* Maidstone College of Art (1986-89, Mike Upton, Peter Morrell, John Titchell), R.A. Schools (1989-92, Norman Adams, Mick Rooney, Roderic Barrett, David Parfitt). *Exhib:* Star Gallery Lewes, Coombs Contemporary, C.A.S., Mercury Gallery, N.E.A.C., R.A., R.O.S.L., N.P.G., *Work in collections:* T.V.S., Chevron (U.K.), K.I.A.D., British High Commission in Nairobi. *Clubs* Reynold's, N.E.A.C. *Address:* 141 Bower St., Maidstone, Kent ME16 8BB.

**WILLIAMS, Glynn,** sculptor in stone and bronze; Prof. of Sculpture R.C.A.; *b* Shrewsbury, 1939. *m* Heather. two *d*. *Studied:* Wolverhampton

College of Art (1955-60, 1960-61 Post Dip.); Rome Scholarship in Sculpture (1961-63). *Exhib:* one-man shows: including Blond Fine A.G. (1982), Bernard Jacobson Gallery (1985, 1986, 1988, 1991, 1994), Artsite Gallery, Bath (1987), Retrospective exhbn. at Margam Park, S. Wales (1992). *Work in collections:* A.C.G.B., Hakone Open Air Museum, Japan, V. & A., Tate Gallery. *Commissions:* Henry Purcell Memorial, City of Westminster (1996). *Clubs:* Chelsea Arts. *Signs work:* "G.W." *Address:* c/o Bernard Jacobson Gallery, 14a Clifford St., London W1X 1RF.

**WILLIAMS, Jacqueline E. E.,** B.A. (Hons.) (1985), Advanced Dip. (R.A.) (1988); artist in oil; *b* Lincoln, 2 Nov., 1962. *Educ:* Downlands School, Hassocks. *Studied:* Glos. College of Arts and Technology (1982-85), R.A. Schools (1985-88). *Exhib:* New Grafton Gallery, Barnes; solo show: Brian Sinfield Gallery; mixed shows: N.E.A.C., R.W.A., R.A. *Work in collections:* Cheltenham and Gloucester Bldg. Soc. H.Q., Contemporary Arts Soc. for Wales. *Clubs:* N.E.A.C., C.G.A. *Signs work:* "J.W." *Address:* Garden Flat, 73 Bath Rd., Cheltenham, Glos. GL53 7LH.

**WILLIAMS, Joan Barbara Price,** A.R.C.A., R.E., R.W.S.; printmaker and painter; *b* Pontypridd, S. Wales. *Educ:* High Wycombe High School. *Studied:* High Wycombe School of Art, Royal College of Art. *Exhib:* R.A., Bankside Gallery, International Biennales of Graphic Art, Ljubljana, Frechen, Germany, Biella, Italy. *Work in collections:* Arts Council, Welsh Arts Council, Sheffield, Oldham, Newcastle, Norwich, Glasgow and Hull Art Galleries and many university collections. *Signs work:* "Joan Williams." *Address:* 1 Upper Mill, Wateringbury, Maidstone, Kent ME18 5PD.

**WILLIAMS, Kyffin,** O.B.E. (1982), A.R.A. (1970), R.A. (1974), Hon.M.A. (Wales), D.L., Hon. D.Litt. Univ. of Wales (1993); artist in oil and watercolour, printing; Winston Churchill Fellow (1968); Hon. Fellow, Univ. College of Bangor, Swansea and Aberystwyth; Cymmrodorion Medal (1991); *b* Llangefni, Anglesey, 1918. *Educ:* Shrewsbury School. *Studied:* Slade School of Fine Art (1941-44). *Exhib:* Colnaghi (1947, 1949, 1970), Leicester Galleries (1951, 1954, 1957, 1967, 1970), Thackeray Gallery (1977, 1979, 1981, 1983, 1985, 1987, 1989, 1991, 1993) and in the provinces; retrospective exhbn. National Museum of Wales (1987). *Work in collections:* National Museum of Wales, Arts Council, Chantrey Bequest. *Publications:* autobiography, Across the Straits (Duckworth, 1973), A Wider Sky (Gwasg Gomer, 1991); illustrated, Gregynog, Kate Roberts (1981), Portraits (Gwasg Gomer, 1996). *Signs work:* "K.W." *Address:* Pwllfanogl. Llanfairpwll, Anglesey LL61 6PD.

**WILLIAMS, Mary,** R.W.A., S.W.A.; painter of landscape, marine and architectural subjects, also of flowers in water-colour and oil; *b* Ottery St. Mary, Devon. *Studied:* Exeter. *Exhib:* R.A., R.S.A., Paris Salon, R.I., R.B.A., etc., and in many municipal galleries; one-man show: R.A.M. Museum, Exeter (1974). *Work in collections:* Exeter Art Gallery, Sunderland Art Gallery, R.W.A. Bristol. *Signs work:* "Mary Williams." *Address:* Dormers, Orchard

Close, Manor Rd., Sidmouth, Devon EX10 8RS.

**WILLIAMS, Peter Ernest,** N.D.D., A.T.D., F.R.S.A.; artist in oils, water-colour, plaster, wood, metal, terracotta, ceramics; formerly Head of Art Department, Oldershaw School (now retd.); muralist and designer for exhbn. and shop-window display; *b* Bebington, 25 Jan., 1925. *m* 1st, Muriel E. Hammer, B.Sc. (d 25 June, 1964); 2nd, Patrica D. Wilson (d 9 Nov., 1988). two *s.* one *d. Educ:* Wirral Grammar School. *Studied:* Liverpool College of Art. *Exhib:* Liverpool Academy of Arts, etc. *Work in collections:* Liverpool University and mural decorations in several churches. *Signs work:* "Peter E. Williams." *Address:* Hedge-Lea, 43 Higher Bebington Rd., Bebington, Wirral, Merseyside L63 2PH.

**WILLIAMS, Susan,** R.A. Schools Dip.; artist in oil and water-colour; *b* Lichfield, Staffs., 23 July, 1944. *m* Ben Levene. one *s. Educ:* Lichfield Central School. *Studied:* Byam Shaw School, R.A. Schools. *Exhib:* regularly at R.A. Summer Exhbn., Spirit of London (prizewinner 1984), Ogle Gallery, Cheltenham, Duncan Campbell Gallery, Waterman Gallery, London. Work in private collections. *Signs work:* "S.W." *Address:* 26 Netherby Rd., London SE23 3AN.

**WILLIAMS-ELLIS, David Hugo Martyn,** R.C.A. (1993), A.R.B.S. (1992); sculptor in clay for bronze and terracotta; *b* Ireland, 6 Apr., 1959. *m* Serena Stapleton; two *s.* two *d* (one decd.). *Educ:* Headfort School, Ireland; Stowe School. *Studied:* in Florence (1977-78, Signorina Nerina Simi), Carrara (1979-80), Sir John Cass (1981-83). *Exhib:* London, Belfast, Paris, U.S.A., Japan, Argentina, South Africa. Many portrait busts and figures in private and public collections. *Clubs:* Arts, Lansdowne. *Signs work:* "D.W.E." dated with signet ring eagle on larger pieces. *Address:* 4 Walham Yard, London SW6 1JA.

**WILLIES, Joan,** R.M.S. (1976) (Eng.), M.A.A. (1995) (U.S.A.), H.S. (Eng.), Mem. Florida (Hon. mem.), Washington and Georgia Miniature Art Socs., U.S.A.; painter in oils, alkyds and water-colours, specialising in minia-tures; *b* Bristol, England, 23 Dec., 1929. *m* Mark Willies. three *s. Educ:* Bristol Commercial College, art studies under private tutors. *Exhib:* R.M.S., R.I., S.W.A., U.A., H.S. (Eng.), U.S.A., Australia, Spain, Germany, Canada, Japan, Tiffanys, U.S.A.; permanent exhbn. Bilmar Hotel, Treasure Island, Florida. *Publications:* The Artist's Workbook 1 and 2; illustrated children's books, St. Francis of Assisi (worldwide prints) I.G.M.A. prints Ohio. Writer of articles, artist magazines; author, 'Miniature Painting techniques and applications' (pub. Watson & Guptil, N.Y. June 1995; English distributors Phaidon Press, London). Awards: numerous U.K. and U.S.A. Teacher: Workshops interna-tionally and private groups at Joan Cornish Willies Studio, 1726 St. Croix Drive, Clearwater, Florida 34619. *Signs work:* "Joan Willies," or "Joan Cornish Willies, R.M.S., M.A.A., H.S." and see appendix. *Address:* P.O. Box 7659, Clearwater, Florida 34619, U.S.A.

**WILLIS, Lucy,** R.W.A. (1993); painter and printmaker in water-colour, oil, etching; *b* 15 Dec., 1954. *m* Anthony Anderson. one *s.* one *d. Educ:* Badminton School, Bristol. *Studied:* Ruskin School of Drawing and Fine Art, Oxford (1972-75). *Exhib:* eight solo shows at Chris Beetles, St. James's, London since 1986; R.A., R.W.A., N.P.G., B.P. Portrait award (1st prize 1992), Mall Galleries, R.W.S., R.E. *Work in collections:* N.P.G., R.W.A. *Publications:* 'Light, How to See it, How to Paint it'; 'Excursions in the Real World' by William Trevor (illustrations); Chris Beetles exhbn. catalogues (1988, 1989, 1994); Light in Water-colour (1997). *Signs work:* "Lucy Willis." *Address:* Moorland House, Burrowbridge, Bridgwater, Som. TA7 0RG.

**WILLS, Joan,** P.V.P.S.W.A., U.A., A.S.A.F., F.R.S.A.; mention hon. (Paris Salon); oil painter; past Vice-Pres., Soc. of Women Artists, Ass. Société des Artistes Français; Council Mem. United Soc. of Artists; *b* Shrewsbury. *m* Major-Gen. J. A. R. Robertson, C.B., C.B.E., D.S.O., D.L. one *d. Educ:* Albyn School, Aberdeen. *Studied:* Sir John Cass College, City and Guilds, London, and privately with the late Kenneth Green and the late Stanley Grimm. *Exhib:* R.O.I., R.B.A., S.W.A., U.A., R.M.S., N.S., Artists of Chelsea, Paris Salon. *Signs work:* "Wills." *Address:* 36 Marlborough Pl., London NW8 0PD.

**WILLS, Richard Allin,** N.D.D., A.U.A.; painter in oil and water-colour, etc.; art tutor; visiting lecturer; *b* Monmouth, 11 Sept., 1939. *m* Vera Elizabeth. one *s.* two *d. Educ:* King Henry VIII Grammar, Abergavenny. *Studied:* Newport College of Art (1956-61, Thomas Rathmell). *Exhib:* R.A., R.W.A., Welsh Young Contemporaries, R.S.P.P., U.A., W.C.S.W. *Work in collections:* British Steel Corp., Welsh Div. British Steel, Rank Xerox. *Commissions:* Welsh Office, Whitehall; Guildhall School of Music, London; Polytechnic of Wales; Yamazaki Mazak Europe; Royal Monmouthshire Royal Engineers; Royal Regiment of Wales. Work purchased: Contemporary Art Society. *Signs work:* "Richard A. Wills." *Address:* The Studio, Mansard House, Vine Acre, Monmouth, Gwent.

**WILSON, Arnold,** M.A., F.S.A., F.M.A.; former Chairman of Trustees, Holburne of Menstrie Museum, Bath, and serves on numerous other Coms.; formerly Director, City Art Gallery, Bristol; *b* Dulwich, 1932. twice married; two *d* by first marriage. *Educ:* Selwyn College, Cambridge, and Courtauld Inst. of Art. *Publications:* author: Dictionary of British Marine Painters (3 eds.); Dictionary of British Military Painters; Exploring Museums: South West England; numerous articles for Burlington Magazine, Apollo, Connoisseur, Country Life, etc. *Clubs:* Bristol Savages. *Address:* 4 George St., Bathwick Hill, Bath BA2 6BW.

**WILSON, Chris,** B.A.(Hons.) (1982), M.A. (1985); artist in oil and collage; *b* Belfast, 27 Dec., 1959. *m* Cindy Friers. one *s. Educ:* Belfast Royal Academy. *Studied:* Brighton College of Art (1979-82), University of Ulster (1984-85). *Exhib:* 'Shocks to the System' A.C.G.B. (1991), 'On the Balcony of the Nation' touring U.S.A. (1991-92), 'Shadows of Light' one-man touring Romania (1992), Bulgaria (1993). *Work in collections:* A.C.G.B., Arts Council of

# WHO'S WHO IN ART

Ireland, Aer Rianta Dublin, Queens University Belfast; private collections in Ireland, England, Germany, U.S.A. *Signs work:* "CHRIS WILSON" or "C. WILSON" with date. *Address:* 44 Victoria Rd., Bangor, Co. Down BT20 5EX.

**WILSON, David,** M.F.P.S. (1976); painter in oil, acrylic, water-colour, etching; *b* Gillingham, Kent, 23 May, 1936. *m* Sheila. two *s.* two *d. Educ:* Sir Joseph Williamson's Mathematical School, Rochester; Joint Services School of Linguists. *Studied:* Heatherley's (Evening classes 1976-77, Terry Shave). *Exhib:* R.A., R.B.A., Royal National Eisteddfod, N.E.A.C., S.G.A., R.Cam.A., F.P.S., and elsewhere in U.K., France and Ireland. *Work in collections:* National Library of Wales, Aberystwyth. *Signs work:* "David Wilson, Bridell." *Address:* Treleddyn Isaf, Bridell, Cardigan SA43 3DQ; and The Studio, 3 Cambrian Quay, Cardigan SA43 1EZ.

**WILSON, Douglas,** R.C.A., D.F.A., F.R.S.A.; painter in oil and water-colour; *b* 1936. *m* Heather Hildersley Brown. one *s. Studied:* Oxford University (1959-62, Percy Horton, Richard Naish, Geoffrey Rhodes). *Exhib:* R.A., R.B.A., R.O.I., R.Cam.A., Vis Art I (prizewinner), Edinburgh Festival, National Library of Wales, New Grafton Gallery, Piccadilly Gallery, Thackeray Gallery, Jablonski Gallery, London; one-man shows: Bluecoat Gallery, Williamson A.G. (1981, 1983), King St. Galleries, St. James' (1983, 1986, 1991), Metropolis International Galerie d'Art Geneva (1985), Phoenix Gallery, Lavenham (1987, 1989), Phoenix Gallery, Kingston upon Thames (1987), Anthony Dawson Artists at the Barbican (1987, 1990), Outwood Gallery (1987), Newburgh St. Gallery (1988). *Publications:* author, Wirral Visions. *Signs work:* "Douglas Wilson." *Address:* 123 Masons Pl., Newport, Salop.

**WILSON, Eleanor Mavis:** see GRÜNEWALD, Eleanor Mavis.

**WILSON, Helen,** S.B.A., B.A. (F.A.) 1996 (Uni.S.A.); painter in oils; working at M.W.A. Centre for Women's Art; *b* Surrey, 1 Sept., 1948. *m* Mua Wilson. two *s. Studied:* City and Guilds of London Art School (1987-88), University of South Africa (1990-95). *Exhib:* solo show at National Art Gallery of Namibia (1996), S.B.A. (1997). *Work in collections:* Telecoms Namibia. *Publications:* Article in "De Arte" (1994). *Clubs:* S.B.A. *Signs work:* "HW" joined. *Address:* 11 Church Rd., Hanwell, London W7 3BJ.

**WILSON, Lorna Yvette,,** B.A. Hons. (1989), Dip.F.A.-R.A. Schools (1992); artist in oil and gouache; *b* Jamaica, 6 July, 1967. *Studied:* Kingston University (1986-89, Derek Hirst), R.A. Schools (1989-92, Prof. Norman Adams, R.A..) *Exhib:* many mixed exhbns. in London. Currently doing series of prints for C.C.A. Galleries. *Address:* 8 Petherick House, 79 Stanley Rd., Hounslow, Middx. TW3 1YU.

**WILSON, Peter Reid,** D.A.; artist in oil paint on canvas; *b* Glasgow, 4 Sept., 1940. *Studied:* Glasgow School of Art (1960-64). *Exhib:* Lamont Gallery. *Work in collections:* Contemporary Arts Soc., A.C.G.B., S.A.C., Sheffield City A.G., Ferens A.G. Hull, Nottingham Castle Museum and A.G., Leicester

Museum and A.G., Glasgow A.G., Kelvingrove, Stoke-on-Trent Museum and A.G., Kettles Yard, Cambridge, etc. *Publications:* Peter Wilson - Paintings 1979-1985 (Third Eye, Glasgow, 1985), Dacapo - Drawings (Arc Publications, 1989). *Signs work:* c within a circle "Peter Wilson" and date. *Address:* 1 The Square, South Luffenham, Oakham, Leics. LE15 8NS.

**WILSON, Susan Ahipara,** B.F.A., Dip.R.A. Schools; Abbey Award to British School at Rome; painter in oil on canvas and hardboard; Fellow of Painting, Glos. College of Art and Technology; *b* Dunedin, N.Z., 22 May, 1951. *Educ:* Westlake Girls High School, N.Z. *Studied:* Camberwell School of Art (1978-82, Arnold van Praag, Tony Eyton, Dick Lee), R.A. Schools (1982-85, John Le Soeur). *Exhib:* R.A., Hayward Annual, Northern Young Contemporaries, John Player Portrait award, N.Z. House Gallery, G.L.C. Spirit of London, Richard Ford scholarship to Spain. *Address:* 51 Faraday Rd., Ladbroke Gr., London W10.

**WILSON, Timothy Hugh,** M.A., M.Phil., F.S.A. (1989), Hon.R.E, (1991), Fellow of Balliol (1990); Keeper of Western Art, Ashmolean Museum, Oxford (since 1990); *b* Godalming, 8 Apr., 1950. *m* Jane Lott. two *s.* one *d. Educ:* Winchester College; Corpus Christi College, Oxford; Warburg Inst. (London University); Dept. of Museum Studies (University of Leicester). *Publications:* books and articles chiefly on Italian maiolica and Renaissance applied arts. *Address:* Balliol College, Oxford OX1 3BJ.

**WILSON, Vincent John,** A.T.D., Mem. Newlyn Soc. of Artists, Penwith Soc. of Arts; painter and etcher; *b* Mold, Flintshire, 24 Nov., 1933. *m* Sheila Richards. one *d. Educ:* Alun Grammar School, Mold. *Studied:* Chester School of Art (1950-54), Liverpool College of Art (1954-55). *Exhib:* R.A., R.W.A., R.C.A., Piccadilly, Thackeray, Penwith Galleries, Celle, W. Germany, Welsh Arts Council (1958, 1974, 1981), Cornwall Now (Sussex 1986), Cornwall in the Eighties (Chichester 1987); one-man shows: Exeter University (1966), Newlyn (1971, 1972, 1980), Plymouth (1979), Taunton (1981), Guernsey (1990), St. Ives (1992). *Work in collections:* Plymouth A.G., Devon C.C., Surrey Educ. Com., Royal Cambrian Academy, Celle, British Foreign and Commonwealth Office (etchings). *Signs work:* "V. Wilson." *Address:* 3 Drakefield Drive, Saltash, Cornwall PL12 6BU.

**WILTON, Andrew,** M.A., F.R.S.A., Hon.R.W.S.; museum curator; Keeper of British Art, Tate Gallery (1989-); Curator, Turner Collection, Clore Gallery (1985-89), Curator of Prints and Drawings, Yale Center for British Art (1976-80), Asst. Keeper, Dept. of Prints and Drawings, British Museum (1967-76, 1981-84); *b* Farnham, Surrey, 7 Feb., 1942. *Educ:* Dulwich College; Trinity College, Cambridge. *Publications:* British Watercolours 1750-1850 (1977); The Life and Work of J.M.W. Turner (1979); Turner and the Sublime (1980); Turner in his Time (1987) and numerous exhbn. catalogues, articles and reviews. *Clubs:* Athenaeum. *Address:* Tate Gallery, London SW1P 4RG.

**WINDSOR, Alan,** B.A. (Lond.), Dip.F.A. (Lond.), N.D.D., D.A.(Manc.);

artist and writer; art historian; Senior Lecturer, Reading University; *b* Fleetwood, Lancs., 10 July, 1931. *m* Elfriede Windsor. one *s.* two *d. Educ:* Audenshaw Grammar School. *Studied:* Regional College of Art, Manchester (1949-54); Slade School, University College (1954-56); Universities of Paris and Aix (1956-57); Courtauld Institute, London University (1967-69). *Exhib:* Young Contemporaries, London Group, Gimpel Fils, Roland, Browse & Delbanco, Pollock, Toronto, New Ashgate, Farnham. *Publications:* Peter Behrens, 1868-1940, Architect and Designer (Architectural Press, 1981); Handbook of Modern British Painting, 1900-1980 (Scolar Press, 1992). *Clubs:* Architectural Association. *Signs work:* "A. Windsor." *Address:* 2 Wykeham Rd., Farnham, Surrey GU9 7JR.

**WINER, Zalmon,** R.B.A. (1984); painter in oil, pastel, acrylic, watercolour; designer, etcher and lithographer; *b* Gateshead, Co. Durham, 21 Nov., 1934. married. one *s.* two *d. Educ:* Gateshead Grammar School. *Studied:* art and architecture at Durham University; etching at Central School of Art and Design. *Exhib:* R.A., R.B.A., P.S., U.A., N.S., Ben Uri Gallery, C.P.S., Safrai Gallery, Jerusalem, Discerning Eye Exhbn. at Mall Galleries (1990), etc. *Work in collections:* Shipley A.G., Oundle Public School Gallery. *Publications:* illustrated Haggadah for the Exilarchs Foundation. *Signs work:* see appendix. *Address:* 53 Shirehall Park, London NW4 2QN.

**WINKELMAN, Joseph William,** B.A. (1964), C.F.A. (1971), R.E. (1982), R.W.A. (1989), Hon. R.W.S. (1996); artist and printmaker; President, Royal Soc. of Painter-Printmakers; *b* Keokuk, Iowa, U.S.A., 20 Sept., 1941. *m* Harriet Lowell Belin. two *d. Educ:* University of the South, University of Pennsylvania. *Studied:* University of Oxford, Ruskin School of Drawing (1968-71). *Exhib:* New Grafton Gallery, R.A., Bohun Gallery, Lumley Cazalet Gallery, Graffiti Gallery, Anthony Dawson, Oxford Gallery. *Work in collections:* Ashmolean Museum, Hereford Museum, Usher Gallery, Victoria A.G., Graves A.G., Bowes Museum, The Museum of London, The Royal Collection, Fitzwilliam Museum, National Museum of Wales. *Signs work:* "J. W. Winkelman." *Address:* The Hermitage, 69 Old High St., Headington, Oxford OX3 9HT.

**WINTER, Faith,** F.R.B.S., Feodora Gleichen Sculpture Award; sculptor in stone, wood, and bronze; *b* Richmond, Surrey, 1927. *m* Col. F. M. S. Winter, M.B.E., F.R.S.A. two *s.* one *d. Educ:* Oak Hall. *Studied:* Guildford and Chelsea Schools of Art. *Exhib:* R.A., R.B.A., R.W.S., Glasgow Academy of Fine Art, Covent Garden and elsewhere in the U.K.; International Centre of Contemporary Art, Paris; Malaysia and Singapore. *Commissions:* include: "The Soldiers" Catterick Camp; "Compassion" Hambro Foundation; The Falklands Islands Memorial relief; The Mysteries of the Rosary, Church of Our Lady Queen of Peace, East Sheen; John Ray statue, Braintree; Air Chief Marshal Lord Dowding and Marshal of the Royal Air Force Sir Arthur "Bomber" Harris statues, The Strand, London; Lennard standing figure 'The

Spirit of Youth', Ontario, Canada; Salters' Hall Coat-of-arms, London; Archbishop George Abbot, Guildford; H.R.H. The Princess Royal, The President of Kenya, Jeffrey Archer, Maria Callas and the late Kamal Jumblatt. *Signs work:* "Faith Winter" (formerly "Faith Ashe.") *Address:* Venzers Studio, Venzers Yard, The Street, Puttenham, Guildford, Surrey GU3 1AU.

**WINTERINGHAM, Claude Richard Graham,** Dip. Arch., F.R.I.B.A., R.B.S.A.; Architect; chairman, Sir Barry Jackson Trust (1982-96); R.N.V.R. Fleet Air Arm Lt. (1941-46), chairman, Solihull Round Table (1956-57), founder mem. and vice chairman, Solihull Civic Soc. (1958-62), president, B'ham Architecture Assoc. (1971-72); *b* Louth, Lincs., 2 Mar., 1923. *m* Lesley Patricia. two *s.* one *d.* Awards: Mason Court Civic Trust (1969), Lichfield City Hall, Civic Soc. Commendation (1976), Lench's Close, Moseley, D.O.E. Housing Design (1983), B'ham Repertory Theatre Architecture (1972). *Clubs:* R.I.B.A. Sailing, B'ham Chamber of Industry and Commerce. *Address:* 7 Sir Harry's Rd., Edgbaston, Birmingham B15 2UY.

**WISE, Gillian,** artist, architectonic reliefs and paintings; *b* London, 1936. *Educ:* Wimbledon School of Art (1954-57). Awards: Unesco Fellowship, Prague (1968); post-graduate, Repin Inst., Leningrad (1969-70); Research Grant, International Communication Agency (1981); Graham Foundation Award, Chicago (1983). *Exhib:* I.C.A. with Anthony Hill (1963), Tokyo Biennale (1965), "British Sculpture in The Sixties," C.A.S. (1965), "Relief/Construction/Relief," Museum of Contemporary Art Chicago (1968), Nuremburg Biennale (1969), Systems (1972), Hayward Annual (1978), R.A. Summer Shows (1981-83, 1986-87), Blom and Dorn Gallery, N.Y.C. (1984-85), Textum Ars, Paris (1990-94). *Work in collections:* Tate Gallery (London and Liverpool), British Council, Arts Council, Contemporary Arts Society, V. & A., Gulbenkian, Lisbon, McCrory Corp. N.Y., Amos Andersonin Taidemuseo, Helsinki. *Commissions:* Architectural: two-storey stainless steel relief for foyer, Nottingham University Hospital; reflex murals, Barbican Centre. *Signs work:* "G. WISE" or "Gillian Wise." *Address:* 3 passage Rauch, 75011 Paris.

**WISHART, Michael,** painter, writer; Knight of St. Lazarus; nominated Academician of Italy with gold medal (1980); *b* London, 12 June, 1928. *m* 1950, Anne, d of Sir James Dunn, Bt. one *s. Studied:* Academie Julian, Paris (1948). *Exhib:* one-man shows: Archer Gallery (1944), Redfern Gallery (1956, 1958, 1960), Leicester Galleries (1963, 1967, 1969, 1973), portrait of Rudolf Nureyev, Royal Academy (1968), Arts Council "Six Young Painters" (1957), Contemporary Art Society "Recent Acquisitions" Whitechapel Gallery (1968), Morley Gallery (1969); retrospective exhbn., "Paintings 1964-76" David Paul Gallery, Chichester (1976); Parkin Gallery (1985); R.A. Summer Exbhn. (1980, 1985, 1988, 1989, 1990); group shows: Parkin Gallery (1985-95). *Work in collections:* Arts Council, C.A.S., Garman Ryan Collection, Walsall. *Publications:* work repro.: Apollo, Burlington Magazine, Studio International,

The Book of Joy, The Observer, Arts Review, Dance and Dancers, La Revue Moderne, Art and Literature, "High Diver" (autobiography), 1977. *Clubs:* Travellers', Chelsea Arts. *Signs work:* "Michael Wishart." *Address:* 34 Brunswick Sq., Hove, E. Sussex BN3 1ED.

**WITHINGTON, Roger,** Dip.A.D. (Graphics) (1966), A.T.D. (1967), A.R.E. (hon. retd.); artist in pencil and water-colour; artist/designer at Bank of England (1983-93), designed new series of banknotes known as Series E; *b* Prestwich, 4 Oct., 1943. *m* Rose-Marie Edna Cobley. one *s.* one *d. Educ:* Barry Grammar/Technical School, S. Glam. *Studied:* Cardiff College of Art (1962-63, etching: Philip Jennings, A.R.E.), Newport (Gwent) College of Art (1963-66, illustration: John Wright). *Exhib:* R.E. Galleries, Bankside Galleries. *Publications:* designed/part author series of booklets to accompany new banknotes. *Signs work:* "R. Withington" or "R.W." *Address:* 51 Garland Cl., Exeter EX4 2NT.

**WITHROW, William John,** Honour B.A., Art and Archaeology (1950), Art Specialist, O.C.E. (1951), B.Ed. (1955), M.Ed. (1958), M.A. (1965); Director Emeritus, Art Gallery of Ontario; Member: Order of Canada (1980), Fellow, Canadian Museums Assoc. (1985), Canadian Art Museums Directors Organisation, American Assoc. of Museums, Assoc. of Art Museum Directors, Canadian National Com. for I.C.O.M., Art Advisory Com., University Club of Toronto; *b* Toronto, 30 Sept., 1926. *m* June Roselea Van Ostrom. three *s.* one *d. Educ:* University of Toronto. *Studied:* University of Toronto (1946-65, Professor Peter Brieger, Professor Stephen Vickers). *Commissions:* Ricard/Withrow report on National Museums, Canada. *Publications:* Sorel Etrog Sculpture, Contemporary Canadian Painting. *Clubs:* University Club of Toronto, Highland Yacht. *Address:* 7 Malabar Pl., Don Mills, Ontario M3B 1A4.

**WOLKERS, Joan Elizabeth Margaret,** N.D.D. (Painting, 1948), Abbey Scholarship (1949), R.A. Silver Medals (1951, 52, 53); retd. teacher; *b* Tunbridge Wells, 28 Aug., 1928. *m* G.L. Wolkers. one *s. Educ:* Lawnside, Malvern. *Studied:* Malvern School of Art under Victor Hume Moody (1945-50) and R.A. Schools under Henry Rushbury, Fleetwood Walker and William Dring (1950-54); Royal Academy, Amsterdam (1954-58). *Exhib:* R.A., R.B.S.A., R.P., N.E.A.C., Brighton A.G., Worcester A.G., Malvern Art Club, Kenn Group, Exeter. Specialises in portraiture. *Signs work:* "J.E.M. Wolkers." *Address:* 37 Powderham Cres., Exeter EX4 6BZ.

**WOLSTENHOLME, Jonathan,** artist/illustrator in water-colour, oil, pen and ink; *b* London, 22 Nov., 1950. *m* Margaret. one *s. Educ:* Purley Grammar School. *Studied:* Croydon College of Art (1969-72). *Exhib:* two one-man shows in London, others in Paris and Brussels. Gallery affiliation: John Campbell Gallery, 164 Walton St., London SW3 2JL. *Signs work:* "Jonathan Wolstenholme." *Address:* Wimbledon, London.

**WOLVERSON, Margaret Elizabeth,** N.D.D., A.T.D., elected A.R.M.S.

(1977); painter of living landscape, portraits etc.; formerly lectured at Hornsea Inst. of Further Education and Stourbridge College of Art; *b* 1937. *m* 1961; one *s.* (div. 1985); *m* 1987, S. Jones-Robinson. *Studied:* Dudley School of Art, Wolverhampton College of Art, Leicester College of Art. *Exhib:* R.M.S., Mall Galleries, Cheltenham Group, Britain's Painters; one-man show Dean Heritage Centre, Workshop Gallery, Chepstow (1997). *Work in collections:* East Riding Collection for Schools, Ferens A.G.; private collections in U.K., U.S.A. *Commissions:* numerous. *Clubs:* Forest Artists Network. *Signs work:* see appendix. *Address:* Sunny Bank, Pope's Hill, Newnham-on-Severn, Glos. GL14 1JX.

**WOLVERSON, Martin,** F.R.B.S. (1971), F.R.S.A. (1976); R.B.S. Silver medal (1971), Trident Television Fine Art Fellow (1977-78), Fulbright Prof. Kansas City Art Inst. (1985); sculptor in wood, stone, metal, lecturer; *b* Wolverhampton, 26 May, 1939. *m* (1) Margaret Smith; one *s.* (2) Sandra Tipper.*Educ:* Wednesbury Boys High School. *Studied:* Wolverhampton School of Art (1956-60, Tom Wright, John Paddison), Goldsmiths' College (1960-61). *Exhib:* widely in the North, London and Kansas. *Work in collections:* Ferens A.G., Hull, Usher A.G., Lincoln, Yorkshire Television, N.C.B., Ecclesiastic Insurance Co. Ltd., Lincolnshire and Humberside Arts, Humberside C.C., Leeds City A.G., and private collections. *Signs work:* "M. Wolverson." *Address:* The Holbrooks, Mount Pleasant East, Robin Hoods Bay, Whitby, N. Yorks. YO22 4RF.

**WONNACOTT, John Henry,** Slade Dip. (1962); painter in oil; *b* London, 1940. *m* Anne Rozalie Wesolowska, B.Sc. two *d. Educ:* University College School. *Studied:* Slade School (1958-63). *Exhib:* Hayward (1974), R.A. Jubilee (1952-77), Marlborough (1981), Marlborough, N.Y. (1983), Tate Gallery (1984), The Foudation Veranneman (1986-87), The Pursuit of the Real, Barbican (1990); one-man shows, Minories, Colchester (1972), Rochdale (1978); touring, Marlborough (1980-81, 1985, 1988), Scottish National Portrait Gallery (1986-87). *Work in collections:* M. of W., Arts Council, Rochdale A.G., Norwich Castle Museum, Tate Gallery, Scottish National Portrait Gallery. *Address:* 5 Cliff Gdns., Leigh-on-Sea, Essex.

**WOOD, Andy,** Dip.A.D. (1970), A.R.B.A. (1980), R.I. (1981); painter in acrylic, oil and water-colour; *b* Porlock, Som., 1947. *m* Katrina Wood. one *s.* one *d. Educ:* schools in Walton-on-Thames, Hersham and Dorking. *Studied:* Croydon and Newport Colleges of Art (1965-70). *Exhib:* R.I., R.B.A., Thackeray Gallery, etc. *Work in collections:* Sultan of Oman; Duke University, N.C., U.S.A.; Central Carolina Bank, N.C., U.S.A.; Lyme Regis Museum. *Commissions:* Sultan of Oman; British Telecom; Southern Gas. *Publications:* Dictionary of 20th Century British Painters, Sculptors and other artists (Antique Collectors Club Ltd). *Clubs:* Chelsea Arts. *Signs work:* "Andy Wood" or "A. Wood." *Address:* Woodside, Hill Rd., Lyme Regis, Dorset DT7 3PG.

**WOOD, Annette (Mrs.):** see GARDNER, Annette.

**WOOD, Christopher Paul,** B.A.Hons. (1984), M.A. (1986); painter in oil on canvas and printmaking mediums; A/L lecturer in Art and Design, York College of Art; *b* Leeds, 10 June, 1961. *m* Simone Abel. two *d. Educ:* Leeds. *Studied:* Jacob Kramer School of Art (1980-81), Leeds Polytechnic (1981-84), Chelsea School of Art (1985-86). *Exhib:* one-man shows: Oldham City A.G. (1986), Sue Williams Gallery, London (1989, 1990, 1992, 1994); mixed shows: Festival Hall (1986), I.C.A. Young Contemporaries (1986), Art London (1989, 1990, 1991), Oldham City A.G. (1989), New Generation, London (1990), Bonhams, Knightsbridge (1991), Rebecca Hossack Gallery (1996), Brit Art (1997). *Signs work:* full signature on back of canvas; initialled on front of paintings - "C.P.W." and date. *Address:* 1 Norfok Pl., Chapel Allerton, Leeds LS7 4PT.

**WOOD, Duncan,** B.A. Hons. Fine Art, Sheffield Hallam University, P.G.C.E., London University, The Inst. of Educ.; artist in oil, water-colour; *b* London, 14 Nov., 1960. *Educ:* Kingham Hill School, Oxfordshire. *Studied:* Gloucestershire College of Art (1980-81), Sheffield College of Art (1981-84). *Exhib:* R.C.A., R.A., City art galleries: Sheffield, Glasgow, Nottingham; galleries: Cardiff, Edinburgh, Birkenhead, London, Fosse Gallery, Stow-on-the-Wold; also exhib. at 'Discerning Eye Exhbns.' (work chosen by Glynn Williams, Prof. of Sculpture at R.C.A. 1992, and by Sir Brinsley Ford ex Chairman of National Art Collections Fund 1991, William Packer, art critic Financial Times, and Martin Gayford, writer and art critic of the Daily Telegraph and Modern Painters 1996). *Work in collections:* throughout the U.K., in London and in the U.S.A., Germany and Japan; public collections: The Finnish Embassy and Sheffield University. Established "The New English School of Drawing" at Nottingham City Art Galleries (1993). *Clubs:* N.E.A.C. (1991). Com.mem.. N.E.A.C. School of Drawing (1995). *Signs work:* "Duncan Wood." *Address:* 1 Church St., Baslow, Bakewell, Derbyshire DE45 1RY.

**WOOD, Gerald Stanley Kent,** M.B.I.A.T. (1968), M.S.A.I. (1977), F.E.T.C. (1978); artist and architectural illustrator in pencil, ink, water-colour, gouache and tempera, perspectivist, architectural technologist, tutor, lecturer; *b* Cambridge, 29 Oct., 1923. *Educ:* Perse Preparatory School, Cambridge, Elmers Grammar School, Old Bletchley, Bucks. *Studied:* under H. J. Sylvester Stannard, R.B.A. (1934-39). *Exhib:* R.A., R.B.A., R.I., R.M.S., N.E.A.C., U.A., N.S., S.B.A., S.G.A., P.S., Contemporary British Watercolours, Pictures for Schools, Britain in Water-colours, Britain's Painters, Lord Mayor's Art Award, Hesketh Hubbard Art Soc., Chelsea Art Soc., Open Salon, Luton Museum. *Work in collections:* Theatre Royal, Haymarket, National Westminster Bank, Theatre Museum; private collections: England, Wales, Australia, Canada, Germany, Saudi Arabia. *Signs work:* see appendix. *Address:* 21 Salisbury Rd., Luton, Beds. LU1 5AP.

**WOODFORD, David,** N.D.D., A.T.C. with distinction, Cert. R.A.S.; painter in oil and water-colour; Royal Cambrian Academician; *b* Rawmarsh,

Yorks., 1 May, 1938. *m* June. two *s*. *Educ:* Lancing College. *Studied:* West Sussex College of Art (1955-59), Leeds College of Art (1959-60), Royal Academy Schools (1965-68). He lives by his painting. *Signs work:* "David Woodford." *Address:* Ffrancon House, Ty'n-Y-Maes, Bethesda, Bangor, Gwynedd LL57 3LX.

**WOODIE:** see RAINE, Sarah Lamar.

**WOODINGTON, Walter,** R.P., R.B.A., N.E.A.C.; painter in oil and water-colour; part-time teacher, Woolwich Polytechnic Art School (1946-60); appointed Curator, Royal Academy Schools (1961-84); *b* London, June, 1916. *m* Jacqueline Murray. *Studied:* Woolwich Polytechnic Art School and City and Guilds Art School under A. R. Middleton-Todd, R.A. *Exhib:* R.A., R.P., R.B.A., N.E.A.C., etc. *Publications:* work repro.: for Hutchinson's and Odhams Press. *Signs work:* "WOODINGTON." *Address:* 5 Kenver Ave., Finchley, London N12 0PG.

**WOODS, Grace Mary,** A.R.C.A.; artist in black and white and pastel, and weaving; *b* Ilford, Essex, 25 Feb., 1909. *m* Sidney W. Woods, A.R.C.A. (decd.). two *s*. three *d*. *Educ:* Ursuline Convent, Forest Gate, E7. *Studied:* West Ham Art School and Royal College of Art in Design and Engraving Schools. *Exhib:* R.A. and other London galleries. Work purchased by private collectors. *Signs work:* "Mary Woods." *Address:* 157 Warren Rd., Chelsfield, Orpington, Kent BR6 6ES.

**WOODSIDE, Christine A.,** D.A. (1968), Post Dip. (1969), R.S.W. (1993); artist in water-colour and mixed media; *b* Aberdeen, 24 Apr., 1946. *m* Samuel Woodside. one *s*. one *d*. *Educ:* Aberdeen High School for Girls. *Studied:* Gray's School of Art, Aberdeen (1964-69, Ian Fleming, Robert Henderson Blythe). Numerous exhbns. *Signs work:* "Christine A. Woodside" and year. *Address:* Garden Cottage, Bellwood, Dundee Rd., Perth PH2 7AL, Scotland.

**WOOLF-NELLIST, Meg,** B.A., A.T.D., F.S.D.C; awarded Exhibition, R.C.A. (1949); formerly lecturer in art, Rachel McMillan College of Educ., Director, Bermuda Art Assoc. School (1950-52); artist in stone, wood, calligrapher; *b* Isle of Thanet, 10 Dec., 1923. *m* Anthony Nellist. one *s*. three *d*. *Educ:* Couvent des Oiseaux. *Studied:* Ravensbourne College of Art, Brighton College of Art (1939-42). *Exhib:* Roland, Browse and Delbanco, A.I.A., R.B.A., R.A., V. & A., Russell Cotes, Hove A.G. (one-man, 1948); with Designer Craftsmen (1968-69), Hornchurch A.G. (1986, 1987, 1989, 1991, 1993, 1994). *Work in collections:* Canada, U.S.A., Germany, Australia. *Publications:* work repro.: Studio. *Signs work:* see appendix. *Address:* 84 Front Lane, Cranham, Essex RM14 1XW.

**WOOLFORD, Harry Russell Halkerston,** O.B.E. (1970), M.A.(Hon.) Dundee University (1976); until 1970 specialist in picture restoration; chief restorer, National Gallery of Scotland; Hon. Mem. Assoc. of British Picture Restorers; *b* Edinburgh, 23 May, 1905. *m* Nancy Philip. one *d*. *Educ:* Edinburgh. *Studied:* Edinburgh College of Art (painting and drawing) and

R.S.A. Life School (Carnegie Travelling Scholarship and Chalmers Bursary, London, Paris and Italy). Fellow, Museums Association and International Institute for Conservation of Historic and Artistic Works. *Address:* 7a Barntongate Ave., Edinburgh EH4 8BD.

**WOOLLASTON, Mountford Tosswill,** artist in oil, water-colour, pen, pencil; *b* Toko, N.Z., 1910. *m* Edith Alexander. three *s*. one *d*. *Educ:* Stratford Technical High School, N.Z. *Studied:* Nelson under Hugh Scott (1930), Christchurch under Len Booth (1931), Dunedin under R. N. Field (1932), and particularly under Flora Scales from Hans Hoffman's School in Munich (1935). *Exhib:* many one-man shows in N.Z., Melbourne and Sydney (1958). *Work in collections:* National Gallery of Victoria, Melbourne, Art Gallery of N.S.W., Sydney, all main N.Z. galleries and universities. *Signs work:* "Woollaston." *Address:* Upper Moutere, Nelson 7152, N.Z.

**WOOTTON, Frank,** O.B.E. (1995), A.A.; President, Guild of Aviation Artists; artist in oil and water-colour, gold medallist, travelling scholarship (1930), official artist R.A.F. (1944-46); *b* Milford, 30 July, 1914. *m* Virginia Cawthorne. two *s*. two *d*. *Educ:* Eastbourne. *Studied:* under Reeve-Fowkes, Eric Ravillious, Eastbourne School of Art. *Exhib:* R.A., Towner Art Gallery, Eastbourne, R.O.I., Imperial War Museum, Paris, Rangoon, New York, Washington D.C., Oshkosh, R.A.F. Museum, London. *Work in collections:* Sussex Collection, Eastbourne; Command Stations, R.A.F.; Imperial War Museum; Smithsonian Inst. National Air and Space Museum; Australian War Memorial, Canberra; National Aviation Museum, Canada. *Publications:* How to Draw Aircraft, How to Draw Cars, Wie Zeichne Ich Autos. The Aviation Art of Frank Wootton, At Home in the Sky, The Landscape Paintings of Frank Wootton (1959), Frank Wootton 50 Years of Aviation Art (1992, 1996). *Clubs:* Royal Air Force. *Signs work:* "Wootton." *Address:* Mayflower House, Alfriston, Sussex BN26 5QT.

**WORSLEY, John Godfrey Bernard,** portrait painter, marine artist, sculptor, illustrator, glass engraver, oil, water-colour, charcoal, ink; Past Pres. (1983-88) R.S.M.A.; Lieut. R.N.V.R. (1939-45), Official Naval War Artist (1943-45); creator of 'Albert R.N.', the dummy P.O.W. escape device (1944); *b* 16 Feb., 1919. *Studied:* Goldsmiths' College (1935-38). *Exhib:* R.S.M.A. annually, R.A., R.P.; one-man shows: Mall Galleries. *Work in collections:* Imperial War Museum, National Maritime Museum, provincial galleries and Exxon Collection N.Y. *Publications:* Drawing Ships, and many children's book and television programme illustrations. *Clubs:* Savage, Naval. *Signs work:* "John Worsley." *Address:* Park Studio, Putney Park La., London SW15 5HD.

**WORTH, Leslie Charles,** A.R.C.A. (Lond.) (1946), R.B.A. (1951), R.W.S. (1959), F.R.S.A. (1992); prizewinner Hallmark International Art Award, New York (1955); painter in water-colour and oil; President, R.W.S., R.B.A.; *b* Bideford, Devon, 6 June 1923. *m* Jane Taylor. one *s*. three *d*. *Educ:* St. Budeaux School, Plymouth. *Studied:* Plymouth School of Art (1938-39, 1942-43),

Bideford School of Art (1940-42), Royal College of Art (1943-46). *Exhib:* Agnews, Mercury Gallery, Wildenstein. Several mural commissions. *Work in collections:* R.A., National Gallery of New Zealand, Aberdeen, Birmingham, Brighton, Burton (Bideford), Rochdale, Southport and Wakefield Art Galleries, Eton College, West Riding of Yorks. Educ. Authority, G.L.C., Admiralty; private collections: H.M. Queen Elizabeth, Queen Mother and several private collections. *Publications:* The Practice of Watercolour Painting (Pitmans and Watson Guptil, 1977, Search Press 1980); magazine articles. *Clubs:* Arts. *Signs work:* "Leslie Worth." *Address:* 11 Burgh Heath Rd., Epsom, Surrey KT17 4LW.

**WORTH, Philip,** M.A., LL.B., Hon. Sec. F.P.S.; self taught artist in acrylic; *b* Gillingham, 23 June, 1933. *m* Jennifer Louise. two *d*. *Educ:* Royal High School, Edinburgh, Edinburgh University. *Exhib:* many one-man and group shows throughout U.K. since 1984. *Signs work:* "P. WORTH." *Address:* The White House, 282 St. John's Rd., Boxmoor, Hemel Hempstead, Herts. HP1 1QG.

**WRAGG, John,** R.A., A.R.C.A., R.B.S.; sculptor in wood; *b* York, 20 Oct., 1937. one *s*. *Studied:* York School of Art (1954-56), Royal College of Art (1956-60). Awards Sainsbury award (1960), winner, Sainsbury Sculpture Competition (1966), Arts Council (1977): Chantrey Bequest (1981). *Exhib:* solo shows: (1963-97), include; Hanover Gallery, Gallerie Alexandre Iolas Paris, York Festival, Devizes Museum Gallery, L'Art Abstrait London, Monumental '96 Belgium; Courcouxand Courcoux, etc.; group shows (1959-93); Bradford A.G., Gimpel Hanover Galerie Zurich, L'Art Vivant, Bath Festival Gallery, Quinton Green Fine Art London, Connaught Brown, etc. *Work in collections:* Sainsbury Centre, University of E. Anglia; Israel Museum, Jerusalem; Tate Gallery, London; A.C.G.B.; Arts Council of N.I.; Contemporary Art Soc.; Wellington A.G., N.Z.; National Gallery of Modern Art, Edinburgh. *Publications:* Neue Dimensionen der Plastic (Undo Kutterman), British Sculpture in the 20th Century (1981), etc. *Address:* 6 Castle Lane, Devizes, Wilts. SN10 1HJ.

**WRAITH, Robert,** R.P.; painter in oil, water-colour, drawing, etching; *b* London, 11 Dec., 1952. *m* Tina. one *s*. two *d*. *Educ:* Stowe. *Studied:* Florence (Pietro Annigoni). *Exhib:* twelve one-man shows, also N.P.G., R.A., R.P.,etc. *Work in collections:* The Vatican, M.C.C., National Trust, Oxford University, fresco in the Church of Ponte Buggianese, Italy, etc. *Commissions:* Many portrait commissions. *Signs work:* "WRAITH" or "Robbie Wraith." *Address:* The Old School House, The Green, Holton, Oxon. OX33 1PS.

**WRAY, Peter,** R.E. (1991), M.A. (1992), P.G.Dip.A.D. (1984), Cert.Ed. (1972); artist in printmaking/painting; Senior lecturer in Printmaking, University College of Ripon and York St. John; *b* Sedgefield, Co. Durham, 27 Oct., 1950. *m* Cecilia. two *d*. *Educ:* St. Mary's School, Darlington. *Studied:* St. Mary's College, Strawberry Hill, Twickenham (1969-72), Goldsmiths' College

(1983-84, John Rogers, Peter Mackarrell), Leeds Polytechnic (1990-92, Geoff Teasdale). *Exhib:* R.E., International Print Biennale, New Academy Gallery, Curwen Gallery, etc. *Signs work:* "P. Wray." *Address:* The Old School, 62 York Rd., Acomb, York YO2 5LW.

**WRIGHT, Bert,** R.S.M.A., F.R.S.A.; Vice President, Royal Soc. of Marine Artists, mem., Wapping Group of Artists who specialise in paintings of the River Thames; marine painter, but also includes architectural subjects and landscapes; *b* 1930. *Studied:* Nottingham College of Art. *Exhib:* R.A., and regularly at major galleries in the London area and in the U.S.A. *Work in collections:* U.K., U.S.A., Far East and the Middle East. *Commissions:* New York Yacht Club, Sultan of Oman, Daily Express, Standard Chartered Bank, British American Tobacco, Mullard Electronics, Beecham Group, Lloyds, Allied Dunbar. *Publications:* listed in '20th Century Marine Art', articles for 'Artist' magazine. Prizewinner Sunday Times/Singer Friedlander Water-colour competition. *Address:* 19 Carew Rd., Ealing, London W13 9QL.

**WRIGHT, Gordon Butler,** F.B.S. Comm., F.Inst.C., Mem. International Association of Artists; professional artist in oils; *b* Darlington, Co. Durham, 2 Apr., 1925. *m* Joan. *Educ:* Gladstone School, Darlington and Kings College, Newcastle. *Studied:* Chichester College of Art (1943-44) followed by two periods of study in Amsterdam and The Hague. Influenced by the Dutch Romantic School. *Exhib:* Galerie Montmartre, Paris, Grosvenor Gallery and Portal Gallery, London, Trinity Art Gallery, Wareham, Whitgift Galleries, London, Recorded in the National Maritime Museum, Greenwich. *Publications:* The Collector's Guide to Paintings as an Investment. *Signs work:* "G. B. Wright." *Address:* 123 Wetherby Rd., Harrogate, Yorks.

**WRIGHT, Valerie Margaret,** B.Ed.Hons. (1977), S.W.A. (1986), S.B.A. (1987); landscape, botanical and wildlife painter in water-colour; *b* Manchester, 6 Jan., 1934. *m* Norman Wright. one *s.* two *d. Educ:* Peterborough High School, Hendon Polytechnic, Coloma College of Educ. London University. *Studied:* Coloma College (Constance Stubbs, Norma Jameson). *Exhib:* R.I., S.W.A., S.B.A., Portico Gallery, Manchester, Manchester Academy, B.W.S., Gorstella Gallery; one-man shows: Chester, Warrington, Bolton Octagon Theatre, Frodsham Arts Centre, Norton Priory. *Signs work:* "Valerie Wright." *Address:* Appletree Cottage, 55 Rushgreen Rd., Lymm, Ches. WA13 9PS.

**WROUGHTON, Julia,** N.D.D. (1957), A.R.C.A. (1960), R.W.A. (1963); painter in oil and water-colour; Principal, Inniemore School of Painting since 1967; *b* Bridge of Allan, Stirlingshire, 24 Oct., 1934. *m* Alastair Macdonald. one *s.* three *d. Educ:* Beacon School, Bridge of Allan. *Studied:* Colchester School of Art (1953-57) under John O'Connor, Hugh Cronyn, Royal College of Art (1957-60) under Carel Weight, R.A., Colin Hayes, R.A. and Roger de Gray. *Exhib:* R.A., one-man show: Torrance Gallery, Edinburgh, Glengorm Castle, Isle of Mull. R.W.A., Malcolm Innes Gallery, Edinburgh. *Work in collections:*

# WHO'S WHO IN ART

Royal West of England Academy, Nuffield Foundation, Mrs. Nelson, Glengorm Castle. *Signs work:* "Julia Wroughton," "J. W." *Address:* Inniemore Lodge, Pennyghael, Isle of Mull PA70 6HD.

**WU, Ching-Hsia,** artist; paintress in water-colour and poetess; Prof. Shanghai Academy of Fine Arts, Prof. Shanghai Normal University; Vancouver Golden Jubilee Chinese Carnival Honorary Prize, Canada (1936); *b* Changchow, China, 11 Feb., 1910. *Educ:* at home and studied art under father. *Exhib:* Shanghai, Nanking, Peking, Rome, Jakarta, Surabaya, Singapore, Helsinki, Tokyo, Hong Kong, Osaka, Paris, Stockholm, Canton, etc. *Work in collections:* Shanghai Art Gallery, Katesan House, Jakarta; etc. *Publications:* Select Work of Wu Qing-Xia. *Clubs:* China Art Society, Shanghai, Accademico d'Europa. *Signs work:* "WU Ching-Hsia," (Wu Qing-Xia). *Address:* 301/3, Lane 785, Ju Lu Road, Shanghai (China).

**WUNDERLICH, Paul,** painter in oil, gouache, lithography; sculptor; *b* Eberswalde, 10 Mar., 1927. *m* Karin Székessy. two *d. Educ:* Berlin High School. *Studied:* Academy Hamburg. *Exhib:* all over Europe, United States, Japan, S. Africa and Australia. *Work in collections:* museums in Europe, U.S.A. and Japan. *Publications:* Paul Wunderlich (Denoel, Paris 1972), Lithografien 1959-73 (Office du Livre, Fribourg Suisse), Monographie 1978 (Filipacchi Paris), Monographie (1955-80), Huber, Offenbach, Homo Sum 1978 (Piper, Munich), Bilder zu Manet (Cotta, Germany 1978). *Signs work:* "Paul Wunderlich." *Address:* Haynstr. 2. D-20249 Hamburg 20.

**WYATT, Arthur Leonard,** T.D. (art pottery), F.F.P.S.; artist in acrylics, mixed media; art teacher (1950-82); *b* London, 6 Dec., 1922. *m* Margaret Sybil Lucy. two *s. Educ:* West Ham Grammar School. *Studied:* Hornsey School of Art (1950's). *Exhib:* 22 one-man shows in U.K., America, Germany, Norway, S. Africa; numerous group shows with F.P.S.; invited exhibitor (11 works) 49th World Sci-Fi Convention, Brighton (1987); Astro-Physics Dept., Queen Mary College, London. *Work in collections:* Pennsylvania Museum of Modern Art, City A.G. Lichfield, Gateshead Municipal Collection, Save and Prosper, Head Office. *Publications:* Illustrated five rambling books (Essex, Herts.). *Clubs:* F.P.S. *Signs work:* "WYATT." *Address:* 1 Kenwood Gdns., Gants Hill, Ilford, Essex IG2 6YH.

**WYATT, Joyce Eileen (Mrs Derek Wraith),** R.M.S., U.A.S., S.W.A., P.S.; Prix Rowland and Mention Honorable (Paris Salon, 1963); Médaille D'Argent (Paris Salon, 1965); Médaille D'Or (Paris Salon, 1969); Member of La Société des Artistes Français (1969); portrait painter in oil, water-colour; *b* London. *m* Dr. Derek Greenway Wraith. one *s.* one *d. Educ:* Copthall School, Mill Hill. *Studied:* Hornsey College of Art, and under Francis Hodge and W. Durac Barnett. *Exhib:* R.A., R.P., R.M.S., R.B.A., Société des Artistes Français, U.A., S.W.A., etc.; one-man shows: Federation British Artists, Edinburgh Festival Exhbn., Rutland Sq., Edinburgh, La Galerie Mouffe, Paris. *Signs work:* "WYATT." *Address:* Archgate, North Stoke, nr. Wallingford, OX9 6BL.

**WYER, Annraoi,** B.A. Hons. Fine Art (1986), Dip. Design Hons. (1985); Greenshield Foundation award, Montreal (1988), President's Gold medal (1987); Prof. of Art, Blackrock College; painter, printmaker, illustrator; *b* Dublin, 7 Sept., 1963. *Educ:* Blackrock College. *Studied:* National College of Art and Design, Dublin, Dublin Inst. of Technology (1981-84, Alice Hanratty, Patrick Graham). *Exhib:* Ljubljana (1987, 1989), Varna (1989, 1991), Taipei (1988), various national exhbns. Work in corporate and private collections. *Clubs:* Assoc. of Artists in Ireland, Black Church Print Studio. *Signs work:* "Annraoi Wyer." *Address:* 146 Upper Glenageary Rd., Dun Laoire, Co. Dublin, Eire.

**WYLES, June,** B.A. (Hons.) Fine Art, M.A. Printmaking; painter/printmaker in oil, charcoal - landscape and the human form; lecturer of art, Berkshire College of Art and Design; *b* Berks., 1955. *Studied:* St. Martin's School of Art. *Exhib:* one-man shows: Dusseldörf, London. *Signs work:* "June Wyles." *Address:* 14a Eldon Rd., Reading, Berks. RG1 4DL.

**WYLIE, Rose Forrest,** N.D.D., M.A., R.C.A.; painter in oil; *b* Hythe, Kent, 1934. *m* Roy Oxlade. one *s.* two *d.* *Studied:* Folkestone and Dover School of Art, R.C.A. *Exhib:* Hayward Annual (1982), Cleveland International Drawing Biennale (1985), Scottish Drawing Competition (1988), Pomeroy Purdy Gallery (1988), Odette Gilbert Gallery 'Women and Water' (1988), Towner Gallery (1991), John Moores (1991), R.A. Summer Exhbn. (1992, 1993, 1997), Towner Gallery 'Interiors' (1993), Harlech International (1994), Norwich Gallery EAST (1994), Seattle Art Fair (1996), Cheltenham Open Drawing (1996), Hunting Art Prizes (1997); two person shows: Odette Gilbert Gallery (1988), Towner Gallery (1994); one person shows: Trinity Arts Centre, Tunbridge Wells (1985), Reed's Wharf Gallery, London (1995). *Work in collections:* Deal Collection, Dallas. *Signs work:* "Rose Wylie." *Address:* Forge Cottage, Newnhan, Sittingbourne, Kent ME9 0LQ.

**WYLLIE, George Ralston,** A.R.S.A., R.G.I., D.Litt.; Fellow, Hand Hollow, N.Y.; sculptor; writer; performer; *b* Glasgow, 1921. *m* Daphne Winifred Watts. two *d.* *Educ:* Allan Glen's and Bellahouston, Glasgow. *Exhib:* (selected): Demarco Gallery, Third Eye, Serpentine, Watermans, Worcester Art Museum, U.S.A., World Finance Center, N.Y. *Work in collections:* (selected): A.C.G.B.; S.A.C.; Glasgow, Whitworth Manchester, Worcester (U.S.A.) museums; U.F.A. Fabrik, Berlin; Getty Foundation. Events: 'A Day Down A Goldmine', Edinburgh Festival, I.C.A., London; 'Tramway', Glasgow; 'Straw Locomotive', Glasgow; 'Paper Boat', Glasgow, London, New York, Antwerp. *Signs work:* "G.R.W." *Address:* 9 McPherson Drive, Gourock, Renfrewshire PA19 1LJ.

**WYLLIE, Gordon Hope,** D.A. (Glas. 1953), R.S.W. (1967); artist in water-colour, acrylic and oil; *b* Greenock, 12 Feb., 1930. *m* Helen Wyllie. two *s.* *Educ:* Greenock High School. *Studied:* Glasgow School of Art (1949-53) under Wm. Armour, R.S.A., R.S.W.; Hospitalfield College of Art (1953) under Ian

Fleming, R.S.A., R.S.W. and Mary Armour, R.S.A., R.S.W. *Exhib:* R.S.A., R.G.I., R.S.W., Compass Gallery, Glasgow; one-man shows in Gateway, Edinburgh, Douglas & Foulis, Edinburgh, Citizens Theatre, Glasgow, Blythswood Gallery, 208 Gallery, Glasgow, Strathclyde University Staff Club, Lillie A.G., Compass Gallery, regular exhibitor Open Eye Gallery, Edinburgh. *Work in collections:* of Argyll, Fife, Renfrewshire, Ross and Cromarty Authorities, Paisley A.G., Lillie A.G., Milngavie and many private collections in U.K., U.S.A., Israel, Germany, etc. *Publications:* at one time part-time illustrator for the Glasgow Bulletin. *Signs work:* "Wyllie." *Address:* 17 Fox St., Greenock.

**WYNNE, Althea,** A.R.C.A. (1960), F.R.B.S. (1994); sculptor in clay and plaster; *b* Bedford, 6 Oct., 1936. *m* Antony Barrington-Brown. one *s.* two *d.* *Educ:* North Foreland Lodge School. *Studied:* Farnham Art School, Hammersmith College, R.C.A. (John Skeaping). *Exhib:* Henley Arts Festival (1994), Margam Sculpture Pk. (1991), Tower Bridge Plaza (1995), Winchester Cathedral (1997). *Work in collections:* 3 horses 1½ x L/size, bronze, Mincing Lane EC1; Family of goats L/size bronze, Barnard's Wharf Rotherhithe; "The Family" group L/size, Walsall Maternity Hospital; "White Horses" L/size resin, QE2 liner. *Address:* Mizmaze, 26c Upton Lovell, Warminster, Wilts. BA12 0JW.

# Y

**YALLUP, Pat,** Dip.Ad.S.A. (1956), S.I.A.D., A.T.D. (1963); artist in watercolour (landscapes and abstracts), oil (portraits); Pat Yallup Studio/Gallery, Llandogo, Gwent, (teacher own School); *b* Johannesburg, S. Africa, 29 Sept., 1929. *m* R. W. Yallup. three *s. Studied:* Witwatersrand, Johannesburg; Byam Shaw School (portraiture). *Exhib:* 35 one-man shows, six in London (1984-94). *Work in collections:* S. Africa, Canada, Germany, America, Australia and New Zealand. *Commissions:* many portraits, landscapes and places. *Publications:* work repro.: Calendars, Limited Prints. *Signs work:* "Pat Yallup" (watercolours and abstracts), see appendix. *Address:* Gallery House, Llandogo, nr. Monmouth, Gwent NP5 4TJ.

**YARDLEY, John Keith,** R.I.(1990); painter, particularly interior and street subjects, in oil and water-colour; *b* Beverley, Yorks., 11 Mar., 1933. *m* Brenda. two *s.* one *d. Educ:* Hastings Grammar School. *Exhib:* R.I., R.W.S., N.E.A.C., numerous one-man shows; awarded Water-colour Foundation prize R.I. (1990). *Work in collections:* Merrill Lynch, C.T. Bowring, A.P.V., and private collections. *Publications:* Water-colour - A Personal View; The Art of John Yardley by R. Ranson; Water-colour Impressionists by R. Ranson; videos: 'Sunlight in Water-colour' and 'Water-colour in Venice'. *Clubs:* Arts. *Signs work:* "John Yardley" in script. *Address:* 5 Evesham Rd., Reigate, Surrey RH2 9DF.

**YATES, Alan,** A.R.B.S. (1976), M.S.D.C. (1973), Cert.Ed. (1969), F.R.S.A. (1973); sculptor in cast bronze and aluminium, art teacher; *b* Bishop Auckland, 30 Nov., 1947. *Educ:* Leeholme School; Bishop Auckland Grammar School. *Studied:* Bede College, Durham University (1966-69). *Exhib:* R.A., R.S.A., R.W.A., Paris, Durham University, York, Grantham, Darlington, Perth, Newcastle Polytechnic, Edinburgh, S. Shields, Swansea University, Stratford, Northern Open Touring Exhbn., Chelsea Harbour, Manchester Academy. *Work in collections:* St. James' Youth Centre, Coundon; Grey College, Durham University. *Signs work:* "A. YATES." *Address:* Leaside, Frosterley, Bishop Auckland, Co. Durham DL13 2RH.

**YATES, Marie,** B.A.Hons (1971); artist; *b* Lancashire, 9 Aug., 1940. *Studied:* Manchester and Hornsey. *Exhib:* Arts Council, British Council, Arnolfini. *Work in collections:* Arts Council, Arnolfini Trust, Cornwall Educ. Com., Plymouth City A.G. *Publications:* A Re-Evaluation of a Proposed Publication (1978). *Signs work:* "Marie Yates." *Address:* 17 Victoria Rd., London N22.

**YATES JONES, Hazel May,** N.D.D., A.T.D., Cert.Ed., B.A.; designer/illustrator/calligrapher, water-colour painter; *b* Hastings. *m* B. H. Jones (decd.). *Educ:* Northampton School of Art (1957-61); West of England College of Art, Bristol University Faculty of Educ. (1964). *Exhib:* Mall Galleries, Liberty & Co., Hitchin Museum, Bedford Central Library, local Galleries in S. West and Somerset. *Work in collections:* Bedford Central Library, County Hall, Bedford, Bingen, W. Germany; Commissioned by N. Herts. District Council, Twinning Documents Letchworth with Wissen and Hitchin with Bingen Am Rhein; by Great Wymondley Parish Council for scroll 'History of Great Wymondley' presented to H.M. Queen Elizabeth II. *Signs work:* "Hazel Yates Jones." *Address:* Chestnut Cottage, Chard Rd., Drimpton, Dorset DT8 3RF.

**YEOMAN, Martin,** R.P., N.E.A.C.; artist in oil, pencil, pen and ink, silver point; *b* Egham Hythe, 21 July, 1953. *Studied:* R.A. Schools (Peter Greenham). *Exhib:* Agnews, New Grafton Gallery, R.A., N.P.G. *Clubs:* R.P., N.E.A.C. *Signs work:* "Yeoman." *Address:* 2a Turquand St., London SE17 1LT.

**YHAP, Laetitia,** D.F.A.(Lond.) (1965); artist; *b* St. Albans, 1 May, 1941. partner: Michael Rycroft. one *s. Educ:* Fulham County Grammar School. *Studied:* Camberwell School of Art (1958-62, Euan Uglow, Frank Auerbach), Slade School of Fine Art (1963-65, Harold Cohen, Anthony Green). *Exhib:* solo shows, Piccadilly Gallery (1968-73), Serpentine Gallery (1979), Air Gallery (1984), 'Life at the Edge' Charleston Farmhouse (1993); 'The Business of the Beach' 1988-89 Touring show organised by Laing A.G., Newcastle-upon-Tyne, 'Bound by the Sea', The Berwick Gymnasium (1994), Maritime Counterpoint (1996), Boundary Gallery, London. *Work in collections:* Tate Gallery, Unilever House, Hove A.G., Hastings Museum, Rugby Museum, Portsmouth City A.G., British Council, Contemporary Art Soc., New Hall

Cambridge, S. East Arts Coll., University College London, Walker A.G., Liverpool, Nuffield Foundation, D.O.E., Arthur Anderson Coll., Yorkshire, Leicestershire Educ. *Signs work:* "Laetitia Yhap." *Address:* 12 The Croft, Hastings, Sussex TN34 3HH.

**YOSHIMOTO, Eiko,** P.S., S.W.A., S.B.A., S.P.F.; artist in pastel, conte, charcoal, oil; *b* Japan, 5 July, 1937. *Educ:* Notre Dame Sacred Heart School, Japan; Diploma from Drama School of Toho Film Company, Tokyo. *Studied:* City & Guilds of London Art School (part-time, 1994-96, Eric Morby), École de Société des Pastellistes de France (Jean Pierre Merat). *Exhib:* P.S. (1986-), S.B.A. (1986-), S.W.A. (1987-), Glyndebourne Opera House (1989, 1991), R.A. (1993, 1994, 1997), N.E.A.C. (1986-), Royal Opera House (1992); solo shows: S.P.F. Paris (1992, 1993, 1995, 1996, 1997). *Signs work:* "Eiko Yoshimoto." *Address:* "Hermitage Lodge", The Hermitage, Richmond, Surrey TW10 6SH.

**YOUNG, Florence,** R.M.S., S.W.A., Associe, Société des Artistes Français; Hon. Mention, Paris Salon (1968), Prix Marie Louise Jules Richard, Paris Salon (1971), Diplôme d'honneur, Biarritz (1971), silver medal, Paris Salon (1981); self taught artist in oil, pastel and water-colour, miniaturist; *b* Preston, Lancs., 19 Nov., 1919. *m* Kenneth Young. one *s.* one *d. Educ:* Farnworth Grammar School, Lancs. *Exhib:* P.S., R.I., S.W.A., R.M.S., R.W.S. Flower Painting, R.I. Galleries Summer and Winter Salons, Paris Salon, S.M., U.A. *Work in collections:* Hillingdon Borough Council, Swedish Tool Mfrs., Kingston, Diaform Ltd. Uxbridge, Public Address Engineers Assoc., Harrow, Barclays Bank, Uxbridge. *Signs work:* "F. Young." *Address:* 1a Maylands Drive, Uxbridge, Middx. UB8 1BH.

**YOUNG, Dr. Joseph L.,** F.I.A.L.; pioneer of reintegration of art in architecture; creator of over 50 cultural landmarks for civic, educational and religious structures throughout America, including works in mosaic, metal, wood, stained glass, concrete, granite, etc.; author of 2 books on mosaics published by Reinhold, N.Y. (1957-63); guest lecturer and artist-in-residence at numerous institutions of higher learning in U.S.A. and Europe; *b* Pittsburgh, Pa., 27 Nov., 1919. *m* Millicent E. Young; two children. *Educ:* Westminster College, New Wilmington, Pa. *Studied:* Boston Museum School of Fine Arts; American Academy of Art, Rome. *Signs work:* "J. Young." *Address:* Art in Architecture, 7917 W. Norton Ave., Los Angeles, Ca. 90046, U.S.A.

**YOUNGER, Alan Christopher Wyrill,** F.M.G.P.; stained glass designer and maker; part-time lecturer, Richmond University; *b* London, 13 Mar., 1933. *m* Zoë Birchmore. two *d. Educ:* Alleyn's School. *Studied:* Central School of Art (1954-57), and in the Studios of Carl Edwards and Lawrence Lee. First prize Worshipful Company of Glaziers (1960), Sir Arthur Evans travelling scholarship (1961). *Exhib:* Centre International du Vitrau, Chartres (1982). *Work in collections:* Durham, St. Alban's, Southwark, Gloucester and Chester Cathedrals, numerous parish churches in Britain including Luton, Tamworth,

Boldre, Haselbech and Monea. *Publications:* The Laporte Rose Window (1989). *Signs work:* overlapping A and Y - see appendix. *Address:* 44 Belvedere Rd., London SE19 2HW.

**YOUNGER, Elspeth Chalmers,** D.A. (1957), Post Dip. (1958); embroiderer, painter in inks, water-colour, gouache; *b* Paisley. *m* John Gardiner Crawford. one *s.* one *d. Educ:* Camphill Secondary School, Paisley. *Studied:* Glasgow School of Art (1953-58, Kathleen Whyte); National Wool Textile Award (1957), Travelling Scholarship, Paris (1958). *Exhib:* one-man shows: 57 Gallery, Edinburgh (1965), Lane Gallery, Bradford (1965), Civic Arts Centre, Aberdeen (1969, 1971), University of Aberdeen (1971), Cornerstone Gallery, Dunblane (1983, 1984, 1988, 1989), Haddo House, Aberdeen (1988), McEwan & Ritchie Fine Art, Dundee (1990), Tolquhon Gallery, Tarves (1992), Cottage Gallery, Newtyle (1993, 1995, 1997); group shows include Glasgow School of Art, S.A.C., S.S.A., Scottish Gallery, R.S.W., etc. *Work in collections:* Aberdeenshire Educ. Authority, Tayside Educ. Authority, North British Hotel, Dundee A.G., and private collections throughout Britain, and Norway, Holland, Germany, France, Australia, Canada, U.S.A. *Publications:* in various publications, and in "20th Century Embroidery in Gt. Britain", Vols. 2, 3, 4, by Constance Howard. *Signs work:* "ELSPETH YOUNGER" and date, embroidery unsigned, label on reverse. *Address:* 34 Strachan St., Arbroath, Angus DD11 1UA, Scotland.

**YULE, (Duncan) Ainslie,** D.A. (1963); sculptor/teacher; Head of Sculpture, Kingston University 1982- (Reader 1987-); *b* North Berwick, 1941. *m* (1) Patricia Carlos (m dissolved). one *d* (2) 1982, Mary Johnson. *Educ:* Edinburgh College of Art. *Exhib:* regular solo and group exhbns. including Whitechapel A.G. (1973), Gubbio Biennale (1973), Silver Jubilee Exhbn. Battersea Park (1977), Fruitmarket Gallery and travelling (1977-79), Angela Flowers (1986), Scottish Gallery (1989-91). *Work in collections:* include Aberdeen A.G., A.C.G.B., Dundee A.G., Leeds City A.G., S.A.C. University of Leeds, Gregory Fellow (1974-75). *Clubs:* Chelsea Arts. *Signs work:* "Ainslie Yule." *Address:* 218 Sheen La., London SW14 8LB.

# Z

**ZALMON:** see WINER, Zalmon.

**ZAO, Wou Ki,** Commandeur de la Légion d'Honneur; Commandeur de Mérite National; painter; *b* Pekin, 13 Feb., 1921. *m* Francoise Marquet. *Studied:* Ecole Nationale de Beaux Arts at Hang Tcheou (1935-41). Professor of Drawing, Ecole Nationale de Beaux Arts at Hang Tcheou (1941-47). *Work in collections:* in Germany, England, Austria, Belgium, Brazil, Canada, Switzerland, U.S.A., France, Hong Kong, Israel, Italy, Japan, Luxembourg, etc. Praemium Imperiale Lauréat (peinture) 1994, Japan. *Address:* 19 bis, Rue Jonquoy, 75014, Paris, France.

**ZEVI, Bruno B.,** Doctor in Architecture; Academician of San Luca; critic and architect; Prof. of History of Architecture, Rome University; President, International Committee of Architectural Critics; Mem. of the Italian Parliament; *b* Rome, 22 Jan., 1918. *m* Tullia Calabi. one *s*. one *d*. *Educ:* Rome and Harvard University. *Studied:* architecture: Cambridge, Mass., U.S.A. *Publications:* Towards an Organic Architecture, Architecture as Space, Storia dell'Architettura Moderna, Biagio Rossetti, Architectura in nuce, Michelangiolo Architetto, Erich Mendelsohn, Saper vedere la città, The modern language of architecture; author of the Voice "Architecture" in Universal Encyclopedia of the Arts; editor of L'architettura-cronache e storia (Rome and Milan), architectural columnist of the weekly L'Espresso. *Address:* Via Nomentana 150, 00162 Rome.

**ZIAR, Elizabeth Rosemary,** painter (water-colour preferred); *b* St. Ives, Cornwall. *m* Ian Ziar, L.D.S., R.C.S. one *s*. *Educ:* West Cornwall School for Girls (art mistress Miss M.E. Parkins of "Newlyn School"); Penzance School of Art (1936-41 James Lias, 1945 Bouverie Hoyton); Leonard Fuller (1945). *Exhib:* over 30 solo shows in Britain, France and Italy with usual complement of mixed international expositions, e.g. Paris Salon, Monaco, Biarritz (Dip. d'Honneur 1973), Juan-les-Pins (premier award Coupe d'Antibes 1979), R.I., R.B.S.A., S.W.A., U.A., Hesketh Hubbard, etc. *Publications:* 'Good Morrow, Brother.' *Signs work:* "ZIAR" or with monogram (see appendix); occasionally: "E. R. ZIAR" or "E.R.Z." *Address:* Trevidren, Penzance TR18 2AY.

**ZYW, Aleksander,** painter; *b* Lida, Poland, 29 Aug., 1905. *m* Leslie Goddard. two *s*. *Studied:* in Warsaw, Athens, Rome and Paris. *Exhib:* Warsaw, Paris, Basle, Milan, London, Edinburgh. *Work in collections:* State Collection of Poland, National Gallery of Poland, Union of Polish Painters, Tate Gallery, Glasgow Art Gallery, Arts Council of Scotland, University of Edinburgh, Scottish National Gallery of Modern Art, Rhodes National Gallery, Salisbury, Carnegie Trust. *Signs work:* "Zyw." *Address:* Bell's Brae House, Dean Village, Edinburgh EH4 3BJ; and Poggio Lamentano, 57022 Castagneto-Carducci (Livorno), Italy.

# MONOGRAMS AND SIGNATURES

Ackroyd,
Norman

Adam-Tessier,
Maxime

Adams,
(Dorothea Christina) Margaret

OR

Arnold,
Phyllis Anne

Atkin, Ann

Auld, J.L.M

OR

Backhouse,
David John

Bailey, Caroline

Baines, Richard
John Manwaring

Baker, Hilary Jayne

Barber Kennedy,
Mat

Barlow, Gillain

Baynes,
Pauline Diana

Beauvais,
Walter John

Beilby,
Pauline Margaret

Beltrán, Félix

Benjamin,
Anthony

Bennett,
William

Bensusan-Butt,
John Gordon

Benton, Graham

Berlin,
Sven

Bewick, Pauline

Blaker, Michael

Blik, Maurice

Bond, Jane

Bransbury, Allan Harry — *Allan Bransbury*

Brasier, Jenny

Brazier, Connie — CMB (water-colours)

CMB (engraved glass)

Brent, Isabelle — *Isabelle Brent.* 

Bridgeman, John

Brindley, Donald

Brody, F.J. — *Brody*

Broughton, Aya

Brown, Neil
Dallas

Brown, Ralph

(drawings)        (stamped)

Bruce, George
J.D.

or

Buck, Jon

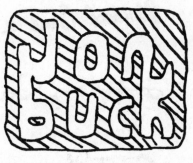

raised letters
on indented
stamp in
bronze

Budd,
Oliver Richard

Budd, Rachel

Bumphrey, Nigel

Burrough, Thomas
Hedley Bruce

Butler, Vincent    or    **V.B.**

Butt, Anna
Theresa

Caine, O.

Camp, Jeffery

Carrick, Desmond

(Up to and including 1979)

(After 1979)

Carrington-Kerslake,
Lynette

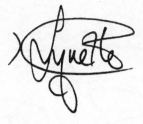

Carter, Joan
Patricia

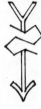

Chang,
Chien-Ying

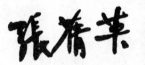  

Chao, Shao-An

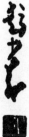

Chatterton,
George Edward

Chauvin, E.

Chesser, Sheila

Clark,
Kenneth Inman
Carr

Clements, Jeff

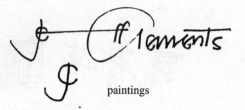

paintings

Clyne, Henry Horne

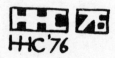

HHC'76

Cochran, Margi

Collins, Michael

Conner, Angela

Conway, Jennifer Anne    (miniatures)    Conway

Cook, David Albert    (paintings)

(pen & ink)

Cook, S.

Cooper, Emmanuel

Coote, Michael Arnold

Corbett, Peter George

Cornwall, Arthur Bruce

Coutu, Jack  Inset silver plate.

Carvings

Cox, Stephen B. 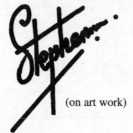 or

(on art work) (on designs/interiors etc.

Cramp,
Jonathan David on oils on some drawings

J. CRAMP or J.C. J. Cramp.

Crawshaw, June

(ceramic signature)

Creber, Frank

FC 91
FC reber 91

Crossley, Gordon

GTC

Crow,
Kathleen Mary

Kw

Crowther,
Hugh M.

Crowther,
Stephen

Cummings, Albert
Arratoon Runciman

Curtis,
Anthony Ewart

Czimbalmos,
Magdolna Paal

Czimbalmos,
Szabo Kalman

Dack, Tom

Dakeyne, Gabriel

Dalby, Claire

Daniel, Brigitte
Elizabeth M.

Danvers, Joan

d'Arbeloff, Natalie    or

Das, Jatin

Davidson Davis,
Philomena

Davis, Michael
Robert

Day, Jane

de Francia, Peter

Demel, Richard

De Vasconcellos,
Josephina

Dickens, Alison
Margaret

Dickson,
Evangeline Mary
Lambart    *small paintings*

Di Girolamo,
Megan Ann

Dowling, Jane

Dring, L.M.

Duffy, Stephen James

Duffy, Terry

or

Dunlop, Jim

Dunne, Berthold

Berthold

Durrant, Roy Turner

or

Eastop, Geoffrey Frank

Edwards, Benjamin
Ralph

Elstein, Cecile

Emery, Edwina

Emmerich, Anita
Jane

Evans, Margaret
Fleming

Evans, Ray

Fakhoury, Bushra

Farrell,
Alan Richard

and dated on
reverse of painting

Faulds. James
Alexander

Faur,
Aurel-Sebastian

Feeny, P.A.

Fei, Cheng-Wu    or

Fellows,
Elaine Helen

Finch, Michael

Fisher, Don
Mulready

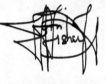

Fisher,
Reginald Stanley

Fleming,
James Hugh    on illustrations
and prints

Folland,
Ronald Norman

Forward,
Hubert W.F.    'HF'    monogram (prints & ceramics)

Foster,
Sir Norman Robert

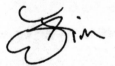

657

Francyn
(Dehn Fuller)

Frankenthaler,
Helen

Fraser, D.H.

Frenkiel,
Stanislaw

Friers, R.B.

Gamlen, Mary

Gatteaux, Marcel

# WHO'S WHO IN ART

Giardelli, Arthur

Gibson, Veronica

Gili, Katherine    some works
signed:

Gilley,
Leonard Christopher

Goaman, Michael

Goodwin,
Leslie Albert

Gow, Neil

Granger, Margaret I.    or

Granville

Gray, Jane
Campbell

Gunn, James
Thomson

Hackney, Arthur

Hampton, Michael

('M' & 'H' WITH GREBES HEAD)

Harrison (née Roberts),
Marguerite Hazel

MR.

Harvey, Jake

Haughton,
Wilfred James

Herman, Josef

Heron, Susanna

illustrations

Herriott,
Alan B.

*Hans Herriott*

and dated

Hickey, Michael

or *M. Hickey*

Hill, Anthony

Hinchcliffe,
Michael

*HINCHCLIFFE*

Hind, Margaret
Madeleine

Hitchcock,
Harold Raymond

19      76

Hoare, Diana C.

Hoflehner, Rudolf    GRAPHIKEN :    PLASTIKEN    HR

Homes, R.T.J.

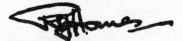

Hooke, Robert
Lowe, Jr.

House, Ceri
Charles

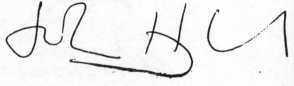

Hoyland, John

Huckvale, Iris

Hudson, Thomas
Roger Jackson

Hughes, Jim

Hundertwasser,
Friedrich

*Hundertwasser*

*Hundertwasser* or HUNDERTWASSER

BRUCE HURN

Hurn, J. Bruce

(oils and acrylic painings)

*Bruce Hurn*

(drawings and gouache paintings)

Huston, John I.

Ibbett, Vera

Irvin, Albert

*Irvin*

Isom, Graham Michael

Jackson, Ashley

Jefferson, Annelise

Jellicoe, Colin

Jenkins, Christopher (potters stamp)

Jennings,
Walter Robin

Jobson, Patrick

Johnston, Duncan    or

Jones, Barry Owen

Jones,
Stanley Robert

Jukes, E.E.

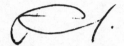

Kalashnikov, Anatolii
Ivanovich

Kanidinç,
Salahattin

S·KANIDINÇ

Kendall, Kay
Thetford

Kennedy, C.

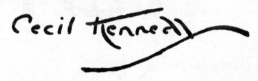

Kern, Doreen

Key, Geoffrey

King, Phillip

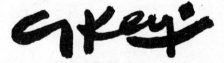

Klein, Anita

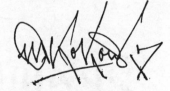

Kolakowski,
Matthew Edmund

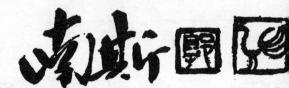

Kuo, Nancy

Lackner, Suzanne O.

Lago, Darren

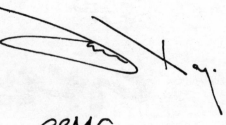

Lake,
C. Elizabeth Matheson

Lambert,
Colin Joseph

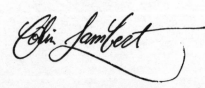

Landers,
Linda Anne

Lang, Wharton

Larmont, Eric

Lauder,
Kenneth Scott

Lawrence,
Gordon Robert

Leach, D.           or           seal in foot of pots.

Leach, Mark Alan

Lee, Rosie                              or           B

Lee, Sidney
Edward

Leech, Raymond

Leigh-Pemberton,
John

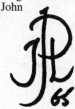

LEIGH-PEMBERTON
. 65 .

Lewenstein, Eileen

Leyden, J.M.

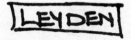

Lilley, Geoffrey
Ivan

LILLEY or GIL

Lim, Kim

Littlejohn,
William Hunter

William Littlejohn or WL.

Lockhart, David

Logan, Andrew

Longbotham,
Charles Norman

Loudon, Irvine

Lucas, Suzanne

Luckas, Joy
Heather

Macarrón, Ricardo

McCarter, Keith　　　　　　(on small works)

McCullough,
George

MacDonald,
Alastair James　　　　or
Henderson

McEwan Reid,
Marjorie

Macey, Leo

McFall, David

McIntyre, Donald

Macmiadhachain,
Padraig

Madgwick, Clive

Maklouf, Raphael

Malcles, Jean-Denis

Mapp, John Ernest

Margrie, Victor

Marr, Leslie

Marriott, Michael

Martin, Marie-Louise

Master, Jean

Matania, Franco

Matheson, Andrew
Kenneth Mackenzie

Mendoza, Edwin

Mendoza, June

Micah, Lisa

Middleton, Renée        10 ℟M·85        (or appropriate date)

Miller, David T.        *[signature]*

Millner, Etienne
Henry, de la Fargue

*[signature]* or *[signature]*

Miners, Neil

Montané, Roger        *[signature]*

Moodie, Stuart

Moreton, Nicolas        *[logo]* (sculpture)

Munslow, Angela E.        *[signature]*

Muszynski,
Leszek Tadeusz

Nalecz, Halima

Neal, Trevor

Nellens, Roger

Ng, Kiow Ngor

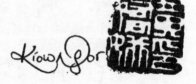

Norland
(Neuschul), Khalil

Ohl, Gabrielle

Padden, Daphne

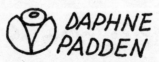

Paes, Rui

Parry,
Sheila Harwood

Parsons,
Denis Alva

Initials
Banker mark based on
hobby of unicycling

Peace, David

Pearson, James E.

Penketh-Simpson,
Barbara

minatures

Piché, Roland

Pincus,
Helen Frances

Pitfield,
Thomas Baron

Potter, Donald

Pullan, Margaret
Ida Elizabeth

Pullan, Tessa

Purnell, John

stamped on sculpture

Pye, William 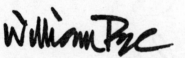 or

Raine, Sarah Lamar
(Woodie)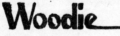

Rank-Broadley, Ian

Roberts,
Phyllis Kathleen

*P. K. ROBERTS*

Roberts,
Walter James

*Walter J. Roberts*

Robertson,
Sheila Macleod

(on still life and flower paintings)

Robinson, Barbara

*Barbara Robinson.*

Rogers, Joseph
Shepperd (Nevia)

*Nevia*

Roper,
Geoffrey John

Roseman, Stanley

Ross, Alastair
Robertson

Roy, Michael

Ryder,
Margaret Elaine

Sahai, Viréndra

Saltzman, William

Sanderson, Roger

ROGER SANDERSON

RS.

Sapieha, Christine     Ⓢ SAPIEHA

Schwarz, Hans

Seal, Norman

Searle, Ronald     Ronald·Searle  or RS. or Searle

See-Paynton,
Colin Frank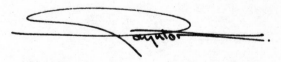

Senft, Nadin          (signature on bronzes etc.)

Seuphor, Michel

Shackleton,
Keith Hope

Shaw,
Barbara Nancy

Shears,
Marcelle Dorothy

OR

Shipsides, Frank

Shorthouse,
G. Sydney

Simpson, Cathy

Simpson, Noelle

Sitwell, Pauline

Smith, Basil

Smith, Edward
John Milton

Snelling, John

Snowden,
Hilda Mary

Soulages, Pierre

Souza, F.N.

Spencer, Claire

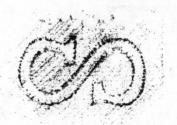

Stokes, Vincent

Storey, Terence

Stuart, Kiel

Sullivan, Jason

Sullivan, Wendy
Lilian Verdin

Summers,
Leslie John

Tajiri, Shinkichi

Tamblyn-Watts,
Harold

Tate, Barbara

Tate,
Barbara and James

Tavener, Robert

Taylor, Alan

Taylor,
Michael John

93

← red

Taylor, Pamela

or

Taylor, Wendy Ann

(prints and work)

Thelwell, Norman

Thomas, M.

Till, Michael John

Tisdall, H.

Tolley, Sheila

Tribe, Barbara

Tuckwell,
George Arthur

Turnbull, William

Turner,
William Ralph

Underwood,
Keith Alfred

Vango, David

Verdijk, Gerard

Vogel, Suzi

Walker, Richard
Ian Bentham

Ward,
Thomas William

Wasim, L.

Watson,
Arthur James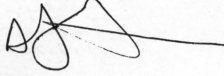

Watson, Heather

Watson-Gandy,
Basia 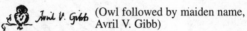 (Butterfly hidden in design)

Watson Stewart,
Avril Veronica  (Owl followed by maiden name,
Avril V. Gibb)

Watts, Dorothy *DOROTHY WATTS.*

Watts,
Michael Gorse  (Generally) (As Septimus Pike)

Watts, Peter

Wattson Dean, Meg  (miniatures)

Wauters, Jef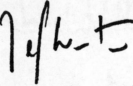

Webb, Elizabeth

Weeks, John
Lawrence Macdonald

Wells, Peter *PETER WELLS* or

Weltman, Boris

Werge-Hartley, Alan

Werge-Hartley,
Jeanne

White, Mary

Whitten,
B. Janice E.

Willies, Joan

Winer, Zalmon

Wolverson,
Margaret Elizabeth

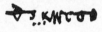

Monogram Stamp

Wood,
Gerald Stanley Kent

Woolf-Nellist,
Meg

Yallup, Pat

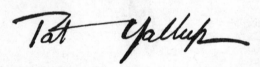

Younger, Alan
Christopher Wyrill

Ziar, Elizabeth
Rosemary

# OBITUARY

ABLETT, Dorothy, F.S.D.C., A.T.D.
ADAMSON, Edward James, F.R.S.A.
ARMSTRONG, Arthur Charlton
BEESTON, Enid, A.S.A.F.
BERNARD, Paul
BICAT, Andre, O.B.E.
BILLINGS, Kathleen Wyatt, R.I., S.M.
BISHOP, Edward, R.B.A., N.E.A.C.
BOYLE, Alicia
BRADLEY, Frank, R.C.A., R.I.B.A.
BRAMMER, Leonard Griffiths, A.R.C.A.
BROADFIELD, Aubrey Alfred (Alan), M.A.
BROADFIELD, Robina Margaret
CLARKE, Peter John
CLEMENTS, Raymon John, F.I.A.L., A.T.D., N.D.D.
COATES, Betty, S.W.A.
COOPER, William Heaton, R.I.
COUVE DE MURVILLE-DESENNE, Lucie-Renée
COVENTRY, Frederick Halford
COXON, Raymond James, A.R.C.A.
CRONYN, Hugh Verschoyle, G.M., F.R.S.A.
DOWNS, Kathleen Mary, S.B.A.
EDGAR, Jennie M., N.D.D., A.R.M.S., S.W.A.
EDWARDS, Iorwerth Eiddon Stephen, C.M.G., C.B.E., Litt.D., F.B.A.
EGONU, Uzo, F.R.S.A.
FAIRCLOUGH, Wilfred, A.R.C.A., R.E., R.W.S.
FISHWICK, Clifford, A.T.D.
GABRIEL, Caroline S., F.R.S.A.
GAMES, Abram, O.B.E., R.D.I., Hon.D.Litt., Hon.F.R.C.A.
GEAR, William, R.A., R.B.S.A.
GENEVER, Margaret
GOODALL, John Strickland, R.I., R.B.A.
GRANT, Alistair, F.R.C.A., R.B.A., R.S.A.
GRAY, Milner Connorton, C.B.E., R.D.I., F.C.S.D., A.G.I., Hon.Dr.R.C.A.
GRIBBLE, Kenneth James, D.F.A., F.R.S.A., A.S.I.A., R.W.A. N.S.E.A.D.

HADDOCK, Aldridge, M.B.B.S., D.Obst.R.C.O.G., M.R.C.G.P.
HARRISON, Eric, A.R.C.A., M.S.I.A., A.T.I.
HART, John
HAWTHORN, Raymond Humphrey Millis, A.T.D., R.E., S.W.E.
HAZELWOOD, David
HOODLESS, Harry Taylor, A.R.C.A., A.T.D.
HORNBY, Anna, N.E.A.C.
HORSNELL, Walter Cecil
HOWARD, James Campbell, S.G.A.
HUYGHE, René
JAMESON, Kenneth, Ambrose, R.C.A., R.D.S., F.R.S.A.
JELLICOE, Sir Geoffrey Alan, C.B.E., R.A., V.M.H., R.I.B.A., P.P.L.I.
JOHN, Anthony T.
JOSSET, Lawrence Leon Louis, A.R.C.A., R.E.
JOWITT, John Alan
LAW, Graham Couper, M.A., A.R.I.B.A., A.R.S.A., F.R.I.A.S.
LEIGH-PEMBERTON, John, A.F.C.
LEVY, Mervyn, A.R.C.A.
LINLEY-ADAMS, Barbara Mary
LUBELSKI, Jan Stanislaw, A.T.D.
MALTHOUSE, Eric
MANSFIELD, Edgar, O.B.E., F.R.B.S., M.D.E., Hon.F.D.B., F.R.S.A.
MARTIN, Pierre Noël
MARTIN, Timothy Stuart, F.R.S.A.
MONGAN, Agnes, A.B., M.A., L.H.D., Litt.D., Dr.F.A.
MORROCCO, Alberto, O.B.E., D.A., R.S.A., R.S.W., R.P., R.G.I., LL.D.
MULLEN GLOVER, Sybil, R.I., R.S.M.A., R.W.A.
MULLINS, Gwen, O.B.E.
NIVEN, Margaret Graeme, R.O.I., N.S.
NOWELL, Stanley, M.B., F.R.C.R., A.R.Cam.A.
OSTLE, Roy John, N.D.D., A.T.D.
OXENBURY, Thomas Bernard, C.Eng., F.I.C.E., F.R.T.P.I., R.I.B.A.
PARK, Alistair, D.A.
PARKER, Herbert, F.R.S.A.
PASMORE, Victor, C.H., C.B.E., R..A.
PATRICK, Marion, N.D.D.
PORTWAY, Douglas Owen
RAMBISSOON, Sonnylal, A.C.P., N.D.D., A.T.C.
REES JONES, Stephen, M.Sc., F.Inst.P., F.S.A., F.I.I.C.
REYNOLDS, Bernard Robert, F.R.B.S.
ROBERTS-JONES, Ivor, C.B.E., R.A.
ROBINSON, Oliver John
RUSSELL, Ena, R.O.I.
SCHAEFER, Carl Fellman, R.C.A., F.I.A.L., C.S.G.A., C.S.P.W.C., C.G.P.

SERRA-BADUE, Daniel F.
SMITH, Norman, N.E.A.C.
STIVEN, Frederic William Binning, D.A., M.C.S.D., A.R.S.A.
SZOMANSKI, Wladyslaw, F.R.S.A., M.C.S.D.
TARR, James C., A.R.C.A., A.T.D.
TENNENT, John Richard Moncrieff, S.WL.A.
WARBURTON, Joan
WEIGHT, Carel, C.B.E., R.A., Hon.A.R.C.A., R.B.A.
WILLIAM-POWLETT, Katherine, S.W.A.
WILLIAMS, Guy R.O., A.T.D.
WILLOUGHBY, Trevor John, R.P.
WRIGHT, Austin Andrew

# QUALIFICATIONS AND GENERAL ABBREVIATIONS

*In using this list of abbreviations care should be taken to split up any compound abbreviation into its constituent parts, e.g., "F.R.S." should be broken into "F." and "R.S.," the equivalents of these letters being found under "F." and "R.S." respectively.*

| | |
|---|---|
| **A.** | Associate; Associate-Engraver (of Royal Academy). |
| **A.A.** | Architectural Association; Automobile Association. |
| **A.A.A.** | Allied Artists of America; Australian Academy of Art. |
| **A.A.D.W.** | Association of Artists/Designers in Wales (disbanded). |
| **A.A.H.** | Association of Art Historians. |
| **A.A.I.** | Association of Art Institutions. |
| **A.A.L.** | Academy of Art and Literature. |
| **A.A.P.L.** | American Artists Professional League. |
| **A.A.S.** | Aberdeen Art Society. |
| **A.B.** | Art's Bachelor (American). |
| **A.B.I.R.A.** | American Biographical Institute Research Association. |
| **A.B.P.R.** | Association of British Picture Restorers. |
| **A.C.A.** | Association of Consultant Architects; Atlanta College of Art. |
| **A.C.G.B.** | Arts Council of Great Britain. |
| **A.C.T.C.** | Art Class Teacher's Certificate. |
| **A.C.W.** | Arts Council of Wales (formerly W.A.C.). |
| **A.D.** | Anno Domini. |
| **A.D.A.E.** | Advanced Diploma in Art Education. |
| **A.D.B.** | Associate of the Drama Board. |
| **A.D.C.** | Aide-de-camp. |
| **A.D.G.** | Architect Diplôme par le Gouvernement. |
| **A.D.M.S.** | Assistant Director of Medical Services. |
| **A.E.C.** | Adult Education Centre. |
| **A.F.I.A.P.** | Artiste, Fédération Internationale de l'Art Photographique. |
| **A.G.** | Art Gallery. |
| **A.G.B.I.** | Artists' General Benevolent Institution. |

| | |
|---|---|
| A.G.I. | Artistes Graphiques Internationales. |
| A.G.M.S. | Art Gallery and Museum Services. |
| A.G.P.A. | Artes Graficas de Pan America. |
| A.G.P.P. | Academia Gentium Pro Pace. |
| A.I. | Auctioneers' Institute. |
| A.I.A. | Academy of Irish Art; American Institute of Architecture. |
| A.I.A.L. | Association of International Institute of Art and Letters. |
| A.I. Archts.(Scot.). | Association of the Incorporation of Architects in Scotland. |
| A.I.C.A. | Association Internationale des Critiques d'Art. |
| A.I.D. | American Institute of Decorators. |
| A.I.I.D. | American Institute of Interior Design. |
| A.K.C. | Associate, King's College. |
| A.M. | Air Ministry; Member of Order of Australia. |
| A.M.A. | Associate of the Museums Association. |
| A.M.C. | Art Masters' Certificate. |
| A.M.I.P. | Associate Member, Institute of Plumbing. |
| A.M.T.C. | Art Masters' Teaching Certificate. |
| A.N.A. | American National Academy. |
| A.O.C. | Artists of Chelsea. |
| A.O.I. | Association of Illustrators. |
| A.P.A. | Association of Polish Artists. |
| A.P.S. | American Portrait Society. |
| A.R.C.A. | Associate of the Royal College of Art. |
| Ariz. | Arizona. |
| A.R.W.A. | Associate of the Royal West of England Academy. |
| A.S.A. | American Society of Artists Inc. |
| A.S.G. | Art Services Grants. |
| A.S.L.A. | American Society of Landscape Architects. |
| A.S.M.A.(Q). | Australian Society for Miniature Art (Queensland). |
| Assoc. | Association. |
| Asst. | Assistant. |
| A.S.T.M.S. | Association of Scientific, Technical and Managerial Staff. |
| A.T.C. | Art Teachers' Certificate. |
| A.T.D. | Art Teachers' Diploma. |
| A.U.C. | Anno Urbis Conditæ (from the foundation of the city). |
| A.V.A.W. | Association of Visual Artists in Wales. |
| Ave. | Avenue. |
| A.W.G. | Art Workers' Guild. |
| A.W.I. | Australian Water-colour Institute. |

| | |
|---|---|
| **b.** | born. |
| **B.A.** | Bachelor of Arts; British Airways. |
| **B.A.A.T.** | British Association of Art Therapists. |
| **B.A.C.** | British Aircraft Corporation. |
| **B.A.D.A.** | British Antique Dealers' Association. |
| **B.Ae.** | British Aerospace. |
| **B-A.S.** | Britain-Australia Society. |
| **Batt.** | Battalion. |
| **B.B.C.** | British Broadcasting Corporation. |
| **B.C.** | Before Christ. |
| **B.C.C.** | British Craft Centre. |
| **B.Chrom.** | Bachelor of Chromatics. |
| **B.C.L.** | Bachelor of Civil Law. |
| **B.D.** | Bachelor of Divinity. |
| **B.E.A.** | British European Airways. |
| **B.Ed.** | Bachelor of Education; Board of Education. |
| **B.E.D.A.** | Bureau of European Designers' Association. |
| **Beds.** | Bedfordshire. |
| **B.E.F.** | British Expeditionary Force. |
| **B.E.N.A.** | British Empire Naturalist Association. |
| **Berks.** | Berkshire. |
| **B.F.A.** | Bachelor of Fine Arts. |
| **B'ham.** | Birmingham. |
| **B.H.P.** | Broken Hill Priority Ltd. |
| **B.H.S.A.I.** | British Horse Society Assistant Instructor. |
| **B.I.A.T.** | British Institute of Architectural Technicians. |
| **B.I.F.** | British Industries Fair. |
| **B.I.I.A.** | British Institute of Industrial Art. |
| **B.I.I.D** | British Institute of Interior Design. |
| **B.I.M.** | (see I.Mgt.). |
| **B.I.P.P.** | British Institute of Professional Photography. |
| **B.I.S.** | British Interplanetary Society. |
| **B.L.** | Barrister-at-Law. |
| **Bldg.** | Building. |
| **B.Litt.** | Bachelor of Letters. |
| **Blvd.** | Boulevard. |
| **B.M.** | British Museum. |
| **B.O.A.C.** | British Overseas Airways Corporation. |
| **B.of E.** | Board of Education. |
| **B.O.U.** | British Ornithologists' Union. |
| **B.P.D.** | British Society of Posters Designers. |
| **B.P.S.** | British Psychological Society. |
| **B.R.C.** | British Refugee Council. |
| **Bros.** | Brothers. |
| **B.S.C.** | British Society of Cinematographers. |
| **B.Sc.** | Bachelor of Science. |

| | |
|---|---|
| B.S.I. | British Standards Institution. |
| B.S.M.G.P. | British Society of Master Glass Painters. |
| B.Soc.Sc. | Bachelor of Social Science. |
| Bt. | Baronet. |
| B.T.A. | British Travel Association. |
| Bucks. | Buckinghamshire. |
| B.W.S. | British Water-colour Society. |
| | |
| C. | Central. |
| c. | century. |
| C.A.C. | Chertsey Art Club. |
| Caerns. | Caernarvonshire. |
| Calif. | California. |
| Cambs. | Cambridge; Cambridgeshire. |
| Capt. | Captain. |
| C.A.S. | Cathcart Art Society. |
| C.A.S.T. | Centre for Art, Science and Technology. |
| C.A.S.W. | Contemporary Art Society for Wales. |
| Cav. | Cavalière (Knight). |
| C.B. | Companion of the Bath. |
| C.B.E. | Commander Order of the British Empire. |
| C.C. | County Council; County Councillor. |
| C.C.H. | Cacique Crown of Honour. |
| C.D.S. | Cambridge Drawing Society. |
| C.E.M.A. | Council for the Encouragement of Music and Arts. |
| C.E.R.N. | Centre for European Nuclear Research. |
| Cert. | Certificate. |
| Cert. A.D. | Certificate in Art and Design. |
| Cert. F.A. | Certificate in Fine Art. |
| Certs. | Certificates. |
| C.F.E. | College of Further Education. |
| C.G.A. | Cheltenham Group of Artists. |
| Chas. | Chambers. |
| Ch.B. | Bachelor of Surgery. |
| C.H.E. | College of Higher Education. |
| C.I. | Channel Isles. |
| C.I.A.D. | Central Institute for Art and Design. |
| C.I.E. | Companion of the Order of the Indian Empire. |
| C.I.H.A. | Comité Internationale de l'Histoire de l'Art. |
| C.I.S. | Institute of Chartered Secretaries and Administrators. |
| Cl. | Close. |
| C.L.A.S. | Calligraphy and Lettering Art Society. |
| C.M. | Master of Surgery. |
| C.M.G. | Companion of St. Michael and St. George. |

| | |
|---|---|
| C.N.A.A. | Council for National Academic Awards (disbanded). |
| Co. | Company; County. |
| c/o | care of. |
| C.O.I.D. | Council of Industrial Design. |
| Col. | Colonel. |
| Com. | Committee; Common. |
| Comdr. | Commander. |
| Conn. | Connecticut. |
| Corp. | Corporation. |
| Cos. | Companies. |
| C.P. | College of Preceptors. |
| C.P.A. | Craft Potters Association. |
| C.P.R. | Canadian Pacific Railway. |
| C.P.S. | Contemporary Portrait Society. |
| Cres. | Crescent. |
| C.S. | Chemical Society; Conchological Society of Great Britain and Ireland. |
| C.S.D. | The Chartered Society of Designers (formerly Society of Industrial Artists and Designers). |
| C.S.I. | Companion of the Order of the Star of India. |
| C.S.M.A. | Cornish Society of Marine Artists. |
| C.S.P. | Chartered Society of Physiotherapists. |
| C.T. | Connecticut. |
| Ct. | Court. |
| Cttee. | Committee. |
| C.U.P. | Cambridge University Press. |
| C.V.O. | Commander of the Royal Victorian Order. |
| C.W.A.C. | City of Westminster Arts Council. |
| | |
| d. | daughter. |
| D.A. | Diploma of Art; Diploma of Edinburgh College of Art; Doctor of Arts. |
| D.A.E. | Diploma in Art Education. |
| D.B.E. | Dame Grand Cross Order of the British Empire. |
| D.C. | District of Columbia. |
| D.C.L. | Doctor of Civil Law. |
| D.C.M. | Distinguished Conduct Medal. |
| D.D. | Doctor of Divinity. |
| decd. | deceased. |
| Dept. | Department. |
| Des. R.C.A. | Designer of the Royal College of Art. |
| D.F.A. | Diploma of Fine Art. |
| D.F.Astrol.S. | Diploma of the Faculty of Astrological Studies. |
| D.I.A. | Design and Industries Association. |
| Dip.A.D. | Diploma in Art and Design. |

| | |
|---|---|
| **Dip.F.A.** | Diploma in Fine Art. |
| **Dip.H.E.** | Diploma in Higher Education. |
| **D.L.** | Deputy Lieutenant. |
| **D.Litt.** | Doctor of Letters. |
| **D.N.B.** | Dictionary of National Biography. |
| **D.O.E.** | Department of the Environment. |
| **Dr.** | Doctor. |
| **D.R.C.O.G.** | Diploma of Royal College of Obstetricians and Gynaecologists. |
| **D.S.** | Dental Surgery; Dental Surgeon. |
| **D.Sc.** | Doctory of Science. |
| **D.S.L.U.** | Association of the Slovene plastic artists. |
| **D.S.O.** | Companion of the Distinguished Service Order. |
| **E.** | East. |
| **E.A.G.M.A.** | East Anglian Group of Marine Artists. |
| **E.C.I.A.** | European Committee of Interior Architects. |
| **Educ.** | Educated; Education. |
| **E.E.C.** | European Economic Community. |
| **E.I.S.** | Educational Institute of Scotland. |
| **E.M.F.** | European Management Foundation. |
| **E.S.** | Entomological Society. |
| **Esq.** | Esquire. |
| **etc.** | etcetera. |
| **Exam.** | Examination. |
| **Exhbn.** | Exhibition. |
| **Exhib.** | Exhibited. |
| **F.** | Fellow; Foreign Member. |
| **F.B.A.** | Fellow of the British Academy. |
| **F.B.S.Comm.** | Fellow of the British Society of Commerce. |
| **F.C.A.** | Federation of Canadian Artists. |
| **F.C.B.S.I.** | Fellow of the Chartered Building Societies Institute. |
| **F.E.T.C.** | Further Education Teacher's Certificate. |
| **F.F.S.** | Fellow of the Franklin Society. |
| **F.G.A.** | Fellow of the Gemmological Association. |
| **F.G.E.** | Fellow of the Guild of Glass Engravers. |
| **F.I.A.L.** | Fellow of the International Institute of Arts and Letters. |
| **F.Inst.C.** | Fellow of the Institute of Commerce. |
| **F.I.S.A.** | International Federation of Works of Art. |
| **Fla.** | Florida. |
| **F.N.C.F.** | Federation Nationale de la Culture Française. |
| **F.P.E.** | Fellow, Philosophical Enquiry. |
| **F.P.S.** | Free Painters and Sculptors. |

| | |
|---|---|
| **F.S.I.** | Fellow of the Surveyors' Institute. |
| **F.S.P.** | Fellow of Sheffield Polytechnic. |
| **F.S.S.** | Federation of Scottish Sculptors. |
| **Ft.** | Feet; Foot. |
| **F.T.D.A.** | Fellow of the Theatrical Designers and Craftsmen's Association. |
| | |
| **Ga.** | Georgia. |
| **G.B.E.** | Knight Grand Cross Order of the British Empire. |
| **G.C.B.** | Knight Grand Cross of the Bath. |
| **G.C.M.G.** | Knight Grand Cross of St. Michael and St. George. |
| **G.C.S.I.** | Knight Grand Commander of the Star of India. |
| **g-d.** | grand-daughter. |
| **Gdn.** | Garden. |
| **Gdns.** | Gardens. |
| **G.E.S.M.** | Group for Educational Services in Museums. |
| **G.I.** | Royal Glasgow Institute of Fine Arts. |
| **G.L.C.** | Guild of Lettering Craftsmen; Greater London Council. |
| **Glos.** | Gloucestershire. |
| **G.M.A.S.** | Miniature Art Society of Georgia. |
| **G.M.C.** | Guild of Memorial Craftsmen. |
| **Govt.** | Government. |
| **G.P.D.S.T.** | Girls' Public Day School Trust. |
| **G.P.Fire E.** | Graduate Institution of Fire Engineers. |
| **G.P.O.** | General Post Office. |
| **G.P.S.** | Glasgow Printmaking Society. |
| **Gr.** | Grove. |
| **G.R.A.** | Guild of Railway Artsts. |
| **g-s.** | grandson. |
| **G.S.** | Geological Society. |
| **G.S.A.** | Glasgow School of Art. |
| **G.S.W.A.** | Glasgow Society of Women Artists. |
| **Gt.** | Great. |
| | |
| **H.** | Hon. Member. |
| **H.A.C.** | Hampstead Artists Council. |
| **Hants.** | Hampshire. |
| **H.D.F.A.** | Higher Diploma in Fine Art. |
| **H.Dip.A.D.** | Higher Diploma in Art and Design. |
| **Herts.** | Hertfordshire. |
| **H.F.R.A.** | Hon. Foreign Academician. |
| **H.L.I.** | Highland Light Infantry. |
| **H.M.** | His Majesty; Her Majesty. |

| | |
|---|---|
| H.M.I. | H.M. Inspector of Schools. |
| H.M.S.O. | Her Majesty's Stationery Office. |
| H.R.H. | His Royal Highness; Her Royal Highness. |
| H.S. | Hilliard Society. |
| H.S.A. | Hampstead Society of Artists. |
| H.S.S. | History of Science Society (American). |
| **Hunts.** | Huntingdonshire. |
| | |
| I.A.A. | International Association of Art. |
| I.A.A.S. | Incorporated Association of Architects and Surveyors. |
| I.A.A.S.B.A. | International Associate, American Society of Botanical Artists. |
| I.Ae.E. | Institute of Aeronautical Engineers. |
| I.A.L. | International Institute of Arts and Letters. |
| I.Arb. | Institute of Arbitrators. |
| I.A.S. | Incorporated Association of Surveyors; Irish Art Society. |
| I.B.A. | International Biographical Association. |
| I.B.D. | Institute of British Decorators and Interior Designers. |
| I.B.I.A. | Institute of British Industrial Art. |
| I.C. | Institute of Chemistry. |
| I.C.A. | Institute of Contemporary Arts. |
| I.C.E. | Institute of Civil Engineers. |
| I.C.O.GRA.D.A. | International Council of Graphic Design Association. |
| I.C.O.M. | International Council of Museums. |
| I.C.O.M.O.S. | International Council of Monuments and Sites. |
| I.C.S. | Indian Civil Service. |
| I.C.S.I.D. | International Council of Societies of Industrial Design. |
| I.D. | Institute of Directors; Institute of Decorators. |
| I.E.E. | Institute of Electrical Engineers. |
| I.E.L.A. | Irish Exhibition of Living Art. |
| I.F.A. | Incorporated Faculty of Arts. |
| I.F.A.W. | International Fund for Animal Welfare. |
| I.F.I. | International Federation of Interior Architects/ Designers. |
| I.F.S. | Irish Free State. |
| I.G.B. | Brazilian Institute of Genealogy. |
| I.I.C. | International Institute for Conservation of Paintings. |
| I.L.E.A. | Inner London Education Authority. |
| I.L.G.A. | Institute of Local Government Administration. |
| **Ill.** | Illinois. |

| | |
|---|---|
| **I.M.B.I.** | Institute of Medical and Biological Illustration. |
| **I.M.C.E.** | Institute of Mechanical and Civil Engineers. |
| **I.M.E.** | Institute of Mechanical Engineers; Institute of Engineers. |
| **I.Mgt.** | Institute of Management (formerly British Institute of Management). |
| **I.M.M.** | Institute of Mining and Metallurgy. |
| **Imp.** | Printer (Imprimerie, Imp). |
| **I.N.A.** | Institute of Naval Architects. |
| **Inst.** | Institute; Institution. |
| **I.O.M.** | Isle of Man. |
| **I.O.W.** | Isle of Wight. |
| **I.P.A.** | Portuguese Institute of Archaeology. |
| **I.P.A.T.** | International Porcelain Artist Teachers. |
| **I.P.D.** | Institute of Professional Designers. |
| **I.P.G.** | Independent Painters Group; Industrial Painters Group. |
| **I.P.I.** | Institute of Patentees and Inventors. |
| **I.P.M.** | Institute of Personnel Management. |
| **I.S.** | International Society of Sculptors, Painters and Gravers. |
| **I.S.C.A.** | International Society of Catholic Artists. |
| **I.S.L.F.D.** | Incorporated Society of London Fashion Designers. |
| **I.S.O.** | Imperial Service Order. |
| **I.S.T.D.** | Imperial Society of Teachers of Dancing. |
| **I.T.A.C.** | Imperial Three Arts Club. |
| **I.T.D.** | Institute of Training and Development. |
| **I.W.S.** | International Wool Secretariat. |
| **I.W.S.P.** | Institute of Work Study Practitioners. |
| **J.H.A.M.I.** | Johns Hopkins University Association of Medical Illustrations. |
| **J.I.** | Institute of Journalists. |
| **J.P.** | Justice of the Peace. |
| **Junr.** | Junior. |
| **K.A.A.G.** | Kirkles Art Action Group. |
| **K.B.E.** | Knight Commander Order of the British Empire. |
| **K.C.** | King's Counsel. |
| **K.C.B.** | Knight Commander of the Bath. |
| **K.C.C.** | Kent County Council. |
| **K.C.M.G.** | Knight Commander of St. Michael and St. George. |
| **K.C.S.G.** | Knight Commander of St. Gregory the Great. |

| | |
|---|---|
| K.C.S.I. | Knight Commander of the Star of India. |
| K.C.V.O. | Knight Commander of the Royal Victorian Order. |
| K.G. | Knight of the Order of the Garter. |
| K.I.A.D. | Kent Institute of Art and Design. |
| Kt. | Knight. |
| L. | Licentiate. |
| La. | Louisiana; Lane. |
| L.A. | Library Association; Los Angeles. |
| L.A.A. | Liverpool Academy of Arts. |
| L.A.M.D.A. | London Academy of Music and Dramatic Art. |
| Lancs. | Lancashire. |
| L.A.W. | Liverpool Artists Workshop. |
| L.C. | Legislative Council. |
| L.C.A.D. | London Certificate in Art and Design. |
| L.C.C. | London County Council. |
| L.D.A.D. | London Diploma of Art and Design. |
| L.D.S. | Licentiate in Dental Surgery. |
| Leics. | Leicestershire. |
| L.G. | Life Guards. |
| L.G.S.M. | Licentiate, Guildhall School of Music and Drama. |
| L.I. | Landscape Institute. |
| Lieut. | Lieutenant. |
| L.I.F.A. | Licentiate of International Faculty of Arts. |
| Lincs. | Lincolnshire. |
| L.I.S.T.D. | Licentiate of the Imperial Society of Teachers of Dancing. |
| L.L.A. | Lady Literate in Arts. |
| LL.B. | Bachelor of Laws. |
| LL.D. | Doctor of Laws. |
| LL.M. | Master of Laws. |
| L.P.T.B. | London Passenger Transport Board. |
| L.S. | Linnean Society. |
| L.S.A. | Licentiate of the Society of Apothecaries. |
| L.S.I.A. | Licentiate of the Society of Industrial Artists. |
| L.S.U. | Louisiana State University. |
| Ltd. | Limited. |
| M. | Member; Ministry; Monsieur. |
| m. | married; metre. |
| M.A. | Master of Arts. |
| MA. | Massachusetts. |
| M.A.A. | Medical Artists' Association; Miniature Artists of America. |
| M.A.F.A. | Manchester Academy of Fine Arts. |

| | |
|---|---|
| **M.A.I.** | Master of Fine Arts International. |
| **Mans.** | Mansions. |
| **M.A.S.-F.** | Miniature Art Society/Florida. |
| **M.A.S.-N.J.** | Miniature Art Society/New Jersey. |
| **M.A.S.-W.** | Miniature Art Society/Washington. |
| **Mass.** | Massachusetts. |
| **M.B.** | Bachelor of Medicine. |
| **M.B.E.** | Member of the Order of the British Empire. |
| **M.C.** | Military Cross. |
| **M.Chrom.** | Master of Chromatics. |
| **M.D.** | Doctor of Medicine; Managing Director. |
| **M.D.E.** | Mitglieder—Meister der Einbandkunst. |
| **Mem.** | Member. |
| **men.** | mention. |
| **Messrs.** | Messieurs. |
| **M.F.A.** | Master of Fine Art. |
| **M.G.P.** | Master Glass Painters. |
| **Mich.** | Michigan. |
| **Middx.** | Middlesex. |
| **Minn.** | Minnesota. |
| **M.Inst.M.** | Member, Institute of Marketing. |
| **M.Inst.Pkg.** | Member, Institute of Packaging. |
| **M.L.** | Licentiate in Medicine. |
| **M.Litt.** | Master of Letters. |
| **Mme.** | Madame. |
| **Mo.** | Missouri. |
| **M.of D.** | Ministry of Defence. |
| **M.of E.** | Ministry of Education. |
| **M.of H.** | Ministry of Health. |
| **M.O.I.** | Ministry of Information. |
| **M.of S.** | Ministry of Supply. |
| **M.of W.** | Ministry of Works. |
| **M.O.M.A.** | Museum of Modern Art. |
| **Mon.** | Monmouthshire. |
| **M.P.S.G.** | Miniature Painters, Sculptors and Gravers Society of Washington D.C. |
| **M.S.** | Society of Miniaturists; Motor Ship. |
| **MS.** | Manuscript. |
| **M.S.M.** | Meritorious Service Medal. |
| **M.Soc.Sc.** | Master of Social Science. |
| **MSS.** | Manuscripts. |
| **M-S.S.E.** | Multi-Sensory Sculpture Exhibitions. |
| **M.V.O.** | Member of the Royal Victorian Order. |
| | |
| **N.** | North. |
| **N.A.** | National Academy of Design (New York). |

| | |
|---|---|
| N.A.A. | National Artists Association. |
| N.A.D.F.A.S. | National Association of Decorative and Fine Arts Societies. |
| N.A.M.M. | National Association of Master Masons. |
| N.A.P.A. | National Acrylic Painters' Association. |
| N.B. | North Britain. |
| N.B.A. | North British Academy. |
| N.B.L. | National Book League. |
| N.C. | North Carolina. |
| N.C.A.C. | New Chertsey Art Club. |
| N.C.B. | National Coal Board. |
| N.C.D.A.D. | National Council for Diplomas in Art and Design. |
| N.C.R. | National Cash Register. |
| N.D.D. | National Diploma in Design. |
| N.E.A.C. | New English Art Club. |
| N.E.C. | National Executive Committee. |
| N.E.C.A. | National Exhibition of Children's Art. |
| N.F.T. | National Film Theatre. |
| N.F.U. | National Froebel Union. |
| N.G.A. | National Gallery of Australia. |
| N.H. | New Hampshire. |
| N.I. | Northern Ireland. |
| N.J. | New Jersey. |
| N.M. | New Mexico. |
| No. | Number. |
| Notts. | Nottinghamshire. |
| Notts. S.A. | Nottingham Society of Artists. |
| N.P. | Notary Public. |
| N.P.G. | National Portrait Gallery. |
| N.P.S. | National Portrait Society. |
| nr. | near. |
| N.R.D. | National Registered Designer. |
| N.S. | National Society. |
| N.S.A. | New Society of Artists; Natal Society of Artists; Newlyn Society of Artists. |
| N.S.A.E. | National Society for Art Education. |
| N.S.M.P. | National Society of Mural Painters. |
| N.S.P.S. | National Society of Painters, Sculptors and Printmakers. |
| N.S.W. | New South Wales. |
| N.U.M. | National Union of Mineworkers. |
| N.U.T. | National Union of Teachers. |
| N.W.A.B. | North West Art Board. |
| N.Y. | New York. |
| N.Y.S. | New York State. |

| | |
|---|---|
| N.Z. | New Zealand. |
| | |
| O. | Ohio. |
| O.A.S. | Oxford Society of Artists. |
| O.B.E. | Officer Order of the British Empire. |
| O.C. | Order of Canada (Officer). |
| O.C.R. | Officer of the Crown of Roumania. |
| O.C.S. | Oriental Ceramic Society. |
| O.D.A.C.A. | Original Doll Artist Council of America. |
| O.H.M.S. | On Her Majesty's Service. |
| Okla. | Oklahoma. |
| O.L.J. | Officer Companion of Order of St. Lazarus of Jerusalem. |
| O.S. | Optical Society. |
| O.S.A. | Ontario Society of Arts. |
| O.S.B. | Order of St. Benedict. |
| O.St.J. | Officer of the Most Venerable Order of the Hospital of St. John of Jerusalem. |
| O.U.D.S. | Oxford University Dramatic Society. |
| O.U.P. | Oxford University Press. |
| O.W.S. | Old Water-colour Society. |
| Oxon. | Oxford. |
| | |
| P. | President. |
| P.A.I. | Paisley Art Institute. |
| P.A.S.I. | Professor Associate of the Surveyor's Institution. |
| P.C. | Privy Councillor. |
| P.C.F.C. | Polytechnics and Colleges Funding Council. |
| P.E.N. | Poets, Playwrights, Editors, Essayists, Novelists Club. |
| Penn. | Pennsylvania. |
| P.G.C.E. | Post Graduate Certificate of Education. |
| Ph.B. | Bachelor of Philosophy. |
| Ph.D. | Doctor of Philosophy. |
| Phil. | Philosophy. |
| P.I. | Portrait Institute. |
| Pk. | Park. |
| Pl. | Place. |
| P.M.C. | Personnel Management Centre. |
| P.& O. | Peninsular and Oriental Steam Navigation Co., Ltd. |
| Pres. | President. |
| Princ. | Principal; Principle. |
| Prof. | Professor. |
| P.S. | Pastel Society. |

| | |
|---|---|
| Q.C. | Queen's Counsel. |
| Q.E.H. | Queen Elizabeth's Hospital School. |
| | |
| R.A. | Royal Academician; Royal Academy. |
| R.A.A. | Runnymede Association of Arts. |
| R.A.A.S. | Royal Amateur Art Society. |
| R.A.C. | Royal Automobile Club. |
| R.A.E. | Royal Aircraft Establishment. |
| R.A.F. | Royal Air Force. |
| R.A.I. | Royal Anthropological Institute. |
| R.A.M. | Royal Academy of Music. |
| R.A.M.C. | Royal Army Medical Corps. |
| R.A.S. | Royal Astronomical Society; Royal Asiatic Society; Richmond Art Society; Ridley Art Society. |
| R.B.A. | Royal Society of British Artists. |
| R.B.C. | Royal British Colonial Society of Artists. |
| R.B.G. | Royal Botanic Gardens. |
| R.B.S. | Royal Society of British Sculptors. |
| R.B.S.A. | Royal Birmingham Society of Artists. |
| R.C.A. | Royal College of Art; Royal Canadian Academy; Royal Cambrian Academician. |
| R.Cam.A. | Royal Cambrian Academy. |
| R.C.G.P. | Royal College of General Practitioners. |
| R.C.I. | Royal Colonial Institute. |
| R.C.M. | Royal College of Music. |
| R.C.N. | Royal College of Nursing. |
| R.C.O. | Royal College of Organists. |
| R.C.O.G. | Royal College of Obstetricians and Gynaecologists. |
| R.C.P. | Royal College of Physicians. |
| R.C.S. | Royal College of Surgeons. |
| R.C.S.E. | Royal College of Surgeons, Edinburgh. |
| Rd. | Road. |
| R.D.I. | Royal Designer of Industry. |
| R.D.S. | Royal Drawing Society. |
| R.E. | Royal Society of Painter-Printmakers (formerly Royal Society of Painter-Etchers and Engravers); Royal Engineers. |
| Regt. | Regiment. |
| Retd. | Retired. |
| Rev. | Reverend. |
| R.F.A. | Royal Field Artillery. |
| R.G.A. | Royal Garrison Artillery. |
| R.G.I. | Royal Glasgow Institute. |
| R.G.I.F.A. | Royal Glasgow Institute of Fine Art. |

| | |
|---|---|
| R.G.S. | Royal Geographical Society; Royal Graphic Society. |
| R.H.A. | Royal Hibernian Academy. |
| R.H.S. | Royal Horticultural Society. |
| R.Hist.S. | Royal Historical Society. |
| R.I. | Royal Institute of Painters in Water-colours. |
| R.I.A. | Royal Irish Academy. |
| R.I.A.I. | Royal Institute of the Architects of Ireland. |
| R.I.A.S. | Royal Incorporation of Architects in Scotland. |
| R.I.B.A. | Royal Institute of British Architects. |
| R.I.C. | Royal Institute of Chemistry. |
| R.I.C.S. | Royal Institution of Chartered Surveyors. |
| Rly. | Railway. |
| Rlys. | Railways. |
| R.M. | Royal Marines. |
| R.M.A. | Royal Military Academy. |
| R.M.I.T. | Royal Melbourne Institute of Technology. |
| R.M.S. | Royal Society of Miniature Painters. |
| R.N. | Royal Navy. |
| R.N.C.M. | Royal Northern College of Music. |
| R.N.I.B. | Royal National Institute for the Blind. |
| R.N.L.I. | Royal National Lifeboat Institution. |
| R.N.R. | Royal Naval Reserve. |
| R.N.V.R. | Royal Naval Volunteer Reserve. |
| R.O.I. | Royal Institute of Oil Painters. |
| R.P. | Royal Society of Portrait Painters and Member. |
| R.P.S. | Royal Photographic Society. |
| R.S. | Royal Society. |
| R.S.A. | Royal Scottish Academy; Royal Society of Arts. |
| R.S.A.I. | Royal Society of Antiquaries of Ireland. |
| R.S.E. | Royal Society of Edinburgh. |
| R.S.F.S.R. | Russian Soviet Federative Socialist Republic. |
| R.S.G.S. | Royal Scottish Geographical Society. |
| R.S.L. | Royal Society of Literature. |
| R.S.M.A. | Royal Society of Marine Arts. |
| R.S.P.A. | Royal Society for Prevention of Accidents. |
| R.S.P.B. | Royal Society for the Protection of Birds. |
| R.S.T. | Royal Society of Teachers. |
| R.S.W. | Royal Scottish Water-colour Society or Royal Scottish Society of Painters in Water-colours. |
| Rt. | Right. |
| R.T.P.I. | Royal Town Planning Institute. |
| R.T.Y.C. | Royal Thames Yachting Club. |
| R.U.A. | Royal Ulster Academy of Painting, Sculpture and Architecture; Royal Ulster Academician. |
| R.W.A. | Royal West of England Academician; Royal West of England Academy. |

| | |
|---|---|
| **R.W.S.** | Royal Water-Colour Society (formerly Royal Society of Painters in Water-colours). |
| **S.** | South. |
| **s.** | son; sons. |
| **S.A.** | Society of Antiquaries; Society of Apothecaries. |
| **S.A.A.** | Society of Aviation Artists. |
| **S.A.A.C.** | Society of Scottish Artists and Artist Craftsmen. |
| **S.A.B.A.** | Scottish Artists' Benevolent Association. |
| **S.A.C.** | Scottish Arts Council. |
| **S.A.E.** | Society of American Etchers; Society of Automobile Engineers (American). |
| **S.A.F.** | Société des Artistes Français. |
| **S.A.G.A.** | Society of American Graphic Artists. |
| **S.A.I.** | Scottish Arts Institute; Society of Architectural Illustrators. |
| **S.A.I.I.** | Society of Architectural and Industrial Illustrators. |
| **Salop.** | Shropshire. |
| **S.A.M.** | National Society of Art Masters. |
| **S.A.P.** | Society of Artist Printmakers. |
| **S.B.A.** | Society of Botanical Artists. |
| **S.B.St.J.** | Serving Brothers of the Order of St. John of Jerusalem. |
| **S.C.** | Senefelder Club; South Carolina. |
| **Sc.** | Sculptor. |
| **S.C.A.** | Society of Catholic Artists. |
| **S.C.F.** | Solidarité de la Culture Française. |
| **S.C.O.R.E.** | Scottish Core of Retired Executives. |
| **Sculpt.** | Sculpture. |
| **s–d.** | step daughter. |
| **S.D.C.** | Society of Designer Craftsmen and Craft Centre (formerly Arts and Crafts Exhibition Society). |
| **S.E.A.** | Society for Education in Art; Society of Equestrian Artists (see S.Eq.A.). |
| **Sec.** | Secretary. |
| **S.E.F.A.S.** | South Eastern Federation of Art Societies. |
| **S.Eq.A.** | Society of Equestrian Artists (formerly S.E.A.). |
| **S.G.A.** | Society of Graphic Art. |
| **S.G.E.** | Society of Glass Engravers. |
| **S.G.F.A.** | Society of Graphic Fine Art (formerly Society of Graphic Art). |
| **S.G.P.** | Society of Graver Printers. |

| | |
|---|---|
| S.G.T. | Society of Glass Technology. |
| S.I. | Surveyors' Institute. |
| S.I.A.C. | Société Internationale des Artistes Chretiens. |
| S.I.A.D. | (see C.S.D.). |
| S.I.D. | Society of Industrial Designers of U.S.A.; Mem. Swedish Industrial Designers. |
| S.I.P.E. | Société Internationale de Psychopathologie de l'Expression, Paris. |
| S.K.M. | South Kensington Museum. |
| S.Lm. | Society of Limners. |
| S.M. | Society of Miniaturists. |
| S.M.O.M. | Knight of Magistral Grace of the Sovereign Military Order of Malta. |
| S.M.P. | Society of Mural Painters. |
| S.N.A.D. | Society of Numismatic Artists and Designers. |
| S.N.G.M.A. | Scottish National Gallery of Modern Art. |
| S.N.P.G. | Scottish National Portrait Gallery. |
| Soc. | Société; Society. |
| Socs. | Societies. |
| Som. | Somerset. |
| South. S.A. | Southern Society of Artists. |
| S.P. | Société Internationale de Philogie, Sciences et Beaux Arts. |
| S.P.A.B. | Society for the Protection of Ancient Buildings. |
| S.P.C.K. | Society for the Promotion of Christian Knowledge. |
| S.P.D.A. | Society of Present-Day Artists. |
| S.P.E. | International Society of Philosophical Enquiry. |
| S.P.F. | Société des Pastellistes de France. |
| S.P.S. | Society of Portrait Sculptors. |
| S.P.S.A.S. | Swiss Society of Painters, Sculptors and Architects. |
| Sq. | Square. |
| s-s. | step son. |
| S.S. | Royal Statistical Society. |
| S.S.A. | Society of Scottish Artists. |
| S.S.C. | Solicitor to the Supreme Court (in Scotland). |
| S.S.I. | Society of Scribes and Illuminators. |
| S.S.N. | Sociétaire de la Société Nationale des Beaux Arts. |
| S.S.S.A. | Society of Sussex Sporting Artists. |
| S.S.W.A. | Scottish Society of Women Artists. |
| St. | Saint; Street. |
| Staffs. | Staffordshire. |
| S.T.C. | Sydney Technical College. |
| S.T.D. | Society of Typographical Designers. |

| | |
|---|---|
| S.W.A. | Society of Women Artists. |
| S.W.A.N. | Society for Wildlife Art of the Nations. |
| S.W.A.S. | Society of Women Artists of Scotland. |
| S.W.E. | Society of Wood Engravers. |
| S.WL.A. | Society of Wildlife Artists. |
| | |
| T. &. T. | Trinidad and Tobago. |
| T.C.D. | Trinity College, Dublin. |
| T.C.M. | Trinity College of Music. |
| T.C.T.A. | Teaching Certificate for Teachers of Art. |
| T.D. | Territorial Decoration; Teacher's Diploma. |
| Terr. | Terrace. |
| T.E.S. | Times Educational Supplement. |
| Tex. | Texas. |
| T.G.C. | Teacher's General Certificate. |
| T.L.S. | Times Literary Supplement. |
| TN. | Tennessee. |
| T.P.I. | Town Planning Institute. |
| T.R.H. | Their Royal Highnesses. |
| T.S.B. | Trustee Savings Bank. |
| | |
| U. | Unionist. |
| U.A. | United Society of Artists. |
| U.A.E. | United Arab Emirates. |
| U.C.H. | University College Hospital. |
| U.C.L. | University College, London. |
| U.L.U.J. | Union of the plastic artists of Yugoslavia. |
| U.S.A. | United States of America. |
| U.S.M. | Ulster Society of Miniaturists. |
| U.S.S.R. | Union of Soviet Socialist Republics. |
| U.S.W.A. | Ulster Society of Women Artists. |
| U.W.A. | Ulster Women Artists. |
| U.W.P. | University of Wales Press. |
| U.W.S. | Ulster Water-colour Society. |
| | |
| V. | Vice. |
| v. | versus. |
| V. & A. | Victoria and Albert Museum. |
| Va. | Virginia. |
| V.A.D. | Voluntary Aid Detachment. |
| V.C. | Victoria Cross. |
| V.D. | Volunteer Officers' Decoration; Victorian Decoration. |
| Vol. | Volume. |
| V.P. | Vice-President. |
| V.R.D. | Volunteer Reserve Decoration. |

| | |
|---|---|
| W. | West. |
| W.A. | Western Australia. |
| WA. | Washington. |
| W.A.C. | Welsh Arts Council (see A.C.W.). |
| W.A.G. | Walker Art Gallery. |
| W.A.S.C.E. | World Art Science and Cultural Exchanges. |
| W.C.C. | World Crafts Council. |
| W.C.S.I. | Water-colour Society of Ireland. |
| W.S.W. | Water-colour Society of Wales. |
| W.E.A. | Workers' Educational Association. |
| W.E.R.P. | Wood Engravers and Relief Printers. |
| W.G.I.H.E. | West Glamorgan Institute of Higher Education. |
| W.I.A.A. | Women's International Arts Association. |
| W.I.A.C. | Women's International Art Club. |
| W.I.A.S. | Women's International Art Society. |
| Wilts. | Wiltshire. |
| Wis. | Wisconsin. |
| Worcs. | Worcestershire. |
| W.W.F. | World Wildlife Fund. |
| Xmas | Christmas. |
| Y.A.E. | Yorkshire Artists' Exhibition. |
| Y.M.(W.)C.A. | Young Men's (Women's) Christian Association. |
| Yorks. | Yorkshire. |
| Y.W.D.A. | Yiewsley and West Drayton Arts Council. |
| Z.S. | Zoological Society. |